STUDENTS' GUIDE TO
COLLEGES

THE DEFINITIVE GUIDE TO
AMERICA'S TOP 100 SCHOOLS

STUDENTS' GUIDE TO
COLLEGES

THE DEFINITIVE GUIDE TO AMERICA'S TOP 100 SCHOOLS

WRITTEN BY THE **REAL** EXPERTS— THE **STUDENTS** WHO ATTEND THEM

CREATED AND EDITED BY
JORDAN GOLDMAN and **COLLEEN BUYERS**

WITH A PREFACE BY **CHUCK HUGHES**

PENGUIN BOOKS

PENGUIN BOOKS

Published by the Penguin Group

Penguin Group (USA) Inc., 375 Hudson Street, New York, New York 10014, U.S.A.

Penguin Group (Canada), 90 Eglinton Avenue East, Suite 700, Toronto, Ontario,
    Canada M4P 2Y3 (a division of Pearson Penguin Canada Inc.)

Penguin Books Ltd, 80 Strand, London WC2R 0RL, England

Penguin Ireland, 25 St Stephen's Green, Dublin 2, Ireland (a division of Penguin Books Ltd)

Penguin Group (Australia), 250 Camberwell Road, Camberwell, Victoria 3124, Australia
    (a division of Pearson Australia Group Pty Ltd)

Penguin Books India Pvt Ltd, 11 Community Centre, Panchsheel Park,
    New Delhi - 110 017, India

Penguin Group (NZ), cnr Airborne and Rosedale Roads, Albany, Auckland 1310, New Zealand
    (a division of Pearson New Zealand Ltd)

Penguin Books (South Africa) (Pty) Ltd, 24 Sturdee Avenue, Rosebank,
    Johannesburg 2196, South Africa

Penguin Books Ltd, Registered Offices:
80 Strand, London WC2R 0RL, England

First published in Penguin Books 2005

10 9 8 7 6 5 4 3 2 1

Editors' Note
Students whose college reviews are published in this book were given the option of using
their real names or a pseudonym and changing their identifying characteristics. The editors
fully support both choices and respect the fact that some students felt the need to protect
their identity in order to speak freely.

ISBN 0 14 30.3558 4
CIP data available

Printed in the United States of America
Set in Stone Serif
Designed by Victoria Hartman

To every student who's hated the stressful
college selection and admissions process:
we've done our best to make it easier,
more honest, and more fun.

✦ *Jordan and Colleen*

To my wonderful family (and amazing parents).
To my best friend, Devin Cutugno.
In loving memory of Ruth Seid.

✦ *J.G.*

To Anjose E. Musas Minhas.

✦ *C.B.*

Acknowledgments

More than thirty thousand students contributed to the creation of *Students' Guide,* and more than one hundred students played a part in assembling it. This book was only possible because these students believed in us, wanted to make their voices heard, and used *Students' Guide* as an excuse to procrastinate when they should have been doing their homework. Thanks to everyone for sharing your thoughts and experiences with us. We hope we've done them justice.

For their hard work and dedication, we'd like to thank our assistant editors: Trina Rose Cutugno, Joshua Poole, and Jessica Rothenberg. We'd also like to thank those students who were instrumental in putting this book together: Thomas Tachibana, Pamela Yang, Terry Wei, Allison Burson, Evan Hulka, Evan Berkow, Emily Crowe, Laura Heggie, Barry Flynn, Emily Ach, and Andrew Sutherland. Our summer 2003 interns also helped shape what *Students' Guide* has become: Lanford Beard, Lindsay Crouse, Elizabeth Currie, Nicole Davidson, Allison Klein, Kathleen O'Campo, Helen McCallister, Bryan Schwartz, and Adina Wise.

College taught us a lot of things, but it didn't teach us how to write a book; we have the following people to thank for that. Thank you Amy Jameson, Richard Morris, and the whole of Janklow & Nesbit Associates—your wisdom and enthusiasm helped us every step of the way. Thank you Richard Price, Jay Seid, and Ralph Figueroa—your guidance and expertise proved invaluable. Thank you Rick Kot, for recognizing our project had merit. And most important, thank you Brett Kelly, our own personal hero, without whom we'd just be two college kids with a crazy idea.

Finally, we'd like to thank the following people for their personal support: Jill Morawksi, David Beare, Richard Walton, Celeste Pelc, Robert Buyers, Janet Buyers, George and Margaret Pelc, Norah Burne Buyers, Larry Buyers, Noreen and Jeff Greenblatt, Kyle Buyers, 30 Fountain, 53 Oak, Aaron Janus, Matthew Eaton, Luka Haven, Kristin Small, Katherine Patterson, Wesley Pederson, Rachel and Marcia Avila, Jesse Whittle-Utter, Melanie Resnick, Craig Resnick, Bill Goldman, Lisa Goldman, Jay Seid, Heather Seid, Stanley Seid, Ruth Seid, Sandy Schreiber, Donna Cutugno, Charlie Cutugno, Paul Brunick, Ben Morse,

Matthew Williams, Andrew Daum, Jon Renshon, David Jay, Ben Shestakfosky, Selina Ellis, Stephanie Carlisle, Kelsey Arnold, Kevin Tyler Hall, Matt Reents, Mike Mckee, Dave Robb, David Azoulay, Mike Cassa, Mike Sudano, Jeff Homan, Bonnie Cassorla, Anthony Lurente, Kate Di Maggio, Mariel Fisher, all the Resnicks, Amanda Goldman, Brandon Goldman, Kyle Seid and Brianna Seid.

Without you, none of this would have been possible.

—Jordan and Colleen

Contents

Preface

The book you're holding in your hands—*Students' Guide to Colleges*—is a fresh and exciting tool that will be invaluable as you attempt to select the school that's right for you.

From 1995 to 2000, I was a senior admissions officer at Harvard. Since then, I've worked as an educational consultant, helping families plan for college. In both capacities, I've read nearly ten thousand applications and worked with hundreds of parents and students who were hoping to find, and get into, the "best" college possible.

However, all too often parents and students have a distorted view of what the "best" college is. They listen to the marketing hype, they pay too much attention to rankings and prestige, and students commit themselves to spending four years at schools that aren't right for them. When making such an important decision as where to go to college, students need to figure out which schools *fit*. They need to discern the stories behind the rankings, to get answers to probing questions about a school's professors, its classes, its atmosphere, and its social life, to find the place they'll enjoy living and learning the most.

Families aren't going to get answers to these questions from biased and blindingly glossy admissions pamphlets, where schools pretend to be all things to all people. They won't get answers from college guidebooks written by journalists and administrators who imagine, but don't know, what it's like on the ground. They will get answers by talking to current college students—the only ones who know the truth. And they will, I'm convinced, get answers from *Students' Guide to Colleges*.

Students' Guide is a new kind of guidebook, created, written, and edited entirely by current college students. Inside, one hundred of the best colleges in America are reviewed. For every school, three students weigh in, each from a different academic and social area of campus, each with a different voice, a different perspective, and different experiences. Together, these students offer detailed, nuanced, personal, and honest portraits of their schools. They give you the stories behind the statistics. They also give you funny and irreverent reviews that are fun to read—the next best thing to spending a week on campus.

Students' Guide to Colleges was started by Jordan Goldman and Colleen Buyers when they were eighteen-year-old college freshman. Goldman and Buyers, from their dorm rooms, created a Web site and an online survey covering every aspect of college life (including questions only true insiders would think to ask, like: What *wouldn't* a prospective student see on a campus tour? What goes on in the dorms at 3 a.m. on a Wednesday night, and how does that differ from school to school?).

In a few months, more than thirty thousand students, all across America, logged on to their Web site. *Students' Guide* quickly became a virtual grassroots movement, spurred on by the power of the Internet, the power of student networks, and students' desires to tell the truth about their schools—both the good *and* the bad. Friends told friends about *Students' Guide*. News of the survey spread from school to school. Students weren't paid to give *Students' Guide* in-depth reports—freshman, sophomores, juniors, and seniors logged on because they wanted to get out the truth and let people know what their schools were *really* like. In the end, *Students' Guide to Colleges* was completely student-created, written and edited—no one involved was any older than twenty-one.

Other college guidebooks offer statistics, sound bites, and out-of-context quotes. They pretend they can give a single, accurate account of what every school is like for every type of person. *Students' Guide* tells you the truth, from three different perspectives, from the actual students. You then have the necessary information to figure out whether each school is right for you.

When students at the top one hundred colleges graduate at the age of twenty-two, they'll be courted by America's top companies for their ability to speak for themselves. But until now, at the ages eighteen, nineteen, twenty, and twenty-one, these students have always been spoken for: by politicians, by advertisers, by college guidebooks written by journalists and administrators. In *Students' Guide to Colleges*, the brightest young minds in America have come together and taken their voices back. They're telling you what it's *really* like at America's top one hundred schools, so you can end up at the college that's right for *you*. They have extremely valuable things to say. I hope you'll listen.

—*Chuck Hughes*

Chuck Hughes was the senior admissions officer at Harvard College from 1995 to 2000, and is the cofounder of Road to College, a leading college and graduate school educational consulting company. For more information on Road to College, please visit www.roadtocollege.com.

Letter from the Editors

Dearest Reader,

You've got a crazy year ahead of you (or two, if you're a junior). We know—it wasn't long ago that we were in the middle of this process ourselves. The countless college tours, the caffeinated blitz to finish applications before the post office closes on December 31, the agonizing wait for that thin or thick envelope while everyone asks, "So do you know where you're going yet?" Yeah, we know what you're up against. This book is our attempt to help you out.

Students' Guide to Colleges was dreamed up in our dorm rooms during freshman year, just after we'd finished the whole process. During one late-night conversation about the ups and downs of our own college searches, we agreed that conventional college guides' two-page summaries were not nearly as informative as talking to actual students at each school we'd visited. There had to be a better way to write college guidebooks.

So we thought we'd give it a try. We decided to create a guidebook written entirely by actual college students, to hear directly from them what it's really like to go to America's top one hundred schools. And as college students ourselves, we realized that everyone experiences each school differently. A single school will be different for a Nebraskan and a New Yorker, an actor and an athlete. When Joe Bloggs finally gets to college, his experiences won't be the same as his roommate's, his hall mates' or his lab partner's. So *Students' Guide* doesn't pretend that we can give you a single objective summary of each institution. Instead, we give you at least three students' contrasting, complementary, and sometimes conflicting perspectives of each college.

This guidebook is designed for critical thinkers. It's designed to help you consider the source of the information you're reading, to consider what *your* experience of each institution might be. How are you similar to and different from each school's student-reviewers? What would *you* think about attending the classes and parties they describe? What else would you like to know?

The college search only starts here: take whatever you learn from this book to college campuses. Stay overnight, make a pest of yourself in the info sessions, ask lots of questions based on who you are and what you're interested in, and then ask some more. Each college truly does have its own multifaceted personality, and while we hope we've given you a sense of each, only you can decide where you'll most enjoy living and learning.

By the time this is printed, we'll both be college graduates. But *Students' Guide* is more than just us—we're among tens of thousands of college students who worked together because we believed you might be interested in hearing what we had to say, and because it was time we finally spoke for ourselves about what it's like to attend America's top colleges. We're delighted Penguin Books agreed with us—and we hope you will, too.

Best of luck in your college search. It's a difficult process. But we've just heard from thousands of students who have successfully gone through the craziness, and they resoundingly agree that it does actually end—and that there's something pretty amazing waiting for you on the other side.

—Jordan and Colleen

Frequently Asked Questions

Are the schools included in Students' Guide to Colleges the best one hundred schools in America?

There are many excellent schools in America. *Students' Guide* reviews the one hundred schools that we feel have achieved a particular level of excellence. We didn't come to our decision lightly—schools were selected for inclusion only after six full months of research, during which we considered more than three hundred schools, spoke with admissions officers, college counselors, and current college students, and evaluated multiple ranking systems. In the end you'll find a broad range of the best schools in the nation, including big schools and small schools, state schools and private schools, expensive schools and less expensive schools, schools located all over America, schools ranked highly by *U.S. News and World Report,* and some lesser-known gems that we think deserve your attention. We couldn't include every school in America in *Students' Guide*—but we think there's something special about each of the schools we did include. We hope you agree.

Did students write absolutely everything in Students' Guide*? Or were there a few journalists or administrators involved?*

Every single school review in *Students' Guide to Colleges* was written by a current college student—more than thirty thousand students participated, and nearly one thousand students are quoted by name.

How did you get so many students to tell you about their schools? Were they paid?

No students were paid to contribute to *Students' Guide to Colleges*—these are real students speaking their minds simply because they wanted to get out the truth.

The content of *Students' Guide* is based on an open-ended survey we developed over a two-year period, drawing on what we cared about as prospective students and what we experienced daily as college students. We took care to structure the survey in a way that would prompt smart, funny, opinionated, and lively descriptions of each school. There were critical questions like "What *wouldn't* a prospective student see on a campus tour?"; creative questions like "On a sunny day, there are four distinct groups of people sitting outside; describe them"; and more standard questions like "Do you receive much personal attention from professors?" You can see the full survey now at www.studentsguide.com. Each school's review is three students responding to the survey.

Then we got on the phone, contacted friends of friends, created flyers and banners for each school to let students know about our survey, had articles run in multiple school newspapers, and contacted student government associations and student group leaders on every campus using student networks extensively. Finally, we put our survey online at www.studentsguidetocolleges.com. And it was a phenomenal success. In one month, more than thirty thousand students logged on.

Once you received filled-in surveys, how did you choose which students to publish?

It wasn't easy. Before we could decide which students to publish, we had to understand each school. So a year earlier, we spent six months researching each of the schools included in *Students' Guide*.

When the surveys flooded in, we read every single one of them and took notes on what was being said over and over again, what fantastic programs, important descriptions, and significant grievances were being continually brought up. We contacted students at every school to ensure our research thus far was accurate.

We selected students whose writing reflected each school, who voiced issues that were being repeatedly brought up by their peers, and who had their own unique voices and things to say. We also looked to select students who had different perspectives on each school, because we recognize that a white, conservative biology major from South Dakota is going to experience a school differently from a black activist English major from New York. We tried to illustrate the myriad of experiences to be had on each campus, while still painting a coherent and accurate picture of each school as a whole.

Did you sanitize these reviews? How were they edited?

Each student's survey was edited for space and redundancy.

Initially, we told students to fill out our survey off the top of their heads, in no more than an hour—and they did (often while procrastinating at 3:00 a.m. on a Wednesday night). So we also cleaned up some punctuation and grammar. Then we contacted individual students when their writing was being considered and again when they were chosen for publication, giving them the chance to edit and add to their entry.

Did you publish students' real names alongside their reviews?

Every student was given the option of using their real name or a pseudonym and if they used a pseudonym, of changing any identifying characteristics. Some students elected to use their real name. Others changed their names because they have a work-study job in the office of admissions but wanted to be critical of their school, because they discussed their involvement in queer organizations but they're in the closet back home, or just because a pen name seemed cool. We fully supported both choices, and respected the fact that some students felt the need to protect their identity so they could speak freely.

A note about facts and statistics quoted by students in reviews:

All statistics on the first page of each school's review were compiled by us, and were, accordingly, rigorously fact-checked. On the other hand, some students cite facts and statistics in their reviews ranging from the male/female ratio of a school to the precentage of students who marry fellow alums. These facts and figures are often part of the campus discourse, passed on from student to student. Their accuracy is not guaranteed. However, we believe the facts and statistics students repeat and hold to be true regarding their institution are often as significant as the numbers the institution itself issues. Consequently, we didn't change or fact-check the numbers students quoted *within* reviews. Instead, we took them (with a grain of salt) as indicative of what students believe and have seen to be true about their school.

"A student referenced something, and I don't know what they're talking about. . . ."

This happens. Students at different colleges often create their own vernacular. But we tried to keep undecipherable references to a minimum. A lot of acronyms have been spelled out, and a lot of college-specific references have been explained. We also trust that you're pretty smart and will quickly catch on that "prereqs" is an abbreviation for prerequisites, "gen-eds" are courses meeting general education requirements, RAs are resident assistants (upperclassmen who live in first-year dorms); and LGBT students are students who are lesbian, gay, bisexual, or transgender. These terms are often used in context, and it should be fairly easy to figure out what they mean.

Technicalities

How did you determine each school's selectivity rating on the first page of its review?

While every school profiled in *Students' Guide* is selective, we thought it would be worthwhile to break schools down into three categories—Most Selective, Very Selective, and Selective. When you're applying to schools, these categories may help you decide which schools are reach schools, which schools are target schools, and which schools are safety schools.

- Schools were designated Most Selective if they accepted 0–33 percent of their applicants.
- Schools were designated Very Selected if they accepted 34–48 percent of their applications.

- Schools were designated Selective if they accepted 49 percent or more of their applicants.

Selectivity was determined based on acceptance rates for the class of 2007.

How did you determine each school's notable programs or majors on the first page of its review?

We asked students at every school which programs or majors were particularly strong, prestigious, popular, or noteworthy. Notable programs and majors features the most frequent responses received.

How did you determine the answers to the bubble grid on the first page of each review?

Size and diversity were determined based on published data. Schools with fewer than 2,500 undergraduates were rated small, schools with 2,501–7,499 undergraduates were rated medium, and schools with more than 7,500 undergraduates were rated big. Similarly, if less than 20 percent of students at a school were ethnic minorities, its diversity was rated low. If 20–29 percent of students at a school were minorities, its diversity statistic was rated moderate. If 30 percent and above of students at a school were minorities, its diversity statistic was rated high. All other evaluations were determined based on students' survey responses.

How did you select each school's Five Words from Students on the first page of its review?

We asked students at every school for five words that they felt summed up their college experience. We then selected collections of five words that we thought were particularly representative based on our research.

How did you select each school's From the School section on the first page of its review?

"From the School" is our attempt to show you each school's official view of itself. We spent hours reading every school's Web site, and, for each school, we selected one or two online paragraphs that we felt were particularly representative and included them in *Students' Guide*.

How did you select the other schools Students May Also Be Interested In on the first page of each school's review?

We asked students at every school what other colleges they looked into when they were in high school. We included the four to six schools that were mentioned with the most frequency.

Finally, are you guys really students? You did all this while you were in college?

Yup. We came up with the idea when we were eighteen and spent the next four years working on the book in your hands. We created and edited *Students' Guide* while simultaneously going to classes, doing our homework, studying for tests, writing theses, and, of course, subsisting on Easy Mac.

I Wish I Knew Then . . .

(Selecting, and Getting into, the School of Your Dreams)

Students' Guide *asked thousands of current college students "What about the admissions process do you wish you'd known when you were still in high school?" This is their advice to you.*

Starting Out

I wish I'd been able to enter the college research and selection and application process with more perspective. The whole thing is frantic—especially if you're like me, studying nonstop and doing ten billion extracurriculars senior year on top of worrying about the whole college thing.

So here's my advice: take a day or two out of your life (yes, an entire day, not just a bit of time here and there) and really think about what you want in a college. Think about your academic interests and determine what gets you legitimately excited, and what just gets you good grades. Think about your extracurriculars and decide which are passions and which are pastimes. Look at yourself and determine what kind of a person you are, and what kind of college environment would make you happiest. Once you figure these things out, try to find colleges where students get excited about the same things you do.

Then visit the schools that interest you and at each one try to find a student (or two) who looks like the kind of person you'd want to be in a couple of years. Buy them lunch or something—talk to them. Seriously. Most students—at least at my school—wouldn't mind at all if you stopped them in the middle of the street and asked them a few questions. And the answers you'll get might make all the difference in deciding where you'll eventually go to college.

One last thing: it's easy to go through high school without learning who you really are—there are plenty of pre-established paths/ruts that students tend to fall into based on their academic/athletic/artistic abilities. Before you decide where to spend the next four years of your life, stop and think about whether you're following your own path, or just a rut left behind by someone else.

—*Craig, Middlebury College*

I wish I'd known how much learning about colleges—and actually seeing colleges in person—would motivate me to work harder my junior and senior years, and to get excited about the whole process. It's easy to put off a process that seems daunting—but once I visited schools, I started finding the process *inspiring*. Seeing the places I'd previously only read about, I really wanted to work hard to get there. Before, I wanted to do well because good grades were good grades, but after seeing and breathing my future I wanted to do well so I could actually live it.

—*Jessica, Williams College*

I wish I'd understood that a prospective student should be impressed by a school. I was so concerned with impressing schools that I didn't realize they were selling themselves to me, too.

—*Kate, Tulane University*

Let me clue you in on a secret well-kept by the college admissions industry: You won't know whether a college is really right for you until you've enrolled and tried it out. No amount of agonizing can change that. And in the end, whether you originally came to get smart or get wasted, every college will mold you, to some extent, in its own image.

When you graduate from college, you'll come to judge all educations by the standards of the education you ended up getting. You will judge college social scenes by the standards of *your* college's social scene. And anyway, by your senior year of college, the school that was your twelfth-grade dream come true may be a grand disappointment. Alternatively, the school that you only reluctantly decided to apply to may become the site of some of the giddiest—if not the happiest—times of your life. Where you are right now, applying to colleges, you just can't know which school would actually be perfect for you. It's impossible.

But don't let this freak you out. Probably, if you actually want to go to college, any college you seriously think of applying to will be just fine.

So, for right now, if you think you want to go to college, the best thing to do is visit a college, talk to some people, sit in on some classes, try to get the gist of the place. Even then, the gist you get may be wrong, totally different from what your experience at that school will end up being—there's just no way of knowing. So don't sweat it.

And books reviewing colleges? They're not that useful. In fact, I'd recommend against them. Remember that somebody stands to make a lot of money off the nervousness of college-bound high school students. Anything you could learn in one of these expensive college books you could learn ten times better from talking to students at the schools themselves. For free. So if you haven't bought this book yet, put it down, leave the store, and go find a real student to talk to.

P.S. If you're going to college because it's expected and you can't think of anything else to do . . . for the love of God, snap out of it! Take a year off. Take three years off. Volunteer at a prison. Work as a janitor. Visit Norway, or better yet, the Third World. You don't need college to be happy. If you don't actually want to be there, college is a very expensive place to spend four years being listless and confused.

—*Mike, Carleton College*

Questions and Considerations

It's really easy to get caught up in asking anything that could help differentiate one school from another. The meal plan is better at School A than School B, but School B has the better gym, and School C is comparable except it has more Nobel laureates—that kind of stuff. But really, are you actually going to choose a college because of its food? Is the difference in gym quality that much of a big deal? If you don't plan on taking classes in the department where the laureates teach, what does it matter? Figure out the things that really matter, that would make you significantly happy or unhappy. Then base your questions on that.

—*Gayle, University of Michigan*

When I visited colleges in high school, I focused on, and asked, all the wrong questions. Now I know things like a college's ranking and its student/faculty ratio are kind of important, but they don't give you much insight into the character of an institution, which is really important. Wherever you go you'll find good students. But beyond just being a good student—what are the *types* of good students you want to spend the next four years of your life with—and what's the type of good student you eventually want to become?

—*Nicholas, Washington and Lee University*

Before asking yourself the "Can I pay for it?"–style practical questions, sit down, smoke whatever it is you high school kids are smoking these days, and ask yourself the more ethereal questions: What kind of school will fit you best? Are you an intellectual? Are you a city person? How far from home do you really want to be? Do you learn best in tiny classes, where the teacher is right up in your face, or in large lecture halls, where you can hide from the professor if you want to? Really, you need to know who you are and what you want. Then you can start looking into the financials. (And, you never know, at even the most expensive school you could end up with more financial aid than you'd anticipated.)

—*Sean, Columbia University*

I really wish someone had told me more about the varied personalities of students at different schools. You hear about all the great things each school offers, but very rarely do you hear about the types of students that predominantly flock to each college. And I think this is key to know, to be sure you'll learn and live with that type of student all four years.

—*Jaime-Alexis, Vassar College*

GEOGRAPHIC PROXIMITY

I had great friends in high school, and we didn't want to risk not being part of one another's lives. We all went to schools close to home, and close to each other. So far it's been great to watch them grow up, to visit their new environments on weekends, and to hang out when we each need the comfort of being around people whom you've known and who have loved you forever.

—*Cory, Amherst College*

Let's be brutally honest for a second, okay? College is hard. It gets to you. And sometimes you break down, you can't stand the piles of laundry stinking up your room, you can't stand the shitty cafeteria food, you can't stand looking at your ugly roommate with his pimply face and the pile of textbooks on your desk. And sometimes you just miss your mom and dad, your brothers and sisters. Those are the times when it's amazing to be close to home. I live a couple hours away, and it's so nice to hop in my car and, not too long afterward, be smothered with love and free food. Sometimes I just need that. After all, I'm only nineteen.

—*Josh, Evergreen State College*

I thought if I had to fly to school, it wouldn't matter where I went—wrong. There's a difference, in both time and cost, between a two-hour flight and two three-hour flights (and if the nearest major airport is a hundred-dollar cab ride away, that makes a difference, too). . . . But above all, I wish I'd known how hard it is to be far away sometimes, to have to choose between seeing family and road-tripping with friends on those few precious vacations; to have to meticulously pack two suitcases weighing no more than FAA regulations of seventy pounds each, instead of just throwing a laundry basket in the backseat of my car and heading off; to missing small holidays, and my little brother's birthday, because it's too expensive to fly home for a weekend. . . . Plus, another part of the country can be a *huge* culture shock! People on this coast can be so rude, and Northeastern winters are long and gray. Sometimes, I just miss home.

—*Liza, Dartmouth University*

I'm very close to my family. Accordingly, I thought a lot about whether I wanted to stray far from South Dakota and being part of my little siblings' lives. And what have I learned? I've learned that college is an opportunity to become an adult, to be on your own, to branch out and explore personally, emotionally, spiritually . . . and geographically. Going to school so far from home taught me to truly be myself, to survive on my own. And it gave me the courage to go even farther: right now I'm writing this while studying abroad in Africa, speaking another language, discovering a new world, a new culture, a new wealth of wonderful people. I think going to school so far from home gave me the courage to go even farther.

—*Andrea, Harvard University*

I finally realized in November of senior year—thanks to much prodding on the part of my guidance counselor—that there were great schools outside of the Northeast, where I grew up. Now I study under palm trees in January at the fourth-ranked liberal arts college in the country—who knew breaking out of the bubble could be so rewarding?

—*Colleen, Pomona College*

I wish I'd understood that it doesn't matter if you're a hundred or a thousand miles away: you won't be going home often. College life is much more independent than high school life, wherever you go. You do not have to go across the country to live—and feel—on your own. I probably would have considered schools on the West Coast, in the Midwest, and in the South if I knew I'd only be coming home once a semester anyway.

—*Meredith, Brandeis University*

SIZE

It's important to ask yourself whether you want a big school, a medium school, or a small school. At a big school you'll have limitless class options, tons of extracurriculars on offer, rowdy parties, and there'll always be new people to meet. You'll also have classes with three hundred plus kids, you might feel lost, and you might not get to know your professors. At a small school, you'll have fewer classes to choose from, a low-key party scene, and people you don't know knowing your business—but you'll make incredibly close friends, have classes with only six other kids, and your teacher will have won a Nobel Prize and will invite you to their house for dinner, where you'll discuss applications of Marx's economic theories on modern-day Southeast Asian markets. A middle-size school would offer some combination of the pros and cons of both experiences. Think about all three experiences, and figure out which one is right for you.

—*Scott, Princeton University*

I always thought the big school/small school question was easy. I hate having professors look over my shoulder, I love being able to miss a class if I have to with no repercussions, I love meeting new people, I hate everyone knowing my business, I love to party. Big school for me! My best friend from high school loves working one-on-one with professors, loves the pressure of never being able to cut class (because the professor will know), and loves being able to say hi to everyone she sees, because she knows everyone on campus. I go to UT Austin. She goes to Macalester. Both of us couldn't be happier.

—*Shelby, UT Austin*

LOCATION

First thing I asked myself was, do I want go to college in a big city, or don't I? If I didn't want to be in a city—did I want to be near a city, or did I want to be isolated? If I went to school in a city (like NYU) I'd have countless internship and job opportunities, constant excitement. I'd also have to spend lots of money all the time, and I'd lose out on the tight-knit college feel. If I wasn't in a city but near one (for example, a school like Princeton), I'd get the best of both worlds— I could escape to the city when I wanted to. But I'd also get the worst of both worlds—I'd often find myself so overworked I wouldn't actually leave campus, and maybe the campus wouldn't be that close-knit because people were always running off when they wanted to have fun. And finally, I could go to an isolated school in the middle of nowhere (somewhere like Williams), where I would know everyone on campus and see all my friends at parties. But then I might feel claustrophobic after a while, and there's really nowhere to go to escape.

—*Scott, Princeton University*

ACADEMIC CURRICULUM

I was looking at schools with large core curriculums, and schools with no core curriculums at all. I eventually chose a school with a large core curriculum, and I couldn't be happier. It turned me into someone who's truly well-rounded. It diversified my interests. It taught me a bit of everything. And it was good for me. I mean, let's be honest—does any eighteen-year-old know what's good to learn? If I'd been given the liberty to choose my classes all along, I might have focused too much on one subject, or missed lots of interesting classes because I heard they were hard and didn't want to bother, or I would have chosen classes so randomly that my education on the whole would have had no coherence. Instead, when I graduate I'll be truly educated: the core here covers every area under the sun, and I'll be comfortable conversing on such a wide range of topics that even Rhodes scholars better watch out, because I'm sure I could take them on intellectual punch for intellectual punch.

—*Jeremy, University of Chicago*

I chose a school with no core requirements because I wanted to be somewhere where I could make my own academic decisions. Really, if you're smart enough to get into Amherst, you're smart enough to shape your own education. What are you interested in? Now's the time to pursue it. If certain classes aren't your thing, why should you be wasting your time with them? And having no core means that, in every class, all of your classmates want to be there—they're students who chose each class from hundreds of options because they were honestly engaged and energized by the topic. That makes such a difference. Then, four years later when you graduate, you'll be able to look back and realize you learned exactly what *you* wanted to learn in college, not what some faceless bureaucrat said you should be learning.

—*Ying, Amherst College*

ACADEMIC DEPARTMENTS

I wish I'd known that some schools with great general reputations have some departments that are positively poor. If there's a possibility your interests will change in college (and really, for whom is that not a possibility?), don't find yourself caught somewhere with strong departments that only match your ex-interests. Make a list of five areas you might want to major in, and apply to schools with more than a couple good professors in each area.

—*Hu, Johns Hopkins University*

It's sometimes helpful to look at colleges with specific majors in mind. If you want to be an English major, see how big or small the English department is at different schools. Are the majors close with each other and the faculty? Are there superstar professors, and how easy is it to take classes with them? Find out about individual departments in individual schools, because even schools with great overall reputations can have poor departments, and if those poor departments are in the areas you'd like to specialize in, you may find yourself one disappointed duck.

—*Claire, Kenyon College*

Know this: going to a top-notch school doesn't benefit you if you're not planning to major in one of its top-notch programs.

—*Lila, Dartmouth College*

I wish I'd known how little top-tier schools differ in the quality of education they offer. Except for maybe science majors (who require resources for laboratory research) and preprofessionals (who require resources for competitive job placement), a liberal arts education is a liberal arts education, and most departments are of comparable quality. Don't waste your time trying to decide whether one sociology department is better than the next.

—*Thane, Lewis & Clark College*

POLITICAL CLIMATE

My school is frighteningly apathetic. No one gets worked up over issues. I don't know if people are Democrat or Republican—I don't think *they* know if they're Democrat or Republican. They don't care enough. I can't stand it. If you're into politics, don't go to an apolitical school or you'll go mad when no one's protesting over major issues.

—*Jim, Wake Forest University*

I wanted a political climate in college where I'd be challenged instead of a climate where everyone would be just like me. I'm pretty far left, so I thought I'd attend a conservative school where I'd meet lots of smart Republicans who could attack my liberal views in a meaningful way. But somehow I wound up falling in love with Bard College, a haven for raging lefties. Here, I've found something surprising: just because everyone's liberal (or conservative) at a school doesn't mean they all agree with each other. To the contrary—coming to a school where everyone agrees on the basics, you get to explore the normally hidden nuances of "left" or "right." I've now had the opportunity to spend four years refining my liberal thoughts, to be deeply and thoughtfully questioned about the minute elements of my opinion in a way that I may never be again. I now realize I'll spend the rest of my life arguing with Republicans; but for now, I'm happy in a liberal utopia.

—*Rayanne, Bard College*

I'm a conservative at a liberal school, and people here think I'm unintelligent, uninteresting, misinformed, and won't listen to me for more than thirty seconds before drowning me out because I voted for Bush. You know what I've found? I've found sometimes "liberal" really just means "close-minded to anyone who doesn't think exactly like me."

—*Leora, Sarah Lawrence College*

I think American schools are fundamentally less educational when they're bastions of liberalism or conservatism. Critical thinking ceases in such a climate. It's better to have both sides represented, so ideas can actually be challenged, and so you can study, and be taught, in an environment somewhat like the real world you're about to enter.

—*Lawrence, Tufts University*

RACE

Just last night I had a conversation with a friend from another school about how deceptive events for prospective students of color can be. Both he and I visited our respective universities during a time specifically set aside for students of color, and we were both left with misleading perceptions of what the student body actually looked like. If I have any advice for high school seniors, it's this: keep in mind that the amount of people of color one sees, even the events that are hosted, are specific to particular times, and may not accurately reflect what your experience at any given university would be. Don't always believe the hype.

As far as general advice for students of color: find a school with a strong student of color community. When considering "community," you have to look past the sheer number of students of color. Is there cohesion among them? A sense of collective identity? Or is the population fractured irreconcilably into different cultural groups and social cliques?

You can usually get a sense of all this by asking students milling around campus, both white students and other students of color. If not, phone an admissions office and ask to talk to a student of color. Most will understand your plight, some will have been through it, and most will be willing to give you an honest answer.

—*Zaahira, Wesleyan University*

RELIGION

I wish I had looked at religious life on campus more to make sure it was a good fit. I didn't realize it would be so important to have friends who share my faith and beliefs. I felt misled when I arrived here, because I'd heard 30 percent of Haverford is Jewish, but the reality behind that figure is that most Jewish students aren't involved in Jewish life on campus. I wish I'd spoken to an actual student about this. This goes for students of every religion—know that a large percentage of (Jewish/Christian/Muslim/etc.) kids at a school does not equal an active (Jewish/Christian/Muslim/etc.) community.

—*Rachel, Haverford College*

CLASS

During the interview and visitation process, I wish I'd known to ask about class in regard to "diversity" statistics. Many schools boast having 15 percent African American students and 15 percent Latino American students, but it turns out these students are mostly recruited from wealthy private schools. I wish I'd known to ask how many nonwhite students came from *non*-upper-middle and upper-class backgrounds. And, generally, I wish I'd known how many kids were wealthy, and how many weren't, to get more of a feel for how I'd fit in, and for how the student body on the whole operated.

—*Doris, Pomona College*

SEXUALITY

When it comes to the LGBT scene, not all colleges were created equal. Few colleges are outright homophobic, and not many are gay meccas—but our little rainbow can be so many shades of gray at the schools in between. Want to know how gay a school is? Talk to queer students who go there. It's scary at first, but you can get in contact with queer students: surf the school's Web site for the gay organization(s), then phone or e-mail whoever they provide as the contact. People running these organizations are always happy to talk with fellow homos, including high-school-aged homos—they were in your shoes not so long ago. If that doesn't work, ask admissions!! Those offices have been notoriously unhelpful to Our Kind in the past (why is it so hard to understand that sometimes when we visit with our parents, we can't ask in front of them what we'd really like to know?!), but you can always call the office afterward (they don't file notes from your conversations in the application—and if you're concerned about whether it's confidential, just ask). People in the office will usually tell you the truth. Or after the tour's over, ask your (seemingly) straight tour guide.

—*Michael, Carleton College*

GENDER IDENTITY

If you're a trans student wanting to find out more info on trans-life on campus, see if there are folks (not necessarily found through admissions) who will give you advice and clue you in on the climate. Health Services is a good place to start. Queer organizations can be helpful. Google search "trans" and the name of the school and see what comes up. Queer studies professors can often let you know what it will be like. Take a look at the forms the school has people fill in— is the space for gender blank, or do you have to check male/female? That's a sign. Is there gender neutral housing? That's a sign, too. If gender neutral isn't an option, you might want to find out how much more expensive a single room would be, and if the college will waive the difference because of trans concerns. A lot of schools have nondiscrimination clauses—check and see if trans is included—if it is, that school is required to accommodate you—don't be bashful about asking whether they actually will.

It's also important to figure out the level of trans awareness on campus. Are there people on campus already educating students about trans stuff? How much work would you have to do yourself, and how much work are you willing to do? Do you want to pass, and do you stand a good chance of doing so, given physical stuff and university housing/name change/etc. issues? These are all good questions to ask. I know this isn't totally comprehensive, but at least it's a place to start.

—*Paige, Wesleyan University*

RANKINGS

I was caught up in economizing colleges: calculating the costs, comparing statistics on class sizes, factoring in every ranking and ratio I could find. In the end, I found that—although some of the above can be important—focusing on it too much makes you forget about the crucial, personal side of each school. By that I mean a school's environment, its students, its social scene, everything that simply can't be quantified. What do I wish I'd known back when I was in high school? That choosing a college shouldn't be a business decision. It should be a personal decision. That's key.

—*Hilda, Haverford College*

I used college rankings a lot—they introduced me to really good schools that I hadn't heard of before. They're also a pretty accurate barometer of a school's reputation, which matters to future employers and grad schools. And honestly? To people like me, I'd love to say a higher-ranked college doesn't impress me anymore than a lower-ranked one, but that's just not true.

—*Laura, Haverford College*

I wish I had understood that "rankings," those annoying numerical strata magazines publish every year, mean very little. I remember all my high school friends fawning over a girl who went to Harvard (the same friends who rode me for wanting to attend Penn State). It turns out Ms. Harvard and I are now going to very comparable law schools, even though I went to a lesser-ranked school as an undergraduate.

—*Sara, Penn State University*

Do you think there's really a difference in the quality of education you'd get at a number three-ranked vs. number twenty-three-ranked school—especially when this year's number three-ranked school will be next year's number seven-ranked school? Are these numbers saying anything about how much *you'll* fit in at these schools, whether you'll like most of the people there, whether its strong departments will actually interest you?

—*Claudio, Yale University*

I wish I'd known that despite the rankings, there are amazing amounts of fools at every university. And incredibly intelligent people everywhere, too. Honestly, throw away your rankings!

—*Noam, NYU*

Research Tools and Techniques

College guides are just one type of resource for looking into schools. Here are a few other resources students found helpful:

1. Read **college brochures**. But realize these are going to be half truth and half lies. Brochures are trying to sell a product to you. Keep that in mind.

   —*Frank, Wabash College*

- Realize brochures never tell the whole story. But don't abandon them. They're useful for the truths they do contain, and for what they imply about every school. How exactly is each school trying to sell itself? What types of students is it looking to attract? What information has each school included—and what has it *not* included—in its materials?

2. When it's time to search for colleges, **the Internet** is your friend!

   —*Molly, Swarthmore College*

   - Fish around on each college's Web site. They list the classes you could take, the sorts of resources available to students, events going on every week. They also have useful links to the student newspaper and to student group Web sites.
   - Search for the university's name using Google and see what comes up. Does one school's research constantly make headlines? Is another one associated with a lot of activist groups?

3. It turns out most college Web sites have a **student activities** page listing different clubs and e-mail contact information for those clubs. Find this page, find a few clubs you might be interested in joining, and contact the club leaders. Don't ask them for a dissertation on their club and their school—college kids are busy!—but do ask a couple questions they can answer quickly. That'll give you a better idea of what that school is like for people with your interests.

   —*Kyle, Davidson College*

   - Kyle said it all!

4. Feel free to **contact individual professors, coaches, religious leaders,** etc., at the schools you're interested in, and talk to them on the phone or through e-mail. Sometimes they won't mind chatting with prospective students, and they can really help you get to know a school better.

   —*Jessica, Hamilton College*

   - If you have interest in a particular area of academic or campus life, ask about it! You can find contact information for faculty, coaches, chaplains, etc., online, or you can phone the admissions office and ask for it directly. Yes, these are all busy people—but Jessica's right: they often don't mind taking a few minutes to answer your questions. Just make it easy for them: avoid "what's the biology department like?" questions that would take them two hours to answer. Instead, ask quick questions that are well thought out and incisive: "Does your lab do research with undergraduates?" Be considerate of their time, and they'll often try to be helpful to you.

5. *. . . And finally, we heard a constant chorus of:*

I wish someone had told me that you can't learn a thing about a college without **speaking to current college students.** I chose where to apply based solely on a book and some Web pages. After I was accepted at a few schools, I began visiting them and talking to the students who go there, trying to figure out where I'd eventually wind up. Only then did I get the real information; only then did I find out that a lot of my preconceptions about each school were entirely incorrect.

—*Eben, Reed*

I wish I'd **talked to more students** because they're the only ones who really know what each school is like on a day-to-day basis.

—*Sarah, Johns Hopkins*

Always **seek out answers from students** because they won't sugarcoat anything.

—*Danielle, Mount Holyoke*

You can research a school's policies, etc., as much as you want before you apply but you will never find everything. It's best to just go to campus and **talk to some random students** and see what they say.

—*Karin, Penn State*

Visiting Campuses

From a current college student to you, here's some advice—it's more important to visit the schools you're interested in than it is to maintain a good high school attendance record. The college decision will shape four years of your life, and getting an actual experience at the colleges you're considering will really affect your choice. So get out there and visit schools, even if you have to take a few days off from high school to do it.

—*Electra, Grinnell College*

PLANNING A VISIT

- Some schools require that you sign up in advance for tours and information sessions.

- Some schools offer overnight visits. Slots often fill up fast, so schedule these early.
- Visit while schools are in session: a campus might look nice in the summertime, but will feel very different when students are actually there.
- Plan to visit no more than two schools in a day, and make sure even that expectation is realistic. College tours often run longer than their officially scheduled hour, and you'll be processing a lot of information at once.

WALKING AROUND ON CAMPUS

Pay attention to posters, because they'll tell you both what you can do on campus that night and whether the school has interests that suit your own. If you're obsessed with drumming and you only see two music posters on five different bulletin boards, you might want to think twice about whether you'd be happy at that particular school.

—Solomon, Caltech

The best thing you can do on a campus visit is sit and watch people. How do students interact with each other? Do they seem excited about what they're discussing? Are kids carrying a lot of books? Are professors and kids mingling? Is everyone in a hurry? What do the posters say? What does the chalk on the sidewalk say? Can you see yourself talking to that kid on the bike? Can you picture yourself as the kid over in the corner, whistling and reading a magazine? Just sit. Watch. Listen.

—Meghan, Colorado College

I wish I had had more flexible impressions of college students. I know it sounds strange, but I expected good students to be carrying stacks of intimidating-looking books while shuffling off to the library for seven hours or so at a time. Now that I'm here, I realize that the most intellectually stimulating and interesting people are the ones that I wouldn't have thought of as smart when I was still in high school. Sometimes the smartest kids are the hippie stoners, or the gorgeous jocks. Observe as much as you can, but keep an open mind.

—Lauren-Anne, Kenyon College

Extracurriculars tend to reflect where students' interests lie—and they're a really big part of campus life. Find out which are the most popular student groups—are they politically charged, artistically oriented? What kind of climate does that create? Are you going to be able to find students who share your interests? And if your interests change, are there a variety of other activities available? Some student bodies spend as many hours protesting and performing as they do studying or partying—how many activities do most students do at once, and what would *your* ideal be?

—*Farrah, Pitzer College*

TAKING A TOUR

If you have the option, try splitting up from your parents on tours. You go on one tour, make them go on another. That way they can ask all the embarrassing questions they want, without your wanting to shrivel up and die. And you have the hour to yourself to walk around campus and envision whether you could live there independently.

—*Zhaoxuan, Evergreen State College*

Hi. I give tours at Antioch. A bit of advice from a tour guide to you: Sometimes parents seem to think that just because I give tours, I have an "in" with all the admissions officers. Please tell your Dad: I don't!!! I'm not going to run upstairs after the tour, pull out your kid's file, and mark somewhere in the margins "Excellent. Father asks good questions. Kid must be admitted."

—*Quinn, Antioch College*

Don't worry: if your tour guide is bad, there are plenty of other ways to get information about a school. It's scary at first, but you should really just try approaching students (use common sense: people who look like they're hanging out are probably a better bet than those who are rushing around late for a class). Students used to be high school seniors themselves, can totally empathize with you, and will usually give you a lot more helpful information than your tour guide ever would. To pass that miserable "this building was built in 1831!" tour, though, make your sister come on the tour with you and spend the entire hour speculating about what kind of tail everyone on your tour would have, if humans had animal tails. It's fun.

—*Adrien, Wellesley College*

ATTENDING AN INFO SESSION

When visiting lots of schools, go to each school's info session and ask the same question. If the question is carefully constructed, the different answers can illuminate a lot about the differences between schools.

—*Herman, Duke University*

Go to info sessions only if your parents make you. The official, manufactured perspective of a school is never what the school is really like. Think about it. Would you go ask a Philip Morris PR guy if you wanted to learn about the effects of smoking?

—*Yaw, Harvard University*

STAYING OVERNIGHT

Did you know you can visit colleges and stay overnight for free? I wish I did! You'll get a much better feel for how students actually live if you get to spend a day with them than you would just parading around the prettiest area of campus on a narrated tour. And it's really only through hanging out with students that you can tell whether you'd fit in. Just be sure, when you're there, to put in extra effort to be as easygoing and outgoing as possible.

—*Daniel, Case Western Reserve University*

When I visited Rice as a prospective, I looked at my host as the Ultimate Answerer of All Questions Pertaining to Rice. While she was a very considerate and thoughtful host, relying only on her limited perspective caused me to misunderstand some important aspects of Rice, and only showed me a partial portrait of the school. So keep that in mind. Even what you see on an overnight isn't definitive or wholly representative.

—*Crystal, Rice University*

TAKING IT ALL IN

Whether you're doing a single whirlwind tour or stretching your visits out over the course of a summer, remember to write down what you liked (and disliked) most about each college after you visit, both so you can differentiate between schools later and so you won't forget the small details.

—*Megan, Bates College*

The Application, Briefly

We received thousands of pieces of advice about how to put together your college application. Briefly, here's what students who have done it before wanted to tell you:

CRAFTING YOUR APPLICATION

Honestly, I was too timid when trying to sell myself. There's this idea that admissions officers will be able to read between the lines—but they only know what you tell them. If you're an amazing person, now's not the time to be modest about it. It's not bragging. It's letting them know exactly who you are.

—*Kaylan, Furman University*

Back in high school, I wish I'd known to toot my own horn. Colleges don't want pompous, but they do want intelligent and unique. Think about it. What sets you apart from everyone else? Now make sure, be absolutely certain, that comes across in your application.

—*Shemeka, College of William and Mary*

I wish I'd known how time-consuming the process of applying to colleges really is.

—*Daniel, Williams College*

START APPLYING TO COLLEGES EARLIER THAN WINTER BREAK. NO, SERIOUSLY!!!!!!

—*Karen, Johns Hopkins University*

EARY DECISION: PROS

- If you're accepted to a school early decision, you *must* attend.
- In applying early, you're telling the school there's nowhere else you'd rather go; they consider your application accordingly.
- If you get into a school ED, you'll know where you're going to college by early December.

EARLY DECISION: CONS

- If you get in early, you miss out on five potentially introspective months, during which you might have changed and discovered a school potentially better suited to your needs.
- You won't be able to evaluate one school's financial aid package against another's. (Financial aid packages can vary widely.)

EARLY DECISION II

- Same as early decision, but with a later set of deadlines.
- If you don't get into a school EDI, you can apply to another school EDII.

EARLY ACTION

- Same as early decision, but not binding.

ROLLING DEADLINES

- Schools accept applicants as soon as applications filter in.
- The sooner you apply, the more spots there are—apply as early as possible.

HOW MANY SCHOOLS SHOULD I APPLY TO?

- Apply to a few reach schools (schools that could well reject you, but you have a shot). It's worth paying the extra application fees—it's an unpredictable process, and kids with low SAT scores *do* get into Ivies.
- Apply to a few target schools (schools where you have a reasonable chance).
- And apply to a few safety schools (schools that regularly accept students less impressive than yourself).
- Apply to too many schools, and you'll drown in paperwork. Apply to too few, and you run the risk of being forced to go to somewhere less than enthralling. Most students said they applied to seven to ten schools.

THE PAPER TRAIL

- If you're financially strapped, you can get waivers so you don't have to pay fees for your applications and SATs. Look into this through the College Board.
- Using the Common Application often saves a lot of time—but don't forget the supplements required by many Common App. schools.
- Applying online also saves time—but *always* save and print your work as you go!
- Make and keep copies of everything you submit to colleges. Schools deal with hundreds of thousands of pieces of paper, and sometimes things get lost. This makes it easy to resend lost information.
- A month after applying, phone admissions offices to ensure they've received everything.
- College admissions officers annually visit most major cities. Phone a college's admissions office and find out whether they're planning to send someone to your area. Make a point of attending their event and speaking with them afterward.
- Admissions officers are people too. And they often honestly care about your future and whether their school would be right for you. Don't be intimidated by them.

ACTS AND SATS

- Schedule your tests early. That way you'll have time to take every test—and if you don't like you scores, to take every test one more time.
- Study hard and study early.

- Prep courses help enforce disciplined studying, but you can save yourself hundreds of dollars by buying and studying a (much cheaper) prep book that covers the same material.

EXTRACURRICULARS

- Don't do extracurricular activities in high school because you think colleges want you to do them—do things because *you* want to do them. Admissions officers are good at discerning honest passions from résumé fillers.
- Some colleges seek well-rounded individuals; others look for students who do individual things extremely well. Don't stress about which you should be. It's a cliché, but it's true: the best thing you can be on a college application is yourself.

THE ESSAY

- Use your essay to tell admissions officers about you as a person. This is your chance to show them how you think, to stress all the human qualities that didn't come through in your transcript and SATs.
- Start your essay in advance so you can work on it, leave it alone for a few weeks, then come back to it with fresh eyes.
- Get input on your essay from a teacher or an adult whose opinion you trust and respect, and who won't sugarcoat his feedback. Go through multiple revisions.
- It's usually possible to just write one essay and slightly tweak it for every school.

LETTERS OF RECOMMENDATION

- If you send more letters of recommendation than colleges ask for, colleges may not read them.
- Some colleges would rather hear from a teacher who knows you worked hard for a B than a teacher who knows you got an A on natural smarts alone.
- Give your teachers plenty of time and ask them in a way that allows them a chance to say no.
- Provide teachers with all the materials they'll need: stamped, pre-addressed envelopes, an updated summary of the achievements and personal qualities you hope your application will convey to college admissions officers, and why you're interested in each school.

- Schedule interviews early; if you can't make it to campus, alumni often do off-campus interviews that hold just as much weight.
- Interviewers make notes, and admissions officers read those notes when evaluating your application. What do you want those notes to say? Keep in mind if you spend your interview regurgitating what's already in your application, those notes won't say anything new to help your case.
- Interviews are the time for schools to get to know you—and for you to get to know each school. Don't be shy about asking lots and lots of questions. This is usually a sign of interest, not ignorance.
- Just be yourself. There are no "right" answers, and being uptight will only keep your real personality from shining through.
- There is no such thing as the Perfect Interview Outfit.

Finding Out

THICK ENVELOPES

If everything goes according to plan, if you get into the school of your dreams, if you wind up with that legendary thick envelope in your mailbox—hey man, congratulations. Nice work. Welcome to college.

—Brian, Stanford University

THIN ENVELOPES

Everyone stresses a lot over whether they'll be rejected. I would have killed to know that I didn't need to worry so much. It's not really about the name of a school; it's about the fit. If you get rejected from a school, you don't need those bastards. You probably would have hated that school anyway.

—Allison, Oberlin College

Everything happens for a reason—even college rejections. Notre Dame wasn't my first choice, but it still ended up being the best thing that ever happened to me. If I could do it all over again, it would be my only choice.

—Alexandra, Notre Dame University

Some of my friends weren't accepted to their dream schools. They were disappointed, and initially very upset, but they adjusted and went to other schools with a positive attitude. Every single one of them has, since then, had an awesome time. I think it's your attitude that can really make or break the college experience.

—Mary-Catherine, Colby College

Public Service Number 1: Venting

We ran a quick analysis and found that literally hundreds of students called the college admissions process "random," "a crapshoot," or "arbitrary." Thought you were alone in your frustrations? Think again! It's utterly gratuitous, but we figured the least we could do was print a page of your peers (who all ended up at very good schools) saying aloud what you were no doubt thinking:

I wish I had known how random it was.

—*Megan, Cornell University*

I wish someone had told me just how random the college admissions process can be.

—*Sarah, Kenyon College*

The process is totally random. No, really, it is.

—*Elliott, University of Chicago*

It's a complete crapshoot.

—*Rachael, Barnard College*

I wish I'd known that it is a total crapshoot.

—*Vanessa, Notre Dame University*

It's a total and complete crapshoot.

—*Thomas, Lehigh University*

I wish I could have actually believed people when they told me how arbitrary it was!

—*Shana, Mount Holyoke College*

It's arbitrary. Ar-Bi-Tra-Ree. Utterly and totally arbitrary.

—*Dana, Bucknell University*

Reasons to Relax

In high school, I wish someone had told me to relax. I felt pressure from every direction; my grades had to be exceptional, my SATs had to be perfect, college is serious, I have to be happy and talented and special, and blah blah blah. Everyone had an opinion for me, whether I wanted to hear it or not. It stressed me out. I honestly wish someone had said to me, "Look Danielle, just go to a school that makes you happy and as long as your grades are decent, you'll be fine."

—*Danielle, Gettysburg College*

I wish I'd known that it's okay not to know! I spent much of my senior year of high school very stressed out because all my friends were applying to schools early decision and choosing preprofessional programs and I felt clueless about my Future Path. Back then, it never occurred to me that it was okay to not know exactly what I wanted out of life at age seventeen.

—*Alexandra, UNC Chapel Hill*

The whole process is overblown. Parents, counselors, fellow students, the whole lot of it. Way too much emphasis is put on the things that are really quite irrelevant when examined in the context of *life*. By college graduation, you will have forgotten your SAT score, and *nobody* will ever ask, for the rest of your life, what you got. Just relax: what college you go to will *not* dictate the rest of your life, only *you* will.

—*Adam, Colgate University*

I wish I'd known that the whole process sucks no matter what, but things work out in the end.

—*Jennifer, Connecticut College*

Public Service Number 2: Stress

In addition, nearly 10 percent of respondents called applying to college "stressful." Hey, nobody said the process was easy. (Literally—nobody.) But there were a ton who did say they wish they knew:

It is the most unnecessarily stressful part of your teenage years!

—*Ben, Colorado College*

I wish I'd known not to stress.

—*Jaime, Colorado College*

Not to stress too much.

—*Lauren, Bryn Mawr College*

Not to stress so much.

—*Jennifer, Penn State University*

Not to stress so much.

—*Tiffany, Harvard University*

I wish I'd known that you don't really have to be so stressed out about it all. I realize now that regardless of what college I went to, I'd have roughly the same experience; everything in life is what you make of it.

—*Ann, Johns Hopkins University*

There is really no point in stressing about it; everything happens for a reason. I never thought I would end up here at UVA, but it turned out to be the best experience of my life (so far).

—*Defne, University of Virginia*

Relax! Once you apply, it's out of your hands. That's when you should stop stressing and let it go.

—*Sandra, MIT*

I wish that I could have enjoyed my senior year of high school more because I stressed over my applications so much—I forgot to have fun, too!

—*Monica, Gettysburg College*

Final Thoughts

I wish I'd known . . . nothing. It's not really all that important. Write a good essay. Be fairly interesting. Don't look like you're about to commit suicide if you get stressed out. I doubt the school wants the liability. Don't think that just because you played with LEGO as a kid that you are born to go to MIT. Everyone plays with LEGO. Just go somewhere that fits, and it'll be great.

—*Nick, MIT*

Enjoy senior year. Try hard, yes . . . but don't stress out and study your whole life away. Do what you love most, and do it well. Don't fill your plate with meaningless and time-consuming positions just to impress admissions officers. Most of the time, they can see through that anyway. Dedicate yourself to something you love, and work your butt off to improve what you love. Be honest in your application and interview; just be yourself, and you'll be more impressive than you could ever be by trying.

—*Lauren, Rice University*

School Indexes

BY SIZE

Small
Amherst College
Antioch College
Bard College
Barnard College
Bates College
Berea College
Bowdoin College
Bryn Mawr College
California Institute of
    Technology
Carleton College
Claremont McKenna College
Colby College
Colorado College
Connecticut College
Davidson College
Gettysburg College
Grinnell College
Hamilton College
Hampshire College
Harvey Mudd College
Haverford College
Hendrix College
Kenyon College
Lewis & Clark College
Middlebury College
Mount Holyoke College
Pitzer College
Pomona College
Reed College
Sarah Lawrence College
Scripps College
Spelman College
Swarthmore College
Trinity College

Vassar College
Wabash College
Washington and Lee University
Wellesley College
Whitman College
Williams College

Medium
Brandeis University
Brown University
Bucknell University
Carnegie Mellon University
Case Western Reserve University
University of Chicago
Colgate University
Columbia University
Dartmouth College
Duke University
Emory University
Evergreen State College
Furman University
Georgetown University
Harvard University
College of the Holy Cross
Howard University
Johns Hopkins University
Lehigh University
Macalester College
Massachusetts Institute of
    Technology
Morehouse College
Oberlin College
Princeton University
Rice University
Smith College
Stanford University
Tufts University
Vanderbilt University

Wake Forest University
Washington University in
    St. Louis Wesleyan University
College of William and Mary
Yale University

Big
Boston College
Boston University
UC Berkeley
UCLA
UC San Diego
UC Santa Cruz
University of Colorado at
    Boulder
Cornell University
George Washington University
Georgia Institute of Technology
University of Massachusetts
    Amherst
University of Michigan
New York University
University of North Carolina at
    Chapel Hill
Northwestern University
University of Notre Dame
University of Pennsylvania
Pennsylvania State University
Rutgers University
University of Southern Cali-
    fornia
SUNY–Binghamton
University of Texas at Austin
Tulane University
University of Virginia
University of Washington
University of Wisconsin—
    Madison

Washington University in
St. Louis
University of Wisconsin—
Madison

South
Berea College
Davidson College
Duke University
Emory University
Furman University
George Washington University
Georgetown University
Georgia Institute of Technology
Hendrix College
Howard University
Morehouse College
University of North Carolina at
Chapel Hill
Rice University
Spelman College
University of Texas at Austin
Tulane University
University of Virginia
Vanderbilt University
Wake Forest University
Washington and Lee University
College of William and Mary

Northeast
Amherst College
Bard College
Barnard College
Bates College
Boston College
Bowdoin College
Brandeis University
Brown University
Bryn Mawr College
Boston University
Bucknell University
Carnegie Mellon University
Colby College
Colgate University
Columbia University
Connecticut College
Cornell University
Dartmouth College
Gettysburg College
Hamilton College
Hampshire College
Harvard University

Haverford College
College of the Holy Cross
Johns Hopkins University
Lehigh University
University of Massachusetts
Amherst
Massachusetts Institute of
Technology
Middlebury College
Mount Holyoke College
New York University
University of Pennsylvania
Pennsylvania State University
Princeton University
Rutgers University
Sarah Lawrence College
Smith College
SUNY–Binghamton
Swarthmore College
Trinity College
Tufts University
Vassar College
Wellesley College
Wesleyan University
Williams College
Yale University

BY STATE

Arkansas
Hendrix College

California
UC Berkeley
UCLA
UC San Diego
UC Santa Cruz
California Institute of
Technology
Claremont McKenna College
Harvey Mudd College
Pitzer College
Pomona College
Scripps College
Stanford University
University of Southern California

Colorado
Colorado College
University of Colorado at
Boulder

Connecticut
Connecticut College
Trinity College
Wesleyan University
Yale University

Georgia
Emory University
Georgia Institute of Technology
Morehouse College
Spelman College

Illinois
Northwestern University
University of Chicago

Indiana
University of Notre Dame
Wabash College

Iowa
Grinnell College

Kentucky
Berea College

Louisiana
Tulane University

Maine
Bates College
Bowdoin College
Colby College

Maryland
Johns Hopkins University

Massachusetts
Amherst College
Boston College
Brandeis University
Boston University
Hampshire College
Harvard University
College of the Holy Cross
University of Massachusetts
Amherst
Massachusetts Institute of
Technology
Mount Holyoke College
Smith College
Tufts University

Wellesley College
Williams College

Michigan
University of Michigan

Minnesota
Carleton College
Macalester College

Missouri
Washington University in St.
   Louis

New Hampshire
Dartmouth College

New Jersey
Princeton University
Rutgers University

New York
Bard College
Barnard College
Colgate University
Columbia University
Cornell University
Hamilton College
New York University
Sarah Lawrence College
SUNY–Binghamton
Vassar College

North Carolina
Davidson College
Duke University
University of North Carolina at
   Chapel Hill
Wake Forest University

Ohio
Antioch College
Case Western Reserve University
Kenyon College
Oberlin College

Oregon
Reed College

Pennsylvania
Bryn Mawr College
Bucknell University

Carnegie Mellon University
Gettysburg College
Haverford College
Lehigh University
University of Pennsylvania
Pennsylvania State University
Swarthmore College

Rhode Island
Brown University

South Carolina
Furman University

Tennessee
Vanderbilt University

Texas
Rice University
University of Texas at Austin

Vermont
Middlebury College

Virginia
University of Virginia
Washington and Lee University
College of William and Mary

Washington
Evergreen State College
Lewis & Clark College
University of Washington
Whitman College

Washington, D.C.
George Washington University
Georgetown University
Howard University

Wisconsin
University of Wisconsin—
   Madison

BY INTELLECTUAL FERVOR

**Students talk academics *all*
the time**
Bard College
Brown University
Bryn Mawr College

California Institute of
   Technology
Carleton College
Carnegie Mellon University
Case Western Reserve University
University of Chicago
Claremont McKenna College
Columbia University
Davidson College
Georgetown University
Georgia Institute of Technology
Grinnell College
Hampshire College
Haverford College
Hendrix College
Johns Hopkins University
Kenyon College
Macalester College
Massachusetts Institute of
   Technology
Northwestern University
Oberlin College
Reed College
Rice University
Sarah Lawrence College
Swarthmore College
Vassar College
Wellesley College
Wesleyan University

Sometimes
Amherst College
Barnard College
Bates College
Berea College
Bowdoin College
Brandeis College
UC Berkeley
UCLA
UC San Diego
UC Santa Cruz
Colby College
Colorado College
Connecticut College
Evergreen State College
Furman University
George Washington University
Hamilton College
Harvard University
Harvey Mudd College
College of the Holy Cross
Howard University

Lewis & Clark College
University of Michigan
Middlebury College
Morehouse College
Mount Holyoke College
University of North Carolina at
    Chapel Hill
University of Pennsylvania
Pitzer College
Pomona College
Princeton University
Scripps College
Smith College
Spelman College
Stanford University
Tufts University
Vanderbilt University
Wabash College
University of Washington
Washington and Lee University
Washington University in St.
    Louis
Whitman College
College of William and Mary
Williams College
Yale University

Hardly ever
Antioch College
Boston College
Boston University
Bucknell University
Colgate University
University of Colorado at
    Boulder
Cornell University
Dartmouth College
Duke University
Emory University
Gettysburg College
Lehigh University
University of Massachusetts
    Amherst
New York University
University of Notre Dame
Pennsylvania State University
Rutgers University
University of Southern Cali-
    fornia
SUNY Binghamton
University of Texas at Austin
Trinity College

Tulane University
University of Virginia
Wake Forest University
University of Wisconsin—
    Madison

**BY INTENSITY OF
NIGHTLIFE**

Intense
Boston College
Bucknell University
Colgate University
University of Colorado at
    Boulder
Cornell University
Dartmouth College
Davidson College
Duke University
Emory University
Gettysburg College
Hamilton College
College of the Holy Cross
Lehigh University
University of Massachusetts
    Amherst
Massachusetts Institute of
    Technology
University of Pennsylvania
Pennsylvania State University
Rice University
Rutgers University
University of Southern Cali-
    fornia
University of Texas at Austin
Trinity College
Tulane University
Vanderbilt University
University of Virginia
Wake Forest University
Washington and Lee University
Washington University in St.
    Louis
Williams College
University of Wisconsin—
    Madison

Moderate
Barnard College
Bates
Bowdoin College

Brown University
Boston University
UC Berkeley
UCLA
UC San Diego
UC Santa Cruz
Carleton College
Carnegie Mellon University
Claremont McKenna College
Colby College
Colorado College
Columbia University
Connecticut College
Furman University
George Washington University
Georgetown University
Harvard University
Harvey Mudd College
Hendrix College
Howard University
Kenyon College
University of Michigan
Middlebury College
Morehouse College
New York University
University of North Carolina at
    Chapel Hill
Northwestern University
University of Notre Dame
Oberlin College
Pomona College
Princeton University
Reed College
Stanford University
SUNY–Binghamton
Tufts University
Wabash College
University of Washington
Wesleyan University
Yale University

Laid-back
Amherst College
Antioch College
Bard College
Berea College
Brandeis University
Bryn Mawr College
California Institute of
    Technology
Case Western Reserve University
University of Chicago

Evergreen State College
Georgia Institute of Technology
Grinnell College
Hampshire College
Haverford College
Johns Hopkins University
Lewis & Clark College
Macalester College
Mount Holyoke College
Pitzer College
Sarah Lawrence College
Scripps College
Smith College
Spelman College
Swarthmore College
Vassar College
Wellesley College
Whitman College
College of William and Mary

BY POLITICAL LEANING

Left
Antioch College
Bard College
Barnard College
Bates College
Boston University
Bowdoin College
Brandeis University
Brown University
Bryn Mawr College
UC Berkeley
UCLA
UC San Diego
UC Santa Cruz
Carleton College
Carnegie Mellon University
University of Chicago
Colorado College
Columbia University
Connecticut College
Cornell University
Evergreen State College
Grinnell College
Hampshire College
Harvey Mudd College
Haverford College
Hendrix College
Kenyon College
Lewis & Clark College

Macalester College
University of Massachusetts
    Amherst
Massachusetts Institute of
    Technology
Middlebury College
Mount Holyoke College
New York University
Oberlin College
University of Pennsylvania
Pitzer College
Pomona College
Reed College
Sarah Lawrence College
Scripps College
Smith College
Spelman College
Swarthmore College
Vassar College
Washington University in
    St. Louis
Wellesley College
Wesleyan University
Whitman College

Split
Amherst College
Bucknell College
California Institute of
    Technology
Claremont McKenna College
Colby College
University of Colorado at
    Boulder
Dartmouth College
Davidson College
Emory University
George Washington University
Gettysburg College
Harvard University
Howard University
Johns Hopkins University
University of Michigan
University of North Carolina at
    Chapel Hill
Northwestern University
Pennsylvania State University
Rice University
Rutgers University
Stanford University
SUNY–Binghamton
University of Texas at Austin

Trinity College
Tufts University
Tulane University
University of Washington
College of William and Mary
Williams College
University of Wisconsin—
    Madison
Yale University

Right
Berea College
Boston College
Case Western Reserve University
Colgate University
Duke University
Furman University
Georgetown University
Georgia Institute of Technology
Hamilton College
College of the Holy Cross
Lehigh University
Morehouse College
University of Notre Dame
Princeton University
University of Southern California
Vanderbilt University
University of Virginia
Wabash College
Wake Forest University
Washington and Lee University

BY DIVERSITY

High
Amherst College
Barnard College
Brown University
UC Berkeley
UCLA
UC San Diego
UC Santa Cruz
California Institute of Technology
Carnegie Mellon University
University of Chicago
Columbia University
Dartmouth College
Emory University
Harvard University
Howard University
Johns Hopkins University

Massachusetts Institute of
    Technology
University of Michigan
Morehouse College
Mount Holyoke College
Northwestern University
University of Pennsylvania
Pitzer College
Princeton Morehouse
Rice University
Rutgers University
University of Southern California
Spelman College
Stanford University
Swarthmore College
University of Texas at Austin
Tufts University
University of Washington
Wellesley College
Wesleyan University
Williams College
Yale University

Moderate
Berea College
Boston College
Boston University
Bowdoin College
Brandeis University
Bryn Mawr College
Carleton College
Case Western Reserve University
Claremont McKenna College
Cornell University
Duke University
George Washington University
Georgetown University
Georgia Institute of Technology
Grinnell College
Harvey Mudd College
Haverford College
College of the Holy Cross
Macalester College
University of Massachusetts
    Amherst
Middlebury College
New York University
University of North Carolina at
    Chapel Hill
Oberlin College
Pomona College
Scripps College

Smith College
SUNY–Binghamton
University of Virginia
Washington University in
    St. Louis

Low
Antioch College
Bard College
Bates College
Bucknell University
Colby College
Colgate University
Colorado College
Connecticut College
University of Colorado at Boulder
Davidson College
Evergreen State College
Furman University
Gettysburg College
Hamilton College
Hampshire College
Hendrix College
Kenyon College
Lehigh University
Lewis & Clark College
University of Notre Dame
Pennsylvania State University
Reed College
Sarah Lawrence College
Trinity College
Tulane University
Vanderbilt University
Vassar College
Wabash College
Wake Forest University
Washington & Lee University
Whitman College
University of Wisconsin —
    Madison
College of William and Mary

MISCELLANEOUS INDEXES

Single-Gender Schools

All-Women's
Barnard College
Bryn Mawr College
Mount Holyoke College
Scripps College

Smith College
Spelman College
Wellesley College

All-Men's
Morehouse College
Wabash College

Historically Black Colleges
Howard University
Morehouse College
Spelman College

Five-Colleges Consortiums

Claremont, CA
Claremont McKenna College
Harvey Mudd College
Pitzer College
Pomona College
Scripps College

Amherst, MA
Amherst College
Hampshire College
Mount Holyoke College
Smith College
University of Massachusetts
    Amherst

Ivy League Schools
Brown
Columbia
Cornell
Dartmouth
Harvard
University of Pennsylvania
Princeton
Yale

PAC Ten Schools
UC Berkeley
UCLA
University of Southern California
Stanford University
University of Washington

Big Ten Schools
Pennsylvania State University
University of Michigan
Northwestern University
University of Wisconsin

AMHERST COLLEGE

Founded: 1821

Location: Amherst, MA

Phone: (413) 542-2328

E-mail: admission@amherst.edu

Web site: www.amherst.edu

Number of Undergraduates: 1,618

Number of Graduate Students: 0

Cost: Approximately $38,000 per year

Application Deadline: December 31

Early Decision: November 15

Rating:	Notable Majors/Programs:
Most Selective	English, Political Science, Psychology

Size:
● Small   ○ Medium   ○ Large

Location:
○ Urban   ● Suburban   ○ Rural

On a Saturday, students talk about academics:
○ Always   ● Sometimes   ○ Never

Nightlife:
○ Intense   ○ Moderate   ● Laid-back

Politically, Amherst leans:
○ Left   ○ Right   ● Split

Diversity:
● High   ○ Low   ○ Medium

Five-College school: Yes!

Students describe Amherst in five words:
- Ivy-caliber liberal arts college
- Very small, intense, cliquish, preppy

From the School

[At Amherst], we believe in teaching as conversation, because the best teaching *is* conversation; except by dialogue we cannot do our work. The college, unlike the university, takes the dialogue of professor and student as a master principle. Neither graduate students nor teaching assistants can spell us in this central portion of our vocation. Our scale and our intimacy, our flexibility in moving across and among fields, our openness to one another and to our students—these are the strengths of a community built on dialogue.

—www.amherst.edu

If you're interested in Amherst, you may also be interested in:
Brown, Harvard, Swarthmore, Wesleyan, Williams, Yale

Name: Nicole
Hometown: Kansas City, Missouri
Class Year: Sophomore
Major: French
Extracurriculars: Amherst Feminists, theater productions (acting), literary magazine staff
Career Goal: Obstetrician

How would you describe Amherst's reputation?

Amherst holds a coveted position; it's among the best of the private liberal arts colleges, and grad schools and employers know it. Despite its strong reputation, however, Amherst cannot escape the small college curse: the further you get from New England, the more often you'll get, "Amherst? Never heard of it!"

Is this reputation accurate?

Yes. I transferred from another small New England college, and I can say for sure that Amherst has something, academically and socially, that other schools do not. The work is tough but interesting, the professors are involved and invested, and the students almost always exceed expectations.

What aspect of your school would a prospective student not see on a campus tour?

On the college tour, they'll tell you that Amherst students work hard and play hard. They won't tell you that playing hard means drinking hard. That said, life at any college invariably involves alcohol. Amherst students are college students, and college students tend to drink when they party.

The Institution

One thing that prospective students may not realize about Amherst is that it has the social perks of a small college but the academic feel of a big university. Amherst is part of the Five College Consortium (Amherst College, Hampshire College, Mount Holyoke, Smith College, and UMass Amherst), where students enrolled at any of the above five schools can take classes and participate in activities at any of the other schools. Because of the Five College Consortium, there are hundreds more students at Amherst at any given time than the official undergraduate population of 1,600 kids (400 per grade). This can inflate Amherst's class sizes, but with good, engaging professors (and most of Amherst's professors are good and engag-

ing), that's not a problem. The bonus of this is that you meet all kinds of different people, and if Amherst lacks an educational or social scene that you want, you can tap into the resources of three nearby colleges and one major university (UMass Amherst). Also, on my first day on campus, I attended a transfer student lunch. The president of the college strolled up to each new transfer, offered his hand, and said, "Hi, I'm Tony!" He was so casual and welcoming that it took me a while to figure out that he was actually Amherst's president. Every administrator at this school, from the president on down, is incredibly approachable.

Amherst has an enormous endowment for a small school. Students can almost always get funding for academic projects and social clubs if they look hard enough, and alumni often contribute to the available funds. Hardly anyone transfers out of Amherst, but many want to transfer in. The school looks out for you, challenges you, and prepares you for the real world, and students are grateful and proud to be at Amherst.

The Education

Professors at Amherst are highly qualified and highly respected. They're also so friendly and collegial that you stop thinking of them as intimidating geniuses and start thinking of them as colleagues. They are masters in leading students in discussions: like orchestra conductors they somehow manage to have the class organically drift toward the culmination of a debate, so that it's the students themselves, not the professor, who eventually voice the main point. Professors are ready and willing to enter into academic arguments, and they take students' ideas seriously. Also, they view education as ongoing, and they regularly publish and attend conferences so that they continue to achieve in their field. It's not unheard of for a professor to critique another professor's point of view in the Opinion section of the Amherst paper—which is always both informative and hilarious.

Fortunately and/or unfortunately (depending on your perspective and on how much those involved have had to drink), Amherst students do talk about their classes on Saturday nights. This can be fun, but it can also be irksome. Amherst kids like to drop names like Nietzsche and words like *existential*. Still, debates about the Red Sox and the Yankees happen just as often, which balances things out nicely.

The Students

Amherst students are politically active, and they are ambitious enough to start organizations on campus to tackle the issues they're passionate about. *The Indicator,* a monthly magazine of political thought, is always brimming with articles from conservative and liberal points of view, and discussions often spill over into the "Letters to the Editor" section of *The Amherst Student* [the school's weekly paper]. I'm from Indiana—Republican in every presidential election since Eisenhower—but I've met more involved and opinionated young conservatives at Amherst College than I did in my Hoosier hometown. That said, they are up against tough competition: there are a plethora of "leftist" groups on Amherst's campus, from the Amherst Feminists to an active and confident LGBT [lesbian/gay/bisexual/transgender] alliance.

The Activities

Here's the light bulb joke for Amherst: How many Amherst students does it take to change a light bulb? Answer: Thirteen—one to change the bulb and an a cappella group to immortalize the event in song. One out of every five students at Amherst participates in music in some way, and most are singers. A cappella concerts are going on all the time; a rehearsal in the lounge of my dorm went on until 2 a.m. last night. Odd as it may sound, kids in a cappella groups are usually the popular, outgoing kids who are never hard up for a date.

At the small school I transferred from, it was impossible for nontheater majors to crack into the close-knit theater department, and students at large universities often run into the same problem. The great thing about the Amherst theater department is that it has excellent professors and a lot of resources but few theater students. This means it's easy for anyone to get into theater, regardless of their majors, and as a result there are student-driven productions happening all the time.

Sports are of course huge at Amherst, although many students complain that we can't seem to turn out crowds to match those of our rival school, Williams. But students here still get excited about big games. Here's an example: a finals basketball game against Williams happened to fall during spring break this year, so the administration set up a satellite broadcast so that students could watch the game no matter how far from campus their spring break took them!

The Social Scene

The Greek system was abolished at Amherst in the eighties, but that only means that frats went "underground." There are still fraternities (but no sororities), and even an off-campus "frat house" (with no official relationship with the school's administration). Since it's no longer official, Amherst Greek life is very low key, but it's still out there—mostly for parties.

Amherst's administration has a strict housing policy and almost everyone has to live on campus. This creates a pretty tight-knit community, particularly within dorms. Living on campus doesn't get too claustrophobic, though—the Five College Consortium brings hundreds of students to Amherst to make life interesting. Also, everything in New England is close to everything else. In one semester, I spent two weekends in New York City, one in Boston, and one in Washington, D.C.

Name: Rachel
Hometown: Buffalo, New York
Class Year: Sophomore
Major: Biology and Spanish
Extracurriculars: Cross-country, track and field, Photography Club
Career Goal: To work in medicine or biology research

How would you describe Amherst's reputation?

I imagined Amherst as a place where everyone studies all the time, and where everyone is stuck-up. The stereotype is that Amherst kids are preppy nerds who are overly focused on academics.

Is this reputation accurate?

Kind of. I mean, we do have a lot of work, and some people do spend most of their time studying. However, most students are always willing to take study breaks and party. And we're not really pretentious. Most students are multifaceted and well rounded, active in their academics, community service, some religious organization, and a sports team all at the same time.

What would an admissions officer at your school probably not tell a prospective student?

They wouldn't tell you that there's quite the party scene at Amherst. Sometimes things get a little crazy. Several times a year you can find groups of students (both drunk and sober) running around campus naked.

The Institution

At first I thought Amherst was a bit too small for me, but I've come to realize that I love being able to walk to class and say hi to twenty or so people every day.

The Education

Very few people talk about grades at Amherst. And most seniors complete a thesis. I myself will be doing an animal behavior thesis this upcoming year. Since there are no grad students at Amherst, I can work directly with experienced faculty and get premium lab space. I can also work on exceptionally interesting projects, like studying the causes of aggressive behavior in Japanese fighting fish. Best of all, there's no core curriculum at Amherst. Think about this. It's amazing. You can take any class you want, at any time. This guarantees that everyone in each of your classes wants to be there and is genuinely interested in the subject being taught. There's also a very high level of student-teacher interaction in most classrooms. For me these were huge selling points.

The Students

There are a million different organizations on Amherst's campus. There are cultural groups like the Asian Student association, La Causa [for Hispanic students], and BSU [the Black Student Union]. There are religious groups like Hillel and the Amherst Christian Fellowship, and a very active LGBT group. There are also a lot of fearless political groups, who love to get involved. There is one group entirely dedicated to expanding national awareness of the situation in Juarez, Mexico!

Everyone is totally willing to meet new people on campus. I can honestly say that I am good friends with at least several people in each class year, so friendships are definitely not limited to your own grade.

The Activities

With nationally ranked sports teams, athletics are very prominent on campus. I love being an athlete at Amherst. My teammates are brilliant and friendly and so supportive—there's a real community—we all frequently hang out outside of practice. Music and art are also very prominent on campus, as we are always bringing in groups to perform or having performances or concerts put on by fellow students.

The Social Scene

Once Thursday afternoon rolls around people begin to relax. On Friday and Saturday people party, or go to games if they're an athlete or a fan. Sunday is hell day, when most people get themselves back into gear and disappear into the dark corners of the library. Amherst does a pretty good job of offering weekend alternatives to the typical drunken college parties. There are FLICS, free weekly movies. There are TAPs (The Amherst Party) with different themes, and these are essentially nonalcoholic sweaty dance parties that happen all the time. Hiking in the nearby woods is another way to relax. The cross-country team uses these trails for training, and there are some truly beautiful areas only five minutes from campus.

> "There's a lot of Burberry and Vera Bradley, but beneath Amherst's white-collar exterior, there beats a good heart."
> + Daryl, sophomore

Name: Greg
Hometown: Salem, Massachusetts
Class Year: Senior
Major: Music
Extracurriculars: Concert Choir, DQ (Coed a cappella group), cabaret performances, Madrigal Singers, Amherst Survival Center (a local soup kitchen)
Career Goal: Nonprofit social work

How would you describe Amherst's reputation?
Rich, snobby, old money, prep school grads.

Is this reputation accurate?
Amherst students are no more wealthy or privileged than students at any other small, well-run liberal arts college in the Northeast. Still, the snobby stereotype isn't entirely made-up . . . sometimes it's hard to be humble when you're surrounded by incredibly intelligent, motivated people.

What would an admissions officer at your school probably not tell a prospective student? What aspect of your school would a prospective student not see on a campus tour?

Prospective students aren't supposed to be told about the underground fraternity system at Amherst, which is funny, because it's such a small presence on campus that it's not worth hiding. Also, I sincerely doubt tour guides mention the fact that Amherst's social life revolves around drinking alcohol, which is true of most schools.

> "School spirit is most noticeable when playing our arch rival, Williams!"
> ✦ Sara, junior

The Institution

Amherst is great, but don't expect a utopia. My biggest run-in with the administration was in the music department, when I served on a search committee for a new professor. Out of five finalists the students unanimously chose the youngest, most inspiring, articulate applicant. The music department then disregarded the students' recommendations and chose an older, more "promising in his field" professor, who was hired and eventually became my adviser. I understand they chose this person because of his indisputable musical talent, but I stand by my original reaction to him, which is that he is skilled in his field, but uncomfortable with students, and unimaginative in the classroom. I am still a bit ticked, but that's my biggest complaint: despite its small size, this kind of stuff happens at Amherst every now and again. That said, this is still a wonderful place.

Amherst has an incredibly powerful and connected network of alums, and they will bend over backward to help students. If you graduate from Amherst, you have friends in high places. If the many benefits of a small school appeal to you, and

> "Western Mass is a tundra from November to March. Prepare for this."
> ✦ Keneka, junior

an open curriculum and a liberal campus sound compelling, Amherst will be a great match.

The Education

One of the things I love about Amherst is the feeling of being constantly surrounded by intelligent people. Discussions on a Saturday night will easily go from local politics to Ultimate Frisbee, from art cinema to Foucault. For the most part, I would say that Amherst's students are as much a reason to attend as its professors. Which is not to say the professors aren't insightful and skilled at teaching—they certainly are. In my academic experience, classes are small, fairly run, and very well taught.

> "Flashing one's SAT scores could probably be counted as one of the clubs on campus."
> ✦ James, freshman

The Students

If you're a Democrat, you'll fit in fine at Amherst. And if you're a Republican, get ready to fight. Students of a conservative mind-set are outnumbered here, and this generally makes conservatives argue louder, provoke more, and lean even more to the right. Some (actually, most Republicans) say that the overwhelming political homogeneity of Amherst makes it a less intellectual place, but I've found that the liberal tendencies of our students and professors result in a more open, accepting classroom environment where conservative students with the confidence and conviction to fight for their beliefs are free to argue their side without condemnation or oppression from the professor.

The Activities

Today's a sunny day at Amherst, and it's also "prefrosh" weekend, so the school is swamped with wide-eyed eighteen-year-olds. Earlier, when I hiked across the freshman quad to get to the gym, I tripped over hordes of kids sitting and reading in the grass; I was nearly ambushed by some eager Frisbee players; I rerouted my path around a student busy taking photos, and walked slowly past a geology class taking place outside and eavesdropped on the lecture. There are four other colleges in a five-mile radius around Amherst, and because kids can easily travel between schools, at any given time at Amherst you can find grad students, hippies, activists, athletic types, singing types, theater types, newspaper types, frat types, and political types. There's an enormous range of people to interact with.

> "There's no core curriculum at Amherst. You take the classes you want. This guarantees that everyone wants to be there, and is genuinely interested in the subject. It's amazing."
>
> ✦ Rachel, senior

The Social Life

People at Amherst tend to fuse into cliques shortly after arriving their freshman year, and stay in those cliques all through college. People pick up friends along the way, but that happens less than you'd imagine. So if you, at some point after your freshman year, want to find a new group of friends, it can be hard. You have to branch out, go to sporting events other than football games, head to off-campus concerts in Northampton, and meet people involved in different extracurricular groups. I tried this, and it worked for me. Alcohol is present, though not mandatory, at 99 percent of the social gatherings at Amherst (no alcohol at school-affiliated events). I really like that Amherst is a big enough school to offer a number of different partying options every night, but it's small enough that all types of students show up at all types of events. Even in unlikely combinations. You'll see hipsters at (unofficial) frat parties, and straight-laced jocks at LGBT gatherings.

Notable Amherst Alumni Include:
Calvin Coolidge, thirtieth U.S. president
Richard P. Wilbur, Pulitzer Prize-winning poet
D. Drew Pinsky, TV talk show host
Burgess Meredith, actor
Melvil Dewey, inventor, Dewey decimal system
David Foster Wallace, author

ANTIOCH COLLEGE

Founded: 1852

Location: Yellow Springs, OH

Phone: (937) 769-1000

E-mail admissions@antioch-college.edu

Web site: www.antioch-college.edu

Number of Undergraduates: 570

Number of Graduate Students: 10

Cost: Approximately $31,000 per year

Application Deadline: Rolling admissions

Early Decision: November 15

Rating:	Notable Majors/Programs:
Selective	Co-operative education

Size:
● Small   ○ Medium   ○ Large

Location:
○ Urban   ○ Suburban   ● Rural

On a Saturday, students talk about academics:
○ Always   ● Sometimes   ○ Never

Nightlife:
○ Intense   ○ Moderate   ● Laid-back

Politically, Antioch leans:
● Left   ○ Right   ○ Split

Diversity:
○ High   ● Low   ○ Medium

Students describe Antioch in five words:
- Radical, relevant, autonomous, experiential, small-town
- Alternative co-op system without grades

From the School

Students are expected to reach beyond conventional learning, plan their own education, and reflect upon their experiences. Antioch requires each student to gain proficiency in a second language, to earn credit for a cross-cultural learning experience, and to complete a senior thesis in their chosen area of study.

—www.antioch-college.edu

Note: **This small Midwestern college has produced seven MacArthur Fellows—as many as Yale and Stanford—since these prestigious genius grants were first initiated in 1981.**

If you are interested in Antioch, you may also be interested in:
Berea, UC Santa Cruz, Evergreen State, Kenyon, Oberlin, Sarah Lawrence

Name: Martin
Hometown: Northfield, Minnesota
Class Year: Sophomore
Major: Communications/journalism
Extracurriculars: Protests, cello, jazzfunk (informal open mike), organic garden, dinner co-op

What is your career goal?

Freelance journalism, but my aspiration is to someday own my own business. Possibly a hostel, organic farm, restaurant, or magazine.

How would you describe Antioch's reputation?

Washed up.

Is this reputation accurate?

Yes and no. On one hand, due to numerous problems over the years, including faculty tension and administrative turnover, Antioch is no longer the radical and relevant educational institution that the college built its reputation on in the late sixties and early seventies. That said, I feel like a lot of students are still getting an invaluable education. Those who thrive on chaos and learn through challenge, those who are willing to create their own authentic communities, those who value experiences over structural involvement, and who can handle eight months of isolation in rural Ohio per year—these are the Antiochians that will come away from the institution with quick street smarts, radical book smarts, and an awareness of how they fit into the world that no other college can offer.

What aspect of Antioch would a prospective student probably not see on a campus tour?

On both of my prospective tours I was told not to go to the president's dorm complex, where most of the second-year students usually live. (Of course) I went, and there I found the fifth circle of Dante's *Inferno*—sex, drugs, and rock and roll. Possessions dispossessed, mold crawling up the walls like two-dimensional stalagmites, overflowing ashtrays, illustrated signs posted over the toilets reminding hippies to flush, glassy-eyed students drinking 3.2 beers, condoms laid out in bowls like Halloween candy, trashcans overflowing with contents indistinguishable from the rest of the room. Hardly surprising that we were told not to go. But this was where I encountered some of the most authentic Antioch perspectives—real students who described Antioch as a dramatic hell and went on to say that there are some things that only a dramatic hell can teach you. My time here has been an ongoing journey to figure out what exactly that means.

The Institution

Our internship (co-op) program is one of the most amazing parts of our curriculum, and, quite simply, is Antioch's biggest draw. Rather than doing one or two internships over the course of a student's education, Antiochians spend no less than five terms off campus, establishing a life based around a co-op position/job in a new place. My first was with Love Makes A Family, a nonprofit queer organization located in Portland, Oregon. I am now working with *Utne Magazine,* out of Minneapolis, Minnesota, as an editorial intern. Most Antiochians do at least two co-ops unrelated to their major, which makes for a very diverse set of experiences—and a student body that knows how to pay bills, find an apartment, do a job search, and bar-hop prior to graduation.

The Antioch environment is one of questioning and deconstructing. We work to dissect privilege and social norms in our community. We also love the fuck out of acronyms, political correctness (Antioch was one of the colleges that P.C.U. was based on), hallucinogens, promiscuity, and attention deficit disorder. And each other.

The Education

Traditional academics are definitely not Antioch's selling point. As an institution, we value nontraditional forms of learning and reject many facets of conventional education (grades, for example) as elitist and unfair. Antioch doesn't have much money to put into its academic curriculum (a consequence of rejecting patriarchy). Thus, most of our faculty falls into two camps. Half the teachers are dedicated leftists, anarchists, Marxists, who have been at Antioch for as long as any of us can remember, and will stay here, out of love or unwillingness to compromise, until they retire or Antioch returns to the primordial idealist sludge from whence it came. The other half are new teachers, fresh out of grad school and making base pay, who will likely leave us (or be forced out by budget cuts) within a year or two. This makes for an unbalanced educational experience.

Those who seek progressive rigor just may be in luck. Timing co-ops intentionally (most faculty do not teach year-round) and selecting classes carefully can result in amazing academic experiences for certain fields (peace studies, for example) that are often unavailable at other institutions. And Antioch is one of only a handful of colleges that have mandatory research experience for undergrads.

The Students

The Antioch student body is diverse, but not as diverse as it should be. People of many gender identities and orientations, people from diverse socioeconomic backgrounds, and people of color attend Antioch. In comparison to other private liberal arts colleges of our size and cost, we are a diverse community. But the student body is predominantly white kids, and admitting more, richer white kids seems to be the administration's intent for fixing the budget. Many students bring racial and sexual baggage that can divide our community. For those who are working to understand their own privilege, this can be a painful yet educational experience. All too often, however, it may be at the expense of community members from marginalized groups.

Obviously, Antioch attracts progressive, radical, idealistic students. On arrival they must find ways to deal with the isolation of living in Yellow Springs, Ohio, and being less connected to the outside world than many are accustomed to. They find connections in the Waffle House and the Steak and Shake, road trips, nasal drugs, and political conversations in many forms.

The Activities

Many groups exist on campus for many needs—people of color groups, queer groups, environmental groups. (Though quite conspicuously, a lasting narcotics and alcohol recovery group has never formed.) Many of these groups are vocal and active in our community government, and outspoken in the community as a whole.

One of our better selling T-shirts is emblazoned with the logo "No football team since 1927." We have a soccer team and/or a women's rugby team. These teams don't exactly have a "league," but they occasionally play similarly informal teams from other schools. At one point, Antioch had an all-male cheerleading squad that "performed" at rugby games. One school now refuses to compete with us based on the squad's behavior: By the end of half time, the entire squad was naked, prancing around the field, and playing leapfrog!

The Social Scene

Antioch's social scene is to the curriculum as urban sprawl is to Los Angeles proper: the latter is always present, but the former is proportionately enormous, terribly confusing, and smoggy with carcinogens.

The value of an education that uses the world as a classroom (after stuffing you into a tiny town in Ohio for four months) cannot be overestimated. Today I am more worldly, more queer, more self-assured, and more open-minded than I've ever been.

> "Antioch's known as a place to make your voice known on issues that you find important!"
> ✦ Hannah, sophomore

Name: Natalie
Hometown: South Kingstown, Rhode Island
Class year: Sophomore
Major: Undeclared
Extracurriculars: (blank)
Career Goal: I would like to be a nurse or an elementary schoolteacher.

How would you describe Antioch's reputation?

It's known as a hippie school. A lot of activists and radicals are said to go here.

Is this reputation accurate?

For the most part it is true.

What aspect of Antioch would a prospective student probably not see on a campus tour?

I give tours to prospective students, so I can answer this question pretty easily. We do not show the dorms. We tell parents that this is because of privacy issues, but I believe it's because the dorms are in poor condition compared to most schools. We also avoid the Student Union because it is equally unattractive to most people's (especially parents') standards. The walls are completely covered with graffiti, and the floors are sticky and dirty. One student's parents said that it looks like the inside of a crack house. I don't believe that's true, but confess the building is in poor condition. There is some charm to the semi-dilapidated campus, but I think it hinders our appeal to prospective parents.

The Institution

This place certainly has a unique charm. Like I said before, it is a bit run down, but still OK. The school and surrounding town are pretty accepting of people who are different. People often call Yellow Springs a liberal oasis in the middle of conservative southwestern Ohio. Antioch has a small campus, which is very walkable and convenient. The location is pleasant, and the weather is usually decent. By and large, people love their school.

At Antioch students are involved in many aspects of administration; they even know the budget of the college. We have an extremely active community government. Students are definitely listened to here. I think people take it for granted sometimes, but if they could see how it is anywhere else, they would realize how much freedom and voice we have here. Horace Mann's famous words, "Be ashamed to die until you have won some victory for humanity," are often quoted and they reflect some of the core values of this school in terms of social activism and human rights.

The Education

Most students are pretty engaged in their classes, but I doubt that's what most people talk about on Saturday night. It really depends on what classes you take, whether you will be totally swamped with work. Generally, first and second year aren't impossible. At Antioch we are not graded unless we want to be. At the end of each term, professors submit written evaluations that give students in-depth feedback with regard to the classes they have taken. And the fun doesn't stop there: students can submit an evaluation of their teachers. It's nice to have these opportunities for reflection.

The Students

Students are generally pretty mature and well rounded because they are required to have experiences outside of the classroom. I would say that the average student at Antioch is a middle- to upper-middle-class white kid who was maybe considered "different" or "quirky" in high school, but now has a place to fit in at Antioch. I think there's a high percentage of out of the closet gay/lesbian students, but there aren't exact statistics on these things.

The Activities

There are several independent, student-run groups at Antioch. Some students are very involved in these, and others are not, but most here are involved in something fun to do! Creativity is hardly in short supply in these hallowed halls.

The Social Scene

There are many different kinds of people at Antioch. Everyone finds a niche.

Name: Rachel
Hometown: Cincinnati, Ohio
Class Year: Junior
Major: Undeclared
Extracurriculars: Theater and dance
Career Goal: I want to find a career that I like and will not burn me out.

How would you describe Antioch's reputation?

Antioch's reputation is not the best for its academics.

Is this reputation accurate?

Well, the school doesn't offer a huge array of majors like other schools. If you want to judge us on that alone—your loss. Antioch has an excellent reputation, however, for the co-op department. As well it should—the system is pretty unique in allowing students freedom to do anything they want to do, regardless of whether it's in your major.

What would an admissions officer at Antioch probably not tell a prospective student? What aspect of your school would a prospective student probably not see on a campus tour?

One thing I don't think is well emphasized is how independent and self-reliant students at Antioch must be to survive. Antioch is not structured like most schools: you make your own degree plan with general requirements . . . and being able to do anything you want is hard for some people who don't know what they want. Co-op is extremely hard for students because you have to find a job, get hired, find your own housing, and then you have to pack and leave. This occurs about every four months because you alternate study and co-op terms. It's stressful. And not everyone can do it. But the people who are successful at it are able to survive almost anything.

The Institution

Antioch is year-round with three terms. By alternating between studying and working in the co-op system, I think students are better able to figure out more about the different types of jobs they could do. The hardest part of adjusting to Antioch was learning to live in an unstructured environment while simultaneously adjusting to small community life—this is a very small school! Because of its size, I know a lot more people than I would at a larger school. Sometimes I feel like I live in a small, gossipy town, but people are friendly. Speaking of small towns, let me tell you about Yellow Springs, Ohio. It is a very cute but very tiny town. It is surrounded by cornfields. It can be very boring. But it can also be very comforting. Everyone in the town is very friendly and welcoming to the students. I even had dinner at a local family's home during orientation.

The Education

Most professors give students a lot of personal attention. They can afford to: classes are quite small. (See a theme developing?) The small class sizes help give students the opportunity to build a relationship with their professors. Depending on subject matter, classes are usually seminar style. Professors don't lecture unless they have to. (Teacher assistants aren't usually present except in the language classes, which they teach basically by themselves.) Professors are extremely active on campus. Many serve on councils with students to help make decisions about the school. With the Renewal Plan that Antioch is going through right now, professors are extremely involved in helping decide the new curriculum.

We don't have letter grades, so there's not a lot of competition. It is mandatory for seniors to complete a senior project—and present it to the community—in order to graduate. The study abroad programs are sometimes difficult to get into, and I've heard they are challenging. Studying abroad is about the same price as the tuition, depending on the program.

The Students

The small student body of Antioch is not racially diverse, and being in the middle of Ohio, surrounded by white people, is not easy for students of color. There are three groups for students of color: BAMN (By Any Means Necessary), UNIDAD, and TWA (Third World Alliance), and these groups provide some support. We have an Office of Multi-Cultural Affairs that is also very involved.

Students here are from all over the United States and are predominantly upper and middle class. A lot of Antioch's students are politically active. We're always organizing groups to go to different protests and rallies all over the United States. A lot of people think that the average Antioch student is a barefoot hippie with piercings and tattoos. Sure, there are quite a few people on campus that fit that category, but there is no average Antioch student.

The Activities

There is a PE requirement for graduation, but Antioch is not a very athletic campus, and I wouldn't say sports are taken too seriously here. The arts, however, play a major role on campus. A lot of students do community service, and while we don't interact often with the surrounding colleges, Wright State University, Cedarville, and Wittenberg are all within a half hour from Antioch.

The Social Scene

People definitely come out to party. Parties usually occur in designated areas, at least once a week. Almost everyone attends at least one party during the weekend. Older students often leave campus and hang out in bars and clubs in Dayton. Some students go out to the movies, out to dinner, or out of town (Cincinnati and Columbus) if there isn't anything going on here.

It is a small campus, and if you want to be social, you will get to know almost everyone that is on campus at the same time as you. Living on campus is very important for the first two years because dorm life is how you get to meet everyone and build a community. Compared to other schools, Antioch was the friendliest campus and town I visited. Walking down the sidewalk people will say hello to you. If they do not know or recognize you, they may stop to introduce themselves or ask if you need directions.

Notable Antioch Alumni Include:
Deborah Willen Meier, director and founder of the
    Central Park East Public Schools, New York
Lisa D. Delpit, teacher and leading authority on
    multicultural education
Mark Strand, former U.S. poet laureate
Stephen J. Gould, paleontologist and author
Sylvia A. Law, civil rights lawyer
Virginia Hamilton (Adoff), writer and author

BARD COLLEGE

Founded: 1860

Location: Annandale-on-Hudson, NY

Phone: (845) 758-7472

E-mail: admissions@bard.edu

Web site: www.bard.edu

Number of Undergraduates: 1,333

Number of Graduate Students: 223

Cost: Approximately $38,000 per year

Application Deadline: January 15

Early Decision: November 1

Rating:	Notable Majors/Programs:
Very Selective	Political Studies, Film, English/Creative Writing

Size:
● Small   ○ Medium   ○ Large

Location:
○ Urban   ○ Suburban   ● Rural

On a Saturday, students talk about academics:
● Always   ○ Sometimes   ○ Never

Nightlife:
○ Intense   ○ Moderate   ● Laid-back

Politically, Bard leans:
● Left   ○ Right   ○ Split

Diversity:
○ High   ● Low   ○ Medium

Bard students describe their school in five words:
- Hipster school for creative rule-breakers
- Small, controversial, intellectual, true individuals

From The School

Bard has developed a new vision and model of the liberal arts college, as a central body surrounded by significant institutes and programs—"satellites"—that strengthen its curriculum. This model is distinctly different from the structure of a large university. While it is flexible enough to include programs for research, graduate study, community outreach, and other cultural and educational activities, the undergraduate program remains its focus. Each satellite program is designed to enhance the undergraduate course of study by offering students opportunities for interaction with leading artists and scholars.

—www.bard.edu

If you're interested in Bard, you may also be interested in:
Brown, Grinnell, Oberlin, Sarah Lawrence, Vassar

Name: Liz
Hometown: Athens, Georgia
Class Year: Freshman
Major: Asian Studies/Psychology
Extracurriculars: Belly dancing, table tennis, Bard EMS (Emergency Medical Services), Sanskrit chanting, peer counselor (Bard's form of a resident adviser)
Career Goal: Professor/child psychologist/expressive arts therapist

How would you describe Bard's reputation?
Oh, those rich, white liberals . . .

Is this reputation accurate?
Because it costs a lot of money to come to Bard, the assumption is that everyone here comes from money and, by association, is a rich, spoiled brat, but this isn't true at all. More than three-fourths of the people I know are on scholarship or came in with a solid financial aid package. And most students do work study to help pay their bills. As for the liberal bit, it's true, Bard *is* very liberal. Bard students are interested in change and progression. It's a campus of students simmering with new ideas and creative insights.

> "Everyone smokes cigarettes at Bard. It really could be classified as an extracurricular activity."
>
> ✦ Scott, junior

What would an admissions officer at your school probably not tell a prospective student? What won't you see on a college tour?
Our admissions officers are pretty open about Bard—they don't sugarcoat the experience here, they want to find students who really fit in with the school and its philosophies. Also, when you're visiting, keep in mind Bard's campus is way too big to cover in an hour tour, so you might not see the dorms, but I'll tell you the truth, Bard offers nice-sized rooms.

The Institution
Bard is located in this gorgeous part of the Hudson Valley, and autumns here are particularly amazing. It's worth coming to Bard simply to experience autumn at its finest. I'm continually amazed by the deliciously red and orange leaves that paint the campus. On the flip slide the winters are pretty hard to bear, but maybe that's because I'm from Georgia.

Bard's small size allows students and professors to develop close and intimate relationships unheard of at larger schools. This is one of Bard's greatest strengths. There's also a close relationship between the administration and students here, which is unusual. Our president is one of the leading progressive educational theorists in America, and he goes out of his way to ensure that Bard is receptive to student concerns. It's rare that Bard students will feel left out of any major administrative decision on campus.

There are roughly 1,400 students at Bard. That's it. On many occasions I've been walking across campus at night, and I've been able to recognize someone moving toward me solely by his/her gait. I like this aspect of Bard, that for four years we live as a tight-knit community of young thinkers. Also, because Bard is so isolated, when you're here you're essentially cut off from the outside world. Luckily, there's always so much to do right on campus that you never need to leave. And if you have a car, you can always take off for New York City [two hours by car].

The Education
One of Bard's defining characteristics is the way its classes are conducted. The average class size is fifteen students; we sit around a table and have discussions with professors. The professors are very cutting-edge, world-renowned thinkers and intellectuals, and they care a lot about students. In class, they move the discussions in certain ways, and insert pertinent facts at the right moments, but for the most part every class feels like an intellectual exchange of ideas, not a rote lecture on boring topics. I leave almost every class feeling involved, motivated, and excited to prepare for the next week's session. Bard does have core requirements, but they're very loose and many students find themselves filling the requirements by mistake. For example, my classes this semester range from Sanskirt to Modern Dance to The Nature and Treatment of Psychological Disorders. That's a few requirements fulfilled right there.

The Students
Students at Bard are very creative in their work, in their clothes, in their art, in all aspects of their

lives. They are who they are, and if they're not sure who they are, they're not afraid to experiment in an attempt to figure it out. Because everyone understands this, everyone is accepted at Bard, no matter who they are, no matter what they're like.

> "At Bard, the Democrats could probably be called the 'conservative' group on campus."
>
> ✦ Tom, freshman

We have a lot of well-integrated international students at Bard, and a very popular International Student Organization that hosts several big parties and a well-attended yearly Cultural Show. We also have many kids who identify as LGBT. Lastly, Bard students are politically active and big on voicing their opinions. We have as many protests and rallies as possible. This is definitely a liberal school, with only a handful of Republicans to be found.

The Activities

Although Bard is not known for its athletic department, we have quite an enthusiastic and growing set of teams, including soccer, volleyball, tennis, rugby, basketball, cross-country, and squash. Many students opt to participate in the intramurals, which include almost everything you can think of, from minigolf to Ultimate Frisbee. There is also a widely applauded cricket club here, which is one of the only teams to have beaten our "pseudo-rival" Vassar College. For some reason, students at Bard love to hate students at Vassar.

Bard has more clubs than there are students. There really is something for everyone. To give you an idea of the range, Bard has a Surrealist Training Circus, a Student Action Collective, Olde English [Bard's highly renowned comedy troupe], Crafty Crafternoon, Bard Prison Initiative, Bard Stained Glass Club, Barbecue Club, Bard UFO Research Society, Black Student Organization, Book Exchange/Info Shop, Contradance Club, Feminist Majority, Hip Hop Movie Club, Video Game Club, WXBC Radio Bard, Asian Film Club, and Equestrian Club. These are just a handful. I suggest going to Bard's Club Web site and taking a look at the rest of the clubs on offer to see how many options there truly are.

All of the artistic productions at Bard are widely attended. There is huge support for the artistic community here. Also, Bard is the home of the American Symphony Orchestra (its conductor is our president), so there are often free concerts offered to all Bard students. If there aren't any tantalizing activities on campus, NYC is only a train ride away. I also spend a lot of my time here taking naps; that's one of the greatest things about college, the naps.

The Social Scene

If you're looking for wild fraternity parties, Bard is not the place for you. If you're looking for creative and inspired bacchanals, Bard has its share. Every weekend night there are always at least two large parties, and then there are countless small gatherings. Dorm life is active at Bard, too; since the dorms are small, everyone bonds and becomes part of the community.

Name: Scott
Hometown: Evanston, Illinois
Class Year: Junior
Major: Political theory
Extracurriculars: Helping my friends with film or photography projects. Job doing specialty makeup at the Fisher Center during the summer opera festival.
Career Goal: I'm not sure.

How would you describe Bard's reputation?

Compared with the schools it most closely competes with—Vassar, Brown, Sarah Lawrence, Hampshire, Wesleyan, and Oberlin—Bard is said to be the most forward thinking, the most progressive . . . I also think Bard is the coolest.

Is this reputation accurate?

Bard College is extremely progressive. Students are pushed here (by their classmates, their professors, and the administration) to always try new things and explore new angles, to do truly original work. And yes, this place is the nexus of "cool" in almost every conceivable permutation.

What would an admissions officer at your school probably not tell a prospective student?

Students here often get so involved in their work, in personal and intellectual introspection, that they wind up exhausted, suddenly wracked with sobs while writing a philosophy paper. Admissions officers might not tell prospective students about that.

The Institution

Bard's campus is a paradise during the warm months; hundreds of acres of pristine gardens, fields, and forests, bordered on one side by the Hudson River, with breathtaking views of the Catskill Mountains just beyond. Also, right near by there are plenty of swimming holes, farm stands, and other country delights. If you enjoy nature, Bard is perfect.

The Education

Bard is one of the few colleges in America that operates on the Oxford system, which divides the school into upper and lower colleges. Every student starts out in the lower college. Then in their sophomore year, people enter into "moderation," which is roughly akin to declaring a major at other schools. Except at Bard you can't just declare, "I'm now an English major." You have to meet with a panel of faculty members from the English department, present them with a piece of original work, and talk to them about why you want to be an English major and what you've done in the past that illustrates your readiness to specialize in the English Department, and what understanding of English literature you'd like to have before you graduate. [This is the case for all majors. English is just an example.] This process isn't easy, it can actually be insanely stressful. But it's also good, because it ensures you don't make a hasty major decision that will impact the rest of your college career, life, etc. Also, not everyone is accepted into every major. In the most competitive departments (film, photography, creative writing), lots of students are deferred, which means they need to go back, reassess, and try again.

Every student at Bard also has to hand in a significant senior project (i.e., a thesis of perhaps one hundred pages or a portfolio of thirty perfectly turned photos) before they can graduate. This is a daunting project, but an excellent indicator of the confidence Bard has in its students, that every student is expected to be capable of such high-level work.

I think both of these educational policies show that Bard is ideal for students who are passionate, driven, and self-motivated. If you're not capable of serious introspection and significant independent work, Bard isn't going to work out for you.

The Students

Bard is unique in that its students all read the newspapers and are capable of sustaining conversation on a very broad range of topics. But they're also, largely, involved in a set of politics that breeds a generalized "damn the man" hatred of the bourgeois capitalist what have you, with an emphasis on protest and complete overthrow. I'm more of a believer in working within the current flawed system to make real positive change, to work toward more concrete, less amorphous goals. But I've, sadly, found myself to be in the minority at Bard over that issue. Most Bard students are pretty bizarre, and they're always in search of ways to be weirder. Campus band names, for example, include Duck Duck Blood, and a club recently devoted itself to building a boat out of trash (the BARDge) and sailing it down the Hudson to New York.

Unfortunately, most Bard students are white. This is because Bard costs $40,000 a year, a hefty sum, and the hard truth of the matter is there are far more white people than minorities in America who can afford the cost. The school absolutely makes an effort to reach out to minority students, though, and compared to many other schools we have a high percentage of minorities on campus.

> "Bard is ridiculously cold in the winter. And the dining hall serves absolutely terrible meat."
>
> ✦ Allison, senior

The Activities

Students can start up any club they want at Bard, and many clubs will receive funding from the administration to get off the ground. A Pirate Club has even been started whose sole purpose is to challenge clubs it doesn't think are deserving of funding to return that money to a general slush fund for parties and shows.

When not starting a club, Bard students take the shuttle to Tivoli, New York [population 1,163], stopping in front of Tivoli's lone bar. Students frequent this bar by the busloads, three or four times a week, ready to consume between one and twelve drinks each time. The bar does its best to accommodate students, putting on a variety of theme nights (there's jazz on Wednesdays, a tightly packed dance floor on Thursdays). My personal favorite Tivoli bar night is Saturday, which I call "eccentric locals night."

In addition to the bar in Tivoli, there's a tattoo shop that's never open, the decent sushi restaurant, the two small book shops, and the three or four other small restaurants. If not Tivoli, you can always go to similar nearby small towns like Red Hook, Rhinebeck, and Kingston that, between them, offer enough variety to keep you going.

The Social Scene

Once upon a time you couldn't paint a portrait of the social life at Bard without talking about the Old Gym, a much-loved, dirty, smoky, dilapidated building that was once the stomping grounds of the Beastie Boys, Chevy Chase, Christopher Guest [all Bard alums], Bob Dylan, Allen Ginsberg, and a litany of other improbably dressed drunkards who spent time there clutching bottles of whiskey, cigarettes dangling from their smirking mouths (and I should have mentioned earlier that everyone smokes cigarettes at Bard. It really could be classified as an extracurricular activity). Old Gym was a major landmark on campus until it was condemned. And it's death has left a damp, burning hole in the heart of Bard, which none of the other unspecial warehouses or barns dotting our vast campus can fill. Bard students have as much fun now, without the Old Gym, as they had with it, but our fun lacks focus, it lacks an inspiring *place*.

Name: Rebecca
Hometown: Radnor, Pennsylvania
Class Year: Senior
Major: Photography
Extracurriculars: My extracurriculars are rather analogous to my curriculars.
Career Goal: I hope to have as many careers as I'll have haircuts.

How would you describe Bard's reputation?

Bard is looked at as a liberal playground full of pseudointellectual hipsters.

Is this reputation accurate?

To a degree, yes. But any generalization will be a biased and reductive interpretation, to which I cannot agree.

What would an admissions officer at your school probably not tell a prospective student? What aspect of your school would a prospective student not see on a campus tour?

Bard has a relatively low retention rate; meaning, many students decide to leave before their four years are up. They might not mention that. On a tour, you'll see Bard's picturesque landscape, the almost haphazard collection of (post and) modern architecture, but you won't see how multifaceted and busy everyone is—our president, Leon Botstein, for example, conducts the American Symphony Orchestra in his "free time." Bard is a campus full of doers.

The Institution

I spent my freshman year of college at Bard's antithesis, Syracuse University, and I basically found most of the institutions on that campus violent and devoid of humanity. I knew I needed a smaller environment with an understanding and accessible administration. Bard students want to be at Bard, and Bard's faculty actually know their students—which is why many choose to leave in the first two years, but is also the reason for the great number of eager transfer students. Bard proved to be the opposite of everything I was used to in a large university and provided me with a student number in addition to, not in place of, my name and face.

Bard is located forty-five minutes from Poughkeepsie, a small city situated two hours north of Manhattan's Grand Central Station via the Metro North commuter train. This proximity to the largest and most expensive city in the Northeast is awesome, but isolating. A great many professors actually live in Manhattan and commute, making the campus very connected to all the resources New York has to offer [field trips to galleries and museums are common occurrences]. Back on campus, Bard College is extremely small and surrounded by hills and sunsets. You should know that on campus everyone knows everyone, and everyone will know you. This is unavoidable here.

The Education

Every department at Bard values original, creative thought. Bard professors (referred to strictly by their first names) regard students as intellectual contemporaries. Students are pushed in their academic writing to constantly probe further, not just to comprehend what's already known but also to add to what's been discovered and stated before. Bard students are taught to question everything, to appreciate hard work, and to embrace ambiguity (because so much of life is ambiguous).

First-year students are inundated in a three-week orientation where they engage in the Learning and Thinking Workshop, attending classes in August while their high school friends are still searching for extra-long sheets for their new dorm beds. L&T is directly followed up with Freshman Seminar, a series of classes taken in a student's first year in which a variety of important classical texts and paradigms are investigated. Due to my transfer status I missed both the Learning and Thinking Workshop and Freshman Seminar, but by observing from the sidelines I am impressed by how hard the administration works to jump-start students' minds after the intellectual malaise many suffer in high school.

The Students

Bardians are idealistic. They fight for what they believe in, and for themselves. They use their work to rail against the problematic status quo in attempts to recreate the world as, they feel, it should be. Bard students have a keen awareness of history, politics, culture, art—you name it—and they use this knowledge as a base from which they can start critical investigations. All Bard students are cultural critics. We all have beef with some aspect of modern America, and we seek answers to our questions through our different academic subjects. We're square pegs. Outsiders. Creative types. Weirdos. Those kids in junior high school that were sent out into the hall for causing trouble or the kids you never heard from very much at all. That's us.

The Activities

Because we're in the middle of small-town America, the school goes to great lengths to keep us entertained. Lectures, film screenings, performances, art openings, poetry readings, class visits, etc., are organized to make sure we're occupied and learning. Professors often get interested in the activities, and it's not uncommon to see teachers and students standing side by side at events.

The Social Scene

Oh, what a scene. We're in the middle of nowhere. On weekends, off-campus students often host parties. Basically Bard students like to combine drinking with most of their leisure-time activities. We play four-square and drink. We go to the movies and drink. Bard students form a lot of bands (with any combination of a guitar, computer, blender, throat, or set of red rhythm sticks) that are met by enthusiastic crowds. As far as sexual relations, the small population here makes sex and dating awkward, as you'll constantly bump into your crush or that vaguely memorable hook-up. The healthiest relationships I've witnessed have been long distance. After a certain amount of time here you've usually burned through your options and you get out your sexual frustration through lighthearted games of spin the bottle or (mostly) platonic fooling around with friends.

Noted intellectuals who have taught at Bard in recent years: Roy Lichtenstein, Elizabeth Murray, Ken Noland, Judy Pfaff, Stephen Shore, William Tucker, Chinua Achebe, William Gaddis, Norman Manea, Bradford Morrow, Mona Simpson, Isaac Bashevis Singer, John Ashbery, Robert Kelly, and Ann Lauterbach

Notable Bard Alumni Include:
Peter Stone, Academy Award–winning screenwriter
Chevy Chase, actor
Walter Becker, musician, member of Steely Dan
Donald Fagan, musician, member of Steely Dan

BARNARD COLLEGE

Founded: 1889

Location: New York, NY

Phone: (212) 854-2014

E-mail: admissions@barnard.edu

Web site: www.barnard.edu

Number of Undergraduates: 2,297

Number of Graduate Students: 0

Cost: Approximately $37,000 per year

Application Deadline: January 1

Early Decision: November 15

Rating:	Notable Majors/Programs:
Most Selective	English, Psychology, Political Science

Size:
- ● Small   ○ Medium   ○ Large

Location:
- ● Urban   ○ Suburban   ○ Rural

On a Saturday, students talk about academics:
- ● Always   ○ Sometimes   ○ Never

Nightlife:
- ○ Intense   ● Moderate   ○ Laid-back

Politically, Barnard leans:
- ● Left   ○ Right   ○ Split

Diversity:
- ○ High   ● Low   ○ Medium

All-women's: Yes!

Students describe Barnard in five words:
- Proud, confident women in Manhattan
- Intense experience for future leaders

From the School

The Barnard experience is inseparable from the New York City experience . . . Barnard is unequivocally dedicated to the success of women. That's immediately obvious in the way issues are considered in almost every field of inquiry, from classical studies to the history of science, or in the prominence of the nationally acclaimed Barnard Center for Research on Women. Perhaps more subtle—but inestimably important to women's success in the long run—is the way Barnard [also] strengthens students' abilities in the sciences and mathematics.

—www.barnard.edu

If you're interested in Barnard, you may also be interested in:
Bryn Mawr, Columbia, Georgetown, NYU, Smith, Vassar

Name: Anne
Hometown: Augusta, Georgia
Class Year: Freshman
Major: Sociology
Extracurriculars: Dinner Club, Opera Club, theater, sign language
Career Goal: I'd like to become a lawyer.

How would you describe Barnard's reputation?

It's an impressive place to go to college. Even though some people still think it's the backdoor to Columbia and world-renowned for attracting angry feminists and ardent lesbians.

Is this reputation accurate?

Barnard *is* an impressive place to be. But a backdoor to Columbia? Preposterous. The two schools are very separate entities, and even though they're next door to one another they offer entirely different feels, administrations, academic philosophies. Full of lesbians? Laughable. There *are* lesbians at Barnard, but no more than any other college. And if being a feminist means you believe women should receive equal pay for equal work in this world, then yeah, Barnard is full of feminists.

What aspect of your school would a prospective student not see on a campus tour?

You wouldn't see the rivalry between Columbia women and Barnard women. It probably stems from the fact that there are only so many Columbia boys to go around, but this is such a superficial rivalry, and it fades away by the time you're an upperclassman.

The Institution

At first I was scared because Barnard is an all-women's college. Most of my friends in high school were male, and I thought I might have trouble with the social scene, but I was so wrong. Barnard women are such incredible people, I made friends right away. Within weeks I'd grown close to people that I'm sure I'll know the rest of my life. And because we're in Manhattan, meeting men outside of class is really no problem at all. Don't worry, you'll have plenty of opportunities to date while at Barnard.

The Education

At Barnard, classes are small (in my freshman year, 75 percent of my classes had fewer than twenty-five students in them). Students come to class prepared and excited, and when class is over, academic conversations continue throughout the day. At 8 p.m. you and your friends will still be arguing about Freud, Descartes, and Shakespeare. And Barnard loves that we have these kinds of continuing discussions, and does everything it can to foster them. For example, the administration will put everyone on the same hall in the same seminar class. That way we all live and learn together. You'll know how well your friends party and how well they can debate.

The interaction between students and professors is also amazing here. After my first semester, I started to apply for summer internship programs. Most of my friends at other colleges had to ask their high school teachers for letters of recommendation because their college professors simply didn't know them well enough. I asked my Barnard seminar professor whom I'd gotten to know and I got into every program I applied to.

The Students

Unfortunately, Barnard is not very economically diverse. It seems there are two types of students—those who have parents who can afford to give them a blank check for their education (the case for most kids at Barnard) and those who get very generous financial aid and otherwise couldn't afford to come here. You rarely meet someone who resides solidly in the middle class. It's very strange. It's also kind of sad, because you can easily single out "Marsha, the rich girl who always wears Gucci and Prada" from "Heather, the poor girl who wears discount clothes from Gap." The upshot is that everyone—rich, poor, white, Asian, black, Indian, straight, lesbian—hangs out with one another, pretty harmoniously. One other thing I've noticed is that Barnard girls are all "hard core" in whatever activity they choose to pursue. No one half-asses things here. There is no group or club for the average kid who isn't superpassionate. Instead, there are tons of groups for active, strong, very opinionated women looking to get big things done in a short period of time.

The Activities

Barnard and Columbia, being directly next to one another, interact fairly often. But the Barnard/Columbia students rarely interact with students at other New York schools. We leave Eugene Lang, NYU, SVA [School of Visual Arts], Parsons, FIT [Fashion Institute of Technology]—and the like—

pretty much to themselves. The one exception would be the queer group on campus, which interacts with queer groups at these other schools. And I guess Barnard's sports teams play against these schools, but I'll be honest, this doesn't really count because athletics at Barnard are a joke.

New York City can be very expensive to live in. But you can make it work. It's all about getting to know the place, identifying where your budget will allow you to go and where it won't, and spending money responsibly. If you watch your wallet, you can go out all the time, have a very "Manhattan" lifestyle, and still spend very little by eating cheap, shopping at thrift stores, and scouting out bars and clubs that don't charge covers to come inside. Winter in New York is miserable: rainy and cold and gray. But the Northern folks don't seem to think it's so bad.

The Social Scene

There isn't much on-campus partying at Barnard, at least not in the Quad, which is where the freshmen live. The Quad has very strict alcohol and drug policies, and most people say, "Screw it, I'll just go to a local bar and drink." There are a good number of bars in the area, and of course there are tons spread throughout the city. That said, most Barnard students really don't drink that much. Students here honestly don't need to turn to alcohol for entertainment, because we're at *Barnard* in *New York City*. There are *so* many things happening on campus and within a ten-minute subway ride. I leave campus a fair amount to hang out.

Name: Anna
Hometown: Chatham, New Jersey
Class Year: Junior
Major: English/psychology
Extracurriculars: Columbia University Club Water Polo Team, lifeguard, office assistant in the Pre-College Programs Office
Career Goal: I want to write for a living and live in a ramshackle farmhouse in upstate New York.

How would you describe Barnard's reputation?

A highly selective liberal arts college for women in the middle of New York City. A hot spot for the best, brightest, and most ambitious women in the country.

Is this reputation accurate?

Absolutely. Barnard is not "the school for girls who didn't get into Columbia." That's idiocy. Barnard is a fantastic school on its own terms. Women leave Barnard with ideals, dreams, and a solid education that will help them turn their ideals and dreams into realities.

What aspect of your school would a prospective student not see on a campus tour?

The maze of underground tunnels. Because Barnard only occupies four city blocks, space has to be utilized as efficiently as possible, so Barnard built underground tunnels (use the tunnels to get from class to class when it snows!).

The Institution

Because Barnard is in NYC, it's very easy to arrange for famous speakers to come to campus. There are so many great speakers coming by on a daily basis that events that would be *huge* at other schools cause only a moderate rustle of interest here. Likewise, the location makes for an *incredible* variety of great internship and job opportunities you wouldn't get anywhere outside of New York. Additionally, there are lots of famous Barnard alumnae (including Anna Quindlen) who are supportive of current students and will hold big dinner parties for freshmen at their houses. I've had six amazing internships in four potential career fields, and I've become friends with people I never imagined I would even meet. I spend half my week interning at an Off-Broadway theater; I'm a research assistant for an author; I take dance classes in midtown; and then I come back to Barnard and play on the water polo team. I work in the Pre-College Programs Office. And because of Barnard's relationship with Columbia, I can take as many classes as I want at Columbia for credit in addition to my awesome Barnard courses. I couldn't be happier. I know all of the above sounds daunting. And it can be. But Barnard helps you get adjusted through its First Year Focus program, and there are lots of resources available for students becoming acclimated with big city life, from the Student Activities Center to the Dean's Office, from the First Year Advisor program to Nightline [the Barnard/Columbia peer counseling hotline]. Our study abroad application process is surprisingly painless. I spent a semester studying in London, and while I was there, Barnard alumni looked me up and took me to lunches, on outings, and invited me to their houses for Thanksgiving dinner. That's how strong alumni connections are at Barnard.

The Education

My first semester at Barnard I took a critical writing course with only eight other students in it, and a fiction writing course with only six other students in it. Amazing. Small classes like this are the norm for Barnard. And the professors are incredible. As trite as it sounds, *professors at Barnard really do care about their students.* A professor you took a lecture class with your first semester will always smile and ask how you're doing when you see them around campus. This past semester I took a fiction writing class with visiting professor Roddy Doyle, an Irish novelist who gave us an enormous amount of freedom. This was exactly what I really needed to really learn how I write, and he was constantly there to reassure me in his office hours and via e-mail that I was on the right track. Though he was only a visiting professor, this style of teaching and level of interaction is typical at Barnard.

> "People dream of living and working in New York. Barnard students don't have to; they're already there."
> ✦ Caroline, sophmore

The Students

Barnard really does have an ethnically and politically diverse student body; and because we're in New York City, hard and fast cliques don't really form the way they do at other small schools. Instead, Barnard students are individuals who are friendly with all different types of people all over campus.

The Activities

I leave campus every other day. I go to benefits and parties organized by my internship, I go to plays on and off Broadway, concerts and lectures around town, to dinner, running in the park. I grab extra acting classes at HB studios, I go to museums and bars and clubs, I walk around aimlessly, I go to the gym, I housesit for professors. I always get really excited when my friends from other schools see what my "school life" is like. They think it's like a vacation (which it isn't quite, be-

cause there is a lot of work and stress), but the stress *does* magically disappear when you're with good friends at a sexy lounge downtown on Friday night!

The Social Scene

Most Barnard students take a very blasé attitude toward alcohol. If you drink, fine; if you don't, fine. Being underage is usually easily solvable through fake IDs or creative strategizing. A weekend night might involve bar-hopping and clubbing, or it might involve doing homework and watching a movie with friends. Some weeks I realize that I've gone out five nights in a row, and sometimes three weeks will go by and I haven't gone out once. At Barnard, it's all about flexibility and personal choice, learning what's right for you and balancing your social and academic life. My only complaint would be [that] while it's not hard to meet new, interesting, friendly people, it can be hard to move beyond the acquaintance phase because everyone is so busy and ensconced in their own lives. You have to make an extra effort to slow people down and let them know you want more than a passing friendship or relationship.

Name: Nadia
Hometown: Madeira Beach, Florida
Class Year: Junior
Major: Economics and mathematics
Extracurriculars: I dabble in everything.
Career Goal: I'd like to teach at the university level.

How would you describe Barnard's reputation?

Academically rigorous, politically and socially liberal women's college, with an administration and faculty truly focused on students.

Is this reputation accurate?

Yes.

What would an admissions officer at your school probably not tell a prospective student?

That Columbia kids think they're better and smarter than us. (They're sorely mistaken.)

The Institution

School spirit at Barnard is rampant. We love it here, and it *really* shows on Spirit Day, when the deans come out to serve ice cream to students and the whole student body celebrates. I love all of Barnard's traditions: the Midnight Breakfast the night before finals begin, the Fall Fest where cider and caramel apples are served, the Sophomore Major Toast and Junior Class Ring Ceremony, the Senior Dinner, the Honors Reception, and so on. Barnard is the best of all worlds: a serene campus in a bustling city, a small liberal arts college for women with the resources of a large, coed research university, and a school that cares about its students but doesn't coddle them.

> "In regards to the meal plan, opt for *points!* Always."
>
> ✦ Jessica, junior

The Education

Most classes are very small and some lend themselves to discussion more than others, but even in lectures, professors are very engaging. Students are not competitive with one another, but they tend to be very competitive with themselves. Professors are great—they teach here and not at a huge research university because they like working with young minds. I've worked on several projects (paid, with free summer housing) with professors. I'm hoping to turn the research I do this summer with the department head into my senior thesis. While not all students have to do theses, many choose to. The academics at Barnard are no joke, and the fact that I know my professors on a personal level makes me ashamed to turn in anything but my best work. Each semester Barnard also offers minicourses, which are fun little classes that provide a break from the more intense academic classes. You can learn to play guitar, knit, belly dance, photography, the ins and outs of wine tasting. It's great.

Additionally, Barnard definitely opens the door to grad school. Women's colleges typically have a high percentage of students that attend grad schools, and Barnard is no exception. It's one of the top ranked liberal arts colleges for the number of students who go on to earn PhDs and having the ability to interact with full professors on a daily basis helps you get particularly strong letters of recommendation.

The Students

Barnard is a women's college, and consequently has a larger percentage of LGBT students than other schools might. Students are, as they tend to be at women's colleges, politically liberal. However, for a relatively small school, Barnard has an extraordinary variety of students. As a somewhat conservative student, I worried that I wouldn't fit in. I was afraid that my peers would all be either staunch activist "wymyn" or giggling salon queens. While both extremes exist here, they are not the norm, and in the middle ground I've made some extraordinary friends.

The Activities

On a sunny day, Lehman Lawn will be covered with students. Most will be reading in small groups, just two or three friends studying in each other's company. There may be a class being held on the lawn, or dancers practicing. Those who don't have any pressing assignments may get some food from the student center and eat lunch with friends outside. There's a club, sport, or activity for just about anyone here at Barnard or Columbia, and student organizations are fully open to students from either school. There are numerous advantages and disadvantages of living in New York City. One of the disadvantages is adjusting to a city-sized room or apartment (smaller than smaller than small). The advantage is, you leave that room and you have the whole world at your fingertips.

> "To be honest with you, my first choice was Columbia, but Barnard ended up being the right place for me—by a long shot. Rather than being a nameless student, I matter. That really makes a difference."
>
> ✦ Madeline, senior

The Social Scene

If you like to drink, there are some Barnard barflies, and they usually don't have problems getting served at bars. But if that's not your scene, it's easily avoidable. It's pretty low key here. You'll make friends in your classes, in your dorms, by seeing people repeatedly in the library. Don't stress—overall, our student body is very open and friendly. And finding a date is easy: Columbia students hang out all over Barnard's campus. We joke that Barnard is the only coed women's college in the world. There will be guys in most of your classes, guys in Manhattan's clubs, guys sitting on Barnard's lawn, and guys in the student center and dining hall.

> "It's always fun when the Columbia boys serenade us at 2 a.m. in the Quad, crooning 'My Girl' at the top of their lungs."
> ✦ Sahar, senior

Note: Studies have found that, by attending women's colleges, women:
- Participate more fully in and out of class.
- Are more successful in careers; that is, they tend to hold higher positions, are happier, and earn more money.
- Constitute 20 percent of women in Congress and 30 percent of *Business Week's* list of rising stars in corporate America, yet only 2 percent of all female college grads.

- Have a higher percentage of majors in economics, math and life science today than men at coeducational colleges.
  —http://www.barnard.edu/about/why.html

Notable Barnard Alumni Include:
Sheila Nevins, executive director of programming, HBO
Joan Rivers, comedian, talk show host
Zora Neale Hurston, author
Anna Quindlen, journalist, author
Cynthia Nixon, actress

BATES COLLEGE

Founded: 1855
Location: Lewiston, ME
Phone: (207) 786-6255
E-mail: admissions@bates.edu
Web site: www.bates.edu

Number of Undergraduates: 1,750
Number of Graduate Students: 0
Cost: Approximately $40,000 per year
Application Deadline: January 15
Early Decision: November 15

Rating:	Notable Majors/Programs:
Most Selective	English, Life Sciences, Social Sciences

Size:
● Small   ○ Medium   ○ Large

Location:
○ Urban   ● Suburban   ○ Rural

On a Saturday, students talk about academics:
○ Always   ● Sometimes   ○ Never

Nightlife:
○ Intense   ● Moderate   ○ Laid-back

Politically, Bates leans:
● Left   ○ Right   ○ Split

Diversity:
○ High   ● Low   ○ Medium

Students describe Bates in five words:
- Close-knit liberal arts in Maine
- Cozy, relaxed, outdoorsy, granola-y and *friendly!*

From the School:
Bates is a college of the liberal arts and sciences, nationally recognized for the qualities of the educational experience it provides. It is a coeducational, nonsectarian, residential college with special commitments to academic rigor, and to assuring in all of its efforts the dignity of each individual, and access to its programs and opportunities by qualified learners. . . . Throughout the history of the College, Bates' graduates have linked education with service, leadership, and obligations beyond themselves.

—www.bates.edu

If you are interested in Bates, you may also be interested in:
Bowdoin, Colby, Dartmouth, Lewis & Clark, Middlebury, Whitman

Name: Randi
Hometown: Milford, Delaware
Class Year: Junior
Major: English
Extracurriculars: Lab technician in neuroscience department
Career Goal: Pediatric psychiatrist

How would you describe Bates's reputation?

Bates is known as one of the friendliest places around, and as a hippie school filled with smart, outgoing kids. However, our closest rivals (Colby and Bowdoin) opine that Bates is a party school with less-intense academics.

> "Bates is *not* 'the weakest of the Maine schools'—I got accepted to Bowdoin and Colby as well and chose Bates because of the more socially diverse and accepting atmosphere."
>
> ✦ Molly, sophomore

Is this reputation accurate?

Bates is easily one of the friendliest places you can find—students and profs alike are always eager to talk to new faces. However, the student body is much preppier than rumors would have you believe. The hippie population is prominent and fairly outspoken, but if you take a look around Commons, the only dining hall on campus, you are far more likely to notice the hordes of New Englanders clad in Abercrombie than the few hippies in the room. As for Colby and Bowdoin: they're right—we are the best partiers and we *do* have the most fun. But what they won't acknowledge is that our strong academic program still rivals any school in the country.

What would an admissions officer at Bates probably not tell a prospective student?

Admissions would not want prospective students to see how bad relations with the town of Lewiston have been over the past few years. The school is trying very hard to strengthen our relationship with the town, but little progress has been made. As security and the administration have made attempts to contain the party scene on campus, students have become far more likely to move their partying to off-campus housing, which further upsets local residents.

The Institution

Be forewarned: Maine weather really is as cold as people say it is. But our spirits are not easily suppressed! We celebrate the first snowfall and stay active throughout the winter. Our campus layout helps—buildings are really close together—which not only makes trekking to class more bearable but also means that there isn't isolation between kids in different dorms and houses. Everyone can easily see each other, despite the subzero temperatures. And while other schools boast about their plentiful choices in dining, one of the greatest aspects of Bates is that there is only one dining hall (discounting lunch on weekdays in the Silo) where everyone gathers for meals; you get to see pretty much everyone you want at least once a day, though it's also equally hard to avoid those you do *not* wish to see, especially after an embarrassing night of partying.

The Education

Classes are stimulating and inspiring, for the most part, and there are few courses that you can coast through. Getting a B in most classes may require simply the basic work, but it requires hours upon hours more work to achieve an A. As an English major taking premed courses, I have found it far easier to get high grades within the humanities departments than within the science departments, meaning many science majors work far harder for lower GPAs. It's a relatively noncompetitive atmosphere, perfect for challenging yourself and seeking help when you need it. Unlike at most colleges, students can work closely with professors in small

> "I don't know a single person on campus who isn't involved in some athletic activity. Batesies like to move."
>
> ✦ Amy, junior

class settings, and while TAs are around to help, they'll never teach the material.

The academic calendar is made up of two complete semesters of school, and then a short term, in which students take only one course for five weeks, and usually select courses that are slightly more offbeat (haiku poetry or espionage, for example), and grades are not entered into the GPA, which allows a laid-back exposure to a unique field. Aside from a few harder courses required for some majors, most students do less work during this time than they do the rest of the year, and may find themselves with little to do besides party *very* hard and take advantage of Maine as it finally begins to warm up in May.

During junior year, people mainly go abroad (it's incredibly hassle-free to apply for these programs at Bates—a quick meeting gave me all the paperwork and information I could need). I was able to study in Denmark, studying in a human health and disease program that allowed me to gain some excellent skills as I prepare for medical school, as well as insight into the Scandinavian approach to health care.

During senior year, most majors require a thesis. Most importantly, the school teaches you how to think and act for yourself, instead of subscribing to anyone else's ideas or thoughts. It really has helped me to find myself, and has given me tools to continue to learn who I am and to discover the beauty in the world around me. Bates encourages you to look deeper into anything and everything.

> "The temperatures this winter were colder than they were in Alaska. Welcome to New England!"
>
> ✦ Andrew, freshman

The Students

Bates really is the stereotypical small, liberal college. Students are generally middle- to upper-class white kids from the suburbs of Boston, but they're also very down to earth. They tend to be caring and compassionate toward everyone and most have a cause they care a lot about. Thus, community service dominates both classroom discussion and extracurricular activities, and tons of clubs are geared toward educating the student body about various courses. . . . Batesies also like to drink. Heavily.

The Activities

Our biggest football game, against Colby, attracts a lot of fans. It's amusing because none of the teams are really that good, so it's just a matter of eking out a win to keep school spirit high. . . . Popular activities range from writing for a newspaper or literary magazine to performing in our great dance programs to participating in our many,

many clubs. . . . On nicer days you'll find the campus bustling with students outside, playing Frisbee or hanging out on the quad. On colder days, you'll easily find someone who wants to hit the ski slopes, which are really close to campus. At night, most people are either working, taking a break at The Den or The Ronj (our sandwich and coffee shops), or taking some illicit substance. There is definitely a work hard, play hard mentality, so when the homework finishes, the partying begins.

The Social Scene

Kids tend to put their academics ahead of their social life, especially as it gets closer to finals. So partying during the week is definitely strained. But come Thursday night, the social life gears up again. Thursdays have become the designated "bar night" as the over-twenty-one crowd strives to get to the most popular local bar, Boondoggles, before the over-eighteen crowd is admitted at 11:30 p.m. Unlike most colleges, it's pretty easy to coast through without ever having a fake ID. Club dances also happen—they usually involve great themes and are a lot of fun. For the rest of the weekend, social life tends to focus on parties. Most nights start with some drinking in the room, followed by an attempt to go to a party on campus, until security breaks it up and the whole campus goes out to off-campus parties. The best tradition at Bates is the "Lick-it" dance, held the night before the annual gala, a formal for the entire campus community. Basically, it involves wearing as little as possible, giving students the chance to be as risqué and unclassy as we can be, before being forced to face everyone at the classiest night of the year.

> "Something like 60 percent of Batesies marry other Batesies. It's out of control."
>
> ✦ Maris, senior

There is very little dating on campus. Most people are either hooking up casually or very seriously involved, with little in between. The social scene is based around a lot of alcohol, and sometimes other drugs, although there is very little pressure to partake in anything except drinking. Since most parties involve very drunk people, non-drinkers usually opt to avoid the scene entirely and participate in chem-free events, which are offered constantly. However, doing so tends to isolate these kids a bit from the rest of the population.

Name: Yang
Hometown: Kuala Lampur, Malaysia
Class Year: Junior
Major: Undecided
Career Goal: Personal satisfaction, via any avenue. Go home to KL, get married, adopt some kids (to ease overpopulation), sell noodles for a living, annoy some people, go to jail, get murdered, win the Nobel Peace Prize, or the Lit. Prize, or both. If you come to Kuala Lumpur, come visit my bookshop. Either that or I'll form a cartel. Or maybe I'll be a schoolteacher like my heroes, or a pastor like my dad. [Shrugs.] Who knows? Maybe I'll join the army and get rid of that *stupid* blue uniform they make our kids wear in the National Service program.

How would you describe Bates's reputation?

It's thought of as a good school. Many peer institutions respect us, including some Ivies. Outside New England, we're almost unknown.

Is this reputation accurate?

Yeah, seems true enough. I've heard talk of how Bates would be ranked in the top ten liberal arts colleges—and would be generally more recognizable—if only we had a larger endowment.

What aspect of Bates would a prospective student not see on a campus tour?

Urban aesthetics—anything dark, damp, somber, graffitied. It's sad that we don't have more of this around here. I have to go off campus to the town to get any real culture. And you won't hear much praise for our location. Bates is located in an abandoned neighborhood, in an abandoned town, in an abandoned state.

The Institution

Bates is still very isolated from the surrounding community, though many Batesies make efforts to mingle. We're on the posh, snobby side of reality. But then isn't this true of all liberal arts colleges? I think the physical layout of the campus is horrible, but I know that they have a twenty-year master plan in the works that is going to change all that. Many students are tremendously optimistic about how this school is preparing them for life, and I agree that this is a very good school overall. I'm

from another country, and what I've gathered about U.S. higher education system is this: Although there is a lot of talk about "liberal education," most institutions are very entrenched in values of academic disciplines that have long traditions and, as a result, academia in this country is much more conservative than it makes itself out to be.

> "My favorite class? Bugs in the system. Did you know for some cultures insects account for a third of their protein intake! We even ate crickets."
>
> ✦ Karen, senior

The Education

The average grade is supposed to be a B+, which means that grade inflation here isn't as bad as it is at, ahem, certain Ivies where the average grade is an A–. They are currently revamping the general education program, which is an excellent move. There are many research opportunities here for undergrads, especially if you're in the natural sciences. Despite the fact that most seniors complete theses, this isn't the school to attend if you like to do things 90 percent independent of curriculum—don't come here if you want a lot of independent study. I think the humanities and fine arts tend to get shafted sometimes, but that may just be my own angry lament.

The Students

People generally get along fine with others.

The Activities

Bowdoin College and Colby College are nearby. We have outstanding relations with the small liberal arts colleges in the area on some days, but on alternate days we hate them and they hate us. Though I'm told after graduation, in the job market, everyone from these colleges seems one big, happy family. Athletics seems to be esteemed almost as highly as academics on this campus. I'm not an artist, so I can't really comment on the arts scene. What do I do when I'm bored? I go for long walks in the surrounding city/town/countryside. Make rice and tika. Take photos. Check out books from the library that I'll probably never read. Listen to world music and follow world news on the Internet. Ditz around on the guitar. Meditate on mindfulness, phenomenology, and kinesthetics. I also design Web sites. Overall, all sorts of things happen here, and that's cool.

The Social Scene

There's no big airy building which is open 24/7—and I think that sucks, especially if you're a loner who prefers to sit in a high space and just watch people. Lots of stuff goes on. People are always doing things. Campus security does a great job dealing with the whiny underage drunk noisemakers (which exist on every campus, mind you).

Name: Kaitlyn
Hometown: Bethel, Vermont
Class Year: Senior
Major: Biology
Extracurriculars: Merimanders (women's a cappella group), college choir, Students in Admissions, junior semester abroad in Costa Rica, intramural softball, senior committees
Career Goal: To be happy no matter what I do, whether it's researching cancer or waiting tables at night to finance skiing during the day!

> "Bates offers wonderful summer internship opportunities. I worked with a Bates alum in Washington, D.C., one summer—and even got to attend congressional sessions at the Capitol."
> ✦ Don, junior

How would you describe Bates' reputation?

An academically strong school comprised solely of liberal hippie-ish students who are very laid-back.

Is this reputation accurate?

Mostly. Batesies work hard and play hard. We take a lot of pride in our work—but we're also pretty relaxed and easy-going. Bates leans toward the left, always being open to everyone, regardless of gender or race, since its founding in 1855, and we're really proud of that.

What would an admissions officer at Bates probably not tell a prospective student?

Even though it's easy for someone to find out on their own, we don't talk about the cost of a Bates education (or at least I never have during my admissions info sessions). It's expensive, and our financial aid office helps out as best they can, but because our endowment is relatively low, we may not have as much money to give as other schools. You also might not hear how amazing our study abroad program is, with its own office and two deans.

> "Study abroad at Bates is *great*! You can go *anywhere* in the world. Mongolia to Mali."
> ✦ Maggie, senior

The Institution

There's a very close-knit community here. With little more than 1,600 students on campus at any given time, you really get to know your classmates. Bring some long johns and boots and you'll be all set. You'll learn to live with the cold, and even to play in it. During Winter Carnival, the Outing Club cuts a hole in "The Puddle" (aka Lake Andrews). People jump in, people freeze, then people warm up by the bonfire. It's a graduation requirement. OK, not really, but we like to say it is. I think Bates does a good job preparing students for life after Bates. The Office of Career Services is great, and being a Bates student automatically connects you to a whole network of helpful alumni—there's a real bond that I've already been able to work.

The Education

We have general education requirements at Bates, which I really like. I think it's important for any student to be versed in a variety of subject areas. One of the best things about Bates is how many classes there are to take—you can never take all the classes you want. The 4-4-1 calendar consists of two regular, four-class semesters, and then "Short Term" (one class) for five weeks, through May. It's a great time to try something beyond your field, or to take something more intense that you'd really like to focus on. One great aspect of Short Term is that you only have homework for one class; one bad aspect is the teachers know this, so they may assign you more homework than normal. But that's not usually the case. Another thing that makes a Bates education unique is that with the exception of one or two majors, you have to complete a senior thesis—and grad schools love that! You'll pick a topic that interests you and work really closely with your adviser. Many ideas come from people's studies abroad, and there are grants that allow you to go back and conduct necessary research. No matter what field you're in, there's always opportunity for you to conduct research with a faculty member—you just might have to take more initiative in certain areas (such as the humanities) than in others (the sciences).

> "Bates doesn't feel as 'crunchy' as it used to be. Birkenstocks and dreads are being replaced by Gucci bags and cell phones. This may just be part of a growing national trend. But I'm concerned.
> ✦ Maggie, junior

The Students

The students at Bates are amazing, and amazingly friendly. That's why a lot of us come here—and certainly what it came down to when I chose between schools. Students are very active on campus, and are also very supportive of each other; all performance events (sporting events, choir/orchestra/a cappella concerts, plays, dance productions, improv comedy shows, etc.) are very well attended by students and faculty alike.

The Activities

One of the biggest student complaints is that there's too much to do on campus, and sometimes it's really hard to choose. What a complaint to have! There are also a bazillion clubs that include sporting (recreational and competitive), political, religious, ethnic, performance (drama, dance, music), service, academic, and many more types of interests that I'm definitely forgetting. Also, if the club you want isn't already here, you can start it! I'd say the majority of students are involved in at least one or two (if not more!) extracurriculars on a regular basis.

The college brings in multiple artists and lecturers every week for events that are open to the entire Bates community, as well as the Lewiston/Auburn community. Every weekend a new movie is playing in Olin—something that's just been in the theaters but hasn't made it out on rental yet (and only costs $1). There's also a shuttle to Lewiston and Auburn: restaurants, the mall, Wal-Mart—you know, the necessities. There's also a free bus on Saturday that takes students to either the Old Port, the Maine Mall in South Portland, the outlets in Freeport, Boston, and Sugarloaf in the winter for skiing. Fun activities during Short Term include a trip to a Sox game, a white water rafting trip, usually a night down in Portland, intramural softball, BBQs every week (you're almost sick of BBQ food by the end of Short Term, if that's possible), and often trips to Popham Beach, about an hour away, or to Range Pond (pronounced "rang") in Auburn, about fifteen to twenty minutes away.

The Social Scene

Ah, the inevitable question. Drinking on campus. Yep, it happens, but no more than at any other school. The college banned hard alcohol after some kids were hospitalized after the Halloween Dance a few years back. If you're caught with it, you'll get a "strike," but it hasn't really put much of a damper on the social scene because there are plenty of other options (if you're of legal drinking age, of course). There's plenty to do if you don't drink. You can attend the same parties (no one's offended if you choose not to partake). But if you're not into the party scene, there's lots happening on campus every night, and sometimes it's fun to just stay in with your roommates and knit, watch movies, and chill out. Dorm life is fantastic—Bates really is a residential community. There's not much of a dating scene on campus—it's mostly people hooking up. Talking with my friends at other schools, they say it's the same way. They say that people do date in the real world after graduation. So that's something to look forward to.

Notable Bates Alumni Include:

Benjamin E. Mays, national civil rights leader, mentor of Martin Luther King Jr., and former president of Morehouse College

Bryan Gumbel, news anchor

Edmund Muskie, congressman, governor of Maine, U.S. senator, presidential candidate, and U.S. secretary of state under President Carter

John Carrafa, choreographer

Stacy Kabat, Academy Award–winning filmmaker, founder of Battered Women Fighting Back

William Stringfellow, peace activist, human rights lawyer, author, and theologian

BEREA COLLEGE

Founded: 1855
Location: Berea, KY
Phone: (859) 985-3000
E-mail: admissions@berea.edu
Web site: www.berea.edu

Number of Undergraduates: 1,595
Number of Graduate Students: 0
Cost: Not available
Application Deadline: April 30
　　　　Rolling admissions

Rating:
Most Selective

Notable Majors/Programs:
Business/Commerce, English, Biology,
Industrial Production Technologies

Size:
　● Small　　○ Medium　　○ Large

Location:
　○ Urban　　○ Suburban　　● Rural

On a Saturday, students talk about academics:
　○ Always　　● Sometimes　　○ Never

Nightlife:
　○ Intense　　○ Moderate　　● Laid-back

Politically, Berea leans:
　○ Left　　● Right　　○ Split

Diversity:
　○ High　　○ Low　　● Medium

Students describe Berea in five words:
- Beautiful Christian tuition-free school
- Intense workload, low-key parties

From the School:
　Adherence to the College's scriptural foundation, *"God has made of one blood all peoples of the earth,"* shapes the College's culture and programs so that students and staff alike can work toward both personal goals and a vision of a world shaped by Christian values. . . .
No student at Berea is expected to pay for tuition out of their own pocket. Tuition at Berea is covered by institutional scholarship, federal financial aid, outside scholarships that students bring with them, institutional grants, and earnings from our work program.

—www.berea.edu

If you're interested in Berea, you may also be interested in:
Antioch, Boston College, Evergreen State, Furman, Wake Forest

Name: Ellen

Hometown: Tecumseh, Michigan

Class Year: Senior

Major: I'm majoring in child and family studies, and minoring in business.

Extracurriculars: Track team, volleyball team, intramural basketball, Habitat for Humanity, teen mentoring

Career Goal: I want to become some sort of community counselor, perhaps working with the Catholic church in Cincinnati.

How would you describe Berea's reputation?

Berea College has an excellent reputation as a strong Christian liberal arts college. We also have a reputation for helping those who need it most.

Is this reputation accurate?

Definitely. Berea may not seem extremely Christian to us as students, but when you compare it to other supposedly "Christian" schools, we really are. I love that I'm able to share my college experience with people who share my faith. And since one of the main tenements of our faith is helping those in financial need, I'm proud that Berea itself stands as an icon of charity: anyone who gets in can come here tuition-free. You still have to pay room and board, but Berea will pick up the rest of your bills.

What aspect of your school would a prospective student not see on a campus tour?

The dorms you see on the campus tour are upperclassman dorms, not freshman dorms; the freshman dorms are quite a bit smaller.

Also, you won't hear about the many hours of homework the average Berea student does—I'd say we do more homework than students at comparable colleges. But it pays off, and because of it, Berea has a reputation for producing particularly hardworking graduates.

The Institution

Berea is the perfect size. You'll know almost everyone you see, but the campus is big enough so that you can hide and see no one at all if that suits you on a particular day. The campus is also notably neat and clean and students work to keep it that way. Sports aren't particularly big, but we have a lot of school pride. Even if they're not jumping up and down screaming "Berea!" all the time, there is an understated, deep appreciation.

Also, even though Berea is free, don't think that the education you'll receive is somehow inferior to the one you'd get at an expensive school—nothing could be further from the truth! Four years spent at Berea are four years spent working hard, learning hard, and getting one of the best educations in the country.

The Education

There is not a lot of competition between students here because classwork is generally so hard that people don't have time to compete—they're too busy working to keep their own heads above water. Even on weekends it's not unusual to stay in studying. We have extensive core requirements. I'd say it's in these core classes that most students do the worst, because they're not always interested in the course topics. And core classes assign a lot of homework—teachers expect that you spend three hours outside of class for every hour you spend in class. That adds up to a lot of hours! I am in twenty-six hours of class a week. That would translate into seventy-eight hours of homework.

The Students

Berea students are very racially diverse, and there are a lot of international students here. Our campus is pretty integrated, and I've loved meeting everyone and getting firsthand knowledge of a wide variety of cultures. Also, nearly everyone here at Berea comes from a working-class Christian background, and nearly every single student has a paid job on top of their studies. I think this brings us closer together. Add to that the fact that most students are from Appalachia and you've got quite a mix!

> "Berea's campus is nestled in the foothills of the Applachian Mountains. It's a very green and beautiful campus that mixes historical buildings that date back to the 1800s with an eco-village which incorporates the most up-to-date sustainable technology available."
>
> ✦ Jon, sophomore

The Activities

Eastern Kentucky University is only ten minutes away from Berea, but since most of us don't have cars our interaction with EKU is very limited. There's plenty to do right here at Berea, anyway—like recreational sports. Lots of students are heavily involved in religious groups. There are also some great community service projects, like teen mentoring (which I do—I love the feeling of making a difference in someone's life).

The Social Scene

Students at Berea don't party very much. If you're awake here on a Wednesday night at 3 a.m., you're probably still doing your homework for your 8 a.m. class. There's very little alcohol on campus—we don't have much of a drinking culture, and no Greek scene—which, in the end, makes this place much safer and friendlier. Typically, Friday and Saturday nights are spent watching movies or meeting with a group of classmates to work on a project due that Monday. You'll meet most of your friends at Berea through your dorm, your classes, and the activities you join. Everyone on campus is very polite and friendly, which makes the process easier; at Berea we hold doors open and say "hi" to people all the time, so it's easy to say, "Hey, you're interesting. Want to grab a cup of coffee some time?" And random introductions like that frequently lead to relationships, then long-term relationships, and then . . . well, marriage.

Name: Paula
Hometown: Jackson, Kentucky
Class Year: Junior
Major: International relations
Extracurriculars: Volleyball, band
Career Goal: I'd like to graduate, head to the Patterson School of Diplomacy, and eventually work for the U.S. government.

How would you describe Berea's reputation?

Berea is an excellent school that is very well respected by those who know of it.

Is this reputation accurate?

Yup. Our professors are amazing, our campus is beautiful, and, if you get in, you don't have to pay any tuition. What more could you ask for from a college?

What aspect of your school would a prospective student not see on a campus tour?

Berea is in a small town, and if you came by on a tour you might think there's not much to do around here. As someone who's lived here for a while now, I can tell there's plenty to do. Berea students are constantly busy.

The Institution

Most classes at Berea are really tiny (we have a 12:1 student-teacher ratio), so you can count on having lots of one-on-one time with your favorite professors. Once you leave Berea, you won't have much trouble finding a job—our school is well known and has been named the number-one school in the South by *Newsweek* magazine quite a few times. I'd say the average Berea student is really friendly. Our motto is "God has made of one blood all peoples of the earth"; the college was founded on this ideal, and students try to uphold it in their everyday lives. Everyone is loved, everyone is accepted. All this sounds kind of religious, and Berea does embrace Christian values, but people of any religion can come to school here, and they'll be entirely free to worship as they wish. There's no pressure to convert or anything like that.

The Education

Most of my classes are discussion-based, which is nice because then everyone gets involved and debates, and otherwise dry issues are covered in a lively fashion. When I first decided to come to Berea, I anticipated this, the small classes, but I didn't anticipate quite how challenging the workload would be. There's a lot of reading and a lot of writing. I guess that just comes with the territory. Luckily, our professors (who all know our names) are very willing to help us out if we're having trouble with the material, or if we're being crushed and have four papers due at once. I definitely have heard of cases where a professor will let a student hand in an essay late because they have tests and papers due at the same time in other classes. Because kids here generally come from families who can't afford to go all over the world otherwise, Berea really emphasizes the importance of studying abroad. We have an excellent program and Berea provides lots of scholarships, so money won't be a factor if you want to apply. Also, Berea's housing is better than what you'd find at most other colleges—most dorms are set up in suites, so you have your own room and then a shared kitchen and living room. Not bad. Lastly, Berea spends hundreds of thousands of dollars to bring in dancers, musicians, politicians, and lecturers to the school, and we actually get class credit for going to see them! It's great. And I forgot to mention, every student at Berea gets a laptop, free of charge!

The Students

Berea was the very first integrated school in the South, and everyone here is very proud of that fact. Currently, we're ranked the thirteenth best school in America for African American students. We have a ton of international students. More than 80 percent of our campus participates in some sort of organization/extracurricular activity. Everyone is welcome at Berea, and all students contribute to the great community feel.

The Activities

I'd say Berea students are known for being "brainy"—but that doesn't mean we don't know how to have fun! All the time, Berea students will leave the library to go to a basketball game, an open mike poetry night, or any variety of other school-sponsored events. There's really always something going on. Also, because Berea is tuition-free, almost every student has to spend ten hours per week working a campus job. Students work in every part of Berea's administration imaginable—from the library to planning on-campus parties, which are always creative and innovative. Drinking isn't big at Berea, so parties have to actually be interesting to succeed.

The Social Scene

Berea students are still college students, so we—like most college students—party just about every weekend to make up for the stress of the weekdays. But again, our parties don't have alcohol and we don't have fraternities or sororities, so our parties are not as wild as ones at other schools. I don't mind this so much because people mix a lot more when they're happy and coherent, instead of drunken and overly rambunctious.

Name: Britney
Hometown: Richmond, Kentucky
Class Year: Junior
Major: English, international relations
Extracurriculars: Entrepreneurship for the Public Good, *BC NOW* news, *BC Live* news, Amnesty International, Buddhist Student Association
Career Goal: Journalism. But before that I'd like to do volunteer work; maybe join the Peace Corps.

How would you describe Berea's reputation?

Put simply, Berea is one of the best liberal arts colleges in America.

> "The student who would be happiest at Berea would be hard-working, friendly, open-minded, and willing to sacrifice four years of drinking for four years of light-hearted times and a lot of studying."
> ✦ Gregory, sophomore

Is this reputation accurate?

I would say so. Berea is very academically challenging, and it has a mandatory attendance policy, meaning you can't ever just skip a class. Students put in a lot, and they get out a lot. Not the least of which is tuition-free college, cheap room and board, and a free computer that you get to keep the rest of your life. I can't stress enough how much of a gift it is to come to this school.

What aspect of your school would a prospective student not see on a campus tour?

I wish an admissions officer had told me just how easy it was to study abroad here! That's a big plus about this place, and one I didn't discover until I was a full-fledged student. Not only is studying abroad easy but [so are] most things that cost money—if you ask, you'll find someone to sign a form and Berea will foot the bill. Berea is so incredibly generous that some kids start to take advantage, try to profit off the school, just because Berea is so trusting, and Berea honestly does want to give students money if that money will allow the student to do something that will contribute to their learning process.

The Institution

While Berea is great because it's so small, it can also be awful because it's so small. You know everyone. Everyone knows you. If you don't like the people you meet, you're stuck with them. But what can you do? You're getting top-notch academics and the tuition is free—can you really complain? Berea is one of the few schools elite enough to be eligible for every major international scholarship, including the Watson, Rhodes, Marshall, Udall, Truman—it's impressive. That said, since we don't have Greek life or sports teams, there's not much school spirit here. The only spirit we can claim is the one that supposedly haunts Draper Hall. Oooooh, creepy. Lastly, Berea's campus is pretty, but it's also a bit disjointed. In the busiest bathroom on campus, someone wrote "CAAW—Citizens Against Atrocious Wallpaper." CAAW doesn't really exist, but it should. Berea does not know how to color-coordinate very well.

The Education

The workload at Berea is considerable, and students spend a lot of time studying. I spend between three and six hours doing homework every night, and we absolutely talk about our academics outside of class. We don't really have social lives to talk about instead. All we know are our academics. So we'll go on and on about Dante and Aristotle. The teachers appreciate our dedication and match it with their own. Professors probably do more work than we do putting together their excellent lesson plans. And every class is taught by a full professor—never a TA. Our professors know us, invite us over to their houses for dinner, and will meet up with us at night for coffee. They care about us.

Also, Berea brings some really important speakers to campus. In the past few years we've had Jesse Jackson, the Dalai Lama . . . At any other school, you'd see someone like Ralph Nader in a big auditorium, and you'd be so far away you wouldn't be able to make out his features, but because Berea is so nice and small, I was able to meet the man, have dinner with him, talk to him, even watch him chew his food. Amazing.

The Students

Most Berea students are middle class to lower middle class, in part because there's no tuition. Most Berea students are staunchly Christian. And I guess most people here get along. One thing that Berea does do extremely well is welcome in black students. We have Black Studies as an academic department, the Black Cultural Center, the Black Music Ensemble, the Black Student Union, and the African Student Association. Black students really couldn't find a more open and accepting college

than Berea, with the exception of an historically black college like Morehouse or Howard.

The Activities

Berea students give their time freely to community service organizations. There are numerous departments on campus whose sole purpose is to coordinate Bereans' community service efforts. In general, Bereans also like their clubs and organizations. They sign up for activities en masse, and actually show up to meetings, and throw themselves into achieving whatever goal the club was set up to achieve. If there's a club you'd like to set up and it doesn't already exist at Berea, it's easy to found it as well.

The Social Scene

So alcohol doesn't exist on Berea's campus. It doesn't matter whether you're over twenty-one, under twenty-one, whatever. No one drinks. Students here don't like alcohol. They seem to fear alcohol. Personally, I don't know what they're afraid of. They think it's the plague or something. Anyway, if you're looking for a college where people go wild on the weekends, you may as well cross Berea off your list immediately. This is primarily a place for sober, vaguely liberal Christians who get together in small groups, know everything about one another, and, in many cases, still giggle when they talk about sex.

Notable Berea Alumni Include:
Harold Moses, director, Vanderbilt Cancer Center
John Fenn, Nobel Prize–winning chemist
Sarah Hamilton, doctor

BOSTON COLLEGE

Founded: 1863

Location: Chestnut Hill, MA

Phone: (617) 552-3100

E-mail: ugadmis@bc.edu

Web site: www.bc.edu

Number of Undergraduates: 8,916

Number of Graduate Students: 4,700

Cost: Approximately $38,000 per year

Application Deadline: January 2

Early Decision: November 1

Rating: Most Selective	Notable Majors/Programs: English, Finance, Psychology

Size:
- ○ Small   ○ Medium   ● Large

Location:
- ● Urban   ○ Suburban   ○ Rural

On a Saturday, students talk about academics:
- ○ Always   ● Sometimes   ○ Never

Nightlife:
- ● Intense   ○ Moderate   ○ Laid-back

Politically, Boston College leans:
- ○ Left   ● Right   ○ Split

Diversity:
- ○ High   ○ Low   ● Medium

Students describe Boston College in five words:
- Prestigious Catholic school for prepsters
- Beautiful, challenging, wealthy, hard partying

From the School:

The Jesuit community at Boston College is committed to maintaining and strengthening the Jesuit, Catholic mission of the University, especially its commitment to integrating intellectual, personal, ethical, and religious formation; and to uniting high academic achievement with service to others.

—http://bc.edu

If you're interested in Boston College, you may also be interested in:
Boston University, Cornell, Georgetown, Notre Dame, U. Pennsylvania, Tufts

Name: Bridget
Hometown: Montpelier, Vermont
Class Year: Junior
Major: History
Extracurriculars: Dance Organization of Boston College, Student Admissions Program of Boston College
Career Goal: I'd like to go into law.

How would you describe Boston College's reputation?

BC's reputation has improved a lot over the past ten years. We used to be known as a party school full of beer-drinking Irish Catholic kids, "J. Crew with a hangover." Now we're far more prestigious and academically serious.

Is this reputation accurate?

Yeah. The competition to get into this school has skyrocketed; we now have twenty-two thousand applications a year.

BC is Catholic, and it leans to the conservative end of the political spectrum. That said, the school's Catholicism isn't too pervasive. If you're really interested in this place, but you're not Catholic, don't let that put you off.

What aspect of your school would a prospective student not see on a campus tour?

I give presentations to high school kids and their parents in the office of admissions. They specifically tell me to downplay the partying and drinking that goes on at BC—but let me tell you, it happens and it happens in full force! Admissions also tells people that living on the Freshman Newton campus, 1.5 miles down the road, isn't bad. But when it's freezing, and you're waiting for the bus, it can feel like forever.

> "BC is known for being a networking school."
>
> ✦ Michael, freshman

The Institution

Since BC is a Jesuit Catholic institution, service and community are very important values here. BC also has two mottos: *cura personalis* (care of the entire individual) and "men and women for oth-

ers," and the school does all it can to make sure every student lives up to them. BC believes that an institution should teach you to be both an academic person and a spiritual person. For those cynics among you, this doesn't mean we churn out strict Catholics; it just means when you leave BC you should be able to argue and defend what you believe and why you believe it, and have the strength of character to live your life accordingly. Also, our campus security is second to none; we have an actual police force trained to the same standards as the Boston PD. They can arrive at any point on campus within sixty seconds of an emergency button being pushed (emergency buttons are everywhere). They take any kind of crime extremely seriously. It's great knowing that we're extremely safe even though we're right in the heart of a big city. On the down side, cost of living is really high here—when doing anything off campus in Boston, be prepared to shell out.

> "Students here are very motivated. Most want to be doctors, lawyers, or businessmen/women."
>
> ✦ Peter, sophomore

The Education

Most classes at BC are discussion-oriented, which I prefer to having a lecturer yabber at me for hours on end. It's nice to be involved in in-class debates with professors and your peers. BC's core curriculum is really huge: there are fifteen required courses, not counting the courses you'll have to take for your major. This is a huge pain, because it cuts down on your ability to take classes you're actually interested in, and sometimes you'll spend days studying for tests in classes you absolutely can't stand, but it doesn't matter because they're part of your core. That said, students generally leave BC feeling glad the core is there. It makes them "well rounded," and they say taking mandatory classes in so many disciplines has helped them narrow down their interests and figure out which major they really want to explore.

The Students

BC is said to have a really homogenous student body. And it's true. We're mostly white, Christian, well-to-do kids. You'll see a lot of what we call "BC girls" around campus—blond, skinny, wearing a short skirt, cell phone in hand, really rich—it's like you've somehow stepped into a J. Crew catalog. Politically, I'd say our campus is split between Republican and Democrat. Maybe the Republicans have a slight edge. *The Heights,* which is our main student newspaper, is widely read—everyone is always talking about the articles. One surprising thing about BC is that there is no Greek system here. Which eliminates a lot of the frustrating social crap you find at schools where everyone is a Delta Delta Delta Kappa Kappa Delta—whatever the hell. I think most BC students appreciate this. Without a Greek scene, you can show up at any party and meet loads of different people, without everyone being segregated by who belongs to which frat and "Oh my god, that's the coolest one!"

The Activities

Students at BC hardly go to other schools to party—students at other schools come to BC because they know we have the most fun. The most interaction we have with any other school is with Boston University—and when we interact with them, we spend most of our time making fun of them. (They're our rival.) BC students wear T-shirts sometimes that say IT REALLY SUCKS TO B.U. Get it?

> "The food here is some of the best you'll find on any college campus—but it will cost you."
>
> ✦ Jason, junior

The Social Scene

When BC students aren't working their butts off, they're partying their butts off. Weekends begin on Thursday nights; Boston bars are packed with BC students from then until Sunday. BC juniors and seniors tend to live off campus, and they hold *biiiig* crazy parties that are lots of fun. We're a big beer-drinking school—at any party you'll find kegs and cans of Red Stripe. When BC students party, they're loud and fun and raucous. When they calm down from the partying, they're polite, they hold open doors for one another . . . if anyone ever stops and asks a student for directions, the student will always help the person out

and usually even walk the stranger to their destination.

Name: Megan
Hometown: Hope Valley, Rhode Island
Class Year: Junior
Major: Communications
Extracurriculars: Undergraduate Government of Boston College, Legislative Director
Career Goal: Broadcast television, perhaps working in programming. I'd love to be the person who decides what to air on NBC!

How would you describe Boston College's reputation?

Boston College is said to be an outstanding academic institution that admits well-rounded students.

Is this reputation accurate?

This is certainly accurate. BC students are intelligent athlete-scholars who involve themselves in many extracurricular activities. BC is also an institution that really cares about promoting Jesuit ideals. The Jesuit "Ignation Society" on campus is strong and offers amazing Kairos retreats to students. I think our Jesuit heritage is appreciated by most students. Then there's BC's Catholic heritage, which is a complicated issue. Most BC students, and most of BC's faculty, are pretty liberal and believe in a range of faiths, but most of BC's upper administration, and most its of trustees, are conservative Catholics. This causes students and administrators to butt heads more than a little and skews people's perception. Some say it's a liberal Jesuit university and others will tell you it's a very conservative Catholic institution.

> "Football traditions: Everyone wears a yellow Superfan shirt. Everyone drinks more than their share. Every time BC gets a point, we toss the lightest girl up in the air!"
>
> ✦ Ronnie, senior

What aspect of your school would a prospective student not see on a campus tour?

A campus tour won't show you the "Mods" (modular apartments where many seniors live). They were built in the 1970s as temporary housing, but they were never torn down. They're pretty hideous, but I've had some great times there. The best parties are at the Mods and I hope they never tear them down. In the center of the Mods is the Shoe Tree; the story goes, every time a senior has sex with a virgin, they're supposed to hang a pair of shoes on the tree's branches. There's also a silly rumor that the golden eagles mounted at the entrance to campus will come to life and fly away if any BC student graduates as a virgin. Lastly, it's good to know that BC is fairly cliquey. Even though we don't have fraternities and sororities, there are certain groups that serve the same functions, and throw exclusive parties that only the "in" crowd can get into.

> "There's a lot of preppy polo shirts with popped collars, Burberry and Gucci bags. Sometimes, when I walk to class, I feel like I'm trapped in a golf or tennis tournament."
>
> ✦ Daniel, sophomore

The Institution

My favorite BC tradition is the "Eleven O-Clock Scream," where, during every day of finals, everyone on campus screams out their window at 11 p.m. It's pretty creepy-sounding—especially in the middle of winter. But it's *verrrry* necessary. Also, I love reading the graffiti in cubicles on the fourth floor of O'Neill Library. Everything from dirty sexual cartoons to polls to elaborate quotes from love songs. It's ridiculous, you can hardly find space to add your own piece of wisdom.

Boston College in the fall and spring is beautiful! Everyone is outside lying in the grass in the Dustbowl (largest grassy area on campus), playing Frisbee, and taking in some rays. Nothing beats it. But by the same token, nothing is worse than having to climb up the stairs from Lower Campus in winter when it's minus 40 degrees outside, and then having to cross O'Neill Plaza in the blistering wind. Except for maybe the Housing Lottery in the late winter/early spring, which many agree is pretty traumatizing. You create a list of who you want to live with the next year, give it to Residential Life, then they stick the list in a giant bingo barrel, then draw lists out one by one. The earlier your list is drawn, the better your housing. It is a

most nerve-racking experience. Lastly, a cool thing we have at BC is Eagle Bucks—dollar credits on our student IDs that let us buy food on campus, shop in the bookstore, and also buy some things off campus, like food at The Wrap and Eagle's Deli in Cleveland Circle.

The Education

BC definitely has its share of amazing professors. It also has "duds." You just have to know how to pick the right classes and avoid the wrong ones. One of the best places to look to find good classes is the UGBC Web site, where students submit comments and critiques of professors they've had. This is a great resource that most students use to inform their class selections. Once you've chosen your classes, class size varies. Most intro or survey classes are large lectures, and as classes become more advanced, they'll become smaller and more discussion based.

On the negative side, advising is horrendous at BC. Well, at least it is in the school of arts and sciences. Our assigned advisers are random professors in our departments who are usually too busy to help us much when we're choosing classes. Instead, they check to see if we're on track to fulfill our core and major requirements, then they send us on our way.

> "In Boston, if you tell someone you go to BC the reaction is either 'Wow, you're smart' or 'Wow, you're rich.'"
>
> ✦ Andrea, sophomore

The Students

I'd say, for better or worse, the average student at Boston College is white and from an upper middle-class background from Massachusetts, New York, or Connecticut. They were probably really involved in extracurricular activities in high school, probably graduated toward the top of their class, with a 3.9ish GPA, and shop at Abercrombie & Fitch, J. Crew, or Banana Republic. On the weekends they will either go to off-campus parties or to parties in the Mods. They might also go to an off-campus bar and get in with their fake ID (fake IDs are everywhere at BC—no student goes out without one). Once out and about, they'll drink a lot, have fun, go to bed, wake up with an obnoxious and painful hangover, fight through it, do school-work all day, then go out again that night.

Princeton Review recently ranked BC number two for schools where "alternative lifestyles are not an alternative." Not too long ago, BC's president came under fire in the *Boston Globe* and the *BC Heights* (our newspaper) for allegedly refusing to hire gay professors. That said, BC students feel completely differently toward LGBT students. Which is to say, we're doing our best to become more and more accepting. Recently, a few BC students put together a program that made and distributed T-shirts that said GAY? FINE BY ME. So many students bought the shirts that the group had to go back and order more. BC students, whenever possible, try to do what they believe is right. At present, lots of students are campaigning for BC's administration to hire more deans and professors of AHANA [African, Hispanic, Asian, and Native American] descent. We don't like the fact that so many professors are Caucasian and have relatively similar backgrounds—we think there's lots to be said for having a diverse faculty.

The Activities

BC students have a ton of school spirit. Most students come to most football and hockey games—they're always a blast, and the bleachers are full of gold Superfan shirts. Really, everyone wears gold BC apparel here. At every sporting event there's a "sea of gold." Also, BC dorm life is great. I'm still close friends with the girls I met on my hall freshman year. Sophomore year I met a group of guys in my dorm, and I still hang out with them as well. Every dorm at BC is a big social community, everyone talks to everyone.

> "Seniors live in the Mods—little town houses with a front yard and everything. It's great in the spring—everyone throws cookouts and house parties."
> ✦ Laura, junior

The Social Scene

Weekends at BC start on Thursday nights (or Wednesday nights if you're particularly devoted). Parties are held either on campus (mostly in the Mods and senior housing), off campus at junior apartments, or at nearby Boston bars. There are quite a lot of bars BC students head to—MaryAnn's, Kinvara, The Kells, Great Scott's, Roggie's, or Cityside. I'd say BC students are pretty devoted to drinking alcohol—particularly beer. And most long-term relationships here start out as drunken hook-ups. Seriously, there isn't a dating scene here so much as a social drinking scene, which turns into a drunken hook-up scene, and before you know it everyone's paired off.

> "BC has issues when it comes to sex: they don't distribute condoms and girls can't get birth control unless they have acne."
> ✦ Alexa, freshman

Name: Alexa
Hometown: Oklahoma City, Oklahoma
Class Year: Junior
Major: History and sociology
Extracurriculars: Rugby, running marathons, volunteering at a health center, student manager of on-campus cafe
Career Goal: Work for a national nonprofit organization and then go on from there.

How would you describe Boston College's reputation?

BC is a conservative, academically challenging school with a lot of really solid programs. It's also looked at as a school for Ivy League rejects.

Is this reputation accurate?

Yes. BC can be very conservative, and it is an academically challenging place populated with students who love it here but originally wanted to go someplace like Dartmouth or Princeton (and didn't get in).

What would an admissions officer at your school probably not tell a prospective student?

BC is problematically conservative when it comes to issues involving sex. They don't hand out condoms on campus, which is a common practice at most other colleges which acknowledge that college students will have sex and want to take measures to ensure it's safe sex. But not BC. They won't even talk about sex.

The Institution

The one big thing that did not meet my expectations about BC was the quality of life for gay students here. I came out freshman year, and I had no support. It wasn't that I was oppressed—the students here are good people, and they would never threaten me or make me feel unsafe for being gay. It was more that they didn't understand me being gay, and the school itself had no structures in place to help students understand homosexuality. It's because the university is Catholic, really—gay and pro-choice students groups don't exist here. They can't. BC won't give any campus groups that go against the stance of the Catholic Church official administrative recognition. If you confront the administration on this, they'll say, "You knew the university was Catholic when you applied. Maybe you shouldn't have come here." To me this sounds like a cop-out—BC acknowledging a problem but refusing to do anything to make things better. Then ducking behind the Church and closing their eyes. It is what it is. Don't come to BC expecting to change the place, because it simply won't budge on issues relating to abortion or sex.

The Education

BC has lots of excellent professors, particularly in the history and accounting departments. I'd say most professors are always there for students, are open to having personal relationships with them, and always encourage students to come to their office hours, to talk about the paper they're writing or just to chat about academics in general. Students, by and large, aren't competitive with one other, except in the premed program, which is kind of cutthroat. I'd say, usually, I do about twenty hours of work per week outside of class, and more than that if I have a paper to write or an exam to study for. Academics are difficult here, but not too difficult. If you set aside a few hours for work every day, and occasionally cram for a test, you'll do well and still have lots of time to have fun.

The Students

The average BC student is white, rich, politically moderate, wears Abercrombie & Fitch, is majoring in business, and is a generally a nice person. There are some students of color, but not as many as there should be. There are several religious groups on campus who get out into local communities and do a lot of volunteer work. There are no fraternities or sororities here, and most big parties are held at off-campus apartments. (Most students are only granted three years of on-campus housing, so they'll elect to spend their junior year in nearby apartments.)

The Activities

BC is right on the edge of Boston, and there are always amazing things happening throughout the city. You can grab a train and head to a movie, the theater, go shopping, go to a great restaurant. BC students can also head to nearby schools like MIT, Harvard, or Tufts, and go to any of their parties or academic events, or even take the $15 Fung Wah bus to to New York City. That said, it's easy to get absorbed in the BC bubble, especially during the winter, and I'd actually venture that most students don't leave campus half as often as they expected they would. There's so much fun stuff going on, there's no need to run off. Right at BC there are football games, parties, plays, lecturers, forums, campus groups, nearby bars . . .

The Social Scene

All freshmen are housed together at BC—and given the dynamics of dorm life, they bond quickly. You also meet people in classes, bring those friends back to your dorms, and everyone's social circle expands. It's great. BC is not known as a dating school, it's more of a hook-up school, meaning people will make out at parties all the time, but that's not really indicative of anything. You can kiss someone drunkenly one night, and it will mean nothing the next night. Or it could be the start of a relationship. You never know. BC's party scene is pretty popular, and it ranges from tiny get-togethers to huge parties in off-campus apartments. Some sports teams throw really big parties with regularity.

Notable Boston College Alumni Include:
Michael C. Hawley, president and CEO, Gillette
Susan M. Gianinno, CEO, J. Walter Thompson
Doug Flutie, NFL quarterback
Chris O'Donnell, actor
Eddie Dowling, musician
Matthew Del Negro, actor

BOSTON UNIVERSITY

Founded: 1839

Location: Boston, MA

Phone: (617) 353-2300

E-mail: admissions@bu.edu

Web site: www.bu.edu

Number of Undergraduates: 17,860

Number of Graduate Students: 9,379

Cost: Approximately $38,000 per year

Application Deadline: January 1

Early Decision: November 1

Rating:	Notable Majors/Programs:
Selective	Social Sciences, Business Management, Mass Communications

Size:
○ Small   ○ Medium   ● Large

Location:
● Urban   ○ Suburban   ○ Rural

On a Saturday, students talk about academics:
○ Always   ● Sometimes   ○ Never

Nightlife:
○ Intense   ● Moderate   ○ Laid-back

Politically, Boston University leans:
● Left   ○ Right   ○ Split

Diversity:
○ High   ○ Low   ● Medium

Students describe BU in five words:
- Huge, eclectic, in heart of Boston
- Independent students; competitive, corporate university

From the School

Boston University—independent, coeducational, and nonsectarian—is an internationally recognized institution of higher education and research located along the banks of the Charles River and adjacent to the historic Back Bay district of Boston . . . As one of the nation's premier research universities, Boston University believes that all students benefit by learning from dedicated teachers who are actively engaged in original research. The University's learning environment is further enriched by an extraordinary array of direct involvements with the broader artistic, economic, social, intellectual, and educational life of the [Boston] community.

—www.bu.edu

If you're interested in Boston University, you may also be interested in:
Boston College, Cornell, George Washington, NYU, UMass Amherst, SUNY–Binghamton

Name: Jared
Hometown: North Richmond, Vermont
Class Year: Senior
Major: International relations
Extracurriculars: BU Students for UNICEF
Career Goal: I want to be part of an international nonprofit agency working on educational development or women's issues in Latin America or Africa.

How would you describe BU's reputation?

BU is a large, highly ranked school in the heart of Boston that's home to every type of student imaginable.

Is this reputation accurate? Why or why not?

Absolutely. Whoever you are, you'll find your place at BU. There are tens of thousands of students here, in seventeen different schools and colleges. Are you a hippie? You'll have a great time in the Arts school with the other hippies. Future businessman or woman? Slap on your designer suit, you'll love BU's School of Management. Not sure where you belong? The College of Arts and Sciences may be perfect for you.

What would an admissions officer at your school probably not tell a prospective student?

An admissions officer won't tell you that you're about to enter into a corporation, not a university. BU does business throughout the city; they own land, buildings, everything. Bostonians have mixed feelings about this. So be prepared to hear about it from the locals and also be prepared to occasionally fight with BU's administration, which sometimes cares more about the corporate entity than it does about BU students.

The Institution

Because BU is a big school, BU students don't have school spirit the way students have school spirit at small liberal arts colleges. No BU graduate will gush, "Oh, I knew *all* of my professors and ate dinner at their houses *all the time.*" But that's not what we at BU are looking for. BU students don't want to be baby-sat by professors or have an artificial life cooped up on a tiny campus in the middle of nowhere. We want to live in the real world and prepare for our futures. We want professors that treat us like adults, and we want to act like adults. I went to a much smaller school my freshman year and transferred here because you just don't grow up in that environment. We have lots of big name professors at BU—five Nobel laureates are on staff, and plenty of professors have Pulitzers, Guggenheims, even Academy Awards—but don't count on having classes with these superstars. Their classes are hard to get into. On the upside, these professors frequently give talks that everyone on campus can come to, along with outside lecturers from all over the world. We even have an African president's roundtable every year where students can stop by and schmooze with former world leaders.

And, if you like cities, BU is right in the middle of one of the best cities in the world. Even if students don't have school spirit, they'll have Boston spirit. The city is clean, the social life is fantastic, it's easy to get around. If you like sports, BU is blocks from the Green Monster at Fenway, so when the Sox are playing, everyone's there. Bostonians love their teams, and it's impossible not to get sucked into the excitement. Step into any Boston bar, and there will be a mix of college students and academics and professionals and whoever. And everyone will get along, because they'll all heartily agree that the Yankees *suck!* Boston winters also suck. But the entire city is giddy once April rolls around.

The Education

Classes at BU can be easy or difficult, depending on which school you're affiliated with. If you're in the College of Communications, you'll have an easy ride. College of Arts and Sciences could go either way. If you're in the School of Management, you'll always be wearing a suit, carrying around a laptop, and fighting a deadline. The education at BU is something of a hodgepodge. You'll have great professors and not-so-great professors. You'll have classes with five hundred kids and classes with fifteen kids. Intro classes are huge, and this can be discouraging; but as you move up into more advanced classes, they get smaller and professors reach out and do their best to be approachable. When you're in a large class, you'll have to reach out to your professor, remind them of your name, and then they'll be, at worst, friendly, at best, inclined to take a personal interest in your studies. The number-one thing to remember is that no one will be checking up on you at BU. If you fall behind on your reading and don't do anything about it in time for an exam, that's your prerogative. BU professors *will* give you a failing grade.

The Students

BU has every kind of student imaginable. There are a whole lot of international students, which is great, especially if you're in the social sciences, because they'll bring entirely different perspectives to the table. Most kids here seem to be fairly liberal. And most seem to be ambitious—BU students have big dreams—even if they're not terribly competitive in the classroom. Greek life exists here, but it's fairly small, and non-Greeks don't take the scene very seriously.

> "Boston University has one of the best academic programs in the world and it's reputation continues to grow."
> ✦ Melanie, junior

The Activities

The Boston area is jam-packed with colleges. Students from BU, BC, Wellesley, MIT, Harvard, Emerson, the Berklee School of Music—all of us mix all the time at clubs and bars. Most people have friends at other schools, and it's really common to date outside of your own university. Plus you can take classes at some of these other schools, too, which provides a great change of pace if you're tired of what BU offers. When it's nice we hang out by the esplanade. There's a path running alongside the Charles River with grassy spots that are just perfect for rollerblading, running, or doing your homework. When it's freezing there are plenty of coffee shops, or, gasp, the library.

The Social Scene

Your social scene at BU will shift and change depending on your class year. If you're a freshman you're likely to do the party scene in Allston (rock city). You will dabble in frat parties and indie-music parties and birthday parties. Hordes of freshmen walk the streets every weekend looking for cheap beer. The on-campus alcohol policy is fairly harsh, so there is very little partying in the dorms. And then there's Lansdowne Street, home to Boston's club scene. You only have to be nineteen at most places and it's always packed. It's fun for a while, but by junior year most kids grow out of it. Juniors are more likely to branch out to private parties throughout the city, they'll take in more live shows, and then when they turn twenty-one

(for real) they can go anywhere. Irish pubs, young professional lounges, swanky hotel restaurants, dive bars, college bars. Boston is a great place to be twenty-one and over. But be warned—our subway, the T, stops running at 12:30 a.m. So when you're out partying, either cut the partying short or save enough money to take a cab home. Lastly, I'd advise against joining a frat or sorority. In the end, it just limits your friendship groups because you'll have so many commitments to your fake (and expensive) new "family" that you'll have less time to meet kids you actually like and get along with.

Name: Lucia
Hometown: Springfield, Massachusetts
Class Year: Freshman
Major: Latin American studies
Extracurriculars: Dance, prelaw, FYSOP (first year service outreach program)
Career Goal: Undecided

How would you describe BU's reputation?

If you ask parents or a guidance counselor they'll tell you they associate BU with a "quality education." If you ask your peers they'll say "You go to Boston College? Awesome! I have a cousin who goes there!"

Is this reputation accurate?

Let's clear this up here and now: BU is a different school than BC. Just because both schools' abbreviations start with the letter *B*, and because both schools happen to coexist on the same portion of Commonwealth Avenue, does not make them the same school. We're our own entity, OK? BU is a school on the rise. Right now, it's not as well-regarded as some of its neighboring schools [BC, Harvard, MIT, and Tufts], but that's definitely changing.

> "Everyone here is ambitious—even if they're not competitive in the classroom."
> ✦ Jared, senior

What would an admissions officer at your school probably not tell a prospective student?

1) There's some grade deflation at BU. 2) Before you declare your major, it is very easy to get lost in BU's bureaucracy. (On the other hand, once

you've declared your major, the school has an outstanding advising system.) 3) A lot of high school kids visit BU and fall in love with tree-lined Bay State Road. Unfortunately, because of BU's housing lottery system and the twenty thousand kids who vie every semester for on-campus housing, it's unlikely a prospective will ever live in a Bay State brownstone. Same goes for the brownstones on Commonwealth Ave. And lastly, 4) BU has a *ridiculous* guest policy. In short, if you ever want to have a weekend overnight guest, they have to be approved by the Residential Life office by 5 p.m. on the Thursday before. Goodbye spontaneity! Have friends in town who might want to crash last minute? Eager to take home some hottie you just met at a bar? Think again, BU won't let them stay overnight. Also, don't count on a late-night study session in your room the night before a test or impromptu snuggling with your honey. Even other BU students aren't allowed into dorms that aren't theirs past 8 p.m. Eight p.m.!?

> "People knock BU for the lack of cultural diversity but the variety of on-campus groups has to be one of the most diverse around. There's a Japanese anime group, a cigar aficionados group, even a meat society."
>
> ✦ Dave, junior

The Institution

BU has a great location. On any given day, you can easily shop at Downtown Crossing and at Copley/Pru, eat dinner in Chinatown, get dessert at Mike's Pastry in the North End, return to drop off stuff at your room, then head out to a party at Tufts, BC, or MIT. Also, many students live within a stone's throw of Fenway, home of the Red Sox.

I think the most difficult thing about being a first-year student here is that there's no one to hold your hand, and it can be lonely if you don't know anyone. But if you get out there you'll be fine. My advice, use The Facebook (www.thefacebook.com), which lets you connect to other BU students and create an online social network. Students list their friends and their friends list their friends, and soon enough you're connected to seven hundred people that you can e-mail to meet you for coffee if you ever get lonely.

At a big school like BU, resources like this can be invaluable.

The Education

Students at BU always talk about classes, but more in the "Damn! This class I'm taking is so hard" vein. BU has both graduate and undergraduate students, so if you're particularly ambitious you can take graduate courses on top of your undergraduate courseload. BU has a lot of core requirements, too, but if you've done well on your IB and/or AP exams, you'll be able to phase out of a lot of them.

> "The guest policy at BU . . . is absolutely ridiculous."
>
> ✦ Karl, sophomore

The Students

You'd think with tens of thousands of students BU would be overflowing with diversity. Well, it's not. Most kids are white, Asian, and Jewish. There are some black and Latino students, but they're rare. There is a large gay population though. And there are some international students, but there are far more kids from New Jersey, Long Island, Manhattan, Massachusetts, and California. I'd also say one out of every four students is on heavy financial aid, and three out of four students have very wealthy parents. Of those who are wealthy, about 50 percent are *insanely* wealthy. And the wealthy range from down-to-earth Polo-wearing, Coach-toting kids to extravagant Burberry-swishing girls who charge down every Boston street like it's a runway.

The Activities

On a sunny day you'll spot the following four groups of kids hanging outside: the students playing Frisbee on Marsh Plaza or BU Beach, sweating heavily, having a great time; the academically focused kids poring over textbooks and trying to soak up some rays while figuring out how to do their problem sets; the students who are wholly devoted to their student groups, desperately trying to raise awareness for an upcoming concert or charity event they're sponsoring; and girls on their cell phones, irritated as they dodge out-of-control rollerbladers and try to maintain perfect hair and makeup. If I'm awake at 3 a.m. on a Wednesday night at BU, I'm probably hungry. The campus convenience store closes from 3 a.m. to 6 a.m., so I'm cursing the fact that I didn't think to get food. Or I'm at a party. Yes, there are parties at 3 a.m. on Wednesday nights at BU and students go to them. If you want to party on a Wednesday night, it won't be hard.

> "If you're caught in dorms with alcohol you can get kicked out and have to move off-campus. BU is pretty strict about this. If you're going to drink, don't do it in your room."
>
> ✦ Lisa, freshman

The Social Scene

People are friendly here, but not overly so. I mean, BU is so integrated with Boston that you *couldn't* just go around saying hi to people. They could be anyone. It's just not practical. But it's still relatively easy to make friends. As I mentioned, people party as often as they want in Boston. If you feel like chilling in a room with a few musicians, smoking pot and drinking, you can always head to the Berklee School of Music. If girls want to drink the night away, they can head to an MIT frat party (they usually give guys a hard time about getting in). If you want free beer and fun dancing, head to Tufts, or Northeastern, or BC where there's always something going on. You just can't drink or smoke in your room. If you're reported twice by a resident adviser for smoking marijuana, you're kicked out of student housing. If you're underage and caught drinking, you usually have to meet with the dorm director and are then put on probation. BU has an extremely strict drug and alcohol policy.

Name: Nicole
Hometown: Brooklyn, New York
Class Year: Senior
Major: Psychology
Extracurriculars: Volunteering, broomball, going to the hockey games, phys ed. classes
Career Goal: Criminal prosecutor

How would you describe BU's reputation?

BU has come a long way. When our parents were in college, it was a party school. But now it's become quite respectable. When I tell someone in their twenties that I'm at BU, they're usually impressed. They also assume that I'm rich, Jewish, and from either New Jersey or Long Island.

Is this reputation accurate?

I'm not rich, Jewish, or from New Jersey or Long Island, but there are plenty of students here who fit that stereotype, as well as just as many who don't.

What would an admissions officer at your school probably not tell a prospective student? What aspect of your school would a prospective student not see on a campus tour?

An admissions officer probably won't tell you each individual BU college's stereotype. The School of Management is academically cutthroat, populated primarily by clean-cut rich kids who dream of driving BMWs, living in New York City penthouses, and wear, even in college, lots of Gucci. The College of Communication, which is one of the best programs in America, is filled with aspiring journalists and people who want to work in the TV and movie industries—they're notorious for hardly having any classes, and when they do, for not going to them. The College of Fine Arts is populated by trendy hipsters. The College of Arts and Sciences is too big to have a reputation—it just has your everyday college kids who, if they bother to change out of their pajamas at all, roll into class in jeans and a T-shirt. And lastly, there's the College of General Studies, which is said to have the most lax admissions requirements, and thus largely full of rich kids who couldn't get into any other parts of BU—but I don't think this is accurate, because all the CGS kids I've known carry a tough course load and are among the hardest-working student's I've met.

The Institution

It's overwhelming at first, there's so much going on. But if you put yourself out there and follow your real interests, you'll be fine. I remember during my first week I heard about this sketch comedy group Slow Children at Play performing nearby. I was interested, but the few people I'd met didn't want to go. So I said screw it and forgot about the whole thing. That was a mistake. When you first get here, you have to branch out, and you have to be social. I should have taken the initiative, gone to the show, and while I was there made an effort to make friends with other people in the crowd.

All in all, most students really like BU. The only major complaint you will hear around campus is in regards to the administration. Up until recently, BU has been notorious for its lack of student-friendly administrators. There have been many changes in the past year or so, however, and great strides are being made in this department. I actually saw changes made after voicing my opinion at one of the recently introduced breakfast meetings with the president. And the dean of students has begun hosting regular gatherings for coffee and conversation with those who want to get involved. I think students are finally getting their voices heard around here.

> "Lunch at BU is golden thanks to the delicious made-to-order burritos. The Myles Standish cafeteria gets the highest marks on salsa. Their pico de gallo is made fresh every morning."
>
> ✦ Joey, senior

The Education

Classes at BU range from lecture-based to discussion-based, depending on the college you're in and your major. The professors are great. One professor, after meeting with me for just a few minutes, went out of her way to set me up with a really exclusive internship. Another professor helped me shape my thesis in a way that tied my academic goals with my career ambitions. And, generally, classes are interesting and well run. BU has a big liberal arts-based core curriculum, but you can get through it. Most students don't complain too much about core requirements.

The Students

There's such a range of people at BU that it's hard to generalize. Students are mostly Northeasterners, but I've interacted with numerous people from all over the country and all over the world—some very rich and some students who were on full scholarships. If you're LGBT or religious, there are a lot of groups and clubs you can join, and these groups and clubs are pretty active. Our political groups are less active, but the campus in general has a liberal vibe. *The Daily Free Press,* an independent student newspaper, is widely read and is often used as a forum for debate on controversial topics.

The Activities

There are a lot of performance groups at BU—there are a million a cappella groups, and everyone goes to their concerts (don't pass up an opportunity to see the Dear Abbeys!). There are also dance, juggling, and sketch comedy troupes. There's a synchronized swimming club, ages eight and up (they play board games), the Vegetarian Society, and the Meat Lover's Society. The Community Service Center on campus helps students volunteer in nearby communities, and The Alternative Spring Break program lets kids travel all over the country working with organizations like Habitat for Humanity.

When students aren't joining clubs on campus, they're out in Boston. Fenway's practically on campus, and the nightlife in that area is fun (and conveniently close, considering public transportation stops running at 12:30). Newbury Street is kind of touristy, but nice to walk around. Boston Common has to be one of my favorite places—the park is wonderful. Faneuil Hall is also a really good time, with all the eateries.

The Social Scene

Most students at BU live on campus, but even off-campus options often feel very similar to brownstone dorms. Greek life really isn't big here. In the first months of the fall semester, you can always see flocks of freshmen wandering around near West Campus, desperate to find a crazy party. Odds are, after a bit of searching, they'll find one. But be careful—the university's alcohol policies are intense, and if you get caught you could lose your housing. Boston is equally intense—fake IDs don't go over very well. Generally, it's harder than at other schools, but if you're determined you'll find what you want. This is probably a blessing in disguise, it'll save you money and you'll have fewer sloppy drunken nights.

Notable Boston University Alumni Include:

Howard Stern, radio personality
Bill O'Reilly, Fox News anchor
Faye Dunaway, actress
Geena Davis, actress
Tipper Gore, forty-fifth second lady of the United States
Jason Alexander, actor

BOWDOIN COLLEGE

Founded: 1794
Location: Brunswick, ME
Phone: (207) 725-3000
E-mail: admissions@bowdoin.edu
Web site: www.bowdoin.edu

Number of Undergraduates: 1,640
Number of Graduate Students: 0
Cost: Approximately $40,000 per year
Application Deadline: January 1
Early Decision: November 15

Rating:	Notable Majors/Programs:
Most Selective	Government, English, Life Sciences

Size:
● Small   ○ Medium   ○ Large

Location:
○ Urban   ● Suburban   ○ Rural

On a Saturday, students talk about academics:
○ Always   ● Sometimes   ○ Never

Nightlife:
○ Intense   ● Moderate   ○ Laid-back

Politically, Bowdoin College leans:
● Left   ○ Right   ○ Split

Diversity:
○ High   ○ Low   ● Medium

Students describe Bowdoin in five words:
- Small, rigorous, beautiful, superstimulating, sleep-deprived
- Isolated, athletic, intellectually intense overachievers

From the School

At Bowdoin, academic learning is paramount, but the learning doesn't end in the classroom. Every aspect of college life is geared toward helping each student reach his or her full potential: personal interaction with faculty; the opportunity to engage in research, independent study, internships, and more; the high standard of facilities and resources; the innovative residential system; the extracurricular clubs and activities; the coaching staff's commitment to academics; the culture of support and growth that reaches across all sectors of campus; the deeply held belief in working for the common good.

—www.bowdoin.edu

If you're interested in Bowdoin, you may also be interested in:
Amherst, Bates, Colby, Haverford, Middlebury, Pomona, Williams

Name: Lucy

Hometown: Saint Albans, Maine

Class Year: Sophomore

Major: Religion, psychology

Extracurriculars: Program director for WBOR (student radio station, and the center of non-Polo-wearing culture on campus). Ongoing research on the development of Theravada Buddhist institutions in the United States.

Career Goal: Religion professor, something in the field of clinical or social psychology, writer, or graphic designer.

How would you describe Bowdoin's reputation?

Prestigious. Selective. Very academically difficult. Work hard, party hard. Rewarding.

Is this reputation accurate?

It's pretty much right on. Sunday through Thursday, kids here work themselves to the point of exhaustion. Then someone flips a switch and kids party themselves to the point of exhaustion. It's unclear how anyone ever actually survives.

What aspect of Bowdoin would a prospective student not see on a campus tour?

Someone on tour might think they were just hiding all the nonwhite, nonkhaki-wearing people somewhere else. I did. I'll spare you the confusion right now: they're not hiding, there just aren't many here. Don't get me wrong, there's enough diversity that anyone could find a crowd (I've found my people and am quite content), but that crowd might be small unless you're from white, upper-middle-class New England and like to play lacrosse. It's a perfectly dealable situation, and an effort has been made to increase racial diversity, but we are still light years behind most colleges.

The Institution

This is the most difficult and most rewarding place I've ever been. It took me a long time to come to terms with Bowdoin, but now that I've settled in, I honestly love this place. It's making me grow in ways I never thought possible. I already feel, as a sophomore, that coming out of here I'll be able to effectively take on any task and succeed. It's so reassuring.

Students are well aware of Bowdoin's prestige. I think, by and large, we're a proud group and strive to do our reputation justice. It creates a comfortable sense of camaraderie. Students and townies virtually do not interact (the sole exception to this rule is the Frisbee team, due to the universal attraction of organized partying disguised as a sport).

The housing is wonderful. The freshman dorms have larger rooms than any other freshman housing I've seen: almost everyone lives in triples that have a common room and a bedroom, so you have a psychological split between your work and your sleep (though there are doubles, too). Since all the upperclass housing is also desirable, virtually everyone lives on campus. You should also know that the dining hall is really good. The food alone makes it worth coming to Bowdoin. People only eat ramen noodles if they have a craving for it.

Oh, and our Career Planning Center provides ample opportunity to get summer jobs, careers, internships, or grants. Like all the other administrative offices on campus, everyone at the CPC is friendly, motivated, and genuinely interested in helping you achieve your goals. They work wonders.

> "When we're bored? Pretend that we're the famous Bowdoin explorers Perry and Macmillan, cook extravagant meals, and talk about where we would travel if we could go anywhere in the world."
>
> ✦ Elizabeth, freshman

The Education

Bowdoin students are truly invested in what they're learning. People throw themselves wholeheartedly into their classes; they don't just plow through the work for the sake of the grade; instead, doing well is a labor of love. Bowdoin students put in a sixteen-hour homework day and don't think anything of it. The workload here is certainly more hefty than at the schools of any of my other friends, including Ivy Leagues. What's more is that kids here take the ideas they're working with in class and apply them to their lives; everyday life and learning are not two separate spheres. That said, people try very hard not to talk about classes on a Saturday night. There's a work hard, party hard mentality here. And there's no competition between students. It's wonderful. People do everything they can to help each other out. After talking to friends at other top-level colleges, I've come to appreciate how rare this is.

We don't have a core curriculum, thank god! Such is the glory of a true liberal arts education. We have distribution requirements, of course, but they're structured so that you have plenty of freedom. I've never been red-taped into taking a class I wasn't interested in. One or two classes are lecture-based, but I've never had one. We have almost all discussion classes. Since we only have undergrads, there are research opportunities for those who want them. We don't generally have TAs, and when we do, it's only in chemistry or bio labs. I receive all the attention I could ask for from my professors. It's incredibly easy to form solid, enjoyable relationships with professors here—they really do take the time to get to know you. There's also a really supportive infrastructure for study abroad here. Nearly half of Bowdoin students go abroad in their time here, and the Off Campus Study office is an indispensable resource.

The Students

We have a lot of rich white people and not a whole lot of anyone else. There are a few kids who don't fit that description, but they're scattered. Students of color don't usually mix with the white kids. Everyone tacitly agrees that the two groups *should* mix, but the barriers have yet to be fully broken down. Also, we only have about ten openly gay people. A ridiculously huge percentage of students here are from the Boston area. I've known people who lied about where they were from freshman year simply because they were tired of saying "Boston" and having people roll their eyes. Bowdoin is a fairly conservative college, but it's still largely Democratic.

People are incredibly involved here, though we're also notoriously apolitical (by and large). Somehow the two are not mutually exclusive. I used to loathe organized student groups, but almost against my will I fell in love with the campus radio station. There's something for everyone here.

The average Bowdoin student wears at least one item of clothing from Ralph Lauren (two or three if they're female). Pearl earrings on females and baseball caps on males. People are overscheduled and so generally move around campus at a frenetic pace, yet everyone is extremely friendly, polite, and willing to help you out if you're in a jam. It's important to note that many people think that "there is no average Bowdoin student." *Anyone* can belong here. I don't have a pair of pearls to my name and that's perfectly fine.

The Activities

The activities board, outing club (a wilderness expedition club), student government, and social houses are probably the most visible student groups on campus, but there're tons of smaller clubs and organizations including minority groups, various dance troupes, and women's groups that throw well-attended events. Athletics are absolutely huge here. Nearly everyone I know plays at least one varsity or club sport, and those that don't go to the gym on a regular basis. And there are at least three major arts events every weekend (and they're usually really awesome); usually kids find the time to attend at least one.

If you're still awake on Wednesday at 3 a.m., it's because you've got work due the next day. To clear your head, walk around campus in the dark—it's safe enough to do that without thinking twice. Cool ocean air rolls across the campus at night, ascending the coastal landscape to make even the shortest walk a relaxing event. My friends and I drive out to the ocean pretty frequently and sit and talk on the bluffs and listen to the waves, or we go to Portland (only a half hour away) and we get reasonably priced sushi, Indian, etc. Granny's Burritos and Flatbread Pizza are also favorites.

To give you a better idea of the types of things on a Bowdoin student's plate, a list of things stressing me out at this very minute:

- twenty-five-page paper due for my cognitive psych lab class
- another paper due for my graduate-level comparative religion theory class
- filling out the necessary financial aid forms for my study abroad program
- finding the time to see one of my friends from home over the weekend while still managing to get all my work done
- thinking of a costume for tonight's party
- making up a playlist for my radio show tomorrow night

The Social Scene

People party Thursday through Saturday nights. Everyone drinks, but there's very little drug use here. Let me reiterate: *Everyone* drinks, and they drink a lot. On what is perhaps a related note, we're famously sexually repressed. People go to parties in hopes of a random drunken hookup—the normal form of Bowdoin romantic interaction. You're either one of the ten campus couples in a long-term relationship or hooking up at the myriad parties, as everyone is eighteen to twenty-two and, accordingly, has hormones to burn. We disbanded the Greek system six or seven years ago. It got too dangerous. The drinking culture is still pervasive, but there's no actual frat culture here. I met most of my friends through classes and freshman year housing. It's small enough here that you just sort of acquire friends through osmosis. You might not know everyone on campus, but you know their name, their face, who they're dating, and what they did last weekend. Everyone says "hi" and holds doors open for each other. It's lovely. Also, Bates and Colby are fairly nearby and we go to each other's concerts or parties occasionally. There's a culture of mutual respect (though everyone knows that we're just slightly better) and playful animosity.

> "The curriculum at Bowdoin is incredibly challenging and I think the intimate connections you forge here are great. The lack of concern for greater world issues outside the Bowdoin bubble . . . not so great."
> ✦ Karl, senior

Name: Benjamin
Hometown: Narberth, Pennsylvania
Class Year: Junior
Majors: Government and German
Extracurriculars: College Democrats, Students for Democratic Socialism, WBOR, *Orient* (newspaper)
Career Goal: I do not want to be a politician, necessarily, but I would love to work in a congressional office or for an interest or lobbying group such as the ACLU or Moveon.org. My goal is to make a truly positive contribution to society by fighting for progressive policies that will reform our political system and lead to a more egalitarian society.

How would you describe Bowdoin's reputation?

Bowdoin has a reputation for being an academically prestigious small liberal arts institution particularly known for its government and biology programs. It also has a reputation for being a school full of rich, preppy white kids.

Is this reputation accurate?

Its academic reputation is very accurate, and I would even argue that every department here—not just gov and bio—is top-notch across the board. As for its student body, Bowdoin is making a concerted effort and getting more and more diverse every year, but it remains true that we draw a large percentage of students from prep schools.

What would an admissions officer at Bowdoin probably not tell a prospective student?

Unfortunately, the college house system—which functions almost like coed fraternities that are more regulated by the administration—is largely dominated by males, and it is not as inclusive as the school claims it to be. Most of their activities are parties, and they do not do enough to attract a wide variety of students. The student body remains pretty divided about the house system.

The Institution

Quite frankly, life at Bowdoin is very pleasant and comfortable, and a lot of students take their excellent quality of life for granted. Housing is outstanding, especially for upperclassmen. My favorite traditions are definitely the lobster bake and the preorientation trips. I don't think too many other schools serve their students lobster. The setting? Beautiful. The forests, mountains, rivers, and ocean are our playground. But the most important thing to mention is the strong sense of community. Bowdoin is truly an intimate, very friendly, and respectful environment where the staff and professors not only know students' names but make an effort to know them. I don't know many other schools where it is as common for students to have beers with their professors or be invited to their houses.

The Education

The academics are truly amazing in every way. And despite the rigorous academics, Bowdoin students are very willing to work collaboratively. There is very little competition, which is refreshing. Professors are highly accessible, always willing to give students extra help. I have had a number of great classes, but my most memorable class was probably The History of Rock and Roll. The professor was very knowledgeable, and it ended up being surprisingly challenging, but above all else, it was pure fun. How many other classes require listening to The Beatles, Led Zepplin, and The Who for homework?

> "The school recently adopted new distribution requirements, asking all students to take a quantitative reasoning class, a class focused on social differences, a natural sciences class, a humanities class, and an arts class."
>
> ✦ Kerry, junior

The Students

Bowdoin is a pretty homogeneous school, with the vast majority of students coming from wealthy New England backgrounds. The average student is also fairly politically liberal and tends to enjoy outdoor activities. In recent years, the campus has gotten much more politically active and vocal, which I see as a very positive development, as there has been a great deal of very honest dialog about issues of race and social life. That being said, I still feel there are some divisions within the student body. Students living in college houses tend to hang out mostly with fellow house members, and many of the varsity sports teams function practically like fraternities.

The Activities

I am a very active member of the College Democrats on campus. I have had a wide variety of positive experiences, but my favorite memory was probably going to a huge rally where Bill Clinton spoke. It was thrilling to see the former president in person and to shake his hand.

The Social Scene

People at Bowdoin work hard and play hard. During the week, everyone hits the books, but lots of people drink on the weekend. Like any school, there is a fair amount of alcohol, but I don't feel that Bowdoin is particularly unique in the way it parties. It is very easy to meet new people at Bowdoin, particularly in the freshmen dorms and through extracurriculars. While it's a small school, you don't know everyone, so there are always new people to meet. At the same time, it's very comforting that you will always bump into friends and acquaintances at any given event. There is a very strong sense of community, and you never feel like you are just a number.

Name: Emily
Hometown: Columbia, Maryland
Class Year: Senior
Major: Biology
Extracurriculars: Ultimate Frisbee, therapeutic horseback riding volunteer, radio DJ
Career Goal: Undecided

How would you describe Bowdoin's reputation?

Competitive in terms of admissions, socially small, academically demanding, politically liberal, poor at football.

Is this reputation accurate?

Fairly. It's true we don't win at football. The school isn't nearly as politically liberal as I thought it would be. Despite a growing activist base there are too many people here with family money for the school to support a really strong political left. Socially, the school is small, and that, more than anything, is what I think turns new students off. The social scene isn't very diverse, but if you want to stake your own territory, there are always willing joiners.

What aspect of Bowdoin would a prospective student not see on a campus tour?

Obviously the partying. Bowdoin kids drink a lot.

The Institution

Bowdoin was the best academic match for me. The only major battles I've had have been with the social scene. Students here are generally intense about work and intense about partying. Because of the intense social scene, people seem to think something is the matter with you if you decide not to go out one weekend. In this way, the school is small. The kids here can also have a very limited worldview, neglecting everything outside their own sphere within Bowdoin, let alone the rest of the campus. That said, all the support systems in this community really allow you to focus on learning. The amount of academic growth I've experienced here, in comparison with my friends at other schools, is really amazing.

Bowdoin, institutionally, is really responsive to student-led initiatives, which builds both confidence and a positive atmosphere. Administrators make themselves available to the student body, and in some, but not all cases, participate in student groups. I feel like this type of interaction is a major benefit of the school's size.

Bowdoin is also a beautiful school. Every year, I forget how unbelievable the campus looks in October when the trees and ivy on the buildings radiate light and color; and again in the winter when it's dead silent after a snow. The dorms, even the freshman bricks, are really nice compared to most schools. Upperclassmen can live in dorms or apartments, or as of junior year, off campus. There's some great off campus housing, especially if you don't mind driving ten minutes out to some really pretty bays and waterways.

The Education

Schoolwork is the center of students' lives, and a lot of our time is occupied with work, or worrying about work. It can be overwhelming. Yet students here are honestly not competitive—I don't even know what kinds of grades any of my friends get, nor do most people. I know several students who don't even look at their grades.

Most people I know stay on campus during the summer to work with professors on independent projects, and research opportunities are abundant, considering the size of the school. I am completing a year-long honors research project, though only about a quarter of students do. There is a definite divide between science students and the humanities students. While the workload isn't excessive, science students do spend tons of time in labs. There's a sort of camaraderie that forms between seniors who have spent 47 percent of their breathing hours in the science building—and who aren't all nerds, thank you very much.

The size and lack of grad school do limit course offerings, however, as really stellar classes I would love to take only come along once every three or four years. But Bowdoin's tiny size works to a student's benefits when it comes to building relationships with lab instructors and professors. My friends at other schools tend to think about their education differently than we tend to at Bowdoin: I think of my time here as nurturing a big leap in intellectual and educational maturity, while they generally talk about the nonacademic things occupying their time.

The Students

The issue of "groups" and "belonging" has really only recently come to the front of people's minds here, in spite of the administration's talk of increasing diversity. It took a racially motivated confrontation to capitulate a lot of the anxieties and frustrations students have about these issues. On paper, we're a tolerant bunch, but there are definitely factions based on group qualities (race, culture, sexual orientation, athleticism). There are plenty of intolerant rich white kids here, and even more just plain rich kids, that seem entrenched in a defensive discourse regarding these issues, which is unfortunate. Most others are just seen as apathetic. Activism is picking up, which is good to see, but because the campus is so small and you want to get along with these people who you have to see and deal with daily, root differences tend to get suppressed in favor of a feigned harmony and civility. For the most part, if you're political, you're a rich white Republican, but if you're left-leaning and political, you're an activist.

> "It isn't as cold as you might think. Brunswick has more sunny days than most points in northern New England."
> ✦ Elizabeth, freshman

The Activities

It's ironic that the college is set up on a hill and that a white church tower marks the end of town and the beginning of campus—talk about a pretty literal "ivory tower." I find it horrifying to learn how infrequently a lot of students venture into town. Brunswick has a really pleasant New England main street (called Maine Street), with a bunch of decent restaurants and a record shop, an amazing coffee shop, natural food store, etc. Highlights include Big Top Deli, Bohemian Coffee, Shere Punjab/Bambay Mahal, Morning Glory, Bull Moose Records, Joshua's Tavern, and Sea Dogs. But there is a separation between the school and the town, in spite of any talk of integration. Most people here have a friend or two at Bates or Colby, or, gasp, USM, but most of the sentiment is one of rivalry, at least academically. We are made to feel superior to these other schools. Athletics here are pretty important, and for those who participate it defines a good deal of their social life. Teams party together, eat meals together, even date each other (. . . or maybe that's just Frisbee). Campus sponsored parties ("campus-wides") are generally attended primarily by freshmen. Concerts of campus bands get a lot of school support.

The Social Scene

Students here drink hard. If you're a freshman and you don't drink, it's not end of the world, but it is harder to connect and find your niche. Weekend nights typically start off drinking in someone's room, then move to larger parties, and if you don't find someone to hook up with, you end up stumbling home when the kegs are kicked. In this type of social scene it is hard to meet new people (class isn't really good for meeting people). That's why athletics may dominate someone's social scene and also why dating relationships are hard to hold onto without exempting yourself from the larger social scene. Living off campus was the greatest choice I made here. The separation between my home and my school really gives me control over when I am "on duty" and when I'm not. I'm also able to have a dog, which is a huge stress reliever; and interacting with people outside the Bowdoin bubble on a daily basis has been invaluable to my own personal sanity and perspective on life, but it has its trade-offs, in that I can't just pop by someone's room unexpected, and so casual friendships are harder to forge.

Nearby getaways:
- Popham Beach, a popular spot when it's warm even though the water is *frigid!*
- Fort Popham, one of the oldest settlements in the United States, older than Jamestown
- Grand City Diner on Maine Street, which serves eggs, toast, and coffee for $1.50
- Nearby Bates and Colby

Notable Bowdoin Alumni Include:
Cynthia McFadden, *ABC News* correspondent
Franklin Pierce, fourteenth U.S. president
Henry Wadsworth Longfellow, writer
Ken Chenault, chairman and CEO of American Express
Nathaniel Hawthorne, writer
Seba Smith, cracker barrel philosopher

BRANDEIS UNIVERSITY

Founded: 1948
Location: Waltham, MA
Phone: (781) 736-3500
E-mail: sendinfo@brandeis.edu
Web site: www.brandeis.edu

Number of Undergraduates: 3,057
Number of Graduate Students: 1,810
Cost: Approximately $38,000 per year
Application Deadline: January 1
Early Decision: January 1

Rating:	Notable Majors/Programs:
Very Selective	Psychology, Economics, Computer Science, Biology

Size:
○ Small ● Medium ○ Large

Location:
○ Urban ● Suburban ○ Rural

On a Saturday, students talk about academics:
○ Always ● Sometimes ○ Never

Nightlife:
○ Intense ○ Moderate ● Laid-back

Politically, Brandeis leans:
● Left ○ Right ○ Split

Diversity:
○ High ○ Low ● Medium

Students describe Brandeis in five words:
- Young, New England activist school
- Small, Jewish, studious, community, PC

From the School

Brandeis University offers the resources you would expect in a world-class research university in the intimate learning environment you would expect in a small liberal arts college. Students at Brandeis experience personal encounters with knowledge through a faculty composed of Mac-Arthur "genius" award winners, Howard Hughes Medical investigators, and proportionally more fellows of America's top scholarly societies, than all but one other university in the country—all of whom teach undergraduate and graduate courses.

—www.brandeis.edu

If you're interested in Brandeis, you may also be interested in:
Boston University, Brown, Cornell, SUNY–Binghamton, Tufts, Washington U. in St. Louis

Name: Meredith
Hometown: Staten Island, New York
Class Year: Junior
Major: American Studies/Journalism
Extracurriculars: A cappella, musicals, Formal Committee, Senior Events Committee, fashion show model, yearbook, newspaper
Career Goal: Editor for a woman's magazine

How would you describe Brandeis's reputation?

Brandeis is very highly regarded, academically. When I go on job interviews, the interviewers are always impressed. But I've also heard it said that Brandeis has a terrible social scene, that it lacks diversity, and is exclusively Jewish.

Is this reputation accurate?

The academic reputation? Totally true. The social reputation? It's a lie. While there are a number of religious and/or studious people on campus, there are just as many people that know how to—and love to—have a great time. Also, Brandeis doesn't lack diversity, and is not exclusively Jewish. In recent years, there's been an equal number of Jewish and non-Jewish students on campus. We have students of all stripes.

What would an admissions officer at your school probably not tell a prospective student? What aspect of your school would a prospective student not see on a campus tour?

Tours don't show prospective students the inside of the infamous Castle dorm because, while the outside looks incredible, the interior is sort of a mess. Tours also bypass dorms in East, where the infamous million-legged "East bug" lives. That said, tours also don't see the really beautiful senior houses.

The Institution

Brandeis is fairly small—we have 3,050 undergraduates—the same size as my high school. I like being in a place like this, where you recognize everyone, get to know a sizable portion of your grade, and never feel like a number. I find that comforting. I also find the range of people here comforting. To be honest, I expected everyone to be middle class, from in or around a city, and Jewish (but not too religious). Instead, I found students here to be of every religion, every race, from all over. Impressive.

Brandeis students—while always enjoying this place—didn't have the most school spirit in the past, but that's changing thanks to administrative efforts. These days we're also more likely to head to campuswide parties, like Pachanga, which is a big dance sponsored by the international club twice a semester. We also have Modfest, a big outdoor party, twice a semester. (It's great; there's free alcohol sponsored by the school and live local bands and DJs.) We also go to the Midnight Buffet en masse (this is a free all-you-can-eat feast the night before finals begin). Best of all are the Louis, Louis Weekend and the Bronstein Weekend. These are nonstop parties from Wednesday to Sunday with constant events, giveaways, bands, music blaring, drunk students, free food, and an amazing amount of fun.

> "Cholmondely's [named for the dog of a Brandeis founding father] is the coffeehouse that inspired "Central Perk" in *Friends*. Co-creators Marta Kaufmann and David Krane went to Brandeis and I've heard the characters on *Friends* were based on their friends here."
>
> ✦ Meredith, senior

The Education

Competition is pretty stiff among premed students, but otherwise students want to do the best for themselves and aren't really interested in how their classmates are faring. Most of the classes I take are discussion-based, with the caveat that the intro classes are almost always lectures. All professors hold office hours and are open to making appointments outside those hours if you have a conflict. Many professors give out their home phone numbers in case of academic emergencies, and most are accessible by e-mail. They're just kind, approachable people. Also, if you're looking to do research in college, you're in luck. Brandeis is really a research university. Psychology concentrators in particular spend lots of time working with professors in labs, and most science majors write theses for which they do tons of research work with their thesis adviser. We also have a graduate school on campus, so students can access graduate-level science facilities and take graduate-level classes if they're so inclined.

Because it's easy to complete core requirements at Brandeis, students here have a great deal of freedom in choosing their classes. And if there's something you want to learn more about, but Brandeis doesn't offer a class on it, find a teacher who's competent in the area and some classmates, and Brandeis will often create the class by the following semester. Lastly, if there's a class you want to get into but it fills up during registration time, write a letter to the professor and you'll probably get in.

The Students

The average Brandeis student is Jewish (but only attends services on high holy days), is white, is upper-middle class, comes from the suburbs, and is liberal-minded, but not necessarily liberal (we've a fair share of Democrats and Republicans). Most students are from Massachusetts, New York, New Jersey, Maryland, Florida, and California. There are, of course, many deviations from this rule: my freshman year I had a Hindu girl, an Orthodox Christian Arab girl, a half Jewish/half Catholic girl, and a gay Jewish boy on my hall. These are also typical Brandeis students. And being in Boston, you've got a wide range of other students to interact with. It's great to be able to keep in touch by meeting your tenth-grade buddies that go to neighboring schools in a nearby bar. Or to meet new people from other schools and be able to see what their campuses are like.

The Activities

There's something for everyone here. While the athletes on campus tend to make athletics their lives, this isn't a sports-oriented campus, so everyone else usually turns a blind eye. If you want to do community service, the Waltham Group facilitates volunteering with senior citizens, the underprivileged, children, etc. Everyone does something and really identifies strongly with it. I perform on and off campus with my a cappella group.

The Social Scene

Brandeis puts a lot of effort into offering fabulous weekend activities, including dances, concerts, movies, and shows, and there are always student-run parties, too. Plus the city of Boston is only a (*free*) half-hour bus ride away.

Name: Josh
Hometown: Norristown, Pennsylvania

Class Year: Freshman
Major: Political Science
Extracurriculars: Triskelion (LGBT group), admissions volunteer/overnight host
Career Goal: Political policy analysis or investment banking

How would you describe Brandeis' reputation?

Brandeis is said to be intensely Jewish, activist/liberal, a safety school for U. Penn and Columbia applicants . . . and JAP-city.

Is this reputation accurate?

Point by point: Not everyone here is Jewish (more than 50 percent of us aren't), but some Jewish kids do come here just to be surrounded by other Jewish kids. Brandeis is pretty liberal. In terms of us being a safety school, I've found that it's an even split. For half our students, Brandeis was their clear first choice and for the other half, they're still furious that they didn't get into an Ivy. As for us being JAP-city, that's not true. We have some JAPs, but no more than you'd find in any top-tier school, and certainly less than you'd find at places like GW [George Washington] or Columbia. Most Brandeis students are concerned with the more substantive things in life. Most of us are really bright, really introspective, and really independent. This is a young school. Those folks that only know of Harvard, Princeton, and Yale are probably going to look at you blankly when you say you go to Brandeis. However, those in the know—people who went to top schools themselves, or who are doing the hiring in major firms—will be impressed. They may also ask you if you're studying to be a rabbi. To which you will *probably* reply, "no."

> "Brandeis is affectionately known as 'the Harvard for Jews.'"
>
> ✦ Jonathan, senior

What would an admissions officer at your school probably not tell a prospective student?

The administration tends to downplay how many Orthodox Jews we have on campus. They make up no more than 10–15 percent of the student body in any given year, but Orthodox Jews have a very rigid way of going about their lives, and, having never been exposed to this sort of thing before, I found it a little jarring at first. Also, the office of admissions has a history of downplaying how many gay students are at Brandeis. But I'll shout it, loud and clear: Brandeis is uber-gay.

> "The campus is white. The campus is Jewish. The campus is liberal. Let's not pretend to be something we're not, OK?"
>
> ✦ Jud, junior

The Institution

At Brandeis students have far more influence in administrative policy than you'd expect. Crime is practically unheard of on campus. Local police are friendly and rarely, if ever, give Brandeis students a hard time. We also have a very laid-back discipline policy. Brandeis treats students like adults instead of large children. If you're responsible for any type of bias/hate-related activity, sexual assault, vandalism, plagiarizing, or cheating, it's taken very seriously, and you should expect to find yourself in a heap of trouble. But if you're caught with alcohol or drugs, you get a slap on the wrist. Brandeis tries to be fair, and the "punishment" for infractions is decided on by a student-majority board. So you don't have to worry about being kicked out for taking a sip of beer before you're twenty-one.

The Education

Because Brandeis is near Boston, we benefit from a proximity effect: if a professor teaches at Harvard, MIT, Wellesley, or Tufts, they probably also teach at Brandeis from time to time. In the classroom, I'd say the amount of attention we get from professors depends on the level of class and on the individual teacher's personality. I've had professors who never even learned my name, and I've also played squash with my economics professor. We do have TAs here, with their level of competence ranging from high to low.

Finally, I love the fact that our core requirements are few and relatively flexible. All we have to do is take three semesters of language classes, a freshman writing seminar, and then a few classes in quantitative reasoning. And if you come into Brandeis with AP credits, you can phase out of

some of those. Another cool thing we can do is take some classes blind pass/fail, which means we're taking a class without being graded, but the teacher doesn't know that. So we're free to experiment in subject areas we're less comfortable with—without the instructor taking us less seriously.

The Students

For whatever reason, there's a huge gay community at Brandeis, which I've enjoyed being a part of. We have a fairly well-organized umbrella group (Trisk) that holds weekly meetings and throws big parties and dances, bringing lots of people together. Even though our numbers are sizable, the gay community still tends to be close-knit—in the "fruit-loop," gossip spreads really fast, so be forewarned. Generally, Brandeis as a whole is incredibly tolerant and welcoming for us. I lie out on the grass and curl up with my boyfriend without encountering even a hint of surprise, disapproval, or shock from those around us.

Brandeis students are predominantly white, Jewish, and from the Northeast. We have some minorities in the mix, but Brandeis needs to work on bringing in even more and not making them feel like "visitors." Luckily the minority students that are here are very vocal and active, and frequently bring in speakers and hold events.

The Activities

What do Brandeis students do when they're not taking sips of beer before they're twenty-one? Well, our athlete teams suck, but no one cares. Somewhere, at all times, some Brandeis athlete is about to perform poorly at an athletic event. Brandeis has a weekly paper, *The Justice,* but it's terrible. I'm told the writers try very hard, but its riddled with errors (misquotes, misspelled names, etc.). I guess we can't expect any better, because we don't have a very credible journalism program here. On the subject of things we're good at, we sing our hearts out in a cappella groups. We have a great Student Union, which is full of egotists, but effective egotists who get lots of money for student activities and have a large role in creating and implementing remarkably fair campus policies.

The Social Scene

Brandeis has a few underground (nonrecognized) frats and sororities off campus, but most people just go to their parties to steal their alcohol and laugh at them. This is far more of a "let's get together with a few of our friends and drink in moderation" campus. Tiny parties with a tiny, low-key social scene. Don't expect big parties. It's more like five friends in a room. A lot of people will duck out of partying on Friday nights for religious reasons. (The dining halls also close early on Friday because they're student-staffed, and people scamper off at sundown.) Thursday is a really big party night. Sometimes Saturday night, too. And on a party night we'll dance, we'll drink, we'll get silly. We'll hook up—some people may say otherwise, but I've found the dating scene to be great (though it's worth noting, a lot of guys are gay or dating a girl at a nearby school, and a lot of girls are not the greatest looking). Nonetheless, most of my friends have been happily paired up at some time or other during their Brandeis years. And speaking of friends, most of the friends you'll make here will live in your dorm with you (Massell and North Quad are on opposite ends of campus from one another).

> "Unless you have a particularly annoying RA, you'll rarely be busted for drinking alcohol or smoking pot in your room here."
> ✦ Megan, sophomore

There are a ton of kids here because they wanted to be around lots of Jewish students. I came for the gay community.

Name: Ariel
Hometown: I was born in Lebanon and my family currently lives in London.
Class Year: Senior
Major: Economics
Extracurriculars: International Club, Hispanic Club, Turkish Student Association
Career Goal: Professor

How would you describe Brandeis' reputation?

Brandeis is known as a Jewish school with a really small, low-key party scene.

Is this reputation accurate?

This reputation is pretty accurate. We're Jewish, we party small.

What would an admissions officer at your school probably not tell a prospective student?

Admissions will downplay how socially liberal we are here, and how often we protest. This isn't an apathetic place—if there's reason to scream and shout and hand out pamphlets, we do. Also, students and parents aren't told how many LGBT students are here. Admissions will also leave out the fact that non-Jewish students are in the minority at Brandeis. On Jewish holidays the campus becomes a ghost town. Admissions will not leave out the fact that we're close to Boston, but then they'll exaggerate how close it is. It can take an hour each way with traffic and parking.

> "Brandeis is *very* open to all different walks of life (except Republicans, of course)."
> ✦ Curtis, senior

The Institution

Our campus food is OK—we always have Kosher options. Our housing is nice enough, because we're a new school, which means we have new amenities. As opposed to some of those crumbling old schools with rusting pipes and such (cough, the Ivies, cough). But most importantly, because Brandeis is small, everyone really feels like they're part of a community. It's wonderful to be a part of and it's really hard to leave.

The Education

The education is where Brandeis really shines: our professors are incredibly distinguished in their fields, and they're extremely approachable. Even our big classes have no more than one hundred students, offering incredible access to knowledgeable scholars. And most professors live right on campus or nearby, so you'll see them outside of class at student events or just walking their dogs on campus. They'll always stop and greet you, let their dog lick your hands. (Once you've been licked by your professor's dog, you can't help but give your all in their class!)

Brandeis is known for its economics, computer science, and biology departments on the undergraduate level, as well as its economics, international business, and arts and social sciences departments at the graduate level. And you can take both a major and a minor here, or a double major and a double minor (which is what I'm doing)—the school will usually do whatever it can to accommodate the path of study you lay out for yourself.

> "Fewer than 10 percent of students ever choose to go off campus and live in Waltham."
>
> ✦ James, junior

The Students

At Brandeis protests are common, and students throw themselves into issues they're passionate about. The LGBT community and the religious community are our two biggest and most vocal contingents. I'm an international student, and I've found my international circle to be vocal as well. While international students tend to hang out a lot with other international students, that crew is also pretty seamlessly integrated into Brandeis and have all kinds of friends.

The Activities

I think everyone I know is a member of at least one club or organization. We have clubs for sky diving, salsa music, theater, politics, the German language, cooking, just about anything you could think of. Students tend to devote most of their energies to a mix of club work and academic work, and then sleep on the side. Sometimes clubs will take precedence, and they'll find themselves not having cracked open a book in a week. And sometimes studying takes precedence, and they'll drop out of sight in their clubs.

Brandeis groups tend to put on some amazing shows. Every year we have a latex show, where students dressed in thongs decorate themselves with latex paint and then dance on stage. The Hispanic campus group puts on a great salsa/merengue show each year, and the International Club hosts big belly-dancing events and food fairs.

The Social Scene

Every weekend upperclassmen throw parties in their suites, and you can usually find a dance, a show, or a movie. But I think most people have fun just hanging out with friends in their rooms. The frat houses are off campus and not a really strong presence here. Greek life doesn't really gel with the general Brandeis mentality.

> "The Brandeis campus is basically a big circle, with dorms on the outside and dining halls, student centers, and academic buildings on the inside."
>
> ✦ Ollie, sophomore

Notable Brandeis Alumni Include:
Thomas Friedman, op-ed writer, *New York Times*
Christie Heffner, CEO, Playboy Enterprises
Abbie Hoffman, social and political activist
Debra Messing, actor
Lettie Cottin Pogrebin, founder, *Ms. Magazine* and author
Tony Goldwyn, actor

BROWN UNIVERSITY

Founded: 1764

Location: Providence, RI

Phone: (401) 863-2378

E-mail: admission_undergraduate@brown.edu

Web site: www.brown.edu

Number of Undergraduates: 6,030

Number of Graduate Students: 1,635

Cost: Approximately $38,000 per year

Application Deadline: January 1

Early Decision: November 1

Rating:	Notable Majors/Programs:
Most Selective	Biology, History, English

Size:
○ Small ● Medium ○ Large

Location:
○ Urban ● Suburban ○ Rural

On a Saturday, students talk about academics:
● Always ○ Sometimes ○ Never

Nightlife:
○ Intense ● Moderate ○ Laid-back

Politically, Brown leans:
● Left ○ Right ○ Split

Diversity:
● High ○ Low ○ Medium

Ivy League: Yes!

Students describe Brown in five words:
- Ivy League with no core curriculum
- Liberal, passionate, creative, aware, prestigious

From the School

Brown University, a leading Ivy League institution, is the only major research university in the nation where undergraduates design their own course of study . . . at the heart of the Brown curriculum are three basic principles: that students are active participants in learning; that acquiring analytical and critical skills is as important as mastering factual knowledge; and that learning requires opportunities for experimentation and cross-disciplinary synthesis.

—http://brownbears.collegesports.com

If you're interested in Brown, you may also be interested in:
UC Berkeley, Columbia, Oberlin, Macalester, Wesleyan, Yale

Name: Micah
Hometown: Lawrence, Kansas
Class Year: Sophomore
Major: American Civilization
Extracurriculars: Editor of *Post* magazine, writer for *Indy* magazine, member of Jabberwocks (all-male a cappella)
Career Goal: Music journalism and cultural criticism

How would you describe Brown's reputation?

Brown is said to be a hotspot for stylish, politically left activists. It's also (unfairly) said to have a huge pot smoking culture and (very fairly) said to have the best looking girls in the Ivy League.

Is this reputation accurate?

There are far fewer Republicans than Democrats at Brown, but that doesn't mean everybody here is an *Economist*-burning hippie. Really, political views run the gamut from the far left to the far right. And while many students do smoke pot while socializing, they don't do so any more than students at other schools. I will say that Brown girls are exceptionally attractive, though. And that we're a pretty stylish bunch.

What would an admissions officer at your school probably not tell a prospective student? What aspect of your school would a prospective student not see on a campus tour?

Most admissions officers would gloss over the fact that Brown is the most poorly endowed Ivy League school. Brown is pretty small, and doesn't have a law or business school, so it's comparatively cash-poor. Really, Brown *University* is a misnomer, considering how few graduate students there actually are on campus, and how strong the undergraduate program is compared to the graduate one. We should be called Brown College.

> "Brown is known as 'the most fashionable Ivy.'"
>
> ✦ Lucus, freshman

The Institution

Brown was founded in 1764. Since then it has been looked at as both the "safety school" of the Ivies and the most popular of the Ivies, the one school that's on *every* bright student's wish list. Because Brown has no core curriculum at all, everywhere you look you'll find creative types, happily freed from the Western canon, exploring such topics as the treatment of transgender inmates in the New York prison system, the politics of West Indian poetry, and hip-hop as a tool of resistance in hegemonic societies.

> "The weather in Providence is never 'OK.' It is either beautiful or terrible, in equal measure."
>
> ✦ Micah, sophomore

The Education

As I said, Brown has no core curriculum, so students never have to take classes they're not interested in, and every class they take, they're taking it because they want to be taking it. This means students are involved, excited, and interested in every single lecture, far more so than students would be at other schools. We love the fact that there's no need to waste our time with generic classes, and throw ourselves into every course we've handpicked! Professors at Brown are also extremely dedicated. Classes range from ten students to four hundred students, but most have about twenty. You get to know your professors, they'll often meet up with you before or after class to talk, and, if there's good reason, most would go out of their way to meet outside of their office hours. All it takes is an e-mail to arrange it. While most professors teach both graduate and undergraduate students, few are consumed with their graduate students, and Brown's TAs (who are usually graduate students) are atypically good. Overall, Brown students do a good job of hiding just how stressed they are about their work. They take their work seriously, and work incredibly hard, but they don't let it interfere with having fun, and on weekends they somehow come off as carefree.

The Students

The real reason to come to Brown—besides the impressive faculty, liberal curriculum, and beautiful campus—is to meet all the other Brown students. Students here are incredibly creative, approachable, and unpretentious. These are people you'll hang out with for an entire year before they'll tell you that, yeah, they double major in neuroscience and philosophy, run their own company through the Internet, play trombone in the orchestra, act and direct plays, and take art classes at nearby RISD [Rhode Island School of Design], all at the same time. These are truly extraordinary individuals. They are also truly diverse: Brown has lots of students of color, queer students, students of different faiths and political leanings, and everyone is accepted and welcomed. I learn more from my friends on a daily basis than I ever thought possible.

The Activities

In high school I was the epitome of the music/band dork. When I came to Brown, I signed up to write music reviews for the campus' weekly arts and culture magazine. Pretty soon I was doing feature stories and coediting a section. Now I am managing editor for the *BDH Post* and I could see myself going into music journalism as a career. This is characteristic of Brown. Kids here experiment, they branch out, they throw themselves into everything they do, and they continually discover new passions. If you come to Brown, don't be reticent about throwing yourself into things. Follow your interests, see where they lead you.

> "As an athlete, one of the reasons I chose Brown was because each of the thirty-seven or so athletic teams receives the same support from fans and the athletic department."
>
> ✦ Allison, junior

The Social Scene

Weekends at Brown typically start on Wednesday night and stretch on until early Sunday morning. Within this time, people can pick and choose which nights they want to have fun, and there will always be a hoard of people packing a house, drinking and dancing, somewhere. There isn't much of a bar scene at Brown, but many kids like to head to the on-campus Grad Center Bar (GCB) to drink, or The Underground, which frequently has live music and stand-up comedy. Many head just off campus

and hit up nearby Thayer Street haunts such as Max's Upstairs. Z-Bar is a favorite, as is Fish Co. I'd say most people party one or two days each weekend. If people party two days, one day will be all-out partying, heading to the spot on campus where they'll find the most students gathered. The other day will be more low-key—they'll meet up with friends, smoke a joint, play Trivial Pursuit, and watch a movie. Brown doesn't have a competitive social scene. Every freshman year a few social climbers pop up, stick out like sore thumbs, and simply don't fit in. The climbers quickly change their evils ways, settle down, and are accepted back into the fold. At Brown, I'd say students from every class year hang out together. There are also lots of transfer students who tend to be more socially and academically zealous than the kids who came as freshmen, because they want to get the most out of their truncated time here.

> "Brown is situated on the top of College Hill in Providence, overlooking the city and within blocks of the Rhode Island School of Design. The surrounding area is quaintly colonial and in the fall, we have the best looking trees in New England."
>
> ✦ Praveen, junior

Name: Allison
Hometown: Los Angeles, California
Class Year: Junior
Major: Judaic studies and history
Extracurriculars: Hillel, yearbook staff, Bruin Club, student member of the Committee on Admissions and Financial Aid
Career Goal: Law school or PhD

How would you describe Brown's reputation?

A bunch of highly intellectual activist-hippies wandering the winding streets of New England in Polo shirts and Birkenstocks—Frisbee in one hand and an advanced chemical engineering textbook in the other.

Is this reputation accurate?

It's an accurate description of the look of a Brown student. But deep down, Brown students aren't activist-hippies anymore. There are still some screaming politicos at Brown, sure. But year by year their numbers have been dwindling. Now you have lots of students who enjoy being thought of as politically active but, in reality, almost never rise up. Which isn't to say these students aren't liberal intellectuals. Brown students are still liberal intellectuals. They're just not activist-hippie liberal intellectuals.

What would an admissions officer at your school probably not tell a prospective student?

I think admissions officers try to downplay the amount of drugs and alcohol on campus. The average student will tell you they can get as much alcohol and pot as you'd want within twenty minutes. That said, students who aren't into smoking or drinking are never pressured to participate. Brown students are nothing if not accepting of other people's decisions.

> "Despite the generally hardcore leftist political leanings of Brown students, we tend to be a shockingly preprofessional lot."
> ✦ Leslie, junior

The Institution

The most overwhelming part of coming to Brown is opening the course catalog. You can take just about any class you want, from thousands of options. It's frightening at first, but also amazing. Honestly, Brown is a really happy place. You can participate in any clubs that inspire you. You are surrounded by students who share your love of learning. Plus Brown is the perfect size—there are always new people to meet, but you never feel lost in the crowd. Sure there will be bad times of the year (I'm talking to you, February) during which you can't feel your toes, you'll have too many midterms, they're serving questionable meat in the Ratty (campus cafeteria), and shit, it's 10 p.m. and you missed your 9 p.m. study session. But that's college in general.

And Brown is in Providence, which is great. They have fabulous restaurants and a vibrant cultural life, or you can just go to the Providence Place mall to unwind. It's also close to Boston (fifty

minutes and about $6 by commuter rail) and New York (about four hours and $50 roundtrip with a student discount on the Bonanza Bus).

I'll just add that Brown has made me proud to celebrate my inner-nerd. I'm proud to be me—a short, Jewish double major in modern American history and Judaic studies, a feminist, a humanist, a Democrat, a pro-choice activist, and a major klutz. Brown gives students the tools to embrace themselves.

The Education

I am always amazed by how approachable Brown's professors are. Brown takes the attitude that a student's education is what they decide to make of it, and a student can go through school having formed no meaningful relationships with their professors, or they can graduate knowing lots of professors extremely well. It's up to the student. If the student does want to get to know their professors, Brown lends an institutional hand—through the Karen T. Romer Undergraduate Teaching and Research Assistantship (UTRA), students are given a stipend to help professors design and prepare for new classes, or do research for a book or project. UTRA encourages students and faculty to work incredibly closely and form a true academic partnership that benefits both parties equally.

> "Our frat houses were built at the exact same time, with practically identical floor plans, so parties are held in identical lounges. Thus if you've been to one Brown frat party, you've truly been to them all."
> ✦ John, senior

Advising programs are also big at Brown. Freshman year, students are given a general adviser. When a student declares their concentration, they're given another adviser in that department. There is also the Meiklejohn Advising Program, where freshmen are given upperclassmen advisers who will tell them which sociology course to take, which professors to avoid, where to sit in any specific lecture hall, how to avoid the dreaded 8:30 a.m. class, etc. First years also have three in-dorm advisers: a woman's peer counselor, a minority peer counselor, and a residential counselor.

These advisers serve as another form of support and guidance during a student's first year at Brown.

About one third of the campus studies abroad, and the Office of International Programs (the OIP), is very efficient. Even if Brown doesn't offer a program in a particular city or country, the OIP will help connect you to a school that does.

> "As everyone knows, Brown has no core curriculum. We have no requirements whatsoever outside of your concentration.
> ✦ Leslie, junior

The Students

I'd say the average Brown student would probably be middle class to upper-middle class, Caucasian, black, Asian, or Latino, Catholic or Jewish, they'll have tried pot once or twice but prefer to drink, they're involved in one extracurricular activity but they might sign up for another, they've switched their concentration three times, they worship at least one professor, and they also listen to rap and Phish. The average Brown student is also pretty opinionated. The school paper—the *Brown Daily Herald*—has a really popular op-ed page, and it's always amusing to give it a read and see what people are going on about.

The Activities

Brown definitely gets its fair share of big-name performers and speakers. My only complaint is that our lecture venues are small. So getting a seat to see speakers almost always involves waiting in long lines or volunteering to staff the event itself just to get in. On a nice day people hang out on the Green—one handful of students eating, smoking, and studying in a big circle, one group of well-dressed guys and better-dressed girls jabbering on cell phones, one batch of kids playing Ultimate barefoot, and a few isolated tie-dyed students protesting something and trying to get more kids involved.

And if you're awake at 3 a.m. on a Wednesday: if you're a freshman, it's because you hardly ever sleep. There's so much work, so many activities, you might miss something! If you're a sophomore, you're drunk. You've accepted that you can't get everything done at once, and it *seemed* like a great idea to open that six pack at 8 p.m. on a Tuesday. If you're a junior, you're studying. It's time to get serious. And if you're a senior, you're working on your thesis.

The Social Scene

Brown has an active Greek scene that collectively throws about two parties per weekend. Most freshmen go to frat parties, but then, as upperclassmen, party more in houses and apartments. A typical Friday night involves a run to Jo's (snack bar), "pregaming" with friends in a dorm, heading to an '80s-themed frat party, going to an invite-only 1 a.m. cocktail party, heading over to an off-campus apartment party, then going back to campus when that party is broken up by the cops ten minutes later. The night then might be finished off with a joint and a call to Via-Via for some pizza.

Name: Stephanie
Hometown: River Vale, New Jersey
Class Year: Senior
Major: Cognitive science
Extracurriculars: Brown Hillel, Kappa Alpha Theta sorority, *Brown Daily Herald*
Career Goal: What? Dear God, I have no idea.

How would you describe Brown's reputation?

Brown has a reputation for being superliberal, filled with green-haired hippies. People think we don't have any grades, don't have to take any classes, and just protest all day.

Is this reputation accurate?

No way! Most of my friends are fairly conservative nonhippies who are serious students but also know how to have fun. As for academics, we take a normal amount of classes, and even though we don't have core requirements, we are always graded unless we take a class pass/fail.

What would an admissions officer at your school probably not tell a prospective student? What aspect of your school would a prospective student not see on a campus tour?

The Admissions office probably wouldn't talk about the increasing animosity between Brown students and Brown's administration. Recently, there has been a significant decrease in student parking, disallowed student storage, and fraternities and other student groups have been prohibited from having large open parties in their dorms. Brown students are not pleased with these developments. On a tour, students will not see New Pembroke Campus, where the dorms are horrible and ugly inside and out. This area, which is surrounded by concrete instead of grass, is called "the ghetto" or "the projects" by students.

The Institution

Brown isn't big on athletics, and we don't have the raucous school spirit that comes with having champion sports teams. We also don't have a campus center, which hurts campus unity. And we don't have as many big traditions as our Ivy League counterparts. That said, we do have one tradition that I wish we *didn't* have, called Naked Donuts. The night before finals begin, a group of students goes to the libraries naked and hands out donuts. Yuck! Our dorms also aren't great. They're mostly old, small, and in desperate need of refurbishing. And the food at the Ratty (what a wonderful name for our cafeteria, right?) is *awful*. The workers try—they make themed dinner nights, with nice tablecloths—and we appreciate their efforts, but we'd appreciate better food even more.

The Education

Most of the classes I've taken, and the professors I've had, have been absolutely incredible. Academics are where Brown really shines. There used to be "guts" (easy classes) at Brown, but as the years have gone by they've been replaced with more challenging classes, which is a good thing. Because Brown students do like working hard, and they do enjoy being challenged. Brown students also talk a lot about what they learned in class outside of class, which is neat. I get to learn about all the most interesting parts of my friends' classes without having to sit through them! There are also tons of research opportunities. Most people I know stayed here at least one summer to work with a professor, and many students work on big projects with faculty members that last a year or more.

The Students

At Brown, there are average, smart, open-minded students who like everyone and try to get along with everyone. Then there are the minority students, many of whom stick to themselves, and there are the queer students, who stick to themselves and think the straight students hate them. Everyone else, as I said, gets along and enjoys the fact that we go to a great school with lots of other interesting, intelligent people. There are a few superliberals who give the campus its reputation. Most students just ignore them, though, and politely step over their sit-in.

The Activities

Students get really passionate about their extracurriculars, and they'll spend large chunks of time getting involved and planning large-scale events that benefit the entire school. The administration is really supportive of funding our efforts—which is great, but, particularly in the arts, it's not enough. Brown doesn't have enough studio and gallery space, nor does it have a concert hall, nor an auditorium that holds more than six hundred to seven hundred people, which is something that I hope changes.

Most Brown students don't leave College Hill all that much. It's a nice place with nearby restaurants, movie theaters, shops, bars. It's almost too bad, because Providence is great. It has superb local theater, great concert venues, some decent minor league sports teams, etc. I almost wish there were less to do right on College Hill so we'd be forced into Providence more often.

The Social Scene

For those that do party during the weekends (most people), there's always a frat party, and lots of people will head in that direction. Everyone is welcome. There's a bar near campus that you can usually get into if you have a halfway decent fake ID, and if you're over twenty-one there are a couple of nice bars in Providence, but most people get together in small groups, go out and meet up with more people, dance and drink, then a few people go back to someone's room, talk, and play a board game into the wee hours of the night.

Notable Brown Alumni Include:
Ted Turner, media mogul
Horace Mann, educator
Mary Chapin Carpenter, singer/songwriter
Lisa Loeb, singer/songwriter
John D. Rockefeller Jr., philanthropist
John F. Kennedy Jr., lawyer, publisher

BRYN MAWR COLLEGE

Founded: 1885

Location: Bryn Mawr, PA

Phone: (610) 526-5152

E-mail: admissions@brynmawr.edu

Web site: www.brynmawr.edu

Number of Undergraduates: 1,322

Number of Graduate Students: 447

Cost: Approximately $37,000 per year

Application Deadline: January 15

Early Decision: November 15

Rating:	Notable Majors/Programs:
Selective	Psychology, English, French, Math

Size:
● Small ○ Medium ○ Large

Location:
○ Urban ● Suburban ○ Rural

On a Saturday, students talk about academics:
● Always ○ Sometimes ○ Never

Nightlife:
○ Intense ○ Moderate ● Laid-back

Politically, Bryn Mawr leans:
● Left ○ Right ○ Split

Diversity:
○ High ○ Low ● Medium

All-women's: Yes!

Students describe Bryn Mawr in five words:
- Community-based, female-only school for intellectuals
- Prestigious, extremely beautiful, very rigorous

From the School

Bryn Mawr teaches and values critical, creative and independent habits of thought and expression in an undergraduate liberal arts curriculum for women and in coeducational graduate programs in arts and sciences and social work and social research. Bryn Mawr seeks to sustain a community diverse in nature and democratic in practice, for we believe that only through considering many perspectives do we gain a deeper understanding of each other and the world.

—www.brynmawr.edu

If you're interested in Bryn Mawr, you may also be interested in:
Brown, Haverford, Mount Holyoke, U. Pennsylvania, Smith, Wellesley

Name: Laurel
Hometown: Glassboro, New Jersey
Class Year: Junior
Major: English
Extracurriculars: the Owl Investment Group, the Women's Club, the Animal Liberation Coalition, the rugby team
Career Goal: Start my own business in cosmetics or fashion.

How would you describe Bryn Mawr's reputation?

Typical misconceptions include: a small school for "rich girls" who believe themselves to be among the academic and social elite; a school for cultish lesbians who don't shower, and run around nude holding gay pride rallies every afternoon; or it's a school full of highly intelligent, overworked, man-starved women who on weekends devolve into horny savages and have sex with any Haverford or Swarthmore boy that steps on campus.

Is this reputation accurate?

Bits and pieces may apply, but the above is mostly fabrication. Yes, there are quite a few rich, perfectly tanned and coiffed girls at Bryn Mawr (including the daughters of some celebrities) that leave campus every weekend in chauffered limousines, some militant lesbians, and some unstoppably horny straight girls, but these girls are obviously the exception. Most people here are just awesome, down to earth young women who are very intelligent, work very hard, and also like to have fun.

What would an admissions officer at your school probably not tell a prospective student?

An admissions officer might not tell you that many of our professors (both male and female) are *very* attractive. Prepare to fall in love with an academic.

The Institution

Bryn Mawr bathroom stalls often have magazines, informational posters, crossword puzzles, or surveys hanging in them—nice if you get bored while going to the bathroom, but a little bit germy if you ask me. But people do go out of their way to make even the most *unexpected* places here feel fun, interesting, and community-oriented. This is a product of our campus being so small; you recognize a lot of people all the time and you're almost always totally comfortable. I personally love Bryn Mawr, I feel so safe here, and it's the most beautiful place I've ever been. Almost every building on campus is Victorian or Edwardian, done in the collegiate Gothic style—most buildings look like gigantic cathedrals or beautiful medieval English castles. At least one building is renovated every year to preserve the old and beautiful exterior and to integrate state-of-the art facilities within. There's the Rockefeller dorm, with its beautiful gargoyles, Rhoads dorm, which looks like an English estate and has a view of a large pond, and Goodhart auditorium, which is like a giant medieval cathedral with flying buttresses. It's magnificent. And the food and dining services at Bryn Mawr are rated as some of the country's best—and it's true, the food is delicious. Lastly, we often get big-name speakers, especially from the creative writing department.

> "There's a *Simpsons* episode where Lisa dreams about the Seven Sister schools—Wellesley claims that you can go there and marry Harvard men, Smith claims that you can play great lacrosse there, and then Bryn Mawr saunters over and kisses Smith on the lips and says, 'You can go to Bryn Mawr and explore.' The whole campus fell out of its seat laughing at that one."
>
> ✦ Jessie, sophomore

The Education

One thing that makes Bryn Mawr students distinctive—like a fine wine, shall we say?—is that we all love to mesh our academic and social lives. Often we'll go out to dinner or shopping, and midway through we'll find ourselves feverishly discussing Judith Butler's theories of sexuality and gender or some new postcolonial literary theorist. We don't talk about these things in our free time because we have to. We do it because we want to, because we're all legitimately interested and involved.

Our professors are also generally astounding, both inside and outside the classroom. That's a big deal—professors at Bryn Mawr aren't only the people you see twice a week in classrooms and hand in papers to. They're also people who are active in campus life, who attend student-run events, eat in our dining halls, and pop up in the library at 9 p.m. before a paper is due to see if anyone has last-minute questions. They're like proud parents and best friends—they want you to succeed, and they are supportive on a personal level. More than a few students find themselves having a hard time not becoming infatuated with their very beautiful, very intelligent professors.

The psychology, English, and French departments are very strong at Bryn Mawr, and allow students to pursue creative and fruitful senior projects/theses. One amazing class that I've taken within the English department is Chaucer's *Canterbury Tales.* We read all of the tales in Middle English, which is like learning a new language . . . and the tales are all filled with sexual commentary and mysterious and supernatural undertones, which made for amazing class discussions.

The Students

There are very large and active Asian, Muslim, Christian, LGBT, and political groups on campus. These groups are composed of students from all races and persuasions, do their best to inform the campus about diversity issues, and frequently sponsor dances, lectures, and fund-raisers. At Bryn Mawr everyone is integrated. You will make friends that are like you, that are unlike you, and that care deeply about things you may have never thought about before. If you come here, open your mind to other viewpoints and prepare to engage with other cultures in entirely new, exciting ways. This school has dismantled my racial and sexual stereotypes, and has taught me to respect, understand, and engage in dialog with minorities of all sorts, with people who are different from me in any way.

> "Be warned: the Haverboys are short and hairy, the Swatties are *not* hotties, and the Villanovan boys have too many cute girls on their campus to ever want to dip their toes into Mawr's waters."
> ✦ Brenda, freshman

The Activities

Let me tell you about the rugby team. They are loud. They are mostly gay. They are incredibly active on campus. And they are fabulous. If you come to Bryn Mawr and want a fun, dangerous way to get rid of your excess energies, join the rugby team. Oh, and they are very big drinkers, so make sure you're ready to down pint after pint of the cheapest beer imaginable. If you can do this without gagging, you'll fit in fine.

There's always *something* to do on campus—be it an event, a small party, someone selling clothing or jewelry in the campus center, a famous speaker lecturing, a band performing, and Bryn Mawr is only twenty minutes away from the King of Prussia Mall, which is one of the largest malls in America. So if we're bored on campus, we can always shop! (Note: the Neiman Marcus at KoP doesn't take Visa.)

> "Bryn Mawr students tend to overuse the word *amazing*. Example:
> Person 1: How was your day?
> Person 2: It was amazing! I had the most amazing day!
> Person 1: That's amazing!"
> ✦ Elaine, senior

The Social Scene

Bryn Mawr girls are generally very friendly and polite. It's very easy to meet new people because everyone is intelligent, funny, and ready to have an intellectually stimulating—or just silly—conversation. There are house parties all the time on campus, some of which will feature alcohol, and if you get bored of those you can head over to nearby Haverford, Swarthmore, or the University of Pennsylvania and party there. You can also go to Philly and go clubbing in any of hundreds of nightclubs. I like this bit: it's always fun to watch the shy, timid girl from your class dress up a little bit for a Bryn Mawr party, a bit more for a club in Philly, and then go overboard and dress like a total hooker for parties with frat boys at U. Penn. Seriously, though, the social scene at Bryn Mawr is definitely *not* lacking, and there's always something stimulating and exciting to do, even if it's just walking down the street to Lancaster Avenue to visit the local shops and bars or grabbing a bite to eat at Minella's (the local diner).

Name: Molly
Hometown: Huron, Indiana
Class Year: Junior
Major: Anthropology; minor: East Asian studies
Extracurriculars: Bryn Mawr/Haverford women's varsity club rugby team, editor-in-chief of Bryn Mawr's yearbook, *Akoue*
Career Goal: Either work for National Geographic or become a CIA agent.

How would you describe Bryn Mawr's reputation?

Where I'm from, hardly anyone knows what Bryn Mawr is, but the few people who do know are *very* impressed. In the professional community it's another story: Bryn Mawr is definitely on the radar for producing capable, intelligent, well-rounded women.

Is this reputation accurate?

The professional community gets it right. I suppose people also say there are lots of lesbians here, because it's an all-girls school, but that's overblown. True, college is a time to experiment, and Bryn Mawr does provide a very accepting and encouraging environment for exploration. Lesbians are totally accepted, and if you want to kiss a girl, go for it. But the majority of students aren't lesbians, and Bryn Mawr doesn't seem any gayer to me than other typical small liberal arts colleges.

What aspect of your school would a prospective

"Bryn Mawr attracts smart and quirky women. BMC on the whole is slightly dichotomous: it's a liberal arts college with booming science *and* English programs, and it's a small school that feels big because its population interacts significantly with students at Haverford, Swarthmore, and U. Penn.

✦ Madeline, sophomore

student not see on a campus tour?

Because of the above-mentioned all-girls school stereotype, a tour guide probably wouldn't talk about Bryn Mawr's gay scene in any depth. If you're interested in hearing about this, though, just ask and I'm sure folks will tell you anything you want to know.

The Institution

One of BMC's biggest strengths is its small size and its relationship with Haverford and Swarthmore colleges. BMC students can take classes at Haverford and/or Swarthmore really easily for full credit if they want to, and classes at all these schools are almost never more than twenty people. Rock on. Haverford is particularly close; in fact, I am actually majoring in anthropology through Haverford's department, not BMC's.

I should also mention that Bryn Mawr's social

and academic honor code is strictly enforced and a big deal on campus. The honor code means you do things like take tests on your own without professors in the room, and you're never allowed to talk about grades. Think about this. It's pretty great. The last bit about grades may seem restrictive at first, but it's a godsend, because you never compete against anyone but yourself.

Also there are no Greek organizations at BMC. That said, there are four big traditions that bind us together (and we are all women here, so BMC itself can feel like a massive sorority, which isn't bad). The four traditions are Parade Night, Lantern Night, Hell Week, and May Day. I'm not going to give anything away—they're too much fun, and it's better if you find out about them once you arrive on campus. Suffice it to say, if you come to Bryn Mawr, you'll eventually have four years of fantastic memories associated with each. And then there are some smaller traditions, like only seniors being able to walk on the "senior steps," and everyone on campus making offerings to the Athena statue in Thomas Great Hall before exams for good luck—which sounds cultish, but it's actually a lot of fun.

Lastly, Bryn Mawr dorms are *gorgeous*—it's like living in a castle. They have hardwood floors, fireplaces, window seats, turrets, spacious bathrooms. Free laundry service. Students rarely live off campus during their four years. And to make the deal even sweeter, the vast majority of sophomores, and all juniors and seniors, are guaranteed singles. So after your freshman year you get to live in splendor *and* you get a whole room to yourself! I wasn't gung-ho about attending an all-girls school. I just happened to wind up at one. But now I'm a huge fan of the all-girls thing—it's been a fantastic experience.

"Dorms here are tiny palaces! At other schools freshmen live in cement-block cells with linoleum floors. I had a fireplace in my freshman dorm room."

✦ Janet, sophmore

The Education

Bryn Mawr is a small school, so you can expect to be in small classes taught by professors (not TAs!) who will know your name and talk extensively with you about your paper on American Modernism three months after you've handed it in. Really, professors are exceedingly concerned with their students' well being and academic progress and will do anything to help you learn and grow. Take advantage of them. Bryn Mawr's deans are also helpful—go to their office hours. They'll typically bend over backward to make your life easier whenever they can.

> "Philly is only eleven miles away, but you'll be so busy you'll rarely make the trip."
> ✦ Alana, senior

The Students

Students at Bryn Mawr are extremely diverse—ethnically, religiously, politically, and culturally. We're a big, fascinating mishmash. Students come to Bryn Mawr from all over the USA and just about every part of the world. There are kids who pay full tuition, kids on heavy student loans, kids in between. To help make tuition more manageable, Bryn Mawr has a great work-study program that helps get the bills paid.

Bryn Mawr is a pretty studious campus—we get assigned a lot of work, and we like doing it. And most people seem to be able to handle their workload enough to still have a social life (though there are recluses who live in their rooms and the library). For those that do go out, there are parties on campus, and there's plenty to do in Philadelphia, which is only a twenty-minute drive away. The only thing I'd complain about is that many kids don't stick with organized extracurricular activities at Bryn Mawr. At the beginning of each year everyone joins teams and clubs, but once academics sink their teeth in, people begin going less frequently, and sometimes groups dwindle away into nothingness. Luckily, both BMC students and the administration are aware of this, and everyone is trying to work together to find a way to boost student participation.

The Activities

I began working on the yearbook staff my freshman year as a photographer, and this year I became the editor-in-chief and it has been a rewarding experience that has taught me a lot about managing and implementing large-scale projects. But mainly my time at Bryn Mawr has been shaped by my involvement with the rugby team and the yearbook staff. The rugby team is the largest team on campus, and our games are the best-attended athletic events. Our motto is "work hard, but play harder," and I really do think rugby helps us cope with Bryn Mawr's rigorous workload. I've worked my way up from being a rookie who had never even seen a game to the president and a starting prop, and for a large portion of the year the rugby team is my life.

The Social Scene

On a typical weekend, the average "Mawrtyr" will go out with friends for dinner or coffee at least once, and probably also watch a movie or attend a campus event and spend some time doing homework, too. If they party particularly hard, they'll drink in someone's dorm, go to local bar, or head into Philly to dance at a club. If they're part of the rugby team, Saturday nights are "social nights," where much beer is consumed and rugby songs are sung. Occasionally students might also venture out to Haverford or Swarthmore and see what's going on there. Large, rowdy, campuswide parties aren't a Bryn Mawr thing, but if you search around you'll find groups of friends having fun in their dorms or apartments.

Name: Jessica
Hometown: Mamaroneck, New York
Class Year: Senior
Major: Political science
Extracurriculars: Campus Republicans, masters swimming, dance, Phonathon, social committee, traditions
Career Goal: International business law

How would you describe Bryn Mawr's reputation?

They say Bryn Mawr is a very academic school, with a liberal student body, a limited amount of parties, and lots of homosexual women.

Is this reputation accurate?

Mostly. Bryn Mawr is very academic and liberal, and it doesn't have an overwhelming amount of campus parties. However, the homosexual women thing, I don't think that's true. Lesbians exist, of course, but not any more than at any other school.

What aspect of your school would a prospective student not see on a campus tour?

On some weekends it's stone-cold dead. If you don't want to leave campus but you want to have a lot of fun, sometimes you're in trouble. This isn't to say people don't socialize, drink, etc. They do that in spades, but in small groups. If you want the big, college-type craziness you see in movies, you don't want Bryn Mawr. It simply doesn't exist here.

The Institution

I chose my school because of its small size, its proximity to Philadelphia, Washington, D.C., and NYC, and its wonderful academic reputation. I also loved the fact that I could take classes at Haverford, Swarthmore, and (with a little more effort) the University of Pennsylvania. Lantern Night, Hell Week, May Day all provide a great opportunity for students to interact with one another, and create a tight sense of community. In fact, one cannot truly understand a "Mawrtyr" until one has witnessed these traditions. When I meet alums there's always an immediate connection and sense of excitement that we both know about this special place and can share a sense of pride.

I'll also add that this is a very, very safe campus, and most of the time people leave their doors unlocked with no fear of theft.

The Education

We do have a core curriculum at Bryn Mawr, but I think that helps make everyone more well rounded. You have to take a freshman writing seminar, three humanities classes, two social science classes, and three natural science classes. We also have most students complete a senior thesis (the length of which depends on the department). A lot of schools are getting rid of senior theses, but I think this is a big mistake. It's pretty incredible for a student to spend their senior year producing a large final body of work representing the sum total of their studies that they can look back on the rest of their life and feel proud of. A Bryn Mawr education is both intellectually stimulating and—dare I say it?—fun. It's great taking interesting classes with other bright kids under the tutelage of professors who feel really close to every single student. And the honor code means everyone respects one another—no one competes, teachers trust us to take unproctored tests—and everyone's here to read and learn and become a better person.

The Students

Bryn Mawr is incredibly diverse. You have students from India, Italy, Ghana, Bulgaria—from every imaginable culture, race, religion, sexual ori-entation, socioeconomic background—and everyone interacts, which is rarer than you'd think. Also, students at Bryn Mawr have a ridiculously diverse set of interests, from clubs specializing in Wiccan religion to baton-twirling trapeze artists. I think the only area in which Bryn Mawr students *aren't* diverse is their politics. Everyone here is a Democrat. Everyone here is liberal. If you're a conservative, and you're thinking about coming to Bryn Mawr, be prepared to argue lots with just about everyone.

The Activities

Bryn Mawr and Haverford are two sides of the same coin. We eat at each other's dining halls, go to each other's libraries. Students do things here, they do things there. Swarthmore, U. Penn, Villanova, and St. Joseph's are also close by. So there's lots of things to do at other campuses. The downside of this is that Bryn Mawr students don't always feel the need to create an active social scene on their own campus because there are so many other social scenes to visit. So a lot of Bryn Mawr campus parties are dead. And on any given day, because students are in their rooms studying, in libraries, in classes, and on other campuses, you can step outside and not see anyone else for ten minutes straight. This is a bit creepy, but once night falls and everyone is back, things pick up again. I'd say Bryn Mawr is a late-night campus, too. At 3 a.m. in the middle of the week, most students will still be awake, polishing an essay or hanging out.

The Social Scene

There's no Greek scene, so people are left to their own means to organize and throw parties. And since everyone is overworked and tired, they just don't that often. And because Bryn Mawr is all women, it's a bit difficult for heterosexual girls to find dates. For lesbians it's great. But for heterosexuals, you have to head over to a nearby school. Luckily, there are plenty of opportunities to do this, and they are all within a fifteen-minute drive.

Notable Bryn Mawr Alumni Include:
Emily Greene Balch, Nobel Prize–winning author
Katharine Hepburn, actress
Marianne Moore, poet
Lee McGeorge Durrell, naturalist, TV presenter
Emily Cheney Neville, author
Edith Hamilton, author

BUCKNELL UNIVERSITY

Founded: 1846
Location: Lewisburg, PA
Phone: (570) 577-1101
E-mail: admissions@bucknell.edu
Web site: www.bucknell.edu

Number of Undergraduates: 3,350
Number of Graduate Students: 192
Cost: Approximately $35,000 per year
Application Deadline: January 1
Early Decision: November 15

Rating:	Notable Majors/Programs
Very Selective	Business Administration, Biology, Economics

Size:
○ Small ● Medium ○ Large

Location:
○ Urban ○ Suburban ● Rural

On a Saturday, students talk about academics:
○ Always ● Sometimes ○ Never

Nightlife:
● Intense ○ Moderate ○ Laid-back

Politically, Bucknell leans:
○ Left ○ Right ● Split

Diversity:
○ High ● Low ○ Medium

Students describe Bucknell in five words:
- Preppy, preprofessional students; gorgeous campus
- Small; intense workload; great parties

From the School

Bucknell University is one of the top liberal arts colleges in the nation, but beyond our broad liberal arts college curriculum we also offer strong professional programs in engineering, business, education, and music performance. With our ideal size of 3,350 undergraduates and 150 graduate students, we are one of the few institutions in the nation that successfully combines the personal attention of a small college with the academic resources of a large university.

—www.bucknell.edu

If you're interested in Bucknell, you may also be interested in:
Boston College, Carnegie Mellon, Colgate, Cornell, Johns Hopkins, Middlebury

Name: Brian
Hometown: Collegeville, Pennsylvania
Class Year: Sophomore
Major: English
Extracurriculars: *Bucknellian* (school newspaper)
Career Goal: Magazine editor

How would you describe Bucknell's reputation?

It's said that Bucknell is in the middle of nowhere, and that, to get by, students have formed a really self-sufficient community. It's also said that Bucknell's campus and students are both gorgeous. And that the students work hard, but play harder.

Is this reputation accurate?

All of that is true. We're this little society, surrounded by farmland, dominated by preppy kids who have been sent away to major in business, psychology, or engineering, to join a fraternity or sorority, meet their future spouse, graduate, and move to a city in the Northeast where they will find a high-paying job.

What aspect of your school would a prospective student not see on a campus tour?

Well, this *is* mentioned on the tour, but it's worth reiterating: Bucknell is located in the middle of nowhere, and because of this, the campus is incredibly safe. There's almost no crime in the area, and, by extension, there's almost no crime at Bucknell. It's great.

The Institution

Bucknell was actually the first, and last, school I looked at, with fourteen other schools in between. The first time I came to Bucknell, I didn't even stay for the entire tour because the tour guide was rattling off random inconsequential facts and trivia, and I got bored. I thought it was the school that bored me, and I left. But as I visited more campuses, I realized it wasn't Bucknell, it was the entire college visitation process in general. And, more importantly, all these little things I'd glimpsed at Bucknell kept coming back to me, and more and more I started thinking, "This place isn't as good as Bucknell was." I knew I wanted a school that bridged the gap, that was small and intimate like a college while still having top-notch facilities and connections like a university. I wanted a school with nice kids, tiny classes, approachable professors, and an active social life.

After visiting fourteen schools I begged my parents to take me back to Bucknell to see it again. And the moment I stepped back on campus (as ridiculous as this sounds), I honestly felt like I'd found my new home. Bucknell is unique in how gorgeous it is, and how hard the university works to keep it that way. The lawns are always perfectly manicured, the snow entirely shoveled in the a.m. after even the most brilliant of snowstorms the night before. Every building is a rich orange-red brick, and both the old and new buildings blend in perfectly with one another.

> "The Mods are located across from the main campus on Route 15. These were originally put up as temporary housing in the seventies, but have been so popular with sophomores that they've remained for almost twenty-five years. They look like trailers, but they're cozy and have great closet space."
>
> ✦ Brian, junior

The Education

Bucknell has two colleges: the College of Arts and Sciences and the School of Engineering. Both have broad core requirements respective to their curriculums, and specialized requirements once you choose your major. Class sizes can range from ten students to three hundred students, and, personally (as a student in arts and sciences), there are usually about twenty students in each of my classes. Bucknellians take their classes very seriously and tend to be active in class, asking questions, doing their work on time, taking notes, and paying attention to everything the professors say. At the same time, they don't take their classes so seriously that they never have fun; for example, if a student wants to watch the premiere of the *O.C.*, but has an exam the next day, they'll study for the exam far in advance so they don't miss the show.

Professors here are also pretty great and inspirational, and they make students want to work hard. Professors don't come to Bucknell to do impersonal research (they'd go to a big research university for that). They come to Bucknell to teach, to be connected to students every day.

Lastly, one of my favorite things to brag about is that we're one of the only universities in the nation that has a Primates Center (where the university houses many baboons studied by students). What a cool feature . . .

The Students

The average Bucknellian is from the Northeast, Baltimore, D.C, or California. They listen to Gavin DeGraw or DMB, own at least one ribbon belt, and know that the "classy" way to wear your collar is up. Most students are from upper-middle-class backgrounds, with an even Republican/Democrat split. I write for the school newspaper, *The Bucknellian,* and I have found that I get tremendous feedback from students on my articles each week, which is so nice because it means that everyone is reading the paper and taking an active interest in what is going on around campus. Generally, students are always friendly and smiling, even under the most stressful conditions. It's hard not to appreciate life in the "bubble."

The Activities

Bucknell does an excellent job of bringing speakers, bands, etc., to campus each semester, including James Earl Jones, Jason Mraz, Eric Schlosser, and Saves the Day (the band). When students aren't going to see speakers and bands, they're usually out watching sports games, since most teams at Bucknell are Division I and really good. On the whole, Bucknell tends to attract an athletic student body. But if you're not satisfied with the arts and sports events on campus, the university also sponsors buses to take students on day trips to Philadelphia, New York, and D.C. a few times each semester.

The Social Scene

It's hard to say which days of the week are the most popular to party. During my freshman year, I would have said Wednesday, Friday, and Saturday, but it really depends on your individual schedule and when getting drunk and hanging out with friends fits into the equation. You make the schedule that suits you.

Greek life is pretty popular here, but personally, I'm an Independent (meaning I didn't go Greek), and I've found that, so long as you're social and outgoing, it doesn't matter if you shun the system. The majority of my friends did go Greek, but I've become a proud GDI (God Damn Independent), and this lets me shape my own life and party on my own schedule.

Lastly, Bucknell has a strict points system re-garding underage alcohol consumption. When it comes to underage drinking most schools look the other way as long as the students aren't doing harm, but at Bucknell, security is always looking to bust kids who are drinking. If you're caught with alcohol, you get assigned certain numbers of points, and there are different penalties for having different numbers of points (for example, when a student has ten points they have to leave Bucknell for a semester). All that said, you shouldn't worry. Bucknell students have come up with many ways to outsmart this system.

Name: Ashley
Hometown: Glenbrook, Connecticut
Class Year: Freshman
Major: Anthropology
Extracurriculars: Club volleyball, intramural volleyball
Career Goal: Undecided

How would you describe Bucknell's reputation?

Bucknell is known to be a school where every student looks like they just stepped out of a J. Crew or Abercrombie catalog. It's said that everyone is preppy and flawlessly beautiful. It's also said that our academics are outstanding, near Ivy League level, and that it's becoming harder and harder to get in every year.

> "I'm obsessed with Bucknell, and I'm not alone."
>
> ✦ Britney, freshman

Is this reputation accurate?

Pretty much. Our academics are top-notch. And our student body is made up of preppy smart kids. If you don't have a pink polo shirt with a collar to pop, you're in the minority, but that doesn't mean you won't be widely accepted.

What aspect of your school would a prospective student not see on a campus tour?

A prospective student might not see, or be told, how large Greek life is here. On a tour or interview you'll hear that there are plenty of alternate things to do if you don't want to pledge or rush. And it's true, alternate things exist (plays to see, concerts to go to), but once night falls, if you want to *party,*

Greek life is where it's at. Also, a major issue for freshmen is the required meal plan, which is illogical and forces students to waste a lot of money. The meal plan is nineteen meals a week—three meals/day during the week, two meals/day on weekends. The problem is, if you miss a meal, you completely lose that meal credit. Breakfast starts incredibly early and ends early, and most students don't wake up in time to catch it. That means every week you may lose five meals that you can't get back, which is $35 gone to waste.

The Institution

Bucknell is the perfect size, and has, literally, the most breathtaking campus I've ever seen, especially in the fall with the colors of leaves changing. I'd say Bucknell is considered by many students to be an *almost-Ivy*. Every year both the average SAT score goes up and the amount of students from the top 10 percent of their graduating high school class rises. Once you're in, the school spirit is amazing. We love sports here (playing them and watching them), and on big football days it's not uncommon to see whole halls group together to spell out BUCKNELL on their chests in magic marker or cover themselves head to toe in blue paint to cheer on their team.

Bucknell has a great freshman orientation where it goes all out for incoming students, with five orientation days packed full of fun—color wars, live music, a giant slip n' slide, a massive dodgeball tournament, carnivals, and a dance party where you're covered in foam and dance on a blow-up dance floor. During orientation you also enter into a lot of great Bucknell traditions. For example, the gates of the stadium are opened once a year to let the incoming freshmen walk in, symbolizing their entrance into the university. On graduation day, students walk out of the same stadium gate to signify the end of their time here. There's also a candle-lighting ceremony before the first day of classes, and senior year you go through the same ceremony the day before graduation.

The Education

At Bucknell you definitely get a great education. The professors are amazing. If you didn't do well on a test, you can go to them and they'll sit with you until you understand the material. They do this because they love teaching, have a passion for their subjects, and really do want to make learning fun. And students work extremely hard. There's always work to be done—as soon as one thing's finished, something else is on your plate.

The Students

Did someone say preppy? Polo shirts with the collar popped, mini skirts, khakis, ribbons in your hair . . . there is a group on campus called "Students Against Popped Collars," but those kids are lonely, as they're in such a minority. Although the majority of students here are upper-class, well-to-do white students, there's an even mix between Republicans and Democrats here, and it leads to some great debates. Both groups occasionally hold small demonstrations to voice their opinions on hot-button issues, and everyone is mature enough to listen to the views of the other group, even if they don't agree with them.

> "Everyone at Bucknell looks like an extra on *Smallville*. The students are gorgeous."
> ✦ Chris, senior

The Activities

Bucknell students are very involved and active. An overwhelming majority of students participated in high school sports, and they continue to in college, be they varsity, intramural, or club sports. Football and basketball games are always big social events. Otherwise, Bucknell provides lots of fun things for students to do. Every week there's a fairly new movie playing on campus for $1, and there are many comedians that come and give free shows. Napping is also popular.

The Social Scene

At midnight on a Monday it's not uncommon for people to ask if you're going to go out and have fun. There's always some sort of party going on here, Monday through Monday. Thursday ("Thirsty Thursday") is a particularly big party night. Drinking is popular at Bucknell, even though the administration is trying to cut down with the points system. Incoming freshmen are now required to take a four-hour alcohol class to teach them how severe the penalties will be if they're caught with liquor. Students still drink plenty, though, both because on-campus parties always have alcohol and because off-campus parties in Lewisburg are nonexistent—there's no off-campus club scene where you can not drink and still have fun . . . so you drink. Frats are a really big presence here. They're somewhat exclusive, and if you're not Greek you can't get into their parties unless you're friends with someone who is. Same thing for the sports teams—they throw great parties, but you can only get in if you're on or good friends with someone on the team.

Name: Sylvia
Hometown: Hillsboro, New Hampshire
Class Year: Junior
Major: Sociology
Extracurriculars: Varsity water polo team, Pi Beta Phi Sorority, Alpha Lambda Delta Honor Society
Career Goal: I'm looking to enroll in Teach for America before going to grad school for communications.

How would you describe Bucknell's reputation?

We're seen as one of the most prestigious non-Ivy League schools on the East Coast. We're known for our engineering program, our active Greek scene, and our stunning campus. However, we have a negative reputation for our homogenous student body.

Is this reputation accurate?

All this is true. We're prestigious, our engineering program is great, Greeks are everywhere, the campus is gorgeous. Our student body is homogenous, but Bucknell is making a real effort to change this, to increase both our racial and economic diversity. And lastly, even though our academics are superb, this isn't an "intellectual" campus, it's more preprofessional.

What aspect of your school would a prospective student not see on a campus tour?

They might not see how completely separate Bucknell is from nearby Lewisburg. Bucknell exists inside its bubble, almost entirely self-contained.

The Institution

Bucknell offers its students a tremendous amount, socially and academically, and kids appreciate everything that's given to them. People tend to be really happy here, and that carries over into their classwork and their personal relationships.

And the people you'll get to form relationships with will be extraordinary—kids who could have done well academically at any Ivy League school, but who chose to come to Bucknell instead because they were active, dynamic, and wanted a multifaceted life that incorporated both the social and the academic. Bucknell is amazing at bringing in interesting and wide-ranging speakers to campus. The cost of living is extremely low, because Bucknell is located in Nowheresville central Pennsylvania.

> "It's unfortunate, but students play little to no role in administrative decisions at Bucknell."
>
> ✦ Matthew, senior

The Education

Because of Bucknell's core curriculum, every first-year student has to take an English course and a math course, as well as a seminar on "foundational skills," which essentially helps you think, write, analyze, and argue more effectively. As a sophomore, students have to take two lab sciences. And before everyone graduates, they need to make sure they've taken four courses in the humanities, two in the social sciences, and three writing courses. Now after all those requirements, take a step back—they're not that bad. You can take *any* course in those broad areas of study. For example, I'm really not a math person, but I was able to take a more interesting computer science course under the Math department and my requirement was fulfilled. Coursework varies here between class years, majors, and even different sections of the same class. For Econ 103, for example, you could end up with a professor who assigns homework every night, or you could have a professor who never gives homework and bases the entire course grade on two tests. Most of the professors I've had at Bucknell have been amazing, though. And even though it's extremely difficult to get into Bucknell, once you're here there isn't much competition between students—everyone gets along and helps one another with their work when they can. There is also wide selection of Bucknell-approved study-abroad programs, which can land you basically anywhere in the world.

The Students

If you come to Bucknell, don't expect an explosive political scene. For the most part, students are apolitical, and while we have some vocal groups, most Bucknellians couldn't care less. Students at Bucknell come from money—I've never seen more Audis and BMWs in a student parking lot in my life—but they're not too snooty. Nonetheless, Bucknellians tend to have parents who are successful in business, and we want to be successful in some sort of career ourselves, and are very focused toward that end.

Intellectualism isn't the thing here—it's more a campus with lots of smart kids pushing pointedly onward toward our eventual lucrative careers.

The Activities

A lot of students involve themselves with campus groups, and there's a big activities fair at the beginning of every year that allows students to see what's on offer and get involved. Bucknell doesn't really interact with the other schools in our area. Athletics are huge. Friday night basketball games are packed, and a lot of students are athletes themselves. Elected student officials have a role in policy development, but it's usually only one student who represents the entire campus, and it's hard for someone that's not this student to affect change.

The Social Scene

Traditionally Bucknellians party the most on Wednesday, Friday, and Saturday nights, but lately Monday nights have begun asserting themselves, too, with lots of fun things to do. Frats dominate, and because of recent alcohol crackdowns, students "pregame" in their rooms before going out to avoid being caught by security with alcohol. There are a number of kids who don't involve themselves in the Bucknell party scene, but there isn't a great crossing over between those that partake and those that do not. As for dating, people are either hooking up and messing around, or they're full blown "going out" for at least a year if not the whole of their mutual Bucknell careers.

Notable Bucknell Alumni Include:
Philip Roth, Pulitzer Prize–winning author
Leslie Moonves, president of CBS
Edward Herrmann, Emmy Award–winning actor
Ken Langone, co-founder, Home Depot
John McPherson, syndicated cartoonist
Jane Brown Maas, creator, "I Love NY" campaign

UNIVERSITY OF CALIFORNIA—BERKELEY

Founded: 1868

Location: Berkeley, CA

Phone: (510) 642-3175

E-mail: ouars@uclink4.berkeley.edu

Web site: www.berkeley.edu

Number of Undergraduates: 23,835

Number of Graduate Students: 8,716

Cost: Approximately $16,000 per year in state; $29,000 out of state

Application Deadline: November 30

Rating:	Notable Majors/Programs
Most Selective	Business, Psychology, English, Molecular Biology

Size:
○ Small   ○ Medium   ● Large

Location:
● Urban   ○ Suburban   ○ Rural

On a Saturday, students talk about academics:
○ Always   ● Sometimes   ○ Never

Nightlife:
○ Intense   ○ Moderate   ● Laid-back

Politically, Berkeley leans:
● Left   ○ Right   ○ Split

Diversity:
● High   ○ Low   ○ Medium

PAC Ten School: Yes!

Students describe UC Berkeley in five words:
- Global powerhouse, large, liberal, tolerant
- Nearly every major is exceptional

From the School

UC Berkeley currently ranks third nationally among all institutions for the number of freshmen who are National Merit Scholars. The campus also produces more graduates who go on to earn Ph.D.s than any other university in the country. However, Cal students share more than strong academic records—they have all demonstrated the potential to add to Berkeley's rich intellectual community and spirit of pluralism.

—www.berkeley.edu

If you're interested in UC Berkeley, you may also be interested in:
Brown, UCLA, UC San Diego, Stanford, Vassar, Wesleyan

Name: Bob
Hometown: Malibu, California
Class Year: Junior
Major: Business and psychology (double major)
Extracurriculars: Asian Business Association, Queer & Asian Society
Career Goal: I'd like to be an ad exec in the high fashion industry.

How would you describe Berkeley's reputation?

Berkeley is supposed to be extremely liberal, extremely political, and one of the greatest research institutions in the country. It's said to be the best school in the UC system, and the number-one public institution in the world.

> "UCB is one of the few big campuses in America that isn't overrun with fast-food restaurants. There are lots of places that serve healthy food at a reasonable price."
>
> ✦ Lorrie, junior

Is this reputation accurate? Why or why not?

All of the above is true. Berkeley students also used to be known as hippies, but there aren't many hippies here anymore—if you walk around campus and take a look, no one's wearing tie-die, no one is any quirkier looking than students anywhere else. Also, Berkeley used to known as a radical political powerhouse, but that's been toned down. Now you'll only see protests once every month or every other month.

What would an admissions officer at your school probably not tell a prospective student? What might a prospective student not see on a campus tour?

The administration probably wouldn't tell you that you're going to have to work harder at Berkeley to get good grades than you would have to at most of our peer institutions. Unlike most Ivies, and the fun-farm across the Bay (ahem, Stanford), we don't have grade inflation. Nor would they mention that Berkeley's Study Abroad office is difficult to deal with. There's a wealth of countries and programs to choose from, that is, if you can get through the seventeen forms, essays, letters of recommendation, and incredibly unhelpful people at the counter.

The Institution

Berkeley is known as *the* University of California. It is the first, the original, the school from which all the other UCs have sprouted. It is a huge place. There are 36,000 students! When you first arrive, expect to feel lost. Then expect to come to terms, sift through it, and eventually find someone just like you. Really, with this many people to choose from, you'll find students you like. Every background, every view, every type of person on earth is represented at Berkeley. You'll pick your friends from this enormous pool, and you'll never run out of people to hang out and socialize with.

Physically, Berkeley was designed to look like a big park. The naturalness compels students to relax after long and stressful days on campus. There are huge fields just a thirty-second walk from every lecture hall door, and students practically pass out every day on the beautiful grassy lawns. Our most popular, Memorial Glade, is situated directly above three enormous underground floors of the main library. Personally, I think there's nothing more satisfying than realizing—while you are sunning yourself on a beautiful grass glade—that there are hundreds of students below you, studying and stressing out.

The Education

Berkeley was declared the number-two university in the entire world by the London *Times*. And almost every academic department is ranked at least top five in the nation.

Within each major, Berkeley students can be incredibly supportive or incredibly cutthroat. If you find yourself in a cutthroat major, be prepared

> "Berkeley's undergraduate business and engineering programs are ranked third best in the nation."
>
> ✦ Zhenia, sophomore

to push yourself to the limit, especially in those classes where professors tell you straight out they're grading on a curve (top 15 percent of students get As, next 25 percent get Bs, etc.). Some advice: choose courses at Berkeley based on the professors teaching them. Find out who the professor is, how they grade, and what they're like and don't waste time in classes where you and your professor are going to butt heads—do the legwork and save yourself the trouble.

As an upperclassman, Berkeley classes get smaller and you get more personal attention from your professors. This semester three of my four professors know me by name, which is pretty good for Berkeley! If you're an underclassman, your average class is going to be monstrously large, and there's little hope of your professors being able to distinguish you from the ninety other kids in the class with brown hair—unless you're smart and take lots of freshman/sophomore seminars. These are great, and too many kids fail to take advantage of them. In short, they're classes that are no more than fifteen to twenty students. They tend to be taught by some of Berkeley's best professors, and they give you an incredible chance to get to know these superstar academics as an underclassman.

The Students

Berkeley students are pretty open-minded. Berkeley is the place you can find yourself, be yourself, and feel at home. If you throw yourself out there you'll meet so many people from all backgrounds and life experiences. Berkeley's openness provided a great space for me in particular when I was coming out freshman year. My dorm mates were super supportive. There was no backlash or homophobia. I even became friends with other gay Cal students. Generally, Cal students are quality people you'll want to meet.

The Activities

At Berkeley there's always something happening on campus. We have ethnic student groups to join, gay student groups, art groups, dance groups, political groups, comedy groups, improv groups, a cappella groups. Everyone joins at least one.

The Social Scene

Berkeley sounds like a big campus, but give yourself a year and it will feel a lot smaller. This is especially true if you become involved in any of the larger clubs on campus (ABA, AAA, Rally Committee, FAST), because you'll know kids from those clubs, from your classes, from your dorm, from friends of friends, and so on.

The big party night at Berkeley—whether you like small house parties or big, frat-row affairs—is Thursday night. And the one big place Berkeley students go clubbing is Blake's on Telegraph Avenue. A lot of my friends also head to this great club on 3rd Street and Folsom, which, on Thursday nights, is the only eighteen and over gay club in the Bay Area. On Thursday nights and Saturday nights, lines form for blocks down historic Telegraph Avenue. On Friday nights, Wheeler Auditorium (the largest lecture hall on campus—it seats over seven hundred students) transforms into a movie theater that offers free sneak previews of unreleased movies, and also plays last month's hottest blockbuster hits.

Name: Analisa
Hometown: Sunnyvale, California
Class Year: Junior
Major: Legal studies
Extracurriculars: When you chill as hard as I do, it's more than an extracurricular activity, it's a lifestyle.
Career Goal: Acting, journalism, law school—in that order.

How would you describe Berkeley's reputation?

My school has a reputation for being very liberal. Berkeley is also said to be (I hate this) a bastion of ugly people in the middle of a state with the most beautiful people in the nation. Coming to California and attending Berkeley, in terms of student attractiveness, is supposed to be like ordering a delicious amaretto chocolate cake and then being served your grandmother's rotten dentures with a thin chocolate glaze instead.

> "If you're homophobic, racist, or averse to spicy food, Berkeley is not for you."
> ✦ Edward, sophomore

Is this reputation accurate?

Berkeley is a very liberal school, but political activism is definitely on the downswing, and conservatives exist in far greater numbers than they did even ten years ago. The two biggest magazines on campus are *The Squelch* (liberal) and *The Patriot* (conservative). Also, there are some ugly people on campus, but there are a lot of attractive people, too. It's more like you order the cake, and you're served the delicious cake, but there's glazed dentures on the side.

What would an admissions officer at your school probably not tell a prospective student?

They probably wouldn't give you much of a sense of Berkeley's social life, which is pretty good. Berkeley kids have fun.

The Institution

The weather here is nice. Berkeley does get cold from November until the beginning of April, but it's a nice, Bay area kind of cold. San Francisco—those twinkling lights in the fog—is just a twenty-five-minute ride across the bay and has amazing shopping, restaurants—pretty much everything—and in Berkeley, you have the gorgeous rolling hills, nature at its finest. My favorite part of Berke-

> "You can get a lovely view of campus and the shimmering Pacific if you climb atop the Lawrence Hall of Science. You need peace and solace like this sometimes, to clear your head from Berkeley's hustle and bustle."
>
> ✦ Frank, senior

ley thus far has been my absolutely amazing adviser. I have no idea how she keeps on top of so many students at such a big school, but she really does everything in her power to make sure I'm always on track, know exactly what classes I need to take and when. In a school of tens of thousands of people, she makes sure I never feel lost. And she is not the exception, either: advising at Berkeley is generally top-notch.

The Education

Berkeley is very competitive. There are thousands of classes to choose from, classes on every subject you could imagine, and they tend to be very big (I take huge classes with 100-plus people). The GSIs [graduate student instructors] run smaller discussions sections, and they're the ones who give you your grades in the end, so get in good with them. Professors, on the whole, will have no idea what your name is, what your interests are, or how you did on that last test. That said, they'll be leaders in their field, their lectures will be good, and at least you get to be in the same room as them once or twice a week.

There are quite a lot of highly ranked graduate schools at Berkeley. I like this, the fact that we're surrounded by slightly older students who come from a broad range of undergraduate institutions and who graduated at the top of their class. You can learn a lot if you make friends with them.

The Students

There are students of every type here, from every walk of life. There's so much you can learn outside of class just by engaging your peers in conversation. Never again in your life will you be surrounded by so many uniformly impressive people and able to count such accomplished individuals among your friends.

> "I wish I'd looked more closely at the various colleges here. When I applied I was undeclared in arts and letters. When I chose to transfer into the College of Engineering, I had to go through the entire admissions process all over again just to change my major within my own school!"
>
> ✦ Paula, junior

The Activities

Athletics are a big deal at Berkeley, and all of our games are well attended. The football team, in particular, rocks out. All the athletes spend a lot of time in the gym, and most kids join them there at some point or another, because our gym facilities are great. I took a boxing class, and through it was able to meet some really cool people I otherwise never would have even seen. And Berkeley is so close to San Francisco, students get AC transit passes, which let you take buses into the financial district of SF for free, so it's easy to escape whenever you feel the urge. And on a sunny day (and it's almost always a sunny day here), if you don't want to leave campus, people sit outside and just do their thing—they read, they write, they watch other people read and write. I originally thought Berkeley was going to be a school of crazies. I actually didn't want to come when I first applied, but after visiting all of my options, something just drew me to this place. Now I love it. There's a whole lot of school spirit at Berkeley, and everyone is involved with the place. There are a million organizations and clubs on campus. If you can't find a club you're interested in, then Jesus, there probably isn't a person alive who shares your interests.

The Social Scene

When classes are over, Berkeley students party. Thursday nights are big, and there will be alcohol almost anywhere you go. Friday is usually spent wearing sunglasses, recovering from Thursday night's debauchery (especially if you have Friday morning classes, you poor fools).

Name: Lorrie
Hometown: Oakland, California
Class Year: Sophomore
Major: Legal studies
Extracurriculars: I work a part-time job and hang out with my friends.
Career Goal: Entertainment attorney. I want to be successful, as an ethnic minority, and I want other minority students to see my career path and feel like they, too, can become successful. I want to work in outreach programs in my spare time and give others the opportunities I was lucky enough to have.

How would you describe Berkeley's reputation?

UCB is an excellent school, one of the best in the country. It's said to be very liberal.

Is this reputation accurate?

UCB is an excellent school. But it's not liberal in the way I thought it would be. In the classroom, UCB is very traditional. Teachers don't have outlandish teaching styles. Not even once has a professor held class with just a black light on. And students are open-minded, but not superpolitical or hippieish. No lovebeads. No tie-dye.

What would an admissions officer at your school probably not tell a prospective student?

Students won't be told that most of your teachers won't get to know you very well, and that it's a good idea to make graduate student instructors your friends (since they'll be doing most of your grading).

The Institution

I didn't have the highest expectations for Berkeley when I accepted a place here, and I was pretty depressed my first semester. I was taking a heavy course load, the size of my classes made me feel like a number, I hadn't made a lot of friends,

and I felt out of place. I prayed a lot, and I reached out to my parents for guidance. They told me to stick with it, that I should get out there and actively involve myself in things. This was, without a doubt, the best advice I've ever received. I made some of the best and most interesting friends of my life. So if you come here, force yourself to be outgoing and get involved. At a school this size, you have no choice.

> "Berkeley's faculty is among the most distinguished in the nation, including seven Noble Prize winners, three Pulitzer Prize winners, sixteen MacArthur Fellows, 139 Guggenheim Fellows, eighty-three Fulbright Scholars, three Fields Medalists . . ."
> —www.berkeley.edu

The Education

There's a great temptation to skip class a lot, especially in four-hundred–person lecture halls. If you do skip class, there generally aren't any real consequences. In some classes GSIs break the class into smaller sections, and these sections have mandatory weekly meetings. These meetings help keep students honest, because going to them will be part of your grade, and it's usually apparent there if you skipped the larger lecture.

At UCB you need to make the effort to meet your professors. Go to your teacher's office hours, try to develop a personal relationship with them. Really, you never know when you're going to need a letter of recommendation for things like internships, scholarships, or grad school. Try to identify three to four professors you'd like to know really well, and then do what you have to to develop a relationship. Last semester I was hospitalized for a serious illness and had to have two separate surgeries. Luckily, I knew both my professors and GSIs, and they understood my circumstances and did what they could to accommodate me. It's only through their help that I was able to make it through the semester and stay on top of things academically.

Also, UCB has lots of DECAL classes going on at any given time. These are small, full-credit, student-run classes that can be on literally anything, from the evolution of the comic book to cheese-making. I'm a big fan; looking forward to classes like this can make all your other big lecture hall classes go faster.

The Students

UCB is not very racially diverse. In a good class, there will be only one or two black or Latino students. UCB's faculty is also mostly Caucasian, and while we do have African American, Asian American, and Native American studies departments, none of them have a wide variety of class offerings. This means students have to take it upon themselves to learn more about other cultures. I have made a firm commitment to dedicate one class each semester to some area of cultural studies, to learn more about my own race and the races of others.

The Activities

There's a lot to do in and around UCB—athletics are pretty popular here (UCB has some great rivalries with Stanford, USC, and UCLA. Basketball games are great, as are football games. "Roll on, you Bears!")—so you have to balance your time wisely. And get yourself an organizer—you'll need one. Professors at UCB do not baby-sit you, and it's your job to know when papers and projects are due. Time is your best friend, procrastination is the enemy.

The Social Scene

Like a lot of people here, I take my academics really seriously, and spend a lot of time rereading notes, or highlighting passages in my textbooks, when students at other schools are giggling and watching *American Idol* in their pajamas. I don't want to give you the impression the students here are constantly pushing up their glasses and tending to their asthma. On Thursdays and Saturdays we put our books away. We drink, we dance, we release steam, we get to know one another better. But the rest of the time, we hit the books.

Notable UC Berkeley Alumni Include:
William Randolph Hearst, newspaper publisher
Abigail Van Buren, "Dear Abby" columnist
Timothy Leary, social activist
Earl Warren, former chief justice, U.S. Supreme Court
Joan Didion, author
Jack London, author

UNIVERSITY OF CALIFORNIA—LOS ANGELES

Founded: 1919

Location: Los Angeles, CA

Phone: (310) 825-4321

E-mail: ugadm@saonet.ucla.edu

Web site: www.ucla.edu

Number of Undergraduates: 25,720

Number of Graduate Students: 4,270

Cost: Approximately $18,500 per year in state; $34,500 out of state

Application Deadline: November 30

Rating:	Notable Majors/Programs:
Most Selective	Premed, Film, Arts, Engineering

Size:
○ Small ○ Medium ● Large

Location:
● Urban ○ Suburban ○ Rural

On a Saturday, students talk about academics:
○ Always ● Sometimes ○ Never

Nightlife:
○ Intense ● Moderate ○ Laid-back

Politically, UCLA leans:
● Left ○ Right ○ Split

Diversity:
● High ○ Low ○ Medium

PAC Ten school: Yes!

Students describe UCLA in five words:
- Excellent, competitive, large, and well-rounded
- Expensive, research-driven, on quarter system!

From the School

Few universities in the world offer the extraordinary range and diversity of academic programs that students enjoy at UCLA. Leadership in teaching, research, and public service make UCLA a beacon of excellence in higher education, as students, faculty, and staff come together in a true community of scholars to advance knowledge, address societal challenges, and pursue intellectual and personal fulfillment.

—www.registrar.ucla.edu

If you're interested in UCLA, you may also be interested in:
UC Berkeley, UC San Diego, U Michigan, NYU, USC, Stanford

Name: Mitch

Hometown: Lawton, Oklahoma

Class Year: Sophomore

Major: American Literature and Culture

Extracurriculars: Cultural studies, weight training, history

Career Goal: Teach English as a second language, preferably overseas (Japan!).

How would you describe UCLA's reputation?

Outstanding. Students are serious about their studies and are very respectful of each other and the academic road that brought them there.

Is this reputation accurate?

Yes. UCLA is a school known around the world, mainly for its enormous medical and research departments. It's selective and it's expensive. However, a UCLA diploma immediately demonstrates that you're a person who strives for excellence.

What would an admissions officer at UCLA probably not tell a prospective student? What aspect of your school would a prospective student not see on a campus tour?

An admissions officer probably would not tell a prospective student that the work is very doable and not as intimidating as it appears. On a tour you wouldn't see all of the students sleeping in the library because they don't get enough rest in their dorms.

> "Going Greek was a great way to make UCLA's big community feel much smaller."
> ✦ Vanessa, sophomore

The Institution

I *love* my school. I applied at UCLA as a reach. I never thought I would be accepted. The day I got my Acceptance Package in the mail from UCLA was the most exciting day of my life so far. UCLA is huge, but not intimidating. The classes are reasonably sized, the students get along, and the advising system is excellent. There are even counselors for counselors. Internship/job opportunities are everywhere. Grad school opportunities are not easy, but there are workshops and counselors everywhere to help you make your plans well in advance. I have

never seen students disgruntled with the administration. Students are very active with decisions on campus and are encouraged to make short appointments with the dean to discuss needs and complaints (if any).

The campus is like a city in a city, but safe. UCLA provides a free on-campus shuttle and the layout is very easy to navigate. The campus is divided into North campus and South campus. "Northies" are the humanities/arts types and "Southies" are the science/engineering types. Housing is expensive, but no surprise there—all of L.A. is expensive. But the weather is damn close to paradise. The school is very tradition-oriented, but not conservative to the

> "The labs here are state of the art and it's amazing to take a class with a professor who can lecture about material they discovered. And the environment is a friendly one."
> ✦ Matt, freshman

point of being stuffy. People are very liberal, respectful, and easy to approach.

The Education

UCLA is on the quarter system and I *love* it. It goes fast, but you never get bored with a subject. It's very challenging at times, but when the ten weeks are over and you have finished three or four classes, it's worth it. Students *live* their classes and are very competitive, but work together to ensure success. The large classes usually have two TAs who head up weekly discussion groups. All of the professors I have had are very approachable, very dedicated, and busy in many aspects of campus life.

UCLA has a *huge* study abroad program and thousands of students take advantage of the program every year, and it's also very doable. I'm going to England this summer to study Shakespeare!

The Students

Students come from every socioeconomic background. There are students of every ethnicity, religion, and sexual orientation. Everyone mixes here and nobody is alone unless they choose to be. An average student on campus is a guy or girl with a backpack, faded blue jeans, UCLA shirt, and thongs. Students usually don't wear sunglasses on campus, so you can see each other's eyes. I really like that. I hate not seeing someone's eyes when I'm talking to them.

The strongest groups seem to be the religious groups. They are the most visible and always have a booth, banner, or flyer somewhere. Political groups, usually from the Democratic party, are constantly passing out flyers and making statements. There are not a lot of protests, but there are some each month.

The Activities

CSU is nearby, and they're our big rival in sports (it's a friendly competition, but they usually win). There is a lot of community service. Just last weekend I joined a group that e-mailed me, calling for volunteers to help with about twelve different nonprofit groups in Los Angeles helping homeless, abused, and low-income families. I painted an apartment for battered women and children, south of downtown, with them. This group is also associated with keeping the environment clean and doing other sorts of volunteering. I always pitch in whenever they e-mail me.

Being located in the heart of L.A.'s most prestigious communities, many big performers and speakers come to Royce Hall every week. I leave campus everyday (I live off campus). I go home and read. I go out on weekends to West Hollywood or Silverlake, which are LGBT areas, but that's not every weekend.

> "Check out www.uclaprofessors.com—the best site for rankings, ratings, reviews. Some students use it to get a general idea of how new professors and their TA(s) are going to be next quarter; other students shape their major around it."
> ✦ Jennifer, sophomore

The Social Scene

A typical weekend night for me is going out to a gay club, or dinner and a movie. Students party on weekends, but within moderation. On holidays and breaks we all cut loose. The rest of the time, students are *very* focused. The party comes second, school comes first, *always*. I don't associate campus life with alcohol; I associate campus life with coffee.

Name: Jess
Hometown: Irvine, California
Class Year: Senior
Major: English
Extracurriculars: *Daily Bruin* newspaper contributor, entertainment editor, PacTies Eastern Philosophy Club, college honors
Career Goal: To become a filmmaker/writer.

How would you describe UCLA's reputation?

UCLA is one of the leading research universities in the nation. It is also known as a place of great diversity, which benefits the lively social scene.

Is this reputation accurate?

Yes, this reputation is accurate.

What would an admissions officer at UCLA probably not tell a prospective student? What aspect of your school would a prospective student not see on a campus tour?

An admissions officer would probably not mention the wild parties in the dorms or in the frat houses across the street. And there are slackers here—just as there are at other universities—that one might not run into during a college tour.

The Institution

To tell you the truth, I chose UCLA based on its reputation without ever visiting the campus. It took me a while to adjust, but in the end I can say that I'm a very proud Bruin. At first I thought the school was *huge.* But then I realized how good I had it. I do recommend a visit and talking to people from your prospective major, if possible.

The Education

Students are always talking about classes—Saturday, Sunday, all the time. Classes can be stressful. Students are generally competitive, especially in premed. Outside of class, I spend about four to six hours a night studying. The TAs are generally fabulous here. They're full of knowledge and very helpful. The professors are usually very happy to help, too, provided you make the effort. If you don't go to office hours, don't expect the professor to find you if you're having trouble. I don't like all of my classes, but I love many of them. For example, I took an amazing life sciences course that blended biology and social anthropology. Why do men cheat? Why are we fat? The class addressed questions like this in depth.

The Students

The university is extremely diverse, and I don't see a lot of segregation going on. Students tend to be extremely motivated, and many talk about going on to graduate or professional schools. I heard UCLA receives the most undergraduate applications of any university in the nation, and there is a reason why: not only do students benefit from the reputation of academic excellence but they also have fun here, too. In most classes you will find yourself surrounded by peers from all over the world. They are bright, vivacious, and earnest students. They take their studies very seriously, but they also know that college is not all about academics. In a given class you might meet a surfer, a gymnast who went to the Olympics, an artist who just had her first exhibit in a gallery, a math champion, etc.

> "This is known as 'the university of Caucasians lost among Asians,' and Asians are everywhere! White people divert themselves to fraternities and sororities while whitewashed Asians find themselves continually asking the question, 'Where do I belong?'"
>
> ✦ Ying, sophomore

The Activities

There are some other schools in the area—lots of community colleges, Loyola Marymount, USC—though we don't necessarily mix much. Athletics is a great part of UCLA life, although it's perfectly fine if you never go to a football game. There are other things to get into: soccer—oh wait, that's still athletics—theater, arts, etc. If it's 3 a.m. on a Wednesday night and I'm still awake, I'm probably studying or up worrying about an impending midterm/final. If I don't go to bed, I'll probably make a list of things to do or study some more.

The Social Scene

Some people party a few times a week; some people never party. It depends. I don't see prob-lems with alcohol on campus. The campus is big enough that you can seek and find whatever floats your boat. If you want to meet people, but don't live on campus, you can still make close ties with people in your classes and major. I've met some great sorority girls, some great nonsorority girls, etc. Everyone is pretty open to making friends with everyone else.

Name: Theresa
Hometown: Thousand Oaks, California
Class Year: Junior
Major: Molecular, cellular, and developmental biology
Extracurriculars: Resident assistant, student researcher, MARC Fellow
Career Goal: I plan to obtain my PhD and become a researcher and college professor.

How would you describe UCLA's reputation?

I think UCLA has a very pronounced reputation as a prestigious research university.

Is this reputation accurate?

UCLA is definitely a competitive school, especially in the sciences. There are thousands of driven, ambitious, and incredibly ingenious people that you will encounter every day. However, there are also the slackers and people of mediocre intelligence. So, while I am convinced that most of the people here are descendents of Einstein, don't think that there aren't plenty of normal people here that you could find at a school whose reputation is not as pronounced as UCLA's.

What aspect of UCLA would a prospective student not see on a campus tour?

Rain. You'll probably visit when it's beautiful. It usually is beautiful. But it rains sometimes, I swear!

The Institution

It's hard to *not* fall in love with such a beautiful campus. UCLA is gorgeous and the local area really caters to students. I love Westwood. There's a lot to do, like going to the local Starbucks and Jerry's Famous Deli. UCLA is also teeming with school spirit! Students are very much into school colors, traditions, and school pride. It is truly amazing.

And maybe it's just because we're in Los Angeles, but there are tons of gorgeous people here at UCLA. There are always celebrities on campus, there's always a movie or commercial being filmed. UCLA feels like it's practically Hollywood sometimes. There's so much to do here. It's amazing.

The Education

Most of my science classes are lecture-based. The professor lectures, then tests you. In situations like that, you really have to be proactive and push yourself to keep up with the classes that only give you a test once every five weeks. Many people don't like the huge class sizes for lower-level courses, but UCLA also offers tons of twenty-student seminars. Many of the humanities classes I've taken have been discussion-based, and your grade is based on papers and your contributions to class discussion, not exams. I really enjoy classes like this, because they train you to think critically.

As a final project for one of my classes on political art, I shot and designed an art exhibit on graffiti in UCLA's Kerckhoff Art Gallery and was fully funded by UCLA's Cultural Affairs Commission. Curating an exhibit was exhilarating, and gave me a whole new perspective to learn from. It was one of the most memorable experiences I've had here.

> "I am the first person in my family to go to college, and I was scared by the size of the place; but I joined the marching band and made dozens of friends immediately."
> ✦ Paula, junior

I'm doing a thesis, but only a minority of seniors complete them. Thesis projects are usually offered as honors credit. These projects entail independent research that can be done in place of electives to go toward your major. There are definitely abundant opportunities for undergraduate research. UCLA has offices and staffs whose goals are to help undergraduates find a professor to work with. I've been doing research for the past year, and I hope to publish a paper with my lab by the end of this quarter!

The Students

UCLA is one of the most ethnically diverse UC campuses, and that's saying something! Even though it's mainly white and Asian with other random sprinklings, UCLA is definitely more diverse than universities with the same prestige.

The Activities

Many students are politically active at UCLA. UCLA has a very active student government, USAC, and active political clubs, such as the Bruin Republicans. As befits a large school, there are so many student groups, activities, events; and our location opens up even more avenues (especially if you have a car): we have Santa Monica to the west, Hollywood to the north, downtown L.A. to the east, and Venice to the south.

The Social Scene

During fall quarter, there are parties in the frat houses and the local apartments every Thursday, Friday, and Saturday night. So UCLA students do love to party—even though it isn't a party school. Dating scene? What dating scene? I'm starting to believe that guys refuse to ask girls out because they are too afraid that the next day they'll find someone who is much better looking on campus. Honestly, UCLA is saturated with beautiful women. However, the population of eligible men is infinitesimally small. Consider yourself warned.

Notable UCLA Alumni Include:
Francis Ford Coppola, director
Jackie Joyner-Kersee, Olympic gold medalist
Jackie Robinson, civil rights pioneer in Major
   League baseball
Johnnie Cochran, attorney
Ralph Bunche, Nobel laureate for peace
Rob Reiner, filmmaker and actor

UNIVERSITY OF CALIFORNIA—SAN DIEGO

Founded: 1960
Location: La Jolla, CA
Phone: (858) 534-4831
E-mail: admissionsinfo@ucsd.edu
Web site: www.ucsd.edu

Number of Undergraduates: 19,088
Number of Graduate Students: 3,465
Cost: Approximately $14,000 per year in state; $28,000 out of state
Application Deadline: November 30

Rating:	Notable Majors/Programs:
Very Selective	Biology, Psychology, Biochemistry

Size:
○ Small   ○ Medium   ● Large

Location:
● Urban   ○ Suburban   ○ Rural

On a Saturday, students talk about academics:
○ Always   ● Sometimes   ○ Never

Nightlife:
○ Intense   ● Moderate   ○ Laid-back

Politically, UC San Diego leans:
● Left   ○ Right   ○ Split

Diversity:
● High   ○ Low   ○ Medium

Students describe UCSD in five words:
- Elite intellectual UC for nerds
- Not actually in San Diego

From the School

Founded in 1960, UC San Diego has grown into one of the nation's leading teaching and research institutions. It has developed an international reputation for scholarship in natural sciences, engineering, oceanography, medicine, social sciences, and the arts and humanities. . . .

[UCSD's] college system combines the friendly intimacy of a small campus with the academic advantages of a major research university. Each college has its own educational philosophy, general education (GE) requirements, housing, social activities, traditions and staff.

—www.admissions.ucsd.edu

If you're interested in UCSD, you may also be interested in:
UC Berkeley, UCLA, Caltech, Harvey Mudd, Stanford

Name: Matt
Hometown: Sacramento, California
Class Year: Senior
Major: Political Science
Extracurriculars: California Public Interest Research Group (CalPIRG) and mock trial
Career Goal: Undecided

How would you describe UCSD's reputation?

1) "Wow, I hear that's a great school!" or 2) "Oh. Party hard!"

Is this reputation accurate?

1) UCSD *is* a great school, especially for computer technology, biochemistry, or political science. 2) UCSD doesn't party that hard. Our neighbor, San Diego State University, does. People get confused. UCSD is less than a partier's paradise. Most students who apply to UCSD think logarithmic differentiation should be declared an Olympic sport.

What would an admissions officer at your school probably not tell a prospective student? What aspect of your school would a prospective student not see on a campus tour?

The admissions officers at UCSD probably wouldn't tell you that we don't have a football team. When UCSD was first opened, the university actively decided against having one because they wanted to be viewed as a serious academic institution. This weakens school spirit, though, and means a lot of UCSD kids are seriously nerdy. On a tour you'll rarely find kids playing soccer on the quad or tossing a Frisbee. Instead, you'll find students discussing *Star Wars* or blinking confusedly from the natural sunlight.

Is there anything about UCSD that's particularly unique?

So I got into UCSD and I thought, "Score. School in San Diego. What more could you want?" Visions of the beach, the nightlife, keg parties at the local fraternity house, and bronzed bodies danced through my head. I packed a pair of flip-flops and some sunscreen and hit the road. Once I arrived, I found UCSD is *not actually in San Diego.* Instead, it's conveniently located in . . . La Jolla. It's a land of rich, uptight retirees, where nothing is open past 10 p.m. except the local TGI Fridays. So, if you want to party and go to the beach, bring a car.

The Institution

The good: Most people like UCSD. Sure, it's in a quiet suburb where your grandmother would feel at home, and the school is packed with Trekkies. But overall, UC San Diego has a bit of everything. We have every type of student, every major you'd want, every student club imaginable, from the Conan O'Brian Appreciation Club to the Snowboarder Club (which, since there isn't any snow, resorts to using its student-allocated funding for alcohol). The campus is beautiful and sprawls over quite a few acres. Students are housed in one of six "colleges," by their major, so you get a bit of the "small school within a big school" feel. You live and learn with the kids in your college and form a little community for yourselves.

The bad: Despite having a strong urban planning department, UCSD seems to have ignored the concept of building *up* rather than *out,* and our campus stretches on and on. So bring some comfortable shoes, because you may have a mile to walk between classes! And the campus police wonder why we keep stealing the janitors' golf carts . . .

Overall, UCSD has been great for me because I learned to force the good times out of it. You have to be very self-motivated, from searching out research project opportunities to finding your social niche. If you don't mind joining random clubs to meet new people and wading through massive amounts of bureaucratic procedures to enrich yourself, UCSD can offer you a great time.

The Education

You just wrapped up a stressful week, with tests in both your biochemistry class and your physics class. All you want is a cold beer. So you collapse in your favorite chair with a Corona in your hand—Corona being the beer of choice for those of us living next to the Mexican playground known as Tijuana—and just then your friends rush in, excitedly babbling about their great biochemistry class, and this amazing physics equation they just learned about. You beg. You plead. No more academics! They don't listen. Welcome to life at UCSD, where nerdy academics are everywhere and inescapable. Your afternoon conversations will range from politics to lectures you've heard, to lab work you've done. Every now and again someone will openly wonder why no one at UCSD gets laid (as if this is some big mystery). We talk about our classes *all the time.*

We also have unique study habits. Which is to say, students have found that UCSD classes (most of which are big lectures, even when you're an upperclassman) tend to summarize what they were supposed to read for class, instead of supplementing the reading. So students often choose to either read what is required by the syllabus *or* attend the massive lectures. You'll rarely fall behind if you do one or the other. Every year, upperclassmen tell this to freshmen, and the freshmen never have the confidence to test the theory first semester. Trust us. It's true.

All in all, UCSD is a big school. So it's very much left to each student to make their own decisions and find the best way to deal. UCSD offers great honors courses, seminars, writing workshops, and research projects with professors. But if you want to get involved in any or all of those programs, you'll have to take it upon yourself to find the start-up materials, petitions, and paperwork. If you slack off or get otherwise preoccupied, you can graduate from UCSD having had a very undistinguished college career.

The Students

If you could put each character from the movie *Clueless* in a blender, you'd have a big mess and a few felonies. But you would also have the average UCSD student. We are *big* nerds who study even on Friday nights, but we'll still find time to smoke weed and drink on Saturdays. We shop at Abercrombie & Fitch, but only after we've spent some time hanging out at a rally against mass consumerism. And we'll read independent newspapers while sipping Starbucks coffee and driving our SUVs (unless we're driving Hummers). UCSD students care about issues and want to change the world. But we don't want to get up before 11 a.m. to do it.

UCSD also has lots of smart kids who were UC Berkeley rejects. All of us try to tell ourselves we're still academically top-notch, and we involve ourselves in lots of activities so we can still sleep at night. This means the main walkway through campus is always packed with representatives of various clubs, bombarding students with pamphlets and leaflets and information about this club or that peer support group. While irritating at times, the general vibe on the main walkway at least provides for an entertaining trek across campus. On the plus side, students at UCSD are really welcome

to do their own thing. I don't know if this is because we're open-minded, or overapathetic, but don't expect many people to care if you decide to make out with a leather-clad transvestite on the center quad. Most students are white and clad in Abercrombie wear, but they don't care if you're gay, black, Muslim, anarchist, whatever. It doesn't matter how you identify yourself, and there is a support group for everything and everyone if you need it.

The Activities

UCSD has a mainstream band come to campus thrice a year (they alternate between rock and rap, for diversity). A lot of community service goes on. Big team sports don't get much support—students are more into individual sports, like surfing and running. That said, don't expect a campus of athletes—on a beautiful sunny day, most students will stay inside and play chess. Unfortunately, there isn't a major social hub on campus, and when you're done with your work and want to have fun, you'll find different groups hanging out in different areas of campus. The student government kids drink on the third floor of the student union and tend to have sex in the student government offices late at night; the jocks and the frat guys hang out at Round Table pizza; and the sorority girls hang out with the surfing club and like to run off and get stoned on random beaches. This is bad, though, this fragmentation. It means you can't just wander around campus and find people—you have to know where to go, where each group hangs out.

The Social Scene

La Jolla has kept an ancient charter on the books that states that a house containing more than four people of the same sex is a "brothel" and illegal. Hence, there are frats and sororities, but there are no frat or sorority *houses* at UCSD, and the cops have absolutely nothing to do on Saturday nights except respond to noise violations. So parties on campus tend to be broken up fairly quickly, even for minor infractions. But worry not! You don't need to party on campus during a weekend, because a car will instantly give you access to everything that San Diego possesses, including tons of students from local state and community colleges (where the money saved from tuition goes directly into the keg fund). Our salvation: nearby

San Diego State University where fraternities have actual houses and throw good parties, and cops have other problems to deal with.

Name: Steven
Hometown: California
Class Year: Junior
Major: Psychology and biology
Extracurriculars: Scientist by training, humanitarian by nature. I'm involved in community enrichment and other volunteer work, both on and off campus.
Career Goal: Clinical neuropsychologist (PhD)

How would you describe UCSD's reputation?

UCSD is garnering more and more respect within the academic community. We have the number-one–ranked faculty in science (according to a Johns Hopkins study), believe it or not. We also have the sixth highest amount of federal funding for research. Socially, UCSD is a bit overshadowed by a local state school with a well-known reputation for partying hard. As a result, and by comparison, we look like a school for nerds.

Is this reputation accurate?

Socially, it's true, we are a bit nerdy. Academically, this is an impressive institution that, I believe, will only be looked at as more impressive as the years go by.

What aspect of your school would a prospective student not see on a campus tour?

Even if UCSD *is* nerdy, students do have a lot of fun partying during weekends! A prospective student might not see that, but it happens, we enjoy ourselves. A lot of kids head to San Francisco whenever possible.

The Institution

There are nineteen thousand students at UCSD, divided into six colleges, each with its own personality. If you're in Revelle, you're a superstudent overachiever. If you're in Muir, you're a stonerslacker. If you're in Marshall, you probably have dreams of saving the world. If you're in Warren, you're an engineer, an athlete, or a total dork. Roosevelt has no real personality, but it's really nice to look at. And Sixth college—the newest, smallest college—is still a bit indistinct.

We're still not a party school, but we're hardly a dead-zone. We have an amazing amount of course options, and more professors to choose from than you could shake a stick at. At the same time, we live in little "college" communities, so we have an area where we get to know lots of faces and feel a sense of belonging.

UCSD is on the quarter system: there's a fall quarter, a winter quarter, a spring quarter, and an optional summer session serving as a fourth quarter. Most students take three or four classes every quarter and each one is about ten weeks, which, if you ever have a terrible class, is great. In ten weeks, it's over. No sweat.

The Education

Professors at UCSD work us hard and they are really top-notch, at least in the divisions of biology and psychology. I didn't have high expectations, but I was pleasantly surprised by the level of support I received when I made an effort to reach out to a professor.

The Students

Unfortunately, most UCSD students are white. And students who aren't white stick to themselves. This doesn't mean minority students are discriminated against—they're not—or that a white student and a black student wouldn't talk and hang out—they would. It's more that you'll see big roving packs of minority students throughout the campus, rather than big roving integrated swarms of all kinds of students. It's too bad.

The Activities

La Jolla and San Diego are eternally "seventy-four degrees and sunny," and while UCSD students spend a lot of time indoors studying, they'll escape every now and again to enjoy the good weather. On a particularly nice day, when even the nerdiest of students can't help but come outside, you'll see students carrying surfboards, BBQs being set up, beach towels being thrown on the grass. This is when most students feel a swell of school pride. We also have more than three hundred fifty clubs and organizations. So if you want to do something with your free time, there are an endless options, and it's always a great way to meet new friends. You can also join a team sport—[but] don't expect the whole campus to be involved, and don't expect your peers to be the greatest athletes on earth. But if you like to play simply for love of the game, you'll be able to find others who do it for the same reason.

The Social Scene

I'm actually a fan of La Jolla, which is a nice little town with a TGI Friday's, a few movie theaters, and a mall. If you're tired and want to get off campus, but you don't want the crazy hecticness of a big city, this satisfies. And then if you want more excitement, you can head to San Diego and feed wild animals at the zoo, drink till you puke at a bar, dance in a high-tech club, go to the theater, watch any number of sporting events. You can also cross the border into Tijuana—if you're under twenty-one, this is the place to go to get as much liquor as you'd want, and no one can stop you. It's perfectly legal. Thanks, Tijuana!

Name: Leslie
Hometown: Clearlake, California
Class Year: Senior
Major: Economics
Extracurriculars: Working at Jamba Juice, captain of the Rec Club soccer team
Career Goal: Undecided

How would you describe UCSD's reputation?

UCSD is known as "that nerdy school near San Diego."

Is this reputation accurate? Why or why not?

Fairly accurate. UCSD students are very studious, and our social scene is dwarfed by the all-the-time crazy party that is San Diego State University.

What would an admissions officer at your school probably not tell a prospective student? What aspect of your school would a prospective student not see on a campus tour?

Prospective students wouldn't be told that a lot of students have a hard time making friends when they first get here. There are just so many students, it's overwhelming. You'll meet someone nice and never see them again. But things do slow down and you'll make friends soon enough. The weather is usually nice, but it's *not* sunny year round; on a tour you might not see the fog that sometimes rolls in and sits over our campus for days on end.

The Institution

UCSD's size is daunting, but once you start meeting people you feel less anonymous. You quickly learn the importance of being proactive and taking the initiative: *You* have to make it a point to get to know your professors, *you* have to seek out friends, *you* have to get involved in different organizations, *you* have to budget your time. *You* have to learn what it really means to "study." If you don't do these things, you're going to be miserable.

I chose UCSD because it had great academics, a good soccer team, and it was in the warmest location of all the schools I got into. Also UCSD is in La Jolla, which I thought would be interesting since it's populated mostly by older millionaires. And Pacific Beach is right nearby—exactly what you think of when the words *college town* are uttered. So if La Jolla isn't working out for you, head to Pacific Beach.

The Education

For a lot of students academics are life. When they're not in class or studying for class, they're talking about class. Monday through Sunday, class class class. The students who really go overboard tend to be really competitive with one another, too. That's not my thing—I try to have a healthy social life. UCSD has a core curriculum, which I've found to be very manageable. You get it done. Similarly, classes are big here, but you learn to go to your professor's office hours and break into study groups, which makes things seem smaller.

The Students

UCSD students are middle class, white or Asian, and left-leaning, but not enough so to really get out there and protest or attend rallies. There are some black and Indian students, but not many, and they stick to themselves.

The Activities

There are four giant colleges in San Diego, and a few smaller ones, so when you go out in the general area you'll always see young people hanging around. For the most part, students from one campus don't spend time on other campuses—but they'll interact with other students in clubs and bars in Gaslamp Quarter and Pacific Beach. It's worth noting that UC San Diego does an *amazing* job of bringing free concerts to campus. They have at least one free concert per quarter. They get *big* names to come entertain us—and equally important speakers. I've seen both Bill Gates and John Kerry. Impressive. I don't live on campus, and I only really go to campus for classes, and even when I did live on campus I had a car, and I'd take off for San Diego about four times a week. Having a car is a good thing here, because otherwise you're totally dependent on public transportation, which is unreliable and a pain. You'll have to pay for expensive parking passes and struggle to find a spot, but having wheels is worth it—it opens up your life considerably.

The Social Scene

Most UCSD students party on weekends. If you're under twenty-one, you'll probably head over to Tijuana, Mexico, first to stock up on alcohol. If you're over twenty-one, you'll probably spend a lot of time at the bars in Pacific Beach and San Diego. You could stay on campus and drink too—there are two on-campus establishments that serve alcohol—but it's more fun to go elsewhere.

Notable UCSD Alumni Include:
James Avery, actor, scholar
Bill Atkinson, computer program designer
Nathan East, musician
Angela Davis, author, social activist
Steve Peace, film writer, producer
Mike Judge, animator, producer, actor

UNIVERSITY OF CALIFORNIA—SANTA CRUZ

Founded: 1965
Location: Santa Cruz, CA
Phone: (831) 459-0111
E-mail: admissions@ucsc.edu
Web site: www.ucsc.edu

Number of Undergraduates: 13,620
Number of Graduate Students: 1,340
Cost: Approximately $17,000 per year in state; $33,500 out of state
Application Deadline: Rolling; November 30

Rating:	Notable Majors/Programs:
Selective	Life Sciences, Psychology, Linguistics

Size:
○ Small ○ Medium ● Large

Location:
○ Urban ● Suburban ○ Rural

On a Saturday, students talk about academics:
○ Always ● Sometimes ○ Never

Nightlife:
○ Intense ● Moderate ○ Laid-back

Politically, UC Santa Cruz leans:
● Left ○ Right ○ Split

Diversity:
● High ○ Low ○ Medium

Students describe UC Santa Cruz in five words:
- 2,000 acres of beautiful campus!
- A strong *alternative* to Berkeley

From the School

UC Santa Cruz students receive an education that combines the resources of a major research university with the advantages of a small college setting. At UC Santa Cruz, undergraduates have the opportunity to engage in in-depth learning while pursuing research and scholarship with leading figures in their fields. Described as one of the most beautiful campuses in the world, UC Santa Cruz has a reputation for excellence, with nationally ranked, rigorous undergraduate and graduate programs.

—http://admissions.ucsc.edu

If you're interested in UC Santa Cruz , you may also be interested in:
UC Berkeley, UC San Diego, Evergreen State, Lewis & Clark, Reed, U Washington

Name: Ken
Hometown: Pacifica, California
Class Year: Senior
Major: Anthropology
Extracurriculars: Working in various labs
Career Goal: Zookeeper!

How would you describe your school's reputation?

All-out hippie party wacky love fest.

Is this reputation accurate?

Nope. While Santa Cruz does have a great laid-back California atmosphere, you have to be a somewhat serious student if you want to graduate. And although the school is very liberal, "outspoken" is a better description; the liberals are loud, the Republicans are loud, and it makes everything more interesting.

What would an admissions officer at UC Santa Cruz probably not tell a prospective student? What aspect of your school would a prospective student probably not see on a campus tour?

They aren't going to tell you how the school is really becoming overwhelmed by new students. There are too many people for too few classes. If yours is a popular major, you might have a hard time getting into all your intro courses. The good thing is that to fill the graduation requirements, you'll need to take a variety of classes, so credits rarely go to waste when you can't take a class for your major. On a tour you really don't get a feel for the classrooms. There are huge lecture halls and there are small rooms with round tables on the fourth floor of buildings surrounded by trees. There are locked computer labs with powerful machines and anthropology labs with ten different monkey skeletons and a cabinet of skulls. You don't see these on the tour, and they're where you end up spending a great deal of time learning and working.

The Institution

People tend to love Santa Cruz fiercely. For a school with almost no sports or frat life, there's a lot of pride flaunted through other means. People get excited when they see our mascot, the mighty banana slug, on any of our oh so numerous wooded paths. We care deeply about our professors, and we have quite a few notable people teaching here. Students really encourage each other to go beyond what is expected in classes; here, you'll be working with dedicated people who care about the material and want to learn. After high school, it feels great to be in an environment of people who like to read!

The college system is genius. Dorms are grouped together into little colleges all over campus, and you pick one to live in as a freshman. It gives you a solid starting place to make friends, join clubs, and go to activities. Each college has its own quirks: Kresge is all apartments with kitchens and no dining hall, Merrill has a pottery room, and everyone at Porter runs naked at the first rain (with students from other colleges joining along the way). Colleges aren't grouped according to majors, although location-wise some might be closer to more of your classes. Since the campus is huge, there are shuttles driving around so you don't have to walk a mile between classes; plus the city bus runs on campus, so it's easy to get around and feel safe at night. But speaking as a person who is easily distracted by birdwatching and general wildlife appreciation moments, it *is* more fun to walk between classes.

> "People party three nights a week. Thursday nights are popular bar nights at Rosie's Irish pub. In terms of weed, some people smoke several times a day, while others graduate without ever having tried it."
> ✦ Katy, junior

The Education

College is harder than high school, and many students don't realize how much harder until they get their first paper back covered in red ink. In one of my introductory courses, every single freshman's paper was handed back and we were told to rewrite them. There's tons of work, and it's tough—but it's important to remember that there is help. Papers can be rewritten, professors have office hours, there are discussion sessions with TAs for almost all the large classes; and there's a tutor for every subject. The liberal arts classes have a reputation for being small and weird—and they live up to it! For my anthropology major, I wrote well over two hundred pages worth of papers last year alone. In another class my final involved the creation and ritual destruction of a sand painting.

Not many people think of UCSC as an engineering school, but we're getting really strong in that department—and since that's a recent development, the equipment is great and the faculty's filled with new professors who know what's going on in the real world.

UC Santa Cruz is actually *very* strong and well-funded in a lot of the sciences. And one of the best things about the science majors is that there's a lot of cooperation; this college does *not* foster a competitive atmosphere. You tend to make a lot of friends in your major, friends who are likely to help each other with homework and research.

The Students

Older professors complain that Santa Cruz students aren't as active as they used to be. Of course, those professors then get mad when the antiwar march closes down roads and when someone dressed as Superman runs through class reminding us to come to the student rights rally. Mixed in with the creative people are a lot of reactionary people who're just protesting for the fun of it. They get on everyone's nerves. There are way too many people just acting like hippies, and not enough thought is put into the activism here. But overall, Santa Cruz students tend to care, deeply, about something—and eventually they might even understand it.

The Activities

UCSC offers activities throughout the year, like wilderness survival courses, surfing classes, weekend backpacking trips, sushi-making seminars, and, my favorite, the semester-long sailing courses. There are performance spaces all over campus. The theater puts on spectacular performances, and there are also smaller student-run plays. Live music is common and often free—read the postings at bus stops to find out what's going on—and at least once a year, some group shows *The Wizard of Oz* with Pink Floyd playing on a big screen. At the end of each quarter, some classes put on shows to exhibit what they've learned and created, and these are not only entertaining but also an excellent way of deciding what to take in the future. The computer labs in Baskin Engineering often have massive unorganized gaming sessions on the weekends, and so do the dorms. Furthermore, it helps that we're in a liberal town with two art house movie theaters, some small concert venues, and a funky downtown that has three big book-stores, a battery of cafes, organic grocery stores, and boutiques. Santa Cruz has the best public transit, which makes it *beyond* easy to get downtown to hang out on weekends. Or just go grocery shopping when you are sick of dining hall food. And there's always the beach . . .

The Social Scene

There is definitely a party scene, although it's up to you how you want to be involved. People talk about the drug scene, but as a nonparticipant, I see more drug use at normal concerts then I do in my daily campus life. The Greek life is all off campus, and doesn't figure in very much, though it's there if you want it. Every full moon there's a huge outdoor drum circle party in the woods, and clubs often organize free movies or events on weekends. Local movie theaters have midnight shows, and there are places like the Saturn Cafe (superfunky, super-Santa Cruz) open late, which can be great gathering places. Overall, there isn't a well organized social scene; it's more of a constant, small-scale thing.

Name: Jordan
Hometown: Plymouth, Minnesota
Class Year: Junior
Major: Psychology, with a minor in education
Extracurriculars: Member of the women's golf team, mentor resident assistant (MRA) for College Nine
Career Goal: Graduate school and eventually work with children within the capacity of clinical psychology.

How would you describe your school's reputation?

The campus is known for its beauty. We're up in the mountains overlooking the ocean and the city of Santa Cruz. Santa Cruz is also known for being liberal. In previous years we were thought to be a "party school."

Is this reputation accurate?

Yes, the campus is absolutely beautiful, the majority of students do seem to be very liberal (although both political sides are represented here). However, partying is no more of a problem here than it is at any other school.

What aspect of your school would a prospective student not see on a campus tour?

Campus tours don't show you the UCSC farm, the arboretum, the numerous trails of nature reserve in upper campus. It also doesn't allow students to see the amazing wildlife that comes out at dusk, including deer, raccoons, and sometimes foxes.

The Institution

UC Santa Cruz is located in a mountain lion habitat; mountain lion sightings don't occur often, but they're something to be aware of. One popular spot on campus is Tree Nine, which is a tree in upper campus that can be easily climbed. At the top, you can see the city of Santa Cruz over the trees and people often leave things at the top for future climbers to find. We also have the Porter caves, but I have not had the opportunity to go down there. The school's size is wonderful. If you like a big school, you get that; if you like a small school, the college system—UCSC is divided up into ten individual colleges in which students live, regardless of major—allows you to enjoy that as well.

> "A friend of mine who graduated with a degree in molecular biology published some of her research, enabling her to get into any medical school in the country."
> ✦ Katy, junior

The Education

With such a large number of students, UCSC does the best job it can in connecting to each student. Many classes are large, often two to three hundred students. However, nearly 80 percent of classes are fifty students or less and most classes require a discussion section each week, which is made up of about twenty to twenty-five students and facilitated by a graduate-level teaching assistant. Sections are designed for students to ask questions and engage in discussion about the material with one another. This format makes students feel like more than just a number in such a large lecture.

The Students

The students on this campus are far more diverse than any group I could've found in the Mid-

west. I would say that the average UCSC student is hard-working and cares about his/her schoolwork. He or she probably has a part-time job to help pay for school, in addition to financial aid and/or student loans.

The Activities

There are *so many* activities. One popular choice is intramural sports and activities through the Office of Physical Education, Recreation and Sports (OPERS). We do have intercollegiate sports here at UCSC, but those athletes receive no special attention or recognition in the classroom. As a member of the golf team, I often have to make the difficult decision of either playing in a match or taking a quiz in a class.

The Social Scene

Most campuses have students who enjoy partying, and we're no different. But if that's not your scene, there are plenty of other students who enjoy just hanging out at night. Residence halls are awesome, and the best way to meet so many people that will be your friends forever.

Name: Cecily
Hometown: Lafayette, Louisiana
Class Year: Junior
Major: American Studies
Extracurriculars: Ambassadors to Africa; Rainbow Theatre/African American Theatre Arts Troupe; African/Black Student Alliance; graduation committees—BlackGrad and Oakes College; PoeticKinetics, slam poetry
Career Goal: Looking to go into entertainment/ sports law.

How would you describe UC Santa Cruz's reputation?

Our school is known for major scientific advances and top-notch professors in every field of the humanities. We're kind of known as a little UC Berkeley. We're also known as a drugged-out hippie school and we've been called the number one party school in America—but that's a big fat lie.

Is this reputation accurate?

The good stuff is true, but the pot-smoking hippie school impression comes from the fact that Santa Cruz is so kicked back it's not even funny and maybe because there are a lot of hippies there, and hippies equal weed . . . or maybe because we're near the beach. We do protest a lot, but that's because after you come here you realize just how many injustices there are to protest.

What aspect of UC Santa Cruz would a prospective student not see on a campus tour?

They wouldn't see the top-secret NASA experiments until they actually come live on campus and see weird stuff in the sky. They wouldn't be told how when a budget crisis hits, the first thing the administration does is jack up student fees/tuition and cut funding to our organizations and support systems. Nor how the humanities programs are the first to lose classrooms, teaching assistants, and staff. And admissions would also make sure that there were some people of color around as well so that you wouldn't be able to tell how lacking in diversity this campus is.

The Institution

Santa Cruz, like most colleges, is a bubble, and you need to learn to take breaks and get away so that you don't burn out. But it's beautiful in another way—it provides you with a space to really learn *how* to think/analyze/understand the world outside.

I came to UCSC to be inspired by top-notch faculty and the small class sizes where learning could be interactive, and I sometimes have to remember that this is an institution. There is a system that you have to master in order to succeed. Learning how to make the system work for you is in itself excellent preparation for the world ahead.

The Education

The quality of education you receive is primarily up to you. Yes, when there's a budget crisis you only have one TA, or class sizes grow tremendously—which makes it more difficult—but how much time you spend reading, researching, and going to talk to professors during office hours determines your success. It's important to do your own legwork and talk to students in the majors you're interested in to find out what the ups and downs are really like. The study abroad programs are excellent; get in on them your second or third year.

UCSC is a research institution, so professors have to continue their own research as much as they teach. That can be tricky especially when they are finishing a book and need their time for that, but it can be a bonus for you since it gives you an opportunity to work with them. That's practically a straight apprenticeship! As far as your required senior project, some folks just take a seminar with other seniors and work on a class project, some choose to go ahead and write a thesis, while some teach their own class! I love having the choice of how to finish up my school career.

The Students

There is no such thing as an average student here! You may think that people are apolitical but I've learned that everything is political! By not standing for one thing, you may actually be condoning another. There are many organizations—mostly political, along with a few social. My biggest issue here is that while the Chicano/Latino population and Asian/Pacific Islander populations are increasing, the black/African American population is very minute. And since cost of living is *high*, students either need to come from money, or have no money and get scholarships.

> "Santa Cruz is different from most schools because we have a quarter system, which means you take three quarters of ten weeks each. I think it's a fantastic alternative to semesters."
>
> ✦ Ken, senior

The Activities

I think sportswise we have a pretty good soccer and swim team; beyond that, no comment. Activities here mostly derive from the student organizations that you're associated with. One of the biggest and best events we have each year is the Multi-Cultural Festival. All the orgs put it on and sell food and clothes, while there's a concert going on. We've had so many top artists perform, and it's free.

When I decide to leave campus, there are a few bars that folks go to on certain nights in town, but I love to go to the Bay Area: Oakland, San Francisco, and South Bay/San Jose. There you find endless possibilities! Public transportation is readily available, and UCSC even has a shuttle to the South Bay. Also, since so many folks here are from SoCal [Southern California], it's easy to catch a ride to Los Angeles/San Diego and Tijuana, Mexico, for a quick weekend.

The Social Scene

The social scene is definitely affected by which dorms/apartments you live in and/or the orgs you are affiliated with. It's somewhat predetermined if you're in a frat or sorority (of which there's been an increase here, no thanks to MTV's *Fraternity Life*). Otherwise, you just find folks that are like you. That way you can live in the same dorm/apartment and you don't feel pressured into, say, dealing with folks who drink, when you don't. There are so many different outlets and events happening on campus that more than likely you'll even end up with multiple groups of friends.

Notable UC Santa Cruz Alumni Include:

Dana Priest, reporter and author

Gillian Welch, singer and songwriter

Julie Packard, executive director, Monterey Bay Aquarium

Kathryn D. Sullivan, first American woman to walk in space

Kent Nagano, conductor of the Los Angeles Opera

Victor Davis Hanson, classicist and neoconservative thinker

CALIFORNIA INSTITUTE OF TECHNOLOGY

Founded: 1891
Location: Pasadena, CA
Phone: (626) 395-6321
E-mail: ugadmissions@caltech.edu
Web site: www.caltech.edu

Number of Undergraduates: 939
Number of Graduate Students: 1,281
Cost: Approximately $32,000 per year
Application Deadline: January 1
Early Decision: November 1

Rating:	Notable Majors/Programs:
Most Selective	Biology, Electrical Engineering, Engineering/Applied Science

Size:
● Small ○ Medium ○ Large

Location:
○ Urban ● Suburban ○ Rural

On a Saturday, students talk about academics:
● Always ○ Sometimes ○ Never

Nightlife:
○ Intense ○ Moderate ● Laid-back

Politically, Caltech is:
○ Left ○ Right ● Split

Diversity:
● High ○ Low ○ Medium

Students describe Caltech in five words:
- Among world's best science schools
- Small, intensely personal, intensely focused

From the School

There are lots of good small colleges. There are also more than a few schools that specialize in math, science, and engineering. . . . But the list of small, elite research institutions that offer undergraduates a first-class scientific and technical education, virtually unlimited research opportunities, and a familylike student community contains only one name: Caltech.

—http://admissions.caltech.edu

If you're interested in Caltech, you may also be interested in:
UC Berkeley, Harvard, Harvey Mudd, MIT, Princeton, Stanford

Name: Vera
Hometown: Stillwater, Oklahoma
Class Year: Sophomore
Major: At the moment, I'm double majoring in applied/computational mathematics and economics. But I change my mind pretty often.
Extracurriculars: Chamber music
Career Goal: Research in either general applied math, theoretical computer science, or theoretical economics.

How would you describe Caltech's reputation?

My school has a reputation of being a haven for big nerds. The office of admissions brags that Caltech is "The World's Greatest Playground for Math and Science." Caltech is also, despite our high standing in the world of scientific research, surprisingly unknown among high school students due to our small size.

Is this reputation accurate?

Caltech is a small school with big nerds. But this doesn't sum up the Caltech experience—for that, you'd have to take into account our amazingly time-consuming homework sets and stress levels that are unrivaled at any college I've heard of. On the positive side, every single student here is extremely intelligent and dedicated to truly understanding the subject they're studying. Honestly, I don't know if there's any other "prestige" school in America where such a negligibly low percentage of people are there for the name. Everyone at Caltech honestly comes to study hard and learn.

What would an admissions officer at Caltech probably not tell a prospective student?

I think Caltech is most secretive about its gender ratio and diversity statistics. Admissions practices no form of affirmative action. This means, for better or worse, there are three guys for every girl on campus, 70 percent of students are Caucasian, 30 percent are Asian, and almost none are African American or Hispanic. This is something that the school does not brag about. Caltech also doesn't talk about the workload and stress levels faced by students. If you ask an admissions officer they'll probably tell you that if you want to party and do lots of nonacademic activities while you're in college, this isn't the place for you. But it's easy to feel like the admissions officer is just exaggerating. Take it from me—they're not.

The Institution

Caltech is different. During freshman orientation, I went on an afternoon kayaking trip with a group of other freshmen. Along the water we came across a nice sandy beach and stopped for a break. Half an hour later we left behind the complete Maxwell's equations written in the sand. And classes hadn't even started! This is the nature of our school spirit. We take pride in the fact our football team is undefeated—because it doesn't exist. Our dorm door whiteboards are covered with math sets, and our schedules consist of five science classes and the single dreaded humanities requirement. Scientists at the head of their fields teach the introductory freshman classes, and almost every undergrad does summer research. We think of ourselves as the MIT that many MIT students weren't fortunate enough to have heard of prior to college. No college can outdo our nerdiness, and we like it that way.

Weather in Southern California is a huge bonus. Housing is also unique—seven "houses" make up the undergraduate on-campus housing system, each housing about eighty students. Each house has a well-defined and unique culture, and students are placed in houses according to their personality and living preferences. In this way, a house becomes a true home away from home for its residents.

The honor code is one of the most loved aspects of Caltech: All tests are take-home, most are open-book, many are untimed, collaboration on homework sets is not only permitted but encouraged, attendance for almost all classes is discretionary, dorm life is almost entirely unsupervised with no rules to speak of, all students are allowed access to every building on campus, and almost no one locks their doors. It's amazing.

Also, since Caltech is so small, I feel like I have a personal relationship with the institution. People in the bursar's and registrar's office know me by name. If I e-mail a big-name scientist who works here, I won't get ignored. I'll often get a response within the day. Where else does that happen?

The Education

A typical day for Caltech students involves rolling unwillingly out of bed at around 9 or 10 a.m., going to a couple lectures, and then spending hours upon hours on the next homework set that's due. Almost all classes are scientific, so a professor lectures (never a TA) and the homework is a weekly problem set. Competition is minimal—collaboration on homework is almost necessary if you want to get it done—and the professors are really accessible—you can knock on the office door of any of the Nobel laureates and other extraordinary faculty members and introduce yourself, and nine times out of ten they will sit down with you and ask that you call them by their first name.

Caltech also has a sizable core. Here's how it works: Freshman and sophomore years, you have to take five terms of math and physics, two terms of chemistry, one term of biology, and two lab courses. Before you graduate, you also have to take a total of twelve courses in the humanities/social sciences.

The Students

Caltech has students from all over the world, and they are all interested in basically the same thing—science. This way of life leaves little room for anything else. No one cares in the least about what someone's race, sexual orientation, religion, or socioeconomic background is. What matters is their dedication to science and learning. In this way, Caltech may be one of the most accepting places in the country for minorities.

> "Many incoming freshmen find themselves to be—for the first time—below average. Luckily, at Caltech even if you're not *the* best, people will work with you so that you can achieve *your* best."
>
> ✦ Tom, freshman

The Activities

Caltech is really cut off from the rest of the world. We rarely venture into Pasadena except for the occasional meal or movie. It's not that it's difficult to interact with the outside world, it's that what most students are interested in is right on campus. Activities on campus are widespread but small. The chamber music program is notable, and at least three active a cappella groups exist, as well as a number of dance troupes. Then of course there are the science activities—DARPA (the off-road remote-controlled-vehicle challenge), the Astronomy Club, the Chemical Engineering student group, the *Caltech Undergraduate Research Journal*, and numerous others.

The Social Scene

There are no fraternities or sororities at Caltech, and as I said earlier, the social scene is very much dominated by the housing system. It's rare to come across an unfamiliar face in the houses, and although of course it's difficult to know all nine hundred undergraduates, it's not difficult at all to meet everyone in your own house. The dating scene is a bit atypical since the gender ratio is so skewed (3:1), but it isn't a huge issue for most people. They're too busy to date. The party scene is also atypical, in that parties don't occur too frequently, but when they do occur they're very creative and tons of fun. As for alcohol, although it certainly exists, it is extremely rare that any individual would drink enough to interfere with their academics.

Name: Billy
Hometown: Bellevue, Texas
Class Year: Sophomore
Major: Physics
Extracurriculars: Prism (LGBT group)
Career Goal: Astrophysicist/researcher

How would you describe Caltech's reputation?

Caltech is a truly excellent—but very difficult—school. It is more devoted to science than any other institution in America.

Is this reputation accurate?

It is pretty accurate. The difficulty and the ubiquity of science at Caltech should be emphasized. You should only come here if you're willing to be immersed in science (or math) almost every waking hour—which is to say 80 percent of all hours since Caltech students don't sleep much.

What would an admissions officer at your school probably not tell a prospective student? What aspect of your school would a prospective student not see on a campus tour?

The fact that you may suffer permanent brain damage from extended periods of staying awake doing problem sets. And on a tour you probably wouldn't see the inside of our student houses. I mean, we're all science majors here. We're smart, weird kids living together in a dorm. We decorate in interesting ways.

The Institution

I chose this school because it was clearly the most scientifically oriented one available. I love it here but I get the distinct impression that much of Pasadena hates the fact that there's a campus full of deviant weirdos right smack in the middle of their socially engineered upper-class suburbia.

> "People stay up all hours doing work. Who needs sleep anyway? Not us. It's not nearly productive enough. You can't do science in your sleep . . . yet. But we're working on it."
>
> ✦ Kat, junior

The Education

Classes are all you will talk about at all times during your four years here, or you will be shot (out of a cannon). Luckily, Caltech has a pleasantly noncompetitive environment. Instead of competing, students support one another. The work is hard so if you don't collaborate, it will only hurt you in the end. As an underclassman at Caltech, when you're learning basic concepts, your classes are going to be big (200–250 students). But that number will decrease sharply as you enter your junior and senior years, particularly if you're in a small major. Physics and engineering students probably have it the worst though, with classes of thirty to one hundred students for all four years. At Caltech it's important that you have good note-taking skills. Professors here talk fast and it isn't always easy to get everything down.

Caltech's also a mecca for undergraduate research of all kinds. The SURF, or Summer Undergraduate Research Fellowship, allows students to work on a project of their choice with a mentor in the field. It's really great. The application process is meant to simulate the process of submitting an actual grant proposal. Aside from SURFs, students have a really easy time getting research jobs—basically, you just need to ask a professor or staff member if you can help them finish projects they're doing in their labs anyway.

The Activities

Caltech students don't have time to get involved in activities. A lot of people, if they have a few minutes, will just play video games or socialize with friends around campus. Occasionally, the Residence Life office will provide subsidized tickets to amusement parks like Disneyland, Knott's Berry Farm, and Magic Mountain.

The Students

There's a fair amount of LGBT students at Caltech. Spiritually, I'd estimate about half of the undergraduates are some flavor of atheist or agnostic, and about one-third are Christian, with the rest being some combination of Jewish, Muslim, Buddhist, and Baha'i. Racially, most students are white or Asian. There's also a fairly high number of students from outside the United States, though the vast majority of students ultimately hail from Earth. We're somewhat left-leaning, but we're not really into politics. If anyone ever tried to start up a protest here, we would let the angry, diseased lab monkeys from the biology department loose in their general direction. Angry, diseased lab monkeys can wreak havoc in no time at all. That would teach those protesters a lesson. Focus on science, people!

Also, dating at Caltech is not great for most people. I'm a gay male, so I'm used to having a small population to choose from. However, for straight males, the 7:3 male to female ratio is a challenge. The pickings are slim, and many females don't like the excess attention males throw at them. And anyway, not to say we're ugly, but a lot of Caltech students are ugly. There are better looking student bodies in the country, you know?

The Social Scene

Parties? What are those?

Name: Stephen
Hometown: Nice, France
Class Year: Senior
Major: Computer science
Extracurriculars: Member of the Institute of Electrical and Electronics Engineers, president of the Hong Kong Student Association
Career Goal: Research in artificial intelligence

How would you describe Caltech's reputation?

Caltech is one of the best schools in the nation, especially for science and technology.

Is this reputation accurate?

This reputation is correct. Caltech is so focused on science and technology, you really should choose Caltech only if you're sure you love science and technology so much that you're willing to make some sacrifices for it (like sleep, for example).

What would an admissions officer at your school probably not tell a prospective student?

Even though a small community has many advantages, it also has shortcomings, including a lack of social activity on campus, limited library resources, and limited variety in the courses offered.

The Institution

Caltech is a very small, research-oriented school. It is so research-oriented that undergraduates sometimes feel they are not in college. I like this kind of environment, in which I get a top-level education while developing close relationships with students and faculty. That said, even though people are proud to go to Caltech, the school's size and heavy workload lead to a lack of school spirit. The house tradition compensates, mixing a bit of frat house culture with a bit of traditional dorm culture. There's also the Interhouse Sports System, where members of each house compete against other houses in sports like basketball, soccer, football—just picture all the science students playing sports.

The Education

Most of the knowledge acquired at Caltech doesn't come from lectures but from doing homework sets. One of the hardest problem sets I encountered was for a theoretical computer science class. Two friends and I spent the whole night brainstorming, and eventually gathered in my dorm's library, scribbling on the whiteboard until the middle of the night. It was very painful, and we spent a lot of time fiddling with numbers until we got it.

Professors at Caltech really do pay attention to each student, and it's not unusual for them to remember your name two or three years after you've taken a class with them. Also, SURF hires about 450 students each summer, from Caltech and other top universities, and gives them the opportunity to do research at Caltech and at the Jet Propulsion Laboratory (JPL), attend seminars, take trips, and get a nice stipend. It's a really valuable experience enjoyed by many Caltech students, which serves as good preparatory work for graduate school.

The Students

Caltech is a small school, but we've got students from all over the world, and financial aid packages are quite good. The school has the repu-

tation of being very generous. I'm originally from France, but came to the United States in high school. That said, I have close ties to the international student community here, and Caltech provides many services to help international students seamlessly integrate into Caltech life. There's an entire office dedicated to providing international students with information, lectures, picnics, and trips. And the nice thing is, scientific communities all over the world know about Caltech—so you can go anywhere with a Caltech degree and find yourself a job working in science.

The Activities

Caltech is conveniently located a few minutes' drive from Old Town Pasadena, where one can find restaurants, clubs, movie theaters. If you want to go to downtown Los Angeles, it's a twenty-minute drive on the 110 freeway. But don't expect to do this often. The workload at Caltech is such that going off campus is a rare luxury. As for academic activities, I'm part of the Institute of Electrical and Electronics Engineers—this keeps me updated with everything connected to engineering, both on and off campus. I'm also president of the Hong Kong Student Association. HKSA is a social club that gathers people who are interested in Hong Kong culture on campus—we go to the beach and to Chinese restaurants and also put together campus-wide events to promote Hong Kong/Chinese culture in the Caltech community.

The Social Scene

There aren't a lot of social activities offered, but there are enough that if you want to have fun and go to most of them, you'll have a great time. Students will sometimes branch out and try to make friends at other nearby colleges—Pasadena City College (PCC) is right across the street and they throw pretty good parties for those times when our scene is lacking.

Notable Caltech Alumni (who haven't won the Nobel) Include:
Frank Capra, film director
Gordon Moore, founder, Intel Corporation
David Brin, author
David Ho, AIDS researcher
Sandra Tsing Lo, author
Harrison Schmitt, astronaut, senator

CARLETON COLLEGE

Founded: 1866
Location: Northfield, MN
Phone: (507) 646-4000
E-mail: admissions@acs.carleton.edu
Web site: www.carleton.edu

Number of Undergraduates: 1,930
Number of Graduate Students: 0
Cost: Approximately $37,000 per year
Application Deadline: January 15
Early Decision: November 15

Rating:	Notable Majors/Programs:
Most Selective	Life Sciences, English, Economics

Size:
● Small   ○ Medium   ○ Large

Location:
○ Urban   ○ Suburban   ● Rural

On a Saturday, students talk about academics:
● Always   ○ Sometimes   ○ Never

Nightlife:
○ Intense   ● Moderate   ○ Laid-back

Politically, Carleton leans:
● Left   ○ Right   ○ Split

Diversity:
○ High   ● Low   ○ Medium

Students describe Carleton in five words:
- Snow and quirkiness equals fun!
- Zany, scrawny, laid-back . . . very Midwest

From the School

Carleton offers a liberal arts education of the highest caliber. Professors are highly respected, leading scholars in their fields, but teaching comes first. With individual attention from your professors and the myriad facilities and resources available to you, Carleton students learn how to learn.

—www.carleton.edu

If you're interested in Carleton, you may also be interested in:
Colorado College, Grinnell, Macalester, Oberlin, Reed, Wesleyan

---

Name: Gus
Hometown: Chicago, Illinois
Class Year: Senior
Major: Classical languages
Extracurriculars: The Non-Career Fair, Radical Bible Study, Alternatives to Violence Project, Campus Advocates Against Sexual Harassment and Assault (CAASHA), Campaign to Stop Coke at Carleton, Coalition of Students Against the War, Mikey Schorsch and the Broken Toe Boys (bluegrass songs about organic food)
Career Goal: Peace activist, small-time farmer, teacher of dead languages, dad—any one or all four of which would make me happy.

How would you describe Carleton's reputation?

Carleton is known for really good academics in a noncompetitive atmosphere. And for being "zany." The zaniness is big.

Is this reputation accurate?

Carleton really is noncompetitive. Nobody ever mentions what grades they get or how high their SAT scores are. A friend of mine just got a Fulbright scholarship and still has only told his girlfriend. That's pretty typical of Carleton. As for the zaniness, I get the feeling some students come here knowing that Carleton is a zany school, and so they kind of force their zaniness at first. They obsess about Frisbee; they write nonsensical phrases in chalk on the ground; some people wear capes. After a year or so, most people drop the zaniness altogether and start thinking about grad school or find something that's more suited to them, instead of doing the typical conformist nonconformist stuff.

> "Where else will you have a discussion with a Jew from Korea, a Cuban Quaker from Kentucky, and a Kenyan on the topic of the sex-change operations of Somali women?"
> ✦ C.J., senior

What would an admissions officer at your school probably not tell a prospective student? What aspect of Carleton would a prospective student not see on a campus tour?

They probably don't tell "prospies" that during the winter, when there's lots of snow, people tend to sculpt giant genitalia in the fields (well, they did once). They probably don't tell students that technically, things like drinking and any kind of sexual misconduct (e.g., sculpting giant snow genitalia) are prohibited and can get you in big trouble—but in practice, there's almost no enforcement of drinking rules and only a little more enforcement on the sexual misconduct stuff, but not much. On tours, you won't see the streakers (despite attempts to quash it, streaking remains a celebrated part of student life). They also don't tell you that there's a good bit of grade inflation. The average GPA has been rising consistently since the seventies. It's not that hard to get all As and Bs at Carleton and it's quite easy to finish in the four years given. Many students actually graduate early without much stress.

The Institution

Carleton students are for the most part totally oblivious to the school's prestige. People mention it when the new rankings come out, but mostly they roll their eyes and complain that moving up in the rankings is going to bring in the elitist riffraff from the East Coast.

Carleton has three ten-week terms. Of those thirty weeks, I'd say fifteen to twenty are spent at or below freezing. Some people say trimesters are hard, because the terms are so short. It's really not that bad, with the exception that Carleton lets out late for a college (early June), so it's often hard to find summer employment.

Carleton students whine about the cafeteria food, but in all honesty it's consistently good, sometimes even really good, it's usually healthy, and the food workers are really nice.

The Education

Carleton students talk about their classes constantly. It's unreal how excited we get about what we're studying. We love to learn, I guess. There is close to zero competition between students, and nearly all humanities and social science classes are discussion-based—though I'm not sure about math and hard sciences, as I avoid those like the plague. Although we have distribution requirements, we do not have required classes, so there is a lot of flexibility in how you fulfill those.

The Classics department has the most collegial and friendly faculty in the school, and, perhaps, the universe. I've been to their homes, been taken out to dinner, gotten permission to throw a dinner party at one professor's house while he was out of town, and actually seen them show up to parties in student housing that they were invited to.

Every senior here completes "comps," or the Comprehensive Exercises, which can be either an exam or a more intense research project or paper. Some comps, like those for history majors, are impossibly hard. Others, say for chemistry, are shockingly easy. Most comps, like those for classics majors, are challenging but not overwhelming and give you the opportunity to do some great, original work and perhaps even get published.

> "It's so cold, some days I'll wear three pairs of long underwear."
> ✦ Andrea, junior

The Students

The average student on campus is from a suburb of either Chicago or the Twin Cities (St. Paul/Minneapolis), or from New England or the Pacific Northwest. He or she votes Democrat but with some degree of cynicism. He or she complains about the dining hall, but can't cook. He or she drinks on the weekends, and doesn't bat an eye at the many students who don't drink. He or she realizes at the end of sophomore year that most of the school's a cappella groups are lame, and that the best thing about a cappella concerts is that someone usually streaks them. The average student loathes the dean of students, but is humbly devoted to the college president.

There's a growing number of minority students here, especially African American students. Unfortunately, there's not a ton of mixing between minority and white students. It's not tense or anything, there's just not a whole lot there. There's a strong network of support for LGBT students, and the student body as a whole is LGBT-positive. Anti-gay speakers have been brought in by conservative student groups, and students (as well as administrators) all show up wearing pride pins. I've known only a few real working-class students at Carleton. For the most part they felt isolated, angry at the sense of entitlement other students have. Being working class doesn't get you much "identity cred" at Carleton. The institutional support is most visibly for racial minorities and LGBT students. No-

body seems to care if you're blue collar. Some people I've known have liked that, and others have been quite annoyed that wealthy black or Latino/a kids get lots of support while poor white kids get little to none.

Carleton is an almost suffocatingly liberal school. The conservatives are active but much maligned. But for all the students' high-minded liberalism, there's a whole lot of apathy. People are self-preserving of their time, and don't want to commit to "causes." I spent a lot of this year trying to organize students around a human rights issue, and it was a struggle every inch of the way, despite the fact that almost everyone I talked to agreed that it was a good cause calling for some action. The most widely read publication on campus is the *CLAP* (Carleton Literary Association Paper). The *CLAP* is about half funny and half moronic. It's often politically incorrect, which has gotten the editors in trouble a couple of times. But most people like it.

The Activities

St. Olaf College is a half-hour walk from Carleton. There's not much interaction, aside from when they crash our parties—St. Olaf is a dry campus; Carleton is completely soaked at times. When not studying or partying, my friends and I usually watch baseball games, brew our own alcohol in someone's closet, write songs about anthropology and organic food products, talk about religion, have extended pancake brunches, and stick it to the man whenever possible.

At 3 a.m. on a Wednesday night, most students awake are either studying, copulating with a long-term boyfriend/girlfriend, or sitting in a dorm lounge playing board games or having intense conversations about Freud, whom they have just learned about in Psychology 110.

The Social Scene

Carleton has absolutely no dating scene. Most people either have a long-term boyfriend/girlfriend or are single and hook up with people at parties when they get lonely, which is frequently. Booze flows freely at Carleton.

Carleton is not particularly cliquish. But there is a group of whacked-out/beautiful people who do drugs and throw lots of parties and are somewhat "cool." But these people are for the most part nice one on one. I do hold open doors and smile at people at Carleton. But I hope that's not unusual.

Name: Kate
Hometown: Minnetonka, Minnesota
Class Year: Junior
Major: Women's and gender studies
Extracurriculars: Copresident, Collective for Women's Issues, Center Associate for the Gender and Sexuality Center, member of AHA!, an AIDS and HIV awareness group, president of American Medical Student's Association chapter, active in theater
Career Goal: To be an OB/Gyn, or some other sort of primary care physician.

How would you describe Carleton's reputation?

One of the top liberal arts colleges in the nation, and grad schools/professional schools/hiring companies know it. We're also known for being a bit left of center.

Is this reputation accurate?

Yes and no. We're definitely highly academically rigorous and curious. However, we aren't quite as liberal as we like to pretend to be—students are so intensely academic, we don't have as much time to be politically active. Still, there's a strong community of progressive activists on campus: last spring I traveled all the way to Washington, D.C., for the big pro-choice March for Women's Lives with thirty-six other Carleton students.

What would an admissions officer at Carleton probably not tell a prospective student?

Admissions plays down how much drinking there is here. We work hard, and we play hard. In fall and spring, it tends to be pretty under control, but in the long, cold winter people can get a bit crazy. You really don't have to drink to be social at Carleton (I didn't drink much freshman or sophomore years), but there is definitely a big drinking scene.

The Institution

Carleton's size is good and bad. It's great to know every other person you run into. It's not so great to run into your ex about every other day. I chose Carleton because of the people. It's a school that attracts quirky, kind of nerdy people who care a bit more about learning than GPAs and get excited discussing their research projects or reading at parties.

Northfield definitely feels small after three years, but Minneapolis is close by, and you're bound to have a friend with a car.

The Education

Academics here are difficult, but for the most part rewarding. I spend probably about four hours a day working, although it varies depending on the point of the term. The term system means you take more classes throughout the course of the year than with the semester system. It also means that finals are always approaching. I'm premed, which is typically a highly competitive group, but not at Carleton. I've studied for exams, shared MCAT practice tests, and discussed problems with fellow premeds often over the past few years.

> "Everyone is so friendly, so Midwest. Even the friendliest schools I visited on the East Coast weren't as friendly as Carleton. I don't even know my profs' office hours because you can go talk to them—in some cases even IM [instant message] them—anytime."
>
> ✦ Becker, senior

As a women's and gender studies major, I'm involved in many disciplines, and none of them seem that competitive to me. All students are academically dedicated, but grading is rarely set up such that only a certain percentage of students could receive As. This leads to lots of cooperative work and, I think, better learning.

The small class size at Carleton is one of the reasons I came here. Although the intro biology classes can be as large as eighty, many of the discussion classes (and there are lots) are as small as five people. My fall term freshman year, I had intro classes as small as fifteen. Carleton encourages professors to get to know students, which is particularly helpful at this point in my career when I need letters of recommendation for medical school. I can count eight professors who know me well enough to write excellent letters for me. I have three profs with whom I've had dinner or appetizers or something else strictly social (in a nonsketchy way). And for a small liberal arts school, because there isn't a grad school, a lot of us get to do research. Last summer I worked in an organic chemistry lab doing metal-catalyst polymerization research. That was just after my sophomore year, and lot of my friends started even earlier than that. Carleton's a great place to get hands-on experience in academia.

For my "comps" project, I am studying the long-term effects of sexual education using a sociological framework; I'm really looking forward to creating something substantial and meaningful. When applying to medical school, Carleton's premed committee was amazingly helpful during the process. Also I did quite well on the MCATs, so I am convinced that Carleton's science courses are of high quality.

The Students

It's easy to forget that the "real world" isn't as accepting as Carleton. I'm a bisexual, feminist, progressive woman, and I feel right at home at Carleton. There definitely are a few homophobic, sexist people here (and they speak up), but Carleton is still the most supportive place I've ever been. I've never been made to feel like I have to apologize for my identity. I think it helps that we have no Greek system. Most of the campus is liberal/Democrat, but there is a strong constituency of conservatives. Of course, a lot of conservatives aren't thrilled with the way the Bush administration is leading the country. The conservatives on campus tend to be old-school conservative; they care about small government and fiscal responsibility, which they don't think Bush is upholding. Also I recently learned that the president of the Carleton Conservative Union is pro-choice, so I'd say we're a pretty liberal-leaning campus. Unfortunately, we tend to be pretty white and upper/middle class, but most people realize that and try to address it.

> "The bathroom graffiti mostly has to do with a fellow named Kyia, who, from what I gather, took maybe six years to graduate, rode a scooter, did a lot of drugs, and was generally an arrogant womanizer."
>
> ✦ Gus, junior

The Activities

Carleton sponsors a convocation once a week. Friday convocation brings really great speakers such as Ben and Jerry, Barrie Osborne, and Maeve Leaky to campus and also gives us a break from classes once a week. Granted, some of us use convo time to study or nap, but if you go to convo, you're definitely going to learn something fascinating.

Mainstream athletics aren't generally that important here, but Ultimate Frisbee is big, rugby is sort of its own society, and we have a football team as well. We have lots of school pride; we just don't place that much value on athletics.

As a campus, we're good at supporting the arts, not so much political causes. Theater productions and concerts usually sell out. Our annual production of *The Vagina Monologues* is wildly popular. Generally, for fun we'll bake bread, play Trivial Pursuit, go for a walk in the arboretum, go to coffee at Blue Monday's, watch movies, make cocktails, head to the cities to go dancing . . .

Northfield is a cute town, even if it is small, and Minneapolis is wonderful and close by. I probably visit the twin cities [Minneapolis and St. Paul] at least once every two weeks. Since I teach Sunday school at the local Unitarian Universalist fellowship, I get to interact with the community more than most students. Northfield people are, for the most part, educated, friendly, and interesting.

The Social Scene

People party every weekend. If it's spring, people also party at Mai Fete on Wednesday nights, a kegger on an island in Lyman Lakes. We drink a lot, but for the most part we're smart about it. Parties are nonexclusive, and many different social groups mix at them. I'm part of many social groups, including a theater group, a science nerd group, a predominantly queer women group, and a more mainstream group, and we all intermingle all of the time. It's assumed that we're all a bit quirky.

Dating can be difficult considering the small size of the school and the fact that we don't have lots of time to devote to maintaining a healthy relationship, but most people manage. Of course, hookups are prevalent and not very stigmatized. I live in Women's Awareness House, so I'm exposed to the most woman-friendly part of campus, but whenever I venture out of it I feel perfectly comfortable. It would be silly to think that things like date rape don't happen here (they do), but Carleton is much more woman-positive than most places.

Name: Jenna
Hometown: Boise, Idaho
Class Year: Sophomore
Major: Mathematics
Extracurriculars: Swimming, Christian community activities
Career Goal: Small-business owner

How would you describe Carleton's reputation?

Unique. It's almost a joke around here because everyone loves to gush about how "special" this place is, but it's entirely true. Students here find interest in all sorts of stuff, popular and alternative.

Is this reputation accurate?

The reputation is totally well received by students and faculty alike.

What would an admissions officer at Carleton probably not tell a prospective student?

There's not much here that people keep a secret.

The Institution

Spirit's big here and largely shown through attendance at musical events, by participating in departmental activities, and by checking in with professors. The football team's not that great, but some people still rally up support, basketball games are pretty big, especially for the girls' games, and home games generally guarantee a good time. In the classroom, students and professors are on a first-name basis, which allows students to feel more comfortable around their professors and to see them more as colleagues.

In addition to freshman orientation, the school offers three prefrosh trips (backpacking, canoeing, or community service) where new students can get acquainted before being thrown into the rigor of school. Carleton is a place where preps, jocks, and *nerds* unite—and what a sweet union it is! There are a number of great traditions including midnight breakfasts during the first night of reading days, as well as the annual bubbles that fall upon the professors as they parade into the school's chapel for the school year's first convocation, and Ebony II, the tri-annual festivity during which students choreograph and perform selected songs for huge audiences.

The Education

All hail trimesters! Three classes at a time for ten weeks—the perfect load, and it makes breaks great because there's almost never any work to worry about. Although we get out later (June), we also start later and have longer winter and spring breaks.

The Students

Students around here are very goal-oriented, whether it's graduate school or landing a great job after graduation. Students participate in a variety of internships and they know how to multitask.

Whether an athlete, a musician, or an involved linguist, schedules are busy—but somehow we figure out how to balance it all without creating the aura that we're stress-heads. Everyone's pretty cool and laid-back despite demanding work, homework, and extracurricular loads.

The average Carl is somewhat politically minded, and generally far left-leaning, but luckily this leaning is done without smothering the conservative minority. Both sides are represented and active, as well as the other groups that fall somewhere in-between.

> "Recently, I got into my top two dream medical schools. Medical school will teach me the technical side of being a doctor, but Carleton taught me the life lessons that will be integral to my practice."
>
> ✦ Kate, junior

The Activities

Just about anything can happen here: people take excursions to the Twin Cities, dinner in town is always fun, parties always exist on weekends, the snack bar's open nearly all the time. The campus was very much addicted to Text Twist last year. There was even a tournament between students and faculty. It's cold here, so we check the temperature obsessively. Thursday's $6 pizza night. Maybe if we're really restless we'll pull a prank, like filling a stairwell with water and goldfish (as performed last spring).

The Social Scene

Though many athletes tend to hang out with teammates, that's not a hard rule and others often join in. Cliques aren't really popular at Carleton. It's cool here to be different. By *different* I mean smart and quirky, and by *cool* I mean everyone else is, too.

Notable Carleton Alumni Include:

Barrie Osborne, Academy Award–winning producer
Christopher Kratt, producer of educational television programs for children
Jane Hamilton, author
Kelly Conlin, CEO, Primedia
Mary-Claire King, genetics researcher
Rush Holt, congressman

CARNEGIE MELLON UNIVERSITY

Founded: 1900

Location: Pittsburgh, PA

Phone: (412) 268-2999

E-mail: undergraduate-admissions@andrew.
cmu.edu

Web site: www.cmu.edu

Number of Undergraduates: 5,340

Number of Graduate Students: 3,000

Cost: Approximately $39,000 per year

Application Deadline: January 1

Early Decision: November 15

Rating:	Notable Majors/Programs:
Very Selective	Business, Engineering, Computer Science, Performing Arts

Size:
○ Small ● Medium ○ Large

Location:
● Urban ○ Suburban ○ Rural

On a Saturday, students talk about academics:
● Always ○ Sometimes ○ Never

Nightlife:
○ Intense ○ Moderate ● Laid-back

Politically, Carnegie Mellon leans:
● Left ○ Right ○ Split

Diversity:
● High ○ Low ○ Medium

Students describe Carnegie Mellon in five words:
- Eccentric, intense, stressed (and sleep-deprived!) workaholics!
- Prestigious arts and technology programs

From the School

The only top twenty-five university founded in the twentieth century, Carnegie Mellon has rapidly evolved into an internationally recognized institution with a distinctive mix of world-class educational and research programs in computer science, robotics, engineering, the sciences, business, public policy, fine arts, and the humanities. The core values that Carnegie instilled in the Carnegie Technical Schools more than 100 years ago—problem solving, collaboration, and innovation—continue to drive the university today.

—www.cmu.edu

If you're interested in Carnegie Mellon, you may also be interested in:
Caltech, Columbia, Georgia Tech, Harvey Mudd, Johns Hopkins, MIT

Name: Andrew
Hometown: Flanders, New Jersey
Class Year: Sophomore
Major: College of Fine Arts; School of Architecture
Extracurriculars: Lambda Sigma Honor Society, National Society of Collegiate Scholars, Student Advisory Committee, a cappella, Departmental Committee on Architectural Curricula, Lecture Series Team, First Year Mentorship Initiative, Singing Ambassadors Alumni Chorale
Career Goal: To pursue an innovative and integrated approach to socially responsible and proactive architecture through regional/urban planning, special interest housing, and architectural education.

How would you describe Carnegie Mellon's reputation?

Carnegie Mellon University has an incredible reputation in scholastic circles. Each one of the colleges in our university is top in its field. Unfortunately, many people have not heard of Carnegie Mellon because of its small size and rather specific programs. It's frustrating—when you say, "Carnegie Mellon University," people either say, "Wow" or "Where is that?" Overall, I feel as if I am riding the wave right before it crests. I think Carnegie Mellon will become an even more widely known and respected name within the next twenty years.

> "A well-known saying at CMU is 'school, sleep, food, friends: choose three.'"
> ✦ Jennifer, freshman

Is this reputation accurate?

This reputation is absolutely correct. Some people feel that the school has a tendency to be filled with "nerdy" engineer types. While we do have our fair share of math and science students, our business and humanities programs are also top in the country. There is an equally active fine/performing arts culture on campus, and *everyone* is proud of being a little nerdy. The environment thrives on the diversity present in an interdisciplinary approach to education.

What would an admissions officer at Carnegie Mellon probably not tell a prospective student?

We have no dining hall, just a measly fast food court! (Though there's a banquet room in the University Center, Schatz, with an all you can eat breakfast every morning, and it's open for dinner on specific evenings.)

The Institution

Our athletics are less than stellar, so pride here is reserved for who we are and what we do in the lab, on the stage, and in the studio. (Our "Sine, cosine, cosine, sine; 3.14159" cheer really does say it all!) We have a distinct Scottish heritage at our school, manifested in a Scottish terrier mascot and the only bag piping minor in the country; hearing the Kiltie Band practicing on the Cut every Monday evening is an experience unique to Carnegie Mellon students. Chalking is also relatively unique: the sidewalks often become changing billboards where students advertise upcoming events. One night several anonymous students wrote over eight thousand digits of pi to celebrate "National Pi Day." That pretty much sums up life here at Carnegie Mellon.

The Education

Not only do we talk about classes on a Saturday night, we often do work into the wee morning hours of Sunday morning! No exaggeration. We usually have a fun time doing it, though, and still manage to find some time to do nonacademic things. We are definitely a "work hard, play hard" school.

Competition is brutal. Everyone here was at the top of their class and we do all try to be on top here as well, but also enjoy working together. Professors (and the courses they teach) are almost always excellent. They are involved both in and out of the classroom. TAs work out pretty well, though a language barrier between TAs and students is a common complaint.

Carnegie Mellon University has one of the most active undergraduate student research populations in the country. And students can also cross register at a number of other Pittsburgh schools, colleges, or professional centers to take classes, like the Pittsburgh Glass Center or Filmmakers' Media Arts Center, for example.

The Students

Carnegie Mellon University is incredibly diverse and open to people of all walks of life. Many groups are active on campus in promoting and sustaining diversity. Most students are preprofessionally oriented. Academics definitely remain the focus of the student population, yet video gaming seems to be one of the most popular outlets for stress. But whether it's jogging or catching a tan in Schenley Park, building a house for Habitat for Humanity, dancing until you drop in Dancer's Symposium, or designing clothes for the annual campus fashion show, students are passionate in their endeavors inside and outside the lecture hall.

> "The worst thing about being a varsity athlete here is that there's very little school spirit for our teams."
>
> ✦ Eric, senior

The Activities

Pittsburgh is a great city in which to attend college. It is manageable, yet still brimming with events and opportunities. Pittsburgh and its inhabitants welcome their college communities (there are at least six nearby schools, though, unfortunately, the only one we remotely interact with is the University of Pittsburgh). While thought of as a dreary industrial city, Pittsburgh is experiencing a renaissance of its cultural and waterfront districts. Students explore the surrounding neighborhood often, patronizing local businesses and events and enjoying half price nightly, when drinks and food are half off after 11 p.m.

Physical activity (working out, running, Frisbee on the Cut, intramurals) is an important part of casual life here. Organized sports are present, but do not monopolize campus culture. There are also numerous free campus events like barbecues, music groups/comedians on the Cut (the major quad) and in small venues, a buffalo wing eat-off, a cappella concerts, improv shows, and an "American Idol" competition.

At 3 a.m. on a Wednesday night I'm working (this is Carnegie Mellon!) and I have another five hours of work to do before my 8 a.m. calculus recitation!

The Social Scene

Dorm life is decent. Housing is equally split among dorms, fraternity/sorority/group housing, and off-campus apartments. Parties happen, but are not a driving force on campus and tend to be reasonably tame. There are just as many people going to the Friday night drama production or a cappella concert as there are people going to the frat party. There's no pressure to drink—a large number of students don't—although the option is certainly there. The community, at large, is quite friendly.

Name: W.J.
Hometown: Pittsburgh, Pennsylvania
Class Year: Sophomore
Major: Music performance
Extracurriculars: Working with animals, various performances with various groups
Career Goal: Broadway, regional theater, concert performances, opera, recording

How would you describe Carnegie Mellon's reputation?

Prestigious.

Is this reputation accurate?

In the arts, I think that it is accurate. Our programs in computer-related fields also have a very high reputation. I do not know a great amount of details about the other schools within CMU, but in Andrew Carnegie's dedication letter, he wrote, "My heart is in the work." I imagine most Carnegie Mellon students carry this on in order to thrive in such a focused and intense learning environment.

What would an admissions officer at Carnegie Mellon probably not tell a prospective student?

They probably would not tell you how many international students there are on campus, or how poor their English is. And on paper, freshmen are guaranteed on-campus housing. What they don't tell you is that "on-campus" housing can be a fifteen- or twenty-minute walk *to* campus! In addition to several dormitories the school also rents space in multiple public apartment buildings that can house Carnegie Mellon students, students from the University of Pittsburgh, and some civilians with no collegiate affiliation. Of the schools that I visited, I found Carnegie Mellon's dorms to be the smallest.

The Institution

I chose CMU because it was close to my home and had such a wonderful reputation. I admire so many musicians who have come out of this school. I like our alumni awards during homecoming and a tradition in the School of Drama, which has now extended to the School of Music: the cast of a show signs their names on the walls of the theater. If you look hard, you'll find the signatures of Holly Hunter, George Peppard, Jack Klugman, Blair Underwood, Christiane Noll, and Hollywood producers Steven Bochco and John Wells.

I feel very secure on this campus. The chief of campus police is always making improvements to an already stable and very present police force. I'm told campus police walk around in plain clothes and patrol the academic buildings dressed as students. The presence of the City of Pittsburgh police, however, has not been as strong in recent months in many areas of the city due to budget problems.

One weekend each spring, the campus shuts down for Carnival. It has a midway, food, games—including the highly anticipated buggy races—and entertainment. In the fall, we have the Wats: On Festival Across the Arts, named after a deceased alumni, which spans several days and features a wide variety of art exhibits, lectures on varying topics in the arts, and dance, music, and theatrical performances. Students are given the first afternoon of the festival off from classes to attend these events.

> "Not *everyone* here is a supercomputer geek."
>
> ✦ Eric, senior

We don't have a dining hall—which many people find hard to believe—but we do have The O. The Original O is located in Oakland, a few blocks from campus, but The O is also conveniently located on the main floor of the UC. Known for its burgers and fries, its menu also features surprisingly good salads, subs (one professor says that The O has the best Philly cheesesteak sub he's ever had), and hot dogs. The fries have spoiled me for life!

The Education

My classes are always on my mind, be that good or bad. My biggest class in my two years here has had twenty people, and I've gotten individual attention from teachers in every class. It feels like high school in that respect. TAs are present and sometimes help in class, but are mostly there for support outside of class. I was surprised at how hard being a music major actually is. It is a lot of work, an incredibly demanding schedule, and lots of rehearsals. As a music student, I wish I had time to take more academic classes instead of just choirs and harmony and many other theory classes. My curriculum is so centered on my own college that it's difficult to benefit from the school's strengths in other disciplines.

The Students

This campus seems to be very accepting of all races, religions, and sexual orientations. I see postings for activities sponsored by different groups, and I have never seen any backlash or rude/degrading remarks made to anyone for the above reasons. That said, people are very concerned with themselves. I can count on one hand the number of times someone has said "sorry" or "excuse me" to me after bumping into me—on one occasion even knocking an armful of books out of my grasp without so much as a backward glance. And there seem to be lots of rich people on campus—many of whom come off as snooty or arrogant. Coming from a middle-class family this was a switch for me. I was not used to seeing a student fly down Frew Street in a custom-detailed, brand-new BMW. I have become more of a pessimist since I came to CMU—the more negative attitude of so many people here has rubbed off on me. At the same time, I think I have developed more of an inner drive than I've ever had.

The Activities

Many students take full advantage our PAT bus passes (included on our student ID) and venture off campus into the surrounding communities. The school is located very close to the eclectic shops and eateries of Shadyside. It's a nice place to walk on a weekend to window-shop or to try a new restaurant. There is also The Waterfront, located in the town of West Homestead. In its heyday the West Homestead steel mills produced large amounts of our country's steel. Some of the industrial towers still stand to this day, as a landmark to the generations of workers who toiled there. Now there are a variety of stores and places to eat in every price range. For entertainment, there is The Improv comedy club and Loews Waterfront Movie Theatre. Our city has much to offer if you like the performing arts. The cultural district in downtown

Pittsburgh has five theaters, the Pittsburgh Symphony, the Pittsburgh Public Theatre, Pittsburgh Ballet, Pittsburgh Musical Theatre, and the Civic Light Opera. The Cultural Trust also brings in a variety of national tours, including Broadway shows, dance companies, and concert acts, and many of these performances have student discounts. Carnegie Mellon students also have *free* admission to all of the Carnegie museums in the city: the Museum of Natural History (be sure to visit Dippy, the Diplodocus statue that stands guard outside), the Museum of Art, the Science Center (complete with a planetarium and Omnimax theater), and the Andy Warhol Museum. If arts aren't your thing, we have the Pirates, the Steelers (or in Pittsburghese, the Stillers), and the Penguins to root for. And if amusement parks are up your alley, we have Kennywood Park, an historical park with rides, multiple roller coasters (three of which are the old-fashioned wooden coasters), and a candy shop that will make your mouth water! And in the warmer months you can visit Sandcastle Water Park, located a little ways past the Waterfront. Sandcastle is noted for its wide variety of water and tube slides.

CMU also shows films in McConomy Auditorium during the week, ranging from classics to new releases (three show times, and admission is $3 and under). Movies are also shown outdoors on Flagstaff hill (a large, grassy, tree-dotted area just behind campus) in the warm months. It's a great place to take a blanket and a picnic dinner.

> "If you're an engineering geek like me, this place is a *paradise*."
>
> ✦ Jared, senior

The Social Scene

Dating scene? Men outnumber women on this campus, but as the saying goes: "The odds are good, but the goods are odd."

Name: Korban
Hometown: Namskaket, Massachusetts
Class Year: Sophomore
Major: Undeclared
Extracurriculars: Intramural sports, Scotch'n Soda Theatre, Sigma Phi Epsilon, CMU Lifesavers

Career Goal: Head an international business using my research in behavioral decision making.

How would you describe Carnegie Mellon's reputation?

We're known for being in competition with MIT and the Ivies. We have outstanding academics across the board. The atmosphere is very intense and it's advertised that way.

Is this reputation accurate?

The reputation is very accurate. But the only problem is that the school does not do a very good job at actually mixing disciplines. Each college sticks to itself. It's difficult to gain a wide and broad education here; everything is very focused.

What would an admissions officer at Carnegie Mellon probably not tell a prospective student?

You wouldn't hear about the sheer amount of work required. Compared to most other schools (according to friends elsewhere), CMU has an extremely rigorous program. No one has it easy or even quasi-easy.

The Institution

The school's size is perfect for me: it's small enough that you always know someone somewhere, and big enough to disappear for a while if you want to. There is more school spirit at robotic competitions and concerts than at sporting events. The best traditions here are painting the fence (the most painted structure in the world, according to the *Guinness Book of World Records*) and Carnival, where we have a buggy race and an elaborate booth competition. The booths that cater to a different theme each year can cost anywhere from $200 to $15,000 apiece to construct. And Buggy is where teams (from different organizations) build these little tear-shaped vehicles driven (usually) by really short Asian girls that are pushed around a course through Schenley Park. The weather in Pittsburgh sucks: then winters are frigid and dark. But when it is nice, the weather is beautiful.

The Education

Unfortunately, school is an all-week event. There is hardly any downtime—there's always a project or homework assignment to work on, so my life revolves around the work I do outside of class. I spend at least twice the amount of time that I do in class on homework out of class. The core curriculum differs from college to college. Once in one college, it is very hard to take courses in other colleges—not because you can't sign up for them but because your necessary course load for your major to graduate on time will not allow it.

You receive individual attention from the professors, but only if you ask for it. The professors are very involved in campus life—it's quite likely when you go to a game or a show, you will find yourself sitting next to your quantum physics professor. CMU does have a rather large grad school, but the grad students and undergrads remain fairly separate. But there are numerous research opportunities and internship, job, and grad school opportunities are way better than average. Big-name companies recruit directly from campus job fairs, such as Boeing, Bose, Microsoft, Apple, Lockhead Martin, Philips Magnavox, JPL, Bell Labs—and those are only the technical companies. There are many more that cater to the arts, humanities, and business sides of things. As for graduate schools, students from here go to all the best schools in the country, including CMU.

The Students

Students here are unlike anywhere else. Most are what people consider "odd"—the ones that never quite fit in during high school. Here they do. Most students know what they want to do with the rest of their lives and busily prepare for that. The student body is ridiculously diverse. In one day I have heard people speaking in most major languages of the world and a plethora of lesser known ones. On your way to class you walk through a mini China, India, Korea, Spanish, Middle East, etc. . . . Politically, the students are liberal but pretty quiet. Individually there are some very strong opinions, but they are not voiced loudly; go down the street to the University of Pittsburgh for that.

The Activities

Most students spend most of their time doing work and don't get into the city much. I try to get off campus as much as possible (usually once a week).

When we're bored, my friends and I reenact the "death to the printer" scene from *Office Space*, play Ultimate Frisbee or football on the Cut, watch movies, visit Barnes & Noble, streak around campus . . . the usual. On the occasional nonrainy day, the groups of people on campus are striking. There is the Goth crowd hanging in their little clump, the Asians smoking and speaking one of their many languages, the computer geeks hurrying from one building to the other to avoid the daylight, and the fine arts students dressed to catch the eye and hanging in the sun.

The Social Scene

An average student on campus works hard and *occasionally* parties hard. There are frequent parties, but a very small percentage of the school's students regularly attend. When they do, the alcohol runs free and people get nuts. But that is only occasionally. Fraternities and sororities are there for your enjoyment and have a large impact on the school in general. People are generally polite and courteous—there is the occasional wacko that will get annoyed at you for holding the door for them, but those people you'll learn to avoid. Many people will say that there is nothing to do here and that Pittsburgh is a lame and dead city. Those people have no imagination.

Notable Carnegie Mellon Alumni Include:
Frank Millero, chemical oceanographer
Holly Hunter, actress
John Nash, Nobel Prize–winning mathematician
John Wells, film producer
Steven Bochco, film producer
Vinod Khosla, cofounder Sun Microsystems

CASE WESTERN RESERVE UNIVERSITY

Founded: 1826

Location: Cleveland, OH

Phone: (216) 368-2000

E-mail: admission@case.edu

Web site: www.case.edu

Number of Undergraduates: 3,460

Number of Graduate Students: 4,050

Cost: Approximately $35,000 per year

Application Deadline: January 15

Early Decision: November 15

Rating:	Notable Majors/Programs:
Selective	Engineering, Premed, Business

Size:
○ Small ● Medium ○ Large

Location:
● Urban ○ Suburban ○ Rural

On a Saturday, students talk about academics:
● Always ○ Sometimes ○ Never

Nightlife:
○ Intense ○ Moderate ● Laid-back

Politically, Case leans:
○ Left ● Right ○ Split

Diversity:
○ High ○ Low ● Medium

Students describe Case in five words:
- Prestigious, nerdy, socially diverse, research-oriented
- Cleveland's sorta conservative academic powerhouse

From the School

Case is a private research university that is transforming itself into one of the most powerful learning environments in the world. This learning environment includes productive partnerships with our neighbors in Cleveland's University Circle and beyond, embracing areas as diverse as medicine, art, music, anthropology, social work, and entrepreneurship. Our new model of higher learning inspires renaissance students who merge the liberal arts with science, technology, and professional education in ways that uniquely position them to serve humanity.

—http://www.case.edu

If you're interested in Case, you may also be interested in:
Carnegie Mellon, Duke, Johns Hopkins, Macalester, Northwestern, Washington Univ. in St. Louis

Name: Sandra
Hometown: Jakarta, Indonesia
Class Year: Freshman
Major: Biomedical engineering
Extracurriculars: Varsity swimming
Career Goal: Surgeon

How would you describe Case's reputation?

Case students are total nerds who never party and stay locked up in their rooms hiding from social interaction all the time.

Is this reputation accurate?

It's true that Case is a nerd school. People joke about physics while playing pool, and one of my friends always tries to prove she hasn't had too much to drink by doing integrals in her head. But the students who do choose to go out and party, party pretty hard.

What aspect of Case would a prospective student not see on a campus tour?

The blue mesh Titanic sculpture would be pointed out, but I seriously doubt the guide would mention its nickname, "the rape cage." Don't panic: no one's ever been raped there. It's just a twisted nickname.

The Institution

Case Western Reserve University began when Case Institute of Technology and Western Reserve University (and a lot of other schools, actually) combined. Recently, as part of the new president's plan, the administration made the decision to drop the Western Reserve, changing the acronym from CWRU (pronounced "crew") to just plain Case. (This caused a bit of an uproar as there are plenty of alumni who graduated from Western Reserve University.) The goal is to make Case "the greatest learning environment in the world." It's a great goal. However, so far, the changes have been the acronym and letterhead, a new Web page, a new style of orientation for incoming classes, a 10 percent raise in tuition, and a lot of construction on new upperclassman dorms. Except for the upcoming curricular implementation of SAGES, I'm just not sure how all this is supposed to affect my learning.

Most of the freshman dorms are coed by floor, except for Pierce and Hitchcock, which are quad-style dorms. Those are the dorms to be in. Freshmen live on the north side of campus, which is great if you're a liberal arts major. If you're not, the walk to the engineering and math classes on the south quad is about twenty minutes. Or you can attempt to take the Greenie (campus shuttle bus), which can be frustrating since it's often packed and is rarely on time, if it comes at all. Case is home to the infamous Peter B. Lewis building, with a severely slanted roof that gives off a glare you can see blocks away. Either you love it or you hate it, but regardless, during winter, the sidewalk next to it has to be closed off because of hazardous sheets of falling ice and snow. Students campuswide are always daydreaming viable methods of climbing the metal roof.

Case is situated directly between one of the nicest areas of town and one of the worst. Three blocks from where the freshmen live, there are shootings reported almost weekly. However, campus security is good. You can't be outside for a full ten minutes without seeing at least one campus security patrol go by. But you do have to pay attention, always have someone with you, and follow all those other rules of common sense that your parents always reminded you of constantly.

Cleveland is definitely different than I expected. I expected a dirty city of factories, and while there are factories, and the river has caught

> "Case is an academic, nonparty school full of engineers and premeds that is known for research with more diversity here than people realize."
>
> ✦ Beth, junior

on fire a couple of times (not recently), there's actually a lot of trees and green space.

The Education

Everyone who goes to Case is a nerd—not in the "pocket protector and coke bottle glasses" sense—but in the sense that everyone at Case is genuinely interested in learning. People here argue about theories and hypotheses they've discussed in class all the time—during swim practice, in the canteen, at parties, sitting out in the common room—*all* the time. If you have opinions and actually like learning, this is an amazing place to be and it's not very competitive between students. My friends at Ivies tell horror stories about how you can't leave an essay alone because it will get stolen (not so it can be copied, but just so that you can't turn it in so it throws off your grade). Case isn't like that at all. There's much more of an us against the work atmosphere. There's no grade inflation here, and the workload is rough, but the students try to help each other keep on top of it. Any time I'm having difficulty with something, I can find someone who understands it and is willing to take the time to explain it to me.

There are plenty of research opportunities for undergrads, even for freshmen. I've been assisting with research in a graduate pharmacology lab in the med school all semester, and will continue doing so for the next year at the very least. I've really enjoyed it, and I'm looking forward to having my own part of the project to research now that I've learned the basics.

If you're interested in medicine, Case has the University Hospitals and Rainbow Baby Center basically on campus. With leading hospitals in cardiac research and infant care, respectively, so close, there're plenty of opportunities to get involved before you get to med school. Volunteer in the ER, shadow a doctor, or get involved with the new Case EMS program. You can even visit the county morgue, just two blocks off campus, for a tour and maybe an autopsy.

The general education requirements at Case have been replaced by SAGES. The SAGES program is a four-semester way to get out of freshman English and fulfill your general education requirements at the same time. All SAGES are small, fifteen students max, seminar-discussion style classes. First semester, you take the first seminar relevant to your area of study. After that, you get to choose from a variety of classes offered by various professors across many fields. In each of the four classes, you do quite a bit of writing, and at the end of the two years, you compile a portfolio. Your portfolio is reviewed, and as long as you have at least a C average, you're given credit for English 150 and all of your gen ed requirements are considered fulfilled.

Case really encourages students to spend a year abroad and/or co-op. A lot of engineering students co-op for a semester. That does add a semester to their graduation date, which may already be more than four years away, but it also gives them a semester of paid work experience. Case's Junior Year Abroad program makes an effort to ensure that any student can go abroad, even premed and engineering students.

The Students

I can talk most about athletes, as sports teams are kind of like cults, and we tend to be a little incestuous. You spend so much time with your team, eating together, studying together, and often living together since you have similar schedules and interests; but playing a sport, or being Greek, doesn't mean all your friends are involved in the same things. I have a lot of friends who aren't athletes, or even in any of my classes. The only people that don't mix with different groups are the ones who stay in their rooms.

> "Little Italy is right next door, and Coventry Village is a short bus ride away. Good eats, and zillions of concerts for whatever taste in music you have. Cleveland rocks!"
> ✦ Beth, junior

The Activities

Just down the street from Case is Little Italy. There are a variety of restaurants, ranging in price. La Dolce Vita has Italian opera every Monday night, which if you've never heard, is definitely worth going to at least once. Restaurants run specials. For five dollars you get salad, bread, and all the spaghetti you can eat. Plus you'll love the gelato.

On a sunny day, there're a few distinct groups of people at Case. There are the people inside playing video games. Then there're the people who really want to be outside, but have too much homework. Next are the people sitting on blankets or picnic benches outside, with books and/or a laptop, trying to do their homework and get a tan at the same time. Then there're the people pretending to be doing their homework, but actually chatting or napping instead. Lastly, there're the people who have homework, but have decided to blow it off, at least for now, and are playing Frisbee or football in the grass.

If you're still up at 3 a.m. on a Wednesday night, it's probably because you've got work to do. This problem might be exponentially bigger if you happen to have been at the Spot until 1 a.m. for wings or a concert. It's also possible that you're bored with your homework and don't have an 8:30 a.m. class, in which case, you're probably playing video games, pool, or just running amok with equally sleep-deprived friends.

The Social Scene

There are different types of parties at Case. There are the frat parties, where people go to play drinking games and dance. Then there are the theme parties, where everyone is supposed to dress up. Then there are the house parties, which are usually somewhat older students. Then there's the get drunk in the dorm room while avoiding your RA party. Those are definitely jumping parties; a knock on the door sends everyone flying for cover. Lastly, there's the nonalcoholic video game/sci-fi marathon, etc., party, which, if you're into that, is fun. As far as dating goes . . . Case is 60 percent guys, although that's slowly evening out to fifty-fifty.

Name: Rob
Hometown: Marysville, Ohio
Class Year: Freshman
Major: Biology
Extracurriculars: Gay Straight Alliance (VP), student newspaper (theater critic), Domestic Partnership Campaign in Cleveland Heights
Career Goal: Research in a genetic or biotech field

How would you describe Case's reputation?

Power school, culturally rich.

> "Joining Greek life here helps tremendously."
>
> ✦ Rupa, sophomore

Is this reputation accurate?

Complete and utter crap! Power school, maybe—but culturally rich? There are many minority students here, but the staff and administration are still very WASPish. The LGBT community is normally ignored by the administration, which makes it hard for us to gain student support. But lately they have been trying to promote more diversity on campus.

What would an admissions officer at Case probably not tell a prospective student?

There are five fundamental drives of a college student: success, food, sleep, social interaction, and sex. Going to Case requires you to pick no more than two to actively pursue.

The Institution

A few tips: the *H* in *Thwing* is silent (*Thwing* rhymes with *swing*). Campus is a full mile north to south, so bring a bike or skates to help get around. The sports teams at Case aren't that great. We are such a geeky campus that the discussion on bathroom walls usually revolves around the existence of God or ridiculous mathematical proofs. A couple restrooms on campus are rumored to be "cruisy," but I have yet to see proof. Students in general avoid the townies—we live on the east side of Cleveland in the middle of the ghetto. Campus security does a decent job, though a rape between two students is swept under the carpet and not prosecuted. Cleveland weather is eternally dismal (think London, but not as intriguing).

The Education

Unless you are completely masochistic (which can be fun, but not in this case), think long and hard before pursuing an engineering degree. The engineering core curriculum is brutal. Be prepared to forgo sleep and food on a regular basis. Chem with Doc Oc is great. Doc Oc is a short, feisty Puerto Rican that knows how to get students to learn. Overall, classes are what you make of them. Supplemental instruction sessions are offered several times each week for major classes and offer review of in-class material and help with any questions you may have.

The Students

Case is a conservative campus, but not viciously so. I have several gay pride buttons on my backpack, and I have yet to even get a comment on them. Our LGBT group, Spectrum, is currently rebuilding from bad leadership in the past, and we have some major events coming up. We have all sorts of groups on campus, including a great improv comedy troupe, and a University Programs Board that schedules entertainers and various trips over school breaks, and the campus TV network airs a lot of student-produced content, including *CWRU Jackass.*

The Activities

If you do come to Case, you can score free or dirt cheap admission to all sorts of fun stuff, including the Rock and Roll Hall of Fame (Rock Hall), Cleveland Museum of Art, The Cleveland Playhouse (the nation's oldest permanently established professional theater company), and Playhouse Square (a group of five theaters downtown that bring in national tours of Broadway musicals and other big-name entertainment). The University Programs Board does bring in a lot of big names: Eve 6, Jurassic 5, Robert Kennedy Jr., for example. The film club is also kickass and brings all sorts of fun movies to campus.

The Social Scene

There are usually all sorts of events on campus on a Friday or Saturday night. Students also go to the Flats (warehouse district), just west of downtown, and hit the nightclubs. A few gay bars and clubs are available near the Flats and can be pretty fun after a week of classes.

Name: Ivan
Hometown: Erie, Pennsylvania
Class Year: Senior
Major: Biology/economics
Extracurriculars: Sigma Chi Fraternity, Gamma Sigma Alpha Honor Society, Undergraduate Student Government, Golden Key International, Mortar Board, Student Turning Point Society, Order of Omega, Interfraternity Congress, Indian Student Association, American Medical Student Association
Career Goal: Practicing physician/researcher

How would you describe Case's reputation?

Case has a reputation as a school very focused upon engineering and premedical majors. The students stereotypically spend all of their time engaged in academic rather than social pursuits.

Is this reputation accurate?

Yes, Case is a very powerful research institution and has had great success in training individuals in engineering and premedical courses of study. But it also has a wide variety of lesser known but excellent academic programs in other fields of study. The idea that students are focused only on study is misleading—there's a diverse student body here, and an equally rich set of extracurricular activities to choose from.

What would an admissions officer at Case probably not tell a prospective student?

An admissions officer would probably neglect to mention that while the school is currently engaged in a master plan which will completely revamp the school's physical structure, the extensive reconstruction will result in multiple inconveniences to the students (such as parking and logistical issues concerning athletics).

> "You have to be aggressive if you want research opportunities here; it's not that there's a lack of opportunities, but no professor is going to come to you."
> ✦ Rupa, sophomore

The Institution

Cleveland, Ohio, is known as a dull or lifeless city. While the weather (generally cold and windy) leaves much to be desired, the city actually affords many attractions. This is especially true for students who take advantage of the many cultural, musical, and social venues in the city—with free or reduced admittance to performances by the Cleveland Orchestra, venues at Severance Hall, the Cleveland Art Museum, the Rock and Roll Hall of Fame, the Cleveland Botanical Gardens, and much more.

The school has a small undergraduate population, which allows for a more intimate relationship among students. Competition is not severe. And while it does not make many efforts to reach out to students, the administration can be extremely helpful to students when approached.

The school has a vast array of well-supported extracurricular activities and many partnerships with institutions in the community. While mixing with the Cleveland population is minimal, the spirit of cooperation among the members of the school and other prestigious institutions such as the hospitals, Severance Hall, and others, is phenomenal.

The Education

The education is phenomenal at Case. With leading researchers and faculty, those who teach are very knowledgeable in their subject matter and generally very interested in the intellectual goals of the students. Many freshman classes are large and lecture-based; however, higher-level classes are generally quite intimate and afford much more individual attention. The presence of top-rated graduate school programs is also a great asset to the undergraduate community, as it affords us the resources of prestigious medical, engineering, law, and business institutions.

As a leading research institution, the opportunities for research are overwhelming; the ambitious student often has their choice among various research positions if he or she so desires. While the workload can be heavy at times, it is manageable, and still allows for the utilization of the school's many extracurricular opportunities as well.

The Students

The students represent many racial, cultural, religious, and socioeconomic groups. With a relatively small student population, each class is encouraged to interact, creating a very stimulating learning and growing environment. While there is a subset of the population that concentrates only on studies, there is a very large portion of the students who are very active within the campus and community, engaging in a seemingly infinite number of extracurriculars. Greek life within the school is very popular, and is one of the strongest in the United States, with more than 30 percent of the students involved in a fraternity or sorority. Greeks and nonaffiliated students mix very well on campus. Despite the small size of its student population, the school provides a niche for almost any personality.

The Activities

The undergraduate student government is quite strong and quite effective at addressing the needs of the student population. Athletics are widely popular, but nonathlete attendance at games and matches is low. The athletic program is, however, being stimulated via the construction of new fields and training facilities as well as efforts by the school to bolster attendance at events. Community service is also popular.

The Social Scene

Most students choose to spend at least half, if not three of the four average years it takes to graduate, living on campus. This is mostly due to convenience and affordable housing as well as access to a pool of other students to directly interact with. However, the city of Cleveland also offers many affordable alternatives to dorm living, with extremely close proximity to campus. The group social scene is not huge on campus, but generally there is at least one party during the weekends, generally held by a fraternity/sorority, athletic group, or other group on campus. While the fraternity/sorority groups generally dominate the social life on campus, it is by no means limited to them. Drinking to excess is not a problem on campus, nor is it taboo.

Notable Case Western Alumni Include:

Alfred Gilman, Nobel prize winner in medicine or physiology

Barry Meyer, chairman and CEO, Warner Bros.

Bruce Cole, chairman of the National Endowment for the Humanities

Dr. Julie Gerberding, director. U.S. Centers for Disease Control and Prevention

Jack Perkins, former NBC News correspondent and host of A&E's *Biography*

Susie Gharib, *Nightly Business Report* anchor

UNIVERSITY OF CHICAGO

Founded: 1892

Location: Chicago, IL

Phone: (773) 702-8650

E-mail: college-admissions@uchicago.edu

Web site: www.uchicago.edu

Number of Undergraduates: 4,236

Number of Graduate Students: 8,159

Cost: Approximately $38,000 per year

Application Deadline: January 1

Early Decision: November 1

Rating:	Notable Majors/Programs:
Very Selective	Economics, Biology, Psychology, English

Size:
○ Small ● Medium ○ Large

Location:
● Urban ○ Suburban ○ Rural

On a Saturday, students talk about academics:
● Always ○ Sometimes ○ Never

Nightlife:
○ Intense ○ Moderate ● Laid-back

Politically, University of Chicago leans:
● Left ○ Right ○ Split

Diversity:
● High ○ Low ○ Medium

Students describe U. Chicago in five words:
- Intense, focused bastion of genius
- Where fun comes to die

From the School

Ever heard of the "Life of the Mind"? Here at Chicago, it's our academic philosophy. It means a constant conversation sparked by the reading and analyzing of original texts from Plato to Foucault. It means small, discussion-oriented classes in the midst of a large research university. It means that academics come first on our campus, and the difficulty of the courses reflects that. Our students learn because they genuinely love learning, while the university rises to meet them with vast intellectual resources.

—http://collegeadmissions.uchicago.edu

If you're interested in U. Chicago, you may also be interested in:
Columbia, Harvard, Northwestern, U. Pennsylvania, Princeton, Yale

Name: Abigail
Hometown: Ridgewood, New Jersey
Class Year: Sophomore
Major: Physics, with a minor in classical Greek
Extracurriculars: Water polo, Knit-and-Bitch Society, University Theater, Sunday school teacher
Career Goal: Earn my PhD and go into scientific research.

How would you describe U. Chicago's reputation?

It's said that the U(C) is an extraordinary place to study economics, and it's also highly respected for turning out a sizable chunk of America's future academics. An average guy on the street might not know the U(C), though.

Is this reputation accurate?

Yup. U(C) is a kickass place to be an economics major, and there are plenty of students aspiring toward academia. Anyone that matters knows how good the U(C) is.

What would an admissions officer at your school probably not tell a prospective student? What aspect of your school would a prospective student not see on a campus tour?

The administration probably wouldn't mention our current housing crunch, as the U(C)'s student body is expanding at a faster rate than housing can accommodate. However, that's minor—and of all the colleges that I visited, the U(C) administration was by far the most honest with prospective students.

The Institution

My friend has a saying: "The University of Chicago is not the place where the high school valedictorian goes. It's the place where the people the valedictorians were intimidated by go to school." And it's true. The valedictorians studied to get good grades, but we spent our days in the library in the name of learning—literally everyone here is pushed by their internal drive to learn, to achieve, to acquire a deeper understanding. Pound for pound, U. Chicago is probably the most intellectual campus in America.

A bunch of years back the somewhat conservative Social Sciences Division commissioned a statue to stand outside Pick Hall. Amusingly, they didn't realize that the sculptor they chose was something of a communist sympathizer. He cre-

ated a big bronze statue which he called "Dialogo." It wasn't until the first of May, after the statue was installed, that everyone realized the statue had been designed so that its shadow would project, on May 1, with that day's corresponding angle of the sun, the communist image of the hammer and sickle onto the ground. There was talk of removing the statue, but in the end it was decided that removing the sculptor's voice would have been worse than removing the message the sculpture carried. This is the sort of place the U(C) is: we have a devotion to listening to all voices, even the unpopular ones.

> "My professor, who left Caltech to teach here, described U. Chicago as 'what happens when you give scientists virtually limitless funds.'"
>
> ✦ Ann, sophomore

We're on the academic quarter system, which isn't used very often in the United States and takes some getting used to. Essentially, we take fewer classes at a time, but classes don't last as long as they would at other schools. In terms of living, housing at the U(C) is based on a house system. Think Harry Potter. Each student is placed into a house of forty to one hundred people. This forms the basis of your social community for your first year at U(C) and beyond. It can be a little overwhelming at first, but the house system really lets students make close bonds with one another early on and increases the general quality of freshman life.

I'll add that the weather here sucks. Full-blown snowy winters, then summers that are hot as hell. We all take a perverse pride in it.

The Education

The University of Chicago has an extensive, comprehensive, hardcore core curriculum. The core takes two to three years to complete for most people. I can never stress enough how important the core is—if you don't like taking classes, and working very hard, in lots of different fields, you will not like the U(C). Everything from the physical sciences to art to linguistics will be covered, and you'll be expected to produce very high quality work in each class. No slacking here. Beyond that, professors and departments at U(C) are extremely flexible and friendly. For example, this year classes in my concentration (physics) and my minor (classical Greek) took place at the same time. For the entire year, the classics department made special arrangements with my professors so that I would still be able to take all of my required courses. I met with all of my classics professors during specially scheduled, one-on-one sessions.

The Students

Like many private colleges across the nation, our student body is mostly composed of upper-middle-class white kids. I'm personally more concerned with the lack of economic diversity here than I am with the lack of racial diversity, though; the lack of racial diversity is a broader social problem, whereas the lack of economic diversity shows the school isn't doing a good job offering fair financial aid packages.

The Activities

I spent most of high school darting from activity to activity to get myself out of my house, and to stay occupied because I didn't really like my classmates. Now that I'm at U. Chicago, surrounded by people I genuinely like and respect, I don't really do the organized activity thing. I'm happy to just hang out. Anyway, there's only so many hours in a day, and it's hard to keep up with academics, friends, sleep, and activities, so for me activities was the one to go. Other people cut out other things. It's a personal choice. That said, for anything you want to do (juggling, Frisbee, mock trial, cooking, etc.), there's going to be a group here to do it with. Plus we're in Chicago. There is always something going on. Some spend a lot of time off campus, some people stay on campus. Public transportation is safe and fairly reliable, so it's easy to get downtown.

> "The library is *the* place to meet people."
> ✦ Judith, freshman

The Social Scene

On most weekends, people pick one night to go out and one night to work/sleep. On the night you go out, there are always parties to find, and we have the city at our doorstep. Additionally, the university has a very liberal alcohol policy—there's

almost never problems with the police or university official-types over that. One last thing: this is the only place I know of where the A-level (first subbasement) of the library is a major social center on campus to see and be seen. This place is as weird as monkeys on nitrous oxide.

Name: Rebecca

> "I hated high school with an abiding passion; here my school spirit is so great that I often explode with random expressions of joy."
> ✦ Adam, junior

Hometown: Boulder, Colorado
Class Year: Freshman
Major: English literature and language
Extracurriculars: I write restaurant reviews for *The Chicago Maroon* (the on-campus, student-run, biweekly newspaper), I'm on the house council for my dorm, and I'm part of the Japanese Anime Society and the Art and Drawing club.
Career Goal: A writer (journalism or fiction), or a lawyer if that doesn't work out.

How would you describe U. Chicago's reputation?

The University of Chicago is known as one of the best "nerd schools" in the country.

Is this reputation accurate?

Best "nerd school" is oversimplifying. It's more that U. Chicago students are fun, outgoing kids who love to learn and pride themselves on their intellectualism. The atmosphere is one of intense interest.

What would an admissions officer at your school probably not tell a prospective student? What aspect of your school would a prospective student not see on a campus tour?

The administration here is actually pretty frank with incoming students. Be prepared to work yourself to the bone.

The Institution

I love U. Chicago's size—about 5,000 undergraduates—which translates into small classes, amazing teachers you get to know on a personal level, and fantastic interaction with classmates. I didn't know what to expect of Chicago—I'd heard stories about the dangerous neighborhoods surrounding the school. But now I know that U. Chicago has one of the largest private university police forces in the country; it's a very secure campus. And I've come to love the city. The Chicago Transportation Authority (CTA) makes it easy to get around.

I love the dorms at U. Chicago. My dorm this year is an historic luxury hotel that's more than a bit past its prime. It's literally begun to fall apart, but there are rooms here that were once lived in by Al Capone, and Elvis used to hang out at the hotel when he was in town, which is wild. The rooms all look different. My room is a triple, with three enormous areas (living room, dining room, and bedroom), plus a private kitchen, pantry, tons of closet space, and private bathrooms. I've painted a mural on our dining room wall and I decorated a table in the dining room as well. It's real cool.

The Students

Students on the whole at U. Chicago tend to be very well read, and it's not unusual to get into a long discussion about a great book or hear about someone's exhaustive self-created summer reading list. We also love to argue—I'm pretty sure we're one of the only schools where impressive argumentation skills is a turn-on. We definitely talk about classes on Saturday nights (as we do every night). And there's not really competition between

> "Most students at U. Chicago are Midwesterners, Ivy League rejects, Ivy League rejectors, or all of the above. Few are pre-professional; many become academics."
> ✦ Adam, junior

students here as much as there is a drive to become a better, smarter individual yourself.

Classes vary between discussion and lecture, but most lectures have discussion sessions where you're free to debate at will. Professors respond to e-mails almost instantaneously, and they're highly receptive to a student's ideas and visits during office hours. I know a lot of students here who do complain about the fact that we have a rigid core curriculum, but it's let me learn so much about so many different subjects I might not have otherwise looked into. I fulfilled my biology topical course requirement by taking a class called "Plagues: Past and Present," and it was really fascinating. As an English major I would have steered clear from a class like that—and now I can quote interesting statistics about plagues. Very cool. I think this school has made me more independent and self-reliant—I now know I can negotiate living in a big city. I've also learned to think more critically, not to be intimidated by other people or their arguments.

The Activities

Loyola and Northwestern are relatively nearby, but there's not too much interaction between our campuses. U. Chicago has decent athletic teams, and everyone enjoys playing on intramural teams and using the new Ratner Athletic Center.

There's also a lot to do that's not athletic. We're close to the downtown museums and cultural centers of Chicago, and we have our own campus movie theater that plays films each night. There are also lectures all the time, especially at the Oriental Institute, which is world famous for its collections of Assyrian, Egyptian, and Middle Eastern archeological artifacts. I leave campus about once or twice a week—my roommate is Chinese and has introduced me, the naive JAP, to the wonders of Chinatown, so now I go there frequently to shop and grab dinner. Sometimes we go to comedy clubs (Second City is in Chicago).

The Social Scene

Our party scene here is mostly frat-oriented, and there's no group that is excluded from that. Apartment parties are also pretty common. If I'm still up at 3 a.m. on a weekend, I'm probably talking to friends in my dorm room. I might have spent some time at a frat house drinking a bit earlier in the night. OK, there's also the possibility that at 3 a.m. I'll be waiting for the late-night van service to take me home from the library—there, I've said it. Happy?

Name: Shelby
Hometown: Philadelphia, Pennsylvania
Class Year: Junior
Major: Law, letters, and society
Extracurriculars: University of Chicago Democrats, Kappa Alpha Theta, Chicago *Quill Magazine*

Career Goal: I want to be involved with some combination of politics, law, and writing.

How would you describe U. Chicago's reputation?

U. Chicago is way underrated by the general population. People think we're a school of huge nerds who do nothing but study.

Is this reputation accurate?

No. U. Chicago is one of the top five schools in the country. And if we are nerds, then we're the cool kind of nerds, the ones that go out and party and have fun while still being cute and smart and cool.

What would an admissions officer at your school probably not tell a prospective student?

They wouldn't mention the huge downsides of being on the quarter system—the biggest being the fact that we don't start school until October, six weeks after all of our friends have returned to college—and then all of our friends are done with college and starting summer vacation, and we still have six weeks left of spring quarter!

Is there anything about U. Chicago that's particularly unique?

My only gripe: the career office here is a bummer. It's called Career and Placement Services, but they have *no* placements. They basically tell you to use MonsterTrak or talk to your parents if you want to find a nonacademic job. That blows.

> "On the way to softball practice the other day, the entire team was blabbing about Freud and Durkheim. That's what it's like here. You're always steeped in it."
> ✦ Andrall, senior

The Institution

Students love it here from day one. I mean, U. Chicago will glide you in, they tell you that you belong, over your sophomore and junior years U. Chicago will show you how much you really do belong, and then senior year they prepare you to leave. It's all so wonderfully smooth that few people choose to "leave" academia—tons just go straight on to graduate school. U. Chicago has one of the highest rates of graduates who go on and receive more education. Everyone eventually gets a PhD.

The administration is really supportive here. There's always someone willing to listen and, if you have a problem, they'll take it as high up as it needs to go until the problem is fixed. My adviser is amazing. She knows me by name and stops me in the quad to tell me to zip my jacket when it's cold out (which it always is). She knows what classes I'm taking. It's the most supportive school. And if you decide you don't want all this support, administrators are also totally willing to back off. Just say the word.

> "U. Chicago *is* Hogwarts."
> ✦ Rebecca, sophomore

The Education

Classes are amazing. Professors, not TAs, teach classes. And the professors are leaders in their field. It's amazing to listen to your professor tell you about this new theory when you know that it's his office-mate's theory and that it's getting national attention at the moment. And these very famous academics want to teach, and want to listen to you, and want to help you learn. Learning is everyone's number-one goal here, from the undergrads to the professors themselves. There's a lot of work, but it's also the most engaging work you'll ever do. The hefty core curriculum really teaches you everything you need to know across a wide range of disciplines to become a well-educated person. Everyone will hate at least one aspect of it, but it will really turn you into a Renaissance man.

The Students

This is an amazingly diverse campus. While some people choose to self-segregate, the majority of students seek friends across racial, religious, and political lines. People are interested in everything, stubbornly committed to nothing. Frats and sororities get a bum rap—overall they really enhance the quality of social life on campus. U. of Chicago students give each other permission to be themselves. People are friendly. *No one is mean.* It's amazing. They let you do whatever it is you do, in peace. It's real nice.

The Activities

On a sunny afternoon—a rare treat in Chicago—people swarm all over the quad. Khaki-shorted boys playing Frisbee, polo-shirted frat boys barbequing on their house porches and drinking beer, girls in flirty skirts with painfully pale legs desperately trying to tan, book discussion groups, impromptu picnics, lots of kids stretched out under trees studying, and every variety of human possible having a good time. And even in bad weather, there's never a day where something isn't going on. Huge philanthrophic events, movie screenings, club sports tournaments, debates. Everything.

The Social Scene

There's always a party if you want one. The Greek scene on campus is starting to grow; it's actually a really open and inclusive community. A lot of underclassmen party on Wednesdays because one of the frats runs a Bar Night then. People of legal drinking age or with a good enough fake ID head toward the Pub or the Woodlaw Top on Thursdays. People party in downtown Chicago on Fridays and Saturdays.

There's not really casual dating. You either go on one date and call it quits, or you stay together for months and months. End of story.

Notable U. Chicago Alumni Include:
Saul Bellow, author
Seymour Hersh, journalist
Susan Sontag, critic
Philip Roth, author
Studs Terkel, author
Mike Nichols, film director, producer, actor

CLAREMONT MCKENNA COLLEGE

Founded: 1946

Location: Claremont, CA

Phone: (909) 621-8088

E-mail: admission@claremontmckenna.edu

Web site: www.claremontmckenna.edu

Number of Undergraduates: 1,027

Number of Graduate Students: 0

Cost: Approximately $37,000 per year

Application Deadline: January 2

Early Decision: November 15

Rating:	Notable Majors/Programs:
Most Selective	Economics, Political Science, Psychology, Joint Sciences

Size:
● Small ○ Medium ○ Large

Location:
○ Urban ● Suburban ○ Rural

On a Saturday, students talk about academics:
● Always ○ Sometimes ○ Never

Nightlife:
○ Intense ● Moderate ○ Laid-back

Politically, Claremont McKenna leans:
○ Left ○ Right ● Split

Diversity:
○ High ○ Low ● Medium

Five-College School: Yes!

Students describe Claremont McKenna in five words:
- Prestigious school for ambitious overachievers
- Small, preppy, political, driven, wealthy

From the School

[Claremont McKenna] pursues its mission by providing a liberal arts education that emphasizes economics and political science, a professoriat that is dedicated to effective undergraduate teaching, a close student-teacher relationship that fosters critical inquiry, an active residential and intellectual environment that promotes responsible citizenship, and a program of research institutes and scholarly support that makes possible a faculty of teacher-scholars.

—www.claremontmckenna.edu

If you're interested in CMC, you may also be interested in:
UC Berkeley, U. Chicago, Georgetown, Harvard, Pomona, Stanford

Name: Katherine

Hometown: Jackson Hole, Wyoming

Class Year: Sophomore

Major: Psychology, Sequence in Women and Gender Studies

Extracurriculars: Admissions Recruitment Committee (VSAC), Associated Students of Claremont McKenna College (Student Government), sponsor (freshman orientation), psychology research assistant

Career Goal: Lawyer

How would you describe CMC's reputation?

CMC is said to be a competitive, small liberal arts college on the West Coast, with a 90 percent acceptance rate to med schools, a similar acceptance rate to law schools, and graduates taking prominent roles in investment banking firms, politics, and government organizations. On the downside, CMC is said to be a bit of an old boys' club, a conservative school for the very wealthy.

Is this reputation accurate?

There's no question that CMC is a fantastic school, and our graduates do disproportionately well getting into the top law and med schools in America. As for our conservative reputation—I think that comes from the fact that some of our more famous departments are pretty conservative (economics and government) and that CMC *was* one of the last schools in America to go coed. Our student body is actually split sixty-forty, with 60 percent being liberal. That said, the conservatives are definitely loud and proud. CMC encourages debate by bringing in lecturers from both sides of the divide.

What aspect of your school would a prospective student not see on a campus tour?

I don't think you'd see how awesome CMC students are—everyone is down to earth and so driven—it makes a huge difference that everyone wants to succeed, but no one wants to do so at the expense of anyone else. This is a place where everyone will talk to you, tell you their dreams, listen to yours, and then immediately start brainstorming ways you can work together.

The Institution

There are about a thousand students at CMC, roughly two hundred fifty new students enter each year. This school is *small*. That said, CMC is in the Five College Consortium [the 5Cs] with Harvey Mudd, Pitzer, Pomona, and Scripps right next door. So all told, there are nearly ten thousand college students within a twenty-minute walk. And on weekends there are frequent "all college parties," with many members of each college in attendance.

This means CMC students get the best of all possible worlds: tiny classes at CMC, big time social life thanks to the 5Cs. Students at any of the 5Cs can also take classes at the other 5Cs, benefiting from each school's resources. Everyone knows CMC specializes in econ, government, and international relations. Interested in science and engineering, too? Take a few classes at Harvey Mudd. Like social and behavioral sciences? Try a class at Pitzer. Natural science or the humanities? Try Pomona. Want an all-girls liberal arts environment? Give Scripps a whirl.

Of all the schools in the 5Cs, CMC is the second most prestigious. (We're ranked one of the top fifteen liberal arts schools in the nation. Only Pomona is ranked higher.) Luckily, though, the prestige doesn't go to our heads. Students are down to earth, they know that life is about how hard you work and what you accomplish, not a name or a number. Also, CMC is in Southern California. It's 90 degrees in January. (Need I say more?) We have a tradition of "Ponding" on birthdays. Here's how it works: as a Southern California school, CMC has several fountains. Without fail, on every student's birthday, their friends will pick them up (no matter how hard they struggle) and that student will end up in a fountain, "ponded," ready to begin their next year of life. Some of our more philosophical students see plenty of symbolism in this, but for most it's just good fun.

On a more important note, for a relatively young school, our Career Services is fantastic. They'll bend over backward to get you a job when your time here is done. I have professors who have written dozens of letters of recommendation for me, and will gladly write more. Really, a lot of schools teach you literary theory, then leave you empty-handed once it's time to get a real job. That's not the case at CMC.

The Education

Because CMC is so small, you can never slack off in classes. Professors notice when you're not speaking up, and they'll call on you twice as much.

And even if you are speaking up, professors expect a very high level of discourse—get ready to defend your opinions, in depth, on a daily basis. This is great as it forces everyone to develop their ideas to a remarkable extent, in a way they wouldn't have to in a 300-plus person lecture class. Does this shock you? Do you want to be able to miss class and not have professors notice? Do you want your ideas to go unchallenged? If so, CMC is *not* for you. On the other hand, if you love to think deeply, want small classes with no TAs, want to learn under professors with advanced degrees who are considered experts in their fields, then this is the place for you. Really, it's not unusual to read an article in a major newspaper, look at the byline, and see that it's been written by one of your professors or turn on the television and see your professors featured as commentators on major network news reports.

One potential downside to our amazing education is that it's an amazingly *structured* education. CMC has a very big core curriculum, put in place to ensure all students graduate with a broad body of knowledge. You need three classes in science and math, three classes in foreign language, literary analysis and civilization, two classes in humanities, three courses in social sciences, and three semesters of physical education. This is all before you start tackling the requirements within your major. It can be annoying at times. Personally, I despise the fact that I'm memorizing useless equations and definitions to fulfill my science requirements. On the plus side, I'll know things I wouldn't otherwise.

Broadly speaking, the strongest departments at CMC are economics, accounting, government, psychology, and joint sciences. If you want to study abroad, just think of a country. Guaranteed, CMC sends students there. And as for the most interesting class I've taken, it's Pitney's Congress class, hands down. We created a mock-Congress: CMC students were on one side of the aisle, Pomona students were the other side, and Pitzer students played the administration. Each side had a handful of bills to pass, and everyone had to work together, make deals, compromises, etc., entirely in character. (If we ever broke character, our grades suffered.) It was such a great class, everyone had to think really hard, and we learned an amazing amount about how bills are actually passed. Lastly, every student at CMC has to write a thesis in order to graduate, and when theses are due you can feel the tension in the air. When the theses are handed in, the entire school lets out a deep sigh of relief and parties.

The Students

CMC students are really political, and we keep up with the news. Most students receive the *New York Times* and the *Washington Post* in their inboxes every morning. CMC students are also *massive* sports fans, so whenever a big game is on, there will be a "screening" that someone sets up— one year we put a projector and a big screen in North Quad so we could all watch the Super Bowl together. CMC does all it can to foster this closeness. Last year, over spring break, the school sponsored a trip to France for every student in the French Department. This past summer a group of students went to China on CMC's dollar. One downside of CMC is that it lacks diversity. Most students are white. This is something the school is working on, but my friends who are minorities definitely say this place is lacking in that respect, and they're disappointed with CMC's efforts thus far to change things.

The Activities

The most popular groups on campus are the Women's Forum, the Chocolate Club, our community service organizations (too many to list), Students for Peace and Justice, Young Republicans, Young Democrats, Under the Lights (theater group), and several a cappella groups. Our on-campus magazines—*The Portside* (liberal), the *Claremont Independent* (conservative), and our multiple literary magazines are also popular.

The Social Scene

Thursday, Friday, Saturday nights are when CMC students go out and have fun. There are always school-sponsored events to go to, dorm parties, club parties, parties in students' rooms, or you can go to the other 5C campuses and see what's going on there. Most students drink—alcohol is plentiful—and we have no frats or sororities because we don't need them. There are plenty of options available as-is. Ninety-six percent of our student body lives on campus all four years, both because housing off campus is super-expensive and because there's so much going on that you wouldn't want to miss anything.

Name: Peter
Hometown: Bremerton, Washington
Class Year: Senior
Major: History
Extracurriculars: Campus paper, honor society
Career Goal: High school teacher

How would you describe CMC's reputation?

CMC is known for being conservative and sports-obsessed. And for throwing really good parties.

Is this reputation accurate?

The political orientation of CMC's student body is fairly similar to that of the nation—almost an even split between the two major parties. However, since students across America tend to be liberal, any campus that has an even split of liberals and conservatives is singled out as an anomaly, and the entire campus is thereafter referred to as conservative. In terms of sports, our reputation is accurate. I read somewhere that one third of CMC students participate in a varsity sport. Add in intramural sports and a good 50 percent of our student body considers themselves to be athletic, if not an athlete. And most colleges throw good parties. That we do, too, shouldn't be a huge surprise.

What would an admissions officer at your school probably not tell a prospective student?

In hindsight, the admissions staff didn't really hammer home just how many general education (GE) requirements we have here. Between completing your major, your sequence (essentially your minor), and your GEs, you're not going to find time to take many electives, and if you change your major even once you probably won't be able to take any.

The Institution

I chose Claremont McKenna because of its location, its small size, and the strength of its academics. I'm incredibly happy with my decision.

There are three distinctly different housing areas on campus that you should know about: there's the North Quad, the Mid Quad, and the South Quad. Each quad offers something a little different in terms of environment, atmosphere, and social scene. North Quad is known as the "party quad" and is primarily sophomores and juniors. It's set up in suites (four double rooms that share a common bathroom), and people in North Quad tend

to spend a lot of money on stereo equipment, and whenever I'm walking past at 2 a.m., I can hear Nelly at full volume, blasting from multiple rooms. Mid Quad is the closest to a "typical dorm." There's a central hallway leading to a communal bathroom, there are students from every class year, and there's a pretty strong sense of community. These dorms tend to be really close-knit, and they're notably quieter than North Quad. Then there's South Quad, which is the newest set of dorms, and, as such, has less personality. South Quad has three towers that have four double rooms and four single rooms on each floor. Everyone shares a common lounge and a common bathroom.

> **How each character in "Scooby Doo" is representative of a Claremont College:**
> "*Pomona* is 'Scooby Doo,' because Scooby Doo holds the gang together, and as the oldest college, Pomona holds Consortium together—without it, the other schools never would have been created. *Harvey Mudd* is 'Velma,' the intelligent one who's always focused on finding mathematical and scientific solutions. *Claremont McKenna* is 'Fred,' the leader of the gang, the hero, the one other people turn to for solid guidance. *Scripps* is 'Daphne,' the strong, sharp woman with a strong, sharp mind. And *Pitzer* is 'Shaggy,' the one who's the most fun, who's always coming up with creative solutions to problems, and the one who always has Scooby snacks to keep everybody happy!"
>
> ✦ Coby, senior

The Education

The professors at CMC are amazing—always available to talk about a paper, give advice on a project, or just chat. Some professors even have their classes over to their homes for dinner. After being at CMC for a while, I take for granted the ability to be so close with my professors. I have some high school friends who went to larger schools, and some of them said they'd never even *seen* their professors outside of class, and if they did see them, the professor probably wouldn't know their names. Not only do all of my professors know my name, most know the other classes I've taken leading up to theirs, the classes I'm planning on taking after theirs to enhance my grasp of the subject, and some even know my dorm and the names of some of my friends.

And CMC students are great about helping one another. I came from a really competitive high school, where everyone backstabbed one another and it couldn't be more different here. If you're struggling, and have friends in the same class, they'll gladly sit down with you and help out.

The Students

I'd say most students at CMC are from the West Coast, with California, Washington, and Oregon being the top three home states. New York, Texas, and Massachussetts are also heavily represented. The great thing about CMC is that it's a small school with the resources of a big one, thanks to the other consortium schools. Joining a club at other schools is also a great way to meet other people, and most have friends and/or boyfriends/girlfriends elsewhere in the 5Cs.

The Activities

Southern California is the place to be, and the great weather makes this campus lots of fun because everyone is always outside playing Frisbee, bronzing, studying. Sometimes we'll even break out the Slip 'n Slide in the middle of the afternoon. You just can't help yourself. One major downer, however, is that there isn't a lot to do in the Claremont area (outside of the colleges), so having a car is a good thing. CMC is just outside L.A., so if you have a car you can go to restaurants and clubs and bars. The beach is also only a forty-five-minute drive, and you can be in Las Vegas within three hours. But even without a car CMC provides lots of opportunities for students to get off campus should claustrophobia hit—the school offers funds to go to Six Flags, sporting events (L.A. Dodgers games), and paintball games.

The Social Scene

Usually there is one major 5C (Five College) Party each weekend. Then, every college has one or two *giant* parties that it throws every year and that everyone comes to. (At CMC ours is called Monte Carlo.) The nearby towns aren't really big on providing events for under-twenty-ones, so most CMC students party on our campus or on one of the neighboring campuses. There are also lots of concerts, fund-raisers, open-mike poetry events, that sort of thing, so you'll never be bored. On a sunny day, if you saw five groups of people outside, they'd be 1) students in their bathing suits heading over to the Scripps pool; 2) athletes playing Frisbee-golf; 3) sunbathers; 4) buff football players with a Slip 'n Slide; or 5) students sitting outside reading on benches all around campus.

Name: Andrew
Hometown: Denver, Colorado
Class Year: Freshman
Major: PPE [politics, philosophy and economics] and government
Extracurriculars: Competitive debater on the Claremont Colleges Debate Union, Claremont McKenna representative of the Claremont Colleges, writer for the *Claremont Political Journal,* research assistant for the Rose Institute of State and Local Government
Career Goal: I might eventually run for elected office in the state of Colorado.

How would you describe CMC's reputation?

Firstly, people say everyone here is a preprofessional. Second, they see our school is all-white, all Republican, and all conservative. I've heard we hinge on being racist. And lastly, that students here will do *anything* to get ahead, and if you don't watch your back, someone will destroy your notes, and your grades will plummet.

Is this reputation accurate?

We *are* overwhelmingly preprofessional. But most CMC kids double major; we like to combine the artsy with the practical. As for us being all-white, all Republican, and all conservative, this has some merit, but not an overwhelming amount. The five colleges collectively have the largest Young Democrats Association in the state of California. So our conservative tendencies are nicely counterbalanced. The racist claim is pure bunk—we are *not* a racist institution—that sort of thing has no place here. Finally, the idea that this place is really competitive is a complete lie. We are *so* not competitive.

What would an admissions officer at your school probably not tell a prospective student?

You might not see the smog from Los Angeles that will drift to the Claremont area and block out the sun. Nor the large amounts of free beer that the school pays for. (Each dorm gets a set of funds for parties, T-shirts, etc., and the dorms can use those funds however they see fit. Most use it for beer.) Also on a campus tour students wouldn't see the amazing pool we share with the 5Cs that is a favorite hangout. At night students sneak into the pool and go skinny-dipping. Yeah nakedness!

The Institution

At CMC, our motto is "crescit cum commercio civitias," which means "with commerce prospers civilization." Accordingly, this is a place for students who want to get out into the world and accomplish big things. A lot of us major in government. Personally, I'm majoring in PPE (philosophy, politics, and economics), which allows me to analyze events from a variety of contexts. Our economics department, and science and math departments, are also some of the best in the country. That makes studying here exciting, but also daunting. We always want to make sure we measure up!

CMC has great academic advising. A lot of other schools have advising systems set up, but they don't flesh out the program and the advisers wind up being clueless and ineffective. In contrast my academic adviser is the head of The Center for the Study of the Holocaust, Genocide, and Human Rights. When I was selecting courses first semester, he sat down with me and said, "I would try this course, because I've read some of your papers and I think you'll really benefit from the way this Professor Daniels makes students write." Second semester, he was saying, "I noticed you really enjoyed your course on political economy. Professor Schwartz, a friend of mine, teachers courses that I think you'd also really enjoy that naturally follow from political economy . . ." In short, your advisers are incredibly helpful, and get to know you on an extremely personal level.

Also amazing is that CMC has a cleaning service, where every weekend someone comes into every student's dorm room, *cleans* their dorm room, and vacuums. That's right. You can leave crap anywhere you want and someone else will bend over to pick it up! Every student really appreciates this service, because without it our lives would be much dirtier and we'd have less time to concentrate on the important things.

CMC is also amazing about bringing fantastic speakers to campus, and then—because our school is small enough—letting students spend real quality time with these celebrities. I've had *dinner* with Tony Kushner, Janet Reno, and Archbishop Desmond Tutu. I got to talk to Tony Kushner about what it was like to grow up gay in the South. Janet Reno and I spoke about the time she appeared on *Saturday Night Live,* and how Will Ferrell was really embarrassed to meet her.

The Education

As to the academic character of CMC, this place is challenging. It's not so much that we're loaded down with work as it is that very high quality work is expected of us, and it takes a very long time to deliver something that your professors will be satisfied with. But professors tend to reward our hard work with great teaching and sometimes quirky (but always interesting) methods; for example, there's one professor here who's known for using old 1950s movies to prove points about calculus.

> "Modeled after the literary and scientific dining clubs of nineteenth-century London, the Athenaeum—15,000-square-foot facility equipped with a living room, a library, and two dining rooms, where meals and conversation could occur—was developed to promote intellectual and social exchange between students, faculty, and visiting luminaries, in an intimate and relaxed setting."
>
> —www.claremontmckenna.edu

The Students

There's a good political mix here: Republicans, Democrats, Greens, and Independents. This allows for some good debates, and people legitimately listen and argue and counterargue in a productive manner, instead of shrill partisan screeching. Because our campus is so political, students feel the need to also be politically aware. Most pay attention to the news, and most read publications like *The Economist,* or any one of the big three: *US News, Time,* or *Newsweek.*

The Activities

A lot of CMC students do research; for example, I work at the Rose Institute for State and Local Government as a research assistant. It is a great job, and seven CMC kids get to do it each year. Together we work with cities in Southern California and California State to conduct oversight, fiscal analysis, polling analysis, and demographic research. CMC encourages this sort of thing. Often, if you get a research position but it doesn't pay, CMC will pitch in and give you money. CMC is giving me $3,000 to campaign on a tight senate race in Colorado.

The Social Scene

I am really enjoying myself here. Between hanging out with my friends at CMC, hanging out with my friends from Pomona and Scripps and Harvey Mudd and Pitzer, heading into LA for parties, and being active in campus groups, every minute of my social life is accounted for. Also CMC pays for students to get involved in a lot of the nearby cultural life, so I've been able to take advantage of genteel culture like operas, plays, and fancy dinners.

Notable CMC Alumni Include:
Mike Jeffries, CEO, Abercrombie and Fitch
Thomas Pritzker, chairman, Hyatt Corporation
Dean Taylor, former general manager, Milwaukee
    Brewers
Robert Lowe, chairman and CEO, Lowe Enterprises
Ray Drummond, jazz bassist
Laura Angelica Simon, documentary film producer

COLBY COLLEGE

Founded: 1813
Location: Waterville, ME
Phone: (207) 872-3168
E-mail: admissions@colby.edu
Web site: www.colby.edu

Number of Undergraduates: 1,830
Number of Graduate Students: 0
Cost: Approximately $32,000 per year
Application Deadline: January 1
Early Decision: November 15

Rating:	Notable Majors/Programs:
Very Selective	Biology, English, Economics

Size:
● Small ○ Medium ○ Large

Location:
○ Urban ● Suburban ○ Rural

On a Saturday, students talk about academics:
○ Always ● Sometimes ○ Never

Nightlife:
○ Intense ● Moderate ○ Laid-back

Politically, Colby leans:
○ Left ○ Right ● Split

Diversity:
○ High ● Low ○ Medium

Students describe Colby in five words:
- Beautiful, cold, secluded, small, close-knit
- Intellectual, hard working, hard drinking

From the School
Colby is a community, and like a city or town it has a governance structure, traditions, communal events, focused interest groups, a wide range of social events, arts and performances, and college teams to play on or to cheer for. Organized around learning and intellectual pursuits, it is a special type of community that stresses discussions, lectures, research, and discovery.

—www.colby.edu

If you're interested in Colby, you may also be interested in:
Bowdoin, Claremont McKenna, Colgate, Dartmouth, Tufts, Williams

Name: Nicole
Hometown: Dublin, Ohio
Class Year: Freshman
Major: Spanish, psychology and creative writing double minor
Extracurriculars: Broadway Musical Review, Colby Dancers, ballroom social dance, Colby Cares About Kids
Career Goal: Undecided. I could teach, become a psychologist, or a translator.

How would you describe Colby's reputation?

Colby is said to be a small, isolated school with very strong academics and a very strong feeling of community.

Is this reputation accurate?

All of that is very accurate. Colby has a fantastic academic program taught by professors who are 100 percent committed to teaching, but who also have a great deal of experience in their fields. Because of its size, it also has a very tight community between students and between students and professors. (I once had a professor host a late-night showing of *The Matrix* in his house, complete with donuts and apple cider, after which we discussed the influence of Descartes on the Wachowski brothers!)

What aspect of your school would a prospective student not see on a campus tour?

There is a large drinking scene at Colby, which I know tour guides don't mention. A lot of people like that aspect of the school. Personally, I don't drink. And I've found that to be okay. I am still invited to parties and I just play Flip Cup and Beirut with water or soda and I don't feel as though I'm looked down upon for not drinking or anything.

The Institution

I looked at twenty-six schools and chose Colby because it struck me as an amazing little community of student-scholars. Colby was the first college I took a tour of, and something clicked. Yeah, Colby's academics are strong, but it was the people I met that made all the difference for me.

Most people here are really respectful of the environment that they are living in and want to maintain it as best they can. Students are also cognizant of the fact that there are a group of very nice, hardworking people responsible for cleaning up after us, and we want to make their lives as easy as possible.

The weather in Maine is harsh: be prepared with layers. I know many people from Florida, California, Fiji, and the Phillippines who have had a rough time, but ultimately survived, and are stronger and better for it. Also be forewarned, the food at Colby is actually so good we gain the freshman thirty! Fortunately, Colby has the largest weight room in the NESCAC [New England Small College Athletic Conference], so there are plenty of opportunities for you to work off those extra pounds.

Lastly, we operate on a 4-1-4 schedule, which means we take four classes in the fall, one class in January, and then four classes in the spring. After freshman year, you can take special one-month internships instead of a class in January. And study abroad is huge at Colby. Two-thirds of all students study abroad at some point in their college careers.

> "Colby has what we call the 'Jan Plan,' a January term where students take one class for the month. You can also use this term to go on a school trip or do an internship. Most students love the chance to narrow their focus for a full thirty days."
> ✦ Deborah, junior

The Education

One of the beautiful aspects of a liberal arts education is that it allows students to pursue the things they know they're interested in, while simultaneously exposing them to new ideas, and subsequently sparking new interests; for example, I'm a pretty hard-core humanities student, but I took a geology course at Colby, and now I can honestly say geology rocks! (pun intended). Maybe now I'll do something having to do with geology one day.

Colby students are a fairly intellectual bunch. Most Colby students read lots, like to talk about what they read, and aren't afraid to come off as dorks. And our professors encourage us to have these discussions as much as possible. Honestly, our professors are very involved—and they do their own research, too—in short, they're superstars. Colby students also do their fair share of fitting it all in. Students on the whole are dedicated to their work, and it is not uncommon or looked down upon for a student to stay in on a Friday or Saturday night to catch up on their academics.

Colby also has a weird core. Courses are divided into six areas. You have to take one course in area I (the arts), one course in area II (historical studies), one course in area III (literature), one course in area IV (quantitative reasoning), two courses in area V (the natural sciences), and one course in area VI (the social sciences). Students also have to take one course on the "issue of diversity" and participate in Colby's Wellness program.

The Students

Students at Colby work together to learn as much as they can and do as well as they can. Study groups are common, books are returned as soon as people are done with them, and the idea that someone would pull a fire alarm in the middle of the night before a big exam (so everyone else would be sleep deprived and do poorly)—which does happen at some schools—is laughable. Also kids come to Colby from all over the world. My freshman year hallmates were from China, Germany, Malaysia, California, Alaska, anywhere you could dream of.

The Activities

Colby's orientation is called COOT, and 99 percent of all first-years participate. My COOT days were among the best of my entire life. Seriously. I went on a theater COOT, where we played improvisation games, sat by a lake and swam, and made friendship bracelets. Other COOT programs include fly-fishing, trail biking, mountain hiking, and civil service. It's a great way to meet people, and makes getting used to college life far less painful. When we're not studying or partying, my friends and I play Frisbee or hackey sack, surf the Internet, play board games, have dance parties, and watch movies.

The Social Scene

People on campus party a lot, and with varying levels of intensity. Some, on the weekends, will break out the beer funnels, other will simply get together with their friends and watch *Newsies*. If you're a big partier, there are big events that go on every weekend. You can just show up, with or without your friends—chances are, you'll know people there. Take note, though, there is no fraternity or sorority scene at Colby. Parties are all thrown by students and student groups, and everyone is welcome. Students of all grades, and all genders, freely party with one another. Lastly, as far as the dating scene goes, it's not too bad.

Name: Andrew
Hometown: Richmond, California
Class Year: Freshman
Major: Government and philosophy
Extracurriculars: Intramurals, Outing Club, admissions volunteer
Career Goal: I want to do something that makes me happy (I don't care that much about money).

How would you describe Colby's reputation?

In the Northeast, Colby is very well known as a fine institution with strong academics. It's also viewed as a "party hard, work hard" type of place, with a lot of rich students who feel, amongst themselves, a strong sense of community.

Is this reputation accurate?

Academically, I'd say Colby is even stronger than people realize. I expected this place to be less challenging than it actually is. To balance off all this challenging work, yes, Colby students party hard. We drink a lot (everyone told me coming in that there wasn't much to do in Waterville, Maine, besides drink—and they were right). The rich kid thing is somewhat accurate—there are plenty of wealthy students—but also [many] who are less well off. And the community thing is definitely right on—most people feel very at home and absolutely love it here.

> "For a small college, Colby has great school spirit. Games like football and hockey really bring out the best in us."
> ✦ Sam, senior

What would an admissions officer at your school probably not tell a prospective student?

Recently, [the administration] has begun cracking down on drinking and partying. A few years back security would never break up parties, and open-container violations were nonexistent. Now you pretty much can't have a party of any notable size on campus without security shutting it down. This has forced all the big parties off campus, which goes against Colby's philosophy of keeping everything in one focused place. Admissions officers talk all about how everyone lives and learns and has fun right on campus at Colby. This just isn't true anymore—those who look to have fun now have to drive ten to fifteen minutes to escape security's overly watchful eye. It also makes students distrust security, which slightly hurts the whole "community feel."

The Institution

Colby is on a beautiful campus in the woods, a short drive from the small town of Waterville, Maine. Nearly every building on campus is red brick and looks like it was built two hundred years ago, despite the fact that the school was actually moved in the forties and every building is pretty modern. We have trees everywhere (which don't have leaves most of the year) and a beautiful pond behind a couple of the dorms that freezes and you can skate or play hockey on it in the winter. You can walk anywhere in ten minutes. I chose to come to Colby because I visited and it instantly felt right. For whatever reason Colby struck me as quintessentially college—it's like a movie set of a college. However, this movie isn't totally perfect—I do wish our school was a bit bigger at times. Most people you see, you know something about. And most people know things about you. I guess you just have to learn to embrace the gossip and drama and move on, since there's no way to avoid it.

Most schools house students by their class year. At Colby, every dorm has students from all four grades living together. This makes it really easy to become friends with people outside of your class. It also makes it easier to settle in to Colby because you always have someone more experienced than you around to talk to about what classes to take or how to best deal with the administration. And Colby dining halls serve some of the best college food in the country. Friends from other schools have looked at the menu online and been utterly blown away.

The Education

Because Colby feels like such a community, competition between students is nonexistent. Everyone wants to get good grades, but students also want to work together and try to help each other out. The professors are awesome here; because we have such small classes you really get to know them, and each one I've had so far has been very willing to meet with me outside of class. It's part of the culture of going to such a small liberal arts school.

The best class I've taken so far was actually two classes that you have to take simultaneously ("a cluster") run by the integrated studies program.

The first was Philosophy of the First Half of the 20th Century, and the second was English Literature of the First Half of the 20th Century. Only eleven kids signed up (the maximum enrollment for any integrated studies cluster is sixteen), and I ended up getting to know my classmates and each of the two teachers extremely well. Professors generally get into the whole cluster idea; they each come to the other professor's section and participate in the discussions so students can more easily make connections between the classes.

> "Colby is relatively near our rival schools, Bowdoin and Bates. Most students have siblings or friends at one of these schools, so there's a lot of interaction and friendly competition between us."
> ✦ Lisa, sophomore

The Students

So Colby is white. Very white. Coming from the San Francisco Bay area, it's pretty weird to be somewhere where there's no real racial diversity. That having been said, there are still lots of (predominantly white) kids from different geographical areas and different monetary backgrounds. Yes, we have rich eastern prep school kids, but we're not as bad as schools like Hamilton and Colgate (from what I've heard), in that we also have not-so-rich kids from Minnesota, Wisconsin, Texas, etc. Colby is also pretty damn liberal, but nothing compared to some places; Republicans actually do exist here! I'd say most Colby students are not pre-professionally oriented. In a nutshell, the average student is probably a reasonably well off white kid from twenty minutes outside Boston. They would be smart but not genius level, they would work hard during the week but drink like a fish during the weekend. They would be athletic and enjoy hiking and the outdoors and skiing, and they would be tough enough not to bitch about how cold it is in Maine. They would be reasonably liberal but not believe in anything enough to really fight for it (a lot of apathy here). And in the end, they would be damn proud to be a Colby Mule.

The Activities

Because Colby is so athletic, the Outing Club is the biggest group on campus; it has something like three hundred members. A cappella groups are also pretty big; I think there are ten different ones that you can join. The school's biggest events are dances and hockey games. (And off-campus parties draw two hundred or three hundred students most weekend nights.) We also have good speakers (Cornel West and Sherman Alexie come to mind) that draw a few hundred students to their lectures. Generally, Colby does a good job of bringing in interesting lecturers, particularly considering we're located in the middle of Maine.

If it's 3 a.m. on a typical Wednesday night, I'm still awake and hanging out with a few of my friends—we're probably plotting something ridiculous, like a way to unhinge and steal a friend's dorm room door from the door frame while they're sleeping. Or we're having a philosophical discussion, debating the concept of free will versus the concept of biblical predetermination. Or I'm working on a paper that's due in the morning, and I'm cursing the fact that I won't get any sleep that night.

> "Most of my professors will do anything they can to captivate students. I had one teacher jump up and down on a desk, and another spontaneously threw his wedding ring in the trash can, just to emphasize a point."
> ✦ Stephanie, freshman

The Social Scene

I'd say about half of Colby goes out every Friday and Saturday night, a third of Colby goes out every Thursday, Friday, and Saturday night, and a tenth of Colby will tell you how they and their friends decided to get drunk on a Tuesday for no particular reason. Though during the Jan Plan month, all bets are off—parties can happen, and will happen (and you will go to them), every day of the week. The main thing to do here is drink: drink to the hard work, drink to the administration telling you not to drink, drink to the winters, drink to the quintessential small college experience . . . drink to Colby.

I met most of my friends at Colby through my dorm; when it's the middle of December, and it's minus fifteen degrees outside, you suddenly find yourself compelled to become best friends with your neighbors so you don't have to step outside to have fun. Because of this, dorm life becomes awesome—everyone is your buddy, and there are always people hanging out in the dorm lounges pretending to do work but really just hoping one of their friends will come by and distract them.

Again, Colby is a small, somewhat isolated school. A prospective student should be absolutely sure they want to go to a small school if they come here. The few kids I know who want to transfer like Colby, but just can't deal with its size and location.

Name: Caroline
Hometown: Brattleboro, Vermont
Class Year: Junior
Major: Geology
Extracurriculars: Varsity women's ice hockey, work at the athletic center, TA for intro geology class
Career Goal: My ultimate goal is to become a hockey coach at the collegiate level.

How would you describe Colby's reputation?

Colby has a reputation for being full of rich kids who (for some reason) don't particularly mind being stuck out in the cold for four years.

Is this reputation accurate?

Yup. At Colby you'll see lots of brand-new SUVs. You'll also see hippies who despise SUVs and wealth, but most of them are equally rich or richer than the SUV kids. And as for the cold thing, Colby is in Maine, so the weather clearly sucks 90 percent of the time. But alcohol can warm the soul . . .

What aspect of your school would a prospective student not see on a campus tour?

A prospective student would see our amazingly beautiful campus, our friendly students, and our genuinely warm atmosphere. They wouldn't see the rabid fights between the administration and the students or the ways in which our president is trying to minimize the importance of athletics here. They also wouldn't see our hard-core party scene. If you don't like to drink, or aren't able to tolerate drunken people every weekend, don't bother with Colby. You just aren't tough enough. Maybe you should look into a wimpier school, like Bowdoin.

The Institution

"Prestige" is not just a word at Colby College, it's a way of life. Drive the right car, wear the right clothes, play the right sports, know the right people. We have an amazingly beautiful school, and we are provided with some of the best, if not the best, amenities available. During the week students work their butts off, and then the weekend comes around and they do some well-deserved partying.

The Education

I'm not exactly what one would call a scholar. I'd rather play sports than go to class. With this in mind, consider the fact that I have professors at Colby who make me enjoy the time I spend with them, and appreciate the words coming out of their mouths. Professors here do their best to be funny, and are easy to relate to. They're in touch with their students, and they understand how we operate. That makes the process of learning so much easier, so much better. Of course there are the exceptions—the professors who were obviously the geeks that got picked on in high school, and are now trying to alleviate their pain by assigning torturous amounts of homework and reading. But you figure out who to stay away from pretty quickly. And, again, the good profs really like to teach. They want you to walk away from their class having learnt something new, something that you will remember. We have small classes, we know our professors and call them by their first names, and they know our first names, too.

The Students

I'm an athlete. That's what most people see me as at Colby. I eat at a specific dining hall, sit in a specific area, and eat with specific kids. People probably think I'm really dumb too, get only Ds and Cs (which is far from true). In the dining halls I'll see tables of other jocks, tables of preppy girls, tables of geeks, and tables of hippies. Let's face it, there are groups at Colby, and most kids, for better or worse, fit into one group or another. In the end, the majority (I'm talking 95 percent) of students are still very happy here.

The Activities

If it's a sunny, warm day outside (hallelujah!), you'll see the jocks playing Wiffle ball or campus golf (most of them play a varsity sport but are in their off season). They've probably already been to the gym that day, or are planning on going shortly. The preppy girls will be delicately sitting or lying on the grass, showing off their new Lilly Pulitzer dress, or decked out in a skirt, a Ralph Lauren polo and their designer sandals. They are most likely checking out the jocks or gossiping about the latest hookups in their group. They've already gone to the gym to work out on the StairMaster for an hour, or else they're so thin they couldn't work out because they'd run the risk of disappearing entirely. The geeks are, well, being geeks. These kids are huddled around one another frantically doing their homework, most likely physics or differential equations math. This group will probably be the most diverse—racially, socioeconomically, and in their appearance. The last group, the hippies, will probably be dirty, playing Frisbee, prancing around happily and enjoying themselves. Some of them might mix with the jocks, but all of them will steer clear of the preppy girls. These kids will rarely, if ever, visit the gym. If they do go, they go to use the climbing wall in preparation for their trip to the third world where they might need to scale a mountain to deliver food to a starving child.

> "You really have to have a sense of humor to deal with Maine winters, because they're ridiculous."
>
> ✦ Jared, junior

The Social Scene

The Colby social scene is pretty much whatever you make of it; some people choose not to drink, and some people drink Wednesday night through Saturday. There are those who leave campus twice a year, and those who go away every weekend on an adventure to the coast or home or to Canada. Athletes tend to stay on campus during the weekend, because that's when sports events take place, and most Saturday afternoons you'll find hundreds of students screaming and shouting to support the Mules when they're playing against a competitor team.

Notable Colby Alumni Include:
E. Annie Proulx, author
Doris Kearns Goodwin, historian
Robert Capers, journalist
Robert B. Parker, author
Benjamin Butler, politician
Stuart Rothenberg, political analyst

COLGATE UNIVERSITY

Founded: 1819

Location: Hamilton, NY

Phone: (315) 228-7401

E-mail: admission@mail.colgate.edu

Web site: www.colgate.edu

Number of Undergraduates: 2,827

Number of Graduate Students: 5

Cost: Approximately $37,000 per year

Application Deadline: January 15

Early Decision: November 15

Rating:	Notable Majors/Programs:
Most Selective	Political Science, Economics, English, History

Size:
○ Small   ● Medium   ○ Large

Location:
○ Urban   ○ Suburban   ● Rural

On a Saturday, students talk about academics:
○ Always   ● Sometimes   ○ Never

Nightlife:
● Intense   ○ Moderate   ○ Laid-back

Politically, Colgate leans:
○ Left   ● Right   ○ Split

Diversity:
○ High   ● Low   ○ Medium

Students describe Colgate in five words:
- Preppy conservative athletes studying hard
- Beautiful, prestigious, wealthy, intelligent, intoxicated

From the School

You will quickly find that Colgate's most cherished tradition is teaching. Intimate classes, research opportunities, and lively debate are the norm. The environment of learning extends far beyond our rich curriculum. It is woven into the fabric that is Colgate. Faculty design and lead twenty-four off-campus study groups to both domestic and international destinations.

—www.colgate.edu

If you're interested in Colgate, you may also be interested in:
Boston College, Colby, Cornell, Dartmouth, Tufts, Williams

Name: Stephanie
Hometown: Pittsford, New York
Class Year: Sophomore
Major: English and History
Extracurriculars: Colgate College Republicans, Pre-law Society, University Orchestra
Career Goal: I'm planning on going to law school. I'd like to do trial law one day.

How would you describe Colgate's reputation?

Colgate has the reputation of being a snobby, rich, white kid school, where everyone drives an SUV, talks on their cell phone all the time, and wears designer clothes—collar *up.*

Is this reputation accurate?

Well, first, people come to Colgate to get an excellent education, and that's exactly what they get. The academics here are truly top-notch. Once that's been said, yeah, there are quite a lot of rich white people here and there are those stereotypical dumb jocks and girls who just come here to bag husbands. It's a little disappointing. But you'll have that at a lot of places, and again, Colgate academics can't be beat.

> "Colgate really stands out in the job opportunity department. If you graduate here with a degree in economics you'll probably end up at a high paying job with JPMorgan or SmithBarney."
>
> ✦ Ann, junior

What would an admissions officer at your school probably not tell a prospective student?

Colgate University is known as a "baby Ivy" because of its stellar academics, which gives the impression that Colgate has a student body of nerds and geeks and dweebs. Let me set the record straight: we study, but when the studying is over, *Colgate is a party school!* Admissions officers and tour guides downplay the amount of debauchery that goes on here, but it's considerable.

The Institution

The brilliant pieces of prose normally found in college bathroom stalls aren't at Colgate. Everyone's too proud of the place. The closest we come to vandalism is when drunken frat boys write their names in the snow whilst relieving themselves. But the school spirit here *is* amazing. It all comes out at sporting events—face paint, signs, half-naked men rolling around in a snow bank, and some of the best trash talking this side of the Mississippi.

The Education

I never *ever* thought I would grow dorky enough to sit around the lunch table discussing an issue from class with my friends. But it happens at Colgate—a lot—and I love it. College forces you to grow up without you realizing it, and before long you find yourself feverishly debating the potential outcome of World War II had Hitler been killed a bit earlier.

There are just over 3,000 students at Colgate. Once you've picked your major, you'll have classes with pretty much the same people over and over (pro: a community of scholars; con: you'll eventually be sick of seeing their scholarly faces). Almost all of your classes will be discussion-based; class participation is usually a huge chunk of your final class grade. It makes you a more eloquent person, though. You'll arrive a freshman answering questions, "uhh . . . like, that guy, right?" but you'll come back as a sophomore easily delivering dissertations on the reach of patriarchial power structures in small town 1950s America.

At Colgate, because the school is small, you receive *a lot* of attention from professors. We don't have a grad school, so full professors teach every class. TAs facilitate discussion sometimes, but they mostly exist to tutor students who need extra help outside of class. And the amount of time you'll spend on schoolwork will really depend on the type of classes you take. I'm an English major, so I do a lot of reading and writing and that takes up a lot of time.

The Students

There are tons of activist groups at Colgate—racial, cultural, LGBT, religious, etc. Maybe that makes up for the fact that most of us are white and rich? This isn't to say that everyone is loaded, though. I do know kids who are paying their own way, and the financial aid office is great at working with each individual to make sure they can afford the education they've earned. There's at least one student from each of the fifty states on campus, and quite a few from foreign countries (*lots* of Bulgarians; no one knows why). Everyone pretty much meshes well with each other.

The Activities

The closest school to ours is Hamilton College. Other than that we're in the middle of nowhere. Colgate is a hockey school—if you play hockey, you're a god. Recently we've grown more football oriented because of our trip to the national championship (we lost; don't ask, we're still bitter). We also have a great music department—lots of a cappella groups, a good orchestra, and plays at least twice a semester. If you're lucky enough to have a car, or a friend with a car, Syracuse is only forty-five minutes away. Utica is a shorter drive but the mall is pretty shabby there, so we don't go much. Lastly, if the sun is out at Colgate, most of the snow is probably melted, and it's probably about 50 degrees. In this case, I guarantee you will see at least one hundred people outside in shorts, sunbathing. We're deprived of warmth during the *long* winter, so we relish the opportunity to be outside when it presents itself!

The Social Scene

People party Wednesday, Friday, and Saturday nights. Not exclusively, but those are the major nights. Pretty much everyone drinks; however, on occasion, it's acceptable to exempt yourself from the festivities everyone else is indulging in like it's religion. (You obviously can't legally drink until you're twenty-one, but as long as you're not stupid you can get away with it.) Frat life is huge, sorority life, not so much (We only have four sororities, and those are more like little clubs.)

I don't know everyone on campus, but if you play that six degrees of separation game I'm sure the whole campus is connected. I met most of my friends through where I lived freshman year. Being a first-year at Colgate isn't hard. You're integrated almost immediately and upperclassmen aren't snobs about befriending you. You get a core group and then you meet people they know and the group just grows and grows. And people in general here are very polite and considerate—unless you add alcohol to the equation—then they're either *more* friendly, or assholes. But this is life.

Lastly, stay away from the townies—you'll know why when you see them. They all have one eye and two teeth.

Name: William
Hometown: Denver, Colorado
Class Year: Freshman

Major: I had originally wanted to double major in Spanish and biochemistry; after a year at Colgate, I've now drifted toward art history and biology.
Extracurriculars: Vice president of the China Club, Eta Bita Pi (not a frat, but a club that helps fight world hunger; get it: eat a bit o' pie?!), and the College Democrats
Career Goal: I'm thinking of becoming either a pediatrician or a cardiologist.

How would you describe Colgate's reputation?

Particularly in the northeast, Colgate is regarded as a very selective, very prestigious school. But at the same time, this small, tight-knit community, full of frighteningly smart, preppy kids, is reputed to turn into a big party school at night. Add to that the fact that it's ranked as one of the most beautiful campuses in the United States . . .

Is this reputation accurate?

It's all true. Particularly the partying bit. Once Friday night arrives, music is blaring, the frats come alive, the local club The Jug is filled to a dangerous capacity. And then Sunday rolls around, when *everybody* and their frat brother disappears into the library to study and prepare for the rest of the week. It's impressive—Colgate students are just the right mix of the healthy, intelligent college student ready to take on the world and the fun-loving individual who knows how to seize the day and party.

What would an admissions officer at your school probably not tell a prospective student? What aspect of your school would a prospective student not see on a campus tour?

Colgate is really good about this: I've volunteered a little bit of my time at admissions, and the first thing they tell us is to answer *everything* a prospective student asks. However, some tour groups do neglect one of the dorms on campus called Gate House, one of the, er, less desired housing options on campus.

The Institution

Colgate is very well maintained. (Even in dorms, if someone throws up at night, it will be cleaned up nicely by the time you wake up in the morning.) Colgate is just the right size for me. It feels very much like an academic community, and you can learn a lot with minimal distractions. Classes are small and discussion-based, professors are interested and involved. And as I was saying, weekend parties offer plenty of opportunities for collegiate debauchery. Very occasionally I'll wish there was a bigger city nearby, but then I realize there's really everything you need either in town or on campus. There's the Barge (local Starbucks/coffeehouse), The Jug (local bar which is disgusting and claustrophobic but everybody still goes there anyway), the Palace (a big party space), Parkside (amazing buffalo chicken wraps), and Slices (can anyone say munchies? Great pizza). The bookstore and movie theater are also pretty close by.

Also Colgate has a ton of school spirit, and we love the number 13. It's rumored that 13 men with 13 prayers founded Colgate with $13. Our address is 13 Oak Drive, our zip code is 13-346, and our biggest a cappella group is called the 13 (third oldest a cappella group in the country). Not since the days of *Sesame Street* have I thought I would have such an affinity for a single number!

> "Getting As at any Ivy is easier than getting them here. I wish I'd gotten into Harvard, I'm sure I wouldn't be working as hard."
> ✦ Brian, senior

The Education

Colgate has a core curriculum, but there are lots of options that fulfill the core, and it's not that extensive—you only have to take two classes in the social sciences, two in the natural sciences, and two in the humanities. If anything, most people find the core fun. And then when that's out of the way, classes are generally small, personalized, and discussion-based. There's a 10:1 ratio of students to teachers, and we get a lot of big name performers/speakers—this year we had Jesse Jackson, Hillary Clinton, Dave Coulier, Ann Coulter, and Sam from *The Apprentice*. If you're into research, Colgate is also the school for you; there are research opportunities open to *everyone*. You just have to apply and something will land in your lap. Also the strongest fields on our campus are political science and economics, neither of which I'm interested in, but my roommates seem to think they're great.

The Students

Come to Colgate and you will see a lot of white, rich, conservative Abercombie-wearing men and women. Oh yeah, and most people come from private high schools, too (though there's *some* public school pride—whoo hoo!). Most students are also from the East Coast and everyone does get along. Also Colgate's not overtly political. There are rarely any protests—in one year I think I only saw one rally, and it was really small, calm, and respectful. I guess the Students for Social Justice Club are the ones that plan big political events, but they often stage their rallies at other schools.

The Activities

There is a whole assortment of activities at Colgate, and I think I've dabbled in almost all of them from picking prizes for Winterfest with the Colgate Activities Board, to dancing with members of the South Asian Culture Club, to greeting in the Office of Admissions. Colgate has a pretty active television station, radio station, and not so great student newspaper (the *Maroon News*). They each voice the opinions of students in their own creative way. Colgate has lots of art history majors, and two main galleries on campus.

Athletics are strong at Colgate, especially lately, when we've been winning lots. It's good to be an athlete here, because students have a lot of school pride and we go out of our way to support our teams. There are always people in the stands rooting for 'Gate, even at tennis matches. And when it comes to hockey or football, forget about it. The entire student body is out in force. Community service is also popular here and comes in many different forms. The frats and sororities will often go out of their way to raise money for charity, or work with the Red Cross to run blood drives. There's COVE, a massive community service office on campus where anyone can step inside and sign up for something service-oriented. Additionally, each dorm has a community council, which works to strengthen the bonds between people in each hall and between each hall and the greater community. Lastly, New York City is only a three-hour drive, so if you're stir crazy, you can wake up early and be in Manhattan by the afternoon.

The Social Scene

People spend Fridays and Saturdays in one of two ways. There's the dry route, which means you'll go to dinner with friends, then go back to someone's room to hang out, watch a movie and play video games. Maybe head into town, sit around at a coffee shop, then head to sleep. Or the wet route, where you'll do the same things but with a beer can in your hand at all times, and at the end of the night you'll find yourself at some frat party or The Jug. At 4 a.m. you won't so much head to sleep as pass out where you stand. And though the frat/sorority scene is a large part of campus life here, it's not like it's Greek Pride Day everyday.

> "Picture nineteenth-century, well-maintained stone buildings, beautifully manicured lawns, and athletic men and women in the primes of their lives. Cover the whole image with snow, drop the air temperature about 60 degrees, put North Face jackets on the students. Welcome to Colgate."
> ✦ Mark, senior

Last thing: Colgate has a lot of cool traditions. For example, on the first night of school the senior honor society, Konosioni, comes with torches and passes them off to freshmen, who then carry them around for hours. It's really cool (and slightly cultish). Another tradition is to have your first Colgate kiss on Willow Path, which is right over Taylor Lake. It's really beautiful, the water underneath, the wind blowing, and it's said that the person you kiss there you'll be with forever. This summer two alums who first kissed there wound up getting married right on the bridge.

Name: Marc
Hometown: Chappaqua, New York
Class Year: Sophomore
Major: Russian
Extracurriculars: Squash team, Volunteer Ambulance Corps, statistics tutoring, I'll write the occasional article for the school newspaper.
Career Goal: I'd like to eventually go into medicine.

How would you describe Colgate's reputation?

Colgate was described to me as *the* place for smart, preppy kids who like to have a good time.

Is this reputation accurate?

Yeah. We get a lot of kids that probably could have gone to Cornell or Dartmouth, but who didn't want to have their heads stuck in books for four straight years. And as for the preppy thing, collar-up polos and khakis really are the standard uniform around here.

What would an admissions officer at your school probably not tell a prospective student?

Upstate New York gets the least amount of sunshine per year in the continental United States. Some locals have to take vitamin D pills to compensate. They always say on the tours, "You guys picked a bad day to come. The weather's terrible today." The thing is, they say that every day, to every tour.

The Institution

The Colgate campus is on a pretty big hill, which overlooks the town and the surrounding valley. It makes for some really great pictures, but it's also a pain to walk up if you're coming from the junior and senior apartments or the town. Fortunately, the administration has implemented a Colgate Cruiser bus system, so kids coming up the hill for classes or coming back from the bars late at night can hitch a ride (the Cruiser runs until 3 a.m. on Friday and Saturday nights). On weekends we call it the "Drunk Bus."

> "I had no idea what the term 'preppy' really meant until I came to Colgate."
> ✦ Martha, freshman

On first-year move-in day, carrying your belongings up the big hill to your dorm is pretty strenuous for first-years and their parents, so every year since anyone can remember, upperclassmen sign up to help the first-years move in. They drive trucks and vans up and down the hill hundreds of times, delivering microwaves, TVs, and anything else to the first-year dorms. During this time, the incoming students can say goodbye to their parents and take care of any last-minute errands. It's an amazing relief for the parents, and it's a testament to the Colgate philosophy of community. Someone helped me move in, so now I'll help someone else. It's how the job system works, too, but we'll get to that later.

Kids here are active. The gym is constantly packed. On nice days almost everyone is outside throwing a Frisbee or playing baseball. The atmosphere of "everyone's here to have a good time" hangs on every sunny, 50 degree day. Some people say they have a problem with the homogeneity here, but the fact of the matter is, that's part of what makes Colgate what it is. The snow isn't the only thing that's white up here. If you're looking for a school with a big minority population, try Howard or Morehouse. You just won't find it at Colgate. On the upside, if you're white and preppy you'll get to surround yourself with 2,800 other people who you probably have a lot in common with.

The Education

At Colgate, you'll end up paying for (and getting) every bit of personal attention you could want from professors. They'll invite you to their homes, out to dinner, or to a special after-class event at least once a semester. That goes for every class. All my professors know my name and where I'm from, and I know where my professors went to college and how many kids they have. The work's hard, but that's just college in general. A friend of mine at Cornell blew through two highlighters in the first two weeks of the semester. Colgate won't run you into the ground like that, but it's not too far off. You're here to get an education and grow as a person, and the professors will make sure you do both. If you write a great paper, but your punctuation sucks, they'll take you aside and teach you where commas are supposed to go, even if it's a chemistry lab write-up. The point is to create people who can succeed in the world after college, and Colgate's filled with professors who have dedicated their lives to that very task.

The Students

A friend of mine goes to Towson and showed me pictures of an exaggerated "preppy party" that her friends threw. Honestly, they all looked dressed-down compared to a typical Colgate student on a weekday, never mind the weekend. But I bet if those kids came here, they'd still make friends, and while maybe they wouldn't be swilling Tanqueray and tonics with the Betas, they'd still have a good time.

Here's a quick recipe for how to make a Colgate student:

2 oz. Brooks Brothers Oxford shirt mix
1 oz. NorthFace fleece
3 oz. vodka
A dash of sea salt from Long Island, Nantucket, or Connecticut
Swirl with a lacrosse stick or tennis racquet, and serve over ice.

Like I said before, you're not coming to Colgate to meet black lesbian socialists who are chaining themselves to trees. And while Colgate isn't the biggest melting pot of socioeconomic and racial diversity, the students and the administration work hard to try and fill the gaps with clubs, events, and guest speakers and are genuinely open to thoughts and ideas outside their realm of experience. A fair amount of Colgate students went to private high schools, and a lot of others grew up in Westchester, Long Island, or Connecticut.

Colgate students are here to have a good time, but they're also looking to the future and to the job opportunities that lie ahead. In that respect, most of the campus here is conservative. There are very few people who don't take their futures seriously, and that leads to a lot of pre-professionalism and high hopes for eventual wealth.

> "I never realized how angry the African-American students here were . . ."
> ✦ Jon, junior

Colgate alumni and their impressive career paths have proven that in many cases students' high hopes are realized. The alumni here are the greatest. They do everything from offering soon to be grads jobs to hosting incoming freshman barbecues at their homes. I have yet to meet an alumnus who wouldn't bend over backward to do a favor for a fellow Red Raider. I was on Martha's Vineyard for the Fourth of July, and my friends and I happened to bump into some alumni several years older than we were at a bar. They handed us business cards from SmithBarney and Morgan Stanley and assured us that after we graduated, we should e-mail them and get in touch if we ever needed jobs. Five minutes into a conversation at a crowded bar, and already these guys were willing to help us find careers. They weren't even drunk. Everyone's your fraternity brother at Colgate, whether you're in a frat or not.

> "I chose Colgate over Brown University for two reasons. One, our writing classes are taught by professors instead of grad students. The other is Colgate's rural location, which I prefer . . . Thoreau would approve."
> ✦ Jeremy, sophomore

The Activities

All college campuses offer every single club (even the weird, outlandish clubs). Colgate's no different. Come to Colgate, join a club, get involved.

The Social Scene

If I had a dollar for every time someone asked me, "Doesn't being in the middle of nowhere suck?" I'd have tuition covered pretty easily. Yes, Hamilton, New York, isn't a bustling metropolis, but no, it certainly doesn't suck to be here. There are parties every weekend. The Jug (a local downtown bar) is a destination for everyone, all the time, and there are enough organized and independent extracurricular activities, sporting events during the days to keep everyone busy until nightfall. It's true that the administration is cutting down on the fraternities, and that kind of puts a damper on the social scene, but there's still very little downtime for your liver.

Notable Colgate Alumni Include:
Andy Rooney, television commentator
Rev. Adam Clayton Powell Jr., politician
Steve Lemme, actor, writer
Charles Evans Hughes, former Supreme Court Justice
William Rogers, former secretary of state
Howard Fineman, journalist

UNIVERSITY OF COLORADO AT BOULDER

Founded: 1876
Location: Boulder, CO
Phone: (303) 492-6301
E-mail: N/A
Web site: www.colorado.edu

Number of Undergraduates: 25,400
Number of Graduate Students: 5,360
Cost: Approximately $11,000 per year in state; $28,000 out of state
Application Deadline: January 15
Rolling Admissions

Rating:	Notable Majors/Programs:
Selective	Journalism, Life Sciences, Business

Size:
○ Small   ○ Medium   ● Large

Location:
○ Urban   ● Suburban   ○ Rural

On a Saturday, students talk about academics:
○ Always   ● Sometimes   ○ Never

Nightlife:
● Intense   ○ Moderate   ○ Laid-back

Politically, UC Boulder is:
○ Left   ○ Right   ● Split

Diversity:
○ High   ● Low   ○ Medium

Students describe CU–Boulder in five words:
- Large research university in beautiful Boulder
- Smart kids leading balanced lives

From the School

Our mission is to advance and impart knowledge across a comprehensive range of disciplines to benefit the people of Colorado, the nation, and the world by educating undergraduate and graduate students in the accumulated knowledge of humankind, discovering new knowledge through research and creative work, and fostering critical thought, artistic creativity, professional competence, and responsible citizenship.

—www.colorado.edu

If you're interested in CU–Boulder, you may also be interested in:
Notre Dame, UC–San Diego, UC–Santa Cruz,
UMass Amherst, UW–Madison, University of Washington

Name: Marilyn
Hometown: Northglenn, Colorado
Class Year: Junior
Major: Finance
Extracurriculars: Work two part-time jobs.
Career Goal: A stable business related job that pays a lot of money.

How would you describe CU–Boulder's reputation?

Well, it was just named the number-one party college in America by the *Princeton Review*. Our reputation has gone down since that happened, but this is honestly not the biggest party school. Their surveys are biased.

Is this reputation accurate?

No, it's been blown out of proportion. People associate partying with stupid students and the assumption that no one studies—and that's just not true. People do party a lot in Boulder, but a lot of people are also very smart around here—proving it's possible to party *and* to study.

What aspect of CU–Boulder would a prospective student not see on a campus tour?

A tour wouldn't show you Boulder itself, which is a great town.

The Institution

The school is great. It's big—almost a bit too big (twenty-five minutes to walk across campus!), and class sizes are too big, too—but Boulder students definitely get the perfect college town experience. There are students everywhere. Boulder is located in the foothills of the Rockies and has a beautiful view. Of course the best thing is that top-notch skiing and snowboarding are only a few hours away! Closer by, there are plenty of things to do, including bars, clubs, and a range of culinary options. And the weather is great, too—summers are hot and winters are cold.

The Education

Part of the upside of a big school is that there's a lot of variation in classes here; you can take a class about any subject of your liking. The downside is that the classes are large (I often attend 400-person lectures), and it's consequently hard to get to know the professors—but at the same time, professors are very accessible. And they're *really* good! Study abroad programs are excellent.

The Students

The average student is laid-back, relaxed. She likes to have a good time and interact with the locals. He's open-minded about everything. The average student is probably white, but I do meet a lot of international and some minority students, too. You've got the frat boys, hippies, science geniuses, entrepreneurs. Anything goes in Boulder. And it's a very creative town—musicians, writers, artists, painters . . . you name it, we've got it.

> "I couldn't have chosen a better college. The campus is beautiful, the town is beautiful, and the weather is beautiful."
> ✦ Lisa, senior

The Activities

There are many sports here, and a great recreation center—it has plenty of instructed classes and excellent facilities, including ice rink, swimming pool, gym, track, exercise equipment, climbing wall, tennis courts, and much more. Food is open *late* here, a lot of places even deliver until three! Boulder definitely does *not* go to sleep early. It is not a quiet town, either (especially around campus). Very loud on Thursday, Friday, Saturday, and Sunday nights especially. Boulder has a great bus system—it's easy to get around. No need for a car. There's plenty to do, but if you like an urban city setting, Denver is only twenty-five minutes away and has a huge nightlife. It's easy to learn the town and the streets. You'll quickly find that people party on the Hill (a huge student hangout) and on the Pearl Street Mall. There are so many different types of restaurants, cafes, coffee shops, bars, piercing and tattoo shops, pipe shops, and just plain weird stores. Everything you ever imagined.

The Social Scene

Big fraternity and sorority life. Lots of alcohol around, but most people are responsible when it comes to drinking and driving. Most people just walk home, which is not too far since everything is so nearby everything else. You have to like meeting tons of different people because you can't escape that here. I meet new people almost every day.

Name: Erinn
Hometown: I'm an army brat, so I don't have one, but my parents live in Colorado Springs at present.
Class Year: Junior
Major: Journalism and theater
Extracurriculars: I'm involved in Catholics on Campus and stage performances at the Theater and Dance Department for the most part.
Career Goal: Someday I'd like to write and direct a movie, but for right now I'm going to be a translator.

How would you describe CU–Boulder's reputation?

Many people believe that it is the liberal capital of the world and that all CU students do is party and cause riots.

Is this reputation accurate?

No. CU's community is made up of different groups of people. If drinking and partying isn't your idea of fun, then you can find a wealth of people who feel the same way—people who would rather spend the evening discussing books, or art, or going to concerts and movies. Believe it or not, a majority of the CU students don't need to get high to have fun; we like to be awake for life, not stoned to death.

What aspect of CU–Boulder would a prospective student not see on a campus tour?

We have some of the best programs in the United States, depending on your subject of interest. A lot of the journalism teachers, for example, have worked at CNN and have covered major events. Our law school is one of the best, as are our engineering school and business school. Also there are three ponds on campus: one by the covered parking lot on the edge of campus, one in the Kitteredge Housing area, and one by the Hale building. These are three of the most beautiful places on campus, but they're well hidden and you won't see them when you visit.

The Institution

CU is amazing because of the people and its embrace of new ideas, which is why one of the biggest events of the year is the Conference on World Affairs, where speakers from every walk of life come to discuss topics ranging from mythology and movies to new scientific discoveries and the question of other life in the universe.

CU is a big campus, but I have never felt lost in the crowd. The school has far surpassed my original expectations. People can be themselves here—whether your parents live in Beverly Hills or the ghetto; if you're here, then that's all that matters.

> "Boulder as a city has been thoroughly 'yuppified' in recent years."
>
> ✦ Terry, junior

The Education

In some of the big lectures we rely more on TAs than on the teachers themselves, but like I said, that doesn't necessarily mean you end up feeling like a number. I'll tell you about two of my most interesting classes. The first is Religion and Dance, which is a discussion of the history of certain dances and how they affect their culture from the perspective of religion. The best part about this class is that one day a week you listen to a lecture, while the second day you actually learn the dance in question. The professor invites teachers from the Boulder dance scene to come in and do guest lectures and teach us their favorite form of dance.

The other one is Creative Technologies: a chemical engineering class designed for people who do not excel in the field(s) of science and/or math. You learn about the latest advances in topics such as artificial intelligence, nanomachines, gene therapy, gene splicing, and the controversy over cloning, etc. The teachers present the material in a fun and interesting way. I highly recommend both of these classes—and the best part is that they both count toward your core requirements.

The Students

Students at CU are pretty open-minded and interested in the opinions of others. Walking around campus any day of the week you can find new discourse on one subject or another. It gives the students a chance to see both sides of an issue; they can talk with people who feel strongly, without being intimidated or feeling someone else's opinion is being forced on them.

The Activities

Since CU is snuggled up against the majestic Flatiron Mountains, we tend to do a lot of outdoor activities that range from hiking to biking to just tossing a Frisbee on one of CU's quads or strolling down to the Pearl Street Mall (a treelined walkway lined with shops). But we are also just a short ride from downtown Denver with its museums and a performing arts center.

The Social Scene

There are six billion different things to do on Friday or Saturday. If drinking and partying is your thing, go up to the Hill and in less than five minutes you will find ten parties. Or go downtown to Penny Lane and recite poetry and play instruments on an open mic night. My dorm experience was awesome! For three years I lived with students from all over the world in the Smith Hall International Program dorm (SHIP). Every dorm on campus sponsors some type of academic or social program; whether you're into political science, art, honor programs, leadership opportunities, music, or antidrugs, you can find a dorm for you. Every two weeks SHIP invites a professor from CU to lecture on their area of passion (for example, Nubian mummies, historic love letters, underdeveloped countries). Then after the lecture, the dorm pays for a dinner specially prepared by Naropa that reflects the guest lecturer's topic country. The dorm also provides the students with new off-campus experiences, from the historic Danshube Teahouse in Boulder to subsidizing most of the ticket price for students to a show in Denver.

> "The sidewalks are usually littered with chalkings (Students Against Cancer! No blood for Oil! So-and-so for Tri-Exec! Join Greenpeace! Stop Chalking on the Sidewalk!)."
>
> ✦ Jayson, senior

Name: Jeff
Hometown: Denver, Colorado
Class Year: Freshman
Major: Urban planning
Extracurriculars: Co-National Communications Coordinator for the Residence Hall Association, member of Freshmen Council, volunteer for the Conference of World Affairs, volunteer for Colorado History Day

Career Goal: Either transporation planner or real estate development.

How would you describe CU–Boulder's reputation?

Supposedly the number-one party school in the nation and a sort of hippieville.

Is this reputation accurate?

Sure we party, but not necessarily any more than most other schools. Hippieville is half true. We definitely have some "Boulder hippies" who drink free trade coffee and make their own clothes—but you could also sit next to the heir to some corporate fortune.

What would an admissions officer at your school probably not tell a prospective student?

They won't mention anything concerning both drinking/partying or about the scandal surrounding our football team a few years back.

The Institution

There is a lot of CU school spirit . . . when we're doing well. People wear school clothing and cheer for the football team, but we're fair-weather fans, you might say. But we all enjoy our football game traditions where (even though it's officially banned) people throw marshmallows and, to a lesser extent, tortillas at each other during halftime.

The Education

Competition between students depends on what level you are at and what your major is in. For example, the science and MCDB (molecular, cellular, developmental biology—essentially premed), engineering, and business schools are particularly strong. The rest of the school is good, but definitely not at the level of those departments. Your core curriculum will depend on the school you are in.

Classes smaller than fifty are discussion-oriented, whereas anything over one hundred is lecture-based (though the teachers sometimes try to combat this, and usually do a good job of doing it). Research opportunities are available for undergrads, and stipends can be received for work done.

My classes have ranged from fifteen people to five hundred people. The only thing that is strange is when you see your professor out of class and you want to say hello but don't because they don't

know you (unless you have introduced yourself). For other people, the big class sizes affect
them.

> "People smoke weed here, but not more
> than any other school. OK, maybe a little
> more."
>
> ✦ Rachel, junior

The Students

Politically the students are mixed. Two-thirds
are from in-state. Unfortunately, CU is one of the
least diverse campuses in the nation. I went to
public schools in the middle of Denver all my life
and was used to a diverse group of people there. I
think a diverse student body is important for understanding the world better and understanding
issues from a perspective other than that of white
middle-class America.

The Activities

Athletics are a big part of this school, but since
it's such a big school and not everyone is doing
Division I athletics, players are not entirely revered
as gods. Students can play a big part in administrative decisions if they get involved and want to be.
For example, I am an executive for the Residence
Hall Association (RHA), and we get to make decisions (or at least have input) on dining menus,

> "Rather than say, 'Don't do it,' which would
> be entirely ineffective, CU's motto is 'Stay
> safe.' As a result, we do."
>
> ✦ Jennifer, sophomore

money spent in the housing department, the up-
dating of campus housing, etc.

The Social Scene

It depends on the person, but usually people go
out on Friday and Saturday, sometimes on Thursday, too. Some people go to frats, but it's not a
huge part of campus—only a small percentage actually pledges.

You certainly don't know everyone on campus,
but if you get involved you can know a ton of
people. I met my close friends in my dorm, but I
have many other good friends from other clubs/
organizations. Everyone has to live on campus first
year, and then most people live off.

Notable CU–Boulder Alumni Include:

Andrew Young Jr., United Nations ambassador
Byron R. White, U.S. Supreme Court justice
Ellis Marsalis, jazz musician
Robert Redford, actor, director, producer
Scott Carpenter, astronaut
Stephen Bechtel, chairman of the Bechtel group of
    companies

COLORADO COLLEGE

Founded: 1874

Location: Colorado Springs, CO

Phone: (719) 389-6000

E-mail: admission@coloradocollege.edu

Web site: www.coloradocollege.edu

Number of Undergraduates: 1,930

Number of Graduate Students: 30

Cost: Approximately $36,000 per year

Application Deadline: January 15

Early Decision: November 15

Rating:	Notable Majors/Programs:
Selective	Geology, Environmental Science, English, Religion

Size:
● Small   ○ Medium   ○ Large

Location:
○ Urban   ● Suburban   ○ Rural

On a Saturday, students talk about academics:
○ Always   ● Sometimes   ○ Never

Nightlife:
○ Intense   ● Moderate   ○ Laid-back

Politically, Colorado College leans:
● Left   ○ Right   ○ Split

Diversity:
○ High   ● Low   ○ Medium

Students describe Colorado College in five words:
- Outdoorsy lifestyle in Colorado Springs
- Smart, laid-back trustafarians. Block plan!

From the School

The people who decided Colorado needed a first-rate, East Coast-style liberal arts and sciences college were visionary mavericks. They came to the foot of Pikes Peak and created a distinctive city and a unique college. Colorado College people are still adventurers—trying new ideas for courses, exploring classical ideas from fresh angles, and venturing out into the community, the wilderness, and the world.

—www.coloradocollege.edu

If you're interested in Colorado College, you may also be interested in:
Carleton, Evergreen State, Lewis & Clark, Macalester, Oberlin, Reed

Name: Alex
Hometown: Columbus, Ohio
Class Year: Junior
Major: English–Creative Writing
Extracurriculars: Climbing wall monitor; intramural hockey, tennis, soccer, Frisbee, rock climbing, road trips, general mountain play, Habitat for Humanity, CLIMB for kids leader
Career Goal: For the book(s)/articles I write to be available in my hometown's library.

How would you describe Colorado College's reputation?

To the small liberal arts college (and outdoorsy) crowd it is considered a backup school to more prestigious institutions on the more crowded, less beautiful East Coast. Within Colorado it is known as a smart (alecky), rich, white institution.

Is this reputation accurate?

To a certain extent. While relatively rich and white we may be, everybody here has something off about them. The women's national freestyle ski team contender is a hell of an artist and also a thug, the frat boy is obsessed with J.R.R. Tolkien, the fake Texas cowboy can freestyle like nobody's business, and the generally hard-core collect coins.

What would an admissions officer at Colorado College probably not tell a prospective student?

That the block plan (which means we take only one class at a time)—while amazing and a godsend and wonderful and able to cover the same amount of material as a semester institution—won't allow you to write a well-researched paper—there just isn't enough time. Also that forming your own major, while doable, is a bureaucratic pain in the buttocks.

The Institution

My main criterion for choosing a school was geography. I wanted mountains. They have them in Colorado. I also wanted a small school. (Small schools, I've found after being abroad at the University of Edinburgh—population approximately 25,000—are very much the way to go.) Campus is compact and communifying and there's almost always somebody you can talk to who has enough authority to fix any problems you might have. The president has open office hours in Warner, the student center/dining hall, one day a week.

The buildings are a hodgepodge of different styles and time periods—Palmer and Cutler are grand, century-old buildings, and Loomis and Slocum, the two kinda crazy freshman dorms, are heinous creations of 1950s architecture. However, you can't beat the view from the back porch of the dining hall, or any west-facing windows for that matter. Pikes Peak looms over campus and looks as if you could be at the top in no time (no time being approximately eight hours). They've tried to create a pretty Eastern university-style quad and have succeeded, I think, even though they water the grass more than they probably should in our climate. You must live on campus for three years unless you figure out how to bypass the system, which is complicated but doable. There are apartments for that off-campus feel, but it just ain't the same. People moan about it but deal with it.

> "How many CC students does it take to change a light bulb? Seventy-six:one to change the light bulb, fifty to hold a protest of the changing of the light bulb, and another twenty-five to hold a counter protest."
>
> ✦ Shanna, senior

The Education

The block plan is wonderful, perfect, and better than a semester system—for some people. I have a hard time multitasking. I'm not very organized. I don't do very well with restrictions. CC is practically Eden for me. You have one thing to do, and it's a lot of it, but it's only one thing. You read a short novel in a night, you discuss it the next day, and then you're done with it, but it works out to more in-class time than a normal university. And the block plan allows for classes that would be impossible at any other place. The block plan equals field trips! For a politics, religion and globalization class we went to CC's Baca campus (a separate, very posh campus in the San Luis Valley) where we visited a Hindu Ashram, meditated with Buddhist monks at their temple at 7 a.m. (the velcro on my jacket has never been so loud), and when we weren't talking with the class, a friend and I got most of the way up a neighboring fourteener [climbing jargon]. There are many classes—all for extra expense, mind you—offering to study art in Paris, architecture in Italy, etc.

The distribution requirements are a pain in the ass. That being said, there are not a whole lot of them and "they're for your own good." Almost all classes are discussion-based. The sciences are intense. Lots of class time. My roommate's a neuroscience major and probably spends three hours in class in the morning, has an hour or so for lunch, then heads back to lab for another four hours. Then homework at night. The block plan is pretty intense any way you go, but the sciences are a particularly burly way, though the science majors I know are all pretty happy. Ecology classes get to go *do* ecology in the field. I'm going to Belize this January to do a combination jungle/marine/cultural ecology course. I won't miss any other classes, 'cause there aren't any. Pretty cool.

Personal attention from professors is profuse, if you want it. But the greatest thing about a small school is class size—the very biggest classes at CC are like thirty-six people. Almost every class is capped at twenty-five. I have been in a class with three other kids and a Ph.D. You call your teachers by their first names, dinners at their houses actually happen, and they get to know you, so if they like you, they can write a properly biased recommendation.

If you don't want to do a lot of work at CC, it's possible not to. And if you want to strike a balance by alternating hard and easy, you can do that. Overall, Bs are pretty easy to get. As are not. Students aren't very outwardly competitive; what they actually harbor in their passive aggressive little hearts I don't know.

The Students

We are, largely, a racially homogeneous campus, but as far as socioeconomic and cultural difference, CC is a bit more flavorful. Students tend to vary in their level of liberalism—are they Communists, Socialists, or straight-up American middle of the road Democrats? That's anybody's guess. Republicans are a minority. My friends include people from Alaska, Hawaii, North Carolina, Minnesota, Massachusetts, Texas, and Ohio. The most vocal groups on campus are the environmental ones. Earth Month (nope, a day isn't enough here) is filled with activities. But for every very environmentally conscious student, there are probably four that do nothing. The Outdoor Recreation Club (ORC) has its own little subculture, and its

inner circle has a tendency to get a little strange and incestuous. They do have an impressive selection of gear you can rent (kayaking gear, backpacking gear, climbing gear), they lead trips most weekends and have access to vans, and the trips are cheap. It is probably the best organized, most well-funded outdoor and recreation program for a school our size in the country. We also have a climbing wall that gets fairly packed on winter evenings. The campus radio station is rad. Overall, students at CC are up for an adventure. We never stop.

> "The average student owns a longboard, wears an article of clothing that he or she made, and smokes a lot of pot."
> ✦ Leslie, senior

The Activities

We get outside a lot. Climbing, skiing, biking, boating, trail running. The opportunities around are huge, but you do need a car for the most part. If you don't have one, you figure out who has a car and likes to do what you do. Then make friends. Block break is the best. You get out of class on the last Wednesday of the block at noon. Two hours later you're in the car and you're going to be sitting there for another eight hours so you can ski, climb, boat or bike further west for three days and then drive back. If it's not block break, you get out of class at noon and drive an hour or two to go climbing and get back at 8 p.m. and then read 150 pages. It's pretty intense, but, golly, it's fun. The administration has statistics on community service, and they're pretty high. Most people I know do something sometime. If you want to get involved in something, just get up the guts and go. But if you don't like to do things outside, I'd imagine the place could get pretty boring. It's cold at night in the winter—no amount of beer will get rid of that; there's not a ton of live music in town, people don't go to bars.

The Social Scene

Most parties have themes and the classic Drag Ball is fun for sightings of fraternity members making out with other men, and general gender ambiguity. Whiskey night (code for Monday) is a venerated institution which must covertly move from host to host in order that the cell is not isolated and smothered. The rest of the time it's down to house parties, going to see movies, or drinking in the ol' dorm room (quietly!). The Air Force Cadets from nearby (it's a big military town) show up sometimes, but I think they just come to laugh at "all the hippies," and CCers tend to almost warily avoid them. There are something like three frats and three sororities. They do play a proportionally large role on campus, but it's not a terribly negative one. A lot of people ignore them. You're not forced into anything socially. As far as the exclusivity thing, yes, it exists on some levels. Where doesn't it, on some level?

Name: Shanna
Hometown: Lakewood, Colorado
Class Year: Sophomore
Major: Sociology, minor in German
Extracurricular: Victim's Assistance Team (VAT), Theatre Workshop, Drama Department, Chaverim/Hillel, tour guide, student host, resident assistant, IM sports, Women's Club Hockey, EQUAL
Career Goal: To go into higher education administration, specifically, to work in residential life, or to go into sexuality education.

How would you describe Colorado College's reputation?

A very strong liberal arts school, with a combination of hippies and preppy trustafarians.

Is this reputation accurate?

I do think we are a wonderful school that provides a well-rounded education. But I also think that we're a lot more diverse than our reputation suggests. There are some students who are hippie-esque, some who drive BMWs, [but] most of us fall in the middle. There are a lot of liberals on campus, and though there have been more conservative students in recent years (last year was the founding year for the CC Republicans), it is predominantly a left-wing school.

What would an admissions officer at Colorado College probably not tell a prospective student?

The admissions office probably wouldn't emphasize the fact that we are not a very racially diverse school (I think we're at about 10 percent racial minorities), even though the minorities we do have are *very* active.

The Institution

I love CC. I had planned on going out of state, but after visiting, I knew there wasn't anywhere else for me. Everyone is so friendly.

We have a lot of spirit for our hockey games. We sell out the student section most nights and blanket it in gold and black. Most theater productions sell out. We have some all-school events, like Llamapalooza (all-day concert with student bands) that draw the school together even more. Since around 80 percent of students live on the campus, and it is such a small school, we are a very close-knit community.

Green and grassy all over, campus ranges from areas heavily populated with trees to large, grass-covered quads (good for classes, IM sports, pickup games of Frisbee, sunbathing). The relationship between students and the administration is wonderful here. And Colorado gets more than 300 days of sunshine a year. We always say if you don't like the weather, wait five minutes!

The Education

Our block system is different than most other schools (only one or two other schools in the United States have it). We are in one class from 9 to 12 every day, for three and one-half weeks, then we take our final, have five days off ("block break"), and then start a new class. We wind up taking four classes a semester, but only one at a time, so we can spend our time focusing on that subject, take extended field trips (especially useful to the geology, Southwest Studies, philosophy, and physics/astromony departments). It does get a little intense, you may have one night to write a paper instead of three weeks, but it just requires discipline in a different kind of way. And you only have to study for one final at a time, instead of four or five. The block plan doesn't work for some people— they tend to transfer out either at semester or at the end of their freshman year; it's not a big issue.

The Students

Students tend to be very outdoorsy, which is hard for me to understand, city girl that I am, but the few of us that don't spend our weekends climbing, hiking, biking, skiing, snowboarding, etc., have no problem being welcomed by the rest of the population. This campus is very open to anything, as long as it's PC . . . occasionally I think it's a little too PC. Everyone interacts, because classes are not by year, so most classes have at least one student from each year. I know people from the Greek system that are resident assistants and people from sports teams that are active in theater. There aren't any exclusive groups on this campus.

The Activities

Colorado Springs is known to be a very conservative city. However, CC is right next to downtown, which is definitely the more liberal area. Just a few blocks from campus, one can get fast food, sushi, a steak dinner, sexy lingerie, smoothies, coffee, imported Nepalese gifts, a hair cut, handmade ice cream, or go see a movie, or head to a club. Students don't go off campus that much, though, because there are *so* many things going on right here. There are some nights when I was in a show, but almost wished I wasn't because I desperately wanted to go to a hockey game, a movie playing in the student center, and a concert on the quad. I'd say the biggest problem people have with activities is trying to do too many at once, especially since it is easy to join everything *and* start your own club.

The Social Scene

Sororities on this campus are completely non-residential, and each fraternity only houses five or so of its members, which makes the Greek system a much smaller player in the party scene. There are only two to three frat parties per block (month). I definitely have two distinct groups of friends: those that party most weekends and those that have movie marathons and play Trivial Pursuit most weekends. I'm an RA in the dorms, in a substance-free hall, so I can't really talk about the alcohol on campus, as I am not usually exposed to it. I will say that most people here don't date per se—they just become a couple, and spend a lot of time together, and hang out in each other's rooms. True dates seem to be a thing of the past in the college scene.

Name: Leslie
Hometown: Boston, Massachusetts
Class Year: Senior
Major: Sociology
Extracurriculars: I write for the student newspaper, I play trumpet for the CC concert band, I volunteer as an English as a Second Language assistant.
Career Goal: Journalist, or work in the nonprofit sector, or some combination of the two.

How would you describe Colorado College's reputation?

The five or so people in this world who have heard of it tend be quite impressed when you tell them you go here.

> "At other schools people feel the need to look good to go out, but at CC theme parties you can get turned away for not looking crazy."
>
> ✦ Leslie, senior

Is this reputation accurate?

I think Colorado College deserves more of a reputation—it's a damn good school and I wouldn't trade it for the world.

What would an admissions officer at your school probably not tell a prospective student?

That the student newspaper is, quite honestly, awful, that the cafeteria food is a recipe for diarrhea, that the arts are vastly underfunded, that the library is ugly, doesn't have enough computers, almost never has the book you need, and that dealing with the Residential Life Office or the Business Office is about as pleasant as a root canal.

The Institution

The place isn't really any different than my original expectations. I read in some college book that it is "Camp Colorado College," and I think that's pretty accurate. It's known as a haven for trustafarians, and while there are a lot of Subaru-driving hippies, there are also quite a few fraternity/sorority/athlete types that I wasn't expecting. CC has school spirit, but not in that "Go Tigers!" kind of way. Everyone just seems to love going to school here, and spirit manifests itself in that way. The best tradition by far is Llamapalooza, which is a day full of bands and beer on the quad.

I do wish my school was more politically active, more diverse. I wish that the school didn't force its students to live on campus for three years, and had a better journalism program (they have a journalism minor only). That said, I love Colorado College. The block plan is wonderful, the professors care about the students, classes are engaging, I love my classmates, I love the location (two hours away from the best skiing in the world), I love the weather, I love the sociology department. And although I have no job lined up for the future, I know that eventually I will put my degree to use.

The Education

I'm so glad there is no grad school here. That would suck. Classes are almost exclusively discussion-based, profs respect our opinions, and in no way do you ever get the sense that the prof's main purpose is research. These profs are here to teach. Sometimes the school brings in visiting professors, who, in my experience, simply don't understand how to teach on the block plan, and tend to be disastrous.

The core curriculum is rather lax—you just have to take a certain number of sciences, language, Western civ classes, classes with a non-Western perspective, humanities, etc. It gives you some requirements, but isn't totally invasive. Most seniors have to write theses or do a senior project. One thing I wished I had known earlier was how much money the school has to give out to students for projects. There are so many grants available, and they are so easy to get. The school paid for me to go to Cuba this past summer to study community development.

The Students

There are the hippie pot-smoking types, the sorority girl/frat boy types, the hockey boys, the athletes, the preps, etc. But if I had to choose the most typical stereotype, it would be: the average student owns a longboard, wears an article of clothing that he or she made, and smokes a lot of pot. This average student drives an SUV and recycles meticulously. He/she is not registered to vote, but expresses frustration with the Bush administration in between bong rips. There isn't a whole lot of ethnic diversity here, and students seem to be racially segregated. The school had an incident a few years back involving racial slurs printed in the April Fool's edition of the newspaper and it really upset me how few white students were outraged by it. African American, Asian, Latino, and Native American students organized and protested, but I heard many white students making comments like "Why can't they take a joke? It's not a big deal." In this sort of climate, it's not hard to understand why minority groups stick together. The LGBT community isn't

huge, but seems to get a lot of support here—people here tend to be more open to different sexual orientations than most people I know. The Drag Ball, which is the queer-straight alliance's main event, is one of the most popular school functions.

The Activities

The strongest student groups are groups that are not political (the improv group, for instance, is quite popular). The Victims Assistance Team (an antisexual violence group) is very vocal. The school publication is barely read, and for good reason: it's awful (and this is coming from a staff writer). Men's hockey is huge. Intramural sports are the best! Touch football and broomball are the best ones. Community service is mildly popular. The frats/sororities are involved in all sorts of bake sales and benefit dodgeball games. The community service office is a great resource, and they have "BreakOut Trips," in which students can do community service over block break. If I'm awake at 3 a.m. on a Wednesday night, I am either: a) writing a paper that I put off to the last minute, b) at a party where the keg miraculously still has beer, or c) up with "someone of interest" whom I met at the previously mentioned party.

The Social Scene

People here party frequently, especially during eighth block (the last block of the year). And different people do party differently—there are the frat parties, and then there are the good parties. I attend the latter. Friday night begins with pre-partying with your friends/roommates as you get dressed up to attend whatever theme party happens to be going on that night. Then you go out to the party as a giant group and drink lots of beer. Then you go home and eat ramen, or, if you're luckier, you don't go home at all. You wake up on Saturday afternoon and watch movies for the remainder of the day.

Notable Colorado College Alumni Include:
James Heckman, Nobel laureate in economics
Jane Lubchenco, ocean ecosystems researcher
Jim Grossman, international surf kayaker
Kenneth Salazar, Colorado attorney general
Lynne Cheney, second lady
Marcia McNutt, president and CEO of the Monterey Bay Aquarium Research Institute

COLUMBIA UNIVERSITY

Founded: 1754

Location: New York, NY

Phone: (212) 854-1754

E-mail: ugrad-admiss@columbia.edu

Web site: www.college.columbia.edu

Number of Undergraduates: 4,180

Number of Graduate Students: 1,770

Cost: Approximately $40,500 per year

Application Deadline: January 2

Early Decision: November 1

Rating: Most Selective	Notable Majors/Programs: Humanities, Engineering, Life Sciences

Size:
○ Small   ● Medium   ○ Large

Location:
● Urban   ○ Suburban   ○ Rural

On a Saturday, students talk about academics:
● Always   ○ Sometimes   ○ Never

Nightlife:
○ Intense   ● Moderate   ○ Laid-back

Politically, Columbia leans:
● Left   ○ Right   ○ Split

Diversity:
● High   ○ Low   ○ Medium

Ivy League school: Yes!

Students describe Columbia in five words:
- Expensive, semipolitical, New York Ivy
- Urban, urbane, intellectual, cultural, independent

From the School

Columbia's undergraduate curriculum combines the breadth of learning provided by general education courses with the solid mastery of a discipline achieved through a major. And because Columbia is a great research university as well as a small liberal arts college, students with the will and ability to pursue their majors to the highest levels of scholarly sophistication are free to do so.

—www.columbia.edu

If you're interested in Columbia University, you may also be interested in: U Chicago, Harvard, NYU, U Penn, Wesleyan, Yale

Name: Sean
Hometown: Colorado Springs, Colorado
Class Year: Sophomore
Major: Neuroscience and behavioral sciences
Extracurriculars: Neurobiology lab, Collision (art symposium), guitar, RA
Career Goal: To actually find a career that I want to stick with. I hope it's in medicine.

How would you describe Columbia's reputation?

Columbia is known for being one of the most academically difficult and one of the most liberal/politically active Ivies.

Is this reputation accurate?

The idea that Columbia's workload is overwhelming needs to be taken with a grain of salt from your next tequila shot. If you can get into Columbia, you will not have a problem with the work, assuming you're willing to study once or twice a week. And yes, Columbia is liberal—and I love it!

What aspect of Columbia would a prospective student not see on a campus tour?

First, you might not see the lack of "central campus unity" that exists here (and at lots of other inner-city colleges). Also, the tour guides are all excited about the different on-campus dining options. But they are all really lame clones of each other, and the food can get bland quickly. However, right off campus there are endless options that are amazing and less pricey. Go to Koronets for a huge slice of quality pizza, Milano Market for ridiculously good sandwiches, Tom's (yes, the *Seinfeld* restaurant) for good milkshakes, and the West End for burgers. www.campusfood.com is also widely used and appreciated.

The Institution

I chose Columbia for two main reasons: the core curriculum and New York City. Coming from

"At another school I would have stayed on my pre-med path and never ventured into something as 'impractical' as philosophy or music, but here I've learned to fall in love with it all."

✦ Luis, junior

cookie-cutter suburbia and never having spent extensive time in a big city, Columbia was great for me to experience a new environment and get away from home. New York is really as much a part of Columbia as Columbia is part of New York. The downside to this is there's an overall lack of school unity. (Though we still have a hell of a lot more unity than NYU.) The campus is beautiful. The main building, Lowe Library, was modeled after the Pantheon in Rome and the Parthenon in Greece. Upon it sits the largest granite dome in North America and across from it lies our equally beautiful Butler Library. The campus is small and easy to navigate. Your farthest class will be a ten-minute walk. It's get up, get out of bed, drag a comb across your head, and get to class–style. The weather is northeasterly and thus crappy. But summer is awesome and New Yorkers take advantage of the warm weather by offering tons of free things to do (movies, kayaking, Shakespeare in the Park, etc.). Housing is good, not great. It's tight, but just try finding something bigger and cheaper in Manhattan! Because of this, students are guaranteed a room all four years and, if desired, a single room for at least two years—the privacy is great. Also, almost everyone stays in campus housing for the duration of their education. The fact that all your friends are close by is great for studying and hanging out. If you're ready to dive into big city life, come aboard. But if you're craving a close-knit college town/community, you might consider other options.

The Education

The core curriculum is what sets a Columbia education apart from all others. (There was an article in the *Harvard Crimson* suggesting a modification of its core to be more like ours.) Each student leaving this place will have taken a year of classical literature, a year of classical philosophy, two years of a foreign language, a semester of music humanities, a semester of art humanities, science requirements, and cultural requirements. In my opinion, the cohesive and well-rounded education forced by the core puts all others to shame. It seems as if I find a new reference to material we covered in class almost daily. The fact of the matter is that almost every great thinker has read and studied what Columbia makes you study. Wonderful education, I could not ask for anything better, except that the core teachers can be hit or miss.

Pretty much everyone who wants to do research at Columbia has the opportunity. To get my job in a neuroscience lab, I just picked the first one that looked interesting, called the professor, and in about ten seconds I had a gig. The summer research program, SURF, is a good way to stay in the city and enjoy not having homework to conflict with going out all the time.

> "The engineering education at Columbia—I would be lying if I said you're not going to work your little butt off."
>
> ✦ Sara, junior

The Students

Premeds here can get a little crazy. I once saw people taking digital pictures of their pig dissections while in lab—I mean, come on, relax a bit. Other than that, I have met some amazing people here. You run into national gymnasts, celebrities, known artists, and has-beens all the time. I feel slightly unaccomplished when I bring out the list of what my friends have done. Being in a pool of perfect SATs and valedictorians keeps you on your toes and everyone learns incredible amounts from each other. But don't worry, the "how did you get ins?" still exist here, just like every other college.

The Activities

Theater is not exceedingly strong besides one amazing production called "The Varsity Show." Every year, this student-written, student-created, and student-directed show astounds everyone who is lucky enough to remember to buy tickets ahead of time. Music and art are popular; athletics and fraternities, not so popular. It's a great thing if you don't really want to change your nationality by going Greek. You will never feel as if you do not fit in if you are not in a fraternity; however, if you love doing keg-stands with your bros, you might only be able to get in one a week at Columbia. As for the music/art scene, there is a killer end of the year art/literature/music party called "Collision." This year 1,600 students came to appreciate the beer and look at and listen to fellow student creations. As for athletics, Columbia is great in . . . well, we are good at fencing! Look at it this way: we have the best athletics of all the schools in the

city, which isn't saying much. Seeing as we are a big name school, we get some pretty big name speakers. Also, if you're a Republican, don't come here unless you love to debate and enjoy being severely outnumbered.

The Social Scene

The [name withheld], a local bar, is the classic social arena for drunken hookups and meeting new people. Lucky for you, the bouncers at the door are very flexible regarding ID. If you write "I am twenty-one" on a napkin with a purple crayon, you are almost guaranteed access. Because of this, the bar is mostly a first-year hangout. After you turn twenty-one, you will head down to the city more often to enjoy the perks of the amazing nightlife New York has to offer. Partying is evident at Columbia and most people drink, but it seems pretty responsible and not too overdone (although that's not what students in the Columbia Emergency Medical Technician organization say). The big nights to party are Thursday and Saturday (no classes Friday!), but if you *have* to do work on those nights, you will not feel alone or like a loser. Everyone studies hard and plays hard. Sometimes it can be tough to leave the Columbia area with work and classes keeping you busy. Do yourself a favor and don't be that student who never goes out and explores NYC.

Name: Ellen
Hometown: Milford, New Jersey
Class Year: Sophomore
Major: Art history
Extracurriculars: American Medical Student Association, Columbia Tour Guide, intern at St. Vincent's Hospital, Columbia Student Wind Ensemble
Career Goal: Physician

How would you describe Columbia's reputation?

Being Ivy League, we are known as extremely selective and extremely challenging academically. We're also known as being very active politically and extremely lackluster in our athletics.

Is this reputation accurate?

To a degree. It is very selective getting here, but the level of academics is completely relative to what major and which teachers you choose. It is true that we are very politically active, with many protests happening each year and active political groups on campus, but our sports are not as bad as they are reputed to be.

What would an admissions officer at Columbia probably not tell a prospective student?

An admissions officer would not tell you about how good the school is at overcharging students for everything from food to pens. Nor that the advising system is poor at best for first-years and sophomores, as only a few deans take a personal interest in their advisees and do not have many helpful answers to questions.

The Institution

New York is everything I expected, but the school has both surpassed and fallen short of my expectations. Life here is much more stressful than I expected: science and engineering classes are extremely competitive, and there is an overall drive to join as many clubs as one possibly can. The dating scene here is much worse than I ever would have imagined. I also wish that my school had more school pride/unity; people only really go to homecoming, so traditional football/basketball/baseball weekends are nonexistent. But despite the areas in which it's fallen short, I generally love my school. It's challenging, prestigious, and in the greatest city in the world.

The Education

There is a good mix of lecture and discussion classes; the first two years, one takes a discussion class each semester (literature, humanities, and contemporary civilization). Personal attention from professors is rare; TAs teach most of the core classes, and recitations for any other classes—but the research opportunities here are extensive in all fields. Barnard students are allowed to register for Columbia classes and sometimes close us out, and Columbia likewise for Barnard. This can be a frustration. I spend *too much* time outside of school on classes, probably about sixty hours a week. Science classes are competitive, period. Academic discussions tend to teem into the social realm—it's not unusual to hear us arguing about books from our core classes at any time of day.

The Students

You won't find an "average" student on this eclectic campus, but students here are mostly from the Tristate area, California, and Texas. Mostly liberals, a few die-hard conservatives. There is a great diversity of ethnicities here, and people are friends with others of all colors and origins. However, there are very some strong ethnic-based student groups that create subcultures that are *very* exclusive. There is good mix of people from all economic walks of life; however, the very wealthy flaunt it at times. Protests are very popular here, from antiwar protests to graduate students picketing for unionization. The daily newspaper here is widely read, as is a sarcastic mock-newspaper, the *FED*.

The Activities

We are a very active student body. Community service is *very* popular—there's a day each spring that the whole campus comes together to do community projects. Internship opportunities abound for Columbia students, and we have an excellent Center for Career Education to help one with job searches of all kinds. NYU, Fordham, Hunter, and the New School are all relatively near Columbia, but little interaction goes on. I leave campus about once a week, to go see an independent film, go to the Metropolitan Museum of Art, shop in SoHo, Fifth Avenue, and the Village, and if it's in the evening, go out to the bars. On a sunny day you can find me chilling on the steps of Lowe Library. You'll hear about the big name speakers on campus, but you probably won't hear that Columbia has a habit of not letting students in to see them. Also the acts they get for fall and spring concerts are usually lackluster unknowns.

The Social Scene

People party Thursday and Saturday nights, and while sometimes frat parties are decent and attended, bars are the better scene. The frat and sorority scene is small and the ones that exist tend to be linked with certain groups: Jewish, Hispanic, homosexual, etc. The dating scene is dismal, because in conjunction with Barnard, females outnumber males by a mile.

Name: Katya
Hometown: Boston, Massachusetts
Class Year: Junior
Major: English with a concentration in writing
Extracurriculars: Photography, *Columbia Review*
Career Goal: I want to do something that involves writing and photography, but I can't say anything more specific than that. It is pretty

scary when you are a senior and realize you have no marketable skills.

How would you describe Columbia's reputation?

It is an Ivy school and it's one of the last schools that still has a core curriculum, so I think people assume it's fairly conservative because everyone is required to study the "great books" and other things of the Western tradition. It also has a history of being very liberal and politically active during the Vietnam War. So I think people see it as being slightly in conflict with itself, or imagine the student body to be particularly liberal and the professors to be fairly conservative.

> "The biggest challenges of being a first-year student?
> 1. learning the New York subway system
> 2. figuring out what classes to take
> 3. getting into neighborhood bars underage."
>
> ✦ Ellen, sophomore

Is this reputation accurate?

I think the school *is* in conflict with itself, at least among the faculty. I think, depending on the department, there is a struggle between the older conservative faculty and the new, more liberal faculty. As for the student body, they definitely don't live up to their history. People expect a lot more activism, but I think apathy is a generational trend sweeping campuses these days, and Columbia is not immune.

What aspect of Columbia would a prospective student not see on a campus tour?

I think the main complaint most people have about this school is the lack of a campus community feeling. Basically, freshman year you make a lot of friends, and after sophomore year people start taking more advantage of the city itself, and you really stop running into people you know because they are all scattered. I'm making it sound more depressing than it actually is—most people are happy, but depending on your major and what kind of graduate school you want to get in to, people's lifestyles here vary greatly, so there is no unified campus feeling.

The Institution

Columbia is funny because I feel like a lot of people are really proud to be going here and proud to be a part of the community, but there is little school spirit. Students bond over how frustrated they are with the school, but they would never want to go anywhere else. I don't think the pride even comes from the school being an Ivy—it's more about the school being in New York. A lot of people I know that go here turned down offers from Harvard and Princeton so they could be in the city. It can set you up for a good job because there are a lot more opportunities here for internships during the school year, and lots of people work or volunteer while taking classes in publishing, fashion, film, and a lot of other things that are centered in New York. And after a while I notice people are proud to come off as "real" New Yorkers, to not react to crazy bums yelling shit at you, or cockroaches the size of turtles, or car alarms. People seem to get a lot of satisfaction from being unfazed.

The security is really intense here: if you have visitors, you have to sign them in, and you need swipe access (from your ID card) to get into all the dormitories. The campus is pretty compact and convenient and the neighborhood is very safe. It is New York, so you do have to be somewhat careful, and there are as many rats as squirrels, but that doesn't faze you after a while. Also because it's New York, it is really expensive, but there are always lots of interesting free talks and readings, if not on campus, elsewhere in the city.

The Education

How much work you do, and what you get out of a class, is entirely up to you. It might be different in the sciences, but in the humanities you can always bullshit your way to a B+. Of course, most people do do the work, because they are paying so much money to learn. People are definitely into their work, and it's nice to listen to people talk about the things they're studying. I'm not saying everyone only talks about the core classes, but it's not uncommon for people to talk about them. Sometimes it can be pretentious, like when drunken boys are quoting Plato, but usually it's not.

The Students

Students here are laid-back but secretly anal and too smart to be too hipster. There are a lot of gay boys on campus. It feels like the male population is predominantly gay because I know a lot more gay boys than straight ones, but this is definitely a good school to be a gay boy in. As for lesbians, I think a lot of them go to Barnard. Barnard is much more segregated from Columbia than they make it seem on the tours. Most people don't take classes there, and most Barnard girls don't take classes at Columbia, unless they are in visual arts or film. There is all this silly fake hostility between Barnard and Columbia girls at first, but people grow out of it pretty quickly.

The Activities

It's hard to talk about campus life because everyone here really does their own thing. In New York you can find things to do at any time. There are a lot of campus groups, or you can get involved more directly with the city. I'm involved with the lit mag *Columbia Review.* They organize student readings at the Bowery Poetry Club or St. Mark's Church, which are really big poetry venues in NY. (The owner of the Bowery Bar actually teaches here.) It's crazy, actually. I was in a used bookstore in New Mexico this spring break and felt like I have met half the authors personally, because they either teach here or I've seen them read at the KGB bar or other places. And it was the first time that it really hit me that if I was going to school somewhere in New Mexico, or any other rural area really, I would not have the same access to amazing people.

The Social Scene

There's alcohol, but because there are other things to do around here than drink, people don't go that crazy with it. There are plenty of parties on and off campus, and there are the local bars that lots of people go to, but older kids tend to either go downtown or have room parties. The Stend (West End) attracts mostly freshmen, frat boys and econ majors go to Nacho Mama's, upperclassmen and film majors go to 1020, swimmers go to The Heights, and the Ding Dong attracts mostly grad students and the more coked-out and artsy undergrads. There is a frat scene, but it in no way dominates. It's a little nontraditional too—there's a gay literary frat—not that many schools have one of those. There's also the rich WASP Saint Anthony's society, but they aren't particularly exclusive with their parties anyway. Dating is notoriously awful here. Everyone is either single and not getting any, or in a very serious committed relationship—at least among the heterosexual community. The gay community is a little different. My Friday or Saturday night is probably really different from most people's here because I am usually just happy staying in with my boyfriend, or hanging around the dorm with my friends. Other people aren't as low-key. And it's really rare, but there are some people that spend Friday and Saturday night studying.

Notable Columbia Alumni Include:

Isaac Asimov, author
Art Garfunkel, musician
Allen Ginsberg, poet
John MacArthur, president and publisher of *Harper's*
Robert Merton, Nobel Prize–winning economist
Max Lincoln Schuster, cofounder, Simon & Schuster

CONNECTICUT COLLEGE

Founded: 1911
Location: New London, CT
Phone: (860) 439-2200
E-mail: admissions@conncoll.edu
Web site: www.connecticutcollege.edu

Number of Undergraduates: 1,897
Number of Graduate Students: 12
Cost: Approximately $30,000 per year
Application Deadline: January 1
Early Decision: November 15

Rating:	Notable Majors/Programs:
Very Selective	English, Psychology, Religion, History

Size:
● Small ○ Medium ○ Large

Location:
○ Urban ● Suburban ○ Rural

On a Saturday, students talk about academics:
○ Always ● Sometimes ○ Never

Nightlife:
○ Intense ● Moderate ○ Laid-back

Politically, Connecticut College leans:
● Left ○ Right ○ Split

Diversity:
○ High ● Low ○ Medium

Students describe Connecticut College school in five words:
- Traditional New England college experience
- Attractive, driven, talented, preppy students

From the School

This highly selective, coeducational, private college offers an outstanding education in the best tradition of the liberal arts and sciences. It also encourages innovations and independence by providing a curriculum and an environment in which change and new ideas can thrive. A commitment to interdisciplinary learning, dynamic student faculty research, and a campus honor code system of shared governance combine to inspire leadership and respect for diversity.

—www.conncoll.edu

If you're interested in Connecticut College, you may also be interested in:
Boston College, Bowdoin, Colby, Middlebury, Trinity, Tufts

Name: May
Hometown: Springfield, Massachusetts
Class Year: Senior
Major: English
Extracurriculars: Dance
Career Goal: Working in the arts

How would you describe Connecticut College's reputation?

We have a reputation for being a pretty good school with sports teams that try hard but are, in the end, pretty lousy. We're also called "Country Club Conn" (referring to our beautiful campus, beautiful students, and the beautiful, expensive things we own like nice cars and designer clothes).

Is that reputation accurate?

We are a pretty good school, and our sports teams do try hard, and do tend to lose . . . badly. Connecticut does kind of look like a country club. Some days on campus all the girls are in white tennis skirts, all the boys are in khakis and button-downs. Everyone's toned, because they frequent the gym. It's just the Connecticut lifestyle—gym, study, class, study, party. Then back to the gym.

What aspect of your school would a prospective student not see on a campus tour?

You wouldn't hear about the ridiculously rigid beauty standards on campus. There are exceptions, but many, many girls are toothpick thin, and many, many boys are ripped. And both parties will insist they never diet or work out, that they "just look this way naturally"!

The Institution

Our campus is beautiful and we do have decent food. Kids come back from being abroad and say, "God, I missed Harris!" (our dining hall). The size of Conn. is something you either love or hate. Conn. feels like a close-knit community and I love it—those that feel it's too small transfer out after freshman year. The best Connecticut tradition is Floralia—a day-long music festival right before the last week of classes in May that lasts from 8 a.m. to 11 p.m. We all set up blankets and chairs on the green as early as 4 a.m., and by 7:30 a.m. people are drinking mimosas. From there on out, drunkenness is key. There are big headlining bands and local bands, bouncy castles and obstacle courses. Basically, Floralia is all about love. The campus safety officers, the cafeteria staff, the students, everyone gets together and has a kick-ass day before the end of the year.

> "The stereotypical Conn. College student went to private school, is from twenty minutes outside Boston, studied abroad in Australia, plays some kind of a sport, and volunteers regularly."
>
> ✦ Christina, senior

The Education

I know all my professors well. They know me by name, and many also know my academic interests and concerns. Almost all classes here are discussion-based, and the professors are amazing. They are genuinely thoughtful people who love to teach. The funny thing about Connecticut is, while I've said all this stuff about physical appearances being important and made us sound superficial, we all work hard, too. Students are very involved in their schoolwork and are genuinely interested in the subjects they study. On a Saturday night, at a huge party, you'll overhear students discussing something that went on in class the previous week, and dinner conversations are intellectually driven. Just because we're beautiful doesn't mean we're dumb (flipping hair off shoulder, winking at the camera).

> "There are coed bathrooms in every Conn. College dorm. Bear this in mind."
>
> ✦ Kayle, sophomore

The Students

People say almost every student at Conn. is from "just outside" Boston or New York City, is attractive, and drives a nice Saab. I would alter that slightly and say that everyone here *looks* like that's their story. In reality, we do have students who are on financial aid. The thing is, you can't usually pick out who is on financial aid and who is not. The rich and the poor are equally buff, equally beautiful, and integrate seamlessly. Also not everyone drives a nice car—I've seen some real beaters out in the parking lot. If you asked me whether Connecticut

College was diverse, I'd say, "Kinda, sorta. The school is doing its best to make the answer, Yes."

The Activities

Arts are big on campus. Dance is particularly popular. The student-run Dance Club puts on one student-choreographed, -produced, and -directed show a semester, and it is *always* sold out. Anyone on campus can try out and over a hundred students usually audition for the Dance Club.

And if you are still awake at 3 a.m. on a Wednesday at Conn., it is because you have a twenty-five-page paper and a project due the next day. You work your butt off until you finish it, and then get right to bed.

> "Conn's endowment isn't as large as those at peer institutions. Accordingly, some of our building projects have been postponed, and some dorms are in need of renovations."
> ✦ Mary, senior

The Social Scene

Conn. parties on Thursday and Saturday nights. We have no frats or sororities, so the social scene is very inclusive. Of course there is drinking, but the general attitude is that drinking is just for fun, not a sport or competition. Getting really wasted is sort of frowned upon, because it means you aren't in control of yourself, and control is key here. Once parties end, most students congregate in the student center to see their friends and the people they'd like to be friends with, and talk about life, classes, or anything over some mozzarella sticks or a pint of Ben and Jerry's. Conn. has great late-night food available; when kids go back to their dorms, the rooms are cushy, and the social scene is vibrant.

Name: Jessica
Hometown: New York, New York
Class Year: Freshman
Extracurriculars: La Unidad Spanish Club, dorm diversity coordinator, literary magazine, ESL on campus, tour guide
Major: English and Latin American studies, minor in Italian
Career Goal: I'd like to go into either journalism or creative writing.

How would you describe Connecticut College's reputation?

Academically challenging, selective, wealthy, and athletic.

Is this reputation accurate?

Perfect.

What aspect of your school would a prospective student not see on a campus tour?

There is no way to really grasp the sincerity, talent, humility, and intelligence of Connecticut College students until you've spent some real time here. They're truly incredible.

The Institution

You can't fall between the cracks at Connecticut. You will be supported and appreciated from every different angle. And there are people here who are so incredibly talented—nationally competing swimmers, people who've lived alone in third world countries, published poets, people who've suffered unimaginable physical and mental trauma and are willing to share their experiences with you, people who have run animal shelters from their garages . . . it's impressive. That said, Connecticut has all the negatives of a small school. People will know when you leave someone's dorm room on a Sunday morning with one shoe and knotty hair. Before you have time to get back to your own room, cell phones will have rung, and there will be a note on your door saying, "Hey, heard you hooked up last night—how'd it go? Are you going to see so-and-so again?"

The Education

Academics at Connecticut really filter into our everyday life. We talk about sociology while we're brushing our teeth in the coed bathrooms, math while we're exercising on the treadmills, and we plan our study-abroad trip while we're doing our laundry. We love our professors—they are a huge part of our lives—and we love what we learn and do. Every course at Connecticut is taught by a professor and not a TA. Students here compete only against themselves, to do better, work harder. The pressure to do one's best can build up, but then it's let out every fall during our dorm versus dorm color war called "Camelympics."

Connecticut College has a core curriculum, which, I think, enhances the academic experience here. Essentially, you have seven broad areas in which you have to take classes: physical and biological sciences, mathematics and logic, social science, critical studies in literature and arts, creative arts, philosophy and religious studies, and historical studies. You'd be taking classes in half of these areas anyway, so the requirements won't bother you too much. Even though math is my nemesis, I took Mathematics of Money this year, and actually got something useful out of it. As for our strongest departments, the English Department is wonderful, psychology, religion, and history are great as well. Feel free to take lots of classes outside of your major. Even if you're majoring in environmental studies and take a classics course just for fun, the professor will treat you like you're the next Cicero.

The Students

Connecticut College is extremely welcoming and firmly believes in the ideals of pluralism and tolerance. Everyone mixes—black, white, Asian, gay, straight, so on. Before freshman year, "Why Do All the Black Kids Sit Together in the Cafeteria?" was on the reading list and the author came to discuss the book with us.

I'd say most Connecticut students are liberal, and those that aren't are comfortable in a liberal atmosphere and open to debate. Most students are politically intelligent, even if they're not politically active. The average Connecticut student would be enthusiastic about academics, talented, motivated, and endlessly friendly.

The Activities

Dance and a cappella groups are extremely popular at Conn. About three quarters of the student body volunteers in local communities. If students feel the need to get off campus, they go to Mystic or Providence or New York for a weekend. But when we're gone, we feel like we're missing out. There's so much happening on campus—you spend a weekend away and it feels like you've missed three weeks' worth of activities!

The Social Scene

There are an unlimited number of ways to party, but a lot of them revolve around alcohol. We're a small school, and we do a lot of intimate dance parties, wine and cheese parties, etc. However, nearly everyone ends up at the student center eating French fries around 2 a.m. on Saturday nights. We don't have frats or sororities but we do have some cultlike sports teams (like the ice hockey team), which put on big events with regularity. If you are looking for a Greek scene, go to U. Connecticut.

If you want extreme liberalism and naked parties, go to Wesleyan. If you want hard drugs, head to Trinity. But if you want the quintessential prestigious New England liberal arts college experience? That's exactly what you'll get at Conn. College. Everyone is really friendly here, always introducing themselves and inviting you to discussions, panels, parties, or poetry readings. Ninety-eight percent of students live on campus, and they love it.

Name: Adam
Hometown: Yarmouth, Maine
Class Year: Senior
Major: Society, culture and documentary studies
Extracurriculars: Student Government Association, gallery assistant
Career Goal: Either pursuing something in urban studies or urban planning or becoming a college professor.

How would you describe Connecticut College's reputation?

Connecticut College is one of eleven schools in the New England Small College Athletic Conference (NESCAC). I think a lot of students from NESCAC schools view us as being like the Ivy League of small colleges.

Is that reputation accurate?

Conn. College does have Ivy-caliber academics. Will I be proud to graduate a Connecticut Camel? Yes, absolutely.

What would an admissions officer at your school probably not tell a prospective student?

Connecticut College is underresourced and, lately, has been having some financial problems.

The Institution

Connecticut College, like many small liberal arts colleges, is a school on a hill. It's separated from the city of New London by Interstate 95, and many students stay on campus and don't cross that divide. I go to town more than most, because I go to the Greek Orthodox Church downtown, and I visit local bars, coffee shops, restaurants, and galleries.

Our relatively small size can be occasionally stifling, and when the desire to get off campus hits me, I travel an hour or so to New Haven, which is a fairly big urban center. I came to Conn. College because it has outstanding study abroad programs, lots of interdisciplinary majors, and a strong honor code that allows students to take responsibility for their own educations. All this has allowed me to create my own student-designed interdisciplinary major (SDIM)—I've become academically well rounded, but I've also been allowed to acutely focus in on my specific interests. I do feel prepared for life after college. I may not have *everything* sussed out, but having gone abroad twice through Connecticut helped me realize and solidify my goals.

> "How many Connecticut College students does it take to change a lightbulb? 1,600. One to change the lightbulb, and 1,599 to complain that if they'd gotten into a better school, the lightbulb wouldn't have burned out in the first place."
>
> ✦ William, freshman

The Education

I talk about classes on a Saturday night because my group of friends is fun, but also intellectual. I don't feel competition among students in the classroom (but that could be a result of my own uncompetitive nature). All of my classes have been taught by professors—we do not have TAs at Connecticut—and I spend a minimum of six hours a night doing reading alone. I have a great deal of work, and I also spend a great deal of time in the lab.

The Students

Students at Connecticut College say they're liberal, but that's mostly just talk. They'll never protest, never get stirred up because of a political issue. Most kids are from New England or the Northeast and are predominantly from the upper-middle class. In general, students from all class years interact. The only real barrier I've noticed to Conn. students interacting is that international students and domestic students rarely hang out together.

The Activities

The U.S. Coast Guard Academy is literally across the street from Conn., but we rarely interact with them. On a sunny day you will see nearly every student outside. You will see guys tossing a football or baseball, you will see hippies playing Frisbee or doing interpretive dance, you will see a group of girls in bathing suit tops, and groups of nondescript students sitting around working or talking. When people do go off campus, there's always something to do, like go to a movie, or Mohegan Sun . . .

The Social Scene

The student center is central to Connecticut's social life. Nights often begin and end at the student center. The alcohol policies are definitely enforced on campus, but that's not to say that students under twenty-one don't drink. Underage students just party behind closed doors. That said, don't come here if you're looking for an Animal House college experience. There is no Greek life, which is generally considered to be a good thing. We tend to party in a more low-key manner. You'll never see someone throwing furniture off balconies. We just think that's dumb.

Notable Connecticut College Alumni Include:

James Berrien, publisher/president, *Forbes* magazine

Agnes Gund, president emerita, Museum of Modern Art

Anita DeFrantz, olympic medalist and vice president, International Committee

> "CCLeft has become increasingly active. This year we've had teach-ins on women's reproductive rights, IMF, and the World Bank, and numerous protests here and in D.C."
>
> ✦ Daniel, junior

CORNELL UNIVERSITY

Founded: 1865

Location: Ithaca, NY

Phone: (607) 255-5241

E-mail: admissions@cornell.edu

Web site: www.cornell.edu

Number of Undergraduates: 20,141

Number of Graduate Students: 5,049

Cost: Approximately $39,000 per year

Application Deadline: January 1

Early Decision: November 1

Rating:
Most Selective

Notable Majors/Programs:
Hotel School, Social Sciences, Biology, Economics/Business

Size:

○ Small   ○ Medium   ● Large

Location:

○ Urban   ○ Suburban   ● Rural

On a Saturday, students talk about academics:

○ Always   ● Sometimes   ○ Never

Nightlife:

● Intense   ○ Moderate   ○ Laid-back

Politically, Cornell leans:

● Left   ○ Right   ○ Split

Diversity:

○ High   ○ Low   ● Medium

Students describe Cornell in five words:
- Largest, busiest Ivy League school
- Ambitious, well-rounded, multitasking individualistic students

From the School

Cornell University represents a distinctive mix of eminent scholarship and democratic ideals. Adding practical subjects to the classics and admitting qualified students regardless of nationality, race, social circumstance, gender, or religion was quite a departure when Cornell was founded in 1865. Today's Cornell reflects this heritage of egalitarian excellence. . . . Both a private university and the land-grant institution of New York State, Cornell University is the most educationally diverse member of the Ivy League.

—www.cornell.edu

If you're interested in Cornell, you may also be interested in:
UC Berkeley, Columbia, Harvard, Northwestern, SUNY–Binghamton, Washington U. in St. Louis

Name: Christopher
Hometown: Salt Lake City, Utah
Class Year: Senior
Major: Human development
Extracurriculars: OUTreach, Ga'Avah Jewish LGBT Student Group, Haven LGBT student umbrella organization, Students Pursuing Teaching Careers, Human Ecology Leadership Initiative, Ultimate Frisbee
Career Goal: I want to become a professor of psychology and eventually open a tuition-free boarding school for teens who are either homeless, abused, or needing to escape destructive environments (i.e., queer youth who live in extremely homophobic areas).

How would you describe Cornell's reputation?

Cornell is an Ivy League school that's said to appeal to academically masochistic students.

Is this reputation accurate?

Yes, for the most part this reputation is accurate. Students here pretend they never work, that they're just your average, slacker, party-going college kids. But head to the library any night and you'll see those same people furiously scribbling notes while working in study groups. No other place on this humongous campus gets visited more consistently than our two main libraries. Everyone spends so much time there because they're busy as hell—and even if they won't admit it, that's just the way they like it!

> "I visited twenty-five schools in the Northeast. I ate at every single one of them, and Cornell's food is by far the best."
>
> ✦ Blake, senior

What would an admissions officer at your school probably not tell a prospective student?

Cornell will tell you that students here don't drink much. "Most Cornell students drink one to three drinks, or no drinks at all, when they party." Sorry, Cornell, I don't think you're pulling anything over on 13,000 of the brightest young minds in the country with that one. Was I hallucinating the other night, or didn't I see three guys pass out while doing a beer bong? I'll tell you the truth, here and now, Cornell students drink. And drink. And drink. Bottoms up!

The Institution

Cornell's admissions propaganda tries to make Cornell sound like it can be everything to every student. "It's a big school with big resources, but it feels like a small school with a small atmosphere." Whatever! Cornell is a moderately large school in a small, crunchy town, and that's exactly what it feels like. If you know in advance that you can't survive if your classes have more than one hundred students in them, Cornell isn't for you. Come here if you want a wide range of big classes, taught by some of the nation's best professors, all located in a cozy little town quite a few hours away from any urban metropolises.

The Education

For an Ivy League school, Cornell has way too many impersonal lecture classes. If you don't want to feel like just a number, make it a point to go to your professors' office hours. Really, not knowing the students isn't the fault of our professors (who are friendly and enthusiastic and eager), it's a practical issue, where there are simply too many students in every class for a professor to reach out to each one. So make it easier on them, stop by their office, chat after class, send them a thank you note after a particularly good conversation. I promise, your professors will love you if you do this, and they'll reward your efforts by knowing your name and your hobbies and your interests. In turn, you'll get far more out of every class. It's allowed me in certain instances to write a research paper instead of taking one of the prelims (prelims equal any test that occurs before the final), and it really pays off when it comes to asking for letters of recommendation down the line.

The Students

On the whole, Cornell students love to learn, and we're not ashamed to be overachievers. The concept of being a nerd doesn't really apply here because we're all nerds. If you're the student who isn't afraid to express your inquisitive side and ask questions, you're going to love Cornell. Cornellians are also ultra-involved in campus activities (hey, Ithaca is a small town), so if you're looking for a school where you can find other people who are obsessed with the mating behaviors of fruit flies, or backpacking in local parks, or designing a student fashion show, or writing a report about pornography (the Cornell library has the largest pornography collection in the academic world), you'll love this place! Also we're quirky. Don't come here if you are obsessed with the status quo. We want your whole, crazy-ass self. If you want a school where you can just be a living, walking version of your resume, go to MIT or Dartmouth. Cornell students tend to be really liberal. The few conservatives are used by everyone else for comic relief. And students also tend to be very diverse religiously, ethnically, and in terms of where they come from. Just the other day, six friends and I were sitting around the table eating strawberry waffles and vegetarian lasagna, and somebody mentioned that we looked just like a picture someone might put on an admissions pamphlet: me, the gay Jewish boy, sitting next to two black women—one African American, the other a mix of all races—an international student from Japan, a white Mormon guy, a bisexual atheist punker, and an Islamic studies-majoring lesbian.

> "You have to climb a large hill to get to class every day, and it can really snow here. On the bright side, you can tell your kids you had 'to climb up and down a big hill, in the freezing cold, in feet of snow, every day.'"
> ✦ Ruby, sophomore

The Activities

You absolutely *must* go to a hockey game before you graduate. Even if you hate sports, they are the place where you'll see more school spirit than anywhere else. Especially at the Cornell/Harvard game. We all sneak a bunch of raw fish into the rink and throw the fish at the Harvard players when they come onto the ice. It's great fun, and it gets a lot of the tension out for the students who really wanted to go to Harvard but didn't get in. There are also a million activities for gay students at Cornell. I came from a small, conservative high school that wouldn't dare mention the word gay, much less have a gay-straight alliance. At Cornell, there are social groups for gay, straight, bi, or closeted students of every possible stripe. There's almost too much to do! We also have several openly gay and

lesbian faculty members, and an LGBT studies major in addition to a very strong feminist, gender, and sexuality studies major. We also have a Queer Prom, which draws students from all over, including hot, straight, frat guys who are completely comfortable hanging out with the feminine gay guys as long as the femmy gays aren't grabbing their asses. Overall, Cornell is sort of a hidden gay paradise! And speaking more broadly, the range of activities and groups for gay students is indicative of the range of activities and groups for *all* kinds of students at Cornell. That's an advantage of this place being so large—there's not only something for everyone, but twenty somethings for everyone.

The Social Scene

It's 3 a.m. on a Wednesday night and you're still awake, as is half your dorm. You'll probably head to the student lounge and vent about your crazy twenty-page paper with the other students who are brewing coffee and dripping Visine into their sleepy eyes. All-nighters happen all the time here. And most Cornell students don't have Friday classes, so if you can just get through a four-day week, you'll be able to get plenty of sleep.

Suffice to say, when I said there are twenty clubs for every type of student, on a weekend night that holds true for parties as well. At a school this big, with this many intelligent students—and, on weekends, with this many intelligent, drunken students—you will never, ever be bored. Ithaca is not a bustling metropolis. Don't expect there to be bars, clubs, good shopping, or fun social outlets in Ithaca. That said, there's so much happening on campus, both academically and socially, that our schedules are already packed full.

Cornell is surrounded by lakes, forests, and gorges. When you're here, you feel like you're living much the way Thoreau did when he "went to the woods to live deliberately." What Cornell lacks in commercial luxury it makes up for in energy. Cornell is this buzzing pocket of intellectual excitement in what often feels like the middle of nowhere.

Also, one thing you should know is that the secret societies on campus (such as Quill and Dagger, the Cornell version of The Skulls) are bullshit. You can't apply to these; you can only be tapped (someone will show up at your doorstep in the middle of the night, wearing a black cape). I was a member of Quill and Dagger, and have since resigned, and I assure everyone that they shouldn't feel bad if they aren't chosen to be a part of the mystery elite snob clubs. The secret societies are so lame. People just get together, network, and gossip about how exclusive it all is.

Name: Gloria
Hometown: Portland, Oregon
Class Year: Freshman
Major: Hotel administration
Extracurriculars: Cornell Hotel Society, employment at the Statler Hotel, Hotelies Volunteering Today, Alpha Phi sorority

How would you describe Cornell's reputation?

There's a saying: "Harvard is hard to get in to, easy to get out of. Cornell is easy to get in to, hard to get out of."

Is this reputation accurate? Why or why not?

I think this is very accurate. From what I've heard, it's pretty hard to get into Harvard, but it's pretty easy for a Harvard student to get As once they're there. Whereas Cornell is (debatably) the easiest Ivy to get into, because we're the biggest Ivy, but professors practice grade deflation, and you have to work extremely hard just to get average grades at Cornell, let alone As.

> "Sometimes there can be a little too much school spirit. Every year, the freshmen rush the field at the first football game to show how much they love this place. This September, a girl in my dorm ran, fell, got stepped on by overzealous students, and broke her arm."
>
> ✦ Lisa, freshman

What would an admissions officer at your school probably not tell a prospective student?

Hidden costs. Everything at Cornell seems to cost something extra: PE classes, campus buses, parking, lost IDs. It's amazing how much you'll spend on extras.

The Institution

The best thing about Cornell is that everyone is so proud to be here. Cornell is a really prestigious Ivy League school, and the only reason anyone got in is because they did something (or many things) incredibly well in high school. But in person, everyone is so humble! Ithaca's weather is rough; it snows December through April. I'm from the West Coast, and the weather-transition was a bit difficult for me. Luckily, Cornell is absolutely gorgeous, one of the prettiest college campuses in the country, and the snow only makes it look even more beautiful.

> "This year I participated in the 'Big Fat Queer Wedding,' a rally/mock same-sex marriage ceremony attended by hundreds of students. When the minister asked if anyone objected to the gay marriage, there was absolute silence. It was one of the most amazing, and affirming, moments of my life."
>
> ✦ Hyun, junior

I actually wanted to go to a small school. I was impressed with the personal attention students receive in liberal arts colleges, I liked the "I know everyone" attitude kids at Amherst and Williams and Wesleyan seemed to have. But now I'm glad that I went to a larger university. There is so much constantly on offer here that a small school, with a smaller amount of resources, just couldn't touch. And as a student in the small hotel school, I feel like I still get the best of both worlds.

Also Cornell has some great food. Freshmen have two dining halls nearby, the Robert Purcell Community Center and Apple Community Center. Each has a gourmet cake station, custom stir-fry, weekly themed dinners, waffle makers, pasta bars, salad bars, ice cream stations, sandwich bars, Asian food, grills, and so on. At the hotel school we have a café called Mac's and the Terrace Restaurant, which makes custom salads and wraps and is *so* good that people come from all over campus to have lunch there.

The Education

I'm in the hotel school, which is, hands down, the best hospitality program in the entire world. Seriously, it's ranked number one every year. My classmates are always, of course (by nature of being "hotelies"), polite, professional, social, and intelligent. It's very comfortable, focused, and everyone takes a wide range of courses relevant to our industry: business communication classes, law classes, information technology labs, and so on. Because the hotel school is so well known, students are constantly being sought after by big name companies. It's rare that a week will go by without an "atrium showcase," which is when a prestigious company sets up a booth in the atrium of the school and answers questions, schedules interviews, etc.

On a broader note: Cornell has a core curriculum, two PE classes, five classes from the social sciences/history/ humanities/arts, and four classes from the physical and biological sciences. Students also have to be "proficient" in a foreign language.

The Students

There are so many different kinds of students at Cornell. I'm not even going to attempt to describe the average student—there are too many of us here to pinpoint a "type"—other than that we're all smart, studious types, all at the top of our high school classes.

The Activities

No single organization or student group dominates campus. There are too many. There are a *lot* of a cappella groups. Our newspaper, the *Cornell Daily Sun,* is pretty popular, a lot of people read it and work on it. And Cornell loves its sports teams, particularly its hockey and basketball teams. Loyal hockey fans are called "The Lynch Faithful," after the name of our rink.

> "The professors are really nice. Despite having won a Nobel prize, your Chemistry 207 professor will gladly make a private appointment to explain redux reactions."
> ✦ Marissa, senior

The Social Scene

Most people go out Thursday, Friday, and Saturday, some go out more. Alcohol is everywhere; you'll never have to worry whether you'll be able to get your hands on a beer or some vodka. Cornell's Greek scene is *huge* and throws most of the good parties on campus, so if being in a fraternity or sorority isn't your thing, you'll still be able to have a social life, but you really might feel left out.

Students who pledge tend to have more fun at Cornell, and get more out of their time here. You don't have to, but if you do, it sure does make things easier.

Name: Ryan
Hometown: Princeton, New Jersey
Class Year: Junior
Major: Government
Extracurriculars: Intramurals (refereeing and playing), some theater, and I was an RA for a year.
Career Goal: I'd like to become a lawyer.

How would you describe Cornell's reputation?

Among the Ivies, we're said to have a party-school atmosphere.

Is this reputation accurate?

Cornell students do have a good time, we have a very active Greek scene, but it's a "work hard, play hard" kind of thing. Students aren't drunk during the week or anything, it's just that, when they do have fun, they like to have big fun.

What would an admissions officer at your school probably not tell a prospective student?

How hard we party. Also—and this is the flip side of Cornell—on the tour they won't show you the inside of the main Uris Library, which is one of my favorite places on campus. It has about fifty million nooks and crannies that I'm still discovering, and every book that you'd ever want to look at. When Cornell students aren't partying, they're studying extremely hard, and it's nice to be able to do so in a gorgeous building like Uris, with everything at your fingertips.

The Institution

Cornell is the single biggest Ivy League school, which means it offers more academically and socially than, say, Brown might—but it's also considerably easier for a student to get swallowed up here, and there are far less people looking out for your well being. If you're pretty independent, this isn't a problem. You'll be able to navigate Cornell just fine. But if you're used to being a bit coddled, you may find Cornell daunting.

The Education

So long as you're willing to work for it, Cornell will provide a fantastic education. Teachers here expect students to give their very best, and that tends to motivate students to deliver. If you want B+'s and above at Cornell, prepare yourself to spend long hours in the library. Particularly if you're pre-med—those guys have ridiculous amounts of work, and, among themselves, are absolutely cut-throat.

One of the nice things about Cornell, though, is that it's so big you can take a course on *anything*. And since Cornell's core curriculum isn't too extensive—it's just large enough to make you take some classes you may not have thought to take otherwise—you'll have plenty of room in your schedule to take fun electives like a wine class or a mythology course.

My classes at Cornell have ranged from two thousand students (the notorious Psychology 101) to fifteen students. When classes are big, you need to take the initiative if you want the professors to know your name. But you might not always want your professors to know you, and that's okay. I actually prefer being anonymous sometimes, because that lets me passively sit back and learn and not have to worry about being impressive on a weekly basis. For those classes where I do know the professor, though, I always take care to know my stuff.

The Students

I'd say the average Cornell student is upper-middle class, from New York, New Jersey, or Penn-sylvania, and from a private or magnet school (or top of their class at a public school). He or she is most likely somewhat liberal and a Democrat, and will often take a centrist position.

The Activities

There are a lot of activities to get involved in at Cornell, but most of them take up large chunks of time. This means most students pick one or two things they're interested in and become heavily in-volved, rather than halfheartedly committing to a smattering of things. And when Cornell students want to get off campus, well, Ithaca College is right nearby, but I've never been there and I don't know anyone else who has. If you have a car, you can always head to Ithaca Commons and shop, or eat out in the really amazing Ithaca restaurant scene.

The Social Scene

Because Cornell is so big, you'll always be meet-ing new people, but you'll never be able to know everyone. The best way to meet people here is through the dorms, where everyone is incredibly friendly and a real sense of community develops. But Cornell students really only do the dorm thing freshman year; by sophomore year people are moving out, and by junior year most students live off campus. So take advantage of the dorm scene while you can. Ithaca is small, so partying, and most of your social life, will take place on campus. And since Cornell is heavily Greek, there are *con-stant* parties, events, lots of fun interfraternity/sorority rivalries and showdowns and showoffs.

Notable Cornell Alumni Include:
Janet Reno, former U.S. attorney general
Christopher Reeve, actor
Kurt Vonnegut, Jr., author
Bill Maher, comedian, actor
Richard Price, author, scriptwriter
Bill Nye, the "Science Guy"

DARTMOUTH COLLEGE

Founded: 1769
Location: Hanover, NH
Phone: (603) 646-2875
E-mail: admissions.office@dartmouth.edu
Web site: www.dartmouth.edu

Number of Undergraduates: 4,079
Number of Graduate Students: 1,291
Cost: Approximately $38,000 per year
Application Deadline: January 1
Early Decision: November 1

Rating:	Notable Majors/Programs:
Most Selective	Biology, Government, Economics

Size:
○ Small   ● Medium   ○ Large

Location:
○ Urban   ○ Suburban   ● Rural

On a Saturday, students talk about academics:
○ Always   ● Sometimes   ○ Never

Nightlife:
● Intense   ○ Moderate   ○ Laid-back

Politically, Dartmouth is:
○ Left   ○ Right   ● Split

Diversity:
● High   ○ Low   ○ Medium

Ivy League: Yes!

Students describe Dartmouth in five words:
- Preppy, sporty/outdoorsy Ivy school
- Small, intellectual, secluded rural campus

From the School

Dartmouth College combines the best features of an undergraduate liberal arts college with the intellectual vitality of a research university. Founded as an undergraduate institution more than two centuries ago, Dartmouth offers excellent graduate programs within the Arts and Sciences and in business, engineering, and medicine. The professional schools, among the first established in their respective fields, have had a historic role in defining the school's intellectual values. Dartmouth encourages a love of learning and discovery in every member of its community.

—www.dartmouth.edu

If you're interested in Dartmouth, you may also be interested in:
Amherst, Bowdoin, Colgate, Duke, William and Mary, Williams

Name: Kristen

Hometown: Brockton, Massachusetts

Class Year: Sophomore

Major: Religion (I was going to be a biology major . . . then I took a biology class)

Extracurriculars: Chinese Dance Troupe, undergraduate Adviser (like an RA), Delta Delta Delta sorority

Career Goal: I want to be a doctor, but I am not doing my premedical curriculum at Dartmouth. . . . I want a broad liberal arts education and don't want to confine myself to one academic discipline.

How would you describe Dartmouth's reputation?

Dartmouth is a small Ivy League school. Those who know us say we're known for our focus on undergraduate education.

Is this reputation accurate?

Dartmouth is focused on undergraduate education, although some will argue that our current president is trying to make Dartmouth more prestigious by turning professors away from teaching and toward impersonal research. But Dartmouth students and alums wouldn't let that happen. We care about our school too much.

What would an admissions officer at your school probably not tell a prospective student? What aspect of your school would a prospective student not see on a campus tour?

The administration wouldn't tell you about our crappy gym. For all the money Dartmouth has, our gym consists of a small weight room with four treadmills. That said, there is so much other great stuff going on at Dartmouth that it doesn't matter . . . our fantastic golf course, our ski slope, the Morton Horse Farm, all the great academic buildings, all the dorms, the museums, the ten libraries. . . . Dartmouth is a small campus, but there's a lot to it!

The Institution

Where else but Dartmouth can you get a top-notch education in a pristine environment, meet amazing and unpretentious people from around the world, mingle regularly with administrators and professors, and participate in a wide range of clubs and activities? Dartmouth College stands alone. After every break, I'm dying to come back. And when the bus pulls up to the campus green and I see the tall steeple of Baker Library, I've never been happier.

The Education

My friends at other schools get to know one or two professors. Here at Dartmouth, I talk to a large handful of professors regularly. Granted, this means you can't miss class because your professors will notice, but it makes your education so much more valuable. . . . And the academic climate carries over to your personal life. I talk about classes on Saturday nights because classes here are wicked interesting. And competition exists—everyone got here because they were pretty smart. But I think what distinguishes Dartmouth from the other Ivies is that the competition here is *healthy*. People compete, but it's good spirited. Classes are smaller and discussion based in the humanities, and a bit bigger and usually lecture/lab–based in the sciences. But in the sciences, there are a ton of research opportunities for students. This school practically throws money at you to do your own research. Take advantage of it.

And we're not really affected by the graduate schools on campus (Tuck, for business; the medical school; Thayer, for engineering) because Dartmouth is, first and foremost, an undergraduate institution. The grad schools, if anything, enhance the undergraduate experience. We have unique opportunities to meet with the grad students, sit in on their classes, etc. But undergrads indisputably rule the school.

The Students

Students have a bigger role in administrative decisions than they realize. I've had the opportunity to meet with the deans and then—to my surprise—see my suggestions play out as major policy changes! It's awesome that Dartmouth lets that happen.

The Activities

A ridiculous number of Dartmouth students go abroad. Unlike Harvard and Yale, Dartmouth makes it easy for us to travel.

The Social Scene

The Greek scene is huge at Dartmouth, probably because we live in the middle of nowhere. Frats and sororities do a lot of philanthropic work, and we are constantly changing and growing. We have twelve Inter-Fraternity Council fraternities and six Panhellenic Council sororities, with a healthy mix of national and local organizations. Our Order of Omega (Greek honor society) has members whose GPAs are among the highest in the nation. We also have

NPHC (traditionally African-American) and NALFO (traditionally Latino-Latina) organizations. Greek life is great. And it's pretty cool when trustees are seen taking a few drinks in fraternity basements.

> "The best tradition at Dartmouth is the eight-story-tall freshman bonfire on the green. Freshmen run laps around it while it burns, spurred on by upperclassmen. It's really fun."
> ✦ Katya, freshman

Name: Blake
Hometown: Lake Forest, Illinois
Class Year: Sophomore
Major: English
Extracurriculars: Men's cross-country, men's track and field, Student Athletic Advisory Committee, mentor at a local elementary school
Career Goal: Writer or teacher of English literature at the secondary or college level

How would you describe Dartmouth's reputation?

Dartmouth was the inspiration for *Animal House*. When people think "Dartmouth," they think beer-pong and fraternities.

Is this reputation accurate?

More or less. The social scene at Dartmouth is rather dichotomous: on the one hand you have the frat scene, and on the other you have the other scene. As a guy who has never touched alcohol and hates to dance, I find myself occupying the other scene—watching movies, going to concerts, playing outdoor sports. Nevertheless, the frat scene dominates. Heck, our unofficial mascot is an anthropomorphic beer keg.

What would an admissions officer at Dartmouth probably not tell a prospective student?

Dartmouth likes to advertise its so-called diversity. Every now and again they take one white kid, one black kid, one Asian kid, and one Hispanic kid, pose them together in a dining hall, tell them to hug, snap a picture and paste it into a Dartmouth brochure. But we're not really that racially integrated, or huggy. It's unfortunate but minorities pretty much stick to their own at Dartmouth. Be forewarned.

The Institution

I love being a Dartmouth student and I love Dartmouth. I may bitch and moan, but the bottom line is that Dartmouth is a great place to go to school. It's intimate, our academics rival Harvard's, our athletic teams are consistently competitive at the national level, and our student body is among the most talented and accomplished in the world. Bottom line: the total experience at Dartmouth is unmatchable.

The Education

Our academic term schedule—the D Plan—is truly one of a kind. Here's how it works—everyone at Dartmouth is required to take classes the summer after their sophomore year. This allows us to take a term off during our sophomore or junior year, and, during that term, we can do whatever we want. We can travel, we can work, we can take an internship. Basically, we get to take a break and manage our own lives in the middle of college, which is both rare and fantastic.

I've had many stunningly brilliant professors. Most are readily available outside of class and enthusiastic about forming strong personal relationships with students.

> "I'm a varsity athlete, and at no other school where I was recruited would I be allowed, never mind encouraged, to study abroad. Here they practically pack for you."
> ✦ Pamela, sophomore

Dartmouth students have to take ten classes in nine groupings to fulfill the core. The groupings are as follows: technological or applied science, international or comparative studies, arts, social analysis, literature, quantitative or deductive science, philosophy, religious or historical analysis, and natural science. Students also have to take a course in U.S. society, European society, and non-Western society. And we have to be proficient in one foreign language.

The Students

There is no "typical Dartmouth student." Everyone that attends this school has their own unique talent that got them here in the first place. I have friends who were admitted for their perfect SAT scores, for performing piano concertos in packed concert halls backed up by professional orchestras, for having written and published their own plays, for being able to run a four-minute mile.

I am also continually impressed at how politically informed and politically active students at Dartmouth are. While Dartmouth's student body is overwhelmingly liberal, the conservative minority is overwhelmingly vocal and has no problem shouting to be heard. You definitely get both points of view.

> "Dartmouth is seen as a bastion of the good-old-boys network."
>
> ✦ Sammy, senior

The Activities

A lot of people don't realize that Dartmouth is what some might call a "jock school." But it's true. We really excel at sports like skiing, lacrosse, hockey, and cross-country. In addition, we've got a kickass intramural Ultimate Frisbee squad. At Dartmouth, everyone plays. If you don't play a varsity sport, you play an intramural. If you don't play an intramural, you play for fun. If you don't play for fun, you're probably a theater major or thinking about transferring.

The Social Scene

As I mentioned earlier, the social life at Dartmouth consists of the frat scene and the other scene. For the most part, students like their parties wild, their Keystones "lite," and their nights late. No one really dates; most everyone "hooks up."

Without exception, students are genuinely friendly. It's almost as if we have an unspoken pact that says, "This college stuff is tough, but since we're all in it together, there's no reason we can't get along." We say hi to strangers and hold the door open for the person behind us. We take time to give back to the community. We deliver newspapers, bag groceries, and babysit our professors' kids. We cheer our friends on at games and support them at performances. We also write theses, isolate DNA, and analyze Machiavelli. We're good kids, ordinary and extraordinary.

Name: Chelsea
Hometown: Neenah, Wisconsin
Class Year: Junior
Major: Government, focus on international government

Extracurriculars: Dartmouth Civil Liberties Union, Amnesty International, Film Society, Epsilon Kappa Theta
Career Goal: I'd like to go to law school, and maybe become a criminal defense lawyer.

How would you describe Dartmouth's reputation?

A school filled with white, beer-chugging, mountain-climbing, book-toting, varsity-letter-earning, oxford-shirt-wearing guys named Chet or Chaz.

Is this reputation accurate?

Admittedly, Dartmouth students enjoy a beer or ten, but for every keg stand we do we read and appreciate ten academic articles or cultural performances or prestigious lectures. As for the white male thing—I think there are a lot of male-dominated spaces at Dartmouth, which frustrates Dartmouth women to no end, and the administration should work harder to neutralize this.

What aspect of your school would a prospective student not see on a campus tour?

As a tour guide, I can tell you that we are very carefully trained not to talk very much about Greek life and alcohol use on campus. The truth is, sure, if you want to be an alcoholic for four years, there's no better Ivy than Dartmouth. That said, most students don't drink themselves into oblivion . . . on weekdays.

> "Tubestock is a massive party where townies and Greeks build rafts made of wood and float them on the Connecticut River. The townies always build great rafts, and the Greeks build rafts that break apart and sink. The Townies then rescue the drunk, drowning Dartmouth students, the Dartmouth students appreciate them, and the goodwill generated from Tubestock keeps students and townies happy till the next year."
>
> ✦ Harvey, senior

The Institution

Dartmouth is for people who love tradition. Running around the bonfire on the green, skinny-dipping in the nearby rivers, listening to the bells on Baker Tower that ring the alma mater every night at six o'clock. . . . On campus, we frequently run into visiting alums from the class of, say, 1950, and we get along so well because we all love Dartmouth. If hearing our motto, *Vox Clamantis in Deserto* (A voice crying out in the wilderness), doesn't make your heart beat faster, you should probably think about transferring.

The Education

Dartmouth students have lives, but they're lives fraught with academia. There's just about *no* competition between students at Dartmouth, to the point where you're not pushed by your peers to do well. You have to decide to do well for yourself. I have no idea what grades my friends get, and no one would *ever* do anything to hurt your GPA to help their own. My professors and I regularly get lunch. I would say every student hangs out with at least one professor as a friend or colleague. One notable econ prof has even been spotted multiple times at campus parties! And every class you'd think to take is excellent. The difference between Dartmouth and other schools is that signing up for a random class at Dartmouth is almost risk free here, because every class is of such a high caliber.

> "I once heard a woman ask a tour guide, 'Hey, where are you hiding all the fat and ugly people?' Everyone at Dartmouth is gorgeous."
>
> ✦ Dora, senior

The Students

Crunchy people—environmental studies, geography, or geology majors that wear only North Face, talk only about rock climbing, they listen to bluegrass, they smell bad, they work at the nearby organic farm, and they looooove each other.

Country club people—Government or economics majors that wear shirts with the collars flipped up, can distinguish among spots in the Hamptons, the latest models of BMWs, and can differentiate between Ralph Lauren Purple Label and plain old Polo. They intern with J. P. Morgan, and they use summer as a verb, as in "Where do you summer?"

Bookers—Astrophysics, philosophy, or computer science majors that come to the library like clockwork at 8:00 a.m. and leave like clockwork at midnight. They talk constantly about writing journal articles and planning their theses, they party once a term, and they think they're really cool for having gone out at all. They have no idea a social scene ex-

ists at Dartmouth. They're really happy, though, because they are utterly intellectually fulfilled.

Socialites—Psychology or English majors that carry cell phones and constantly check their e-mail. They work for political campaigns or retail establishments, if they work at all. The girls wear Uggs, the boys wear wrinkle-free khakis and aviator sunglasses. They're at every party, but they are different than the alcoholics, in that they're good-looking.

The Activities

There are tons of things to do at Dartmouth, from mundane to weird to weirder, from being a member of the flute choir to being a member of the Citrus Alliance (a club for people adapting to the cold weather in Hanover, New Hampshire). It's so easy to get involved in things. I rarely, if ever, leave campus. You can go hiking, skiing, swimming, rock climbing, horseback riding . . . or just sit on the green and sunbathe. Nature is a big part of our campus. But even if you are not a nature person, you can still appreciate the natural beauty of the area.

> "Dartmouth is located in the beautiful mountains of New Hampshire, bordering Vermont and surrounded by woods and the Connecticut River. It is a rural school, but it is a lively and busy campus. The autumns are colorful and breathtaking, the winters sugarplum perfect, the springs are rainy but dazzlingly green, and the summers are gorgeously relaxed and fun."
>
> ✦ Ralph, junior

The Social Scene

Come here if you're a social butterfly. If you had a whole crew of casual friends in high school, you'll be ecstatic at Dartmouth. This is the single most important requirement. Also, during orientation, take a freshman trip! Three days of hiking, kayaking, horseback riding, etc., and you'll make the greatest group of friends.

Notable Dartmouth Alumni Include:
Robert Frost, poet
Theodore Geisel (Dr. Seuss), author
Andrew Shue, actor
Salmon P. Chase, U.S. Supreme Court justice
C. Everett Koop, U.S. surgeon general
Daniel Webster, orator and statesman

DAVIDSON COLLEGE

Founded: 1837

Location: Davidson, NC

Phone: (704) 894-2000

E-mail: admission@davidson.edu

Web site: www.davidson.edu

Number of Undergraduates: 1,700

Number of Graduate Students: 0

Cost: Approximately $35,000 per year

Application Deadline: January 2

Early Decision: November 15

Rating:	Notable Majors/Programs:
Most Selective	Life Sciences, Social Sciences

Size:

● Small ○ Medium ○ Large

Location:

○ Urban ● Suburban ○ Rural

On a Saturday, students talk about academics:

● Always ○ Sometimes ○ Never

Nightlife:

● Intense ○ Moderate ○ Laid-back

Politically, Davidson leans:

○ Left ○ Right ● Split

Diversity:

○ High ● Low ○ Medium

Students describe Davidson in five words:
- Grueling southern liberal arts college
- Honorable, academically charged, and charming

From the School

Davidson College is dedicated to intellectual and cultural growth in the broadest sense. Davidson prides itself on a student body made up of the nation's most talented young people, chosen not only for their academic promise but also for their character. Davidson is a highly selective independent liberal arts college for 1,700 students. Since its establishment in 1837, the college has graduated 23 Rhodes Scholars and is consistently ranked in the top ten liberal arts colleges in the country by *U.S. News & World Report* magazine.

—www2.davidson.edu

If you're interested in Davidson, you may also be interested in:
Dartmouth, Emory, Harvard, Swarthmore, William and Mary, Williams

Name: Reid
Hometown: Austin, Texas
Class Year: Junior
Major: English
Extracurriculars: Crew
Career Goal: Professor, journalist, filmmaker

How would you describe Davidson's reputation?

We're known for attracting reasonably intelligent students mostly from the South and the East Coast, introducing them to an Ivy-esque atmosphere, and then proceeding to work them to death. We're also known for our Division I athletics and free laundry service.

Is this reputation accurate?

Warning: the workload is no joke. However, most students adjust and manage to find a good balance. Despite its competitive athletic programs, Davidson rarely cuts any academic slack in the admissions process for athletes. And yes, laundry service is free.

What would an admissions officer at Davidson probably not tell a prospective student?

Davidson admissions officers like to push the image that everyone on campus is ridiculously friendly toward each other, and while the school isn't without its southern charm, the whole "nice as can be" atmosphere is a bit of a fake-out. Students are outwardly polite, but competition is intense and cliques form just as easily as they do anywhere else.

The school also tries to conceal the party-hardy nature of its students. Davidson is no party school—not by a long stretch—but when students here do let loose, they do it in droves. Fraternities and eating houses are not an overwhelming presence on campus, but students find their own ways to binge drink, even on weeknights.

The Institution

The campus has an "Ivy of the South" image—redbrick buildings surrounded by redbrick sidewalks and lush greenery. In the fall it's beautiful as the leaves change color and coat the ground. New buildings like the Union and our newer dorms, mesh well with the old ones, and the gym and fields are well kept. Chambers, the main classroom building, has been recently renovated. Only the library seems out of place, with its tacky lime-green carpeting.

Campus is small, isolated, and very tight-knit. While some may feel anxiety about going to school more than twenty miles from the nearest city (Charlotte), the quiet town life is refreshing, even through the eyes of this city dweller. The school traditionally has a very good relationship with the surrounding town. Townspeople often flock to campus for various speakers and concerts (of which there are many), just as students invade local businesses and attend events on the charming town green.

The school's small size is a shock for some but a relief for most. Many students come from smallish private schools and are used to an environment where gossip spreads like wildfire and you know almost everyone's name by the end of the first year.

Students and faculty get along remarkably well, but there is some real tension between students and certain administrators, especially the Residence Life Office and Public Safety.

The Honor Code is perhaps the most unique aspect of life at Davidson. All students sign the code during orientation, and its benefits soon become apparent. Hardly anyone locks their doors. Professors routinely give take-home or unproctored tests, and finals are all self-scheduled. While the atmosphere of trust is a breath of fresh air coming from a stifling and gestapolike high school, the system is not without its flaws. Most students generally refrain from stealing or cheating, but vandalism is an unfortunate pastime here. It's nice to have people trust one another but it's equally valuable to exercise *some* caution in how much trust you put out there.

The Education

Davidson, at times, fosters too much intellectual spirit for its own good. Students almost never fail to put work before anything else. They're in the library at all hours, and when that closes, you'll find them huddled en masse at the Union or crouched in the corner of a hall lounge, working solo. I might label competition as Davidson's weakest aspect. Virtually all students here came from the top of their respective high schools and are used to being the best. When students like this are placed alongside one another, disaster strikes, especially at a place like Davidson, where you wouldn't expect such strong competition (as opposed to an Ivy, for example). Students here always try to flex their intellectual muscle, even and especially outside of the classroom setting.

Professors at Davidson exceeded all of my expectations. With very few exceptions, faculty members are open to differing opinions. Professors frequently take part in various aspects of campus life, including organized debates on political issues, cultural demonstrations, and even special social events open to all (the exam week Ice Cream Social is a favorite).

There are ten core requirements: one history, one math, one literature, two social sciences, one lab science, one non-lab science, one religion, one fine arts, and one philosophy credit. Also, freshmen are required to take specialized writing classes ("W-courses"), and every student must satisfy a foreign language and cultural diversity requirement.

I've already mentioned the workload, but it bears repeating. Do not come to Davidson expecting work outside of class to be easy. There's no sense in stressing yourself out too much, and despite that complaining about work is a favorite Davidson pastime, anyone with a good work ethic should be able to navigate it pretty easily.

The Students

Davidson is a very homogeneous place in terms of its students' racial, economic, and social backgrounds—but to be fair, admissions officers and other administrators continually do their best to increase diversity. Despite the high WASP ratio, there seems to be little hostility on campus toward other cultures or ideas. Students join groups dedicated to the appreciation and study of various cultures (the Asian, Middle Eastern, and International groups are particularly popular). The Young Democrats is one of the most popular campus groups, followed by the ever-vocal College Republicans.

Students at Davidson do their best to perpetuate the image of "southern charm," as I mentioned earlier, but it just doesn't ring true. There are many friendly students at Davidson, but genuine friendliness is virtually impossible in a place where competition and personal betterment are stressed above all else. How can you expect to get truly close to someone whose only concern is getting a higher GPA than yours or looking good in front of professors? Academics are important, but college should be all about making lifelong personal connections also.

The Activities

The Union abounds with giant hand-painted posters advertising the coming week's activities. The Davidson outdoors program is immensely popular and includes rafting, backpacking, and horseback trips. Numerous cultural and political groups give students the chance to speak up about social matters that affect the world on a daily basis. The Union Board recently created a new group called Recess, dedicated to letting jaded college kids relive their glory days of elementary school with massive organized kickball, dodgeball, and foursquare tournaments. The arts programs are also very popular. The growing theater department produces several shows per year, and students all over campus are excited about the upcoming residency of the Royal Shakespeare Company. There are many dance and musical groups as well, with concerts just about every week. There are also two major concerts each year, in the fall and spring. Recent performers include John Mayer, Dave Matthews, and Ben Folds.

The Social Scene

Davidson is home to seven national fraternities (including Alpha Phi Alpha, a historically black fraternity), four eating houses for women, one coed eating house, and a black student coalition. These organizations make up a ring of small houses in the center of campus known as Patterson Court. There are parties on the court just about every weekend, and they are the major social destination for students looking to dance, hang out, or just unwind. But partying at Davidson is not limited to the court. Some students have even been known to schedule late classes on Tuesdays and Thursdays so they can party on Monday and Wednesday nights.

Alcohol is a major force on campus, but not so much that you have to drink to fit in. Res life offers substance-free housing, but most people that do choose to drink do so in each other's rooms and rarely off campus (even those who are of legal age). Beirut (beer-pong) can almost be considered an unofficial varsity sport. The school is fairly strict in its enforcement of the alcohol policy, but the rule of thumb at Davidson is that if you get in trouble with the campus police for drinking, you usually deserve it.

Dating at Davidson is a daunting and much maligned practice. Because of the school's small size and the sheer workload here, the vast majority of relationships do not last beyond a single semester and people usually just hook up.

Name: Ryan
Hometown: Charlotte, North Carolina
Class Year: Sophomore
Major: English
Extracurriculars: Theater, Writing Center tutor, college newspaper (film critic)
Career Goal: I would love to teach, most likely at the college level.

How would you describe Davidson's reputation?

Outsiders think of Davidson as a slightly conservative, overly homogeneous, and an academically charged version of such northern liberal arts schools as Amherst and Williams.

Is this reputation accurate?

For the most part, yes. Although faculty and students at Davidson still lean to the left, I would say that the political cross-section here is more balanced than at most schools of this type. Also, "diversity" is definitely not Davidson's middle name. But Davidson could challenge any Ivy school in a throw-down of grueling academics.

What aspect of Davidson would a prospective student not see on a campus tour?

It's amazing how, during Parents' Weekend and Discover Davidson programs, the food at the cafeteria suddenly becomes exponentially better. It's almost as if it were that way all the time! But it's not.

> "I feared that I was entering a bastion of southern conservatism. This was only partly true. While the Right tends to be more vocal, the Left is a large and growing contingent on campus."
>
> ✦ Sami, sophomore

The Institution

A financial tiebreaker sent me to Davidson instead of Dartmouth, and I haven't looked back since. I arrived at freshmen orientation knowing *no one*, and I credit the college for quickly amending that situation. Many of my friends at enormous schools just feel lost, constantly wondering, "Where do I begin?" Davidson has such a warm, charming, and accessible atmosphere it's impossible not to make good friends. The campus is stunning. Not the pretentious kind of beautiful that

you find at Duke. No, Davidson has a real charm and serenity to its beauty—like you're living in a postcard. People take the honor code very seriously, and as a result, the Davidson College campus is so safe it could be a thief's paradise—no one has to worry about the security of themselves or of their personal effects.

And regardless of how students feel about the undergraduate experience, a Davidson diploma means only one thing: you're in business! Career Services is a fantastic resource, and a degree in any department will serve you well in the job market. Davidson gets a lot of slack for handing out bad grades like Halloween candy, but employers know what a Davidson diploma means, so an average GPA here will serve you better than a 4.0 at a mediocre school. And I guarantee that you will learn a lot more here in the process. If you want straight As, go to Harvard. If you want an occasional A that actually means something, come here.

I'm an English major with a theater minor, and I have no concerns about my career situation once I graduate. It takes a certain amount of guts to have the least practical major-minor on record and still be able say that.

The Education

This is a school defined by its grueling-and-verging-on-impossible expectations and the overall lack of grade inflation is often very unrewarding for the amount of work we put into our classes. Yet Davidson acknowledges its borderline academic fascism, and as a result it strongly encourages extracurriculars as an outlet. The Dean Rusk Study Abroad Office is the crown jewel of the Davidson experience. Because the school recognizes the limitations of its small size, it does everything it can to get its students out in the world. I'm off to Greece, Turkey, Egypt, and Italy and my roommate spent the summer as a medical assistant in Kenya. A school can make you ship out for one of two reasons: either (a) because it sucks or (b) because the opportunities abroad are too remarkable to ignore. Luckily, Davidson fits in the latter category.

The Students

At first glance, you'll think that the typical Davidson student is a white type-A goal-oriented Christian, dependent on Daddy's checkbook, and very in shape—typical CEOs in training, concerned with getting good grades, planning youth-group activities, and organizing weekend excursions—

who drink mightily on the weekends, carry a Nalgene bottle on the weekdays, and enjoy a good theme party any day of the week. But even if you cannot find the superficial diversities here, people are different where it counts. Athletes, singers, dancers, and actors all appear in great abundance for such a small school.

The Activities

The activities are expansive here, but there are a few holes:

1. Musical theater—as an actor, it is frustrating to have a tremendous theater department that mostly ignores musical theater. Some have transferred because of this major gap in the performing arts.
2. Rivals—with regard to sports, Davidson has very few true rivalries. This hurts both school spirit and turnout at athletic events with the exception of basketball.

The Social Scene

Each dorm has its own personality, and freshman halls tend to stay closely knit throughout the four years here. Most people live on campus, and seniors are treated to some beautiful apartments for their final two semesters.

If you like alcohol, loud noises, and sweat, the frat scene on Patterson Court pretty much covers that. (There aren't sororities, but gaggles of giggly girls instead pledge their allegiance to the institution of eating houses, which are basically sororities parading as alternative cafeterias. About 60 percent of females choose to join an eating house, while fraternity pledging hovers around the 50-percent mark and is not at all a necessity.) If you prefer fun that ends around 12:30, you have to be a bit more creative. Luckily, Davidson rests at the tip of Charlotte's suburban sprawl, so there are plenty of restaurants, movie theaters, and shopping centers to keep us less rowdy folk amused.

Name: Page
Hometown: Macon, Georgia
Class Year: Sophomore
Major: Political science
Extracurriculars: *The Davidsonian* (newspaper), Davidson Young Democrats, intramural softball, men's basketball manager, Student Advisory Committee, Just Peace
Career Goal: To work in an embassy

How would you describe Davidson's reputation?

Growing. It's known as a pretty tough school, but isn't as well known by people outside the South, though that's changing. Davidson was ranked the number seven liberal arts school in the country, and those who actually know we exist also know how true that is.

Is this reputation accurate?

Very. Davidson is a really tough school but it's a great place to be. A Davidson degree really means a lot nowadays in the workplace, and it's academically one of the best.

> "Though we are located in the South, Davidson lacks that 'good ol' boy' Southern feel some may associate with Southern schools."
> ✦ Leida, senior

What would an admissions officer at Davidson probably not tell a prospective student?

They might not talk about how little diversity there is. I know that it's something the administration is working really hard to fix, but generally Davidson is a pretty homogeneous campus.

The Institution

I joke that I chose Davidson because of the good-looking tour guide I had, but in truth, there are very serious reasons why I applied early decision to Davidson. It has amazing professors, the largest class I've had had thirty students, and that's the largest I will ever have. I also chose Davidson because of its location in a tiny and quaint little town. I am amazed by how much students and townies interact. I will walk down Main Street and will be greeted by many townspeople I have never seen before. The shopowners love the students and create such a welcoming atmosphere.

The weather at Davidson is typically southern, which means it can change dramatically in the course of a day. However, most days, especially in fall and spring, are gorgeous.

Our Res Life Office uses the Myers-Briggs personality test to match you. I have only known of a few people who have had a problem and had to switch rooms. I've grown to know many members of the administration on a very personal level, and that's really important to know there will be someone there to help me out when I need it. I once had to take a friend to the emergency room, and while I was in the waiting room, one of the deans walked in—he'd driven down to the hospital to make sure my friend was okay. She was fine, but he sat with me and talked to her and was so amazingly kind. I just don't think that sort of thing happens at other schools.

Sometimes I wish that the school wasn't so religious. It makes it a little difficult for students who aren't into the whole churchgoing thing. Some of the religious groups can be a little pressuring. But even if you're not very religious, you won't be excluded; there are plenty of secular people here.

The Education

The classes are a nice mix of lecture and discussion and are, simply put, amazing. I think the most interesting class I've ever taken was Religion in the Movies. We watched films I'd seen before but had never noticed their religious undertones. I really learned a lot about religion and also how to better watch a film.

I think our core is really beneficial: it allows students to get a feel for many different subjects, from finite math to Latin American history, and therefore have a much easier time choosing their major.

> "The average student here is upper middle class, was high school class president, lettered in at least two varsity sports or dominated their music-drama programs in high school. They have a strong work ethic, are deeply Christian (most likely Presbyterian), and volunteer once a month if schoolwork permits."
>
> ✦ Kirk, sophomore

The Students

We do not have a large number of gay and lesbian students, but those who are are almost never excluded or judged. The campus is generally accepting of minorities, and I have heard of few instances when intolerance was a big problem. Many students are preprofessionally oriented (mostly premed or prelaw).

Davidson has a good balance of Republican and Democratic students, and I do not feel that there is an overwhelming majority for either party. Conservatives and liberals mix freely as long as they don't discuss politics too much. We have very few protests or rallies, and most political events are very low-key.

The Activities

Davidson has a pretty good theater and music program, and the larger theater productions are generally well attended. We also have three a cappella groups that always pack the house. The Davidson Dance Ensemble performs once every semester. All dance shows are student-choreographed, and often sell out quickly.

Community service is a very important prerequisite for getting into Davidson, so it is no surprise that it's stressed once you're here. The most popular form is probably tutoring local schoolkids, and we actually have a student-run Homework Lab on campus that students from the community can attend to get help for any subject.

Most students are usually around on weekends because there's always something to do. Sometimes we'll drive about twenty minutes to the Concord Mills mall. Or to the Birkdale area, which has a movie theater, great restaurants, and wonderful shopping.

When the weather's warm, guys throw footballs or play Frisbee or Wiffle ball. The musical crowd strum their guitars and provide great music on the lawn. Other kids have their laptops and notebooks in front of them on the grass.

The Social Scene

There is always some sort of party to go to on the weekends with bands or DJs, and many have cool themes like '80s night or a Tacky Party. Alcohol is the drug of choice and people tend to drink pretty heavily on the weekends. The administration is pretty weak on its alcohol enforcement, so people are safe and don't usually get into too much trouble.

I live in a substance-free hall and it's great. People are usually considerate of other people and try not to be too loud or obnoxious if others are trying to sleep. People at Davidson are very polite. Being here makes you feel really special because everyone is so nice and always tries to make everyone else feel at home.

Notable Davidson Alumni Include:
Dean Rusk, U.S. secretary of state
Henry Louis Smith, former Davidson president and producer of one of the first X-ray photographs
Patricia Cornwell, author
Sheri Reynolds, author
Woodrow Wilson, twenty-eighth U.S. president
Wyche Fowler, senator

DUKE UNIVERSITY

Founded: 1838
Location: Durham, NC
Phone: (919) 684-3214
E-mail: askduke@admiss.duke.edu
Web site: www.duke.edu

Number of Undergraduates: 6,206
Number of Graduate Students: 4,416
Cost: Approximately $37,000 per year
Application Deadline: January 2
Early Decision: November 1

Rating:	Notable Majors/Programs:
Most Selective	Biology, Economics, Psychology

Size:
○ Small   ● Medium   ○ Large

Location:
● Urban   ○ Suburban   ○ Rural

On a Saturday, students talk about academics:
○ Always   ● Sometimes   ○ Never

Nightlife:
● Intense   ○ Moderate   ○ Laid-back

Politically, Duke leans:
○ Left   ● Right   ○ Split

Diversity:
○ High   ● Low   ○ Medium

Students describe Duke in five words:
- Very prestigious, southern, sports rule!
- Rigorous workload, great school spirit

From the School

The mission of Duke University is to provide a superior liberal education to undergraduate students, attending not only to their intellectual growth but also to their development as adults committed to high ethical standards and full participation as leaders in their communities.

—www.planning.duke.edu

If you're interested in Duke, you may also be interested in:
Colgate, Dartmouth, Harvard, Northwestern, U. Pennsylvania, Princeton

Name: Karen
Hometown: North Andover, Massachusetts
Class Year: Sophomore
Major: Psychology and religion
Extracurriculars: Alliance of Queer Undergrads at Duke (AQUADuke), InterVarsity Christian Fellowship
Career Goal: Undecided. I might go into pastoral counseling or work with LGBT youth.

How would you describe Duke's reputation?

Polo shirts and southern belles, with a little basketball thrown in. The Harvard of the South.

Is this reputation accurate?

Yes and no. Basketball is *huge* at Duke, you'll find that out right away. But "Harvard of the South"? Harvard is the "Duke of the North." The only difference is that you won't find as much brutal academic competition (even though we have the same brilliant minds), and Duke in the spring is *beautiful*.

What aspect of your school would a prospective student not see on a campus tour?

Duke is a little heavy on the frat-sorority end of things. Durham can be a little boring if you don't have any friends with cars. Duke tends to be closed off from the "real world"—heck, we're surrounded by a forest. But otherwise, life is pretty good. Isn't that pathetic? I wish I had more dirt to dish!

> "Basketball is, of course, king at Duke."
> ✦ Sean, sophomore

The Institution

School spirit is *oozing* out of Duke students. You will learn to love being a Blue Devil as soon as you arrive. The campus is marvelous—it took me all of two seconds to realize that Duke is basically the prettiest campus in the world.

That's not to say it's all sunshine and roses here. Duke can be a little isolated if you don't have a car to get around town and beyond. And yeah, we are a bit "hoity-toity" in the sense that a lot of the students here come from money. But you'll get over that. Classes are the great equalizer, making everyone realize that the wealthy kids don't have any more smarts than the rest of us Average Joes, and then the playing field is even.

As a freshman at Duke you need to learn how to love buses, because the east and west sides of campus are separated. (All freshmen live on the east side.) First-years have to roll out of bed a few minutes earlier to get to class on the west side on time. But living on the east side is worth it in the long run.

Lastly, some students from the North (where I'm from) might be apprehensive about coming to Duke because it's in the South. Don't be! You'll learn more than you can imagine.

The Education

At Duke, you will learn—hopefully about things that inspire and interest you—and under professors who are among the most noteworthy in their field. Currently, I'm taking a class called Gender, Pain, and Coping, which is a lecture course on the physiological and psychological differences in pain perception between men and women. My professor is world renowned, and he's brought in guest lecturers to speak to us who are famous enough to make your jaw drop. I've also taken fantastic classes with titles like Hinduism, Introduction to Human Memory, Women and Mental Health, and Women and Sexuality in the Christian Tradition. These courses have really broadened my little world.

If I was to complain about anything academic here, it would have to be the core curriculum. There are six different areas of study: arts and literature, natural science, social science, foreign language, quantitative reasoning, and civilization. Pick the area of your choice and disregard it—you won't have to take any classes in that area. Five areas left. In one of them you'll have to take two classes. In each of the other four areas, you'll have to take three classes. It adds up, and it makes it hard to double major. So, if you want to go to Duke, you're going to have to live with this, but you wind up "well rounded," I suppose.

The Students

Good: I am a Christian, lesbian, vegetarian, Republican northerner. You might think this is a weird collection of traits. At Duke, it's not. Here, you'll find people of every conceivable mix of race, religion, creed, sexual orientation, political affiliation, and plain ol' attitude. And all of these kinds of people—they hang out, they butt heads, they have a good time. Duke is a big school, and everyone generally respects one another. It's big enough so you'll be exposed to people that don't think like you, and it's also big enough that you can count on finding people who think just like you do. Between these two extremes, rest assured, you'll make some really solid friends, no matter who you are.

Bad: Frats and sororities are *huge* at Duke. If you're into that scene, great. If you're not, the amount of people who are can be intimidating. Also, I've found that a lot of women at Duke have eating disorders. It's sad.

But on the whole, you take the good with the bad here, just as you would at any other school. As long as you come to Duke with a pretty stable sense of self, and you have a desire to become your own person, you'll be OK.

> "Cameron Indoor is an experience. Duke is all about synchronized cheering. And if any player on the opposite team has ever done anything wrong, ever, Duke students do their homework, they will find out, and they'll scream about it at the top of their lungs during every game."
>
> ✦ Lesley, senior

The Activities

Being gay, I'm fairly active with the campus LGBT association. Duke's administration is very open to LGBT activities, and we are blessed to have an entire LGBT center right on campus. What else do we have? Well, what else do you want? Hoof and Horn produces excellent musicals all year long. There are more campus publications than you could ever dream of writing for (e.g., *Duke Blue, Newsense, Thread, The Chronicle, Carpe Noctem*, and more). We've a huge Community Service Center. And if you're looking for athletics . . . *come on,* we're DUKE! Basketball is our middle name. Seriously.

The Social Scene

If you're less into organized activities and more into good old-fashioned partying, then you can go to any number of frat or sorority parties. They're open to pretty much whoever, and if you go party hopping with friends, you're sure to have a good time. And afterward, you can head on over to Rick's, the local twenty-four-hour diner.

A word about alcohol. If you want it, it's everywhere. No one is forcing it down your throat. I know a few people at Duke who are entirely straight edge, meaning they won't consume any substances whatsoever. And everyone I know thinks they're *awesome,* but the point is, as much as school security tries to crack down on drinking, if you're smart, and you want to get drunk, you'll find a way. And if you got into Duke in the first place, well, you're probably smart.

Name: Russ
Hometown: Charlotte, North Carolina
Class Year: Sophomore
Major: Political science
Extracurriculars: College Republicans (state treasurer); vice president and rush chair, Delta Kappa Epsilon Fraternity; student government senator; Quad treasurer; Relay for Life Logistics Chair; President's Advisory Council on Resources; Interfraternity Council Vice President of Community Interaction
Career Goal: Politician

How would you describe Duke's reputation?

We're consistently ranked as one of the top five schools in America, we're an athletic powerhouse, and we have a really strong social scene. This combination makes Duke a one-of-a-kind institution. Whether you're in a room full of academics, sports fans, or partyers, if you mention that you went to Duke, people will be wowed.

Is this reputation accurate?

This reputation is 100 percent accurate. Duke is, quite simply, an incredible experience.

What aspect of your school would a prospective student not see on a campus tour?

You probably won't see Central Campus, which is mostly student apartments. At first glance they look dark and dingy, but the apartments are actually pretty nice on the inside.

The Institution

Everything Duke students do, they do with intensity. We work hard. We play hard. We cheer hard at sports games. We study like fiends . . . and, at Duke, you'll never be looked down upon or thought of as a nerd for studying, even on Friday or Saturday nights. Everyone understands that schoolwork comes first. . . . Unless, of course, there's a basketball game. If it's at Cameron Indoor, then you should not only be watching it, you should also have spent the past few weeks camping outside Cameron, guarding your place in line to make sure you get good seats.

There are more than twenty restaurants on Duke's campus, so you'll never want for culinary variety. The administration is really great here, taking pains to be responsive to student concerns. It's not uncommon for the president of the university to schedule lunches with individual students, student groups, or fraternities, just to keep track of the tone on campus. We get lots of big name speakers and performers. On the downside, premajor advising is terrible at Duke, very disorganized and unhelpful. You're pretty much on your own to figure out what you want to major in and which classes to take freshman year. But once you've declared a major, you're assigned a suitable adviser within your department, and they'll work hard to help you shape your education. No complaints there.

> "There are a disturbing amount of expensive cars in the Duke student lot, but luckily they're constantly being driven to local soup kitchens, independent bookstores, grammar school tutoring sessions, and research labs."
>
> ✦ Antonio, junior

The Education

Academic panels, featuring both professors and students, are commonplace at Duke. These run the topical gamut, covering everything from slave reparations to the politics of Tibet. And, because Duke has so many fantastically knowledgeable professors, students can put together panels themselves on just about anything and easily find professors who can speak intelligently and eloquently on that topic.

The stacks at Perkins Library close at 2:00 a.m.; and although there are several twenty-four-hour reading rooms on campus, 2:00 a.m. is the time everyone goes to Rick's Diner. This nearby twenty-four-hour restaurant (which features breakfast food all the time) is a late-night center of student life. Some students do homework by themselves with papers and books spread everywhere, others sit in groups, talking about issues that have come up in their classes. Still others just finished partying and are looking for a late-night bite to eat. At 2:00 a.m. the atmosphere at Rick's is intellectual, a buzz of people talking about their studies, debating feverishly, trying their best to learn more.

The Students

The majority of Duke students are from the Northeast, Texas, or North Carolina. But broadly, there are students from every state in America, and 10 percent of the student population is made up of international students. That means, in every class, one of ten students will have come from some far-off corner of the world. How amazing is that! I've found that the international students really contribute to student life at Duke.

That said, Duke does self-segregate a bit, with different ethnic groups largely sticking to themselves. Lately, some Duke students have begun to actively try and break down these barriers. For example, many fraternities and sororities now have frequent mixers with NPHC sororities and fraternities (which are historically African American).

And I'd say the average Duke student is well informed about the world at large. Duke's student government provides free copies of *USA Today,* the *New York Times,* and *Durham Herald-Sun* all over campus. The *Chronicle,* Duke's student newspaper, is also available everywhere, and the entire student body consumes it greedily each day. It's a well-written paper, with a good mix of national commentary and Duke-specific articles. It also lists the good parties to go to (though you can also find out about those from the banners hanging over the Bryan Center Walkway).

The Activities

The University of North Carolina is eight miles down the road from Duke, and my friends and I head down there for parties all the time. It's nice to have a big campus nearby whose students are somewhat similar to Dukies . . . the fraternities and sororities at Duke and UNC mix frequently. There's a bus that runs back and forth between the two campuses all day long. We're also about twenty miles away from North Carolina State University, but we spend less time there.

I'd say, if you come to Duke, plan on having lots of late nights. Going to bed before 3:00 a.m. here is considered going to bed early. But don't worry about being sleep deprived—if you don't want to ever have a class before noon, that's an option. You can just take all your classes in the afternoon, and all will be well.

The Social Scene

There is a three-year residency requirement at Duke, so everyone lives on campus for at least three years, and most stay on all four. The dorms are really nice, the campus housing is well located, all your friends are nearby. Why would you really want to leave? You're also closer to on-campus parties if you stay. And, speaking of parties . . . people at Duke party whenever they want. There's something going on just about every day. Which isn't to say you'll be able to appreciate parties every day—it's more that, some weeks, you won't be able to go out at all. You'll have a crushing amount of work. Then the next week it'll ease up considerably, and you may decide to party four days in a row. Good for you!

> "It's a beautiful day outside, with perfect blue skies and those Duke students not throwing Frisbees on the quad are . . . holed up in the stacks, cramming for tests, jittery on their fourth cup of coffee, wondering if they'll ever sleep again."
> ✦ Rory, senior

Fraternities, which throw lots of big events and are located on main west campus, have parties every Friday and Saturday night, and they're open to all Duke students, regardless of whether they're Greek. The alcohol policy is very lenient here, with the caveat being Public Safety will bust you if you're drinking from a beer bottle outside—so don't do that. Pour the beer into a cup.

At Duke, being a freshman feels different than being a sophomore, junior, or senior. As a freshman you live on East Campus, with all the other freshmen. You see freshmen everywhere, you go to freshman parties, all freshmen eat at the Marketplace for dinner during the week. It's a unique experience, and it allows students to make great, close friends in a short period of time that will last them all four years.

Name: Manny
Hometown: Platteville, Michigan
Class Year: Freshman
Major: Linguistics and literature
Extracurriculars: AquaDUKE (queer undergraduate alliance); Duke Allies (gay-straight alliance); theater; Progressive Alliance, writing for publications (*Thread* and *Matter*)
Career Goal: I'd like to teach someday, perhaps as a high school or college professor.

How would you describe Duke's reputation?
A de facto Ivy with a great basketball team.

Is this reputation accurate?
Well, the fact is, Duke is becoming increasingly selective every year. Unfortunately, rather than saying, "Things are on the up and up, if we hold the course, we'll do fine," the administration is saying, "What can we change to continue our rankings upswing?" Their answer, for now, seems to be cracking down on partying. We used to have keg parties in the middle of the quad, for instance. That doesn't happen anymore. There used to be a big bar on campus—now there's a tiny bar in the basement of a nearby restaurant. None of this, however, changes the fact that our basketball team kicks ass.

What aspect of your school would a prospective student not see on a campus tour?
As I'm sure other students have mentioned, Duke is divided into East Campus and West Campus and the school provides a free bus that goes between the campuses. Tour guides downplay the hassle of having to commute from one end of campus to the other. It's not always "only a seven-minute bus ride." And when 150 people run for the bus in the winter, most will be left out in the cold. It can be a nightmare.

Also, Duke's administration and Duke students don't always get along. Students tend to yell at the administration for outsourcing jobs to nonunion workers, providing substandard dining options for freshmen, for not having enough political diversity among Duke's faculty members, and for hiring in the housing office the most difficult, inefficient, insensitive, inflexible, unreasonable people on earth. Students love Duke. I love Duke. But, like anyplace else, it's not perfect. Don't expect it to be.

> "Durham ranks higher than New York in per-capita crime, so students need to watch out for themselves."
> ✦ Mark, freshman

The Institution
Duke is a funny place. I'm a gay freshman, and I heard this place was going to be really homophobic because (a) it's in the South, and (b) there was once an article on the front page of the *Chronicle* about lesbians kissing, which provoked a donnybrook of angry

editorials, and the word spread that there was homophobia at Duke. At first administrators shivered, and then they—to their extreme credit—worked really hard to make Duke a more accepting place. Today—despite what I expected—Duke is great for gay students. There's an active queer undergraduate group, and active queer groups in all the grad schools, as well as an LGBT training program for allies (called SAFE), which is so highly regarded that Duke now sends its training DVD to hundreds of other schools across America. If I have a boyfriend, I can kiss him in public without feeling at all self-conscious.

Duke also has a long-standing tradition of passionate student-led workers' rights campaigns. Students often bring issues of workers' rights to the administration, and the administration usually responds responsibly and does the right thing. Duke's administration, with a little nudging from students, also practices socially responsible investing and will (for the most part) only do business with vendors and companies that are known for being ethically sound.

I think all this says something about Duke. In short, it's prepared to evolve, change, and improve itself (when given a push to do so). And that, when Duke decides to change, it won't half-ass the change—it will change thoroughly, brilliantly, and in a way that's respected all throughout America. Three cheers for my alma mater!

> "Duke's admit rate is pretty high given its top five ranking in *U.S. News.* Even if you don't think you'll get in, apply. You may be pleasantly surprised."
>
> ✦ Christian, junior

The Education

Duke has a great program called FOCUS. You choose an academic theme when you start school your freshman year, and you follow that theme for the next nine months. You then get placed in dorms with other people who have chosen your same theme. Everyone in your dorm bonds academically and socially. All your FOCUS professors talk to one another, classes complement one another, and you get to know some great professors extremely well. FOCUS is a lot of work, I'll say that. But it brings all Duke's freshmen together, and it's worth it.

Also worth noting, Duke is a research institution. You can't go to Duke and not do research.

Even as an undergrad, you *will* do research, no matter what you're majoring in. So get ready to buckle down and read lots of dusty old books.

The Students

At Duke, all kinds of students mix and get along. Freshmen, sophomores, juniors, and seniors mix. Greeks mix with non-Greeks. Conservatives and liberals bite their tongues and mix. Kids who turned down Ivy League schools to come to Duke mix happily with those who still hold a grudge that Dartmouth, Harvard, and U. Penn rejected them.

I'd say the largest cultural groups on campus are the Black Student Alliance, Mi Gente (the Latino group), and AquaDUKE. All three are very active and very vocal.

The Activities

First, if you come here and don't love basketball, you'll learn to love it. It's that simple. Second, Duke interacts a lot with nearby UNC. Kids from each school go to the other school's social functions, you can take classes at either school, and UNC is generally a cool nearby resource to take advantage of. Third, while there's plenty to do in general, there is little to do on Duke's campus after 2:00 a.m. (unless you go to Rick's Diner on West Campus—East Campus has nothing).

The Social Scene

All freshmen must live on East Campus. All sophomores live on West Campus. Juniors may live in apartments on Central Campus, and seniors have the option of living off campus. Sororities have no housing . . . frats have been moved off the main quad. The parties have been moved off the main quad with them. The reasons behind these strict housing rules implemented in recent years are unknown to us. We suspect it has something to do with the administration trying to tone down our party scene. Good thing that'll be impossible. Duke's party spirit is impossible to kill, no matter how much the administration moves us around. We love our parties too much!

Notable Duke Alumni Include:
Charlie Rose, talk show host
Grant Hill, NBA player
Kenneth Starr, prosecutor, U.S. Office of Independent Counsel
Dan Abrams, MSNBC news anchor
Mike Gminski, CBS sports analyst
Elizabeth Dole, U.S. senator

EMORY UNIVERSITY

Founded: 1836

Location: Atlanta, GA

Phone: (800) 727-6036

Email: admiss@learnlink.emory.edu

Web site: www.emory.edu

Number of Undergraduates: 6,285

Number of Graduate Students: 4,981

Cost: Approximately $37,000 per year

Application Deadline: January 15

Early Decision: November 1

Rating:	Notable Majors/Programs:
Very Selective	Premed, Biology, Political Science, Business

Size:
○ Small ● Medium ○ Large

Location:
● Urban ○ Suburban ○ Rural

On a Saturday, students talk about academics:
○ Always ● Sometimes ○ Never

Nightlife:
● Intense ○ Moderate ○ Laid-back

Politically, Emory is:
○ Left ○ Right ● Split

Diversity:
● High ○ Low ○ Medium

Students describe Emory in five words:
- Beautiful, hardworking, traditional, and fun
- Demanding, Coca-Cola, underrated, and unique

From the School

Emory University is known for its outstanding undergraduate college of arts and sciences, its highly ranked professional schools, its demanding academics, and its state-of-the-art research facilities. Along with dramatic increases in research support in recent years, the university has maintained its long tradition of fine teaching. Emory has a long-held commitment to public service and a concern for the ethical implications and use of knowledge.

—www.emory.edu

If you're interested in Emory, you may also be interested in:
Duke, Georgetown, Northwestern, UPenn, Tufts, Washington U. in St. Louis

Name: Brian
Hometown: Matawan, New Jersey
Class Year: Freshman
Major: Comparative literature and economics
Extracurriculars: *Lullwater Review* (literary magazine), Volunteer Emory, student admissions representative
Career Goal: Successful writer and/or businessman

How would you describe Emory's reputation?

Emory is somewhat—though not strikingly—prestigious.

Is this reputation accurate?

Pretty much.

What aspect of your school would a prospective student not see on a campus tour?

A prospective student wouldn't see just how racially segregated Emory is. There are lots of minority students here, but they all stick closely together in cliques. It's rare that you'll see a black student and a white student interacting. In the cafeteria (known as the DUC), you'll see multiple tables of all white students, then a few tables of all Asian students, a few tables of all black students, and a few tables of all Indian students.

The Institution

Emory's size is perfect and it's in a prime location right outside of Atlanta, it's got a beautiful campus, as well as a well-regarded business program. It's always amazingly sunny outside. Campus security is excellent. If you're ever in trouble, you can call the campus police from any of the numerous blue pole phones and they'll arrive almost instantly.

The Education

Emory has a great freshman orientation in which all incoming frosh are assigned a FAME (Freshman Advising and Mentoring at Emory) "group" consisting of two upperclassmen advisers, one faculty adviser, and one staff adviser; this group meets once a week and will show you everything, from where to get the best cup of coffee on campus (Starbucks, Caribou, or Dooley's Den), to which classes to take so you don't get stuck with boring professors. Emory students take four classes each semester—lecture or discussion-based. It's usually pretty clear in the course catalogue which classes are taught using which methods, so you can choose the mix that suits you best. If you're into discussion classes, you'll spend a lot of time at Emory sitting around a large table hashing through topics with your classmates and your teacher. After class, you'll spend a couple of hours doing homework each day—particularly if you're premed or majoring in political science, which are two of the most difficult and prestigious programs here.

For a pretty big core curriculum, our "general education requirements" are relatively easy to fulfill. We need courses in the natural sciences, history, aesthetics and values, writing, and phys ed. All students are also required to take a Freshman Seminar—typically an excellent experience. Internships are plentiful here because Emory has strong ties with most big corporations in Atlanta.

The Students

Thirty percent of Emory students are minorities, but, as I said, they do their own thing on this campus. I'd say the average female Emory student is white, Jewish, wealthy, from either New York, Chicago, or Massachussetts. She frequently wears Bebe skirts and clutches a Prada handbag, and studies a lot but still makes time to visit the clubs, bars, and frats three or four times a week. The guys are the type that you would expect to date these girls.

The Activities

The most popular activities to get involved with would have to be Greek life, a cappella groups—Aural Pleasures and No Strings Attached are the biggest—student government, Volunteer Emory, and *The Emory Wheel* (our widely read school newspaper).

If you're an athlete, you may be a bit disappointed. We don't have a football team at all, and, for the teams we do have, there isn't much student support—with the exception of maybe soccer and tennis. Students here who really want to go to sporting events visit Georgia Tech or the University of Georgia, where athletics are taken more seriously. MARTA, Atlanta's public transportation system, has six stops close to Emory's campus, so it is very easy to get out and about in Atlanta. I'd say I leave Emory's campus two nights a week, and once a week during the daytime to go to nearby clubs, bars, restaurants, to the Lennox Mall. Just to clear my head. When I come back, my dorm, Longstreet, is really social and there are always people hanging out in the lobby ordering food or clowning around in the halls and rooms.

The Social Scene

Emory parties far harder than I thought it would. On weekends, kids really go crazy, even though the administration has cracked down on alcohol lately (students find ways to sneak their bottles of vodka in, anyway). I'd say Emory students party in one of three ways: (1) we'll go to a club in Atlanta, and often run into—and drink with—celebrities, (2) we'll head to a bar (Park Bench is the bar most freshmen head to, because it's low key and close to campus), (3) or, the most popular option—Frat Row. Greek life is alive and well on this campus, and if you want a big party, the frats will never disappoint.

Name: Megan
Hometown: Tampa, Florida
Class Year: Junior
Major: Neuroscience and behavioral biology
Extracurriculars: Laboratory research, tour guiding, a few philanthropic organizations
Career Goal: I'd like to do research and teach as a professor at the university level.

How would you describe Emory's reputation?

Emory is a high-ranking school with strong academics. It's a Research I university. Some look at us as a party school, too.

Is this reputation accurate? Why or why not?

Emory's a tough school that expects a lot of its students, but it's not so tough that it's unmanageable. It's also not so tough that we have to party our brains out, like the kids do at Harvard. We're more balanced, more Zen. At Emory you work hard and also have a lot of fun.

What would an admissions officer at your school probably not tell a prospective student?

An admissions officer wouldn't tell you that a lot of kids are *overly* politically correct at Emory. I got sucked into this and I started thinking differently, becoming offended by everything. Anyway, I've since tried to stop myself from going PC-overboard, and I now think with both the academic world and the real world in mind.

The Institution

I came from an overcrowded, underfunded public high school, and I've been surprised at how efficiently Emory is run. If there's ever something wrong with your dorm room, put in a work order and it will be fixed immediately. If grass turns brown or a tree dies, the greenery is immediately replanted. Aesthetically and structurally, Emory's an impressive place. And academically . . . well, see below.

The Education

All of my professors are incredibly good. They all do a lot of research, but they're never distant in the classroom. My organic chemistry professor, for example, doesn't have to teach—he's developed some really important AIDS drugs, and he could live quite comfortably on the royalties alone. But he *wants* to teach—undergraduates no less—because he really likes teaching. He's not the exception, he's the rule. Professors at Emory take an honest interest in their students, and students, in turn, learn an amazing amount during their time here.

The Freshman Seminar system, where freshmen have small discussion-based classes with senior faculty members, is amazing. Take advantage of this program. I did, and my freshman seminar professor became my mentor here. She even helped me find a position working with a world-renowned primatologist at the Yerkes National Primate Research Center.

Also, if you're looking to get research experience as an undergraduate, this is the place to be—there are three affiliated hospitals on campus, a nearby Center for Disease Control and Prevention, the Carter Center, the Yerkes National Primate Center, the Emory Vaccine Center, CNN, ESPN. . . . If you're willing to send out a few e-mails and go to a few interviews, you'll find yourself with more opportunities to intern and research than you'll know what to do with.

The Students

Emory students are about 75 percent liberal, 25 percent conservative. The conservatives are vocal though, so if you were only on campus for a brief visit you might get the impression that those numbers should be reversed. Also, a lot of Emory students come here intending to be premed and prelaw, but by their sophomore year they change gears because of the heavy workload involved. About a third of Emory students also decide to go Greek. There are quite a few fraternities and sororities (though not as many as at state schools). And the Greek culture is fun—plus, they throw great parties (which anyone can attend).

The Activities

President Jimmy Carter comes to campus every fall and speaks to students. Every fall. Everyone on campus comes to see Carter, gets really excited over it, and Carter always puts on a great show. Odd, right? Only at Emory. Other things: Emory sports are Division III, so academics come first. Students support teams, but work takes top priority.

Because Emory is so close to Altlanta, there are always things to do off campus . . . with or without a car students can attend sporting events, go to concerts, see shows, go to dance performances, symphonies. There are a lot of small, hip, unique areas with quirky shops and great restaurants that students will head to so they can take a load off, replenish, and enjoy themselves.

The Social Scene

Emory is big enough that every type of social scene is represented. Want to go to bars and clubs in a big city setting? Head into Atlanta. Want to go to a rowdy frat party? We have those in spades. Want to hang out in your room with close friends and watch movies? That's always an option. Want to stay in the library and study all weekend so you'll ace your test on Monday? You may be a bit lonely, as our library is far from packed on weekend nights, but your friends won't look down on you for studying—they'll even stop off at the library on their way to whatever and bring you snacks to keep you going. Whatever scene you want, Emory shall provide.

Name: Daniel
Hometown: Bedford, New York
Class Year: Sophomore
Major: Theater and philosophy
Extracurriculars: Web administrator for EmoryVision (campus TV station), assistant layout editor for *The Spoke* (campus humor magazine), Ad Hoc Productions (musicals), Theater Emory, Emory Dance Company
Career Goal: Lawyer

How would you describe Emory's reputation?

In the South, Emory is viewed as an excellent school. Elsewhere, not many people have heard of it. Except for doctors, who know the medical school.

Is this reputation accurate?

This is a top-notch institution, with a lot to offer. The teachers are fantastic, the academics are rigorous. I think it's only a matter of time before word spreads to the Northeast that Emory is a school on the rise.

What aspect of your school would a prospective student not see on a campus tour?

They wouldn't see how much time we spend in the library or in our dorm rooms, studying. There's constant cool stuff going on here, but I'd say you're going to be forced to miss out on at least 50 percent of it because of your academics. At least you're learning . . . *C'est la vie!*

The Institution

Emory's campus is laid out extremely well—everything is central, and easy to get to, and shuttles run constantly between the far ends of campus. In the spring and summer, Atlanta has one of the highest pollen counts in the nation; buildings have been known to literally turn yellow from all the pollen. Hay fever aside, Emory students have a lot of school spirit, and we all rally behind our weird mascot—Dooley, a walking skeleton. Supposedly, Dooley roams Emory's campus all the time, and there are members of a not-so-secret secret society who claim to commune with Dooley and function as his mouthpiece. Every spring, we have Dooley's Week on campus, where, if Dooley enters a classroom, professors are supposed to let every student out early. Weird, right? That's Emory.

I visited Emory and immediately fell in love with its gorgeous campus right in the middle of Atlanta. When I started looking into Emory's academics, I found myself pleasantly surprised—almost every department was strong. This was important to me, because I have a lot of different interests, and I didn't come to Emory with my career mapped out. I wanted to be able to explore, to take interesting classes in lots of disciplines, and Emory offered that option. As a student, it's been great. I take classes all over the map, and I've yet to find a weak department. I also like Emory's size—5,000 undergraduates, roughly 1,250 incoming freshmen per year. That's just enough people to provide for good dating and social options, but way smaller than a monster-sized school.

The Education

Emory professors are not the professors who hurry off after a lesson or roll their eyes when students show up at office hours. Instead, they're the ones who welcome student contact and who will meet with students at just about any time, if you schedule it in advance. We have TAs here, too, but I've found them to be just as knowledgeable as our professors, and exceptionally well-trained.

My favorite class has been Astronomy 141. This class took place in our planetarium, which was built in 2001. The class had an evening lab where we got to use a high-powered telescope and to look at stars, planets, moons, and galaxies.

Emory also has amazing arts departments, which too many students overlook. Our visual arts are strong, our music department brings in local Atlanta musicians to give private lessons to students in any instrument you could think of, and both the dance department and the theater department have professional companies that students can audition for, and their productions are very well attended.

The Students

Emory students tend to cross all racial-cultural-socioeconomic-religious-political divides. We really are a diverse group. The Office of Multicultural Programs and Services and the LGBT office are both very influential and are constantly putting on interesting programs. We've got Young Democrats, College Republicans, Campus Libertarians, and Greens, but don't expect most Emory students to care about what goes on in these groups—politically, we're pretty apathetic. Most students don't read national newspapers, they just read *The Wheel,* and that's just so they can comment on how bad it is.

The Activities

There's always something fun to get involved in at Emory. We have a sold-out student musical every semester, lots of a cappella music groups, and group concerts the first Friday of every month. Every year we have three Band Parties (homecoming, fall, and spring) that are big bashes, and lots of students get involved in planning them. Community service is also a big thing at Emory. Volunteer Emory, EmoryREAD, and Habitat for Humanity are all popular. Outdoor Emory (OEO) is another big group, running up to eight trips per weekend. They get discounts for everything, and the skydiving, skiing, and paintball trips alone are worth the price of membership. *The Wheel* (which pays student journalists), the once-a-semester humor magazine *The Spoke,* the *Emory Political Review,* the literary magazine *Alloy,* and Emory's student-run radio station (WMRE) and television station (EmoryVision) are also fun to be a part of.

The Social Scene

Most Emory students party on Friday and Saturday nights, with the occasional Thursday thrown into the mix. The university is strict about not allowing alcohol in dorms, so when students want to drink they'll usually head to Frat Row, an off-campus house-apartment: the Park Bench (a bar within walking distance from campus); or one of the various clubs in Atlanta, usually in the Buckhead area. Of those four options, most students will just head to the frats—33 percent of the student body is Greek, so there are always lots of options to choose from, and anyone can come in, get drunk, dance, have fun, and leave.

Emory is generally a friendly campus, and it's easy to make new buddies. We have this great online forum here, called LearnLink, which provides chat rooms and message boards for students, and if you're ever bored you can log on, have a good conversation with a total stranger, and meet up with them for coffee minutes later.

Notable Emory Alumni Include:
Howard Lamar, former president of Yale University
Kenneth Cole, fashion designer
Newt Gingrich, former Speaker, House of Representatives
Sam Nunn, U.S. senator
Claude Sitton, journalist
David Brinkley, TV newscaster

EVERGREEN STATE COLLEGE

Founded: 1967

Location: Olympia, WA

Phone: (360) 867-6170

E-mail: admissions@evergreen.edu

Web site: www.evergreen.edu

Number of Undergraduates: 3,840

Number of Graduate Students: 277

Cost: Approximately $10,000 per year in state; $20,500 out of state

Application Deadline: March 1
Rolling Admissions

Rating:	Notable Majors/Programs:
Selective	Environmental Studies, Social Sciences, Media Arts

Size:
○ Small ● Medium ○ Large

Location:
○ Urban ● Suburban ○ Rural

On a Saturday, students talk about academics:
○ Always ● Sometimes ○ Never

Nightlife:
○ Intense ○ Moderate ● Laid-back

Politically, Evergreen leans:
● Left ○ Right ○ Split

Diversity:
○ High ● Low ○ Medium

Students describe Evergreen in five words:
- Quirky, liberal, laid-back, flexible students
- No grades + no majors = progressive.

From the School

The Evergreen State College is a public liberal arts college serving Washington State. Its mission is to help students realize their potential through innovative, interdisciplinary educational programs in the arts, social sciences, humanities, and natural sciences. In addition to preparing students within their academic fields, Evergreen provides graduates with the fundamental skills to communicate, to solve problems, and to work collaboratively and independently in addressing real issues and problems.

—www.evergreen.edu

If you're interested in Evergreen State, you may also be interested in:
Antioch, Berea, UC Santa Cruz, Lewis & Clark, Reed, Sarah Lawrence

Name: Katie
Hometown: Kirkland, Washington
Class Year: Senior
Major: We don't have majors
Extracurriculars: Women's soccer team
Career Goal: Graduate school counseling–social work

How would you describe Evergreen State's reputation?

It's a very new and progressive school that promotes a very new and progressive way of learning. I think people in the community fear this change. They fear the uncertainty of an education that doesn't follow the standard rubric. It introduces very current and controversial issues and encourages students to question everything. . . . And as far as the cliché assumptions go, most people understand Evergreen to be a place where hippies live in the woods and smoke pot.

Is this reputation accurate?

Absolutely. Diversity looks incredible from a distance, but sure, it can be a little scary to step outside of one's comfort zone and experience it up close. As for the pot-smoking hippie deal: although I can't say there isn't a hint of truth to this assumption, I challenge people to look a little deeper to find out what the school is truly about.

What aspect of Evergreen State would a prospective student not see on a campus tour?

The incredible academic energy that occurs in the classroom. I wish any potential TESC student could be a fly on the wall for just one seminar session. Seminars are a time for students to make meaning out of what they're learning in the program, to respond to, dissect, analyze, and question content. The tour also doesn't show that this amazing intellectual energy continues outside the classroom. Working with such small class sizes, students become passionate. One semester my class became so engrossed that we continued our discussions every Thursday evening at a local pub with our professor.

The Institution

TESC is a liberal, experimental college that allows students a great deal of freedom and flexibility in their learning. Choice is endless at TESC. Credit can be awarded for anything from making art out of garbage found at the local dump, to analyzing global perspectives on masculinity and femininity, to studying the societal struggles in the works of Steinbeck, to learning how to juggle.

TESC is a relatively small school, only four thousand students, which makes it much easier to connect with your peers. Professors and students are very open to new ideas academically. There are no grades at TESC, just evaluations. There are no exams. There are no majors. We call professors by their first names. There is no football team, and there are no sororities or fraternities. You can take classes titled "Baseball: More Than a Game," "The Fungal Kingdom: Lichens and Mushrooms, Nature's Recyclers," and "Labyrinths." We have a student-run organic farm. Pyramidal, multicolored skylights illuminate the library entryway. Both Courtney Love and Matt Groening attended TESC. Did I mention our mascot is a geoduck? It's a clam of immense size (can weigh two to ten pounds), so

> "I received a full ride scholarship for any college or university that I desired. Evergreen was the only school that I applied to. That has to say something!"
> ✦ Sarah, sophomore

naturally, athletes here take an ironic sense of pride in this.

I don't know about school spirit, but I think there is a sense of unity among Evergreen students that isn't found on many other college campuses. Education at Evergreen is such a unique experience, I think students recognize this and connect with one another because of what we share. Every June the graduating class at Evergreen races to the annual Mud Bay Run. Clothing is optional. As a senior about to walk away from Evergreen, I feel as prepared as I can be for life after college. Whether it be graduate school, a career, or traveling abroad, Evergeen has opened my perspective on many social, cultural, and political issues that continue to affect our country and world today.

I chose Evergreen after attending a much too large university freshman year. Being one of ten thousand students made me feel like a number, and with two midterms and a final exam for each class, I found I wasn't absorbing the information because I wasn't applying it to anything outside the classroom. . . . I chose Evergreen because it offered the opportunity to analyze, question, and discuss topics that were introduced instead of regurgitating what a professor told me.

The Education

TESC has a very nontraditional approach that truly enhances awareness about the world in which we live and prepares students for making change. The class theme for this year's graduation was "You must be the change you wish to see in the world" (Gandhi). Through interdisciplinary and collaborative learning, TESC students are able to link theory to practice when it comes to real situations.

It's common to talk about classes on a Saturday night or go to a pub or a coffee shop with a group of students and a professor or two in order to continue class discussions. The traditional hierarchal status of a professor is broken down here, and instead students and professors treat each other as equals. Learning is done together. Instead of grades, students and professors write evaluations for one another documenting what they did in their program, what they learned, and how they can take what they have learned and apply it to their future. It's a very honest process.

Evergreen does a great job promoting and encouraging students to study in other parts of the world. Although set programs and organizations are not always accessible financially to college students, as they can be very expensive. Evergreen students have the opportunity to create our own abroad curriculum through independent contracts. If you can get a professor to sponsor you, you can plan your own program abroad for a much more reasonable price.

The Students

A typical stroll through Red Square may include watching a feminism class writing bold statements in chalk on the sidewalk in front of the library; saying hello to a fellow student in patchwork pants as he continues to prance to class with a smile; viewing the student group Carnival theatrically performing a scene from *Planet of the Apes* in the grass; and perhaps being encouraged by a student group to sign a petition to preserve and protect the environment.

Evergreen students and faculty could make more effort to integrate diversity on campus. Being such a liberal, politically active school, the majority are aware of the need for diversity but are not

> "You get a lot of, 'Isn't Evergreen that weird school where all the hippies go to do drugs, have tie-dye, dreadlocks, and slack off because they don't get real grades?' People need to know that you can get an amazing education, without spending thousands more dollars to attend an Ivy."
> ✦ Sarah, sophomore

always responsible when it comes to embracing and accepting it.

The Activities

Playing for the TESC women's soccer team has been a really enriching experience. It gives me a sense of connectedness. I've formed some really wonderful friendships with teammates, and the level of competition is ideal for me—I'm challenged, but I still have fun because there's no intense pressure to win. The teams we play have cheerleaders with clean uniforms, synchronized routines, and generic spirit songs, while enthusiastic TESC fans beat conga drums and shake their tambourines.

The first protest I attended at Evergreen was in opposition to the war in Afghanistan, and I have to admit I was disappointed. Rather than discussing the war and our opposition to it, bongo drums were being played and massage circles being formed. I felt disconnected. I think Evergreen students have the knowledge and skills for creating social and political change, but they don't always apply them well.

The seven sisters tree in the woods, an immense tree that branches out into six other trees at the top, is an excellent cradle for someone to sit and contemplate the day. The roof of the library building—with the new pyramidal skylights—is fascinating. Old School Pizza is a great place to hang with friends. The Eastside Tavern on a Thursday night has pool, darts, air hockey, and a plethora of excellent beers on tap. Mud Bay Coffee Co. is a mellow place to get some studying done. And the drive-in always has a double feature and free dog biscuits!

The Social Scene

Dorm parties usually consist of cheap beer, the scent of Nag Champa, and a lot of old Michael Jackson hits. There are also full-moon parties in the woods, where students usually make a big bonfire, play drums, and dance in the moonlight. The best is perhaps the Foreign Exchange parties in the mods, which always make for an exciting evening.

Name: Joseph
Hometown: Moses Lake, Washington
Class Year: Freshman
Major: Film
Extracurriculars: A little bit of this, little bit of that
Career Goal: My goal is to create or act in films.

How would you describe Evergreen State's reputation?

Evergreen is looked down upon—especially where I come from—given its very liberal reputation. Where I come from, *liberal* isn't a very admired word.

Is this reputation accurate?

Yes—and it's exactly what I love about it.

What would an admissions officer at Evergreen State probably not tell a prospective student?

I suppose a prospective student won't see what tours at any school won't show you: parties, drugs, alcohol, and especially at Evergreen, a cigarette butt or trash lying on the ground.

> "We are known for our abundance of pot usage. But show me a college that is drug free. Evergreen is no more or less of a 'pot school' than anywhere else."
>
> ✦ Tracy, freshman

The Institution

The institution is great, and I have no complaints. I am friends with townies and a gazillion people in the school. For a small liberal arts college with this atmosphere, TESC is a pretty substantial size. I really like that here, I am similar to the majority. I'll be different from the mainstream for the rest of my life; for once (four years, to be exact), it's nice to just fit in. In a world where people hate what they don't understand, and where the hated need to find solace . . . there is Evergreen: the school of freaks, the school where everyone is weird, the school where everyone's views and opinions are different from the norm. What bliss!

The Education

Sure, I've talked about classes on Saturday nights. Evergreen students are pretty serious about their studies and interested in applying them beyond the classroom. However, we're also laid back enough to know how to take it easy on a weekend. Most of the classes are discussion based, and I feel like everyone can offer their opinion. It's nice to experience the intellectual views from smart kids in such a liberal atmosphere. I spend twice as much time on homework than I spend in class—but this is how it is at all colleges. You wouldn't come here if you weren't expecting to work hard. Evergreen also has a really strong film department—that's what I came here for.

The Students

I have never been to a place with such a wide range of people!

The Activities

There are lots of entertaining things to occupy your time here at Evergreen. The school presents a lot of entertainment for their students. We have pretty big names visit and give lectures and concerts. Olympia's also the capital of Washington, so the town ain't bad, either. You don't need to try hard to make a lot of friends here—people are so friendly, they'll say hello to you even when you don't say hello to them. There's always something to do and somebody to do it with.

The Social Scene

There is a party on campus every single weekend where you can witness all kinds of people entertaining themselves in, well, the typical fashion for people aged eighteen to twenty-five. Kids really need a break from the extreme dullness of constant studying, and I believe that socially meeting people in a drunken state is the perfect vacation away from reality.

Name: Carolyn
Hometown: Grosse Pointe, Michigan
Class Year: Sophomore
Major: We don't have majors; my focus is in classical philosophy and ethics

Extracurriculars: Cooking, baking frivolous desserts, and playing kickball

Career Goal: Classical education that emphasizes philosophy and ethics

How would you describe Evergreen State's reputation?

Evergreen is a renowned liberal arts college that moves progressively beyond popular education by emphasizing learning and scholarship over grades. It is a perfect environment for independently ambitious thinkers.

Is this reputation accurate?

Yup.

What would an admissions officer at Evergreen State probably not tell a prospective student? What aspect of your school would a prospective student probably not see on a campus tour?

Admissions would probably neglect to tell you that there are not many new programs offered after the fall quarter, and if you want to switch out of a program it's difficult because there's a limit on what you can switch into. On a tour a prospective student would probably not see the areas of housing that are infested with bugs and/or mold.

The Institution

Evergreen is certainly a unique place. It surpasses any notion of "weird" or "strange" that I had ever known. This is exactly the reason why I was attracted to Evergreen in the first place, and the reason most others are, too! It is a haven for people who aren't average, and it represents progressive thought and freedom of ideas in an age when materialism and capitalism are dominant.

> "The campus is beautiful! A thousand acres of land, tons of trees!"
> ✦ Tracy, freshman

The Education

People do not come to Evergreen because they want a prestigious-looking diploma, because they want to make a lot of money, or because they like football. People come here because they desire knowledge and because they have a sense of duty to their community. There is a general consensus that we benefit the world most by being actively informed and knowledgeable.

The relationship between students and the profs at Evergreen is outstanding. Since class sizes are small, professors spend lots of time connecting with students. You'll find students talking with their professors over tea, and faculty members regularly have meetings with each individual about their work in class. This sets Evergreen apart from any other institution. In many ways, I think Evergreen's lack of grades makes it far more academically challenging. An A means nothing. The concept of an A isn't good enough. I remember turning in a paper that was well thought out, logical, fluid, and grammatically perfect. My professor wrote me a letter that was almost a page long—single-spaced—in response. She could sense that I had a superior grasp on the text I was writing about, but I hadn't set up a great enough challenge for myself. She wanted me to push myself to more complex ideas because she knew what I was capable of. Now *that's* what learning's all about.

The Students

Evergreen is very diverse in age. Almost 40 percent of the student body is over the age of twenty-five. This adds a richness of ideas and experiences to the classroom that would be lacking in a traditional college where students are predominantly eighteen to twenty-four.

Students at Evergreen were the rebellious and/or quirky kids in high school that knew better than to worry about social popularity or fashion trends. Students at Evergreen are very liberal and certainly live up to the stereotype of being protesters: about *everything*. The most vocal groups on campus are usually the political awareness groups, and groups that support the diversity of sexual orientations on campus. Environmental groups are a huge part of the Evergreen campus as well, and they help to sponsor events that raise environmental sustainability awareness and activism.

The Activities

Evergreen is known for potlucks. Classes have potlucks. Teachers have potlucks. Students have potlucks. Everyone has potlucks—all the time. Evergreeners enjoy laid-back activities that involve organically grown food and/or time spent in nature. Though sports exist at Evergreen, they represent a small part of campus life and few people go to athletic events. Evergreeners are more concerned with playing bluegrass or attending poetry readings than watching basketball games. The best sports at Evergreen are pickup games of soccer, Frisbee, or kickball that attract an array of students with differing athletic abilities. Sports at Evergreen are just for fun.

> "Before Evergreen, I was a habitual class skipper. But here classes are definitely worth waking up for."
>
> ✦ Sara, junior

The Social Scene

There are no fraternities or sororities at Evergreen. Parties tend to be smaller affairs, often including . . . a potluck! This is not to say there are never parties. They just aren't like the ragers seen at larger universities after football games.

Campus is pretty small, so meeting people is easy. Campus life is also for the younger community at Evergreen (eighteen to twenty), while off-campus life is generally for the older crowd. Dorm life is generally loud, but one of the best ways to meet people.

Evergreen State Notable Alumni Include:
Bruce Pavitt, founder of Sub-Pop Records
Lynda Barry, cartoonist
Matt Groening, cartoonist, creator of *Life in Hell, The Simpsons* and *Futurama*
Michael Richards, actor (Cosmo Kramer on *Seinfeld*)
Rachel Corrie, activist
Saab Lofton, author and activist

FURMAN UNIVERSITY

Founded: 1826
Location: Greenville, SC
Phone: (864) 294-2034
E-mail: admissions@furman.edu
Web site: www.furman.edu

Number of Undergraduates: 2,654
Number of Graduate Students: 506
Cost: Approximately $29,000 per year
Application Deadline: January 15
Early Decision: November 15

Rating:	Notable Majors/Programs:
Selective	Psychology, Chemistry, Political Science, History

Size:
○ Small ● Medium ○ Large

Location:
○ Urban ● Suburban ○ Rural

On a Saturday, students talk about academics:
○ Always ● Sometimes ○ Never

Nightlife:
○ Intense ● Moderate ○ Laid-back

Politically, Furman leans:
○ Left ● Right ○ Split

Diversity:
○ High ● Low ○ Medium

Students describe Furman in five words:
- Beautiful, prestigious, challenging, small, friendly
- Southern, conservative, rich, white, fun

From the School

From its inception, this institution has assumed that intellectual inquiry and spiritual reflection can thrive together. The Latin motto on the university seal declares that Furman exists "for Christ and for learning." Over the years, Furman has broadened its mission and revised its programs—and it has been blessed by the presence of female students since its merger with Greenville Woman's College in 1933.

—www.furman.edu

If you're interested in Furman, you may also be interested in:
Davidson, Duke, UNC at Chapel Hill, Vanderbilt, Wake Forest, Washington and Lee

Name: Donna
Hometown: Greensboro, North Carolina
Class Year: Sophomore
Major: Undecided
Extracurriculars: Baptist Collegiate Ministry, church-related vocations, Alpha Kapola Fermata
Career Goal I think I'll wind up teaching.

How would you describe Furman's reputation?

Furman is known as one of the best liberal arts colleges in the Southeast. Nearby schools look at us like we're a bastion of liberalism. But that's only because these schools are *so* right wing everywhere else looks liberal by comparison (*cough*, Bob Jones University, *cough*).

Is this reputation accurate?

Furman is an academic gem. The Music, Chemistry, Political Science, Psychology, History and Foreign Languages Departments are particularly strong here. And politically, well, there are a few liberal students, but most students proudly voted for Bush. This is the South. Conservatism is in our blood.

What aspect of your school would a prospective student not see on a campus tour?

A visiting student probably wouldn't see the huge variety of activities going on every night of the week here. We're a small school, but we have visiting speakers, foreign films, concerts and recitals, political activities, improv shows, discussion groups, religious groups. There are literally at least five activities to choose from every single night.

> "This place is absolutely gorgeous. I feel like I'm living on a resort."
> ✦ Joshua, junior

The Institution

Furman is exceptionally pretty—the architecture is impressive, the buildings are all old and brick, there are lots of wide open green spaces with huge oak trees, there's a nice lake, a Japanese garden, a picnic and walking area. . . . I love Furman. The students are all very open and friendly, as are the professors and staff (except maybe the dining

hall staff). We even have Lake Monsters: Incredibly huge trout with fins that stick ominously above the water as they glide around the campus lake. They really are *huuuuuge*. But the lake is still beautiful, and full of ducks and swans and geese. There is a tradition of throwing birthday boys and girls in the lake.

The Education

You should know there's a kooky three-term system at Furman—over the course of the year you'll have one twelve-week term, one eight-week term, then another twelve-week term. That's how your academic life will be broken up. More madness—in the two twelve-week terms you'll be taking three classes, and in the eight-week term you'll only be taking two classes. But in the eight-week term, your two classes will last a half hour longer than your classes did in the twelve-week term. This all sounds weird, I know. But it's actually nice, because the year gets broken up in interesting ways.

At Furman people talk about their classes fairly often, but they're pretty good about having a good time on the weekends, and usually weekend discussion of classes is limited to, "Okay, I've got to study for this test before we go to the movie." And that's that. You study, you go to your movie, done. In class, professors are stimulating. You feel connected to them, comfortable going to them for help, saying hi to them in the hallways. They really are, in a sense, your buddies. This type of atmosphere is ideal if you want to do lots of research as an undergraduate, since all you have to do is find a professor you want to work with and ask them if you can. Odds are, they have some sort of project on the backburner that they'd gladly let you help out with. There are especially good opportunities for research in the chemistry and history departments. Most of the classes I've taken have been lectures, with a nice bit of discussion mixed in. And you should study abroad if you come to Furman. The opportunities are varied, numerous, and affordable. Almost everyone takes at least one trip. I managed to take a term off to go to Germany, which was one of the best times of my life.

The Students

I'd say the typical Furman student was in the top 5 percent (at least) of their high school class, got a 1250 SAT score, and grew up in the Christian conservative South. Furman students are serious about overachieving, but pretty good about keeping a sense of humor about themselves (even during hellish midterm season).

The College Republicans are the largest group on campus, which should tell you something. But even the most hardcore CR is pretty accepting of those out of the typical Christian, conservative, southern mindset. Difference is definitely tolerated here.

> "A number of girls here are more concerned with getting their MRS. than their BA."
> ✦ Nicholas, junior

The Activities

There is a lot going on in the Furman "bubble." Seriously, a lot of kids never leave campus. So, if you want to stay in the Furman bubble on weekends, our Student Activities Board is fabulous and keeps us entertained with every mix of activity you can dream of. There are also constant fraternity parties to go to. But if you want to escape, go for it! Discover Greenville! It's only ten minutes away and full of artsy shops, places to eat, a great county library, a little theater, an art museum, a concert hall–hockey stadium and yet another theater-concert hall, the Slab (great ice cream!) and Coffee Underground, which is one of the coolest, yummiest places to hang out . . . really, the *yummiest*. Otherwise, we play crazy, loud, fast card games. We play music, Frisbee, watch Disney movies, make up scavenger hunts for each other, have huge outdoor pillow fights.

The Social Scene

Furman is officially a dry campus, so most fraternities have their houses right outside Furman's property lines. Brightly colored flyers will appear in your mailbox advertising their parties. I think about a third of our students are Greek, and the Greeks seem to hold lots of formals and semiformals and informals, or whatever. I'm not a Greek myself, and I have a fine social life. Hanging out, going downtown, going dancing. You'll do OK, too, if that's not your thing.

Name: Loren
Hometown: Franklin, North Carolina
Class Year: Sophomore
Major: Music education

Extracurriculars: Collegiate Music Educators' National Conference, marching band, symphonic band, concert band, brass quintet, symphony orchestra, basketball pep band, Sigma Alpha Iota Women's Music Fraternity
Career Goal: I want to teach high school in a somewhat rural area of the South.

How would you describe Furman's reputation?

Furman is known for being a "prestige school" with hardcore academics. In the brochure you'll see lots of information about our liberal arts program and study-abroad opportunities, alongside photographs of our stunningly beautiful campus.

Is this reputation accurate?

All of the above is accurate. . . . But there's so much more to this place! Our athletic programs are diverse and our facilities are top-notch. We have an awesome community service program that's entirely student run, and our fine arts program has just started to come into its own, attracting regional attention.

What would an admissions officer at your school probably not tell a prospective student?

The one sad thing about Furman is its homogeneous student body. The administration will tell you that Furman is diverse, blah, blah, blah. The truth is, we're a former southern Baptist school that's incredibly white, incredibly Christian, and incredibly southern. We're conservatives, here . . . we're conformists.

The Institution

Furman is the perfect size. Any smaller and you'd feel trapped. Any bigger and you're a number. Three thousand students, to my mind, is just right.

Furman used to be located in downtown Greenville, but now we're set apart from the town a bit. But memories remain, and the town still looks at us like we're a part of their daily life. Community and college are unusually intertwined. Being a music major, it amazes me how much of the community actually comes to support the university's performing ensembles. There's this one elderly couple that seriously comes to every single senior recital! We know them by name. I just think that's awesome.

Also, though Furman isn't very well known outside the South, in the South it's a powerhouse.

The students here realize they go to a very prestigious school, and it goes to their heads a little bit. How can it not?

Because Furman is small, you really get to know the teachers and administrators. Each fall the president of Furman throws individual pool parties for each freshman residential hall—at his house! You get to eat barbecue and talk to him while in your swimming trunks. At what other school could this happen? Also, less cool but worth noting, our Greek rush events don't start until the winter, so the freshmen really have a chance to get settled in before all that starts. If you're going to rush, you'll appreciate this, as you'll have time to organize your life before frat and sorority madness sets in.

The Education

This Clemson guy calls me up on a Tuesday night—he's having a party, and do I want to come? My answer—yeah, right. I'm studying! Everyone in my dorm is! Sorry, buddy. During the week, this is life at Furman. There's a lot of work here, and you have to have a lot of self-discipline to get it done. This isn't to say that we never have crazy fun. We do. On weekends. During the week, we are studying and being taught by fantastic professors. They know all of our names, and they're very eager to discuss things outside of class. This goes for professors both inside and outside of your major—even professors who teach your core classes. And speaking of core classes, one of my favorites ever was Psych 21 (general psychology); it's known for being one of the hardest classes on campus, period. And it was. But it was so interesting that it was worth every minute of missed sleep. See, that's the Furman mentality. We take the hardest classes and buckle down and get them done with a smile on our faces. Welcome to college.

The Students

Furman is noticeably a southern school, full of southern hospitality. Everywhere you go you'll see smiling people and hear polite hellos. Even if you're having a terrible day this sort of thing will cheer you up. You won't be able to stop yourself from smiling back. I'd say, roughly 20 percent of our students were valedictorians or salutatorians in high school. That's a lot of overachieving perfectionists in one place! It's also a lot of stress balls. Many Furman students had never gotten a B in their life. Then, when they get their first B–, they go crazy. Absolutely nuts.

The Activities

The campus closest to ours is Bob Jones University, and sometimes students go to visit their library or art museum, but other than that we leave them be. Clemson is also down the road and we'll interact occasionally.

Other things: Furman's community service corps, CESC, is particularly active. May Day Play Day is sponsored by CESC. It's a day when kids and exceptional adults from nearby come onto campus and play games, have arts and crafts booths, and it's great for community bonding.

> "In keeping with Furman's unwavering commitment to Baptist ideals, it's a dry campus with *enforced* alcohol prohibition. On one hand, the lack of hypocrisy is refreshing (I have friends that go to 'dry' schools where the alcohol is abundant). But, on the other hand, Furman is *dry*!"
> ✦ Tamara, senior

The Social Scene

There are *some* random people at Furman who will get absolutely trashed on a Tuesday night. But they're the exception. For the most part, Furman's social scene lies dormant during the week. Students are studying, rehearsing for plays and performances, working on the school newspaper. It's on Friday and Saturday night that we bust loose. Our campus is "dry," so frat parties are held at local clubs or at the fraternity houses off campus. While I respect the idea of a "dry" campus in theory, there's a greater likelihood of people going off campus and then driving home drunk, which is unfortunate but a reality.

For some, the dating scene at Furman is weird . . . there seems to be a lot of pressure to find someone, settle in, get engaged and be married by the time you graduate. There's the "two-function assumption" at work here, where if you take the same person to two different parties or events you're an item, and a wedding ring is supposedly imminent within the next three years. I hate that pressure.

Name: Melanie
Hometown: Athens, Georgia
Class Year: Sophomore

Major: Neuroscience
Extracurriculars: Furman's Finest, Delta Delta Delta, Alpha Epsilon Delta, Phi Eta Sigma
Career Goal: General dentist

How would you describe Furman's reputation?

If you've heard of Furman, you know that it's incredibly academically challenging. You might also think a lot of Furman students come from wealthy families. And also, you might be one of the people who are perpetuating the myth that Furman students only get married and never just date, ever.

Is this reputation accurate?

Furman definitely places a challenging workload onto each student's plate. It takes some getting used to, but it's not impossible. And sure, some kids here are loaded. But plenty of people are on financial aid here, too. And, of course people just date!

What would an admissions officer at your school probably not tell a prospective student?

They won't tell you how hard the middle (winter) term is. Essentially, during that term we cram three months' worth of work into two months. Fine, we take one less class, but it's still ridiculously hard and it hits most students like a brick. Do I need to explicitly state that I'm not a fan of Furman's winter academic schedule?

The Institution

Furman's size is perfect. And because Furman has a beautiful campus, during the fall and spring townies come onto campus for walks, to enjoy the scenery, to be around us college kids. I think that's great; it really makes you feel like a part of the nearby community, not just a member of some imposing nearby institution of higher learning. For four years, at least, we're all residents of Greenville. (Doesn't Greenville sound idyllic? It is.) The only strange thing is that Furman has these squirrels. They're everywhere. You can't walk ten feet without dodging a squirrel. If you like squirrels, this is great! Otherwise, it's gross.

The Education

Most students at Furman were at the top of their class in high school, and you don't get to the top of your class unless you're more than a bit competitive. That carries over to college life, and

Furman students definitely compete for the best grades. Competition spurs you on, makes you work harder. I don't think that's a bad thing. I once had an organic chemistry test on a Tuesday, and I stayed up studying through Saturday and Sunday, just so I'd have an edge on everyone else who spent the weekend partying. Not everyone does this though. Lots of students don't look at their books from Friday morning through to Sunday night.

Most of the classes I've taken at Furman have been discussion based, even though I'm a science and math kid. This means you can rarely skip class or not do your reading, because your professors will know. And you don't escape your professors once class ends—you'll see them around campus a lot, and many professors are also advisers for fraternities and sororities and other campus groups. So do your work and you can really make great friendships with professors, and they'll go out of their way for you.

Furman has a core curriculum, but I think it does an OK job with it. Each student has to complete a few general education classes and it's really doable. And once that's out of the way, every department at Furman is a pretty strong. You'll probably spend two hours a day on schoolwork if you don't have a test or paper due. And when you're a senior, you'll take "senior seminars," where you meet with faculty members and do high-level research and course work. Lastly, Furman has great research facilities for biology, chemistry, and psychology classes. Many stay at Furman during their summers to do research, which sounds miserable but isn't, since Furman's campus is *so* beautiful.

> "I love being a part of a nationally renowned college choir, and having the chance to make beautiful music with one hundred of my closest friends."
> ✦ Jeremy, sophomore

The Students

Let me be blunt—Furman is not racially diverse, religiously diverse, politically diverse, and it's barely socioeconomically diverse. Most students are white, Christian, Republican, and while incomes vary, no one is really poor. That's just how it is. But at least we all get along. And if you don't fit in the above groupings, you'll probably still be fine. The only people I can imagine having a really hard time at Furman would be atheists. The concept of religion plays a real part in student life here. I believe in God, and I like the fact that most people here do also. If you don't believe in God at all, that could be a problem.

> "Furman is white. White, white, white. White."
>
> ✦ Cian, freshman

The Activities

Athletics are not a big part of campus life. I mean, we have athletes, and people know who they are, but they're not worshiped, and if their names are mentioned on ESPN once or twice people don't drop to their knees in their presence. Instead it's just like, "Oh, you play sports, good for you. Keep throwing those balls around." Most campus activities are planned by the FUSAB (Furman University Student Activities Board). They get things rolling, and then you have outside activities planned by religious groups, political groups, ethnic groups. There's plenty to do. Personally, I tend to head into town on the weekends to grab dinner and a movie or something.

The Social Scene

Everyone has to live on campus all four years at Furman. I like this, because it makes everyone feel like they're part of the community, and you're never going to live far from any of your friends. Generally, the dorm rooms are fine, too. And when you're a junior or senior, you get a two- or four-bedroom apartment. It's just unfortunate that Furman is a "dry" campus. It can be annoying to walk all the way back to your dorm room from someplace off campus, drunk. People at Furman party on Friday and Saturday nights either at frat parties or some other function. And while maybe the dating scene isn't *great* at Furman, it's not terrible! It's not half as bad as people make it out to be! You *can* date here and *not* get married!

Notable Furman Alumni Include:
Betsy King, golfer
Mark Sanford, politician
Richard Riley, former secretary of education
Charles Townes, physicist
John B. Watson, psychologist
Ben Browder, actor

GEORGE WASHINGTON UNIVERSITY

Founded: 1821
Location: Washington, DC
Phone: (202) 994-1000
E-mail: gwadm@gwu.edu
Web site: www.gwu.edu

Number of Undergraduates: 9,950
Number of Graduate Students: 10,766
Cost: Approximately $41,000 per year
Application Deadline: January 15
Early Decision: December 1

Rating:	Notable Majors/Programs:
Very Selective	Political Science, International Affairs, Business

Size:
○ Small   ○ Medium   ● Large

Location:
● Urban   ○ Suburban   ○ Rural

On a Saturday, students talk about academics:
○ Always   ● Sometimes   ○ Never

Nightlife:
○ Intense   ● Moderate   ○ Laid-back

Politically, GW is:
○ Left   ○ Right   ● Split

Diversity:
○ High   ○ Low   ● Medium

Students describe GW in five words:
- Opportunity-rich, politically aware, preprofessional, oh-so-bustling!
- A monumentally expensive, worthwhile experience

From the School
Our academic prowess is expressed in a myriad of ways: in the classroom, in the laboratory, in the study group, in the studio, online, in the library, on residence hall academic program floors, in academic and honor society clubs, and in academic or departmental social gatherings.

—http://gwired.gwu.edu

If you're interested in George Washington, you may also be interested in:
Boston University, Case Western, Cornell, Georgetown, NYU, Tufts

Name: Julie

Hometown: Harrisburg, Pennsylvania

Class Year: Junior

Majors: Biology and political science

Extracurriculars: Band, Alpha Chi Sigma, Habitat for Humanity, Circle K, International Affairs Society, College Democrats, freshman advising, Major Advising Cabinet, intramural floor hockey

Career Goal: Earn PhD in molecular oncology and conduct cancer research at a major private not-for-profit laboratory

How would you describe George Washington's reputation?

I think GW is generally thought of very highly—a lot of people even think it's an Ivy League school (hey, I'm fine with that!).

Is this reputation accurate?

Well, of course GW is not an Ivy League school, but we do get a great education. Plus, I've met a lot of students, myself included, who were accepted into Ivy schools and came to GW instead.

What aspect of George Washington would a prospective student not see on a campus tour?

The red-tape hassles (though I'm sure that's common at most schools). Prospective students on a campus tour do not see some of the older, deteriorating classrooms—just the nice, new ones . . . it's not until you're here that you realize the bad state of some of the buildings.

The Institution

I love GW. Since we are a city school and lack the standard campus, everyone is a little more independent and more willing to do their own thing. Campus security is great—maybe because we're so close to the White House—but UPD is always there right away when you need them. And, internship opportunities are phenomenal, regardless of what you are interested in going into. Coming to GW was the best decision of my life in terms of finding internships and career goals to point me in the right direction—I have already interned at the House of Representatives and am now doing research at the Institute for Genomic Research.

The Education

A common misconception is that GW is only good for international affairs or political science. Being in D.C., it naturally offers an excellent curriculum in both—but not only in these. Professors here are still active in their fields outside of teaching—some may view this negatively, since they are not full-time, but I view it as incredibly positive because they're still involved and are so up-to-date. I take classes with PhD researchers at the National Cancer Institute—some of the top researchers in the nation. Competition between students can get rough depending on majors—in biology, all the premed students are fighting for spots into medical school, and that goes the same for prelaw. Occasionally teachers add to this by declaring that "only the top two students in my class will get As." Unlike many schools these days, GW doesn't practice "grade inflation," so you have to work harder, but it is definitely more rewarding. I actually *learn* in my classes—about things which will be very relevant for me in graduate school.

Most students have no problem fulfilling the General Curriculum Requirements right along with their major, as many major requirement courses also count toward GCRs, and each of the seven colleges within GW has different GCRs.

Freshman year intro classes can number up to two hundred students, but this is rare—most intro courses are kept to under one hundred. Typical lectures are kept under fifty, and lab courses are usually kept under twenty-four students. And any course with over fifty students is broken down into discussions, usually with fifteen to twenty students, and a PhD TA. For people like me who dislike discussions, most larger classes, such as intro political science courses, also offer a smaller section without discussions and only fifty students. And lastly, thesis requirements vary by department, but most have them as an option for students wishing to graduate with honors.

> "The fact that I am woken up by the presidential motorcade or the Marine One helicopter flying overhead is exhilarating. I really am living in Washington, D.C."
> ✦ Dagan, freshman

The Students

Everyone knows that the largest groups on campus are College Democrats and College Republicans. Three-fourths of the students on campus are a member of one or the other, even if they never show up to meetings and don't participate in the events. Being in D.C., we are surrounded by politics and news, and as a result I feel that GW students are often more aware of the world around them than students at most other schools. CNN is on in the student center round the clock and nobody ever complains. You will hear that all students at GW are rich and Jewish—definitely not true, although those that are do make their presence known. Rumors fly that everyone is from boarding school, etc., but there are also lots of middle-class students from diverse backgrounds. Only about 20 percent of campus is Greek, and there is not a large divide between Greek and non-Greek. I opted to not join a sorority, but several of my close friends did, and this has not affected our relationships.

The Activities

GW has minimal interaction with surrounding universities. Georgetown students tend to think GW stands for "Georgetown Waitlist," and although some students did apply to Georgetown and were not accepted, most students honestly had no interest in going there. Athletics are not a huge part of life—not too many students attend events other than basketball—but lots of students play intramurals, from flag football and Ultimate Frisbee to Wiffle ball and floor hockey. There are *loads* of performance groups on campus, several theater companies that put on lots of plays (including the annual twenty-four-hour play: within twenty-four hours, an entire play is written, casted, produced, and staged—lots of people are involved in this one, and it's supposed to be a lot of fun), many music ensembles (from the general symphonic band open to all to the exclusive wind ensemble, the a cappella groups, etc.). GW also sponsors several days of community service each year, and they are well attended. Students have the opportunity to factor into administrative decisions, if they so choose, by serving on the influential Student Association Senate or within the Executive Committee. Otherwise, D.C. has some amazing places to visit: the National Zoo or the Spy Museum, the galleries in Dupont Circle.

The Social Scene

People at GW party—but not wild and crazy, like at state schools. Weekends it's not hard to find something going on, whether it's a group going to a club or parties at a frat house. Even if you're not Greek, you're always welcome at frat parties—but most of the time they comply with UPD rules and card at the door. Lots of people just hang out on weekends, however, and I've never been in a situation where I have felt obligated to drink.

The dating scene is standard, lots of individuals are in relationships, but lots of individuals prefer just the weekend hookups. Unlike a lot of schools, it's not standard for upperclassmen to live off campus, and those who remain in dorms are not the unpopular or uncool kids.

Name: Rachel
Hometown: Wayzata, Minnesota
Class Year: Junior
Major: International affairs
Extracurriculars: Amnesty International, Transfer Student Organization, internships in D.C., Writing Center
Career Goal: To work at a nonprofit human rights organization

How would you describe George Washington's reputation?

A politically active, liberal-minded school filled with wealthy, Jewish, would-be politicians from New York and New Jersey.

Is this reputation accurate?

For the most part, but there are many students who do not fit this mold. The campus is *very* politically active—most students intern on Capitol Hill, watch CNN, especially *Crossfire*—and most students are politically liberal, though a conservative minority makes its voice heard. While many students are from the Northeast, there are students from every state and many foreign countries. Roughly 40 percent of the students are Jewish, but other religions are prominent as well. And while an atmosphere of entitlement does exist on campus, there are plenty of students on financial aid and students who work part-time to afford Washington's high living costs.

What would an admissions officer at George Washington probably not tell a prospective student?

The red tape, long lines, and forms are unbearable. To get anything done on campus you have to speak with at least three departments or offices, who all send you somewhere else. I feel like it is harder to get *into* my classes than it is to *pass* them.

The Institution

Of all of the universities in D.C., GW has the best location. The main freshman residence hall is located just blocks from the White House, the International Affairs building is across from the State Department, and another dorm used to be the Howard Johnson's across from Watergate. GW is also a short walk from Georgetown, Dupont Circle, and the National Mall. While other D.C.-based universities require a shuttle bus to get to the nearest metro station, GW's metro stop resides on campus. Big-name speakers are common, and major political announcements often occur on our grounds.

Housing at GW is excellent! The residence halls are mostly old hotels and apartment buildings. GW has built a few residence halls in the past few years as well. Almost all residence halls have a bathroom for each room, freshmen have housekeeping, and almost all sophomores and upperclassmen have a kitchen in their rooms. You'll find some students complaining about their assignments, or saying that the major problem with housing at GW is the Community Living and Learning Center (the residential life office), where the staff is really out of touch with college students. They do a lot of work, but that doesn't mean they're very student-friendly.

Being an urban campus, GW has to work hard to create community. The university has an excellent freshman orientation program, which works to immediately welcome students to GW. All in all, I'd say GW's motto, "Something Happens Here" is an understatement to the opportunities and experiences that students gain by living and studying in the heart of the nation's capital.

> "What you're really paying for at GW is location, and the only way to put value behind your degree is to intern."
> ✦ Eli, sophomore

While GW has many positive aspects, it is not perfect. The university sometimes loses track of the reason it exists: to educate students. Also, everything at GW is about money, and the university tries to extract more of it from students whenever possible. The administration invests a lot of money in real estate and buildings, rather than in professors. Class sizes should be smaller and professors should be paid more. Some people joke about how the university is basically a cover for a tax-free real estate agency. And administrators at GW are distant, having little if any contact with students—few students have ever met the president of the university or any of the deans. Also, the university's obsessed with making the "Top 50 Colleges List"; it will do whatever it takes to get on this list, regardless of the impact on students.

The Education

To get an A in a class, most students have to invest considerable time and effort into learning the materials. While students do study, rarely do they spend a Saturday night in the library.

GW has many adjunct professors (experts in their fields who are often professionals in Washington, D.C.), and few tenured professors. The con of this is that it is hard to build lasting relationships and to really get to know your professors, as they may only be on campus a few days per week.

Internships are integral here. Most students do at *least* one internship during their time at GW, and many have a different internship each semester. Our location makes it easy, and students hardly need to major in political science to get a good internship here. There are numerous opportunities in computer science, media, psychology, and the arts as well.

Lastly, study abroad at GW is huge! Between one-third and one-half of the junior class studies abroad each year. The one negative aspect of study abroad at GW is that while abroad, students have to pay GW tuition, GW housing, and GW board. I am studying abroad in Costa Rica this fall and there is no way that food and housing in Costa Rica will be as expensive as they are in D.C. On the upside, your financial aid and scholarships still apply while you are abroad.

The Students

The students who are best suited to GW are those who seek out their own opportunities. The ambitious student will get more out of the GW experience than will a student who waits passively for opportunities to happen to him or her. There are resources on campus to help students achieve their goals, but students have to seek them out.

The Activities

GW has over three hundred student organizations, ranging from cultural groups to clubs devoted to cigar smoking and popular television shows such as *West Wing*. Our Student Association is more corrupt than the U.S. government. They have election scandals, resignations, and recounts. The Student Association buries itself in worthless crap and spends so much time pretending to be important that it accomplishes nothing. Their only real purpose is to distribute student funds to student organizations, a task they have nowhere near mastered. And Greek life at GW is what you make of it. It exists (the University recently built several townhouses that house most of the frats and sororities) and it can be a large part of your college experience, but if you're not interested in Greek life, you barely notice it. Same with sports.

The Social Scene

Many people go clubbing or to bars on weekends. If they aren't clubbing, students often go to dinner in Georgetown or go see a movie. Being on the East Coast makes it easy for students to travel to New York for the weekend, so some students do that once in a while. Here, you don't know everyone on campus, but you know enough people. There are enough students so that you don't know every detail about everyone.

Name: Kaleb
Hometown: St. Louis, Missouri
Class Year: Senior
Major: Political science
Extracurriculars: GW Students for Fair Trade, College Republicans, National Federation of Young Republicans, Beta Theta Pi Fraternity, Cigar Smokers Forum
Career Goal: Engage in education policy advocacy for a couple of years, attend law school, work for the Department of Education

How would you describe George Washington's reputation?

George Washington University has the reputation of being the waiting list for Georgetown.

Is this reputation accurate?

Sure, a lot of students who are wait-listed or deferred from Georgetown may end up attending GW. However, this idea dramatically underscores the benefits GW has over Georgetown. Whereas Georgetown is located on the outskirts of town, not really a part of the city at all, GW is located in the heart of D.C. and in the heart of the political world. It gives students greater opportunities for internships and overall real-world experience. So while some may view us as Georgetown's AAA baseball team, eagerly awaiting the call up to the majors, I say we're the ones playing in the major market, getting the scouting attention from employers.

What aspect of George Washington would a prospective student not see on a campus tour?

You won't see an all-white campus. What you will see is an urban campus with a large amount of diversity. All races, creeds, and religions are represented here, and you should know that unlike some other schools, we don't have to doctor photos to make it seem that way.

The Institution

Going to the George Washington University is like playing for the Milwaukee Brewers: you're in the majors (at a good school academically), you're in a decent market (D.C. being a decently populated city with good job opportunities), but there's no team spirit because you know there's always another losing season on the horizon. School spirit is an anomaly at GW. This may be the result of having no football team, having a basketball team that hasn't produced a competitive season in God knows how long, or the fact that we've been waiting to crack the top fifty on the *U.S. News & World Report*'s college ranking for the past eight years. You'll find more chants of "go Maryland Terps" than you will "go Hippos/Colonials" on this campus.

The Education

The professors in the Political Science, International Affairs, and English Departments are well respected in their respective fields, attentive to students' interests and needs, and overall a solid core of teachers. If you want to focus your studies in any of these areas, you'll have plenty of opportunities to get to know your professors, learn a great deal about life after college, and get help in starting off your own career. If you want to pursue your education in anything else, get ready for a bumpy ride. The Mathematics and Statistics Departments here are notoriously known for employing individuals who are bright but don't have a solid grasp of the English language. I think you'd have more luck striking up a conversation about calculus with a cab driver than you would with your calculus professor.

The Students

You'll meet a myriad of people at GW, but a good 30 to 40 percent of them will be effectively the same person: "Hey, I'm from New Jersey/New York, attend Temple weekly, am majoring in political science/international affairs, and have a trust fund that would allow me to buy and sell you three times over." Most students have a strong political orientation and are active in an extracurricular organization. There is some sense of competitiveness among students, but most aren't cutthroat. I think close to 25 percent of students are involved in the Greek community. There's Greek Row on campus, and you'll see a number of students wearing letters and attending fraternity or sorority dinner hours. The most important thing about Greek life is that it's hazing free. The university is strict about this. You may still be subjected to binge drinking and mind games, but as long as no one gets hurt, there's no harm in that, right?

The Activities

There is an abundance of student groups at GW, and all are active in the community. Community service, fund-raising, and political advocacy are big things on GW's campus. These groups often coordinate with similar groups from Georgetown, American, Catholic, and the University of Maryland, allowing these groups to reach beyond just GW's campus. The one problem with D.C. is that it shuts down after five o'clock on most days. Sunday through Wednesday, after five o'clock, you can get the feeling that the campus is the only thing operating in the entire district. But, at the same time, GW students enjoy three-day weekends, usually with the absence of Friday classes.

The Social Scene

Alcohol and everyone's favorite little plant are abundant on GW's campus. But avoiding these substances isn't a problem either. A number of students take a more laid-back approach to the weekend. The club scene in D.C. is huge, but that can leave a dent in your wallet. Some frats have house parties with the standard three or four kegs, rarely on Greek Row, which is university owned. If you want to watch your spending and enjoy yourself, apartment parties are the way to go, and there is little problem finding these. Also, there are a number of bars in the area that have relatively cheap drinks. Watch where you use your fake ID—there are a few stores and bars where fakes aren't a problem, but like any city, you can easily get busted. Otherwise, we just stay in and enjoy a friendly game of Hold 'em or Omaha.

Notable George Washington Alumni Include:

Abe Pollin, owner and chairman of the Washington Wizards

General Colin Powell, U.S. secretary of state and chairman of the Joint Chiefs of Staff

J. William Fulbright, U.S. senator

Jacqueline Bouvier Kennedy Onassis, former first lady

Kenneth W. Starr, attorney

Syngman Rhee, first president of South Korea

GEORGETOWN UNIVERSITY

Founded: 1789
Location: Washington, D.C.
Phone: (202) 687-0100
E-mail: n/a
Web site: www.georgetown.edu

Number of Undergraduates: 6,270
Number of Graduate Students: 3,880
Cost: Approximately $40,500 per year
Application Deadline: January 10
Early Decision: November 1

Rating:	Notable Majors/Programs:
Most Selective	International Affairs, Business, Social Sciences, Languages

Size:
○ Small   ● Medium   ○ Large

Location:
● Urban   ○ Suburban   ○ Rural

On a Saturday, students talk about academics:
● Always   ○ Sometimes   ○ Never

Nightlife:
○ Intense   ● Moderate   ○ Laid-back

Politically, Gtown leans:
○ Left   ● Right   ○ Split

Diversity:
○ High   ○ Low   ● Medium

Students describe Georgetown in five words:
- Cosmopolitan, politically astute, résumé junkies
- Washington D.C.'s most prestigious school

From the School

Founded in 1789, the same year the U.S. Constitution took effect, Georgetown University is the nation's oldest Catholic and Jesuit university. Today, Georgetown is a major international research university that embodies its founding principles in the diversity of our students, faculty, and staff; our commitment to justice and the common good; our intellectual openness; and our international character.

—www.georgetown.edu

If you're interested in Georgetown, you may also be interested in:
Columbia, George Washington, Harvard, NYU, Notre Dame, U Penn

Name: Nicole

Hometown: Bethlehem, Pennsylvania

Class Year: Senior

Major: American studies, minor in InterArts

Extracurriculars: Arts and entertainment critic for *The Hoya;* producer and singer for Georgetown Cabaret; member of Mask & Bauble

Career Goal: Officially: to work in PR, communications, or publishing in arts and entertainment. Unofficially: to pursue all intellectual interests and passions and still be able to eat

How would you describe Georgetown's reputation?

Georgetown has a lot of cachet because of the SFS program and its political connections. The campus attracts powerful and important speakers, distinguished faculty, and is a great springboard to working on Capitol Hill.

> "The words that instantly come to mind are *preppy* and (thanks to the Jesuits) *conservative.*"
>
> ◆ George, junior

Is this reputation accurate?

It's true, but it doesn't tell the whole story. If you're passionate about the arts, we have a strong music program and one of the oldest dramatic societies in the country. One great thing about Georgetown is that even though it's a medium-sized school, it allows a lot of people to shine. If you want it to happen, you can make it happen here. Whatever it is.

What would an admissions officer at Georgetown probably not tell a prospective student?

An admissions officer wants you to think money is divvied out in a way that affects every student fairly, but that's not the case. One of the most common complaints here at Georgetown is the administrative red tape. As a student in the arts, I could not use the art studios, equipment, or photography labs unless I was enrolled in a class. As a musician, it was a struggle to get practice space and other types of support. The charity rock concert I was involved in had to pay for rehearsal space. However, if you can form a relationship with a professor, there's a large chance that he or she will go to bat for you.

The Institution

Georgetown is the oldest Catholic university in the United States and the oldest college in Washington, D.C., and it's world renowned. I came to Georgetown for the American studies major, which is self-designed and culminates in a senior thesis. It gives motivated students a chance to pursue their passions. I created a concentration on media, psychology, art, consumerism, and women's cultural history, and the American Studies Department paid for me to travel to New York City so I could go to galleries and museums and complete my research. If you're looking to go into politics, law, or business, Georgetown has an amazing job network built up. If you're someone more like me (arts), they are less helpful because no one really recruits for communications or the arts.

I love the weather in D.C. It rains a good deal, which is unpleasant, but in the spring it can't be beat. As soon as the weather gets nice, everyone goes out onto the front lawn, and lies out on blankets, with their stereos, bikinis, and books or plays volleyball or Frisbee. Georgetown housing used to be tricky, but with the completion of the Southwest Quad it's possible for a lot more students to live on campus. What I loved about the housing is its large number of apartments. Apartment living is fab; you throw parties, have large dinners, and host big movie nights. It's so grown-up. One housing highlight is Village A, a complex of apartments, the top floors of which are most coveted. Commonly referred to as the "rooftops," Village A offers a beautiful view across the Potomac. It's also where all the huge parties are when the weather is nice. Freshmen migrate up there often, but it's tolerated.

Last bit of advice: learn the fight song as soon as you can. When I say *hoya,* you say *saxa.* And when someone asks you, "What's a hoya?" Reply, "WHAT." (*Hoya saxa* means "What rocks.")

The Education

Most people follow this rule of thumb: "Georgetown: hard to get As, easy to get Bs." It's a question of what you want from your education. I did everything I was assigned and worked for my As, but I have friends who didn't even buy the books for their classes and wound up with Bs.

People go abroad generally in junior year, and

best of all is the villa. Georgetown owns a villa overlooking Florence, Italy. And you are actually allowed to live there. It's the most amazing experience to wake up, look out your window, and see the Duomo. Best of all, you live with about twenty-five students from Georgetown who will become your best friends abroad and then at home in D.C. You don't have to know Italian to go, but you will learn the language, art, and culture in your time there. People usually say that going abroad changed their lives, and it's true—it does.

> "Gtown was named the second best non-black college for black students, but it's still only about 5 percent black."
>
> ✦ Josh, senior

The Students

Much of Georgetown feels cookie-cutter. It's frustrating. We call them Jane and Joe Hoya. Jane Hoyas are pretty girls with ribboned ponytails, short skirts, and cute sandals. The guys wear trousers or pressed khakis and polo shirts with the collars flipped up. That's not to say that they aren't good people or serious students, just that you have to actively seek out the cool individuals.

The Activities

Most colleges nowadays are grossly expensive, but D.C. offers up some of the best options for living on a budget. Museums are free, concerts and plays are discounted for students, public transportation is reasonable. Basically, there's a ton to do if you don't want to break the bank. However, if your gang has a taste for the finer things, it might be harder to keep up.

As I mentioned, the front lawn is a huge spot on campus. Less explored is the Observatory, which is set near the field house, far from campus. It's quiet and has a beautiful garden. Hoyas are also fond of the Esplanade, a grassy rooftop over the student center with a great view of the campus. Often barbecues and concerts are held there. Our new cafeteria, lovingly referred to as Leo's (for Father Leo O'Donovan), is also a hot spot.

My favorite place? The Tombs, our local bar with great cheap eats and a student staff that will know your name if you become a regular. I also

love Halloween. The traditional Georgetown Halloween begins with a screening of *The Exorcist* in Gaston Hall, and everyone applauds when Georgetown appears on the screen. Then, in full costume regalia, you parade down to M Street, which is packed like Mardi Gras.

All in all, you have to find where your passions fit at Georgetown: if you love to act, join Mask & Bauble, one of the oldest dramatic societies in the country; if you're interested in medicine, volunteer for GERMS, a student-run EMT program. Edit a newspaper, write your own play and see it produced, hold an exhibition in an art gallery.

One more thing: you may hear talk of secret tunnels that run under the campus. Don't be cajoled into exploring them. They're mud holes with the atmosphere of a sauna.

The Social Scene

No one dates here. Okay, maybe one or two people. But don't count on it. I know a few couples who met in their dorms freshman year and remained "married" all four years. At a competitive school like Georgetown, it sometimes means that people are reluctant to form relationships that would tie them down. On the flip side, because not many people are in pursuit of the Mrs. degree, it's easy to form a large coed group of friends to have fun with.

My friends are pretty obsessed with theme parties, but we'll also go dancing in Adams Morgan, catch a jazz show at the Kennedy Center or Blues Alley, walk to the waterfront and have drinks, go to Thomas Sweets and get their famous ice cream, go to the Virginia twenty-four-hour IHOP, or just play drinking games to *The Muppet Movie*. Everyone picks a Muppet. When your Muppet makes an appearance, you drink.

Name: Joe
Hometown: Sunrise, Florida
Class Year: Junior
Majors: English, Spanish
Extracurriculars: Student government, Residence Life
Career Goal: To study law and ultimately pursue a career in real estate law

How would you describe Georgetown's reputation?

Georgetown has an excellent reputation in academic circles. Unfortunately, lately the school has taken some fairly deserved criticism for its lacking athletics. Don't expect your gym coach to put Georgetown at the top of his or her list.

Is this reputation accurate?

The academic reputation is certainly accurate: it is rigorous and very theory centered. It really embodies the Jesuit concept of educating the whole person, from the inside out. Georgetown is the sort of school that makes critical thinking a graduation requirement of sorts. You will be smarter when you leave than when you came. No exceptions.

The Institution

Georgetown is the academic center of Washington, D.C.; accept no substitutes. The campus is beautiful, with a very traditional old stone and Ivy feel, and yet it's constantly changing with new buildings emerging as modern adaptations of that classic charm. Green space abounds, as do flowers and squirrels. Georgetown certainly deserves the awards it's won for its aesthetics.

I applied to a number of schools with "Ivy" and little else in mind; if I had known at the time how little those places' surrounding communities offered in comparison to Georgetown's Washington, D.C., backdrop, I would have saved myself a few hundred bucks in application fees by not applying to them at all! Georgetown's D.C. location offers its students a great many opportunities for intellectual and employment opportunities "beyond the Healy Gates." I just wish Georgetown had a better internship-career center. Nevertheless, a student looking for D.C. experience will certainly be able to find it on his or her own, and, truthfully, there is something to be said for going it alone.

> "The best class I took was a seminar on the Booker Prize, where we actually went to London for five days to do research, meet the authors, and see the Booker Prize being awarded at the British Museum . . . all because of a few very generous alumni."
> ✦ Lauren, senior

The Education

I came into Georgetown gung ho about international politics and eager to study at the Edmund A. Walsh School of Foreign Service. I found that most of the students within that college were initially quite enthused about it, too, but I eventually left the SFS because, in its own way, it helped me to realize the drawbacks to a very narrowly focused education.

I joined the Georgetown College of Arts and Sciences instead and found the transition between the schools very smooth and worthwhile. I needed (as more students than are willing to admit it do) both the diversity and the rigor of a liberal arts education. Georgetown College offered me that, and I am very much the better for it.

Students of the School of Foreign Service rightfully, albeit arrogantly at times, boast about the brilliance of the school's faculty. People I play tag with on the Copley Lawn take classes with Madeleine Albright and Donna Brazile. There are a number of former and current ambassadors in the school, and they usually have no reservations about letting students in on their experiences in the field.

The Students

Georgetown's student newspapers of record might tell the story differently, but, in my opinion, Georgetown is probably the most political (and spiritual and moral . . .) campus I have come across. Sure, the university itself—since it is a Catholic school—is obligated to uphold some of the church's doctrines on community issues, particularly in relation to gays, lesbians, and bisexuals, but this should not be mistaken for a campus-wide phenomenon. If anything, the university's students (perhaps not the parents of these students, true) are as liberal as they are conservative. Is Georgetown more conservative on the whole than, say, UCLA or NYU, yes, probably, but the opportunity for liberal students to interact with students whose views are diametrically opposed to their own really ought not be thought of as a detriment to their education. Education, like politics, is about conflict and resolution.

The Activities

My schedule might be a little different than most: I try to arrange my schedule so that I have class only two days a week. That makes for two horribly long days and five wickedly relaxing days off. But come Monday and Wednesdays nights, the nights before my two days of classes, I'm very consistently in the Leavey Center at Sellinger Lounge all night working. Though the facility is not technically open past 2:00 a.m., the cleaning crews will usually let me slide until about three.

The oldest student-run business in the country, "The Corp," has had a lot to do with keeping me up as well. The Corp runs, at present, three on-campus coffee shops as well as two small grocery stores, a photo shop and a video store. The coffee is adequate, I suppose, and it certainly does get the job done.

> "As an African American bisexual woman, I think I pretty much satisfy every requirement for marginalization, but here I honestly have not encountered ignorance often."
>
> ✦ Abony, junior

The Social Scene

There aren't traditional frats here, but you won't miss them—there's plenty to do on a Friday night, and Georgetown students *do* know how to relax from time to time. My friends and I play a lot of video games and we watch cartoons. Drinking and partying happen, true, but we really get rid of our stress with games and cartoons.

Name: Virginia
Hometown: Everywhere
Class Year: Senior
Major: Spanish
Exracurriculars: Writing, women's rugby, theater (acting and production staff), teaching SAT courses
Career Goal: Writer and teacher

How would you describe Georgetown's reputation?

A prestigious school, with a large international population and a very strong language program, amazing political connections, and the best school of foreign service in the world. It's also supposedly very integrated for such an old, would-be Ivy League school.

Is this reputation accurate?

Parts of it are. There are a lot of international students. You can't really beat the language and linguistics school here. That's why I came, and it hasn't disappointed. The School of Foreign Service is certainly impressive, and not a week goes by that we don't have some important international political figure on campus for some reason or another.

However, the school is only as integrated as you make it.

What aspect of Georgetown would a prospective student not see on a campus tour?

There's a whole lot of drinking and partying here that you won't see on a tour. In the middle of the day campus looks just as pleasant and sterile as the tour guides would like parents and kids to believe. But at night the campus turns into your typical college campus, no different than your average party school. You don't have to partake. It's not all-encompassing. That's the nice thing about D.C.: there's always something else to do if you don't want to drink, but it's always there if you do.

The Institution

There are a number of schools in D.C. and in the D.C. area, but none of them has the feel that Georgetown does. You're right at the edge of the city, in one of the nicest areas of Washington, but you're also on a secluded campus. If you wanted to, you could spend your entire time on campus and not once set foot outside. Or, by simply passing Healy Gates and going down a few blocks to M Street, you put yourself smack in the middle of one of the nicest commercial areas in the District, and just a short bus ride away from the rest of D.C. and all of its theaters, museums, tourist attractions, restaurants, bars, clubs, and, let's not forget, major political leaders.

Georgetown just finished building some amazing new dorms. You're required to live on campus freshman year. I live in Darnall Hall, which is supposed to be one of the worst dorms on campus, and I have to say, it's actually quite livable. And the rest of the dorms (a lot of which are apartments) are great. Off-campus housing (while expensive) can be very nice, quiet, and quite convenient, but if you are loud and like to have lots of house parties, you are actually probably better off *on* campus.

I had wanted to come to Georgetown since junior high. I was really excited about Spanish, and I was excited about other countries and cultures, thus Georgetown's international population and language programs became my main attraction to the school. I didn't get in and ended up going to one of my backup schools, then transferred to Georgetown for the start of my junior year. I came here first and foremost for the language program, and it has not disappointed me.

I was surprised at the ease of the transition as a transfer student. The people here, and the general atmosphere of the institution, made it easy to get into the swing of things. There are a huge number of people who come from very diverse backgrounds (despite the fair number of Joe and Jane Hoyas walking around), and people are so used to meeting new and "strange" people that it's fairly easy to settle into the community here.

> "Our gym is a dank pit, and the general consensus on campus is that the only way to make the library a more enjoyable and attractive place would be to blow it up."
> ✦ Dan, junior

The Education

One thing that Georgetown boasts, and lives up to, is its rigorous academic programs. No one here will tell you that they've got it easy and are never stressed out by how much work they have to do. There are no easy As here. The upside is that you are always academically challenged. The downside is, it can be very stressful, and some of the students don't take it as well as others, and it shows.

One thing that surprised me about the academics is how serious everyone is about their GPA, not to mention how competitive. I made Dean's List my first semester here, thought that was pretty cool, and never made it again. I'm more concerned with getting as much out of a class as I can, but everyone else I know is paranoid about getting Bs. They think that's the end of the world. It's kind of funny to me to hear people talking about "bombing an exam," then finding out that they got a B+. That's something I expect to hear from the kids in grad school, but not from the undergrads. But, perhaps the proximity of the undergrads to the grad students has some effect on this attitude.

The professors here are generally great. At least in the humanities (I have very little experience with the sciences here) they are always available for help outside of class and particularly willing to meet with, and help, students. I've spent the last two years taking grad-level courses in Spanish, and intensive German courses. The language professors here are the best I've experienced. The professors I encountered for most of the "general require-

ment" courses weren't nearly as good. However, they weren't all awful either.

Since all of the grad schools, except for the law school, have their classes and programs on the undergrad campus, it's a very mixed group. It's very easy for undergrads to take grad courses (if they have the background for them), and there are a number of grad students who take (for fun or interest) or TA (for credit or income) the undergrad classes. I think the mixture of the programs adds a lot to the feel of the courses, and I also think it makes grad school seem more appealing and less daunting (even though it is daunting).

The Activities

There's a general enmity between GW, AU, and Georgetown, but nothing I would consider a rivalry. Duke used to be our big basketball rival, but I'm not sure that's a big deal anymore. We're decently self-contained and, aside from running into people from other schools while out at night in Adams Morgan, Dupont, or here in Georgetown, we don't see much of them. I suppose the D1 athletes have a lot more exposure to them than your normal student, and the club sports too for that matter. But only a very small percentage of the students here play any kind of competitive sport. . . . Don't be deceived; the rest of the world gets out and mingles, albeit not necessarily with people from other schools, because the location here is optimal for getting out and seeing the rest of the city. (Except for our lack of a metro stop, but that's a whole other story, and a Georgetown political war to boot.)

> "As a visitor from Brown once said, 'WOW! I've never met a *real* conservative!'"
> ✦ Hiroki, senior

The Social Scene

I should start off by explaining that getting drunk with a bunch of strangers in someone's overpacked campus apartment is not my idea of a good time. However, that seems to be the nightlife for a large percentage of the Georgetown students. I'm one of those rare seniors who doesn't go out every weekend, who prefers wine to beer and civil conversation to loud music punctuated by the shouting of overexcited frat boys. I suppose that makes me a geek of some kind, but hey, it's a title I'm willing to bear.

When I do go out, I go to bars, go dancing or out to eat in Adams Morgan, an area of town that boasts a million different national cuisines. It's great date territory. You can go to a nice dinner and enjoy the international cuisine of your choice, then go for dancing and drinks in whatever style (and price range) you wish. Really, there's something for everyone here: from a night out at the Kennedy Center to a big bash in someone's apartment to a quiet night with friends.

Notable Georgetown Alumni Include:

Antonin Scalia, U.S. Supreme Court justice

Bill Clinton, forty-second U.S. president

Charles Cawley, president and CEO, Bank of America

Dikembe Mutombo, professional basketball player

Pat Buchanan, presidential adviser and political pundit

Robert M. Hayes, founder, National Coalition for the Homeless

GEORGIA INSTITUTE OF TECHNOLOGY

Founded: 1885

Location: Atlanta, GA

Phone: (404) 894-4154

E-mail: admission@gatech.edu

Web site: www.gatech.edu

Number of Undergraduates: 11,456

Number of Graduate Students: 5,385

Cost: Approximately $10,000 per year in state; $21,000 out of state

Application Deadline: January 15
Rolling Admissions

Rating:	Notable Majors/Programs:
Selective	Industrial Engineering, Mechanical Engineering, Electrical Engineering

Size:
○ Small   ○ Medium   ● Large

Location:
● Urban   ○ Suburban   ○ Rural

On a Saturday, students talk about academics:
● Always   ○ Sometimes   ○ Never

Nightlife:
○ Intense   ○ Moderate   ● Laid-back

Politically, GT leans:
○ Left   ● Right   ○ Split

Diversity:
○ High   ○ Low   ● Medium

Students describe Georgia Tech in five words:
- Factory producing the finest engineers
- Often Tech is painfully difficult

From the School

From the academic challenge of undergraduate research to the big-time college sports and hundreds of campus activities, to the cutting-edge technological education, to the dynamic social atmosphere and professional opportunities offered by Midtown Atlanta, choosing Georgia Tech means that you can rely on us for support as you create the college experience that will best prepare you for the future.

—http://www.enrsrv.gatech.edu/

If you're interested in Georgia Tech, you may also be interested in:
Caltech, Duke, MIT, UNC at Chapel Hill, Stanford, UVA

Name: Andrew
Hometown: Lillington, North Carolina
Class Year: Sophomore
Major: Industrial and systems engineering
Extracurriculars: None; I work too hard to have extracurriculars
Career Goal: CEO of an industrial-technical company

How would you describe Georgia Tech's reputation?

Georgia Tech has a reputation as a superb, but extraordinarily difficult, engineering school brimming with dorky, antisocial, computer-geek guys, and women (what few there are) with major attitudes.

> "GT trains engineers. It doesn't have an English Department. Don't be surprised by this."
>
> ✦ Mart, sophomore

Is this reputation accurate?

Yup. Georgia Tech is one of the finest public schools in the nation, with a reputation for engineering excellence. We work hard to be the best, and if you come here you'll see some of the world's brightest students studying under the supervision of the world's brightest faculty.

What aspect of your school would a prospective student not see on a campus tour?

They wouldn't tell you that you'll be spending most of your waking hours here doing homework and studying, and that in order to have an active social life one might have to sacrifice getting good grades. The study halls are always full, the dorms are always dreary, and the food is always as bad as it looks.

The Institution

On the bathroom walls, students write the places that they are from: Georgia, California, Europe, Asia, Africa, the list goes on and on. I chose Georgia Tech because of this, because everyone in the world wants to go here because of its outstanding name and reputation, particularly in the field of engineering. I was looking for a prestigious school that would challenge me; I found exactly that in Georgia Tech. School spirit is an interesting

thing here, we all bitch and moan, but hardly anyone transfers. If we spent half the time working that we do complaining, we'd have a lot more free time.

GT's study-abroad programs are amazing, and the workload abroad is more tolerable than it is at Tech. Study abroad provides an amazing opportunity to travel and learn before you have to enter into the workforce, and—if you're paying hand over fist for college—you may as well visit the Great Wall and the Colosseum along the way.

Our co-op program is equally amazing, being the largest nonmandatory co-op program in the nation. The program allows us to get school credit while doing real work for real pay and to gain real experience that will provide us with an advantage when the time to compete for jobs comes around. The co-op helped me land a job with one of the premier companies in my field as a freshman, and I have one friend who has co-op'ed in Asia for an international corporation.

The Education

I generally study every day of the week, except maybe Friday nights (though studying on a Friday night is not uncommon). In general, students take the approach of "us against them" regarding classes, so we work together to get things done and don't really compete for grades. Most of the time professors don't grade on a curve anyway, so it typically doesn't do any good to stab someone else in the back. All of our engineering departments are amazing, especially at the graduate level. Of particular interest is our industrial engineering program, which is consistently ranked number one in America; however, few of our programs aren't in the top ten or twenty.

The Students

Well, 70 percent of Tech's students are white males. We're mostly politically conservative and Christian. Roughly 35 percent of Tech students go Greek, and Greek life is a major presence on campus. The average student is from Georgia and pursuing a degree in engineering so that he can eventually get a job and make excessive amounts of money. Despite our collective brilliance, we certainly have far more than our fair share of guys who enjoy sitting around in their underwear playing computer games online at all hours of the day and night. "LAN Parties" (that's *local area network*) aren't something that people only joke about at

Tech, and a careful analysis of Tech's male population reveals a large group of unusually unusual individuals who would truly rather play Dungeons and Dragons than socialize and meet women.

The women at Tech are also, generally, brilliant, but also either unattractive or stuck up. We have a term for their behavior—TBS—Tech Bitch Syndrome. What happens is that a moderately attractive girl will come to Tech and will instantly get more attention from guys than she's ever had in her life. The women get spoiled by the attention, and before long they're stuck-up and full of themselves.

However, and I cannot stress this enough, there are many guys and girls on Tech's campus who are the epitome of excellence: intelligent, outgoing, driven, attractive, and fun. And it's not so hard to find them—you just have to leave the computer lab and get to the gym or hit up a party. Georgia Tech may be a haven for geeks, but it is certainly not devoid of people who break that mold and are truly a joy to be around. And really, even our geeks have their positive attributes . . . you just can't be turned off by their greasy hair and pale skin. Warm up to them. Besides, they just might be your boss someday.

The Activities

Emory and Georgia State University are right by Georgia Tech, but the schools don't really interact. There's a lot to see and do in Atlanta, including museums, shows, bars, concerts. But in general, if you're up at 3:00 a.m. on any given night, you're not doing fun things—you're up because there's a test in electromagnetism the next day, or you're finishing up a digital signal processing lab. If you don't go to sleep soon, you'll just pull an all-nighter and sleep one day . . . eventually.

The Social Scene

There's a social scene at Tech? With girls? Wow, wouldn't that be amazing!

Name: Sean
Hometown: Orlando, Florida
Class Year: Junior
Major: Mechanical engineering
Extracurriculars: Connect with Tech Overnight Host, GT tour guide, Delta Upsilon Fraternity, Interfraternity Council, American Society of Mechanical Engineers (ASME)
Career Goal: I'm hoping to enter the world of bio-

medical engineering and perhaps do research for a pharmaceuticals firm.

How would you describe Georgia Tech's reputation?

GT supposedly houses lots of male geeks, nerds, dorks, and other such overachievers who study all the time and never have fun, even though they're in the middle of one of the most vibrant cities in the Southeast.

Is this reputation accurate?

It can be. It all depends on you. Some people complain constantly about the geek factor, the school, the city, and their workload, but they're usually the ones who never leave their dorm room, and their faces have taken on a neon sheen from all the computer games they play. Those that do make an effort to balance business and pleasure, like myself, can have a good time here, so long as they're willing to occasionally sacrifice a Saturday night party for the good of their calculus grade.

What aspect of your school would a prospective student not see on a campus tour?

Someone might mention that classes are "rigorous" here, but it doesn't sink in that that means you'll be studying X hours per weekday and then again on weekends if you want to get a good grade. . . .

> "Don't bother bringing a bike to Georgia Tech. It *will* get stolen."
>
> ✦ Josh, senior

The Institution

Georgia Tech is unique in two ways. First, it is located in the heart of Atlanta, a major city. This means city life is there for you if you want it. Second, and this is what most people don't realize, is that GT has been and remains an "institute of technology." This means we don't have majors like criminal law or secondary-school education. We're far more focused and specialized. If I really thought about it, I could probably name all the undergrad majors here off the top of my head because we have so few. So, if you come to Georgia Tech, do so because you want to specialize and work hard.

I'll add that GT's co-op program was a huge selling point for me. Lots of students involved in the co-op get hired by top firms immediately after graduating, and even those that don't get hired straight out have an amazing resume with up to five semesters of experience in their field!

The Education

You come to GT to get a superior education, and, ultimately, it's impossible to escape that education. Some weekends, fun is going to have to take a backseat to your studies. On most nights, there are at least two hours of classwork to be completed, not counting studying for any upcoming tests you might have. And when you see your friends, your academic life definitely sneaks into your conversations. Normally, whenever that happens, we all just kind of stop talking, look at each other and shake our heads, realizing just how much Tech is affecting us.

Tech has really rigorous core requirements (calculus, programming, chemistry, another science, history, etc.), and you might think this means taking core classes is rote and boring. But I've found the opposite to be true. The classes are really well structured. Professors tend to lecture three times a week, and TAs teach recitation the other two days, reviewing the concepts the professor went over and solving problems in small groups. TAs often grade tests, but most professors demand that you talk to them if you have any issues with anything, and they tend to be really receptive.

> "The best thing about Tech is that everyone is a dork, and proud of it. Students write AIM away messages in CSS code. Half of our sports cheers mention differential equations. It's great."
>
> ✦ Matt, senior

While there are grad students on campus, I'd say the most dominating presence is the Research Institute (GTRI). Georgia Tech is first and foremost a research institution, and it gets billions of research dollars from defense contracts, biotechnology grants, and the automobile industry. Sometimes a professor will be really involved with GTRI, and they'll seem to care more about their staff of grad students and their research than they will about teaching. But that's the exception rather than the rule, and, particularly in lower-level classes, the professors teach first and do research if they have time.

As you might have guessed, GT has a fantastic engineering department, where even its individual classes are nationally respected. For example, there is a required class for mechanical engineers called "Creative Decisions and Design" that has been copied at places like MIT and CalTech. It's primarily a lab class; each week students are assigned to a different lab group and given a task, such as building a cantilever with nothing more than a roll of masking tape and a box of spaghetti. Or we're told to write instructions on how to build a very sturdy tent out of nothing but old newspapers. At the end of the semester each lab group is given a massive final project that involves a broad range of principles in electronics, machinery, and design.

The Students

GT is a politically conservative campus. The students work hard, party sometimes, and get along well.

The Activities

Athletics are the biggest activity on Tech's campus, and the most unifying. However, there are occasionally large nonathletic events that bring out most of the campus. The student government has tried to make it a point to create more of these activities, like school-sponsored concerts and Tech Night at Six Flags.

If you want, you can also find groups for everything here. People use groups as their escape from academics, and, thankfully, the administration has made it pretty easy to create groups and get funding. There is every sort of racial, cultural, ideological, international, and social group you can imagine, from the GT Buddhists to the GT skydiving team.

The Social Scene

Tech's social scene is unique because it's a technical college with traditional D1 sports located in the center of a bustling metropolis chock-full of cultural events and interesting places to go. Within walking distance of campus are the ballet, the orchestra, an art museum, an arena, a stadium, and numerous restaurants and bars. However, on campus, the social scene is dominated by Greek life, though the vast majority of the parties are open, and more likely than not you'll know someone who is Greek who can always get you in.

Name: Kelsey
Hometown: Dunwoody, Georgia
Class Year: Senior
Major: Management
Extracurriculars: A cappella, Alpha Delta Pi, GT Orientation Leader (FASET), Freshman Council member
Career Goal: To become a successful business-woman in either international finance, sales, marketing, or general management. I want to be respected by my employees and my peers for being fair, honest, loyal, and dependable.

How would you describe Georgia Tech's reputation?

Academically challenging, dorky-nerdy.

> "If you come here, go Greek. But keep in mind, Greek at Georgia Tech wouldn't be Greek at other schools. Here the brothers don't drink, they reenact Godzilla destroying Tokyo by building a city from cardboard boxes."
>
> ✦ Heidi, junior

Is this reputation accurate?

It is academically challenging here, and there are some dorks, but there are also lots of "normal" people. GT offers programs that attract a wide variety of students.

What would an admissions officer at your school probably not tell a prospective student?

They wouldn't tell you that a lot of our professors are hired for their research skills, and these profs teach as a side note. When you get one of these professors, it's disappointing and you notice the difference.

The Institution

Georgia Tech is full of traditions. We're called the Ramblin' Wrecks, and our fight song is great. (*I'm a ramblin' wreck from Georgia Tech and a helluva engineer!*) We also have an animal on campus that every student knows and loves—Sideways, the dog. No one knows where Sideways came from exactly, but students always see him, and he pops into classes and sleeps in a different dorm room every night. It's said that you'll have good luck if Sideways shows up to sleep on your floor.

GT has an absolutely beautiful campus located in the heart of downtown Atlanta. Recently the campus has expanded, creating facilities on the east side of the I75/85 highway. This expansion, part of the Capital Campaign, has created Technology Square, which is home to GT's very own hotel and conference center, its stock exchange, its management department, and its newest research buildings.

The Education

Georgia Tech is challenging—over the course of a semester, there are definitely crunch times during which stress and irritation levels rise. However, GT students know they're in it together, and we support one another throughout our four years. In the classroom, sizes vary from three-hundred-person lectures to twenty-student discussion seminars, which isn't bad at all. And attending class is a must at Tech—it's essential to learning and understanding course material, and a lot of professors make attendance a portion of your grade, particularly if you're in nonengineering classes.

The Students

Georgia Tech has an extremely diverse student population, representing over one hundred countries and many, many ethnicities. GT's Student Government Association (SGA) is very active. The Greek students are generally campus leaders, involved in organizations, clubs, and community service, but at Tech that level of involvement usually means your grades are going to suffer a bit. The average GPA of a Greek student is a 2.8, and the average GPA of a non-Greek student is a 3.2.

The Activities

Community service is a huge part of life at Georgia Tech. We have students tutoring underprivileged children in the TTP program, students in the big brother–big sister program. . . . GT Panhellenic sponsors Halloween festivities for children in the Atlanta area through its annual Run & Hide program. Various other organizations have events where they contribute their time and effort to helping. If you like to give back (when you're not doing engineering problem sets), GT is the school for you.

The Social Scene

If partying is your thing, you'll have a blast at GT. With over fifteen thousand students, there's always something going on. You can choose from fraternity parties, off-campus parties, small get-togethers, Atlanta bars and clubs (which are great fun all weekend long).

Most students live on campus, too, which adds to your social options. East Campus is mainly freshmen with a few sophomores mixed in. West Campus is mostly upperclassmen, has apartment and suite-style dorms, and is located right next to our award-winning Campus Recreation Center, the Couch Building (our amazing music center), and Under the Couch (UTC), our concert venue, also equipped with a sound and recording studio.

Overall, GT is an amazing school with so much to offer. People need to know that going to college is about more than just partying and having a great time. College is about preparing yourself to succeed, creating life goals and fulfilling dreams. College is about finding yourself and finding life-long friends who will support you and push you to do your best and be at your best.

Notable Georgia Tech Alumni Include:
Jimmy Carter, thirty-ninth U.S. president
Jeff Foxworthy, comedian, actor
Arthur Murray, dance instructor, businesman
Jason Varitek, professional baseball player
Kevin Brown, professional baseball player
Randolph Scott, actor

GETTYSBURG COLLEGE

Founded: 1832

Location: Gettysburg, PA

Phone: (717) 337-6000

E-mail: admiss@gettysburg.edu

Web site: www.gettysburg.edu

Number of Undergraduates: 2,550

Number of Graduate Students: 0

Cost: Approximately $37,500 per year

Application Deadline: February 15

Early Decision: November 15

Rating:	Notable Majors/Programs:
Very Selective	Business, Political Science, Life Sciences, Psychology

Size:
● Small ○ Medium ○ Large

Location:
○ Urban ● Suburban ○ Rural

On a Saturday, students talk about academics:
○ Always ● Sometimes ○ Never

Nightlife:
● Intense ○ Moderate ○ Laid-back

Politically, Gettysburg is:
○ Left ○ Right ● Split

Diversity:
○ High ● Low ○ Medium

Students describe Gettysburg in five words:
- Preppy, Greek, small, secluded, beautiful
- TONS OF FUN in Pennsylvania

From the School

Gettysburg's size and residential setting have provided close contact among students and faculty for nearly 170 years. In recent years, Gettysburg College has moved to enhance its learning environment in order to offer an innovative liberal arts education attuned to the needs of students preparing for the twenty-first century. At the core of our efforts has been a commitment to the principle of active learning.

—www.gettysburg.edu

If you're interested in Gettysburg, you may also be interested in:
Bucknell, Colby, Hamilton, Lehigh, Penn State, Trinity

Name: Jessica
Hometown: San Antonio, Texas
Class Year: Sophomore
Major: Psychology
Extracurriculars: Chi-Omega, intramural sports, campus hosting
Career Goal: I want to find a job that I love—either in psychology, public relations, or maybe even human resources. I've also been looking into Forensic Psychology.

How would you describe Gettysburg's reputation?

We're known as a good school but the administration wants to drop the "party school" reputation we have and replace it with "Ivy League caliber," which doesn't seem to be working well. We are also known as being not very diverse.

Is this reputation accurate?

Yes and no. Gettysburg is an academically good school, without question. And even though we party a lot, we really aren't a "party school." We are definitely lacking in diversity, and the administration hasn't taken great action to improve this.

What would an admissions officer at Gettysburg probably not tell a prospective student? What aspect of your school would a prospective student not see on a campus tour?

An admissions officer would never tell a prospective student about the amount of partying that goes on here, especially during the week, or that people here drink with such frequency. A campus tour would definitely not allow a prospective student to see how much fun they could have here. I would recommend an overnight stay.

The Institution

First off, I am from Texas, so I find the weather to be unbearable. So if you are from Maine, then you can just skip over my complaints. It is always rainy and windy here. The school, however, is gorgeous and exceeded my expectations in many ways. My friends from home convinced me that I would be churning butter with the Amish. I'm not.

The school is small, so the athletic events are not as much fun as they would be at a big school and everyone always knows everyone else's business. Greek letters are written all over the busiest bathroom stalls, library cubicles, desks . . . Greek life is very important here. Guys tend to join be-

cause if they don't then they sometimes aren't allowed into parties. Girls can get away with going wherever, even if they're not in a sorority, but I found that it is a lot of fun to be in one.

The food is really good, best cafeteria food I have ever had. I was obsessed with the BBQ sauce we had freshman year but they replaced it sophomore year, so I wrote an e-mail and complained. The purchasing manager sent me a whole box of little jars of the old BBQ with a nice note. Now those are results! Housing is nice even for the freshmen and available all four years, though seniors can live off campus.

The Education

No one really talks about class on a Saturday night, but that doesn't mean Gettysburg isn't a competitive school. Everyone here is striving to do well because they know if they don't, then they won't be here much longer. I spend a couple hours every day on my work, but it really depends on the classes that I am taking and what point I am at in the semester—midterms and finals are always busy times, of course. And some classes require more reading than others. Most of the classes are lecture based, but all of it is done by the professors. TAs provide extra help sessions but do not teach the classes. The professors are easily accessible when you need to talk about how you're doing in class or about anything on your mind. The core curriculum is really good. It makes you take classes you wouldn't think of taking and overall you receive a very well-rounded education.

The Students

We don't have a very diverse campus. Racially, culturally, and probably religiously, everyone is about the same: Caucasian, Italian or Irish, and Catholic. Obviously this is a very extreme generalization, but it seems to me that most people here fit into one of those categories or another . . . I do, anyway. We have few international students, and as far as socioeconomic standing goes, many people here are quite well-to-do. Politically, my guess is there are mostly liberals but people don't talk about politics much; I've never seen a riot or rally since I've been here. The average female student is good-looking, does well in school, and knows how to have fun. The average male student is preppy, does more work than he will ever admit, and likes to have a good time. I feel like some people are very exclusive, but it really just depends on who you hang out with. I think the groups that are least likely to mix are the fraternities, which don't get along with each other. There aren't as many problems like this between the sororities though.

> "It seems this institution has two fetishes outside the academic arena. One is renovating things, and the other is putting up phallic-looking statuary."
> ✦ Whopper, sophomore

The Activities

There are a number of schools around here, but we don't really interact with them very often, aside from sporting events. Community service seems to be very popular—we even have a campuswide day in the fall when everyone volunteers. It's called GIV day (Gettysburg Is Volunteering), and the people who participate divide into groups and go out to help different areas of the community.

I barely ever leave campus. If I do, I go to D.C. to a concert or something like that for a night. This is not a suitcase school; people hardly ever go home. Gettysburg gets really good entertainment. At 3:00 a.m. on a Wednesday I would probably be asleep or at a frat party; and if I didn't go to bed after that, I'd go to 7-Eleven for a snack. I might also be studying or talking online.

The Social Scene

I attend mostly fraternity and sorority events. My favorite tradition is Springfest, which is a weekend of parties. The weather is nice, there's a carnival outside, and there's a concert. It's a really good time just to relax, drink, and hang out with friends before finals begin. And since joining a sorority, I've found that Springfest is an even bigger party when you are Greek.

Name: My Frisbee name is Whopper
Hometown: Gettysburg, Pennsylvania
Class Year: Sophomore
Major: Philosophy and anthropology
Extracurriculars: Ultimate Frisbee
Career Goal: Hobo or Pirate

How would you describe Gettysburg's reputation?

I think that this school has two different reputations. Among parents, it's seen as a good academic school, but among students, it's seen as a big party school . . . and most people in town see it as a big, rude transplantation of New Jersey.

Is this reputation accurate?

I would say that this reputation is pretty on the mark—there are a limited number of students who are here to learn, but most seem to want to join Greek life and party.

What would an admissions officer at Gettysburg probably not tell a prospective student?

Admissions probably won't tell a prospective student about the homogeneity of the student body, both in terms of demographics and ideas. Despite the college's best efforts, about 90 percent of the student body is still white, and the atmosphere borders on oppressive when it comes to being different or outspoken.

The Institution

I think Gettysburg College is an institution with a great setting and a good curriculum, both of which are lost on most of the people enrolled here.

The physical layout of the campus is excellent: almost everything is within a couple minutes of everything else, and the buildings themselves are very nice. People in Gettysburg generally hate most of the college students, and the college students seem to ignore the town except for Beer Mart.

The Education

Most professors are easily accessible, and a good number are involved in campus social life. Overall, I have been satisfied with most of the classes I have taken—they're well taught and well sized. I've had two or three professors whose classes I've especially enjoyed, and I've actually come into job opportunities because of my connections with them. Still, the focus at this college does not seem to be on academics, especially on Friday and Saturday night. The library seems to be where people go when they want to be interrupted from doing work rather than actually doing work. At the same time, the library is by far one of the best parts of the campus, with great collections of literature and movies, and plenty of nice spaces to enjoy them in.

The Students

Most of the students seem to be conservative WASPs from New Jersey or "outside Philadelphia" majoring in management (for the boys) or psych (for the girls) to please their parents long enough so that they can go back home and work in the family business.

There are a few smaller niches people can run to if they don't want to be part of Greek life and whatnot, but these aren't always easy to find. The Ultimate Frisbee team is what keeps me sane here; we are not ultracompetitive and have a great group of friends between us. GBLTQ students; students with liberal viewpoints; nonfraternity and nonsorority students; and nonwhite students seem to be the least-encouraged groups on campus.

> "Carson from *Queer Eye* went to G-Burg . . . but you wouldn't know it. This place is *dripping* with Republicans."
>
> ✦ Korbin, junior

The Activities

Generally it seems that the extent of student involvement in administrative decisions is when the administration makes a decision, it will ex post facto ask the students their opinions on it, rather than in advance. I think this is probably also the fault of the Student Senate, which is largely ineffective. There is a small group dedicated to community service on campus, but most people don't seem to have the time or concern. Big-name performers and speakers are almost nonexistent here; the concerts the college has are mostly attended by fifteen-year-old girls, and the speakers are generally conservative and attended mostly by residents of the town.

The Social Scene

People mostly party on Friday and Saturday nights, a lot of which takes place at the fraternities, and almost all of which involves alcohol. As far as dating goes, I think it's hard for either gender to meet intelligent people. Of course, this works out well for some people, but for the few of us who are here on merit and value our brains, it's rather dis-

couraging. This school has made me more cynical (can you tell?).

Name: Elena
Hometown: Hagerstown, Maryland
Class Year: Freshman
Major: Double major in religion and visual studio arts
Extracurriculars: Senate, dance ensemble, Japan Club, WZBT Gettysburg College Radio, small group Bible study, small independent band, Student Global AIDS Campaign, recruitment events for Sorority Rush 2004
Career Goal: Right after graduation I hope to work either for the Peace Corps or the Catholic Relief Services to aid victims of the AIDS pandemic, brutal civil wars, acts of inhumanity, etc. Afterward, I hope to attend graduate school, where I intend to focus on a small aspect of religion and religious life so that I can become a professor.

How would you describe Gettysburg's reputation?

I don't think Gettysburg is as well known as it should be. Generally when people ask me "Where do you go to school?" and I say "Gettysburg," they respond, "Where's that?" Sheesh, you'd think that a school located in probably the most famous Civil War site would be slightly better known!

Is this reputation accurate?

What's missing from Gettysburg's reputation is the quality education that we receive here, the great attitudes of the caring faculty, and the amazing amount of opportunities we have.

What would an admissions officer at Gettysburg probably not tell a prospective student?

Admissions officers most likely don't tell students that partying is a schoolwide issue. Alcohol is really present on campus, but you don't know it until the first weekend of the fall semester.

The Institution

To sum up G-Burg in one line: It's a crazy little place that I call home nine months outta the year. I love my school. The only thing that I would change about Gettysburg is its location. I would transport my campus to the middle of Hagerstown, MD—just because that's where I'm from and I miss living there.

> "The average Gettysburg student is one of three people: (1) the frat boy majoring in management so that he may inherit Daddy's Fortune 500 company; he likes drinking, smoking weed, taking advantage of freshman girls, and wearing pink shorts he calls "Nantucket Red"; (2) the sorority girl majoring in something her sisters suggested; she likes mixers, tanning, "Easthampton beach party casual" attire, and watching her boyfriend play lacrosse on his frat-house lawn; and (3) the student who avoids gender stereotypes—and also avoids types 1 and 2 at all costs."
>
> ✦ Sam, freshman

The Education

I always heard that in college you can either go to class or not go to class and it won't matter either way cuz it's the papers and tests that equal your grade. Well, here there are strict attendance policies. Participation is a huge part of your grade.

I have only ever met one TA, who is simply in class to give extra assistance on papers when it is needed and to add to the classroom discussion. I have found that most of my classes are lectures open to discussion, and every professor that I have had so far enjoys it far more when the class discusses the material or debates something than when fifteen exhausted faces are fixed in a stare.

The Students

The average Gettysburg college student: (1) takes four to five classes a semester and plans on traveling abroad at least once, (2) enjoys the twenty-four-hour services of our library and the coffee cart that is available from midnight to 6:00 a.m., (3) needs twenty-four-hour services of the library due to procrastination or overinvolvement in activities, either or both of which lead to lack of sleep and study time, (4) is involved in at least one campus activity (i.e., fraternity, sorority, intramural sports, campus-sponsored sports, Senate, political activist group, etc.), (5) enjoys at least one party a weekend, be it frat house or chillin' with friends, and (6) feels that Servo (our cafeteria) brunch on Sundays is heaven and hates missing it.

The Activities

I'm going to list as many campus groups as I can think of: men's and women's rugby, Tae Kwon Do Club, Senate, International Affairs Club, Peace Club, Young Democrats, Young Republicans, Gettysburg Campus Christian Fellowship, Disciple Makers, fraternities, sororities, APO—the coed service frat on campus, marching band, jazz band, chorus, dance ensemble, WZBT Gettysburg College Radio, Art Society, Habitat for Humanity, French Table, Amnesty International, theater, Allies, Japan Club, intramural soccer, GRAB—on-campus resource for camping, caving, hiking, climbing gear, and trips, just to name a few. . . .

> "We tend to attract a lot of Civil War buffs and also diehard reenactors. Last night at the bar, I saw a guy dressed up like a Confederate soldier, singing karaoke."
>
> ✦ Aron, junior

The Social Scene

The party scene on campus: if you're twenty-one, the Attic serves alcoholic beverages and there are a few bars to go to, but 75 percent of our campus parties are at the frats on Fridays and Saturdays (though there are some parties on weeknights). . . . Everyone on campus is courteous . . . holding doors open for people, smiling, etc. Dorm life is just that: dorm life. People up late, loud music, pizza delivery and Chinese take-out, crazy occurrences such as an RA's door being blocked by massive amounts of duct tape, etc. . . . I don't think there are any seriously exclusive elements in the Gettysburg social scene.

Notable Gettysburg Alumni Include:

Bruce Gordon, president, Verizon Communications
Carol Bellamy, executive director, UNICEF
David Hartman, first blind person to graduate from medical school
Fred F. Fielding, former deputy White House counsel
J. Michael Bishop, Nobel Laureate in medicine
William Sunderman, author and oldest practicing doctor in the United States until his death at age 104

GRINNELL COLLEGE

Founded: 1846

Location: Grinnell, IA

Phone: (800) 247-0113

E-mail: askgrin@grinnell.edu

Web site: www.grinnell.edu

Number of Undergraduates: 1,485

Number of Graduate Students: 0

Cost: Approximately $ 31,000 per year

Application Deadline: January 20

Early Decision: November 20

Rating:	Notable Majors/Programs:
Selective	English, Anthropology, Business, Economics

Size:

● Small   ○ Medium   ○ Large

Location:

○ Urban   ○ Suburban   ● Rural

On a Saturday, students talk about academics:

● Always   ○ Sometimes   ○ Never

Nightlife:

○ Intense   ○ Moderate   ● Laid-back

Politically, Grinnell leans:

● Left   ○ Right   ○ Split

Diversity:

○ High   ○ Low   ● Medium

Students describe Grinnell in five words:
- Dorky liberals in rural Iowa
- Passionate, progressive, politically correct, creative

From the School

The college aims to graduate women and men who can think clearly, who can speak and write persuasively and even eloquently, who can evaluate critically both their own and others' ideas, who can acquire new knowledge, and who are prepared in life and work to use their knowledge and their abilities to serve the common good.

—www.grinnell.edu

If you're interested in Grinnell, you may also be interested in:
Carleton, Colorado College, Macalester, Oberlin, Swarthmore, Washington U. in St. Louis

Name: Mary
Hometown: Fayetteville, Arkansas
Class Year: Sophomore
Major: English and French
Extracurriculars: Quiz Bowl, Grinnell Review, Feminist Action Coalition
Career Goal: I'd like to become an English professor.

How would you describe Grinnell's reputation?

Grinnell is a tiny island of rampant liberalism in the middle of a bunch of Iowa cornfields. We're also well respected academically, ranked in the top fifteen by *U.S. News* for the past handful of years.

Is this reputation accurate?

Yes. We are a small school of thirteen hundred incredibly left-of-center students. And our academic reputation is well deserved. I haven't had a single bad class at Grinnell.

> "The other day I was hanging out with the football guys in the weight room, and all they wanted to talk about were titrations and chem class. . . ."
>
> ✦ Devin, senior

What would an admissions officer at your school probably not tell a prospective student?

Admissions officers don't tend to tell prospectives about the cabin fever that sets in during the winter, when Iowa is covered in snow and there's nowhere to go and nothing much to do besides homework. Prospective students also don't tend to see the inner workings of the dining halls. This is relevant because most Grinnell students wind up working in Dining Services at one point or another while they're here.

The Institution

Grinnell has a compact but beautiful campus, and the college does its best to bring in interesting speakers and performers so students forget that they're in rural Iowa, an hour from any city of notable size.

I also prefer Grinnell dorms to those at every other campus I've seen—they have wide hallways, and Grinnell makes an effort to put students from every class year on every hall. This means, at all times of the day, people hang out in the hallways, the freshmen learning from the upperclassmen, the upperclassmen wishing they were underclassmen so they'd have more time to spend here. . . .

Every bathroom on Grinnell's campus is covered with scrawled lists of beautiful and wonderful people, poetry, whiny rants about this and that, interesting sketch drawings, quotations from songs or professors, and social commentary. The school paints over the bathroom walls a couple of times each year—so stall drawing is a largely temporary form of art—but it's still practiced by most students on campus, and most of the time you can even recognize the handwriting on the wall . . . which brings me to my next point, the smallness of Grinnell is fantastic. You love everyone you meet and recognize everyone you see. Granted, it can feel incestuous and the rumor mill on campus is alive and well.

The Education

Generally, Grinnell professors are always willing to talk to students outside of class. They'll even let you do summer research with them if you ask nicely, and that's usually paid. Oh, and a big plus of coming to Grinnell is that there's no core curriculum here—you only learn the things you want to learn. And it's easy to go abroad—at Grinnell, instead of worrying about taking those classes you didn't want to take anyway, you can be dashing around in London or Africa or Asia.

If you're planning on being a science major at Grinnell, get ready to work particularly hard. Really, science majors just live in the science building, and they're resigned to that. On occasion someone will start up a game of midnight Capture the Flag in the science building, just so the poor bio and chemistry kids can have a little fun in their lives. . . . And if you're planning on being an English major, let me tell you, I'm in love with Grinnell's English Department. Who isn't? Even the non-English-loving people agree that our English professors are fantastic beyond words.

Lastly, if you don't like talking about your classes when you're not in class, you won't like Grinnell. Students here will ramble on about their favorite subject for hours, even on a Saturday night. We love to think, and we love to get our friends to challenge our notions of this and that. Intellectualism rules at Grinnell! Students can be a little pretentious, too, in their academic strivings. Luckily, we mock ourselves for this; on weekends, we'll get drunk and giggle over our unhealthy obsession with that philosophical issue, or our roommate's mad quest to solve their linear algebra equations.

> "Grinnell is 'the Harvard of the Midwest.' I've heard we have more homework than every undergraduate school in the United States except for MIT."
>
> ✦ Jenni, senior

The Students

I'd say most Grinnell students are from the Midwest—which makes sense—and there's a wide range of accents from Wisconsinese to Ohioan, all of which amuse me, being a southerner. Most students are Democrats or Greens, and there are a number of political events every week: speakers or protests or meetings of campus groups or postering in support of one party or another. The school newspaper is a bit weak at times, but the parody newspaper and the satirical *Grinnell Underground Magazine* (GUM) are both fantastic, and the *Grinnell Review* (the literary magazine) publishes some excellent pieces every semester.

There is no Greek system at Grinnell, which is a relief. Who needs the Greeks? Since academics rule here, geeks and hippies and jocks all get along, as they're all in the same classes and they all know and respect one another's intellectual prowess. I'd say the average Grinnell student has a healthy GPA, an interest in community service and/or politics, and—when they're done working—a love for partying. It's also fantastic that our tiny school in the middle of Iowa has so many international students and such a strong LGBT community. The LGBT student group and the International Student Organization are some of the largest groups on campus, and they both hold some very popular events.

The Activities

Grinnell's student government is very influential—we have a say in a good number of the school's policies, and the SGA president speaks frequently with the president of the college, the board of trustees, and the academic steering committee.

We also have some great yearly parties, including the Haines Hall Underwear Ball and the Mary B. James Drag Ball. There are also two yearly Waltzes, for which students dress up and actually waltz! It's like prom, only better.

On a sunny day at Grinnell, everyone is sitting outside. Hippies are sprawling on blankets on South Campus. Jocks are playing Frisbee on North Campus. Those who have a lot of homework are reading books and watching the hippies or the jocks, and some people are just sleeping. And if you to want to leave campus, Des Moines or Iowa City are both only an hour away, and there's a free shuttle to each on weekends.

The Social Scene

Every weekend at Grinnell there are parties and concerts and movies and social events, and everything is free. You barely spend any money at Grinnell! I can literally go weeks without taking cash from an ATM. I'd say our campus is pretty fond of alcohol, but for those who don't drink, the administration arranges nonalcoholic events and alternatives to hardcore partying so they'll have something to do.

> "The swim team is really good and also *really* big. Just about every twentieth person you'll meet at Grinnell will be on the swim team."
>
> ✦ Jeff, sophomore

Name: Jeremy
Hometown: New Ulm, Minnesota
Class Year: Junior
Major: Political science
Extracurriculars: Mock Trial, Alternative Happy Hour
Career Goal: That's a little too scary for me to think about right now.

How would you describe Grinnell's reputation?

Those who do know Grinnell know that it's a tough school that produces amazing individuals who have nothing but love for their alma mater.

Is this reputation accurate?

Yeah, I think it's pretty accurate. Come to Grinnell. You'll like it here.

What would an admissions officer at your school probably not tell a prospective student?

An admissions officer probably wouldn't talk about the social scene, which is a world unto itself.

The Institution

Grinnell is in Iowa, and living in Iowa is wonderful; it's a surprisingly beautiful state. They frequently bring in speakers and performers from all over the world, so even though we're living in the middle of Iowa, on eight square blocks, we don't feel isolated at all. Our classes are small, which means students and professors get to interact more closely and build stronger relationships. Our campus is also tiny, which means you can live on the opposite end from your best friends and still see them every day with very little effort. You can count on one of your friends being in the Forum or the library every time you drop in to do (or pretend to do) homework. Grinnell's campus creates a very close-knit community where everyone cares about one another. When you graduate from Grinnell, you don't just miss your friends—you miss Grinnellians as a whole.

> "There's only one rivalry at Grinnell—between North and South dormitories. The South are supposedly tree-huggers, hippies, and druggies. While those living in North are jocks and gym bunnies. But the rivalry is all in jest."
>
> ✦ Lillian, junior

The Education

Most Grinnellians are big dorks, whether they'll admit it or not. They love to read. They love to write long academic papers. They'll spend hours debating whether to do the most basic things (like partying on a Tuesday or going on a bakery run), weighing every potential ramification, every pro and con. They'll have long arguments about politics over dinner. They'll dominate classes with discussions and debate (as most don't like being lectured at for an entire period). And since we don't really have a core curriculum, students can explore their interests in multiple areas, all the time.

Personally, I think I'm far more able to convey my opinions and ideas than I was before I came to Grinnell. I attribute this mostly to learning that if I want a word in during a discussion, I have to think quickly, clearly, and intelligently. Grinnell helps its students to really think things through, take strong positions, and argue them effectively.

The Students

Grinnell's population is fairly diverse. Politically, many Grinnellians lean toward the left, enough so that we're often categorized as a campus of "flaming liberals." Racially, Grinnell is still fairly white, and we're also fairly gay, with plenty of LGBT students.

Grinnellians are very opinionated, and we tend to turn anything we can into a forum for expressing our views. The school paper, *The Scarlet & Black,* almost always has a long list of "Random Rants." On the whole, if Grinnellians are passionate about something, they stage protests, put up signs and posters, attend conferences, and scream about whatever it is from any rooftops they can get themselves onto.

The Activities

On a sunny day, people are sprawled all over MAC field, Cleveland beach, Forum beach, Central Campus, and the loggia. They're throwing footballs, playing Frisbee, reading for class, listening to their music, laughing with friends, sleeping. These are the best days at Grinnell. You can tell who didn't have class that afternoon, because they'll come into the dining hall bleary eyed and pink from having been outside for hours. There is almost nothing in the world better than being at Grinnell on a beautiful day.

The Social Scene

Since Grinnell is so small, we really do form a community. We live with all of our friends. We study with them, party with them, depend on them. There is almost always something to do, and if there isn't anything formal going on, people find ways to occupy themselves. We study hard and we balance that by doing our best to have a good time when we can. In addition to parties and things of that nature, there are often concerts, either given by Grinnell groups or groups that the school brings in. Every weekend, there are free movies shown at Harris. Also, substance-wise, no one at Grinnell will ever force someone to go out and do things if they don't want to—everyone is free to do what they want without fear of being looked down upon by other students. I have met very few people who are genuinely unhappy at Grinnell. Nearly everyone can find a group of people who has similar interests and goals.

Name: Electra
Hometown: Seattle, Washington
Class Year: Junior
Major: General sciences
Extracurriculars: World drumming, instructor of belly dance, instructor of a peer-based sex education class.
Career Goal: Naturopathic physician, Sex-Positive advocate and educator (w/ PhD)

How would you describe Grinnell's reputation?

Grinnell College is one of the top fifteen liberal arts colleges in the nation, and it has a longstanding reputation for excellence. A certain kind of student thrives here—a student who's studious, who's liberal, and who's more than a bit weird.

Is this reputation accurate?

Yeah. We're mostly studious, liberal, weird. Check.

What would an admissions officer probably not tell a prospective student?

The trustee board makes a lot of choices that affect the life of the average Grinellian, and many feel that certain recent decisions haven't been the best ones. Unfortunately, the trustees have a lot more power than the students do, and they've gotten their way on more than one hotly debated issue. This is a big sore spot right now.

The Institution

The bathrooms of Burling, our library, were designed with the notion that students will write on the stall walls. So we do. My favorite "stall piece" is a list in the third floor bathroom stall—Sexiest Geeks on Campus. Its numbering system is an "array" (this is a computer science term, for those not in the know, where counting begins at zero and some of the numbers in the list are redefined). Yeah. See what I mean? We're all so weird here. It's great.

Also, our study-abroad programs are excellent. A huge ratio of students (somewhere between one third and one half of the campus) goes abroad for a semester or a year. Also, Grinnell has two weeks of spring break and a month or more of winter break. Nice.

The Education

Grinnell has a lot of interesting academic programs—my favorites are MAP (Mentored Advanced Projects), Summer Research, and Special Topic courses. MAP is where you do advanced coursework in a one-on-one capacity with professors of your choice. Summer Research is what it sounds like—both MAP and Summer Research allow students grad-school-style research opportunities, and Grinnellians often produce very impressive results in each program. In many cases, those results are published and shared with the entire Grinnell community.

And Special Topics are relatively new, very particularized classes that star professors teach. For example, Gospel Singing as Higher Art, Japanese Fiction and Film from the Meiji Period to the Present, and Social Control of Reproduction Rights. A Grinnell education is very eclectic. You take classes across the board, limited only by your interests. The only downside being, you'll leave Grinnell with a list of about thirty classes that you wish you could have taken.

The Students

Grinnell is a pretty integrated campus. There are some conservatives on campus who probably feel a bit uncomfortable. But for everyone else, things are great! Even for the Republicans, it's not that bad. I'm sure they're wonderful, intelligent people behind their flawed political viewpoints. So long as they're not constantly talking politics, most people will still be friends with them. Also, don't choose a college based on its prestige—choose a college that really fits your personality and style of learning. If you like liberal, active, fun, weird kids, brilliant professors, and a comfortable, close-knit environment (and you don't mind living in Iowa), think about choosing Grinnell.

The Activities

Grinnell is about sixty miles from anything terribly interesting, so the school provides its own entertainment. There is probably a minimum of three activities every weekday to choose from—and that shifts to five or six activities per day on the weekends. And this isn't counting the impromptu gatherings of friends and parties that crop up. Despite the fact that we're in the middle of Iowa, someone has to *try* to be bored at Grinnell. Grinnell also arranges trips to nearby city centers, and it's easy to find a friend or alumnus who will drive you somewhere if you're going nuts and *need* to get off campus. Lastly, Grinnell provides lots of funding for student groups to take trips and retreats.

The Social Scene

Every weekend, Grinnell has a student-DJ'ed dance or concert in the Harris Center (which has a concert hall, movie theater, and lounge). These dances and concerts are usually themed and provide both alcoholic and nonalcoholic beverages and snacks. There are three or four movies per weekend: two mainstream movies and multiple independent films. There is an Experimental College system where students and community members can teach weekend classes on things like Wine & Food Appreciation, *West Wing* Analysis, Ballet, Martial Arts, and the Theory of Role Playing Games. There is the Grinnell Outdoor Recreational Program, which organizes camping, horseback riding, and mountain climbing trips, and the huge Physical Education Complex is also open to everyone. And if all that isn't enough, you can start any club you want, and the school will likely fund the effort.

Notable Grinnell Alumni Include:
Morgan Taylor, Olympic hurdler
Robert Noyce, inventor of the microchip
Herbie Hancock, jazz pianist, composer
Gary Cooper, actor
Thomas R. Cech, chemist
James Norman Hall, author

HAMILTON COLLEGE

Founded: 1812
Location: Clinton, NY
Phone: (315) 859-4011
E-mail: admission@hamilton.edu
Web site: www.hamilton.edu

Number of Undergraduates: 1,760
Number of Graduate Students: 0
Cost: Approximately $39,500 per year
Application Deadline: Jan. 1
Early Decision: Nov. 15

Rating:	Notable Majors/Programs:
Most Selective	English, Life Sciences, Social Sciences, Chinese

Size:
● Small   ○ Medium   ○ Large

Location:
○ Urban   ○ Suburban   ● Rural

On a Saturday, students talk about academics:
○ Always   ● Sometimes   ○ Never

Nightlife:
● Intense   ○ Moderate   ○ Laid-back

Politically, Hamilton leans:
○ Left   ● Right   ○ Split

Diversity:
○ High   ● Low   ○ Medium

Students describe Hamilton in five words:
- Frozen tundra in rural locale
- Work hard; play really hard

From the School
At Hamilton, students are accorded freedom to pursue their own educational interests within the broad goals of a liberal arts education. In intensive consultation with their advisors, Hamilton students regularly plan, assess and re-assess their educational progress and their success at fulfilling the ideals of the liberal arts.

—www.hamilton.edu

If you're interested in Hamilton, you may also be interested in:
Bates, Colby, Colgate, Gettysburg, Middlebury, Vassar

Name: Jennifer
Hometown: Syracuse, New York
Class Year: Senior
Major: Chemistry and women's studies
Extracurriculars: Gamma Xi Sorority; swimming; chamber ensemble
Career Goal: PhD scientist doing research to improve the quality of women's health

How would you describe Hamilton's reputation?

Hamilton is considered a "safety" school for many who do not get into the Ivy League.

Is this reputation accurate?

Sure some students once thought they'd rather go elsewhere—but for most, there's nowhere else they'd rather be. People apply here early for a reason. The classes are small and very discussion based, and the student-professor interaction is incredible. It's a great little school where you can really learn a lot.

What would an admissions officer at Hamilton probably not tell a prospective student?

Academics at Hamilton are split. You can work very, very hard to get a B+, or slack off and go out a lot and wind up with a B–. It is hard to get As at Hamilton.

The Institution

I chose Hamilton because it just felt right when I came here. I liked that people said hi to my tour guide as we were walking around and that people smiled and seemed to like being here. The prestige of Hamilton is also a plus because a lot of employers and grad schools know of Hamilton. I just applied to graduate schools on the West Coast, and all of them had heard of Hamilton and commented that it was a really good school.

The campus is beautiful but bring lots of sweaters. The weather in upstate New York is not the best. We get a lot of snow, and it is really cold from November through March. However, the spring and fall are sufficiently beautiful that it makes it bearable. The campus is divided into a light and a dark side. The light side houses the new science building and tends toward the more science-based courses, and the dark has many of the more liberal artsy courses and the bohemian culture (to the extent there is one here) that comes with it. And, Clinton is a cute little town. Park Row looks like a Norman Rockwell scene. There're a

couple of good restaurants and the most adorable movie theater *ever*.

The Education

It is definitely rigorous! There's supposedly no core here, but there are a few roundabout requirements that you need to fulfill. Most classes are discussion based, which I like. However, sometimes the class length is insufficient for everyone to say what they want to, which can be frustrating. The attention from professors is great. Sometimes they are overly attentive! One time freshman year I overslept and woke up to a phone call from the professor asking if I was OK, and if I needed any-

> "Hamilton is clique-central. And if you don't look like the group you want to join, you probably won't fit in. The segregation here is intense."
>
> ✦ Kioshi, sophomore

thing. Guilt got the better of me, and I arrived in class fifteen minutes later.

I'm so glad that Hamilton is just undergrads. After having visited huge universities, I can't imagine having gone to any of them. I would have gotten lost in the crowd and never gone to class. The biggest class I've had here is thirty (Intro Calculus). My smallest was four, in a research seminar. My favorite classes have been Theories of Sexuality (women's studies), Contemporary Moral Issues (philosophy), Introduction to Chemical Research (chemistry), and Intermediate Ballet (dance). As you can see, there's strength in a variety of fields here. Lastly, the honor code is taken very seriously at Hamilton, and offenders have to appear before the Honor Court. Make sure you read the code, because not knowing the stipulations is not a valid excuse in court.

The Students

Students are mostly white, upper-middle class, Abercrombie, J. Crew, and Patagonia-wearing kids with an appreciation for the great outdoors (the Adirondacks are a big draw here). We're smart and studious but really know how to let loose when the time comes. We're not known for being overly warm, but hey, this isn't California. Go West, young man, if that's what you're looking for, because you won't find sun and laid-back students welcoming you with open arms here. However, I do believe most students are genuinely nice people once you talk with them.

The Activities

I leave campus pretty regularly; good restaurants and bars are close by. If I have insomnia, I IM my friends or go to the diner for late-night breakfast and to hang out.

The Social Scene

Parties are very well attended. There is a lot of drinking on this campus, so if that bothers you, Hamilton might be no good. The administration is trying to minimize the amount of underage drinking and the quantity consumed. We'll see how that pans out. The party scene at Hamilton is largely dominated by Greek societies. Almost all of the parties here have a theme, e.g., '80s, jungle juice, Studio 54, golf pros and tennis hos. Greek or not, all parties are open to everyone, and you will still have a fun social life.

There are no society houses, but after freshman year you can live with your friends in pulls, and that's what most of the society members do. The Greeks here are really proud. And although we don't have a house, joining a sorority was one of the best things I did in college. Nearly everyone lives on campus. Some of the dorms on the dark side are not the best, but by the time you are a junior or senior, you can get really nice housing. One of my favorite things about Hamilton is how everyone says hi to each other, says please and thank you, and always stops you on the Quad to chat.

Name: Gabrielle
Class Year: Sophomore
Hometown: Portland, Oregon
Major: Economics
Extracurriculars: Political activism, member of Rainbow Alliance (GLBT organization)
Career Goal: PhD and teaching, or working with an NGO

How would you describe Hamilton's reputation?

Looking at a *U.S. News & World Report* ranking, I'd say it's pretty reputable. If one merely looks at the selectivity of the school, or the achievements of some of its graduates, it looks pretty solid.

Is this reputation accurate?

I don't believe statistics or figures accurately gauge my school's real academic environment. My school's full of either the smartest stupid people, or the stupidest smart people I've ever met. People at Hamilton, considering that so many of them come from elite schools or are supposed to be a part of the next generation of this country's leaders, are, sadly, very apathetic and not particularly intellectual. I think the fraternity and general social scenes on this campus have negative influences over academic environment. Finally, I feel as though this school does not encourage any more thinking than is required inside of class. Outside class, I find very few people interested in talking about anything of much substance. Many people who realize this apply here as their "safety."

> "Undergraduates here are in a premier position to get a glimpse at research projects and equipment that they would normally never see until grad school. They've invested a lot of money in the sciences here of late."
>
> ✦ Carin, sophomore

What would an admissions officer at Hamilton probably not tell a prospective student?

The aspect of this school that the administration tries to hide is the level of drug and alcohol consumption on campus and the consequences that they foster. A recently created commission made a number of recommendations for this problem, but I doubt its efforts will come to fruition. I'd say that 80 to 90 percent of the school opposes the recommended measures.

The Institution

The school's size doesn't affect a person much, unless they're part of a minority group that feels like they can't relate with enough people in their demographic, or when it comes down to the number of opportunities for students to receive grants or research opportunities. Then it's rough. However, the small size helps students receive internal opportunities that would be much more competitive at other schools. One of my friends is getting a grant to do some research on some esoteric topic—coffeehouses in seventeenth- or eighteenth-century Europe and their effect on political discourse, or something. For those kinds of opportunities, Hamilton is excellent.

I have trouble with the way administrators regard the students. They really don't seem to take student input into consideration. The college's materials speak of how it fosters and demands personal responsibility, but I haven't found that to be particularly true. When students go to administrators with serious concerns—about its disability policy, the level of racial tension or homophobia on campus, or how overenrollment has led to students living in former study lounges—they tend to brush them off. Overall, this school acts too much like a business and too little like an academic community. I think it places *looking* reputable above *being* reputable, and especially above improving the well-being of the students.

> "I never thought I'd meet so many people from Connecticut in one school. . . . Do they send college recruiters to the yacht clubs there?"
>
> ✦ Florence, junior

The Education

I'm quite certain I can't find the five-student classes I've encountered at Hamilton anywhere else. A few of my classes, particularly those that are esoteric or unpopular, have had a very small number of students, which really helps in terms of student-faculty interaction. Also, one benefit of a small campus in a rural area is that professors are always close by. This allows people to meet on short notice, and once in awhile, the professors invite students over.

Since I take classes in both social sciences and mathematics, about half my classes in a semester are lecture based and half are seminar based. I would say that the strongest departments at Hamilton, by far, are the mathematics and philosophy departments. Both have incredibly competent professors who are not only friendly but willing to assist you for hours.

Nicely enough, there are no distribution requirements! For a student like myself, who attempts to work toward a broad education with my own interests in mind, this works out perfectly! Strangely, however, we do have five physical education requirements.

The Students

One in every ten people here feels like misfits of some sort, and I fall into that category. I'm from a very progressive "left-coast" city, and I've never seen more explicit racism or homophobia than I've seen on this campus. I find the level of substance and alcohol abuse quite frightening as well. I find the students here rather unfriendly and not particularly interested in "embracing" diversity. I never felt "Latina" or "queer" before I attended Hamilton. This campus is very intolerant. I'd say most students aren't out. Many people use words like *fag* or *faggot* and simply say that the word doesn't reflect its homophobic roots anymore, when questioned about it. So high school of them.

Overall, the school's composed of generally upper-middle to upper-class students of a relatively privileged background. Probably around half of the students on campus pay the full $40,000-per-year tuition. Less affluent students like myself tend to be good at hiding their socioeconomic background when necessary. I'd say this campus, overall, consists of apolitical, relatively conservative students. They're not particularly enlightened on issues surrounding identity or the economic realities of this country. They're not particularly concerned about social, political, or environmental issues that don't directly concern them.

The Activities

I have a friend who's very involved on campus, and talks about how 5 percent of the students seem to do 95 percent of the nonsporting activities. However, the Student Assembly has a $250,000 student activities budget, and this allows the small groups of students who do organize into particular groups to receive lots of funding. This means that groups can go on expensive junkets to different cities and dine on expensive Thai food, spend money on crepes, and stay in nice facilities. No joke. Kind of nice, right?

The Social Scene

On Saturday night, depending on which niche you fit into, you're either drinking or hanging out. There isn't much to do on campus, and it's far from any major city with much to do. So, generally, students have to find their own means of entertaining themselves. A lot of students clearly have a great time together, and everyone loves their friends, but the Northeastern chill extends beyond the weather. When I return home, I find it amusing to find people waving and saying hello or holding doors open for each other. This place is definitely not for everyone.

> "Hamilton is like a big country club with PhDs wandering around instead of golf pros. Lots of pastels here. When spring finally comes this campus looks like an Easter basket exploded."
> ✦ Lucas, sophomore

Name: Larry
Hometown: Ellsworth, Maine
Class Year: Senior
Major: Economics
Extracurriculars: Swimming
Career Goal: To become the owner of a technology business

How would you describe Hamilton's reputation?
Very good to excellent.

Is this reputation accurate?
Yes. The professors are readily accessible and class sizes are small. Each student gets a lot of attention, and the faculty do take care that you learn to communicate well and think critically.

What would an admissions officer at Hamilton probably not tell a prospective student?
The fact that the weather is *miserable* for six of the nine school months! Positively dreary.

The Institution
I chose the school partially for its size. The school is definitely too small to remain anonymous, which has its drawbacks and benefits, as you might imagine. The most difficult thing about being a first-year was that the housing situation was terrible. My mother, who is by no means affluent, asked (almost seriously) whether my cramped freshman room was legal. Four guys who barely knew each other being forced to live in such tight quarters was extremely difficult, even though we all got along.

And despite administrative attempts at diversity, the school remains very ethnocentric, and *very* WASPY. Most students wear pastel dress shirts with collars popped. It is too preppy for my taste, too small, but the education is *definitely* excellent. As with any situation, you have to take the good with the bad. So it is with Hamilton.

The Education
Two nights ago I participated in a conversation with a few housemates that would, if witnessed by prospectives, make them loooove to come here (if they're very intellectual). We discussed the history of Europe from the rise of Rome all the way to the beginnings of capitalism. It was wonderful. But prospectives won't see this often. Because, well, this doesn't happen often. In fact, I think it hardly ever happens; that night was a chance occurrence. Don't get me wrong: Hamilton students are smart. We're just not crazy intellectual or super geeky in that way.

I spend less time on schoolwork than most students out of class, about two hours a day. Generally, I think most students spend roughly three hours a day on work. But we all put in long-haul study or writing sessions at least once per week. Competition is moderate. Since I am an economics major, most of my classes are lectures, but as a government minor, I can attest to the fact that there are some very high-quality intensive discussion-based classes here. You can have your pick. I have been approached only once to do research with a professor, but if you get to know your professors well, the opportunities are nearly endless for research. And, almost all seniors do a thesis within their major and are required to do a "senior project." Whether that involves a long paper (thirty to one hundred pages) just depends on the major.

The Students
The students are generally from affluent families. I heard that 80 percent come from prep schools, and I don't doubt it. I came from a rural public high school and feel a little out of place because of it.

The Activities
The cost of living is minimal here. It is so isolated that there is hardly any need to spend money, aside from an occasional cup of coffee. The economy in upstate New York is so bad that prices are depressed and things are cheaper than in other areas of the country. People complain there's not

enough to do, but there's a fair amount of activities on campus: film screenings every weekend, a whole bunch of student groups, occasional concerts or comedians. Al Ham Weekend, the spring carnival, is great.

I'm on the swim team. We play in NESCAC, Div. III, so athletics are quite competitive while still allowing you to be a student and have a life outside their sport. Even if not on a varsity team, most Hamilton students are pretty athletic.

The Social Scene

Many students at Hamilton drink heavily; aside from the drinking culture, there isn't much of a nightlife, which I find depressing. The geographical location of the college makes getting off campus even less desirable. Hamilton's been transitioning for the last decade from a removal of fraternity houses to creation of alternative social spaces, and the result is the social scene has gone from huge all-campus parties to smaller gatherings of friends. Some people like the transition.

Notable Hamilton Alumni Include:
A. G. Lafley, CEO, Procter & Gamble
B. F. Skinner, behavioral psychologist
Ezra Pound, author
Paul Greengard, Nobel Prize winner in medicine
Terry Brooks, author
Theodore Dwight Weld, abolitionist

HAMPSHIRE COLLEGE

Founded: 1965
Location: Amherst, MA
Phone: (413) 559-5471
E-mail: admissions@hampshire.edu
Web site: www.hampshire.edu

Number of Undergraduates: 1,267
Number of Graduate Students: 0
Cost: Approximately $37,000 per year
Application Deadline: February 1
Early Decision: November 15/Early Action: December 1

Rating:	Notable Majors/Programs:
Selective	Social Sciences, Creative Writing, Film, Theater

Size:
● Small   ○ Medium   ○ Large

Location:
○ Urban   ● Suburban   ○ Rural

On a Saturday, students talk about academics:
● Always   ○ Sometimes   ○ Never

Nightlife:
○ Intense   ○ Moderate   ● Laid-back

Politically, Hampshire leans:
● Left   ○ Right   ○ Split

Diversity:
○ High   ● Low   ○ Medium

Five-College school: Yes!

Students describe Hampshire in five words:
- Idiosyncratic, experimental, rock 'n' roll
- Independent, progressive, liberal, worth it

From the School

It takes some extra time to understand Hampshire, especially the way in which students develop their academic pathways in the absence of formal majors. Hampshire's interdisciplinary approach means that the basis for each student's academic program is her or his interests, rather than requirements imposed by academic departments and majors.

—www.hampshire.edu

If you're interested in Hampshire, you may also be interested in:
Bard, Brown, Oberlin, Sarah Lawrence, Vassar

Name: Donald

Hometown: Shreveport, Louisiana

Class Year: Junior

Major: Philosophy

Extracurriculars: Student Government, United Students Against Sweatshops, various antiwar organizing activities

Career Goal: Librarian

How would you describe Hampshire's reputation?

Hampshire's known as a left-wing college with a free-thinking educational philosophy. We're also known for having a lot of hippies and smoking a lot of weed.

Is this reputation accurate?

Yes. Hampshire College was created to radically challenge traditional pedagogical methods. There are no grades, and there are no tests, as they are often antithetical to free and critical inquiry. Instead, there's an emphasis on receiving verbal and written feedback from faculty, meant to stimulate us and help us become better students. And yeah, there are some hippies and I think there might be some weed on campus, but the hippies are all so nice, and the weed *does* support independent farmers in Vermont, so . . .

> "If my friends at more prestigious schools were working in a lab sophomore year, they were washing test tubes. Meanwhile I was extracting DNA and doing research independently on a project of my own design."
>
> ✦ Becca, junior

What would an admissions officer at your school probably not tell a prospective student?

The administration might not tell students that the Pioneer Valley (where Hampshire is located) is one of the major centers of the academic left in America. This has made more than a few conservative students uncomfortable. Also note: New England winters are a curse sent by a higher power to punish New Englanders for once burning old women at the stake and giving smallpox-ridden blankets to Indians. Really, they're terrible, especially if you're from California or something.

The Institution

Once upon a time, I was a good student who was becoming increasingly competitive with my peers. I wasn't self-motivated; I wasn't being creative. I was also becoming someone who wanted wealth and status just to have it. Then I read about Hampshire. And I knew that's where I had to go. It would make me the type of person I wanted to be and steer me away from the type of person I feared I was becoming.

There's no competition at Hampshire. There's a lot of creativity. You don't do your work because you have to; you do it because you're engaged with the subject matter. A big part of many classes at Hampshire is completing a final project, and this helps, because completing a project is really intellectually challenging and satisfying in a way that memorizing answers to questions, or writing some formulaic essay, isn't. Instead, you create something really cool, something to be proud of.

The Education

At Hampshire, students have to satisfy a fairly general distribution requirement their first year, taking classes in four broad subjects. Then, students sit down with their faculty adviser, talk about their interests, and spend their next three years taking whatever classes they want that will help them learn more about their interests. Instead of being forced to fulfill someone else's conception of what a "major" should be, Hampshire students get to arrange their studies around themes they find compelling, and they're free to take *any* classes that address those themes with *no* externally imposed restrictions. And everyone else is so genuinely interested in what everyone else is doing that you can get into a three-hour discussion with literally anyone on campus, and only talk about academics, and it will be among the best discussions you've ever had.

The most popular things to study at Hampshire are the cognitive sciences, physics, environmental science, sustainable technology, sustainable agriculture, anthropology, public health, progressive history (labor, women's rights, etc.), development studies, cooperative economics, Continental philosophy, political philosophy, urban-rural studies, film, and dance. Lastly, every senior at Hampshire produces a large final project that represents the culmination of their studies. This could be original scientific research of publishable quality or a hundred-page paper dissecting a literary text, or you could write and produce a full-length play or make a movie. If you come to Hampshire, most of your final year is going to be consumed by the final project, but when you leave, you'll have a massively impressive *something* as proof of your efforts.

> "Our campus is very '70s. The buildings are 'artistically industrialized,' which means they're ugly and concrete."
>
> ✦ Nuala, senior

The Students

Students at Hampshire are generally liberals or leftists of various stripes, but they aren't too pushy about it. People read the *New York Times* a lot, and we have a decent campus paper. There aren't really groups of people who don't mix. There are many strong identity-based groups (cultural, ethnic, sexuality groups), which get a lot of support on Hampshire's campus. Generally, we're very white, but we're steadily becoming more diverse. We don't have fraternities or sororities. People usually have no idea what they're going to do after they graduate, but we end up sending many to graduate programs. We also send lots of kids into the NGO sector. Very few if any of us become business students, but we churn out a good number of entrepreneurs.

The Activities

Hampshire is in a consortium with Mt. Holyoke, Smith, Amherst, and the University of Massachusetts–Amherst, which means we can take classes at any of these schools for credit. It works out well, because it means our class options are virtually unlimited (since we have five schools' worth of course catalogues to choose from), and, since each of those schools is less than fifteen minutes away, it's easy to campus-hop, and our social life can be really large if we want it to be. Generally, Hampshire kids like UMass kids a lot. We also like Smith and Mt. Holyoke students, who tend to be pretty chill, but sometimes have a bit of an upper-class-girl-at-finishing-school air to them. Amherst has good professors, so we go there for classes, but

we generally despise Amherst College students, because they're often obnoxious, arrogant snobs who treat us like trash.

Hampshire's strongest sport is Ultimate Frisbee. We have lots of outdoorsy programs, mountain climbing and kayaking and such. People also take lots of martial arts (aikido, karate, judo), yoga, dance, and frequently go to lectures on campus, political rallies, music recitals, and improv comedy shows.

Hampshire has some great traditions. First and foremost there's Hampshire Halloween, a giant and infamous costume party the whole campus comes to, with fireworks and breakfast served at 2:00 a.m. by Hampshire's president himself—this thing is part concert, part fair, part *Through the Looking-Glass*. Then there's the Final Project Parade, where people in the midst of their projects dress up as whatever they're producing and parade themselves around campus, joined by the school deans and Hampshire's president. And then the Bell Ringing, which happens each year when people hand in their final projects—seniors throw a giant party on the school commons in front of the library, and they ring an incredibly large, loud bell. Breakfast with the president is also fun—Hampshire's president has breakfast in the dining commons every Monday, so any student can speak with him about any issue they'd please and get immediate feedback.

The Social Scene

Hampshire is a small school, so the parties are pretty standard—there's music, drinking, dancing, mind-altering substances. You know, the usual. Most of the time, really, we don't even party, we just nerd it up with our friends. There's no Greek scene here, so we don't get crazy in the traditional frat-sorority way, that's for sure.

Also, some people think the postmodern culture studies–film students create the closest thing to Hampshire's "social elite." I think that's a bit of a stretch, though.

Name: Anne
Hometown: Albany, New York
Class Year: Junior
Major: Musical Theater/video
Extracurriculars: I act in some Hampshire productions; I also sometimes help people with their video projects.

Career Goal: I'd like to become either a casting director, a singer, or an actress.

How would you describe Hampshire's reputation?

People look at Hampshire as a pothead, hippie-carnival college. Lots of drugs, little work, Just smelly people smoking all day.

Is this reputation accurate?

This isn't the reality of the situation at all! Sure, there is a lot of pot smoking here—maybe a little more than you'd find at other schools—but it's not as in your face as you'd expect. And it doesn't prevent us from working *hard*—really, I went to a well-reputed state school before transferring to Hampshire, and I used to do a lot less work. I mean, for any given class at Hampshire, you're expected to write between eighty and one hundred pages in papers each semester. No slacker's going to be able to pull that off! Also, people aren't smelly here. They're very clean. I promise.

What would an admissions officer at your school probably not tell a prospective student?

Well, admissions officers always get mad at students when they run around naked. Not everyone at Hampshire runs around naked, mind you, but packs of naked students have been known to pop up. Also, Hampshire's a relatively new school, and it doesn't have the ridiculous monetary endowments other schools do, so sometimes the financial aid packages offered won't be as generous as you'll find elsewhere. Lastly, Hampshire students can take classes at any of the other five colleges in the Five College Consortium (Amherst, UMass–Amherst, Smith, Mt. Holyoke), but sometimes if you want to study something specialized, you'll still find yourself at a loss. For example, I'm studying musical theater right now—or trying to—but there's been only one musical theater class in the five colleges in the past year, and I've already taken it.

The Institution

Students complain about the food all the time, but I don't think it's worse than any other cafeteria food. And if you don't like the food, you can always live in the Mods (apartmentlike structures with kitchens). One good thing about Hampshire housing is that the rooms are 80 percent singles, so your chances of having a single, even in your first year, are pretty smokin'. Everyone thinks Public Safety is sort of campy because they take themselves really seriously.

Hampshire's also supportive of studying abroad and internships. Anyone who wants to go somewhere will be encouraged to go to that somewhere. In Hampshire's bathroom stalls, you'll find lots of political writing, lots of queer theory examining gender issues, quotes from world leaders, poetry, and, of course, the usual poo humor. Half the time you'll recognize the handwriting in the bathroom stalls, and one of the poo jokes will have been written by a friend of yours. And you'll recognize handwriting at Hampshire because this place is small and cozy, and people get to know one another really well. You never feel lost, professors and students are on a first-name basis.

I chose Hampshire because I liked that it has no core curriculum and lets students design their own majors, and I liked that I would never have to take another math class, ever, ever again, if I came.

> "The average student on campus wears Birkenstocks, plays guitar on the grass, smokes weed, is well educated about Middle East conflicts, hikes in the woods in winter, is vegan, and is *very* friendly."
> ✦ Brian, freshman

The Education

One of the best things about Hampshire is that it has no core curriculum after your freshman year. I would go mad if I was always taking bullshit courses that I hated and wouldn't remember in a year just so my university could tell everyone else that it had farted out another anonymous "well-rounded" graduate. I came to Hampshire to use my time well, to take all the things I'm fascinated by past the point of casual interest and into the realm of earnest study. And that's exactly what I've done. I'd say the amount of work you'll do at Hampshire will vary—you can spend a half hour on homework each night and you'll get by. Your professors might not respect you, but you'll get by. You can also spend four hours on homework each night and be really thorough, and engage in an honest dialogue with your professors, who will notice what you've done and commend you accordingly. It's all up to you. You'll receive a lot of attention from every Hampshire professor you'll have, and they'll certainly notice the quality of your approach.

I think the best departments at Hampshire are in the sciences, the social sciences, film-photo, theater, and creative writing. Professors in these areas are top-notch, and our graduates have gone on to do some truly amazing things. My one complaint is that almost every class is called "Something Something and Race" or "Something Something and Gender" or "Something Something and Class" or "Something Race and Something Gender in Something Class." It's a bit much!

The Students

The average Hampshire student is a clean (not smelly!) Birkenstock-wearing white kid who misses class at least once every two weeks, considers him- or herself to be very liberal, isn't terribly religious, and has probably smoked pot at least once in the past month. Most students are also from upper-middle-class families—probably because the tuition here is so exorbitant—and there are a surprisingly large number of international students. You won't see as many minorities as you'd hope. That said, all minority students are seamlessly integrated at Hampshire. And as for LGBT kids—it's been said that everyone at Hampshire is at *least* bisexual. So, if you are LGBT, prepare to get laid more than you've ever been laid in your life.

The Activities

Hampshire students don't really do athletics. We're more the kids who laughed at the athletes in high school while sitting in the corner applying a third coat of black nail polish to our nails (if we had a Goth phase). We do have a popular Ultimate Frisbee team—that would be the one exception.

> "Near the soccer fields, down toward the edge of the woods, there's a narrow path. Take it across a rickety log bridge and then follow the creek. You'll emerge in a clearing and all around you there'll be cairns built of stones from the river, round rocks balanced carefully one on top of the other by Hampshire students over the years, for no reason other than 'because.' That's Hampshire."
> ✦ Josh, senior

There are lots of student groups here, covering just about anything you'd want a student group to cover. (Except musical theater, dammit.)

The Social Scene

Hampshire students like a heavy dose of fun mixed in with their academics. So, when weekends come around, we don't just roll over and keep on studying—we take a break and party. And the party options are limitless. We can stick to Hampshire's campus and see what our classmates have cooked up, which could be a themed party, "Starlets of the 1950s," or an impromptu campuswide chess tournament, or a big outdoor sleepover. We could smoke a bit and just hang out in someone's room, talking; we could hang out in Northampton, our little nearby hippie town, and eat at nice restaurants, go to some bars and dance clubs.

Name: Rochelle
Hometown: Daytona Beach, Florida
Class Year: Senior
Major: Postmodern theory
Extracurriculars: Femme Group, Queer Community Alliance, Drag Ball organizer, teaching assistant
Career Goal: To become the queer Oprah

How would you describe Hampshire's reputation?

This place is chock full of queers, hippies, postmodern scholars, and generally very intelligent and creative folk.

Is this reputation accurate?

Sure. That's us, guilty as charged. Note, in the above description I didn't say say that we were "activists." Because we're not. This campus sounds like it would political, but it's actually disappointing in that arena.

What would an admissions officer at your school probably not tell a prospective student? What aspect of your school would a prospective student not see on a campus tour?

The administration won't tell you that a lot of the housing at Hampshire is decaying and in need of repairs, but Hampshire doesn't have the money at the moment to get those repairs done. And they won't show prospective students the on-campus apartments, the "Mods," which are old, filthy, and falling apart.

The Institution

The buildings that make up Hampshire are hideous examples of 1960s architecture. But the grounds and the surrounding area are absolutely stunning in autumn and late spring. So that's the trade-off you'll have to make.

Hampshire has a pretty unique educational philosophy, which I'm sure others have already spoken about. This philosophy sounds great in theory, but can be kind of awkward in practice. Let's be honest, some students need more guidance than "take any class, any time." Too much structure is a bad thing. But just a little structure wouldn't be so bad. That said, the type of people who are drawn to Hampshire precisely because there isn't structure make this place what it is. Hampshire is really progressive. Particularly when it comes to gender. Nearly every bathroom on the entire campus—in dorms, administrative areas, and academic buildings—is gender-neutral.

The Education

Hampshire has what we call a Division system. What this means is that when students are freshmen, they have to complete course work in the four schools of Division 1—humanities and arts, natural science, social science, and cognitive science. Then there's Division 2, when you meet with your adviser sophomore year, figure out your core interests, and formulate a plan of action where you'll take classes that speak to those interests. Finally, there's Division 3, where you produce a senior project that reflects all you've learned over your four years. Most classes you take are going to be small, ranging from four to twenty students. You'll get to be close with your classmates, your professors, and close with Hampshire's library, because you'll be expected to do several hours of reading on a daily basis, and lots of research papers and projects. Get ready to start typing, folks.

The Students

You know that "unique-weird" kid from high school who was artsy and a little bit annoying, but if you ever spoke to him you found out he was also interesting and fun in a good way? That's the kid who winds up coming to Hampshire. These are kids who love to be challenged, who hate the status quo, who not only think outside the box, but get theoretical trucks full of explosives, park them outside of the box, then blow that box up so that it's never seen or heard from again. These are the most brilliant, amazing, and innovative people I have ever crossed paths with.

The most active groups on campus would have to be those allied with the queer and transgendered communities at Hampshire. Coming in a close second would be those groups involved in anticapitalism protests and drug-policy protests. Students here are liberals, period. Maybe there's one Republican on campus, and I don't know why she's still here, we told her we'd cut out her tongue months ago.

The Activities

Hampshire students play Red Scare Frisbee, and that's it for sports. No football, no baseball, no basketball, no soccer. . . . Students at Hampshire call this place "the bubble," because it's such a self-sufficient, enclosed, idealistic little community. If I do leave the bubble, it's to briefly head to Amherst for lunch or to buy some clothes at the thrift store.

The Social Life

Hampshire students love alcohol. We're definitely boozers. We also love pot. We may even love pot more than we love booze. We don't have any fraternities or sororities here, thank the good Lord, so our social scene revolves around our own creativity. We'll have a lot of great dance parties on weekends with amazing music. Everyone is really uninhibited and just looking to have fun. If the on-campus scene gets dull (which it rarely does), you can also head into the nearby town and see what it has to offer. I go to the local gay bar in Northampton called Diva's a lot, just to add diversity to my social schedule.

Dating is always a bit awkward because Hampshire is so small. There's just over a thousand students at Hampshire, which means you know everyone, and after a while you've slept with all the people you want to sleep with, and they've all slept with one another, too. That said, I'd still like to stay here forever.

Notable Hampshire Alumni Include:
Elliot Smith, musician
Naomi Wallace, playwright
Ken Burns, filmmaker
Jon Krakauer, author
Lucy-Ann McFadden, astrophysicist
Alex Rivera, video artist

HARVARD UNIVERSITY

Founded: 1636
Location: Cambridge, MA
Phone: (617) 495-1551
E-mail: college@fas.harvard.edu
Web site: www.harvard.edu

Number of Undergraduates: 6,649
Number of Graduate Students: N/A
Cost: Approximately $38,000 per year
Application Deadline: January 1
Early Action: November 1

Rating:	Notable Majors/Programs:
Most Selective	Government, Biology, Economics, English

Size:
○ Small ● Medium ○ Large

Location:
● Urban ○ Suburban ○ Rural

On a Saturday, students talk about academics:
○ Always ● Sometimes ○ Never

Nightlife:
○ Intense ● Moderate ○ Laid-back

Politically, Harvard is:
○ Left ○ Right ● Split

Diversity:
● High ○ Low ○ Medium

Ivy League: Yes!

Students describe Harvard in five words:
- The world's number one college
- This ain't college—it's *Harvard*.

From the School

Students learn in classrooms and labs from professors who are leading authorities in their fields; all members of Harvard's large, diverse, and accomplished faculty teach undergraduates. Just as important, Harvard offers its undergraduates the privilege of studying with exceptionally talented and motivated peers from all over the globe.

—www.admissions.college.harvard.edu

If you're interested in Harvard, you may also be interested in:
Amherst, U. Pennsylvania, Princeton, Stanford, Yale, Williams

Name: Rich
Hometown: Hackensack, New Jersey
Class Year: Senior
Major: English and American literature/language
Extracurriculars: Chinatown ESL/Citizenship, the *Harvard Crimson*
Career Goal: Harvard Law School, specializing in international law

How would you describe Harvard's reputation?

Students here don't tend to tell people right up front that they go to Harvard. They'll say "I go to school in Boston—well, in Cambridge." Then they'll watch the other person's eyes widen and their mouth grow a little bit slack. "Harvard?" they'll ask. And you have no choice but to say "Yeah," sheepishly. We call that "dropping the H-bomb." And, once the H-bomb has been dropped, you know they've started thinking of legacies, subversive geniuses and future presidents, brilliant professors and redbrick buildings.

Is this reputation accurate?

Harvard is just a school. It's just a school. Say it with me. It's a school that has some good professors and some smart students who got lucky and received a thick envelope in the mail when they were still in high school. In the flesh, Harvard students are, for the most part, down-to-earth. I'm best friends with an anime aficionado, a cross-stitcher, a Scrabble addict, a beach bum, and an '80s dance freak.

What would an admissions officer at your school probably not tell a prospective student?

When you get into Harvard, you immediately dream of being in small, specialized classes with famous faculty members. This happens, eventually . . . but certainly not your first year, when you'll be taking a lot of core and intro classes, both of which are likely to be big and impersonal. You'll also be assigned an academic adviser, but they're likely to be a grad student, new to Harvard themselves and, frankly, just as lost as you are.

The Institution

Harvard has a lot of great traditions, including Primal Scream (where students streak naked around Harvard Yard the night before exam period begins), athletic and social rivalries between Harvard and Yale, and the rivalry between the *Harvard Crimson* and the *Harvard Lampoon*. Students tend to love it here, being part of a school with so much history. It's actually daunting, trying to live up to the accomplishments of the people who have studied here in the past—but we're all determined to give it our best shot.

Harvard freshmen live in the Yard, which has dorms with long, social hallways and stairwells in just the right locations so students can roll out of bed and end up in class minutes later. Upperclassmen housing is a bit different, though—rising freshmen divide themselves into eight-person "blocking" groups and are assigned a house accordingly. And once you're assigned an upperclassmen house, life becomes relatively staid. Almost too staid, as there are only two or three rooms to a floor, the plus side being the rooms you'll live in off these empty, echoey hallways will be huge and beautiful, with private bathrooms and guaranteed singles.

The Education

At Harvard, professors aren't going to be knocking on your door, demanding to get to know you better. They're at the top of their field, and they're usually pretty busy themselves. That said, if you take the time to go to a professor's office and ask to sit down and chat, most will gladly have a conversation with you. You have to take the initiative, but that initiative is usually rewarded. And as you spend more time at Harvard, you'll find more ways to cozy up to your professors—you can work as their research assistants, you can take small seminar classes, and if/when you write a thesis, you're guaranteed lots of one-on-one time with your thesis adviser. Really, once you get to know professors here, their impressive résumés are matched only by their impressive dedication to their students. I've been *very* happy with the number of professors I've become close with.

Also worth mentioning—Harvard has a very unique exam schedule. At the end of the first half of the year, you don't take finals in your classes. Instead, you go home. You have a monthlong break. Your exams hang over your head the entire time. Then, you come back to Harvard and have a two-week reading period, where you're supposed to bone up on anything you might have forgotten over the break. Then—*finally*—you take your finals from the previous semester. Once that's over, your new semester's classes can begin. Students, by and large, hate this.

But, once you're a senior and getting ready to go into the real world, Harvard makes sure you're taken care of. Professors will provide excellent advice on going into academia, if that's the route you see for yourself. The Office of Career Services will help you get into anything else, from nonprofit work to investment banking. Harvard also has excellent resources to help you apply to medical, business or law school.

The Students

Harvard students are pretty extraordinarily diverse. Students are of every religion, every ethnicity, from every single country in the world. Harvard's enormous endowment—$19.3 *billion*—means that it can offer generous financial aid packages to those in need, and, while the student body is still predominantly wealthy, any student who gets accepted but can't afford tuition will be taken care of. Politically, Harvard students run the spectrum—we have loud and proud liberals and rabid conservatives. It's not unusual for liberal and conservative students to argue late into the night, but all such conversations have underlying currents of affinity and respect. "That's what I love about you guys," a friend commented after a recent, particularly heated debate. "We can yell and fight and scream, but when the argument's over we can still happily play video games together."

> "I chose to go to Harvard because of its prestige. A Harvard degree is like a good insurance plan—it'll carry you anywhere."
> ✦ Felicia, sophomore

The Activities

From the *Harvard Crimson* to the Harvard Lovers of the Garden State (HLOGS), this college offers a plethora of groups and clubs to join. Both traditional and nonconformist students find their niche here—and, if you find yourself in any way dissatisfied with what's on offer, you can just go through the relatively painless process of finding an adviser and filling out a grant form; before long, you'll have a club of your own.

Harvard also has plenty of fantastic speakers coming to campus on a regular basis, and any time an issue of national importance arises, you can be sure the person you saw speaking on CNN will be headed to Harvard.

Harvard also has lots of newspapers and publications that are always being distributed throughout the campus and are widely read. The only annoying bit is that if you want to join the staff of one of these publications, you often have to go through a semester-long "comp" process. This comp process can be just about anything. For example, the comp process for the *Harvard Crimson*—which takes place in November and is called the Turkey Shoot—involves a monthlong trial where candidates must submit multiple papers on a variety of issues and must go through several schmooze sessions with current editors to prove their social skills. Candidates are finally chosen or turned away based on secret deliberations—the contents of which often become public, causing hurt feelings and resentment among those not chosen.

The Social Scene

There isn't much of a Greek scene at Harvard, so students turn to clubs and sports teams for a sense of belonging. You really do become associated with the groups you join, and you'll find yourself spending most of your time hanging out with the kids you do volunteer work with, sing a cappella with, and so on. You get the picture.

Name: Andrea
Hometown: Salem, South Dakota
Class Year: Sophomore
Major: Concentration (no majors at Harvard!): social studies, with a language citation in French
Extracurriculars: Volunteering (student-run homeless shelter and mentoring), Model UN, Kuumba (choir based in Af-Am culture and spirituality), Christian Fellowships
Career Goal: I'm not sure. I can see myself working with developmentally disabled children, writing for *National Geographic,* being a social worker for troubled teenagers, or dancing in a Mickey Mouse costume at Walt Disney World.

How would you describe Harvard's reputation?

Stellar. But also very stereotyped. Everyone the world over has a preconceived notion of what Hahhhvahd is: a school reserved solely for geniuses and the sons of the ridiculously wealthy. People also think Harvard isn't just difficult to get into—it's impossible.

Is this reputation accurate?

In truth, Harvard is a very good school that houses some pretty good students. Everyone here is smart—some happen to be geniuses, but many aren't. Some kids at Harvard are the children of the wealthy, but others grew up in really poor areas and made it here just the same. All in all, Harvard is a school like any other, and it's not impossible to get in.

> "The meal plan is amazing compared to other schools', because it is completely covered in your tuition. You get unlimited meals."
>
> ✦ Greg, freshman

What would an admissions officer at your school probably not tell a prospective student?

They won't tell you that once you do get into Harvard, you're going to start feeling pressured to do well to show that you didn't get in by accident. In school, at home, with your family, with everyone—you'll have this Harvard-sized weight on your shoulders. People start expecting brilliance. How will you ever deliver? This is something that a lot of students here have come to resent. Also, they won't tell you that when libraries stay open twenty-four hours a day during reading and exam periods, students literally move into them, studying constantly, sleeping there, leaving only to shower and eat. I don't consider myself a crazy studier—I've got other things to do!—but I've spent more than one night sleeping in the library.

The Institution

There are two entities at play here: there's "Harvard" as a whole, counting all the graduate schools, and "Harvard College," the part of Harvard where undergraduates live and learn. "Harvard" is the place that's always in the news, because new discoveries are being made at the med school or because some hotshot law school professor will be doing work that resonates nationally. As a member of "Harvard College," I'll read about this stuff but it won't really impact me much outside of that. Members of Harvard College and members of each of the grad schools do very different things here.

That said, I think Harvard College's size is perfect. Everyone knows lots of people and feels connected to other students through friends of friends, and there are always certain traditions that bring us together. My favorite Harvard tradition is Primal Scream, as a freshman I was too nervous to join the parade of nudity, but this year I decided if I didn't go through with it I'd be a complete wimp, so I found some friends and we all joined in. It was one of the most invigorating things I've ever done. Once you've run naked with hundreds of your peers, you can't help but be more at ease with them, and with yourself.

Because of traditions like this, Harvard students have a lot of school spirit. Whenever alums come back to visit campus, they're always so happy to talk to current students and to offer to help them in any way they can. There's just so much Harvard pride!

Harvard's campus is spread all over the city of Cambridge, which allows for a unique mix of college people and "real" people. The main, most recognizable bit of Harvard is the Yard, where most freshmen live and undergraduate classes are held. Then, about a mile away you have the Quad, where about a third of sophomores and juniors live. And then not too far from the Yard you have the Upper-Class Houses, which are scattered around a bit. I'd say 98 percent of Harvard students live on campus, both because living off campus is expensive and because Harvard housing is absolutely fabulous.

In the past, if a Harvard student wanted to study abroad, they'd have to go through a *lot* of beauracracy and red tape. Lately, though, a lot of changes have been happening to make studying abroad more accessible and more of an integral part of the Harvard experience. So, if you do want to study abroad, odds are you'll be able to arrange it now.

And, everyone at Harvard is basically forced to buy unlimited meals up front, so any time you're hungry you can head to a dining hall and eat whatever you want. This also means everyone eats together—it's not as though the rich kids go off and buy steak at fancy restaurants every night while the poor kids live off of peanut butter.

The Education

Harvard kids can be nerdy. Really, we talk about classes a *lot.* All the time. I'd say some students at

Harvard compete a lot, particularly those in the premed or preprofessional tracks. You're at Harvard; it happens. Professors are neutral on this—they don't encourage competition, but they don't *discourage* it either. I think our professors are good teachers more often than they're not, and they're very active on campus politically, always getting involved in the latest debates. Overall, the education I'm getting here is pretty good. Be forewarned, it's not all that it's cracked up to be, and it's certainly not as stellar as the general public would assume. But it's good; most people are challenged to think for themselves, and that's really the best gift a college can offer.

The Students

I'd say most Harvard students are pretty political (with slightly more liberals than conservatives), from a broad range of religions, and very LGBT friendly. Most Harvard students are also amazing (pretty often I'll feel like I got in by mistake, because everyone else is so extraordinarily talented!). I think that's a common sentiment here, feeling like you got in because the admissions officer fell asleep on the job. As my (student) tour guide told me on my pre-frosh tour, "I haven't won a Nobel Prize, I'm not an Olympic athlete, and I haven't written a best seller yet—so don't worry! There are some near mortals at Harvard!" And there are, though there are just as many ridiculous achievers in our midst.

The Activities

Harvard has a lot of varsity sports, and if you're an athlete you'll have a great time. That said, most students aren't too enthusiastic about attending games, so be prepared for empty bleachers—unless we're talking about the Harvard-Yale football match, or the Harvard-Cornell hockey game—both of those are extremely well attended. If you're into the arts, there are shows and concerts going up every weekend; it's often hard to choose which group or show to support! We even have an Arts First weekend, where multiple artistic performances go on all day in different locations for several days.

Harvard students are also quite active in public service. We have the nation's only student-run homeless shelter (something I've been blessed to be involved in for the past two years and which has shaped my college career immensely! I'm now a work-contract director at the shelter, and I help

certain guests maintain employment and manage their money as they work toward finding and paying for their own long-term housing).

The Social Scene

Harvard's party scene seems to be dominated by room parties and Finals Clubs. Finals Clubs are old, elitist single-sex organizations—Harvard has about twelve all-male finals clubs, and two all-female ones; the male Finals Clubs are housed in ridiculously extravagant buildings. For the most part, every kind of student parties together at Harvard. The only exclusive element I can think of is the previously mentioned Finals Clubs, which are a bit shadowy over who they decide to let in and who they don't.

No one cares about underage drinking at Harvard. Technically, alcohol isn't allowed in the frosh dorms, but plenty of people bring it in and it's never a big deal. In the upper-class houses everyone has alcohol, and people throw parties there all the time where students get *very* intoxicated. Harvard doesn't try to bust people—it tries to make people feel safe should they ever drink too much and need help.

Name: Felicia
Hometown: Cleveland, Ohio
Class Year: Sophomore
Major: African American Studies
Extracurriculars: Kuumba Singers of Harvard College, Association of Black Harvard Women, Black Students Association, tutoring
Career Goal I'd like to work in education, potentially creating educational policy from Washington, D.C.

How would you describe Harvard's reputation?

Harvard is said to be one of the best, most prestigious schools in the world. Students are thought to be very focused and very academic.

Is this reputation accurate?

This reputation is somewhat accurate. When you go to Harvard, it's hard to believe it's one of the best schools in the world, just because a notion like that is hard to get your head around. But I think kids from less privileged backgrounds get it the most. They're the ones that are very focused and academic and who work the hardest, because they really appreciate the chance to be here. For a lot of the more privileged students Harvard always seemed within reach. And so, these are the kids who are more inclined to slack off.

What would an admissions officer at your school probably not tell a prospective student?

They won't tell you that the quality of housing ranges *tremendously*. Almost everything is livable but your dorm room can be anything from a little cinderblock cell to grand parlors with fireplaces and private bathrooms.

> "Harvard says there are no fraternities or sororities on campus, but that's not true and Harvard knows it."
> ✦ Felicia, sophomore

The Institution

Harvard is big and impersonal. No student is here because Harvard "fit," and certainly no student is here to get lots of one-on-one attention. They're here because Harvard is Harvard. I chose to come to Harvard for that very reason. A Harvard degree is like a good insurance plan, it'll carry you anywhere for the rest of your life. Because Harvard's name was the only reason I chose to come here, I didn't have the highest expectations. And I haven't been disappointed *or* pleasantly surprised. Some things have been really good, some things have been really bad. It balanced out, so I've been satisfied. I've had an adequate experience here.

The Education

Just about every concentration at Harvard is strong. I'd say the most common concentrations are in the sciences, in economics, and in government. Classes at Harvard are challenging but they're certainly not crushing. I know plenty of people who don't work very hard throughout the semester, cram for two weeks before finals, and still ace their tests. Others, who seem to care about knowledge for knowledge's sake (I'd say there's a fifty-fifty split between these two types) will read every book they can get their hands on throughout the semester and won't care all that much how they do on the final because it's just a grade. Also, students tend to work together at Harvard, so before a test study groups will form and each student will create an extensive summary of, say, four texts that they've read over the course of the semester. Together, all of the texts will get summarized and each of the kids in your group will have all the materials they need.

The Students

To Harvard's credit, there's every imaginable type of student here. Students of every ethnicity, from every part of the world, from every conceivable background. And everyone hangs out with one another, from the kid who grew up in the projects in Brooklyn, struggling his whole life to make it here, to Al Gore's kids, to an Olympic gold-medal winning athlete, to that shy, pretty girl from New Jersey. It's impressive. At a lot of other schools, each of those kids would have their own defined cliques and rarely interact. Not so at Harvard.

Also, Harvard students tend to be of two types—they're either overachievers or geniuses/nerds who stay up all night reading not just what's been assigned for a class, but also comparative texts, and if there are ideological opponents who think the assigned reading is bunk, and if *they* wrote a book, the nerds in your class will have read them, too. Then you have the overachievers, who got into Harvard because they were president of every club in high school. At Harvard they're at every party, every event because these kids think, in the long run, they'll get farther ahead by knowing lots of Harvard students (who will become successful Harvard graduates) than they will if they graduate with a 4.0 GPA. So they study enough to do decently well, but socialize their brains out.

The Activities

There are about a million and two clubs and groups to join at Harvard, and everyone seems to join at least two of them. If you want to get a job on-campus while you're a student at Harvard, you're covered. There are tons of them, and they all pay $10+ (there are more jobs than people to take them). And if you want to work at Harvard and live on campus during the summer, that option's open to you.

The Social Scene

While everyone gets along, I've found white students and black students do things a bit differently when the sun goes down on weekends. Which is to say, at 10:00 p.m. on a Saturday, white kids at Harvard tend to get together in big rooms and drink a lot. Whereas, at 10:00 p.m. on the same Saturday, black kids at Harvard tend to get together in big rooms and dance a lot.

Harvard says there are no fraternities or sororities on campus, but that's not true and Harvard knows it. Greek organizations exist, students pledge, all of that happens, Harvard just refuses to recognize any of it. I don't understand this. Why let Greek organizations exist if you don't want them? And, if you do want them at Harvard, then why won't you just recognize they exist? So silly.

As far as interpersonal relations, students are generally nice to one another within Harvard's gates. But once you step outside into Cambridge, it's a cold, cold world. If you're from the South or the West Coast, expect to be shocked at how people will treat you when you're walking around outside. They won't say hi or greet you in stores. Also, expect to be shocked at the way Harvard students treat non-Harvard students. Meanwhile, Harvard students are nice to other Harvard students and think they're above just about everyone else. I think *they* think they've earned their aloofness. Whatever.

Notable Harvard Alumni Include:
John Adams, second U.S. president
Franklin Delano Roosevelt, thirty-second U.S. president
John Fitzgerald Kennedy, thirty-fifth U.S. president
Henry James, author
W. E. B. DuBois, author, educator
T. S. Eliot, poet

HARVEY MUDD COLLEGE

Founded: 1955

Location: Claremont, CA

Phone: (909) 621-8011

E-mail: admission@hmc.edu

Web site: www.hmc.edu

Number of Undergraduates: 703

Number of Graduate Students: N/A

Cost: Approximately $38,000 per year

Application Deadline: January 15

Early Decision: November 15

Rating:	Notable Majors/Programs:
Very Selective	Engineering, Computer Science, Physics

Size:

● Small   ○ Medium   ○ Large

Location:

○ Urban   ● Suburban   ○ Rural

On a Saturday, students talk about academics:

○ Always   ● Sometimes   ○ Never

Nightlife:

○ Intense   ● Moderate   ○ Laid-back

Politically, Harvey Mudd leans:

● Left   ○ Right   ○ Split

Diversity:

○ High   ○ Low   ● Medium

Students describe Harvey Mudd in five words:
- Engineers and scientists who party
- Way, way better than Caltech

From the School

If you are looking for schools with outstanding reputations for technical science, look no further. You have probably noticed that many are subsets of universities or research institutes. Unlike these places, HMC is an undergraduate college where you will get the full attention of our faculty without standing in line behind graduate students.

—www.hmc.edu

If you're interested in Harvey Mudd College, you may also be interested in:
Caltech, Cornell, Georgia Tech, MIT, Rice, Stanford

Name: Audrey
Hometown: Marin, California
Class Year: Sophomore
Major: Biology
Extracurriculars: Freshman Orientation Director 2005, Freshman Mentor and Peer Counselor for the Office of Institutional Diversity, volunteer tour guide, Planned Parenthood volunteer, aikido, Shotokan karate, and taking care of a pet hamster and a succulent plant
Career Goal: Medical research

How would you describe your school's reputation?

Harvey Mudd is known as one of the top schools in the nation for those who would like to become scientists, mathematicians, and engineers.

Is this reputation accurate?

Absolutely.

What would an admissions officer at your school probably not tell a prospective student?

An admissions officer wouldn't tell students about the big party scene at Harvey Mudd. In short, students subscribe to the "work hard, party hard" philosophy here. So, after spending an entire week doing homework and lab work, and sleeping little, students spend weekends partying all night long.

The Institution

Harvey Mudd is a small school within the larger Claremont Consortium—a group of five undergraduate colleges (Harvey Mudd, Scripps, Pitzer, Claremont McKenna, and Pomona) and two graduate schools (the Claremont Graduate School and the Keck Graduate Institute) that are all incredibly close to one another. The 5Cs, as they are called, share one another's facilities—meaning students can take classes at any of these schools, eat in any of their dining halls, take books out of their libraries, use their student unions and pools, and join their clubs and activities.

Harvey Mudd has a very strict honor code. All students must live by it, and, in return, we're basically trusted to act responsibly on our own with no one looking over our shoulders—we get to take all of our tests at home; we have access to all academic buildings, including research and computer labs twenty-four hours a day; we don't have RAs enforcing dorm rules—we just have proctors with

no authoritative powers. The honor code is an extremely serious part of living at Harvey Mudd. If anyone violates the honor code, there's a judiciary and disciplinary board composed of students who hear cases and dictate (potentially serious) consequences.

Also, our mascot is named Wally Mudd, and he is a "wart," which is this architectural accent that appears all over the school on every building. Weird, right? Our main rival is Caltech, whom we have bested in the past in many ways. Harvey Mudd students love to prank Caltech; one favorite was stealing their giant cannon (in broad daylight, I might add).

The Education

At Harvey Mudd, professors aren't intimidating; they're our mentors and friends. They're deeply devoted to undergraduates. Their office doors are always open, students can see them any time, and there are no classes taught by TAs. If you want to get involved in a serious research project with one of your professors, all you have to do is ask, and when the results are published your name will appear on the same line as your professor's. Outside of the academic sphere professors are our friends. They attend our parties, eat in the dining halls (sometimes with their families), and, once we graduate, they open their houses and homes to us if we ever need a place to stay.

> "Mudd's campus is one block wide by about ten blocks long, with the academic buildings at one end of campus, the dining hall in the middle, and the dorms at the other end of campus. We have two fountains on campus, one a koi pond outside of the main lecture hall and one a small waterfall at the entrance to the Activities Center."
> ✦ Joshua, junior

First semester of freshman year all classes are taken "pass or fail" to encourage students to become involved in activities outside of academics and to give them a chance to adjust to college life. There is adjusting to be done—there's zero grade inflation at Mudd, meaning, for the first time, you're going to fail tests. This is often a shock, and some students drop out of Mudd after studying hard and still failing their first three or four tests and papers. Everyone else realizes that this is simply part of going to an extremely difficult school. They bond over this, work harder, and their grades eventually improve.

Harvey Mudd offers ten majors: biology, chemistry, chemistry-biology joint, computer science, computer science–math joint, engineering, mathematics, mathematical biology joint, physics, or a major of your own design. Everyone is required to do a capstone project before they can graduate, and this is either a year of research culminating in a thesis or a year and a half of work in a clinic, during which a company will sponsor a small group of students to complete a project. Many theses earn students renown as budding scientists, and clinic sponsors will often hire participants from their sponsored teams right after they graduate.

Classes at Harvey Mudd tend to be tiny. Even large lectures (which occur only in core classes) always have smaller recitation sections, where there's a maximum of twenty students per professor. Teachers will know you by name, and closely follow your progress over the course of the semester. You're expected to know the material taught in classes inside and out, an enormous quantity of very difficult homework is often assigned, and tests are taken very seriously and are very, very difficult. Everyone at Mudd is intelligent (most graduated in the top 10 percent of their high school class), but many will get only 50 to 70 percent of the questions correct on an exam.

But your hard work will pay off. The alumni network makes it simple to find summer internships, and well-respected faculty members will bend over backward to get you shining recommendations for summer research applications; and come graduation, we have one of the highest acceptance rates to graduate schools in the country.

The Students

Harvey Mudd is very diverse. Our honor code and our community say that we are all different individuals with different lifestyles, and that we must all respect one another for our choices. All religions are respected, and no one forces their beliefs on anyone else. The minority community is fully integrated. LGBT individuals are also entirely accepted here.

Freshmen, sophomores, juniors, and seniors live together in the dorms all four years and mix a lot, helping one another out. Our dorms really do become like families, partially because everyone is so stressed out from work that they have to stick together. This bizarre form of camaraderie develops between Mudders, and no one else can really understand it.

The Activities

Almost any type of activity a student would like to participate in is available in the 5Cs. For sports, we play in conjunction with Claremont McKenna and Scripps Colleges, forming Claremont-Mudd-Scripps (CMS) sports teams. If you're into ballroom dancing, theater, and music (orchestra, band, small jazz, rock, and ska), there are plenty of opportunities to get involved. There are political clubs and community service groups. Lots of people get together to play poker or bridge weekly, and there are well-attended games of hide-and-go-seek played at midnight on Fridays in the tunnels. LAN parties are also held in the academic computer labs every Saturday night, and HALO/HALO 2 are played on the big screens in the lecture halls for thirty-six-hour stretches on weekends. There are also tons of trips sponsored by the Dean of Students to go into the "real world" to places like Disneyland, the San Diego Zoo, the movies, and baseball games.

Los Angeles is also only a forty-five-minute train ride, so oftentimes students go to concerts in the city or, if they have access to a car, to beautiful downtown Pasadena for dinner. In the winter, it is a half hour drive up Mt. Baldy to go skiing, and when it's slightly warmer the beach is just an hour away. Getting off campus is important to life at Mudd, because it reminds us that there's more to life than just schoolwork.

On campus, when we have time, "hanging out" is a relaxing activity. Since it is beautiful in California, we have couches outside all the dorms, where we sit and work in the afternoons and evenings.

The Social Scene

Honestly, when it's time to have fun, Harvey Mudd is known for throwing the absolute best parties in the 5Cs. Parties are hosted by dorms, and every party gets extensive funding from the dorm's budget and from the Dean of Students. Every party has to have a gimmick that makes it fun for everyone, including those who want to have a good time without getting drunk. Some of our traditional parties include Casemass, a holiday party thrown by Case Dorm where the dorm pays nearly $1,000 to have snow trucked in to cover every inch of the surrounding area, and Trick or Drink, a Halloween party thrown by West Dorm, where, instead of candy, drinks are served to students who knock on doors dressed in costumes. One of our parties, a classy affair called Long Tall Glasses, hosted by North Dorm, was named one of the top ten college parties of the year by *Playboy* magazine.

You can always find alcohol on Mudd's campus, and marijuana is easily accessible too. Not very many students smoke cigarettes, a larger percent smoke marijuana, and I'd say at least 50 percent of students drink every weekend. There are also harder drugs on campus, but they're not very commonly used. And if you're not comfortable with substances, no one will ever force you into anything.

Name: Meghan
Hometown: Mercer Island, Washington
Class Year: Sophomore
Major: Biology
Extracurriculars: Campus tour guide, Society of Women Engineers, Barnstormers Aerospace Club, Mudd Creative Collective Art Club
Career Goal: To be a program manager/lead engineer in an engineering design firm

How would you describe Harvey Mudd reputation?

Mudd's known as *the* place for those rare smart kids who want to study the sciences but also have outgoing, fun personalities.

Is this reputation accurate?

Absolutely. Mudders are far more social and fun than our counterparts at CalTech and MIT.

What would an admissions officer at your school probably not tell a prospective student?

The admissions office definitely downplays the party scene on campus, where dorms throw huge, extravagant bashes.

The Institution

Because Harvey Mudd is so small, it feels like a giant family. You know all the other students. They know you. In your classes, you gets tons of personal attention from faculty members. Even members of the administration will know you by face. When you're having a terrible day and you're overwhelmed with work, it's great to see friendly, smiling faces who will tell you it's all going to be all right. And when all this smallness gets to be too much, you can take classes at other colleges, join sports teams at other colleges, work out in the gym at other colleges, and diversify your social scene. Mudd is in Southern California, where the weather is awesome year-round. Sunny, seventy-degree winter days are something we all take for granted around here.

Our meal plan situation is pretty nice because Mudd is in a partnership with four other Claremont Colleges, so we're able to eat in the dining hall at any campus. This means we have seven decent dining halls to choose from for every meal, and their daily menus are online.

We're a young school, only founded in 1955. That said, we're still ranked the sixteenth best liberal arts college in America. We're also ranked as having the second best undergraduate engineering program in America (at schools where the highest degree is a bachelor's or a masters). Pretty impressive, right? Our Career Services Center is constantly sponsoring job fairs and getting companies to come and recruit students on campus. Last year's job fair was full of such top companies as Microsoft, JPL, Rainbird, Amazon.com, Sandia National Labs, Raytheon, Honeywell, Expedia, the CIA, and tons of others. I am by no means an astounding student here, yet after only my sophomore year I was able to get an engineering internship at Boeing.

The Education

Since academic life at Mudd can be ridiculously rigorous at times, it's not uncommon to hear people talking about their classes at any given hour of any given day. Luckily, the workload tends to bring students together, rather than drive them apart—most everyone here does their homework in groups, which makes things more manageable.

It's not uncommon to find professors in their offices late at night, and you can knock on their doors if you're having trouble with a homework assignment. Relationships with professors tend to become friendships over the course of the years here.

Mudd has pretty intense core requirements, which you'll complete by the middle or end of your sophomore year. Luckily, the core is well planned, and you'll find yourself applying just about everything you learned through the core in your upper-level classes. There's also an important part of the core that differentiates Mudd from other technical schools, and makes us a full liberal arts college—this is the humanities requirement.

Essentially, you're expected to take at least a third of your classes in nontechnical areas. This is part of Mudd's mission statement, to craft well-rounded scientists who are also competent in a broad array of social sciences, humanities, and arts areas—because what's the use of being brilliant if you can't relate to anyone? Most students use the humanities requirement to get off campus and take classes at the other 5Cs, which allows us to expand our social circle.

The Students

Although our campus isn't nearly as diverse as the huge public universities in California, like Berkeley or UCLA, we definitely have many different kinds of people. Our financial aid program is incredible and ensures we have a spread of students from different socioeconomic backgrounds. We also have a good number of Asians, Pacific Islanders, Hispanics, African Americans, and students from overseas, and a noticeable portion of LGBT students and students from different religious backgrounds, and everyone is very accepting.

> "The quality and amount of work that will be expected of you will leave you with very little time to figure out who you are. If you already have a strong sense of self, you'll be okay. But be prepared to work very hard."
>
> ✦ Audrey, senior

The Activities

There are a ton of schools in Southern California, but Mudd mostly interacts with the other Claremont Colleges, particularly when it comes to sports and activities. Music productions, 5Cs football and rugby games, art shows, theatrical performances, and guest speaker events are all always packed. Great people come to the 5Cs to speak and perform. Ray Kurzweil, a leading scientist in the field of artificial intelligence and virtual reality, gave a lecture recently—from his office in Boston! I have no idea how it worked, but he was able to

project a 3-D image of himself into our lecture hall and give the talk. (No joke, it was unbelievable!) Besides college-scheduled activities, I usually leave campus every weekend to go on day trips, to head to the beach, to do a little shopping in San Diego or Pasadena, or to go camping in the desert or rock climbing in Joshua Tree.

The Social Scene

The social scene at Mudd is whatever you want to make of it. There are tons of activities going on every week in the 5Cs, but if you want to stay in your room and play video games with your friends or watch *South Park* or *Futurama*, you can do that too. If you really like to get out there, there are small parties going on every night of the week and big dorm parties on the weekends. All the dorms at Mudd have large central courtyards, which makes partying even easier. And, for our big parties, we get very extravagant. It's not at all uncommon to encounter a mechanical bull, a lemon-batting cage, hundreds of roses, or an insane amount of foam. . . .

Name: Jeremy
Hometown: Big Bear City, California
Class Year: Junior
Major: Mathematics
Extracurriculars: Math Club
Career Goal: High school math teacher

How would you describe Harvey Mudd's reputation?

Harvey Mudd is a small liberal arts college that is also one of the best math-science-engineering schools in the nation.

Is this reputation accurate?

Yes.

What would an admissions officer at your school probably not tell a prospective student?

They might not mention the fact that Mudd has a completely student-run freshman orientation. Literally everything in freshman orientation is decided by us, from the food to the social activities to the talks. This means orientation is fun, inventive, and informative. Nothing extraneous is covered, all the information given is very much on target, because it's Mudders telling other Mudders exactly what they need to know.

The Institution

All the dorms at Mudd are relatively nice (and made out of cinderblocks, like everything else on campus). There are eight dorms: four inner, older dorms and four outer, newer dorms. All dorms are arranged in suites of rooms, with two doubles or two singles sharing a bathroom. The average double is 210 square feet, and the average single is 132 square feet. Students are almost guaranteed singles as juniors and seniors. Half of the dorms have kitchens. Each dorm also has its own personality—we have the jock dorm, the party dorm, the raver dorm, the computer-gamer dorm, and they all have their own friendly rivalries with one another. Because we live on campus together all four years, upperclassmen in the dorms love to hassle and play pranks on freshman and make freshman do work for them. This is all good-hearted fun (for upperclassmen, at least). And the prankees eventually become the prankers. . . .

The Education

Mudd as an institution exists entirely for undergraduates. This means there are no grad students teaching recitation sections, and all the research opportunities go to undergrads. Mudd has a core curriculum that consists of two semesters of chemistry (with lab), three semesters of physics (with lab), four semesters of mathematics, one semester of systems engineering, one semester of biology, one semester of computer science, and two semesters of humanities courses. All of these core classes have to be taken by the time you finish your sophomore year, which means your first two years will be mostly filled with required coursework. Also, because we're a liberal arts college, you have to take ten humanities courses (in addition to the two humanities courses mentioned in the above core). This requirement may not sound too hard to fulfill, but sometimes it's frustrating when there's a math or science class you really want to take but can't because you need to fill your humanities quota. . . .

Mudders do a ridiculous amount of work. A typical courseload is sixteen units, which means five full courses and a four-hour lab. Most courses have homework sets, due weekly or twice weekly, that are usually worth about 25 percent of your grade. Many courses are also project oriented, where you'll have to create something on your own or with a team. On top of all that, there are also papers, midterms,

and presentations. If you're thinking of coming to Mudd, be prepared to work harder than you've ever worked in your life. It rarely lets up.

Lastly, before graduating, every student must complete a thesis project and paper or a clinic project. Those opting for a clinic project (all engineering students *must* take a clinic) complete a real-world project in a team of four to six students. They work with real companies to solve existing problems. The end results vary, but some clinic projects in the past have resulted in patents and have allowed for important networking between students and the companies that sponsored them.

The Students

Mudd is fairly liberal. We have an active LGBT community. And intolerance is (notably) not tolerated here. Dorms are a big part of the social scene. While we don't have fraternities or sororities, the dorms have such well-defined personalities they might as well have Greek letters associated with them. All the dorms are coed and mix underclassmen and upperclassmen. During the first year it's likely that a student will interact with students from lots of other majors and years because of the dorm system.

The Activities

In the 5Cs there are a wide variety of activities to choose from—there are groups and clubs for just about everything, and if a club you want doesn't exist (which is unlikely), you can just start it on your own. Also worth noting, Claremont McKenna hosts talks from notable speakers three times a week at the Athenaeum. The Athenaeum is great: you hear famous people speak and then sit down and have a meal with them. Harvey Mudd puts on similar events under the Nelson Series, bringing science and technology people in to speak. Pomona has a great theater and produces several impressive productions every year.

Lastly, just south of the 5C campuses is the Claremont Village. This is a small collection of shops and restaurants (also a post office, banks, and public library). It's well within walking distance, and students often walk there for a meal out with friends.

The Social Scene

There are parties every weekend, both at Mudd and at the other colleges. I tend to really like the parties at Mudd because I know almost everyone in attendance, but it's also necessary to branch out to the 5Cs. The ratio of guys to girls at Mudd is tough. The fact is, there are about three guys for every girl here. This means that guys have a harder time finding dates, as do lesbians, I suppose. It also means that you don't have as many female friends and you'll probably take at least one class where there's only one girl in the room. Scripps, right next door, is all girls, so that helps, but not having a lot of women around changes the atmosphere slightly in a way that's hard to explain. It's certainly not a sexist atmosphere; it's just different.

Notable Harvey Mudd Alumni Include:
George Nelson, astronaut
Richard Jones, U.S. ambassador
Jonathan Gay, creator, Flash software
Michael G. Wilson, producer, James Bond films
Walt Foley, founder, Accel Technologies
Sage Weil, inventor, WebRing concept

HAVERFORD COLLEGE

Founded: 1833

Location: Haverford, PA

Phone: (610) 896-1350

E-mail: admitme@haverford.edu

Web site: www.haverford.edu

Number of Undergraduates: 1,105

Number of Graduate Students: 0

Cost: Approximately $38,000 per year

Application Deadline: January 15

Early Decision: November 15

Rating:	Notable Majors/Programs:
Most Selective	Biology, Economics, English, Psychology

Size:
● Small ○ Medium ○ Large

Location:
○ Urban ● Suburban ○ Rural

On a Saturday, students talk about academics:
● Always ○ Sometimes ○ Never

Nightlife:
○ Intense ○ Moderate ● Laid-back

Politically, Haverford leans:
● Left ○ Right ○ Split

Diversity:
○ High ○ Low ● Medium

Students describe Haverford in five words:
- Quirky Quaker community of scholars
- Students create honor code here

From the School

Haverford is a coeducational undergraduate liberal arts college founded in 1833 by members of the Religious Society of Friends (Quakers). While the College is not formally affiliated with any religious body today, the values of individual dignity, academic strength, and tolerance upon which it was founded remain central to its character. . . .

—www.haverford.edu

If you're interested in Haverford, you may also be interested in:
Amherst, Bryn Mawr, UPenn, Swarthmore, Wesleyan, Williams

Name: Caitlin
Hometown: West Milford, New Jersey
Class Year: Freshman
Major: Political Science, with a concentration in peace and conflict Studies
Extracurriculars: Women's varsity cross-country; women's varsity indoor track; women's varsity outdoor track; customs person for 2004–05 (our equivalent to an RA)
Career Goal: Politics or law

How would you describe Haverford's reputation?

Haverford is a top-ten liberal arts college near Philadelphia that's often applauded for its student-run structure and open atmosphere.

Is this reputation accurate?

This reputation is most definitely accurate, especially in terms of the college being largely student run. Here the student body undertakes much of the administrative work—at the beginning of each semester we have an event called Plenary, where students get together and establish an honor code and an alcohol policy. Then, the entire student body sticks to the policies created. It's as simple as that. We identify our academic and social objectives for the year, set in place rules that reflect those objectives, and then, as a class, have the maturity and strength of character to do what we say we will.

What would an admissions officer at your school probably not tell a prospective student?

The honor code isn't foolproof. While it is true that the honor code is embraced by the majority of the student body, and that students at Haverford honestly respect one another, and that this is a fantastic place, you're still going to be confronted with occasional indecencies—theft, a shouting match, a big fistfight. We do our best, but we're not perfect.

The Institution

As I mentioned, the honor code influences every corner of student life, from our academic work to the social scene. Teachers allow students to take their exams unproctored because students have promised never to cheat, and teachers believe them. Final exams are self-scheduled. In the same vein, people leave their doors unlocked, their bags outside the dining center.

Haverford also places a big emphasis on public discourse. There is a Comment Board in the campus center and on Haverford's Web site, and students are encouraged to say and write whatever they think and feel, so long as they're confident enough about their words to sign their name to them. Topics of conversation range from campus diversity to athletic rules and change *does* happen based on what's said. A single student can bring up an important issue, it will be fully and honestly debated by most of the campus, and then at Plenary, decisions will be made that reflect the outcome of the debate and that will, one hopes, make things better.

Haverford offers the best of all possible worlds. We have the hustling, bustling city of Philadelphia within reach, but our campus is beautiful, peaceful, and calm, situated on acres and acres of land. (We have a nationally recognized arboretum—originally landscaped by William Carvill.) We can take classes at Bryn Mawr, Swarthmore, and the University of Pennsylvania, so you never feel claustrophobic or academically stifled. Students are academically involved and actively engaged with the world, and we're also from every corner of that world that you can imagine (my roommate is from Tobago!). We have constant interaction between faculty and students, and upper- and underclassmen. Haverford is unlike anywhere else because what happens here matters. I am becoming exactly who I want to be, while surrounded by people who care enough to help me on my way.

> "They call it the Haverbubble for a good reason—everything is so safe! We leave laptops out in the library, we leave backpacks in the foyer of the dining center and nothing gets stolen. The honor code really is taken seriously."
>
> ✦ Foster, sophomore

The Education

One of the best things about being at a small school is the accessibility of the professors. Many live on campus, and if they don't, they live very close to it. As a first year, I've gone to professors' homes to meet with them on more than a few occasions, had dinner with their family, played with their kids, and then headed into their living room to discuss political theory late into the night.

Another great thing about academics here is the lack of competition; we're all motivated by our individual drive to learn new things and understand the world around us—not because we want to graduate with a better GPA than the next student. We take what we learn in the classroom everywhere we go, and there is rarely a meal or movie that can escape a philosophical or moral discussion at Haverford.

The Students

Haverford tends to attract down-to-earth (but intellectually hungry) students who are more interested in people's beliefs, and how their beliefs influence their actions, than they are in the size of someone else's wallet or the size their own wallet may someday be. In other words, the life of the mind rules here—preprofessionalism and social climbing is looked down upon.

And because it's the mind that rules, Haverford is open and generally accepting of all avenues of student life—those who are minorities and those who are not, those who are straight and those who are gay, those who are athletes and those who aren't . . . the list could go on and on. Nearly everyone gets along at Haverford, and no one is ever discriminated against.

> "This is a small school, so not many recruiters come to the campus to hire students for post-graduation jobs. . . ."
> ✦ Jacob, sophomore

The Activities

Haverford is right near Philly, and nearby scores of other schools. So when you exhaust the things to do at Haverford, there's no lack of other places to go. The students recently organized a bus to provide transportation to and from Philadelphia on weekends, free of charge.

There are countless student orgs: the Republican and Democratic groups that meet regularly, along with several other political groups that run the spectrum in between. The *Bi-Co* newspaper, printed in conjunction with students at Bryn Mawr, is really popular. The Sex and Gender Alliance (SAGA) meets on a regular basis; and there is a group called Street Outreach that travels into Philadelphia weekly to feed the homeless.

The Social Scene

Parties at Haverford are a big part of the social scene, but, like I said, there's so much out there between Haverford, Swarthmore, Bryn Mawr, UPenn and Philly. We don't have any frats or sororities, so parties tend to be smaller and held in dorms, houses, or apartments.

Name: Peg
Hometown: Sante Fe, New Mexico
Class Year: Junior
Major: Sociology
Extracurriculars: Student Council, Women's Center, yearbook, Haverfest Committee
Career Goal: Sex-crimes prosecutor/corporate litigator

How would you describe Haverford's reputation?

Most would say Haverford is fiercely intellectual. Liberal. Pacifist. Ruled by the honor code.

Is this reputation accurate?

Sure. To elaborate, our honor code is life altering—it's really made me change the way I think about everyday social situations. Haverford kids are, as I said, fiercely intellectual and liberal (hippie-vegan types). We're also kind, accepting, and friendly. I'm the white upper-middle-class blond-sorority-girl type. At first glance, you wouldn't think I was the typical Haverford student. But at Haverford, no one judges you on the first glance—my friends are so diverse, my views have been changed by them on a multitude of issues, and I've never been happier.

What would an admissions officer at your school probably not tell a prospective student?

Haverford is small—only 1,100 students—and while most of the time it's great that you get to know every single person on campus, at times it can feel claustrophobic. If you are the type who wants constant excitement from college, if you love to always have the chance to meet new people at parties, Haverford might not be for you.

The Institution

Ninety-eight percent of the time, I love my school. Everyone here is so uniformly intelligent and open. I come from Phoenix, and people are a lot more closed-minded out there. The party scene at my high school was full of chauvinistic jokes and stories of terrible date rapes. You'll never find anything like that at Haverford. The men here, even when drunk, are intelligent, respectful, kind, and understanding. They're like some new, evolved species of man. The Haver-man. I'm a big fan!

> "Students here rarely admit to wanting jobs that will make money. Instead, they want to pursue opportunities that will change the world."
>
> ✦ Dorian, senior

The Education

Here are some interesting numbers: at Haverford, 100 percent of my classes have been taught by full professors. Ninety-nine percent of my classes have had fewer than twenty students. Half of those classes had fewer than ten students. The largest class you could possibly take at Haverford would have only seventy-five students, and you will call half of your professors by their first name.

And on the more qualitative end, everyone at Haverford is a nerd, whether they look the part or not. It's refreshing. This is a campus full of students with an honest passion for learning. And the numbers I cited above mean that that passion will be accommodated by brilliant professors on a daily basis.

The Students

"Most students at Haverford are Democrats, but they won't be when they get older." That's the running joke here. We're all open-minded and intellectual. But when you dig a bit and get to know Haverford students' backgrounds, you find a disproportionate number of us with upper-class, incredibly successful parents. Sometimes "astronomically successful" comes to mind. So even though we all profess liberal views, there's a vague suspicion that more than a few of us will, somewhere down the line, sell out and conform to our parents' ideals, our own boarding-school backgrounds, and even turn into Republicans.

Nonetheless, everyone reads the *Bi-Co* (our student publication), we have a liberal protest or rally at least once a month, and have a very active LGBT group. We also have BSU, Sons of Africa, a great Women's Center, Men Against Sexual Assault and Rape. Unlike other campuses, apathy isn't even close to a problem. . . .

The Activities

Haverford is part of something that we call a Tri-Co. This essentially means that we're very close with Bryn Mawr College and Swarthmore College—we can attend each other's classes, as well as parties, events, and rallies. . . . We're also able to take classes at UPenn. Though sports aren't huge at Haverford, lacrosse and baseball are popular, and our cross-country team is award winning. The rest of our teams are just okay. But that's fine by us; we have plenty of fun just playing. About 50 percent of campus is involved in at least one sport.

And at 3:00 a.m. on any given night, I'd say everyone on campus is still awake. That's generally right when people come home from the library, and they're gossiping with friends on their hall about their day and organizing a late-night run to the WaWa for food.

The Social Scene

If you're a freshman, and it's Friday night, here's a likely gameplan—the library closes at 9:00 p.m. on Fridays, so you're going to get in every last bit of studying that you can, then you'll head back to your room and study just a little more. At about 11:00 p.m., you'll start to pre-party. In your dorm, the hallway is crowded, kids are grabbing beers and downing shots of vodka, the music is turned up, and everyone is wearing their most fun clothing. When you're good and ready, you'll head out at midnight, and you'll probably stay out until 4:00 a.m. More likely than not, you're going to head to Yarnall or Drinker, which are the two party houses on campus. And you're going to have an absolute blast.

> "Haverkid's were all quasi-nerds in high school, whether we were in the closet about it or not."
>
> ✦ Sarah, junior

On Saturday, you'll work and go shopping during the day, then party again that night. Once the end of the school year rears its head, people party even harder. I'd say most of Haverford students drink, and a fair number smoke weed. There are harder drugs too—just as there are on any college campus—but I go out a lot and I only see harder drugs once in a blue moon. So that's Haverford. Work hard, think hard, dream hard during the week. Then have as much fun as you could hope for on the weekend!

Name: Sam
Hometown: Princeton, New Jersey
Class Year: Freshman
Major: Art history/religion
Extracurriculars: College Democrats, honor code orientator, copresident, Outdoors Club, Photography Club, lacrosse goalie
Career Goal: I'd like to get my PhD in art history so I can either teach or work in a museum or private foundation.

How would you describe Haverford's reputation?

I've heard people call Haverford "an elite school where all anyone ever does is work."

Is this reputation accurate?

I have been nothing but impressed by the caliber of the teaching, and of the student body, at Haverford. I have friends at similar colleges, like Williams and Amherst, and I'm convinced Haverford is at least as good as the number one and number two ranked liberal arts schools. (And Haverford is waaaaaay better than Swarthmore could ever hope to be . . . take *that,* rival school!) We do work hard. Sometimes we'll have three papers and an exam due in a three-day period, and we won't see the light of day for seventy-two hours straight. But, for the most part, we do find time to hang out, play Frisbee, go into Philly.

What would an admissions officer at your school probably not tell a prospective student?

Because we set our own rules here, thanks to the honor code, we've deemed it okay to drink on campus. Campus security will never bust you for drinking a beer at a party. Students can pretty much drink whenever and wherever they please, and often the school will provide the alcohol for free. Surprisingly, this policy is rarely abused, and if anything, it allows students to feel more comfortable when they're drunk and need to call security to help them out. Generally, drugs and alcohol are our own business here—we pledge to deal with both responsibly, and the university allows us to live up to that pledge.

The Institution

Haverford is a pretty special place. Our campus is beautiful, our students are idealistic, and we're just minutes from Philadelphia, so it's easy to take advantage of the city both in the context of our classes and in the context of our social lives. At Haverford, we debate endlessly, philosophize constantly, and try to figure out life's big questions. Some people talk about the "Haverbubble," the feeling that we've created a little utopian community on our campus that's very unlike the "real world." I think it's great that Haverford is set apart from the "real world" in that everyone is genuine, intelligent, and caring. Now all we have to do is expand the Haverbubble, make its ideals spread to Philadelphia and the rest of Pennsylvania, the rest of America, and the rest of the world. . . .

> "Haverford doesn't have the greatest-looking guys. We have some gems, but everyone fights over them like crazed animals."
>
> ✦ Essie, sophomore

The Education

You can't escape academics at Haverford, and that's the way we like it. Just the other day, I stood on the sidelines at my lacrosse practice and had a great discussion with a teammate about race in America. There's also almost a complete lack of competition here. Because of the honor code, we're not allowed to talk or ask about someone else's grades. This caused a classmate to once note, "Because I don't know how any of you are doing in this class, I treat you all as my equals." That's how it should be.

I'd say the sciences and economics are our strongest departments at Haverford. We don't have an art history major. Bryn Mawr does. So I'm doing my major through Bryn Mawr . . . we're interestingly intertwined, HC and BMC. Look into the ways this might work to your advantage.

The Students

Haverford and Bryn Mawr produce a newspaper together, the *Bi-Co News,* and everyone on both campuses reads it. Most people read the *New York Times,* too. We lean to the left here. Heavily. A lot of us call ourselves Democrats, but could really be classified as members of the Green Party. And at Haverford, everyone hangs out, whether you're an underclassmen or upperclassmen or whatever. We all mix. I don't even know what grade some of my good friends are in.

The Activities

One of the most prominent groups on campus is STAND, the club for social activism. They send buses to rallies in Georgia and D.C., and a large proportion of students get involved and protest and scream and yell about their favorite new cause. Aside from STAND, a very high number of Haverford students are involved in club or varsity athletics, and often Haverford athletes are the smartest kids here. There are no "dumb jocks" on this campus, just active, well-rounded, sporty kids.

And every fall and spring we have Plenary, where the whole campus gets together and passes resolutions that, for the remainder of the term, we'll abide by. We make our own rules, our own honor code and alcohol policy. And no faculty members are present at either Plenary—they trust us to pass rules that are fair and that make sense. We do everything we can to live up to their trust.

The Social Scene

Like I said earlier, our alcohol policy is really cool. At Haverford we think age is an arbitrary way to judge one's readiness to drink. It's more a question of maturity, and we all pledge to drink maturely. At Haverford, if you pledge something, you mean it. Haverford has a certain relationship with the local police, so what happens on campus stays on campus, and we're free to do things like make our own rules about drinking.

Notable Haverford Alumni Include:
John Whitehead, assistant secretary of state
Dave Barry, author, comedian
Juan Williams, author, reporter
Joseph Taylor, Nobel Laureate in physics
Gerald M. Levin, chairman and CEO, Time Warner Inc.
Norman Pearlstine, editor in chief, Time Inc.

HENDRIX COLLEGE

Founded: 1876

Location: Conway, AR

Phone: (501) 329-6811

E-mail: adm@hendrix.edu

Web site: www.hendrix.edu

Number of Undergraduates: 1,040

Number of Graduate Students: 0

Cost: Approximately $22,500 per year

Application Deadline: Rolling Admissions

Early Action: December 1

Rating:	Notable Majors/Programs:
Selective	Biology, Psychology, Social Sciences, Business

Size:
- ● Small   ○ Medium   ○ Large

Location:
- ○ Urban   ● Suburban   ○ Rural

On a Saturday, students talk about academics:
- ● Always   ○ Sometimes   ○ Never

Nightlife:
- ○ Intense   ● Moderate   ○ Laid-back

Politically, Hendrix leans:
- ● Left   ○ Right   ○ Split

Diversity:
- ○ High   ● Low   ○ Medium

Students describe Hendrix in five words:
- Beautiful libarts community in Arkansas
- Eccentric, challenging, small, well-kept secret

From the School

Hendrix students come to live and learn in an environment that challenges conventional wisdom and common assumptions. We value the individualism and the distinctiveness that each person brings to our community. Whether you are interested in our extraordinary undergraduate research opportunities, our thriving social life, our nationally known faculty, or our students' academic achievements, you are sure to find what you are looking for at Hendrix.

—www.hendrix.edu

If you're interested in Hendrix, you may also be interested in:
Antioch, Davidson, Emory, Lewis & Clark, Pitzer, Washington U. in St. Louis

Name: Tyler
Hometown: Frederick, Maryland
Class Year: Sophomore
Major: History
Extracurriculars: Hillel, Russian Club, Historical Society
Career Goal: Professor of history

How would you describe Hendrix's reputation?

Hendrix is known in Arkansas and throughout the South as the finest college in the state and one of the best in the region. It's less well known elsewhere, but this is changing.

Is this reputation accurate?

If it were located in the Northeast, Hendrix would be much more well known and more difficult to get into. This little liberal arts college is a well-kept secret, but it won't be for long, especially if the administration has its way.

What would an admissions officer at Hendrix probably not tell a prospective student?

I found admissions officers reasonably forthcoming, but they did gloss over things like Internet connectivity (and how often outages occur) and the limited friendliness and accessibility of some administrative staff (like residence life).

The Institution

I regard Hendrix as my home—and Conway as my prison. It's in a dry county, and the town is not exactly intellectually stimulating. Most locals regard Hendrix students with a mixture of disdain and apathy. Letters to the editor of the local paper have expressed outrage at students' apparent unpatriotic desire to oppose war. But on campus there is definitely a close feeling of community. It's small but not so small that you have to constantly see people you dislike. I chose Hendrix for a number of reasons. Hendrix gave me a great scholarship, but above all, I came because I felt that at Hendrix I'd be a part of something. Hendrix is, more than anything, a warm, supportive, and friendly community. I feel comfortable here. As a Yankee (or what passes for one in Arkansas—I'm from Maryland), it certainly took a little bit of adjustment, but not too much. Arkansas can feel a little isolated, but you get used to hanging out on campus (and really, how often do you end up leaving most campuses anyway?), and there's plenty to do in Little Rock as well. It's also a really beautiful state.

The Education

Students don't generally compete with each other—most would prefer to collaborate on papers and support each other. When students sit around outside class, you can generally find them discussing academic topics. The faculty is the single best thing about Hendrix: the professors are never too busy for students—their primary goal is teaching, not getting published or becoming stars in their field (although many of them do and are). There are no classes taught by TAs and no grad program to distract professors. The distribution requirements are demanding, but they truly do complement the "unto the whole person" motto (although Journeys, the required freshman course, is boring and basically useless).

The Students

In my experience with other colleges there are really bright people and really dumb people everywhere—from Ivy League schools to community colleges. I couldn't rate the intelligence of my peers at Hendrix; what's more important is that they have a real desire to learn. And that's what I respect about them most.

> "Hendrix used to be this little hidden gem, but the secret's out, and we're getting a ton more people from out of state."
> ✦ Dan, senior

There are plenty of student activists, and Hendrix students are generally left-leaning and concerned about the world, but rarely concerned enough to actually do anything. The minority of conservatives generally perceive themselves as persecuted by the rest of the student body, and perhaps there is some truth to this. But people are generally very civil even if they disagree. LGBT students are widely accepted at Hendrix, although it's untrue that the school has an abnormally large gay population. They're just more comfortable to express it here. Students tend to be reasonably well informed about campus issues but are often ignorant of news in the outside world.

The Activities

Many students participate in community service activities through VAC (Volunteer Action Center). A lot of Hendrix students are religious, although not necessarily in a fundamentalist manner. I personally helped to found a Hillel (Jewish student organization) at Hendrix my freshman year. I have found the college chaplain and administration extremely helpful in all that Hillel has done.

The Social Scene

People party on the weekends and sometimes during the week as well. Different groups have their own parties, but the whole student body comes together at many events, and everything is very inclusive. There is no Greek life, so students feel comfortable partying together. Though it's true that students feel *very* strongly about their own dorm's "personality," and sometimes this can take on a ridiculous fratlike quality. People at Hendrix are extremely friendly. They will say hi even if they don't know you (although virtually everyone knows each other anyway).

Name: Lori Ann
Hometown: Conway, Arkansas
Class Year: Freshman
Major: I'm designing my own interdisciplinary study major called Urban Ministries. It combines a lot of religion and sociology classes, as well as some from the psychology and politics departments.
Extracurriculars: Future Preachers of America, flute choir, pep band
Career Goal: Urban ministries/missions—I want to work with at-risk youth in an inner-city setting. I'm not planning on making much money, but I am planning on doing something that matters a lot more than material possessions and social status.

> "Since I was premed, I thought that I would spend all my time in science classes. However, Hendrix provided me with the opportunity to build my own major."
>
> ✦ Ali, senior

How would you describe your school's reputation?

Hendrix is well known for strong academics in the arts and humanities, and less well known for its strengths in math and science. Hendrix is also known for its liberal population; Hendrix students make sure their voices are heard on issues important to them. I suppose a lot of Arkansans consider Hendrix weird.

Is this reputation accurate?

About the academics, I think so. Hendrix is a very strong school academically. As for being weird, that just depends on what you mean by weird. We may not be mainstream Americans, but thank goodness for that!

What aspect of your school would a prospective student not see on a campus tour?

There's a lot of partying here on campus. I guess Hendrix may even have somewhat of a reputation for that . . . but you won't see it on a tour.

The Institution

Everyone who visits Hendrix comments on how beautiful the campus is. The grass, flowers, and trees are well kept. It's fairly small; I can walk from my residence hall, Raney, which is on one end of campus, to Trishemann, a building pretty much on the other side of campus, in five minutes or less. The new art buildings are a bit farther away, but I haven't had any experience with them. The campus is also full of cute little squirrels, who love the campus as much as we do. Arkansas humidity is hard to bear, but the well-air-conditioned buildings keep you cool, sometimes too cool.

Hendrix is for the person who is willing to step outside his or her comfort zone and is unafraid to meet challenges. It's also for people who are willing to get help rather than go it alone. There's a real sense of support and community. On your birthday, the workers in the dining hall get everyone to sing "Happy Birthday" to you, and they bring you a cake to share with your friends. And then your friends throw you in the fountain!

Campus security is really nice. You can call for an escort if at any time you feel unsafe. I've never felt uncomfortable walking around campus at two in the morning, though. It's a pretty safe place. Arkansas humidity is harsh, but the beautiful campus and well-air-conditioned buildings make it bearable.

The Education

Friends and I talk constantly about interesting stuff we've been learning in class while just sitting at lunch or hanging out in the Burrow (the student hangout). I've learned a lot about science, business, and history through my roommate, boyfriend, and neighbors; I've never taken a class in any of those subjects! Now, academics isn't all we talk about, but you'd be surprised at how often things we've learned in class do find their way into our conversation. I've even eaten with professors, sometimes talking about class, sometimes not. I love the professors and the classes here at Hendrix, and I really like the advising system here. Also, the career center isn't well publicized, but it's there in Buhler and open to help you out! There are so many internships and jobs, career-relevant workshops, and mission trips that are readily available.

> "My two favorite things about Hendrix: (1) We don't have a Greek system; (2) we have an annual campuswide toga party anyway."
>
> ✦ Marcus, junior

The Students

Hendrix students always seem to be getting involved. Fair trade, environmental issues, homelessness, and so forth, are on the minds of the students and the faculty, who are often involved with student organizations, too. Hendrix hosts a lot of foreign exchange students, and each semester I've gotten to know several students from backgrounds very different from mine. Students here are from all different backgrounds. When I went to work in an inner-city church in Chicago for a spring-break mission trip, I went with a girl from Russia, one from Finland, someone from New Hampshire, some people from Texas, and just three or so from Arkansas. There's a group for everyone here, and the great thing is, you're not going to be restricted to one group.

The Activities

Buildings are all open until at least midnight. I know I've been in the music building until midnight, and once I went in the Lilly Office at Mills to the little prayer room after 1:00 a.m. The Burrow is usually open, and it has board games and things. Different groups at Hendrix, like SoCo (the social committee) and MDC (multicultural development committee), plan lots of events throughout the year that are fun and free. The Hendrix

Olympix, at which we mock other schools' Greek systems by pretending to divide into fraternities and sororities (Hendrix doesn't really have any) and compete throughout the week. There's also Campus Kitty, a giant fund-raising week that everyone, faculty included, gets involved in. We don't bring in big-name bands, but smaller groups come in often, and all performances are free!

The Social Scene

For a dry county, people do party a lot. I'm not into that, though, and don't feel any pressure to join in. There are a kazillion other things to do on campus, and they're always free. Sometimes we'll go to the Burrow (there's food, pool, table shuffleboard, a TV, couches). Downtown is less than five minutes' walk from campus, so late at night (or really any time) we'll walk to the little coffee shop, Something Brewing, where they have outdoor movie showings and Toad Suck Daze, like an annual fair, or we'll just walk around and shop.

Name: Barrett
Hometown: Batesville, Arkansas
Class Year: Sophomore
Majors: English and politics
Extracurriculars: Hendrix Pre-Law Society, Hendrix Model UN, Hendrix Big Buddy program, United Methodist Youth Leadership scholar, resident assistant
Career Goal: I want to practice law in Little Rock, Arkansas.

How would you describe Hendrix's reputation?

Hendrix has a very prestigious reputation. We are trying hard to become known nationally, since our professors are nationally ranked. Hendrix has something of a controversial reputation within Arkansas—it is a very liberal environment in the middle of a conservative state.

Is this reputation accurate?

Yes. Hendrix is a prominent educational institution. The "controversial" reputation of Hendrix is deserved, as it strives to be a liberal learning environment.

What would an admissions officer at Hendrix probably not tell a prospective student?

We're fairly up front and honest, but prospective students might arrive here without realizing how liberal Hendrix is. I do not personally see this as a bad thing, but I know some people do.

The Institution

I think all types of people can be happy at Hendrix. This small, liberal arts atmosphere strives to provide students with as many opportunities as possible. Hendrix is a college of about 1,100 students on a really nice, safe, and small campus. Hendrix is a very accepting institution, where students can be whatever and whomever they want to be; this is a great environment to explore who you are. We have a diverse crowd, and so the level of school spirit is dependent upon whom you talk to.

There are many housing options open to Hendrix students. The college owns apartments that are technically on campus, but aren't really in the middle of campus life. There are two male residence halls, three female residence halls, and one coed hall. Hendrix also has four New Houses, which have a GPA requirement, and one is alcohol free. Every dorm here has an identity, which compensates for our lack of a Greek system.

> "The Shirttails Serenade is my favorite tradition. Girls and guys alike dress up in guys' white dress shirts and usually boxers, and go to each other's dorms and sing for each other."
>
> ✦ Lindsey, sophomore

The Education

Hendrix is not a very competitive campus. Some premed students do take their standing in certain classes more seriously, as some have bell-curve grading, but for the most part, a Hendrix education is about the individual. Classes are pretty well a mixture of discussion and lecture, and usually have around ten to thirty students. Depending on the class, I find myself spending a reasonable chunk of free time doing work. Hendrix has endowments for undergrad research; I know we have grad school programs here, but those people are not really a part of campus life. We have *lots* of opportunities to study abroad. Hendrix emphasizes outside learning and is currently investigating a system that would almost require every undergrad to try some sort of outside learning experience. All majors require a thesis or project for seniors. The

general graduation requirements guarantee that a student receives a decent liberal education—you cannot be effective in the humanities if you do not understand how the other side works. All classes are engaging, to some degree; professors challenge students to think critically, and most classes expose students to a wide range of ideas.

If you are premed, Hendrix is definitely for you. We have a lot of premed students, and I believe our acceptance rate into UAMS (University of Arkansas Medical School) is the highest in the state.

The Students

Hendrix students are an interesting group and are typically open-minded and diverse by nature. Hendrix students strive to be aware of global and national issues of importance. Our campus was talking about free-trade coffee *long* before Starbuck's picked up on it. No matter where you come from (a lot of students are from Arkansas, but a rapidly increasing number are coming from out of state), there will be a Hendrix student that will challenge your thinking. There are more Democrats on this campus, or at least liberal-leaning people, than there are conservatives. However, this just makes the conservatives more outspoken.

The Activities

Hendrix has a group for seemingly every area of interest. No club is exclusive here, except for the national honors societies, of course. We have a school newspaper that everyone reads, *The Profile*. The Student Senate has an unprecedented amount of power and influence in school affairs, and it budgets a huge amount of money annually to its various committees. Students play an integral role in policy development and general student life. There is a lot of volunteering on campus. Every Saturday there is a Volunteer Action Committee event. And as an officer in the Pre-Law Society, I have been able to network with professional attorneys and judges throughout this region. I have also had a chance to refine my own search for a field of law. Our sports program is probably our weakest area, as no scholarships are given for sports.

The Social Scene

There are two other colleges in Conway: UCA, a very large state school, and Central Baptist College, an extremely small private school. There is as much or as little interaction with them as you desire.

Dorm life is dependent upon where you live. I live in the "party dorm," and so I see a lot of partying. Hendrix parties every Friday. Social life is diverse and fairly rich. There is always something to do, and in a number of varying social circles. People form their own cliques, but we are an accepting campus. Alcohol is widely used here and is officially tolerated in rooms when the consumer is twenty-one and the door is closed. There are *no fraternities or sororities*. And keep in mind, Hendrix has something like a two-to-one ratio of guys to girls.

Notable Hendrix Alumni Include:

Craig Leipold, owner, Nashville Predators

Harry Meyer Jr., developer of the vaccine for German measles

Jo Luck, president and CEO, Heifer International

Kevin Wilson, playwright

Mary Ann Gwinn, Pulitzer Prize winner for journalism

Sarah Caldwell, first woman to conduct the Metropolitan Opera

COLLEGE OF THE HOLY CROSS

Founded: 1843

Location: Worcester, MA

Phone: (508) 793-2011

E-mail: admissions@holycross.edu

Web site: www.holycross.edu

Number of Undergraduates: 2,750

Number of Graduate Students: 0

Cost: Approximately $38,500 per year

Application Deadline: January 15

Early Decision: December 15

Rating:	Notable Majors/Programs:
Very Selective	Social Sciences, Premed

Size:

○ Small   ● Medium   ○ Large

Location:

○ Urban   ● Suburban   ○ Rural

On a Saturday, students talk about academics:

○ Always   ● Sometimes   ○ Never

Nightlife:

● Intense   ○ Moderate   ○ Laid-back

Politically, Holy Cross leans:

○ Left   ● Right   ○ Split

Diversity:

○ High   ○ Low   ● Medium

Students describe Holy Cross in five words:
- Inebriated, religious, well-rounded, hard-working, steep!
- Very Irish Catholic. Very Massachusetts.

From the School

Holy Cross is an exclusively undergraduate college with a liberal arts curriculum and an active Jesuit culture of learning and faith. Our faculty members are dedicated to teaching you to think critically, make connections among disparate ideas, and communicate effectively with others. As you learn these skills, which will serve you throughout your life, you also discover a sense of purpose and direction in the world.

—www.holycross.edu

If you're interested in Holy Cross, you may also be interested in:
Boston College, Connecticut College, Georgetown, Gettysburg, Notre Dame, Trinity

Name: Bron
Hometown: West Hartford, Connecticut
Class Year: Freshman
Major: Biology/premed
Extracurriculars: Bishop Healy Multicultural Society, Black Student Union, INDIA, Multicultural Peer Education, Biology Society
Career Goal: Neurosurgeon, psychologist

How would you describe Holy Cross's reputation?

The name kinda throws you off at first. Some people think it's some intensely religious college. But it's got a huge drinking reputation. And of course, it's known for its men's basketball team.

> "'Men and Women for Others' is the school motto, and it shows. Volunteering and the urban development program are very popular."
>
> ✦ Jane, senior

Is this reputation accurate?

The religious part, I don't know. Sunday's an "I'm-sorry-God-I've-been-so-caught-up-in-school-and-chillin'-with-my-friends-and-oh-yeah-getting-wasted-for-the-last-three-nights-that-I-couldn't-find-an-earlier-time-to-pray" kind of day. It depends on the individual, more than anything. The booze reputation is pretty accurate, but that applies to any other college that's in a city half as "exciting" as Worcester. The basketball team is amazing.

What would an admissions officer at Holy Cross probably not tell a prospective student?

One thing any AO would not tell a prospective would probably have something to do with the two billion hours of homework and studying we have to do every week. The workload at HC is insane. Also, when a prospective comes here, usually for an open house or some kind of organized tour, the food they serve is amazing. Don't be fooled.

The Institution

The winter season lasts for eight *long* months in Worcester and Mount Saint James. Get used to it. The cost of living is also ridiculously expensive, not only because we live in Worcester, which really has no exceptional entertainment to offer, but also because we seriously must have only about six or seven months of actual school. We basically pay HC to go on vacation every month. Of course, we don't complain about the breaks, just the tuition.

Holy Cross is only about 2,700 students strong, which is great at times (small classes, easier to get to know people), but it can also be frustrating. It's practically the job of an HC student to know everything about everyone on campus. However, I chose this school over BC (Boston College—a very similar school with respect to reputation, academics, and Jesuit identity) simply because it's so small and the lectures have a maximum of forty-five students.

The Education

Holy Cross emphasizes "cooperation over competition" in its catalog, but I wish I could see more of that. All the students here were in the top 5 to 10 percent of their high school classes, and they want to stay up there when they come to college. Coming to HC has made me a much more easygoing person. I'm more chill about a lot of things that would've had me flipping in the past. In high school, I'd expect nothing below a 95 on anything. Here, I'm happy with a 70 on a chem exam.

Most of the professors that I've had, I'd say 95 percent, are very passionate and knowledgeable about their field of study. They know what they're talking about and try their best to help us understand. If we don't, they always encourage us to come to office hours and make study plans with them. They take a pretty active interest in their students, as far as their courses go, and some professors really become good friends.

The workload is crazy. But not all of us talk about classes on Saturday nights—a lot of us here aren't sober enough. We do so much work during the week that we like to keep all of that out of our minds for at least one day.

> "The best bathroom on campus is in the basement of Dinand Library. It's called the Ozzy stall, a tribute to Ozzy Osborne."
>
> ✦ Colin, freshman

The Students

Most of the students here are from upper-class, more privileged families. You can usually tell this by looking at the parking lot, which is packed with really nice cars that most students received as presents from their parents. I don't think there's an "average" student, but most people would say that the campus is predominantly white Irish Catholic and preppy (Abercrombie & Fitch), which is true. However, we've got a large percentage of minority students as well, and they add greatly to the diversity at HC. As in most other small colleges, the minorities tend to stick together—you'll see this in the dining hall: most of the black, Hispanic, and Asian kids will be sitting if not together, then in the same general area, while others will be scattered throughout. Fortunately, we have no frats or sororities.

The Activities

Athletics are a huge part of campus life, especially baseball (not the school teams, but the Yankees and the Red Sox) and our men's basketball team. The biggest organizations on campus are SGA (Student Government Association), CAB (Campus Activities Board), and BSU (Black Student Union). They end up bringing in most of the speakers or putting on the biggest events, although other clubs, usually the multicultural organizations, contribute to campus activities too.

If I'm up at three in the morning on a Wednesday, the only reason would be because of all my homework, whether it's religion, English, or preparing for biology or chemistry lecture or lab.

The Social Scene

The weekends at HC are said to run from Thursdays to Tuesdays. Everyone goes clubbing on Thursdays, which was a little weird to me initially, because I thought that's what weekends are for. But most people arrange their schedule so that they don't have any early morning classes on Friday, and can go out Thursday night to any of the big clubs in Worcester without having to be back until early Friday morning.

There are definitely different types of parties on campus. A lot of the "smaller" athletes—soccer, field hockey, lacrosse, and track—tend to go the sports houses on a nearby street, and all the girls who obsess over those male athletes follow them there. It's like having two different sections in a club, one for techno music and the other for rap, hip-hop, and R&B. That's basically the categories that the parties—and the students—break into.

Worcester also has something like nine to twelve other schools around here, although I can't name half of them. We've got WPI, Clark, and Worcester State, to name a few, and because of open-invite parties, plenty of HC students go to at least one of them over the course of the year.

Name: Courtlyn
Hometown: Bremerton, Washington
Class Year: Junior
Major: Economics with a minor in German
Extracurriculars: Cocaptain, Holy Cross Color Guard; Pep Band (alto sax)
Career Goal: My dream is to teach economics at a private college.

How would you describe Holy Cross's reputation?

There unfortunately is the belief that Holy Cross students are a bunch of white Irish Catholics whose conservative nature oppresses anyone different.

Is this reputation accurate?

This is not the case. Holy Cross is an open environment that accepts you whether you are black, white, purple, gay, straight, unsure . . . anything. It is true that there are some bigoted people on this campus, but there is plenty of support to overcome their cowardly ways. There are a bunch of us liberal types who give the conservatives a run for their money.

> "I'm half-Indian, and half-Irish, but I grew up in an all-white suburb feeling very white and suburban. But here, because I have tanned skin and a nose ring, everyone expects me to identify as a minority student—even though I'm a fan of the Irish Catholic feel, and that was a reason I came here."
> ✦ Mark, sophomore

What would an admissions officer at Holy Cross probably not tell a prospective student?

The Admissions Office will lead you to believe that Holy Cross students are all friends—but there is a select group of spoiled, superficial people who will judge you on how many Coach purses you have or what kind of car you drive. But spoiled, superficial people exist everywhere in America, so Holy Cross is no exception.

The Institution

Holy Cross is the campus that never sleeps: at any time of the day you can find a protest, a party, a sports game, or a study group. The campus strongly supports the different athletic teams, either through posters, giveaways, clothes, or attending various sporting events in elaborate costumes and face paint. The student body is always clad in the purple and white. Nine out of every ten students is wearing something that says "Holy Cross" every day. One tradition at this predominantly Irish school is the annual St. Patrick's Day T-shirt competition. The sports teams all compete to come up with the coolest shirt that combines Holy Cross, Ireland, and drinking. The result is a green, purple, and white campus come March 17th.

The campus is gorgeous, and as for its layout: "Freshman 15"? What's that? After going up your 20 millionth stair of the week, you'll be asking the same question. And the small size makes for a community feel, especially within your major. Also, be forewarned: we get lots of snow here and the winters are cold.

The Education

People thrive off the competition at Holy Cross. When you attend a prestigious school that is known for large workloads, you can't escape competing not only with other schools, but with fellow students. That said, it is impossible to not become friends with your classmates. Classes are small, tight-knit, and you are also guaranteed a quality education because you learn from only the best: the professors themselves, who are involved in all facets of campus life. Many of them serve on the executive boards of numerous student programs/organizations. They also provide excellent research opportunities for undergraduates. The professors like to take a hands-on approach to teaching, and they believe that you don't just learn in the classroom—you learn in everything you do and they want to be a part of that.

Lastly, if you are looking for a hassle-free way to party, then Study Abroad is for you. Sure this program offers the opportunity to tour different countries, explore various cultures, and learn new languages, but it also offers light workloads and plenty of easily accessible alcohol.

The Students

Although the majority of students on this campus are upper-middle-class white kids, almost all other racial and socioeconomic groups are represented. There is no absence of cultural clubs that double as support groups for the minorities on campus, and these clubs put on some of the best programs and events. It is true a large portion of the campus is Republican, but members of the Democratic Party and even the Green Party can find supporters here. Since Holy Cross is a very politically active campus, the split in political opinions can lead to boisterous demonstrations, active protesting, and educational panels.

The Activities

Community service is popular on this campus. The Student Programs for Urban Development (SPUD) offer numerous sites where you can donate your time and energy. Many different types of people participate in SPUD, and you can make some unlikely friends while volunteering—these people sometimes become your closest friends on campus.

Holy Cross is lucky to be part of a consortium comprising seven colleges in Worcester. Students from these colleges can take courses for credit, borrow library books, and participate in student organizations at any of the other colleges. We're also fortunate to have many distinguished alumni who ensure that we are always guaranteed excellent speakers throughout the year.

> "I really thought there was going to be way more schoolwork than I actually have. It's all about time management, people. Don't wait until the last minute and you will be set."
> ✦ Kelly, senior

The Social Scene

There is no doubt that Holy Cross is known for its drinking, and a student from Holy Cross can drink most other people under the table. Our stress levels combined with our location in the middle of nowhere might explain why so many people party at Holy Cross. However, there are numerous people who don't drink, and no one forces anyone to do anything. Parties are always available to you and are enjoyable whether you're sober or not—every weekend.

With the obscene amount of student-organized programs, such as dances, concerts with local bands, and pub night, meeting people is a cinch (as long as you put yourself out there). The coed dorms also give you the chance to meet people. Dorms tend to act like large cliques; you can often characterize people by the dorm they live in.

Name: Pete
Hometown: Santa Monica, California
Class Year: Freshman
Major: Undeclared
Extracurriculars: Multicultural Peer Educators, Multiethnic Identity Xploration (MIX), Student Health Advisory Board
Career Goal: Undecided

How would you describe Holy Cross's reputation?

Very reputable but fragile. With the general public, we've a great reputation. Within the local Worcester community, we're plagued with the reputation of being a school with serious binge-drinking issues.

> "We're known for drinking like fishes, but don't be fooled. If you come to Holy Cross, be prepared to do lots of work."
> ✦ Anthony, junior

Is this reputation accurate?

Very. The school does provide one of the best academic programs in the country, no doubt about that; it's just that the social issues are a serious concern. However, HC does a good job of covering up all the dirt that really goes on here.

What aspect of Holy Cross would a prospective student not see on a campus tour?

On tours they very quickly gloss over Wheeler—the party dorm—and move on to the next part of the tour because it's also the oldest building and doesn't look as nice as the others.

The Institution

Holy Cross's size is small, and it's great to be a big fish in a small pond. There's a lot of great school spirit—but once you go out into Worcester, you tend not to flaunt your HCness because the local Worcester community hates HC. We live up on our hill in our gated community, and like good little Jesuits, we go out into the community every week and do good service and events. On one particular day of the year, Holy Cross Cares Day, we do tons of service for the good of the community (which is often misinterpreted by Worcesterites, who see it as us just making ourselves feel better).

The Education

Best academic education you'll receive!

The Students

There's a general sense of racism and homophobia, but other than that, it's fine. Much like every school, we have our issues, but the school always comes together in some fashion when a horrible event happens: We just held a rally against homophobic hate crimes and more than two hundred people attended. When we had racist epithets written on walls, we had more than four hundred attend a march and more than two hundred attend a rally speech.

The Activities

Even more valuable than the formal classroom experience here is the education you receive outside of the classroom, with cultural programs and events. This school should be ranked number one in terms of extracurricular activities. MIX is the most active and full-of-potential group. They've put on more programs and events than any other group on campus this year.

I never leave campus unless I want to go shopping, to eat, or to the movies. We've got *so* many things on campus, from comedians to films. There are always meetings and events all week, but come weekend time, it's Parties-R-Us! It's a shame, but too much drinkin' goes on here.

The Social Scene

People party all the time. Generally Thursday through Saturday, but you always have the occasional morons who drink from Tuesday through Saturday. HC has no Greek system but is compensated by athletic teams and their parties. There are things to do on weekend nights, but they always end by midnight, so people tend to go back and party if they haven't already done so. People don't have relationships here. No one dates, they hook up. It's just a drunken make-out fest.

Notable Holy Cross Alumni Include:

Anthony Fauci, director of the National Institutes of Health
Billy Collins, U.S. poet laureate
Chris Matthews, talk show host
Clarence Thomas, U.S. Supreme Court justice
Joseph Murray, Nobel Laureate in medicine
Robert C. Wright, CEO, NBC

HOWARD UNIVERSITY

Founded: 1867

Location: Washington, D.C.

Phone: (202) 806-2763

E-mail: admission@howard.ed

Web site: www.howard.edu

Number of Undergraduates: 6,892

Number of Graduate Students: 1,785

Cost: Approximately $17,000 per year

Application Deadline: February 15
Rolling Admissions

Early Decision: November 1

Rating:	Notable Majors/Programs:
Selective	Biology, Psychology, Radio/TV/Film

Size:
○ Small ● Medium ○ Large

Location:
● Urban ○ Suburban ○ Rural

On a Saturday, students talk about academics:
○ Always ● Sometimes ○ Never

Nightlife:
○ Intense ● Moderate ○ Laid-back

Politically, Howard is:
○ Left ○ Right ● Split

Diversity:
● High ○ Low ○ Medium

Historically black college: Yes!

Students describe Howard in five words:
- Legacy, leadership, fashionable, political, challenging
- Number-one historically black college

From the School

At Howard, the core curriculum calls attention to the many achievements of African Americans in literature, history, criticism, philosophy, and every other area of academic study. African-American achievement isn't a side issue at Howard or something relegated to a department of African-American studies as it is at many universities. Here, the contributions of African Americans are tightly interwoven into all course work.

—www.howard.edu

If you're interested in Howard, you may also be interested in:
Columbia, George Washington, Georgetown, Morehouse, NYU, Spelman

Name: Tamyra

Hometown: New York, New York

Class Year: Junior

Major: Finance

Extracurriculars: New Yorkers Unlimited; University Fashion Council; *The Hilltop* (student newspaper), contributing writer; *The Bison* (yearbook), staff writer

Career Goal: I'd like to go into fashion, particularly in the areas of merchandising or sales so I can apply what I've learned in the finance major.

How would you describe Howard's reputation?

Howard is known as "the Black Harvard" because a disproportionate number of black intellectuals and leaders choose Howard as their college. Also, because Howard is located in Washington D.C., it's strongly tied into the political scene in the nation's capital.

Is this reputation accurate?

This reputation is definitely accurate. The Howard name really does hold a lot of weight, too—if you mention to affluent black individuals that you're an alum, you will most often open doors for yourself. Howard students are usually movers and shakers, people who want to succeed and will be important. Everyone has an agenda; everyone wants to be a star.

What aspect of your school would a prospective student not see on a campus tour?

Prospectives wouldn't see that almost all the teachers in our Math Department are foreign, meaning they have heavy accents and their English isn't the best. This makes it really hard for students and foreign math professors to communicate effectively, if at all.

The Institution

Howard has educated so many famous black people from the worlds of entertainment, law, and politics. The most successful black figures in American life either went to Howard or think extremely highly of it. I chose Howard because I felt it could push me into the upper echelons of whatever career I choose. As I said, this is a school for leaders, for people who take initiative and want to go places. Accordingly, this is a big networking school—those students who get the most from Howard are the ones who are active in clubs, who meet and keep in touch with lots of people, who know the other movers and shakers and go through life (even after Howard) calling them regularly.

Three important things to note are (1) housing is seriously overcrowded here, and while freshmen are guaranteed housing, no matter what year you're in, make it a point to send in your housing forms early because if you're late, you'll be out of luck. (2) Howard has lousy visitation rules. On weekdays, visitors can only be in your room between 12:00 p.m. and 12:00 a.m., and on the weekends it's from 2:00 p.m. to 2:00 a.m. This is regardless of how old you or they are and regardless of whether they're a fellow HU student or not. There is no visitation allowed on holidays, and extended visitation is usually limited to homecoming time, and then you cannot sign in a member of the opposite sex. Only one dorm (the East Towers) and certain individuals (RAs, GAs, etc.) are allowed more lenient visitation rules. (3) As our Alma Mater states, Howard is "proudly there on hilltop high." So be prepared for the long climbs up and down campus. But aside from all that, people really do enjoy their time here and have lots of school spirit. It's almost guaranteed that an average student will wear a Howard University sweatshirt, T-shirt, or hat at least one day of every week, especially off campus.

The Education

The biggest classes at Howard have sixty to more than a hundred students, and you'll experience a few of these while satisfying your freshman-year requirements. After that, you'll have lecture-based classes with thirty to fifty other students. And class size will shrink to no more than twenty-five to thirty students as you make your way to higher-level and more specialized courses.

Throughout, your professors will really be excellent, and even in the largest classes if you take time to ask professors for advice or help, they'll gladly oblige. In fact, even if you don't need much help, ask for it anyway because you'll get to know your professors better, and knowing your professors will, in the long run, prove to be an asset.

Remember, they are important people, with many important friends. From somewhere in your professors' social networks they can usually help you land a good job or internship if you're ever in need.

Every student at Howard is required, in the first two years, to take an African American–oriented class (black politics, black diaspora, etc.), a humanities, a phys. ed., an English, and a math class. These requirements aren't too bad, and they can be filled by taking *any* class within these departments—Egyptian mythology, tae kwon do, you name it. Then, once you declare your major as a junior, you have a new, major-specific set of requirements. For example, engineering majors have to take virtually every math course available. Journalism majors take English- and history-heavy courses.

For the most popular schools within Howard, like the School of B (business), School of C (communications), and Arts and Sciences, the competition is incredible. As you get higher up in classes, student-to-student rivalries can become cutthroat. You really do have to become smarter, faster, and stronger than your peers in order to stay at the head of the pack, which can, in some cases, ruin friendships. As I said previously, there are a lot of preprofessionals here, and everyone wants to be the best.

The Students

Howard is a big melting pot of varying accents, slang, personalities, and values. The students and people that call Howard home are from all walks of life and many different countries all over the world. We have a lot of students from Africa and the Caribbean. A good 90 percent of the students who attend Howard are from out of state, and there are large numbers of students from California, Georgia, Texas, and all over the East Coast. Most everyone is from middle- to upper-middle-class families. There are a lot of gay and lesbian students, and they're very accepted. On the downside, even though Howard is very diverse, students tend to hang out mostly with other students from their part of the United States or the world.

> "Soulfood Thursdays in the main cafeteria are always good."
> ✦ Kristina, freshman

There are five general "types" of Howard students. (1) The models wear designer clothes, shades, shoes, and look like they're on their way to a photo shoot. (2) The activists hang by "unity tree," spouting on and on about ending "the establishment," heavily dressed in red, black, and green, sporting "a natural look." (3) The preprofessionals dress impeccably in suits or business casual; they usually are on their cell phones talking about stocks or jobs or politics. (4) The thugs/thugette males dress in stocking caps while "chirping" others on their Nextels, and the females wear the "ghetto styles," like multicolored hair and back-length cornrows, and they're loud. (5) The balanced ones are the students who are a healthy mixture of all or some of the above and the most open-minded of the groups mentioned.

The Activities

There are tons of clubs to join at HU, with our state clubs being extremely popular, the biggest being the Georgia Club, Texas Club, and California Club. We have tons of social and special-interest organizations like Campus Pals, BLAGOSAH, National Society of Black Engineers, and so on. All these organizations hold fund-raisers, clothing drives, and food drives and host parties. The biggest political groups on campus are the student government/council that helps run the school, the dorm councils, the school councils, the Howard University Student Association (HUSA), and the Undergraduate Student Assembly. We also have a school publication, *The Hilltop,* which has national distribution and is the single most widely read student newspaper in the country. Every Tuesday and Friday new issues come out, written and edited entirely by students (including myself). There really is an organization that represents everyone here.

Howard is located in an urban area, minutes from downtown D.C. Because we're in a city setting, there's public transportation readily available, and it's easy to go from the heart of D.C. to places like Virginia or Maryland. Since the immediate area around Howard's campus offers little in terms of restaurants, clothing stores, and entertainment, when you have free time you'll travel elsewhere in D.C. for fun (like clubs). You can easily take the Metro to malls, movie theaters, monuments, and museums, or Adams Morgan—an eclectic hangout-get-drunk area where the nightlife is huge. After a night of clubbing at Adams Morgan ends, most head to get a slice of "big-face" pizza—they sell huge foot-long slices for about $3.50. If clubbing isn't what you're after, Georgetown is always good for upscale shopping, as is Pentagon City.

Back on campus, on a warm, sunny day, you'll see one or two people ciphering (freestyle rapping) at one end of the Yard, you'll see people hanging out in front of Blackburn at the other end of the Yard, and in between people will be converging and talking, trying to avoid heading to class.

The Social Scene

Howard's social scene is lively, to say the least. As the end of the week approaches, miraculously, hundreds and hundreds of flyers appear, promoting a club or a house party. Since you have to be twenty-one to drink at clubs, underage students head to house parties, almost all of which are then shut down by police between 1:00 and 2:00 a.m. Beer isn't as popular here as it is at predominately white schools. Instead, top-shelf shots and mixed drinks are everywhere and usually free. On the weekend many people go to house parties for the free drinks before they head to clubs like Dream, Republic Gardens, Platinum, D.C. Tunnel, Azteca, and Killi's.

> "The ease with which Howard students can get jobs and internships is great. I'm not even a business major, and I was flown to NYC for an interview with a major investment bank."
>
> ✦ Masai, senior

There's also a strong Greek presence at Howard (many national black fraternities and sororities began here). The most important Greek houses are referred to as the Divine Nine, and these houses are very particular and exclusive. If you want to be part of them, you have to spend a lot of time impressing their members, otherwise don't waste your time; a halfhearted effort will get you nowhere. On the plus side, if you do get in, you're assured a lifetime of friends, and connections, and like I said earlier, a big part of coming to Howard is making connections, opening the right doors, getting your name out there.

Lastly, as a freshman, dorm life is incredibly important. In Quad and Drew in particular, people always keep their doors open, a sort of gesture showing that they're willing to meet new people. A trendy freshman thing to do at Howard is to "rep" your floor and your dorm with hand signs

and calls when at school functions. With that grow rivalries between the dorms and between floors within the same dorm. As you get older this happens less and less, though, and you also make a core group of friends and leave your door open infrequently, and you care less about what dorm you live in or its reputation.

Name: Kristina
Hometown: Oakland, California
Class Year: Sophomore
Major: Film
Extracurriculars: WHBC's "Welcome to the Show," EPP (Endustry Power Players), HUFO (Howard University Film Organization), California Club
Career Goals: Filmmaker and singer-songwriter; in short, I want to be the Gordon Parks of this generation.

How would you describe Howard's reputation?

Howard is looked at as the best HBC (historically black college). Our School of Business is one of the best in the nation, as is our student newspaper, *The Hilltop*.

Is this reputation accurate?

Yes, all of it.

What would an admissions officer at your school probably not tell a prospective student?

The office of admissions sometimes loses things of great importance. I've learned to make copies of everything I hand in and receive, just in case. And I always call to make sure they've received things from me, and I call again a week later to be sure they didn't misplace it.

The Institution

Howard University has a rich history, which students are reminded of every day by the sight of gawking tourists. Our lecturers really admire this place, and our fellow students are truly impressive. Every day I hear stories about my classmates starting their own companies, recording their own albums, creating their own films and documentaries, and other amazing things that make me say, "Dang, I need to start doing something!" This place is truly special, not just a university but a place where great things have happened, and great things are still happening, history in the making. That's why I came here, because I knew if I graduated from Howard I would be able to do something big for myself.

The Education

Howard professors are incredibly prominent throughout the world, and it's not unusual to hear a professor lecture and see them that night on the news. And these same professors, if you ask them, will give you lots of personal attention after class. If anything, when you speak with them they're glad that you're taking an interest in their subject and treating it seriously. One of my professors, Dr. Ramsey, said that talking to students after class helps her lecture better in the long run. She really enjoys being challenged and getting into involved discussions with us.

Students at Howard work really hard. I'd say I spend at least fifteen hours a week outside of class on schoolwork. If there's a test coming up, I'll spend at least twenty-five hours studying to prepare. This can include studying on weekends—it's not unheard of for Howard students to give up partying to focus on their academics.

The Students

I've come into contact with all different kinds of people at Howard—people who dress differently, who have different attitudes, heritages, religions, political views; people who are gays, lesbians, and heterosexuals. And, for the most part, everyone gets along, everyone's respected.

I'd say a lot of Howard students get part-time jobs off campus. It's pretty easy finding a job. Back in California getting a job is difficult, but in D.C. you can go to a well-known mall area called Pentagon City and get a job like *that*. You can also go to the McDonald's right across the street from campus and work there.

The Activities

At least once a month, if not once a week, a famous artist, musician, businessperson, historian, writer, or poet drops by Howard to speak with us. It's great. I'd say the most active group on campus is HUSA (Howard Student Association). HUSA promotes school spirit at Howard, functions as a liaison between the administration and students when trouble arises, and organizes large-scale community service events. Howard's NAACP chapter also goes far toward preserving Howard's activist legacy. Even in a city like D.C., I still sometimes feel discriminated against; for example, sometimes I can't catch a cab in D.C. without me and my friends standing right in front of the car, and when I'm in Georgetown people will give me looks and follow me around in stores to make sure I'm not trying to shoplift; it's horrific.

Last thing, there are a lot of other schools near Howard—American, Georgetown, George Washington, University of Maryland, University of D.C., and George Mason University. Howard students head to these other schools for parties, and we'll usually protest with them if we're being political, or we'll organize massive community service drives in conjunction with other schools.

The Social Scene

Living in a dorm freshman year is a lot of fun; you make new friends and get to know everyone really well. The only problem is you're then living in close proximity with people who will play loud music, occasionally act stupid, and occasionally get attitude with you. You'll also have an RA looking over your shoulder. If you live off campus, you don't have an RA on your back, you have your own personal space, you can drink alcohol whenever you want, and you're closer to grocery stores and malls, but it's harder to see friends, you have to commute to and from campus, you might have vermin, and rent can be high. So it's a trade-off.

Name: Zenobia
Hometown: Atlanta, Georgia
Class Year: Freshman
Major: Graphic design
Extracurriculars: I do a little bit of everything.
Career Goal: I'd like to work as an art director at an urban or fashion magazine, documenting culture through photography and design.

> "Howard is full of students who are quietly planning great things."
>
> ✦ Kane, junior

How would you describe Howard's reputation?

It's said that Howard is home to the best and the brightest, boasting some of the most reputable African American alumni in the country—no, the *world*—and is the *mecca* of African-Latino-Asian culture and education. It's also said that *all* students wear fashionable designer clothes, shoes, and jewelry to class.

Is this reputation accurate?

Sure. People do come from all over the world to attend Howard University. Lots of famous people, dignitaries, and members of the "black elite" send their children here. However, Howard does coast on its legacy a little bit . . . and there have been recent budget cuts and poor planning that have left more than a few programs underfunded.

As for fashion, it is safe to say that our student body is pretty well dressed. Not everyone involves themselves in the fashion display, though—some people spend their days, nights, and money putting together the perfect outfit, others couldn't care less.

What would an admissions officer at your school probably not tell a prospective student?

When you first come to Howard you might not realize how broke you'll soon be. But living in a big city can be expensive! College is always costly, with tuition and food and books, but then add going to clubs, buying drinks at bars, paying for the metro, and the need to keep your "gear tight" at Howard U, and you may find yourself desperately needing a part-time job.

The Institution

Howard is known for its School of Business, School of Communication, and its medical schools (dentistry, pharmacy, etc.), so these are the programs that usually receive the most funding. Howard isn't really a big sports school, but we have all the basics: football, basketball, soccer, swimming, etc. I'm in the School of Fine Arts studying graphic design, and even though the program is underfunded (i.e., no printers, slow computers, etc.), great professors and small classes more than make up for lack of resources. And, in the end, Howard is as much about networking outside of class as it is about performing well inside of class. There's a lot to be said for the phrase "It's not what you know but *who* you know"—since so many of your classmates will go on to hold important and prominent roles in business, politics, entertainment, etc. Good connections will often get you further in the long run than a good GPA.

The Education

The education you receive at Howard is pretty amazing, both inside and outside of class. Be proactive about making yourself a better, smarter person. Sometimes professors will actually hinder this; for example, I've had more than one professor here who only erratically showed up to class. I would drag myself out of bed and run to get to a lecture on time only to find a note on the door saying the professor had to make an important speech or simply got caught in the traffic and won't be showing up at all. That's the point at which you have to go into Washington and educate yourself. Don't waste any time. Don't be afraid to hit up Howard's libraries. And if a professor doesn't show, when they *do* show, go to their office hours and make up for lost time (plus, professors will love you if you come see them outside of class).

> "Howard homecoming is one of the most anticipated events of the school year. People from all over the country travel to D.C. to be part of it. Celebrities flock from all over America to host parties in the area and be a part of Yardfest, which is a big five-hour show where big names in hip-hop and R&B perform."
>
> ✦ Tamyra, junior

The Students

When the weather is nice, students can be found on the Yard, the huge grass square in the middle of the main campus. Couples lay in the grass talking. The stairs of the fine arts building could double as a stoop in Brooklyn; guys are perched there to holler at the girls walking by. Friends gather all over to discuss the day's events and figure out what's going down for the weekend. In the background you can hear the chanting and calls of any one of the Greek sororities/fraternities on campus. Upperclassmen congregate in the Punch Out to watch the flat-screen TVs and get some food. Underclassmen and most athletes will retreat to the Café for meals. Students all over the green will be perusing *The Hilltop* newspaper for the latest campus and world news. On the surface this looks chill but it's not *all* fun and games. Never forget that Howard University puts the HU in hustle. All these people are steadily "grinding"—even as they look like they're relaxed and having fun, they're really making plans for their collective futures and discussing the best way to accomplish their goals.

The Activities

Howard has all kinds of events and activities going on. A lot of stuff is poorly advertised, so you really have to check *The Hilltop* and the *City Paper* every week to find out what's happening. Overall, I'd say the best part of living on campus is getting off . . . campus, that is. There are campus shuttles that will take you to Meridian Hill, a dorm that's walking distance from one of D.C.'s coolest areas, Adams Morgan. Everyone eats at the Diner and catches the shuttle back to campus later at night. If you want to go farther than Adams Morgan, you can also catch a bus to New York for $35 round trip or to Philly for only $28 round trip.

The Social Scene

The social life at Howard is what you make of it. If you're one for sitting in a room, chillin', you can do that. If you're a true party person who loves getting drunk and dancing till the wee hours of the morning in clubs, you can do that, too. Every week the campus is littered with flyers for club parties "with shuttles leaving from the quad and the annex every 30 minutes after 10." You can also opt for house parties. Both house parties and clubs are cool options; just know that at either you'll be in for lots of loud music, sweating, and liquor. If you're looking for a more upscale scene, you can head out to Adams Morgan or downtown to one of the many "lounges," but you better bring an ID if that's your plan because most of these places are twenty-one and up. Also, the main campus is walking distance from the 9:30 Club, a concert venue where artists like Talib Kweli, Mos Def, NERD, and Jill Scott have been known to play.

Lastly, a note to the ladies: D.C. is a big city, and Howard isn't in the best neighborhood. The local guys have been known to come on a little strong. If a guy tries to stop you in the street, politely say you have to go and keep it moving. It's best to travel in groups at night. Just make sure you keep your eyes open and avoid crazy situations.

Notable Howard Alumni Include:
Thurgood Marshall, U.S. Supreme Court justice
Toni Morrison, author, Nobel Laureate in literature
Andrew Young, former mayor of Atlanta
L. Douglas Wilder, former governor of Virginia
Phylicia Ayers-Allen, actress
Jessye Norman, opera singer

JOHNS HOPKINS UNIVERSITY

Founded: 1876

Location: Baltimore, MD

Phone: (410) 516-8171

E-mail: gotojhu@jhu.edu

Web site: www.jhu.edu

Number of Undergraduates: 5,524

Number of Graduate Students: 1,576

Cost: Approximately $38,000 per year

Application Deadline: January 1

Early Decision: November 15

Rating:	Notable Majors/Programs:
Most Selective	Biology, Chemistry, Engineering, Creative Writing

Size:
○ Small   ● Medium   ○ Large

Location:
● Urban   ○ Suburban   ○ Rural

On a Saturday, students talk about academics:
● Always   ○ Sometimes   ○ Never

Nightlife:
○ Intense   ○ Moderate   ● Laid-back

Politically, John Hopkins is:
○ Left   ○ Right   ● Split

Diversity:
● High   ○ Low   ○ Medium

Students describe Johns Hopkins in five words:
- Competitive powerhouse for medical research
- Pretty campus in urban ghetto

From the School

The first research university in the United States. Founded in 1876 . . . its aim was not only to advance students' knowledge, but also to advance human knowledge generally, through discovery and scholarship. The university's emphasis on both learning and research—and on how each complements the other—revolutionized U.S. higher education. Today . . . it remains a world leader in teaching, patient care and discovery. Please explore our university. We hope you'll discover something for yourself.

—www.jhu.edu

If you're interested in Johns Hopkins, you may also be interested in:
Duke, Harvard, MIT, UPenn, Princeton, Yale

Name: Jake
Hometown: Sugarland, Texas
Class Year: Sophomore
Major: Premed
Extracurriculars: HAPA (multiracial student organization), Filipino Students Association
Career Goal: Physician

How would you describe Johns Hopkins's reputation?

Johns Hopkins is considered to be an elite school, an "almost Ivy" that's too young to be "establishment–blue-blood," but too prestigious to be pedestrian. HopKids are also said to be both antisocial (because of their workload) and academically cutthroat.

Is this reputation accurate?

Hopkins is an academic stronghold that is consistently ranked as one of America's top fifteen schools by *U.S. News & World Report.* It's home to one of the world's best hospital-and-medical schools, and it also has top creative writing and international studies programs. All HopKids are not competitive, but most are. And while there are definitely students here who never seem to crawl out of the library, recent years have seen more social, fun-loving people matriculating.

What would an admissions officer at your school probably not tell a prospective student?

JHU doesn't stress that our school is really close to Washington, D.C., and that Hopkins is located right between a ghetto and an upper-class neighborhood in Baltimore, Maryland. It's weird. Within a five-mile radius, students can both hobnob with Balitmore's social elite and buy drugs from sketchy crack dealers.

The Institution

Hopkins exists in its own little world. Everything you could ever need is a walk, a phone call, or a free ride away. It's a small school; almost everything on the Homewood (main) campus is within a ten-minute walk from everything else. So students tend to know one another (or have at least heard of one another). But despite the close-knit feel, school spirit is almost nonexistent until lacrosse season starts in the spring (then everyone cheers twice as hard to make up for lost time). I chose Hopkins because it has incredible professors and a world-renowned academic reputation.

The Education

Hopkins is regarded as über-cutthroat—a school where every student is vying to get ahead of the next student, and no one will ever help out anyone else. This is kind of true. I won't go into detail, but I've witnessed some of the most intense examples of academic competition imaginable here. But if that's not your thing, you can avoid it. There are plenty of students who despise the "competition mentality" and band together to give one another the academic love and care everyone else here misses out on.

There are quite a few graduate schools at Hopkins—the Peabody Institute (School of Music), the School of Public Health, the School of Advanced International Studies, and the School of Medicine—and undergraduates can often take classes at each, under some truly brilliant scholars. These classes can often lead to fantastic research opportunities. But the research opportunities come at a price—you don't get offered them unless you're doing phenomenally well, and you don't do phenomenally well unless you're driven and able to spend *nearly all* your time outside of class in labs, in study groups, and in the library poring over books.

> "One of the best things about Hopkins is 'the beach'—a big grassy sloped area at the front of the campus. We all hang out there when it's nice."
>
> ✦ Stephen, junior

The Students

Hopkins students are, for the most part, exceedingly driven, successful, and talented. When you put hundreds of students like this together in a dormitory—well, let's just say late night discussions are riveting, all with beers in hand and chocolate chip cookies baking in the oven. Students also come from such diverse backgrounds—from the highest socioeconomic echelons (we have a considerable number of those) to those families who straddle the poverty line. Most students are left-leaning, but one of the most active (and therefore, vocal) groups on campus are the College Republicans and the pro-life group. So a casual visitor might conclude that this is a conservative campus.

The Activities

The Baltimore Collegetown Network tries to get the dozens of schools in the area interacting, but, to be honest, it fails—kids from Hopkins rarely hang out with kids at nearby schools. We do our own thing. There are lots of cultural and community service groups right on campus that organize events during the week. The Greek organizations throw big parties on the weekends. Our student government is particularly active and sometimes efficient—it's filled with the ambitious achievers who want to eventually see their names gracing the front page of the *Wall Street Journal* or the *New York Times*. There are a lot of night owls at Hopkins, so being awake at 3:00 a.m. on a Wednesday night is pretty common—if you're up, you're probably cramming for an upcoming midterm, watching movies for no particular reason, or you've decided to start your weekend early and are just coming back from a local pub.

The Social Scene

Hopkins parties take place in frat houses, in clubs, in bars, and in dorms. Specifically, frat parties tend to be composed of freshman and frat brothers, with a few straggling sophomores and juniors here and there. As HopKids get older, they have smaller and smaller gatherings, all of which are haunted by the specter of graduate school applications and advanced standardized tests (LSATs, GREs, and MCATs). It's also worth noting, *Playboy* is rumored to have ranked schools by the attractiveness of the girls enrolled. It's safe to say that this is one ranking where Hopkins would not have shone.

Name: Amy
Hometown: Rockville, Maryland
Class Year: Sophomore
Major: Psychology
Extracurriculars: I play a lot of piano, and I write creatively when I have free time.
Career Goal: Ten years from now, I'd like to be solving violent crimes for the FBI.

How would you describe Johns Hopkins's reputation?

JHU is known to be incredibly nerdy, incredibly hardcore, and incredibly cutthroat. It's also kind of known as the school for Ivy League rejects.

Is this reputation accurate?

Somewhat. Yes, JHU students are nerdy, but not in a pocket-protector kind of way. It's more that people have interests that fall outside of the mainstream and pursue them with lots of passion. As for our reputation of being a hardcore, cutthroat campus—yes, we have grade deflation here, and yes we work very hard and have very difficult classes. But I think that it all builds character. Life is not handed to you on a silver platter; there will always be people smarter than you, and it's good that Hopkins shows us this now. And if you can make it through, you will have developed incredible resilience and a great work ethic that will stay with you throughout your life.

And the Ivy League reject thing—nah. It's every bit as hard to get into Hopkins as it is to get into an Ivy League school, and Hopkins graduates go head-to-head—and often beat out—Ivy graduates when it comes to getting jobs and grad school placement.

What would an admissions officer at your school probably not tell a prospective student?

The administration probably wouldn't tell a student about the intensity of the workload here because people would get scared away. Hopkins can be a lot of fun if you are outgoing, but it is definitely a *lot* of work. And because everyone is really intelligent here, you'll work for hours and hours and hours and still not be anywhere near the top of your class. It's humbling.

> "Hopkins can be cutthroat. Some people will lie and tell you a test has been postponed so you don't study and they'll do better on the curve. They will rip out pages from textbooks. . . . These people exist and they suck."
>
> ✦ Richard, sophomore

The Institution

Hopkins is a great size—small enough that you don't feel lost, but large enough that you are always meeting new people. The professors (that I've had) have been friendly and very approachable. Students and townies don't usually interact—the area around Hopkins is very depressed, so there are not a lot of commonalities between the two groups.

Hopkins organizes some fantastic activities at freshmen orientation to ensure you make friends instantly. Also, your first semester freshman year, every class is pass or fail. This policy is key because it allows you to adjust to Hopkins's workload, and if you find things harder than you expected (which you will), it gives you time to start revamping your study habits without destroying your GPA right out of the gate. This also means that first semester, you can try classes in new areas you aren't familiar with (and might not do so well in) without any real long-term consequences.

> "LGBT students and African American students exist in small numbers at Hopkins."
> ✦ Chistopher, senior

The Education

I am a psychology major, so most of my classes are lectures (very interesting). But I live for the type of classes where you can express your opinions, get into discussions. These exist at Hopkins; you just have to work to find them. I recently did the legwork and enrolled in discussion-based Moral Philosophy and Islamic Studies classes, and I loved the group discussions and writing involved. I found it developed my skills far more than taking in information from a lecturer would have.

There are no core requirements at Hopkins. Instead, there are broad "distribution requirements," where you have to take a number of classes distributed across a few key academic disciplines—natural sciences, historical social sciences, engineering, quantitative sciences, and so on. Within these key disciplines, you can choose any of hundreds of classes and your distribution requirements will be easily fulfilled. This is great, because it pushes you in all different directions, so you're forced to get a well-rounded education and explore new subjects, but the requirements are broad enough so that you never have to take a class that you're not actually interested in.

The best class I took at Hopkins was Advanced Expository Writing. There were only eight people in the class, and it was taught by a graduate student. We wrote a great deal over the course of the semester, and I was really pleased with the results.

The Students

I would say there are three main types of students at Hopkins: (1) the rich, snotty kids who more or less stay in their rich, snotty cliques; (2) the super-nerdy kids who have few social skills and twitch when you talk to them; (3) the relatively normal people who are nice and friendly.

People at Hopkins say that we're a politically apathetic campus, but from what I've seen, the ACLU is pretty active, and every year the pro-life group puts together a silent protest. There are also a lot of cultural groups on campus that hold parties that are open to everyone and are generally a whole lot of fun.

The Activities

The Peabody Conservatory is fifteen minutes away from Hopkins. In addition to classes, Peabody also puts on lots of musical recitals and performances that many Hopkins students go to. Otherwise, I don't leave campus too often, unless I'm heading over to the Inner Harbor—an area with lots of good restaurants, an aquarium, Ravens Stadium and Oriole Park—or Towson Town Center, where the mall and cinemas are. Baltimore is not a utopian city, but it can be a wonderful place and it has a lot of character.

The Social Scene

The biggest complaint I hear about Hopkins is that it has no social scene. I've *never* had any trouble having fun at this school. Freshman year, my friends and I went to a lot of frat parties (the frat scene is pretty big here). But they can be too big and kind of dirty—so now, as an upperclassman, my friends and I will chill at somebody's place in a small group or head to a big house party and drink till we all have Irish brogues. There definitely is widespread alcohol consumption here, but no more than you'd find at any other college.

People here are not superoutgoing or friendly, so it's kind of hard to make new friends unless you know someone who knows someone and formal introductions are made. This is probably the case elsewhere too, but I do wish HopKids were a little friendlier. Also, the dating scene is kind of nonexistent. I'm lucky enough to have a long-term boyfriend, but I'd imagine it's pretty frustrating for people who are single.

Name: Tami
Hometown: Liberty Center, Ohio
Class Year: Freshman
Major: Sociology
Extracurriculars: Outdoors Club, Red Cross, Phi Mu
Career Goal I'd like to become a doctor.

How would you describe Johns Hopkins's reputation?

Hopkins has a very good reputation. It is an excellent research institution, and it prepares you for graduate work in just about any field. It's also one of a small handful of schools that are known both nationwide and worldwide.

Is this reputation accurate?

Absolutely. It presses its students to be the very best they can be, and students live up to the challenge. I'm quite proud to be here.

What aspect of your school would a prospective student not see on a campus tour?

The workload! I don't even watch TV anymore. Our unofficial motto is "Johns Hopkins University: where your best hasn't been good enough since 1856."

The Institution

Hopkins's campus is really beautiful, and the university does an excellent job of maintaining it. Also, JHU housing is really excellent. Freshman dorms are large and well designed. You're provided with lots of furniture, and it's all in good condition. Some freshman dorm rooms even have a kitchen and a bathroom. My only complaint is that when it rains, the marble staircases and walkways get really slippery and need to be navigated with the utmost caution. A few kids slip and hurt themselves every year.

Hopkins is a good size—big enough so you don't know everyone, but small enough that you'll randomly run into your friends. Professors don't know everyone by name, but, if you're a standout student, they'll know who you are. Many of the premed classes in your freshman year will be quite large (150 to 200 in each class), but as the years go by, and you start taking advanced courses within your major, classes will shrink considerably.

I chose to come to Hopkins because it has a stellar reputation in the sciences—there really isn't a better place to come to prepare for a career as a doctor. That said, lots of people want to be doctors, and most people won't do very well at Hopkins. If you're looking for easy classes and crazy college life, you'll fail out and be left behind. If, on the other hand, you're determined, focused, confident, and willing to be sleep deprived, you'll do fine. Really, we work till we bleed here. I'd say those majoring in science here have it the hardest, and among the science students, those who study biomedical engineering earn the most respect. The school will drop loads of work on you, but it will also set up help sessions with TAs, student study groups, drop-in tutoring, and group tutoring sessions, so, if you fall behind but have the strength necessary to get back on your feet, the school will do all it can to help you up.

> "Baltimore isn't that bad. There is a high crime rate. But as long as you're smart (and sober) you shouldn't have any real problems."
>
> ◆ Dean, junior

The Education

There is an unbelievable amount of competition here. Everyone at Hopkins is used to being the smartest in his or her high school, and they don't like the idea of falling behind now. People are always asking how you did on a test just to see if they did better. It is intimidating knowing you are competing against such intelligent people; however, it feels extremely good when you find yourself outperforming your very bright peers.

Professors, on the whole, are very well respected in their fields, and are extremely intelligent and expect a lot from their students. I spend four to six hours on homework each night—including Friday and Saturday nights—and I'm not the exception; I'm the rule. You will always have a lot of work, but it will eventually pay off. Particularly if you're a major in one of Hopkins's most prestigious departments (biology, chemistry, engineering and—strangely enough—creative writing). Do extremely well in one of these disciplines and you're set for life.

The Students

Hopkins is diverse ethnically, but not economically. Most students are wealthy and have either attended boarding school or private school. Most seem to be from the East Coast and California as well. In general, students associate primarily with those of their own race and social class. The frats and sororities are predominately white, and there are Asian and Jewish frats, but these last two are not officially recognized by the administration.

The Activities

Lots of kids at Hopkins play lacrosse, and going to watch JHU lacrosse games is always a blast. Lacrosse starts up in spring, and when the players hit the fields, everyone feels a resurgence of pride for JHU. Also, student groups get a wide variety of well-known people to come speak on campus.

The Social Scene

JHU's party scene is restricted to Friday and Saturday nights. Fraternities put on basically all of our parties, and they never charge a cover for girls. Joining a frat or sorority pretty much guarantees you a social life, and almost everyone that goes out on a regular basis is in one. Our dating scene is pretty pathetic—most people just hook up. But then kids at Hopkins are generally not the most attractive bunch. And many students are stuck-up and academically superior. They don't say hi or even look at you when you pass them. But you don't come to Hopkins for the social scene . . . you come for the academics!

Notable Johns Hopkins Alumni Include:
Allan Huston, president, PepsiCo
Michael Bloomberg, mayor of New York City
Madeleine Albright, former secretary of state
Morris Tanenbaum, president, CEO, AT&T
John Astin, actor, director, producer
John Barth, author

KENYON COLLEGE

Founded: 1824
Location: Gambier, OH
Phone: (740) 427–5776
E-mail: admissions@kenyon.edu
Web site: www.kenyon.edu

Number of Undergraduates: 1,576
Number of Graduate Students: 0
Cost: Approximately $35,000 per year
Application Deadline: February 1
Early Decision: December 1

Rating:	Notable Majors/Programs:
Very Selective	English, Psychology, Political Science

Size:
● Small   ○ Medium   ○ Large

Location:
○ Urban   ○ Suburban   ● Rural

On a Saturday, students talk about academics:
● Always   ○ Sometimes   ○ Never

Nightlife:
○ Intense   ● Moderate   ○ Laid-back

Politically, Kenyon leans:
● Left   ○ Right   ○ Split

Diversity:
○ High   ● Low   ○ Medium

Students describe Kenyon in five words:
- Quirky liberal poet-scholars study here
- Beautiful, isolated campus, close-knit community

From the School

Why Kenyon? Because Kenyon is one of the nation's finest liberal-arts and sciences colleges—and more. Because it's rigorous and collaborative at the same time. Because it's a place where people reach beyond their grasp—and cheer when others do the same. Because it's a learning environment that uniquely blends creativity and ambition.

—www.kenyon.edu

If you're interested in Kenyon, you may also be interested in:
Carleton, Claremont McKenna, Grinnell, Macalester, Oberlin, Vassar

Name: Jordan
Hometown: Dale City, Virginia
Class Year: Freshman
Major: Synoptics major
Extracurriculars: Hillel, United Students Against Sweatshops, Activists United, Humane Society
Career Goal: I'm not sure. Maybe law, with a focus on the environment. . . .

How would you describe Kenyon's reputation?

Kenyon is known as *the* school for poet-scholars.

Is this reputation accurate?

Absolutely. Kenyon is a place for sensitive, artistic, original thinkers. Our English Department is one of the best in the nation—no other institution that I know of focuses as much on language and poetry. Our Drama Department is also top-notch.

What aspect of your school would a prospective student not see on a campus tour?

Kenyon students, finding themselves stuck in the middle of Ohio for four years, often decide to fill up their free time with hardcore partying. This means, be prepared to do some drinking and pot smoking. (Note to parents: Don't worry. Honestly, alcohol and pot are on every campus in America, and everything is done in moderation here. Some students even choose to refrain from drinking/smoking entirely.)

> "There are a lot of frat boys at Kenyon. But Kenyon frat brothers aren't typical . . . they're nerdy, artistic, poet frat brothers."
> ✦ Jonah, sophomore

The Institution

Kenyon is a small school, and this is a good thing. If Kenyon wasn't so small, the students wouldn't all know one another so well. The teachers wouldn't have us to dinner at their houses. Campus leaders wouldn't stand out as much. The maintenance staff wouldn't know you by name. You couldn't walk into the campus deli and say "the usual" and get your favorite sandwich, exactly how you like it. The size of this campus is what makes life here so unusual and extraordinary.

The meal plan is also extremely great. We're the only school in the country that has an honor-code-run meal system. Basically, you pledge not to take more food than you can eat. So you never have to swipe a card or show your ID; you just eat whenever and wherever you're hungry. It's great!

Middle Path is the area in the center of campus where students from every academic discipline and social scene come together and hang out. In the winter, when Middle Path is covered in a sheet of ice, you'll find English majors and neuroscience majors slipping and sliding everywhere. When the weather is good, preachers from nearby towns will come to Middle Path and hand out flyers, often inspiring a lively debate. Hillel members will be at a table nearby, making peanut butter and jelly sandwiches to help feed the homeless in Mount Vernon. Really, Middle Path embodies Kenyon—it's the place where everyone converges, where ideas are in the air, and you'll always see one of your friends.

Off campus, you'll quickly find that Gambier exists for us. Students outnumber the residents of Gambier by three to one and of the six hundred full-time residents of Gambier, I'd say five hundred are professors or administrators at Kenyon. On the downside, Ohio weather is insane. Prepare for random snow in the middle of spring, and seventy-degree days in the middle of winter.

The Education

Professors at Kenyon are very informal and flexible, nothing like the anal, tight-lipped, mustached "college professors" of the movies. Many Kenyon professors ask you to refer to them by their first names. One Sunday afternoon I stopped by Sunset Cottage, the adorable little dwelling that houses the English Department. One of my professors was in her office, grading papers, and she stopped what she was doing to chat with me for an hour. On a Sunday afternoon. Try doing that at Ohio State.

The Students

The average student on campus wears a North Face jacket and Ugg boots, is an apathetic Democrat, drinks and smokes pot occasionally, writes poetry, and is from either Ohio or the D.C. area. At Kenyon, poets, economists, biologists, actors, daddy's-little-girls, beer-guzzling frat boys, pot-smoking hippies, guitar-playing indie hipsters, and environmental activists blend together in a relaxed, individualist small-town atmosphere. The most vocal student groups at Kenyon are Hillel, the Brown Family Environmental Center, and Kenyon After Dark, but students are—unfortunately—apathetic when it comes to politics. There are almost no protests or rallies on campus, which differentiates us from similar but more active schools, like Oberlin.

The Activities

The arts are everywhere at Kenyon—poetry, theater, a cappella groups, student-run comedy troupes. Creative energy abounds. Community service is very popular, from volunteering at the local elementary school to becoming a dog caretaker at the Humane Society. And if a freshman drama enthusiast finds him- or herself without a major part in a faculty-run play, he or she can easily direct or act in any of the myriad of student-run productions going on in the Black Box Theater. At Kenyon, it's so important to get involved. If your passion is watching independent films, come here and start an Independent Film Society. The campus will give you funding; all you have to do is fill out a form in the Student Affairs Office. It's so easy.

In our spare time we watch movies, go to frat parties, go for walks on Middle Path, go to the Brown Family Environmental Center and walk around the butterfly garden, go to the bookstore (the largest independent college bookstore in the country), or the twenty-four-hour diner in Mount Vernon. Oh right, and we work sometimes, too.

The Social Scene

In the freshman quad, on any given day, you'll fine a lone poet under a tree reading a book or writing, a group of neo-hippies smoking pot on a bench, girls piled next to each other on towels tanning and talking to the boys they hooked up with the previous night, and a group of just regular "college" kids chatting. Pretty much everyone finds their group here and happily sticks to it.

Wednesday, Friday, and Saturday nights are the party nights at Kenyon. The south part of campus is where all the parties are, and where the frats are. The north part of campus is the more artsy side, where people stay in on weekends to paint or write or talk. If you drink, you'll drink. If you don't drink, you can take the shuttle to Mount Vernon to see a movie for a dollar, go bowling at Deerfield Lanes, go to Columbus if you have a car, or just chill in a friend's room. Everyone at Kenyon chills a lot. If you want to spend your college days going

to clubs, dressing up in black pants and tight shirts, then don't come to Kenyon.

Name: Brandon
Hometown: Portland, Oregon
Class Year: Sophomore
Major: Philosophy
Extracurriculars: Debating, theater, Kenyon Film Society
Career Goal: I'd like to become a professor. Maybe a professor at Kenyon? That could work. I'm certainly going to graduate school.

How would you describe Kenyon's reputation?

Kenyon is a rather prestigious school. It's particularly well known for its stellar English Department.

Is this reputation accurate?

Yes. But it's also important to note that although Kenyon has a hardworking student body, it's by no means the hardest-working student body in the nation. If you want an extremely rigorous education, you may find Kenyon somewhat disappointing. While you can work hard here, you'll be surrounded by an uncomfortable number of "talented slackers."

> "There is no need for keys on campus at Kenyon, no need for student IDs, no need for cell phones, and no need for money. Doesn't that sound great?"
> ✦ Kyle, sophomore

What would an admissions officer at your school probably not tell a prospective student?

I doubt they'd mention that Kenyon's social scene revolves, to a large degree, around drinking.

The Institution

Kenyon's campus is absolutely beautiful. Architecturally, it's very well designed—a handful of prominent buildings clustered around a central path. I've seen quite a few schools across America, and Kenyon is among the most beautiful I've laid eyes on. It looks, and feels, exactly as "college" should. For better or worse, Kenyon is located smack in the middle of nowhere. The closest *real* town is Mount Vernon. And Mount Vernon houses Nazarene Bible College. Kenyon students and Nazerene Bible College students don't, shall we say, see eye to eye. So Kenyon students largely avoid Mount Vernon and the NBC. This means Kenyon students are essentially confined to campus. And, because we're an enterprising lot, we take what we're given, make the best of it, and create our own fun. There are parties every weekend, and, frequently, during the week. There are clubs and activities to join, so many of them that you won't have difficulty choosing something to do—you'll have difficulty choosing what *not* to from many, many appealing options.

Kenyon is super laid-back. Sports and other school-spirit activities are not the Kenyon scene (I was here about five months before I even knew we *had* a football team) . . . although our swimming team stands out somewhat, in that they throw a rather infamous yearly party called "Shock Your Mama." (Yes, that party is every bit as good as it sounds.)

The Education

For the most part (exempting the previously mentioned "talented slackers"), Kenyon students are eloquent, well read, opinionated, and intelligent. They're always up for an argument, an intellectual battle, a long discussion. I've had more conversations at Kenyon that start in the early afternoon and end at 3:00 or 4:00 a.m. than is healthy, considering the large amount of work that has to be done on a daily basis! But at Kenyon, that's just how it works.

Kenyon employs some of the best teachers in the nation because, institutionally, it insists professors teach first, publish second. This draws teachers who *love to teach*—and students in every discipline benefit. Another big draw is that the classes are small, intimate, and are typically a mix of lecture and discussion. And while you'll have homework in every class, the amount of homework you'll have is really up to you—some professors assign an hour's worth per class, others five hours' worth per class. Ask around, find out which professors assign what, and choose classes based upon the level of involvement you'd like to have.

The Students

It seems every upper-middle-class community in the world sends students to Kenyon. New York, California, England, China . . . you name it. This means your classmates at Kenyon will be from everywhere in the world. And they'll also be, more often than not, a member of the upper middle class. Kenyon realizes this, and they're currently offering many more scholarships with the hope of bringing more socioeconomic diversity to campus.

That said, if you've managed to pay for Kenyon and aren't upper middle class, you'll fit in fine—no one judges anyone else based on economic status. Equally, minority students are very integrated at Kenyon, and GLBT students are free to make out in the middle of campus without anyone blinking an eye. Really, the only group of people at Kenyon who could qualify as an oppressed minority are Republicans. There aren't many of them here. And, by and large, we like it that way.

> "People here don't really compete. They say 'I want to do well, but I want you to do well too!' It's a big family."
> ✦ Logan, senior

The Activities

Kenyon students are calm, cool, collected, laid-back. And Kenyon clubs and groups are the same way. They're fun, well-attended, nonstressful gatherings. They have a purpose; that purpose is worked toward on a weekly basis, and then group members will head back to someone's room to have a glass of wine and talk into the wee hours of the night.

The Social Scene

Parties happen all the time at Kenyon. Some are small, social, intimate . . . others are big, loud, and, from afar, look like riots. I'm not much of a partier outside of Kenyon, but I do my share here—it's such a small, tight-knit campus that no matter how big, how small, or who's throwing the event, you'll typically be surrounded by friends having good times . . . the whole thing will feel less anonymous, more comforting.

Name: Sarah
Hometown: Los Angeles, California
Class Year: Senior
Major: English
Extracurriculars: Pealers (ringing chapel bells), voice lessons, yearbook, Peer Writing Tutor
Career Goal: Elementary education

How would you describe Kenyon's reputation?

People have either never heard of Kenyon or know absolutely everything about it because their friend/niece/doctor's-second-cousin went here, loved it, and couldn't stop talking about the place.

Is this reputation accurate?

Kenyon is top-notch. And while it's still not a household name, it's interesting, it's evolving . . . Kenyon just finished building brand-new, cutting-edge science facilities, which are far better than those that can be found at most other liberal arts colleges.

What aspect of your school would a prospective student not see on a campus tour?

Although Kenyon's campus tour is relatively comprehensive, the best way to experience Kenyon is to stay overnight with a student in their dorm and sit in on their classes. Listen to what any given student has to say—in their casual discussions and in their classes—and you'll know exactly why Kenyon is so unique.

The Institution

Kenyon has one of the most beautiful campuses in the country. The buildings are delightfully Gothic (down to the gargoyles), and the layout is neighborly and welcoming. Kenyon really does feel homey. . . .

My high school had only five hundred students in it, and I loved the way that felt—my classes were small, I knew all of my teachers, and students really got close to one another. I knew I wanted my college experience to be similar. I'm not a nameless face here; I'm a member of an actual college community. And because Kenyon is in tiny Gambier, Ohio, when I'm at the grocery store buying cucumbers and lettuce to make a salad, I'll often look up and see administrators and professors on line just in front of me.

The Education

One of the great things about Kenyon is that all classes are small and taught by full professors. The only courses that have assistant teachers at all are the languages; on top of regular class time with professors, there are review classes run by ATs. But otherwise, you're interacting directly with notable professors who are often famous within their field! You know them, they know you. On the downside, you can't just skip class, because the professor and your fellow students will notice. On the upside, you'll become very involved in your academics, and you'll find yourself happily involved in many after-class conversations about great thinkers such as Dante, Aristotle, and Shakespeare.

Kenyon has a roster of fantastic professors with quite a few stars with whom everyone tries to take at least one class before graduating, particularly in the English Department. And Kenyon's core requirements are really quite manageable. You are expected to complete two semesters of classes in each of the following four areas: fine arts, humanities, social sciences, and natural sciences. You also have to complete at least one major, and all majors have a "senior exercise," which varies from department to department.

The opportunities for studying abroad, and getting financial aid for it, are abundant. Kenyon is affiliated with lots of excellent, hassle-free study-abroad programs. Also, Kenyon has also brought in some amazing speakers in the past few years—Oliver Sacks, Jared Diamond, Patricia Ireland, and Alan Keyes, to name just a few.

> "Kenyon is haunted. There have been a number of tragic fires in the older dormitories and numerous reports of ghosts. Stephen King visited Kenyon once and wouldn't even get out of his car."
>
> ✦ Rhadha, junior

The Students

I would say most Kenyon students are liberal or moderate, with a small handful of conservatives mixed in for fun. There are many student- and college-run groups focused on cultural, LGBT, religious, and racial issues, and they run the gamut from very vocal and visible to private and confidential. Kenyon students tend to be very individualistic. . . . I think my favorite statistic about Kenyon is that 60 percent of alumni marry other alumni, with about half of those people meeting while they were students, the other half meeting at reunions and at homecoming events. The experience of having gone to Kenyon is really amazing, and I think you form an immediate bond, for the rest of your life, with others who have had the Kenyon experience too!

The Activities

Kenyon tends to interact only with other nearby schools for sports purposes; otherwise, we're pretty isolated on our Hill, and we like it that way. Sometimes people will head into Columbus, Ohio, for a day or so, but Kenyon is definitely not a "suitcase school," where the dorms empty out on the weekends. People stick around because there is always something exciting going on, whether it's a faculty drama production, a famous lecturer, a professor reading his or her own work, a mock game show or a film screening. Lots of students become involved in community service in the area around Kenyon, such as volunteering at the local women's shelter, building homes with Habitat for Humanity, taking care of dogs and cats at the Humane Society, and helping with HotMeals.

I've personally come to rely on the Kenyon Pealers for de-stressing at the end of every week. The church on campus has a bell tower with nine bells in it that can be played using hand levers. Every Friday, the Pealers gather in the bell tower and play running patterns, hymns, and secular songs ("Scotland, the Brave" and the *Star Wars* theme are a few favorites) for a full hour. We have a lot of fun, and there's nothing quite like slamming down the levers and ringing a bell to help you forget the paper you turned in that day.

The Social Scene

There is a great deal of alcohol on campus, and kids do get drunk and act stupid. However, there really is no pressure to get involved in the drinking-party scene if that's not your thing—there are lots of other options, and many areas of campus are designated alcohol free so nondrinkers can feel comfortable.

The coffee shop, Middle Ground, is open until 2:00 a.m. during the week, serving gourmet organic soups, sandwiches, and salads and with student art hanging on the walls, space-age decor, and regularly scheduled live performances by visiting artists. It's a bit expensive, but the atmosphere is great, and everyone goes there—it's a great late-night study-break hangout.

One huge negative of Kenyon, though, is that there is almost no "dating scene." I certainly didn't go to college expecting to find my future husband in the first month, but I've been here for quite a few months now, and neither I nor my friends have gone on any traditional "dates." Most of the couples I know are either in very casual, "no-strings" kinds of relationships or they're in long-term, committed relationships that they've been in since forever, with not much going on in between those extremes.

Notable Kenyon Alumni Include:
E. L. Doctorow, author
Rutherford B. Hayes, nineteenth U.S. president
Paul Newman, actor
Allison Janney, actress
Mark. C. Rosenthal, president and COO, MTV Networks
John Snow, secretary of the U.S. Treasury

LEHIGH UNIVERSITY

Founded: 1865

Location: Bethlehem, PA

Phone: (610) 758-3100

E-mail: admissions@lehigh.edu

Web Site: www.lehigh.edu

Number of Undergraduates: 4,685

Number of Graduate Students: 2,053

Cost: Approximately $35,000 per year

Application Deadline: January 1

Early Decision: November 15

Rating:	Notable Majors/Programs:
Very Selective	Mechanical Engineering, Finance, Industrial Engineering

Size:
○ Small   ● Medium   ○ Large

Location:
● Urban   ○ Suburban   ○ Rural

On a Saturday, students talk about academics:
○ Always   ● Sometimes   ○ Never

Nightlife:
● Intense   ○ Moderate   ○ Laid-back

Politically, Lehigh leans:
○ Left   ● Right   ○ Split

Diversity:
○ High   ● Low   ○ Medium

Students describe Lehigh in five words:
- Prestigious and challenging college experience
- Conservative, preprofessional students partying hard

From the School

Lehigh is larger than typical liberal arts colleges yet smaller than most other research universities. You have many options in science and engineering, business, humanities, social sciences, education, and the arts—or a combination of these areas. In addition, you'll have absolute flexibility, so if your interests change or you're curious about a particular discipline, you have the latitude and the opportunity to pursue other coursework. . . .

—www3.lehigh.edu

If you're interested in Lehigh, you may also be interested in:
Boston College, Bucknell, Carnegie Mellon, Colgate, Cornell, NYU

Name: Laura
Hometown: Wynnewood, Pennsylvania
Class Year: Senior
Major: Marketing, with a minor in English
Extracurriculars: Women in Business, Marketing Club, college yearbook editor, Outing Club
Career Goal: I would like to become involved in marketing consumer goods.

How would you describe Lehigh's reputation?

When people hear the name *Lehigh,* they usually think of smart, conservative, preppy, and affluent students. They might also think "party school."

Is this reputation accurate?

It used to be one of the biggest party schools in the nation, but every year, Lehigh leaves its party school days further and further behind, replacing them with a continually increasing devotion to academic excellence. For most students, this has been bittersweet, but the administration is certainly happy—they've vowed not to rest until we reach Ivy League levels of recognition and achievement. And as for the rest of it—we're definitely intelligent; most students narrowly missed getting into their Ivy League first-choice schools, and there are lots of rich, preppy, and conservative students here, but there are also students who don't fit that mold.

> "Lehigh's campus is gorgeous, very all-American, exactly what you imagine college to look like."
>
> ✦ Craig, junior

What might an admissions officer at your school probably not tell a prospective student?

Students who visit Lehigh probably wouldn't be told (unless they specifically asked) about the recent spate of crimes that have occurred off campus. Crime on campus is minimal, but there have been some troublesome events right off campus.

The Institution

Lehigh is, in two words, *absolutely gorgeous.* The size is perfect and friends from home who have visited me here just couldn't get over how beautiful the campus is. The architecture ranges from modern to Gothic. There are trees, flowers, grassy greens, and cute pathways everywhere. The frats at the top of "the Hill" are incredibly old and beautiful. At Lehigh's highest points you can get a great view of the city lights at night. Rathbone dining hall is located at one of these points, and it has huge windows so students can look out on the campus and the city of Bethlehem while they eat. The food isn't great at Rathbone, but it's worth going there just for the view. Overall, though, Lehigh's food is pretty decent. We have three dining halls (I prefer the UC), and there's also a food court and multiple restaurants and eateries. The school has recently implemented a great system with off-campus restaurants and shops where students can use Gold Plus money (a Lehigh account that works like a debit card) instead of cash.

The Education

Lehigh is most proud of its engineering and business schools, both of which are extremely prestigious and consist of students who work remarkably hard. For business students, I would describe their work like a parabola. Sometimes there isn't much physical work assigned (technically you should always be reading the texts, but it's not enforced), and at other times there is an insane amount to do, and tests and papers are naturally always due at the same times of year. To be successful in the business school, you can either work continuously at a decent pace throughout the semester and never have to break a sweat, or you can cram at the end and be very stressed when deadlines loom. At the other end of the spectrum in the engineering school, students are constantly doing massive amounts of work that never lets up. Unlike business students, engineers have homework due almost every day, and it usually includes material they haven't covered yet (they have to teach themselves a lot) and/or extremely difficult versions of things they learned in class. If you can't cut it in the engineering school, you usually switch into the business school or the school of arts and sciences.

Overall, classes at Lehigh start out large (introductory classes) and then become smaller (specialized or advanced classes.) Professors are top-notch. I've never had a professor I've disliked in the business school—every one I've come across has been extremely knowledgeable and enthusiastic about teaching, and they have all worked in the industry as well as in academia, so they have a broad understanding of the subjects they teach. They encourage discussions in class and practically bend over backward to help out, urging students to visit them outside of class during their office hours.

Considering the large number of people who graduate from Lehigh and go on to become CEOs, vice presidents, or presidents of companies, you'll find yourself with excellent networking opportunities once you graduate. The Career Services Department is extremely helpful if you're looking on the East Coast, putting you in touch with people and teaching you necessary skills like interviewing, writing résumés and cover letters, etc. If you're looking at other regions, it's a little trickier. And since most of the on-campus interviews they schedule are for accounting and finance majors, if you're a business student, you're practically guaranteed a job, but if you're not—even if you're an engineer—well, there are no guarantees.

Unfortunately, while Lehigh is great on the preprofessional front, it doesn't have the unique, fun classes you'd find at a small liberal arts college. If you want to study basket weaving or African dance when you're not crunching numbers, Lehigh will disappoint. It just doesn't offer classes like that. But overall, Lehigh is the perfect place to get a top-notch education and have a fun social life. It's also a great stepping-stone for students who were bright in high school but didn't apply themselves as much as they should have. Professors here really draw you out and show you how to apply your intelligence and creativity in order to operate at your best.

The Students

The students at Lehigh never cease to impress me. They are all intelligent and work extremely hard. Typical stereotypes don't really apply here. Most athletes have very good GPAs, and sorority girls, if anything, tend to be perfectionists when it comes to their work. At the same time, there's a major work hard–play hard mentality at Lehigh, and students reward themselves when the weekend rolls around.

Lehigh isn't the most diverse place in the world. Most students are from Pennsylvania, New York, or New Jersey. We don't have many quirky individuals. Sometimes it's hard to tell the girls apart—they're all hot, blond, thin, and dress extremely well. Coach, Louis Vuitton, and Burberry bags are the norm, as are Ralph Lauren turned-up collars. The guys all look like they just stepped out of an Abercrombie ad, and you'll be hard pressed to find a Lehigh male without at least one Polo or Lacoste shirt in his closet. Fine, most kids are rich, white, and conservative, but they're also very tolerant of differences, and interesting and intelligent when you get to know them.

The Activities

Lehigh has its share of athletic events, and frat brothers attend in large numbers, but this isn't a school where everyone heads to every football game. There's a decently large audience and tailgate scene, for sure, but it lacks the intensity of state schools'. I guess the exception would be wrestling—students have a large interest in attending wrestling matches here because Lehigh has one of the best teams in the nation, but it is extremely difficult to get tickets because there is only a small section for student seats. If you're lucky enough to get seats, go. It's an awesome cheering, chanting, stomping experience.

We also have a campus movie theater that shows recent films nearly every weekend. And, there are theater shows and musical acts each week in the Zoellner Arts Center. And Lehigh hosts a lot of well-known comedians and impressive guest speakers. (When Michael Moore came, there was a lot of protest . . . the only two organized protests in my tenure here have been an antiwar demonstration and an anti-Moore demonstration.) There's also a big musical festival at the end of the year, with big-name bands.

> "Lehigh is built into the side of a mountain, so everything's angled at about 45 degrees. By the time you graduate you'll have very toned calves."
>
> ✦ Lucie, junior

The Social Scene

Making friends is very easy during your first year here. You'll become close with people in your hall, in your classes, or during rush. . . . There's a decent party scene at Lehigh when the weekends roll around, but it's limited. The school has started cracking down on drinking and general craziness. The frats feel the crunch, and now they sometimes make their parties closed events to stay out of trouble. This means, once the open-house rush period is over, frats will sometimes invite only one or two sororities to a party, and if you're not invited, you have to do something else with your weekend. This has introduced a weird element of exclusivity to Lehigh's party scene. If you're in the Greek system, you won't have to worry. If you're not, then you can always go to off-campus parties, small gatherings with your friends, or to one of the three bars that are right next to campus and usually full of Lehigh students. Also, if you have a car, we're about an hour and a half from both Philly and New York.

Name: Sumit
Hometown: North Brunswick, New Jersey
Class Year: Senior
Major: Electrical engineering
Extracurriculars: Delta Phi fraternity
Career Goal Engineer

How would you describe Lehigh's reputation?

Lehigh's unofficial motto is "Work hard, play hard."

Is this reputation accurate?

Extremely accurate. People come to Lehigh for both a great education and great times. This is a place for the kids who almost but didn't quite get into Ivy League schools, or kids who got in but decided they wanted to have a little more fun in their college years.

What aspect of your school would a prospective student not see on a campus tour?

A prospective student would not grasp how filthy rich a lot of students at this school are. You might see the numerous A4s, M3s, and SUVs in the student parking lot, but then the tour guide would walk in another direction and insist that Lehigh is, indeed, diverse. In my experience, this place is 70 percent white, and most of my friends have parents who make at least $200K per year. Lehigh is *incredibly* generous with its financial aid packages, more generous than *any* Ivy League school, so it's not hard to come here if you don't have the funds, but once you are here, it might feel harder to fit in.

The Institution

The weather is hot and humid in the summer, amazingly nice during spring and fall, and horribly snowy during the winter. Lehigh is (quite literally) on the side of a mountain, so be prepared to hike everyday. All the on-campus housing—freshman dorms, upperclassmen apartments, and frats—are at the top of the mountain, and all the classes are at the bottom. The walk down to class isn't bad, but the walk back up is. Luckily, buses run back and forth about every ten minutes. When it snows,

> "On Friday or Saturday night Lehigh students will head to the Hill, a group of over twenty Greek houses on . . . a hill."
> ✦ Stuart, sophomore

however (we'll frequently get a foot or two), even SUVs aren't going anywhere.

Because there aren't enough upperclassmen apartments, housing is a problem after freshman year. All the rising sophomores enter into a lottery in hopes they get assigned housing. If they don't, they have to move to an off-campus apartment (most kids move to 5th Street, Hillside, and Birkel). Or they can join a fraternity or sorority (members get guaranteed housing in the frat or sorority houses until they graduate, and the frat and sorority houses are amazing—think twenty-bedroom mansions with private kitchens, dining rooms, living rooms, party rooms, pool rooms, big-screen TV rooms . . .).

I chose to come to Lehigh because it offered the best value in terms of education and price (like I said, if you qualify, the financial aid is amazing and can make this place just as affordable as a state school). And in the end, if you make it through Lehigh, you'll be rewarded with a great job.

The Education

For your first two years here, most of your classes will be lectures with seventy other kids. After that, class size will drop dramatically to ten to twenty other students. Once this happens, the academic setting feels intimate, and hanging out with professors after class is not uncommon. Lehigh does have a core curriculum, which unfortunately means you'll spend a lot of time during your first two years here fulfilling assorted basic requirements. These classes aren't always the most stimulating, and some make the mistake of not paying attention and, in the end, failing them.

This only means you'll have to retake the class. Luckily, Lehigh has a policy where if you do fail a class, once you retake it Lehigh drops the fail and replaces it with the new grade (so failing a class won't hurt your GPA in the long run). Ironically, failing in certain cases will actually help you (I know some who have failed classes on purpose because they weren't doing well, knowing the second time around they could get a really good grade that would end up boosting their GPA).

The Students

At Lehigh, you'll find *a lot* of preppy kids, but there are also a number of students from foreign countries, which is neat because it means you get to interact with people from Ghana, Pakistan, China, etc., and this gives you a better view of the world.

Lehigh has a great reputation in the Northeast, but—unfortunately—outside of the Northeast it's not terribly well known. So most graduates wind up in the tristate area, especially NYC, where our degree is respected and other graduates–business contacts are abundant.

The Activities

Lehigh has an incredibly active Greek system. The Greeks do everything from throwing parties on campus to running massive food drives and doing volunteer work en masse. If you don't think you're the type to pledge, well, that'll change when you come to Lehigh and you see how great it is.

The Social Scene

When Lehigh students aren't working hard they're playing hard. Every weekend the Hill is packed with tons of parties. If you're in with the scene, on a typical weekend you can stroll into maybe a dozen fraternities houses that are each holding amazing events. And parties go on all night long. Don't be surprised if you see kids still playing Beirut at 7:00 a.m. the next morning, having still not gone to bed.

A note on the meal plan: Do *not* choose twenty-one meals/week—you won't eat all those meals; it's just a waste of money. Go for the four-teen meals/week and ask your parents to load up on Gold Plus (which is Lehigh currency that's accepted at dining halls as well as off-campus sub shops and pizza places throughout the local area).

Name: Aliza
Hometown: New York, New York
Class Year: Sophomore
Major: Journalism, with minors in public relations and English
Extracurriculars: Writer for *The Brown and White*, Alpha Chi Omega, Girl Scout troop leader, and nursing-home volunteer
Career Goal: I'd like to be in public relations, or become a magazine editor.

How would you describe Lehigh's reputation?
Lehigh is said to be a work hard–party hard school with a huge emphasis on Greek life.

Is this reputation accurate?
This reputation is definitely accurate. Students party all the time here, but when it's time to buckle down we know how to do that, too.

> "Lehigh has a lot of formal support groups for our sports teams. There's the Hawk's Nest, a cheering-section comprising more than eight hundred students in T-shirts that say, 'Don't Mess with the Nest,' and the Lehigh Guys and the Mountainhawk Maniacs, smaller groups of students who paint their chests brown and white and scream their lungs out."
>
> ✦ Jeremy, freshman

What would an admissions officer at your school probably not tell a prospective student?
An admissions officer would definitely leave out the fact that if you're not involved in Greek life, there's not much to do on weekends. If I weren't Greek, I think my social life would just disappear. And it's not like off campus has a great scene—there's just some bars and movie theaters. Bethlehem is kind of a sketchy little town.

The Institution

I think Lehigh is the perfect size for a university—a nice happy medium. So far, I don't think I've met anyone who doesn't love it here. Freshman year was so much fun, my guy friends rushed and pledged fraternities, I went to all their parties, then I rushed and pledged my own sorority. Once I was part of the system, every Saturday in the fall I was able to go to Morning Cocktails with a fraternity, then we would all head to the football field and tailgate before games.

The area surrounding Lehigh is OK, not great. It has everything you need, at the least. But if you're looking for city life, you'll have to travel a bit. Luckily, New York City and Philadelphia are only an hour-and-a-half drive away, which means you can be in Manhattan by dinnertime.

The Education

The education that one receives at Lehigh depends on the college they're in. There are four colleges to choose from: Arts and Sciences, Business, Education, and Engineering. Arts and Sciences is commonly referred to as "Arts and Crafts," the College of Education is the newest and smallest college, and the P. C. Rossin College of Engineering is the most well-known and respected college, with a first-year core curriculum infamous for weeding out those students who don't really want to be engineers.

Every college has a different core curriculum, but in general, freshman year you have to take two English classes, a freshman seminar class, and "Choices and Decisions" (sessions with your adviser). Before graduation, you have to have taken at least three credits of mathematics, three credits of arts and humanities classes, eight credits in the natural sciences (including a lab), and eight credits in the social sciences.

I'd say I spend about eighteen hours a week on work when I don't have exams or big papers due. My friends in the business and engineering schools definitely work harder than I do. Generally, at Lehigh, classes aren't discussed on Saturday nights—weekends are for *not studying,* unless it's exam time.

The Students

Lehigh isn't very diverse and the different racial groups on campus tend to stick together, so there isn't much integration between whites and nonwhites. We have some students from the South, Midwest, and West, but most students come from the Northeast. We're not a very political campus—apathy is the norm. And there isn't much rallying behind student groups here, none of which are very vocal. The only student group that springs to mind as having any influence at all would be the school newspaper, *The Brown and White,* which is fairly well read and covers issues of importance on campus.

The Activities

There are some schools close by—Muhlenberg (ten minutes away), Lafayette (thirty minutes), and Penn (forty minutes). There's not much interaction, though, aside from the Lehigh-Lafayette football rivalry.

Lehigh puts on a lot of events every year in our large theater, the Zoellner, and these are always well attended. We have a variety of well-known speakers who come to lecture on a regular basis. We also have lots of theater and music events, but more people head to athletic events than head to theater and music events.

The Social Scene

By the time you graduate from Lehigh you'll be a partying aficionado. Partying is an art form here, and students quickly become adept at getting incredibly wasted in incredibly short periods of time. Fraternities are the nexus of the campus social life, and when frat parties aren't broken up by the police, they're a lot of fun. The alcohol flows like water, and you can always find a game of Beirut (beer-pong) being played. If you're not in a frat or sorority, you can still go to registered Greek parties and have fun. I think the Greek scene is great, but there are other facets to Lehigh. I have several friends who aren't in a fraternity or sorority, and they're perfectly happy with their life here. It's up to you to figure out what you want to get involved in and to realize there's a social niche for everyone.

Notable Lehigh Alumni Include:
Nora R. Slatkin, former executive director, CIA
Herbert J. Siegel, CEO, Chris-Craft Industries
Lee A. Iacocca, former CEO, Chrysler Corporation
Roger Penske, CEO, Penske Motors, Penske Racing
Terry Hart, NASA astronaut
Warren V. Musser, CEO, Safeguard Scientifics, Inc.

LEWIS & CLARK COLLEGE

Founded: 1867

Location: Portland, OR

E-mail: admissions@lclark.edu

Phone: (503) 768-7188

Web Site: www.lclark.edu

Number of Undergraduates: 1,750

Number of Graduate Students: 570

Cost: Approximately $33,500 per year

Application Deadline: February 1

Early Decision: November 15

Rating:	Notable Majors/Programs:
Selective	Premed, Social Sciences, English

Size:
- ● Small ○ Medium ○ Large

Location:
- ○ Urban ● Suburban ○ Rural

On a Saturday, students talk about academics:
- ○ Always ● Sometimes ○ Never

Nightlife:
- ○ Intense ○ Moderate ● Laid-back

Politically, Lewis & Clark leans:
- ● Left ○ Right ○ Split

Diversity:
- ○ High ● Low ○ Medium

Students describe Lewis & Clark in five words:
- Intimate, hardworking, woodsy, passionate, free
- We color outside the lines

From the School

If these sound like you, we encourage you to explore Lewis & Clark College:

- An academic achiever
- An independently minded scholar who loves a challenge
- A planner with the ability to carry through on projects
- A creative and collaborative thinker
- A multitalented individual with diverse interests
- A committed and open-minded member of the global community.

—www.lclark.edu

If you're interested in Lewis & Clark, you may also be interested in:
UC Santa Cruz, Evergreen State, Macalester, Pitzer, Reed, Whitman

Name: Jon

Hometown: Sandy, Oregon

Class Year: Senior

Major: English

Extracurriculars: *Literary Review* (annual publication); copresident, Spanish Club; varsity basketball (first and second year of college); peer tutor; Oregon Bus Project volunteer; SMART volunteer.

Career Goal: To delay the finding of a "real" career for a few years by traveling overseas to teach English

How would you describe Lewis & Clark's reputation?

We have a bad rep because our former president invested $10.5 million of the school's general fund in an environmental company that went bankrupt. Oops. That's bad, but what's worse is that he wasn't fired; he'll just teach here now. Besides that, I think in general we're thought of as a hippie school.

Is this reputation accurate?

The hippie reputation is bunk. True, we have a lot of environmentally conscious students and we run a naked mile every year, but our "hippies" are merely the scraggly college kids on every campus with beards and long hair who throw Frisbees, smoke weed, listen to Bob Marley, Phish, Ani DiFranco, and talk about peace, oppression, and drugs. There are also a lot of hipsters, indie rockers, athletes, mathletes, stoners, and overachievers; and they all participate in the Environmental Affairs Symposium. They're not hippies—just college students.

What aspect of Lewis & Clark would a prospective student not see on a campus tour?

They'd be told, "Lewis & Clark is a fantastic liberal arts institution with small class sizes, engaging professors, a wide array of campus activities, and an impressive mix of people from around the world." I know because that is what I was told. But a prospective student would not see many people from "around the world." He also would not see downtown Portland (one of the best things about the school) or the packed computer lab at 8:30 p.m. He would not see me because I'm graduating.

The Institution

The campus is beautiful. It's big enough to have variety but small enough to get everywhere by foot. Mount Hood is visible from campus, and there is a nice balance of old buildings that offer inspiration and newer buildings that offer technological advances. The weather isn't bad, if you don't mind the rain. I don't because the moisture (along with our exceptional landscaping crew) keeps everything green and lush.

The Education

I think what's great about this school is that most of my friends don't see education as a burden. People want to have fun and sure, we get fed up with classes and the work and professors, but the majority of the student body is genuinely interested in learning, and this sentiment extends beyond the classroom. It's not uncool to talk about our studies over dinner, while drinking a beer, or on the weekends.

More than half of the student body spends at least a semester overseas—Africa, China, Cuba, or Spain, for example. We have a great reputation for our study-abroad programs, which are great for experiencing other cultures as well as escaping the claustrophobic atmosphere that can occur here.

> "We have a fairly large contingent of hippies, as well as students who love to get naked."
>
> ✦ Maggie, sophomore

The Students

There's someone from every social circle represented on campus. Students at Lewis & Clark are socially and politically aware, and they use this knowledge to get involved in the community. Some students like to display their liberalism by going to class naked on our clothing-optional campus. I think this would have been more interesting to see when I was in junior high and nudity was still a forbidden excitement. Now, I wish these people would put their clothes back on because it's hard for me to take notes in a class when two breasts won't stop staring at me.

The Activities

There are very few religious activities, and our sports teams suck. However, there are a lot of fun things to do on campus, if you make the time to seek them out and attend. When my friends and I are bored, we make movies, ride tiny bikes down the huge hill that goes up to the zoo downtown (it's called "zoobombing"), make big, elaborate dinners and eat them, or drink tasty Northwest beer.

The Social Scene

What can I say? It's college. Everyone has to go to class. Most people do their homework. Most people drink too much at first and then wise up. Some people smoke weed. Some people party; some people don't. It's what you'd expect at a small liberal arts college anywhere in America. There is something for everyone, and it's just a matter of finding it.

Name: Liv
Hometown: Oslo, Norway
Class Year: Junior
Majors: English literature
Extracurriculars: Debate Team, vice president of International Students of Lewis & Clark (ISLC), 2004 International Fair Coordinator, Third-Culture-Kid board member, salsa dancing, "Amica" volunteer
Career Goal: I'd like to work in education in a job that would allow me to combine travel, writing, reading, and cross-cultural communication.

How would you describe Lewis & Clark's reputation?

Lewis & Clark is known for its "tree-hugging hippies." It's rumored that everyone dresses in tattered homemade organic clothing, has dreadlocks, and is busy smoking pot. If you're not on the laid-back side, you're in line with the activists who petition for everything from global warming to the detriments of wasted chalk. The stakes are high, and political and personal views are flamboyant. All this happens with a friendly smile, paint, poster paper, petitions—and if all else fails, protest.

Is this reputation accurate?

It holds some truth. Lewis & Clark is known for being very active and vocal. There are many different viewpoints and opinions cropping up in the form of a lecture, must-see documentary, brown-bag lunch, discussion, or even a revolutionary dance once or twice a year. But no one is as stereotypical as they seem—the school is a big community, filled with enthusiasm, skepticism, and one too many

social gatherings for the benefit of society as a whole.

What would an admissions officer at Lewis & Clark probably not tell a prospective student?

Ethnically, Lewis & Clark is not very diverse, but internationally there is a wide range of people from different countries.

> "Athletics are not big here; I wish more people would show up at games and meets."
>
> ✦ Whitney, senior

The Institution

Lewis & Clark is located on a little hill on the outskirts of Portland. We're nicely surrounded by trees, scenery, a little creek. Being in this domelike forest, and being a smaller school, you feel safe walking around late at night.

It's a superfriendly place and there are all types of support services and groups, which range from social to more political. As an incoming international student, I was embraced by the administrators, guided through the bureaucratic paperwork, and practically escorted to every corner of the campus during my first three days here—welcome help for a dazed freshman!

The disadvantage of this small school is the lack of connection with the outside world. Going to the store seems a very odd thing to do. While most students will head down to a concert, catch a movie or go eat, we're not very much in touch with such simple things as dealing with people on very basic levels. I think that once people leave here, they will have to learn a lot about socializing with different types of people—especially those that hold different (nonliberal) opinions.

The Education

Some of my favorite classes have been ones in which different disciplines are brought together, such as African Politics and Literature. I was able to take my passion for literature and use it to read into the politics of apartheid. Classes here can also have a lot of depth to them: I took a Theater and Society class that called for us, in the course of one semester, to put on a production, to write a script of our own, to write a regular analytical paper, to take on an impromptu Dadaist performance—and I even got to see my professor do an interpretive dance atop a table.

It seems that certain barriers between students and professors are broken down, and the friendships can be informal and laid-back. I was surprised by this. At Lewis & Clark, a professor is really just a human being interested in listening to your ideas and getting you to push yourself harder than you think you ever could. Their office doors are mostly open. On occasion, a professor will tour the art gallery with you, accompany you on a nature walk, sit down and discuss Blake over a cup of coffee, or even let you bake in the sun while they lecture to you on the soft green grass.

The Students

A few weeks ago there was a survey in the school paper asking "What religion are you?" The majority of the school answered that they had no religious affiliation. And while no one defined religion really finds a secure home at Lewis & Clark, students are still spiritual. They all have their own ways of dealing with religion. There are religious groups on campus, but they tend to be pretty soft-spoken.

> "Downtown Portland is hugely fun, with great independent record stores, bookstores, and thrift stores."
> ✦ Whitney, senior

There are *a lot* of other groups on campus. You have a womyn's center, an ecological group, Third-Culture-Kids, student governments, activists, Amnesty International, swing dancing, etc. I've spent a fair amount of time on the debate team, which is an intense ride. And I'm also inclined to stick to identity groups such as the Third-Culture-Kids, where people who have lived all over the world, or who have been moved from their own culture due to their parents' work, go to the movies and have dinners together. This group tends to be more supportive and not as popular as some of the more vocal ones.

Occasionally when a big issue arises, such as the war in Iraq, people pledge silence or walk around naked in protest. You'll hear about this a lot. But you should also know that not everyone, luckily, is about shocking the rest of the community.

> "On a tour, you won't see the very dirty outdoor pool or the completely ridiculous classrooms under the gym."
> ✦ Lizzy, senior

The Activities

It's 3:00 a.m. on a Wednesday and everyone's still up. Some come waltzing back into the dorm after several hours of a role-playing game, others have sat through two movies and can't sleep. Some of us are getting some of those things we put off all week ready for class the next day. I'm finishing my PowerPoint presentation, which didn't seem that important after my classes ended at 6:00 p.m. So instead, I went to get some dinner after my classes and to two activity meetings. Then I decided I should probably go for a swim for an hour. I headed back to my dorm at around 9:00 p.m., when the resident advisers have organized a study break—more food, mocktails, cookies, and chocolate. I've socialized for an hour when my friend wanders in and wants to know if I'll see the latest Spanish film with her, one in a series of several throughout the year presented by the Spanish Club. When I get back around midnight I check my e-mail and then realize it's midnight and I have to do homework! *Arg!!!!!* And all I really want to do is get some sleep before my 8:00 a.m. class.

The Social Scene

If there isn't a party in someone's basement with illegal alcohol, there's definitely something else to do. Portland is not a big night city, but it has a fair share of options, from hanging out in the local coffee shop (not recommended) to going to concerts, plays, movies, etc. It also has a really big bookstore that sells all sorts of comics, travel guides, literature, and academic work. If you're not big on walking through the small streets of Portland, the school has movie nights, performances, a quasi–Dead Poets' Society, rock bands, or if you're daring enough, there is always midnight swimming in the reflecting pools on campus (not officially permitted).

Name: Carmen

Hometown: Rutherford, New Jersey

Class Year: Sophomore

Major: English

Extracurriculars: Vice president of French Club, WRAP volunteer (Write Around Portland)

Career Goal: I hope to become a writer and a professor of English (focusing on science fiction and astronomy in literature).

How would you describe Lewis & Clark's reputation?

Lewis & Clark College has the reputation of being a very good liberal arts college, which has its own unique taste. A bunch of hippies who smoke pot but still study very hard.

Is this reputation accurate?

Lewis & Clark is definitely not a party school. We are all very focused on our studies. We do have some neo-hippies, but we have *a few* neocons.

> "Unlike my last school, where it was all about lip gloss and football at dinner, you hear discussions about racism, gender bias, social inequities."
>
> ✦ Dana, junior

What would an admissions officer at Lewis & Clark probably not tell a prospective student?

I know that the admissions office has tried to be careful about exposing parents to some of our activities. We occasionally have some naked events, and once a tour group did have the pleasure of seeing a naked soccer game (which was not scheduled), but that hasn't happened again. But they also wouldn't tell you about everyone's amazing sense of humor here. I am laughing a lot of the time, which helps reduce stress considerably.

The Institution

Being a Northeasterner in the Northwest is interesting. I am teased a lot for my "accent." At first, I definitely felt a culture clash, but I really appreciate the culture of the Northwest. It is much more relaxed and not quite as judgmental.

The physical layout of the campus is one of the main reasons that I came to Lewis & Clark. The grass is this amazing green, and the architecture is gorgeous. If Wordsworth were alive, he would definitely agree that this campus is a Romantic's paradise.

At Lewis & Clark, each student is required to spend two years on campus. First year, you can request which dorm you'd like and you usually get your first choice. The second year, students have more choices and can have a single. There are also apartments on campus for juniors and seniors, though most opt to live off campus. But all the housing's very nice compared to many other schools I've seen—it's kept very clean and, for the most part, students have a lot of living space.

I chose this school because I wanted to be in a college community where students want to study and explore their interests and not just get a degree to get a job. I also wanted a school that would make me comfortable: able to meet new people and not be judged. I truly think that Lewis & Clark has filled these two criteria. I love it here.

The Education

Grades are not as important to Lewis & Clark students as learning is. We learn from each other as well as from the professors. Compared to other schools, Lewis & Clark has a large workload—at orientation they described it as a full-time job, which seems about right: I spend about forty-five hours a week on work, including time spent in classes.

Because we are a liberal arts school, we have a number of core requirements. And since I am an English major with a physics minor, I do get to see both sides of academia at Lewis & Clark. The humanities student spends a lot more time writing papers and often needs silence in order to ponder. The science student spends more time in classrooms and labs. Plenty of research opportunities exist in the sciences. For example, in the Physics Department, students can work in the observatory or help with the chaos study that one of our professors is working on. The science departments also keep their students informed of research opportunities outside Lewis & Clark.

The Students

There is no "average" student here. The college prides itself on having international students. I'm first generation Polish-American and my current roommate is a TCK, or Third-Culture-Kid—she was born in South Africa and lived in Japan and Singapore. Many students are from California, but I often meet people from the East Coast and from the Midwest. The most vocal groups on campus are ISLC (International Students of Lewis & Clark) and BSU (Black Student Union). Our school is mostly Naderish liberal, though quite a few students do feel that conservative and other arguments should be considered more carefully. I think most students aim to form opinions after researching all the sides of an argument.

> "I've been overwhelmed by the quality of the faculty; they refuse to settle for anything less than their students' best work."
> ✦ Christine, freshman

The Activities

We have athletics, but students usually go to other student-activities events like Casino Night and to hear bands that play on campus. Students try to get off campus about once a week. I usually like to take a walk to my favorite part of Portland: NW Twenty-third Avenue. I like walking to Washington Park, the largest park in Portland, to get a good view of the city, and the views from the hillsides are amazing, especially at night.

The Social Scene

Parties are pretty common, but usually are on the weekend. I think a lot of students when they go to college expect a huge drinking scene, as displayed in many American movies about college. However, at Lewis & Clark, many students drink alcohol, and many do not, and the two populations tend not to mix together regularly. Lewis & Clark does not have frats or sororities, so most house parties are off campus and composed of upperclassmen. They're pretty fun, but difficult to get to without a car.

Meeting new people is not very difficult, as long as you are willing. Even if I don't know someone, saying hi is perfectly fine, and smiling is very common. I met my closest friends because we lived right across the hall from one another our first year. I met other friends from going to events at French Club and in class. I also try to eat with different people at mealtimes when I get the chance.

Notable Lewis & Clark Alumni Include:
Christopher Roberts, president, Polygram Records
Doug Greene, associate director, Peace Corps
Earl Blumenauer, Oregon congressman, governor
Keith Lindner, CEO, Chiquita Brands
Lewis Sharp, director, Denver Art Museum
Markie Post, actress

MACALESTER COLLEGE

Founded: 1874

Location: St. Paul, MN

Phone: (651) 696-6357

E-mail: admissions@macalester.edu

Web site: www.macalester.edu

Number of Undergraduates: 1,840

Number of Graduate Students: 0

Cost: Approximately $32,000 per year

Application Deadline: January 15

Early Decision: November 15

Rating:	Notable Majors/Programs:
Very Selective	Psychology, Biology, Economics, Political Science

Size:
● Small   ○ Medium   ○ Large

Location:
● Urban   ○ Suburban   ○ Rural

On a Saturday, students talk about academics:
● Always   ○ Sometimes   ○ Never

Nightlife:
○ Intense   ○ Moderate   ● Laid-back

Politically, Macalester leans:
● Left   ○ Right   ○ Split

Diversity:
○ High   ○ Low   ● Medium

Students describe Macalester in five words:
- Progressive intellectuals freezing in Minnesota
- Small, respected, international, political, liberal

From the School

Macalester has a long history of strong academics, a global student body, and involvement in the issues of the world. The Macalester Seal, which originated in 1885, portrays the college's belief in the harmony of nature and revelation, represented by two robed figures. One holds a telescope and represents science investigating nature; the other holds God's word, representing revelation.

—www.macalester.edu

If you're interested in Macalester, you may also be interested in:
Carleton, UChicago, Middlebury, Oberlin, Swarthmore

Name: Maura
Hometown: Galesburg, Illinois
Class Year: Junior
Major: English
Extracurriculars: Student newspaper (*Mac Weekly*)
Career Goals: I'd like to earn a living as a writer.

How would you describe Macalester's reputation?

Macalester is a prestigious, academically focused school that's said to be full of pot-smoking hippies, wealthy liberals, and homosexuals.

Is this reputation accurate? Why or why not?

Prestigous? Yup. Academically focused? Yup. Do we have pot-smoking hippies, wealthy liberals, and homosexuals? Yup. But we also have a fair amount of conservative students, and a *lot* of international students. So factor those into the mix.

What aspect of your school would a prospective student not see on a campus tour?

A prospective student might not see how well everyone at Macalester gets along. Everyone here is really friendly, and our social climate is very relaxed.

The Institution

Macalester is in Minnesota. (Why, I'll never understand.) Essentially, the weather is unbearable. In the winter you'll have to wear long underwear and a hat every day. It's the price we pay for an extraordinary education. Also, the food is actually pretty good. If I had any complaints at all, I'd say there are *too many* vegetarian and vegan options on offer. I like my meat!

Macalester is pretty small, and though you end up knowing everyone (and quite a lot about everyone), our size is a good thing. There is a real sense of community here, and it's nice to walk across campus and see your friends. It's also nice to be around so many people who are so uniformly intelligent—I come from a small, conservative, closed-minded, religious town, and Macalester is an amazing change from my high school days. And not just the school, but the town we're in as well—a lot of Macalester grads settle down here, breed, and then send their kids right back to Macalester. So students generally get on well with the locals because lots of the locals were once students themselves!

I think the best tradition here is the Midnight Breakfast. This happens every semester during finals, and the entire Macalester student body shows up at midnight at a predetermined location for this amazing meal. And every year a big group of students runs naked through the Midnight Breakfast crowd (mind you, it's freezing *with* clothes on!). The naked kids chant the Macalester fight song, everyone laughs, it's fun. The annual Queer Union dance is also a great tradition. Everyone dresses in drag or in their most revealing clothing—it's a whole night of debauchery!

> "A sign on the boys' bathroom reads: Single-sex Bathrooms Oppress Transgender Students."
>
> ✦ Nate, senior

The Education

Students at Mac are not very competitive, which I appreciate. Most classes are discussion based, and everyone receives personal attention from professors. We're such a small school, there's no reason *not* to receive personal attention. There is a lot of schoolwork assigned, but you can get away with doing a surprisingly small amount and still get OK grades. I guess it's like any college, where there are people who work nonstop and people who never work, with most students falling somewhere in between the two extremes.

The best courses I've taken here were Acting I, which was an insane 7.5-hour-a-week course that helped me understand what acting is fundamentally about; The Regional Geography of Africa, which focuses on the culture and landscape of Sub-Saharan Africa; and Catholicism, where we visited different types of Catholic churches and discussed church doctrine and the issues affecting modern Catholicism.

The Students

Most students at Macalester are liberals. Even the Republicans are probably the most liberal Republicans you'll ever meet. The Mac Democrats and the Mac Greens are really popular student groups, and the Queer Union (the LGBT group) is extremely active. Minnesota's Twin Cities (St. Paul and Minneapolis) host lots of protests and rallies, and Mac students come to them en masse and play a crucial role. We're a fairly politically active campus.

Our student body is mostly upper middle class, coming from all over America and many different countries throughout the world. Everyone is tolerant of everyone—even the hardcore jocks show up at the Queer Union dances, fully decked out in drag. And the queer kids show up at jock parties, downing beer with the best of them. If I had to pick a cooler group on this campus, the queer kids or the jocks, the queer kids would win hands down. It's like high school in reverse.

The Activities

Though Macalester is in the Twin Cities, most students don't head off campus much. The Twin Cities are both really sprawled out, so they're not the types of places you can head to and just walk around. You need to have a very specific destination in mind. It's all more trouble than it's worth, and most students just stick to Mac, where there are always things going on: plays, dances, sporting events, etc. On any given afternoon, students are hanging out, playing guitar in the dorm hallways, drinking beer in someone's room, or when it's warm, dancing and drumming outside in the courtyard. I'm in a rock band, and we play lots of shows all over campus, especially in the basement of "football house" (an on-campus house that's almost always occupied by football players). Spring is, by far, the best time at Mac, when students are outside all day and all night, playing Frisbee, foursquare, or whiffle ball, just lying in the sun, thanking God because the snow has melted!

> "We talk about our academics constantly."
> ✦ Sho, junior

The Social Scene

There are no frats or sororities at Mac, so the party scene is less intense than, say, what you'd see in *Animal House*. For the most part, we have lots of small parties. Most people drink, but few people overindulge. A typical Friday or Saturday night would involve hanging around with your friends, wondering what to do. Usually you'll all head to the liquor store, then go to some academic event on campus. Then, you'll head over to a party. Around 2:00 a.m., you and your friends will go back to someone's dorm and talk or play guitar and sing until 4:00 a.m. It's all very cozy, very lovely.

Last thing, most juniors and seniors live off campus at Macalester because the upperclassmen dorms are not very nice. This means, when you're an upperclassmen, you'll party more off campus than on campus. And, accordingly, there's a schism between the upperclassmen and underclassmen social life.

Name: Luke
Hometown: Santa Fe, New Mexico
Class Year: Junior
Major: Religion
Extracurriculars: Macalester Protestants, Council for Religious Understanding, Knight Moves Chess, and Go Team, Community Service member (leader for the Lilly Project and volunteering at Hmong American Partnership)
Career Goal: I'd like to be a teacher, social worker, or minister.

How would you describe Macalester's reputation?

Macalester is academically rigorous, socially conscious, and politically progressive.

Is this reputation accurate?

It is accurate. Macalester students work very hard, they care about the world around them, and—since people like U.N. Secretary-General Kofi Annan are counted among our alums—Macalester tends to attract progressive-minded individuals.

What would an admissions officer at your school probably not tell a prospective student?

An admissions officer might downplay how cold it gets here . . . really, it's like the White Witch from *The Chronicles of Narnia* decided to curse us all. Minnesota is freezing!

The Institution

My first week of Macalester, everyone on my hall started talking to one another right away. We stayed up all night three days in, finding out where each person was from, what their pasts were like, what brought them to Macalester. There's a really strong community feeling here, and it gets to the point where, if you head home for a weekend, you can expect multiple notes under your door when you return saying, "Hey, missed you this weekend, let's get lunch! Hope you had fun." All this leads to a very strong sense of community, and lots of (what I hope will be) lifelong friendships.

The comfort you feel with friends here crosses over to professors, too. One semester I decided that I wanted to research ancient Egypt for a creative writing nonfiction project. With a phone call, I arranged a meeting with the chair of the Classics Department, who eagerly pointed me in the right direction.

> "Once there was this spontaneous pow-wow outside my window at 1:00 a.m. Fifty people had congregated with drums and other musical instruments, and everyone started dancing and singing and joining in."
> ✦ Sasha, senior

The Education

At Macalester, we *love* the phrases "postmodernism," "post-Colonialist discourse," and "hegemony." Be prepared to say each phrase multiple times during any given week. Almost all your classes at Macalester will be extremely small and discussion based, even in the hard sciences. Generally, Macalester professors strive to get students thinking, considering the ideas thrown out, and coming up with ideas of their own. And our professors are known for being able to bring even the most boring topics to life—I can still vividly recall walking into Literature of the Americas, a class that examined a movement called negritude and its evolution. I thought this class was going to be incredibly boring, but from day one I was hooked. The professor was energetic, she broke down even the most complex subjects in no time, and, with her help, I was able to rip through incredibly heavy readings, finding and considering every philosophical point. In class, any time someone would offer their thoughts she'd tie their thoughts into the text and complement the student. Students *hated* missing class. This is how it goes at Mac. If you choose your professors well, you'll have a shockingly good time with your academics.

The Students

Macalester students are really socially conscious. Macalester is *very* gay-friendly. The LGBT/ Queer Union is one of the largest student groups on campus, and they throw great parties that everyone attends. It's wonderful how many of my peers here have an honest and profound desire to try and make the world a better place. Some join activist groups, some join student government, others do community service. But almost everyone gets involved and makes a difference. Most students also love to talk about their academics outside of class . . . you'll start off discussing Foucault and Derrida, which will segue into discussions of morals, which will segue into something else, and something else, until you find yourself heatedly debating whether carbonated beverages should be called "pop" or "soda," and it's 4:00 a.m.

The Activities

Macalester is right in between St. Paul and Minneapolis. Both cities have lots of clubs and bars, movie theaters and sports arenas, paid jobs and impressive internship opportunities, but students don't really leave Macalester's campus that often. We have too much fun right where are, with all of our friends and all of our extracurriculars. The majority of students, if they frequent the Twin Cities at all, go there only for their academic resources (lots of libraries) or because there's lot of good community service to be done in urban areas.

There are a million clubs at Macalester to join, and if there's a club you really want to be part of but it doesn't exist, you can start the club yourself. Case in point: when I first got to Macalester I was excited to join the chess team only to find out Macalester didn't have a chess team. So I started my own. Now the club has more than fifty members and has played matches against University of Minnesota undergraduates and law students. Some of my friends were walking around in downtown Minneapolis one day when a random idea popped into their heads: "We should start a club that serves soup." Within a month MacSoup had plenty of members, and now they meet once a week to make, and hand out, soup to anyone who wants some. When you put intelligent, creative kids in the middle of Minnesota, you never know what they'll do!

The Social Scene

Sure, we drink like students do at every college in the country, and a large handful of students smoke pot. But Mac students drink and smoke in moderation. There's no excessive puking every Saturday night at 4:00 a.m., and then sleeping until 4:00 p.m. on Sunday. Instead, this is the place where people will get a bit buzzed, then host Scattergories tournaments where the winner gets a homemade trophy. We'll throw pirate-themed parties, or get-togethers where we'll plow through six episodes of *Buffy the Vampire Slayer,* supplying heavy commentary. We also tend to play a lot of late-night Foosball on weekends, and a lot of late-night pool.

Name: Matthew
Hometown: Black Earth, Wisconsin
Class Year: Sophomore
Major: Biology
Extracurriculars: Orchestra, swing dancing, Macalester Christian Fellowship
Career Goal Research in biology—possibly in cellular biology

How would you describe Macalester's reputation?

Macalester is supposed to be a very liberal college with a lot of international students and a lot of self-styled "intellectuals" . . . in the middle of Minnesota.

Is this reputation accurate?

To the letter.

What would an admissions officer at your school probably not tell a prospective student? What aspect of your school would a prospective student not see on a campus tour?

An admissions officer probably wouldn't tell people the reason Macalester attracts so many international students is because it offers them significantly more financial aid than they would get at other schools. And on a tour, prospective students wouldn't see all the late-night studying that goes on in the dorms and the very tired students who show up for class at 8:00 a.m. every morning.

The Institution

Macalester College sits over a span of about four blocks. It's a pretty campus, with a strange mix of redbrick buildings and modern, glassy structures. And while we may complain about the weather, students love it here. We love the decent housing options, from the big, six-story Dupre Hall to the nice, antiquated Wallace. We love most of our classes, which have between ten and twenty students in them. We love that we know all the cafeteria workers by name, and people notice when the guy who usually makes the omelets hasn't been around in a while. Even when Macalester's

administration is being frustrating—sometimes the Residential Life Department is particularly annoying—odds are we'll still know the administrators who work there, and we can go into their office, sit down with them, and tell them our concerns. This might not accomplish anything . . . but that everyone knows everyone else makes problems seem somehow less problematic, and daily life nicer and more friendly.

> "Imagine a sophomore English class where a professor wearing a plastic pastel 'Hello Kitty' backpack will lecture for fifty-five minutes straight, cover and erase the white board with notes three to four times, call on every student to contribute to the heated discussion, and will climb onto/jump up and down on his desk, to make an important point, twice."
>
> ✦ Robert, sophomore

The Education

Not everything is roses at Macalester—we do have professors who are duds. That said, if you ask around, it's easy to find out which professors you should avoid like the plague and which you should beg for on your hands and knees. When you have the latter type of professor, sometimes they're good enough to make you want to change your entire major. This one chemistry professor I had was so wonderfully nerdy and enthusiastic that I felt guilty not living for chemistry as well. When you hear about great teachers like this, I'd really recommend you take their classes, even if they're on a subject you're not too interested in. The best teachers here make *anything* worthwhile. And it's always good to diversify your courses. Last semester I took a random class in linguistics—Sounds of Language—in which we learned to produce most of the sounds used by languages around the world. I may never get a job using what I learned in that class, but it will definitely make me a more interesting person to talk to in the future.

One potential downside to a Macalester education, though, is that it's very antipreprofessional. Many joke around that they can't possibly get a job right out of Macalester—they've just spent so much time learning the theories behind every educational field, rather than the educational fields themselves, that they leave this place having lots of knowledge around subject areas but very little knowledge *in* subject areas. For that reason, a Macalester education is very helpful if you want to go into academia. But it's a bit hard, I'd imagine, to convince someone in a major law firm to hire you based on your expertise at deconstructing traditionalist literary tropes.

The Students

I'd say the average Macalester student is a tiny bit insane. Students are pretty socially and politically active here. We don't wear designer clothes—partially because we're concerned with keeping warm and partially because we're laid-back and we know "clothes don't make the man" and all that. I have a suspicion most Macalester students weren't part of the popular crowd in high school—they were probably more of the bookish kids who (unbeknownst to the popular kids) looked down on the popular kids for not being terribly interesting. Then, all these bookish kids come to Macalester and it's a nice old nerdfest! Just how we like it.

The Activities

There is so much to do and be a part of at Macalester that it can be a bit overwhelming. Last weekend I wanted to go to a karate show, a bagpipe concert, a dance concert, a flamenco guitar concert, and a play about an intramural water-polo team. But all of it was going on at the exact same time, so I had to choose! It's like this constantly.

The Social Scene

There are parties all over Macalester's campus every weekend, and big dance parties are particularly popular. Most students drink, but if you don't—I don't—no one will look down on you for it. A lot of students here get so caught up in their studies that they almost don't want to party on weekends. I know sometimes I only party because I know I should, that it's healthy to get my nose out of the books. I just really like what I'm learning.

Notable Macalester Alumni Include:

Catharine Deaver Lealtad, physician (Macalester's first African American graduate in 1915)
Walter Mondale, vice president, U.S. senator, and U.S. ambassador to Japan
Kofi Annan, U.N. secretary-general and recipient of 2001 Nobel Peace Prize
Shawn Lawrence Otto, screenwriter
Charles Baxter, author
Tim O' Brien, author
DeWitt Wallace, cofounder, *Reader's Digest*
Stephen Paulus, composer

UNIVERSITY OF MASSACHUSETTS AMHERST

Founded: 1863

Location: Amherst, MA

Phone: (413) 545-0111

E-mail: mail@admissions.umass.edu

Web site: www.umass.edu

Number of Undergraduates: 18,060

Number of Graduate Students: 5,600

Cost: Approximately $15,000 per year in state; $24,000 out of state

Application Deadline: January 15

Rating:	Notable Majors/Programs:
Selective	Business, Engineering, Social Sciences, English

Size:
○ Small ○ Medium ● Large

Location:
○ Urban ● Suburban ○ Rural

On a Saturday, students talk about academics:
○ Always ● Sometimes ○ Never

Nightlife:
● Intense ○ Moderate ○ Laid-back

Politically, UMass leans:
● Left ○ Right ○ Split

Diversity:
○ High ○ Low ● Medium

Five-College school: Yes!

Students Describe UMass Amherst in five words:
- Huge, bustling, social, exciting, semi-apathetic
- Biggest of the Amherst colleges

From the School

Academically, UMass Amherst is the place for you if you want a broad array of majors and classes to explore, faculty who are the best in their fields, the opportunity to dive into high-level research as an undergraduate, and significant academic support to keep your ambition fueled.

—www.umass.edu

If you're interested in UMass Amherst, you may also be interested in:
Boston University, UC Berkeley, UMich, Rutgers, SUNY Binghamton, Tufts

Name: Alissa
Hometown: Brookline, Massachusetts
Class Year: Freshman
Major: English
Extracurriculars: Jewish a cappella group, University Chorale, St. Jude Children's Research Hospital
Career Goal: I want to be the head of an influential environmental policy organization.

How would you describe UMass's reputation?

UMass Amherst is a state school, but it has a reputation for being a good education at a low price. The UMass Amherst campus is known as the flagship campus among the UMass schools, being by far the largest and the only one to have an honors college, so it attracts those looking for "the biggest and best" the Massachusetts public university system has to offer. Commonwealth College, the honors college, raises the reputation certainly, with its guarantee of smaller and challenging classes. The Five-College System is another big draw. It allows UMass students to cross-register for courses at Mount Holyoke, Smith, Hampshire, and Amherst Colleges while only paying UMass tuition.

Is this reputation accurate?

There are many large classes, which is to be expected at all big schools, but Commonwealth College definitely makes the price attractive. It's important to note that even if you're in the College, you'll only take two or three honors courses in a semester; expect to take "regular" classes with the mainstream students, too. Five-College courses have restrictions and can be difficult to register for, but the effort is usually worth it. Bottom line: the education is as good as each student makes it.

What would an admissions officer at UMass probably not tell a prospective student?

Budget cuts are inevitable on the UMass campuses. The smaller programs are especially at risk, but classes, faculty positions, and even departments sometimes wind up on the chopping block.

The Institution

Although UMass–Amherst can seem a vast and overpopulated campus, the truth is that residence areas help foster closeness and a home-within-a-home at the university. There may be eighteen thousand undergrads, but living at one end of campus, you won't see or feel their presence. The chancellor and vice chancellor of student affairs make sure we're always entertained, either with Homecoming Weekend, the Winter Ball Dance, or an end-of-the-year barbecue outside the library. They make the "institution" of UMass feel smaller and more personal.

> "Southwest is described by the university as the 'city living campus' and houses nearly half of the student body in its five twenty-story high-rise dorms."
>
> ✦ Rita, sophomore

As for the size of the campus itself, people say, "It's like a city!"—but the truth is that UMass–Amherst feels smaller than it seems at first glance. Most living areas and their residents (except for the poor, isolated souls in Sylvan, the suite apartments in "the boonies" of campus) are near at least one dining hall and the main part of campus where classes are held. The Student Union, W. E. B. DuBois Library, and Campus Center are practically next to each other, and these three buildings will take care of your every school-related need. The main drawback is that the Mullins Center, in which basketball and hockey games take place, as well as concerts and other grand events, is at the bottom of campus and a twenty-minute walk from most living areas.

I was looking at top-tier private schools, and applied to UMass as a "safety." I ended up choosing between two private schools and Commonwealth College at UMass. While debating which private school to attend, my mom suggested I visit UMass, just in case. I did, and I fell in love with the class I attended that day. The young instructor was extremely knowledgeable and lively and inspired heated debates and intelligent conversation among the students. Remembering the dull and tired atmospheres of the classes I had visited at the private schools, I chose UMass on the spot. I haven't been disappointed.

The Education

Competition between students, even at the honors level, is nonexistent. Professors are usually available for help or a chat, with most classes having Web sites complete with professor contact info, homework assignments, and lecture notes. Schoolwork itself doesn't take up much time, but extracurriculars can make you feel like there are only fifteen hours in a day. The advising system is difficult to navigate as a freshman—I found myself with three different advisers in two semesters, none of which contacted me of their own volition. I was not impressed.

> "The food is horrible and there will more than likely be vomit in the dorm bathrooms every weekend morning."
> ✦ Rita, sophomore

The Students

Students are inevitably mostly from Massachusetts, and Red Sox versus Yankee battles can be heard up and down campus come October. Most come from white middle-class backgrounds, and diversity is lacking probably more than the administration would like to admit—although student-run organizations supporting diversity abound.

The Activities

As a singer, I've joined UMass's Jewish a cappella group and the University Chorale in order to get a well-rounded vocal experience. You don't have to be a voice major to audition for these groups, and another huge plus is that, with the Five-College System, you can audition for choirs at the four other schools—and that goes for plays and dance groups, too.

The Social Scene

It's impossible to know everyone, but it's not hard to meet new people, if you make an effort. Dorm life is great if you have something in common with the people in your hall. Commonwealth College lets freshmen sign up to live together in Learning Communities and take two classes in common, which is great for making instant friends and having study buddies across the hall. In terms of socializing, "Thirsty Thursday" is when the weekend officially begins at UMass, whether that means parties, bar-hopping (valid ID is required around these parts), or frat fests. The Hippodrome, half an hour away in Springfield, is the only real dance club around and fills up on Saturday nights. Depending on where you live, Sunday night can be counted as the weekend as well. There is no pressure to join a frat or sorority, although the

Greek houses are always good for entertainment. Also, upper- and underclassmen mix easily.

Name: Carla
Hometown: San Juan, Puerto Rico
Class Year: Junior
Major: Double major in marketing and economics with an International Relations Certificate
Extracurriculars: UMass Volleyball Club, UMass Ballroom Dance Club, Undergraduate Leadership Council, Marketing Club, Association of Latino Professionals in Finance and Accounting, Habitat for Humanity
Career Goal: Masters in public relations and later, law school

How would you describe UMass's reputation?
U-MASS = ZOO-MASS

Is this reputation accurate?
It can be. It all depends about where exactly you decide to live on campus and whether or not you happen to be in the right place at the right time.

What would an admissions officer at UMass probably not tell a prospective student?
UMass–Amherst is a state institution with something like twenty-five thousand students. You will never be able to get the classes you need when you need them. Registering for classes will challenge your patience.

The Institution
I chose UMass because it is a kind of best-value-for-your-money school. It is fun and has a sense of community. The students are the town and the town is the students: everything you need is here (accessible and affordable). School spirit? You just have to check out the bar crawls, athletic riots, and Hobart Hoe-down. Would you dare get naked with everyone else on Streak Night? Or just go and have free popcorn and see a new release movie at Something Every Friday?

The most difficult thing about being a first-year student is figuring out how to get a fake ID so that you can get into the bars, learning how to do a keg stand, winning a game of beer-pong, and convincing your parents to let you go off to Cancun for spring break.

The Education
You get homework every day from almost every class. Group studying is quite popular, and there

are very nice study areas for that all over campus. Classes are rather large, there are lectures by professors and discussions by the TAs. At UMass if you need an A, you need the TA. The TAs are your most trusted learning tool—take advantage of their unconditional help. Professors are very accessible: they work with an open-door policy, and the first thing you should do is introduce yourself at their office hours during the first two weeks of class. You have to put yourself out there. But you will feel like the king of the world if they call you out by your first name in a three-hundred-student auditorium.

A big school has its drawbacks. You have to work to stand out and there's a lot of red tape.

> "UMass's size provides unparalleled opportunities, both social and academic, that are otherwise unavailable to the other colleges in the area."
>
> ✦ Levi, sophomore

The Students

Most students are from the Northeast. The Asians stick together and don't mess around with that; African Americans own South West and are very friendly; Latinos have the best parties; LGBT have a very active community on the fourth floor of the Mary Lyon Building, and they are extremely welcoming to all; socioeconomic differences have never been an issue. The biggest thing on campus is railing against the state government budget cuts and the fee increases. The *Collegian* is an institution; you will read it before, during, or after class because you will find copies of it everywhere.

UMass is not a show-off school. You can comfortably go to class in pajamas, but you cannot survive without jeans and one UMass sweatshirt.

The Activities

I do go into Boston about twice a month, but here you have students everywhere: Amherst, Smith, Hampshire, Mount Holyoke. I personally don't know any—the twenty-five thousand at UMass are enough.

Basketball games at the Mullins Center are recorded for ESPN and make you just feel lucky that you got in. Ice Hockey games are a UMass experience *not* to be missed. There are plenty of

music concerts and dance exhibitions if you are into that sort of thing. Most attended event: Spring Concert. Campus group I'm most passionate about: being the loudest table in the dining hall at six p.m. every day with my group of Puerto Ricans. Outside on a sunny day you'll see girls in their bikinis trying to get a tan and some male attention; guys barefoot and in their shorts playing Frisbee; the UMass professional volleyball players spiking it in the beach volleyball courts, shirtless of course, (among them my own dear brother Rene); the residence council lighting up the barbecue for a student cookout. If you're awake on a Wednesday night at 3:00 a.m., you (a) got out of the Monkey Bar at 1:00 a.m., went to an afterparty in Puffton, so now you are waiting for your delivery of DP Dough, or (b) you have an exam at 9:00 a.m., so you are pulling a typical all-nighter.

The Social Scene

People party every day. Frats are a big part of life at UMass, but it all depends on how involved you get with them. There isn't a clubbing scene to speak of. People are different, so of course they party differently: some parties are about drinking, others about dancing, others about pot smoking, others I don't know. . . . Meeting new people is a daily hobby. Most people are in their rooms with the door open, with the music blaring so you just stop to say hi anytime. Juniors and seniors live off campus. And you all meet up late night on Main Street in town, when all the bars close and hundreds of students get thrown into the street.

Name: Christopher
Hometown: Barre, Massachusetts
Class Year: Sophomore
Major: Finance (primary) and Chinese (secondary) (double major)
Extracurriculars: International Relations Club, student government
Career Goal: To work on trade relations between the United States and China

How would you describe UMass's reputation?

The University of Massachusetts–Amherst has a mix of reputations. We have one of the best computer departments in the country, an excellent business school, and our Chinese program ranks in the top ten. However, we also have the reputation of being a party school.

Is this reputation accurate?

Absolutely, our academic programs are very good. For our reputation as a party school, it's true in some aspects. But then again, any college is bound to have parties.

What aspect of UMass would a prospective student not see on a campus tour?

A prospective student would not see the 450-person lectures.

> "People party every day here."
> ✦ Carla, senior

The Institution

I chose to go to my school because it has a very good business program and an excellent Chinese program. In high school I took Chinese and wanted to make it part of my life. Here at UMass, I'm shaping my life and career at the same time and am enjoying it tremendously.

About ten thousand students live on campus. There are lots of dorms to choose from at UMass. There are five major residential areas on campus, each with its own characteristics. The residential area I lived in last year was Northeast, where the buildings have a 1930s look to them. You need to live there a while to qualify for a single, but the two-person rooms are a good size.

The administration at UMass is huge. As such, it can take a long time to get something done. Patience is definitely a must.

The Education

One of the nicest things about the university is the number of courses you have to choose from. For example, there are so many languages offered, either through the departments or through a special program that allows students to learn a language with the assistance of a native speaker. I plan on learning Czech this fall. And the Five-College System allows you to take courses elsewhere without paying extra money, which increases your options even more. Despite the fact that I'm enrolled in a 450-student lecture, I can go to my professor for help, just as I can in my 15-student discussion class. It's up to each student to make the most of the classroom experience. All the professors for my business classes were excellent, especially my statistics and business law classes. I can safely say that the professors at the Isenberg School of Management will go to great lengths to help willing students. Also, the alumni support (financial and moral) for Isenberg is top-notch.

The Students

The University of Massachusetts provides a lot of opportunities for students of all backgrounds and interests to get involved. There are over 160 student organizations, the most vocal being ALANA (for minorities) and the SGA (Student Government Association). Students are mostly Democrats—but that doesn't quash discussion beause there are all kinds of Democrats. I participate most in the International Relations Club. I would say about half of my friends are from the club.

The Activities

Each residential area has its own special event for the year. Mine has Streak Night. Once upon a time people streaked, but now the student government has sponsored food and movies to take its place, giving the would-be streakers something to do instead. (Note that the student government never condoned the streaking. Campus police also patrol the area at night to arrest anyone who streaks. If arrested, a person could be forced to register as a sexual offender, according to Massachusetts law. We take streaking seriously here!)

There is at least one protest every month at UMass. The reasons range from tuition increases to political issues (e.g., Iraq). However, I have never heard any reports of the protests becoming violent.

Also, the Fine Arts Center holds a lot of theatrical and cultural and special performances, usually with student discounts on tickets. I got to see the Moscow Ballet perform *The Nutcracker* last December.

The Social Scene

People party frequently. I honestly think a student could find a party going on any day of the week.

Notable UMass Amherst Alumni Include:
Bill Cosby, entertainer
Catherine Coleman, astronaut
Jack Canfield, author
Jeff Taylor, founder, Monster.com
Natalie Cole, singer
Russell Hulse, Nobel laureate

MASSACHUSETTS
INSTITUTE OF TECHNOLOGY

Founded: 1861

Location: Cambridge, MA

Phone: (617) 253-1000

E-mail: admissions@mit.edu

Web site: web.mit.edu

Number of Undergraduates: 4,110

Number of Graduate Students: 6,230

Cost: Approximately $41,000 per year

Application Deadline: January 1

Early Decision: November 1

Rating:	Notable Majors/Programs:
Most Selective	Engineering, Computer Science, Life Sciences, Social Sciences

Size:

○ Small　● Medium　○ Large

Location:

○ Urban　● Suburban　○ Rural

On a Saturday, students talk about academics:

● Always　○ Sometimes　○ Never

Nightlife:

● Intense　○ Moderate　○ Laid-back

Politically, MIT leans:

● Left　○ Right　○ Split

Diversity:

● High　○ Low　○ Medium

Students describe MIT in five words:

- Innovative, humbling, inspiring, masochistic, off-the-wall
- MIT's most popular term is IHTFP, which can mean either: "I hate this f*cking place" or "I have truly found paradise"

From the School

　The essence of MIT is our appetite for problems—especially those big, intractable, complicated problems whose solutions make a permanent difference. . . . If you like a good tussle with a tough problem, you've come to the right place.

　　　　　　　　　—www.admissions.mit.edu

If you're interested in MIT, you may also be interested in:
Caltech, Carnegie Mellon, Georgia Tech, Harvard, Harvey Mudd, Stanford

Name: Jonathan
Hometown: Mequon, Wisconsin
Class Year: Senior
Major: Economics and management (double major)
Extracurriculars: Varsity soccer, Interfraternity Council, Delta Kappa Epsilon fraternity, novice crew, undergraduate economics association
Career Goal: To be happy with what I'm doing

How would you describe MIT's reputation?

Very nerdy. Frail. Very, very, smart. Scary smart. See *Good Will Hunting* or *The Recruit*. Very mathematical. Socially inept.

Is this reputation accurate?

A lot of it is earned—there're a lot of strange people here: people who don't wear shoes or spend all day playing with robots. They have things like "integration bees," which make the normal people here cringe. An "integration bee" is like a spelling bee, only for students who take calculus—I can feel your eyes rolling already. But actually, not everyone is a nerd here. If you want to hang around seminormal intelligent people here, you can.

What would an admissions officer at MIT probably not tell a prospective student?

They probably wouldn't talk about the suicide rate, or that the workload is sometimes ridiculous.

> "Rather than priding ourselves on sports, we pride ourselves on our reputation as engineers. Such pride is the basis for traditions such as 'The Engineer's Drinking Song' and the annual measurement of the Harvard Bridge . . . in human lengths."
>
> ✦ Alvin, senior

The Institution

We don't have a traditional sense of school spirit, unless you count "nerd pride." In general, MIT does not have a "campus feel" like other universities. The campus is very long and narrow, haphazard and bizarre. The campus architecture is a number of different shades of ugly. The main building, which is *huge,* is pretty on the outside, but inside there's a gruelling maze of dark hallways and pipes. They hired some fancy architects to design a new dorm and computer science facility, but both look awful. The dorm looks like a sponge, and the computer science facility looks like a heap of scrap metal.

That said, we're not here for ambiance. I chose MIT for the prestige. May not have been the best deciding factor: it certainly isn't the school where you are going to have the most fun—unless doing lots of math or designing things is an erotic experience for you. The most difficult thing about being a first-year is getting used to failure. Every student comes here from the top of his class, used to being smarter than our peers and having class be very easy. Getting a 40 percent on your first physics test comes as a shock. But when you're a senior, you definitely feel prepared for life after college as job opportunities are better here than at most other schools. A lot of students become engineers, investment bankers, consultants, or work in government.

The campus is pretty secure, but Cambridge in general is a little sketchy. As a rule, your bike (if you own one) will almost certainly be stolen once. And ugh, townies!! Their credo is to get drunk and fight people. Their accents are hideous. We don't interact with them . . . And weather in Boston is nasty from mid-November to mid-April. It's a long, frustrating winter. Lots of wind . . .

The best tradition at MIT is the "hacks"—pranks that are supposed to be highly visible, provocative, and (of course) well engineered. Many of the hacks involve the great dome in the middle of campus. One year, a group of students placed a replica of the Wright brothers plane on the dome to honor the one hundredth anniversary of flight. Another year, a police car replica was placed up there, complete with mannequin holding a box of donuts. It's also been turned into R2D2 and a working telephone booth(!). (See http://hacks.mit.edu for a complete list.) There are rumblings about the unfairness of how the hacks' masterminds are fined (if caught) while their hacks are publicly praised—and publicized. I think it's pretty crappy that MIT benefits from all the good press surrounding the hacks while simultaneously punishing the students who engineer them. MIT's policy on this matter is silly.

The Education

The term system is 4-1-4. The "1" is a January period called Independent Activities Period (IAP). It offers a lot of noncredit workshops and seminars that give students a chance to try things they wouldn't normally during the term or cram in a class for credit if you really want to. Some students, like myself, don't participate in the IAP activities, and thoroughly enjoy having what becomes a six-week winter break. But many do.

Students here, for the most part, can never get work off the brain. Too many here are Type A personalities (i.e., very competitive) who talk about school at the wrong times (i.e., Saturday night).

Research opportunities for undergrads are abundant. This is something that MIT does very well. There's a large and awesome program called the Undergraduate Research Opportunities Program (UROP), which coordinates this type of work. Most students (80-90 percent) participate in a UROP at least once while at MIT.

Top Ten Strange Things About MIT

10. Our class ring is called the "Brass Rat"
9. All of the buildings are numbered
8. All of the majors are numbered
7. All of the courses are numbered
6. Students get more excited about the autonomous robot competition than the football team
5. Some students go weeks without showering . . . or wearing shoes!
4. The school's cheer, the Beaver Call, contains calculus and trigonometric functions
3. Our newest dormitory resembles a sponge
2. The school's unofficial motto is IHTFP (I hate this f-----g place)
1. Yet despite all of this, we have elite athletes, the reigning Miss Massachusetts, and raging fraternity parties. . . . Go figure!!!

✦ Jonathan, junior

The grad students are a very large part of the campus (six thousand grad students versus four thousand undergrads). Some departments are incredibly graduate focused (such as economics). It can be frustrating when it seems as if most of the attention and money are directed to the graduate students, but other departments teach the undergraduates very well.

The core curriculum is good prep for the scientists and engineers (about 80 percent) and a bore for the rest of us (like me). Every student takes two se-

mesters of calculus, two semesters of physics, a semester of chemistry, and a semester of biology. There is also an eight-class humanities requirement that frustrates a lot of the more technically oriented.

Very few students study abroad relative to other schools both because MIT is pretty stubborn about not accepting most of your foreign credits and because students don't study foreign languages here, so they are less prepared to study abroad.

Sometimes, going to MIT can seem like "drinking water from a fire hose," but if you make sure to keep balance in your life, you will preserve your sanity.

The Students

This campus is very diverse. You can find every type of racial, cultural, LGBT, international club imaginable. We even have the reigning Miss Massachusetts. The campus political environment is very liberal. Antiwar protesters are also very vocal here. Students by and large aren't that politically involved, though.

The Activities

There are tons of schools in the Boston area (Harvard, Boston University, Simmons, Tufts, Northeastern, Wellesley, Boston College, to name a few). Every student knows some students at other local schools. Our sports are D-3 and no one cheers for them—athletics are just not a prominent part of campus life. Many people participate in athletics (we have around forty varsity sports) but they mostly compete in anonymity. The MIT symphony is quite good. There are also good student-directed plays, which are generally well attended. A cappella is also quite popular. The MIT Logarhythms, an all-male group, is the best, and they play to a packed house twice a year. People also go see the Dance Troupe, although that gets mixed reviews and every year for Spring Weekend, MIT gets a big-name band slightly past its prime.

The Social Scene

People generally party on Fridays and Saturdays, but there are a lot of antisocial types who just stay in their rooms and study all of the time. MIT students like to drink, but the administration's actively been curtailing that since 1997, when a student died from drinking at a fraternity event.

In our free time my friends and I generally hang out, play pickup football and basketball, go bowling, play video games and poker, catch up on sleep, crack open a couple of beers, go into Boston, hang out at other schools.

Name: J. Wan
Hometown: Saskatoon, Canada
Class Year: Sophomore
Major: Electrical engineering and computer science
Extracurriculars: Varsity men's volleyball, Committee on Student Life, Theta Chi fraternity
Career Goal: Technology management (i.e., making six figures)

How would you describe MIT's reputation?

In general, we are seen as *wicked smaht* kids (or *turdy geniuses*).

Is this reputation accurate?

It's true for the most part. It's nice to be able to deal with smart people for a change; however, be warned that when you return to the Real World, you will realize just how fucking clueless the rest of the world is. Did I also mention that we are very humble?

What would an admissions officer at MIT probably not tell a prospective student?

They won't tell you about the twenty-four-hour lab hours because students are up till dawn doing problem sets and grunt work in the labs. They won't tell you about test averages of 40s and getting an A on an exam with a 65 percent score. Thank God for the curve!

The Institution

Simply stated, MIT is one of the most efficient campuses on earth. There are no fancy redbricks like Harvard down the road, nor do we have a twenty-thousand-capacity football stadium. This is a school built on technological inspirations, and we have a campus that models itself after our purpose. Our aptly named "infinite corridor" stretches for a goddamn long distance, and a student can move from class to class without having to go outside. Hence, we have a lot of pale kids. At MIT, you have the option to be as involved as you want to be: you can choose to spend your four years as a hermit and work in your Macgregor single without anyone ever knowing who you are; or you can easily get involved in numerous student offices across campus. MIT loves forming committees for the most retarded things, and you can surely find one to boost your résumé.

The Education

It is pretty common to have to do two problem sets after a night of drinking. It's all about compromise—and certainly no one's willing to compromise their college years for sleep. Thus, we sleep an average of five, six hours a day. Everyone brags about how little they've slept and how wasted they got. I'd say that we are pretty much the dumbest smart kids in the world.

But make no mistake: academically, the people here are talented. Our engineering majors account for a third of the school's population. We pride ourselves on our ability to take on a large quantity of work, persevering with no sleep and a whole lot of caffeine.

Note: people suck at English here, and our literature department is a joke.

Top Four Stereotypes at MIT
1. Popular: Asian with dangly cell phone antenna ornament and Armani Exchange outfit.
2. Frat guy: tall white guy in Puma jacket hiding long hair underneath baseball cap.
3. Loud Course 6 (EECS): pasty-faced computer nerd in XL "Generic City Name" hoodie.
4. Normal Course 6 (EECS): student in a single-breasted suit and solid Brooks Brothers tie, rushing off to interview with Goldman or Merrill.

✦ Mike, sophomore

The Students

It is refreshing to step back sometimes and see for yourself that your friends at MIT are not only your Beirut partners, they are also some of the smartest fuckers you've encountered in your life. At MIT, there is always someone better than you at everything you do. Few can claim they find their four years of school easy or trivial.

The Activities

Fraternity and sorority life is huge around campus. Something like 50 percent of the student body is involved in Greek life. The fraternities dictate much of the weekends, with parties, community service events, and mixers. Otherwise we drink, watch movies, cause trouble, and figure out ways to make money.

The Social Scene

Girls love their frat parties at MIT. Most frat guys like to stay at their own house and drink like fishes. Typically, MIT gets a lot of traffic from nearby Boston schools, since no other school has a Greek life like MIT—which is kind of ironic given our academic intensity and geeky reputation.

Name: Jessica
Hometown: Lake Oswego, Oregon
Class Year: Freshman
Major: Chemical engineering
Extracurriculars: AXO sorority, MIT Swimming and Diving Team, development of a campus bike share program
Career Goal: Doctor and astronaut

How would you describe MIT's reputation?

It is one of the best schools in the world. People dream of coming here. We have some of the brightest students in the country, and we work hard.

Is this reputation accurate?

Yes. I have never met so many smart people in my life. This place is tough, but there are people here who find it too easy. My friends sometimes challenge themselves by taking six classes at a time just because they're bored (the rest of us who find the regular courses to be über difficult stare on in amazement). But what people forget is that kids at MIT don't just work hard. We play hard, too. Not at the same caliber of a state school, but nonetheless, our parties rock—and students from all over the many Boston schools know this and travel to party with us.

What aspect of MIT would a prospective student not see on a campus tour?

Students in the computer clusters at two and three o'clock in the morning still studying. I always tell prospectives about our tons of clubs, sports teams, and other activities, but what you won't hear is that you'll probably have time for only one or two.

The Institution

I love the size of the school. I can walk through Infinite Corridor and say hi to twenty people I know or not see anyone I know at all. I like how all the academic buildings are clustered together and that I don't have to go outside if I don't want to. I can pass by the ocean engineering department and look at all the boat models and still get to class on time.

The pass/no pass record for first semester freshmen helps kids adjust to the difficult-caliber classes, but not performing well is still very frustrating. You'll get used to it, though, and there are ways to get help if you suck up your pride and ask for it. MIT makes it hard for a reason. The average person probably never takes differential equations or cares about inductance or Markovinkov addition, but in order for us to do the high-tech stuff we do after graduation, those are just the basics. That's why MIT graduates get so much respect: they *earn* it.

In the winter we get the month of January off. It's called IAP (Independent Activities Period). Students can use it as an extended winter vacation before starting second semester. Winter sports teams are called back to practice; my swim team goes to Puerto Rico every two years. Some freshmen classes require you to stay during IAP to finish the course. There are lots of seminars offered (credit and non-credit) to keep you busy, as well as the option of taking an intensive twelve-unit class in the one-month time period.

I like MIT because I can be the person that I want to be here and I am accepted. This place is a challenge, and everyone is doing amazing things. Colin Quinn did a stand-up show on campus and he joked, "Someone asks you what school you go to and you say 'Harvard,' they say 'Asshole.' If you say 'MIT,' they say 'No shit!?'"

> "The best bet to staying socially viable is to find a fraternity—fast."
>
> ✦ Brockton, senior

The Education

Students are only competitive with themselves. Premed students tend to be uptight about their grades, but that's typical at most institutions. We don't talk about grades, except to say that we didn't do as well as we had hoped. I personally don't discuss classes on weekends unless I'm doing homework.

The Students

We are *so* diverse at MIT. (I'm from Oregon and my high school had the diversity of a box of Cheerios.) But there are people from everywhere here! It's amazing. Everyone is friends with everyone. There are some racial cliques, but we all take the same classes so we mix and mingle all the time. The international students are the smartest ones by far—MIT only takes *the* very best of the world population. I love how I've met people from all over, and learned so much about other cultures. My freshman roommate is originally from Sweden, and I've even learned a little Swedish because she speaks it in her sleep.

> "There are some people who are so smart that all they can do to keep from exploding is to take an insanely large number of classes."
>
> ✦ Molly, junior

The Activities

Everyone loves *The Tech*, the student newspaper, and they love our a cappella groups. The Logs, the all-male group, are the equivalent of basketball players at Duke. Everyone plays sports here, and we're not that bad for a DIII school and we have more teams than any other school (forty-one varsity teams), but we don't have a lot of school sprit when it comes to going out and supporting them. We don't have time.

The Social Scene

Smart people are attractive. At MIT I don't have to worry about a guy I date being "stupid and unmotivated." They're all brilliant! (Maturity, however, is another issue.) As for dating, if you don't live in the same dorm or have any of the same classes, it's hard to find time to see each other.

We're not a dry campus, but MIT does a lot to make people aware of alcohol abuse and how to keep each other safe. Parties start on Wednesday nights each week at the fraternity houses across the river and run through the weekend. A couple different houses have weekly parties or a weekly pub night. The safe-ride bus (a free MIT shuttle) stops running around 4:00 a.m. on weekends, 3:00 a.m. on weekdays.

I joined a sorority. They are all dry here. I'll live there next year—it's a beautiful house across the river in Boston. Greek life is a large part of my social scene, but it isn't the case for everyone. I have friends who have never been to a fraternity party, so it's not that important.

Notable MIT Alumni Include:

Benjamin Netanyahu, former prime minister of Israel

George W. Santos, pioneer in bone marrow transplantation

Robert Metcalfe, entrepreneur, founder of 3Com

Whitfield Diffie, pioneer of public-key cryptography and the Diffie-Hellman protocol

Larry Kahn, tiddledywinks champion

William C. Ford, chairman and CEO of Ford Motor Company

UNIVERSITY OF MICHIGAN

Founded: 1817

Location: Ann Arbor, MI

Phone: (734) 764-1817

E-mail: ugadmiss@umich.edu

Web site: www.umich.ed

Number of Undergraduates: 24,350

Number of Graduate Students: 12,090

Cost: Approximately $16,000 per year in state; $34,000 out of state

Application Deadline: February 1
Rolling Admissions

Rating:	Notable Majors/Programs:
Selective	Business, Premed, Engineering, Psychology

Size:
○ Small ○ Medium ● Large

Location:
○ Urban ● Suburban ○ Rural

On a Saturday, students talk about academics:
○ Always ● Sometimes ○ Never

Nightlife:
○ Intense ● Moderate ○ Laid-back

Politically, Michigan leans:
○ Left ○ Right ● Split

Diversity:
● High ○ Low ○ Medium

Big Ten school: Yes!

Students describe UMichigan in five words:
- Competitive, difficult, exciting, large involved
- Loud, smart, not intellectual, spirited

From the School

At Michigan, students can have the best of both worlds—small classes in the first year and access to the vast opportunities of a world-class research university. Michigan's size provides resources for students not available at smaller schools. These include one of the largest library systems in the world, extensive computing resources, opportunities to work with faculty on research projects, special interest programs, and a diverse student body from around the world.

—www.admissions.umich.edu

If you're interested in U Michigan, you may also be interested in:
UC Berkeley, UCLA, Duke, UPenn, UT at Austin, UW—Madison

Name: Marisa

Hometown: Rancho Santa Fe, California

Class Year: Sophomore

Major: Political science

Extracurriculars: Delta Epsilon Chi, Campus Day, Project Community, Team Blue football intern

Career Goal: To be the first African American female Supreme Court judge or president of the United States. I'm aiming high.

How would you describe UMich's reputation?

Academic powerhouse.

Is this reputation accurate?

It is true that we work hard and take advantage of the academic excellence, but we all know how to unwind and have a lot of fun.

What would an admissions officer at UMich probably not tell a prospective student?

They won't tell you that while the classroom is extremely diverse, campus is pretty much socially segregated. Much of this can be seen in the stratification of our residence halls—many African American students live in one res hall, most of the Jewish students from the East Coast live in another, etc.

The Institution

The University of Michigan is a helluva place to learn, discover yourself, and find your niche in the world if you can keep your eyes open and your hangovers at bay. It can be tedious navigating this campus as a freshman. With more than 25,000 undergraduates, it can be easy to get lost in the shuffle. You have to be proactive in seeking out resources and extra help. Everyone loves (of course) Football Saturdays, tailgating and watching our favorite Wolverines with 110,000 of your closest friends. (On Football Saturdays, Michigan Stadium is the 186th largest city in America!)

Our terms are short, so most students are here from September until late April, which pretty much means that you get about six weeks of good weather. The other six months or so, you should definitely expect to wear hats, boots, gloves, and thermal underwear. On the upside, job opportunities are fabulous, as Michigan has the largest alumni base in the world, but you *have* to be proactive about seeking out contacts yourself.

Overall, Big Ten athletics, midsized surrounding suburban community, and a diverse student body make this a great place to enjoy your four years of freedom and personal exploration.

The Education

It never ceases to amaze me how great a school this is academically and how many truly dumb people go here. But since learning is at your own pace, both the bars and the libraries are crowded on Tuesdays and Fridays. Go to Club UGLI (second floor of the undergraduate library)! It's a great place to socialize and pretend that you're doing homework.

The competition level between students varies highly depending on your major. Political science students for the most part work together because we are all lazy and would rather talk about what we should be doing than actually do it.

Must-take classes include UC 151, Human Sexuality and Gender Issues (your parents will be shocked at your knowledge of sexually transmitted diseases and sex toys on your first weekend home from school); Political Science 432, Law and Public Policy (taught by U of M's general counsel, who argued the affirmative-action decisions in front of the Supreme Court, and he also brings in renowned speakers and political bigwigs); Sociology 389, Project Community (where undergraduates facilitate sections on community-based learning, ranging from volunteering at a prison or elementary school, to helping with AIDS education or tutoring non-English speakers).

The Students

Michigan used to have a reputation for being a political campus where protests occurred often—not so much the case anymore. Michigan students on the whole care more about their Prada bags and Gucci sunglasses than the war or racial equality. I hear over half our students come from a household income of over $200,000. Shocking. We have a lot of closet Republicans, and the general tone of campus is relatively liberal. Ann Arbor really helps this. If most people had to depict the average student, they would probably draw a sorority girl in a North Face puffy jacket with Tiffany jewelry, designer sweatpants, and a cell phone. But that's just the image that stands out—the truth is, with more than 25,000 students, there is *no* average student.

The Activities

There are almost a thousand student organizations on campus, so there is something for everyone. We even have a squirrel club that goes around on Sundays and feeds the squirrels. But sports is life here. Get season tickets to football, basketball and hockey; if you decide you don't like them or don't want to go, you can always scalp them. And pick up the *Michigan Daily* only for "Boondocks," and the *L.A. Times* crossword puzzle to do in lecture. The paper, though respected, is good for little else.

The Social Scene

There is a social event every night of the week. Alcohol is a relatively large part of campus and tends to be the social elixir of choice before going out. Freshmen year is dominated by frat parties, which get old *real quick*. But as you get older there are a lot of house parties hosted by friends, and bars once you turn twenty-one.

Student organizations can be the best way to meet friends—most of my close friends and roommates have come from organizations we were in together. I guess the jocks tend to be popular, as at any school, but because there are so many students, there are friendship cliques, not "popular" ones.

Name: Jennifer
Hometown: Northbrook, Illinois
Class Year: Sophomore
Major: English and psychology
Extracurriculars: Yearbook, sorority, Hillel
Career Goal: To be editor in chief of a major magazine

How would you describe UMich's reputation?

Michigan is known for being an academically competitive as well as an athletically involved school.

Is this reputation accurate?

Fairly. Every student at Michigan is an extremely hard worker. Whether they are on a sports team, involved in a certain club, or just studying, everyone is really motivated. Michigan is stressful, but what school isn't? College is about the friends and experiences, not just grades, and students at Michigan know that.

What would an admissions officer at UMich probably not tell a prospective student?

They may not mention how hard everyone works. Whether it is sports, clubs, or academics, every student works their butt off. It creates a very competitive edge that pushes everyone to do even

better. I was especially surprised when I walked into the library to study for finals and could not find a seat.

> "There's a superstition that if you walk on the brass *M* in the Diag before your first blue-book exam, you'll fail it. Even seniors avoid it like the plague."
>
> ✦ Val, senior

The Institution

Big Ten football games, frat parties, walkouts, diversity, home . . . there are many ways to describe the University of Michigan, but for me, it means community. It means thousands of students screaming blue and maize at football games. It means my sorority sisters volunteering at a nursing home. It means over thirty thousand students coming together to learn, live, and enjoy themselves for four years.

The Education

Michigan is an academically demanding school and makes sure to challenge how you think by making you take a variety of courses. I always thought that being in such a big school, it would be hard to get individualized attention from my professors. However, I can say that I have met with most of my professors one on one. It is all about making the effort to search them out.

The Students

When applying to college, I wasn't sure what I was looking for, but when I walked on campus at U of M, I knew it was where I belonged. I know it sounds cheesy, but what attracted me most was that there are so many different types of people. You cannot pin a stereotype on our campus because you find a variety of students everywhere—students of different backgrounds, ages, races. Michigan is very diverse. I have also found that Michigan students do know how to balance their social and academic lives. We study when we have to and when we feel confident everything is done, then we go out . . . whatever day that may be.

The Activities

Everyone is really involved on campus. Whether it is athletics (the whole town as well as students come together every Saturday to scream rabidly for the Wolverines), community service, or student publications, students find activities that make them happy and then pursue them. I ran an after-school program for inner city students in Detroit, I volunteered at a juvenile delinquent center, and I even helped run a conference on the Holocaust at Hillel. Most organizations at some point take part in our tradition of painting the rock: A huge rock off campus is painted every night by various groups to show off their group. Every night, the student group has to make sure to get to the rock early enough to claim it, so no one else will.

The Social Scene

People constantly go out at Michigan. The Greek scene is fairly big on campus—there are roughly fifteen sororities and thirty fraternities, allowing people to always find a party until you're old enough to go to bars. The dating scene is not huge at school. People tend to hang out in groups more often. But everyone is friendly and loves to meet new people. What I especially love about Ann Arbor is that it is not just a college town—within a five-minute drive, there are art museums, jazz clubs, nice restaurants, and even a martini bar.

I rushed as a way to meet people. I was nervous at first and I pictured sororities as a bunch of obnoxious, annoying, ditzy, self-centered girls. I slowly learned that my stereotype was wrong. There are sororities at Michigan for every type of girl: the athlete, the drama queen, and even me.

Name: Mike
Hometown: Grand Rapids, Michigan
Class Year: Senior
Major: English
Extracurriculars: Tons of social activism and social justice work (e.g., something called the Prison Creative Arts Project—www.prisonarts.org); Students for Choice; the Genre Evolution Project (a research project where a couple professors collaborate with undergrads); soccer.
Career Goal: Organizer for a labor union (already have a job set up)

> "If you want a big school, this is the best university I can think of."
> ✦ Jill, sophomore

How would you describe UMich's reputation?

Berkeley academics and social activism with Big Ten athletics and a Big Ten feel.

Is this reputation accurate?

In general it is, but I think people think that Michigan is harder academically than it really is. It varies. Some departments inflate grades more than others. But the reputation of a great school for the quintessential college experience is right on. It's the kind of place where any type of student can thrive.

What aspect of UMich would a prospective student not see on a campus tour?

The campus tour should be a tour of Ann Arbor because there's no real difference between U of M and Ann Arbor. The campus and city are one, and it has got to be the best college town in the nation.

The Institution

While Ann Arbor is amazing, the cost of living here is atrocious (the university hasn't built undergraduate housing since the late sixties, demand for housing has pushed the cost of rent up enormously), especially considering the condition of most off-campus housing. Most students move off campus after their first or second year, and many of the apartments and houses that students live in are actually closer to academic buildings than the dorms. Better alternatives such as renting with a large group or the Co-Op houses are often solutions for students who can't pay high rent.

Campus security is generally good, and Ann Arbor is relatively safe as well. Most of the crime on campus is minor (theft). Some students would say that bigger problems, like date rape, aren't addressed by the university to the extent that they should be. The university administration recently reorganized the university's Sexual Assault Prevention and Awareness Center (SAPAC), despite strong student protest. The administration's policies regarding Sexual Assault services remain controversial.

The relationship between students and administration (especially Student Affairs) is tenuous at best. The head of Student Affairs has made several big decisions with what some describe as little or no student input, and student government is regarded as a joke because it seems to have no effect on the university.

The Education

Weekends, starting Thursday night, are observed religiously—that is, unless you're in engineering. Then all bets are off. U of M is too big for there to be much competition between students (again, unless you're in engineering). For the most part, students work hard but have plenty of time for parties and football.

There are too many GSIs (graduate student instructors) in general. But if you try, you can make connections with professors. As far as research, UROP (Undergraduate Research Opportunity Program) is known nationwide for its excellence in getting first- and second-year students involved in professors' research.

The distribution requirements are reasonable, though some students take issue with the language requirement. I think most students appreciate that the administration gives professors a lot of academic freedom, especially in creating unusual and creative classes like the controversial English 317 course, "How to Be Gay: Male Homosexuality and Initiation," which examined this theme in literature. It landed the university in some hot water politically, but the administration wholeheartedly supported the professor's right to teach it. This culture of academic freedom doesn't go unnoticed by students.

Advising at U of M could use improvement. I only saw my concentration adviser twice, when I declared as an English major and just now, when I'm about to graduate, for a combined total of probably seven minutes. This is an aspect that U of M needs to improve. Also note, the study-abroad program looks good on paper, but there are never enough spots to guarantee going to the country where you want to go (even the same continent).

> "Our engineering school is one of the hardest academic experiences available. I spend fifteen hours a day studying and doing work."
>
> ✦ Ben, senior

The Students

There is often tension between in-state students (who have jobs) and students from the East Coast, especially the NYC area (who have the Greek system). In-staters are seen as naive and East Coasters are seen as snobs. There's also tension between social activists and the Greek system. African American and LGBT students definitely have a voice on campus—LGBT students are out and proud. Protests on the Diag are practically weekly occasions. Anti-War Action teams up with the Ann Arbor Committee for Peace often to organize protests (one of many examples of how Ann Arbor residents and students generally get along and work together).

The Activities

In the fall, football is king. Big Ten athletics are huge, especially in the fall, but lots of students shun them and aren't worse off. There's never a lack of alternative things to do. You can go smoke at a hookah bar, shop at little independent clothing stores, or eat at the Earthern Jar, a vegetarian South Indian buffet. There is never any reason to leave downtown Ann Arbor. Lots of students have cars, but only because they're too lazy to walk for fifteen minutes. Public transportation is incredible, with a new bus service called the Link that makes a loop around downtown Ann Arbor. It's the kind of place where any type of student can thrive.

The Social Scene

Greek students party at Greek houses, activist students party at Co-Op houses, and nearly everybody parties at house parties. There is never a charge for alcohol at parties—to impose one would mean social death. Thursdays are club or bar nights; Friday and Saturday nights, students party. Saturday afternoons are spent exercising or watching sports, and on Sundays, students frantically try to catch up on schoolwork.

Students in the Greek system generally don't socialize with other people, and other people are fine with that. I've met most of my friends through my activist student organizations. And I think dorm life is underrated—people form bonds in the dorms that last four years and longer, and you can always find someone you want to know.

Notable UMich Alumni Include:
Arthur Miller, playwright
Clarence Darrow, attorney
Gerald Ford, thirty-eighth U.S. president
Gilda Radner, actress and comedian
Raoul Wallenberg, Holocaust rescuer
Tony Fadell, "father" of the iPod

MIDDLEBURY COLLEGE

Founded: 1800

Location: Middlebury, VT

Phone: (802) 442-5000

E-mail: admissions@middlebury.edu

Web site: www.middlebury.edu

Number of Undergraduates: 2,420

Number of Graduate Students: 0

Cost: Approximately $40,500 per year

Application Deadline: January 1

Early Decision: November 15

Rating:	Notable Majors/Programs:
Most Selective	English, Life Sciences, Language, Social Sciences

Size:
- ● Small   ○ Medium   ○ Large

Location:
- ○ Urban   ○ Suburban   ● Rural

On a Saturday, students talk about academics:
- ○ Always   ● Sometimes   ○ Never

Nightlife:
- ○ Intense   ● Moderate   ○ Laid-back

Politically, Middlebury leans:
- ● Left   ○ Right   ○ Split

Diversity:
- ○ High   ○ Low   ● Medium

Students describe Middlebury in five words:
- An endometrium for inspiring potential
- Beautiful, cold, active, super-demanding, darn–good

From the School

The Middlebury College faculty is composed of outstanding, dedicated teachers who are also accomplished scholars. Students have many opportunities to work closely with their teachers, and intellectual exchange with the faculty goes on outside the classroom as well as during class. The liberal arts education offered by the College is designed to enable students to lead rewarding lives of ongoing intellectual and spiritual growth and to prepare them to meet the challenges of responsible citizenship in a complex, changing world.

—www.middlebury.edu

If you like Middlebury, you may also be interested in:
Amherst, Bowdoin, Dartmouth, Davidson, Swarthmore, Williams

Name: Kira

Hometown: Andover, Massachusetts

Class Year: Junior

Major: Spanish (with minors in environmental studies and psychology)

Extracurriculars: Classical Dance Middlebury (ballet), Middance (jazz), On Tap (tap-dancing troupe), Middlebury College Figure Skating Club

Career Goal: To work in the environmental education/advocacy field and to use my Spanish skills to reach the Latino community about these issues

How would you describe Middlebury's reputation?

Middlebury has a very strong academic reputation, particularly in the languages. In terms of its student body, Middlebury is often described as a school for J. Crew–sporting, friendly, attractive white kids.

> "It is so freakin' cold here in the winter . . . but the skiing is awesome, and the spring and fall are absolutely gorgeous!"
>
> ✦ Colby, senior

Is this reputation accurate?

It is true that Middlebury's language programs are top-notch, but this often casts a shadow on its other strong academic departments. Middlebury really excels in the sciences, boasting a beautiful state-of-the-art science center that is the second largest building in the state and has the comfiest chairs in Vermont. Also, while Middkids do tend to be friendly, attractive, conservatively dressed, and white, we have a high number of international students on campus, who really enrich class discussions, and I believe Middlebury has become more diverse over the past few years.

What would an admissions officer at Middlebury probably not tell a prospective student?

They would probably not tell you about the complaints about the Commons system. This system (modeled after Yale's) divides our already small 2,300-student campus into five groups of dorms called Commons, each with their own dean, staff, and activities. While there are certainly benefits to these smaller communities, they somewhat limit the number of people you will live with over your tenure here. Despite many administrative attempts, the student body as a whole is still not entirely on board with the concept.

The Institution

In a nutshell: 2,400 hardworking, happy, Ben & Jerry's–loving, college kids in Vermont. One of the things I love most about Middlebury is the close-knit community that comes with being a member of this campus. Middlebury students get along very well, and I think the college does a great deal to foster this, providing student groups with great opportunities to bond. Last year the college sent Classical Dance Middlebury (one of the groups of which I'm a member) down to Boston to see the Boston Ballet perform. Little things like that really distinguish Middlebury from the larger, more impersonal institutions.

It would also be a true injustice to not mention Middlebury's food. So very, very good. Middkids choose from four main dining halls, each of which has its own distinct menu posted online daily (which comes in handy when it's 40 below out). Also, every Friday night, one of the smaller dining halls is converted into a student-run gourmet restaurant called Dolci. A candlelit five-course meal is served—all free to any student with the fortitude to wait in line for a pair of tickets the night before.

The Education

I think it goes without saying that the academic experience here is excellent. Don't even consider Middlebury if you don't want to work hard for four years (it is worth every single late night). At Middlebury, you'll get a liberal arts experience like nothing else. Next semester I am taking astronomy, economics, sociology, and photography—and I'm a Spanish major. Almost without exception, the classes here have been outstanding—nearly all are small and discussion based, and the few lectures all have discussion components to them.

Even more than the classes themselves, the professors here—and our day-to-day interactions with them—really make this place special. I babysit for my adviser and teach skating to the children of several of my other professors. I've been invited over to a faculty or staff member's house on numerous occasions. The student-professor connection here is incredible.

In terms of academics, Middkids are serious about their work, but we don't dwell on it to an extreme degree. We do our reading, study for our exams, then dash off to the meetings for the bazillion other different activities we do. I like that most of the other students truly care about their education, yet they also know how to relax and have fun on the weekends. It's a very healthy balance. We're not competitive; we don't peek over one another's shoulders when exams are returned or obsess over our GPAs. In fact, except for the honoring of a valedictorian, Middlebury doesn't even rank its graduating students. Our semester plan, 4-1-4, is extremely unique. During our J-term—the J is for *January*—we take only one course for the month. It's allowed me to take American Sign Language my sophomore year, and I spent this J-term in Spain on my own. During the month, numerous extracurricular workshops are also available, including anything from improvisational fiddling to Indian cooking to to self-defense.

Middlebury offers academic courses in Spanish, French, Latin, German, Italian, Portuguese, Arabic, Greek, Hebrew, Chinese, Japanese, and Russian, in addition to winter workshops in anything from American Sign Language to Swahili. The college also offers an excellent opportunity to practice your newfound language skills while you eat. In Cook Dining Hall, each table is devoted to one language, and fluent waiters serve family-style meals to students and faculty while they converse only in that language.

The Students

Middlebury College is a relatively politically active left-leaning campus. Middlebury students are from all fifty states and some seventy countries. Seventy percent of our students come from outside New England. Environmental and social activism—justice initiatives are common. Students demanded fair-trade coffee in the dining halls this year, which we were told we could have if we made up for the additional cost by reducing food waste accordingly (a successful venture). Last year, a group of Middlebury students drove cross-country in a bus they had converted to run on biodiesel fuel. (We are a relatively green campus.) We also have a diverse group of active cultural and political groups, including AAA (African American Aliance), FAM (Feminist Action Middlebury), ALC (Alianza Latinoamericana—Latin American Alliance), MOQA (Middlebury Open Queer Alliance), College Dem-

ocrats, College Republicans, Women of Color, International Students Organization, etc., and numerous religious groups, including the Intervarsity Christian Fellowship, Hillel, the Unitarian Universalist Society, though I wouldn't characterize religion as particularly popular here.

The Activities

Middlebury is located in the dead center of rural, cow-filled Vermont. (Of course, this also means we're near both the Ben & Jerry's and Cabot factories and are guaranteed 365-day-a-year gorgeous panoramic views of both the Adirondack and Green Mountains!) The winter playground that is Vermont also makes J-term a wonderful time to ski (the college owns its own slope, and a free shuttle makes the half-hour trip regularly) or ice skate at our rink or just plain enjoy the gorgeous mountain views. Be forewarned, however, that the closest college is probably the University of Vermont, in Burlington (Vermont's largest city—a whopping 42,000), which is a good forty-five-minute drive from Middlebury. No fear, there is *plenty* to do on this campus. Our activities board prevents weekend boredom by regularly bringing in all kinds of entertainment from comedians to jugglers to casino nights, to murder-mystery dinners to free movies. On rare sunny days we play Frisbee or catch on Battell Beach (what we call the big grass quad in the center of campus because, well, this is a land-locked state). It's also a five-minute walk downtown to the movie theater.

> "Roughly a hundred people in each class are 'Febs,' people who start their first year in February. It's a good option for some (you can request it when you apply)."
> ✦ Naomi, freshman

The Social Scene

While Middlebury does not officially have sororities or fraternities, we have "social houses," which are essentially the coed equivalent. A very small number of students are members, and the houses just provide an additional party spot for the weekends. While Middlebury's reputation of being a large beer-drinking school is relatively justified, I've lived in a substance-free hall all three years here and have had no trouble finding other people who share a similar concept of having fun that doesn't involve just getting drunk every Friday night.

People here do date, but casual dating is somewhat of a rarity. Everyone here is super-friendly—maybe it is because Vermonters in general are so warm and friendly. The vast majority of students here live on campus (you actually need special permission not to), and the housing here is *amazing*—you are even guaranteed a single starting your sophomore year. We've just finished the construction of three new senior apartment buildings, which are suites of four or five singles with spacious living rooms, bathrooms, and kitchens. The college also owns a number of former private homes on the fringe of campus that seniors (with good enough draw numbers) are lucky enough to live in.

Name: Felipe
Hometown: Mexico City, Mexico
Class Year: Freshman
Major: Film and media culture
Extracurriculars: Board of reading and contributor to future literary magazine
Career Goal: To become a full-time writer of fiction, drama, and cinema

How would you describe Middlebury's reputation?

Middlebury College is a beacon of multilingual development. It is a place where written and oral expression in the most widely spoken tongues is richly nurtured.

Is this reputation accurate?

Extremely. English is officially abandoned during the summer language schools (students sign a pledge, committing to give the English language a temporary burial), and so for a few months the college becomes a playful slice of foreignness that makes one feel welcome.

What would an admissions officer at Middlebury probably not tell a prospective student?

They won't tell you about the lack of diversity here.

The Institution

The setting is simply gorgeous: the quiet of Vermont's mountains, the school's enormous green fields, and the trees that turn to the thousand colors of fire during the fall evoke and invoke boundless places and times. The rock-brick outer architecture of the buildings, with some effort, can resemble castles. Unsurprisingly, these very surroundings inspired Robert Frost's poetry and became the home of Middlebury's Bread Loaf Writers Conference, one of the most prestigious in America.

Through the Commons system, events are organized throughout the year by the Commons Council, ranging from lectures to Hawaiian luaus. It's so nice to learn about Etruscan linguistics and wear a coconut bra in the same week in the same place! I lived in Ross Commons my freshman year (short cut to Milliken fifth Floor). It's got the newest dorms on campus, which some call impersonal and oppressive. I've been told they were designed by an architect who specializes in prisons, which explains the riot columns, but I find their light-colored walls and general uniformity pleasant.

The Education

First Year Seminar is worth mentioning. FYSs are for freshmen only and are small discussion-based courses. My seminar, "Physical Immortality: Hopes and Dangers," dealt with the question of what "human life" really is, as treated by such authors as Homer, Plato, St. Thomas Aquinas, Shakespeare, and Jorge Luis Borges, to name a few. Our professor devised the seminar to reveal the greater benefits of a liberal arts education—in his words, a liberal arts education "empowers us to locate the strings of the recursive web of knowledge so we can become a little wiser."

> "Twenty minutes from Snow Bowl, forty-five minutes from Sugarbush, two hours from Montreal, and forty-five minutes from Burlington places Middlebury *exactly* where you want to be in Vermont."
>
> ✦ Chris, sophomore

The Students

Middkids are great, and a statistic I heard tells me I am liable to get very friendly with them. According to a program assistant during my freshmen orientation week, 60 percent of Middlebury College students end up marrying each other.

The Activities

The most vivid memory from my freshman year at Midd was a faculty-directed staging of Anton Chekhov's *Cherry Orchard*. The text was already extremely exciting, thought-provoking material, but the way everything came together made for one of the most enjoyable teamwork experiences of my life so far. The production was lavish (the set included two flights of stairs equipped with air tanks and wheels; the combination made both pieces seem to fly across the stage), but what I truly relished was the process. Not only was I given the chance to get involved in the kind of creative work I love in my first semester here, I also met some extraordinary people that I'm sure the drama world will hear from in the very near future. Every rehearsal was a delight. Faculty productions here are always highly sought-after, big-budget worthwhile enterprises, but with some initiative, a Middkid can mount his or her own show.

The Social Scene

During the college's AIDS awareness week, two friends of mine toured every single party being thrown on campus during a Friday night and distributed free condoms. I fell behind, and spent the night trying to catch up with them. Their trail was unmistakable: I kept stumbling into houses where rubbers littered the floor, along with plastic cups, beer bottles, and was led through everything from a glow-in-the-dark black-light party to pitch-black swimsuited festivities. It was pretty surreal—and really showed me what the social scene here has to offer.

Name: Sarah
Hometown: Palo Alto, California
Class Year: Sophomore
Major: Undeclared
Extracurriculars: *Also* (campus magazine); tour guide; I just pledged a fraternity (yes, we're the alpha chapter, we can admit girls and do whatever else we want!), Hillel
Career Goal: Rabbi

How would you describe Middlebury's reputation?

We're well known on the East Coast as a top-level educational institution with a particular emphasis on foreign language and international focus.

Is this reputation accurate?

Yes, but we're more than just a language school.

What aspect of Middlebury would a prospective student not see on a campus tour?

You wouldn't see how secretly multitalented everyone is. Just by looking, you wouldn't know that someone was an opera-singing downhill-skiing environmentally friendly history major who has lived abroad.

The Institution

I love the community here—small enough so that you can always see friendly faces, but not so small that you feel like you know the entire student body after one semester. Having small classes and professors who really care about you also helps to make the campus really close.

> "The cops should be avoided at all costs because they *really* don't like Midd kids."
> ✦ Chris, junior

As a Californian, I felt very much at home in the liberal atmosphere in Vermont while still being able to experience a completely different part of the country. Fall leaves, blizzards, and thunderstorms are only the beginning of the exciting differences between the Northeast and home! It gets cold. Really cold. But we deal. The cold brings us together, especially during J-term, which is the best scheduling idea ever. An entire month of taking one class, skiing, spending time with friends, and also having the opportunity for unique internships and travel is absolutely amazing. It makes you (almost) forget about the cold. Some of my best friendships were solidified during J-term, and my most exciting classes were during that time.

This is the safest campus I visited as a pre-frosh. We leave our doors unlocked, laptops lying out for extended periods of time, and walk alone late at night, and we have rarely had problems. There's a real sense of community at Middlebury, and that includes trust and safety. The food is amazing. (Think free Ben & Jerry's in every dining hall at every meal. Beware the Freshman Fifteen!)

The Education

The freshman seminar is one of the greatest aspects of the academic system. In my seminar, Frost Country, we read and analyzed Robert Frost's poetry, and we also went on field trips to Frost's cabin and a hiking trail dedicated to him, went apple picking, and had dinner twice at our professor's house. It was one of the best academic experiences of my life and a great way to get acquainted with Vermont and college life.

The Students

There is no "average" Middkid. People classify the student body into three categories: jocks, hippies, and internationals, and while we do have quite a few who fall into those categories, most of us are somewhere in between. Midd is very environmentally conscious, maybe because of its location in rural Vermont. It's also a very community-service-focused school. I heard a statistic that more kids from Midd go into the Peace Corps than from any other college. I don't know if that's true, but I believe it.

> "The average student is a little preppy, a little outdoorsy, and a little drunk."
> ✦ Chris, sophomore

The Activities

One thing I didn't know before coming to Midd is how athletic the campus is. Almost everyone has some kind of activity—from varsity football to Ultimate Frisbee to dance to backpacking to just going running with friends; being active is a priority for Middkids. Hockey games are very well attended, really spirited and exciting.

I'm on the board for Hillel at Middlebury, which is expanding rapidly. We have a core group of twenty or so kids who come to most of the events, but our turnout for Friday night services (and especially dinner, home cooked by one of the students) has been more like forty every week, which is awesome. We have a Passover Seder, High Holiday Services, themed Shabbats (luau in the snow), Spring Break community-service trips (this year I went to Honduras to build a school), lectures, movies, and at least two big open parties a year, including our extremely popular Bar Mitzvah party—like seventh grade, only better!

The Social Scene

There is usually some kind of party going on on campus—sponsored by one of the social houses or other on-campus organizations, so my friends and I will usually go out and party at least one night a weekend. Drinking is pretty widespread. But there's plenty else to do with your friends, like go to the Grille—a combination juice bar–coffeehouse–grill-type restaurant–study space, the Grille is the hangout for procrastinators, studiers, student performers, pool and Foosball players, and sports-game watchers.

Notable Middlebury Alumni Include:

Ari Fleischer, former White House press secretary

James Davis, founder and president of New Balance athletic shoes

John Wallach, author, journalist, and founder of Seeds of Peace

Julia Alvarez, author

Robert Stafford, former U.S. senator (VT)

Ron Brown, former secretary of commerce and chairman of the National Democratic Party

MOREHOUSE COLLEGE

Founded: 1867

Location: Atlanta, GA

Phone: (800) 851-1254

E-mail: admissions@morehouse.ed

Web site: www.morehouse.edu

Number of Undergraduates: 2,738

Number of Graduate Students: 0

Cost: Approximately $22,000 per year

Application Deadline: February 15
Rolling Admissions

Rating:	Notable Majors/Programs:
Selective	Engineering, Business Administration, Biology

Size:
○ Small ● Medium ○ Large

Location:
● Urban ○ Suburban ○ Rural

On a Saturday, students talk about academics:
○ Always ● Sometimes ○ Never

Nightlife:
○ Intense ● Moderate ○ Laid-back

Politically, Morehouse leans:
○ Left ● Right ○ Split

Diversity:
● High ○ Low ○ Medium

All-men's: Yes

Historically Black College: Yes!

Students describe Morehouse in five words:
- Warm, challenging, southern, stately, unique
- Prestigious all-male historically black college
- Martin Luther King studied here

From the School
No institution has achieved greater success than Morehouse College—the nation's only private, historically black, liberal arts college for men—at preparing young men, particularly African American males, to be exemplary models of leadership, manhood and citizenship.

—www.morehouse.edu

If you're interested in Morehouse, you may also be interested in:
Brown, Emory, Georgia Tech, Howard, UPenn, Washington U. in St. Louis

Name: Leon
Hometown: Delton, Florida
Class Year: Sophomore
Major: Business administration, with a concentration in finance
Extracurriculars: Student Government Association, Morehouse College Senate, Morehouse College Young Republicans, Model United Nations, Morehouse Business Association
Career Goal: Corporate attorney, with hopes to eventually become a United States senator

How would you describe Morehouse's reputation?

Morehouse is known as a very traditional, all-male, historically black college that has educated many, many intellectual middle-to-upper-class black men. It's also known for producing alumni who go on to do great things.

Is this reputation accurate?

All of this is true—particularly that we've produced, and continue to produce, outstanding alumni. But we don't *only* educate middle-to-upper-class men—Morehouse caters to a more diversified student body than that. There really are *all* types of students here, from those raised in extremely wealthy households to those from poor inner-city areas who have struggled to be here. If you think Morehouse may be for you, don't hesitate to apply, regardless of your economic circumstances.

What aspect of your school would a prospective student not see on a campus tour?

On a campus tour, a student wouldn't fully grasp that academic competition at Morehouse is, in a word, *fierce.* Everyone is here to succeed and get ahead, and it really doesn't let up. Also, a prospective student wouldn't hear about the (ridiculous) stereotype that everyone at Morehouse is homosexual. Totally untrue.

The Institution

Morehouse puts out more black (male) lawyers, doctors, and engineers than any other school in the country. We were ranked twenty-ninth by the *Wall Street Journal* for sending students to Ivy League and top-twenty graduate schools. And *Black Enterprise* ranked us as the number one college in the world for educating black students. Students have a ridiculous amount of school spirit. They respect and are proud of their school, tout

the colors, reputation, mascot, and traditions constantly. Many Morehouse students have close family members who also went to Morehouse. Incoming freshmen here are taught both how to be a man and how to be a Morehouse man. Teachers and administrators will often recite the quote by the great Howard Thurman: "Over the heads of her students, Morehouse holds a crown, which she challenges them to grow tall enough to wear."

It's also worth noting that Morehouse and Spelman (the historically black all-girls college across the street) have incredibly strong ties to each other. In many ways, the institutions operate as one, especially during big events like homecoming.

Also, we only have one cafeteria on campus (which students get sick of), so bring extra cash to eat off campus. Study-abroad programs are great, and if you have a scholarship, it will pay half your study-abroad expenses.

> "Morehouse College has repeatedly been named the number one school for educating African American men."
> ✦ Willis, sophomore

The Education

Morehouse is a relatively small school (around three thousand students), which has its pros and cons. On the plus side, you have small classes, you get to really know your professors, they get to know you, and you know all of your peers by both name and reputation. On the minus side, you always have to do all of your work or your professors will notice, students are more competitive because they know who their rivals are and how everyone else is doing, and everyone knows everyone, so you can kiss your anonymity good-bye. Rumors spread fast here, but back to the workload—on the weekends students enjoy themselves, but during the week it's all work. Students can major in a wide variety of areas, but the strongest majors are probably business, engineering and biology. I know biology majors have a lot of opportunities to do research with their professors. And if you're a business student, you get to take LPD (Leadership and Professional Development), which is pretty helpful and will teach you the ways of corporate America.

Morehouse has a sizable core curriculum that every student has to complete, including four humanities classes; an art, music, religion, and philosophy class; two social sciences; two semesters of intermediate foreign language; two math classes; two composition classes; world literature; and a semester of a lab science.

The Students

About 97 percent of Morehouse is African American. Most students are either Christian or Muslim, though all religions are accepted. Most students are Democrats, but because Morehouse is a very traditional institution, and because most students are religious, they tend to be conservative Democrats, which also means they aren't as accepting of alternative lifestyles as students are at less traditional institutions.

Socioeconomically, most Morehouse students are either very well-off or very much dependent on financial aid. Those who are well-off pride themselves on the fact that their parents are both professionals (usually doctors, lawyers, businessmen or women), and they'll brag about how many generations of their family attended college (which is a big deal in the black community, considering blacks have only had the same educational opportunities as whites for the past forty years or so). On the other end of the spectrum, those on financial aid pride themselves on their Jack and Jill upbringings, the fact that they've worked particularly hard and been particularly ambitious to get to Morehouse.

I'd say the average Morehouse students are business majors, fairly conservative in their views but Democrats on paper, probably graduated from a predominantly white high school, and come from a two-parent household where one or both parents attended a four-year college or university.

> "Since arriving here, I've met a student who's released his own CD, a student who already has a book in print, and a student who's acted in several films. These are the kinds of people that come to Morehouse."
> ✦ Charles, senior

The Activities

Morehouse College, Spelman College, Clark Atlanta University, Morehouse School of Medicine, and the Interdenominational Theological School are each within walking distance and, together, they make up the AUC (Atlanta University Center). All five schools collaborate in various activities (though snobs from Morehouse and Spelman think that they're better than students from the other schools).

On all the AUC campuses, Greek life rules. Generally, at predominantly black schools Greek organizations run the entire social scene, and Morehouse is no exception. Four fraternities at Morehouse generate Morehouse's social life. Most students find themselves drawn to these organizations, and the organizations, in turn, have become incredibly exclusive. Accordingly, the process of applying and becoming a brother has become so grueling and time consuming that a lot of students either flat-out give up, or find themselves not making the cut after months of effort. It's too bad.

Life at Morehouse is pretty balanced. Students spend half their time doing community service, studying, going to class and being productive. And they spend the other half of their time partying, sleeping, clubbing, and being otherwise unproductive. We get great bands to perform throughout the year.

The Social Scene

When schoolwork is done, students here party like it's their job. They'll go to ritzy clubs in the area, nearby bars, and house and frat parties here and at Emory, Agnes Scott, Georgia State, GeorgiaTech and Spelman. A typical Saturday night will include pre-gaming at someones place, hitting a club in Buckhead, a house party in Cascade, then chillin' at someone's house until you're ready to pass out. When not partying, I've met friends through classes, through my dorm. I've also met a lot of friends because I saw them in Martha's Vineyard or Nantucket during the summer.

Name: Thomas
Hometown: Austin, Texas
Class Year: Senior
Major: Political science
Extracurriculars: *The Maroon Tiger, The Torch* (yearbook), Student Government Association, Deputy Homecoming Director, Student Senate, Student Court, Elections Committee, Pre-Law Society, Political Science Club, Morehouse Young Democrats, Morehouse Black Think Tank
Career Goal: United States congressman, a high-ranking official in the Democratic Party, or the editor in chief of *GQ* or *Esquire* magazine

How would you describe Morehouse's reputation?

Our most famous alum, Martin Luther King Jr., casts a shadow over every Morehouse student (we try hard to live up to his legacy). Morehouse's world-renowned reputation was built on the efforts of such great men and is strengthened by the brilliant students that leave Morehouse every year.

Is this reputation accurate?

Absolutely. And it's impressive to note how small Morehouse is, just under three thousand undergraduates. We have a saying, "Never before have so few done so much with so little." Think about it. Morehouse is this tiny little school for men in the South, with a tiny student body, and it's produced some of the most important leaders the world has ever known, regardless of race or nationality. Morehouse does something special to produce such men.

> "My advice to any new student at Morehouse is to get to know the campus police fairly well. They'll always help you out."
> ✦ Alfred, sophomore

What would an admissions officer at your school probably not tell a prospective student?

Morehouse is hard and Morehouse is competitive. Every single student here is held to a standard of excellence that's very hard to live up to. I've been classmates with two Morehouse Rhodes Scholars, one Morehouse Marshall Scholar, and one Morehouse Fulbright Scholar. These kids weren't breezing through Morehouse—they were working every day, and they got where they are because of hours of sweat and tears. If you tell prospective students just how difficult Morehouse is, they'll either have the daylights scared out of them, or they'll be inspired to walk the same path as those who came before them and do their best to do even better.

But Morehouse is also caring, loving, and nurturing. On a college tour, a visitor wouldn't see the love students here have for one another, or how we go out of our way for our Morehouse brothers, both while we're here and once we've graduated. This is something you can't see on a tour, you can only experience it as a student. Some call it the Mystique, others don't know what to call it, but it binds us . . . forever.

The Institution

Morehouse is a small campus on a hill at the highest point in Atlanta. It's kind of like going to Lehigh, but in the hood. Most of the buildings are brick, which makes the campus feel historic. The main street that runs through campus goes up the hill and behind Graves Hall. (The original building of Morehouse College that once housed classrooms, administrative offices, and dorm rooms. Graves Hall is where Martin Luther King Jr., Samuel L. Jackson, and Maynard Jackson once lived.)

Atlanta weather changes by the moment, so be prepared. Campus security officers are nice if you treat them like your friends; do this and your stay at Morehouse will be far nicer. Morehouse's food is, shall we say, always improving. Morehouse has the best big-name performers and speakers in the country because everyone wants to come to King Chapel and speak where Martin Luther King went to school. Use this to your advantage, meet as many CEOs, entertainers, presidents, kings and queens, and various celebrities as you can. Morehouse students get some of the best internships and jobs in the country. Our grads also go to the best grad schools—Harvard, Yale, Columbia, Johns Hopkins, Brown, Penn, Duke, Chicago, Cal and Stanford, Georgetown, NYU—you name it.

Morehouse is a small school, meaning teachers are more accessible and every student feels like they matter, like Morehouse is really a part of them. School spirit is, accordingly, overwhelming. There are many traditions here, with my favorites being New Student Orientation, homecoming, A Candle in the Dark, and graduation—at each of these, beautiful, educated African American people gather together to celebrate their efforts and their success. They're all fantastic sights to see.

The Education

Students are always talking about classes at Morehouse. Classes are rough. Teachers are demanding. Some teachers are so demanding they're known throughout the school for the rigor of the work they assign. That said, those same teachers are usually known throughout the school for providing a great deal of personal attention and really caring for their students—if they make their classes difficult, it's only because they want us to push ourselves and rise to the challenge. The strongest departments here are biology, chemistry, economics, English, math, music, physics, political science and psychology. As a political science major, I've been able to complete a very lengthy thesis, and I've had some excellent classes and professors along the way.

The Students

I'd say the most influential and vocal group on campus is the school's newspaper, *The Maroon Tiger*. The biggest group on campus is the Morehouse Business Association. Most students are from the South, with many from Georgia. Most students are Democrats. The average Morehouse student has a cell phone, lives on campus, is a business major, and has a 3.0. He wants to be in a fraternity, does some community service, dates a young lady from Spelman, and probably has a car.

The Activities

Morehouse students spend a lot of time interacting with students from Spelman College, and vice versa. We're all males; they're all females. It's natural. Morehouse and Spelman go together like yin and yang. When Morehouse students aren't chasing girls, athletic events are very well attended. Community service is also very popular, especially through a variety of programs like the Bonner Scholars and the Emma and Joe Adams Public Service Institute.

The Social Scene

Morehouse students go to a lot of house parties. They also party all over Atlanta, from Buckhead to Midtown to Downtown to Downtown Decatur to Austell. Morehouse is a dry campus, with no alcohol allowed, but Morehouse students still drink a lot; they just do it off campus and at private residences.

The dating scene here is pretty great. There're plenty of people to meet in Atlanta, and we're across the street from Spelman, next door to Clark Atlanta. While walking to the library, you literally bump into beautiful women every step of the way.

Name: Alexander
Hometown: Bronx, New York
Class Year: Freshman
Major: Dual degree in Engineering
Extracurriculars: Student Government Association, NSBE
Career Goal: Architect

How would you describe Morehouse's reputation?

It's one of the best liberal arts colleges in America, known for educating outstanding black men.

Is this reputation accurate?

Absolutely.

What would an admissions officer at your school probably not tell a prospective student?

That the process by which students register for classes at Morehouse is rather tedious and requires patience. Generally, tasks at Morehouse where students have to interact with the administration are frustrating. There's far too much bureaucracy. But you'll get used to this and learn to deal with it.

The Institution

The small size of the school allows for extensive interaction between students and professors. I chose Morehouse because I was impressed by its overall presentation. The brotherhood at Morehouse that everyone always speaks of actually exists. There are students from every socioeconomic background, from different countries and cultures all over the world. The school spirit here is great. Also, study-abroad programs, internships, and grad school opportunities at Morehouse are phenomenal. NSO (New Student Orientation) was probably one of the best experiences of my life. We all have incredibly fond memories of NSO; it's the beginning of being a Morehouse Man.

The Education

Morehouse provides a very competitive academic environment. I spend between four and six hours a day doing homework and studying. There's an even split between discussion- and lecture-based classes at Morehouse. Lecture classes in science and mathematics and discussion-based classes in English, history, and the humanities. Biology is by far the hardest department here, followed by engineering. Do not major in biology or engineering! They'll kill you! (Just kidding, they're challenging, but not impossible.)

Lastly, Morehouse's large core curriculum means every student leaves Morehouse with a wide range of knowledge, prepared to go out into the world and make something of himself. There's very little anyone can get over on a Morehouse man; he has a wide body of knowledge at his disposal.

The Students

There is no average student at Morehouse College. There's so much diversity here—the inner and outer differences radiate from every member of the student body. There's such a variety of cultures, professional styles, and personalities that keep our campus vibrant.

The Activities

Morehouse interacts with Spelman and Clark most frequently. There are always activities on all of these campuses, though, that are open to students from all over the AUC. This makes students feel like they go to a big school even though Morehouse is rather small. Community service is encouraged and well participated in by Morehouse students, and since Morehouse is basically located in the slums of West End, Atlanta, there is always plenty of community service to be done.

The Social Scene

As a freshman, live in a dorm. This will help you build strong friendships and craft a support system, so when the workload gets rough, people are there to help you through it. Most upperclassmen live off campus so they can escape the many rules in campus dormitories, but dorm life is otherwise great. People party all the time at Morehouse. There's always something to do, both on campus and off. Because Morehouse is in downtown Atlanta, you can always meet new people, and you never feel suffocated by Morehouse's size. I think I meet someone new just about every day.

Notable Morehouse Alumni Include:
Martin Luther King Jr., civil rights leader
Julian Bond, civil rights leader
Samuel L. Jackson, actor
Sanford D. Bishop Jr., Georgia congressman
Edwin Moses, Olympic gold medalist, track and field

MOUNT HOLYOKE COLLEGE

Founded: 1837

Location: South Hadley, MA

Phone: (413) 538-2000

E-mail: admission@mtholyoke.edu

Web site: www.mtholyoke.edu

Number of Undergraduates: 2,100

Number of Graduate Students: 10

Cost: Approximately $40,000 per year

Application Deadline: January 15

Early Decision: November 15

Rating:	Notable Majors/Programs:
Selective	Life Sciences, English, Social Sciences, Psychology

Size:
● Small   ○ Medium   ○ Large

Location:
○ Urban   ● Suburban   ○ Rural

On a Saturday, students talk about academics:
○ Always   ● Sometimes   ○ Never

Nightlife:
○ Intense   ○ Moderate   ● Laid-back

Politically, Mount Holyoke leans:
● Left   ○ Right   ○ Split

Diversity:
● High   ○ Low   ○ Medium

All-women's: Yes!

Five-College school: Yes!

Students describe Mount Holyoke in five words:
- Smart sexy women go here!
- Tradition-based, hardworking, empowered, progressive MHC-lovers

From the School

Mount Holyoke College reaffirms its commitment to educating a diverse residential community of women at the highest level of academic excellence and to fostering the alliance of liberal arts education with purposeful engagement in the world.

—www.mtholyoke.edu

If you're interested in Mount Holyoke, you may also be interested in:
Amherst, Bryn Mawr, Scripps, Smith, Vassar, Wellesley

Name: Shana
Hometown: Brattleboro, Vermont
Class Year: Freshman
Major: Undecided
Extracurriculars: Concert choir, SHE (Sexual Health Educators)
Career Goal: I could see myself working in a museum.

How would you describe Mount Holyoke's reputation?

You could get a reaction anywhere from, "Oh, it's just a bunch of rich girls looking for husbands at Amherst" to "Be careful, all those militant feminists might turn you into a lesbian!" When I first told people that I was applying to Mount Holyoke early decision, they seemed surprised. Someone said to me, "How are you going to go to a school with just girls?" The emphasis tends to be on the fact that there are no guys at Mount Holyoke, rather than on the academics.

Is this reputation accurate?

Never having visited or really known a Mount Holyoke woman, people tend to grasp the stereotypes, which is a shame. Sure, there are wealthy students and yes, there is a large gay population, but that's not all there is to it. They're overlooking the fact that Mount Holyoke is a very highly regarded liberal arts college and that women here will do many great things with their lives. How else would we boast famous alumnae like Frances Perkins, the first woman to be appointed to a presidential cabinet, or Pulitzer Prize–winning playwrights Wendy Wasserstein and Suzan-Lori Parks?

What would an admissions officer at Mount Holyoke probably not tell a prospective student?

There is a large emphasis on the Five College Consortium community, but an admissions officer probably wouldn't talk about how the flip side is an empty campus on weekends.

The Institution

I think one of the most striking aspects of Mount Holyoke is its devotion to tradition. I'm not talking about donning high heels and dresses to dinner, but the fun ones like M&Cs (milk and cookies), where we get snacks each night at 9:30 and "elf-ing," where a sophomore leaves presents and decorates a first year's door during a week in the beginning of the year. The week of elf-ing was such a thrill for me. My elf was awesome. She called me one night and sang me a lullaby. That she was so into the tradition got me really excited. I will be a sophomore this fall and I am psyched to be able to "elf" a firstie! As for the campus itself, it looks like a movie set in the autumn when the leaves are turning colors. Most of the buildings are constructed out of old brick. It's very New Englandy. The size is fairly small. It doesn't take more than ten minutes to get anywhere on campus, and it is very safe, even late at night. Instead of one big cafeteria in the middle of campus, our dining halls are in the dorms. Some have closed due to budget cuts. It's too bad, but not terrible, as we still have a number of choices of where to go to catch up on the day's news with friends.

The Education

Because MHC is a liberal arts college, science and humanities students are forced to get a taste of the opposite's subjects while completing requirements. My friends who are premed and take many science courses do seem satisfied with their academic experiences.

> MHC's slogan: We're not a girl's school without men, we're a women's college without boys.

The Students

Another aspect of being a Mount Holyoke student is being surrounded by overachievers 24-7. Everyone here is involved in a billion different activities. I even had a friend who had to schedule showering time into her date book! Overall, the people here really do want to learn. They aren't at college just to party and meet boys. They are here because they know that MHC will give them what they need to succeed in life and achieve their goals.

If there is one thing I love about Mount Holyoke, it is its diverse community. Coming from a completely Caucasian rural community, where diversity meant eating Indian food once a month, I found Mount Holyoke to be a breath of fresh air. As someone who is half Japanese, I feel completely comfortable here—it turned out my next-door neighbor was half Japanese as well! There are many cultural groups to join on campus, and the

LGBT groups are very vocal because it is a safe atmosphere for people to come out. Also, the campus tends to be more liberal and activism is very strong here, so whatever your cause is, you are likely to find others who will support you.

The Activities

The Five College Consortium is something that is beat into your head during the info sessions and campus tours at any of the five colleges, and it is an advantage for classes and weekend activities, but the extent to which you participate is up to you. The town of South Hadley doesn't offer much, but there is a deli, café, pizza place, and bookstore. Amherst and Northampton are the great places to go on weekends for food, shopping, or just a change of scenery, so having a car is definitely a plus for getting around to the more exciting areas.

The Social Scene

On the weekends campus is dead. Once in a while there will be a large event, but otherwise I wouldn't recommend the parties in Blanchard Student Center because they consist of usually about twenty people or so with some odd guys standing around thinking they're God's gift to women because they are on the campus of a women's college. The dating scene tends to be better if you're LGBT than if you are straight, for obvious reasons. But that shouldn't be discouraging because I know many people who have dated guys at Amherst and UMass.

Name: Amber
Hometown: Monterey, California
Class Year: Sophomore
Major: History
Extracurriculars: Yearbook, volunteer teaching in elementary school
Career Goal: To become a professor of history or archaeology

How would you describe Mount Holyoke's reputation?

MHC's reputation varies between a finishing school complete with traditional values and a hotbed of lesbian and radical liberality.

Is this reputation accurate?

Honestly, both of them are. It's a bit of a strange mix—we like tradition here and guard it fiercely, but we also love being liberal and progressively minded.

What would an admissions officer at Mount Holyoke probably not tell a prospective student?

That there is a *huge* workload here, and this is not like any other college—if you want to party, you really have to search for it. There aren't many keggers here.

> "The all-women atmosphere drives me mad!"
>
> ✦ Jos, junior

The Institution

The size of the school seems big at first, but after a year here, you start to recognize many of the same faces and a web of acquaintances begins to emerge, so as time goes by, the student body begins to feel smaller and smaller. The campus is absolutely beautiful. I don't think that as many students would matriculate here if it weren't for the campus—with all of the work and stress that we have, it's one of the main reasons a lot of us stick around. The most difficult thing about being a first-year student is that you have to adjust to being in an all-women environment—it's a little disconcerting at first, but then you forget about it and find yourself slipping into a routine of classes and work.

As for the interaction between students and townies, there are basically two kinds of interactions: our talking to the dining hall staff, since we see them every day and they feed us; and girls going out with guys from the major city nearby, Springfield, or the occasional desperate firstie who will find a guy from South Hadley High.

Honestly, if you make it past first year (and don't transfer, which a lot of people do, since Mount Holyoke definitely isn't for everyone), you end up absolutely loving the school and having a great connection with it and everyone associated with it.

The Education

I love January term. It's a great opportunity to focus on one course or work on an independent project while the campus is quiet and glittering with icy beauty. We definitely all love to study here—I talk a lot with my friends about what we're studying. I just now got back from lunch with a friend, and we were discussing Hawthorne, as well as Greco-Roman conceptions of deity (on a Saturday!). There isn't much competition among students. The preprofessionals have it hard here. The premeds work their tails off, and the other preprofessions don't really have their own programs and have to take off-campus classes (like accounting) that we don't offer. We're in the Five College System, so Smith, UMass, Amherst, and Hampshire are very close by. A lot of people take classes at those colleges, and their students take classes here, so there are connections between the colleges. Some of my friends take a class off campus every semester, though I never have.

TAs are really just for first-year seminars and for science classes—humanities and social sciences almost never have TAs. As for lecture or discussion, it depends. Professors pretty much keep out of student life on campus, but they give us lots and lots of opportunities to work as research assistants, no matter the subject field.

As much as distribution requirements are annoying, they are good because they give us a chance to find out what we really like. If it weren't for distributions, I would have never taken anthropology, and it's totally changed my thesis.

> "We have the most beautiful library I have ever seen! The main reading room is modeled after Westminster Abbey."
> ✦ Reena, senior

The Students

There are quite a few students from Massachusetts, but then there are more Pakistani girls on campus than girls from Ohio, so it's really pretty diverse. Pretty much everyone here has a cause, so it's hard to get people outside of your group to attend rallies. All of the different minority groups on campus are very vocal, and most have their own houses off campus. Most students are very liberal—and the College Republicans on campus do have to keep pretty quiet to avoid being attacked for their party affiliation.

The average MHCer is excellent at procrastinating, always has loads of work to do, enjoys partying hard when the chance comes along, has a few close friends and a huge network of acquaintances, focuses hard on her work and has that strange mix of valuing tradition and the past with a progressive and optimistic outlook on the world. We all think that we can change the world for the better. The missionary spirit is still here.

The Activities

The most vocal campus groups? The a cappella groups! For those who participate in athletics, it takes up a big part of their lives and for those in the arts, time in the studio does absorb inordinate amounts of time. I am the editor in chief of the yearbook, and it takes up a huge chunk of my life. The hardest part about it is not the production but getting people to join and stay interested. There are so many worthwhile organizations and causes available that many students overdo it, then have no time for anything. Community service isn't in your face here—but almost everyone does something and there's a sense that we owe a lot to the community and should do something to give back. Unfortunately, students have little place in administrative decisions here. The SGA is considered a bit of a joke on campus. Most student participation in administrative decisions comes after the decision has been announced and there is a student outcry.

The Social Scene

People usually party on Thursday and Saturday night—strangely, Friday isn't the hugest party night. This goes for most of the valley. During the winter and during finals and midterms, there are next to no parties. However, once the weather is nice, people celebrate and throw quite a few loud shindigs. Most parties are just groups of close friends having fun with some vodka and maybe some rum. Typical Friday: chill with friends and see a movie, go to a concert, play pool. Typical Saturday: go to a party at a friend's room, hang out.

The dating scene: if you are straight, then you can either (a) get lucky and find a boyfriend or a one-night stand at another college or (b) bury yourself in work and become chaste for four years. Most straight girls strike a note somewhere in between. If you are gay, then it's totally different because there is a sizable lesbian population on campus, and consequently more opportunities for hookups. Beyond that, I don't know too much about that scene. Since it's pretty hard to get approval to live off campus, everyone lives in dorms and hopes that they get good lottery numbers to live in the "good" dorms on the green. Everyone is very friendly and fairly considerate of one another, and besides the faint cliquishness of the minority groups, everyone pretty much hangs out together.

Name: Jennifer
Hometown: Houston, Texas
Class Year: Sophomore
Majors: German studies and theater arts
Extracurriculars: Art, theater
Career Goal: Professor

How would you describe Mount Holyoke's reputation?

A stuffy, lesbian-filled, academically challenging, best-of-the-best women's college.

Is this reputation accurate?

It's not stuffy or lesbian filled! Yes, it *is* academically challenging, and yes, we *are* the best of the best, but I forget all the time that I'm at a women's college; gender becomes a nonissue and one less obstacle when it comes to focusing on your studies and, more importantly, focusing on yourself.

> "Some students refer to nearby Northampton as 'NoHo,' which inspired students to then call the school 'MoHo' and themselves 'MoHos.'"
>
> ✦ Michelle, junior

What would an admissions officer at Mount Holyoke probably not tell a prospective student? What aspect of your school would a prospective student not see on a campus tour?

They wouldn't tell you about the political activism on campus. When we don't like something, we let the faculty and administration hear about it. We can unite as a community to effect changes, and it's awesome to behold. And a prospie wouldn't see the scary, older-than-your-parents elevator in Buckland Hall or the steep, outdoor, ice-covered dungeon stairs that lead to the basement lecture hall of Clapp.

The Institution

Soooo pretty! The campus is like Hogwart's on a good day (all the snow included, much to the dismay of this Texas-born-and-bred student!) and full of character—you can practically imagine Emily Dickinson still walking around here. MHC definitely has a prestigious reputation, and people do have prejudices about it (we must all be rich to go here; we're snotty; we're all lesbians; we're all man haters). But it really isn't like that at all; we are strong women and proud of our heritage as a school, and we celebrate our diversities as individuals.

The Education

Most of the professors here are dedicated and passionate about their subjects. As a theater and German double major, I work closely with all of my professors to integrate my interests and still meet basic requirements. They have been nothing but helpful and enthusiastic. It's more than just office hours—they're always responding promptly and helpfully to e-mails, chatting with students after class, and setting up class-related excursions. They really want you to love what you're doing as much as *they* love what *they're* doing.

Study abroad is *huge* here—many good programs, lots of funding, very good reputation. You can also design your own major—a wonderful convenience. Professors here really want you to pursue exactly what interests you. There are about eight core requirements—but they're there for a reason. I came to MHC thinking I'd be a classics and English double major. I took Intensive Elementary German to get out of having to take a two-semester-long foreign language course, because everyone must have eight foreign language credits, and now I'm a German major. I know this sounds like a testimonial on a TV infomercial, but it really is the truth. It's good to have to stretch yourself academically in ways you may not necessarily want to, because it really might open your eyes to a whole new set of interests.

The Students

Students are smart: intelligent, inquisitive, and very hardworking. We all tend to take on the world—too many classes, extracurriculars, work-study, etc.—so it's hard to find a student with too much time on her hands. *Everyone* works hard. It can be hard to relax here; everyone is so accomplished, it's easy to get caught up in that and forget to just *enjoy* learning.

The Activities

A day in my life: 3:00 a.m. on a Wednesday—I got back from play rehearsals around 11:00 p.m., did my work-study job of taking out the trash from 11:15 p.m. to 11:30 p.m., showered around midnight, watched the Cartoon Network's *Adult Swim* with a couple of friends in the TV room, practiced German with my friend (complaining about the German homework I haven't done yet), chatted with a French foreign exchange student about accents for twenty minutes in the hallway; finally around 1:15 I started my homework and around 2:00 gave it up in favor of sleep.

The Social Scene

People are pretty laid-back here. Not a big party school, though MHC women can go wild. We're polite and friendly—people hold open doors, smile, shout to friends across campus, chat with professors as they walk to and from classes. No sororities; MHC is like one big sorority. Dorm life is important—the TV room's a great place to hang out, and M&Cs every night are a very welcome study break at 9:30 p.m.!

Notable Mount Holyoke Alumni Include:
Elaine Chao, U.S. labor secretary
Emily Dickinson, poet
Frances Perkins, first woman U.S. cabinet member
Nita Lowey, U.S. congresswoman
Suzan-Lori Parks, Pulitzer Prize–winning playwright
Wendy Wasserstein, Pulitzer Prize–winning playwright

NEW YORK UNIVERSITY

Founded: 1861

Location: New York, NY

Phone: (212) 998-4500

E-mail: admissions@nyu.edu

Web site: www.nyu.edu

Number of Undergraduates: 19,490

Number of Graduate Students: 15,348

Cost: Approximately $39,000 per year

Application Deadline: January 15

Early Decision: November 1

Rating:
Most Selective

Notable Majors/Programs:
Business, Social Sciences, Directing,
Creative Writing

Size:
○ Small   ○ Medium   ● Large

Location:
● Urban   ○ Suburban   ○ Rural

On a Saturday, students talk about academics:
○ Always   ● Sometimes   ○ Never

Nightlife:
○ Intense   ● Moderate   ○ Laid-back

Politically, NYU leans:
● Left   ○ Right   ○ Split

Diversity:
○ High   ○ Low   ● Medium

Students describe NYU in five words:
- Trendy, diverse, alive, challenging, eye-opening
- Something to write home about

From the School

NYU is a major private research university renowned for its unparalleled resources, faculty, and scholarship. Our students choose from 160 areas of study and over 2,500 courses each year. We have eight libraries with more than four and one-half million volumes, as well as study-abroad sites in Florence, Ghana, London, Madrid, Paris, and Prague . . . [and] NYU and New York City are inseparable. There is a palpable exchange of energy and ideas that flows seamlessly from one to the other. Every day you spend at NYU is a day in the real world where you will benefit from all that New York City has to offer.

—www.admissions.nyu.edu

If you're interested in NYU, you may also be interested in:
Brown, UC Berkeley, Columbia, Georgetown, Sarah Lawrence

Name: Rachel

Hometown: New Canaan, Connecticut

Class Year: Freshman

Major: Romance Languages and Journalism (double major)

Extracurriculars: Founding sister of the Alpha Sigma Tau sorority.

Career Goal: Editor of a newspaper or magazine, or a broadcast journalist.

How would you describe NYU's reputation?

NYU is supposed to be a bastion of liberal students. It's also supposed to have a lot of students who are artsy, eccentric, and unique.

Is this reputation accurate?

NYU students are definitely (and overwhelmingly) liberal, but the notion that every student is also rebellious and quirky is a bit off the mark. Really, NYU has such an enormous student body that it's hard to make generalizations. But, of course, just from living in New York City, you're going to pick up some quirks if you didn't have them beforehand.

What would an admissions officer at your school probably not tell a prospective student?

You will receive a laughable amount of financial aid at NYU, if you receive any at all, and your tuition will climb each year to renewed epic proportions. On a tour, you would see the nicest freshman dorm, which has high ceilings and carpets and a Starbucks right in the building. This dorm is in stark contrast to *most* freshman dorms, which are cinder-block cells.

The Institution

That said, *every* dorm room at NYU has its own private bathroom. That was a huge selling point for me, and it's been wonderful. The physical layout of our campus is a huge part of student life here at NYU, because we *have* no campus. Dorms and classes are in apartment buildings sprawling all over the city. While freshmen are mostly placed in dorms around oh-so convenient Washington Square Park, upperclassmen are shunted to either Chinatown or South Street Seaport (where you'll have a lovely view of the Brooklyn Bridge but a twenty-five-minute commute to class).

The cost of living is astronomical. Not only does NYU have the second highest tuition of any private university, but New York is unbelievably expensive in itself. What with paying for taxis and subways, dining at restaurants/delis/diners, buying show tickets, paying cover charges at clubs (always at least ten dollars), museum admissions, and shopping, I spend at least a hundred dollars every week. Be prepared to run yourself into *massive* debt.

That said, there is no better place than New York City to find internships and job opportunities at the most important corporations in the world. If you intern frequently while you're a student at NYU—and you should—you'll leave this place with a glowing résumé students at other schools simply won't be able to touch.

I'd say the hardest part of being a freshman at NYU is the first week, when you haven't made friends yet and you're feeling kind of lost and alone. It's during this time that people wonder whether they made the right decision to come, and when some of the suicides happen. Don't worry, though. Things will get better. You'll make some friends, and before long you'll be having the best time of your life. NYU has the largest student body of any private university, which suits me fine. Being from a small town, I wanted the opportunity to meet thousands of new and different people, and I got my wish.

NYU's massive size does make it hard to socialize, though, because you'll meet someone one day and then never see them again. You have to really put yourself out there in order to stay in touch with that fantastic person you just had a random and great conversation with. NYU's big size also makes students feel jaded. For example, most of our student body was largely unaffected by the rash of student suicides we had recently because the people who died were people we had never heard of before—many didn't even know anyone who had known them. Because there's all this anonymity, I've found it useful to join a sorority and get involved in the Greek system, which actually does a good job of tying you to other people and giving you a solid group of friends to fall back on.

The Education

I've found the workload at NYU to be very manageable. I take four to five classes, and I only have about two classes each day. And the only tests assigned are usually midterms or finals. For some classes you have to write one-page papers once a week, but many classes require no papers at all.

Almost all of my classes at NYU have been lecture based. For certain classes there's a recitation section, which meets once a week and breaks down into groups of twenty students or less for discussions based on the lectures. TAs (called "preceptors" here) teach these recitation sections as well as some of the core curriculum classes and some basic low-level classes, such as beginner language courses. For the most part, I have been very satisfied with the level of teaching here, and with the fact that TAs only teach the classes they're qualified to teach (rather than important upper-level classes).

NYU's core curriculum, referred to as MAP (short for Morse Academic Plan) is a huge pain, but it is a necessary evil and there are ways of skirting around it. For example, thanks to my AP classes in high school, I passed out of the math, science, and foreign language requirements, which saved me a full semester and made my double major/double minor possible. And then, some of the requirements are actually enjoyable, like the Writing the Essay class that everyone has to take. A lot of requirements are history/literature–based, and I'm currently satisfying one of those by taking Russia Since 1917, taught by Stephen Cohen, one of the leading Sovietologists in the country.

> "NYU's campus *is* New York City. While most administrative NYU buildings are around Washington Square Park—which has a few trees, grassy fields, a fountain, some regular chess players, and bums sleeping on benches—NYU classrooms are everywhere, scattered across the city, as far as midtown, Chinatown, and the Seaport—anywhere you see a purple flag."
> ✦ Joseph, junior

The Students

NYU students are predominantly liberal, and a lot of students are Jewish and LGBT. We're also pretty political—protests are held on the sidewalks almost every day. The current biggest political debate on campus is between the pro-Israeli student group and the pro-Palestinian student group.

The Activities

It's very easy to interact with students from other Manhattan schools, because all the students in the city go to the same clubs and bars. I've met people from Pace, the New School, Hunter, Fordham, and Columbia.

Both athletics and Greek life are very minimal parts of overall student life. Sports are Division 3 and events are not well attended at all. NYU is the antithesis of a football college, like Notre Dame or USC. The arts, however, can play a large role if you want them to. Both the Tisch and Steinhardt schools are always putting on productions, and there's always Broadway/off-Broadway or any kind of performance art you can imagine in the city.

The Social Scene

People at NYU do not "party" very often, in the sense of big parties that are full of rambunctious NYU students. It's more that groups of NYU students meet up in bars, where there will also be plenty of nonstudents. On a typical Thursday/Friday/Saturday night (Thursdays are big because NYU rarely schedules classes on Fridays, so most people have four-day weeks), small groups of friends will either have some drinks or go to a club to dance. Clubs are tricky though, because (a) they're less likely to accept fake IDs (everyone at NYU has a fake ID), (b) the cover charges are astronomical, anywhere from ten to thirty dollars just to get in, and (c) clubs tend to be frequented by sketchy men looking for younger women. It's not as bad as it sounds; you just have to keep your wits about you when you go out in New York.

When we get back from partying, everyone hangs out in the dorms. Dorm life is pretty wonderful here; dorms are very tight-knit. I love being able to walk down the hall at two in the morning and hang out with my friends only ten feet away. My freshman year I lived in Goddard, which is right in the middle of "campus." That's the dorm with high ceilings and carpets and a Starbucks right on the first floor. If you get assigned to Goddard, you've lucked out. The main classroom building is directly across the street, so it took literally two seconds to walk to most of my classes.

Finally, the intra-NYU dating scene is nonexistent here. The joke is that 50 percent of NYU guys are gay, 25 percent of the straight guys already have girlfriends, and 50 percent of the 25 percent who are straight and single have STDs. Most people wind up dating folks they meet around the city, who either go to another college or live in Manhattan.

Name: Jennifer
Hometown: Abington, Massachusetts
Class Year: Freshman
Major: Studio Art
Extracurriculars: DCA (Dancers and Choreographers Alliance).
Career Goal: I don't have much of a career goal right now other than to do something with art and not starve.

How would you describe NYU's reputation?

It's funny, because even though NYU is considered to be this great school—almost up there with the Ivy Leagues—when I say I go to NYU a lot of people back home in Boston ask, "Now what school is that again?" Maybe NYU isn't as well known as I thought it was? Or maybe this is just Bostonian ignorance?

Is this reputation accurate?

I think NYU is well known—regardless of whether or not NYU is well known in Boston—and it deserves to be.

What would an admissions officer at your school probably not tell a prospective student?

They won't tell a prospective about the suicides (unless you were on that one tour that actually witnessed a kid jumping to his death), the occasional robberies, how the tuition will continually get jacked up, how there are movies and television shows constantly being shot around the area—which makes it hell to get to class on time—about NYU's bitchy security guards, the Children's International people who are always badgering students for donations, the dorms that are thirty minutes off campus, that the sophomores get screwed out of *everything* at NYU, that a lot of New York City apartments are actually cheaper than staying in NYU dorms, that cabs *will* run you over if you're in their way, that you *must* buy an umbrella, and that you will at need at least one good pair of boots.

The Institution

If there's one thing about this college that is different from a lot of other colleges, it's that there isn't much of an NYU "community." There isn't a campus, so formal social gatherings are few and far between. This means you can't rely on friendship-

making opportunities falling into your lap—you'll have to manufacture them on your own. This is where kids lacking social skills may struggle. But if you're outgoing, you'll do all right. Between the kids in your dorm, the kids in your classes, and the kids you'll randomly meet around the city who don't even go to NYU, you'll find people to hang out with.

It's also worth noting that, when you apply to NYU, you apply to an individual college: Gallatin School of Individualized Study, where you "create your own major"; the College of Arts and Science; the Stern School of Business, where you prepare to make lots of money; the Steinhardt School of Education; the School of Health and Nursing; the School of Social Work; or the Tisch School of the Arts, which is pretty famous for film, writing, and acting. Every different college also has different core requirements.

> "The student who would be happiest at NYU would be an 'individual'—a fashion whore, a drama queen, a world traveler, a savvy businessman, an existential artist, a film nerd, a kid who couldn't stand another second living in his/her boring suburban home."
>
> ✦ Jessica, senior

The Education

I'm an art major, and one thing the art department is good for is providing some wild professors. I was always under the impression that art professors were pretentious and cruel; here, they're the complete opposite, this weird mix of down-to-earth, friendly, and totally out of control. Most of them, for example, won't hesitate to drop a four-letter word regardless of whether they're speaking to students or parents. They also like giving ridiculous assignments. Once, in Fundamentals of Digital Art, our teacher gave each of us two photographs of our classmates that she'd taken at the beginning of the semester. She then walked up to the front of the room and said, "Okay, class. Everyone have their two images? I am going to give you two words, and you must use Photoshop to transform the person in the picture to fit the words. Okay? First word: Sexpot. Second word: lecher. GO!" Needless to say, we all had a great time.

Now for my complaints: the equipment we have in the art department gets the job done, but it's far from top quality. Considering the money that I, and the other thousands of students, dish out to this school, it makes me wonder why we can't get a slightly better photo lab or at least an elevator that doesn't require a human being to operate it in the art department. Things like this make me think twice about my decision to come to NYU when I could have gone to Harvard for less money and come out with a degree from an Ivy League school.

The Students

What I do like about this school as opposed to a lot of the schools back in Massachusetts is that a large portion of the student body is from out of state. It's fun to meet people from different states and to see how different their lives have been from mine. It's also been fantastic meeting so many friends from out of state because now I have lots of places to crash if I ever want to go on some crazy road trip. And last, don't be surprised if you have a celebrity in your class, or the kid of a celebrity on your hall or in one of your classes; it's that kind of a place.

The Activities

There's so much going on around NYU that students usually come for the city every bit as much as they come for the school. Whatever you're interested in, you can find it here. I rarely go to on-campus events. I'm really into music, so I go to a lot of music shows. I've made a lot of friends in "high places," so every so often I get invited to some crazy parties with celebrities or other bigwigs (this is actually a common thing that happens around here, students making friends with celebs).

I hate kids here who sit around and say, "I'm so bored . . . there's nothing to do tonight. . . ." Bullshit. You're in the city that never sleeps. There's *always* something to do, whether it's going to a club, getting tattooed, visiting art galleries, skateboarding in Union Square Park, watching break-dancers in Washington Square Park, or eating hot dogs at 3:00 a.m. (Crif Dogs—the best hot dogs in the country). The phrase "nothing to do" is obsolete here. For about a month straight, a few of us were always spending time with a Brooklyn artist who was doing a project where people would pay him to kidnap them in very specific ways that they'd lay out in advance. When a kidnapping wasn't taking place, we would participate in crazy skits that included my roommate pretending to be a crack whore and rampaging through the city. There aren't words to describe how wonderful all this has been.

The Social Scene

When I think "social scene," I think of the people I encounter on a daily basis on the streets of Manhattan, not just NYU students. Not being on a traditional college campus, I see a lot of the same people every day, and most of them are not students. Despite what you may hear, a lot of New Yorkers are really friendly—a lot friendlier than people in Boston. I pass by this haircutting school every day on my way to the art building, and I always get a friendly hello from the people inside. And I definitely think it's beneficial, making friends outside of the university—they can show you things about the city that most students couldn't.

So, if you want a typical college experience, do *not* come to NYU. This is not a place where you're going to go to a frat party every Friday night, attend a free concert on the campus green, and go to the football game proudly sporting your school colors. If you are not an individual or a free spirit, you will probably have a hard time at NYU! But if you want to spend four years in the middle of the greatest city on earth, this is the place to do it. NYU rocks. I mean, the Olsen twins go here; what more do I have to say?

Name: Matt
Hometown: Roxberry Falls, Connecticut
Class Year: Junior
Major: Screenwriting through the Tisch School of the Arts
Extracurriculars: Fraternity (DKE), rock climbing, drama groups
Career Goal: To become a screenwriter. I've also thought of editing films, going to law school, or maybe going to graduate school for something more academic.

How would you describe NYU's reputation?

NYU is said to be an excellent school that caters to a wide variety of interests. It's pricey, but it's said to be well worth the cost.

Is this reputation accurate?

NYU *is* an excellent school, with "star" professors in every academic discipline who have a lot of knowledge to impart to their students. That said, there's not always a direct correlation between how famous your professors are and how much you'll learn. A case in point: I learned more in one class I took here taught by a grad student than I did in another taught by a published, tenured faculty member. Nonetheless, the education you'll receive at NYU will be top-notch. NYU is expensive, and right now it can still be argued that the cost is worth it. But if tuition goes up much more, people might begin to think and say otherwise.

> "Studying abroad at NYU is absolutely incredible, since NYU has five actual campuses in Europe. They encourage us to go, and make the process so-o-o-o easy. You really can go anywhere."
>
> ✦ Ashley, sophomore

What would an admissions officer at your school probably not tell a prospective student?

An admissions officer probably wouldn't tell a prospective that it's possible to have only fifteen minutes to walk ten to fifteen city blocks between classes (I've been late to several classes all semester because of this). And since classes are spread throughout a *huge* range of buildings in lower Manhattan, there's really no way to predict where your classes will be when you first sign up for them; they could be anywhere.

The Institution

Well, first, this school is huge—just try to get into an elevator in the main building without having to wait in line for a half-hour. In some respects you can't help but feel like you're just a number at NYU, even in some of the smaller programs/departments. This means you have to try hard to find a good group of friends so you don't feel lost. Personally, I hang out with NYU's rock-climbing community, the other guys in my fraternity, and a group of others who share my taste for pubs and sports bars. Others have found friendship groups through their dorms, through their classes, through drama groups, or just through being friendly when walking through Washington Square Park. If you come here, try to identify the types of people whom you get along with best, and then seek them out. This school is big enough that all "types" are here, somewhere—you just have to find them.

Precisely because NYU is so big, it's impossible

for any of us to have "school spirit" in any traditional sense. But that's not to say we don't all feel connected. We do. We're all here because we wanted to come to a big school like this. I was never attracted to the idea of having a college quad, a gated campus, all that. I wanted independence, a chance to study while living in the real world. Most students here felt the same way, and, while many students frequently bad-mouth NYU (we have a noticeable anti-authoritarian streak), most would agree that, as far as college goes, there's no place they'd rather be.

Note: if you don't have air-conditioning in your room, New York can be almost unbearably hot in the summer. Winters can also range from just cold to being unbearably frigid (especially on those fifteen-block power walks between classes). Also, the housing is rather expensive and not all the dorms are created equal—if you can find an apartment for roughly the same price, you'll probably be happier there than in a dorm.

The Education

I'd say the education you'll receive at NYU will range from very good to excellent. You essentially get to choose whether you'll be in discussion- or lecture-based classes. That said, I'm not much of a talker, and I've taken small discussion classes (ten to fifteen people) and said absolutely nothing. Ironically, this speaks volumes about NYU students—generally, there are enough students in any discussion class who are willing to talk and ask questions and be involved that, if you don't feel comfortable speaking, you won't have to.

Also, because there are so many students at NYU, there's almost no feeling of academic competition between them. There's no reason to compete. Not only are there so many students here that the odds of you becoming valedictorian are virtually nil, but you will rarely have the same people in enough classes to be able to establish any kind of meaningful rivalry.

One of the more unfortunate aspects of our large size is that any given teacher won't know what's going on in the university as a whole, doesn't necessarily care, and as a result seems rather unconcerned with things outside the immediate scope of their classes. This isn't to say teachers aren't there for students outside of class—to the contrary, most go out of their way to accommodate students during their office hours. It's more to say that professors seem to be almost "academic cowboys," there to impart knowledge and then ride off into the sunset.

The Students

Because NYU is so expensive, most students tend to be from upper-middle-class families. Other than that, though, there's no "typical" NYU student. Kids are from every race, every ethnicity, every religion, every sexual and political orientation. We're all tied together by the fact that we're all very independent.

The Activities

Students at NYU tend to spend a lot of time at our great gyms—most will spend at least one day a week playing basketball, weight lifting, running on the treadmill. You'll see NYU athletes at the gym all the time, too, but at NYU, athletes are just students who happen to be good at throwing a ball around. They're not gods on earth, like a basketball player might be at Duke. And most students don't go to see athletes play . . . no offense to the athletes, but we're in the middle of New York! We have so many better things to do than watch NYU lose.

The Social Scene

NYU parties tend to be either small and closed, a few friends hanging out in a dorm room, or really big and raucous, advertised via flyers and word of mouth, and then everyone shows up and it gets a bit wild. NYU dorms have really restrictive sign-in policies, though, which makes it hard to easily/quickly get in and out of them. So this means most of your partying, really, will be done in bars, in clubs, in lofts, in warehouses, in any number of random locations throughout Manhattan.

And, last, dating at NYU . . . well, it doesn't happen all that often. Many students find themselves dating that guy or girl they met in that club, who's probably not an NYU student and could be any age at all. There are quite a lot of eighteen-year-old-college-student/thirty-year-old-investment-banker relationships going on. And then, a lot of other NYU students have no interest in dating. They're here to go out, hook up, have fun, meet people, develop themselves, learn, start a career. To each his or her own.

Notable NYU Alumni Include:
Charlie Kaufman, screenwriter
M. Night Shyamalan, director
Spike Lee, director, actor
Alan Greenspan, chairperson, Federal Reserve Board
Judith Smith Kaye, chief judge, New York Court of Appeals
Ang Lee, director, screenwriter

UNIVERSITY OF NORTH CAROLINA AT CHAPEL HILL

Founded: 1789

Location: Chapel Hill, NC

Phone: (919) 966-3621

E-mail: uadm@Email.unc.edu

Web site: www.unc.edu

Number of Undergraduates: 15,961

Number of Graduate Students: 7,857

Cost: Approximately $11,000 per year in state; $24,000 out of state

Application Deadline: January 15

Early Decision: November 1

Rating:	Notable Majors/Programs:
Very Selective	Biology, Business, Psychology

Size:

○ Small   ○ Medium   ● Large

Location:

○ Urban   ● Suburban   ○ Rural

On a Saturday, students talk about academics:

○ Always   ● Sometimes   ○ Never

Nightlife:

○ Intense   ● Moderate   ○ Laid-back

Politically, UNC leans:

○ Left   ○ Right   ● Split

Diversity:

○ High   ○ Low   ● Medium

Students describe UNC in five words:
- Large, traditional, with school spirit
- Gorgeous, great sports and academics

From the School

We offer an elite education in a nonelitist environment—a community known for its friendliness and its commitment to the public good. We pursue state-of-the-art research, including research in the basic and applied sciences, while maintaining the feel and the focus of an outstanding liberal arts college. We serve our home state while opening our doors to the rest of the nation and the world.

—www.admissions.unc.edu

If you're interested in UNC, you may also be interested in:
Brown, Davidson, Duke, Harvard, University of Virginia, Wake Forest

Name: Adam

Hometown: Virginia Beach, Virginia

Class Year: Junior

Major: Journalism and Mass Communications

Extracurriculars: Works for student newspaper and a local radio station, campus tour guide, a cappella group, a social fraternity, and an honors fraternity, Hillel.

Career Goal: To get a graduate degree in journalism, then work as a niche reporter.

How would you describe UNC's reputation?

Other schools might be described as designer pairs of jeans, made to impress people. In contrast, UNC would be your favorite pair of sweat pants, the ones that just feel right. This is a place that is known to feel just like home, where you can be happy doing whatever it is you want to do.

Is this reputation accurate?

Yes. UNC is nice, comfortable school just overflowing with Southern charm. Factor in the fact this place also has amazing academic resources. UNC is the place where you'll work hard and have the time to play hard, too. Time to develop your talents, explore your interests, and play a lot of Texas Hold 'em, as well.

What would an admissions officer at your school probably not tell a prospective student?

Truthfully, administrators here really try to be open and not hold anything back, I think they'd do their best to answer any questions you had.

The Institution

I first knew UNC was for me when I saw "The Pit" (the main gathering place on campus) lined with smiling, happy people on a campus tour. The sky was this perfect Carolina-blue. Behind everyone was this beautiful redbrick campus, with tall white pillars rising up toward the sky, accented by big trees and flowers in bloom. It was raw, unstaged, real UNC. Now, as a student, every time I go to The Pit between 10:00 a.m. and 2:00 p.m. on a weekday, I see what I saw that first time and get the same feeling.

UNC is three blocks away from downtown Chapel Hill. It is full of big beautiful buildings, lots of greenery, and designed so students can walk everywhere. The classrooms are equipped with state-of-the-art technology that allows teachers to integrate multimedia and computers into any learning experience. The campus is incredibly safe, and you don't have to buy a meal plan—I love this place. And I'm not alone. At Carolina it's cool to be spirited. Every day people wear UNC shirts. When basketball season comes around, we go wild! Students are there in the bleachers for game after game after game. When we lost in the NCAA tournament last year, I found my friend in his room crying!

The Education

UNC has more than fifteen thousand undergrads—which makes it even more impressive that it feels homey and cozy. This is a testament to the warmth and friendliness of professors, administrators, and students.

As with most big schools, UNC has a core curriculum. It's medium-sized, and doable. Most don't mind it much, and finish the core by the end of their sophomore year. At that point, students start applying to professional schools in their major. (We have schools here for Business, Education, Journalism and Mass Communications, Law, Information and Library Sciences, and Social Work, among other things. We also have the Division of Health Affairs, which encompasses the schools of Dentistry, Medicine, Nursing, Pharmacy, and Public Health.) Once you're in a professional school, class sizes range anywhere from large lectures with four hundred students, to small, intimate classes with only fifteen or twenty kids and a professor.

UNC also has a large graduate school, which I think enhances the UNC experience for everyone because our grad schools draw big-deal professors from a wide variety of fields that undergraduates can often take classes with. In the end, just about any subject that you'd want to take a course in is available at UNC.

The Students

UNC is a very liberal, open, and accepting place. Slights made toward any minority are taken very seriously and usually cause quite a stir. There is also an open climate for LGBT students despite a good number of Southern students with overbearing religious convictions. While LGBTQ students are safe on campus, and they have big, well-functioning organizations, there are some students who still feel uncomfortable around them. That said, diversity is an important ideal at this school.

The Activities

One of the great things about UNC being public is that students have complete control of student activity funds. So, any club your peers decide is worthwhile gets funding, and lots of it. This means political groups and a cappella groups abound, and they have plenty of cash at their disposal. This also means you can create your own group and get resources to make it fun and exciting if it passes the test of your peers. Aside from clubs, athletic events (mainly basketball) are a big deal on campus. And UNC has a thriving arts community, with several arts-related performances every week. We even have a unionized theater company located on our campus. And knowing what is going on is always easy because we have a top-notch television news organization on campus, not to mention the school newspaper, which comes out every day. Unlike some schools that put out a substandard rag, UNC's paper is award-winning and everybody reads it.

My typical day at UNC is as follows: I wake up. Berate alarm clock. Think: "Well it's almost ten. I should get up and start my lab report so I can get it done in time for my physics lab." Toil away for four hours. Stress over getting everything printed out by 2:00 p.m. Lab, 2–4 p.m. Think: "Wow, there are so many better ways I could spend my time than in a lab." OK. Finish lab, then it's off to voice lessons for an hour. At 5:00, get to the library and study physics for an hour before meeting up with friends for dinner. Spend two hours eating and chatting. Yum. Then hurry to a 7:00 p.m. meeting of the downhill skiing club! After that, there's an 8:00 p.m. newspaper meeting, and a late-night meeting at 10:00 p.m. for the fraternity. By midnight, I'm back in my room, ready to study and do homework for two hours. Rinse, repeat.

The Social Scene

Students at UNC party, just like students party at every college in America. Thursdays and Saturdays tend to be our big nights out. And while we have a fraternity and sorority scene, their parties are open to all, so you can be non-Greek, show up, and still have a great time. Everyone is super-nice. If you're from this part of America, you can't help but have ingrained Southern charm. And even if you didn't grow up here, other people's Southern charm will wear off on you. Everyone's polite at UNC, and everyone is always eager to lend a helping hand.

Name: Allison
Hometown: Danbury, North Carolina
Class Year: Junior
Major: Art History and English
Extracurriculars: Tour guide, staff writer for the *Daily Tar Heel*, member of the Order of the Bell Tower, member of the Shag Club, Ackland Art Museum volunteer.
Career Goal: To work in an art museum or an auction house.

How would you describe UNC's reputation?

I was always a bit dubious about UNC. It struck me as a big, preppy state school, and I had doubts about the quality of its academics. Also, having grown up ninety minutes away, I didn't know if I'd find myself surrounded by my hometown/high school friends, which was not what I wanted out of a college.

> "UNC's *Daily Tar Heel* paper really has cachet! My student reporter credentials got me into the 2004 Republican Convention, and I couldn't believe the people I was able to talk to as a twenty-year-old reporter. If you're a newspaper buff, UNC is for you."
> ✦ Megan, freshman

Is this reputation accurate?

Well, I was right that UNC is preppy, and that it's big. And I was wrong about everything else! The academics here have been more challenging that I ever dreamed, my professors have been incredible, and while a few other kids from my high school did wind up coming to UNC as well, this is a big place, and I've made friends from all over North Carolina, the United States, even the world.

What would an admissions officer at your school probably not tell a prospective student? What aspect of your school would a prospective student not see on a campus tour?

Prospectives probably aren't told enough that at UNC you have to make yourself known. There are so many opportunities here, but no one is going to push you to find them—you have to get out there and take the initiative. Also, as a tour guide, I'm never sure if the prospectives I show around really understand the level of school spirit here. The number of people donning Tar Heel apparel is staggering. Students camp out and stand in early-morning lines for sports tickets here, even when our teams aren't having great seasons. We particularly love our basketball team, and when Roy Williams was hired to coach it, all the merchants and restaurants on Franklin Street had balloons in the air and banners saying "Welcome home, Roy."

The Institution

Well, this is North Carolina, so the first few weeks of the fall semester, it's going to be pretty muggy. If you don't have air-conditioning or a fan during that period, you may be an unhappy kid, but I promise it only lasts a few weeks. And come spring, Chapel Hill is truly one of the most beautiful places I've ever seen: blue skies, dogwoods in bloom, and people studying and playing all around. It is a truly special place. Charles Kurault put it best: "It is as it was meant to be."

The Education

Out of the twenty classes I've taken here over the last two years, only four have had more than thirty students in them. Really, even though it's a big school, it's very easy to find small classes at Carolina, even as a first-semester freshman. You just have to search them out. The majority of professors I've had have been wonderful teachers as well as esteemed scholars. If you make an effort to get to know them, they will reciprocate. The workload here is challenging, but manageable. Professors have high standards, but they're also fair. The only classes I've been disappointed with have been my foreign language classes—the language departments here focus too much on textbook grammatical exercises and not enough on the culture, the language, and how to really speak it.

The Students

Carolina is a big school, and students come from pretty diverse backgrounds. So there's a lot of opportunity for mingling and integration. Unfortunately, if you walk into the dining hall at any given time, you'll still see that students tend to sit with people of their own ethnic group. This isn't to say minority students are treated differently here, because they're not. Intolerance is not accepted, period. It's just that, for whatever reason, each racial group is most comfortable hanging out only within their racial group, and no one is really sure how to remedy this.

The Activities

I started on the the *Daily Tar Heel* staff as a freshman. Unlike most college papers, it's one of the best in the country, with a circulation of 39,000. On my first day, having never written an article before, I was told to call the U.S. Department of Education, as well as several state representatives, to interview people on some controversial issue. A few weeks later I was writing stories about congressional committee appointments and going to Raleigh to cover the state General Assembly. It was such an amazing trial-by-fire experience. For anyone with any interest in journalism or writing, I can't recommend working at the *DTH* enough.

"Chase Dining Hall, on South Campus, had a very distinct odor to it—imagine if you combined the smell of a fast-food restaurant with a middle-school locker room—it was legendary. They tore it down recently and now The 'Ramshead' is opening in its place. But I suspect the smell will live on. . . . when you enter the Ramshead, take a good, long sniff, and if you detect something pungent, that's the ghost of Chase you smell."

✦ Allison, junior

The Social Scene

The weekend scene in Chapel Hill varies depending on seasonal sporting events. If there's a big game, it probably figures into our schedule, as does schoolwork, eating on Franklin Street (it has a lot of martini bars, sports bars, dance clubs, and good restaurants), and possibly shopping at nearby Southpoint Mall. Alcohol does play pretty heavily into the social life here, but it's not a problem if you don't drink. At night students hang out with friends in dorm rooms or apartments, go to whatever frat is having a party that weekend, or go visit friends at N.C. State, Duke, or Wake Forest (our "rivals" with whom we interact fairly often). We have one of those social scenes where there's always something fun going on. With more than fifteen thousand undergrads, it's going to be a good time.

Name: Sarah
Hometown: Smithfield, North Carolina
Class Year: Freshman

Major: Public Policy Analysis

Extracurriculars: Public Service Scholars, Safe Ride Program, Dance Marathon, office assistant in the Olde Campus Upper Quad Residential Community.

Career Goal: I would like to first be an attorney, then a United States senator.

How would you describe UNC's reputation?

UNC is well known both around the country and around the world, for both basketball and our great academic opportunities. Carolina is often referred to as the Southern Part of Heaven, and I think this is a pretty fair assessment.

Is this reputation accurate?

Yes, Carolina is a very prestigious place to go to school academically. As far as being known for basketball, I think former coach Smith said it best when he said, "This is a women's soccer school. The women's soccer team is far better than our men's basketball team." And this is true. Basketball is definitely a part of Carolina, but it's not everything. There's so much more, athletically and otherwise.

What aspect of your school would a prospective student not see on a campus tour?

As a tour guide, I work closely with the admissions office, and honestly, UNC does its best to be honest and truthful in all circumstances. Even on campus tours, you really get to see it all.

The Institution

There are many legends at Carolina, but the most unique is the legend of Davie Poplar—a tree that was planted not long after the university was founded—which states that as long as Davie Poplar stands, so shall the university. Davie Poplar has been struck by lightning three times, survived various North Carolina hurricanes, ice storms. . . . Today Davie Poplar is filled with cement and is tethered to one tree. (Just in case something happened to Davie Poplar, a seedling was taken from it, and we now have Davie Poplar Jr., and at the bicentennial celebration of UNC in 1993, President Clinton planted a second seedling, known as Davie Poplar III. . . .

Carolina, can be as big or as small as you'd like it to be. I've chosen to make it small, by being involved in small organizations, and by creating a really tight group of close friends. I chose to come to Carolina because when I came to visit, it felt like home right away. UNC has many schools very close by. Duke is just eight miles away. North Carolina State and North Carolina Central are no more than thirty minutes away. While rivalries are shared (especially between Duke and Carolina, and N.C. State and Carolina), there is also a lot of collaboration between the schools. Duke and UNC share a scholarship program that allows students to be enrolled at one university and to live and take classes at the other university for a semester. Any student from UNC is also able to enroll in classes at Duke, and our libraries all work together to provide a massive number of educational tools for the students from each of the schools.

The Education

At a school with fifteen thousand undergraduates, many people would assume that a majority of the classes would have three hundred people in them and would be taught by TAs. This is not the case at UNC. Only 5 percent of the classes have more than one hundred students. Many classes in popular departments are capped at twenty to thirty students. In large classes, such as introductory classes, the professor lectures, and then TAs lead recitation sections or labs with only about twenty students in them. Professors have mandatory office hours, and you are highly encouraged to go visit them. Some professors will tell you to come by to talk about the class, your major, life, etc. They're very accessible.

The most interesting class I've taken has been in American Studies, "The Emergence of Modern America," with Professor Joy Kasson. In the syllabus the class seemed like it would be really dry, but Professor Kasson used paintings, photographs, movies, and songs to make it really interesting. This class is what made me decide to double-major in American Studies.

The Activities

UNC has more than five hundred student organizations on campus, so there's an option for everyone. If you have a particular interest in something and there's not already an organization, it is very easy to start one. Carolina is very diverse, and has many ways to get involved.

Athletics, namely men's basketball, are important to a lot of people. However, there are some people who, as seniors, have never been to a single basketball game. It's a choice, and it's not an essential part of UNC if you don't want it to be.

The Students

At many universities, there is a typical student; not at Carolina. UNC has a diverse campus with many ethnic and cultural groups, LGBTQ groups, Republicans, Democrats, and pretty much any other classification you could think of. There's a place for everyone at Carolina; you just have to find your niche.

Differences in students can be seen in the way that people dress. Some people sport the preppy look, with clothes, hair, and make-up perfectly primped. Others wake up five minutes before class and go to class in sweatpants and a T-shirt. Still other students walk around in Carolina-blue clothing purchased from the student stores. There really isn't a typical Carolina student, other than the fact that our blood runs that pretty shade of Carolina blue.

The Social Scene

Some people don't party. I have a friend whose roommate has never been out after 11:00 during her entire time at UNC. Some people party every night. In Chapel Hill, you can go to clubs, hang out with friends in their suites, or go to fraternity houses. Around 15 percent of the students are involved in a social fraternity or sorority. Rushing one of these organizations is an easy way to meet people, but there are definitely other options. And anyway, many Greek parties are not limited to only fraternity or sorority members, so even if you don't join, you can still benefit from having them around.

Last, Chapel Hill really is a college town. Just off campus is Franklin Street, which is home to shops, restaurants, a movie theater, clubs, and many other things to do. Buses in Chapel Hill are free, so it is easy to hop on one and go to one of the local shopping centers or malls.

Notable UNC Alumni Include:
Thomas Wolfe, author
Michael Jordan, professional basketball player
John Edwards, senator
James K. Polk, eleventh U.S. president
Mia Hamm, professional soccer player
Andy Griffith, actor, writer, producer

NORTHWESTERN UNIVERSITY

Founded: 1851

Location: Evanston, IL

Phone: (847) 491-7271

E-mail: ug-admission@northwestern.edu

Web site: www.northwestern.edu

Number of Undergraduates: 7,946

Number of Graduate Students: 6,876

Cost: Approximately $38,000 per year

Application Deadline: January 1

Early Decision: November 1

Rating:	Notable Majors/Programs:
Most Selective	Chemistry, Economics, Political Science, Engineering

Size:
○ Small   ○ Medium   ● Large

Location:
○ Urban   ● Suburban   ○ Rural

On a Saturday, students talk about academics:
● Always   ○ Sometimes   ○ Never

Nightlife:
○ Intense   ● Moderate   ○ Laid-back

Politically, Northwestern leans:
○ Left   ○ Right   ● Split

Diversity:
● High   ○ Low   ○ Medium

Big Ten: Yes!

Students describe Northwestern in five words:
- Driven students tackling rigorous academics
- Quarter-system nerds. Chicago's cold.

From the School

Northwestern combines innovative teaching and pioneering research in a highly collaborative environment that transcends traditional academic boundaries. It provides students and faculty exceptional opportunities for intellectual, personal, and professional growth in a setting enhanced by the richness of Chicago.

—www.northwestern.edu

If you're interested in Northwestern, you may also be interested in:
University of Chicago, Columbia, Harvard, Princeton, Stanford, Yale

Name: Maggie
Hometown: Los Angeles, California
Class Year: Freshman
Major: English major, Spanish minor
Extracurriculars: Delta Gamma sorority, peer advisor, Jewish United Fund College Campaign.
Career Goal: I'm not sure. Journalism? Elementary ed? Law? There's time, right?

How would you describe Northwestern's reputation?

Northwestern is considered to be an academically challenging university where students are driven but nerdy. NU is the only private university in the Big Ten and is located in what most consider a cold part of the country.

Is this reputation accurate?

Yes, but allow me to clarify. Chicago isn't cold, it is *freezing*! We are in the Big Ten but our teams tend to disappoint. (My least favorite tradition involves Northwestern students shaking their car keys at the opposing team when we're losing, implying, "You may be better athletes, but you'll be parking our cars someday.") Academically, this is a challenging and prestigious school and students *are* nerds . . . or, at the least, we're not very social. This is because we're on the quarter system, which means classes end more quickly, our semesters are faster paced, and we simply have less time to socialize. And, during the winter, the weather isn't conducive to going outdoors, so lot of kids stay inside for months on end.

> "Northwestern has a system that scans every single academic paper and tests it for violations of the honor code. Turn in a paragraph of an old paper in a new paper, and you can get put on academic probation. Don't try to cheat here! It won't work."
> ✦ Kevin, junior

What aspect of your school would a prospective student not see on a campus tour?

Campus tour guides don't make it clear that the dorms are really spread out. This may not seem like a big deal, but in the winter it is. I met some awesome people who I would have loved to get to know better, but I live on North campus, and you couldn't *pay* me to walk twenty minutes to South campus to see them when it's negative 20 degrees out with wind-chill. We do have a shuttle system, but it's rarely on time and it doesn't run as frequently as it should.

The Institution

I love, love, love the fact that Northwestern is on the quarter system. Each quarter lasts only about ten weeks, which means you'll never get sick of a teacher or subject area. Also, this means you can take as many as twelve classes each year (at most schools you only take eight a year), so you get the chance to explore plenty of new subjects while still satisfying your core and major requirements. The only downside is that your academic calendar will be different than your friends' at other colleges.

Now, the meaning behind some commonly uttered NU phrases:

The Rock: A big rock between three big academic buildings that gets painted on a regular basis by different student groups.

The Plex (aka Foster-Walker Complex): The only good dining hall on campus.

SPAC: Sports Pavilion and Aquatics Center, a huge, gorgeous gym on North Campus with weight and cardio machines, basketball and squash courts, a pool, and everything else you could ever want in a gym.

The Deuce: Nickname for the Mark II Lounge, a dive bar—you have to take a taxi to get there so none of us really know what city it's in, but it's not in Evanston. Everyone goes there on Thursday nights (karaoke night—and we like our karaoke).

The Education

I study English and Spanish, so most of my classes are small and discussion-based, and I'm primarily taught by professors rather than TAs. But it really depends on your area of study. Science classes are far bigger, for example. I love all of my classes this quarter; my professors are extremely accessible. Three out of my four professors are female, which is impressive—most big universities are dominated by males, but that's not the case here. And I've found that, within departments, Northwestern can be really cozy. Your major department becomes a comfortable reprieve from the bigness of the rest of the school, if you're in a good department. (Look into this! Different major departments at NU have different sizes, different feels.)

I'd say there's a ton of work to do here. When I take a full load of four challenging classes in one quarter, I rarely have a day off. I always have a book to read, a paper to write, a midterm to study for. But if you are academic enough to get into Northwestern, you'll be able to handle it—there is no more work than there is at any other top-tier school.

The Students

Students at Northwestern are members of one of six colleges—the College of Arts and Sciences, the School of Music, the Medill School of Journalism, the School of Speech, the School of Education and Social Policy, and the McCormick School of Engineering and Applied Sciences. Because a lot of these schools are oriented toward the pre-professional student, a more wishy-washy English major can sometimes feel a bit lost—but hey, what can you do?

Northwestern is a Big Ten school, and I thought that meant there would be a lot of school spirit. But everyone here is so academically driven that they don't have much time for the typical rah rah antics. We'll go to football games, but plenty will leave by halftime to get back to the library.

I'm a freshman, so, granted, I haven't met everyone yet. But thus far, Northwestern doesn't seem very diverse. It seems like it has "fake diversity"—which is to say everyone's white. But if you grill people, you find out, Oh, you moved from Russia when you were two, or they're a quarter Portuguese, so on paper, we're very diverse. But we're mostly white, well-off Christians from the Midwest. I'm not too diverse myself, but I'm at least Jewish (and I'm the first Jewish person some of my peers have ever met).

The Activities

About a quarter of the students here read the papers. Northwestern students are not very politically active. I can recall a handful of protests—"NU: No Place for Hate"—which was a rally in response to anti-Semitic phrases graffitied on the walls outside the student center and Kellogg School of Management, and there was once a demonstration, and a counterdemonstration, about abortion.

There are quite a few volunteer-oriented student groups, though, and community service is

relatively popular, but the biggest philanthropies (which also have the best publicity) are Dance Marathon (the biggest student-run philanthropic event in the nation) and the Suitcase Party.

Also, there's the tradition of painting "the Rock" that I mentioned. Almost every day, someone will try to paint the Rock and will often stay up all night guarding it so no one paints over their handiwork. Then they'll finally fall asleep, and someone new will paint over it. There are all sorts of reasons to paint the Rock—to make a statement, to bond, to advertise a philanthropic event. If you go on the Northwestern Web site, there's actually a Webcam set up so you can see what the Rock looks like at all times.

> "There are two Northwesterns—Northwestern in the spring, summer, and fall, with its beautiful grassy quads and trees sprawling toward the lake, and Northwestern in the winter, when it's dead, gray, freezing, windy, quiet."
>
> ✦ Jared, sophomore

The Social Scene

Thursday is the big night to go out and have some fun at NU. Fridays and Saturdays, students are out there, too, but Thursday is our crowning achievement. When you're a freshman, the big thing to do is to head to frats and apartment parties and get drunk and irresponsible, but as kids get older, they tend to move into a more mature bar scene, mostly going off campus to Evanston. Almost everyone has fake IDs—even the nondrinkers have them so they can head to bars with their drinker friends—and I've seen kids get away with having some pretty shoddy fake IDs.

Greek life is really big here. Thirty to forty percent of NU students go Greek. But that's because the Greek scene is laid back, more intelligent. It's not the party-hard mindlessness you'd picture. Seriously, so many people come here adamant that they will *not* go Greek, and two years later they're president of their sorority. I was one of these people. If you come here and you still think Greek life is lame, you're not forced into joining at all. But Greek parties are somewhat exclusive—meaning, if you're not Greek and a great party is being thrown at a fraternity, you may be turned away at the door.

Unless you're incredibly good-looking. Finally, for whatever reason, there is no dating going on at this school. People are either practically married and unavailable, or they're dedicated to a casual hook-up lifestyle. I have some gorgeous single girlfriends who are *begging* to couple up, but they haven't dated at all here because no one does.

Name: Joseph
Hometown: Homewood, Illinois
Class Year: Sophomore
Major: Chemistry
Extracurriculars: Undergraduate Chemistry Council
Career Goal: I'd like to go to graduate school and work toward a doctoral degree in chemistry and eventually teach at the high school or college level.

How would you describe Northwestern's reputation?

Northwestern is very well-respected school, particularly in the fields of journalism, theater, medicine, and scientific research. The social life here is supposed to be just fair, though.

Is this reputation accurate?

Yes. Some of our academic programs are ranked in the top five in the country, and students work very hard. We work so hard our social life sometimes suffers.

What would an admissions officer at your school probably not tell a prospective student?

They might not tell you that you can't take extra classes each semester and graduate early without paying what the school calls "an acceleration fee."

The Institution

NU is the perfect size, not too big and not too small. Walking from one side of the campus to the other, I usually run into at least fifteen people I recognize or know. When it's sunny you'll see students everywhere handing out flyers for the new opening at the Block Art Gallery, or for a new contest or club or party. There will also be flyers all over the sidewalk and advertisements for events hung from the branches of trees.

But Northwestern isn't perfect. Registration here is a giant pain. Just last year, CAESAR (the registration program) malfunctioned for some registering freshman. And then when it started working again, every single class was full. I wound up rushing around campus frantically, begging teachers to put me on the wait list for their classes, and the administration had no sympathy for me (some faculty were outright mean). I eventually got everything sorted out, but the process was incredibly frustrating.

The Education

Northwestern has great science departments, particularly in the fields of chemistry and nanoscience research. Because the departments are so fantastic, lectures are jam-packed. Want to take Intro to Chemistry or Intro to Biology? Get ready to be in a lecture with three hundred other students. This seems to be the case at every school in the sciences—big, impersonal intro classes, nothing you can do about it. Luckily, teachers do have office hours, and if you go they'll be more likely to call on you in class and give you whatever personalized attention they can. And once you're out of intro courses, the classes get smaller and professors more accessible—my upper-level organic class has thirty-five students, and the professor knows all our names and even some of our little quirks.

Students in the sciences at NU also work together, which is worth noting—in a lot of schools the sciences are really cutthroat. Here, we help one another out whenever we can, and we also spend a lot of fun time with one another outside of class. And because NU is a research university, it tries to get every undergraduate involved in significant lab work that prepares us for future high-level research (since most of us will go on to grad school), and grad students are always around to talk and to give us advice about our futures. I think my favorite class so far has been my Organic Synthesis laboratory, in which we had to synthesize a molecule with a specific amount of starting product and then fully analyze the product with IR, C NMR, and H NMR spectroscopy. You learn both lab techniques and how to fully interpret data, which is extremely useful for future work.

Also, NU has some very selective honors programs that are worth looking into. Students who participate in the honors program in Medical Education, for example, are guaranteed entrance into the Northwestern Medical School. Other honors programs are in Engineering, Integrated Science, Mathematics, and Mathematics in the context of the Social Sciences.

The Students

There are many different kinds of students on campus. You have the upper-class overachievers (many of whom join frats and sororities). You have the lower-middle-class students who have struggled to make it this far and are working extraordinarily hard. You have the eccentric theater students who insist on putting on productions of *The Vagina Monologues* every year, and the music students who are always rambling on about Beethoven. You have the students in the Public Affairs Residential College, who debate anything and everything. You have the stereotypical "Greek" students who study hard but really view their schoolwork as an annoying disruption of their partying. The best thing, though, is that all of these students hang out together. Most students at Northwestern honestly do get along.

> "Everyone here is freakishly talented and plays at least one instrument, like the mechanical engineer who was first-seat all-state for bass clarinet."
>
> ✦ Coral, senior

The Activities

NU students venture into Evanston, but they don't really interact with students from nearby Loyola or DePaul. I think this is because Loyola and DePaul students are very homogeneous, the same types of kids from the same parts of the world, whereas Northwestern students are from all over the map. Just walking to the student center today, I came across my friend from Honduras, a friend from Japan, a friend from Los Angeles, and a friend from New York. Northwestern offers more than you could ever soak in.

The Social Scene

The weekend starts on Thursday night at NU. This is when the sorority girls and frat boys head into Evanston en masse with their fake IDs, and start drinking. I'm not a big fan of Greek life on this campus, and I think most students here are better off not joining the Greek scene. I like hanging out in small groups, with people I like and respect. If we want to hang out in my room and watch a movie, we can do that. If we want to head to a bar, we can do that too. But we never have to consult with the greater body of our "brothers" to see if they'll okay our weekend plans and follow us in a big group like sheep.

Name: Sarah
Hometown: Tuscola, Illinois
Class Year: Senior
Major: Anthropology
Extracurriculars: Women's Coalition, Women's Center Advisory Board, Jewish Theater Ensemble, Rainbow Alliance, NoWAR, Progressive Alliance
Career Goal: I want to get my PhD in Anthropology and either teach and research at a university or curate at a natural history museum.

How would you describe Northwestern's reputation?

Northwestern is known for having strong academics and a weak social scene.

Is this reputation accurate?

This is only partially true. It is a great school, almost always ranked as one of the top fifteen universities in America. But that doesn't mean everyone here is wildly intelligent and committed to their work. I'd say there's actually a disappointing number of students who take easy majors, breeze-through classes, and study as little as they possibly can. Luckily, they aren't the majority and they're counterbalanced by those of us who put in a lot of effort so we can get the most out of our education, and who push ourselves to work as hard as we possibly can. As for the social scene—it can be bleak. However, I would much rather attend a small party with my close friends than a huge kegger, anyway. And small parties with friends happen on this campus in spades.

What aspect of your school would a prospective student not see on a campus tour?

Northwestern will downplay exactly how *much* crime there is in Evanston. At night, the streets are *dark*, and it's absolutely not safe to walk home alone. Even walking back to my dorm from the library at 10:00 p.m., I don't feel safe. The university does have an escort car service to give students rides after dark, but on busy nights wait times can be longer than three hours, and the service shuts down at 1:00 a.m. And the administration has done nothing about this.

Also, the closest grocery store to campus is

about two miles away, so unless you want to live on Osco's chips and canned soup, you're going to have to travel. And waiting for a bus with your groceries is a hassle, so you find yourself stuck having to either take a cab or bother your friends with cars if you don't have wheels of your own.

And last, they won't tell you that there were a lot of racist incidents on campus in recent years. All were nonviolent but still disturbing. Most included highly offensive graffiti being written on dorm doors, including the words "sand nigger," and "slut." These incidents were handled well by the administration, but at the same time, this type of behavior doesn't make for a totally safe and effective learning environment.

The Institution

NU's campus is pretty compact, so even going from the north end to the south end will take you only twenty minutes. The campus is well divided, though—science and tech classes are on the north end, and that's where science majors tend to live. Liberal arts classes are on the south end, and that's where liberal arts majors tend to live. This way, students generally don't have to walk back and forth the length of the campus every day. Our student center, which is a popular meeting place, is right in the middle of campus. Then, to the east, there's the beautiful Lake Michigan, which students will hang out by in big groups and have picnics.

Now, the bad stuff: My first year at Northwestern was, to put it bluntly, terrible. This school is big, and I felt dwarfed by it. Being shy, I had no friends. I seriously considered transferring, but I made myself stick it out for the year and, luckily, things got better. The key, really, was joining a lot of extracurricular activities, where you're introduced to people who you might otherwise not meet, and you're doing fun things that get everyone talking. I made friends and that's really the key to happiness in college: good friends to share your educational experience with. (Could I get any more sappy?)

NU has some interesting traditions. Some of them I hate, like primal scream (at 10:00 p.m. on the Sunday night before exams begin, everyone goes to their front porch and screams. So annoying). Others I love, like big groups of kids jumping into the lake. Dillo Day and Philfest (big, yearly concerts on campus). Take Back the Night (annual march/rally against assault). The yearly production of *The Vagina Monologues*. Edward 40 Hands (se-

niors strap full, forty ounce malt liquor bottles to each hand and can't remove either bottle until both are empty). The Spare Rib performance arts festival.

The Education

Northwestern's core is pretty sizable. Every student has to take two quarter classes from each of six distribution groups—Math, Natural Sciences, Social and Behavioral Sciences, Historical Studies, Values, and Literature/Fine Arts. Freshman also have to take two writing seminars. This is all a lot of work, but you come here to do work.

Most seniors at Northwestern wind up writing theses, and I just wrote mine this year. I really enjoyed the experience, and the feeling you get when you print out that last page is just amazing. You hold it in your hands and think, "My god, I wrote a damn book." Writing my thesis pushed me to my academic limits, and I love that I have something tangible to show for it.

Top ten things to do before graduating from NU:

10. Make the drivers at Norshore Cab hate you.
9. Go and see the Christmas lights in Chicago.
8. Wake up to a traveling bar in Bobb on game days.
7. Get written up by your RA.
6. Dirty rush or get dirty rushed.
5. Paint the Rock.
4. Road trip over to Madison for Halloween.
3. Close down the Deuce.
2. See Waa-Mu.
1. Make amazing BFFs.

✦ Maggie, junior

The Students

I'm pretty liberal and politically active, and during my time here I've made friends with others of a similar mind-set. I kind of just assumed *everyone* at Northwestern was as liberal and political as I was. But last year, when I was meeting with the VP of student affairs, he made a comment that he was shocked more students weren't taking a stand on

Iraq. I was surprised because I'd been protesting, writing newspaper columns, holding teach-ins, doing everything I possibly could. But after he made that comment, I stopped and looked around, and realized the activist community really is a small group on campus. It exists, but it's small.

The Activities

The biggest groups on campus are For Members Only (the black students union), the Women's Coalition, Associated Student Government, Dance Marathon (which organizes the largest student-philanthropy event in the nation), Studio 22 (the film organization, which annually gives students several thousands of dollars in grants for filmmaking), College Republicans, College Democrats, and the Arts Alliance (an umbrella student theater group). We also have lots of student bands on campus.

Every student has to pay a hundred-dollar student activity fee which is then pooled into a fund (usually around a couple hundred thousand dollars). Then, every student group submits a proposal to the funding board to get a piece of the pot. The student senate votes on those requests, based on your group's past performance, how many students attended your events, whether you've filed your paperwork correctly, and so on. It's an interesting system, and if you know to play your cards, you can get thousands of dollars for your student group.

The Social Scene

Students head to bars all the time. Evanston has a nice little variety of establishments, from college bars that freshman sneak into with their fake IDs, to nice Irish pubs and upscale bars. If you can't find a bar that fits your style in Evanston, Chicago's only a short L ride away, and you can find just about anything you'd want there.

There's at least one frat party per weekend on campus. And there are plenty of student group fund-raising parties. It's also not unusual for a group of ten friends to forgo a big party in order to just sit around an apartment and hang out. And while there are a few couples that are dating, everyone else is part of a hook-up culture, where there's lots of random sex, few commitments. It's worth noting, though, that the people with the best odds of having a good, long-term relationship here are gay men. There are lots of them on campus, and they seem to pair off in large numbers.

Notable Northwestern Almuni Include:
Richard Gephardt, U.S. representative
Warren Beatty, actor, director
Brent Musburger, sportscaster
John Cameron Mitchell, actor, director, screenwriter
Cindy Crawford, model
Charlton Heston, actor, gun enthusiast
Garry Marshall, producer, filmmaker
Julia Louis-Dreyfus, actor
David Schwimmer, actor

UNIVERSITY OF NOTRE DAME

Founded: 1842

Location: Notre Dame, IN

Phone: (574) 631-5000

E-mail: admissio.1@nd.edu

Web site: www.nd.edu

Number of Undergraduates: 8,300

Number of Graduate Students: 2,520

Cost: Approximately $37,000 per year

Application Deadline: December 31

Early Discipline November 1

Rating: Most Selective	Notable Majors/Programs: Business, Architecture, Engineering, Performing Arts, Theology

Size:
○ Small   ○ Medium   ● Large

Location:
○ Urban   ● Suburban   ○ Rural

On a Saturday, students talk about academics:
○ Always   ● Sometimes   ○ Never

Nightlife:
○ Intense   ● Moderate   ○ Laid-back

Politically, Notre Dame leans:
○ Left   ● Right   ○ Split

Diversity:
○ High   ● Low   ○ Medium

Students describe Notre Dame in five words:
- Proud, spirited, conservative, tough, Irish!
- Community, tradition, football, academics, service

From the School

Students come to Notre Dame hoping to leave better prepared for their chosen professions; through their experience of a broad education taught by caring faculty who encourage research, service learning, and global travel, they leave here better prepared to continually pursue knowledge and to share it, no matter the direction their lives take.

—www.admissions.nd.edu

If you're interested in Notre Dame, you may also be interested in:
Boston College, Georgetown, Holy Cross, University of Michigan,
University of Southern California, Vanderbilt

Name: Megan
Hometown: Akron, Ohio
Class Year: Junior
Major: English
Extracurriculars: Class Council, Interhall Athletics, Service, Hall Government, employee in ND Sports Information Office.
Career Goal: To be a writer.

How would you describe Notre Dame's reputation?

Most view Notre Dame as a healthy blend of academics and athletics with a strong Catholic tradition. A lot of people see it as a second-rate Ivy League school, and sometimes as a second-rate athletic powerhouse because of the high academic standards demanded of our athletes.

Is this reputation accurate?

Yes, in a sense. Notre Dame combines academic strength and athletic prowess, but we're not "second-rate"—it is just that instead of focusing solely on one goal, such as academics *or* athletics, there are many other things ND strives to cultivate. Notre Dame's focus is on forming a well-rounded person, and the school is constructed to facilitate connections between all aspects of life—academic, social, spiritual, athletic—to really encourage its students to *think* about their expectations of themselves and of their lives, their values (not just in the religious sense, but in all areas of their lives), and what life should really be all about.

What would an admissions officer at Notre Dame probably not tell a prospective student?

They would not mention that not everyone fits the Notre Dame mold. There is a profound sense of pride, identity, and support in "the Notre Dame family," which really is a wonderful network, but the extreme school pride can bewilder a student who is unhappy with some aspect of the school. I came here with extremely high expectations, only to find out that the school isn't perfect (no school is). Certain rules are a pain. And despite efforts to increase minorities on campus, the student body is not that diverse, which was difficult for me at times. Also, many students feel that their voices go unheard by the administration. Others think many students take protests too far and that when they agree to come to the university they are agreeing to the rules already established by the administration. Groups like the Progressive Student Alliance are currently working to try to improve relations.

The Institution

I chose ND because of its school spirit. The sense of school pride is astounding. Football Saturdays are probably the best-known tradition. There are also the notorious Rally in the Alley at the beginning of the school year, signature dorm events like the Alumni Wake, the Keenan Revue and the Dillon Pep Rally, which is the unofficial rite of passage where upperclassmen take the frosh running through the Stonehenge fountain. The campus lingo itself is a tradition, calling upon heroes of the past in reference to buildings like "The Rock" (Knute Rockne Memorial) and nicknaming almost every campus landmark (O'Shag, LaFun, the Huddle, DeBart, etc.). ND even hosts its own annual midnight reenactment of the Civil War on the night after the first big snowfall, pitting North Quad against South Quad in an all-out snowball fight.

> "School spirit is through the roof. Everyone is extremely proud to be Irish and won't let anyone forget it!"
>
> ✦ Kyle, junior

Another great thing is that there is *always* a Notre Dame connection available if you need it. The Notre Dame family (i.e., network of alums called Domers, current students, or just any ND fan or affiliate) is incredible. I met a priest in Rome who made a group of us stand in a circle and sing the alma mater with him. A friend once got bumped up from coach to first class on a plane because he had an ND sweatshirt on. And the ND connection never hurts in the job search, either. The downside: some people get on your back when the football team is in a slump. But it's all in good fun, and I wouldn't trade it for the world.

The Education

Classes *may* be brought up on a Saturday night, but it's not likely. If you were to casually mention that C you got in chemistry, no one would pummel you, but you might get a beer shoved in your face and be told to save it for the morning. If you mention that A-minus that should've been changed to an A, you might get that beer dumped on your head. Students are extremely dedicated to their academic lives for the most part, but they are more competitive with themselves than with other students; ND focuses a lot on encouraging collaboration among students.

The core curriculum really adds to the whole experience. Requirements allow a student to get a taste of disciplines outside their majors and also add an interdisciplinary approach that aids students in becoming thinkers, not just studyers. I'll admit that freshman year I was a little disappointed in a few of my professors in general-requirement courses. Ever since then, however, I have been nothing but impressed. Profs at ND know their stuff and love to share it with you, and they are also enthusiastic about hearing students' own views. The workload can be heavy, depending upon your major, but it's all what you make it.

Study-abroad programs are absolutely *amazing*. I spent a semester in Rome and met up with ND students throughout Europe on several weekends, and ran into others randomly in the Roman Forum, Paris, and Interlaken.

The Students

Diversity is a widely discussed topic at ND because many claim that it is nonexistent. People complain that certain ethnic/racial/gender groups cling together and don't branch out. While certain groups do seem to naturally gravitate toward each other, there is nothing exclusive or threatening about it. The university has recently been taking strides to increase the number of minority students, and everyone seems supportive of creating a more diverse campus.

One of the other biggest campus complaints deals with gender relations. (Warning: If you are seen eating dinner with someone at a two-person side table in the dining hall, it will be concluded by students you may or may not know that you are on an SDHDD—South Dining Hall Dinner Date. Approach said situation with caution.) Students complain that single-sex residence halls create a tension between the genders—a sense that when a girl approaches a guy or vice versa, everyone is watching them and wondering if one or the other is "interested." Girls complain that ND boys lack social skills. Boys complain that the girls aren't that good-looking—it's a vicious cycle. Overall, though, by the end of sophomore year, gender relations are much less of an issue and everyone realizes it is completely possible to be "just friends"

with members of the opposite sex and that it's equally as acceptable to be "interested" in someone. Maybe this realization would occur much earlier in coed dorms, but you won't be seeing those at ND any time soon.

It is difficult to say what the socioeconomic atmosphere is really like here—many people seem to believe the student body is composed solely of rich kids, yet no one claims to belong to that category. Students tend to be proud of their financial aid packages, while those not receiving financial aid insist that they really should be. For the most part, money is not a big issue. ND sweats and T-shirts and the relatively standard dorm room even things out, whatever economic differences there may be.

> "How many Notre Dame students does it take to screw in a lightbulb? Fifteen: one to screw in the lightbulb, two to discuss Notre Dame's tradition of lightbulb screwing, one to write a Viewpoint article about it, one to light a candle for the lightbulb at the Grotto, and ten to check espn.com the next day for Notre Dame's ranking in lightbulb-screwing."
> ✦ Alexandra, senior

The Activities

Campus can be a mean wind tunnel in December and January (bring a serious parka), but when spring rolls around campus is an entirely new place. Everyone is on the quad, and many of the dorms have stereos in the windows and couches on the lawn, and you see an occasional Slip 'n Slide or kiddy pool on the quad. Campus is an extremely active and fun place all year round, but especially when the weather gets nice.

If it's 3:00 a.m. on a Wednesday morning and I'm awake, it's because I just got back from a Quarter-Dog run with the girls. QDs can be found at the Huddle—ND's on-campus grocery store (where the prices are beyond inflated; however, you can use your Flex Points, available with one of several meal plans, to shop there)—located in the LaFortune Student Center. Every night at midnight, the Huddle starts selling hot dogs for a quarter—thus, "Quarter-Dogs." Freshman year, a group of girls in my dorm started a tradition of going for QDs at midnight on Wednesdays to break up the monotony of homework, chill with each other, and just relax.

Notre Dame may be the easiest place in the world to get involved in campus activities. There is never a shortage of opportunities. Clubs, residence halls, and academic departments all provide students with endless events such as the Mr. and Ms. ND pageants and Irish Idol, ND's spin-off of TV's *American Idol*, which have recently joined the ranks of the more experienced Black Cultural Arts Council Fashion Show, Asian Allure, and Latin Expressions.

An Irish blessing, Notre Dame style:

> May Juniper Road rise to meet you,
> May Touchdown Jesus look always over your back,
> May the South Bend zephyr take it easy on your frozen face,
> And snow fall soft upon your respective Quad (whether it be South Quad—the best—North Quad, God Quad, West Quad, or Mod Quad).
> And until we meet again (i.e., tailgating at the ND vs. BC game next October),
> May Notre Dame Our Mother hold you safe in the shadow of the Golden Dome.
>
> ✦ Megan, senior

The Social Scene

ND students follow one main guideline: work hard, play hard. Whether or not "playing hard" involves alcohol, everyone finds time to seriously unwind, kick back, and make their college years the best that they can. ND is obviously the home of the Fighting Irish, and the Irish take pride in their drinking enzyme. Partying can play a big role in your college experience if you want it to. Students can definitely be found out at bars on any given night of the week. On the other hand, students (though significantly smaller in number) can also be found in the Hesburgh Library on any given night of the week. The very same student you see out on Monday until 3:00 a.m. you may encounter in the library at 3:00 a.m. on Tuesday, studying for a cell bio test. Other students aren't all that academic yet choose to have fun without drinking. There is no Greek life at Notre Dame and

it is wonderful. Instead, residence halls serve this function, sponsoring events and mixer-type dances without anyone having to take an oath. Hall unity provides a pool of almost-assured friends, if you want it. There is a tremendous amount of residence hall pride.

Name: Matt
Hometown: Charlotte, North Carolina
Class Year: Sophomore
Major: Management Information Systems, History
Extracurriculars: Student International Business Council, Student Managers Organization, Hall Council.
Career Goal: Consultant for a Big-Four firm in Chicago

How would you describe Notre Dame's reputation?

Notre Dame is the most well-known Catholic university and is one of the top schools in the country.

Is this reputation accurate?

Very. The school has more than a hundred Masses on campus each week and students are among the most intelligent and athletic in the nation.

What aspect of Notre Dame might you not see on a college tour?

Life in South Bend is very uneventful. The winters are long and boring, but that does make the beautiful falls and spring much better.

The Institution

Words cannot describe what football means to the school. By Thursday of every home football weekend, thousands of people descend on the school. Game day is full of tailgating, marching-band concerts, marching Irish Guard members, and various other activities.

Notre Dame is a great size in that you end up recognizing most kids on campus, although you don't have to bother knowing them all. Dorms act as the center of social life and most students live in the same dorm for three years before moving off campus. The campus is self-contained and small compared to many schools, and made more beautiful by the Gothic architecture and the large, open quads. The dining halls actually have good food! There's even a twenty-four-hour restaurant on campus, Reckers, where they serve great smoothies, onion rings, and pizza.

South Bend is the only downside to ND, as it offers nothing other than a string of bars, and since the campus is closed, there is little interaction with townies.

The Education

Like most schools, your major will determine your workload. Most engineers find themselves working countless hours six days a week. Business and Arts and Letters students manage to enjoy themselves more often. Everyone here seems to have been competing for the top of their high school class, so it's usually an even playing field. Class sizes vary from more than a hundred to fourteen. Freshmen usually have two to three very large lecture classes with a discussion group and then smaller seminar classes. Some professors are better than others, but all are generally approachable and care for their students. While students are on their own to seek academic support, a plethora is available. The career center is very active, bringing companies to school throughout the year (with a few large career fairs). It holds workshops providing help from resume writing to mock interviews. The university tries to give students every possible service required (including laundry), but once again, that support is not mandatory.

The Students

Notre Dame is not diverse. While everyone comes from a different background (one of my roommates was born in China and the other hails from Slovenia), the majority are whites from the Midwest who attended Catholic schools. This is not to say there are no minorities at Notre Dame, but they do stand out. At least one out of five people you meet will either be from Chicago or have family there. It's a very conservative campus with a large Republican backing. Most students have an active social life, play dorm sports, do volunteer work, and drink a lot. While plenty of students don't drink, the Irish in everyone comes out eventually.

The Activities

In the fall, football rules. Profs generally plan their syllabi around the schedule and many students travel for away games (including Southern Cal and Boston College). Chicago is less than two hours away, and many people leave for the weekend during the winter or spring for Cubs games, concerts, and various other activities.

Being rather conservative, students at ND don't often demonstrate. The most active club is probably the Leprechaun Legion—essentially the basketball team's cheerleaders. Members research other teams to find information about players, create specific cheers, and print and distribute "jeer cards" before each game.

The university has decided to place a large emphasis on the arts. The new DeBartolo Performing Arts Center opened in 2005, and while I wouldn't say the majority of students strongly support the program (ticket prices are high), more arts-minded students are being attracted to ND.

> "I think it's very difficult for women (and many minorities) to feel a part of the ND community. While forming the first feminist club on campus (in the twenthy-first century people!), I was explicitly told by the administration that *if* there was to be a feminist club on campus, it wouldn't be allowed to address issues of abortion, contraception, or homosexuality. Students are definitely more liberal than the administration, but still . . ."
>
> ✦ Morley, senior

The Social Scene

People generally go out two or three nights a week. Dorm parties are a unique Notre Dame experience for freshmen. You would not believe how many people can fit into a nine-by-twelve-foot room when the furniture is cleaned out. Drinking is allowed in the dorms as long as it stays in the rooms (some dorms are stricter than others, though). Apartments within walking distance provide a place to party any weekend night, and houses generally have parties.

Name: Alexandra
Hometown: Houston, Texas
Class Year: Junior
Major: English
Extracurriculars: French club, Texas club, Ms. Wizard Day

Career Goal: Earn a PhD in English and become a professor of Shakespeare.

How would you describe Notre Dame's reputation?

Knute Rockne. The Gipper. The Four Horsemen. Notre Dame belongs to the legends of great college football. . . . Oh, and it's pretty good academically too.

Is this reputation accurate?

The strong academic side of Notre Dame usually gets lost behind the kelly green and the blue and gold, but it's definitely what also makes Notre Dame Notre Dame—even if more people talk about the score from Saturday's game than Notre Dame's ranking among the top twenty colleges in the country.

What aspect of Notre Dame would a prospective student not see on a campus tour?

Gender relations are a real problem at Notre Dame. Only coed for about thirty years, ND still seems to have trouble with interaction between the sexes. Also, say good-bye to the sun after October because it's not coming back until April. Get ready for 0-degree winters and snow, snow, and more snow. On the plus side, the campus looks beautiful in the snow.

> "Notre Dame is definitely full of policies that are intolerant of LGBT students; however, there's a significant number of students who'd like to change that."
> ✦ Adrien, senior

The Institution

Saturday afternoon football games at Notre Dame have a mythic quality that reflects its spirit and community. As a first-year student at ND on your first football weekend, you get an indescribable feeling walking around campus and seeing so many alumni and fans who have driven, flown, or bused their way to campus. You have so much pride for Notre Dame when you hear the marching band play the greatest of all university fight songs for the first time. Finally arriving in the stadium and standing in the student section (you never,

ever sit at a football game), you feel how tightly knit the Notre Dame family really is. Nothing can describe the first time you see the gold-clad players take the field. Finally, when you yell out with eighty thousand fellow fans, *"we are ND!"* you know you've made the right decision.

Notre Dame has two famous campus features—the Golden Dome on top of the main building and Touchdown Jesus, the mural on the side of Hesburgh Library (in which Jesus's arms are outstretched . . . and it just so happens to be next to the stadium—an extra demonstration that our victories are truly blessed).

Housing at Notre Dame is pretty unique: all dorms are single-sex and ruled by the infamous parietals system. Parietals mean that no one of the opposite sex is allowed in your room after midnight on weekdays and after 2:00 a.m. on Friday and Saturday. Without fraternities and sororities, these single-sex dorms become your replacement for the Greek system—but they, along with parietals, seem to perpetuate the infamous gender-relations problems on campus.

The Education

Freshman year means, for most students, fulfilling university requirements, including one class each in math, science, history and social science, English, philosophy, and theology. If you're taking care of these subjects freshman year, you might have one or more classes in the biggest auditorium on campus, DeBartolo 101. It might be a bit of a shock to learn chemistry or math in a classroom that fits three hundred people (and then get your questions answered by a TA in tutorial), but don't worry—most classes after the initial introductory ones are considerably smaller. As a liberal arts student, I usually have classes with about twenty students or less.

There are numerous research opportunities on campus for students in the sciences, working with professors on projects and in labs. There are also grants available to undergraduates to do summer research.

Notre Dame has a plethora of study-abroad opportunities in major cities all over the world. As good as the pasta stir-fry is on campus in North Dining Hall, it doesn't compare to the pasta you can get while studying in Rome for a semester. Granted, I wouldn't say the food in England was a selling point for me I when I spent junior year there studying at Oxford University, but the opportunity to study Shakespeare and the Elizabethans in depth was a good trade-off.

The Students

Unfortunately, one of Notre Dame's weakest points is its lack of diversity. The typical student is upper-middle class, white, and owns a full wardrobe from Abercrombie & Fitch. Over 80 percent of the campus is Catholic—but being Catholic is not a prerequisite. Despite the cookie-cutter image, students are generally very tolerant. Be prepared, though, for occasional vehement exchanges in the opinion section of the student newspaper, the *Observer,* about hot issues. There are always people on campus (usually older alumni or professors, but sometimes the occasional student) who will write in at some point with extremely conservative Catholic viewpoints about abortion, homosexuality, and topics in the news.

The Activities

Aside from football, there's support for teams like men's basketball. Hockey, volleyball, softball, cross country, and lacrosse have much smaller attendance records and there are often special giveaways (T-shirts, mini-volleyballs, etc.) to increase student interest.

We live in the so-called Notre Dame bubble. Sure, you'll take the occasional trips into South Bend to go out to dinner or make that all-important Meijer run (a twenty-four-hour super-store), but the events you'll attend will more than likely be on campus.

> "Many Domers are practicing Catholics— every residence hall has a chapel, or students can attend Mass in the Basilica of the Sacred Heart (located in the center of campus, on 'God Quad')."
>
> ✦ Erin, junior

There are an amazingly large number of activities during the week. Clubs and organizations (academic, social, religious) number in the double digits and cover a number of interests (the biggest being service and social awareness). Comedians, music groups (including U2 a few years back), and plays are frequent occurrences, so there's always something to do. Nearly every weekend a different dorm is sponsoring a formal dance or, more often, a less formal SYR (Screw Your Roommate), which refers to the old, now-defunct tradition of roommates setting up their roommates with less than appealing dates.

The Social Scene

Typically, the weekend starts for business students (the group with seemingly the least amount of work on campus) on Wednesday. However, the rest of the campus usually waits for Friday—maybe Thursday if you're not a science, engineering, or architecture student. There are all kinds of partyers on campus: heavy drinkers, moderate drinkers, and nondrinkers. Notre Dame has a rather troubled relationship with alcohol—there is a lot of it on campus, and the new alcohol policy has not done much to curb it. The trend seems to be that if the alcohol is in your dorm room, then you're generally okay, but if you are caught off campus with alcohol and you're under twenty-one, then you are in big trouble. It's a rather maddening double standard. However, there is usually no pressure to drink if you don't want to. As a nondrinking freshman, I did not have a problem at all.

Dating seems more difficult at Notre Dame than at other universities because of the rules and housing, but it's certainly not impossible. And despite the strange rules, overbearing administration, and frigid temperatures, Notre Dame is a great place. The spirit and community feeling of the student body is unparalleled. You leave after four years a Domer and part of the worldwide Notre Dame family.

Notable Notre Dame Alumni Include:

Condoleezza Rice, national security adviser and secretary of state to President George W. Bush

Edward J. DeBartolo, businessman and former owner of the San Francisco Forty-niners

Eric Wieschaus, Nobel Prize-winning biologist

Nicholas Sparks, author

Regis Philbin, television personality

Father Theodore Hesburgh, Congressional Gold Medal winner and world record holder for most honorary degrees received

OBERLIN COLLEGE

Founded: 1833

Location: Oberlin, OH

Phone: (440) 775-8411

E-mail: college.admissions@oberlin.edu

Web site: www.oberlin.edu

Number of Undergraduates: 2,880

Number of Graduate Students: 20

Cost: Approximately $39,000 per year

Application Deadline: January 15

Early Decision: November 15

Rating:	Notable Majors/Programs:
Very Selective	Music Conservatory, Life Sciences, Social Sciences

Size:

○ Small   ● Medium   ○ Large

Location:

○ Urban   ○ Suburban   ● Rural

On a Saturday, students talk about academics:

● Always   ○ Sometimes   ○ Never

Nightlife:

○ Intense   ● Moderate   ○ Laid-back

Politically, Oberlin leans:

● Left   ○ Right   ○ Split

Diversity:

○ High   ○ Low   ● Medium

Students describe Oberlin in five words:

- Counterculture, political, busy, relaxed, brilliant
- Carnegie Hall's and Woodstock's lovechild

From the School

[Oberlin] uniquely combines an outstanding professional school of music with a leading undergraduate college of arts and sciences. The two divisions reinforce each other. The Conservatory provides flexible programs to prepare students as professional musicians and teachers of music. [T]he College of Arts and Sciences offers a rich and balanced curriculum in the humanities, social sciences, and natural sciences. Within that framework the College expects that students will work closely with the faculty to design an educational program appropriate to their own particular interests, needs, and long-term goals.

—www.oberlin.edu

If you're interested in Oberlin, you may also be interested in:
Brown, Carleton, Grinnell, Reed, Vassar, Wesleyan

Name: Andrew
Hometown: Washington, D.C.
Class Year: Sophomore
Major: African American Studies and Politics
Extracurriculars: Bike Co-op, WOBC, the *Grape,* Concert Sound.
Career Goal: Cultural theorist/pop culture critic.

How would you describe Oberlin's reputation?

Oberlin is best known as a drugged-out, über-liberal haven in the middle of nowhere, filled with brilliant, crazy students knowledgeable in every field imaginable.

Is this reputation accurate?

Yes. We are a bunch of stoners and are, for the most part, super-liberal and in the middle of nowhere (which just happens to be only forty miles away from Cleveland, so it's fairly easy to escape from the town). Everyone I know is brilliant and full of all sorts of useful knowledge, whether it is an awesome band that you should listen to, or an awesome book about destroying the military-industrial complex.

What would an admissions officer at Oberlin probably not tell a prospective student?

If you don't have a car, you're essentially stuck in Oberlin, which can be a mixed bag. Some nights, there may be something very interesting occurring on campus, like electronic musicians performing in the Tappan Square gazebo, a performance/dialogue with poet Saul Williams, or a reading by Billy Collins. Other nights, not a damn thing happens, not even a conservatory concert (of which there are many). On one of these nights, you may notice that the ceiling of your room is primed, not painted.

The Institution

The Administration: As time has progressed, the administration seems more concerned about its bottom line than about the students. Thanks to the administration, Oberlin has switched from a need-blind to a need-sensitive admissions policy, which has created a clear campus dynamic shift, bringing in preppier students who don't quite fit the Oberlin dynamic, and that's tragic because they just aren't politically active enough.

The Protests: This is Oberlin. The image that you have built up in your mind about Oberlin—with everyone always trying to save the world, protesting every imaginable issue possible—is true. Students for a Free Palestine, Save the Tongass National Forest, Transgender Awareness Week, Tell the Senate to Vote No on the Central American Free Trade Agreement—these are all actual groups/protests that have occurred on campus.

The Housing: There are two options for dormitories: student-run co-ops and college-run housing. Just like most colleges, housing ranges from good to bad. Most of the housing at Oberlin is aesthetically unattractive and mentally unsettling, as it was built to resemble military barracks. There are two different vibes, but as everything goes at Oberlin, you'll find your own place to fit in. The campus is pretty small; everything can be reached by foot, but a lot of people, myself included, prefer to ride a bike. It's a good option, as Ohio's really flat. There're tons of good and bad architecture here. There are buildings done by Cass Gilbert (think Stanford and Harvard), and there are buildings (most dorms on campus) that were built in the fifties and sixties.

> "We're known as the Haight-Ashbury of the Midwest: a school in the middle of a cornfield where the dreds are locked and the doors are always open."
> ✦ Jessica, sophomore

The Sports: For two years Dill Field and the north fields have been just outside my dorm room window. I've spent more time cursing at the teams for waking me up than actually watching them. I went to one football game, once . . . for five minutes . . . with two gay men who commented not on the travesty of a football game here, but on the tight pants. . . . We used to go laugh at the football team, but now they're getting better. The women's rugby team is as close as Oberlin comes to a frat. They're amazing.

The Weirdo Factor: It's kind of true (nontraditional people who didn't feel comfortable in a traditional high school environment tend to be very happy here). But actually, everyone's been commenting on how many "normal" kids have been coming here lately, which is kind of disturbing.

There's a new trend that we like to call the hipsters, who've overtaken the hippies in influence. They love obscure bands and pointy shoes and trucker hats. It's a little scary. The hipsters are pretty exclusive. But I don't want to hang out with them anyway! Silly hipsters!

The Education

Oberlin isn't a place for half-assers. The education is intense. You can't skate through and not do the work; the professors know how to bite you in the ass especially hard if you slack off. In addition, you cannot expect to get through classes at Oberlin and not talk. Almost every class at Oberlin is under 50 students and discussion-based. Even in larger classes, there are discussion sections—groups of fifteen to twenty-five students talking about the reading with the professor (there are almost no TAs). If you're the lecture type, Oberlin is not the place for you at all.

> "Mudd Library is the trippiest place on the face of the planet. It's like a Smurf ate confetti and then puked it up in a place of higher learning."
>
> ✦ Alli, junior

There are a lot of classes available for a school of Oberlin's size. They are not difficult to get into, or get out of; you should be able to take anything that you want at Oberlin as long as you're appropriately qualified. The requirements are pointlessly easy to fulfill. There is a 9-9-9 requirement. Each student has to take nine credit hours in each of the college's divisions: Arts and Humanities, Social and Behavioral Sciences, and Natural Sciences and Mathematics. It's easy when there are so many strong departments. Both of my majors, in the African American and politics departments, are really strong to take classes in. The same goes for the chemistry, biology, neuroscience, English, art history, and environmental science departments. Hooray for liberal arts! In addition, there is a nine-credit "cultural diversity" requirement. I'm not really sure what this term means anymore; it's supposed to be non-Western/European thought and history, but I got it for Marxist theory. While meeting the 9-9-9, you can meet the writing proficiency requirement for the college and probably the quantitative proficiency for the college as well.

The Students

At first, Obies come across as cold, distant, and intimidating, but in reality, we are really, really nice people to talk to and be friends with. The students here are all of the activists/social outcasts/ crazy kids that you knew in high school and thought were cool but strange. When I see a kid wearing Urban Outfitters, I am alarmed. That's the kind of school that Oberlin is.

The Activities

Just hanging around is always the main event on campus. If it's warm, hang on Wilder Bowl; maybe you'll smoke a bowl or drink a brew. All the students (except the athletes) have fun shooting the shit, talking about something postmodern. It's always possible to just stroll around and just throw down with a few people on any day, whether it's 0 or 70 degrees out. It's really cool.

Students really have a lot of control at the school. The gay kids are really loud at Oberlin, as are the minority groups. There is a community service center that many people are involved with, which is great. The radio station is unstoppable, and it's totally student-run. Students also have a role in deciding which professors come here and which don't. A lot of people read the student publications— especially the *Grape*—and complain about the quality, which is fine because that means they read it.

The Social Scene

The party scene is vibrant. Every weekend, there are at least a couple of parties. If there is no party, you can always work, hang out with friends, smoke a bowl, whatever. Since there is no Greek scene, the parties revolve around individual people's houses. And meeting people is super-easy at Oberlin, but due to the social ineptness of everyone on this campus, myself included, it takes a little while to get to that level. Chivalry is not dead at Oberlin, but I think some students are jerks and don't hold doors or look out for others. But most Obies are awesome—you can talk to anyone for hours. It's sweet.

Name: Fairlie
Hometown: Dover, Delaware
Class Year: Senior
Major(s): Biology and English

Extracurriculars: Anime Club, volunteering at the dog shelter.

Career Goal: I think I might want to be a science writer for a newspaper or magazine.

How would you describe Oberlin's reputation?

A generally good school, with a lot of leftist hippies and potheads, and an elitist music conservatory.

Is this reputation accurate?

It is, although we don't get enough credit for academics being a big part of everyday life here. You're far more likely to overhear someone debating what Kant or Hume would think of Karl Rove than bragging about how wasted they were Saturday night.

What would an admissions officer at Oberlin probably not tell a prospective student? What aspect of your school would a prospective student not see on a campus tour?

They would probably not tell you we have a really low freshman retention rate, possibly due to the fact that we attract smart but socially awkward people. On the campus tour, they are unlikely to show you any of the co-ops, some of which are embarrassingly dirty and run-down. They aren't all bad—I love eating at Asia House and Old B whenever I can—but most of the co-ops would never make it onto an Oberlin promotional poster. (Just step into Harkness, the "hippie co-op," and you'll know what I mean.)

The Institution

I think Oberlin inspires people to be different and innovative. Professors reward original ideas that may be half-formed rather than perfectly worded parroted responses. This makes English classes a lot more fun than they were in high school . . . for me, at least. I wrote every single paper for Intro to Cinema Studies on (admittedly bad) science fiction movies, and it was the only class in which I ever got an A+.

The traditions here go along with the "I'm unique just like everyone else" mentality. There's skinny-dipping in the old reservoir, a freshman favorite. Or there's painting the big rocks in Tappan Square with an imitation Van Gogh or some obscure inside joke. The busiest bathroom on campus (in the library basement) has sheets of paper up for people to whine on. You get the predictable lists of "hottest profs on campus," but also really long debates about, say, why *fluid* is a more descriptive word for some people's sexuality than *bisexual* because it implies multiplicitous gender possibilities.

There's a lot of disdain directed at the administration these days because of the financial trouble the school has been having recently. They had to fire people and cut budgets to keep operating, and stepped on a lot of toes in the process. I think a lot of the anti-administration rhetoric is just part of the culture of the school, not because they are doing anything to annoy students on purpose. I mean, Oberlin's administration has a history of helping the students in times of crisis. After the Kent State shootings in 1970, when all the other schools were closing down and sending their kids home, Oberlin's administration organized buses for the students to go and protest.

> "We've got a lot of trust-fund activist hippies and a lot of pretentious hipsters, but most people aren't at either extreme."
> ✦ Alli, junior

The Education

Everyone I know here claims never to have worked in high school, yet they all work decently hard on their classes. Besides the few big intro classes, there's a peer-perpetuated feeling of pride about turning in good academic work. And classroom concepts get discussed outside of class *a lot*. A good joke will often involve Freud or Lacan or Marxism.

There are tons of opportunities for people to get involved in extracurriculars or research with professors. The science faculty is made up of nearly all research scientists, which is exciting because they keep up with their fields and discuss recent breakthroughs, even in intro classes. Typically there will be assignments that involve reading published scientific papers or seeing a visiting lecturer (of which there is usually one per department per week). I ended up caring a lot more about the sciences, and research science in particular. The professors are, for the most part, really approachable, and even though biology is the biggest major on campus, everyone who wants to put in the effort to do a senior honors project is allowed. (I've been working with a professor and three other students on a molecular biology project, and it's a lot of fun.)

Our term system includes a winter term during January, and because it is horribly cold in Oberlin at that time of year, it's a great opportunity to go abroad, or to learn a weird skill like basket-weaving and get college credit. But I'd only recommend staying in Oberlin for winter term if you like being alone. It is snowy and windy all month, and people deal with the isolation by acting even stranger than normal. Should you leave, our study-abroad programs are pretty amazing—there are countless countries to visit and directly Oberlin-run programs in London and Japan.

All in all, Oberlin has changed me into someone who can't stop overanalyzing everything. I can't write papers now without spending half of them defining the main terms used in my thesis. Anytime anyone makes some sort of generalization in conversation ("Voice majors are so spoiled," "Capitalism is bad"), I can't stop myself from saying, "That's not entirely true. . . ."

> "We like our music. Jazz, rock, electronic, and some *serious* organ music."
>
> ✦ Alli, junior

The Students

There are a lot of politically minded people on this campus. Quite a lot. It seems like people are always angry about something. The most amusing is when particular groups are angry at themselves, like when the LGBT Union temporarily disbanded over issues of sexuality and gender identity, and then reformed under the nondescript (but all-inclusive) title "the Union." Or last year, when the Sexual Assault Support Team accused *themselves* of being racist in their policy, and decided to shut down. Overall, though, I think everyone here is extremely open-minded, and most of these debates are just petty squabbling. We have a higher percentage of people with purple hair than do most schools. You're much more likely to see a bald girl with a nose ring sitting next to you in a computer lab than a blond girl with a pink shirt (there must be some of them around, but I can't think of any I've seen recently). I had a friend who claimed he could tell Oberlin students from visitors and prospies by their shoes. We do get a lot of

criticism for being "rich hippies" who think it's cool to pretend to be poor and shop at Goodwill and stuff, but I know a lot of students with large financial aid packages—so we're not all rich.

The Activities

It's a small campus, and people leave very rarely. I'm not much of a sports fan, but everyone loves the Ultimate Frisbee teams (they throw good parties). Of course, there are always concerts on because of the conservatory, and we get a lot of big-name musical performers and famous jazz musicians coming through, because this is such a musical campus. Our little student-run dance club is able to attract some immensely popular indie bands (The Rapture and Deerhoof), and we have at least three film clubs that are always showing good movies (which always conflict with each other, damn them).

The Social Scene

It is hard to meet new people after freshman year, although there are lots of extracurricular groups to join, or social excos. I think a lot of people become isolated as the years go by, as the work gets harder and your friends from freshman year drop away.

Name: Meghan
Hometown: Humble, Texas
Class Year: Freshman
Major: Biopsychology (neuroscience and psychology)
Extracurriculars: American Civil Liberties Union, lacrosse, soccer, Newman Catholic Community, Hall Council Secretary, Boys and Girls Club volunteer, America Reads–Head Start, RA.
Career Goal: To become a child psychiatrist with an emphasis on alternative medicine. I hope to have my own private practice but volunteer my services to homeless youth and other underprivileged groups.

How would you describe Oberlin's reputation?

Oberlin has a reputation for being very liberal and activist, with a very high homosexual rate. There is also a reputation for just loving to learn.

Is this reputation accurate?

Yes, Oberlin is liberal and full of activists; most people admire those who take risks and are different and everyone has an opinion (my best friend here said she thought less of me because I own an SUV and was less energy-conscious by leaving the lights on when I left the room). And loving to learn? Definitely accurate. I just wish Oberlin's reputation as a high-quality school was more nationally known. No one in my home state of Texas knows about the school. They're like, "Overland? Where's that?"

> "Oberlin is sold short by a lot of the guidebooks. It's often pegged as an oddity more than an actual rigorous academic environment. Yet I've visited friends who go to Ivy League schools, and they generally have a lot less work to do than I do."
>
> ✦ April, senior

What would an admissions officer at Oberlin probably not tell a prospective student?

An admissions officer might not tell you how unlikely it is that you will leave Oberlin during the academic year. It gets pretty humdrum sometimes, being in the middle of nowhere.

The Institution

Oberlin is a haven for laid-back liberal kids who enjoy life while they're figuring out how to change the world. That laid-backness pervades the atmosphere here, to the extent that everyone takes time for granted—no one is ever on time for anything!

I like how all the dorms are located around one of three quads. Unless there's snow, you can always look out and see someone playing out there. Our co-ops are amazing. I haven't eaten or lived in one, but they're a good way to reduce your room and board costs and provide a sense of unity.

The college is divided into two parts. All the Connies (students in the conservatory) tend to live and attend classes on South Campus, while the mathletes and/or science majors live on North Campus. So, if you're not careful, you could end up only knowing one or the other.

Although the town is only two square miles, there really is not that much interaction between the town and the school. I walk to the Boys and Girls Club, which is two blocks from campus, and everyone says, "Where is that?" My job through the Community Service Learning Office allows me to get to know the town better. Oberlin, the town,

has the highest poverty rate in the poorest county in Ohio, but the town also has the most PhD's per capita in the United States.

Bike theft is the highest form of crime at Oberlin. Kids will steal your bike just to ride it down the street. This happened to me, and then I got a weird note telling me where to get it back.

Career services set up a cool system through eRecruiting, where you can stay with alumni in other cities and do whatever interests you. This past winter I stayed with an alum in Seattle and worked with homeless youth in a health-care clinic.

The Education

Most people here major in the humanities, but each year more students become science majors, due to the new science center. I felt that my intro bio lab was primitive compared to the one at my public high school, where we dissected cats. But the chemistry labs were amazing; I'd never seen such high-tech stuff before.

Since the school is so small, everyone with an okay GPA has the opportunity to do research, either on their own (as an honors project) or with a teacher. This year, I participated in a psychology study (how your brain reacts when it sees a picture of yourself) and fell in love with the project. I e-mailed the professor during finals week and asked if I could help with his research next year. He replied the next day.

"Excos" are courses taught by anyone, and by "anyone," I mean *anyone*: students, professors, townies. All they have to do is get it approved. Such courses include the "sexco," water polo, stilting, a *Sex in the City* exco, and many, many more.

The Students

Most students are from the D.C. area, New York, and California. Students come from all income levels, although most are middle class. People dress in casual, comfy clothes; T-shirts and jeans work best. Most of the food co-ops are vegetarian (the co-ops make their own food, although they sometimes get shut down because they don't meet health requirements); about half of the Oberlin population is vegetarian, and a large number are vegan. Although Oberlin was one of the first colleges to offer an education to African Americans, there are still (faint) social lines of division between ethnic groups. There are very few Hispanics, but there are a lot of international students.

The Activities

Marches and protests are the most common activities. An article in a Republican online magazine said we send two hundred people to every protest; that's not *entirely* true. Music is a big deal on campus, and many students are active in musical groups even if they're not attaining a bachelor's degree in music. There are about five student-run a cappella groups and seven theater groups.

Club sports, like rugby and Ultimate Frisbee, are common, but varsity sports are not. Most people don't know where the fields are; I play soccer and lacrosse, and even I had a hard time finding the softball field.

There's only one movie theater in town, which costs two dollars on Tuesdays and Thursdays and three dollars the other days. The movie is changed every week, and if enough people request it, you can get one to come back. Also, sometimes my friends and I will take a short (twenty-minute) drive to Lake Erie and go swimming.

The Social Scene

There are a lot of events on campus, often advertised by flyers and chalkings on the sidewalks.

Hardly anything costs more than five dollars, and most events are free. There are no frats on campus. There is an on-campus "dance club," called the 'Sco, which also serves alcohol. If you don't drink, no one tries to pressure you, and everyone is open and receptive. The two main social functions on campus are Safer Sex Night and Drag Ball. On Safe Sex Night, students dress in almost nothing, learn about safer sex, and get free condoms or dental dams. Drag Ball is a bigger deal. Everyone dresses up as the opposite sex and watches shows performed by students and real drag queens.

Notable Oberlin Alumni Include:

Bill Irwin, actor and clown

David Brown, founder of the art movement Actualism

Jane Pratt, creator of *Sassy* and *Jane* magazines

Liz Phair, musician

Ed Helms, senior correspondent for Comedy Central's *The Daily Show*

Jeffrey S. Ross, medical director of BioGenex Laboratories, Inc.

UNIVERSITY OF PENNSYLVANIA

Founded: 1740

Location: Philadelphia, PA

Phone: (215) 898-5000

E-mail: info@admission.uago.upenn.edu

Web site: www.upenn.edu

Number of Undergraduates: 9,840

Number of Graduate Students: 7,200

Cost: Approximately $39,500 per year

Application Deadline: January 1

Early Decision: November 1

Rating:	Notable Majors/Programs:
Most Selective	Business, Life Sciences, Engineering, Social Sciences, Pre-Law

Size:

○ Small   ○ Medium   ● Large

Location:

● Urban   ○ Suburban   ○ Rural

On a Saturday, students talk about academics:

○ Always   ● Sometimes   ○ Never

Nightlife:

● Intense   ○ Moderate   ○ Laid-back

Politically, Penn leans:

● Left   ○ Right   ○ Split

Diversity:

● High   ○ Low   ○ Medium

Ivy League: Yes!

Students describe Penn in five words:
- High-achieving, super–preprofessional, mind-expanding, coffee-infused, fun-as-hell
- Work hard, play hard, period

From the School

Somewhere in each of us is the unabated love of learning for its own sake. Students throughout the University have the singular opportunity to explore virtually any aspect of the human experience with some of the world's most knowledgeable, thoughtful, and highly respected teachers as their guides. In our culture (and in our hearts) we hold the conviction that knowledge deepened to critical, integrated understanding in these areas is the hallmark of the well-educated man or woman. To those who have the foresight to build a career on such a foundation, and to those who seek merely to know and understand, Penn extends a warm welcome.

—www.admissionsug.upenn.edu

If you're interested in Penn, you may also be interested in:
University of Chicago, Columbia, Georgetown, Harvard, Princeton, Yale

Name: Dana
Hometown: Lansdale, Pennsylvania
Class Year: Senior
Major: Political Science
Extracurriculars: President of the Penn political science honor society; residential college house manager and house technical support; research assistant.
Career Goal: To work in national security and intelligence.

How would you describe Penn's reputation?

The forgotten Ivy League school who graduates its students with impeccable business suits and a desire to be either an investment banker or professor.

Is this reputation accurate?

In general, yes. Friends of mine who have come to Penn from the artsy communities have been converted to J. Crew–wearing, résumé-minded future i-banking consultants or law school students. I am one of very few people looking at "life-changing" jobs after graduation, like the Peace Corps and teaching English in foreign countries. Most here—especially from the Wharton business school—head straight for Wall Street, Corporate America, Capitol Hill, or graduate school.

What aspect of Penn would a prospective student not see on a campus tour?

Penn is a school of nerds, but in a good way. People who were overachievers in high school come here, and become popular in a community of fellow overachievers. As a fellow nerd, I felt totally comfortable here.

The Institution

I was warned that Penn was big and that I'd have trouble finding a niche here. *So* not true. The university is big, but it's broken down into smaller components—i.e., academic departments, college houses, frats/sororities, clubs. And its size makes it liberal, in the democratic sense. For example, during the first two weeks of class, the professors have to "perform" well, like dancing monkeys, because those are "class shopping" weeks when students go to a variety of classes and choose the ones they like best—and drop the bad ones. It reflects poorly on a professor who has half of his/her class drop in the first two weeks. This process of "adding" and "dropping" is incredibly easy compared to other schools (from what I've heard)—it's the click of a mouse.

Students really do run the school. Student representatives sit on the main university committees. Each academic department has an "undergraduate advisory board." The student union organization is very active in putting on student activities—especially the famous "Spring Fling"—and getting renowned speakers, such as Madeleine Albright and Billy Joel.

> "Penn is often confused with Penn State. Let me set the record straight: Penn is the Ivy League, top-tier institution with renowned faculty, a beautiful campus, and exceptional students."
>
> ✦ Jaime, junior

The Education

I said this before, and I'll say it again: Penn students are overachievers. We talk about classes way too much. We don't usually debate political views or current affairs, but we love to debate the upcoming midterm questions. It is unfortunately easier to get your TAs to know you than professors, especially at the freshman and sophomore level—which hurts when getting recommendations. Most of the intro classes are lecture style, but by junior and senior year, you start taking the discussion-based classes and interacting with the professors more. Certainly, for the undergraduate with ambition, it is possible to become very involved with professors: do research for them, take them out to lunch, visit during their office hours and ask questions, attend their speaking engagements. So I'd say getting to know professors isn't easy—it doesn't come naturally—but it certainly is doable. Penn rocks for research opportunities; I've spoken to transfer students who came to Penn for this reason exclusively. Penn tends to produce Rhodes, Marshall, and Fulbright scholars, and lots of students decide to do independent studies in their major or work with a professor on his/her research. It has been very easy for me to get university funding for any research I've wanted to undertake.

The Students

There's a great diversity of thought here. As far as other types of diversity: I have close friends who are Indian, Hispanic, Asian, Catholic, Jewish, and atheist. Certain ethnicities tend to form cliques, especially the orthodox Jewish community (because of the amazing Hillel resources), the Asian community (with Asian frats and clubs), and the Indian community. They're not really exclusive, though.

Penn is not an activist university. The last major outrage was against the quality of dining hall food and against the mice in our college dorms. We only mobilize when an issue affects our quality of life. That said, we have been known to recycle on occasion, if it's on the way to class.

The Activities

Drexel University is nearby, but there is little interaction between the two campuses. They see us as snobby elitists, and we see them as bitter because they couldn't get into Penn. As for the activities at Penn, there are so many campus groups competing for officers and members, it's amazing. The biggest of these are performance groups advertising for their concerts, frats pushing their parties, or community service groups trying to raise money. Most people attend events sponsored by their friends, or those where there's free food. Our newspaper has been rated the most widely read of all university papers (but that's because we all like to have the *Times* crossword puzzle to do during that really boring class).

The Social Scene

Two main places to party: frats and the Quad (a series of dorms with a lot of freshmen). Partying in the Penn sense usually involves drinking, although nondrinkers have recently founded their own organization to show that not drinking is still a valid choice at parties. The drink of choice at frat/dorm parties is usually beer and/or rum and Coke. There really is no pressure to join a frat or sorority. Still, frats are the place to go on Thursday night for a party—not necessarily to join but to make friends.

Senior year is notorious for making drinkers of those that never really drank, myself included. My friends and I, in our senior year, have been known to go get drunk after finishing major projects. We work hard but play hard.

Name: Cezary
Hometown: Franklin Park, Illinois
Class Year: Sophomore
Major: Philosophy and Management
Extracurriculars: Parliamentary debate team; Student Federal Credit Union; Sigma Nu fraternity; intern at American Lawyer Media; two work-study jobs on campus.
Career Goal: Composer/conductor.

How would you describe Penn's reputation?

One of the best in the nation; consistently in the top five nationally.

Is this reputation accurate?

Definitely. People recognize the Penn logo as much as they do the Nike swish. You can't not land your dream internship with the Penn name and reputation backing you, along with simply the best career services department in the Ivy League. Last summer, for example, I interned for a senator. It's hard not to know someone here who's had an internship at Goldman Sachs or Citigroup or some other top Wall Street firm.

> "Penn is a competitive college where students tend to pack their schedules with various résumé-building activities—but they always make time to party."
> ✦ Lirra, sophomore

What would an admissions officer at Penn probably not tell a prospective student? What aspect would a prospective student not see on a campus tour?

Penn is a diamond in the rough of West Philadelphia. It isn't yet as safe a campus as I'd like it to be. It's not because Penn doesn't have enough police on duty—I see police and patrolmen all over the place—but they can't be everywhere at once. Studying in an urban environment has its risks and rewards, and crime is one of the risks. But I believe the benefits far outweigh the risks. So don't be scared off; just be vigilant, and be smart. Also, it rains often, and it is cold most of the year. If you tour campus on a sunny day, keep in mind that it is the exception, not the rule.

The Institution

Penn is a great university when it comes to creating a sense of community. I feel as if I attend a small liberal-arts college, even though this is a major national university. The social circles are tightly knit but very much interconnected; I feel as if I know everyone. The faculty and administration also do a great job of interacting with students via lunches, seminars, speaker series, and the like. The best part, though, is that no matter what you decide to major in, you will encounter faculty who are the best in their fields and super-knowledgeable (yet down-to-earth and approachable). I once asked my philosophy professor a question, and his answer began with, "Well, I've written a book on this subject. . . ." You'll hear that a lot from faculty at Penn.

As far as housing, the college house system fosters a true community environment, in which your residence is not merely the place in which you live, but also your home among friends. There are dances, trivia nights, trips to Philadelphia landmarks, nights at the orchestra, outings to restaurants, scavenger hunts, movie nights, study sessions, picnics, and faculty dinners—all sponsored by the college house. It's hard to *not* get to know everyone who lives in your building.

> "I do wish I had known Penn's stance on AP credit, which is as follows: "f——that . . . we're gunna make you take it again."
> ✦ Jess, sophomore

It is a bit futile describing Penn's campus, since by the time this book goes to print, it will look totally different. Penn's campus is in a constant state of flux. It has changed dramatically—for the better—since I became a freshman: a movie theater opened, scores of new restaurants have sprung up around campus, new buildings like Huntsman went up, student dorms have been completely renovated on the inside and outside, the landscape in Hill Field has been completely redone, and so much more. New renovations are planned for various buildings, including the law school and construction just started on a new building for the engineering school. In fact, Penn's credit rating with Moody's decreased because it has spent so much of its cash, more than any other Ivy, renovating and improving its real estate. The campus will also become even larger in the future because Penn just purchased a large parcel of land next to the Schuylkill River.

Architecturally, Penn is greatly varied; it has Gothic buildings, a library designed by Frank Furness, collegiate buildings by Frank Furness, and, of course, some brick-and-concrete monstrosities from the 1960s. When you put it all together, I think it gives the school character.

Penn's urban setting makes it possible to enjoy all that Philadelphia has to offer, since you are just a cab ride away from all the best spots for nightlife, the Avenue of the Arts, South Street, and many other Philly hot spots. Or you can just walk; none of it is far away. So I guess the best way to describe it is as a large, diverse urban campus that keeps getting larger and better.

The Education

Penn is divided into four undergraduate schools—the School of Nursing ("Nursing"), the School of Engineering and Applied Science ("Engineering"), the College of Arts and Sciences ("College"), and the Wharton School ("Wharton"). One of the first questions Penn students ask each other when they first meet is, "What school are you in?" The College is by far the largest, followed by Engineering, Wharton, and Nursing. Wharton students are really the only ones who try to make themselves stand out and get special attention because they go to Wharton; in the end we're all Penn students, especially since there is a lot of crossover between the different schools. For example, I am in Wharton and the College.

Penn makes it exceedingly easy for you to get as many degrees as you want, given you're willing to put in the time and effort to get it done. I have a friend who entered Penn in all four undergraduate degree programs. You *can* do that . . . it just depends on how much you value sleep. There are also special programs such as the Huntsman Program (combines College and Wharton) and the Jerome Fisher Program in Management and Technology (combines Wharton and Engineering) that synergize different degree programs and disciplines, so you graduate with two degrees and a wealth of specialized knowledge.

Many of the TAs in Wharton and economics courses, as well as the engineering program (from what I've heard), seem to have a very limited understanding of the English language. Also, I've heard many students complain about subjective grading in large lecture courses: an answer could be right in one recitation course, and wrong in another section, depending on the TA. Most professors in the College are chill and very approachable, highly knowledgeable, and intellectual; same for Wharton, except that I find the lectures more on the boring side, but maybe that's because it is hard to get students riled up about topics such as logistic regression. If you're into doing research, you will find plenty of opportunities and funding for it here at Penn; I'm only a sophomore, but I've already written a complete research thesis via the Penn Humanities Forum. And Penn has several great honors programs, such as Joseph Wharton Scholars and University Scholars.

The Students

Penn students are quality people. In general, you hear a lot about young people here and there being future leaders. But when the Penn president told my freshman class at Convocation that we are the leaders of the future, I really believed her, and I still do. As a criticism, though, I think that Penn students tend to be somewhat self-segregating racially and ethnically. You will find entire clubs here at Penn that are entirely Asian or entirely Jewish, not by official club decree or anything, but simply because the members choose new members whose backgrounds resemble theirs. Penn students also tend to associate themselves with their Greek organizations a bit too much; I'd like it if they thought of themselves more as Penn students, as opposed to "insert Greek letters here" Penn students. Politically, Penn has a strong liberal slant, but the conservative bunch tends to be more vocal.

The Activities

There are an amazing number of student organizations—one for every purpose—and it is impossible not to find your niche at Penn via a student group. There's a sport or activity for everything. I'm part of the Parliamentary Debate Association here at Penn; we debate well, we travel to tournaments every other weekend, we're all friends and have tons of fun together.

The Social Scene

One of the reasons I chose Penn was because it is located in Philadelphia, where the beer flows freely, on into the night. Being in a major city like Philly makes it *extremely* easy to have fun on a Friday night. 'Nuff said.

Name: Katherine
Hometown: Sandy, Utah
Class Year: Senior
Major: Molecular Biology and Economics
Extracurriculars: Tap dance, Drummer in Penn Band, Student Committee on Undergraduate Education (SCUE), cofounder of Cognitive Science Undergraduate Advising Board
Career Goal: I want to be a professor of psychology so I can teach at the university level and perform research in the field.

How would you describe Penn's reputation?

Academically, Penn has an excellent reputation, but often only among other elite schools. To the average Joe, "University of Pennsylvania" is a state school, not an Ivy League institution. We even have T-shirts in the bookstore that say "Not Penn State" on them.

Is this reputation accurate?

I'd say that Penn is underrated by the general public. Most people don't realize that it's an Ivy League school, although, in my opinion, it's in the top half of the Ivy League in terms of academics. On the other hand, certain aspects of the school (like Wharton, the business school) are overrated.

What would an admissions officer at Penn probably not tell a prospective student?

1. The elevators in the high-rise dorms are so slow that you usually have to factor in an extra 15 minutes to get to class when using them in the morning.
2. The dining hall food is pretty bad, yet meal plans are required for freshmen.
3. Everyone is required to join the gym for a yearly two-hundred-dollar membership fee.
4. Despite campus diversity, students tend to self-segregate.
5. The pilot curriculum sounds cool, but in practice, the team-teaching system just doesn't work.

The Institution

Penn has the best traditions of any school:

1. Toast at football games. At the end of the third quarter, thousands of pieces of toasted bread rain from the Penn stands in the middle of the playing and singing of a school song. The lyrics are as follows: "Drink a highball, at nightfall / Be good fellows while you may / For tomorrow may bring sorrow / So tonight, lets all be gay! [or '. . . get laid'] / Tell the story of Glory/ Of Pennsylvania / Drink a highball / And be jolly / Here's a toast to dear old Penn!" We throw toast when the song hits the word "toast." Why? It's a tradition! The tradition used to be to drink a toast at this time, but alcohol has long been prohibited in the stands. We've tossed toast since the early 1970s.
2. Penn-Princeton basketball. In the past forty years, either Penn or Princeton has won the

Ivy League title (including ties) thirty-eight times. The rest of the Ivy League games are essentially practice sessions for the two rivalry games that Penn and Princeton play against each other (one at home, one away). Nearly every Penn-Princeton game is sold out, and since the schools are close to each other geographically, there is always a good visiting crowd. There is nothing like thousands of Penn fans chanting in unison or cheering at a game-winning buzzer shot. It is college basketball at its finest. And when Penn scores 100 points or more at a home game (happens maybe once every two years), Abner's doles out free cheesesteaks to every ticket holder from the game.

3. Hey Day—Penn's best tradition. Every year on the last day of classes (a Friday toward the end of April), graduating seniors spend the morning and afternoon drinking, juniors parade around campus to the beat of the Penn Band, and nearly the whole rest of the school observes and cheers them on. Seniors taunt the juniors at Locust Walk (the main walkway of the school), throwing things like shaving cream and silly string. The parade culminates in front of College Hall, where the juniors are addressed by the president, who makes them "officially" seniors. They all wear red Hey Day shirts designed by the class board, and carry canes, to symbolize that they are now "old." The most important part of the costume is the Styrofoam hat. It is tradition to take bites (don't swallow) out of your friends' hats. By the end of the day, your goal is to have as little left of your hat as possible.

> "The competition at Penn can be brutal."
> ✦ Mateo, junior

Housing at Penn is a bit idiosyncratic. There is the typical quad, which is old and where many freshman live. Rooms are dormitory style, the architecture is brick/gothic (typical "college" building), and the building encloses a large green space. Two other primarily freshman dorms (Hill House and Kings Court) also have enclosed spaces and Hill houses a dining hall. On the western end of campus, there are three enormous apartment-style high-rise buildings that house mostly upperclassmen). A lot of students live off-campus. Because so many houses are off-campus, this allows for a more vibrant party scene.

The Education

Students at Penn are much more preprofessionally oriented than students at similar (Ivy League) schools. The College is designed to give students a liberal arts education, but even many of the students in the College are focused on going to medical school, law school, vet school, or business school. Despite this, there is a vibrant community of undergraduates interested in the arts (performance, publishing, etc.), public service, teaching, academia, research, and other alternative careers.

Penn students are pretty competitive, but the amount of competition you will experience varies on what field you go into. If you are in Wharton, you are automatically pitted against your peers. Premeds are also exceptionally competitive. In general, I'd say that students aren't nasty toward each other, even in curved classes when you are in direct competition with people. However, they are nasty to the TAs and professors. Every Penn student thinks he/she is above average and deserves As. They often go to their professors or TAs to get re-grades or to "discuss" the paper.

Because of the size and diversity of the academic offerings, the amount of schoolwork per student really varies. Some departments (communications, Spanish, English, urban studies, education) offer lots of "joke" courses, where you can do practically no work and get an A. Other departments (all of engineering, biology, chemistry, physics, math, etc.) are made up of mostly difficult courses that require lots of high-quality work in order to do well. Engineering students usually either spend more than thirty-five hours on homework each week or have poor GPAs.

Penn is one of the top schools for research opportunities, including for undergraduates. For students who want to go on to get PhD's, these opportunities are priceless. They are also quite valuable to students who want to go on to professional school or straight into a job. Many seniors complete theses, but this is not required, and many of these projects turn into publications in top journals. And since Penn is a major research institution, top researchers in each field come to give colloquia on a regular basis. Most departments have colloquia at least once a week, each given by a famous researcher.

The Students

The "Penn Girl" stereotype—she is a rich Jewish girl from Long Island, New Jersey, or the Main Line (wealthy suburbs of Philly), her father went to Penn, she belongs to a sorority (probably SDT), wears black pants all the time, either has an eating disorder and is too skinny or is too fat but exposes her midriff anyway, and is just at college to get her "Mrs." Degree—is horribly inaccurate and outdated. In reality, only a minute percentage of Penn students are even remotely like this girl. Penn is a huge school with many types of people. It is true that a large number of the students come from Pennsylvania, New York, or New Jersey because these places are the most proximate. However, students come to Penn from all states and usually about a hundred different countries.

Because Penn is liberal, it is a relatively comfortable environment for many people who would be discriminated against elsewhere (gays, blacks, Jews, etc.). However, the environment is more comfortable for some than others. While blacks are not directly discriminated against, sometimes they don't feel "at home" in the wider Penn community. The LGBT community has become increasingly large, vocal, and welcoming in the past few years, but some homosexual students are still ostracized by anonymous drunk frat boys every once in a while. As for religion, the Jewish community is enormous and, indeed, dominant on campus.

The Activities

There are *many* different types of student activities (government, performing arts, athletics, community service, cultural groups, Greek societies, academic groups, etc.) at Penn, and students are *very* involved in them. Most students belong to at least one group of some sort, and many students belong to multiple groups. Athletics aren't as big at Penn as they are at some schools, but they are still a pretty big deal, and student athletic involvement is pretty high. Penn has about thirty varsity sports, so there are opportunities for many different types of athletes. While Penn's music department is not outstanding in the performance area and there are no academic courses on dance, the performing arts community at Penn is huge, with more than forty groups ranging from a cappella to dance to music to theater. There's an all-male Indian dance troupe, a Jewish comedy troupe . . . there is something for everyone. However, because of this, performing arts groups are always competing for rehearsal/performance space, audiences, and even members.

Penn's oldest existing student organization, founded in 1813, is also one that is unique to Penn. It is called the Philomathean Society, and it is dedicated to the pursuit of knowledge and appreciation of the arts and sciences (essentially, a literary society).

Off campus, students can get to the center of Philadelphia in ten minutes. People go out to eat at the hundreds of award-winning restaurants in the city; they also go to the opera, ballet, Kimmel Center, museums, bars, clubs, everywhere. However, because people are busy and there's a lot to do on campus, most students don't go downtown more than once a month.

The Social Scene

Penn has a pretty average-sized Greek system, involving about 30 percent of the population. This is a very manageable number—you don't feel in the minority if you are in the system or if you aren't. No one feels left out, and no matter what you want to do when you come to Penn, you won't feel pressured to join or not.

The typical weekend usually starts on Thursday because a lot of students don't have classes Friday. Most students go out at least one night a week. Whenever you want to go out, there is never "nothing to do" because *someone* is always having a party, be it a frat, an off-campus house, or your friend down the hall in the dorm (though dorm parties are less common). Even during the week, there is at least one party on campus every night. Conversely, you'll find people in the library every night, even Saturday. Spring Fling is just about the only time you'll have a hard time finding anyone studying.

Notable Penn Alumni Include:

> "Wharton has a bad reputation for being snotty and pretentious, but that's really not the case. Wharton students are just . . . more focused."
>
> ✦ Allen, sophomore

Candice Bergen, actress
Charles Addams, creator of *The Addams Family*
Donald Trump, billionaire financier
Kwame Nkrumah, first president of Ghana
Martin Luther King Jr., civil rights activist
Noam Chomsky, linguist and theorist

PENNSYLVANIA STATE UNIVERSITY

Founded: 1855
Location: University Park, PA
E-mail: admissions@psu.edu
Phone: (814) 865-4700
Web site: www.psu.edu

Number of Undergraduates: 34,060
Number of Graduate Students: 6,790
Cost: Approximately $16,000 per year in state; $26,000 out of state
Application Deadline: Rolling

Rating:	Notable Majors/Programs:
Selective	Architecture, Engineering, Sciences

Size:
○ Small ○ Medium ● Large

Location:
○ Urban ○ Suburban ● Rural

On a Saturday, students talk about academics:
○ Always ● Sometimes ○ Never

Nightlife:
● Intense ○ Moderate ○ Laid-back

Politically, Penn State leans:
○ Left ○ Right ● Split

Diversity:
○ High ● Low ○ Medium

Big Ten school: Yes!

Students describe Penn State in five words:
- Four: We are . . . PENN STATE!!!
- Fun-filled, football-loving, party-going, educational heaven

From the School

Penn State is a multicampus public land-grant university that improves the lives of the people of Pennsylvania, the nation, and the world through integrated, high-quality programs in teaching, research, and service. Our research, scholarship, and creative activities promote human and economic development through the expansion of knowledge and its applications in the natural and applied sciences, social sciences, arts, humanities, and the professions.

—www.psu.edu

If you're interested in Penn State, you may also be interested in:
Gettysburg, Rutgers, University of Southern California, University of Texas at Austin, Tulane, University of Wisconsin–Madison

Name: Kathleen
Hometown: Gilford, New Hampshire
Class Year: Freshman
Major: Biology with Vertebrate Physiology Option
Extracurriculars: Blue and White Society, Silver Wings, Red Cross Club, Habitat for Humanity, UMC choir
Career Goal: I would like to enter the Peace Corps, and after serving, I plan to attend medical school.

How would you describe Penn State's reputation?

We are a drinking school with a football problem. Yet a degree from this university is considered top-notch. Everyone knows about Penn State and the alumni are closely affiliated with the school.

Is this reputation accurate?

Yes, there is a lot of drinking and a lot of sports enthusiasm. There is also a lot of school pride and the academics are rigorous. We know how to party hard and study harder. It's all about learning the balance.

What aspect of Penn State would a prospective student not see on a campus tour?

Prospectives wouldn't be told about the level of drinking on campus, or the constant construction. Also, most prospectives don't see the conditions of the elevators and bathrooms.

The Institution

WE ARE . . . PENN STATE! It doesn't take a special occasion to hear these words yelled across the street, down the hall, or out the dorm window (with an airhorn!). We bleed blue and white here, and we know that the reason the sky is blue and white is because God is a Penn State fan! We have tons of traditions, such as the Blue and White game, guarding the lion shrine, Homecoming, Thon, and eating the creamery's ice cream. Even though Penn State is gigantic, somehow you find your niche with close friends and the clubs you join. The school seems like home in no time at all. Rarely do I walk across campus without waving to somebody I know. We are in the valley—Happy Valley—and beauty surrounds us every step we take. Some days I just take a book outside, sit on the steps of Old Main, and take in the beauty around me. . . . The school never has a dead moment, so you'll feel pretty safe walking around; there'll always be someone outside tossing around a glow-in-the-dark Frisbee.

> "People are afraid to come to Penn State because of its size. To those people I say: the more people there are out there, the more people that can be your friends—and they don't call State College 'Happy Valley' for nothing."
>
> ✦ Tom, junior

The Education

Most of the classes I've had are lecture-based with separate sections that meet later in the week. The TAs are extremely helpful and answer most questions. However, if they are unable to answer one, the professors are more than willing to meet with you individually. The professors are active inside and outside of the classroom. I have run into some at football and basketball games as well as cultural events. If you make the effort to meet them, they reciprocate.

Due to the size of the school, students get the opportunity to take a variety of classes. For example, next semester I'll be taking Swahili along with the general organic chemistry and genetics courses. If you want to take an interesting class, then the advisers are able to make sure that the course will fit into the major and will work out any of the quirks. We have the basic Gen Eds, but there is a lot of variety in how to fulfill them.

Having a science major at PSU is very different from having a liberal arts major. I study a lot, drink a lot of coffee, and learn more than I thought possible in a short period of time. For classes such as O-Chem, receiving a 55 percent on an exam is equivalent to receiving a C, which should help you determine the difficulty of some of the science courses. On the flip side, many of the liberal arts majors I know don't need to study as much, drink as much coffee, or stress as much as I do, and, the curves in the humanities courses aren't as high as in the science courses.

Penn State offers many undergraduate research positions. I have a friend working for the biology deptartment who helps determine gene sequences. PSU offers many other job opportunities for students, such as grading papers, proctoring exams, aiding professors, working in the dining facilities, etc. All you have to do is ask and a job will likely be available to you!

The Students

Students here are from across the globe. Every Wednesday night, a group of girls comes into my dorm room to watch *The OC*; I am white and the minority in this group. When I look around, I see a Puerto Rican/Korean, African American, Cuban, and Indian. I wouldn't want it any other way. These ladies have taught me a great deal over the last year, and the different cultures have strengthened each of us with a greater global perspective.

There are also rallies such as "Take Back the Night" march regarding sexual assault and some during homosexual/bisexual week that enlighten students and the public about global issues. Opinions are not stifled. We learn from each other.

We have our strong Republicans and our strong Democrats as well as every other political group out there.

The Activities

Penn State has its share of jocks and geeks. However, the jocks are the most notable group on campus. Our football stadium holds around 110,000 people, so you can't even imagine how crazy football weekends are unless you've been here. Don't get me wrong, though. We don't just chant and sing the alma mater. There are clubs designed to suit everyone's needs. We have community service, singing, religious, academic, and hobby clubs. Also, you can create a club yourself if you get twenty friends to join.

We have many performance art events on campus. The Bryce Jordan Center hosts the popular-culture musical and comedy acts, while Eisenhower Auditorium hosts more theatrical performances. Downtown at the clubs are the more "underground" acts. And you can tell by the cowboy/girl hats when country singers come to town. And big-name performers and speakers are always coming to campus.

The Social Scene

People party anywhere they can. Fraternities and sororities are normally open to all. However, the best parties are normally at the houses or apartments. Alcohol is available to everyone if they try to find it. After a party, it's amazing how many numbers are on your cell phone the next morning labeled "good kisser," "awesome hair," and "sexy!" But then again, Penn Staters are generally friendly even without the alcohol. Men hold doors open and it's not uncommon to say hi to people you pass everyday. If you're friendly, you'll make more friends than your buddy list can hold!

Name: Steven
Hometown: Staten Island, New York
Class Year: Senior
Major: American Studies
Extracurriculars: Founder/editor in chief, *ALT.news* magazine, student government, TA, Delta Chi
Career Goal: I hope to be able to provide for my family, exercise my political agendas, have medical coverage, see friends, have vacation, continue to be creative, pursue hobbies, and be my own boss.

How would you describe Penn State's reputation?

We are known for sports and parties.

Is this reputation accurate?

Completely. Because our school is in the middle of nowhere, there are very few things to do except watch/support our sports programs and drink frat beer.

> "Penn State is arguably one of the top party schools in the country. We have great bars, an extensive Greek system, and people who party like it's their job."
> ✦ Tom, junior

What would an admissions officer at Penn State probably not tell a prospective student? What aspect of your school would a prospective student not see on a campus tour?

This question reminds me of a news report where a black student from another school found himself on the cover of his school's admissions packet. The student was amid a sea of white faces at a football game. The idea was to send prospective students the message that the school was diverse. Turns out, though, the student had never been to a football game and was Photoshopped into the photo and he sued the university. An incident like that parallels how Penn State also misconstrues the campus environment. According to some statistics you'll hear, Penn State is diverse, but in reality, the campus atmosphere feels much different. There is a vast polarization of ethnicities and races throughout campus, and it should also be noted that there have been three to five nationally covered hate crimes in the four years I have been here, in which *really* serious threats were made against presidents of cultural/lifestyle organizations. Turns out there are more than fifty white supremacy groups within the Centre County region. . . . You'll never hear about this during your official campus visit.

Another statistic that you won't get the full story about is the four-year graduation rate. Somewhere around 37–43 percent of incoming freshman will graduate on time. Worst yet, if you're one of the majority of students who do not graduate within this span, the PHEAA grant (which is the loan afforded to students from the state of Pennsylvania) actually expires when a student passes the four-year mark. This is tough for those who take a semester co-op or go abroad.

The Institution

Because I was raised in New York City, I chose Penn State (over a damn good scholarship elsewhere) to be part of the big college experience. Penn State has it all. We have a huge sports culture (some organization recently voted us the most athletic school in the country), a party culture (consistently on several Top 10 lists for party schools), Greek life (one of the biggest in the country), more than five hundred student organizations, and a grand alumni base (again, one of the biggest in the country). Penn State doesn't just typify what college is—it leads the way. Here you can expect an anthology of eighties classics to be belted out as loudly as possible by the resident drunkards.

Job fairs are only good here if you don't have skills relating to creativity. However, if you're a good little robot (i.e., an engineer or business major), expect to have numerous opportunities from school investors such as MBNA, Johnson & Johnson, and Raytheon. And I do recall one graduate school fair . . . one.

Housing for freshmen is terrible but it's a lifetime of memories . . . if you can remember it. A loft here, a *Scarface* poster, and some Christmas lights and presto—it's home. In my first year, buying a couch was out of the question, so my roommate and I "rented" ours from the cafeteria for the year. Once you're not living in the freshman dorms or "East Halls," class is easily accessible by

foot, although I mostly used my bike to get around. On cold days when I was a freshman, I never made it to lectures because the dorms were so far from the classrooms.

> "The school is large, but through activities and clubs, it is easy to find your place here."
> ✦ James, sophomore

The Education

I've learned a lot during college but very few things at class. Two maxims that I took from my education are (1) We're all going to die, and (2) C's get degrees. In my opinion, education is about understanding the real-life problems surrounding the world today, as well as applying material to our own personal situations. The way college students stress over college exams and other academic situations is a little absurd to me. Stress for me isn't an exam. Real stresses are having a family in poverty in the Philippines, or learning an immense amount about the war in Iraq, being against it, and still seeing your country bomb the shit out of it. Not only do these issues and many others like it take a priority in my life, but I would almost always choose throwing a Frisbee around, laying on the lawn with a girl, or biking around State College than sitting though a class that I felt was mundane. Learning about truth tables and how to do chi-squares in statistics aren't exactly on the top of the list as practical solutions to things I care about. But if *you* do, you can certainly have a good academic experience here.

The Students

I have always thought of college as a very big high school, except there are no bullies. There are still plenty of the same types of groups to choose from here. There are the student government people (both liberals and conservatives, and both do little of value), the jocks (kids in the navy Nike jumpsuits), the nerds (these are the kids who not only still play Magic and Dungeons and Dragons but also run the late-night events at HUB—our student center), the international students (always in the Boucke building, the chem building, and the newly built IST building), the minorities (who are broken up into Greek, activist, urbanite), the hippies (they're over on West College . . . many dare to travel to those parts), and last but not least, the GDIs and the Greeks. The GDIs dwell in the apartment complexes, while the Greeks live in mansions—well, at least the males do—while the females live in dorms for an extra year. Greeks laugh at GDIs and dismiss them as former "rush failures." I was only an independent for two semesters. While I had fun as an independent, being Greek allows for networking beyond belief. Not only is there a constant barrage of social options, but the choices of whom to study with are endless. IFC and Panhellenic Greeks have a higher cumulative GPA than that of non-Greeks. Amazing, considering the stereotypes.

Repeatedly I have had friends and acquaintances who have felt discriminated against for whatever reason. They might be overly sensitive at times, but I think if one has to be on guard like that constantly, then it can be said that our campus isn't exactly the bastion of diversity.

> "We are truly in the middle of nowhere . . . you're driving along: cow, cow, cow, forty thousand people, cow, cow."
>
> ✦ Jake, senior

The Activities

We are known for two things: parties and sports. Chess tournaments aren't exactly playing to a sold-out crowd.

People get up as early as 7 a.m. to commence tailgating/drinking for games at noon. When the football game starts, many of the participants go back home instead of attending the game. The fanaticism is ironic; at least in my tenure here, we've never had a decent football team. If we did, I think there might be a riot. But don't worry; we still have other excuses to riot.

Like when the Penn State's men's basketball team made it to the Sweet 16 in the NCAA tournament—there was a riot then. And then there are the Arts Fest riots. Arts Fest is when students migrate back from their hometowns for a festival where all the local artists present their works. It's basically a reason to get together and drink. And it's amazing how many people come back for it! My first riot was my freshman year, during my first Arts Fest. Everyone was pepper-sprayed, and, needless to say, it was wild.

Someone once told me, "You can really see college kids' intelligence come alive in the many ways they figure out how to drink." It's so true—ask about frat parties like the Meatball, the Sailor's Ball, and the Pig Roast. On St. Patty's Day, people wake up at five in the morning to drink at the only Irish Pub, the Phyrst. I guess this all should be in the Social Scene category—but for Penn Staters, partying is the number 1 activity around.

> "People don't seem to have too much trouble finding girlfriends/boyfriends— State College is, after all, the nation's capital for singles."
>
> ✦ Kris, freshman

The Social Scene

I've been to a few other colleges, and our social scene blows theirs out of the water. On campus, there are these posters that say, "70 percent of Penn Staters drink smart." This supposedly means that during the course of the night, students consume fewer than four drinks. I don't know where they got that bullshit. I have never gone through a weekend where someone didn't throw up either in front of my house or on the toilet, or where someone I knew didn't get an underage citation, or get into a drunken brawl of sorts. Smart drinking? I don't know about that. . . . Smart pot-smoking, maybe?

Otherwise, when you live in a fraternity house, there is never a dull moment. Either there are pledges to do your chores, brothers who are playing video games, sorority floors to visit, or girls who are over to hang out; or you can just play no-limit Texas Hold'em with textbook money.

Name: Rafael
Hometown: San Francisco, California
Class Year: Sophomore
Major: History
Extracurriculars: President of the History Roundtable, member of Political Science Association.
Career Goal: College professor of history.

How would you describe Penn State's reputation?

Depends on who you ask. Penn State has a great academic reputation and some really elite departments. However, it also has a party-hard reputation.

Is this reputation accurate?

Yes. The academics are very strong, and my professors very accessible. Also, the party reputation is right, too. When you have forty thousand students all around age twenty and within a few square miles of each other, partying cannot really be prevented.

What would an admissions officer at Penn State probably not tell a prospective student?

Stupid restrictions in the dorms, such as the firewall they put up. Supposedly the computer firewall is to protect us from viruses, but I get viruses e-mailed to me several times a week from the Penn State server itself! The only thing it does is block file sharing, and they say that was by "accident." Bunch of boloney!

The Institution

Q: What do you get when you throw thousands of young adults smack-dab in the center of PA (which is dominated by cow pastures), add a football stadium and a few bars, give them some classes, and add snow for most of the year? A: Penn State! School spirit is incredibly strong here—everyone loves the Nittany Lions and owns multiple pieces of Penn State gear. You cannot go ten yards without seeing someone wearing something with Penn State pride.

> "Classes are easy here at Penn State—once you're in, it's cake."
> ✦ Candace, sophomore

Yell "WE ARE" anywhere on campus and someone will answer "PENN STATE!" Half the students hold season football tickets—which means more than eighty thousand people (nonstudents) travel to Penn State on game days. The student sections stand the entire game, taking a seat only between quarters and at halftime. Outside the stadium, it's tailgating as far as the eye can see, RVs and cars from many neighboring states; and some people come just to tailgate, without even entering the stadium! The game day scene is downright unbelievable until experienced.

Penn State is huge in size, but that's great because it provides so many different opportunities. There are always many events going on, student clubs and organizations for almost any interest, and campus is very much like a vibrant small town. There are huge career fairs for plenty of internship opportunities. Most of my friends have gotten multiple internship offers for this summer already.

> "The majority of the students are either coming to PSU for the in-state tuition or a specific program that is nationally/internationally known."
> ✦ Joe, junior

It doesn't snow too much, but it's almost always overcast and cold most of the year. But when it's sunny, it's gorgeous!

The Education

Penn State is a big school, but as a sophomore, I've found that most of my classes are twenty-five students or less, professors are easily accessible, and with so many people around, it is easy to find your niche. Students help each other through classes rather than try to bring their competition down. I do think semesters are way too long and they need to give time off before finals for studying.

One of the best classes I took here was a history class on the civil rights movement. It met once a week for eight weeks, we had a coordinating professor, and each class we had a discussion with a different professor, thereby providing the students with a different perspective each week. The best part of the course, however, was the mandatory bus trip through some of the major civil rights sites in the South, such as Greensboro, Birmingham, Selma, Montgomery, and Atlanta. Not only did we immerse ourselves for one week on an excellently coordinated trip with jam-packed days, but we met many of the leaders who were actually involved in the civil rights movement. One of the best guests was Johnny Carr, who was still involved in the Montgomery community at age ninety-four. We also met Lewis Brandon III, who helped organize the Greensboro sit-ins and the first cousin of Dr. Martin Luther King Jr.

The Students

Lately, groups have been raising a lot of awareness about issues on race, sexual assault, and the

LGBT community. People here are very conscious of their bodies. Almost everybody is in great shape. Penn State girls have a reputation for being gorgeous. That is definitely true, especially come that first sunny day after winter, when the lawns are littered with hot women wearing very little. Girls here are beautiful! And the students here are very friendly and fun-loving.

The Activities

We may be in the middle of cow country but there are always speakers coming to Penn State. Some of my favorites have been Jesse Ventura, Spike Lee, and John Nash III. Academic departments always sponsor speakers, as do student organizations. Finding a campus group you're interested in is easy; there are so many. The most vocal student groups here are racial groups, women's groups, and LGBT groups. There are a variety of viewpoints presented, though, and often conservative groups will put together a big rally or events as well.

The Social Scene

On Friday and Saturday nights, the town is taken over by dressed-up college students going out to party. Forty thousand students concentrated into a small area makes for a wild town on party nights. I think the party scene has died down a bit recently, but bar nights are getting bigger.

Notable Penn State Alumni Include:

Carmen Finestra, producer
Donald Bellisario, creator of *Magnum, P.I., Airwolf, Quantum Leap, JAG,* and *Navy NCIS*
Guion S. Bluford, first African American in space
Kerry Collins, football player
Paul Berg, Nobel Laureate in chemistry
William Schreyer, chairman and CEO of Merrill Lynch

PITZER COLLEGE

Founded: 1963

Location: Claremont, CA

Phone: (909) 621-8000

E-mail: admission@pitzer.edu

Web site: www.pitzer.edu

Number of Undergraduates: 940

Number of Graduate Students: 0

Cost: Approximately $40,000 per year

Application Deadline: January 15

Early Action: December 1

Rating:	Notable Majors/Programs:
Selective	Media Studies, Social Sciences, Psychology

Size:
● Small ○ Medium ○ Large

Location:
○ Urban ● Suburban ○ Rural

On a Saturday, students talk about academics:
○ Always ● Sometimes ○ Never

Nightlife:
○ Intense ○ Moderate ● Laid-back

Politically, Pitzer leans:
● Left ○ Right ○ Split

Diversity:
● High ○ Low ○ Medium

Five-College School: Yes!

Students describe Pitzer in five words:
- Globally aware, liberal, outgoing students
- Intellectually engaged, interesting, beautiful campus

From the School

Pitzer offers a curriculum that embraces the best of both tradition and innovation. The Pitzer education is a rigorous course of study, firmly grounded in the traditions of learning and intellectual debate found at the great colleges and universities of the world. At the same time, we offer our students the opportunity to design, with the assistance of concerned faculty advisers, academic programs that are truly creative and support and enhance individual interests and aspirations.

—www.pitzer.edu

If you're interested in Pitzer, you may also be interested in:
Antioch, UC Santa Cruz, Lewis and Clark, Pomona, Stanford, Whitman

Name: Bertha

Hometown: Honolulu, Hawaii

Class Year: Sophomore

Major: Undecided—interested in Environmental Studies/Science, Anthropology, and Art

Extracurriculars: Ecology Center, Student Senate (Aesthetics Committee), Claremont student news magazine (design team), Babes and Blankets (club that knits blankets for children's hospitals and such), Hawaii Club, On Tap (tap dancing club).

Career Goal: Bring people back to earth/nature in order to help preserve the native Hawaiian environment (plants and animals . . .) and culture.

How would you describe Pitzer's reputation?

Largely unheard of. One of the first things I heard from someone who actually knew Pitzer was that the *P* in Pitzer stood for pot. Others who have heard of Pitzer often know of it as the most liberal of the Claremont Colleges (5Cs), with a student body of crazy, artsy hippies, activists, and people who couldn't get into the other Claremont colleges.

Is this reputation accurate?

Somewhat. When Pitzer was founded in the sixties, it was the rebel college of the Claremont Consortium. It was—gasp—the first to abolish curfews for female students and the first to create Black and Chicano Studies programs and although the spirit of progressive activism is still present, it is perhaps not as strong as it was during Pitzer's founding years. Despite the few conservative students, Pitzer remains quite liberal, and there are a good number of "hippie"/artsy, environmentally friendly, peace lovin' students. But the part about the student body who couldn't get into the other Claremont colleges is largely untrue. The students here are very intelligent and just because they sometimes smoke pot doesn't mean they don't know what's up.

What would an admissions officer at Pitzer probably not tell a prospective student?

They probably wouldn't talk about the weed smoking, which I don't think is actually any more prevalent than at any other college. But it is definitely the drug of choice. I, myself, don't smoke or drink, and am quite happy at Pitzer. So there is obviously a niche for those like myself.

The Institution

I love Pitzer. I chose Pitzer because it's a small (but not that small, if extended to the consortium) liberal-arts college in California with good educational goals. The general education requirements at Pitzer are relatively small, too, which I saw as great because it leaves more room for personal exploration—which I am needing right now as an undecided major. I also like that I recognize almost everyone, and the professors know who you are. And I don't know how it is at other schools, but at Pitzer we call most of our professors by first name and are even invited to their homes. And I like that we're more down to earth than students at other schools. (Po-*cough*-mona.)

It is easy here to talk to faculty and staff to get things done. If there is a club you want to start, it's easy to start one; if you want to implement a policy change—get larger recycling bins, whatever—it is easy to talk to different groups on campus and see what they think. When issues come up, like the recent changes in external studies or changes to the art policy, Pitzer students get really excited to voice their opinions and share their ideas. It's really cool.

Pitzer is part of a five-college consortium—Pitzer, Pomona, Scripps, Claremont McKenna College, and Harvey Mudd. Each college has its own personality, but what people don't understand is that the colleges are right next to each other, like one big continuous campus, and you can eat at any of the dining halls and take classes at any of the colleges. They're very close knit. Right now, I'm taking Chinese at Pomona, and my roommate is taking drawing at Scripps and art history at Pomona. It is difficult to view or describe Pitzer as a stand-alone college, independent of the other Claremont colleges. Much is brought to each of the 5Cs through our consortium.

The townies are mostly old people, and we don't interact that much. It's an upper-class neighborhood, and right next to the colleges is The Village, a quaint little shopping area, which is really cool, but really expensive. Being from Hawaii, I get a little cold sometimes in Claremont, but I'm told that's just me. This is definitely some of the best weather to be found on the mainland United States unless you like to see major season changes. The only bad thing is the inevitable smog which blows in from Los Angeles once in a while.

People paint murals on campus and sometimes we have "chalk the walk" days where the art collective puts out buckets of sidewalk chalk for anyone to scribble on the sidewalk. The themes of the murals are things like civil rights (Chicano rights, women's rights), the environment, a Bob Dylan quote, a joke, abstract shapes. . . .

The Education

There is no competition, which I kind of miss. My high school was very competitive and it is more difficult for me to motivate myself; competition drives me. For others, Pitzer's is a better environment.

Pitzer classes are mostly discussion-based, minus the pure science and math classes. The only TAs I've had were chemistry and biology lab helpers. Science students are somewhat separated from other Pitzer students because their core classes are taken through the consortium's joint science department, not at Pitzer. As a side note, the joint science department (which includes Scripps, Claremont McKenna College, and Pitzer) is a very good program. It pissed me off when I saw a college guide book that raved about Scripps's science department and railed on Pitzer's. It's the *same* program. Hello? Yes, there are research opportunities. In my first semester of biology last year as a freshmen, our professor started a DNA research project and included top students from my class as her assistants.

It is really neat to go to a school where they emphasize interdisciplinary studies. I really enjoyed taking biology and learning about the environment from a Western science perspective and then taking an ethnoecology class and learning about the environment from an indigenous peoples' perspective. This kind of holistic learning is, I believe, one of Pitzer's strong points.

Pitzer's study-abroad program is also really great. It is based on the cultural immersion model and put together by Pitzer faculty. Pitzer sees intercultural learning as an important part of one's education.

The Students

Aside from the fact that almost everyone is liberal and Democratic, the student body is quite diverse—in terms of ethnicity, socioeconomic background, and interests. The students here are very laid-back—you can wear PJs to class, people walk around barefoot. I also don't think it is most Pitzer students' main aspiration to make a lot of money, but rather, to improve the state of the world.

The Activities

The strongest group on the Pitzer campus is either POA (Pitzer Outdoor Activities) or the Art Collective. POA goes on all kinds of awesome affordable trips all the time (camping, surfing, hiking—to Joshua Tree National Monument, Sequoia National Park, Baja [Mexico], Havasupai [Arizona]—fall break, spring break, every weekend). Last spring break I spent a whole week camping on Catalina Island (part of the Channel Islands) for the low price of $25 and we had good food and kayaks—*everything.*

Pitzer athletics are combined with Pomona College's athletics, making the Pomona-Pitzer Sagehens. I'd say probably only 15 percent of the teams (minus rugby) are from Pitzer, so no, athletics do not play a big role in campus life. Community service is popular in the form of JumpStart—a program that works with preschool-age children one on one. And at Pitzer, student government plays a big role in policy and administrative decisions compared to most other schools.

I personally don't leave campus that often because I don't have a car. (And by "campus," I mean the whole five-college consortium.) The times my buddies and I ventured off campus last year, besides shopping trips, were to LACMA (Los Angeles County Museum of Art), USC, and Huntington Gardens. The Los Angeles county subway has a stop a couple blocks away from campus. The MetroLink is clean, cheap, and easy to use, making the city of Los Angeles easily accessible.

Pitzer has Groove at the Grove every Thursday. The Grove House is a chill little cottage in the middle of a citrus grove; upstairs is a little art gallery, the EcoCenter, and the Women's Center, while downstairs is the kitchen (where they serve up yummy cookies, limeade, sandwiches, and such during the day), and a living room–type area. Oranges and limes are available for anyone to pick. And we also have open mic night there, too, as well as rockin' parties. If I was up at 3:00 a.m., I would probably be writing a paper due the next day. But most likely, I would be snoring away. Most Pitzer kids would be sleeping—or chatting it up in the halls.

The Social Scene

Since we have four sister schools, there are parties at every campus open to everyone. Claremont McKenna College starts partying on Tuesdays at 4:00 p.m., but at Pitzer, not so much. I think it's because our love of beer is not as great, though it's not hard to find beer at Pitzer. My view of this might be a little skewed—I've been put in the substance-free hall for the past two years.

We have no fraternities/sororities—thank God. We do have the PGS (Pitzer Gentlemen's Society), previously PMS (Pitzer Men's Society—can you believe it took so long to change the name?). But they don't have any sort of hazing week, and PGA is open to anyone, even if you don't play golf. (That was a joke. No one at Pitzer plays golf.) Mostly, they do community service and drink beer.

Name: Chris
Hometown: Westport, Connecticut
Class Year: Sophomore
Major: Political Studies/Environmental Policy
Extracurriculars: Student Senate, Outdoor Club, volunteer at local juvenile detention center, admission tour guide, residence-hall government.
Career Goal: Undecided. I have lots of ideas. I want to live lots of places and cannot see holding one specific job for more than five to six years at a time.

How would you describe Pitzer's reputation?

It depends on what part of the country you are from. Pitzer has achieved prestigious status among many circles of high school students on the West Coast, but is not all that well known on the East Coast. Within the Claremont Colleges, Pitzer is often referred to as the "conscience of Claremont" because of students' tendency to be left-leaning and politically active. Each Claremont college is associated with certain stereotypes, and in the case of Pitzer, that label would be drug use—particularly pot.

Is this reputation accurate?

Pitzer is a community of individuals, much more so than the other Claremont colleges. That said, sure, there's drug use on campus. And while students overwhelmingly lean left of center, I know conservatives and they tell me they feel free to express their views inside and outside of class.

What would an admissions officer at Pitzer probably not tell a prospective student?

An admissions officer would not talk about the popularity of recreational drugs on campus—not because they are trying to hide anything, but be-cause it's not something you would be aware of, unless you're a student.

The Institution

I chose Pitzer because of the limited core requirements and resultant flexibility. I could take courses that interested me right from the beginning. Coming from an East Coast boarding school, my first semester was quite a culture shock. But you get used to it. With weather like this, how could you not? At Pitzer you can start your morning at the Gold Center pool, make it up the slopes for skiing, and out to the beach for surfing in the same day. Claremont is an upscale town, full of boutique stores and fancy restaurants, on the edge of Los Angeles County. The cost of living is high; while most students live on campus, you might save money by living in town. Do students and townies interact? No!

There is a ton of school spirit—but you are more likely to find it in common causes such as a student hunger strike to unionize dining hall employees than at an athletic event. Pitzer is a young school, which means: (1) the campus is beautiful, but don't expect Thomas Jefferson to have carved his name in the cement or anything—it's a different aesthetic than that northeastern brick-and-ivy; (2) Students are not at all affected by the school's prestige; it's not really an issue yet—come back in ten years. That said, Pitzer has become increasingly competitive in recent years with the largest percentage increase in applications among the Claremont colleges. This is an exciting time for students to be here.

The dorms are outdated, but the rooms are huge and have tons of storage space. Pitzer is in the process of building new residence halls that will open in fall 2007.

I bet that students and administrators at Pitzer have a closer working relationship than any other college in the country. Students are voting members of every standing committee at the college—that includes the Faculty Executive Committee, which deals with tenure and promotion, to the Campus Life Committee, which allocates funds for parties, and everything in between.

The Education

All of my classes are discussion-based—no TAs at Pitzer. Anything talked about in class is fair game for dorm discussion, especially hot-button political issues. Students work hard, but the environment is laid-back—nobody will ever ask you what your grade was on a paper. There's no honor code. Very little cheating. Pitzer's atmosphere encourages self-respect.

In terms of political activism among professors, the same teacher you have for sociology might be leading a 50-mile workers' rights march later the same day. Pitzer does not have departments per se, but field groups. Students often consider the strongest to be Political Studies, Sociology, Psychology, Premed, and Media Studies (this is the department Pitzer takes the most pride in).

Virtually every junior and senior I know has studied abroad. Students that have completed both SIT and Pitzer programs prefer the Pitzer one. Pitzer is known across the country for its strong experiential yet academic study-abroad programs. One of Pitzer's graduation requirements is Social Responsibility for which you must complete fifty hours of community service.

From 2001–2004, Pitzer students were awarded:
- Sixteen Fulbright Scholarships
- Three Rotary Ambassadorial Scholarships
- Two Freeman Asia Fellowships
- Two Watson Fellowships
- Two Coro Fellowships
- Two American Sociological Association Minority Fellows
- One Udall Fellowship
- One Woodrow Wilson Foundation Award
- One teaching/study grant awarded by the French government

The Students

Pitzer is super-accepting of minority groups and students with nontraditional lifestyles. A handful of students are religious, but for the most part, students at Pitzer do not attend worship on a regular basis. Most of the students I know seem to be either paying full tuition or receiving a huge financial aid package—there is little middle ground. About half of the student body is from California. Other states heavily represented include New York, Oregon, Washington, Connecticut, Maryland, and Texas—all blue states, with the obvious exception of Texas. Count on Pitzer students being up to date on world events. I have friends that read multiple international papers every day.

The Activities

We are always up to something. A 3:00 a.m. walk through campus on a Wednesday night might reveal students finishing a thesis, a movie being shot, a party, people getting high, lots of students studying for exams, and maybe even the occasional streaker, screaming to wish you a happy Wednesday.

The Pitzer campus could be described as a big piece of art. Any wall or building side throughout the campus is available for students to paint on. The Campus Aesthetics Committee allocates space—I have never heard of anyone being denied.

The Social Scene

Freshmen tend to party a lot more than other students. While there are on- and off-nights, you can find distractions every night of the week. Traditional big party nights are Tuesday, Thursday, Friday, and Saturday. Friday is often more low-key than Thursday or Saturday nights. Most parties occur in public spaces on campus, or in dorm rooms.

There's no Greek system at Pitzer and we like it that way. It's super easy to meet new people and change groups if you get in with a scene you don't like. I met most of my friends through living in the dorm. Dorm life at Pitzer is great, and it's where you will definitely want to live at least through your junior year. A large number of seniors choose to live in the surrounding cities. They have the independence of having a house, but end up spending a good deal of time on campus because that's where all the events are.

Name: Javier
Hometown: La Jolla, California
Class Year: Freshman
Major: possibly Human Biology and Dance
Extracurriculars: Student Senate, Pomona-Pitzer hip-hop dance team, Pitzer's Hiphopanonymous Club.
Career Goal: I hope to either pursue my MD or PhD. Or I'd like to go into research: biomedical or genetic engineering.

How would you describe Pitzer's reputation?

Pitzer is a great school with great academics. It is one of the most diverse colleges in the nation.

Pitzer's joint science program with two other Claremont colleges is also a distinguished program. It's a very classic liberal-arts college.

Is this reputation accurate?

Yes. Pitzer's students come from many different backgrounds, and most of Pitzer's students study abroad. Its academics are reflected in how a high percentage of students who apply to medical school are accepted. Pitzer definitely has a renowned standing among other liberal-art colleges.

What aspect of Pitzer might a prospective student not see on a campus tour?

There is nothing to hide about Pitzer. When prospective students come on campus, they see everyday life. That is one reason why Pitzer becomes every one's first choice after they visit the campus.

The Institution

Pitzer's size is great. You get a close experience with your professors due to the small class sizes. Everyone knows each other and there is a great bond and comfortable feeling among the whole student body. The surrounding area is quiet, peaceful, and really nice. The weather is really nice, especially if you are from a cold area. The physical layout of the campus is exceptional—it seems like everything is connected, and the college is a big family, with easy access anywhere. The relationship between students/administration is great. There are great internship programs here, and you get a big foot in the grad school door. What a fantastic place! Pitzer definitely met all of my expectations.

The Education

Classes are talked about 24/7; it is funny (and scary) to say that in most conversations we have, someone always *has* to relate the topic to one of their classes. This shows that the education here is not just ingested but really applied, making us better, smarter, and more critical thinkers.

The Students

There is a ton of diversity here on campus. Everyone gets along well since we have the same goals in mind—to better the community—and the small living environment brings us close to other students. The religious support here is really big, too. The student body tries to observe most religious holidays. I can say that here on Pitzer's campus students are very liberal, mostly Democrats. Students are from all over the United States, and we also have many international students.

The Activities

Here at Pitzer, everything is for the students, by the students. Student Senate plays a big role in decisions and policy development, and students vote and make happen what they want to see on campus.

When students are not working, we are into an adventure! Usually involving food. Either in search of food . . . or really, anything that is edible.

The Social Scene

Party. Well, that sure is one word always mentioned on weekends. Every weekend there's something to do. There's no reason to go off campus—the 5Cs contribute to much of the social life. The parties here are safe, and students go to have a fun time. Everyone gets along well at the parties and can definitely meet a lot of people there.

Everyone is *very* friendly, courteous, and respectful. When my friends from elsewhere came to visit me, they were very surprised to see that everyone walking down the halls or sidewalks said hi, even though my friends were weird strangers on campus. After a while, they got so used to it that they thought the ones who didn't say hi to us were the weird ones.

Notable Pitzer Alumni Include:

Anne Archer, actress

David Bloom, NBC journalist

Debra W. Yang, first Asian-American woman to serve as United States Attorney

Fabian Núñez, Speaker of the California State Assembly

Jessica Hurley, writer

Thomas T. Perls, professor, geriatrician, and author

POMONA COLLEGE

Founded: 1887

Location: Claremont, CA

Phone: (909) 621-8000

E-mail: admissions@pomona.edu

Web site: www.pomona.edu

Number of Undergraduates: 1,530

Number of Graduate Students: 0

Cost: Approximately $39,000 per year

Application Deadline: January 2

Early Decision: November 15

Rating:	Notable Majors/Programs:
Most Selective	English, Life Sciences, Social Sciences

Size:
- ● Small   ○ Medium   ○ Large

Location:
- ○ Urban   ● Suburban   ○ Rural

On a Saturday, students talk about academics:
- ○ Always   ● Sometimes   ○ Never

Nightlife:
- ○ Intense   ● Moderate   ○ Laid-back

Politically, Pomona leans:
- ● Left   ○ Right   ○ Split

Diversity:
- ○ High   ○ Low   ● Medium

Five-College school: Yes!

Students describe Pomona in five words:
- Really happy, intellectual, laid-back students
- Best of the Claremont Colleges

From the School

The heart of a Pomona education lies in training the mind broadly and deeply, in developing the kind of intellectual resilience that equips our students for lifelong learning. . . . In short, Pomona strives to create intellectual entrepreneurs—people who are equipped to lead, able to see beyond the status quo, and prepared to stake out new directions, whether in the arts, in business, in the academy, in government, in old or new media, or in education.

—www.pomona.edu

If you're interested in Pomona, you may also be interested in:
Amherst, Claremont McKenna, Davidson, Grinnell, Reed, Stanford

Name: Colleen
Hometown: Summit, New Jersey
Class Year: Senior
Major: English
Extracurriculars: swing dancing; admissions office (tours, interviewing, etc.); kabuki.
Career Goal: undecided.

How would you describe Pomona's reputation?

Pomona isn't very well-known by laypeople—even people in the neighboring towns think Pomona is a community college! By other colleges, graduate schools, and large employers, however, we're very well-respected—quite a few companies come on campus to recruit, and our medical school acceptance rate is through the roof.

Is this reputation accurate?

Yes. Pomona is a great school; it's a shame that no one's heard of it.

What would an admissions officer at Pomona probably not tell a prospective student?

Pomona's acceptance rate has seriously decreased over the past few years—it's under 20 percent now—and that's often downplayed by the officials. We also (shh!) have "modular housing units," meant to be temporary; "Trailer Clark," as it's sometimes called, isn't on any of the campus maps, and admissions officers do their best to avoid mentioning our shameful residential secret.

The Institution

Aside from the trailers, housing is *amazing!* Two-thirds of rooms on campus are singles or two-room doubles; a quarter of freshmen get singles; and the rooms are great! Many rooms have private (two-person) bathrooms, and fireplaces and built-in bookcases are also pretty common. The campus is very green and pretty (it should be; the gardeners are always ripping out anything that isn't blooming and installing new, flowering plants), and, although it's meant to look East-Coast-College-y, it's also very typically Southern California, with red tile roofs and low-slung stucco buildings. And the weather is not to be under-rated—while my friends on the East Coast are snowed in in their dorm rooms, I'm at the beach. The two outdoor pools are open all year, and Frisbee and volleyball are always popular.

Freshmen are particularly well taken care of, with a unique sponsor group program—twelve to twenty-two freshmen are placed in a hallway with two sophomore sponsors, who become parents/advisors/best friends. Sponsor groups, which are typically organized around lifestyle and interests, become extremely close and most students remain friends with their sponsor groups throughout their time at Pomona. The instant family and security of the sponsor group is pretty special, and makes transitioning to college easy.

The college gates are a big part of Pomona tradition. As a freshman, you run through the gates following Pomona's mascot, Cecil Sagehen, chirping for the first time in your college career. "Let only the eager, thoughtful, and reverent enter here," the gates read, quoting a past president. And that is exactly what the college expects from its students: eagerness, thoughtfulness, and reverence (well, respect, really) for the academic institution and the people in it. As a senior, you exit the gates, promising to bear your "added riches in trust for mankind." Most Pomona students take this very seriously; you tend to see Pomona graduates taking idealistic, save-the-world type jobs instead of making lots of money on Wall Street (although some certainly choose that route also). The gates without question define the types of students Pomona seeks, and, cheesy as it sounds, most Pomoniacs stay true to those words.

The institution at Pomona is quirky and fairly accessible. Three faculty members and three deans live on campus, along with the president, and it's common to see Dean Quinley strolling (or being dragged) around campus with her four Jack Russell terriers, or to receive a formal invitation to the president's house for dinner. Although there are some areas that could be finessed—most notably, study abroad and the registrar—Pomona as a whole is a warm and welcoming place.

> "Pomona's name will get me as many opportunities as Harvard."
> ✦ Dale, sophomore

The Education

Pomona prides itself on its discussion classes, and prospective students should be aware that they will be expected to speak up—often. As a humanities student, I can count on one hand my nondiscussion-based classes—even in Introduction to Psychology (which is generally more lecture-oriented), professors expect frequent student participation and interaction. Pomona's small size and small classes makes it less intimidating to participate, but still, this isn't a place for kids who like to simply sit back and take notes. Without any graduate students, contact with professors is very high, and science and social science professors especially recruit primarily undergraduates for their research.

Work here is hard, but manageable—except during April, when senior theses are due. Professors are dedicated, though—my thesis advisor marked passages in books for me, answered any e-mail question no matter how trivial, and returned my entire thesis with ample corrections and suggestions within twenty-four hours during the final week before the deadline. I've been blown away by the commitment and enthusiasm from the professors here, as well as the depth of their intelligence.

Pomona is a member of the Claremont Colleges, so Pomoniacs are free to enroll in classes at any of the other schools in the consortium; however, Pomona, as the largest school, has the greatest diversity of curriculum, so most students tend to stay on campus for their classes.

> "The worst situation to be in as a freshman at Pomona is not to get along with your sponsor group."
>
> ✦ Andre, senior

The Students

I chose Pomona for its people—this was the only campus I visited where students greeted me, a li'l ol' prospy, and seemed genuinely happy on campus. The average student is articulate, friendly, and intelligent—I'm constantly amazed by the quality of conversations I overhear. People I might have stereotyped in high school as jocks or prom queens turn out to be multidimensional and multitalented. That was one of the biggest surprises for me—seeing the high-school hierarchy totally abandoned and realizing everyone around me was interesting, smart, and friendly—even the biggest nerds are cool at Pomona.

Freshmen are particularly well taken care of, although there are definitely some class divisions on campus, since upperclassmen tend to live on a different part of campus than the lowerclassmen. Academics are also often polarized by class—freshmen into the usual smorgasbord of introductory classes, and seniors into their upper-division seminars and thesis meetings.

The Activities

The five-college social scene affords a pretty endless array of parties, lectures, concerts, etc. Getting off campus is a little tougher—Southern California's public transportation system is laughable—but luckily, with 5,000 college kids on adjoining college campuses, there's always something happening, and always new people to meet. Involvement levels range from me (extremely lazy) to my suitemate ("Let's play Frisbee!" "Let's go to a senate meeting!" "Let's eat at Pitzer tonight!"). But there's definitely something for everyone. And no matter how busy they may be, everyone remembers to take time to just hang out.

The Social Scene

Yes, there is alcohol at Pomona. That said, pressure to drink is virtually nonexistent—I've asked for Shirley Temples at parties, and no one's given it a second thought. Partying is one aspect of the social life, but a fairly small one. Pomona doesn't really do the frat thing, so most parties are open to the whole 5C student body.

Sponsor groups are the first source of friends at Pomona, the instant social network and security blanket; after that, it's kids from Shakespeare class, fellow AAMP mentorees, friends of sponsor group friends, etc. You quickly start to recognize everyone at Pomona—it's just not a big school—but that still leaves four other colleges of fresh faces at which to find friends. I don't get tired of the small community—I'm constantly reevaluating my opinion of people I already know as well as starting a conversation for the first time with someone I've recognized since freshman year.

Name: Eldon
Hometown: Phoenix, Arizona
Class Year: Senior
Major: English, with creative writing emphasis
Extracurriculars: Student AIDS Awareness Committee, Queer Resource Center, Queer Questioning and Allied Mentor Program, Resident Adviser.
Career Goal: Teacher/novelist.

How would you describe Pomona's reputation?

It's very well known and respected in liberal-arts circles, not very well known by the wider public. Students are known for being laid-back yet hard-working and the school for having rigorous academics.

Is this reputation accurate?

Compared to other schools, I think so. I've taken classes at the other four colleges and abroad and our academics are definitely challenging and rewarding. I also feel that the campus atmosphere is laid-back and all of the people are friendly.

> "Townies leave their retirement communities to attend our lectures and concerts, but other than that, they just stay home and call the police for noise complaints."
> ✦ Carmen, sophomore

What would an admissions officer at your school probably not tell a prospective student?

That it's not as easy to get into Los Angeles as one would expect . . . but they're working on that.

The Institution

I love Pomona. I chose to come here because of the small liberal-arts feel, coupled with the feel of a bigger school due to the four other colleges in the Claremont Consortium (CMC, Scripps, Pitzer, and Harvey Mudd). I also chose it because of the sponsor program that puts twelve to twenty freshmen together in a hall with two sophomores who serve as mentors—it was really helpful freshman year to have an immediate support network.

The surrounding town, Claremont, is more conservative and aged than the colleges and doesn't really cater to college students. But there's enough to do on campus that this isn't really a problem. The school is split up into North and South campus, and students have a tendency to become lazy and feel that they're far away from each other and don't like walking to the other campus. But in reality, they aren't far apart at all.

As a senior, I feel very well supported by the career development office in my search for a job and confident in my abilities to find a job I'll like. The career development office is rated one of the best in the country and there are a bunch of internship and job opportunities on and off campus.

The Education

The academic life at Pomona is one of cooperation as opposed to competition, which was a big deciding factor in my search for colleges. Most classes are discussion-based and the professors really take the time to engage their students and help them understand the material. Professors are active in the life of the college and regularly give extracurricular talks and lectures on their research or current events.

Study abroad is really easy to do here because it's the same cost as tuition, but some people complain that it would be cheaper if they did study abroad independent of the school.

The Students

Everyone at Pomona is generally open-minded, liberal, generally politically apathetic, friendly, and polite. This means that sometimes issues of diversity that need to be discussed are overlooked. Last year we had a number of racial incidents and there was a lot of divided discussion on campus. But when there was an event that appeared to be a hate crime, the community really pulled together. Even though it turned out to be a hoax, the show of solidarity was inspiring. While I do believe that some people only pay lip service to diversity, I think we're a community that does care about each other. All groups on campus, like the Queer Resource Center, the Office of Black Student Affairs, and the Asian American Resource Center, try to be inclusive, but the students in the majority sometimes assume they aren't welcome, which isn't the case. Students generally mix along all sorts of lines, ranging from their sponsor groups to sports to activities; there are no definable "cliques."

The Activities

Athletics are not a big part of campus life—people play them, but games aren't attended en masse. An organization that I'm passionate about is the Queer Resource Center (QRC). They put on events that address the needs of the queer community on campus. While the campus atmosphere is generally tolerant of LGBT students, the community is fairly small, and students not involved with QRC events or QQAMP generally blend into the general population and have to find their own support network.

I go to the other 5C campuses fairly often, though it is also possible for people to sequester themselves in their own campus. Concerts are pretty well attended depending on who's performing. We have a lot of big-name performers; since I've been here, people like John Mayer, Beck, Ben Harper, Jurassic 5, Maroon 5, and the Black-Eyed Peas have come to campus. We've also had big-name speakers like Senator Barbara Boxer. There's also a movie theater on campus that plays movies that have recently left mainstream theaters. There are some big dances like Harwood Halloween and Smiley 80s. Students have input into policy decisions, and there are usually committees formed that include students. If it's 3:00 a.m. on a Wednesday night and I'm still awake, I'm probably writing a paper and looking for food to help keep me awake.

> "The weather is unbeatable. Where else can you have an 80-degree day in the middle of winter?"
>
> ✦ Bryson, junior

The Social Scene

The majority of people party on Fridays and Saturdays, though Thursdays can also be party days, and really, any day of the week is prime party time. Most people drink alcohol, and on the weekends they generally go to a school-sponsored party. There are also other events like movies and trips to amusement parks or museums. Some people do homework on weekends, and this can vary depending on workloads. There are no official frats or sororities here, but there are some "social clubs" that basically mimic frat drinking culture without the community service or any other redeeming qualities. They aren't taken too seriously.

The dating scene is pretty nonexistent—people either hook up or act like married couples. It's not too hard to meet new people; I've met most of my friends through living near them in the dorms. Dorm life is really nice. You really feel a sense of community. This is partly because around 98 percent of people live on campus.

Name: Anne
Hometown: Pawtucket, Rhode Island
Class Year: Junior
Major: History

Extracurriculars: Work at the Organic Farm and with the Peace Coalition.
Career Goal: No idea. Something noncorporate, noncubical, non-sell-out. Maybe work for an NGO abroad. Maybe a nonprofit here. Farm? Set up a community center? Teach at a progressive school?

How would you describe Pomona's reputation?

We have a reputation for being very liberal and very happy.

Is this reputation accurate?

I think that the reality of liberalism on a campus is hard to judge. I know that once I leave the Pomona Bubble, there are going to be far fewer people who hold the same views that I do. So sure, we are a liberal place. In terms of happiness, it's hard to say. The weather helps a lot. Pomona feeds us a lot. We have snack every night and you can always find free beer. But obviously there are other realities. There are people who don't feel comfortable here; there are people who are unhappy, or depressed, or worse. But all in all, here people smile a lot.

What would an admissions officer at Pomona probably not tell a prospective student?

That there are realities of racial prejudice and homophobia here. It's been in the news—some crazy incidents where individuals or groups express hate toward more marginal groups on campus. People are scared. Some people feel really silenced. There are people who don't care. There are people who don't think about these realities after the teach-ins and rallies have ended. The way that the community has responded is also something that can't be seen on a tour. I really think that the resulting community building and direct response have strengthened us. There is something really powerful going on here. People are becoming active.

The Institution

Well, I think Pomona is pretty amazing overall. Weather is basically always sunny and warm. It gets cool at night, so you can whip out the scarf and mittens if you want (I do). Snack five nights a week is quite nice. Free beer six nights a week. Also nice. We have a symposium every other week with more gourmet treats and wine.

It's a funny place. Things are very clean. And newish. And then there are all these crazy smart twenty-somethings buzzing around. Full and drunk.

Or not. Lots of skateboards. Lots of inside jokes about the school itself or administrators or teachers. Like, "Oh man, so-and-so looks like he is about to melt he is so old." And everyone knows what you're talking about.

I'd like to take a moment to give general recognition to the *amazing* people here. Everyone knows that we are in an incredible community. The students here astound me again and again.

It's like we're all in this sort of parallel universe of faux perfection and intellectual intensity and youth. And we all know this. It's fun to look out of the bubble and realize how bizarre this place actually is. But it's also very normal in other ways, I suppose. Just depends on how you look at it.

The Education

The education is amazing. So rigorous, so inspiring. As a history major I am so impressed. Classes with these wise, wise professors letting you in on a bit of their knowledge. I'm taking this class in the religious studies department that's all about approaching life, really. We meditate and pray and read and talk in order to figure out who we are in this world. I mean, that is amazing! With this man who is incredible—who you want to be like. As for the number of professors that I have had who I genuinely want to model myself after in one way or another, I think it's pretty much all of them. Well no, but close. Professors are there for you. To work with. To talk with. I have grown so much as an individual in this crazy, crazy world because of this education. I am able to look at the world and deconstruct these institutions that run it. I've been taught to question. To be critical. To not sit back and take things as they are. It's been incredible. I wish I could stay here for four more years.

The Students

We've got kids from all over the place. I have friends from almost every state. Which is great for planning cross-country trips. Lots of kids are from California and the West Coast. But it's definitely not the overwhelming majority.

Diversity is a hard thing to describe. I guess that, statistically speaking, this is a very diverse school. I don't feel like there's so much interracial flow. Most of my friends are white. I think that there is a lot of acceptance or integration of LGBT kids with the "straight" community, but that might just be my take on it from the people that I spend time with.

It's not the most activist school. We try. There are waves. Certainly in terms of dispositions, it's pretty progressive. Lots of talk. I'm not sure what that says. There're little communities that are very active. The Farm community is active in a very different way from the Queer Resource Center or the Asian American Resource Center. It's there in pockets.

The average Pomona student: very very very smart, progressive, challenges the traditional systems of thought, works hard and parties hard, a little odd, and has no idea what to do with his/her life.

The Activities

We party a lot, and have themed events, like radical Fridays. Lots of meetings of various groups on campus. Lectures are well attended. Little bands and big bands. Farm parties. I am most involved in the Farm, so it's easiest to talk about that. Some good work outside in the dirt. Nibbling greens and talking about what's going on in the world or on campus or in the day. We have parties on Fridays a lot. Good food. Music sometimes.

Kids hang out in their groups. Mingling definitely occurs. But people seem to have pretty tight friend groups, I guess personality-based mostly. But as the years have gone by, I see my class getting closer and closer.

When hanging out, my friends and I go to the pool. Walk up to Pitzer to the cactus garden. Go hiking on Baldy. Rally and go to Joshua Tree. Watch movies. Talk. Smoke. Drink. Nap because we stay up too late working or partying.

The Social Scene

People are pretty outgoing and friendly here. Open to the quirks of very, very smart people. Kids come out for the beer and enjoy each other. There are also the kids who work all the time and don't come out much. Or the kids who are not so party- or substance-oriented. But we're sort of this large family. The scene is just excellent. I love the people here.

Notable Pomona Alumni Include:
Bill Keller, executive editor of the *New York Times*
John Cage, experimental music composer
Kris Kristofferson, country music songwriter, singer and actor
Paul Fussell, cultural historian, author
Richard Chamberlain, actor
Robert Shaw, conductor

PRINCETON UNIVERSITY

Founded: 1746

Location: Princeton, NJ

Phone: (609) 258-3060

E-mail: uaoffice@princeton.edu

Web site: www.princeton.edu

Number of Undergraduates: 4,779

Number of Graduate Students: 2,012

Cost: Approximately $37,000 per year

Application Deadline: January 1

Early Decision: November 1

Rating:	Notable Majors/Programs:
Most Selective	History, Economics, Politics, English

Size:
○ Small   ● Medium   ○ Large

Location:
○ Urban   ● Suburban   ○ Rural

On a Saturday, students talk about academics:
○ Always   ● Sometimes   ○ Never

Nightlife:
○ Intense   ● Moderate   ○ Laid-back

Politically, Princeton leans:
○ Left   ● Right   ○ Split

Diversity:
● High   ○ Low   ○ Medium

Ivy League: Yes!

Students describe Princeton in five words:
- Best undergraduate education in America
- Intense, elite, prestigious, historic, gorgeous

From the School

[Princeton University] seeks to provide its students with academic, extracurricular and other resources—in a residential community committed to diversity in its student body, faculty and staff—that will permit them to attain the highest possible level of achievement in undergraduate education and prepare them for positions of leadership and lives of service in many fields of human endeavor. Through the scholarship, research and teaching of its faculty, and the many contributions to society of its alumni, Princeton seeks to fulfill its informal motto: "Princeton in the Nation's Service and in the Service of All Nations."

—www.princeton.edu

If you're interested in Princeton, you may also be interested in:
Amherst, Harvard, MIT, Stanford, Yale, Williams

Name: Natalie
Hometown: Riverdale, New York
Class Year: Junior
Major: English and Theatre
Extracurriculars: I do a lot of theater on campus, both performing and directing, everything from Shakespeare to *The Vagina Monologues*.
Career Goal: Ideally, I'd like to become a world-renowned playwright. For now, the short-term goal is to get into theater administration and lose myself in some tiny, obscure theater company in Manhattan.

How would you describe Princeton's reputation?

People think it's become this terrible bastion of snobbery, wealth, grade inflation, and J. Crew–worship.

Is this reputation accurate?

I think Princeton's image has spun out of control and out of all rational proportion. If the above *was* accurate, I would have transferred out a long time ago. Do we have wealthy students? Of course. Will you encounter snobbish students during your four years here? Find me a top-tier school where you won't. But those types are the exception. For the most part, the people that go here—the people *I'm* friends with—are just very intelligent middle-class college students trying to have as much fun as possible while not getting put on academic probation. In short, don't be dissuaded from applying because your family doesn't own a yacht and possess flawless diction. Mine doesn't either, and I get along fine.

What aspect of your school would a prospective student not see on a campus tour?

We have this rare breed of highly aggressive squirrel that fears no man, woman, or child. They're a force to be reckoned with. After four years, you kind of come to appreciate them. Some particularly ambitious students try to tame them and keep them as pets, but that's not really advisable; if you try this, your odds of being mauled are pretty high.

The Institution

Princeton's campus is absolutely gorgeous. It's like living in a fairy tale. As a senior, I am lucky enough to live in Cuyler Hall, which is a castle. A real castle. You have a view of a stone courtyard from your window. Every now and again, you wake up and think, "Where am I? How in the world did I end up here?" School spirit runs rampant at Princeton. (Orange and black isn't just for Halloween anymore!)

> "Princeton is a powerful campus with a powerful alumni network, and alums definitely look out for undergrads. Need a job or internship? It's yours, kid."
>
> ✦ Jonah, sophomore

The Education

Competition between students exists here, but it's not particularly severe. You'll never find yourself in a position where you have to worry about classmates/roommates sabotaging your work. It's more that, at Princeton, you always feel a nudge to keep up, to be on top of things, to stay at your peak. You compete mostly with yourself, and vaguely to make sure you're still staying at the top of the pack.

And the academics here are great, the teachers dedicated and intelligent. I've taken some truly incredible classes because of them. Particularly interesting ones include: a lecture in the Near Eastern Studies department on the Bin Laden phenomenon; a class on the origins of and experiments in musical theater from Gilbert and Sullivan to Lars von Trier; and a playwrighting course with Erik Ehn, author of *The Saint Plays*.

Princeton does not have a core curriculum, but it does have ten "distribution areas" that you satisfy by taking any class in certain departments: HA (Historical Analysis—one class), EC (Epistemology and Cognition—one class), ST (Science and Technology—two classes), QR (Quantitative Reasoning—one class), LA (Language and Arts—two classes), EM (Ethics and Moral Reasoning—one class), SA (Social Analysis—two classes). Most people complete their distribution areas sometime during their junior year; it seems like a lot, but it really isn't. Classes you want to take for fun more often than not will hack away half your distribution requirements and you'll barely feel any pressure to complete the remainder. There's also a foreign language requirement, but depending on your AP scores and how you perform on the placement exams at the beginning of your freshman year, you may test out of that.

The thesis. Princeton requires every senior to write a thesis in order to graduate. Writing a thesis is both fun and manageable. It's a nice culmination of all your academic work at Princeton, and it's also something that you're pretty much prepared for by the time it rolls around. As a junior, everyone writes one to three Junior Papers (except engineers), and these are like mini-theses that help you get up to snuff. Also, the thesis can take lots of forms. In the English department, for instance, students in the creative writing or theater tracks can write novels or plays (I'm doing the latter).

Also, last thing: Princeton has a bizarre midyear break schedule. The first half of the year ends the second week of December, and everyone goes home for three weeks. Then everyone comes back to Princeton at the beginning of January for a weeklong "reading period" before taking all of our finals from the previous half of the year (yeah, our finals are *after* the break). Then we go home *again* for something called "intercession," then we come back to Princeton and classes start for real. It's weird, but you'll get used to it.

The Students

From what I've seen, the average Princeton student . . . considers a ten-minute walk from their dorm to class to be a long walk (our campus is beautiful, but relatively small!) . . . is a member of an eating club . . . is from New York, New Jersey, or California . . . participates in a sport (be it varsity, intramural, or club) . . . is majoring in Economics, Politics, English, or is at the Woodrow Wilson School (our strongest departments) . . . knows that the campus center stops serving pizza at 2:00 a.m. . . . knows the nearby WaWa staffers by name . . . has a car, or knows someone who does . . . can speak at least one language other than English . . . has never had a lecture taught by a non-professor . . . knows the exact price of a New Jersey Transit ticket from Princeton to New York City . . . and more than occasionally wonders how in the world he or she got into Princeton.

There are a lot of white students on this campus, and there is some noticeable white/nonwhite segregation. Everyone is working on this, though. The Princeton University Band, for instance, has recently formed a friendship with the Black Student Union. "Spectra" is a fledgling organization created for students who want to hang out together without putting themselves into a single ethnic box. And for students who do want to have a more direct celebration of their culture and heritage, the sheer number of campus "cultural" groups—everything from the classical Indian

dance troupe to the Black Student Union—is impressive. I should also mention that the theater community at Princeton is incredible. As a theater kid, you really can pursue your passion for performance/directing/design. And New York isn't that far away. Most Princeton students don't go there often, but it's easy to take the train once every month to Manhattan to see a Broadway play.

The Activities

On a sunny day, you'll see the following people sitting on a lawn at Princeton, hanging out: (1) The sunbathers; you wouldn't believe how many people will lie on a lawn in the middle of New Jersey in a bathing suit when the weather rises above 75 degrees; (2) The Frisbee folks; these guys play their hearts out, while ostensibly doing their best not to hit the sunbathers with their Frisbees; (3) The crazy creek'ers—the ones who bring half of their books out onto the grass outside their dorm, set up a Crazy Creek camping chair, and try to get some work done in the sunshine.

Finally, if I'm awake at 3:00 a.m. on a Wednesday night—God, I don't know if I remember the last time I *wasn't* still awake at 3:00 a.m. on a Wednesday night—that's the point where I'm bleary-eyed, still attempting the three gazillion hours of reading I've been assigned. Or I'm watching dating shows on TV, pretending to be doing the three gazillion hours of reading I've been assigned.

> "Princeton is extraordinarily safe. I can leave my laptop and books on the library table while I take a break for dinner, and when I return I know all my belongings will be right where I left them."
>
> ✦ Clair, senior

The Social Scene

Although I'm sure some students at Princeton choose to live off campus, I've yet to meet them. It's just not practical and the dorms here are so nice. Why leave?

"Parties" at Princeton are basically confined to the eating clubs, with only a small number of room parties happening on a weekend. Depending on which eating club you belong to, your "party" experience will be entirely different. Some are more chill—a bunch of people standing around and listening to music while sipping beer. In other clubs, it's all about Beirut, quarters, robo, and a host of other random drinking games. And at others still, it's all about the music, be it a live band or a well-known and well-loved DJ. Every eating club has a distinct personality. And all together, they eclipse all other aspects of Princeton's social life.

Name: Sophie
Hometown: Redondo Beach, California
Class Year: Sophomore
Major: I major in Environmental Engineering, but I take as many liberal-arts classes as I can. In my free time I sing, I dance, I read, I write. I chose Princeton in part because I could major in the sciences and still do these things—unlike at a tech school, like MIT.
Extracurriculars: Engineering Council, Princeton Materials Research Society, Society of Women Engineers, Flavor (ethnic food club), Epicurious Gourmet Club.
Career Goal: I'm not entirely sure yet.

How would you describe Princeton's reputation?

U.S. News & World Report often ranks Princeton number one as the best school in America. We're said to have brilliant professors, gifted students, and amazing monetary resources, with a beautiful campus thrown into the mix. On the downside, some say Princeton students are rich, snobby, elitists.

Is this reputation accurate?

Mostly. Princeton is one of the best schools in America, our campus is breathtaking, our professors are dedicated, and, through the Freshman Seminar Program, students can take interesting courses—the Physics of Ice Cream, the Physics of Music, the Natural History of Food, Shakespeare in Love, and Public Education in America—that are taught by "celebrity professors." And as far as Princeton students being rich, snobby, and elitist—there are some pockets of that, sure, mostly clustered around the eating clubs.

What aspect of your school would a prospective student not see on a campus tour?

A tour guide wouldn't show prospective students The Street. That's where the eating clubs are, and Princeton doesn't really like to tell prospective students about the eating clubs, and their impact on campus social life.

The Institution

If you're trying to decide whether or not to come to Princeton, think about the following: Princeton is a liberal-arts university. You can't be prelaw, you can't be premed, you can't be a part of a business school. If you're incredibly preprofessional, Princeton might not be right for you. This isn't to say that Princeton graduates don't go on to be doctors, lawyers, or businessmen—they do, and Princeton helps them out with on-campus career advisors. Princeton students just don't feel the need to dive directly into their eventual profession while they're undergraduates. They happily study lots of things instead. Make sure you have diverse interests if you think you'd like to come here.

Look into major departments, and contact students within those departments to find out what they're really like. Every department has a different level of student-teacher interaction, different monetary resources, and different thesis requirements. Princeton may be perfect for you if you study thing X, but not if you're into thing Y. So do some legwork and find out what's what. Also, find out if the department you have your eye on allows cognates; these are courses in other departments that can be counted toward your major if you can demonstrate they're somehow related. Cognates give you a lot more academic freedom in the long run.

Last, even if you get into Princeton, your life isn't going to be perfect. You're still going to face competition, and you're still going to have to deal with rejection. You might not get into a specialized school within Princeton (like the Woodrow Wilson program, "Woody Woo"). You might not get into that a cappella group, and you might get hosed (lingo for being rejected from an eating club). Having a set definition of what your Princeton life is going to be like in advance is a big mistake. Be flexible.

The Education

In a way, the fact that Princeton is often ranked number one colors everything about it. Princeton's administrative decisions are national news, Princeton students are the basis for wild generalization about our generation (see David Brooks's article, "The Organization Kid," *The Atlantic Monthly,* April 2001), and students who live halfway across the world and have never seen Princeton's campus want to get in more than anything else. It's strange. Your classes are all going to be top-notch, and they'll be staggeringly difficult. Your classmates are going to be smart and interesting, and sometimes they're so much smarter and more interesting than you that you begin to feel like you're a failure. It's a lot to put on your shoulders. But it also makes for an incomparable four years.

Princeton has two 12-week semesters, whereas most schools have two 15-week semesters. This means semesters really fly by. Get ready to do lots and lots of work in relatively short periods of time.

Big-name speakers are invited to campus fairly often. We've had Sandra Day O'Connor and Colin Powell just this month. You get to see some of your heroes in the flesh. Also, because we're a top school, we have great placement into top grad schools. (Though recently Princeton's administration started a grade inflation-reduction campaign, which might end up lowering our collective GPAs and making us less favorable candidates as compared to our competition at other top-tier schools. We'll see.)

> "Unlike other Ivies, Princeton has no professional graduate schools on campus, so Princeton gives its undergraduates its complete attention. My freshman seminar professor e-mailed me daily—and this is a man who has written over forty cover stories for *Time* magazine."
>
> ✦ Jonah, sophomore

The Students

Princeton students mix pretty well. There are some small schisms between engineers (the closest Princeton gets to a preprofessional major) and liberal-arts students, between bicker and sign-in eating clubs (meaning the ones you apply and are accepted to versus the ones anyone can go to). But really, none of these are huge issues.

Freshman year, your biggest social scene is going to be in your dorm, and dorms at Princeton vary widely. This upsets some freshman, who see beautiful Rocky and Mathey on their tours, then find themselves assigned to Butler. And though you really have no say in your residential college assignment, here's a quick rundown: Rocky (Rockefeller)—best housing, Gothic, recently renovated. Mathey—Like Rocky, but less tight-knit; all gothic. Forbes—used to be the Princeton Inn; pretty nice, but far from the center of campus, though sometimes you can get a private bathroom. Wilson—

down-campus, more modern, but with huge rooms and great facilities, and because the rooms are bigger, the parties here are bigger. Butler—the ugliest dorm, dubbed "the Butt," but you can get a single if you want one. You can get very, very lucky, or very, very unlucky.

The Activities

You can do just about any activity you can think of at Princeton, and I'd say most students are happy. Students appear to get along with the administration, too, with the campus upstart being the *Tory,* a conservative magazine that does its best to stir up trouble. If you want to see the flip-side of Princeton's glossy, optimistic admissions brochures, get a few issues of the *Tory,* then maybe read some of the editorial columns in our campus paper, the *Prince.*

The Social Scene

Everyone lives on campus, and housing is guaranteed all four years. This makes Princeton really feel like a community of students. The dating scene is made up of joined-at-the-hip couples and sketchy, random, drunken hook-ups. Or you're asexual because of your extreme workload.

The eating clubs are a big thing at Princeton. They're places that you eat, that are more expensive than dining halls and not fully covered by financial aid, and they have various (sometimes snobbish) criteria for membership. In their defense, they're all coed, they're quite nice places to kill time between and after classes, and they're all uniquely different from one another: some are really low-key, others resemble very wild fraternities, and some go out of their way to be classy and exclusive, like tiny country clubs minus the golf courses. They're easy to ignore when you're a freshman. But in your sophomore year, the eating club selection processes—sign-in and bicker—dominates. The Street, where the eating clubs are located, becomes your life. The whole process causes a great deal of anxiety, both for those choosing the sign-in eating clubs (what if your friends all wind up choosing different clubs?) and for the bickerees (what if you get rejected from an eating club outright?). The clubs definitely divide up the student body because they have various levels of prestige, they hold frequent members-only events, and because on a campus where everybody is very busy, people look at meals as their only time for socializing, and you really only eat meals at your eating club. Because of this, if you and your freshman-year friends choose different eating clubs, it's very likely you will drift apart.

Name: James
Hometown: Amherst, Massachusetts
Class Year: Senior
Major: German and Politics
Extracurriculars: Pride Alliance (student-run LGBT group), Brown Food Co-operative (only omnivorous co-op on campus), German Cultural Society, mountain biking.
Career Goal: Save the environment single-handedly, and become an ambassador to an insignificant but rich nation such as Luxembourg.

How would you describe Princeton's reputation?

Princeton is the forgotten number one. People are wowed by its name in the United States, but abroad it carries less cachet than Harvard and Yale. It is renowned for being the "Southern gentleman's school in the North," which is true to some extent.

Is this reputation accurate?

It's pretty close to the truth. There is an air of Southern gentility, a rich, snobby subculture, the physical embodiment of which are the exclusive on-campus eating clubs where students are served multicourse gourmet-style meals by black-suited waitstaff. (If that doesn't bring to mind "old boy entitlement," I don't know what will.) Princeton just oozes money. Students bring their Lexus SUVs to school by the dozens. And according to the school paper, over half the students go into banking and finance after graduation. In effect, if you want to make oodles of money, Princeton's a good bet. You'll make all your connections right here.

What would an admissions officer at your school probably not tell a prospective student?

Princeton tries to downplay the wealth of its student body. When I was visiting campus, the dean of admissions refused to tell my father the percentage of Princeton freshman who had attended private schools, or provide any statistics about the income distribution of those students' families. As a current student, let me tell you—this place is overrun with rich, private-school types.

The Institution

I did not choose to come to Princeton. My parents chose it for me. I am a fourth-generation Princetonian. However, I don't go to eating clubs. (You don't have to do that here if you hate that sort of thing.) I'm a die-hard member of an awesome food co-operative instead.

> "Almost everyone at Princeton has a skill or talent. The quiet, skinny kid who never speaks up in class? He's a published author and/or world-class pianist. The big, All-American meathead? He's a gifted mathematician who has already invented an influential mathematical theorem. These people do exist. They're at Princeton."
>
> ✦ Lyman, senior

Like most schools, Princeton is a bubble. Many students never leave campus. They rarely go to New York City (an hour away by train, which stops right on campus), or even into town. Princeton has no connection to New Jersey, or, more broadly, to the real world. The campus is populated with hardworking students from all over the world who come here because the name Princeton opens doors. Students here produce, and Princeton encourages productivity. Princeton is not an arts school, and there are not many artsy people here. Princeton students will work hard and do their best to get the answers right. Unfortunately, there's not much experimenting in-between.

The Academics

Princeton offers a good mix of classes, taught by professors who range from competent to brilliant. There's a wide range of majors to choose from, and you have a lot of flexibility in choosing classes to satisfy your major. And then each academic department is different from the next; before choosing your major, check out how big the department is, how well-funded, how close-knit.

Also there is a strict honor code at Princeton, which in many regards resembles the English Star Chamber in that it has none of the guarantees of a modern judicial system. A friend of mine was forced to leave the university after being found guilty of cheating—something she strenuously denies; five professors came out to support her, but to no avail. Don't get on the honor code's bad side; they'll kick you out in a heartbeat.

The Students

Princeton students are often so (voluntarily) overworked that they don't have time for dating, playing, or going to the dozens of academic and cultural events held on campus every week. Instead, they study. Ditto for typical collegial goofing off—you won't find too much of that here. Either "work hard, play hard," or "study all day and occasionally drink like mad" could be our motto.

There is also not much political activism at Princeton. You rarely see a protest, or find people overly concerned with political issues. They just don't have time. You also won't find many LGBT students. LGBT group officers (myself included) have almost given up trying to foster an LGBT social life on campus, because there's no one around to take advantage of it. Everyone's either straight or deeply closeted. I guess it's not much better if you're straight—Princeton's straight dating scene is, in a word, nonexistent.

Top-tier schools don't differ so much in the quality of education they offer. What separates one from the next are the programs (Princeton, for instance, doesn't offer majors like environmental studies or art) and the students themselves. Go to a school where the students seem to be people whom you'd want to be friends with. At Princeton, students are by and large workaholics, relatively conservative, and kind of socially conformist. Because of this, if I had to choose my college all over again, I'm not sure that I would have come here.

> "Since 1975, eighteen alumni and faculty members have won the Nobel Prize."
> ◆ Craig, junior

The Social Scene

Princeton is in a yuppie suburban town in the middle of New Jersey. When you step five minutes outside of campus, you're surrounded by boutiques selling overpriced clothing and chocolates. If you like that sort of thing, perfect. If you don't, get a car so you can escape to Philadelphia, New York, and beyond.

Princeton's administration is pretty liberal and progressive—notably more so than the students themselves. And the administration does its best to put on scores and scores of events. There's always a lecture, a film, a play. Unfortunately, most people don't have time to take advantage of this.

The eating situation at Princeton is pretty unique. Juniors and seniors do not eat in the dining halls of the residential colleges (which house the freshmen and sophomores). There are eleven eating clubs, which are private entities, and juniors and seniors eat there. Eating clubs provide everything from three meals a day to live bands at night. . . . They have wood-paneled taprooms, velvety red carpets, suited waiters. . . . And they cost upwards of $6,000 a year on top of the money you're already paying for tuition and room and board and books and all of your other expenses. Some students adore the eating clubs. Others, like me, find that they monopolize the social life of the campus, divide kids by their social class, suck the life out of smaller, student-created programs or parties, and are by nature even more elitist than Princeton itself.

If you hate the eating clubs, you can elect to be "independent." But then you don't eat with any of your friends who are part of the clubs, and you have to fend for yourself on a campus pretty much devoid of kitchens, and in a town empty of grocery stores within walking distance. You're forced to eat in the student center (which is prohibitively expensive), or you can join one of the two food cooperatives on campus: 2D is vegetarian; Brown is omnivorous. I'm part of the food co-op. The co-ops are warm communities that cost next to nothing and offer good food. The people in the co-ops are fantastic, my kind of people. However, the demand to be in a co-op is greater than the spaces available, so sometimes you'll find yourself shut out.

Finally, students at Princeton are relatively chaste. Sex is a big taboo on campus, among members of all sexualities, and it rarely happens. If you want to have lots of sex in college do yourself a favor—go to some liberal, pro-sex school like Wesleyan or Brown. Steer clear of Princeton.

Notable Princeton Alumni Include:

Woodrow Wilson, twenty-eighth U.S. president
Ralph Nader, politician, activist
Steve Forbes, president and CEO, Forbes Inc.
Bill Bradley, former NBA Star, U.S. senator
David Duchovny, actor
Dean Cain, actor

REED COLLEGE

Founded: 1911
Location: Portland, OR
Phone: (503) 771-1112
E-mail: admission@reed.edu
Web site: www.reed.edu

Number of Undergraduates: 1,284
Number of Graduate Students: 30
Cost: Approximately $37,000 per year
Application Deadline: January 15
Early Decision: November 15

Rating:	Notable Majors/Programs:
Very Selective	Life Sciences, English, Social Sciences

Size:
● Small   ○ Medium   ○ Large

Location:
○ Urban   ● Suburban   ○ Rural

On a Saturday, students talk about academics:
● Always   ○ Sometimes   ○ Never

Nightlife:
○ Intense   ● Moderate   ○ Laid-back

Politically, Reed leans:
● Left   ○ Right   ○ Split

Diversity:
○ High   ● Low   ○ Medium

Students describe Reed in five words:
- Eclectic, top-tier, rambunctious, Northwestern, amaaaazing
- Intelligent, intellectual, critical, rigorous—intense

From the School

The curriculum at Reed is highly structured and extremely rigorous. The four basic elements—the required humanities sequence, the breadth of study requirement, junior qualifying examinations, and the senior thesis—mix a strong component of interdisciplinary work with study of traditional majors. . . . The effectiveness of such an educational experience as a foundation for widely varying careers is indicated by the outstanding records of Reed graduates in scholarly pursuits, business and industry, the professions, public service, teaching, and fine arts.

—www.web.reed.edu

If you're interested in Reed, you may also be interested in:
Brown, UC Berkeley, UC Santa Cruz, Oberlin, Stanford, Whitman

Name: Kendall
Hometown: Duluth, Minnesota
Class Year: Junior
Major: English
Extracurriculars: Student Senate, Residence Life, Office of Admission, Office of Communications, volunteering (with environmental groups, literacy groups, animal rights groups), horseback riding, creative writing for the Reed College *Creative Review.*
Career Goal: Writer

How would you describe Reed's reputation?

Academically rigorous, liberal, full of creative and drug-addicted students.

Is this reputation accurate?

I think that Reed is extremely academically rigorous, and it is a fantastic intellectual environment. Most Reedies do tend to be extremely liberal, and incredibly creative (if perhaps not in completely constructive ways). I find the drug reputation almost completely undeserved and ridiculous. Sure, "Reed" does rhyme with "weed," but you don't do drugs here if you don't want to. And there's also this weird perception that all Reedies smoke a lot of cigarettes and wear only black, which isn't true at all.

What aspect of Reed would a prospective student not see on a campus tour?

Multiple aspects, namely the full creative force of Reed students—something that needs to be either experienced or left up to the imagination.

The Institution

Reed is a beautiful place filled with wonderfully intelligent and (sometimes) motivated people. "Graffiti" in the bathrooms here ranges from a full-scale Dr. Seuss mural downstairs in the library (which must be seen to be believed) to comments on the nature of time to Beck lyrics to discussion of who you'd like to make out with to serious conversations about issues like birth control.

Reed didn't stray too far from my initial expectations (it is truly a wondrous place), though sometimes the students can be a bit more apathetic (about nonacademic issues only; academic work is always taken very, very seriously); this apathy is probably the main thing that I would like to change about Reed.

Portland is a fantastic city with many volunteering/activism opportunities as well as many entertainment opportunities, and it's also conveniently located for enjoyment of the natural world (it's well under a two-hour drive to either the Pacific Ocean or Mount Hood). There is a sort of Reed "bubble" effect at times, but your involvement with the greater Portland community is as extensive as you make it.

Reed has an honor principle that governs all members of the community here, and it's important to understand and research the honor principle before coming to Reed. There is also an immense amount of amazing school spirit at Reed. If you don't think you could grow to love the honor principle, the Doyle Owl, the thesis tower, CHVNK bikes, Canyon Day, and other amazing aspects of Reed, you may not want to come here. If you don't love Reed, Reed won't love you—and an unloving relationship with Reed can be harsh.

> "Reed *does not* participate in the *U.S. News & World Report* rankings program. They try to rank us anyway, and we always get graded super-low because of it. While the external, quantitative recognition of how great we are might be nice, I don't think we need anybody else to tell us how great Reed is."
>
> ✦ Robert, freshman

The Education

Reedies talk about classes and work constantly; we immerse ourselves in the life of the mind (clichéd, but true). There isn't significant competition as far as grades go, but Reedies definitely love to argue and can become very convinced that they are right (if you thought there wasn't room for disagreement among a bunch of liberal intellectuals, think again). You can have an intense intellectual discussion, have a casual discussion, or smoke a cigarette with a professor at any time (provided he or she isn't teaching a class at that time, of course). You can even fix a professor's bike tire if she or he has a flat. TAs? What's a TA? We ain't got those here. Professors aren't quite as active in the campus social life as they might be, but then again it could be kind of creepy to see your professor at a party—I kind of prefer to have professors involved in mostly the academic portion of my life, personally.

There are countless opportunities for undergraduates. I love that we don't have a grad school (we do have a Master of Arts in Liberal Studies program, but it's not particularly visible or intrusive in any way). I love that Reed is all for me. Expect to spend at least four hours on homework each day outside of class (*at least*). Also, all seniors write theses. English and biology are probably the largest departments, but each department has its amazing and not-quite-amazing aspects.

The Students

There is no average Reedie. Reedies can have purple hair or blonde hair (or both within the span of a few weeks), black clothes or pink clothes, scary facial piercings or no piercings, tattoos or toe rings, Abercrombie jeans (*maybe* we'll tolerate those) or no clothes at all. Though we probably have too many rich white liberal hippies here, there's no limit to what you can be or—more importantly—*become* at Reed. Reedies love academics, individuality, and Reed itself, and that's about all that's required.

Geographically, many students are from California and Oregon, but we have students from all fifty states and dozens of foreign countries. The "preprofessional" Reedie doesn't exist, at least not in my experience—thankfully! We don't have a business major. No journalism or "communications" major either.

The Activities

Activities are up to you. Wanna do it? Do it. Nobody else is doing it? Who cares? Start a trend. *Any* student can plan *any* activity and get funding (if the student senate deems the activity worthy of funding) from the student body funds. Community service is not quite as popular as it might be, but there is a decent volunteering organization on campus called SEEDS (Students for Education, Empowerment, and Direct Service), and there are many student groups that launch service projects (often with student body funds).

If I'm awake at 3:00 a.m. on a Wednesday morning—which isn't necessarily that unusual—it's probably because I'm reading or writing a paper. If I leave campus, I go wherever I want.

The Social Scene

Partying. *If* there's drug use, the best thing about it is that (generally) Reedies are pretty aware of what they're doing to their bodies and really study up on substances' potential effects (both positive and negative). This responsible approach is something I can appreciate. Of course, that doesn't mean that the occasional stupid thing doesn't happen; stupid stuff happens everywhere, but it's stupider, more dangerous, elsewhere. Drinking occurs. People get drunk. I find the most disappointing thing about drunkenness at Reed is the mess that the drunk people sometimes leave in their wake—a little more responsibility in that department might be nice.

Name: Kevlyn
Hometown: Batesburg, South Carolina
Class Year: Senior
Major: Classics
Extracurriculars: Working at the Admissions Office and on-campus coffee shop.
Career Goal: Public information for a government agency or nonprofit, working in communications for a U.S.-based company or government agency elsewhere in the world.

How would you describe Reed's reputation?

The three usual reactions in ascending order: (1) "Wait, is that some community college?" (2) "They do a lot of drugs there," and (3) "That's one of the most academically challenging colleges in the country."

> "Reedies pursue education to its highest level, especially in the sciences and through research and fellowships around the world. Go us."
>
> ✦ Joshua, senior

Is this reputation accurate?

The last one is most correct, I think. Reedies may look (and occasionally smell) funny, but we do not mess around when it comes to academics and we accept no messing around from others.

What aspect of Reed would a prospective student not see on a campus tour?

A prospie probably would not see the student union after one of our large parties; come on, though, it's a college—people spill beer on the floor. This is not terribly unusual. Other than that, I worry that the Admissions Office portrays us as a paradise;

it's not at all. There are pompous, ignorant people here just as there are at other great colleges, and I sometimes feel stupid, lonely, depressed, etc., but it certainly makes the final achievement sweeter.

The Institution

Hard-working, left-leaning smart kids make for an interesting campus. The cold, rainy weather makes me miserable from November until April, but I'm from the South and spoiled. Housing is wonderful due to cheap, safe, and plentiful off-campus options. Our bathroom graffiti is the best—plenty of talk about favorite books and theories, plenty of fun, empty banter about various people on campus, but most interestingly a mix between the two ("top ten sexiest historical figures," "Reed women who'll make great profs some day").

My only real problem with the school has been the career center—it's just too small to help out much unless you're staying in the area, but luckily professors and employers here have helped me get everything I need (and probably provided more personalized and invested guidance than even a top-rate career center would have). If you're continuing in your field (rather than doing something silly like jumping from classics to communications), our departments are extremely supportive and work hard to make certain that you get what you need to move on.

The Education

My brain has been completely overhauled since arriving here; I analyze everything I see, from novels to cereal boxes. It takes over, and you don't realize how hard you're working academically because everything you do fits into this big mental game. At this point I sort of enjoy spending six hours a day in the library, even on the decreasingly occasional Friday or Saturday night, and the classics department feels like a second family. The value of my Reed education wasn't clear to me until I studied classics in Rome for a semester; most of my classmates abroad were as intelligent and hardworking as the average Reedie, but they lacked the desire to truly understand what they were translating and relate it to the world as a whole, classical or otherwise.

The Students

Sadly, after four years I have grown tired of most Reedies. My close friends are the most wonderful people I've met, and I get on well with most

of the students in my year, but the overall tendency to try to be as unique as possible at all times is driving me up the wall. Reedie individuality can still be great in many instances—Renn Fayre (see "the activities" section) is amazing. But please, give it a rest for class, would you? Nobody wants to hear about your foot fetish or your goofy sub-par art-rock band during Spanish 311.

I am also sick of hypocritical Reedies. There is a select group on campus that cries foul if anything vaguely suggests homophobic or racist leanings but then gets up and cheers every time someone makes a joke about Jesus having sex with dogs or something. It's juvenile and offensive. Luckily, most Reedies seem to have more sense than this.

> "How many Reedies does it take to screw in a lightbulb? One, and she doesn't even need a ladder because she's wearing platform Birkenstocks. (Hell yeah!)"
> ✦ Lauryn, senior

The Activities

Between academics and my two jobs, I don't really have time for clubs or organizations. Many Reedies, however, make time for campus activities, and lazy bums such as myself reap the benefits. Students frequently obtain school funding to organize interesting activities such as lamb roasts and midnight spaghetti feasts in the center of campus. Also, the small campus means that a large percentage of the students attend formals and other events. Our biggest event each year is Renn Fayre, the end-of-thesis celebration each spring; it begins on a Friday with Thesis Parade, when seniors torch their rough drafts and march through the library while other students spray them with champagne. On Saturday night comes fireworks and Glow Opera, a student-created musical performed with glow sticks in the pitch dark. In between are various other activities. Last year the theme was old-school video games. Someone made an eight-foot-tall papier-mâché Bowser from Super Mario and put it in the mailroom—it was amazing.

We don't have any varsity sports, but we do have a couple of savage rugby teams. Ironically, I hated sports while attending public high school in central Georgia but have grown rabid over Renn Fayre softball at Reed—we have a tournament at the end of every year between poorly organized teams whose names are generally tacky puns (the Cunning Linguists, the Biohazards). Team Classics conquers, of course.

The Social Scene

Seriously, I try to be in bed by 11:00 p.m. every night, so I'm not the one to ask about the party-hardy scene—but potlucks, films, rock shows, fancy dessert places, and bad television are well within my realm. My friends, and most Reedies, are great at finding fun, unorthodox things for college students to do: the zoo, cooking enormous pieces of meat, holding ugly-bird drawing contests, independent gallery openings, etc. The library, particularly the lobby, tends to be the social center of campus on any given night. Living off campus is a good idea—people who stay in on-campus housing for four full years can get a bit loopy from overexposure.

Name: Eben
Hometown: Wellesley, Massachusetts
Class Year: Junior
Major: History, with a focus on China
Extracurriculars: I helped organize Paideia, a week of informal classes called before spring semester taught by students, faculty, and staff. Classes this year included sewing sock monkeys, making liquid nitrogen ice cream, and learning to speak Elfish.
Career Goal: I would like to have one. Perhaps in another country.

How would you describe Reed's reputation?

In general I think we have a reputation for extremely rigorous academics and radically leftist politics. I think some people see us a school full of stressed-out library dwellers, while others view us as crazy pinko-commie-hippies. Fortunately, among academics, Reed has a reputation as a breeding ground for highly intelligent, thoughtful individuals.

Is this reputation accurate?

Yes and no. Reed is academically focused, but we also have a lot of opportunities to have fun. Even when you do have a lot of work, ideally you should be enjoying it. This is a school for people who love to learn. In general the Reed student body is left of center, but Reedies are just too cerebral to fall into cliché ultra-leftist categories. If we all held the same far-left view, then we wouldn't be able to argue with each other. Where is the fun in that?

What would an admissions officer at Reed probably not tell a prospective student?

The much-beloved policy of no grade inflation gives us an underwhelming average GPA of 2.9 at graduation. Fortunately, most of the best grad schools know about Reed's policies, and the high quality of Reed grads.

> "Reed is one of the few places where you can walk across campus at two in the morning and end up talking to someone about foreign economic policy, Nietzschean ideals, or high-energy mass orbitals."
> ✦ Adam, sophomore

The Institution

We are a small school, but that is fine by me. I actually went to a public high school of less then a thousand people, so it seems kind of large to me. I like that when I walk around campus I can tell when someone is a guest.

Reed is full of traditions, but I would say my two favorite are "Renn Fayre" and the Doyle Owl. The Doyle Owl is a large concrete owl that periodically shows up on campus and drives people insane. All Reedies desire to possess, not just touch, the two hundred-plus-pound concrete lump, so when it shows up on campus, large mobs of normally rational students go nuts and surround it trying to get it into a car. Once you own the owl, you must display it, once again setting off another scramble for the owl.

Roughly 42 percent of students live off campus. There are a variety of "Reed Houses" that have always been rented to students. This saves us *lots* of money. Though the school is in a residential area of the city, there is a state fish and wildlife preservation in the middle of campus known as the "canyon." Lastly, it rains all winter—which can be hard for freshmen, but you get used to it.

The Education

Academics are the focus of most things at Reed College. Everywhere you go, people talk about classes, professors, books, and ideas. My living room has been home to a semester-long, ongoing debate about "functional variability" in psychology. I think this is fantastic. I don't want to give the impression that we don't have other ways of having fun—there are lots of other things to do on and off campus, and people do take advantage of them—but we definitely have a lot of fun debating, arguing, and studying.

Most classes at Reed are conference-style. This means that the professor usually talks for a few minutes at the beginning of class, but after that it is up to the students to talk with each other about the material. Some classes have lectures apart from the conferences, but no class is entirely lecture-based. In the sciences there are TAs only in the lab, and they are just upperclassmen who help students with lab-related problems. Professors give lectures and run the conferences, not TAs.

There are plenty of research opportunities for undergrads. I have three close friends who have grants to do research between their junior and senior years. One friend has a grant to conduct a psychology experiment at the airport. Another has a grant to travel to China with her art history professor to compare mountains and their representations. A third will be traveling to Ireland to interview immigrants.

As a freshman the senior thesis requirement seemed really scary, and I must admit as a junior it still makes me anxious, but I feel very well prepared.

> "When fall rolls in, it's kind of a shock how often it rains here, but by spring, you realize the flip side: it keeps our world green. Really green, all one hundred acres of this place. All year long."
>
> ✦ Erica, senior

The Students

I have heard that Reed College has the most diverse assortment of white people at any school. This is not particularly fair, but also not particularly false. In my three years at Reed, students of color went from being practically nonexistent, to being a small visible minority on campus. That said, Reed is really white. The discourse of diversity has been taken up in a really big way by the administration. There has been a lot of time, money,

and energy invested in trying to recruit students and professors of color. This project seems to be almost universally supported by the student body, which is a rarity for any administration policy. Socioeconomic diversity at Reed is alive and well and geographically, Reedies come from all over the country, with the largest groups coming from the coasts.

There is no stereotypical Reedie. When I first came to Reed this was very evident in the way people looked: lots of piercings, strange clothing, dyed hair, etc. What I loved about Reed was that these people were judged by their words and deeds, not these superficial traits. Nowadays the campus looks a little bit less exciting than it once did, but students are still not judged by their appearance, and some people still find exciting ways to dress. It's just not the norm anymore.

The Activities

There are a lot of ways to get involved on campus. Every semester there is a campus-wide election called funding poll. Any student may start an organization and enter it into the funding poll. The student body votes on which organizations they support, and then the student senate uses that information to distribute money to the various organizations. The last funding poll had over eighty different organizations on the ballot.

One thing I hate about "college books" is that they always say that Reed has no sports. This is a lie. What Reed does not have is football. While I played some football in high school, I can not understand how it has come to be the only appreciated college sport. At Reed, while we have no football, we have a variety of other intercollegiate sports. You can compete in soccer, Ultimate Frisbee, basketball, squash, fencing, and rugby. Our women's rugby team is probably the most popular team on campus. They are NCAA Division One, and they have gone to the championship tournament two years in a row.

The Social Scene

The social scene at Reed is what you make of it. If you want to sit alone in your dorm room and study, go for it. No one will look down on you for it. If you want to go out partying a lot, that's cool too. As freshmen, many people just hang out with their "dormies," but as people get older they tend to branch out and meet more people. This can be easy if you manage to overcome the general awkwardness that seems to come standard with being a Reedie. The best places to meet people are probably the library and the Paradox, the student coffee shop.

There are parties both on campus in the Student Union and off campus at Reed Houses. SU parties will usually feature a band and lots of dancing, while off-campus parties feature a keg and lots of people milling around outside talking. Both can be a lot of fun. In the past year or so, Reedies somehow learned to dance. I think this may be the best thing that has happened to Reed socially since I arrived.

Notable Reed Alumni Include:
Barbara Ehrenreich, writer and social critic
Dr. Demento, radio personality
Emilio Pucci, fashion designer
Gary Snyder, poet
James Russell, inventor of the compact disc
Peter Norton, creator of Norton Utilities

RICE UNIVERSITY

Founded: 1912

Location: Houston, TX

Phone: (713) 348-0000

E-mail: N/A

Web site: www.rice.edu

Number of Undergraduates: 2,860

Number of Graduate Students: 2,040

Cost: Approximately $27,206 per year

Application Deadline: January 10

Early Decision: November 1/Early Action: December 1

Rating:
Most Selective

Notable Majors/Programs:
Architecture, Engineering, Life Sciences, Social Sciences

Size:
○ Small ● Medium ○ Large

Location:
○ Urban ● Suburban ○ Rural

On a Saturday, students talk about academics:
● Always ○ Sometimes ○ Never

Nightlife:
● Intense ○ Moderate ○ Laid-back

Politically, Rice leans:
○ Left ○ Right ● Split

Diversity:
● High ○ Low ○ Medium

Students describe Rice in five words:
- Intellectual, quirky, crazy on weekends
- One word for you: *exhausting*

From the School

Rice University strives to create on its campus a rich learning environment in which all students will meet individuals whose interests, talents, life-experiences, beliefs, and world-views differ significantly from their own. To encourage our students' fullest possible exposure to the widest possible set of experiences, Rice seeks through its admissions policies to bring bright and promising students to the University from a range of socioeconomic, cultural, geographic and other backgrounds.

—www.futureowls.rice.edu

If you're interested in Rice, you may also be interested in:
Davidson, Duke, Emory, Stanford, Washington U. in St. Louis, Yale

Name: Crystal
Hometown: Torrance, California
Class Year: Senior
Major: English and History
Extracurriculars: Students Organized Against Rape, Women's Resource Center, Student Alumni Liaison Committee, miscellaneous theater productions, mentoring, tutoring.
Career Goal: To be a corporate lawyer for a Fortune 500 company and possibly enter public service as a political candidate. If I can make time to work on women's rights legislation, or earn enough to purchase my own small private island, I'll be happy.

How would you describe Rice's reputation?

People in Texas usually say, "Oh, you must be smart." As a matter of fact, the campus bookstore even sells bumper stickers stating, "I go to Rice. I must be smart." These stickers can be seen displayed (proudly upside down) on any number of cars in Rice parking lots. But despite Rice's growing reputation, it still lacks the name-brand recognition of other, similar-caliber private schools. Academically, we're best known as an engineering school. Less widely known is that Rice is also home to top-ranked music and architecture schools. Something like two-thirds of each incoming freshman class declares engineering or natural sciences majors, and two-thirds of each graduating class leaves as social sciences or liberal arts majors.

Is this reputation accurate?

Yes. You cannot afford to slack off at Rice if you have any ambition of doing well here. Students are smart and driven. Since Rice is a reasonably affordable private school, fewer students come from wealthy families, and these kids are determined to move to the next tax bracket. They know there's no safety net if they fail.

What aspect of Rice would a prospective student not see on a campus tour?

It's difficult for prospective students to understand the full ramifications of the residential college system. Many go to Rice overjoyed that there is no Greek system. They're wrong. We do have one: we just call it the college system, and everyone gets in. In fact, everyone has to be in a frat, er, college. Essentially, the college system is like the house system at Hogwarts in the *Harry Potter* books. Everyone is randomly assigned a college; each college has a dorm, dining facilities ("the Commons"), and faculty and staff who live in the dorm serving as administrators, buddies, and surrogate parents for the college and its members ("Masters" and "Resident Associates" or "RAs"). Each college has its own self-run government, with a budget to spend, a judicial system, a set of elected officials and a constitution to regulate it all. You eat in your college's Commons, study in its library, hang out in its common spaces to play pool and video games (all owned by the college), and chances are, most of your friends are from your college. Some colleges have newer, better facilities, and some are making do with renovating original buildings, and in colleges with fewer common spaces connected to high-traffic areas, it can be difficult to make friends. Additionally, each college has its own quirky traditions that are fairly incomprehensible, if not altogether unknown, to members of other colleges.

For some, the college system is an easy way to transition to university life and make friends, providing an automatic social network. For others it's claustrophobic, since the college system is the predominant means of socializing for most Rice students and makes a small school like Rice feel even smaller.

> "Houston has essentially two seasons: (1) hot and (2) hot as hell. Also, beware criticisms of country music, SUVs, and the word 'y'all' (and variations thereof)."
> ✦ Crystal, sophomore

The Institution

Rice is weird. What else do you expect when you take some of the nation's best and brightest and fence them off from the rest of the world on one city block surrounded by hedges? But Rice likes the fact that it's weird. To illustrate: Twice a month random volunteers run around campus wearing only shaving cream, a tradition known as Baker 13. This passes for risqué and adventurous at Rice. It's exciting and funny to watch at first, particularly if you are armed with a bucket of water, and then it gets so routine you completely forget and are only reminded when you see the shaving-cream butt prints on the library windows the next morning.

The "best day of the year" for many students is Beer Bike, an annual bike race between the colleges that is celebrated with a weekend of drinking. On Beer Bike morning, most of the people from my college are so trashed that they don't even make it to the race at noon. Prior to the race, a "parade" is held, wherein trucks for each college laden with thousands of water balloons travel from the front of the school to the stadium parking lot in back, stopping at intervals to allow students to approach the truck, get balloons, and throw them at other people, preferably individuals from other colleges.

Willy Week is a week of festivities preceding Beer Bike (one such festivity: Beer Debates, wherein a panel of professors answers random student questions throughout the night while simultaneously finishing off as many pitchers as they can), but more important, Willy Week is one of the only times when it is acceptable to play "jacks." A "jack" is generally a prank played on a college (unleashing farm animals in another college's green space, stealing things [like the Masters' children]. The most famous jack occurred when engineering students designed a contraption to turn the statue of our university founder, William Marsh Rice, 180 degrees. They were able to accomplish this feat in but one night. To undo their actions, the administration had to hire a contractor who not only required an entire day to move the statue back, but also scratched it in the process. The students were forced to pay for the contractor's services and raised the fees by selling T-shirts bearing the image of Willy's statue facing the library (instead of Lovett Hall) and a copy of the police blotter from that week noting the incident, as printed in the *Thresher*. The shirts were so popular that they made a sizable profit, which they stashed in a savings account to pay for future upkeep of the statue, which is still being used to this day.

The Education

The perennial slacker does not win points for being cool at Rice. Any university has its share of less-motivated individuals, but at Rice, academic laziness is considered a major vice. From two weeks prior to midterms until the end of finals week, a marked sense of despair and dejection pervades the campus, increasing exponentially as the end of the semester draws ever nearer. The line at the coffee house gets longer. The dark circles under everyone's eyes get darker. Suddenly there are people at the library, apart from those who work there. During this time, Rice students like to play a little game during meals. This game is unofficially called "I Have More Work Than You Do. . . ."

I can't speak much about an engineering or natural sciences education, but I know that the bulk of it is spent on problem sets, exams, and mandatory labs. Music and architecture students spend most of their time in their respective buildings, slaving over instruments and sheet music or diagrams and models. Though the liberal arts aren't the major selling point of the university, there's no reason to believe that they aren't up to scratch. Analytical ability, originality of thought, and precision and elegance in expressing such thought are the end products of a Rice liberal-arts education taken seriously. As with any other university, the individual department, not the university as a whole, determines the quality of your education.

> "Don't expect people to hold your hand and guide you through everything, or you will be disappointed. Rice expects independence and intelligence to guide you. . . ."
> ✦ Erik, senior

If there is one thing you really must know to get through four years at Rice, it is: do not, under any circumstances, mess with the Honor Code. Remember, you are at a nerd school. Were your lab partner to discover that your GPA is .1 higher than his/hers because of your cheatin' heart, there would be hell to pay. Honor Council trials are rare, so they tend to make headlines at the school newspaper, the *Thresher*. The Honor Code is taken so seriously that incoming students are lectured and quizzed on its workings.

The James A. Baker III Institute for Public Policy is excellent. It invites political players from around the world to hold forums and speak on policy issues. Notable former guests have included Nelson Mandela, Alan Greenspan, and Vladimir Putin. It's exciting to have such influential individuals so relatively available. Of course, it's more difficult to get tickets to see the big names, but it's definitely possible, and the Ambassadors program allows selected student volunteers to help run Institute events, and sometimes Q&A sessions are set up exclusively for Ambassadors.

The Students

Rice may be a private school, but Ivy League it is not. I am hard-pressed to think of another place where you can get away with creating your entire wardrobe from free T-shirts collected from campus events. You can tell the freshman girls from the seniors by how much more polished the former are in appearance.

The Activities

Sports aren't huge here. The athletic department has to bribe students with free food and raffle drawings to get students to come to games and meets. The paradox of Rice is that most individuals are actively involved in something, but the student body as a whole cares about very little. Rice students are known for their apathy, political and otherwise. Any college campus has its activists, but the majority of the student body largely ignores their efforts. With merely a couple thousand students on campus, most organizations cannot hope to have hundreds of members. As a result, there are numerous little subcultures at Rice revolving around one or another organization or club. Most students will simultaneously try out at least one other extracurricular. In fact, many aspects of student life are student-run initiatives, like the weekly Coffeehouse where students can showcase their performing talent and college-based tutoring services. In that sense, we're not exactly apathetic and self-centered. We care about certain things quite a great deal; we're just cynical enough to realize that no one else does.

The Social Scene

Even though Rice is in the fourth largest city in the United States, many students do nothing beyond the confines of the campus. We describe the closed nature of Rice life as "inside the hedges," coined for the hedges outlining the campus's perimeter. (The Career Services guide for graduating seniors is titled "Beyond the Hedges.") But there's always plenty to do around campus for the students who never want to leave, since almost everyone lives on campus (except for those who have rejected the dorm lifestyle or even—gasp—the cult of the college). What little socializing people do, between their myriad extracurricular activities and mountains of homework, tends to involve one common denominator: alcohol. Rice is the only "wet campus" in Texas, meaning that it's the only Texas university where alcohol can be served to students of age at public functions. There are two pubs at Rice, one for the grads (Valhalla) and one for the undergrads (Willy's Pub). Colleges can (and do) purchase alcohol to serve at parties; students can have minibars in their rooms; and many colleges host wine- and beer-tasting classes for their senior members. The most basic Rice party consists of two or more people and some alcohol. Any alcohol.

Name: Aurora
Hometown: Tulsa, Oklahoma
Class Year: Freshman
Major: Psychology and Religious Studies
Extracurriculars: Intervarsity, yearbook, tour guide, hosting prospective students, student government, Native American Student Association.
Career Goal: Clinical psychologist with an emphasis on family therapy.

How would you describe Rice's reputation?

Very prestigious and consistently top-ranking, though some people haven't ever heard of Rice.

Is this reputation accurate?

Of course it is! And we are *not* the "Harvard of the South." If anything, Harvard is the "Rice of the North."

What aspect of Rice would a prospective student not see on a campus tour?

They wouldn't hear all of the residential college cheers. Rice is very open about showing prospective students what really goes on here; sometimes, my campus tour groups will run into students playing beer-golfing games, so I just explain the alcohol policy and move on. The one thing we don't flaunt is the fact that nearly all the residential colleges have obscene words strewn throughout their cheers.

> "William Marsh Rice is actually buried on Rice's campus. Also, Rice students consider it to be good luck to sit in the lap of Willy's Statue. Exiting the campus through the Sally Port (an archway that is the main entrance), however, is considered bad luck unless you are doing it during your graduation."
> ✦ Minerva, sophomore

The Institution

I *love* my school. I love the atmosphere because the size really helps everyone get to know each other, and the college system facilitates that even more. I think the most difficult thing this year has been really to buckle down and study, because there are just so many interesting people and so many things to do that work really comes second. It feels like a summer camp, but the work is real and you have to do it.

> "In every way—from the beautiful architecture, to the outstanding professors, to the fantastic opportunities to study abroad and find internships, to the crazy-cool student body—Rice *will* rock your face off!"
> ✦ Lauren, junior

The residential college system is the coolest thing ever. It's the best of the Greek system without the ostracism, or dorms without the strict rules and unisex codes. The campus is beautiful and relatively small. The longest walk you will *ever* have is 15 minutes, tops. The weather has its pros and cons. The cons are that it's super-hot in Houston, and also super-rainy. The pros are that you can tan in January, and instigate a great game of mud soccer.

I've never worried about my safety while on campus. It is super-safe. Tons of people leave their doors taped so that they never close, let alone lock. It is *so* safe! The school is basically student-run. We have created our own alcohol policy and honor code. Our administration is *really* supportive. Our president and vice president host study breaks during finals and have shown up in full boxing attire. Our VP even memorizes every single person's name, and at least three facts about them, before they matriculate. Freshman Orientation Week is the best week *ever*.

The Education

The classes are amazing. They're generally very small and the professors are also amazing! I've had one give me a home phone number and another complain that no one was coming in for his office hours. Rice has some really unique classes (I took a class on Tolkien last semester), and the fact that you have to take certain "distribution" classes really doesn't bother anyone, because most people

here are well-rounded enough to choose classes from all different areas on their own. Not having general requirements is *awesome*. We have a rockin' honor code. It's marvelous to be able to take a test in the middle of a field, underneath a tree, or at three in the morning in the library (which is open twenty-four hours), because you are trusted to follow the instructions and not cheat.

Although classes are tough, I yell at people if they talk about them on a Saturday night. I try my best to make sure that everyone avoids it and has fun on a Saturday.

The Students

Rice is probably one of the very few liberal campuses in Texas. All cultures and groups interact very freely in this accepting atmosphere. I went to a diverse high school (half of the students were black and half were white or other), and yet coming to Rice showed me *so* much about other cultures. In my room alone I live with an Indian (I'm Native American, so it always confuses me that people here say Indian and mean people from India), a Jew, a Mexican, an Italian Catholic, and a viola major (who is white and thus ethnically challenged—just kidding). I don't think you can say that there is an "average" student at Rice. There's really not a Rice mold.

The Activities

Students get very involved and go to many of the student productions. The Philharmonics (an a cappella group), Spontaneous Combustion (the improv group), and Rice Dance Theatre are just some of the more popular productions to attend. Since we have a music school, students often go to those performances and thus get to hear beautiful symphonies and watch amazing operas. Also, baseball is big, so many students go to that or to the intramural games. We leave campus about once a week just to go eat. There's usually stuff to do here, so it's really not necessary to go anywhere.

The Social Scene

We have some great parties. Since Rice is a wet campus, all of our drinking is done on campus rather than off, which creates a much safer atmosphere. Different colleges have different parties every weekend. A fair amount of drinking goes on, but it is usually very safe. And if anyone gets too out of hand or sick, the Rice Emergency Medical Service is always on call to help (remember to call

6000!). Of course, the Texas drinking age is twenty-one, so underage drinking is breaking the law. However, if a student is under twenty-one and drinking in his/her own room, not disturbing anyone, then no Rice University police officer is going to come and bust you. That really makes the decision up to you when it comes to drinking. Many different types of people party. It is not restricted to a certain group. I love not having sororities or fraternities. I think it makes the campus a lot stronger.

Name: Joshua
Hometown: Kingston, Jamaica
Class Year: Junior
Major: Mechanical Engineering
Extracurriculars: AIAA (American Institute of Aeronautics and Astronautics), ASME (American Society of Mechanical Engineers), NSBE (National Society of Black Engineers), SAE (Society of Automotive Engineers).
Career Goal: Aerospace, power generation, or technology R&D executive.

How would you describe Rice's reputation?

Rice is very prominent in the Southwest United States. People view the school's academics as almost legendary, and also tend to think that Rice students eat, sleep, and breathe their schoolwork. On the athletic side of things, the football and basketball teams attract some attention but, having won the 2003 College World Series, the baseball team is the real star of show. It also might be thought of as a rich-kid school.

Is this reputation accurate?

Yes, it is. Rice is truly one of the most prestigious and intense academic institutions in the country. But as for the rich-kid view of Rice, few things could be further from the truth. While the average family income is high, Rice students are not a bunch of fashionistas who roll around in German autos and tote Chanel bags. Generally speaking, this is *not* a fashion school or a place for show-offs. As a matter of fact, showing off is more likely to garner isolation than acceptance.

What would an admissions officer at Rice probably not tell a prospective student?

This place is supposed to be diverse. It is, on paper. However, the dominant culture here is decidedly Caucasian, upper-middle-class, suburban.

Discrimination is nonexistent, but those who aren't in tune with or able to adapt to the status quo here might find it hard to fit in. For me (I'm one-quarter Jewish, one-eighth East Indian, three-eighths black, and one-eighth Scottish, so I'm pretty diverse myself) it's not an issue. I love it here and I wouldn't rather be anyplace else. Also, this is Houston, Texas. People here are naturally religious and conservative (when they're not apathetic). Activism is tolerated, but good luck finding much concrete support.

The Institution

Everyone loves to be a Rice student, but school spirit is dampened by the apathy that results from the homicidal workload. It's difficult to get people involved in anything that doesn't get them a grade—unless of course it involves alcohol.

The Education

Coming from a competitive Jesuit high school, I thought I'd already seen the toughest schoolwork and the highest academic quality of my classmates. Wrong, wrong, wrong. Welcome to Rice.

A Rice education is much like Navy SEAL training for your mind, except that it lasts four years while SEALs get out of their training much, much sooner. All-nighters, indecipherable problem sets, tons of tests, and mountainous projects will become your life (except on Friday and Saturday nights, when most people decide to take a break, and the awesome parties happen). If you thought you were smart in high school, prepare to take a massive kick in the pants. Classes here are *not* easy, although people will tell you that they're o.k. just so they can sound smart and defend their egos. If you're a premed or science and engineering major, prepare to discover new limits of endurance and performance that you never imagined you had. The school has good liberal-arts and social sciences departments, but one look at the companies that recruit here will tell you that this is primarily a science and engineering institution.

The Students

Besides the academics, I'd say that the people at Rice are the school's next best selling points. First up: everyone here is very smart. You *will* be blown away by the abilities of the person next to you.

As I said, although Rice is diverse, the culture here is Caucasian-upper-middle-class-suburban. Nothing's wrong with that; everywhere has its own flavor, and that's just how it is here. However, those who find it difficult to adjust to this or "go with the flow" might find fitting in a bit of a challenge. The saying "When in Rome, do as the Romans do" applies well here in that regard. Most students will claim to be either Republican (most common) or Democrat, but in reality they're almost all apathetic. This is Texas, and Rice is run by conservatives. There are vocal conservative (whether Christian or political) groups here, and occasional conflicts do arise. Ideas for public parties (which must be approved by local residential college government) can be and have been struck down for being too offensive.

The Activities

Almost any activity you could imagine is available here. If it isn't, starting it is easy. A friend of mine started a juggling club in freshman year that is now a thriving organization with regular meetings. Intramural sports is a big deal, but it isn't high school. Everyone gets a chance to play and to feel like an integral part of the team. Club sports (mainly lacrosse, Ultimate Frisbee, soccer, and rugby) are available for those who are more athletic than most but not Division 1A material. Of course, if you are an athlete, this *is* a Division 1A school.

The Social Scene

There is almost no exclusivity. Those who try to be cliquish are more likely to isolate themselves than become popular. Formal gatherings are few and very far between; Rice students are loath to dress up for anything. Currently there are only three formal balls per year: Esperanza, Rondolet, and the newly instituted and successful E-ball (held by the engineers, but general admission is encouraged). Attendance at these events rarely exceeds a third of the student population. Toga parties and the famous Night of Decadence require considerably less attire. Parties are standing-room only, with loud hip-hop or techno (rare) and oceans of alcohol.

Notable Rice Alumni Include:

Mary Johnston, editor of *Fortune* magazine and responsible for origination of the *Fortune* 500

Robert Curl, Nobel laureate in chemistry

Ron Bozman, producer

S. I. Morris, architect

Sam Reed, CEO of Keebler Cookies

Vivian Vahlberg, first woman president of the National Press Club

RUTGERS UNIVERSITY

Founded: 1766

Location: Piscataway, NJ

Phone: (732) 932-4363

E-mail: admissions@asbugadm.rutgers.edu

Web site: www.rutgers.edu

Number of Undergraduates: 28,070

Number of Graduate Students: 7,577

Cost: Approximately $14,000 per year in state, $20,000 out of state

Application Deadline: Rolling

Rating:	Notable Majors/Programs:
Selective	Psychology, Biology, Economics

Size:
○ Small ○ Medium ● Large

Location:
○ Urban ● Suburban ○ Rural

On a Saturday, students talk about academics:
○ Always ● Sometimes ○ Never

Nightlife:
● Intense ○ Moderate ○ Laid-back

Politically, Rutgers leans:
○ Left ○ Right ● Split

Diversity:
● High ○ Low ○ Medium

Students describe Rutgers in five words:
- Large, bustling, diverse, Public Ivy
- High quality education—minimal cost

From the School

Rutgers' commitment to educational excellence throughout its rich and enduring history has allowed it to become a premier public research institution and a public "ivy" of national distinction. Chartered in 1766 as Queens College, Rutgers is one of the original nine colonial colleges and is distinctively recognized as the eighth oldest institution of higher education in the nation. Today, seven of the nine colonial colleges (Harvard, Yale, Princeton, University of Pennsylvania, Columbia, Brown, and Dartmouth) are private and two (William and Mary, and Rutgers) are public.

—www.admissions.rutgers.edu

If you're interested in Rutgers, you may also be interested in:
Boston University, Cornell, George Washington,
University of Massachusetts at Amherst, Penn State, University of Virginia

Name: Karen

Hometown: Marlboro, New Jersey

Class Year: Senior

Major: Communications, with a minor in Political Science and a certificate in Criminology

Extracurriculars: Rutgers College Program Council (special events chair, president, vice president of marketing); Cabaret Theatre (actress); Villager's Theatre (stage manager).

Career Goal: I'd like to become an attorney specializing in international family law—adoptions and custody cases across international borders.

How would you describe Rutgers' reputation?

Rutgers is looked at as the Ivy League of state schools. The farther you get from New Jersey, the better Rutgers is perceived.

Is this reputation accurate?

Rutgers is one of the oldest schools in America. In New Jersey, because Rutgers is a state school, people tend not to take it as seriously as they should. When you get away from NJ, though, people don't know that it's a state school; they just know that it's a great school, and look at it very favorably.

What would an admissions officer at your school probably not tell a prospective student?

Rutgers is a big school, and because of it, there are lots of administrative mishaps. If you come to Rutgers, at some point in time, you personally will be the victim of an administrative mishap. Students call this the "RU Screw." They're generally minor computer glitches that are easy to straighten out, but they happen with alarming frequency.

The Institution

One of the things I love about Rutgers is that it has such a rich history; founded in 1766, it was the eighth in America to open its doors. Then it had only one professor and a handful of students. These days, Rutgers University is quite a bit bigger—a whopping 30,000 undergraduates and 20,000 graduate students. To make Rutgers feel a bit more personalized, it's been broken up into several smaller colleges, each with its own campus and personality. Rutgers College is for students specializing in liberal arts. Cook College is a professional school specializing in agricultural and environmental sciences, Douglass College is the largest all-women's college in the country. Livingston College is for the social sciences, and is said to be particularly diverse. University College is for nontraditional students and is the only school that allows part-time enrollment. There are also a few preprofessional colleges, like the Mason Gross School of the Arts, the School of Engineering, the Ernest Mario School of Pharmacy, the School of Nursing, the School of Business, and the School of Communication, Information, and Library Studies (SCILS). (Students adverse to traveling, take note: If you come to Rutgers, you're going to have classes on multiple campuses that are part of the larger New Brunswick/Piscataway Rutgers campus. Because of this, you're often going to have to take a free campus bus to get from class to class; traffic can be rough, so try to avoid back-to-back classes on different campuses.)

I transferred here second semester freshman year. (FYI: the school no longer accepts freshman transfers.) But I wish I'd been here from the beginning. I've found my professors to be staggeringly intelligent and my classes to be both interesting and well-taught. I'm going to be attending a top law school this fall, and I can't imagine anyone being any better prepared than I am.

Before I move on, some more Rutgers history/trivia: the first-ever college football game was played at Rutgers, against Princeton. Rutgers won the first game, but went on to lose the series (the school usually likes to leave that little tidbit out). During that first game, Rutgers fired a cannon from the Revolutionary War every time Rutgers scored a touchdown. Princeton students, annoyed, stole the cannon from Rutgers. Since then, there have been several attempts made by Rutgers students to steal the cannon back from Princeton (all unsuccessful). Frustrated, Rutgers just got a new replica cannon, and every year before graduation Rutgers College seniors break a clay pipe over the cannon to signify breaking childish habits and trading in "pipe dreams" for the real world.

> "I've been able to do a lot of undergraduate research while at Rutgers, and, because of the work I've done, I've been accepted into several top-ten graduate schools."
> ✦ Jonathan, junior

The Education

I love the fact that Rutgers is big enough to offer lots of different classes in many fields of study. In four years I've been able to complete a major in communication (through the School of Communication, Information, and Library Studies), a minor in political science, and a certificate in criminology. Great classes I've taken here include: Crimes against Humanity and Political Terrorism and International Law. In each class we studied international law and wrote a major thesis paper (twenty-five to thirty pages long). Both courses were taught by the same professor, a permanent representative to the UN for the International Association of Democratic Lawyers (he was also one of Nelson Mandela's attorneys). Not only were the courses both topical and interesting, but we got to take them under a professor who was currently practicing what he taught and who, between classes, represented clients in international tribunals.

> "Rutgers is considered a 'Public Ivy.'"
> ✦ Jen, freshman

The other great class that stands out in my mind was called Leadership in Groups and Organizations, offered through the Department of Communication. In this course, we worked directly with Rutgers's Housing Department. After submitting résumés, we were "hired" by the managers whose divisions could most benefit from each student's skills. Then, the Rutgers's Housing Department gave us the issues they were dealing with—like how to best respond to student's needs, or how to enhance the image of the Housing Department—and each division's group had to prepare reports on how to fix things, or make things better. I thought this class was fantastic—it really forced us to think outside of ourselves, and we got some great experience working in an organizational setting.

Here's a tip: Rutgers offers a ton of classes, but the most popular ones fill up incredibly quickly. This is especially true for courses in communications, business, and in other cases where there are only one or two sections of a class offered in a semester. To make sure you get the classes you want, wake up as early as possible the morning of online registration. Really, set your alarm for 7:00 a.m. and be among the first people at the registration center.

The Students

Rutgers is a very politically active school. Students are constantly going to rallies, setting up tables and handing out information, heading to protests, and writing articles for the school newspaper to bring attention to their cause of the week. Some of the most active political groups on campus are New Jersey Solidarity (a pro-Palestine organization), Hillel (a pro-Israel organization), and the *Medium* (a very political student newspaper that is often criticized for being offensive). I'd say most students at Rutgers do come from New Jersey, but there are still students from other states (New York, Massachusetts, Hawaii, Connecticut, and Pennsylvania) and other countries (Brazil, Israel, and Greece.) This school is large enough that every type of student is represented, and everyone will find their clique.

The Activities

Rutgers College holds an Involvement Fair at the beginning of every academic year to provide student organizations the opportunity to recruit new members. This fair is a great place to learn about the different things you can do at Rutgers. Most student groups at Rutgers are very active, especially the cultural organizations. For some groups, anyone on campus can sign up and get involved. Other groups are open only to members of a specific college.

> "Unfortunately, introductory-level courses are like factories here. Information is mass-produced and mass-distributed. You're not a name, you're a number."
> ✦ Spencer, senior

For the past four years, I've personally been a board member of the Rutgers College Program Council (RCPC). The RCPC puts on all sorts of events at Rutgers—we hire comedians, novelty acts, organize variety shows, cultural shows, coffeehouse poetry slams, spoken-word shows, trips, lectures, visual and performing arts, etc. The RCPC has a board of twenty students and four advisers, and we do a lot to make Rutgers an exciting place. We put on between twenty and thirty programs (aka, big, fun events) each semester, usually. And it's great experience for us, because we organize every aspect of every program we put on, from thinking up the idea, writing the proposal to get funding, putting together contracts and tech riders, contacting agents, advertising the event, setting up on the day of implementation . . . and so on.

Last, a lot of big schools say their inner workings are too complex to be comprehended and don't give students much say in administrative policy, but that's not the case here. The administration, in my experience at least, has been very receptive to student concerns and works with the student body to make things better.

> "Rutgers is so big, it can take a half-hour of driving to get from campus to campus, and from class to class."
>
> ✦ Susan, sophomore

The Social Scene

I'm not a big drinker/partier and tend to get most of my social life through my involvement in extracurricular activities. At one point I also pledged a sorority, but I chose not to continue with that because I simply didn't have time between classes, my job, and RCPC. As it is, I'll be in class until 4:00 p.m., work at my off-campus job until 7:00 p.m., go to meetings of the RCPC until 10:00 p.m., then head to nearby bars (where there's a huge party scene) until midnight, before heading home and starting my homework. I don't think I could fit more in if I tried!

Name: Kristin
Hometown: Bellmawr, New Jersey
Class Year: Junior
Major: Sociology and Psychology
Extracurriculars: Rutgers College Governing Association, Rutgers Community Outreach, Rutgers High School Outreach
Career Goals: I'd like to pursue a career in public relations.

How would you describe Rutgers' reputation?

A lot of Rutgers students tried, and failed, to get into more "prestigious" schools and they come here with a bit of a grudge. Rather than looking at what a great place this is, they'll badmouth Rutgers at every opportunity because it's not whatever they chalked up Georgetown or Cornell to be in

their heads. So, yeah. I guess a lot of people would describe Rutgers as the safety school they found themselves enrolled in full-time.

Is this reputation accurate?

This is completely ridiculous. Just because (a) Rutgers is a state school, and (b) Rutgers is large enough that it can accept most qualified applicants instead of turning away three out of every four qualified applicants like the Ivys do, people think it isn't as good. But the truth is that this has no bearing whatsoever on the quality of the education you receive here—which is fantastic. I've also found that many of my high school friends who *did* get into these expensive "prestige" schools simply aren't having as good a college experience as I am, and I'm paying half the price. Many at Rutgers just don't realize how good they have it.

What would an admissions officer at your school probably not tell a prospective student?

An admissions officer would never utter the words "RU Screw." But really, things like the RU Screw happen at all large universities. And the new president has done a great job of lessening the instances of the RU Screw.

The Institution

Rutgers has everything I wanted in a school. It's thirty minutes away from New York City and forty-five minutes away from gorgeous beaches at the Jersey Shore. It has Division 1 sports and all the school spirit that comes with having top-notch athletic teams. It has absolutely fantastic professors who are very concerned with their students. There are thirty thousand undergraduates, which means you'll *never* outgrow this place. It's really a city made up entirely of college students. Think about that. Picture some big city, and everyone is eighteen to twenty-two years old. Amazing. You'll never run out of people to meet and things to do.

Campus security is absolutely amazing here. There are patrols 24/7, and there are also free RUPD self-defense seminars in case you want to learn what to do should any trouble arise. Rutgers provides late-night escort/taxi services free of charge in case you ever have to go far late at night. In addition to having one of the safest "urban" campuses and an incredibly low crime rate (compared to other urban schools), we also have the best late-night sandwiches ever served by the (in)famous "Grease Trucks." When the sun goes down, the

Grease Trucks open. At 2:00 a.m., when you have the munchies, the Grease Truck Fat Sandwiches are the best things you could possibly hope to eat!

The Education

It's funny—there are some students who think that Rutgers is going to be easy simply because it's big. They spend their first semester here barely going to classes, not doing their reading, really just scraping by. The professors don't breathe down their necks to work harder, so they think they're getting by okay. But then their first-semester grades come in, and they've failed. Because the academics are challenging here, and there's *no way* someone can get good grades without putting in the hours. First-semester slackers don't last. They drop out. You have to work hard here to succeed.

Also, because this school *is* big, a lot of popular classes are going to be lectures, just so Rutgers can fit in as many students as possible to learn together. But this doesn't mean the professors are unwilling to get to know individual students; go talk to the professor when lectures are over. Take advantage of their office hours after class. E-mail them when you have questions about the reading. Nine out of ten times, they'll get right back to you. Rutgers professors admire students who are dedicated to succeeding, and will help you reach your goals.

> "The deans here really get to know the student leaders, and there's an entire staff dedicated to helping students develop leadership skills."
> ✦ Matthew, sophomore

The Students

Being at Rutgers is like being in a city, with all types of students—black, white, conservative, liberal, gay, straight, Catholic, Jewish. This isn't like other schools where all the girls are blond and dressed to the nines and all the guys are football players. We have your hippies, your punks, your athletes, your indie rockers, your prepsters. Really, whoever you are, you *will* find a crowd of other people just like you.

A lot of students have school spirit here. Even though our football team isn't the greatest, games are still well-attended. Our basketball team also always gets a good turnout. I actually think that school spirit is on the way up: our new president really cares about this university, and he's been proactively taking steps to make it even better than it already is. I think students recognize this, and see that Rutgers is only becoming more exciting from one year to the next.

> "We're one of the nation's largest and most up-to-date research universities, and also one of the nation's oldest schools, with important and fascinating traditions that have been carried out for generations."
> ✦ Cody, junior

The Activities

We have every group you can imagine represented here; there are literally hundreds of different clubs and organizations to join, Division 1 sports, club and intramural sports, strong Greek life, and a bustling downtown area. There are several large community service groups, as well as lots of smaller ones. Cultural groups hold the most events, which are always entertaining. There is always an opportunity here to learn about students different from yourself. We also have lots out-of-staters and international students, and tons of different venues in which to meet and interact. We are also sandwiched in between two lively and enriching cities: New York City and Philadelphia.

The Social Scene

Rutgersfest is the biggest yearly event at Rutgers, and it draws thousands of students for a massive carnival/show. In the past, Redman and Methodman, Fuel, Ludacris, and Kanye West have played at Rutgersfest! As for partying . . . Rutgers doesn't really party on Thursday nights. Instead, we save up our energy for the weekend, when there are always big parties at fraternities and off-campus houses. Some, inevitably, get out of hand, but the RUPD is always there to keep us in check, and most Rutgers parties are good fun. Greek life here is big, but it doesn't dominate. If you're a guy, I guess being in a fraternity helps just because that guarantees you easy entrance into big parties. If you're a girl, though, there's no need to join a sorority, because any and every party is open to you! No frat will ever turn you away.

Then, if you ever get sick of Rutgers, you can always jump on a train and be in New York City in under an hour. Organizations are always on campus promoting plays and concerts in the city, giving students great discounts. And if you want an on-campus escape from campus, head to the strip called Easton Avenue. It's full of bars and late-night pizza joints, and on weekends it's the greatest place to get a bite to eat and meet interesting people.

Name: Kevin
Hometown: Medford, Massachusetts
Class Year: Junior
Major: Double major in Biochemistry and Journalism
Extracurriculars: Rutgers College Planning Committee, Rutgers' New Student Orientation, and I volunteered at the Robert Wood Johnson University Hospital.
Career Goal: If my MCAT scores are high enough, I'd like to go to med school and become a physician.

> "Rutgers is thirty minutes away from New York City, forty-five minutes away from the beach, has excellent sports teams (NCAA Division 1), and great academics. What more could you want?"
>
> ✦ Gina, senior

How would you describe Rutgers' reputation?

When I told people I was going to be attending Rutgers, the most common response was, "Wow. Good school?" Rutgers is odd, because it's an extremely old school with a great reputation. But it's also the state university of New Jersey. So people who only know the first bit look at Rutgers highly, and sometimes lump it in as an almost Ivy League school. And people who know only the second bit tend to think it's just your typical, second-rate state school, filled with STD-ridden students that do nothing but party.

Is this reputation accurate?

I guess because Rutgers is so big, in the end it's both of those things. We do have the students who are only here because it's cheap, and they do party and have lots of sex and ignore the academic opportunities. And we have the students who realize the potential of this place, put in lots of work, and

leave Rutgers with an amazing education. Really, you can get an amazing education anywhere if you're dedicated.

What would an admissions officer at your school probably not tell a prospective student? What aspect of your school would a prospective student not see on a campus tour?

Admissions officers probably wouldn't tell prospective students that there are some professors at Rutgers who are terrible. Really, I've had professors who made me want to jump out the classroom window just so I wouldn't have to keep hearing their voices. Prospectives probably also wouldn't see any of the gigantic introductory lectures we're forced to sit through, particularly if we're studying anything having to do with the sciences. A prospective also wouldn't see how you can't park anywhere on this campus, and how completing a simple administrative task at Rutgers can often mean having to sift through piles and piles of bureaucracy.

The Institution

There are many different colleges and campuses that make up Rutgers, and every college/campus has it's own reputation. Busch, for example, is meant to be the "science campus." A lot of people also see it as the "Asian campus." Therefore, it is assumed that East Asian students and science students all live at Busch. . . . Or that anyone who lives at Busch is East Asian or studying science. (Of course, this isn't really true.) But if you come here, you'll find each campus is laden with bizarre, untrue associations, and you'll probably find yourself fighting against whatever associations other people project on you because of what/where you're studying.

The Education

When you look through the course catalog at the beginning of every semester, it's incredibly difficult to assemble a simple class schedule from a veritable sea of thousands of interesting course listings. It can take hours and hours just to narrow down your options!

Rutgers is a different experience for students involved in different majors. I have a double major, so I've gotten to see two very different academic worlds. This past semester I had a journalism class on College Avenue, which had maybe twenty people in it and at the beginning of every class the professor would say, "What's new?" He knew everyone by name, and the atmosphere was light and jokey. Then, on the science end, I had a four hundred-person lecture for my Molecular Biology and Biochemistry class taught by five different professors, none of whom would know me from Adam. In the journalism department, e-mails get sent out about internships and jobs once a day. In the MBB department, you get one lecture at the end of the semester called "Jobs in Biochemistry." It all goes to show that if you're going to go to a big school, figure out first what you might want to major in and contact the school. Figure out how big that major is and what it's like. From school to school, and from department to department, this will vary widely. Likewise, some colleges have big cores, others small ones. Go to the Rutgers Web site and check out what each college's core looks like if this is a big deal for you.

The Students

The most vocal students on campus are almost definitely the black students and the Jewish students. In general, we do have lots of protests and rallies, but then again we have students from every single ethnicity and background imaginable, so it's hard not to offend *someone,* and as soon as the offense registers, whoop! There's a rally. Nicely, though, all these different groups of students do get along for the most part. You don't see segregated groups of white kids and black kids and so on—you see integration. To paint a picture of Rutgers's diversity: my apartment this year houses a black basketball player, a British exchange student, a Jew from Massachusetts, and a Turkish Muslim from northern New Jersey. The four girls next door are of Chinese, Indian, Colombian, and European dissent. Having people this diverse around means all of your conversations are always going to be fiendishly interesting. On any given topic, if you find ten different people, you'll be able to have a great conversation encompassing ten different points of view rooted in ten very different upbringings.

The Activities

I've been involved in a whole pile of campus groups. It took me a long time to find ones that I actually enjoyed, but I was determined to keep on trying things until I felt comfortable. This means I went to salsa club meetings, outdoors club meetings, kendo club meeting, Hillel meetings . . . all kinds of meetings. In the end, the clubs I've liked the most have been primarily social and secondarily task oriented. This year, in particular, my favorite club has been the music arm of the Rutgers College Planning Committee. Here, students planned, organized, and implemented concerts for the entire student body. There was a small group of maybe fifteen or twenty of us, and we became close friends. We also put on some pretty amazing shows. There's something about a club that involves actually creating something that I like a lot more than a club that gets together for a lot of sit-and-talk meetings.

The Social Scene

We *drink.* The fraternity scene is pretty big around here; Union Street is "Frat Row," and on Thursday, Friday, and Saturday nights, that's where you'll find a great deal of Rutgers students. Things can get kind of crazy there, with parties sometimes getting broken up by the police and people getting in trouble. But as long as you're smart about your partying (don't attempt three keg-stands in a row if you know that you get drunk from one 12-ounce can of beer), then you should be fine and in for some great times. Personally, I'm not into frats, which is why it's great that there are also a lot of bars, restaurants, house parties, and other things that I can go to when I'm in the mood for fun (crazy or laid-back, depending on what I want out of the evening). Then, when you go home, dorm life is great because you meet lots of people, and there are always folks around to talk to. Even at four in the morning there's probably someone sitting in the lounge, listening to music. I've met most of my close friends from dorm linkages (most have lived on my floor or been friends with people who lived on my floor). I think the most difficult thing about being a first-year is finding your place here. It's hard, but everyone gets through it, so you will, too. But it's still hard.

Notable Rutgers Alumni Include:
Joyce Kilmer, poet
Calista Flockhart, actress
James Gandolfini, actor
David Stern, NBA commissioner
Milton Friedman, Nobel Prize-winning economist
Ozzie Nelson, actor, director, composer, producer

SARAH LAWRENCE COLLEGE

Founded: 1926
Location: Bronxville, NY
Phone: (914) 395-2510
E-mail: slcadmit@sarahlawrence.edu
Web site: www.sarahlawrence.edu

Number of Undergraduates: 1,226
Number of Graduate Students: 314
Cost: Approximately $41,000 per year
Application Deadline: January 15
Early Decision: November 15

Rating:	Notable Majors/Programs:
Very Selective	Creative Writing, Theater, Literature

Size:
● Small ○ Medium ○ Large

Location:
○ Urban ● Suburban ○ Rural

On a Saturday, students talk about academics:
● Always ○ Sometimes ○ Never

Nightlife:
○ Intense ○ Moderate ● Laid-back

Politically, Sarah Lawrence leans:
● Left ○ Right ○ Split

Diversity:
○ High ● Low ○ Medium

Students describe SLC in five words:
- Oxford-style education puts students first
- Tiny, gorgeous, alternative, near Manhattan

From the School

We care deeply about what is taught and how it is taught. We believe that true learning best occurs in an academic environment that promotes dialogue between teacher and student and in which each student's talents, insights, interests and needs help to determine the focus of her or his own work. Students are thus encouraged to use their own interests as the key to engaged involvement with the subject matter. As a result, they work ambitiously, take greater responsibility for their endeavors, care deeply about their studies and are better able to remember and apply what they have learned.

—www.slc.edu

If you're interested in SLC, you may also be interested in:
Bard, Brown, Hampshire, Oberlin, Vassar

Name: Archie

Hometown: Fayetteville, Arkansas

Class Year: Senior

Major: Sarah Lawrence doesn't have majors. Everyone graduates from Sarah Lawrence with a generic SLC degree, no major specified. This lets all SLC students have a true liberal-arts education. I study women's history, poetry, visual arts, literature, fiction writing, economics, and philosophy. Basically, I always take the classes that sound interesting with the professors I want to work with, rather than artificially focusing my attentions by "majoring." Sarah Lawrence encourages this. Badass, right?

Extracurriculars: Internships in publishing

Career Goal: I'm not sure. I might want to edit children's books. Maybe I'll live in Brooklyn, which is the new postgraduate SLC dorm.

How would you describe Sarah Lawrence's reputation?

Sarah Lawrence suffers from stereotyping. Mostly, when people think SLC, they think the following things:

1. Prestigious
2. Expensive
3. All women
4. Gay, gay, gay, gay
5. Hard drugs

Is this reputation accurate?

These stereotypes range in degrees of truth:

1. True: Sarah Lawrence is one of the best schools in America, with innovative programs, amazing professors, and small class sizes.
2. True: It's the second most expensive school in the country (I'm on heavy financial aid). Luckily, there are good reasons for our expensive price tag: We only have professors, none of that TA crap. We have the lowest student to teacher ratio in America (6:1 and only three hundred students per grade). And SLC has to charge more because it has a fraction of the endowment of most schools. (Because we are a fairly young college, and a lot of our alumni can't afford to give back tons because they don't work for "the man." Instead of money, grads send photos of themselves living in cardboard-

box art installations in the middle of rain forests, smiling happily away.)
3. False: We used to be a women's college, but now we are 30 percent male.
4. True: We do have a very high gay population. But, more important, Sarah Lawrence is a place where everything—sexuality included—is accepted.
5. True/False: There are some that do drugs here, but not all that many. This isn't the '80s. The days of abundant lines of coke littering our campus are long gone.

> "In high school, all of the artsy flaming-liberal kids have to stick together, so they all do theater. Then these kids get to Sarah Lawrence and realize they don't need to do theater because everyone here is essentially a flaming-liberal drama kid."
> ✦ Nicholas, junior

What would an admissions officer at your school probably not tell a prospective student?

The administration probably wouldn't tell a high school student that it's really hard to date here—no matter what your sexuality. For a straight girl, the straight boys are limited and conceited. For a queer student, the queer community is kind of moody. For a straight male, well . . . then you have it made it in the shade.

The Institution

I first arrived at Sarah Lawrence a starry-eyed eighteen-year-old girl from Arkansas. Freshman year, first semester, was exciting and scary and shitty and hard. I went from being one of the more creative and "out there" people in my high school to a little country bumpkin at SLC, surrounded by beautiful college folk. Luckily, everyone on my hall was dealing with the same situation, so we were dorky together and adjusted together. I had a monster crush on my RA, and knew that we were destined to be together (his boyfriend disagreed). I struggled with my writing (one teacher handed back a paper and told me, "This was really good . . . for a high school student"; I cried). But all of those freshman year travesties went away or got better. It's just a lame period that you survive—

you eventually become an amazing college student. SLC helps you get through it.

The Education

I have always loved Sarah Lawrence's education philosophy, which is remarkable for the following reasons:

1. We have no core curriculum, no majors. Sarah Lawrence doesn't control our academic life—instead, it provides knowledgeable professors and worthwhile classes, and students can study anything that interests them, all four years. This means every class you take will be full of people who want to be there. You are 100 percent in control of your academic life.
2. We have no tests. Cramming for a test isn't a particularly productive way of learning. And most students cram—whether they'll admit it or not—for most tests. So we don't take tests at all at Sarah Lawrence. Good riddance.
3. No TAs. We don't have TAs because our classes are so small that we don't need them. You'll never have a class with more than fifteen other students at SLC, and most classes have far fewer students than that. This means you get to be ridiculously close to every amazing professor you take a class with.
4. The conference system. Through the conference system, you'll be meeting with every professor outside of class right from the start to develop some sort of project that will incorporate everything you've learned and eventually mark the course's completion. Usually it's a long paper. Sometimes it's an internship or a play. Sometimes people do performance art. It's just another way to tie in learning with your personal interests. It's also an opportunity to spend time alone with amazing, brilliant professors.
5. At the end of every course, you'll know how you did because teachers will write a one-page evaluation of your work. We never receive letter grades, although they are recorded on our transcripts. (I've never seen mine and I never will—most people never ask to see their "official" grades.) Written evaluations are so much more valuable than a lousy letter or number, anyway. Grades and numbers don't help you learn. I'd much prefer to hear a teacher's actual, thought-out opinions on my work.
6. At Sarah Lawrence, you choose each teacher you have through the interview system. A week before classes begin, you get to roam all over campus and sign up for interview spots with teachers. Then, you meet with teachers and you can ask them questions like "Why do you teach this course?" and "Can I do this (fill in the blank) for my conference work?" My major rule is that my teacher and I need to get along and both of us need to laugh at some point during the interview. Then I can take the professor's class.

> "Our library is hideous. It makes me horribly angry. Good thing the rest of our campus is so gorgeous."
>
> ✦ Evan, junior

The Students

We've had some students that were once celebrities. For example, at one time there were three kids from the movie *The Mighty Ducks* attending SLC. Why? No one knows. We also have some pretty famous alumni who reappear on campus every once in a while, like Barbara Walters, Vera Wang, and Yoko Ono. But mostly our students aren't famous (which is a good thing). Instead, they are interesting and different. Here's a sampling:

Brad—a freshman boy who wanted to weld two shopping carts together, fill them with glow sticks, and throw it off the roof of the science center for a conference project. By the end of his first year he held the distinction of being on every kind of probation that exists at SLC, and his photo is on every security guard's clipboard.

T–r–h—she bends gender so much that she had to get rid of the A's in her name. She was in love with a theater boy freshman year, then got her first girlfriend; now she prefers to date trannie-boys. She's from privileged Vermont and expounds beautifully on the classist implications of the term "ghetto."

Peter—a six-foot-five-inch red-haired Scotsman who hooks up with a different girl every week while being a dedicated and talented student of philosophy and Middle Eastern history.

Emma—a fashionable photo and writing student who interns for posh magazines and only wears Marc Jacobs and pink stilettos. She never uses a dull verb in her fiction stories and has a knack for making mix CDs.

Brian—Mr. Gay Sarah Lawrence, who is a safer-sex educator (we all know the safest methods of fisting now) and makes dresses out of Polaroid pictures for credit while studying the cultural implications of the metrosexual.

Greg—a gun-carrying Texan, king of beers, president of the senior class, hates New York City.

The Activities

SLC only has 1,200 students but, there is always something do to. In the last few weeks, I: attended a play about a boarding school during WWII that was a friend's senior thesis project; saw a dance concert where a girl wore a tiny tennis dress and shouted "Go!" a lot; ate a barbecued piece of pig served by SLC's People Who Eat Tasty Meat Club; cheered for an a cappella singing group; stayed up all night in the library; went to my internship in New York City twice; drove into New York City to see friends perform at a Prostitute's Union benefit and skateboarded through Wall Street at midnight; swung on the SLC swing set and talked about Virginia Woolf's true feelings on war; ate dinner with my classmates at my teacher's dazzling Upper East Side [Manhattan] apartment; sat on a blanket with candles on one of the back lawns and whispered secrets; laughed at all the people dressed up for the choir concert; and went for a two-hour Sunday brunch in the cafeteria.

The Social Scene

As I'm sure is true for everywhere, we have every kind of partyer here. We have the kids that don't party at all. We have the kids that get drunk once a month, once a weekend, or once a day. We have the kids that sell prescription drugs in the library. We have the kids that play glow-in-the dark Frisbee at midnight. What we definitely don't have are fraternities or sororities (although there was rumored to be a lesbian frat with a topless fight club for a while).

Name: Ahonui

Hometown: Anahola, Hawaii

Class Year: Senior

Major: Music, Architecture

Extracurriculars: Chamber Choir, French Club.

Career Goal: I'd like to be a composer or an architect—probably a composer who works as an architect to actually make a living.

How would you describe Sarah Lawrence's reputation?

A place for really weird, gay people. And if you're not really weird or gay, you will be soon.

Is this reputation accurate?

No. We're not that weird or gay. Sarah Lawrence is just an extremely fun, open, accepting place. We just like people here.

What would an admissions officer at your school probably not tell a prospective student? What aspect of your school would a prospective student not see on a campus tour?

Well, the administration would hide the fact that there's drinking and drug use on campus, though it's not any more prevalent at SLC than it is at any other school. SLC is college. Drinking and drugs exist.

> "The biggest social event on campus is the Coming Out dance—last year, I made out with twenty-six people (thirteen female, thirteen male). I also broke my toe."
> ✦ Marissa, sophomore

The Institution

Sarah Lawrence is rather small—about 1,200 students. I, for one, like this, though I think going abroad for your junior year is a must. Four years living with the same people would get difficult and kind of cramped. This way, you leave, see the world, then get excited to come back and learn some more.

Sarah Lawrence is located in Bronxville, which is a really lame, ultra-conservative, ultra-rich town. Students and townies mutually dislike one another, but since SLC is so close to New York City, this isn't really a problem. If tensions rise, students leave. Then the townies calm down.

My favorite SLC tradition is registration, which is unique in that students interview professors for classes. You can see if a professor is willing or particularly able to help you out if you have a particular conference idea. That way, you never have a wasted class here. You always know what you're getting into.

Broadly, going to SLC teaches you a lot about how to do real work—not just cramming for finals ('cause we don't have 'em), but how to plan and prepare for a project that is due months and months in the future. It's one thing to study for a final a few days before you take it; it's another to enter into a contract with one's professor, saying I will have a twenty- to thirty-page paper about this specific topic in your hands three months from now. It makes you realize you can do big things, and it helps you learn how to make a long-term plan for yourself and stick to it.

> "Half of the dorms on main campus are lovely, traditional-style buildings, full of ghosts and interesting corners."
> ✦ Alexa, senior

The Education

I think courses and conference work are the two biggest topics of conversation at SLC. We're all a bunch of nerds who love studying whatever the hell it is that we're studying. Since SLC has managed to do away with finals and since there is no emphasis put on grades, it's really difficult to compete with other students, too. Because of things like this, I cannot overstress how amazing SLC's education system is. It's modeled after the Oxford University system, where every student has a don (an academic adviser, not to be confused with the head of the mob). Your don, or adviser, is everything, from the guy who helps you cope with adjusting to college life, to the guy who suggests what courses you should take, to the guy who listens when you're having trouble with your math course.

Also following Oxford tradition, SLC places emphasis on group discussions and the individual. Seminar classes are limited to fifteen students. Here is a sample of the different class-end conference projects from a class called the Literature of Hawaii:

a study of the cruise industry and the places cruise ships visit; a critique of the Hawaiian sovereignty movement, comparing it with the Rhodesia move to Zimbabwe; the social and cultural significance of the tattoo in Polynesian cultures; the sex-trafficking industry in the Philippines. Again, all these projects were for the same class, based on each student's individual interests.

The Students

SLC is a very open place, or at least I've found it to be so. Sometimes students tend to fall into the category of "being so open-minded, you're closed minded," or however the saying goes. But in general, I feel the student body is very accepting of you, whether you're LGBT, Christian, Muslim, black, Asian, white, whatever.

People here are mostly white though, and only 40 percent of the students are on financial aid. At a school that costs over forty grand a year (including housing and fees and all that fun stuff), that should tell you a lot. Students come from forty-eight states and something like twelve countries, so it's a geographically diverse place. Fifteen percent of the students are from New York State (not just Manhattan and the surrounding area), and 12 percent are from California.

Students are mostly Democrats. If you're right-wing, expect to explain exactly why, and to explain this well. There aren't many protests on campus. SLC suffers from severe lack of motivation on the political front. We live happily in a liberal bubble.

The Activities

You can be an athlete at Sarah Lawrence, but you have to understand that sports aren't a very big deal here. I mean, you'll have fun, you'll have lots of institutional support, and you'll have great coaches. But don't expect students on the whole to get too excited about your sports games.

There are a lot of crazy events here—many themed cabarets, including a Coming Out dance in October, which started out as a celebration of gay pride but has now devolved into more of a debaucherous spectacle of scantily clad students. It's fun; anything goes. There's also an auction every year to raise money for student scholarships. People put up items ranging from chocolate-chip cookies, to dinner for four at a trustee's house, to Zac Posen and Vera Wang dresses, to walk-on roles on various sitcoms that are written or produced by SLC grads.

Students play such a *huge* role in administrative decisions and policy development that it can pretty much be classified as an activity here. I mean, students write evaluations for each course that are read by the administration and the faculty members (*after* they've submitted your evaluations and grades). And when professors are up for tenure or rehiring, students are invited, and encouraged, to come say something assessing the prof's performance.

One year, some students disagreed with a policy enacted by the new president of SLC. They protested and wrote her a letter explaining their thoughts on the situation, and asked that she respond and hold a schoolwide debate (called a town meeting). SLC's new president set up the debate within the week.

The Social Scene

I tend to leave campus less and less as the years go by. But NYC is only twenty minutes away. There's also a crapload going on on campus, ranging from dance parties and live performances to poetry readings and hang-outs. And the theater department is insane. They put on 30 productions a semester, and these are open to all students.

SLC doesn't really party. People have "gatherings." If you're looking for raging keggers, look elsewhere. There is no Greek life, either, so if your hope is to be a sister or a brother, sorry. This isn't the place for you.

The male/female ratio at SLC is about 30/70. And since the campus is so small, dating is difficult if you don't want to see your sweetie all the time. I suggest not doing it. The city is so close. If a relationship is what you need, it'll be better coming from Manhattan.

Name: Elissa
Hometown: Los Angeles, California
Class Year: Junior
Major: Liberal Arts
Extracurriculars: FLUX co-founder (Feminism. Liberation. Unity. Xylophone), theater production, 'zine writer.
Career Goal: Writer? Librarian? Maybe archivist? I'm not sure.

How would you describe Sarah Lawrence's reputation?

All-girl militant feminist lesbian school.

Is this reputation accurate?

Sarah Lawrence hasn't been an all-girl school since the '60s, yet for some reason that is the most common misconception. As for us being feminists—a good number are, though not as many as is assumed, and among the feminists, there aren't that many "militant" feminists. We are a queer-friendly school, but I don't think that we have any more queer students then any other college. (Queer refers to students who are gay, lesbian, bisexual, transsexual, transgender, etc.)

What aspect of your school would a prospective student not see on a campus tour?

I work in the admissions office as a tour guide and make it a point to be completely honest with anyone visiting the school, so there's not much that I wouldn't tell a student or parent.

The Institution

I chose Sarah Lawrence because there was a handwritten note at the bottom of my acceptance letter commenting on my application and expressing how much the administration wanted me, in particular, to come and study. I knew right then that SLC was a different kind of school, where the administration really cares. I came from a small high school where I knew all of my teachers on a relatively personal level and they knew me. It was great, and that's exactly the kind of environment I wanted in college. I wanted a small school, with people who were weird and with whom I could have the freedom to experiment. And all those expectations have pretty much been fulfilled here.

We have a great administration. Most of our staff is completely open and most students form incredible relationships with them. Our school is so small that everyone knows your name or at least your face and that's wonderfully comforting.

The Education

SLC is a great place for learning for the sake of learning. It's not a school with the intention of training you for a specific career or job or future. In fact, most students have no clue what they're going to do after they graduate (seniors included). But that's okay. We find our paths eventually.

I've had amazing teachers here—people I consider my friends before I consider them my teachers. I can talk to them about my personal life, about my goals, my dreams, about sharks, anything. We don't ever need to see our grades and there's no competition here. You have to be incredibly self-motivated to be here. No one is going to push you along; you have to do it yourself. You might have a few teachers who will kick you in the ass if you're not doing your work, but in the end it's really up to you.

The Students

Sarah Lawrence's motto is, "You are different, so are we," and to a certain extent that's true. The school does attract the type of student that might have been ostracized in high school, the kid that always felt a little out of place—the Dungeons and Dragons kids, the theater kids, the queer students, the radical feminists, etc. However, when you get all of those kids into one school, you feel more at home.

We are mostly white, middle-class, liberal artists here. Those who are really different (Republicans—I can name the three we have) are usually the majority out in the "real world." There's a reason our satirical newspaper is called the *Bubble*—SLC is a bubble. We are all the weird kids from high school thrown into one school—which is amazing, but it's also not reality.

The Activities

There's always something happening on campus—theater performances, dance and music concerts, poetry readings, movies, etc. This is not to say that all of them are good or even decent, but there's always something to do.

We have tons of clubs because we don't need a faculty advisor to start one. However, not all of our clubs are active because people are busy and it's usually hard to get someone to commit to anything around here. There's something for everyone, but, because of our small size, it might just be you and one other person.

The Social Scene

Our weekends usually start on Thursday night because there are very few classes on Fridays. People get drunk in small groups, usually with their friends, and some of them stumble around campus being obnoxious, but for the most part people are very respectful and smart drinkers.

The dating scene on campus is awkward. Some people form great relationships here, but for the most part, if you're a straight woman, you're celibate; if you're a lesbian, you might do a little better; if you're a gay man, your dating pool will be the same small incestuous group of people; and if you're a straight guy, you could do real well, but possibly graduate with the reputation of being a complete jerk. Don't come to SLC with the intention of dating; if its important to you, just don't come here.

Notable Sarah Lawrence Alumni Include:
Barbara Walters, first female TV news anchor
Jon Avent, director
Alice Walker, author
Janice Simpson, editor, *Time* magazine
Jean Baker Miller, psychiatrist, author
Susan Meiselas, photographer

SCRIPPS COLLEGE

Founded: 1926
Location: Claremont, CA
Phone: (909) 621-8149
E-mail: admission@scrippscollege.edu
Web site: www.scrippscollege.edu

Number of Undergraduates: 810
Number of Graduate Students: 20
Cost: Approximately $38,000 per year
Application Deadline: February 1
Early Decision: November 1

Rating:	Notable Majors/Programs:
Selective	Life Sciences, English, Psychology, Studio Art

Size:
● Small   ○ Medium   ○ Large

Location:
○ Urban   ● Suburban   ○ Rural

On a Saturday, students talk about academics:
○ Always   ● Sometimes   ○ Never

Nightlife:
○ Intense   ○ Moderate   ● Laid-back

Politically, Scripps leans:
● Left   ○ Right   ○ Split

Diversity:
○ High   ○ Low   ● Medium

All Women's: Yes!

Students describe Scripps in five words:

- I hate questions like this. In lieu of five words I will simply say this: Every so often a magazine profiles some up-and-coming young woman who is changing the face of politics, business, her occupation. . . . These women come from Scripps.
- Confident, individualistic, unique, beautiful sisterhood

From the School

As one of the founders of the Claremont Colleges Group Plan, Scripps is a principal contributor to the university community. Scripps emphasizes high aspirations, high achievement, and personal integrity in all pursuits, and it expects students, faculty, staff, and alumnae to contribute to Scripps and to their own communities throughout their professional, social, and civic lives. Scripps believes that this form of challenging and individualized education will best prepare women for lives of confidence, courage, and hope.

—www.scrippscol.edu

If you're interested in Scripps, you may also be interested in:
Barnard, Bryn Mawr, Mount Holyoke, Pomona, Smith, Spelman

Name: Katherine
Hometown: Renton, Washington
Class Year: Sophomore
Major: Cognitive Neuroscience
Extracurriculars: Vice president of the Claremont Colleges Ballroom Dance Company, a tour guide for Scripps, and I am doing research with the Adult Development Project.
Career Goal: To obtain a master's degree, possibly in teaching, and teach high school science before going on to grad school, or obtain my doctorate in neuroscience straight away and go on to teach and do research at a college or university. Not sure.

How would you describe Scripps's reputation?

Scripps is known to produce women who are well-educated and ready to take on the challenges of tomorrow.

Is this reputation accurate?

Absolutely! We are one of the only women's colleges on the West Coast, and certainly one of the best. Somewhere around 80 percent of the Scripps students who apply to medical schools get in, and law school is about the same.

What aspect of Scripps would a prospective student not see on a campus tour? What would an admissions officer at your school probably not tell a prospective student?

A campus tour can only give you the feel of the buildings at Scripps. The flavor of campus life, however, can be felt if you stay the night. You also might not get a feel for just how integrated the 5Cs are—how often we go up to Mudd, down to CMC or Pomona, or across to Pitzer to eat, take classes, visit friends.

Also, I talked with one of the admissions officers when I came for my interview here, and she told me that it was fairly easy to have a double major, even in different concentrations, and while it is possible (she wasn't completely wrong), it's *really not* the easiest thing to do, especially if you want to double major in a science and a humanities area.

The Institution

Scripps College is a women's college, but that doesn't mean there are no men around. Being one of the five Claremont schools does have its advantages in terms of mixing student bodies. Scripps was founded in 1926, and was the second of the Claremont colleges to be built. It started off as one building where students and professors lived, worked, slept, and ate, surrounded by a wall and orange groves, and has gradually expanded to a nine-dorm, multibuilding campus. There were originally dorm mothers who would serve tea and cookies from a silver service every day. We do still have tea, but only once a week, in Seal Court on Wednesdays, and you can have as many cookies as you want. Speaking of cookies, we do have fresh-baked cookies in our dining hall every day: chocolate chip, peanut butter, sugar, and macadamia nut too. They're delicious, and we have a wood-burning pizza oven, so the pizza is always good as well. Not to brag, but we have some of the best food on the 5Cs, so lots of people come to eat at Malott, our dining hall.

We have a little over eight hundred women on campus: small enough that you get to know a large variety of people whom you see on a regular basis and who create a feeling of community, but large enough that you won't meet absolutely everyone— and especially with the other colleges around, there are definitely people you still won't know after four years. About 99 percent of our students live on campus all four years, because we have really nice dorms, and if you're off campus, you're just too far away from everything.

> "On a campus tour, they don't show how evil the olive trees can be. Sure, they look neat, but in the fall they launch olives at your head—those things hurt more than you would think."
>
> ✦ Amelia, sophomore

The campus is built in Mediterranean-style architecture and is absolutely gorgeous. We have approximately sixteen fountains on campus, some hidden away in little courtyards inside the dorms, and we have Margaret Fowler Garden, which has a sixty-year-old wisteria in it that is beautiful when it blooms in the spring. Margaret Fowler also holds a mural by Alfredo Ramos Martinez, who passed away while he was painting it. They've left it unfinished so that artists from around the country can come and study his techniques. We also have a graffiti wall, which consists of murals from every graduating class going back to almost the beginning of the school; in front of the wall is the rose garden, which is planted with roses so that we can pick them and take them back to our rooms or give them to people. We have a library that looks like a gothic chapel. Urban campus legend has it that the woman who donated the money wanted a church, but we compromised and built a library that looks like a church.

Our president likes to walk her dogs around the campus, and the deans and faculty and administration eat in the dining hall with the students, so there's always a time to talk to them. It's a wonderful set-up.

The Education

Classes are relatively small. The largest class you'll ever have here is Core 1, which is your first semester here. Every other day you'll have lecture or discussion, and the lectures are comprised of the entire first-year class, around two hundred people. But you get to sit in comfy velvety chairs. It's co-taught by thirteen professors; each lectures on a specific day and then the next day leads discussion for a smaller group of students, probably fifteen or so. Core 2 and Core 3 complete the Core program, each one getting more focused. The cool thing about Core 1 is that it's interdisciplinary, so there's something for everyone—and it's a true bonding experience because everyone's going through it at the same time. So you have late-night study sessions and debate core issues with people over dinner.

Other classes are open to everyone in the 5Cs, and most number around five to fifteen people. Intro science classes are a bit larger, but still they max out at about thirty people, which is still very much smaller than you'll find at most universities. It's so nice, because you get to know your profs and they know you, and you can go to their offices and talk to them and meet them for lunch and get invited to their houses. If you don't want individual attention, it's probably not the best place for you.

Cross-registration with the other campuses is really easy: you simply go to our registrar and give her the paper with what you want to take on it, and she types it in and tells you whether you got everything you wanted or not. The chance of not getting a class that you want is very low. I've had it happen only once in two years here, and I know very few people who have had a class close before they could get into it.

Since Scripps is only an undergrad institution, we have no TAs. We have research opportunities all over the place for students as early as your first year. Classes are fairly intense. Work outside of classes depends on what you're taking; I know people who can go out and lie on the grass in the sun every afternoon, and I know people like me who spend lots of time indoors getting things done. It's totally up to you and what you want to do with your time here.

> "The women here are strong individuals and some are great to debate with."
> ✦ Amelia, sophomore

The Students

The students here are fabulous. Of course I'm biased, being one of them, but really, it's a good place to be. To be brutally honest, we don't have a huge minority population, but what we do have is active and strong. The majority of us are white middle-class women. But we're trying to change that to some extent. The people who come here are friendly and kind, and are from all kinds of places and backgrounds. Our students range from being highly political (mostly liberal, although there are conservatives as well) to indifferent, but you can always find something for any interest and a group of people interested in the same thing. And if Scripps in particular doesn't have something, one of the other colleges is sure to. We don't have any sororities or fraternities (I guess the latter would be obvious, since we have no men). All the dorms are mixed classes, so you have seniors in with the first-years, and they can tell you which classes you want to take and that kind of thing.

The Activities

There are all kinds of activities at the 5Cs. As a member of the Claremont Colleges Ballroom Dance Company and the Claremont Colleges Orchestra, I know the most about those, but we also have groups for minorities, groups for politically minded people, religious worship groups, and intramural sports, as well as sports teams through the school. There's always something. We get daily e-mail updates so you can decide whether you want to go see a movie down at Pomona, or go to a party at Mudd, or go to the Motley (our coffee house) to hear a band—it's all there. There's no need to go off campus—however, if you do, there are all kinds of places to go, providing you can catch a bus or have a friend with a car. Pasadena is about forty-five minutes away; one of its many offerings is a Thursday night swing club that's really fun! And L.A. isn't far away either. If you don't have a car, the Village is a fifteen-minute walk away, where there are banks, coffee shops, bagel shops, a café, a Sunday morning farmer's market, and the best part, Bert and Rocky's, an ice cream and candy emporium.

The Social Scene

The social scene at Scripps isn't overly present, but is definitely there. If you want to find a noisy party, most of the time you just have to walk across the street to Mudd, but you can come back here and do work, and sleep, and no one's going to bother you. We do have an escort policy in the dorms, which requires that any visitor, male or female, be within about ten feet of you, and visitors can stay for only four nights in your room, but it's not a hassle. It is enforced, and it's just for our safety; sometimes it would be nice to let the boys walk out on their own, but . . . it's not horrible, and it could be worse.

Name: Lindsey
Hometown: Lakewood, Colorado
Class Year: First
Major: English and Gender Studies
Extracurriculars: The *Voice* school newspaper, theater, Claremont Student Union, Naughty Revolution.
Career Goal: For now, I plan on going into the publishing industry; I'd like to eventually become a magazine or book editor.

> "How many Scrippsies does it take to screw in a lightbulb? Two: one to hold the Diet Coke and the other to yell out, 'DADDY!!!!'"
> ✦ Lindsey, senior

How would you describe Scripps's reputation?

Of the five Claremont Colleges, Scripps is considered to have the most spoiled "Daddy's girl" students, but also the girls who get most of the attention from the guys on the other campuses. Scripps is also the most feminist campus.

Is this reputation accurate?

There are definitely a handful of those "Daddy's girl" girls on campus, but that doesn't mean they can't change the world; they probably will. There are definitely a lot of feminists on campus, but that doesn't mean they shy away from guys. These are liberated, sexually aware, empowered women.

What would an admissions officer at Scripps probably not tell a prospective student?

[He/she] probably wouldn't tell them about the frustration of financial aid. The financial aid office is tricky. While some have had positive experiences with financial aid, I was not one of them.

The Institution

The most difficult thing for me about being a first-year student here was the lack of sociability in the dorms. Since first-years are spread over all the dorms, there's no "Freshman Hall" where everyone can make new friends. The upperclassmen don't usually try to interact with the first-years, which was disappointing. But housing is beautiful! And this is definitely the most beautiful campus if you like flowers, greenery, and fountains. The campus is small and easy to get around.

The Education

The small class sizes are one of my favorite things about this school. Six of the eight classes I've taken as a freshman have had under twenty people. Of course, that means you have to keep up with your work and you can't disappear into the background, but you get a lot more out of the classroom experience. Because of this setup, there are hardly any tests except for the occasional midterm and finals, and a whole lot of writing goes on, at least in the humanities. I have had only one lecture class so far; most classes are discussion based and everyone's opinion counts. We have no TAs, which I think is great, because the professors are more willing to discuss even menial things with you.

There was definitely a sense of competition among the first-years first semester, because so many of us were at the top of our class during high school. That died down soon after we got our first set of grades and realized all of us could succeed in college without the competitiveness.

All seniors have to complete a senior thesis or project, which sounds pretty intimidating, but it speaks to the ability of the graduating class and its great preparation for those people going on to grad school.

I love the variety of classes that are offered here. The one class that always gets strange looks when I mention I'm taking it is "Feminist Introduction to the Bible," but it's a great class and I've put to use a lot of the concepts I've learned from it toward other classes. There's also a class called "Communities of Hate," which is about genocide in the twentieth century; it's definitely a sad class, but it's something everyone can learn from.

The Students

Most students are from the West Coast. There are a lot of people from California, but at times it seems that Seattle has the most representation here. Most of the girls here are upper-middle class, but there is definitely a fair share of girls who are close to the poverty line but have gotten great financial aid. Scripps has a liberal flavor to it, especially when it comes to women's issues and queer issues; on other issues, it's a mixed bag. There are a bunch of politically active students, but also just as many who could care less.

The Activities

The Claremont Colleges—the 5Cs—form basically one giant school, with small subdivisions based on interest. We all interact during class (you're allowed to register for any classes within the 5Cs), but especially during the weekends. Claremont McKenna and Mudd have the best parties by far, often themed. Pomona is the one campus that sometimes excludes itself from the rest of the 5Cs. They have a reputation (deserved) for being snobby to the other schools' students. Athletics might as well be nonexistent here. Of course, they exist if you want to play, but don't expect anyone to go out and watch you. School is much more important to the students here.

If you don't have friends with cars, it's hard to get out as much as you'd like, as public transportation here is lacking, but the Metro-rail is close, so students use that to get down to L.A. to see the sights, or go to the beach (forty minutes away).

The Social Scene

Partying starts on Thursday and ends early Sunday morning. The majority of students don't have classes on Fridays, so some of the best parties are on Thursday nights. Scripps doesn't have a lot of parties (maybe two per semester), but the ones we do have are fun. Harvey Mudd has some great theme parties, like Wild West (complete with mechanical bull), while Claremont McKenna specializes in the typical college parties. There are only a

handful of fraternities, which aren't even based on campus, so no one really knows about them. Instead of frat houses throwing parties, usually specific dorms throw parties. It works better that way—no stupid, dangerous hazing process. Most of the parties are outside, thanks to the great California weather, so that makes it a lot of fun and usually leads to bigger gatherings. About a quarter of the parties actually card, but you can always find someone to get you alcohol.

Name: Amy
Hometown: Fillmore, California
Class Year: Senior
Major: English
Extracurriculars: Lead computer consultant for the Scripps computer lab.
Career Goal: Not sure. Currently considering something in political organizing.

How would you describe Scripps's reputation?

A little odd. Most people have either never heard of it or assume it is part of the Scripps Oceanographic Institute in San Diego. Those who do know of it, however, know it to be an upper-tier private school with the high academic standards expected of an Ivy but without (thank God) the snootiness.

Is this reputation accurate?

Absolutely. I attended University of California my first year of college and consequently have a better understanding of why Scripps is so unique. People here *want* to go to school. The students also aren't stuck up like some of the Ivy Leaguers or the Pomona students down the street. We're high quality but not well known, which gives us a certain sense of humility.

What would an admissions officer at Scripps probably not tell a prospective student? What aspect of Scripps would a prospective student not see on a campus tour?

An admissions officer probably would not tell you that we have recently had a lot of issues regarding diversity. A large faction of the student body is opposed to having a predominantly white community. Funny thing is, no one ever bothers to argue for the rights of poor students. . . . Black or white.

A student on a campus tour probably wouldn't see the administration's distant handling of the student body or the animosity the students and administration feel toward one another.

The Institution

Because Scripps College is so small, you know nearly everyone. This small size and close community was something I was looking for when I was looking to transfer from my former college.

The school and the city of Claremont do not get on too well. Our biggest problem is people calling in noise complaints and the refusal of most business owners to consider the needs of the students. The Village, the small and quaint shopping center, sells very few items that are practical for a college town—it is mostly art stores, high-priced restaurants, and antiquaries. Claremont has planned to build a club district; however, it is likely that said club will be intended for eighteen-year-olds and up, and left to the high school crowd. (You'll know the high schoolers in Claremont by sight—they are the ones in the grunge clothes bitching about capitalism before getting into their BMWs.)

The housing here is amazing, rooms are large, most people have singles, and the dorms are not filled with losers cranking their stereos up to maximum volume. Recent changes in acceptance policy have made it so first-years and sophomores live in doubles and juniors and seniors in singles, but previously, and perhaps again in the future, you could expect to have a single from sophomore year on.

> "The Claremont Colleges are considered the Ivy Leagues of the West Coast; I think this holds pretty true. . . . There's *such* a wonderful academic community here."
> ✦ Saida, freshman

The Education

Academic fervor is strong at Scripps, although competition is limited. Very few students discuss their grades with others; in fact, the only time it comes up is during Senior Academic Awards period. Most of the week is dedicated to study and weekends are dedicated to alcohol-fueled parties at Mudd and the other 5Cs.

All seniors complete a thesis—I just completed a seventy-nine-page original work myself. Theses are unusually difficult at Scripps but not something the average Scripps student cannot overcome. Theses will be most difficult for those who are not self-directed learners (which is a shame because everything else is set up for those who want academic hand-holding). Because I completed my thesis pretty much on my own, I feel prepared to go into most careers.

Also, the classes here are not terribly interesting (they were more interesting at my former college) but they will certainly give you a good overall education and will definitely prepare you for almost any course of graduate study. Do not expect to "find yourself" in the coursework here—we're a school made for those who know what they want and are good at getting it.

Over half our students study abroad for at least a term; this is a *huge* percentage of study-abroad scholars.

The Students

We have a small contingency of racial minorities and an extremely small contingency of financial minorities (there are few very rich people and fewer poor people). Despite being small, the racial minority groups are vocal, as are the LGBT students. If you want to protest, you should head over to Pitzer College (where dwell those who hate capitalism unless it comes in the form of Daddy's gold card) or join the Asian American Student Union (which is extremely active on all 5Cs). There are a number of lesbian students, but lesbian rights are widely accepted without protest or comment; most people here are liberal enough to simply assume gays and lesbians deserve full and equal rights. Students are usually Democrats, and Scripps can be very intolerant toward those who identify themselves as Republicans. Greek societies are nonexistent (we're practically an 800-person sorority anyhow). Most people expect to go into the professional world or become mothers (active mothers, the kind that teach their children Bach in the womb), but very few of them expect to become famous doing it.

The Activities

We have lectures, loads of them, which sadly I do not go to simply because I am lazy. When we're bored, we go to Target. It sounds stupid, but it is THE PLACE for social interaction outside in-room gatherings. If it's after ten at night (when Target closes), we go to one of the on-campus eateries—usually the Hub at CMC or the Mudd Hole at Mudd. As a nondrinker I find the social life disturbing; if you don't drink, there is very little to do on the weekends and, no, these are not parties you can go to and not drink.

The Social Scene

Most of the student body (something like 98 percent) lives on campus, which helps with the community feel. Scripps has few parties, but you can find one or two parties on any given Friday or Saturday night. The "hardcore" parties are at Mudd (across the street) and include rather unique themes (just envision *Animal House* with a cast of nuclear physicists and you have Mudd). There are times I wonder if Scripps's goal is to found a generation of alcoholics. Alcohol is provided by the school and there are only the most limited attempts to ensure said alcohol is distributed to those who are of age. But don't worry, you'll find friends no matter what you choose.

Notable Scripps Alumni Include:
Barbara Cook Wormser, founder and president, Inland Harvest
Louise Francesconi, president, Missile Systems
Molly Ivins, journalist, author
Nancy Cook Aldrich, physicist and engineer
Nancy Neighbor Russell, environmental activist
Pamela Corey-Archer, Colin Powell Diplomat in Residence, UNC–Chapel Hill

SMITH COLLEGE

Founded: 1871

Location: Northampton, MA

Phone: (413) 585-2700

E-mail: admission@smith.edu

Web site: www.smith.edu

Number of Undergraduates: 2,680

Number of Graduate Students: 480

Cost: Approximately $39,000 per year

Application Deadline: January 15

Early Decision: November 15

Rating:	Notable Majors/Programs:
Selective	Social Sciences, Life Sciences, Engineering

Size:
○ Small ● Medium ○ Large

Location:
○ Urban ● Suburban ○ Rural

On a Saturday, students talk about academics:
○ Always ● Sometimes ○ Never

Nightlife:
○ Intense ○ Moderate ● Laid-back

Politically, Smith leans:
● Left ○ Right ○ Split

Diversity:
○ High ○ Low ● Medium

All Women's: Yes!

Students describe Smith in five words:
- Empowering, funky, aesthetically very pleasing
- Passionate, progressive, academic, social, hard-core!

From the School

Smith develops within its students the capacity to lead and change the world. For more than 125 years, Smith women have thrived in fields that women have not typically entered; they have broken new ground and set new standards. And the college continues to forge new paths, offering a curriculum based in the humanities, arts and sciences, but with an emphasis on globalism, practical learning and leadership skills.

—www.smith.edu

If you're interested in Smith, you may also be interested in:
Amherst, Barnard, Bryn Mawr, Mount Holyoke, Wellesley, Wesleyan

Name: L.B.
Hometown: Westford, Massachusetts
Class Year: Junior
Majors: Architecture/Spanish
Extracurriculars: Tour guide, museum volunteer, Habitat for Humanity.
Career Goal: I hope to someday to find myself in an architecture-related or business field.

How would you describe Smith's reputation?

Smith has a reputation for being a competitive all-women's college. I think a lot of people perceive the women here to all be politically active (even politically crazy), liberal, tree-hugging lesbians.

Is this reputation accurate?

To some extent. Academically, Smith is definitely challenging. So many people here are over-achievers that you have to work very hard to stand out. At the same time, I wish people didn't generalize about the student body. Sure, there are a lot of people who dress weird, pierce their faces, and dye their hair pink (blue, green, and red)—but there are also plenty of your typical New England preppies: Reef sandals, polo shirts, pearl earrings, and all. Sometimes, I think it's these mainstream gals who get lost in the shuffle.

What aspect of Smith would a prospective student not see on a campus tour?

On my tours, I usually don't play up how many lesbians there are here. As a straight student, I find it both an asset and a turn-off how active the lesbian student population is. Sometimes I feel very educated and proud that I am part of such a diverse student body and other times I think it's insane and that all these girls talk about is lesbian sex. Hopefully you know this before you get here—otherwise you are in for a big awakening!

The Institution

Smith's prestige can make you feel like you are awesome. Being part of such a great school and surrounded by so many successful women is almost too much to handle on a daily basis. So many of the women I now study with will go on to hold positions of power and prestige. Seeing all the amazing things people do around campus is like listening to a motivational speaker every day. Smith has given me a motivation to achieve my dreams that I don't think I could have gotten any-

where else; I just want to go out and be one of those amazing Smithies!

School spirit changes daily from "Smith sucks" to "Smith is bliss." And the reality is that Smith sucks and it is bliss. I love the school's size, like having small classes, profs that know my name, and small houses to live and eat in. I never considered a larger school and I'm damn glad. Plus, Smith gets the best of both worlds because you can always take a class at UMass or head to their crazy frat parties on the weekends.

The Career Development Office here is amazing. I cannot say enough good things. They will bend over backwards for you until you are standing tall exactly where you want to be.

> "Smith is a small school, and it can get claustrophobic. Eventually, you can connect yourself to anyone else on the campus: 'Nice to meet you, Alex; aren't you my roommate's best friend's ex-girlfriend's lab partner?'"
>
> ✦ Sarah, senior

Housing here is amazing. With a baby grand piano and an electric fireplace, the living room in my college house is nicer than my one at home. Plus, the bathrooms are so clean here. We have Corian countertops and tile floors you could eat off— just one upshot of not having guys at the school.

Sometimes I do wish Smith would go coed. For many, the lack of guys can be a little annoying. For others, the plethora of available lesbian women is just what they are looking for. But inevitably, Friday comes and the PVTA (transit system) sends all those Amherst boys our way, or us to them, and we realize that maybe being at an all-girls school isn't quite so bad—in fact, it's pretty awesome! I attribute my friendships and academic accomplishments largely in part to Smith being all women. There is just so much petty stuff I don't have to deal with on a daily basis, so I can keep my head clear for all the important stuff.

The Education

Smith has no core requirements; however, you are required to take 64 credits outside of your major, and to be eligible for Latin Honors you must complete a class in all seven different sections (i.e., arts, foreign language, historical studies, literature, math and analytical philosophy, natural science, social science).

The Students

Smith girls can range from bitchy to sweet to lesbian to guy-crazy to funny to just plain weird. You will find that no matter how different the students are, everyone learns to get along and learn from one another. It's a pretty inspiring environment, especially for someone who came from a very homogenous, preppy, "Gap-clone" high school. The student body ranges from those preppy, Reef sandal- and polo shirt-wearing Saab-driving women, to the hard-core punk rockers who still really like heart-shaped Post-its and drive a black Jeep SUV (that Dad bought for their sweet sixteenth), to tree-hugging lesbians who came to Smith because life would be better without guys, and who ride bikes. And the best part of it is that there are also all the other 2,497 students. Nobody is the same and everyone somehow seems to get along.

The Activities

Northampton is a fantastic town. If you are prone to spending a lot of money on coffee, food, and funky gift-type stuff, you will definitely fall victim to downtown Northampton. For such a small town, the variety of restaurants, ice cream stores (you *must* visit Herrell's), and funky gift stores is amazing. There are so many places to hang out with friends or grab a coffee or a bite to eat that downtown never grows boring.

The Social Scene

It's all about the five-college consortium, baby. You might think Smith sucks if you're straight. Actually: it's great. You are hot a commodity to those males at UMass, Amherst, and Hampshire. And you are always just one bus ride away from men who think Smith girls are a break from the norm at their schools. Amherst and Hampshire are only about two thousand strong; the guys get pretty sick of seeing the same girls every day. They love making friends with Smith girls and showing you around the parties and fun things to do on their campus. Downtown Amherst also has lots of bars, which facilitates interaction. Put it this way: if you are a lesbian, Smith has a lot to offer; if you are straight, learn the bus routes and I promise you will never have any trouble meeting guys.

Name: Anne
Hometown: Southlake, Texas
Class Year: Senior
Major: Biochemistry
Extracurriculars: Triathlete; special studies lab work on exercise-induced changes in skeletal muscle; computer lab consultant; Smith Democrats.
Career Goal: Short(er)term—to work in an industrial biochemical research lab, specifically in proactive therapeutic development for life-threatening diseases. Long(er) term—to work toward a law degree in the field of intellectual property and "rewrite the books" with regard to scientific technologies and the law.

How would you describe Smith's reputation?

A women's college has its own reputation, well before academics are considered. Smith graduates are well-regarded, highly recruited, smart, able, and vocal. The alumnae network is stellar (which was the selling point for me, four years ago) and academic rigor is at the perfect level—not killer but still first-rate and the hard sciences are particularly esteemed. Here in Massachusetts, however, Smith is seen as a haven for those "repressed women" that attracts a very wide variety of people; Smithies are seen as threatening not because they're violent, but because they're vocal.

> "The average Smithie is way too overcommitted, has at least one 'pet' issue, is loyal to one and only one a cappella group, has an Irish-level of warmth and hospitality, is addicted to Ethernet, has been told by public safety at least once to put clothes on, lives for the *Daily Show*, watches TLC with one eye out for antifeminist sentiment and the other for cool styles, and could successfully organize and run the entire world and be home in time for Friday tea."
> ✦ Sarah, senior

Is this reputation accurate?

I think so. Smith is friendly to many forms of diversity (sexual, racial, geographical, socioeconomical, etc.), and some of this friendliness is further accentuated by the vocalness of the student body.

What would an admissions officer at Smith probably not tell a prospective student?

The first-year retention rate is significantly lower than most other schools. Concerns about social life (Friday and Saturday nights, generally) have been cited by the student body, though these concerns are being addressed. Smith is higher pressure than other schools I know of, which also causes some to transfer. You generally either love or hate it here. (Those that hate it just transfer.)

The Institution

The school's size is wonderful; intro classes are larger, giving some rigidness to the class structure, whereas more advanced classes are smaller (I think my smallest class had six people), more intimate (I had class at a professor's house on Monday nights a couple of semesters ago), and extraordinary. A bigger college would provide too much anonymity for my tastes, yet a smaller college wouldn't be able to offer the breadth of classes available.

School spirit is a funny thing. If there's one thing I miss, it's football games, large stadiums, lots of people screaming for the team. But I think Smith has a different form of spirit. It's much more evident when you're away from campus: if you meet another Smithie in your travels, you instantly form a rapport with them.

Rather than living in dorms, we live in houses, all of which have their own style, traditions, and student makeup. House size can range from thirteen to about one hundred; co-ops are available for those interested, as are on-campus apartments. I've lived out in the Quad for the past four years, primarily because after the first year, I'm guaranteed a single (which is a godsend). And with dining and living rooms downstairs, coupled with traditions, it truly is like living in a house. Also, we don't have meal plans—food is made by cooks and chefs in the houses, providing a great meal for up to about 80 students per kitchen. If there's one thing Smith is famous for, it's housing and food.

Overall, I think I'm prepared for anything that happens after college, which will hopefully include finding a job (probably the thing I'm *most* prepared for), but from there, I have not an idea. I'll probably contact the Smith Club wherever I go, just for psychological support.

My Smith wish list:

1. A social life that doesn't include policing by the administration
2. A little less political correctness from the student body
3. Better town-gown relations (which aren't awful, but could be better)

> "Going to Smith doesn't 'make you' or 'turn you' gay, and gay students don't go here because they want an endless supply of dates. College is about getting an education."
>
> ✦ Carolyn, senior

The Education

I've been particularly impressed with the hard sciences here at Smith, as are many employers. While Smith isn't known as a research institution, Smith excels at grooming science majors, particularly in chemistry and biochemistry, due to the liberal-arts leanings and a top-shelf faculty available to the students. For the past two years, I've worked in the laboratory and will (hopefully by graduation) publish my work; this opportunity wouldn't have been available to me in many other places.

The time I spend on schoolwork varies depending on the material. I do know the meaning of a good night's sleep, as well as the meaning of an all-nighter.

My favorite class(es):

1. Biochem Cancer Seminar. Absolutely the most intriguing class I've ever had. I could die academically happy afterward, except that I'm really into the field now, and have too many questions and projects I want to pursue. (We had a guest speaker, the Tufts director of pathology, who brought in thirty-some-odd samples of normal and cancerous organs. If you've never touched a liver irreversibly damaged by alcohol, or never held sections of a brain of a stroke victim, or never had to smell the lungs of a thirty-year chain smoker who died of lung cancer, honest to God, you've never lived.)
2. Immunology. The first day of class, the professor said, "This class is going to be like learning a foreign language, and it's gonna be taught with a medical school curriculum." Sure enough, we used a book generally reserved for the upper echelon of

medical schools and the class was probably the most difficult, yet most rewarding, of my Smith career.

3. Organic chemistry. I should state that nobody (except the sadists who become professors) particularly enjoys organic chemistry, but this professor was *phenomenal*.

The Students

Let me first start with the answer to an obvious first question everyone seems to have (except me—I thought Smith some perfect 1950s sitcom or something when I visited): Smith is not a large group of man-hating, fire-breathing, neo-Nazi dykes. Your daughter will not become a lesbian if she attends Smith—if she comes out while here, it's probably been a long time coming. (This was my father's greatest fear about me going to Smith, though he had absolutely nothing to worry about.) Truthfully, I don't think the statistics for such populations is much higher than anywhere else; we're just a little more vocal about it.

Socioeconomic and geographic makeup are incredibly diverse; I've met people who live(d) in a car and people who are longtime legacies that give plenty of money to the institution (though neither were admitted on those standards, believe me). And we've got people from all around the world and throughout all the states. I think I can safely say that my immediate circle of friends don't share a "geographic home" in common, and once we get past the "coke/pop/soda" wars, things are peachy between us.

> "One of the main reasons I chose Smith was that I felt really comfortable here: While I was on my tour, people kept walking by with huge smiles on their faces yelling, 'Come to Smith!' And so I did."
> ✦ Jessica, freshman

The Activities

When I feel like procrastinating, I have a friend who will jump in the car with me and go to the supermarket around midnight. Bejeweled (an online game) is dangerously addictive, and the Daily Jolt generally gets strange between the hours of 1:00–7:00 a.m. If you're available during more normal hours, there's something like forty restaurants

within three square blocks (including five coffee shops), three non-mainstream movie theaters, plenty of music halls/clubs, a few bars, and a plethora of strange shopping experiences to be had (I can't walk out of Faces without buying something).

The Social Scene

One great tradition at Smith is that each house serves tea on Fridays at 4:00 p.m. in the living room, and it's a time for the house members to meet, mingle, and discuss issues while enjoying cookies, fresh fruit, crackers and dip, tea, and whatever else the chef felt like making that morning. Issues discussed vary, depending on campus "goings-on," or focus on various group tea themes (Sex Ed tea, Diversity tea, Professor tea, Family tea, etc). It's not mandatory by any means, but definitely a wonderful way to end the week.

Name: Cary
Hometown: Northampton, Massachusetts
Class Year: Junior
Major: Psychology (with focus in abnormal psychology), Studio Art minor
Extracurriculars: Member of D3 lacrosse team, writing, reading.
Career Goal: Attend grad school for psychopharmacology with a neuroscience focus and some day work at the National Institute for Mental Health developing new medications and therapies to help those with mental illnesses.

How would you describe Smith's reputation?

Very good. Not only is Smith regarded as one of the best private schools in the country, but as a student here I always feel challenged to perform and to push myself. I have never heard a Smithie say she doesn't feel challenged. It's a good feeling to reach a new plateau of learning.

Is this reputation accurate?

Yes. Intellectually we're on par with Ivy League colleges.

What would an admissions officer at Smith probably not tell a prospective student? What aspect of your school would a prospective student not see on a campus tour?

Currently the thirty plus dining areas on campus are being downsized to only ten to twenty dining halls. This has caused many heated feelings on campus, since with the previous system of a kitchen-in-every-house, the dynamics of the house were reinforced, and mealtimes were a time when everyone was present and you were able to catch up on the day's events. While you are on a visit or tour at Smith, you should try to avoid the usual tour and make some new friends. This past semester, my friends and I were eating lunch in our house when a prospective student asked if she could sit and eat with us. She was on her own, simply trying to get a feel for Smith, and I thought to myself, "She would fit in great here." By going off on her own and having the gumption to find honest and unbiased answers to her questions about the school, she proved to not only be brave, but intelligent and level-headed as well.

The Institution

Even though Smith is in the middle of a great, liberal, artsy town, there are so many great events on campus that it's very hard to leave our isolated little campus. But there's definitely a lot of interaction between the town and Smith; people from the town will even attend our theater productions and sporting events in the springtime. The athletic fields are actually a great place to see non-Smith people—they're connected to the old state hospital grounds right near campus, so there are lots of joggers with cute dogs, and also a river which is great for swimming on those hot New England days.

> "One of things that frustrates me about Smith is the huge amount of competition between students."
>
> ✦ Aubrey, sophomore

The houses can be very similar to sororities: you come to know every person in your house, and there are exclusive house rituals and also a feeling of pride in your house. Smith has many traditions. A couple of big ones are convocation and the Celebration of Sisterhood. Convocation, which is the celebration to start off each new school year, is held at John M. Greene Hall on campus. You attend convocation with your house, usually costumed in a theme outfit, such as pirates, royalty, or even saran wrap if you feel like it (it all depends on how crazy you want to get). The president speaks during this event and everyone cheers and it's a big to-do. Celebration of Sisterhood is a tradition

held in the Quad, and involves a series of skits (one from each house that wants to be involved). The skits and songs all are aimed toward acceptance of everyone and diversity on campus. This event is always well-attended and it reinforces the feeling of unity and trust on campus. It was started about

> "There is a wide range of social lives on the Smith campus. You can party every night here or at another school, or you can play Scrabble with a few friends on Friday night. No one thinks twice about it."
>
> ✦ Lydia, junior

ten years ago after some homophobic and racist events occurred on campus.

Smith's campus is beautiful. It's situated in western Massachusetts, where we have hot summers, freezing winters, and the most amazing fall foliage you'll ever see. The architecture is mostly old brick buildings from the time when the college was founded (1871), although there have been additions to campus that don't seem to fit with the New England theme because the founder of the college, Sophia Smith, stated that every new building built on campus must be built in "the style of the times."

The Education

Sometimes my friends and I make fun of the fact that we spend so much time talking about classes. We're not total bookworms—we just happen to talk about our classes a lot, whether it be a class that really interested or inspired us, the cute new psych professor, or a really funny lecture. The workload can be intense, which may be one of the reasons why we focus on it. Weekends can be busy with more work than socializing, depending on the time of year, but as long as you have an outlet it shouldn't be an issue. The campus is an intense intellectual arena, and while it is great to be pushed in classes to think for yourself and understand complex theories, it can also be frustrating. I have several friends at the nearby UMass Amherst campus who are also psych majors, and they talk about how easy their major is and how they ace all their tests. Smith's psychology department is challenging—there's no coasting through classes here. Your fellow students in class are part of the concentrated atmosphere—there are often debates in class and discussions of personal ideas, so be sure to know what you're talking about before you make a controversial comment in class.

The professors here can also be very good or very bad, but it is guaranteed that during your stay at Smith you will meet and become comfortable with at least one. While there are some profs that ignore their scheduled office hours and return papers late, the majority of profs are not only available often, but always welcome students dropping by to chat or for advice.

Smith has no core classes, so you have a wide variety of classes to choose from. While you still have to take 64 credits outside your major, these subjects can be virtually anything offered.

Junior year abroad is a very common thing at Smith—it is almost expected. I went to Galway, Ireland, for my fall semester, and Smith made it very easy to travel—you can apply to any abroad program (even though Smith runs several programs of its own), and you pay the usual Smith fees. While abroad I was able to see amazing parts of the world, meet new people, and experience a new and ancient culture. Studying in Ireland gave me a break from the tough Smith schooling and allowed me to know myself better.

> "Smithies are never bored. We're always out causing some kind of ruckus."
> ✦ Caylin, senior

The Students

Although there's a very strong Republican group on campus, students are mainly Democrats. The area is mainly Democratic; Northampton is a safe place known for its strong lesbian community—we were one of the first places in which gay marriage became legal, and everyone is pretty damn proud of that. There are a ton of organizations at Smith, everything from LGBT groups to the Republican Club to Ceramics Club. The different groups on campus will frequently throw open parties and have events to further their cause. The Smith Democrats were voted the number one Democratic college group in the United States, which is a huge deal.

Parents ask whether there is a noticeable difference with no men on campus; the answer is Yes!; the atmosphere at Smith is socially relaxed, and in classes I feel free to speak my mind. Attending an all-women's school has helped me gain self-confidence in situations where I used to feel uncomfortable and I've carried that into my life outside of Smith.

The Activities

Lacrosse has been one of the most rewarding activities I've partaken in while at Smith. It has helped me to meet a bunch of new girls, make great new friends, and basically just do a lot of silly things with my teammates. We are a Division 3 school in the NCAA, and that suits me. Being in D3 is nice because you still get to play and get all sweaty on the field, but it doesn't cut into your studies.

Smith has an amazing new art museum (even the bathrooms were designed by artists) that is always having events and new installations, and we'll often host famous artists who give talks and show their work. There are also so many talks on campus from distinguished authors, poets, speakers, activists, and even from controversial political figures that you feel guilty because it is impossible to go to them all. And, there are two concerts every year that a Smith group puts on; in the past we've had everyone from Busta Rhymes to Ani DiFranco to Counting Crows to Pink—they're huge events and always packed full.

The Social Scene

Smith is a small school (about 2,500) and yet there are still a lot of faces I don't know. There's some sense of camaraderie, like we are all here for the common purpose of learning and having fun while we do it. The fun part of Smith is definitely the house parties; about twice a semester each house on campus will have a wild party. Students from all around come and it's a lot of fun: kegs, dancing, hors d'ouevres, and new people. There are also the more mature cocktail parties linked to musical performances, like an a cappella group or live piano music. Normally the parties get pretty crazy, and in general they are a safe place to let loose and have a fun time with your friends.

Notable Smith Alumni Include:
Anne Lindbergh, author
Catharine MacKinnon, feminist and author
Gloria Steinem, feminist and journalist
Julia Child, chef
Madeleine L'Engle, author
Nancy Reagan, former first lady

UNIVERSITY OF SOUTHERN CALIFORNIA

Founded: 1880
Location: Los Angeles, CA
Phone: (213) 740-2311
E-mail: admitusc@usc.edu
Web site: www.usc.edu

Number of Undergraduates: 16,240
Number of Graduate Students: 2,980
Cost: Approximately $39,500 per year
Application Deadline: January 10

Rating:	Notable Majors/Programs:
Most Selective	Business, Engineering, Film

Size:
○ Small   ○ Medium   ● Large

Location:
● Urban   ○ Suburban   ○ Rural

On a Saturday, students talk about academics:
○ Always   ● Sometimes   ○ Never

Nightlife:
● Intense   ○ Moderate   ○ Laid-back

Politically, USC leans:
○ Left   ● Right   ○ Split

Diversity:
● High   ○ Low   ○ Medium

PAC Ten: Yes!

Students describe USC in five words:
- Driven, proud, conservative, crazy fun
- Great academics, competitive, supportive, social

From the School

A unique strength of USC is its integration of liberal and professional learning. Students are encouraged to develop "breadth with depth" by pursuing academic minors that are far afield from their chosen majors or by combining USC's strong liberal arts program with its wide range of professional training. However, USC doesn't just impart the best in academic tradition to its undergraduates, graduates, and professional students. As a major research institution, USC is committed to discovering new knowledge and to actively contributing to what is taught, thought and practiced throughout the world.

—www.usc.edu

If you're interested in USC, you may also be interested in:
UCLA, University of Michigan, NYU, Stanford, Tulane, Vanderbilt

Name: Ryan
Hometown: New Orleans, Louisiana
Class Year: Freshman
Major: Theater—Stage Management (BFA)
Extracurriculars: Various independent theatre organizations; LGBT Assembly.
Career Goal: Stage-managing productions on Broadway and on national tours.

How would you describe USC's reputation?

USC is easily recognized as one of the country's "elite" schools. Students from all over the world come to 'SC because of its strong academic reputation and great location in the middle of Los Angeles. Mention "I go to USC" and prepare to be greeted with a flash of recognition and possibly even a hearty "Fight On!" For whatever reason, SC has a fairly conservative political reputation—people seem to think that the school is a breeding ground for Young Republicans.

Is this reputation accurate?

Yes. However, the conservative reputation of the school is questionable; the administration and faculty can be conservative, but the student body is fairly middle-of-the-road and even liberal. It may not be as liberal as the University of California schools (USC is private—*not* part of the UC system), but neither is it as staunchly conservative as a lot of southern schools—so it's fairly balanced.

> "USC has the perfect mix of amazing academic programs, social life, and school pride."
>
> ✦ Nila, junior

What aspect of USC would a prospective student not see on a campus tour?

When I first toured USC, I was impressed by the honesty—they showed us lots of the less-impressive aspects of the school, and didn't try to gloss over the fact that the neighborhood isn't so great. However, they did neglect to mention that housing is only guaranteed to freshmen, and that everyone else is thrust upon the mercy of the housing renewal lottery, which puts returning residents in random order to choose their spaces for the next year—at least until all the spaces are filled up, at which point you have to scavenge for one of the hundreds of apartments close to the campus. Also,

they won't show you the great parties that are constantly happening within just a few hundred yards of school. At least not if your parents are around.

The Institution

The school's really big, and it's easy to get swept up in the crowd and become anonymous, especially if you're in one of the larger colleges (Letters, Arts, and Sciences; Business; or Engineering, for example). Taking smaller classes your first semester (like the Category V general education classes or the freshman seminars) really helps you to get to know a few people and not feel lost in a giant lecture hall. However, as a freshman living in the dorms, there are lots of opportunities to get involved with other students and to get out and about in the city of Los Angeles and have fun. Going to football games and being involved in Trojan pride is a big part of campus life here, although you can survive without it—I certainly have. Also, there's a lot of peer pressure at the "University of Spoiled Children" to wear the same designer labels as everyone else and to drive the same expensive cars, although you can be perfectly happy here without spending your entire bank account on material possessions. It's beautiful in L.A. pretty much year-round—even when it's cold. I love living in the City of Angels and I think the school thrives on the energy and life flowing through the area.

The Education

As a student in the theater school, I'm taking mostly smaller, interactive classes, with lots of involvement from the professors, staying with a tight, close-knit group of students. It makes it really easy to get interested in the subjects, especially with fun professors and great TAs (who are mostly graduate playwriting students). The classes vary in difficulty, but none of them (so far) has made me consider suicide. The hardest part about taking difficult classes as a theater major is balancing reading and studying time with the twenty plus hours a week of rehearsal time, but as long as you don't goof off too much, that's not a problem. The general education classes are the hardest part of USC, though—most of them have a minimum of fifty pages of reading per hour of class time, so they can be very intense, especially with their papers, exams, and presentations. There's a lot of variety, though, so it's not hard to find a general education class that either interests you or is closely related to your major.

The Students

USC is a *very* Greek campus, so everyone is either in a frat/sorority or knows someone who is. The various frats and sororities are very visible as well, and they have their own little rivalries and reputations, although they also mix fairly well with the other cultural and social groups. A lot of the groups are very fluid, with members identifying with lots of different social circles and intermingling with them; there's not as much of the "clique" atmosphere as you'll find at some schools.

The Activities

USC's closest competitor is, of course, UCLA. There's a long-standing rivalry between the two universities that gets kind of ridiculous sometimes, but it makes for entertaining football games and some occasional pranks. The school's definitely athletically dominated; performance and arts groups don't get nearly as much attention or attendance as the various sports groups do. If you look, though, there's usually a cultural event of some sort, either musical, artistic, or theatrical, every weekend, if not every night. There's always something to do. I love the convenience of having the entire city of Los Angeles right outside. Even if there's nothing to do on campus (which is a rare occasion indeed), there's always a club or a show or something to do within driving distance. . . . That is, if you don't mind fighting with L.A. traffic.

L.A. is a fairly expensive place to live, but it's worth it to live in the center of the entertainment industry in a huge metropolis.

Campus organizations are great at using USC's reputation (and the combined buying power of thousands of students' Student Programming Fees) to attract great performers—and most of these events are free to students and well-advertised, so there's no excuse for not seeing everything that the Programming Board has to offer.

The Social Scene

USC's a fairly big party school, especially amongst the frat/sorority scene. Various different groups have their own social events, though, and it's not hard to have a very busy social calendar.

There's usually some sort of gay-and-lesbian-friendly event (or, as several of them are termed, "Big Gay Parties") on or near campus once a week or so, and they're usually a lot of fun. Also, there are the dozens of clubs in Los Angeles that cater to the young gay crowd: Tigerheat, Rage, and Micky's are some of the most popular for eighteen plus kids, and the Abbey is definitely the place to be for the over-twenty-one crowd. The LGBT community on campus is pretty close-knit, though, so everybody's either dated everybody or is dating somebody's ex.

Name: Portia
Class Year: Senior
Major: Biomedical/Mechanical Engineering
Extracurriculars: USC Fencing Club, USC Archery Club, horseback riding, SCUBA diving (we have some of the best diving sites off the coast in the Channel Islands), Society of Women Engineers, Associated Students of Biomedical Engineering.
Career Goal: Consulting.

How would you describe USC's reputation?

Premier athletic and academic research institution. Sometimes referred to as the "University of Spoiled Children."

Is this reputation accurate?

Absolutely. USC has one of the largest funding bases in the country for its research. Working in labs or on different national projects is very easy to do here; even entering freshmen can contact some of the USC professors and can apply to volunteer in their labs. From an athletic standpoint, we don't just have a trophy case, we have an entire trophy *building* with more alumni Olympians than I can count. Even the non-NCAA sports clubs and teams are incredible and often take national championships in their respective sports.

At USC we really are spoiled; my average class size in my major has had about twenty students with one professor teaching, two teaching assistants, and a class grader. The faculty and department staffs take their jobs seriously and bend over backwards to ensure that each and every student is happy and able to learn.

> "On game day it's hard to walk through campus without having a drunk student, alumnus, or parent spilling a beer or cocktail on you."
>
> ✦ Nila, junior

On a more superficial note, our campus is one of the most beautiful in the country, with old buildings from the 1800s and lush flowerbeds and fountains everywhere. Being in such a beautiful area makes it easier to relax and study.

What would an admissions officer at USC school probably not tell a prospective student?

The fact that USC students are sometimes mugged or burglarized and that most of the crime is not reported. Coming from a quiet and very safe community to the middle of L.A.'s South-Central was a big change for me. You can't treat it like it's a safe place or you'll become a victim. If you leave your bag somewhere, you probably won't find it again. What the school reps will tell you is that the Department of Public Safety (DPS) puts out an annual report on campus crime that is accessible online. Buy double U-locks for your bicycle and use one for each tire. Have a bike shop put a cable that locks your seat in place too. If you want to go out and party or need to go home late, call a Campus Cruiser or take the school trams. Campus Cruiser is a free late-night personal taxi service that has a radius that extends several miles around the campus. Whatever you do, do not walk alone and never leave your door open or unlocked. The Department of Public Safety puts on free awareness and self-defense classes, but they can only help you if you actually go to them. DPS is very good but they can't crack down on local crime because it's not their jurisdiction. By just being aware, you'll probably not be a victim and will have an incredible experience at USC.

The Institution

I adore my school! It has its bad points, but so much about it is unbelievably good! I love the school camaraderie and the way that there are always intelligent, upbeat people to talk to. If you like to be dull and not involved, then don't come here, because you won't like it. If you do like reaching personal goals and constantly learning with a great group of people, then you will probably love being a Trojan.

The weather is gorgeous! Our version of cold is 50 degrees Fahrenheit. In the summer, temperatures reach 100 degrees Fahrenheit. USC's main physical drawback is the fact that it doesn't have much space to spread out. For this reason, many parking areas and recreation spaces have been bulldozed to put in more buildings. I really didn't like the fact that most recreational sports groups needed to go off campus to practice. The fact that the nearest horse stable was about an hour away was really inconvenient for me. On-campus sports were also limited in the amount of time that they could practice because of space constraints.

Housing is very hard to get. It's typically done on a lottery system and is not guaranteed to upperclassmen or transfer students. Be sure to go on a campus tour and find out which housing options allow second-year students to return to them without going into the lottery. Also make sure that your room doesn't back up to Figueroa or Jefferson streets; the fire department is near those streets and responds (complete with horns and sirens) 24/7 to emergencies.

Last, adding the phrase "USC" to your job application can really get you places. Students like to call it "The Trojan Network" and "The Trojan Family." Trojans always take care of their own.

The Education

The most highly admired departments on campus are the Marshall School of Business, the School of Cinema, the Thornton School of Music, and the Viterbi School of Engineering. Interstudent competition is not a big issue here, as students place high value in helping each other. Professors also encourage group interaction and place an emphasis on always trying for greatness. The engineering school offers a free tutoring program to its students, taught by other students who have received A's in the same classes. Supplemental Instruction, a free group tutoring program, is available for several of the "hardest" first-year classes, while places like the Writing Program and Math Center are free, open, and staffed year-round to all students. Expect to work incredibly hard if you are an entering science or technology major, but also know that the school will try its best to help you if you are willing to put in the effort to help yourself. Mandatory advising every semester is required for engineering students because the department likes to live up to their standard of students actually graduating in four years. Other specialty advising—like career, premed, prelaw, honors, etc.—is always available.

The Students

Yes, you really are seeing a Ferrari parked next to a Corolla in our parking garage.

The Activities

If you come to USC and want to do a specific activity and we don't have it yet, then you can always start your own organization. We already have several hundred student organizations, though, so you will probably find several that you will enjoy and make tons of friends in.

One of the largest organizations on campus is the Recreational Club Council. Called the RCC for short, it is actually a representative body of over forty non-NCAA sports organizations. They offer everything from archery to Olympic weight lifting, and are open to all students regardless of experience level in the particular sport.

In the fall, everyone is excited about Football. Everyone gathers in the middle of campus next to the Tommy Trojan statue and cheers as the "Spirit of Troy"—the best collegiate marching band in the world—belts out our favorite USC songs. We then march down the campus behind them in a massive horde across Exposition Blvd. and into the Coliseum where we watch the football team decimate our rivals in sports.

The Social Scene

For those inclined to party, the Row (frat/sorority) is a great place to be. Since we're also right next to downtown L.A., there are tons of clubs, performing arts presentations, sporting events, and restaurants to go to. USC students can get discount tickets to many local events through the USC ticket office.

You don't need a car to have a good time, although it is still convenient. The DASH bus system that runs through the cultural centers of the city is inexpensive and easy to ride. USC also has a tram service that can get you to the train station if you need it to go long distances.

It's not hard to meet people on campus since it's a very diverse and friendly place. I have met people from all over the world here and have learned a lot about overseas cultures. Overall, people are courteous to other Trojans but enjoy giving UCLA Bruins, Cal people, and Stanford "Trees" a very hard time when they are spotted on campus.

Name: Christopher
Hometown: Orange, California
Class Year: Senior
Major: Urban Planning

Extracurriculars: Student government, LGBTA (gay rights organization), planning student association.
Career Goal: Public policy analyst or lobbyist in the urban planning and policy arena. This could take the form of civil service work, private sector advocacy, or governmental/political staffer and adviser.

> "Students party Monday through Thursday."
> ✦ Nila, junior

How would you describe USC's reputation?

The school has a fair to good academic reputation and it is well deserved. For the most part the school is full of bright students who perform well. The school also has a social reputation for being rich, conservative, spoiled, and white, with students who party all the time and suffer no consequences.

Is this reputation accurate?

The academic reputation is accurate and classes and students are getting better each year. The social perception could not be more inaccurate—students are not overly conservative, are ethnically diverse, do not party more than anywhere else, mostly do not come from money, and are on major financial aide.

What would an admissions officer at USC school probably not tell a prospective student?

There are a large number of commuter students—thus the population on campus falls during the weekend. When I was a freshman, I thought this very upsetting because I'd been told what a connected place the campus was, only to find it becomes a ghost town on weekends.

Also, the university has a very troubled relationship with the neighborhood—they don't tell you this but instead point to all the community service done by students (this is correct). I sometimes feel very uncomfortable going to a school that promises community job development and shopping centers on a site and then builds exclusive basketball arenas, that purchases affordable housing and converts it into luxury student housing, and the list goes on.

The Institution

The school is far too big and abuses its power to get what it wants politically and in the community. I feel very prepared for my career—I have grown greatly as a person and I feel I have been exposed to as much as I could handle in four years.

The Education

The deal is, the education at USC varies greatly by discipline; some are easy (Spanish, sociology, communications), some are difficult (planning, biochemistry, architecture), but you all get a degree with the same university name on it. I'm not sure that that is fair. GEs are huge and usually (some exceptions include classics courses, planning, and Judaic studies) insultingly easy, but most classes are small; I love that.

The presence of the grad school seems to be a good thing; many high-profile graduate professors also teach an undergraduate course. The passion of many professors is really impressive.

I have never had trouble getting the classes I need. Advisers are only helpful if you know what you need and ask them questions. There is an opportunity for undergrads to sample grad courses so they know if grad school is right for them.

The Students

As a gay man I'm not sure my experience has been standard, but I would describe it as good but definitely could be improved. There is a core group of students who are involved in everything: I see the same people at gay events I work on as at political events as at academic discussions. This is not to say other students are anti-anything; they are simply apathetic or uninvolved, or they are involved elsewhere. We are in the middle of Los Angeles: there are a lot of choices.

There is no typical USC student. There is a fairly even distribution of Democrats and Republicans, the Greek system is fairly small but very visible, the school paper is always far right of the student body but seems ingrained in being so. The religious groups pose a problem: the most conservative (Campus Crusade, Victory, etc.) are so aggressive and offensive that it's very hard for liberal Christians to show their faces. For example, I belong to United Ministries, which is a main-line Protestant group that works for full rights for LGBT persons in the church, and I feel very intimidated to ever mention God or church on campus because the far right groups have provided such a bad and unavoidable picture to everyone on campus about what a religious group is about. The school is also so large that it lends itself to cliques—in the gay community, it's hard to have mass gatherings because the gay activists want to have their events, and the gay Asians their events, and the gay film students their events.

The Activities

Community service is very, very, very important and almost everyone does it. People leave campus often—there is too much to do in the city to not explore.

The Social Scene

There is a lot of alcohol, no way to get around it. The fraternity scene is a vestige of a white, rich, exclusive USC of the past—with the exception of the Asian and black fraternities (and how sad it is they need separate frats). The Greek scene is much of what the university used to be. Thank goodness we have LA as an outlet!

Notable USC Alumni Include:

Gen. Norman Schwarzkopf, United States Army four-star general
George Lucas, director
Marilyn Horne, opera singer
Neil Armstrong, astronaut
Paul Orfalea, founder of Kinko's
Ron Howard, actor and director

SPELMAN COLLEGE

Founded: 1881
Location: Atlanta, GA
Phone: (404) 681-3643
E-mail: admiss@spelman.edu
Web site: www.spelman.edu

Number of Undergraduates: 2,140
Number of Graduate Students: 0
Cost: Approximately $23,000 per year
Application Deadline: February 1
Early Decision: November 15

Rating:	Notable Majors/Programs:
Very Selective	Engineering, Life Sciences, Premed, Prelaw

Size:
● Small ○ Medium ○ Large

Location:
● Urban ○ Suburban ○ Rural

On a Saturday, students talk about academics:
○ Always ● Sometimes ○ Never

Nightlife:
○ Intense ○ Moderate ● Laid-back

Politically, SLC leans:
● Left ○ Right ○ Split

Diversity:
● High ○ Low ○ Medium

All women's college: Yes!

Historically black college: Yes!

Students describe Spelman in five words:
- Supportive, progressive, nurturing, spirited, challenging
- Black women are empowered here

From the School

[At Spelman] our goal is to provide you with countless opportunities to expand your mind to the edges of the universe. Whether you're interested in the humanities, social sciences, mathematics, the arts or the natural sciences, we have a program tailored to meet your needs. . . . No matter what field you choose, you will come to know outstanding faculty and staff who care, who push, and who help you maximize your potential.

—www.spelman.edu

If you're interested in Spelman, you may also be interested in:
Howard, Mount Holyoke, Scripps, Smith, Wellesley, Wesleyan

Name: Charli
Hometown: Maplewood, New Jersey
Class Year: Senior
Major: Sociology and Anthropology
Extracurriculars: Student newspaper, Peer Educators Program, Zeta Phi Beta Sorority, Inc.
Career Goal: Magazine editor.

How would you describe Spelman's reputation?

A small black college, notorious for attracting young and wealthy black girls from all over the world and turning them into man-eating feminists, full-fledged lesbians, or stuck up, spoiled, and educated brats.

Is this reputation accurate?

Hell no! Granted, Spelman women do come from all over the world, but we definitely don't all think a certain way. There are feminists, and lesbians, and even a few overprivileged princesses, but in reality, the Spelman experience breeds a young woman who embraces her differences and her womanhood, and uses her life experiences and education to make things happen. Spelman women don't just sit around ragging on men, or plotting to take over the world, and there is not one single course offered that focuses primarily on men. Sorry fellas, but we've got lots more on our minds!

What would an admissions officer at Spelman probably not tell a prospective student? What aspect of your school would a prospective student not see on a campus tour?

A walk across campus may proffer the impression that there's an abundance of that sisterhood the college so boasts of having. But the truth is, friends aren't handed out inside your freshman orientation packets. You will bond with your fellow students, and you'll find the same amount of drama, pettiness, and backstabbing behavior on this campus that you would at any other. And an admissions officer probably wouldn't tell you that the Spelman experience extends well beyond Spelman's gates. Many major Spelman events are held off campus, because our campus is so small. And most students must venture off campus to fulfill basic needs: getting your hair done, grocery shopping, and even using the library. The city is your playground. You'll find more Spelmanites in one place off campus than you ever would on. But re-

ally, that's *so* not a problem. Campus shuttle buses and Atlanta's MARTA train will get you everywhere you need to go. And during your visit you won't see many guys around but don't be alarmed: there are plenty hanging on campus during the day—especially on Fridays.

> "It's generally thought that you must be brilliant, community oriented, and way above average to be here. And it's true. You see this in the courseload, and in the emphasis on service and excellence."
> ✦ Jeni, sophomore

The Institution

Spelman was my dream since childhood! I couldn't have imagined attending another school. I wanted to attend an all-girls college because I was sick and tired of males in the classroom intimidating females, stealing the spotlight, and belittling my opinion. Spelman gave me a chance to be heard and to shine. I never have to worry about what I wear to class, how I feel about something, or what I have to say.

Spelman is a very small and traditional school, and our school spirit is absolutely excessive. It's like a mini-cult, built on tradition, love, and a common understanding of what it means to be a young, gifted, and educated African American woman.

Upon leaving those Spelman gates, I'll be more prepared for life's obstacles than I ever thought I could be. The career services department is so amazing that you're practically guaranteed a job walking out of here.

The Good:

The campus: It is clean, neat, cozy, and very well organized. It's like a small suburban town in the middle of a giant urban city. You can roll out of bed and make it to class in under five minutes. If you ever caught an episode of *A Different World*, back in the '80s, you know exactly what Spelman looks like—it's a very historic campus: many of the buildings are old and beautiful, circa 1800s. But there has also been a lot of work done recently—the dorms have been modernized, and the majority of the classroom buildings are fairly new. The campus is one big oval, with a cobblestone road riding through and neat, trimmed green lawns. When you enter those gates, it's like driving into heaven—especially compared to the poverty-stricken West End community outside the gates. Spelman is in the middle of downtown Atlanta, but when you're on campus you forget. Spelman is a true haven.

The Bad:

Freshman Orientation: The freshman orientation program asks more of you than your parents ever will. You simply won't believe the times they wake you up and the seminars you must endure.

And the Ugly:

Housing: If you were an only child growing up, or you've never shared a room, you may want to consider living off campus when you come to Spelman. The freshman dorm rooms are almost unbearably tight. The absence of air conditioning, coupled with Atlanta's sweltering late-summer heat, can starve you for a breath of cool, fresh air. But knowing that the upperclassmen dorms are a huge improvement, and commuter students have all the fun, will somehow get you through it.

Finally, the professors and the higher-ups at Spelman are absolutely amazing people to work with, but the administrative staff and assistants that support them have major attitude problems. If they can get off the telephone long enough to ask why you're there, you might be told exactly what month to come back before they can help you!

The Education

The education that Spelman offers is outstanding. All the professors are well-known and established in their fields, and can offer you a lot more than just the theory behind what they teach. Because of the small class sizes and intimate major programs, your professor will most likely know your pet's name, where you're from, and your part-time schedule. They're always available for extra help, always around, and always willing to chat.

There are very few lecture halls at Spelman. Everything about the classroom experience is interactive. And most class discussions will later turn into fun dorm debates or cafeteria discussions. If you're stuck on something, or need help studying for a test, there's always someone who can and will help. Every department is strong and requires your

best work. Most seniors are required to produce some sort of final project or thesis in order to graduate, but what you chose to do is totally up to you.

The Students

The Spelman woman is always the first to speak up when something just doesn't seem right and the last one standing up for her cause. She wants to learn as much about her heritage and where she comes from as she does about her major. Second place is never her style, and everything she does makes a difference. She is the epitome of a well-rounded student, and time management is her specialty. There's something about her that makes her stand out in any crowd. She will never compromise who she is to get where she is going. You'll probably see her at a party, a step show, or even having a few drinks with friends, but the one place you'll always see her is in the library making sure she's prepared for class. You'll find a Spelman woman anywhere: on *American Idol,* atop the *New York Times* bestseller list, or even standing alongside the nation's president.

> "There's no question that Spelman is academically top-notch, but I think the sisterhood could use a bit of a revival. . . . Spelman students are so motivated, so competitive that if you do not know someone coming in, you will most likely not be able to participate fully in campus leadership."
>
> ✦ MacKenzie, senior

The Activities

Spelman is part of the Atlanta University Consortium, otherwise known as the AUC—five historically black colleges and universities (Clark Atlanta University, Spelman College, Morehouse College, Morris Brown College, and the Interdenominational Theological Center). All five campuses touch each other, and students share lots of social clubs and events. You can pretty much join a club for anything at Spelman. I was a member of the New Jersey Club, and the Tri-State Club, so I got to meet and work with most of the AUC students from my area. AUC schools take homecoming events very seriously. Major artists and celebrities come out to perform and support, and the coronation shows look like something right out of a Broadway play. Fashion shows, spoken-word nights, poetry slams, and comedy shows are the norm. Because of Spelman's famous reputation, major scholars and celebrities frequently come to visit: Nikki Giovanni, Method Man, and Oprah, to name a few.

On any given day, you can catch the following campus cliques floating around: the "I can charge anything on my parent's credit card" divas; the homogenous sorority gals; the "I made my entire outfit and come see my exhibit this weekend" girls; the "Come march with me, sister, or at least sign this petition real quick" crew; or the "I don't have time to eat, sleep, or go shopping with you, I have homework, three projects, two tests, and a paper due next month" students.

The Social Scene

You'll hear a lot of "hellos" on Spelman's campus. We're all pretty friendly. Sorority life dominates, but although many of the sorors will never admit it, your time at Spelman will be just as much fun without three Greek letters. When you arrive at Spelman as a freshman, you're assigned a brother (or two) on Morehouse's campus at a ritual ceremony during your first week at school. You may not keep the one you were assigned, but I guarantee that by the time you graduate, you'll have at least two or three that you'll swear were lost at birth and you couldn't imagine your life without. There's lots of dating in the AUC, but there really isn't as much couple action as there would appear to be. With so many talented and attractive young people running around, it's pretty hard to pick just one.

Name: Moya
Hometown: Fayetteville, Arkansas
Class Year: Junior
Major: Comparative Women's Studies
Extracurriculars: PopandPolitics.com contributing writer, *Fierce* magazine writer/intern, dean of Enrollment Student Advisory Committee, Afrekete treasurer, Sisterfire facilitator, National Alliance of Radical Prison Reform Youth Action coordinator, WireTapmag.org staff writer, Cofounder of Student Activists Leading Alternative Diets (SALAD), Atlanta University Center Peace Coalition, Feminist Majority Leadership Alliance president to name just a few.

Career Goal: An MD/PhD running a free clinic for women.

How would you describe your school's reputation?

Bourgeois black girls trying to get their Mrs., not a BA.

Is this reputation accurate?

Not completely. A lot of Spelmanites are getting degrees to help their respective communities after graduation. And not all Spelmanites arrived with a silver spoon in their mouths.

What would an admissions officer at Spelman probably not tell a prospective student? What aspect of your school would a prospective student probably not see on a campus tour?

That Spelman is seriously lacking when it comes to amenities. We don't have a real post office and we are behind the curve with student access to information technology. A prospective student won't be able to see the sisterhood that exists in the campus community. She won't be able to see the way the first-year class bonds, or the unique and wonderful traditions that set Spelman apart from other institutions.

> "I can't imagine a better place for a black woman to be. It's nurturing and challenging. It allows for you to be all that you are, and not a stereotype. It's life changing and it's empowering."
>
> ◆ Moya, sophomore

The Institution

For black girls who were tokens at majority high schools: this is your haven. For black girls who went to predominantly black high schools: this is a second home. For black women, period: it's the place to be.

There's nothing like Hotlanta. It's a very diverse city, if you know where to look. Spelman and Morehouse are sometimes thought of as one coeducational environment. Clark Atlanta as well. The other Atlanta schools are a little bit more removed. Spelman has serious school spirit; people fly from around the country to go to the Morehouse/Spelman Homecoming. It's quite an event, and so inspiring.

Public Safety is so serious! You will memorize this number, so let me just give it to you now: 525-6401!

The first rule of Freshwoman Week is you do not talk about Freshwoman Week, . . . but it's amazing, and it only happens here!

The Education

Do we talk about classes on a Saturday night? As a first-year, absolutely! The required ADW, or African Diaspora in the World, class will keep you talking even over Christmas break. ADW is a reconceptualizing of history, from the perspective of the colonized. The matrix of domination, as expressed through the interlocking systems of race, gender, and class oppression, is discussed. It will change how you see the world. Guaranteed.

There isn't really any competition between students—we try to help each other out. We also get a lot of help from professors. You and your professors are as close as you want to be—I even have a couple of profs' cell numbers. And there are *no* TAs.

Science students have it rough. They *live* in the science center, which isn't so bad, because it's a brand new building. They seem to get a little tunnel vision over there, but the teachers are working on changing that. My sciency friends seem quite academically satiated, though.

Every department I know of has groundbreaking research in which students participate. The Women's Studies Department is the bomb! It's the only one at an HBCU (Historically Black College or University), and definitely worth checking into. Black women who are vanguards in their field come to Spelman all the time. Sometimes they like it so much they stay. Examples: Bernice Johnson Regan, Ayoka Chenzira, Gloria Wade Gales, and more!

With regard to study abroad, Spelman women go everywhere! The Netherlands, Japan, and everywhere in the African Diaspora.

The Students

The school was founded with a strong tie to Christianity, but many faiths are represented in the campus body. The vast majority of the campus is black, with maybe about 8 percent being divided among African, Asian, and European students. There are a few U.S. white students. The student body is purported to be mostly middle class but in actuality is much more working class. A lot of students are from Georgia, California, or Illinois. There's good mix from nearby Southern states too. Most students are Democrats, and they're definitely preprofessionally oriented. Of all the students, I'd say the groups least likely to mix are the Greeks and non-Greeks.

The Activities

Sorority events, pageants, and forums on hot-button issues are the most well-attended campus events. The typical college protest scene doesn't happen here too often. But the Feminist Majority Leadership Alliance was responsible for the "Nelly Protest" last year, which got international press. But do students play a role in our administration's decisions and policy development? Not large enough! Is community service popular? Very! A majority of students have on-going community service projects.

The Social Scene

Every weekend, people party. People party off campus at clubs and at house parties. Different crowds may be different places, but I wouldn't say there are separable crowds at Spelman that predictably do totally divergent things each night. I feel like I know everyone on campus. I met most of my friends through clubs and organizations . . . Though oh, my goodness, as a freshwoman, dorm life is so much fun! Everybody's so warm and welcoming, . . . most definitely, Southern hospitality at its finest!

Name: Rashida
Hometown: Woodhaven, Michigan
Class Year: Senior
Major: Psychology
Extracurriculars: Glee Club, Cheerleading, Peer Education Program, Psychology Club, Alpha Kappa Alpha Sorority, Inc.
Career Goal: I plan to obtain my masters in social work and work as a clinical social worker in the nonprofit sector.

How would you describe Spelman's reputation?

Excellent. Spelman has a reputation for positively influencing the lives of African American women, unlike an experience you can get anywhere else.

Is this reputation accurate?

Spelman benefits each individual academically and personally. Spelman women are infused with a great sense of pride, awareness, responsibility, and a commitment to our communities.

What aspect of Spelman would a prospective student probably not see on a campus tour?

A prospective student would most likely be unaware of the community's activism, in part because a lot of our service and involvement takes place off campus.

The Institution

I like Spelman because it's really a close-knit community. Upperclassmen are directly involved in freshman orientation on a very personal level, so every student can say that someone personally welcomed them to Spelman. I would not trade my Spelman experience for anything. Despite the size of the institution, it offers countless opportunities. I definitely feel prepared for life after college, and I owe a lot of that confidence to Spelman.

The Education

The best part of getting a Spelman education is taking African Diaspora and the World (ADW), a two-semester sequence that is part of the core requirements. ADW is a great class which is annually updated and revised to include the best and new information. The class is supplemented by presentations throughout the year, on topics ranging from civil rights to the effects of migration on the development of blues music.

The Students

A very interesting thing about Spelman is how there's still much diversity within the student body, despite the fact that it's a historically black institution for women. Spelman students come from different states, regions, and countries and represent different socioeconomic groups. Many students come from Africa and the Caribbean. The student body is also comprised of different religious faiths, including but not limited to Christianity, Islam, Bahai, and Judaism. There are clubs which provide support to and activities for students of various backgrounds.

The Activities

All students at schools in the AUC can cross-register at other schools in the AUC, and most of them are in walking distance, so there's a lot of interaction between students. Spelman also has a direct relationship with Morehouse College, which is directly across the street. Morehouse is an all-male institution, so at the start of your freshman year, Spelman and Morehouse students are brought together for socials and are introduced to another student who will be their Morehouse Brother or Spelman Sister.

Spelman's motto is "Women who serve," so community service is strongly encouraged and is very popular here, and is mandatory during the freshman and sophomore years.

The Social Scene

All freshmen are expected to live on campus, unless they are from Atlanta and can commute. Most people meet their close friends in their freshman dorm, but their social circle changes over the years. There are parties all the time in Atlanta, but there aren't a lot *on* campus. I'd say everyone's quite friendly and it's not hard to meet new people.

Notable Spelman Alumni Include:

Alice Walker, Pulitzer Prize-winning novelist
Audrey Forbes Manley, former U. S. Surgeon General
Aurelia Brazeal, ambassador, Ethiopia
Marian Wright Edelman, founder and president, Children's Defense Fund
Mattiwilda Dobbs, opera singer
Ruth A. Davis, director general of the Foreign Service

STANFORD UNIVERSITY

Founded: 1885

Location: Stanford, CA

Phone: (650) 723-2091

E-mail: admission@stanford.edu

Web site: www.stanford.edu

Number of Undergraduates: 7,360

Number of Graduate Students: 9,748

Cost: Approximately $38,000 per year

Application Deadline: December 15

Early Decision: November 1

Rating:
Most Selective

Notable Majors/Programs:
Computer Science, Engineering, English, Biology

Size:
○ Small ● Medium ○ Large

Location:
○ Urban ● Suburban ○ Rural

On a Saturday, students talk about academics:
○ Always ● Sometimes ○ Never

Nightlife:
○ Intense ● Moderate ○ Laid-back

Politically, Stanford leans:
○ Left ○ Right ● Split

Diversity:
● High ○ Low ○ Medium

PAC 10: Yes!

Students describe Stanford in five words:
- Prestigous, always sunny, resort-esque
- Challenging academics, happy laid-back students

From the School

Stanford has one of the most renowned faculties in the nation . . . here in large part because of Stanford's extraordinary students—men and women of all races, ethnicities and ages—distinguished by their love of learning and desire to contribute to the greater community. . . . The pioneering spirit that inspired Jane and Leland Stanford to start this university more than a century ago and that helped build Silicon Valley at the doorstep of the campus encourages boldness in everything we do—whether those efforts occur in the library, in the classroom, in a laboratory, in a theater or on an athletic field.

—www.stanford.edu

If you're interested in Stanford, you may also be interested in:
Claremont McKenna, Duke, Harvard, MIT, Pomona, Yale

Name: Ryan
Hometown: Santa Monica, California
Class Year: Sophomore
Major: History
Extracurriculars: Dorm Government, Talisman (World music a cappella choir), Tap Dance
Career Goal: I'd like to work for a nonprofit arts foundation. I'm also interested in teaching and writing.

How would you describe Stanford's reputation?

Academically rigorous.

Is this reputation accurate?

Stanford *is* academically rigorous—but at the same time it feels laid-back. Students aren't bogged down by work, they're inspired.

What aspect of your school would a prospective student not see on a campus tour?

Sure, Stanford's buildings are beautiful, and the academic programs are excellent, but talented students are what really makes Stanford special. If you're touring Stanford's campus, find a student and ask them to get lunch with you. They'll tell you everything you need to know.

The Institution

My school is physically large (the second largest campus in the world, second to the University of Moscow), but the community of students feels small. There are only 6,500 undergraduates—about 1,600 students in each class year—and you never get lost in the crowd. I love that most students live on campus their entire four years and remain in constant close contact with one another. I feel at home here at Stanford, surrounded by palm trees and fantastic architecture.

The Education

Stanford's faculty is amazing and accessible. There is a 7:1 ratio of students to faculty members. About 75 percent of Stanford's classes have twenty students or less. There is also something called the Freshmen and Sophomore Seminar Program, where you get to take small group seminar classes with noted faculty. This way you can be sure to interact with faculty in close quarters and meet your peers in an intimate setting from the time you first step foot on Stanford's campus. Fall quarter of my freshman year, I took The Worst Journey in the World: What Drives Polar Explorations? My professor had my tiny class read literature on Arctic and Antarctic expeditions during the early 1900s. I, of course, had never even heard of the famous explorers that I ended up becoming obsessed with. Throughout the course, my (famous) professor treated us to lunch at the Faculty Club and later cooked dinner for us at his house with his family. At the end of the class, we took a field trip to the Sierra Nevadas to cross-country ski through the mountains. We learned how to survey for avalanches, build snow shelters, and melt snow to make water. We also cooked on a cast iron stove before spending the night in the hut we'd built. I thought I would die—the winds were blowing between fifty and sixty miles per hour. But I made it through alive and had the time of my life. Thank you, Professor Dunbar, for creating such an innovative class. Thank you, Stanford, for funding the whole trip. And for making experiences like this the norm.

Also, Stanford has a core, where you have to take courses in each of the following areas: Science, Technology and Math, Humanities and Social Sciences, and World Culture, American Culture, and Gender Studies. Students also have to take courses in writing and foreign language.

The Students

About 48 percent of Stanford's students are from California, 47 percent from out of state, and 5 percent from outside of the United States. So, yeah, our student body is culturally diverse. I appreciate the opportunity this gives me to learn about new cultures and traditions. Students are very active in racial, cultural, Lesbian-Gay-Bisexual-Transgender, religious, socioeconomic, and international groups on campus. We have a great arena available for political demonstrations: White Plaza. From the occasional religious evangelist to Reverend Jessie Jackson, White Plaza is open to all who seek to rally support for their causes. It's also the site of our cultural and activities fairs.

The Activities

Community service is very popular at Stanford. There are several student organizations that offer tutoring to the local (and underprivileged) elementary, middle, and high schools. There are also programs that allow Stanford students to teach tennis, piano, dance, and much more to younger children from the community. Many of the religious groups on campus also perform community service.

The Social Scene

I've met most of my friends through my dormitory, classes, and my a cappella choir. I love to hang out. I love to watch movies. I love to dance, I never feel pressured to do anything illegal to have a good time.

Name: Kyle
Hometown: Burbank, California
Class Year: Junior
Major: Product design (mechanical engineering and art)
Extracurriculars: A cappella, Musical Theater, American Sign Language Club
Career Goal: I want to design theme parks for Disney; their Imagineering Division is a great place to be both creative and technical at the same time.

How would you describe Stanford's reputation?

I think many people view Stanford as a relaxed but competitive California school where a love of learning is shared by both the faculty and the student body, and the warm, sunny weather ensures even the most diligent students occasionally step outside to be social.

Is this repuatation accurate?

This is entirely accurate: Stanford students love to work and learn, but also enjoy occasional respites from their studies.

> "The campus is a Disney-style utopia—(almost unnaturally) pristine, with chlorinated fountains, perpetual sunshine, beautiful brick buildings, and thousands of palm trees."
> ✦ Charles, junior

The Institution

Stanford University is a school of 14,000 students (6,500 undergraduates and 7,500 graduate students), which generally classifies it as a medium-sized research institution. Even though the university is larger than a small liberal arts college, the campus feels very intimate. It's not uncommon for me to say "hi" to more than five friends on my three-minute bike ride to class in the morning, or to run into a professor while waiting in line at one of the on-campus eateries. In all, a student can choose to either get lost in their studies or feel like they know everyone on campus. It's great.

Stanford's got every type of housing that an undergraduate could ever want on campus: Greek houses, dorms that look like castles, suite-style arrangements, apartment living—the university's housing options are spacious and endless. What's best is that every undergraduate is guaranteed four years of housing right on campus and within steps of their classes. Almost everyone takes advantage of this.

Our food is also wonderful here; the other day, I went to visit a friend at a state school and was horrified by the dining choices they were given. All of our dining facilities employ professional chefs to provide high-quality meals at reasonable prices.

> "When I tell people where I go to school, they usually say something like, 'Wow, you must be really smart.' And I stand there awkwardly, wishing I was actually smart enough to come up with a graceful reply."
> ✦ Jon, sophomore

The Education

Stanford's housing department is called "Residential Education" because of the number of academic programs that are offered by the dorms. On any given day, inside a dorm, you might walk in on Stanford's dean of admissions speaking with freshmen about the details of their college application, or a student-run program about body image, or a full-blown cultural show, sponsored by a student-group, complete with songs and dancing. Living and learning is really integrated here.

All of our classes at Stanford are taught by professors, with larger classes broken down into sections of five to twenty students, facilitated by TAs (usually doctoral students). In TA sections there is never any new material presented to students. Instead, it's a time to discuss what was previously presented by the professor. All professors hold open office hours (at least four time slots per week) and give out their e-mail addresses so students can ask them questions about class material, the professor's research, or about life in general. Stanford professors are warm, friendly individuals who tend to treat their students like peers and are always willing to give advice.

By the way, I love Stanford's Freshman and Sophomore Seminar Program. When I was a freshman, I took a class titled The Mechanical Design Issues of Sports Equipment, which was taught by an associate professor in the Department of Mechanical Engineering. The class looked at the physics of golf and how engineers at leading companies such as Callaway Golf design their products to maximize a player's performance on the range. Students were able to hit a few balls ourselves, and we talked with an industry expert about being in research and development at a large sports equipment manufacturer. It was a really great opportunity for us to get to know a preeminent member of the university's faculty while exploring a real-world application of the field we were studying. And when it was all over, I was convinced that I wanted to be a mechanical engineer.

The Activities

There are over six hundred student groups on our campus, ranging from a knitting club to club sports to a cappella singing groups. And if a student group doesn't already exist, it can easily be started up by gaining the written support of five other students. Because of this, most students are involved in *some* sort of extracurricular activity.

The Social Scene

Because 96 percent of our undergraduates live on campus, the social scene at Stanford is based in dorms and houses. Somebody is sure to have a party every Friday and Saturday night, and much of the campus heads out to have fun. Alcohol is almost always available at parties here. The university believes that students are adults that are capable of making intelligent decisions for themselves about alcohol consumption, and doesn't require house staff members to file a report every time they see underage drinking. As a consequence, there is very little closed-door or binge-drinking at Stanford, and things are much safer and more moderate because of it. And there are many students on campus who choose not to drink at all—a choice that is widely respected, and all parties have EANABs (Equally attractive nonalcoholic beverages) readily available.

Name: Mark
Hometown: Tampa, Florida
Class Year: Sophomore
Major: Human biology and film studies

Extracurriculars: Filmmaking, political/social activism, mentoring LGBT freshmen, taking trips to San Francisco
Career Goal: I am planning on going into film or doing grassroots work for a human rights organization. I also hope to do a lot of traveling.

How would you describe Stanford's reputation?

People look at Stanford as a very "happy" school. In the fall and spring, students really take advantage of the great weather, reading outside, rollerblading, going for hikes in the foothills. Stanford also has fantastic academics.

Is this reputation accurate?

Stanford students do have fun, but we'll also disappear indoors for days on end when we have to indulge our serious, studious side. Students who major in Stanford's strongest departments—Computer Science, Physics, and Engineering—are particularly studious.

What would an admissions officer at your school probably not tell a prospective student? What aspect of your school would a prospective student not see on a campus tour?

Stanford loves to tell people that the student body is racially and ethnically diverse. And it's true. But Stanford isn't racially and ethnically *integrated*. Students of different ethnicities often form their own social circles and stick to themselves. It's too bad. I wish there was more interaction here.

> "Everyone at Stanford seems laid back, but they're really working very hard. It's called 'Floating Duck Syndrome,' where a duck seems calm and content when its floating on the water, but under the surface that same duck is paddling furiously so it doesn't sink, half-exhausted at all times."
> ✦ Linda, senior

Is there anything about Stanford that's particularly unique?

Strangely enough, students here don't seem to be affected by Stanford's prestige. If anything, I'd say that most of them don't give themselves enough credit, despite the fact that it's not uncommon to have an Olympic athlete, an accomplished artist/musician, and a math genius in the same room at any given time.

The Institution

The campus is beautiful and one of the best decisions I've made here is to walk to class instead of riding a bike—sometimes students get so caught up biking from place to place that they don't take the time to appreciate how breathtaking Stanford's scenery and architecture really is. But it's great—lots of trees, archways, gorgeous buildings with giant red roofs. It's exactly how college should look.

Most Stanford students take similar four-year paths: freshmen meet new people and take obscure, interesting-sounding introductory seminars; sophomores get depressed and feel the sophomore slump, which happens at every college (though Stanford's nice weather makes things easier); juniors go abroad or take some time off from school to independently pursue their interests; and most seniors realize how much they love Stanford, get sad, take advantage of their dwindling time as a student, and party a lot, particularly at Senior Pub Night.

> "There does seem to be a strong emphasis on making money after graduation—seniors are actively courted by investment banks, consultancy firms and tech companies."
> ✦ Bill, senior

The Education

Stanford has some really strong departments, with the strongest being computer science and engineering, which is great for people who want to go into those fields, but intimidating for those who just want to dabble and take an intro course. Science classes as a whole at Stanford are pretty competitive.

If you are a science kid, though, I have to recommend the Human Biology program. It's really unique—I'm finishing up the thirty-unit core right now, and I feel like I just took a crash-course in life. I got to dip my feet into such disparate fields as sociology, psychology, anthropology, economics, political science, public policy, ecology, chemistry, and developmental biology—which all ended up being tied together through relationships to the human predicament.

I'd say that the classes are split fifty-fifty in the sciences between large, lecture-style classes and small, seminar-style classes. I have not found it difficult to forge relationships with my professors, but it definitely doesn't just happen, you have to make an effort to talk to professors outside of class.

> "Stanford is home to Hoover Tower, a conservative right-wing think tank that majorly influences policy in the White House. I think this is a dangerous hawk-run institution. It scares me."
> ✦ Andy, sophomore

The Students

As a gay student I have found it very easy to be out at Stanford. The LGBT center on campus (which is celebrating its thirtieth anniversary this year) is amazing, and there is a great mentor group for LGBT freshmen that organizes social events, takes trips into San Francisco, and generally makes the transition to life as a queer/questioning college student both painless and (dare I say) fun. Stanford's proximity to San Francisco is also a huge advantage and a good number of LGBT upperclassmen go into the city on a semiregular basis to hang out at clubs in the Castro, coffee shops in the Mission, or shops/restaurants in the Haight. Sororities/fraternities are visible at Stanford but, for the average student, they exist for the sole purpose of going there for parties on the weekends—most don't get too caught up in them. While the majority of Stanford students are liberal Democrats, I wouldn't call the student body an activist one by any means—since everyone tends to be in agreement over social/political issues, protests and rallies seem almost futile.

The caliber of the students at Stanford is no different from that at other top schools—what distinguishes Stanford is its laid-back, laissez-faire attitude, idyllic weather, and overall positive atmosphere. It's hard not to walk around campus without thinking that this is what people think of when they imagine their dream school.

The Activities

Some of the more popular extracurricular activities here include a cappella groups (of which there are currently nine) and intramural/varsity sports.

Most students also take advantage of Stanford's idyllic weather (sometimes you actually look forward to a rainy/cloudy day) by spending much of their time outside, either reading or exercising. Palo Alto is definitely not a college town, but the Stanford campus is almost a little village unto itself—and the student union (Tressider) is actually quite nice (it recently underwent a huge renovation project), and it now includes a gym, two coffee shops, a Mexican restaurant, a Subway, and a Jamba Juice. The sports teams definitely garner a lot of support from students, and the big athletic events are really well attended. That being said, I think most Stanford students see sports as a great escape from schoolwork rather than their central, motivating force.

I've spent a lot of time this year with the Stanford Film Society, which spends most of the year preparing for the Stanford Student Film Festival in May. For any student interested in filmmaking, the film society is a huge asset—not to mention the fact that Stanford's campus is a beautiful setting for any film. While Stanford doesn't have a film department per se (although you can major in Film through the Interdisciplinary Program in the Humanities), the administration is currently in process of hiring lots of film professors, and hopes to make Stanford more art/film-friendly over the course of the next few years.

The Social Scene

Stanford students seem to put all of their time and energy into academics and extracurriculars and, consequently, the dating and relationship scene is small. That being said, we definitely take advantage of the weekends to relax and unwind and multiple parties happen every Friday and Saturday night—usually either at the (few) fraternity houses or on the Row (the premiere undergraduate housing option). The alcohol policy is fairly lax, especially compared to other schools, but that does not mean there's excessive, uncontrolled drinking—on the contrary, most Stanford students are pretty responsible and take care of each other when the need arises. Dorm life is vastly different depending on which style of housing you live in— Row houses are fairly social but tend to be filled with juniors and seniors; Mirrielees (apartment-style housing) is a good option for those students who like a more relaxed, laid-back time; Toyon is a posh all-sophomore dorm, great for those lucky enough to get into it; and Wilbur/Stern are your typical freshman dorms. Most people tend to make friends in dorms, through classes, or through extracurricular activities.

Notable Stanford Almuni Include:

Ken Kesey, author
bell hooks, feminist, author
Herbert Hoover, thirty-first president of the United States
Jennifer Connelly, actress
Ted Koppel, TV journalist

Ten Things You Must Do at Stanford before You Graduate

1. Kiss someone at Full Moon on the Quad
2. Go Fountain-hopping
3. Go on a Scavenger hunt in San Francisco
4. Take a ski trip to Tahoe
5. Dance with the band to "All Right Now"
6. Go for a run in the foothills
7. Go to Wednesday night happy hour at the Enchanted Broccoli Forest (a dorm)
8. Read in the Oval
9. Watch Gaieties (the student-run musical) on Big Game weekend
10. Take a road trip to Los Angeles

✦ Mark, junior

SUNY–BINGHAMTON

Founded: 1946
Location: Binghamton, NY
Phone: (607) 777-2171
E-mail: admit@binghamton.edu
Web site: www.binghamton.edu

Number of Undergraduates: 10,378
Number of Graduate Students: 2,822
Cost: Approximately $11,000 per year in state; $16,000 out of state
Application Deadline: Rolling

Rating:	Notable Majors/Programs:
Very Selective	English, Political Science, Engineering, Biology

Size:
○ Small ○ Medium ● Large

Location:
○ Urban ● Suburban ○ Rural

On a Saturday, students talk about academics:
○ Always ● Sometimes ○ Never

Nightlife:
○ Intense ● Moderate ○ Laid-back

Politically, Binghamton leans:
○ Left ○ Right ● Split

Diversity:
○ High ○ Low ● Medium

Students describe Binghamton in five words:
- Quality academics without the price
- Ivy League of SUNY system

From the School

Binghamton has earned a reputation for innovative academic and student life programs, outstanding students, faculty and staff, and the highest graduation rate in the SUNY system. For 50 years, we have been sustained by a vision of excellence that has earned us accolades as the "crown jewel" of New York State's public university system. From unheated Quonset huts offering returning GIs the chance to attend a public liberal arts college to the soaring glass walls of our new academic buildings, Binghamton has made that vision a reality.

—www.binghamton.edu

If you're interested in Binghamton, you may also be interested in:
Columbia, Cornell, U. Michigan, University of Pennsylvania, Penn State, Rutgers

Name: Amber

Hometown: New York, New York

Class Year: Junior

Major: English and cinema studies

Extracurriculars: Student government, Senior Class Council, resident assistant, honor societies

Career Goal: Elementary school teacher

How would you describe Binghamton's reputation?

Binghamton is the best school in the SUNY system, delivering a very high quality education at a very low cost.

Is this reputation accurate?

Absolutely. Everyone at Binghamton was a top student in high school and many got into extremely prestigious private universities, but turned them down to come here because our education is top notch *and* our price tag doesn't make you want to collapse onto the floor crying. Cornell, for example, is just a half hour away, and many Binghamton students applied there and got in, but chose Binghamton so they could graduate with a hundred thousand dollars less in debt.

> "The town of Binghamton definitely has everything you need. You get a downtown bar strip, an insanely large Wal-Mart, a movie theater, and a good, solid variety of take-out (Adriano's delivers pizza till 4:00 a.m.!)."
> ✦ Vanessa, senior

What would an admissions officer at your school probably not tell a prospective student?

They probably wouldn't tell you that Binghamton is a cold, rainy place most of the year. Binghamton is also in the middle of nowhere—hours away from any major city. We're surrounded by woods. If you're the type that needs to escape college every now and again, make sure to bring your car to campus.

The Institution

I first looked at Binghamton because the price was right and then when I came to visit, something just clicked. I knew this place was for me. As I said, it made financial sense. Binghamton is known as the "Ivy of the SUNY's," so the academics fit. I came from a large high school (four thousand students), so going to a college more than twice that seemed like a nice step up. And while Binghamton's campus is big enough that you'll never feel claustrophobic, it's also small enough that you can walk from one end of campus to the other within ten minutes. The only downside is that it's not the prettiest campus in the world. It's well designed—it's a big circle—and while it's functional, aesthetically, it's not inspiring.

Binghamton has a full-fledged University Police Department, which is a branch of the New York State Police, which always makes me feel safe. Also, on campus, it's pretty easy to go days on end without spending much money. Everything is reasonably priced (except for books, but that's at any school).

Binghamton's dorm facilities are separated into five different "living communities," and each has a different reputation, a different vibe, and they allow students to feel a small-school sense of community while still a member of Binghamton's sprawling campus. The five communities are called: Newing (the party dorm that most Greeks live in), Dickinson (the most diverse living community), Hinman (said to be for the more serious, studious kids on campus), College in the Woods (rumored to house the druggy community), and the graduate dorm (which you can only live in as a junior or a senior). I live in Hinman, and I really do find it to be a reprieve from the otherwise overwhelming bigness of Binghamton. When I'm walking around elsewhere and I notice people from Hinman mixed in the crowd, we smile at one another and feel connected.

The Education

During freshman year, Binghamton classes are big. You're mostly going to be taking intros to biology, chemistry, psychology, organic chemistry, and so on. But don't worry, this won't last forever. Once you get going in your major, your classes will get smaller. And as classes get smaller, professors will get more accessible, and if you take the initiative they'll meet with you outside of class, at office hours.

At Binghamton academics are what you make of them. If you slack off you'll find yourself staring at impossible tests three months down the line, and your grades aren't going to make you (or your family) very happy. But if you show up to class, pay attention, and do your homework on time, you'll find the workload to be pretty reasonable. Every now and again you'll find yourself in an incredibly easy class where you honestly can get by doing nothing at all, or a killer class where you have to move into the library if you expect to do well. But on average, classes are very manageable so long as you put in a couple of hours every week. My favorite classes here have been: Shakespeare; Pop, Rock, and Soul; Literature and Medicine; Cinema and Violence, The Love Story in Literature; Mathematics in Action; Jazz 1 and Jazz 2 (dance classes); Swimming for Fitness; and Aerobic Kickboxing. Binghamton also has a grad school, and students can take graduate classes if they want to, which is a great option if you really want to challenge yourself.

> "Fitspace has two weight rooms, one for normal students with the typical variety of machines that you can use to keep in good shape, and one for the Greek Gods and Goddesses of our campus, who lift the eight thousand plus pounds of weight in this other room with unnatural ease."
> ✦ Devin, sophomore

The Students

Binghamton's campus is surprisingly diverse. I expected everyone to be white, Catholic, and liberal. Instead, there are students from all ethnicities, from all religions, and every political belief. You learn so much more when you're surrounded by students different from yourself than you would if you were surrounded by clones. And all types of students mix here, you'll rarely see a black-kid, white-kid, Indian-kid, Asian-kid divide. It's more like everyone hanging out together, talking, laughing, partying. My one complaint is that, since we're a state school, almost everyone is from New York. It would be nice to know more people from California and Texas and all over the world.

The Activities

At Binghamton I've really thrown myself into the student government organization in my living community. Hinman has something called the Hinman College Council, and there are a handful of students that make up the board. I'm a member of the board, and we all plan programs and activities for everyone in our living community, and attend them with one another. We talk every day and often late into the night. It's worth it to involve yourself in an activity like this here, because you'll get to know people incredibly well and it will allow you to set up a tiny support group in this otherwise big school.

The Social Scene

Binghamton doesn't really have one "scene" that dominates on weekends. We have jocks that have big jock parties and watch sports and talk about sports and get drunk. We have super artsy types that lounge around in their rooms and listen to obscure music while running their hands through their jagged/expensively-cut-but-made-to-look-like-it's-not expensively cut hair. We have big Greek organizations, so frats will throw massive parties and sorority girls will giggle to their sisters that Bobby from Beta is really hot. Every scene exists, and whichever scene is your ideal, you'll find it.

I really like living on campus, but a lot of juniors or seniors move to off-campus apartments(a five-to-eight-minute drive away), as many seem to like moving into a "real-life" atmosphere when they become upperclassmen.

Name: Pauline
Hometown: Staten Island, New York
Class Year: Senior
Major: Sociology and biology
Extracurriculars: Black Student Union, Charles Drew Pre-Medical Minority Society, Counselor at U-Turn (a maximum security juvenile detention center), EMT with Harpur's Ferry Volunteer Ambulance at Binghamton University, Wilson Hospital Emergency Room Volunteer
Career Goal: To become a doctor and open a free clinic in the West Indies

How would you describe Binghamton's reputation?

A fine research institution that is also considered a "public Ivy League" school.

Is this reputation accurate?

Yeah. Binghamton has fantastic research facilities and any undergraduate who wants to get involved in research will find a professor to work with. And Binghamton does offer a rigorous curriculum and great professors, so we do deserve our public Ivy reputation.

What would an admissions officer at your school probably not tell a prospective student?

I'm sure admissions officers don't tell prospective students that the quality of on-campus food ranges from blissfully tasteless to dear-God-what-did-I-just-put-in-my-mouth.

The Institution

The size is just right. When I first arrived I thought the campus was huge and that I would get lost in the sea of people, but I haven't found that to be the case at all—if the school was any smaller, I think I'd feel boxed in. And everywhere I go, I see people who greet me by name. I also like that townies tend to be on campus a lot, and that we see them when we're on buses to and from campus, in the mall, at parties. It makes us feel like we're more than just college students, that we're also residents of Binghamton. The diversity of the student body here is also amazing. One gripe I have is that there's not much school spirit. Sure, we occasionally go to basketball games, and within every living community when there are traditional activities like dorm wars, semiformals, and carnivals, everyone says "I love Binghamton!" But otherwise it's rare that you'll hear spontaneous declarations of school love. Maybe it's because we don't have a football team? Another gripe is that I don't particularly like dorm life at Binghamton. I don't like sharing a bathroom with twenty other kids, people knocking on my door and being rowdy in the hallways at all hours of the night. Plenty of people love it and stay on campus as long as possible, but it wasn't my thing. It's just a matter of preference. People who live on campus enjoy the convenience, I think. While people who live off campus enjoy their privacy.

The Education

Students at Binghamton belong to different academic colleges—either the College of Arts and Sciences, the School of Nursing, the School of Management, the School of Education and Human Development, or the School of Engineering and Applied Science. Every school has its own core requirements, but, on average, you'll find yourself having to take one writing class, two physical education classes, one course in the arts, one in

pluralism, one in global studies, and one in communications. I think the core is great—you're not mindlessly fulfilling requirements, you're exploring and learning different things you may not have otherwise been exposed to. In fact, I would probably not have taken biology at all if it weren't for the core, and now it's one of my two majors!

I'd say the strongest departments at Binghamton are English, Political Science, Engineering, and Biology. Students are serious about their work, but this isn't a place where students talk about their classes on a Saturday night out of pure intellectual joy. That's not our scene. Instead, we enjoy our classes, work to get good grades, and that's that. And we don't *compete* to get good grades—it's pretty common to see big groups of kids studying together or helping one another with term papers so everyone does well.

I'd say most classes at Binghamton have three separate components. For example, in my science classes, the professor has everyone meet in a massive lecture hall three times a week, and they'll go over new material. Then, once a week, students will break into small groups and meet with TAs to talk about the professor's lecture. Also once a week, small groups will meet up with TAs to do labwork. In this way, we get the big-school atmosphere mixed with small-school personal attention. If you want to do research as a undergrad, there are lots of opportunities, you just have to be aggressive and corner your professors, demanding a piece of the research pie. They usually oblige, and if you do good work, you can continue with them four years. I was a research assistant and it was a great opportunity to get some hands-on experience.

> "There are probably a thousand computers all over campus available for student use. You can use them to work, surf the net, or print papers. All Binghamton students also have solid Internet connections, and you can get six channels of HBO right in your dorm room."
>
> ✦ Roger, junior

The Students

Most Binghamton students are from the New York City area. Racially, I'd say we're 50 percent white, 30 percent Asian, 10 percent Indian, 5 percent Black, and 5 percent Latino. (That's based on what *I've* seen.) Even though students of different ethnicities interact very frequently, there are still very strong ethnic student groups on campus. I'd say the biggest (and most vocal) are the JSU (Jewish Student Union), the BSU (Black Student Union), and CSA (Caribbean Students Association). All of these groups hold frequent rallies and protests on a variety of issues. They never work together, though. I think they'd all be more effective if they teamed up. But that's for them to decide.

I'd say most students here are pre-professionally oriented, too. A lot of people are premed, prelaw, into nursing or management, very future oriented. It's rare to find Binghamton kids who are wishy-washy on where they'll be ten years from now, or who are so engrossed in their academics that they can't see the bigger picture.

And, lastly, I suppose bathroom-stall-writing isn't the most credible way to assess the collective political thoughts of the student body, but "Fuck George Bush" was written in big letters in one of the bathroom stalls on campus and it sure does feel like most people hate this particular president, and the impacts of his policies that will be felt for years to come. While we have our share of Democrats *and* Republicans—there is a strong anti-Bush sentiment 'round these parts.

The Activities

Community service is strongly encouraged here, and takes all forms. There are blood drives, breast cancer walks, book drives, clothes drives, a dance-a-thon, and volunteer slots at the local hospital. I volunteer at a facility for young men with the Black Student Union, and have really enjoyed being able to help shape lives and change them for the better.

> "Binghamton has more than 80,000 living alumni spread throughout the world. The alumni network is a big help when you're looking for a job upon graduation, or if you're trying to network."
>
> ✦ Lee, sophomore

The Social Scene

Depending on what's on offer, students party on-campus or off-campus. Thursday, Friday, and Saturday tend to be the nights to have fun, and most go out two, or all three of these nights. Be warned, Binghamton has started cracking down on underage alcohol consumption, and now you'll see lots of campus police around on weekend nights, searching for underage students with beers, or intoxicated morons stumbling toward their car with their car keys in hand.

On a typical Friday, students will go to the library and study until 8 p.m., then head home, take a shower, eat, maybe take a nap, then wake up and get ready to have fun. Usually there'll be a good off-campus party that everyone's heard about, and students will head there at 11:00 p.m. and leave around 3:00 a.m. There also might be a good frat or sorority party to head to—the frat/sorority scene is big here, not necessarily because everyone joins up and becomes Greek, more because Greeks throw big parties that anyone is welcome at, and most students here have participated in a bit of Greek debauchery. The Greeks also do a lot of community service in the nearby area, and hold a lot of fund-raisers, too, so the rest of us admire them for that.

Name: Adam
Hometown: Matawan, New Jersey

> "Binghamton is located right near this great nature reserve. A lot of students will hang out in the wooded area, and some will . . . ah . . . use the wooded area as a shield of sorts, to do things the administration wouldn't approve of."
>
> ✦ Adam, freshman

Class Year: Junior
Major: Psychology
Extracurriculars: Golden Key National Honor Society, Psi Chi Honor Society (psychology), Hall Government, Intramural Volleyball
Career Goal: Obtain a Ph.D. in neuroscience, studying the psychopharmacology of addiction.

How would you describe Binghamton's reputation?

Binghamton offers a good bang for your buck. It's full of high-quality professors and students.

Is this reputation accurate?

Yeah. SUNY Binghamton delivers a great education at a manageable price. It's not too aesthetically pleasing—certainly not as aesthetically pleasing as most private schools—and it's often wet and cold outside. But students graduate with a meaningful diploma and no loans hanging over their heads, so I think it's well worth it!

What would an admissions officer at your school probably not tell a prospective student? What aspect of your school would a prospective student not see on a campus tour?

An admissions officer probably wouldn't tell a prospective student that Binghamton has taken up some aggressive building projects lately, and, because of them, Binghamton doesn't exactly have money to spare. So now students don't get things like paper syllabi; we have to go online to read class descriptions. Little things like this are happening left and right so Binghamton can save money.

Also, prospective students probably wouldn't be told that the town of Binghamton itself isn't exactly thriving, and there's not too much for students to do there.

The Institution

I chose Binghamton because it offered a quality education at a reasonable price. I've really enjoyed my time here, but I've been disappointed with the fact that, because it's a state school, most students are from New York City or upstate New York, and everyone reminds me of the people I went to high school with. My friends who went to more diverse private schools met people from all over the world, who had very different experiences growing up. That's not going to be the case here. Also, a lot of Binghamton students have a very high school approach to their education. They go to class and study to get good grades, not to learn, and it's rare that anyone will talk about their classes for fun, or because they found something they read to be extraordinarily interesting. Students also, in only working hard enough to get a good grade, will gripe endlessly if they find it *hard* to get a good grade in a course. Everyone at Binghamton graduated toward the top of their class, so they're not going to allow themselves to get a bad grade. But they don't expect to work too hard and rather than reveling in the challenge, in a hard class they'll bitch and moan and moan and bitch about how much time they're being forced to spend in the library.

The Education

There are many large lecture-based classes at Binghamton. That said, there are also some pretty great upper-level classes and seminars where you are in a room with only ten other students and you get to become close with your professors. And even in large classes, if you go to your professors' office hours and ask them if you can do research, you'll be able to get personal attention. I did this, as a psychology major, and I was actually able to enroll in an independent study with a professor to function as a research assistant in the psychology labs. I learned so much through this position, and because of it I've decided to go on to grad school to obtain a Ph.D. in neuroscience.

I've also found that Binghamton has top-rate study-abroad programs, which are also subsidized by the school, so anyone can study abroad regardless of whether they have money to burn. Last year I studied abroad in London, and had a really incredible time.

> "There's a Hooters not too far from Binghamton, and the customers there have amazing mullets. In some cases, a standing ovation really would be appropriate. Business in the front, party in the back. The Binghamton mullet is evolved, advanced, a true art form. Brilliant."
>
> ✦ Michael, senior

The Students

Students at Binghamton are varied in the sense that they're all from different towns in Long Island. Our more exotic students are from the boroughs of New York City and upstate New York. Most students are white, but there are substantial communities of Asian and Indian students, and less substantial communities of Hispanic and African American students. While Binghamton on the whole is pretty apathetic toward social and political issues, the ethnic and multicultural groups do their fair share of shouting and protesting.

I'd say the average Binghamton student is from an upper-middle-class Jewish family, born and bred in Long Island, and they decided to come to Binghamton because their parents said they could either go to a private school and get no car, or go to a state school and get the car of their choice. This average student works pretty hard in their classes and complains constantly if their GPA is below 3.2. In their spare time and on weekends, this student will go to a lot of bars and drink a lot of alcohol.

The Activities

Binghamton students mostly stick to themselves. There aren't other schools close enough for us to interact with. I guess Cornell is less than an hour away—and Binghamton does provide occasional transport there—but students from Cornell and Binghamton don't interact enough for the proximity to be considered significant.

The Social Scene

The Binghamton social scene is a big mix. Some students focus on their studies and rarely party. Others party every weekend, and still others party ever night. Some party on campus, but the school has started cracking down on underage drinking and pot smoking, so it's become a bit more difficult to smoke/drink casually, and this has driven many students to spend more time partying off-campus. There are lots of frat/sorority parties, which are big and rowdy, so if that's your thing, Binghamton won't disappoint. There are house parties, which tend to only be good if you know the people who live in the house, and if the police don't find the party and break it up. And finally, a lot of people party downtown, where Johnny Law isn't breathing down everyone's neck as much. "Downtown" is really just one block with about seven bars on it, but of those bars only two are strict with IDs, so it's easy to get into the majority of them with a fake ID or with nothing at all. Most of these bars get really crowded on the weekends, and have drink specials during the week (like fifty-cent mugs on Wednesdays and a beer pong tournament on Thursdays). A lot of students will also head to the Ale House, which is a nearby bar where students of legal drinking age can do the tour and get their name on a plaque if they can down portions of about ninety different beers from all over the world. There's also Cheers, which is popular on Thursday nights.

Notable Binghamton Alumni Include:

Camille Paglia, author, political columnist
William Baldwin, actor
Michael Convertino, composer
Gary Kunis, executive, Cisco Systems
Paul Reiser, actor, comedian
Tony Kornheiser, sportswriter

SWARTHMORE COLLEGE

Founded: 1864

Location: Swarthmore, PA

Phone: (610) 328-8000

E-mail: admissions@swarthmore.edu

Web site: www.swarthmore.edu

Number of Undergraduates: 1,480

Number of Graduate Students: 0

Cost: Approximately $39,500 per year

Application Deadline: January 1

Early Decision: November 15

Rating:	Notable Majors/Programs:
Most Selective	Life Sciences, Social Sciences, English

Size:
● Small   ○ Medium   ○ Large

Location:
○ Urban   ● Suburban   ○ Rural

On a Saturday, students talk about academics:
● Always   ○ Sometimes   ○ Never

Nightlife:
○ Intense   ○ Moderate   ● Laid-back

Politically, Swarthmore leans:
● Left   ○ Right   ○ Split

Diversity:
● High   ○ Low   ○ Medium

Students describe Swarthmore in five words:
- Intensely rigorous, friendly, and awkward
- Small, brainy, liberal, super-intellectual community

From the School

Swarthmore prepares students for full, balanced lives as individuals and as responsible citizens through exhilarating study supplemented by an exciting array of extracurricular activities. We're dedicated to helping you realize your fullest potential, to become a valuable member of society with a deep sense of ethical and social concern.

—www.swarthmore.edu

If you're interested in Swarthmore, you may also be interested in:
Harvard, Haverford, Reed, Wesleyan, William and Mary, Williams

Name: Bryan
Hometown: Exeter, New Hampshire
Class Year: Junior
Major: Chemistry
Extracurriculars: Wind Ensemble
Career Goal: vague

How would you describe Swarthmore's reputation?

Swarthmore is well known in certain academic circles. It has a reputation for dazzlingly brutal workloads and an unconventional social scene. The students, I think, are more or less approached as freaks or geeks. But the typical response I get when I tell folks I'm from Swarthmore is a blank stare.

Is this reputation accurate?

By and large I think the school's reputation is accurate, inasmuch as one sentiment can really describe an entire (small) population of diverse, different, and amazing people. Yes, the work is very difficult, but it is often administered with care and understanding from professors, and the student approach to the workload is just as intense as the volume of work we're faced with. As for the social scene, we live in a dry suburb of Philadelphia, surrounded by students who are just as likely to get enveloped in a good book on a Saturday night as they are to wind up at a dance party.

> "As a person who forewent the larger schools of the Ivy Leagues for 'the Harvard of liberal arts schools,' I am thankful for Swat's small, intimate size and accepting environment, but I'll admit that the size is sometimes simultaneously the source of much frustration."
>
> ✦ Yoshi, senior

What would an admissions officer at Swarthmore probably not tell a prospective student?

Generally admissions would not tell you that the town of Swarthmore is far and away the worst college town outside of Beirut.

The Institution

I was really really excited to be at Swarthmore my freshman year. I had a perpetual grin on my face (the dark circles and sallow complexion had not yet settled in). Armed with a backpack, pens and pencils, and what I considered a liberal humanistic approach, I could take on anything. Two years later I find myself returned from studying abroad, acrimonious, overworked, addicted to cigarettes, possessing an unhealthy approach to drinking, desperately single, and generally unmotivated. Who's to blame? I want my freshman year back!

> "The bathroom stalls mostly have intellectual debates, with the occasional 'Your mom' comments thrown in for good measure."
>
> ✦ Will, senior

The Education

Professors are genuinely available, in and out of class. They are largely approachable and friendly, interact well with students, and go out of their way to demonstrate this. Some even show up at parties, even drag parties. I haven't decided whether or not this is a mark of a cool prof. Academics truly invade the social experience here. Whether it's misery poker at every meal, or dissecting arguments over a gin and tonic on a Saturday night, you will find it hard to mentally get out of class. Students are very passive-aggressively competitive. It's somewhat gauche to be demonstratively so, and mentioning grades, GPAs, and test scores is frowned upon. But there are very few students who are not secretly grinding axes to get to the head of a class.

The Students

Largely left of center student population. A friend of mine once claimed that "Everyone at Swarthmore is either queer or Jewish. Or left-handed." In general, if she had added "oppressed," she'd have a universal statement. Students typically mix pretty well. There are too few of us not to. Still, I think there is a significant amount of polarization between black students and students of other racial backgrounds. This is not unilateral, but it is present. LGBT groups on campus are strained, but welcoming. Because Swarthmore as an institution is actively queer-supportive, and the student population is tolerant if not actively interested in queer issues, the groups are sort of superfluous, and find themselves catering to the confused bisexual freshmen girls and the sex-radical transfeminist advocates. While the place is seemingly open, it's very rare that anyone comes out after freshman year. This may be due to cliqueyness, though I can't really justify it. Personally, I've found Swarthmore to be a great place to come into my sexual identity; I just wish there was a larger dating/whatever pool to splash around in. The average student: wears sandals nine months out of the year; voted Democrat in 2004, but for Nader in 2000; is wealthier than they would have you know; wishes they were as cool as that girl with the boots; has a radio show; drinks too much coffee; prefers hard liquor to beer; doesn't smoke cigarettes, but can be convinced to take a hit.

> "I was petrified that I was going to die under the stress of work when I first came to Swarthmore, but it's all really quite manageable. Eventually, Swarthmore students *do* have free time and *do* have fun, contrary to popular belief."
>
> ✦ Martyna, freshman

The Activities

When I leave campus, which is rare, it's usually to the liquor store. Or to Philadelphia/UPenn. There are no bars in Swarthmore, and while the college policy on alcohol is very progressive, sometimes being seen drinking a classy drink outweighs the price tag.

It's 12:30 on a Wednesday night right now, and I'll be awake for a while. Most likely I'll be working for a few hours, I'll slam back some NyQuil, and wake up at the crack of dawn to TA an orgo lab. If it was a weekend, and I had my senses about me, I'd probably take a walk in our beautiful arboretum. There are usually some great late-night conversations going on, it's the only way to get your mind off the utter lack of food after midnight.

The people sitting outside on a sunny day are: (A) The freshmen who go to every multicultural event and feel the need to really make you know that they are getting a lot out of this school. (B) The athletes throwing a Frisbee around, not terribly anxious about work. Some people find them attractive—hmmmm. (C) The kids who wear capes, read fantasy, and juggle. They're a hoot. And they'd prefer that I said "cloaks." (D) Hipper-

than-thou arts/theater/radio/NYC crowd, lounging about with affected accents, their anthropology books sprawled about, trying to say "fuck" as often and loudly as possible. They're a good time.

The Social Scene

Party situations are typically available Thursday, Friday, and Saturday nights. Most people only pick one night a week. This campus approaches alcohol strangely. You have teetotalers, the moderates, and the problem drinkers. We all get along. Friday night starts with a room party. Loud '80s music, shared drinks. Then we probably see a movie on campus, or just take a nap to make up for the two hours of sleep the night before. After an hour or so of prepartying, we head off to the dance party, for a night of sweaty bad dancing to hip hop and top forty delights, hoping to get groped by the right people, and hoping that the condom that's been in that back pocket for three months might get some fresh air.

> "Campus is a nationally recognized arboretum = gorgeous, but lots of allergies. (One word: Clarinex.)"
>
> ✦ Martyna, freshman

I feel like I know just about everyone on campus, by sight if not reputation. It's a burden—news travels SO fast. My friends who are abroad right now are often cluing me in on some gossip I've missed while buried in the basement of the science library. Unless you are intimately familiar with someone, you do not say "hi" to them on the sidewalk. "Hey, you're in my math class. How's it going?" (deer in headlights). I hold doors open for other people, though.

Name: Katherine
Hometown: Princeton, New Jersey
Class Year: Senior
Major: Biology
Extracurriculars: field hockey for three years, tutoring
Career Goal: Ph.D. in some area of biology

How would you describe Swarthmore's reputation?

Really hard and intense with lots of weird people.

Is this reputation accurate?

Pretty much—it sounds very negative but if you want an intellectual experience, this is the place to come. Although there are a lot of really weird people, most are weird in a good way. It all depends on what you want. Swat isn't some place you come just to get a degree.

What would an admissions officer at Swarthmore probably not tell a prospective student?

How many socially awkward people there are. Also they wouldn't tell you that if you are applying to law school or more mainstream jobs (i.e., investment banking, consulting sorts of jobs), I think a lot of those places won't have heard of Swat and won't know that your 3.2 GPA is like a 3.8 at Harvard.

The Institution

I chose Swat because I wanted to go to an intellectual college. I could also play field hockey here, which was a nice bonus, although it wasn't why I decided to come. I wanted to take a year off between high school and college, and Swat was the only place that said it was not a problem when I asked if I could defer.

People here tend to complain a lot about Swat, which I think is unfair. It is definitely incredibly hard and there are a lot of awkward people here, but I think we'll be surprised, when we get into the real world, at how much better prepared we are than everyone else. Workwise, pretty much anything after this will seem easy, or at the very least bearable. And it is probably the last time in my life I will be surrounded by people who are so intellectually stimulating. People here are actually interested in what's going on in the world. They don't look at you funny because you read the *New York Times* and like foreign movies. It's a unique experience. Overall I'm happy I decided to come here.

The Education

We always talk about classes. If we're drinking or something, we'll at the very least mention how we should be doing work. You should always be doing work. But I never ever do work on Saturday evenings. I have some friends that do, but *I* need to unwind. Incredibly for such a hard-core place, there isn't very much competition among students here. I remember in high school my friends and I would always compare grades, but I can't remember the last time somebody asked me what I got on

a test at Swat. Everyone has fallen flat on their face at least once since they got here, so we know better than to ask.

If you are in the natural sciences, you have great opportunities afterward to go to grad school. People have definitely heard of Swat in the natural sciences, and most principal investigators I know say that some of their best grad students have been Swatties. And at least for science students, research opportunities abound for undergrads. Even though we don't have a grad school, most students do research at least one summer. I have done some sort of biological research every summer since my freshman year. And it's paid off: although I had very little experience with molecular and cellular biology, I got a job in a lab doing just that because I had so much other research experience.

The Students

Coming from a private school in Princeton, Swat seems incredibly diverse to me. And I think it actually is, in comparison to most private colleges. We have quite a few international students, considering how small we are—every once in awhile I'm just amazed at how many people I know from so many different countries: Bolivia, Nepal, Venezuela, Italy, France, Palestine, the list goes on. But there is definitely self-segregation between different racial groups. And although most people are middle class or wealthier, people certainly don't flaunt their money; there's no prestige in being wealthy here. In fact it's the opposite: no one wants to admit that they don't get financial aid or don't need to work. The campus is incredibly liberal: everyone knows the five Republicans on campus (that's only a slight exaggeration). Just about everyone reads the *Phoenix* and most people read the *New York Times*. Also popular are CNN.com, BBC.com, and the *Economist*.

The Activities

Supposedly we are part of a tri-college consortium with Bryn Mawr and Haverford. However, the only time I have ever been on their campuses was for a sports event. Occasionally you'll have a student from one of those schools in your classes or at one of your parties, especially the Bryn Mawr girls. I'm sure there are some Swatties who hang out at those schools but I never have.

People really don't pay much attention to athletics at all. Although a fair number of people play either a varsity or club sport, most people can't be bothered to attend games unless a good friend is playing.

I probably get off-campus about once a week. Every once in awhile I'll go into Philly for dinner or something but most of the time I just go and get coffee with a friend or go to the movies. Everything is free on-campus so there isn't much of an impetus to get off-campus.

It's a sunny day and there are four groups of people:

1. Activist hippies: at least one would have dreads, one guy would be wearing a skirt, one person would be on a scooter.
2. Frat jocks: most likely lacrosse or baseball players. One would have his shirt off. There would be a couple of well-dressed preppy girls flirting with them.
3. Rhythm and Motion crowd: mainly black and Hispanic kids dancing to African or hip hop music. Most of the guys would be gay.
4. Chill hipsters: talking about indie rock, girls would be wearing Ugg boots, the guys would be wearing obscure band T-shirts. They would be smoking (probably weed) and drinking beer out of bottles.

The Social Scene

People party starting on Thursday—although it depends on the workload. Most people preparty with friends in their rooms, drinking beer or cheap alcohol, although by senior year we don't drink totally crappy alcohol. If there is only one party on campus everyone will go there, but if there's more than one, groups will split up. The hip indie rock crowd will go to Olde Club where they have bands play about once a week, the frat/jock crowd will be at the frat parties, and everyone else will be at Paces. There isn't a lot of dating. People either hook up or have serious relationships. At such a small school you're going to run into someone numerous times a week, so there really isn't any point to going out on dates. Not to mention most people don't want to spend the money.

Not very many people live off-campus. They tend to get sort of isolated because most people don't have cars and the social life is very much centered on campus.

I don't say "hi" to strangers, but I certainly hold doors open for them. There aren't obviously exclusive elements of the social scene at Swarthmore; people find their group and stick with it.

Name: Meredith
Hometown: Menomonee Falls, Wisconsin
Class Year: Senior
Major: Psychology
Extracurriculars: Swarthmore Protestant Community; Varsity Swimming; Varsity Track; I also work for eight to twelve hours a week
Career Goal: I aspire to be a family practice lawyer, specifically working with children's rights and/or adoption law.

> "This is the kind of place where everyone is encouraged to be original and to express themselves as comfortably and freely as possible. Want to see a guy in a cape? In a skirt? Wearing Abercrombie pants? You can find it all at Swat."
>
> ✦ Saed, junior

How would you describe Swarthmore's reputation?

Liberal, intense, expensive, and prestigious.

Is this reputation accurate?

Swarthmore is all of those things and more. It is liberal, but I myself identify as conservative and have found the liberal environment to be stimulating and welcoming. Swarthmore is intense, but it's only as intense as you make it. I feel like I've had a great social life here, have gotten good grades, and have found a wonderful balance between great academics and fabulous people. Swarthmore is expensive, but they also have a fantastic aid program that makes it affordable—I am far from wealthy and have attended Swarthmore with reasonable financial sacrifice. Finally, Swarthmore is prestigious. It only accepts one out of five applicants, so the odds are against getting in here. But if you do, it's wonderful!

What would an admissions officer at Swarthmore probably not tell a prospective student? What aspect of Swarthmore would a prospective student not see on a campus tour?

Swarthmore doesn't have the big-name recognition that you're going to get with the Ivies, but it has a lot of special things to offer that you're not going to get at the Ivies, either. I think the phrase is that it's "the best school you've never heard of." Be okay with that if you're going to come here. On a tour, I feel like a lot of times they forget to emphasize that we have fun here! It's a great place to be.

The Institution

We have something called the "Swarthmore Swivel"—it's meant to warn you to check first that the person you're talking about isn't standing behind you. We are a small school, but it doesn't feel confining. It's nice to see familiar faces and know half of the student body. The school's prestige is sort of interesting; there's the running joke that "everyone thinks they're an admissions mistake" because no one feels that they actually belong among all of these intelligent people, and yet

> "Students here have a lot of say in what goes on in the community. This stems back to the Quaker heritage and belief in decision making based on consensus."
>
> ✦ Saed, junior

everyone *does* belong. They don't let you in if you can't cut it, and it's crucial to remember that.

We are a very contained community. Ninety percent of people live on campus and I really like that—all of your friends are close by, the dorms are fabulous, and hall life is usually great, especially for underclassmen. The best bathroom to see on campus is the women's one in the science library. There are huge sheets of paper with pencils attached, meant for writing anything and everything. There are polls, summer plans, reflections, inspiring quotes, class recommendations—you find yourself staying in there much longer than necessary!

Swarthmore has fantastic internship opportunities, especially the ability to get financing for them because we have a very large endowment—know that, and seek out that money! They want to give it to you. I do feel prepared for life after college, but I am incredibly sad to be leaving all of these wonderful people.

The Education

Swat probably isn't the place for you if you don't love learning. We always talk about classes. But you certainly don't have to—you can never get away from it, if that's what you want, or you can think about academics at an extreme minimum. And contrary to popular belief, there isn't competition between students. We aren't rated and nobody talks about grades. It just doesn't matter.

The core curriculum is very reasonable and helps ease you into the college workload. Class size depends on the department and what kind of class you take, but we have large (for us: one hundred student) lectures, small discussions, small lectures, even classes with only four people. I feel as if I am actual friends with a few professors I've met here; it's virtually impossible to come away from Swarthmore without at least one close professor relationship. You'd have to be avoiding it.

The Students

I think the average Swarthmore student is from the East Coast or California, liberal, academic, an activist, and definitely a Democrat (something like 96 percent of students identified that way in a newspaper poll). And yet I'm from Wisconsin, conservative, Republican, and don't think I could be described as activist at all. I love it here and almost all of the people I've met here. Don't let preconceived notions deter you from going to a school. Had I been more informed about Swarthmore's profile, I'm not sure I would have come here—and that would have been one of the biggest mistakes of my life.

The Activities

In addition to the Tri-Co (Tri-College Consortium) and our ability to take classes at U. Penn, there are tons of colleges in the Philadelphia area; we compete athletically at almost all of them, but those three are the ones with which we have academic ties. Athletics have been central to my time at Swat but are not central to the lives of the average student. We don't get a whole lot of student support, but most athletes didn't come here just for the athletics.

One of our best traditions is "Screw Your Roommate." It's an annual dance in which everybody 'screws' their roommate by setting them up with a blind date for the formal that evening. In order to meet your date, you have to perform in some way in the cafeteria for the public. Usually, the skit or costume is personally relevant and almost always embarrassing. It's all in good fun, and watching people get screwed is a blast. It's also absolute mayhem in the dining hall on that particular day—not much eating gets done, and they only put out the plasticware.

The Social Scene

We're pretty accepting of alcohol. That might have freaked me out in high school, but it's really just not an issue. Drink if you want to, don't if you don't. Most people drink here, and getting drunk with your friends is a fun thing to do on the weekends. That's pretty much where it stays, though. You can't come here and drink every night and expect to graduate—it's just not going to work out very well.

We don't have sororities, and there are only two frats, which most guys aren't a part of. They host a lot of the parties, but those are open to everyone. A frat party is just like any other party here; nobody lives in the frats, so they're not huge influences even for their members. The dating options are pretty much hook up or get married.

Notable Swarthmore Alumni Include:

David Baltimore, Nobel laureate for physiology or medicine

Edward C. Prescott, Nobel laureate in economics

Eugene M. Lang, philanthropist

James Michener, author

Michael Dukakis, former governor of Massachusetts

Molly Yard, founder, National Organization for Women

UNIVERSITY OF TEXAS AT AUSTIN

Founded: 1883

Location: Austin, TX

Phone: (512) 475-7440

E-mail: frmn@uts.cc.utexas.edu

Web site: www.utexas.edu

Number of Undergraduates: 39,611

Number of Graduate Students: 11,297

Cost: Approximately $10,000 per year in state; $16,000 out of state

Application Deadline: February 1
Rolling Admissions

Rating:	Notable Majors/Programs:
Very Selective	Business Management, Communications, Engineering

Size:
○ Small　○ Medium　● Large

Location:
● Urban　○ Suburban　○ Rural

On a Saturday, students talk about academics:
○ Always　● Sometimes　○ Never

Nightlife:
● Intense　○ Moderate　○ Laid-back

Politically, UT Austin leans:
○ Left　○ Right　● Split

Diversity:
● High　○ Low　○ Medium

Students describe UT Austin in five words:
- Huge, vibrant campus in Austin
- Fantastic scholars teach spirited students

From the School

[The University of Texas's] undergraduate and graduate academic programs rank among the best in the country. . . . Austin, an attractive city that offers natural beauty, abundant outdoor activities, sophisticated culture, lively arts and musical entertainment, and a spirited political atmosphere. The University community and Austin culture make an irresistible combination.

—www.utexas.edu

If you're interested in UT Austin, you might also be interested in:
UC Berkeley, Duke, George Washington, NYU, UNC at Chapel Hill, U. Virginia

Name: Leah
Hometown: Pasadena, Texas
Class Year: Junior
Major: Mathematics, acturial science
Extracurriculars: Kappa Phi Gamma Sorority, Inc. (South Asian Sorority), Indian Students Association
Career Goal: Actuarial consultant

How would you describe UT Austin's reputation?

UT Austin used to be a generic state school that students went to by default. Lately, though, UT Austin has distinguished itself from the pack and made the leap to "prestige" status, and now it's known throughout the country for offering top-notch academics. It's also said to have a great football team, and—partially because it's in Austin, one of the most liberal areas of Texas—UT Austin is said to be a hotbed of liberalism.

Is this reputation accurate?

Most students will agree that UT does offer a fantastic education at an affordable price. And students love it here. When football games are on, you'll see everyone wearing burnt-orange T-shirts that say UT Austin. And if cheering at sports games isn't your thing, you can cheer as part of any of the more than 750 student organizations at UT, ranging from the Texas Spirits to the Out of State Students Association. Lastly, though UT is a pretty liberal place—particularly in relation to the rest of Texas—there are pretty big pockets of conservatism thriving here, so don't expect a liberal paradise.

What would an admissions officer at your school probably not tell a prospective student? What aspect of your school would a prospective student not see on a campus tour?

Well, when you first apply to UT you apply to a "college" that corresponds with the major you'll eventually declare. Once you're on campus, if you decide you want to switch majors to an entirely unrelated subject, well . . . prepare yourself for a fight, because this is difficult to do. I know a couple people that have tried, and failed, to stop being Natural Science majors and switch into the College of Business. It doesn't always work out. Also, admissions won't talk about the fact that some kids have a difficult time adjusting to our giant campus. Really, UT is one of the largest universities in the nation, with more than fifty thousand students—it's easy to get lost and to feel alone if you're not the outgoing type. You can make friends here, but they won't just fall into your lap, you have to get out there and *make* friends.

The Institution

Originally I really didn't want to come to UT because it was a state school and I was convinced that meant it would be subpar. Boy, was I surprised! Now I love the place. I love that no matter where I am, I tell people I go to UT and they're impressed, be it because they know of the school's academics, because they like the school's football team, or because they know one of our alums who's gone on to do big things. I love that our alums are so proud, that our students are so happy, that you can go to a football game and cheer in the stands with *thousands* of other UT kids. The noise is deafening. And, in all these circumstances, you can't help but feel deep love for your alma mater.

It's also worth noting that the cost of living at UT is pretty minimal. If you're a Texas resident, tuition costs next to nothing. Even if you're not, you can easily find housing for three hundred dollars a month, which will save you a large chunk of change. Also, there are buses that UT provides to transport students to and from campus, so you never have to worry about bringing (and paying for) a car at this school.

The Education

Yes, UT Austin is big, and yes, you're going to find yourself in some huge, three-hundred-person introductory classes. But professors here are conscious of this and do everything they can to make their lectures dynamic and interesting. And in every big class, there are multiple TAs that teach small-group review sessions later in the week, so you never feel like you're missing the opportunity to ask questions or have discussions with your peers. Also, once you're a junior or senior you segue into far smaller upper-division classes, with between twenty and fifty other students. At that point all of your professors will know you by name.

Nicely, UT Austin has highly ranked undergraduate *and* graduate schools on campus. This works out well for undergrads, because, if they want to challenge themselves and take an occasional graduate-level class, they can. If an undergrad thinks they want to stay on at UT for grad school, they can get to know graduate faculty and ask them questions about the admissions process. And there are also some specialized programs that you can apply to that allow undergraduates to get both a BA *and* an MA from UT in five years. The Professional Program in Accounting is one of these programs, where you concurrently take lower- and upper-level classes as an undergraduate and leave UT ready to jump right into top positions at accounting firms throughout the country.

Now, two random UT academic facts: before finals every year there are "dead days," which are days when the university is closed and everyone is given time to study and prepare for their final exams. These dead days are great, because they really let you focus (and let you do any reading you missed out on) before taking any potentially GPA-altering exams. Also, at UT, professors only take attendance in 50 percent of classes. This doesn't mean you should make it a habit to skip class. But it does mean you have the liberty of not going to a nonattendance-based class if something important comes up, and you won't have to worry about being penalized.

The Students

Austin, Texas, and UT Austin are both pretty liberal, but neither is perfect. About two years ago, there were a couple of instances where students dressed up in blackface and yelled racial slurs at minorities at campus events. Of course the entire student body condemned these actions, the campus organizations which encouraged students to dress in blackface were penalized, a large handful of students were forced to attend seminars about racial equality, and, generally, UT's faculty and staff went to great lengths to put policies in place to ensure nothing like that would ever happen again. Nonetheless, the fact that it happened in the recent past is worrying and shows that UT isn't perfect.

The Activities

There really is always something to do at UT. There are constant theater productions (both student-run and professional), there are frequent on-campus concerts like the Forty Acres Fest (which is free and has featured performers such as Ludacris, Vertical Horizons, and Bubba Sparx), there are huge concerts in Austin that attract tens of thousands of people, and small musical venues in Austin that only have room for a hundred people. Individual departments at UT bring fantastic lecturers in to speak with students, and UT as a whole has a speaker series that has brought in people like Bill Clinton and Spike Lee. There are parks all over the city to walk through, and, in nice weather, you can go canoeing or kayaking on the river that runs through the center of Austin. If you're ever bored on campus and want to find out which twenty activities are going on that day, just head to West Mall, where organizations always have tables set up and are giving out tickets and flyers and pamphlets. West Mall is also where protests and rallies tend to take place, so as you're planning your night, deciding between far too many attractive options, you'll have the voices of energized and political students ringing in your ears.

The Social Scene

When most UT kids want to party, they'll head over to Sixth Street, which has everything you'd need—lots of bars, clubs, hotspots. On weekends, Sixth Street is always packed and overflowing with students. City officials even close the streets to traffic on Saturdays and Sundays so kids can congregate in the middle of the road and not have to drunkenly dodge traffic at the end of the night. And if the manic energy of Sixth Street is a bit much, students can always head to Fourth Street, which has a similar range of things to do, but everything is a bit classier, more expensive, and upscale. UT's administration has acknowledged what great and popular hangouts Sixth and Fourth Streets are, and they provide shuttles there, and shuttles back to campus, every Thursday through Saturday, between 10:00 p.m. and 3:00 a.m. So you never have to worry. And if, for whatever reason, you did happen to bring your car and you're drunk and it's past 3:00 a.m. and you don't know what to do, UT has a designated driver program where someone will be dropped off at your location and drive you and your car safely home at no cost.

UT also has a really big fraternity/sorority scene. Only 12 percent of UT is Greek, but that still translates into more than five thousand students! Every weekend there are multiple big frat parties that are open to all, and if you like loud music and gyrating bodies in a small space with beer everywhere, you'll love UT frats.

Lastly, be *sure*, 100 percent sure, to live in a dorm your freshman year. This is where most students make friends, and friends are crucial if you're going to get by in this place. I know some people who decided to live in off-campus apartments freshman year, and every single one of them has regretted it. Sure, the UT dorms are small, and you don't have a kitchen so you'll be forced to eat mediocre campus food. This is the case at every college in America, though; just bite your lip and live in a dorm. You'll thank me.

Name: Foster
Hometown: Rowlett, Texas
Class Year: Junior
Major: Theater
Extracurriculars: Theater. It's all-consuming.
Career Goal: I want to become a professional performer.

How would you describe UT Austin's reputation?

It is said to be a diverse school filled with students of every religion, race, sexuality, and political orientation.

Is this reputation accurate?

Absolutely. Have you ever seen a straight-laced conservative sit down comfortably next to a black lesbian with a mohawk and then launch into an interesting and open debate about the pros and cons of America's two-party political system? Well, if you come to UT, you'll see that sort of thing. All the time. We're such a big school, *every* type of person under the sun is here. And everyone interacts with one another. It's great.

> "UT Austin was recently named one of the top fifteen universities in the world by the *London Times*, our undergraduate program is incredibly strong. UT's law and business schools are among the best in the nation."
> ✦ James, senior

What would an admissions officer at your school probably not tell a prospective student? What aspect of your school would a prospective student not see on a campus tour?

The administration won't tell you that you'll never be able to find a parking space at the university, or in the whole city of Austin. Ever.

The Institution

Whenever I think of my time at UT, I can't help but feel I've experienced something remarkably similar to the college life you see in the movies. UT is the place where everyone is always wearing their school colors and heading off to football and basketball games to cheer their hearts out. UT is the place that every type of student comes to, and every type of student gets along. It's the place where you can't walk through the center of campus without being bombarded with fliers for a geopolitical rally, a string quartet concerto, and an all-night tailgating kegger. It certainly doesn't hurt that all of these things happen under the gorgeous Texas sky, where it's almost always sunny and comfortably warm outside.

And then there's Austin, which is this vibrant and fantastic young city. UT and the city of Austin are, in a sense, the same thing. By that I mean to say, fifty thousand UT students look for fun in Austin every weekend, and Austin colors UT students' feelings toward their college years to a remarkable extent. And, because every year new young faces flood into Austin thanks to UT, Austin has remained a young and dynamic city—really, we're the ones keeping the all-night diners, the theaters, the concert halls, the exotic clubs, the themed bars, the everything—we keep everything in Austin in business.

The Education

I'd say the most difficult dilemma any UT student will face is whether or not to go to their classes. Because there's so many other things to do! Between the city of Austin and the constant sensory overload of student life, when given the choice between going to a big lecture class called Age of Dinosaurs, or going to a screening of the new Quentin Tarantino film and meeting Quentin Tarantino afterwards, well, it's tempting to skip the lecture. You have to fight that temptation, though, because it's very easy to do well here if you go to class, and very hard to do well if you don't. And if you go to class and find that it *isn't* easy to do well, the university offers free tutoring, and a free writing center that will help you get your papers up to snuff. Go to both! They're fantastic resources.

The Students

I'd say UT is predominately white, but every third person is black, Asian, or Indian. That's pretty impressive—at most schools it's every sixth or seventh person. And every year, UT is becoming more culturally and ethnically diverse. UT is also becoming more politically diverse; if you took a poll of UT students you'd find very large numbers of Democrats, Republicans, Independents, and Greens. Interesting political debates go on all the time, since so many sides are represented. There are also a lot of political activists on campus, and you'll see protests and rallies at least once every two weeks.

The Activities

There are quite a few other schools right near UT. Both Austin Community College and Southwestern University are within a half hour's drive. Baylor University is right over in Waco, and Trinity University is in nearby San Antonio. I'd say that there is some interaction that goes on between these universities, but, for the most part, students have their hands full right at UT. If you're in the mood to see new faces, you don't have to travel, you can just step outside your dorm room.

As for what students do on campus—well, a lot of students head to nearby playhouses. There are hundreds of theaters in the city of Austin, meaning there's plenty of plays to watch, or—if you're an actor, dancer, musician, or writer—plenty of performances to get involved in. On campus there's Bass Concert Hall, which gets big-time national touring shows, and any student can get discounted tickets. Nearby there's also the popular "No Shame" open mic night, where anyone can get up on stage and say whatever they'd like for five minutes. Sporting events are extremely important to student life (particularly sporting events having to do with the UT football team). If you wake up on the day of a UT football game and decide you have errands to run, well, you might as well just go back to sleep and wait twenty-four hours, because you're never going to make it to the store through the huge hordes of drunken students prepping for the game, or celebrating after the game, or skipping the game just to block sidewalks and scream about UT. Every street for miles and miles is going to be congested with cars and standstill traffic. We live for football here, and everything else falls to the wayside on big game days.

The Social Scene

UT students party in many different ways. Some drink (and some drink in excess), but plenty abstain. Some go to massive all-night keggers. Others prefer hanging out in small, intimate groups, playing board games and watching *Willy Wonka and the Chocolate Factory*. Sororities and fraternities are popular, but if that's not your scene, there's no pressure at all to be involved with them. If you like going off-campus, you can head to Sixth Street, which is littered with things to do, or Fourth Street, which is littered with the same things to do but with a more adult vibe.

There are so many students at UT that you'll graduate not knowing the vast majority of your classmates. Most likely, you'll become friends with those students who are in the same school of study as you, which makes sense. A lot of people also make friends from their dorms. Personally, I lived in a dorm (Jester) for one week and found dorm living to be terrible, so I moved off-campus shortly thereafter. But if dorms are your thing, friends will only be a cinderblock wall away.

Name: Lindsay
Hometown: Eastland, Texas
Class Year: Junior
Major: Journalism
Extracurriculars: KVRX Radio DJ, *Texas Travesty*
Career Goal: Work for a music magazine or a record label

How would you describe UT Austin's reputation?

It's said to be a *huge* school filled to the brim with crazy atheist liberal students, all with purple Mohawks and joints hanging half-smoked from their mouths. It's said our teachers are indifferent, our classes are huge, and every student is just a number.

Is this reputation accurate?

Not at all! There are fifty thousand kids here. You can't classify them as one thing or another! We have a lot of atheists and a lot of Christians and a lot of liberals and a lot of Republicans and a lot of pot smokers and a lot of kids who are stone-cold sober. Same thing on the teacher front—we have teachers who are indifferent and teach big courses and never learn the names of any of their students. We also have professors who are warm while teaching big courses, who reach out to individual students, who are some of the most experienced and dynamic people at UT, and who lead extraordinary classes of all sizes.

What would an admissions officer at your school probably not tell a prospective student? What aspect of your school would a prospective student not see on a campus tour?

An admissions officer won't tell a prospective student that it can be really hard to meet people here and that every student is responsible for getting things taken care of and finding their own niche.

The Institution

I'm from a small town, so coming to giant UT Austin really took some getting used to. To be blunt, those first couple weeks sucked, and some people get so depressed they immediately drop out or transfer. I held back from taking steps that drastic and actually found that, once I got through the initial shock, I was able to be proactive and make friends, and then I started to enjoy myself. Once you make even one friend it becomes easier to go up to groups of people and things snowball (in a good way) from there.

All that said, UT *is* a really beautiful place to go to school. It's really green, with all these patches of grass we call "malls" where students lie down and play Frisbee. Most UT building are Spanish-style with reddish-orange rooftops. There are statues all around the school of famous graduates, and there's this big old clock tower right in the middle of campus that glows orange whenever UT sports teams win a big game. Also, at 12:50 every day the tower's chimes play songs.

The Texas weather is pretty nice, but it can turn on a dime. The meal plan is terrible. Also, freshman orientation here is a sad, unhelpful charade. Many a lost freshmen sits alone at meals during orientation, wondering if they made the right decision to come to UT. It took at least a month at UT for me to feel like I'd made the right choice. So get out there.

> "Jester is the world's largest university dorm. Which means it has the world's grossest dorm bathrooms."
> ✦ Anna, sophomore

The Education

UT doesn't really have a "core" curriculum. Instead, when you first get to UT you're put into a college that corresponds with your academic major. Every college then has its own curriculum, which I'd imagine is a modified version of some pure "core" that UT students never get to see. Having spoken to a lot of my friends from different UT colleges, it seems the average all-round core is two

required classes in English, two required classes in math, two required classes in history, and two required classes in government.

The Students

An unfortunate consequence of having so many people is that many students actively search out others like them, become part of a clique, and then stay within that clique for the majority of their time at UT. Because every clique has it's own identity, and identity is formulated on what a clique *isn't* as much as on what a clique *is*, every clique quietly wages war on its opposite. So the hipster kids will mock the sorority girls and frat boys painting themselves for a pep rally. And the sorority girls and frat boys will shout "Go UT" right in the hipsters' faces to prove their unabashed school pride. Which only makes them a bigger and easier target for the hipsters. This happens with a lot of cliques at UT, this weirdly antagonistic and symbiotic relationship.

In the above scenario, at least, I definitely take the side of the hipsters. Frat boys and sorority girls at UT are as annoying as hell. The Greeks on campus try their hardest to separate themselves from the rest of the student body, because they think they're better than everyone (those who go Greek also tend to be the richest students on campus) and the rest of the student body lets them separate themselves, because they're so pathetic. It's too bad, because right in the middle of all the frat and sorority houses on campus there are these co-ops full of hippie kids who just want to do their own thing and spend a lot of time making homemade hummus. But they're interrupted all the time by the sounds of frat boys screaming and puking up their alcohol at 3:00 a.m.

There's also a fairly big LGBT community at UT, but LGBT kids stick to themselves and are pretty cliquey. There are a lot of gay bars and clubs in Austin, and they'll head there on most weekends to party and hook up with one another.

The Activities

Some students are insane about sports here, but I don't really care about athletics, so I'll move on. There are countless music groups to go hear in Austin. Every year Austin puts on the Austin City Limits Festival, which is amazing; more than a hundred thousand people show up. There are lots of hiking trails and a big river right in Austin too. People go down to the river and go tubing with their cases of beer, then come back drunk and sun-burned. When Austin is warm it's a fantastic place to be. Everyone is so relaxed and chill.

UT's student publications are pretty amazing, and most are also award-winning. I'm a member of the *Texas Travesty,* the official humor publication on campus. Everyone involved in the *Travesty* is good friends, but we're very professional and work hard when it's time for a new issue to come out. We want to make the best possible publication, and we recognize that having a student publication at UT on your résumé is a huge deal. Honestly, former *Daily Texan* writers can be found at nearly every major newspaper in America. The editor of the *Daily Texan* has the pick of jobs at graduation.

The Social Scene

There's always plenty to do here: West Campus holds crazy parties, the co-ops always have bands playing, and joints are liberally passed around. Sixth Street is full of drunk kids stumbling in the direction of some club or other, Miguel's la Bodega is a fun nearby bar that everyone heads to for salsa dancing, Emo's is an all-ages place with a different live band every night (including *lots* of bands that heavily scrape the bottom of the talent barrel). The nearby Alamo Drafthouse is always doing bizarre things like hosting Mary Kate and Ashley Olsen nights, where they show clips from every one of Mary Kate and Ashley Olsen's movies. Austin's gay scene is also adequate if not great, and most head to Sidekicks, the Boys Attic, and Oil Can Harry's.

Notable UT Austin Alumni Include:
Earl Campbell, NFL football player
Renée Zellweger, actress
Sandra Bullock, actress
Ricky Williams, NFL football player
Roger Clemens, Major League baseball player
Matthew McConaughey, actor

TRINITY COLLEGE

Founded: 1823
Location: Hartford, CT
Phone: (860) 297-2000
E-mail: admissions.office@trincoll.edu
Web site: www.trincoll.edu

Number of Undergraduates: 2,150
Number of Graduate Students: 180
Cost: Approximately $40,000 per year
Application Deadline: January 15
Early Decision: November 15

Rating:	Notable Majors/Programs:
Very Selective	Social Sciences, Engineering, Life Sciences

Size:
● Small ○ Medium ○ Large

Location:
● Urban ○ Suburban ○ Rural

On a Saturday, students talk about academics:
○ Always ● Sometimes ○ Never

Nightlife:
● Intense ○ Moderate ○ Laid-back

Politically, Trinity leans:
○ Left ○ Right ● Split

Diversity:
○ High ● Low ○ Medium

Students describe Trinity in five words:
- Preppy, athletic, friendly, beautiful, joyful
- Elite, moderately liberal, suburban, hard-working

From the School

At Trinity, students have the chance to fully share in our faculty's knowledge, passion for teaching and love of learning—an approach that affords them invaluable opportunities to learn through example. It's no wonder, then, that Trinity College graduates are better equipped to reflect on their life experiences, challenge assumptions, welcome fresh points of view, think critically, make well-reasoned choices and proceed confidently.

—www.trincoll.edu

If you're interested in Trinity, you may also be interested in:
Boston College, Boston University, Connecticut College, Hamilton, Holy Cross, Tufts

Name: Anna
Hometown: Baltimore, Maryland
Class Year: Junior
Major: English literature
Extracurriculars: Varsity softball team; Admissions Day host
Career Goal: My career goal is to become the English teacher whom you still remember when you are forty.

How would you describe Trinity's reputation?

Many people think it's a party school for preps.

Is this reputation accurate?

I don't think I would still be at this school if that were true. I have met some of the most intelligent, open-minded, and multifaceted people here that I could ever hope to meet.

What would an admissions officer at Trinity probably not tell a prospective student? What aspect of your school would a prospective student not see on a campus tour?

I don't think that an admissions officer would play up our school's diversity because, well, there really isn't much to play up. It is getting better—I have seen a greater diversity of student body with every incoming class since my first year, and I can only hope that trend will continue. Additionally, the surrounding city is a deterrent to prospective students. Downtown Hartford might be a bit of a shock for some. But Trinity does not hide the fact that it's a city school; it embraces that fact. You cannot get to Trinity without being aware of the fact that you are immersed in a distinctly urban experience.

The Institution

I chose Trinity on a whim. I didn't know what I wanted to be, nor did I have the faintest idea of where I wanted to go. I did know, however, that I wanted to play college softball. I sent my recruiting tape to a bunch of schools, and a handful called me back about it. I was particularly interested in Trinity because it was very close to where my sister went to school, Yale. So when the coach of the team called to ask me on a recruiting trip, I accepted. I am shy. The girls on the Trinity College varsity softball team were *not*. Each one of them made an effort to learn my name the first time they shook my hand. They looked directly into my eyes when they spoke. A few offered to introduce

me to their favorite professor. I liked the girls, but perhaps more importantly, I liked the passion they had for their school. They could never say enough good things about Trinity, but they didn't hide anything either. They were all very proud to be Trinity students. Now I am, too.

I recognize that no one school is for everyone. But Trinity fit me perfectly because I wanted a school where I could successfully be a student athlete, have a close relationship with my professors, have crazy weekends, and most importantly, feel that I was a part of a community. It's also a place that is interested in my future after graduation, a place where you can make up your own major, a place where you can go into the city and see good theater or go to a good restaurant.

The Education

Having gone to a private high school, I was used to having small classes and frequent attention from my teachers. I was prepared to have professors not notice me in class. I was prepared for them to never learn my name. It didn't turn out that way. I have never been in a class at Trinity in which the professor hasn't learned my name or had time to meet with me outside of class. But what I *really* appreciate is the fact that I have actually taken a class in which we listened to rap music and used it as an educational tool. That's my favorite part about Trinity. I took a class entitled American Popular Music which not only includes a trip to Graceland, but also listening to 2 Live Crew's early nineties hit, "Me So Horny."

Trinity wants well-rounded students, and in the spirit of this, there are five very basic core curriculum requirements. The college requires that you take a class in the humanities, like a history or English class. Also required is a class in the natural sciences, like biology, or for the less science-y types, Science in Art. Also, a class in numerical sciences like math or computer science. And, of course, a class in fine arts, like my music class. And finally, a class in the social sciences like psychology or sociology.

The Students

I suppose most of my life I have thought of myself as weird. This isn't necessarily the ideal forum in which to divulge one's innermost secrets, but in the name of edification, I'll do it: I am an English Literature major, a film studies minor, and am considering a second minor in music. I am a varsity athlete. I am a good student. I am a bit of a party girl on occasion. I am a moderate Democrat, and I am openly bisexual. That might come a surprise to anyone who thought of the Trinity population as a bunch of rich, preppy, white kids. I'll tell you what else: I have never felt out of place at Trinity. I have never encountered any form sort of discrimination or hatred. Then again, I am what you might call a femme—that is, without knowing me personally, you wouldn't imagine I was anything other than heterosexual. The point of all this is that Trinity looks a little bit homogeneous on the surface, and it may take a little digging to discover that the campus is actually full of very complex, interesting people. I can't say enough about the amount of intelligence, talent, and motivation to succeed on this campus.

You don't *have* to belong to a fraternity of sorority to belong. You don't *have* to be on a team or in a club. Most people do some sort of activity associated with campus, but you don't have to in order to get to know people. Because the classes are so small, it is easy to meet people.

All right, now that I have said all that good stuff, I wouldn't be entirely honest if I didn't tell you that there are potential drawbacks to this utopia of student love. There is a reason that Trinity is sometimes labeled a rich, white kid's school. That reason is that there are a lot of rich, white kids here.

> "In retrospect, I might've liked an 'artsier,' more liberal school better. I mean, this is a rich white school, drawing most of its students from Boston and Philadelphia suburbs—pretty standard stuff. Never in my life have I seen more blonds, more flipped-up polos, Tod's loafers, Lily Pulitzer, and CK Bradley gear than at Trinity. There are definitely diamonds in the rough, but you've gotta be a miner."
>
> ✦ Sophie, sophomore

The Activities

Because Hartford is, in many ways, a city rebounding from disenfranchisement, Trinity places emphasis on student involvement in community service and civic involvement. Trinity is the only school in the country with a Boys and Girls Club on the campus, for example. There is a yearly event known simply as "Do It Day" which makes it easy for students to sign up for a day of community service with their friends. There are numerous opportunities for students interested in education to tutor at neighboring public school which, having done it myself, is an invaluable experience.

The students on campus are vocal: if there is an opinion on campus, you are bound to know about it. It seems there are forums on nearly everything. They sometimes lead to many positive changes.

I think most people on campus enjoy exercise—if they are not on a varsity team, they at least make use of the gym or participate in the intramurals (a favorite on campus is softball). I am a college varsity athlete as well as being a full-time student. Division III athletics are designed so that they do not rule your life. This is not to say that they do not take up a good deal of your life, don't get me wrong! I recently filled out a survey that asked how many hours you spend a week preparing for sports and how many hours a week you spend preparing for classes, and I found myself answering that the two numbers were about the same.

The Social Scene

Partying at Trinity. We do it well, that is true. We do it often, this is also true. We have to do it? Untrue. Unlike larger schools at which fraternities and sororities are a mainstay of the campus, a must for students who want to get to know people on campus, Trinity's social scene does not revolve around frats and sororities. Instead, groups of friends develop in strange ways, from your first year dorm floor, to your athletic team, to your first English class. Instead of ruling the social scene, frats and sororities provide a forum for late night life, if the late night life should choose to travel there. There is a building on our campus (formerly "the Party Barn") now known officially as the Vernon Social Center, which is used for visiting comedy acts, parties hosted by the college, and the mandatory incoming first year math test [insert diabolical laugh]. If there is one universal experience at Trinity, it is the moment a first year steps into the Party Barn, very drunk, and utters the words, "I took a math test in here this morning!" The renaming of the Party Barn is inexplicable, if not rather amusing. The administration of Trinity College decided that it would be appropriate to rename our beloved Party Barn, Club V. Why? It remains a mystery to this day, but the point of the story is that there are social traditions at Trinity, the first of which being: one never calls the Party Barn anything else. Second: old habits die hard, and Trinity still parties hard.

Dating? Don't expect to do it your first year. There is a little phenomenon, don't know if you've heard of it, called hooking up. It is often followed by another of my personal favorite college phenomena, the walk of shame.

Name: Tyson
Hometown: Boston, Massachusetts
Class Year: Senior
Major: Classics
Extracurriculars: Coordinator at on-campus movie theater, co-vice president of Trinity College chapter of the International Lions Club, Sexual Assault Response Team, *Other Voice* magazine, Tripod Online
Career Goal: Unsure, going to graduate school for masters in teaching.

How would you describe Trinity's reputation?

Conflicted. Trinity has a reputation among academic circles as being a fine institution of undergraduate learning, among the majority of students "in the know" as a preppy party school (though widespread belief is that this has now been toned down somewhat), and among a vocal student minority as deplorably lacking in its race/town-gown relations. It is certainly an interesting place at times, to say the least.

Is this reputation accurate?

It's hard to say for certain just what in this multifaceted reputation is accurate. In my experience, Trinity will not fail to meet the expectations of any student wishing and actively seeking to be academically challenged in the classroom. This may not occur in all the lower level courses, but no serious student will be disappointed by the depth of study available in any given field he/she pursues. The guest-lecture series are top-notch and very diverse. The arts do flourish here. Sadly, many students do not seem to care to take advantage of many of these things, and often express a typically high school attitude toward shirking work and a general noninvolvement or unwillingness to put effort toward helping create and enjoy the extracurricular offerings.

What aspect of Trinity would a prospective student not see on a campus tour?

Some of the racial tensions (real or imaginary) might be glossed over.

The Institution

To be honest, I chose Trinity because it was the best school that accepted me, not for its social opportunities. On the bathroom walls, you get the usual slew of antihomosexual and derogatory slurs about girls and professors scrawled about here and there. Students and townies have very little interaction. And how can they, when a large portion of the locals only speak Spanish? Almost no one here, not of an ethnic minority background, knows or speaks regularly with anyone who does not work on campus.

Housing is pretty decent. Freshmen, of course, get the short end of the stick, but the bonding experience is great. There is no problem getting a single room or a quad after that, and with theme housing and cooking units, there is plenty of room to shop around. I think the career services office is almost completely useless to anyone not interested in law or finance. There are plenty of resources, but almost no guidance whatsoever about using it. Professors and other administrators have unofficially taken on the role of career/grad school advising in many instances. The new president of the school is planning to look into it, however.

> "It's been difficult to be a first year student here—Trinity is elitist in many ways and there is a very distinct class and social structure here that can greatly determine your college experience if you can't learn to adjust."
>
> ✦ Elizabeth, junior

The Education

I wish the school held students to higher standards. More required courses, required extracurricular involvement, and stricter punishments for violation of college policy would attract a better crowd. Call me old-fashioned, but college ought to maintain some modicum of tutelage over students, to give them guidance and build them into better and more self-sufficient and introspective human beings. I know there's a big push for "allowing students to express themselves," "sharing ideas from different backgrounds," and "independence," but it ought to really be better balanced on a strong, well-rounded, and structured college learning, in and out of the classroom. Professors are active in campus life in varying degrees. Some are very politically active on campus, others religiously. All of them in my experience have been ready and willing to help individual students whenever asked.

The Students

Hmm, like I said: I think sometimes Trinity students are prone to treating this as a post–high school playground. And it's true that students are quite preppy, and they like the ways that this could be called a party school. But there are many smart people, many serious people. Come visit, meet them, and judge for yourself.

The Activities

There is a lot of possibility for involvement in different activities on campus, it is sadly a very small percentage of people who sample things outside the narrow three flavors of extracurriculars: fraternities, sports, and private parties. An upshot is that students who do venture out into the less-popular venues often find themselves quickly being offered leadership positions in these other activities, but this should be noted as a sign of lack of interest more than an open-mindedness about new people.

Trinity holds some really great parties, if you are into that sort of thing. Personally, I am not. Most serious students who find their leisurely enjoyment in interesting reading, attending performances, and other activities that do not involve alcohol and blaring music, are generally disappointed outside of the classroom—as has been my experience. There are some good arts here, and downtown Hartford does offer a few attractions, but c'mon, it's the insurance capital of the world. Would you really expect such a place to be hoppin'?

The Social Scene

People here party everywhere/time/way they possibly can. Almost everyone consumes alcohol to some extent. Parties occur Thursday through Saturday night at frat row, sometimes even more often. Themed parties sponsored by the college occur regularly but are sparsely attended, save for a

few exceptions. Many just have private gatherings in their quads. It's pretty easy to meet new people at these smaller parties, and it is very possible to have a complete party life without ever joining a fraternity. The hook ups are rampant and traditional dating is all but dead, despite a few attempts at revival.

Only a few percent of students live off campus, and even then, they're often within one to two blocks. Dorm life is fun and crazy for freshmen, with various dorm activities and an all-freshman cast grouped by first-year seminar, but the upperclassmen dorms are more like apartment complexes, everyone at various stages of the game doing their own thing.

Name: Wilson
Hometown: Mill Valley, California
Class Year: Senior
Majors: Economics and political science
Extracurriculars: Division III wrestling team, InterVarsity Christian Fellowship, PRIDE mentor, Asian American Student Association, Do-It-Day, Hartford Parks and Bikes Pre-Orientation, Halloween on Vernon Street, Fun Fair, staff and faculty technical assistant, student admissions associate
Career Goal: Earn a Ph.D. in economics with at least a minor in econometrics. Apply it to either the marketing research or international development arena.

How would you describe Trinity's reputation?

The difference between a freshman and a senior is the difference between embracing or rejecting the school's outdated stereotype, respectively. This applies to the stereotypes about both the school's party image and the students' interactions with the city. For example, I would say that freshmen jump into the fraternity party scene wholeheartedly. By senior year, one's tastes become a little more refined and local bars, nightclubs, and a little more restraint seem to typify the Trinity experience. Overall, I think that senior year affords students the retrospect to both realize that the intense fraternity scene is not the be-all, end-all, of Trinity life (as is the stereotype), and embrace increasingly the city of Hartford for its varied offerings.

Is this reputation accurate?

Please see above.

What would an admissions officer at Trinity probably not tell a prospective student?

The tough questions for us in the admissions office are about safety on campus and the party scene—there have been some terrible incidents on Trinity's campus. There is no doubt that there've been some assaults, some muggings, and some cause for concern. But as someone who walks back from the library one to three nights a week at 4 a.m. from the library's twenty-four-hour zone, I can tell you that the administration has been proactive (albeit somewhat slower than hoped) to address issues of safety. In four years I've seen: Alpha Chi Rho offer a walking escort back from any location on campus, campus safety offer walking escorts and driving escorts back from any location on campus, an improved on-campus shuttle system, a consistent off-campus shuttle system, and a lighting scheme on Vernon Street that has been dubbed "the landing strip."

In regard to the party scene, let me be forthright first and add stipulations later. The on-campus party scene mostly revolves around alcohol. The weekend fillers, whether sponsored by the school, an extracurricular organization, or by the frats, have alcohol available for those who are of drinking age. But once the alcohol leaves the bar, it's anyone's guess to whom it goes. For students committed to staying completely dry, this may make the Trinity experience uneasy, and I have certainly met my share of students who just found it overwhelming. But Trinity is now far removed from what was the heyday of *Playboy*'s top party school list.

The Institution

I was pretty tenacious about my college search. I used three guidebooks and weeded out anything that wasn't on the top fifty liberal arts colleges or top fifty national universities (according to *U.S. News & World Report*)—searching for an academically prestigious, yet small school with wrestling. So I did my research.

Four years later, it will not be my struggles with the social atmosphere or the frats that I'll remember most, but all the opportunities that Trinity afforded me. Some of the most memorable include: the opportunity to work amazingly close with my applied econometrics professor (my favorite course at Trinity), meeting up with a professor I had two years ago for ice cream in West Hartford, having intellectual conversation with a professor at the political science senior majors dinner, and many other accomplishments I've been afforded in my time here.

The internship office is outstanding. As the preeminent academic institution in our area, the office has previously established relationships with many firms. It's practically an expectation that one or two economics majors work at Smith Barney each semester. Another great example is that one economics professor's senior seminar worked with the Connecticut Policy and Economic Council to do a cost-benefit analysis of various city services. The chances to work in the city are just astounding. In a slow economy, many of my friends have found sanctuary by competing for jobs *in* Hartford.

The Education

First-year mentors are assigned to every first-year seminar to aid in coursework both related to and unrelated to the seminar. They are trained in the academic computing necessary for first-year students, advising students on course loads, and so on. Although I've met academic mentors who did not give their mentees guidance on the preregistration process, I've also met those who are still in touch with their mentees four years later (myself included).

There are some departments at Trinity with exceptional notoriety and academic pull. The Human Rights department (as the only Human Rights minor in the country and with the first Human Rights major graduating this year), is very well connected internationally and the Economics Department also has an amazing degree of academic prestige. Albeit, not all our professors herald from the University of Chicago, but speakers include Steven Moore, of the CATO Institute, and Geoffrey Hodgson, labeled as one of the most influential economists of the century, have come. It speaks volumes that such prestigious individuals would stop by a small college of 2,200 in this little city.

The Students

Yes, they're homogenous. But Trinity students are a very driven, motivated group. There's no bunch of kids I'd rather be in school with.

The Activities

It is often said that Trinity students are apathetic. Trinity is a far cry from our liberal NESCAC competitors that are purported to be inundated with politically active students. Conversely, one would be hard-pressed to argue that those students who participate in Do-It-Day (some three hundred plus students this past year), volunteer at one of the three local hospitals (within walking distance), do scientific research on campus over the summers, volunteer at the Boys and Girls Club, or live in the community service dormitory on campus are apathetic students. One would be better off arguing that Trinity instead does not effectively foster and encourage this participation through adequate public recognition.

The Social Scene

Trinity works hard on a Sunday through Thursday week, but makes good use of the weekend (whether it is or isn't really intended to be three days long). I would never purport to overstate the value of a work-hard, party-hard environment, but it seems to be the consensus that it produces students who are also very sociable. One need look no further than alumni networking events to know that, historically, our students tend to be go-getters.

Notable Trinity Alumni Include:
Edward Albee, playwright
George F. Will, columnist and Pulitzer Prize–winning author
Linda A. Wells, editor-in-chief, *Allure* magazine
Thomas M. Chappell, founder of Tom's of Maine
Tucker Carlson, host, CNN's *Crossfire*
William C. Richardson, president and CEO, W. K. Kellogg Foundation

TUFTS UNIVERSITY

Founded: 1852

Location: Medford, MA

Phone: (617) 628-5000

E-mail: admissions.inquiry@ase.tufts.edu

Web site: www.tufts.edu

Number of Undergraduates: 4,870

Number of Graduate Students: 1,280

Cost: Approximately $40,000 per year

Application Deadline: January 1

Early Decision: November 15

Rating:	Notable Majors/Programs:
Most Selective	Engineering, International Relations

Size:

○ Small ● Medium ○ Large

Location:

○ Urban ● Suburban ○ Rural

On a Saturday, students talk about academics:

○ Always ● Sometimes ○ Never

Nightlife:

○ Intense ● Moderate ○ Laid-back

Politically, Tufts leans:

○ Left ○ Right ● Split

Diversity:

● High ○ Low ○ Medium

Students describe Tufts in five words:

- Challenging, passionate, brown and blue!
- Elite, conservative, liberal, cosmopolitan, academic

From the School

Tufts' rigorous academic programs are designed to teach students to make decisions, think independently, solve problems, take intellectual risks, challenge conventional wisdom, communicate effectively and explore the latest knowledge and research in all fields. The academic environment at Tufts extends beyond the classroom as well, through study abroad opportunities, continuing education and summer learning programs, conferences, lectures and workshops, and much more.

—www.tufts.edu

If you're interested in Tufts, you may also be interested in:

Brown, Cornell, Johns Hopkins, Vassar, Washington U. in St. Louis, Wesleyan

Name: Abigail
Hometown: Boston, Massachusetts
Class Year: Senior
Extracurriculars: Political Science and Women's Studies, Tufts Community Union Judiciary, Women's Union at Tufts, Tufts Feminist Alliance, Tufts Dance Collective
Career Goal: Lawyer

How would you describe Tufts' reputation?

Tufts somehow got the reputation of being a backup school for all the kids who didn't get into an Ivy.

Is this reputation accurate?

This isn't exactly true. There *are* kids here who came because they were rejected from Harvard—but you'll find them anywhere. I applied to Tufts early decision, and so did a lot of my friends. There's nowhere else we'd rather be.

What would an admissions officer at Tufts probably not tell a prospective student?

An admissions officer at Tufts wouldn't talk about the political tensions on campus. The liberal versus conservative debates are constant and often really intense.

The Institution

Tufts' size is perfect. With about 4,500 undergrads, it sounds really big—but because all classes are centralized on the hill, the entire student body seems to know each other. It is impossible to meet a fellow Jumbo and to *not* have a friend in common! Tufts isn't a gated community. Also, because housing isn't guaranteed after sophomore year, the majority of juniors and seniors live off-campus. The result is a lot of interaction with townies and local residents, and it isn't good. Tufts doesn't have a good relationship with Somerville and Medford; local residents tend to resent Tufts students and the university as a whole. Major Tufts traditions that all students embrace include painting the cannon and the Naked Quad Run—a mass mile-long run on the first night of Reading Period, just before final exams in December. It's cold! The food at Tufts is *good!* We have two main dining halls, one uphill and one downhill, and students are really loyal to their favorite—it's kind of an identity.

The Education

The core curriculum here is intense. It requires two credits each in arts, humanities, social sciences, natural sciences, and mathematical sciences, as well as six semesters of a foreign language and a world civilization class. Tufts undergrads are fortunate to share the Medford campus with grad students in many departments as well as those from the Fletcher School of Law and Diplomacy. Grad students are often involved with undergrad student organizations, as TAs or fellow students in classes. They are a fantastic resource for anyone who wants to learn more about pursuing something in their major after Tufts. Students at Tufts aren't scarily competitive; however, your peers *will* hold you up to certain academic standards. The people here are really smart, and expect a lot from each other.

The Students

Tufts is incredibly diverse—and although the university prides itself on having a high percentage of international students, there's even more ideological diversity, which is great. People here are very passionate about their political/religious beliefs, and there are constant forums sponsored by student groups to debate current global issues. The majority of the campus is very liberal, although the conservative population has grown considerably more active since my freshman year. Despite the constant rallies

---

Top Ten Complaints Heard at Tufts:

10. The townies suck.
9. I lost my Nalgene.
8. I lost my North Face.
7. Why don't they have sushi with low-cal, air-puffed whole wheat brown rice?
6. The *Primary Source* (conservative newspaper) is really mean, and it's not even that funny anymore.
5. I'm oppressed by the white man. We should have more queer/Asian/Latino/Polka-dot/Midget studies courses.
4. Ugh, I don't want to walk to the T.
3. Why do people think we'd actually want to go to Harvard?
2. President Bacow doesn't want us to have any fun because he saw a kid die at MIT.
1. I almost got run over for the thousandth time.

✦ David, freshman

---

and campaigns, people are generally pretty open-minded; most people are much more eager to know what you think about an issue than to get mad because you don't agree with them. I have definitely learned more about the world and different perspectives from other students, more so than in class.

The Activities

Tufts is only a T ride away from BU, MIT, Harvard, Boston College, Northeastern, Brandeis. As a result, there are many events/conferences/activities that unite students at different campuses, as well as a plethora of resources, libraries, and classes to choose from. Davis Square and Harvard Square are the most popular hangout spots.

Community service is very popular here. The Leonard Carmichael Society (LCS) is the largest student organization at Tufts, and is made up of at least forty subgroups, all with different service-oriented focuses, from teaching economics in local elementary schools to cleaning up the Mystic River to peer-leading young girls around Somerville. Tufts also sponsors "Kids Day" every April, when hundreds of local kids come to campus for the day to be entertained by Tufts students. Everyone gets involved.

The Social Scene

People party at Tufts. "Frat Row" is the popular destination most Thursday, Friday, and Saturday nights, especially for freshmen and sophomores. The I-House (International House) throws really hot parties, and the alterna-crowd parties at the Crafts House and Arts Haus. But everybody parties. And people really socialize with one another, they don't just stick to their one social group—I met my best friend during a Saturday night out, when we just happened to be partying in the same dorm room. Of course, we had mutual friends: the Tufts rule is that there is never more than two degrees of separation between any two students (even if one is an engineer). You really get to know everyone.

Name: David
Hometown: Plainview, New York
Class Year: Junior
Major: Political science and community health
Extracurriculars: Tufts Democrats, Tufts Transgendered Lesbian Gay Bisexual Collective, *Tufts Daily* (newspaper), Tufts Amalgamates (a cappella), Tufts Hillel, Student Health Advisory Board, Tufts Dance Collective
Career Goal: Health policy and law

How would you describe Tufts' reputation?

Tufts has a reputation as being just-under-Ivy and also has an academic reputation of very strong for international relations and premed.

Is this reputation accurate?

Partially. A lot of us, myself included, turned down Ivies. Some of us didn't even apply to any because we just had no desire to go there. The academics are just as rigorous as some of the Ivies, if not more. Yes, there are some Ivy rejects here, but there are Tufts rejects at Ivies, too. Our International Relations (IR) program is indeed very strong, and it's also the largest undergraduate major. However, as an undergraduate program, it is multidisciplinary and draws on faculty from political science, history, economics, anthropology, and the languages. While there are great courses offered in these departments in non-IR fields, there aren't that many courses on the American experience in those departments. For U.S.-based classes, you have to look at child development, some political science, urban and environmental policy, community health, American studies, and sociology. Our premed program is all right, but nothing unusual for our peer group. There are a lot of research opportunities at the Medical Campus, though, which is in downtown Boston.

What would an admissions officer at Tufts probably not tell a prospective student? What aspect of your school would a prospective student not see on a campus tour?

They probably would not tell a prospective student that town-gown relations are fairly poor and that the administration is very focused on raising money and prestige and not on improving the internal situation. On a tour, you wouldn't see some of the poorer dorms and academic facilities that exist in some places, or even the average Tufts student. I think admissions offices in general hide average students and highlight some that they think are spectacular. The average Tufts student is usually white, middle-class, suburban, fairly intelligent, and involved passionately in at least one nonacademic pursuit, although he or she may not make headlines for that passion.

The Institution

Tufts is a mutt of a school, half liberal arts and half large university. I chose Tufts based on its size, location, and the general atmosphere. I actually had no idea how close Tufts was to Boston, so much closer than many of the other suburban schools. I felt Tufts was a place where I could do lots of things—academic and otherwise—and feel no pressure to choose one. Also, Tufts is a place where there isn't any huge academic competitiveness, even though the work is hard. People seem happy here, and nice!

It seems like everyone has some kind of internship in the Boston area before they graduate; the Tufts name carries big clout here. It's easy to get downtown, but underclassmen tend not to because there's so much to do right here.

The campus is small even though on first glance it seems huge. There are two main residential areas: uphill and downhill. Each hill has it's own dining hall and the food isn't contracted out so it's really good. The English and humanities buildings are uphill and the math and science buildings are downhill. Housing is a big issue, in terms of the conditions and availability, and the administration hasn't really made any big progress in a while.

We have a lot of big performers and speakers come to campus, particularly for a small school. In my three years so far we've had former presidents Bush and Clinton, Vice President Gore, Desmond Tutu, Spike Lee, Billy Joel, Virginia Coalition, the Roots, Robert Randolph Family Band, Sugar Hill Gang. There's also a big concert festival "Spring Fling" right before exams, which is an all-day party on the President's Lawn, and then several smaller concerts throughout the year.

Some students have great relationships with some members of the administration, but most students never have anything to do with administrators. The lower-level administrators tend to have open-door policies and will go out of their way to help you. But the dean of students, president, and the provost seem to only interact with students when there are problems, which I think is sad. I think they're focusing more on external relations.

The Education

We don't necessarily talk about classes themselves outside classrooms, but we talk about academic topics and our favorite professors. It also depends on the student; it really ranges here from totally intellectual to intellectual-sometimes. But there is no competition between students at all. The class work is much harder than I ever thought it would be, but it really depends on what courses you take. Most people work fairly hard during the week, and then loosen up on the weekends.

As a freshman, I had some big lectures, but just in some introductory classes—and now, most of my classes are totally discussion based. A big class at Tufts is a medium-sized class at other schools. The largest class here is the introductory bio class, and it's only about 250. Professors tend to be very involved in their students' lives. There aren't many big grad programs, so departments really focus on undergraduates, which is great. It also means that many undergrads serve as research assistants for grad students. In some departments, a lot of people do theses, but it really depends on the department. Tufts is one of the smallest research institutions in the country, and there are lots of research opportunities for undergrads. The administration is really trying to promote undergraduate research with special programs and funds.

> "I wish that Tufts was *in* the city of Boston."
> ✦ Apurvi, sophomore

The Students

The campus is fairly liberal, but the conservatives make a big stink about everything, even though they represent a tiny part of the student body. This is a campus where it's very easy to be LGBT. No one cares if you are or not. Most of my friends are straight, and I've never heard anyone say anything bad about LGBT students or administrators. There unfortunately isn't that much outreach, though, so a lot of students, particularly guys, stay closeted. Racially, the campus is fairly segregated. There are a lot of people of every group, so they seem to seldom feel the need to mix up. I think the number of cultural organizations has kind of had a negative impact by dividing up the campus. Also, it seems socioeconomic status is largely tied to race. If I had to generalize, I'd say that the black and Hispanic students tend to be lower-income and first-generation college students, while the white and Asian students tend to range from middle-class to upper-class. The international students definitely seem very rich and tend to stay together.

The Activities

There's no one kind of group that's big. Sports aren't that big on the varsity level, but most people are involved in something. People love a cappella and dance performances, and they'll go to theater shows (although I don't think they're generally on par with dance and a cappella). Community service is *huge,* ranging from direct service in soup kitchens, to running our own programs, to interning at social service organizations, to going into the Peace Corps or doing policy and advocacy work after graduation. The TCU Senate, our student government, seems to have no influence on major decisions whatsoever. Individual advisory boards (appointed) have much more clout, but it depends on the area. Everyone reads the *Daily* every day, and it's where much of the campus debates and dialogues occur.

The Social Scene

Of Thursday, Friday, and Saturday, usually people drink one night, do something cultural the other night, and veg the other. Those who do like drinking tend to drink a lot, but most people don't. The frats and sororities aren't huge. They provide parties for freshmen and those who choose to go Greek. Going Greek isn't a huge deal. Most parties for upperclassmen are in the on-campus apartments or off-campus. You meet most of your friends from classes (so much group work!) or your activities. The dorm life varies a lot from year to year and building to building.

> "Prospective students would not be told that the majority of students at Tufts are spoiled kids—they are told that we are very diverse, but the majority has lots of money and is quick to remind you of it."
> ✦ Lauren, senior

Name: Jordana
Hometown: Longmeadow, Massachusetts
Class Year: Sophomore
Major: Political science and philosophy
Extracurriculars: The *Primary Source* (conservative publication), Tufts Republicans, Political Science and Philosophy, Women's Crew (three semesters), Tufts Dance Collective, Tufts Community Union Judiciary, Ballroom Dance Team (starting fall 2004)
Career Goal: Law school, to study and then pursue constitutional law.

How would you describe Tufts' reputation?

Diverse and welcoming.

Is this reputation accurate?

It's diverse in terms of race but still extremely segregated. We have "culture houses" that divide people up and our "culture groups" are the largest and most segregated organizations on campus. The school is obsessed with diversity unless it means ideological diversity. Nonliberal thinkers are clearly not welcomed and when it comes to student government—you're guaranteed a win as long as you're a minority student. Everyone here claims to be "underrepresented" and "oppressed" and any time the word *gay* appears on a whiteboard it's classified as a bias incident and anyone present in that dorm is required to attend mandatory sensitivity training. Anyone who displays a conservative or even libertarian belief is a hatemongerer and students expressing nonliberal beliefs have been victims of libel, slander, and even assault by the campus Left.

What would an admissions officer at Tufts probably not tell a prospective student?

Prospective students will not be told about Vulvapalooza and Sex on the Hill, or about how "womyn" have "reclaimed" the word *c-nt* and plaster it all over campus with explicit pictures of female genitalia. They won't be told about the restrictive speech codes Tufts has tried to enact in the past, nor will they learn anything of the antidemocratic election rules our elections board has enacted.

The Institution

We don't have too much in the way of tradition here. Except maybe the Naked Quad Run and the cannon. The cannon was a gift to Tufts for winning the first collegiate football game ever played, and is pointed vaguely in the direction of Harvard University. At night, students paint the cannon to commemorate birthdays, advertise events, or celebrate sports victories, and guard their work until sunrise.

The campus is built on a hill and excellent for sledding in the winter (students steal lunch trays from the dining halls), but watch out for all the trees! The hill is also home to Spring Fling, where the concert board pays through the roof (on our student activity fee's dollar) for a few mediocre bands no one will care about since they'll be too drunk to even stand up straight.

Off-campus housing is ridiculous—we have terrible town-gown relations. Off-campus residents will face neighbors who seem to exist to make life difficult. They will call the police if students' cars are parked on the street for two consecutive days, or if they can hear students talking in their own homes.

> "Being a premed student, I was apprehensive about a cutthroat, overly competitive atmosphere, but Tufts students are not like that at all."
>
> ✦ Kate, senior

Boston is a very small city but a great place to go if you're a college student. Something like 50 percent of the population of Boston during the school year is comprised of college students (due in part to really large schools like Boston University and Northeastern). MIT frats throw the best parties, and there are a multitude of events geared for college students in the greater Boston area, and our dance clubs are pretty classy and a great place to meet people and dance. And for the more ballroom-inclined we also have a number of places for salsa, jive, swing. The North End is home to some great Italian restaraunts and Mike's Pastry, which always has a line out the door. The Boston Duck Tours are the perfect way to see our city, and the Charles River is home to the head of the Charles Regatta every year where crew teams from all over the United States will come to compete, and we also have Fenway Park, home of the Boston Red Sox, which is where we all gather together to cheer on our team to the shouts of "Yankees Suck!" This phrase is also shouted at other sporting events that do not involve the Yankees or baseball, on the Boston Common during Hempfest, in the theater during intermission, or while standing on the Harvard—a.k.a. SMOOT—Bridge that connects BU to MIT.

We have a shuttle that takes us from the campus center and a couple uphill stops to Davis Square, where we can catch the T (Davis is on the Red Line) to take us straight into Boston. On Friday and Saturday evenings we also have a Boston shuttle for those not wishing to make alternate arrangements to get home after the T closes around 1:00 a.m. Everything in Boston closes at 2:00 a.m. (we have a number of Puritan Blue Laws that do not allow businesses to stay open as late as they'd like to, alcohol purchase only became legal on Sundays a few months ago, and there are citywide smoking bans in Boston, Cambridge, and Somerville). Since drinking is illegal for those under the age of twenty-one, most students choose to drink on campus in their rooms and at frat parties. A large number of students also smoke marijuana, but harder drugs are pretty rare to come by.

The Education

Some students here are very academic and will debate in the dining halls and at parties. Professors here tend to be pretty active in politics. Some of our professors are good, but others should be shot and put us all out of our misery. We have a number of distribution requirements that are reasonable, with the exception of the language/culture requirement that's far too excessive (six semesters) as well as a world civilization requirement that excludes the entire Western world (is that to say Europe is uncivilized?). Asian American and African American and Latino American studies all count toward the "foreign culture" requirement despite the word *American* in their very title.

With the exception of engineers, students are all required a minimum of six semester of a foreign language. This may seem unreasonable—and it is. Luckily, some students can test out of it or fulfill half of the six course requirement with a "culture" option. There's also an English requirement (which you can sometimes avoid through a decent AP score) and a world civilizations requirement. Some of the requirements do make some sense, such as requiring two courses each for math, natural science, social science, humanities. There's some talk that this should be reduced to one class each, which makes sense for students juggling three majors who really don't want to have to take the joke classes Math of Social Choice and Symmetry to fulfill their math requirements when they're trying to do International Relations, a language, and economics.

The Students

Students here are *obsessed* with diversity and culture. Culture is exclusive, however (white people have no culture, apparently). Conservatives are the vast minority on campus and are treated poorly by the general student body. Most students are from eastern Massachusetts or someplace foreign. You can tell the difference fairly easily: one group wears Red Sox T-shirts and jeans; the other you can just barely see their Gucci spiked-heeled shoes and cell phones amidst the cloud of cigarette smoke.

Postscript: Tufts had made me resent diversity, since it seems to only apply to minorities. Tufts tries to make me feel guilty for being white, or straight, and I think it's sickening. All that said, and as cynical as I might sound, I actually find humor, entertainment, and satisfaction in being an (ideological) campus minority. You might not believe it, but I actually love Tufts. My classes are challenging, the majority of my professors are truly dynamic, and I have found that there is a club for just about anything I might want to do.

> "The most difficult part of being a first-year student is letting go of the first year—it's been the best year of my life!"
>
> ✦ Anna, junior

The Activities

We have many many student groups that cover a wide variety of interests. Our community service organization, Leonard Carmichael Society, is the largest group on campus. The most active groups are the far-Left political groups, which are known for crashing April Open House to protest janitors' wages, making obscene gestures at former president George H. W. Bush, desecrating the U.S. flag, and causing their own demise from disorganization. Our most vocal campus groups are Voices for Choice, the Coalition for Social Justice and Nonviolence (which includes the Student Labor Action Movement and Tufts Coalition Opposing the War in Iraq), and the Bias Response Team.

I was a varsity athlete for three semesters (women's crew team). I gave it up, since it's very difficult to be an athlete, a student, and be active in other organizations. Although Tufts is Division III, athletes take their sports very seriously, almost as seriously as their drinking. Athletics can be a great experience, but they can also be very detracting to other opportunities because they are so time-consuming.

Performing arts at Tufts is very impressive. We have many different dance, theater, and musical groups that satisfy just about every niche. Some of these groups are very popular and sell out their shows the day tickets go on sale. Other groups perform to half-empty rooms. These groups are known for being very cliquey, but that's the nature of performing arts in general.

The Social Scene

There is no such thing as dating at Tufts. We have a hookup culture. Parties are generally packed with people standing around drinking beer, with a band or DJ in the basement. The classier students choose to go off-campus.

Notable Tufts Alumni Include:

Daniel Patrick Moynihan, U.S. senator, ambassador, administration official
Guster, musicians
Hank Azaria, actor
Joseph Neubauer, CEO of Aramark Corporation
Pierre and Pamela Omidyar, founders of eBay
Tracy Chapman, musician

TULANE UNIVERSITY

Founded: 1834

Location: New Orleans, LA

Phone: (504) 865-5000

E-mail: undergrad.admission@tulane.edu

Web site: www.tulane.edu

Number of Undergraduates: 7,830

Number of Graduate Students: 2,930

Cost: Approximately $39,000 per year

Application Deadline: January 15

Early Decision/Action: November 1

Rating:	Notable Majors/Programs:
Selective	Engineering, Architecture, Business

Size:
○ Small ○ Medium ● Large

Location:
● Urban ○ Suburban ○ Rural

On a Saturday, students talk about academics:
○ Always ● Sometimes ○ Never

Nightlife:
● Intense ○ Moderate ○ Laid-back

Politically, Tulane leans:
○ Left ○ Right ● Split

Diversity:
○ High ● Low ○ Medium

Students describe Tulane in five words:
- Beautiful, *fun,* laid-back, *fun,* challenging
- Trendy, quasi-indifferent smarties in N'Orleans

From the School

There are many ways to augment and enrich your degree at Tulane. The university's international programs give students new perspectives, internships afford valuable career-building experience, and Tulane's honors program enables participation in special seminars and innovative courses. Early acceptance programs allow guaranteed acceptance into Tulane's medical or law school. Integrated graduate and professional studies help students obtain bachelor's and master's degrees in only five years. And for those looking for an unconventional course of study, interdisciplinary and joint-degree programs, as well as self-designed majors, are also available.

—www.tulane.edu

If you're interested in Tulane, you may also be interested in:
Duke, Emory, UNC at Chapel Hill, USC, UT at Austin, Vanderbilt

Name: Rachel
Hometown: Tulsa, Oklahoma
Major: Biomedical engineering
Extracurriculars: Soccer, sorority, academic, and professional clubs
Career Goal: Attend medical school

How would you describe Tulane's reputation?

That Tulane, a top-notch academic school very much embedded in the deep South, is primarily a bunch of really rich Yankees. You'll hear that the student body as a whole is very trendy, and it's not just the girls: you're just as likely to see the guys sporting Prada or Burberry. Tulane is also known for being very social and a *huge* party scene—this is New Orleans, after all.

Is this reputation accurate?

Oh yes. Students with money = lots of designers (we're talking Prada, Gucci, LV, etc.) + lots of alcohol (top shelf). Academically, it's definitely tough, but I know I'm getting a great education.

The Institution

School spirit, ha. It's getting better, slowly. I don't think some students even knew we had an athletic program. It doesn't help that the football team plays in the Superdome. Even if the entire student body were to go (which would *never* happen), that's fewer than ten thousand people in a dome meant for sixty thousand, but this doesn't mean students here don't love Tulane. It's true that students here can be stuck up, about their social status and especially about going to Tulane.

The hardest thing about being a first-year student is learning to balance schoolwork and going out. With bars everywhere (even on the way to the library), it's hard to pick! New Orleans is an amazing place to live, and an even more awesome place to go to college. Ninety percent of the time, the weather is absolutely amazing here—you can lie out on the quads February until mid-October. But when it rains, watch out—parts of campus flood after a good thirty-minute downpour!

The Education

Competition between students, in my major, can be fierce. I had a class that was graded by the bell curve (10 percent A, 20 percent B, 30 percent C, etc.), and after being in lab for three hours, my partner and I could not figure this electronics

thing out and asked another pair for help. One kid tried to help us until his partner grabbed him and said "don't help them! remember the curve!" But not to freak you out: other than that incident, we studied in big groups, and did want everyone else to do (almost as) well (as us). But my profs are awesome and helpful and really want me to both succeed and understand the material, and my relationships with them are awesome, too. I had a teacher work with my group from 5 p.m. until 11 p.m. until we solved an assignment!

There are lots of research opportunities for undergrads—most of the time you just have to ask your prof. Lots of seniors write theses—and in biomedical engineering it's a requirement to graduate, I think one of only a handful of institutions in the country with such requirements.

I think our strong departments are Biomedical Engineering (you say that and the immediate response is "you must be really smart"—it's kinda nice), Chemistry, Architecture, and Environmental Studies. But then again, I'm a biomedical engineering student so you may have to ask someone else for a different perspective. Everyone calls the Business School the A & B Free school; people who have friends in there (and that's everyone) never see them do work.

The Students

Tulane is indeed a bunch wealthy white kids, primarily Yankees. Our nickname is Jewlane, not kidding. Neither of which are necessarily a bad thing! Everyone tends to hang out together, upper and underclassmen, Greeks and non-Greeks. But I guess if you're an athlete, you tend to live in a bubble and hang out with other athletes only, unless you joining a Greek organization to get a break from everything. It's a really small school so you can't be that picky.

Everyone here wants to go to grad school, whether it's engineering, MBA, law, or medical school. I actually don't know many people entering the job market after graduation.

A Tulane girl wears the latest jeans or a micro mini, bright colored high heels, layered tank tops, hair is either scrunched or straightened, carries the latest Louis Vuitton, which contains her cell phone, lipgloss, and a pack of cigarettes. A Tulane boy also wears the latest jeans, Gucci belt and shoes, Lacoste or Burberry polo with the collar turned up.

The Activities

When friends and I are bored, we go to the levy (where the Mississippi River runs) and hang out. Go shopping at all the boutiques on Magazine Street. Eat at one of the amazing cafés/restaurants in the city. Go walk through the French Quarter, listen to some jazz. If its 3:00 a.m. on Wednesday night and I'm still awake it's because I'm at the Bulldog drinking beer. The thing about New Orleans is that its an experience in itself. Going to Tulane, you cannot be bored, there is just too much to do.

The Social Scene

People party 24/7. At Tulane, if people aren't drinking in their dorm or their apartment, bars are a dime a dozen and open all night. Every campus activity is centered around alcohol: kegs on the quads on Fridays, Happy Hour. It helps that New Orleans is the cheapest city ever.

Thursday is the scene. You start at ten or eleven and head out to one bar that has cheap drinks, then you jump in a cab (or have a designated driver) and go to another, followed by the last bar where *everyone* goes. We drink and dance until 5:00 a.m. or so, when we either stumble home or head to the campus bar (the Boot) and then stumble home.

Name: Kylie
Hometown: Dallas, Texas
Class Year: Sophomore
Major: Marketing, minor in Spanish and media arts
Extracurriculars: Media Chair (oversees all undergraduate and grad student media), Council head to undergraduate student government, layout editor of magazine, staff editor of *Hullabaloo* (newspaper), Chi-Omega sorority, intramural softball
Career Goal: Graphics artist for a newspaper or advertising executive

How would you describe Tulane's reputation?

There is a huge image that Tulane is a party hard, work hard school. I think most people in the country think that we are a bunch of rich kids from the northeast who come to New Orleans to party.

Is this reputation accurate?

I think it would be too easy to say that about Tulane. Students here are from all over the country, though there is a lot of southern pride here and the culture is addictive. As for the party reputation, sure it's true—but in order to stay here you have to work hard.

What would an admissions officer at Tulane probably not tell a prospective student?

The admissions people do a great job covering up student apathy by calling it "New Orleans's laid-back atmosphere." I don't think a student would realize what it means to go to a school that is in the Big Easy. The appeal of a slower atmosphere does seem nice, but it also means that it's difficult to get the student body to do anything unless there's a keg.

The Institution

I think the size of the school is perfect: it progressively gets smaller and by senior year, everyone on campus can be linked within two or three degrees of separation. I have friends in different groups, as opposed to a larger university where I'd be more inclined to stick to the same five best friends. I come from a very competitive private high school, so I didn't want a huge university campus where I was a number. I think this is the perfect college for the high school student who was a bit of an overachiever and needs a little break.

Something unique about Tulane is that the administrations of the liberal arts colleges are separated by gender: Newcomb College for women and Tulane College for men. The classes are all integrated, as are the faculty, but the administrations are separate. They both have very different identities. For orientation, Newcomb has a number of programs that match up incoming freshman with upperclasswomen. They have a mentoring program and a big sister/little sister program, which matches a freshman with an upperclassman who takes her little sister out and helps her adjust to college life. The pinning ceremony introducing the big and little sis is a fifty-year tradition, and the little sister gets a pin unique to her year. I do wish the individual colleges worked together instead of having repeated turf wars over new courses and majors.

The most difficult part of first year is realizing that there are so many bureaucratic administrations working out of one university that it is next to impossible to get anything accomplished if it requires the support of more than one bureaucracy. There are too many ears on campus that hear your complaints, and not enough hands to act.

> "There is a lot of interaction between locals and students. Some of the coolest people I've met have been students from New Orleans and their friends from high school. They are a totally different breed from anyone else in the country."
>
> ✦ Kerry, senior

As for the local community, they love to hate Tulane with a passion. The city is consumed with LSU fans and its dwellers tend to feel that Tulane students are spoiled Yankee alcoholics. But the university does employ a fair amount of the community, local bars certainly miss the students during the summer, and when it comes down to getting a good job in Louisiana or anywhere in the country, the locals will concede Tulane is the best.

I really regret the lack of housing for upperclassmen. It polarizes the campus when half the students don't live there. After freshman year, the chances of getting a dorm are slim. The neighborhood around Tulane is nice and housing isn't unreasonable, but to get a house within walking distance takes work and a little more money.

I think the campus security is a joke. The Tulane campus police do not respond to pressing issues. There have been a few violent crimes on campus that seemed to be ignored; instead, the campus police pursue every freshman with a brown paper bag in his hands, thinking it's alcohol. The weekly police reports include everything from the occasional rape or robbery to students being arrested for stealing caution tape and golf carts.

The Education

I would say one of the best things about Tulane is that you are never a number. I am only a sophomore and know all of my teachers, have had coffee or dinner with at least two of them this semester alone, and their doors are *always* open. My teachers are truly here to teach me, not do research or help grad students. I spend a moderate to heavy amount of time on schoolwork. There will be weeks, even a month or two when I don't leave the

library—and then there are weeks where I don't leave the parties. It comes in waves and overall I would say it's appropriate for a competitive, prestigious university.

The Students

Politically, students are pretty apathetic overall, except for maybe the same group of a hundred students who seem to run everything, and are the most passionate and outspoken. Protests are rare, and student government would rather debate over who sounds smarter than what really matters. Last year we had Howard Dean speak and there was more arguing over the use of student funding for a perceived political purpose than over the politics themselves. The campus Republicans seem to dominate campus, but I think it seems that way because they just shout louder. Yeah, insofar as it's political at all, I'd say the campus is relatively balanced politically.

The *Hullabaloo* is really popular. The editor-in-chief gets flooded with letters, and it is an award-winning newspaper. Considering there is no communications school, and the major might as well not exist, the student media at Tulane is excellent. WTUL is a radio station that serves far more than the university; they do a lot of programming in the New Orleans area. There is a literary magazine that covers gender issues, and a well-recognized prose magazine.

The upside to student apathy is it is incredibly easy to get leadership positions in most student organizations. By sophomore year, I got to be a staff editor, which probably wouldn't have happened at a large university until senior year.

There are definitely different social groups, but they are easy to mix with and it is very possible to be friends with everyone. The Greeks, the motivated, the partiers, the studiers all seem to make it to the Boot for happy hour.

> "Social scene? Hello! It's New Orleans. Bourbon Street, French Quarter! Need I say more?"
>
> ✦ Jed, junior

The Activities

If I'm awake on a Wednesday at 3:00 a.m., it's because I am sending out e-mails to my organizations—I guess I'm part of that small group of students who are really passionate about student life. Students have been more enthusiastic in the past about athletics, but that was until the cops started handing out MIPs. Tulane students will turn out occasionally for events like homecoming and any baseball game against LSU.

There is never a dull moment at Tulane. There's always a party, a bar, a new part of New Orleans to explore. The city has so much culture and history that there is always a new museum, art gallery, or street with amazing little shops.

The Social Scene

Alcohol and the university have been in a very long-term abusive relationship. The administration tries to make Tulane more academic by attempting to curb underage drinking, but it doesn't keep the library open past 8:00 p.m. on a weekend night, or on three-day weekends. The administration knows that New Orleans has been around a lot longer than Tulane, and it isn't going to change any time soon. It is very possible to have a social life regardless of Greek affiliation. While it opened a lot of doors for me, I think I would have still been happy if I had not been Greek. Most students here are ridiculously friendly and polite 90 percent of the time. Those who come here from anywhere other than the South, learn southern hospitality real quick! The dating scene is probably like most college campuses: a long-term relationship essentially means hooking up with the same person more than four times in the same semester.

Name: John
Hometown: Virginia, Illinois
Class Year: Freshman
Major: Architecture
Extracurriculars: Phi Gamma Delta (FIJI) fraternity, RHG New Doris Hall 2nd Floor Representative
Career Goal: To major in architecture and eventually become a fully licensed architect

How would you describe Tulane's reputation?

A big party school since it is New Orleans, but also quite highly ranked in most of the academic programs such as business, architecture, law, and engineering.

Is this reputation accurate?

Yes—very big on partying, with some distractions from the city, but when everyone puts their minds to it, they put out good, quality academic work.

What would an admissions officer at Tulane probably not tell a prospective student? What aspect of your school would a prospective student not see on a campus tour?

An admissions officer tries to hide the fact that we have fun and party quite a bit, and you wouldn't see this on a campus tour.

The Institution

I think school spirit is decreasing because of Tulane's poor athletic track record in many sports except baseball—but who watches college baseball anyway?

The school's size is great: big but not too big. Every day I see someone I know walking through campus, and I also see many people whom I do not know yet. The campus is laid out very well—everything is within a fifteen-minute walk and even closer with the use of a bike. The weather is just as nice as advertised: very warm, not very rainy.

I chose Tulane University because it was the perfect fit for me—I loved the architecture program, especially how the students get involved in the design process, the weather is great, the campus is beautiful, and the atmosphere of the city is unlike anywhere else.

The Education

Saturday night is strictly for partying—classes aren't heard of on the weekend, except on Sunday, which is set aside for homework and recovery. I'd say there is some competition between students, especially to get a higher GPA. Most of my classes are lecture-based, except my architecture studios, which are very hands-on. TAs mostly do grading, but not much teaching. The research opportunities for undergrads are amazing. Many engineering students, at least, are able to research quite early. I usually spend three to four hours on schoolwork outside of class but I have an easier class schedule and all my architecture work is done in the studio class. There are many quality study abroad programs offered for the junior year.

The Students

There seems to be quite a small Asian community compared to many other campuses around the nation. Many of the African-American students at Tulane seem strongly involved in the athletic sports and programs offered. There does seem to be quite a large number of Jewish people at Tulane. It has been said that one in every four people at Tulane is Jewish, although I am not sure how true that really is. Students come from all across the United States and even some from across the world. I think that being able to meet and have good friends from all over the place is a big plus, for both Tulane and myself. An average student at Tulane is quite well educated and keeps to his/her studies—and also has a big party attitude when the weekend rolls around.

The Activities

There are other schools around: Loyola is right next door (literally a step off of campus), University of New Orleans is near the lake, Xavier (an all black school) is in town, and Delgado (a small community college). Tulane students and Loyola students often interact with shared programs and parties and at bars.

Athletics are a bit sad at most times but Tulane tends to do decent in football and basketball and above average in men's and women's tennis and very good in baseball. Art is very popular at Tulane with the Newcomb Art Gallery featuring highly recognized exhibits.

Community service is popular among many groups, particularly CACTUS (a strictly community service group at Tulane University). There is a very active undergraduate student government that has a strong hand in making decisions at Tulane.

There are several big name performers that come each year—mainly comedians and several good bands and New Orleans is full of many top touring performers. I leave campus to go to parties/bars, get food (Subway, Wing Zone, and Frostop to name a few good ones), and to go downtown for Bourbon Street or shopping or movies.

> "There are a lot of people who'd rather get drunk on a weeknight than see a great foreign film. But then there are folks who love New Orleans for its art and its culture, its music, and unique spirit. It's the balance that makes Tulane great."
> ✦ Amanda, sophomore

The Social Scene

A person's partying ranges from never or once in a while to four or five days a week. Different types of people party differently: some stay in and drink in their rooms (although not legally), others pregame in the rooms and then go to bars, and others just go to bars or frats off-campus.

The fraternity/sorority scene is quite strong at Tulane—I would say about 30 to 40 percent of the student body participates in them. The frats and sororities are quite small and I imagine different compared to larger campuses.

The dating scene is quite sleazy and easy if one tries. I feel it is quite hard, especially freshman year, to meet good, quality people to date—but I am not into the whole thing, sadly, myself.

Dorm life is a lot of fun but exhausting at points—it seems hard to get away and be alone, although the nice, urban park across the street is useful for that. All freshmen live on campus for their first year.

I say "hi" to many people on campus but not always to complete strangers; I do always hold the door open for people after me.

Notable Tulane Alumni Include:
Bob Livingston, congressman
David Filo, founder of Yahoo!
Jerry Springer, television personality
Michael DeBakey, heart surgeon
Eleven governors of Louisiana
Five Pulitzer Prize winners

VANDERBILT UNIVERSITY

Founded: 1873

Location: Nashville, TN

Phone: (615) 322-7311

E-mail: admissions@vanderbilt.edu

Web site: www.vanderbilt.edu

Number of Undergraduates: 6,240

Number of Graduate Students: 3,580

Cost: Approximately $40,000 per year

Application Deadline: January 2

Early Decision: November 1

Rating:	Notable Majors/Programs:
Very Selective	Life Sciences, Engineering, Education, Music

Size:
○ Small ● Medium ○ Large

Location:
● Urban ○ Suburban ○ Rural

On a Saturday, students talk about academics:
○ Always ● Sometimes ○ Never

Nightlife:
● Intense ○ Moderate ○ Laid-back

Politically, Vanderbilt leans:
○ Left ● Right ○ Split

Diversity:
○ High ● Low ○ Medium

Students describe Vanderbilt in five words:
- Intelligent, beautiful, respected—simply Vandy
- Charming, in the southern sense

From the School

Vanderbilt offers undergraduate programs in the liberal arts and sciences, engineering, music, education and human development, as well as a full range of graduate and professional degrees. The combination of cutting edge research, liberal arts and a distinguished medical center creates an invigorating atmosphere where students tailor their education to meet their goals and researchers collaborate to solve complex problems affecting our health, culture and society. Vanderbilt provides a gateway to greatness, drawing the best and brightest students from across the nation and around the world.

—www.vanderbilt.edu

If you're interested in Vanderbilt, you may also be interested in:
Duke, Emory, UNC at Chapel Hill, Tulane, U. Virginia, Wake Forest

Name: John
Hometown: Louisville, Kentucky
Class Year: Sophomore
Major: Economics, Spanish
Extracurriculars: Varsity athlete; captain Cross-Country Team, Alternative Spring Break site leader
Career Goal: Excel at something I have a passion for.

How would you describe Vanderbilt's reputation?

Very well-respected academically—however, many people up North still describe it as a "Good Southern School" and not just a plain good school. It seems less well-known in the North, but carries a lot of notoriety in the South. I was born in the North and raised in the South (Kentucky), and I think the North definitely sees the South as inferior when it comes to education. It is known for being pretty conservative for a top-twenty school. Also, we are seen as rich, smart, beautiful (mainly the women), party-happy, spoiled, superficial, homogenous, and not socially conscious.

Is this reputation accurate?

It is definitely a very good school (and it does has a more southern flavor than other top schools down here like Duke, Emory, or Wake Forest). However, the entire nation needs to view us as an excellent school *period*, without needing the southern qualifier. I think being on the conservative side of the college political spectrum is a good thing because you'll find more balance here—our political demographic is much more realistic, allowing for more mature, civil, and less judgmental political debate than you'll find at the extreme left-wing schools comprising most of the top tier. We don't make nearly as much noise as a Berkeley or Brown would, but this seems a healthier political environment; honestly, college politics on the whole are a bit out there. Generalizations don't come out of thin air, of course, but the last sweeping generalization I listed above is far too limited to be a true representation. The student body is very well-off on average, and the social system is a bit elitist at times, and the Greek system is very influential—but there are still plenty of alternative cultures here. It's just that the social Greeks are the loudest and most conspicuous.

What would an admissions officer at Vanderbilt probably not tell a prospective student? What aspect of your school would a prospective student not see on a campus tour?

Probably would not focus on how strong the Greek influence is here or the sort of true stereotype of the Vandygirls and Vandyguys. They might also not focus on how school sport spirit is quite a bit lower here than other SEC (Southeastern Conference—our sports league, as good as any in the nation) schools, mainly because football has struggled for so long.

The Institution

There is school spirit if you want it—there are some incredible fans here, such as the Memorial Maniacs. It's a student fan club for men's and women's basketball (they play in Memorial Gym), and they stand up front at games in "the pit" and everyone wears the same shirt. Vanderbilt's version of Duke's Cameron Crazies, about two hundred members, the Memorial Maniacs' influence and involvement has grown tremendously the past four or five years. Not bad, but I do wish there were more school spirit.

There isn't huge interaction with the community; we talk about the "Vanderbubble" because this place isn't really the real world. The campus has a very friendly, cheerful, and rich landscape, full of trees and shrubs, as nice as you'll see anywhere—a definite southern feel. The main campus seems small at first but it as a whole ends up being a lot larger than it initially seems. It's set in an area similar to downtown; Nashville doesn't have a big city feel. This is a very pleasant place to be, except that it rains a ton in February—to the extent that it induces seasonal affective disorder in some people. My advice is to get outdoors and exercise nonetheless—doing so can be fun and will raise spirits.

The Education

Learning here has a more laid-back feeling than most top schools, I'd say. It's less cutthroat, with many students willing to help each other out and share info on assignments; students don't seem too obsessed with class rank. Students seem to talk about classes a good bit, but you won't see a lot of super-brainy philosophical debate (which you could still find if you wanted to). Students are pretty social and the workload is certainly not overbearing, allowing pretty much any student plenty of time for sports and extracurricular activities (for me at least—econ and Spanish double is probably about average in terms of difficulty, premeds and many engineers obviously work a good deal harder). A lot of students are pretty smart to begin with, but plenty weren't superstars at their high school, more like top 10 percent types.

The College Program in Liberal Education is the basic nonmajor set of requirements necessary to graduate from the College of Arts and Science, such as a history component, math, foreign language, humanities, English and writing, lab and nonlab science. Some complain about how time-consuming and cumbersome it is, especially if they don't have AP credits. Those who do come in with a good amount of AP credits usually blow right through, and I had no problem with it. I've heard that the program is currently being amended and that AP credits will not be accepted as much, if at all, in the future. The workload here is manageable. I spend three hours, maybe four some days, and get it all done. They don't try to kill you here. Even doing a double major, I never feel overwhelmed by school. Work is mostly meaningful, not much busywork from my experience. A good number of seniors do a thesis or an honor thesis but I didn't.

"Vandyguy: Preppy southern guy, from private or maybe boarding school, who joins a fraternity and cares a good deal about social status. Rich and conservative, drives an SUV, has little if any understanding/concern for social issues. Could be viewed as a junior version of The Man. Some truth to the stereotype, but it's not a necessity to be a Vanderguy to find a solid niche here.

Vandygirl: The more infamous of the two; a rich, southern, very attractive (blond) white girl who loves to shop, spends a lot of money. Joining the right sorority is of utmost importance, and she's excessively superficial, with little social concern. Vandygirls got a real extreme portrayal a few years ago in *Seventeen* magazine—the lady who edited the piece was a bitter ex-Vanderbilt student.

The myth and stereotypes are entertaining and hold a degree of truth, but are certainly blown out of proportion. They're not nearly the airheads they are sometimes portrayed as being. Please don't overdo or play up these stereotypes in the book. It's just not that true.

✦ John, sophomore

The Students

I'd say the average student here is pretty academic but laid-back and quite social. Vanderbilt seems to attract social students who did very well in high school; there seems to be a lower proportion of oddballs here than at other private schools of our size and academic prestige.

There is definitely growing diversity and LGBT community. They're getting bigger without much tension and are well accepted, I'd say. Many just let them be. Races tend to keep to themselves mainly, but that is true almost anywhere and is not a hard-and-fast rule. The socioeconomic makeup is about as well-off as you'll ever find (supposedly we have the lowest percentage of students not on financial aid) but you will find many, many students on aid. Geographically, it seems like every other student is from Georgia or Texas but there are a considerable number from the Northeast and West too, but they tend to become more southern once they're here!

Activism is relatively low here, but it is very civil and no side can really dominate (again, more like the real world). Particularly liberal students may be frustrated here with the student body, but your average student should feel comfortable expressing his/her political opinions. There was plenty of good dialogue at the onset of the Iraq war, with a large silent protest and some more vocal ones, and there were many students in support of the war, yet it was all very civil. I was proud to see this—and am still proud how evenly distributed opinions are in the *Hustler* (student paper). Columnists can express strong conservative viewpoints and not get bashed (they will certainly be challenged, but not bashed). I enjoy hearing equally from both sides, and developing from that an informed, reasonable, independent opinion.

The Activities

There is a very good Army ROTC program here, with a strong presence. This school is accepting of military activities and they have an excellent recruiter.

The facilities for athletes here are very good. Potential athletes are scared off a little bit by our athletic department restructuring, thinking that we are trying to leave the SEC or weaken our programs, but that is not the case. The athletic department has very ambitious goals and practically every team has improved substantially over the four years I've been here. Athletes are well taken care of by the Athletic Department (but not necessarily overindulged), and they're legitimately concerned with your academic progress, not just staying eligible until your days are up.

The Social Scene

Well, we did receive a top twenty-five party school rating from *Playboy* and maybe another publication, but I wouldn't say partying is out of control. Some people go out several nights a week, but they still get their work done.

As far as partying habits, open fraternity parties in the fall are very big for freshman and sophomores. In the spring, fraternity parties are much more closed (freshman pledge in spring here, not fall). Parties in upperclass dorms and suites/apartments are popular because most students live on campus, though there's not the abundance of house parties and off-campus parties you'll find at other schools. Many upperclassmen can be found at bars in town (Flying Saucer, Sams, Sportsmans, Buffalo, Tin Roof, and Lonnie's are some) on particular nights of the week. If you like live country, this is a great place; if you don't, you'll probably learn to like it (I did!); if you still don't, then I guess it's somewhat avoidable. The main strip of downtown bars is about two miles from campus.

The Greeks are quite a presence here (30 percent males, 50 percent females). I've never been involved with the Greek system, but my close friend was part of a prestigious fraternity and depledged, and he says there's a very sharp contrast between his social life then and now. He feels a significant loss of social status—and he got a lot more interest from sorority girls back then. So I guess if you're really into top-flight sorority girls, then you should be part of a good fraternity. But it is very important to realize that this stereotypical social scene is not the end all/be all here. There is plenty more. Also, the importance of it dwindles; it's most important for the middle two years. By senior year, it can be seen as a bit juvenile.

Also of note is how the most prominent athletes here are not as big a deal as you would think. Social prestige supercedes athletic prestige here, unlike at other SEC schools. I don't see much formal dating here at all, hardly ever. You can meet new people but I've stuck with friends from freshman year and my teammates. You won't know everyone on campus, which I think is good. I wouldn't want this school to be any smaller. Sometimes you'll meet someone and then not see them

for months; I see people all the time whom I don't recognize. But if you don't hold the door for someone and say "hi," you won't come across very well.

Name: Laura
Hometown: Milwaukee, Wisconsin
Class Year: Sophomore
Majors: Child development and psychology
Extracurriculars: Vanderbilt Hille; Alpha Phi Omega Service group; Alpha Delta Pi Sorority; ALD, PHS, KDE Honor Societies
Career Goal: To get my Ph.D. and be a child psychologist.

How would you describe Vanderbilt's reputation?

Work hard, play hard. Also one of the most incredible up-and-coming schools in the nation.

Is this reputation accurate?

Yes, for the most part. You can find just about any extracurriculars that you are interested in and "play hard" only if that's what you are looking for. This school is making huge strides to emerge as the best of the best, and is really coming into its own— as well as becoming more liberal than in the past.

What aspect of Vanderbilt would a prospective student not see on a campus tour?

All of the amazing opportunities that await its students with so many different organizations. The tour only shows the main campus and there is no way to see all that is available unless you really explore from the inside out.

The Institution

The school's size is ideal: all the benefits of a major research university but with no way to get lost in the system. There is a lot of school spirit, even when the teams aren't on the favorable side of the scoreboard! Everyone loves it here! I don't know anybody who has transferred. How can you possibly be down, when every place that you walk is more beautiful than the last and smiling faces are all around you? Whether it's needing to find a class in the first few days of school or changing your major, everyone is there to help you, with a smile. To get an incredible education on top of all that is, well, incredible!

The Education

We know how to take breaks on the weekends, and the competition between students isn't high at all. We want everyone to do well. There is always personal attention, and the faculty are more than accessible. Classes are generally small but some of the introductory classes are slightly larger. All of these larger lectures do break down into small discussion groups once a week, though. Science- and humanities-oriented students take different core classes but also come together for their CPLE classes. Vanderbilt is unique because of all the different schools and types of people that you are exposed to on a daily basis. I have both Peabody and Arts and Science classes every day, but I've also taken engineering classes and have some of my best friends in Blair! Vanderbilt offers a variety of unique majors and I truly feel that it's only because I am at Vanderbilt that I've found the right major for me. There are numerous research opportunities available on campus. No matter what your field, the faculty has a place for you and wants you involved. The schools even run meetings to help you get started. Students can easily get involved even in their fist semester on campus.

> "This place is really manicured. All around."
> ✦ Michael, freshman

The Students

Diversity is ever-increasing on this campus and this has been wonderful for Vanderbilt. This diversity seems to be very well respected and, at least from a religious standpoint, is very much accepted and encouraged by the students and faculty/administration alike. Hillel has had very open and friendly discussions with the Muslim Student Association and other groups do these types of things as well. All groups are likely to mix and interact with one another.

The Activities

Community service is very popular and there are some other schools in the area that many organizations partner with in these endeavors. The Hillel board that I am VP of plans and instigates all activities that it puts on. We have guidance but the fact that it is a student-run organization is highly respected.

The Social Scene

While many people do enjoy the party scene, there are plenty of people who do not and are still very happy here. There is a place for everybody. It is so easy to meet new people, that you will have many friends by the end of move-in day. Most people live on campus and, especially freshman year, everyone is out to meet new people. All first-year students live in freshmen dorms together and housing is done by lottery for upperclassmen. About half of all freshmen live in singles and most juniors and seniors live in apartment-style dorms. The majority of students live on campus all four years.

Name: Michael
Hometown: Westlake, Ohio
Class Year: Freshman
Major: Political science
Extracurriculars: *Vanderbilt Hustler* (newspaper), Student Government Association
Career Goal: Corporate attorney, public office

How would you describe Vanderbilt's reputation?

As *Playboy* said, it is the place where we are smart enough to work hard all week then party like there is no tomorrow on weekends.

Is this reputation accurate?

I'd say it is accurate for the most part regarding fraternities (a huge part of life on this campus), but half of the campus isn't involved in them.

What would an admissions officer at Vanderbilt probably not tell a prospective student?

The admissions officer probably wouldn't tell a prospective student that their office is recruiting minority students above and beyond affirmative action, I think—Vanderbilt has the reputation of being too white.

The Institution

Vanderbilt's a really interesting school if you want to learn how to be independent and have fun at the same time. The administration and staff doesn't really watch over the students too much. Part of this may have to do with the fact we have a reputation as a very rich student body, but not everyone here is snobbish or even rich themselves. As a freshman, I found it difficult to interact with other students and upperclassmen without truly going out of my way because of the seclusion of freshman in separate dorm rooms.

The Education

Vanderbilt is extremely competitive in a very good way. People don't talk about their grades on a daily basis, but there is an understood level that most people strive to achieve. Getting good grades at Vanderbilt is tough unless you study a lot—the professors don't "inflate" grades like other Ivy-esque schools. The student body is fairly conservative, while the professors are fairly liberal, often setting up interesting class discussions. But in my experience, no student has been hurt by expressing their viewpoints in class; in fact, discussing important issues is one of the hallmarks of professors—they try to encourage discussion amongst the students as if we were their peers. One of the best parts of Vanderbilt is the fact that we have an Honor Code. It's a unique bond between students that makes it quite clear that we intend to live our four years here honorably and with integrity.

The Students

Students may be fairly conservative, but they're not intolerant. Because university students are normally known to be liberal in nature, Vanderbilt might seem like a shock at first, but you'll find most students here are open to new ideas. We have the reputation of being too white, but there are a significant number of minorities on campus and they make their voice heard. LGBT life on campus is interesting: while students aren't normally harassed, it is not a university that is generally radically accepting of the LGBT lifestyle. Furthermore, there are not many places off campus to go for LGBT students, so most spend their time interacting in one or two places on campus.

The Activities

There are many activities to participate in on campus. If someone truly wanted to get involved, there are numerous avenues to do so. The problem is, however, that many students are apathetic when it comes to anything other than maintaining their 3.5 GPA and drinking on the weekend.

The Social Scene

The fraternity scene is pretty dominant on campus, and is where most people hang out on Friday and Saturday nights—especially first semester when students are rushing. But there are numerous places off campus to go to for fun, like bars, restaurants, and clubs. If you want to do something, Nashville has it, for the most part.

Notable Vanderbilt Alumni Include:

Amy Grant, musician

James Sasser, former senator and U.S. Ambassador to China

Muhammad Yunus, pioneer of microcredit

Robert Penn Warren, Pulitzer Prize winner

Roy Neel, campaign manager for Howard Dean, deputy chief of staff to Bill Clinton, and chief of staff to Al Gore

William Douglas Parker Jr., chairman, president, and CEO of America West Airlines

VASSAR COLLEGE

Founded: 1861

Location: Poughkeepsie, NY

Phone: (845) 437-7300

E-mail: admissions@vassar.edu

Web site: www.vassar.edu

Number of Undergraduates: 2,472

Number of Graduate Students: 0

Cost: Approximately $38,000 per year

Application Deadline: January 1

Early Decision: November 15

Rating:	Notable Majors/Programs:
Most Selective	English, Psychology, Political Science

Size:
- ● Small ○ Medium ○ Large

Location:
- ○ Urban ● Suburban ○ Rural

On a Saturday, students talk about academics:
- ● Always ○ Sometimes ○ Never

Nightlife:
- ○ Intense ○ Moderate ● Laid-back

Politically, Vassar leans:
- ● Left ○ Right ○ Split

Diversity:
- ○ High ● Low ○ Medium

Students describe Vassar in five words:
- Liberal, quirky students, breathtaking campus
- Earthy, nonconformist, intellectual, friendly, passionate

From the School

After declining an invitation to merge with Yale, Vassar decided to open its doors to men in 1969. In keeping with its pioneering spirit, Vassar was the first all-women's college in the country to become coeducational: men now represent 40 percent of the student body. . . . The unique traditions upon which the college was founded continue to be upheld today: a determination to excel, a willingness to experiment, a dedication to the values of the liberal arts and sciences, a commitment to the advancement of equality between the sexes, and the development of leadership.

—www.admissions.vassar.edu

If you're interested in Vassar, you may also be interested in:
Bard, Brown, Carleton, Oberlin, Macalester, Wesleyan

Name: Jessica
Hometown: New Rochelle, New York
Class Year: Sophomore
Major: English
Extracurriculars: Helicon Literary Magazine, Editorial Board. Miscellany News, Assistant Editor.
Career Goal: Journalist

How would you describe Vassar's reputation?

Vassar is known as a small, prestigious school with one of the most liberal student body's in the country.

Is this reputation accurate?

Yes. Vassar is small—only 2,400 students—and it's consistently ranked as one of the top fifteen liberal arts colleges in America. And I'd say our student body's devotion to rampant liberalism is roughly equivalent to the pope's devotion to Catholicism. (We have a student-run porno magazine on campus called *Squirm*, for god's sake.) We're essentially a school of idealistic white kids who believe we can save the world from the evils of corruption, capitalism, and poverty—all from the comfort of our dorms.

> "Mike-D of the Beastie Boys was expelled for throwing kegs off the roof of Jewitt, one of our dormitories. We have connections to the *Simpsons*, the Muppets, and the Beastie Boys—what more could you ask for?"
> ✦ Jessica, sophomore

What would an admissions officer at your school probably not tell a prospective student? What aspect of your school would a prospective student not see on a campus tour?

If you were taking a tour of Vassar, you probably wouldn't see signs advertising some of Vassar's more interesting events, like our sex-toy auctions. You probably also wouldn't see the dorm called Noyes, which is an art-deco monstrosity. Instead, you'd be directed toward the dorms lining our quad, which are all aesthetically pleasing Victorian relics. Freshman often choose to live in these dorms, and brag about their spacious rooms when friends from other schools come to visit.

The Institution

Vassar's campus is jaw-droppingly gorgeous. The Rockefellers used to send their daughters here, and they donated a lot of money to ensure their offspring were educated in a pristine environment. Vassar is also a nationally registered aboretum, which means we're surrounded by literally hundreds of varieties of strange and exotic plants. It doesn't get any nicer than that.

And, best of all, the students who live amidst all this splendor are uniformly unpretentious. Vassar's a place where two students walking past one another will almost always both smile, even if they don't know each other. (Which is both really comforting and vaguely creepy.) If you're looking to make friends, and you come to Vassar, you'll have an easy time. I'm über-timid, and I've had great luck meeting people.

Dorms at Vassar are also extremely social, and function as small, tight-knit communities (which you can live in all four years if you so choose). At Vassar we have Student Fellows instead of R.A.s in dorms, and these are upperclassman who live with, advise, and generally help out younger students. When you're first settling in at Vassar, Student Fellows are a great help, coordinating study breaks, setting up peanut butter and jelly making sessions and organizing field trips. They help you bond and find your niche.

Off-topic: Vassar's main dining hall, the All Campus Dining Center (AC/DC), was used as a backdrop in the movie *The Muppets Take Manhattan*. When I first arrived on campus, I took great comfort in the fact that Kermit the Frog, Miss Piggy, and Gonzo (what exactly is he supposed to be, anyway?) each came to Vassar and lived to tell the tale.

And, Vassar's been referenced four times in the *Simpsons* so far. My personal favorite exchange:

Lisa: At this rate I'll never get into an Ivy League school. I probably won't even get into Vassar.
Homer: I've had just enough of your Vassar-bashing young lady!

Even Homer Simpson loves Vassar!

The Education

At Vassar, there are only three (loose) requirements—you have to take a writing class freshman year (though there are ways to make this class math- or physics-based if you hate writing), you have to take a quantatative science *or* math class at some point over your four years (you can take a psych class to satisfy this, and psych classes aren't all that different from humanities classes), and you have to take one class in a foreign language (with a broad array of languages to choose from, including Swedish, Italian, Arabic, and Old English). Once these requirements are filled, you can take any classes you want. Go nuts. You control your education at Vassar.

And Vassar professors are generally intelligent, articulate, and accessible people. Our English department is top-notch, and I love the fact that they don't grade papers—they just "evaluate" them and give you extensive amounts of feedback. Sure, we get a grade at the end of every class, but professors are far more focused on helping you learn than they are on assigning you a number or a letter. I think that's great.

There's also absolutely no competition between students here. Just the other day, eight people in my dorm all got together to study for an intensive comparative politics midterm. We helped one another outline essays, we stayed up all night discussing assigned readings. All told, it was incredibly helpful.

> "Vassar is probably not the college to come to if you're ultraconservative, homophobic, sexist, racist, or a snob. Just thought you ought to know."
>
> ✦ Donna, senior

The Students

Although Vassar likes to talk about diversity a lot, most students are wealthy and white. This is really too bad. Vassar students are wealthy, white, wear Birkenstocks, smoke pot, and eat vegan. We're liberal, friendly, generally agnostic, and a fair share are gay. Conservatives, jocks, and religious folk exist, but they tend to be a small presence on campus.

The Activities

Vassar students study a lot. But when they're not studying, they do everything else you can think of, including: playing Frisbee, tossing flam-

ing bowling pins high into the air, hammering out tunes on xylophones, debating life's most important issues (does the word "puke" have more interesting uses as a noun or verb?). If there's anything you think you might like to try one day, come to Vassar and an upperclassman will show you how to do it while jumping on one foot and juggling.

The Social Scene

On weekends, most kids at Vassar party in the dorms. This is fun for a while, but it can get boring. Particularly in the winter months, when Poughkeepsie is covered in snow and kids don't leave their dorms as much, the same people throw parties and it can be disappointing to hang out in the same small room three Saturdays in a row.

If you do want to venture past the dorm scene, there's always the Mug, Vassar's on-campus club and bar. Alcohol flows freely there, and you can find nerds drunkenly "bumping and grinding" to bad '80s New Wave music on a nightly basis. I'm not a big fan, though—at first it's amusing to watch the tall, thin kid who eloquently condemned apartheid in your class twelve hours prior now sloppily kissing a random girl in the corner. But that wears off, and the Mug gets boring quick.

Overall, Vassar's a small school, so the party options aren't too extensive. My advice: come to Vassar if you're happy just playing cards and telling stories with your friends on weekends. I think that can be great fun.

Name: Marissa
Hometown: Bainbridge Island, Washington
Class Year: Junior
Major: Psychology
Extracurriculars: Vassar Volunteers (we walk dogs, read to second graders), Varsity soccer team, student athlete mentor, and I work with a local nonprofit helping people with developmental disabilities
Career Goal: I'm not sure, I'd like to go to graduate school and study public health, occupational therapy, or education.

How would you describe Vassar's reputation?

People generally know that Vassar is one of the top fifteen liberal arts colleges in America. I hear conflicting reports about our social scene—older generations think Vassar is still a training ground for upper-class white women, whereas younger generations see it as a typical liberal arts college filled with quirky, laid-back students passionate about changing the world.

Is this reputation accurate?

Academically, Vassar's reputation is sound. Socially, the younger generations have a better sense of what Vassar is all about. Our diverse student body enjoys a tolerant environment where students of any background or sexual orientation exist in harmony. Vassar is a place where intelligent, passionate, critical thinkers can lie in a field and play acoustic guitar and excel in the classroom with equal ease. (And 40 percent of those intelligent, critical thinkers are male.)

> "The students and administration are tight here."
>
> ✦ Peter, freshman

What would an admissions officer at your school probably not tell a prospective student? What aspect of your school would a prospective student not see on a campus tour?

A prospective probably wouldn't get a real sense of how much drugs and alcohol are a part of campus life at Vassar. That said, I've met quite a few people who have survived their four years here with nothing more foreign in their bodies than caffeine.

A prospective also might not notice that the bathrooms in our dorms are coed, and that you typically share every dorm bathroom with thirty other students. Most people at Vassar wind up living in dorms for three full years, so this is something you'll have to get used to.

The Institution

Let me be blunt—if you're looking for a bustling campus located in the heart of a big, entertaining city, you're going to be disappointed with Vassar. However, if you want a close-knit campus where professors know your name and you walk around as a senior feeling like you've really made an impact, then Vassar might be ideal.

Personally, I love it here. I love seeing my friends everywhere I turn. I love being able to walk to class in no time at all. I love going to the Mug (our campus dance club) and seeing people who never talk in class sweating it up and going crazy—

I wouldn't be experiencing any of this if Vassar was some big school in an anonymous city. Some find all this stifling after four years. I find it comforting.

And even the town of Poughkeepsie—most people say it's terrible, that the townies hate the students and vice versa, but this doesn't have to be the case. If you put even a little effort into interacting with the town, you'll find it pays off. Join Planned Parenthood. Sign up to tutor at a local school. Volunteer at a community farm. I worked at an off-campus job for three of my four years at Vassar, and it really made me feel like a part of the greater community. I would highly recommend this to anyone with the urge to venture past Vassar's gates.

The Education

Every student at Vassar has to take three required classes. Once those are out of the way, you are free to take any classes you want (not counting requirements for your major). This allows students to have a really fantastic and unusual amount of control over their education. Take only the classes that interest you. Add our fantastic professors to that mix, and you've got a winning combination.

Without a doubt the education Vassar offers is its biggest strength. As I said before, there are few requirements. In classes, professors are extremely respectful of students and by senior year classes feel more like a collaboration between colleagues than some sort of power struggle between a babysitter and children. I didn't think I'd actually wind up spending time in professors' homes, munching on homemade chilli, discussing psychological theory with leaders in the field. But at Vassar, this happens!

> "My favorite Vassar tradition is Serenading where freshman and seniors go down to Sunset Lake and the dorms have a sing off. It sounds kind of crazy, but it's one of the best days of the year."
>
> ✦ William, junior

I'm a psychology major, so I can talk most specifically to prospective students interested in the sciences. If you're looking to go into the sciences at Vassar, you should know that classes are both time-consuming and demanding. For better or worse, you'll often find yourself spending more than seven hours a week in a class/lab that will yield as many credits as a two-hour-and-fifteen-minute English course. As a chemistry, biology/biochemistry, or physics major, you'll find yourself pulling frequent all-nighters to finish lab reports and papers. On the plus side, the sciences have smaller than average departments at Vassar, and this tends to encourage a tight, collegial atmosphere. You'll get to work directly with fantastic intellects (both your fellow students and your professors). During the summers, many students stay to work with professors on various projects. It all works out in the end.

> "One of the biggest groups on campus is called The Barefoot Monkeys. They're a juggling and circus group, and you'll frequently see them juggling with fire and riding unicycles on campus."
>
> ✦ Gayle, sophomore

If you're interested in psychology at Vassar, don't let Intro Psych, which tends to be the least in-depth class, discourage you from experiencing the deeper 200 and 300 level courses! Great classes include Physiology of Behavior, Physiology Research Methods, and Comparative Psychology. For those interested in the social aspect of psychology, there's Social Psychology and Personality Theory. In the middle, you have Learning and Behavior, Developmental Psychology, Abnormal Psychology, and Statistics. In my experience, psychology professors were fairly lenient about allowing students from other majors to enroll in their classes, so I would always give it a shot if you see a class that piques you interest.

The Students

People have high intellectual standards at Vassar. But they also know when to close the books and play a game of Frisbee (or a computer game if it's cold outside). And, even though it's hard to believe, I've found Vassar to be much less stressful than my public high school. I think it stems from the fact that Vassar's student body is a highly confident group. Most know that they're smart, and therefore don't feel the need to constantly prove themselves, don't feel compelled to overachieve

on every single assignment. There's a general feeling of respect and ease on this campus.

I don't think there's really a typical student at Vassar; the only thing I can see that binds us together is intellectual curiosity and a wry, somewhat cynical sense of humor.

The Activities

I'm an athlete, so I spend a lot of my free time at Vassar playing sports. If you're an athlete, know that sports are not a very big deal on Vassar's campus. Play because you love the game, not because you want or need the attention of the entire student body. Practically speaking, if you're going to play sports at Vassar you'll have to travel to meets on other campuses, and this means you'll miss a few classes over the course of the year. It is extremely important that you inform your professors this will be the case as soon as possible, and give them exact dates—they will usually do their best to work with you. In my years on the soccer team I only heard a couple stories of professors who absolutely would not let their students miss class for a game/meet. Coaches understand, knowing that academics come first.

Again, Vassar students don't care much about sports on the whole, and this means you may play a great game but look up and see empty bleachers. Rumor has it the administration is attempting to change this; they've done a great job with the new athletic complex, and have been noticeably admitting more athletes each year. Over my four years, I've felt that the sports programs have become stronger and more recognized schoolwide, so this is a trend to keep an eye on if it's important to you.

Oh—there's a line of cute cafés and restaurants within walking distance of campus. They're worth checking out! And when the weather is nice, Poughkeepsie has some great nearby mountains. If you're into rock climbing, they're ideal.

The Social Scene

Most people at Vassar party in a low-key fashion, mostly in the dorms. If you want to party harder, Manhattan is only an hour and a half away. It's easy to get there and back, and a lot of students go once or twice a month.

Name: Aiden
Hometown: Creve Coeur, Missouri
Class Year: Senior
Major: French, with a minor in history

Extracurriculars: Queer Coalition, French Club, intramural sports

Career Goal: Travel writer, professor

How would you describe Vassar's reputation?

Different people would tell you different things about Vassar. Younger people see it as an academically challenging haven for trendy rich kids who are also frequently drug addicts and/or homosexuals. A member of an older generation would probably say it's a highly prestigious liberal arts college famous for accepting students from old money families and playing a part in creating the almost-mythical figure of the "Vassar girl." One thing both groups would say is that Vassar is very politically active.

Is this reputation accurate?

For the most part, the youngsters get it right. Vassar's moved on from its finishing school days, and now its educational punch is enjoyed by sizable communities of (smart) hipsters, homosexuals, and drug users. The political thing, though—Vassar students, when it comes down to it, are surprisingly apathetic. Or we're all so liberal that we leave it at that. We've scared all the conservatives away and have fallen into happy complacency, adopting an overarching live-and-let-live ethos that's rarely disturbed by rants or raves about any political issue.

What would an admissions officer at your school probably not tell a prospective student?

I doubt an admissions officer would talk about how insular the Vassar community can be, how your entire social life will revolve around hanging out in the same handful of dorm rooms.

> "The weather in Poughkeepsie sucks."
> ✦ Nancy, senior

The Institution

I love Vassar for all the same reasons that I hate Vassar. Vassar is a small school that offers a close-knit community that can be truly amazing and supportive. That said, it can also be kind of suffocating. Intense, close bonds form between students (and between students and professors) and before long you feel like you know everyone in the entire school. But, again, this makes it that much harder to escape and be anonymous when you're having a bad day. Vassar students are fun loving and cosmopolitan, and on breaks from school they'll travel the world with you and go to the most interesting places at the drop of a hat. But this also means that they're everywhere—for example, I went to Portugal on my own over spring break to clear my head, and, to my horror, there were five or six Vassar students on my plane. Vassar is a small school, but Vassar students hang out in the same places, domestically and internationally. Can you ever escape?

Coming to Vassar from small-town Missouri was also a big leap for me, particularly because I'm gay. Back in Missouri, it's incredibly hard to be openly homosexual. Whereas Vassar is probably the most open, accepting place I've ever been. This can cause problems, though—when I go home, after having been at Vassar for a few months, it's hard to settle down and fit in again. You forget that the whole world isn't liberal and tolerant, and that can really mess you up. Even now, as a rising junior, I still have problems going from Vassar to Missouri, or vice versa.

The Education

First and foremost, you come to Vassar to get a top-notch education. All of my classes have been pretty spectacular. With one exception, they've all been discussion-oriented and incredibly small (usually ten or fifteen students). In fact, even that one exception, the large course with more than a hundred students had a professor who made an effort to foster intense, rewarding class discussions. I know all my professors at Vassar; they know me. I babysit for my history professor (and I work for his wife as a research assistant), and it's not uncommon to get an e-mail from a prof who's just checking in one or two semesters after you've taken their class. I'm a French major with a minor in history, and I can't praise either department highly enough. The English courses I've taken have been equally amazing, and from what I hear the English department is ridiculously rigorous. At Vassar, I always feel like I'm getting a lot of academic bang for my buck.

The Students

Vassar students are also a reason to come here—they're a strange and (for the most part) wonderful bunch. They're all over the board, but most will be from the East Coast, possibly gay, liberal, and wearing something from Urban Outfitters. In general, Vassar students are friendly. Some are pretentious and rich, which can make a lower-middle-class kid from Indiana like me feel slightly out of place in certain situations (though I have to say most kids aren't flashy with their money. In fact, it's almost like they pay to grunge-down and look poor).

It is worth noting that something almost all Vassar kids talk about nonstop is sex. I mean, hell, we have *Squirm,* the student-created and run porno magazine, which Harvard totally stole from us, so in your eye, Harvard. Vassar did it first. (I apologize for that outburst.)

> "Vassar's property extends far beyond the areas with housing and academic buildings—there's an entire, expansive 'Vassar Farm' area which provides welcome respite for those who wish to take a quiet walk, run, or for those who derive scholastic pleasure from studying organic farming and soil content."
>
> ✦ Marissa, junior

The Activities

As far as clubs go, there are a ton of them, and everyone does something. From the Asian Students Alliance to the Barefoot Monkeys (a group that twirls fire and stuff), everyone does things that make them feel like they belong. Dorms often sponsor parties and events, and the Halloween Bash is the best dorm party—everyone goes, and everyone wears great costumes. Founder's Day is the granddaddy of campus activities, an all-day gathering on Sunset Hill with bands, games, and rides. Its finale is a projected movie and fireworks set off over the lake.

Right now I'm focused on Vassar's study abroad program because, as a French major, I'll be spending both semesters of my junior year at L'Institut d'Etudes Politiques de Paris, one of France's most well-regarded universities. It's because of Vassar's connections that I've been given such an incredible opportunity, and it speaks to Vassar's position on the world stage that L'Institute would let me attend for a year. Three cheers for the international reach of my alma mater. (This isn't to say everyone in the world knows Vassar—they don't—but through Vassar's International Studies department, you can study just about anywhere you'd like.)

The Social Scene

Because Vassar's so small, people spend a lot of time hanging out in dorm rooms. To make life more interesting, a lot of students drink and smoke pot, and I've seen a fair amount do harder drugs. Particularly on weekends. Really, I don't know what nonsubstance users at Vassar do for fun—on Saturdays, just about everyone drinks or smokes.

If it's their scene, some kids go "dancing" in the Mug (the popular on-campus club/bar). And the most awkward moment for many Vassar students is when the lights at the Mug come on at the end of the night, exposing intoxicated, sweaty kids who will grab someone (anyone) to hook up with, bring them home, then, the next morning, awkwardly attempt (and fail) to avoid all interaction with them while eating breakfast in the dining hall. At Vassar, people either frequently hook up or are practically married, and not much goes on in between. It's the same for gay kids, but I have to say that Vassar earns my highest praises for the fact that I can hold hands with my boyfriend at any time and kiss him in public without having to be afraid a broken bottle will be hurled in my direction. Vassar is incredibly, unbelievably gay friendly.

Notable Vassar Alumni Include:
Meryl Streep, Academy Award–winning actress
Lisa Kudrow, actress
Jacqueline Kennedy Onassis, former first lady
Jane Fonda, actress
Lloyd Braun, co-chair, ABC Entertainment Group
Geraldine Laybourne, president, Oxygen Media, Inc.

UNIVERSITY OF VIRGINIA

Founded: 1819

Location: Charlottesville, VA

Phone: (804) 982-3200

E-mail: undergrad-admission@virginia.edu

Web site: www.virginia.edu

Number of Undergraduates: 12,909

Number of Graduate Students: 7,617

Cost: Approximately $12,000 per year in state; $28,000 out of state

Application Deadline: January 2

Early Decision: November 1

Rating:	Notable Majors/Programs:
Very Selective	Politics, Premed, Economics, Psychology

Size:
○ Small   ○ Medium   ● Large

Location:
○ Urban   ● Suburban   ○ Rural

On a Saturday, students talk about academics:
○ Always   ● Sometimes   ○ Never

Nightlife:
● Intense   ○ Moderate   ○ Laid-back

Politically, UVA leans:
○ Left   ● Right   ○ Split

Diversity:
● High   ○ Low   ○ Medium

Students describe UVA in five words:
- Traditional, gentlemen, gentlewomen, sundresses, honor-code
- Preppy, historic, intelligent, friendly, mathletic

From the School

As a state institution, U. Va. serves the Commonwealth of Virginia. Yet it is national—indeed, international—in the scope of its student body, its faculty research, and its cultural, commercial, and political influence. U. Va. is known for its rich history and traditions, yet its students, alumni, and faculty are among the world's most inventive, creative, and original thinkers.

—www.virginia.edu

If you're interested in UVA, you may also be interested in:
Boston University, Duke, Georgetown, George Washington, UNC–Chapel Hill, William and Mary

Name: Mark
Hometown: Warrenton, Virginia
Class Year: Junior
Major: Psychology
Extracurriculars: Fiji Fraternity and the Car Club
Career Goal: I own a small business right now. When I graduate, I'd like to expand it, perhaps nationwide.

How would you describe the UVA's reputation?

The University of Virginia has been repeatedly ranked the number one public university in America. We have the reputation of being preppy, snobby, and "frat-tastic." We're thought of as a Southern school with tradition.

Is this reputation accurate?

UVA is ranked as the best public university for a good reason, this is a fantastic place. Everything else is accurate only for about 10 percent of the student body. In general, I am in awe of all the students around me at the University of Virginia. They are the brightest, kindest, most friendly people I have ever met. Almost everyone is tolerant of individual differences and is usually eager to learn more about someone else's religious practices, ethnicity, or other characteristics. That said, we do have our fair share of southern princesses and frat dogs.

What would an admissions officer at your school probably not tell a prospective student? What aspect of your school would a prospective student not see on a campus tour?

UVA's administration will go on and on about our superb academics, long roster of traditions, and fantastic athletics. But they won't tell a prospective student just how much fun everyone has here. For a bunch of smart kids, UVA folks know how to throw a party. And an admissions officer certainly won't talk about Rugby Road, home of the Greek life on campus and *the* party place for those who like more than a little bit of vodka with their tonic water. Rugby Road is the greatest. If you come to UVA, you and Rugby Road will have many a good night with one another.

The Institution

UVA is a big school. Come here, and you'll be surrounded by twelve thousand of America's best and brightest minds. You will also be surrounded by twelve thousand unbearably good-looking people. Really, the only thing on earth that could interrupt my male classmates' heated discussions of Jacques Lacan is an incredibly good-looking female UVA student. And there are *plenty* of them. But every hot girl has a lot going on upstairs.

UVA's Honor Code is really important to both students and administrators. When you accept a place at UVA, the administration sends you a corny video in the mail that explains the Honor Code, and tries to depict the ways the Honor Code influences everyone's life here on a day-to-day basis. You'll watch the video, you'll roll your eyes, then you'll come here and be incredulous because everything that's in the video is actually *true*. The Honor Code is alive and well at UVA. Students are always leaving expensive laptops, iPods, book bags—the things they would normally chain to their wrists—unchained, in open air, in the middle of the library. The owner of these objects will then go downstairs to the bathroom, run into their friends, chat, slowly make their way back upstairs. And everything will still be there when they return. Honestly. At UVA, you can trust everyone around you to respect your belongings.

So, if you come to UVA, respect the Honor Code, be prepared to be surrounded by gorgeous people, and—last thing—get used to abbreviating everything and using strange UVA terminology. For example, during my first year I lived in Tuttle House across the street from the AFC and next to O-Hill. Now I live off-grounds on JPA and can catch UTS to MEM if I feel like lifting. Don't worry, when you get here you'll figure it out soon enough.

The Education

UVA is the biggest small school out there. Yes, there are twelve thousand students, but every single professor makes an effort for us to feel like we go to a small liberal arts college. For example, once, in a class with three hundred students, my professor invited *every single student* to a barbecue at his house. When Thanksgiving rolls around, most professors will invite students to their houses to share in the festivities. Most professors live on or very close to campus, and consider this place to be their home. They do everything they can to make us feel like it's our home, too.

Because it's such a big school, UVA has lots of departments, and it offers classes in just about anything you'd want to learn. I don't think there's a single weak department here, so you can feel safe and secure taking just about any class, in any discipline. And there are lots of famous professors here as well. I once had class in the middle of the afternoon, and then saw my professor on the national news that night. Incredible. And the stu-

> "The University of Virginia is known as Mr. Jefferson's University. It is a campus of beautiful colonial-style brick buildings accentuated by white columns and colonnades, snuggled into the Virginia countryside. The Blue Ridge Mountains traverse our skyline and make for extraordinary sunsets."
>
> ✦ Kenneth, junior

dents, let's face it, we're dorks. Cool ones, yes, but really . . .

The Students

The greatest lesson I've learned at UVA is to never judge someone based on the way they look or the crowd they hang out with. Freshman year I lived in the same dorm as Jason Clarke, a 6'8" strong forward on our varsity basketball team. I expected this guy to be totally aloof—instead he was friendly, goofy, a fantastic guy. I've met many gorgeous blondes who look lighter than air in the intellect department, and then they speak, and you find they're fluent in four languages and translate Old English texts for fun. Here every "nerd" is cool and every football player has brains. Really, every single student here has something that makes him or her special. You feel blessed and humbled every day to be surrounded by such amazing people.

The Activities

Sports are huge at UVA. Football games in particular bring everyone out of their dorms and to the stadiums, dressed in their Sunday best. There was a great quote from a DC radio station about UVA and its football games—he said he came to see the game, but was awestruck by the students in the bleachers. In short, he said he'd never seen so many dorks in ties surrounded by so many beautiful girls in his life. That's just how it is here.

Students at UVA also seem to like combining running and philanthropy. Fiji Fraternity's "Run across Virginia" raised over $36,000 last year for the Jimmy V Foundation. One sorority's annual run consistently raises $15,000 to fight breast cancer. I guess combining running and philanthropy makes sense here, because everyone is always exercising and running anyway. It's kind of like harnessing hydroelectric energy. The water's already running, so you might as well put a wheel in front of it and profit from the whole endeavour.

The Social Scene

If I'm awake at 3:00 a.m. on a Wednesday night, I won't be bored, there's still plenty of stuff to do! Someone else in my dorm is definitely awake, and likely hungry—I can get them to go to a twenty-four-hour restaurant with me. Or I can head to the library, which is still open, and I can offer much-needed distractions to my more hardcore student friends who probably need a break from their textbooks and caffeinated beverages.

On weekends, UVA students party. Here's a statistic—one third of UVA students are in either a sorority or fraternity. That's a lot of kids in a lot of sororities and fraternities. Because of this, there are tons of parties every weekend at UVA. Some parties are small, some are large. All have alcohol there, if that's your thing.

Last thing—it's really easy to make friends at UVA. Everyone here is friendly, and people seem to just get friendlier as the sun goes down and the beer cans go up. Regardless of the time of day, though, you can always expect a smile and a "hello" from strangers. Everyone here always seems ready to meet new people. This is kind of rough sometimes, because, for example, if you ever plan on studying in one of our many libraries, you have to plan on spending half your time hanging out with friends and potential friends. The other half of the time, *maybe* you'll study. It's just hard to get work done when you're surrounded by such great people!

Name: Georgia
Hometown: Hampton, Virginia
Class Year: Junior
Major: Biology
Extracurriculars: Biology Department representative, layout editor for *Vital Signs* (UVA's only premedical newsletter), program director for Medical Services (UVA ER Chest Pain Center),

volunteer, Charlottesville Free Clinic, Adopt-a-Grandparent

Career Goal: Doctor

How would you describe the UVA's reputation?

UVA is known as one of the best public schools in the United States.

Is this reputation accurate?

Yes, but it doesn't tell the whole story. You hear "best public school in the U.S.," and you think of socially stunted students wasting away until 5:00 a.m. in the library, every night of the week. That's not the case at UVA! We work hard, then we play hard. Most students party as hard as they study here!

What would an admissions officer at your school probably not tell a prospective student? What aspect of your school would a prospective student not see on a campus tour?

Well, here are some annoying things about UVA that a prospective student might miss on a campus tour:

- UVA is big, and buses take students all over campus. But there aren't enough buses, and the ones that are around are always full. You'll get fed up waiting for a bus and decide to walk home way more than is reasonable. And your university housing may be a twenty-minute walk from where you are! In the rain or snow, not fun.
- A lot of the science classes are huge—two to three hundred people. If you are premed or a science major, you will probably spend your first two years in huge classes where the professors will not know your name unless you take some serious initiative.
- The advising system is not very helpful at all. At the start of your first year, you are assigned to a random adviser who usually does not know anything about your major. You'll have to fend for yourself—this random adviser is not going to do much for you.
- There always seems to be construction projects going on here. Get used to seeing work crews and hearing jackhammers.
- And finally, if you bring a car, parking is a pain. If you want to park your car, you either have to buy an expensive parking spot (which is never guaranteed after 5:00 p.m.)

or you have to go to the parking garage, which is far away and expensive as well.

Is there anything about the UVA that's particularly unique?

UVA sponsors class trips, and department trips, all over the world! I went on a trip with the biology department to San Salvador. It was a great experience, and I basically got to spend three weeks on beautiful beaches with a lot of fun people. And we learned things too. Yeah. Sure we did.

The Institution

Right now I love UVA. There have definitely been times when I haven't, though. I've spent many late nights in Clemons Library cramming for difficult exams. I've been in too many big classes where my professor had no idea who I was, and no inclination to find out. But those experiences just taught me to work harder and to be more independent. Now, I study for exams far in advance of the exams themselves. When I'm in a giant class, I make it a point to stop by my professor's office hours, introduce myself, and make sure, by the end of the semester, that they know me by name.

The size of UVA impacts your social experiences, too. I'm constantly walking through a sea of people whom I don't recognize. That said, it's rare that I don't see someone I know after a minute or two. I think that's common, that the sea of anonymous students is almost always punctured by a friendly face.

All in all, most students love their time at UVA, and everyone has a lot of school spirit. All you need to do is come to one football game and you'll see just how much we appreciate our alma mater. Really, everyone gets dressed up, and when the team scores everyone wraps their arms around one another and belts out "The Good Old Song" at the top of their lungs. It's definitely a unique experience!

The Education

I have to admit, I have definitely talked about classes on a Saturday night, and I've even been in the library some Saturday nights. The premed program here is really competitive, and I always have to keep up with my work. Most of my classes are lecture-based. I've never had a science discussion. Also, as a science major, I have to take a lot of labs, which are incredibly time-consuming. For example, my organic chemistry lab lasts four hours every week! I've had a lot of non-English speaking TAs in my science labs, which has been frustrating, because my work sounds practically like a foreign language even when it is spoken in English. No one wants to be in lab for four hours anyway, and it's ten times more miserable when you can't understand a single word the TA is saying. On the plus side, there are lots of research opportunities here, you can even do research for credit. And the close proximity of the UVA Medical School and Hospital definitely adds to the research opportunities.

One last negative—the premed requirements are pretty intense here, and, at UVA, every student is subjected to our large and rigorous core curriculum. When you combine the two, premed students don't wind up with time to take many electives. So, if you're looking to be premed here, resign yourself to the fact that you'll have very little choice in deciding which classes you'll be taking all four years.

> "I know it sounds sort of weird, but kids dress up for football games here. It's tradition and it's fun. We haul out our shirts, ties, blazers, sundresses, and heels, join hands, and sing the 'Good Old Song.' I promise, everyone who does this can't stop smiling."
> ✦ Erica, junior

The Students

Unfortunately, there isn't much diversity amongst the students at UVA. Most students are white, from upper-middle-class families, and from Virginia (specifically northern Virginia)—unless they're from New Jersey. For some reason, if someone *is* from out-of-state, you can be pretty sure they're going to say they're from New Jersey.

The Activities

UVA students love our athletic teams. Almost everyone goes to the football or basketball games (when we're doing well!). Community service is also really popular, and it's one of the things I really respect about UVA. Even though the students here are so busy, it's hard to find someone who doesn't give at least a little of their time to help out. Madison House is the volunteer center here, and they make it incredibly easy for students to sign up and get involved. Madison House personally set me up working at the Charlottesville Free Clinic, which has helped keep me grounded, and made me realize just how much I'd like to become a doctor.

The Social Scene

Because I'm premed, my classes tend to have the same people in them from year to year. So I've gotten to know my classmates really well. I've also stayed in close touch with my freshman year hallmates—halls are really social at UVA, and the friends you make from living with people tend to last. Really, I'm a UVA-housing pro at this point. I've lived on the grounds for three years now—the first year I was in a dorm and the last two I have been in university apartments—and I am happy to announce that I will be moving off-grounds next year to a real person-style house. Hey, it's a slow transition to the real world! UVA actually makes it pretty easy to find housing off campus if that's the route you want to take, though, so you never have to worry about being homeless, unless that's your thing, then by all means run with it.

I'm not big on the campus party scene, and when I want to get away from my studies I tend to go into Charlottesville with my friends. Really, Charlottesville is a great, diverse place, and I love it. Too many students get overinvolved with UVA, which is easy to do, there's always something going on, but it's sad that they get involved to the extent that they graduate having never experienced the things Charlottesville has to offer. There are a lot of Spanish-speaking people in Charlottesville, which is great if you're looking for a practical application of what you've learned in your Spanish language classes (if you happen to be taking those, that is).

One more thing, if you like to hike or mountain climb, then UVA is the place for you—we're right in the Blue Ridge. Excellent. Lots of students spend weekends out in the mountains being athletic together.

Name: Alice
Hometown: North Glenn, Colorado
Class Year: Junior
Major: Politics and French
Extracurriculars: Jefferson Literary and Debating

Society, 4th year Trustees' Project, Internship at Virginia Women's Health Center
Career Goal: International human rights law

How would you describe UVA's reputation?

UVA is said to be full of smart conservative people who like to have fun.

Is this reputation accurate?

Yes, to the T.

What would an admissions officer at your school probably not tell a prospective student? What aspect of your school would a prospective student not see on a campus tour?

An administrator at UVA wouldn't tell a prospective student how overcrowded classes here can get. They also wouldn't mention how hard it can be to get into popular courses with star professors—most students don't get into one of these until at least their junior year.

Is there anything about UVA that's particularly unique?

> "UVA isn't Berkeley, but for central Virginia we're really open-minded!"
> ✦ Warren, freshman

If you are not from the South, your first two months at UVA might be unbearable. Seriously, I'm from Colorado, and for those initial sixty days I thought I was drowning 24/7 from the humidity. I couldn't wear makeup for quite a while here, I would just sweat it right off. Now that I've been here for three years, I have a proper southern "glow"— but I'll never forget those first two months, thinking that I'd moved to a swamp.

The Institution

UVA's campus is really beautiful. Everywhere you go you're surrounded by marble columns and red brick. It really makes this place feel stately. Football games continue with that feel—you wouldn't imagine that, I know, you think football games and you immediately picture rowdy students shouting and screaming. But at UVA, football games are social dress-up events. Girls wear dresses. Guys wear a suit and tie. And yeah, maybe they still get rowdy

and scream, but even as they shout they still look like they're full of southern charm.

The Education

UVA is the perfect combination of the academic and social powerhouse. On the academic end, professors here are always open to talk to students and to spend time with them during their office hours. Classes are large, but professors really do strive to give every student personal attention, and if you want to get to know a professor really well, they're usually open to having an individual relationship with you. If you really enjoy an undergraduate-level course a professor is teaching and you want to be part of their graduate-level course as well, they'll usually say okay.

UVA has a very large core. Outside these requirements, I've taken a lot of classes in the politics department, and I can honestly say our politics program is second to none. Really, it's one of the best politics programs in America, and our teachers are first-rate. Which all makes sense. After all, this *is* a school founded by Thomas Jefferson, and we count former President Woodrow Wilson and Senators Robert and Edward Kennedy among our alumni. (Edgar Allen Poe and Katie Couric went here, too!) Politics and UVA go hand in hand.

Also, a lot of students at UVA complete individual research including a senior thesis at the end of their four years. If you're looking to do research most professors will gladly let you assist them with any project they're working on.

The Students

UVA students can be divided into two groups: Greek, and non-Greek. Take your pick which you want to be! Your social life will vary accordingly.

I'd say most UVA students are conservative, most are Republicans. The occasional Democrat (like me!) rears their head every now and again, and the Cavaliers for Kerry was a pretty prominent organization this past fall. But, for the most part, the Republicans have the upper-hand 'round here.

The Activities

Thomas Jefferson's original vision for a university was one in which community service was key—a place where students recognized and appreciated the notion of giving back to those less fortunate. In keeping with this vision, students at UVA do all they can to help others. During the first week of school, UVA puts on an activities fair, and among the most popular student groups to sign up for are those that do community service.

There are also other, less altruistic clubs, dedicated to everything under the sun, from the Disciples of Bob Barker club to the Virginia Dance Company. And it's easy to become a member of a club, all you have to do is put your name down on the e-mail list and you're in.

Other than clubs and activities, there are amazing speakers every week at the Miller Center for Public Affairs and Philanthropies. If a political/artistic/entertainment figure of any merit comes to the nearby area, you can be sure they'll stop off at UVA and give a speech. We also have a cappella performances, plays, and dance shows going on almost every single weekend.

The Social Scene

UVA has a pretty busy social scene. Freshman year, most students stick to the frats, which always party hard. This is an appealing option for freshman, because—unlike in the bars—there won't be any bouncers between eighteen-year-olds and a few cups of warm beer. Once students are sophomores, juniors, and seniors, they tend to keep on with the frats, plus do some pretty impressive bar-hopping on and around campus, plus they go to Greek formals and other social events that you're only really invited to once you've begun to meet lots of people and become ingrained in the UVA scene.

Notable U. Virginia Alumni Include:
Edgar Allen Poe, author
Katie Couric, host, NBC's *Today*
Tina Fey, head writer, *Saturday Night Live*
Valerie B. Ackerman, president/founder, WNBA
Timothy A. Koogle, former CEO, Yahoo! Inc.

WABASH COLLEGE

Founded: 1832
Location: Crawfordsville, IN
Phone: (765) 361-6100
E-mail: admissions@wabash.edu
Web site: www.wabash.edu

Number of Undergraduates: 860
Number of Graduate Students: 0
Cost: Approximately $29,500 per year
Application Deadline: Rolling
Early Decision: November 15
Early Action: December 15

Rating:	Notable Majors/Programs:
Selective	Premed, Business, Social Sciences

Size:
● Small ○ Medium ○ Large

Location:
○ Urban ● Suburban ○ Rural

On a Saturday, students talk about academics:
○ Always ● Sometimes ○ Never

Nightlife:
○ Intense ● Moderate ○ Laid-back

Politically, Wabash leans:
○ Left ● Right ○ Split

Diversity:
○ High ● Low ○ Medium

All men's: Yes!

Students describe Wabash in five words:
- Tradition, integrity, Wabash always fights!
- Respect, trust, passion, unity, discipline

From the School

We believe that the public school's goals include the education of young people by providing them with a broad general education, one which helps each student to develop the intellectual, social, and moral tools to live happy and productive lives within this society. Specifically, schools strive to educate lifelong learners, those who can solve a range of life's problems by thinking reasonably, critically, and creatively about issues and events, both personal and abstract. Finally, we are aware that today's public schools attempt to address with sensitivity the holistic needs of the students as developing human beings who, increasingly, come from more diverse backgrounds and social contexts.

—www.wabash.edu

If you're interested in Wabash, you may also be interested in:
Davidson, Emory, Macalester, Morehouse, Northwestern, Washington & Lee

Name: Alex
Hometown: Indianapolis, Indiana
Class Year: Sophomore
Major: History
Extracurriculars: member of the football team, president/captain of Wabash Lacrosse Club, member of Phi Gamma Delta
Career Goal: I am not as sure about what I want to do with myself after I leave here anymore, but I do know that whatever I do, I will be very well prepared for it

How would you describe Wabash's reputation?

Being an all-male school, there are many reputations we're given. We are first and foremost one of the most academically challenging schools in the state, if not the country. Wabash teaches you how to be not only a man, but a gentleman, by learning how to think critically and take responsibility for your own actions. We are also known as a party school, because we work hard during the week and party hard during the weekends. Correspondingly, girls come to Wabash because they know that they will be treated right when they are here. There has also been a rumor that we bus the girls in on the weekends for parties.

Is this reputation accurate?

Yes, except that we do not actually bus girls in—they come on their own.

"While the idea of a single-sex education may seem old-fashioned and scary for many, it frees students from the distractions of women and creates a truly unique place to learn."

✦ James, sophomore

What aspect of Wabash would a prospective student not see on a campus tour?

One thing that a prospective student might not see on a tour would be the fraternity life at Wabash. Being all-male, the fraternity system is an important part of the lives of many Wabash men.

The Institution

Crawfordsville is a small town, kind of out in a cornfield. The campus is fairly small; I can wake up about fifteen minutes before class starts, get dressed, eat breakfast, and still make it to my farthest class on time. The school facilities are all brick, reminiscent of New England architecture, arranged around the mall, with the focal point of campus being the chapel.

Tradition and spirit at Wabash are very important. The most important part of homecoming week is the Chapel Sing on the steps of our chapel, which is the focal point of campus. Each pledge class links arms to show their pledge class unity (though some independents participate, too) and yells the school fight song for forty-five minutes. This activity has been the most important and meaningful thing that I have done at Wabash (which includes an undefeated football season with a trip to the quarterfinals of the national championship tournament for Division III football). Chapel Sing is such a moving experience that it cannot fully be explained in words—you need to experience it to understand. The raw power and emotion that you feel as you are yelling with your pledge brothers is something I will remember for the rest of my life. Chapel Sing bonds the pledge classes together, and is a visual symbol of not only the pledge class's unity, but also their school spirit and loyalty. Surprisingly, you only get through the song a few times, because we have to have one of the world's longest fight songs.

Another important tradition that every Wabash man, both past and present, takes a great interest in, is the Monon Bell Football game between Wabash and DePauw. The game is played for the Monon Bell, which is a three-hundred-pound brass railroad bell. It is one of the oldest rivalries in the country, and I am happy to say that I was a part of the Wabash football team that gave Wabash the overall edge: Wabash leads the series 51-50-9. The whole week leading up to the Bell game is very exciting. The school that has the Bell has to protect it, because in the past there were several times when the Bell was removed from the DePauw campus in the middle of the night, and brought back to its true home, Wabash. Freshman pledges stay up all night to guard the Bell—each fraternity house has a different night, and some professors and alumni walk around and talk to the students on guard.

It's amazing that not only the students and staff support every aspect of Wabash, but the alumni can only be described with one word: crazy. No matter where I am, if I run into an alumnus and he realizes that I am from Wabash, he'll instantly ask what house I'm in, and he'll usually talk about the success of our football team, especially in the Monon Bell game. The support for athletics is amazing, from the students, faculty, and administration; everyone comes out to support Wabash athletics.

The Education

Academically, Wabash is second to none. The classes at Wabash are hard. At Wabash, you will learn to read, write, and think critically. Students write many, many papers at Wabash. Naturally, Wabash students have loads of work to do during the week, but there are no weekend classes, so we work hard, but play hard as well. Did I mention that we write a lot of papers at Wabash? It should be mentioned again: if you learn nothing else at Wabash, you will be able to express yourself and your thoughts in writing much more concisely then you ever thought possible.

At Wabash, the focus is on the student. Each class is taught by professors; there are no TAs at Wabash. The professors genuinely care about your progress in their course, and will stop in the hall to talk with you and bend over backward to help you out. Most of the professors have open-door policies, and I have personal relationships with each professor that I have had at Wabash.

Another thing that is unique about Wabash is a class that every Wabash man must take and pass in during his sophomore year, Cultures and Traditions. C&T, as it is known, is one thing that all graduating classes have in common, and many of the materials that are discussed are the same: classic styles of writing and thinking are read, and then discussed during the next class period. This class teaches all Wabash men not only to be able to form an opinion, but to be able to defend it against opposing opinions from the professor and other students.

The Students

Wabash students are intensely competitive when it comes to sports, and any kind of competition really, even in the classroom.

The Activities

Students at Wabash are extremely involved in extracurricular activities. It's not hard, with about 70 percent of the population being members of a fraternity, and the fraternities being very active on campus. The majority of clubs and activities on campus are completely student run. There is a Student Senate that allocates funds to student clubs. The Senate is completely student run, with no faculty involvement. Most students are active in multiple clubs and sports—not to mention the intense rivalry between the living units for the intramural sports championship. The school closest to Wabash is DePauw, and they have been our archrival in every possible aspect for over a hundred years.

The Social Scene

The weekends at Wabash are for the student to unwind from his hard academic week. On Saturday nights, there is almost always at least one party at a fraternity. The catch is that usually you need to be in a fraternity to get into the party. The fraternities generally have good relationships with each other, other than the occasional good-natured rivalry. But there is a split between independents and the fraternities; the majority of the parties on campus and all of the big parties on campus are thrown by the fraternities, and it's difficult for an independent to get in, unless they are good friends with someone in the specific fraternity.

Obviously, it is a little difficult to meet girls at Wabash, yet we still manage to do well for ourselves. The main reason for leaving campus is to go where there are girls, but if there are big parties, the girls will come here, and we do not need to leave campus. The big parties coincide with the football schedule, with the biggest parties being on the biggest football game weekends.

I know just about everyone on campus because of the size of the school, and because of my involvement on the football team and as a member of my fraternity. As a whole, the Wabash campus is a friendly place, guys will say "hi" to each other on the way to class, and you will always see someone that you know, wherever you are going.

Name: Patrick
Hometown: Springfield, Illinois
Class Year: Freshman
Majors: Biology/art double
Extracurriculars: Alpha Phi Omega, WNDY radio station DJ, Biology Society, volunteer at Southern Illinois University School of Medicine
Career Goal: I plan to become a doctor—though at the moment I am leaning in the direction of a medical degree, I may seek a Ph.D. and do research. This school is the best place to prepare

me for medical and graduate education, and to become a successful scientist.

> "You will have a great time here if you are white, middle class, heterosexual, and Christian. I do not fit into these categories. Unsurprisingly, I am having a, er, difficult time."
>
> ✦ Tom, senior

How would you describe Wabash's reputation?

Wabash is a place that can be defined by the Gentleman's Rule. The Gentleman's Rule states that "A Wabash Man is to conduct himself at all times, both on and off campus, as a gentleman and responsible citizen." This is the single rule that has governed Wabash men since Wabash was founded in 1832. Another aspect of Wabash that caused me to be drawn instantaneously was the camaraderie. People here look out for one another, and the bond between students is something that is stronger than any other school.

Is this reputation accurate?

The Gentleman's Rule has held strong, encouraging a student to be at his best at all times. Students are allowed to learn from their own mistakes instead of being tirelessly reprimanded for them. The dedication among the students to one another is something so remarkable that upon visiting other campuses, I was surprised to *not* see the same level of fellowship among students.

What would an admissions officer at Wabash probably not tell a prospective student?

An admissions officer at Wabash would not tell a prospective student what type of living unit he should reside in while he stays at Wabash. It is left up to the student to visit all of the five residence halls and ten fraternities, and decide for himself where he fits.

The Institution

At Wabash there's no "bar code effect." What I mean by the bar code effect is that upon admission to a large public school, students are easily lost in the woodwork. At Wabash, every administrator and professor you will have will know your name, which makes you a person, not a set of features assigned to some identification number.

The Education

The opportunities for Wabash students to perform research are endless. Every summer and every academic session there are many research projects going on, especially in the science departments. All departments here are very strong, and require a level of thought and conceptualization unattainable at a state school.

The internship opportunities available to Wabash students are amazing. One can find an internship through the college that ranges from giving historical art tours in New York, as one friend of mine is doing, to purification of reverse transcriptase right down the road. Summer internships with the school are also widely available, and give students the opportunity to excel in their fields of study. Wabash has about 90 percent acceptance rate for dentistry, medical, veterinary, and other graduate schools.

Lastly, the Gentleman's Rule is something that the words Honor Code cannot possibly describe— the Gentleman's Rule goes much deeper than that; but before you think that Wabash is a school full of pompous men required to wear suits to class and speak with the utmost formality to professors, think again. Wabash men are taught here to think critically, act responsibly, lead effectively, and live humanely. These are the very words that have been in the mission statement of Wabash for over 170 years.

> "Some campuses are dry. Some are wet. Wabash is saturated. That said, no one in *my* house has ever been forced to drink."
>
> ✦ Andrew, junior

The Students

Wabash has students from all over the world and United States. Most Wabash students plan to attend graduate or professional school. Because of the remarkable camaraderie among students at this small and private school, there is rarely much separation of social groups. If people are isolated from others, it is because they choose to be. The majority of my friends share no common grounds—I know people in fraternities and I know independents—besides the fact that we come together as Wabash men.

The Activities

With DePauw, Ball State, and Indiana universities nearby, as well as schools in and around Indianapolis, intercollegiate interaction is very much a part of Wabash social life—not just socially, but across organizations, too. The organizations here have events in cooperation with other schools, pool resources, and contribute to their respective purposes. I am a member of shOUT, the LGBT organization, or gay-straight alliance at Wabash. The organization is very active in promoting awareness of LGBT issues and has sponsored such speakers as Dr. Patrick Dilley from Southern Illinois University and writer and poet Mark Doty. Wabash has sponsored several other influential speakers and musicians here on campus, including SIU's Dr. Patrick Dilley, conservative writer Ann Coulter, the Eroica Trio, and Mexican folk singer Lila Downs to name a few. There are organizations at Wabash that cover every aspect of the spectrum, and if there is no organization for your particular interest, funds may be appropriated for the formation of your proposed organization. Things are very flexible here; the school works with students to create an ideal learning and living environment.

Sugar Creek is great for canoeing and nature hikes. The great thing about Crawfordsville is that it is not a huge city, and for this reason there are not malls in which one can waste away his mind, but for those who enjoy the phenomenon known as shopping, Lafayette (and Purdue University) are about a forty-minute trip away.

The Social Scene

It often seems to outsiders that meeting members of the opposite sex would be an issue here. However, because of our campus involvement with other campuses in the area, meeting people is not as difficult as you'd assume.

Most students choose to live on campus, in order to decrease the already minute amount of time needed to make it to class (it takes less than fifteen minutes to traverse the campus). As far as saying "hi" to strangers goes, there are very few people I do not know, or am not at least familiar with while walking across campus.

Name: Mike
Hometown: Ardmore, Indiana
Class Year: Junior
Major: Speech
Extracurriculars: Football, Lambda Chi Alpha Fraternity, Sphinx Club (Community Service/ Campus Unity Club)
Career Goal: Football coach

How would you describe Wabash's reputation?

A small, close knit, all-male school with rigorous academics, and students filled with school pride.

Is this reputation accurate?

Yes. Nearly every single student would agree with how Wabash is portrayed. The school is small enough that we all know each other, and nearly everyone here loves the school and the people running it.

What aspect of Wabash would a prospective student not see on a campus tour?

They wouldn't show you a fraternity on Sunday mornings at 8:00 a.m. The aftermath of a party is not something to be seen by the faint-hearted, especially parents.

The Institution

The reason I choose my school is the same reason I am writing this, and the same reason I write as much as I can every chance I get: I love this school. It is a school deep in traditions and school spirit, and every student gets into it. As stated, the school only has 850 students, but the Monon Bell game draws up to ten thousand fans. Alumni come back, family travel great distances, and most importantly, *every single* Wabash student attends the game.

Being one of only two all-male schools with no sister school associated, makes us unique, but our Gentleman's Rule makes us amazing. Also amazing is our alumni support (we have a $350 million endowment fund for 850 students) and the close student relationship with professors.

The Education

I figured out how lucky I was to gain acceptance to Wabash when I moved into my fraternity on the last day before classes. I was sitting around talking to my soon-to-be pledge brothers about why we chose the school, and where we also got accepted. One student was an Eli Lilly scholar, meaning he could go anywhere in Indiana for free. Another student chose Wabash over DePauw because they offered him twice as much financial aid (he had a plus 1500 on his SATs). Finally, a kid from California described how he picked Wabash over Columbia, even though he had a full-ride scholarship. I looked around and thought, wow, how did I get in here? Each day I'm here, I understand why top high school students attend: small classes, usually ten to fifteen students, no TAs, only professors with doctorates, friends going on to graduate school at an unusually high rate. However, it does not come easily: students never, never stop studying.

> "One of the most incredible things about the Wabash experience is the opportunities for international exploration. The school sponsors several spring break immersion trips to different countries—housing and transportation fully paid for."
> ✦ Dunmomi, freshman

The Activities

Wabash has forty-two intramural sports and 850 students. Everyone gets involved. We have 110 members on the varsity football team, so that's over an eighth of the campus. Upon arrival on the campus, every freshman completes a community service project, which is integral to the mind-set here: A Wabash man supports the community at every opportunity. Because of the Gentleman's Rule, the students, not administration, take the active role in governing the student body. Our school newspaper is read by everyone, and always sparks interest—and at least once a year, it will spark a debate that the entire school engages in.

Wabash is refreshingly unique when it comes to Greek life. While most college administrations are pushing to remove fraternities from campus because they are causing nothing but bad publicity, Wabash moves in the other direction. Seventy percent of students live in fraternities. Most move in as soon as school begins freshman year. They are not like those described in *Animal House* or *Old School*; instead, they're an environment that fosters aca-demic growth and support. Students in these houses can always turn to an upperclassmen in their major to help them with work. Independents are not that different; although they are the minority, they also help each other whenever they can.

The Social Scene

Since nearly everyone is involved in something outside of the classroom, the whole campus seems to operate as one close-knit family. The men I play football with are the same I go to class with, and do other activities with. By the end of four years, you feel like you know just about everyone on campus.

Social life at an all-male school would seem to be pretty dull, unless they knew someone from Wabash. The rules are simple: Sunday through Thursday, the Wabash man will study. Friday and Saturday are times to release the tension of rigorous academic life. These are the times to party, which we do with a fervor that I'd like to think can compete with any school in the country. Greek or independent, black or white, Democrat or Republican, all Wabash students can tell you about a great party they've been to. Fraternities seem to hold the biggest bashes: live music, a DJ, and contrary to popular belief, lots and lots of girls. I tell prospective students this: "If you were a girl at a school where parties were always busted, and guys were all jerks, then you found out there is an all-male school close by, where you are treated like a queen, what would you do?" Simple: go to Wabash, party like a rock star, and be surrounded by gentlemen.

Notable Wabash Alumni Include:

Dan Simmons, author

Fred Wilson, president and CEO of Saks Fifth Avenue

John Bachmann, managing principle, Edward Jones

Kevin Clifford, CEO of American Funds, Inc.

Robert Allen, CEO of AT&T

One-eighth of Wabash alumni are presidents, CEOs, or chairmen

WAKE FOREST UNIVERSITY

Founded: 1834

Location: Winston-Salem, NC

Phone: (336) 758-5201

E-mail: admissions@wfu.edu

Web site: www.wfu.edu

Number of Undergraduates: 4,045

Number of Graduate Students: 1,396

Cost: Approximately $34,000 per year

Application Deadline: January 15

Early Decision: November 15

Rating:	Notable Majors/Programs:
Very Selective	Business, Psychology, Biology

Size:
- Small ● Medium ○ Large

Location:
- Urban ● Suburban ○ Rural

On a Saturday, students talk about academics:
- Always ● Sometimes ○ Never

Nightlife:
- ● Intense ○ Moderate ○ Laid-back

Politically, Wake Forest leans:
- Left ● Right ○ Split

Diversity:
- High ● Low ○ Medium

Students describe WFU in five words:
- Preppy, southern, affluent, athletic, spirited
- Small, competitive, driven, very difficult

From the School

Wake Forest is, without apology, a university shaped by faith and reason. The values that grew from our religious affiliation and from our founding in a small Southern town have given us a community that seeks more than just the creation of knowledge. Our motto, *Pro Humanitate*, embraces the values of service to others, compassion and attention to the individual, as well as excellence in intellectual pursuits.

—www.wfu.edu

If you're interested in WFU, you may also be interested in:
Davidson, Duke, Furman, UNC at Chapel Hill, Vanderbilt, U. Virginia

Name: Thomas
Hometown: Brooklyn, New York
Class Year: Senior
Major: History major/religion minor
Extracurriculars: Athletic equipment manager, resident adviser, guest contributor to our college newspaper
Career Goal: I'd like to become president of the United States.

How would you describe Wake Forest's reputation?

Wake Forest is a small university with an outstanding academic reputation.

Is this reputation accurate?

Wake Forest is a small college on a pristine campus. It was originally created to be a close, tight-knit community of scholars, dedicated to advancing their minds for the good of all humanity. (Our motto: *Pro Humanitate*.) Integral to Wake's mission were small, intimate classes where the leaders of tomorrow could study under the tutelage of the brightest academic minds of today. And, nowadays, we have the brightest academic minds of today in spades. Put simply, the professors at Wake are world class. And yes, on top of all of this, Wake has a big time athletic department. It is very rare to have a small university be so successful in sports, yet our teams—all of them, not just basketball—consistently perform above and beyond anyone's reasonable expectations.

What would an admissions officer at your school probably not tell a prospective student?

An admissions officer probably wouldn't tell a prospective student that a lot of Wake kids come from wealthy families, and that they can be spoiled and bratty. I don't know. I came from a solidly middle-class suburb on the East Coast. Rich southerners act quite a bit differently than people did back in my hometown. It was a bit of a culture shock.

The Institution

Four years in, I never cease to be amazed by this place's beauty, especially Wait Chapel late at night or early in the morning. The weather is wonderful from August to late October; it never gets too cold (below 25 degrees), and, since southerners can't handle snow, classes are cancelled if there's so much as frost on your windshield.

Wake Forest offers students a tremendous opportunity to grow and learn. I cannot even begin to detail all the amazing things that I've been able to do at this place, but highlights include my time spent traveling around the country with the football team as their student manager, my time spent in my favorite professor's house, chatting about where my life is headed, and the unbelievable semester I spent in Vienna, Austria, looking at the world and realizing for the first time how interconnected it all is. For me, someone who is usually concerned with the big picture, with where I'm headed, where I'll be five or ten years from now—Wake Forest showed me how to slow down and appreciate life day-by-day. It's shown me how to challenge myself to think hard and deep, to question everything and come up with solutions on my own that are morally, spiritually, and intellectually satisfying.

It's also worth noting Wake's really excellent study abroad program. Fifty percent of students partake and Wake makes it really easy to study abroad, because it has amazing houses purchased all over the world, and you can easily spend a semester or a year in a Wake house, with other Wake students, being taught by fantastic Wake professors, but surrounded by whatever you choose. Have a fancy for London? Want to study in a Viennese mansion? How about Venice, on the Grand Canal? And Wake takes great pains to ensure everyone's study abroad experience is fantastic. I'm an alumnus of Flow House, in Vienna, and I had the absolute best time of my life.

> "Wake Forest is a microcosmic bubble, a fictitious land where Ralph Lauren meets Steve Urkel, mixed together with good old southern hospitality, and stirred with a few bronzed, talented athletes."
>
> ✦ Leigh, junior

The Education

For some Wake kids, the library is home. For others—particularly those enmeshed in fraternity and sorority life—academics are secondary, all they want is to get their B's so they can focus on the next golf pros/tennis hoes party. For the majority of students, life is a mix of the two extremes.

Most students work, and play, in equal measure. Or maybe they work a little more than they play—this place isn't called "Work Forest" for nothing, after all. Our classes are hard. Our professors are demanding. Our Divisional Requirements are intense—students must take fifteen or sixteen core classes (from a standardized selection), which is one of the toughest core curriculums in the country. Luckily, once you satisfy the core and reach the upper-level classes in your major, you're rewarded with really small classes—three or four people besides yourself—with professors who will rock your world. This semester, for example, I am in an honors seminar examining Greek democracy with only four other students. Our professor is one of the leaders in the field, I call him by his first name. He calls me by mine.

> "Whenever Wake Forest's sports teams win a game, everyone runs outside and throws toilet paper over all the trees in the quad. This is known as 'rolling the quad.'"
> ✦ Josh, sophomore

The Students

The average Wake student was the popular, intelligent, socially active, preppy kid in high school. These types of kids usually get along with similar kids, and most at Wake Forest enjoy one another's company. Wake has a really excellent student newspaper, one of the best in the nation, and it does its darndest to get students involved in important social and political issues. But students here are, on the whole, morally upright but politically unresponsive. Editorialists beg and plead. Students don't listen. Our campus isn't diverse, they'll say. Look around you, everyone's white! Look around you, everyone's rich! (the paper will say). Shouldn't we have more socioeconomic diversity? There are far too many BMWs in our campus parking lot, doesn't that register as "weird"? No response. Wake students can be schizophrenic. Everyone's bright, everyone's idealistic, everyone's bothered by the things that are wrong in the world around them, but they'll rarely get organized and take political action. They're smart, they're capable, but while they're in college they're more interested in inventing new beer games than they are in

coming up with ways to make the world a better place. In the classroom, they're incredibly intelligent, sometimes bordering on brilliant. Every now and again a student will say something that will give a professor pause, and you can see how pleased they are to be around such bright kids. But at the same time I think Wake students are extremely hardworking underachievers, with lots and lots of potential. I've spoken to a few alumni, and from what they've said Wake students "wake up" and accomplish great things within ten years of graduating. It's just a bit frustrating as a motivated student, to see everyone when they're still in their early, apathetic years.

The Activities

Admissions officers tend to downplay the importance of the Greek system at Wake. Around 65 percent of our campus is Greek, and since Winston-Salem isn't exactly a cultural mecca, Greek life is where it's at. People go to Greek houses during the day to hang around, play foosball, have a beer, watch the game. Occasionally Greek houses will host charity events, and everyone will get involved. Then on weekends, they'll transform into the rowdy social center of campus.

Sports are also a very big deal here. If you come here, you'll learn never to mention that you like Duke or Chapel Hill. God, for your sake, I hope you'll learn. Wake students are extremely spirited, and they love their Demon Deacons and hate our rival teams with an incredible passion. Really, when we're having a big sports game, it's not uncommon for die-hard fans to line up and camp out for hours and hours and hours to get good tickets.

The Social Scene

The Greek life is vital to the social life on campus, in that if there were no Greek parties, there'd be no parties. Winston-Salem is a weird little town and although there are some bars in the nearby area, "Wake Bars" as we call them, most have been territorialized by the fraternities and sororities to such a degree that they're not an alternative to the Greek scene so much as an extension of it.

On Wednesdays, if students don't have much work to do, they'll hit the aforementioned bars, or search around until they find a tiny, small-scale frat party. Fridays are the big days (with Saturdays coming in a close second), and that's when everyone will head to a big frat party and drink a lot and get rowdy. Lately, the administration has taken note that students drink in the lounges in fraternities, and has sent public safety officers to give summons to anyone who's caught drinking. This hasn't been too successful, though—now students just predrink in their rooms and show up at the parties drunker than they have to be, instead of what it was like before, where they drank just enough at the party and then enjoyed themselves. Lastly, Wake has a very weird dating scene. We don't "date." And we don't hook up. We do some weird mix of both. Often, instead of meeting a person, going out on a date with them, and then messing around, Wake students will mess around with someone at a drunken party on a Friday night, then go out on a date with them the next day so they can finally meet them. At this point, they feel guilty for messing around with the person in the first place, but guilt is kind of hot, and then they'll mess around again. Before long, these two kids are "dating," but not in any traditional sense. It's more that they're messing around and messing around and messing around, each hookup tied to the next by that sexy thing called "guilt," and in the end they'll call it all "dating" so they can continue without running the risk of violating their Christian values. Being from New York, I have to say southerners can be very, very weird.

Name: Melissa
Hometown: Cleveland, Ohio
Class Year: Senior
Major: Psychology/neuroscience
Extracurriculars: I really just focus on my studies.
Career Goal: The master plan: start my career in the pharmaceutical industry, in the research sector, then, when the time is ripe and I have a few more degrees under my belt, switch over to management. Before long, I'll be the one pulling the strings.

How would you describe Wake Forest's reputation?

Wake is a somewhat prestigious school with the nickname "Work Forest" because everyone here is said to be working their brains out.

Is this reputation accurate?

Yup. Wake is somewhat prestigious. (I can't understand why it isn't more prestigious, though. Seems there's a pervading myopia amongst those who rank universities, but I suspect this will

change in the next few years. They can't ignore us forever.) And as for Work Forest—it's true this place feels like a labor camp, but that's what we're here to do. Students are here to work hard at a topnotch school. So when we graduate, we'll have fantastic work ethics, and the skills to take top positions in firms all over the world.

"Interesting fact: almost one in every eleven students at Wake Forest is a varsity athlete (myself included)."

✦ Zach, senior

What would an admissions officer at your school probably not tell a prospective student?

Well, Wake Forest is totally Aramark's bitch. (Aramark is the school's main dining company.) Aramark produces most of the food on our campus, and it's absolutely terrible stuff. And it's expensive. There's better, cheaper food elsewhere— anywhere—but students at Wake use their Deacon cards to buy food, and you can only use your Deacon card to buy Aramark food. So we're pretty much stuck. Not a good situation. Also, most Wake Forest students are white and upper class. Most Aramark employees are nonwhite and not upper class. Let's just say the employees don't tend to like the students too much, and this causes a little bit of a hostile vibe on campus.

Lastly, when you come visit campus you'll see and hear (and be stunned by) the beautiful skinny creatures we call "students" at Wake Forest. What you won't see and hear is the cacophony of mucus-hocking, belching, and vomiting that resounds in stereo through the toilets at Wake Forest every day after lunch. There is an eating disorder epidemic at Wake. I suppose it's the price we pay for having such a gorgeous student body.

The Institution

Location is so important when you're deciding what school to go to. You're choosing to spend four years of your life somewhere. Know exactly what that will mean! I think I failed to get what it would be like to spend so much time in Winston-Salem. Don't misunderstand me, our campus is absolutely gorgeous, and there's so much going on around campus that you're never bored. But I spent my junior year abroad in Sydney, Australia, and realized that I'm just a city person. Coming back to Winston-Salem has been hard, being confined in a tiny little town for another year. If you're a suburb person, this place is great. If you're a city person, think twice.

Wake Forest has a pretty flexible administration. (Our school is small enough that it should be flexible.) This works out well, though. For example, if you have more than two exams on any given day, you can usually talk to a teacher and move one of them to keep you sane. Finally, a word on breaking Wake's Honor Code—don't do it. Or at least be *really* crafty about doing it. There are few who can get away with cheating or plagiarizing without being burned in the process.

The Education

Everyone at Wake Forest is really smart and when smart kids go head to head with other smart kids, someone's going to sink to the bottom, so some smart kids are going to find themselves with frighteningly low GPAs at the end of their freshman year. Don't fool yourself and think this won't be you—it might be. Wake Forest teachers are also notoriously hard graders, so steel yourself in advance that your previous 4.0 lifestyle might become a humbling 3.0 reality. C's require some work around here, B's are quite good, and A's are pretty hard to come by. I'd say, if you work really hard, you can expect a B+/A- average. Work extraordinarily hard, and A's will pop up on your transcript every now and again. That said, most students at Wake Forest don't compete, instead they'll work together to study for most exams. In class, everyone feeds off one another, since most classes are small and discussion-based. And, in class, professors tend to be really engaged. You'll find yourself in a terribly named class that you'll expect to be a bore, and then some stellar teacher will make it shockingly interesting. It really is true that when professors are passionate about a subject that passion tends to transfer by osmosis to all the students, and that's often the case here.

Outside of class, students spend a lot of time on schoolwork, especially if they're majoring in the sciences, business, or English. I'd say our most prestigious majors are the premed track, the business track, our neuroscience program, and anything in the Romance Language Department.

As a senior I can honestly say I've had a really well-rounded and satisfying education. In the sciences I've been granted a lot of lab time, doing things that some grad students at other schools don't have the opportunity to do. I've gotten to know my professors in all my classes, most of whom are quite well-known in their respective fields, and I know that my degree will always be looked upon highly.

The Students

Students here are infuriatingly good-looking and appear to have stepped straight out of a J. Crew, Abercrombie, or Banana Republic catalog. Gossip here spreads like wildfire. If there's a juicy rumor, half the campus will know about it within the day. You learn to deal with it, though. At some point, everyone here gets a singed ear because of some gossiping and back-stabbing, and everyone learns to give it as good as they get it. No rumor goes unpunished, everyone is constantly on their Instant Messenger and checking their e-mail, so as soon as you find a rumor being spread, you can get online and strike back.

I'd say most students here are white. That's too bad. I'm not white, and while I get along with everyone, I wish there were more minority students on campus. Also, prehistoric high school cliques walk the Forest here and there, but most have evolved enough so that we'll have our cool kids and our nerds, but they'll play together far more than the same kids would have in eleventh grade.

Finally, most students here also have a relatively good grasp on their futures, and while you may see John or Jane out partying hard at the bars on the weekend, during the week they're studying and getting good grades. We're not the kids who don't see past this exam—we're the kids who are preprofessionally oriented with plans for bigger and better things after Wake, and we know every grade counts, even on the weekends when the beer goggles and blackouts come into play.

The Activities

People here love the outdoors and we'll spend a lot of time getting out there to tackle the world (white water rafting, skydiving, camping, etc.). Plus, Pilot Mountain is only half an hour away, and it's ideal for climbing or hiking on a nice afternoon. Runners take advantage of the cross-country trails around campus and in nearby Reynolda Gardens, which is absolutely gorgeous in the spring. If it's 3:00 a.m. on a Wednesday morning and you're still awake, you're not alone. For sure, a big handful of kids are also awake—studying or drinking, most likely.

I used to be a lot more involved in the entire vista of university life when I was an enthusiastic freshman. But as I've gotten older, I've pared down. Now that I'm a senior, all I have time for is schoolwork (papers, labs, presentations, exams), making enough money to pay the bills (mommy and daddy still love me, but they have to let go of their baby girl, and yours will too eventually), and Beer Pong (my skills are sick).

> "Wake's campus is beautiful. Except when it rains, because Wake has drainage problems. This means, every time it rains, Wake's campus turns into a giant lake with two to three inches of standing water. But what can you do?"
>
> ✦ Brian, freshman

The Social Scene

Did I mention we like to party at Wake Forest? With lots of alcohol? 'Cause we do. On the weekends, kiss your sobriety good-bye. We have some truly crazy parties that have to be seen to be believed.

A typical Wake Forest Friday involves going to class and finishing up your academics around noon, then sitting around to watch the game over a few beers with friends. Hours later, when dinnertime rolls around, we'll head to a local Mexican place (there are a lot around here) and grab some eats and a pitcher of margaritas. Then, back to a friend's apartment to "pre-game." At 10:30, we'll shoot over to the bars or to a frat party or both. We'll keep drinking until a late night crew forms to head to IHOP to satisfy our drunken munchies. Everyone calls it a night around 4 a.m. or so, if they're still standing. On Saturday, we'll wake up and get some type of hangover relief from Chesapeake Bagel. Or we'll wake up and immediately start drinking again, through DAM (DAM is Drinking in the a.m., a Saturday social event put on by a frat where everyone rolls out of bed and launches into full party mode). When Sunday rolls around, the library fills up and the cycle of work begins again!

Name: Leigh
Hometown: Winston-Salem, North Carolina

Class Year: Freshman
Major: Business (and premed)
Extracurriculars: Cycling instructor at Wake and a local YMCA, women's lacrosse (club), Wake Forest catholic community, ballroom dance club
Career Goal: To go to a five-year MD/MBA program, and specialize in nutritional psychiatry, eventually going into private practice. Eating disorders are a prevalent issue on college campuses, and have affected many of my friends, so I feel that working with eating disorders will hit close to home and be really fulfilling.

How would you describe Wake Forest's reputation?

A small, fantastic school with Division I athletics, said to be populated by trust-fund babies who are there not so much to work hard as they are to get an expensive private education from a "name" school on daddy's dollar.

Is this reputation accurate?

I was right that Wake is a small, fantastic school with Division I athletics. As for the rich kids—sure, they're here, with their Polos and khakis, cardigans and pearls. But they work hard (our unofficial motto here is: "Work Forest, where your best hasn't been good enough since 1834") and there are other types of people here too, with their own, nonpreppy dress code. But this shouldn't put you off, because Wake fits everyone in somewhere.

What would an admissions officer at your school probably not tell a prospective student?

Well, Wake Forest's admissions officers ask for your picture on your application, and they never tell you exactly why. I've heard a rumor that Wake Forest was ranked third for having the most beautiful college students in America. Maybe admissions is using the pictures to weed out the uglies? There certainly aren't many of them here. Also, when you come to campus to visit as a prospective student, the administration will give you free food. But it's not just to woo you—Wake Forest is always giving catered lunches and pizza to boost attendance at campus events. This school loves to feed us.

The Institution

Having grown up in Winston-Salem, the daughter of two alums, I've heard about Wake Forest since I was knee-high to the Demon Deacon.

When I was a junior in high school, I started thinking about the things I wanted in a college, and spent a lot of time on the Internet taking compatibility tests. That's when I started noticing Wake kept coming up as a perfect match when I said I wanted a small school with rigorous academics, tough but not so tough that I'd never have time for anything but studying. I also wanted a school with Division I athletics, because I loved cheerleading in high school, and I love the way sporting events can bring people together, give them something common to cheer about. Wake Forest, on paper, satisfied all of my requirements for a school. And it has done the same in person.

It's the perfect size, people are respectful and friendly. When you enter the front gates of Wake Forest you'll be greeted by an empty security station that looks like a miniature house, landscaped with an array of colorful flowers (we were recently named one of the best landscaped campuses in the country!). Continue along the entrance road, you'll see woods on either side of you. Then you'll come upon Davis Field, which will inevitably be dotted with members of the marching band, sunbathers, or ultimate Frisbee addicts. Regardless of the season or time of day you'll see runners making use of the sidewalks which criss-cross campus, jogging off on the trail that connects campus to Reynolda Village.

> "From what the polls say, we have the second highest workload in the nation, but I could swear we have the most."
>
> ✦ Ami, senior

Once you're on campus proper, you'll see Georgian architecture, a medium-colored brick with black wrought-iron accents. It's beautiful. The clock on the chapel steeple can be seen from almost anywhere on campus, and is sort of the North Star of Wake Forest. The campus is then divided in two, into North and South campus, by Reynolda Hall, the administration building. North Campus is home to the main quad and upperclassmen housing. South Campus is home to freshman and the majority of our academic buildings. Regardless of where you are, you'll never be more than about a ten- to twelve-minute walk from the farthest point on campus. The campus has blue light phones everywhere, and if you call security from one of them, they're there within seconds. I always feel pretty safe. I go jogging after dark and nothing's happened to me yet. The rooms here are huge! My freshman single was bigger than a normal double at other schools. If you come here, request Bostwick on your housing application! Such a nice, big, friendly dorm to live in.

The only other thing you should know is that North Carolina has really spazzy weather. Really, it's totally unpredictable. It's a clear day, and then it's a loud, scary thunderstorm. No warning.

The Education

The professors are people at the top of their fields and they will know your name, your interests, and in class they'll say "Joe, did you do the reading, because your comment on industrialization in the early twentieth century was good, but it was also refuted on page 240 of Parker and Boyles, and I'm surprised you didn't point that out." These professors work incredibly hard to give us good lectures, and they expect us to work hard to earn their good lectures. No slacking allowed 'round here. That said, if you are having trouble with the considerable workload, there are free writing tutors who will walk you through your papers and make sure you're communicating effectively, and we also have a writing center where you can workshop papers with your peers.

Wake has a big core curriculum. You have to take three "core" courses in each of four broad areas: literature and arts, natural sciences and math, history, philosophy, and religion, and social and behavioral sciences. Every student also has to take one writing course, and they have to fulfill a foreign language requirement. If you have AP credits from high school you can phase out of some of our core classes—for example, I started college just one class shy of being a sophomore, which has given me considerable leeway in jumping the core and choosing the classes I really want to take.

Finally, the workload is difficult. But if you choose classes well—don't take three or four classes that are notorious for giving a lot of work, take one or two of those and then one or two more moderate classes—you'll be fine. Also, don't take this to the opposite extreme. I have friends who scrape by doing the bare minimum of work, taking "football player class" after "football player class," and they are going to regret wasting their education one day.

The Students

A lot of people will complain that students at Wake Forest are all conservatives and are all white. But if you come down and visit this place, you'll find our professors are mostly liberals, and that our homecoming queen this year was a minority student. Diversity is in the eye of the beholder. I think this place is diverse. You make up your own mind.

The Activities

Really, there are groups here for every kind of student. It's more a matter of having the time to join and stay involved in a group than it is of finding something you're interested in. You'll only be hindered by how many hours there are in the day (and, at Wake Forest, you'll wish there were far more! Why does your body need sleep, there are so many cool things you could be doing with those eight extra hours!).

The Social Scene

Wake Forest social life is dominated by Greek life, and every frat/sorority has a slightly different personality, so you'll have fun figuring out which one is which, and which one best suits you. And if Greek life isn't your thing, though, no one will pressure you to join. I'd say students who elect to remain independent are one of three types— they're the kids who "shoulda been a brother, just didn't want to pay to pledge," the kids who are too busy studying around the clock to get involved in organized activities, and the kids who are nerdy theater buffs, so caught up in their thespy social scene that there's no need for Greek life. But really, everyone parties together anyway on weekends. We're a small school, so students all run into another. Especially during basketball season, when Wake wins, everyone on campus is best friends and the alcohol flows like water.

Notable Wake Forest Alumni Include:
James Forrester, senator, deputy Republican leader
Robert L. Ehrlich, politician, governor of Maryland
Philip E. Berger, senator, Republican Caucus secretary
Arnold Palmer, professional golfer
Tim Duncan, NBA basketball player
Penelope Niven, biographer

UNIVERSITY OF WASHINGTON

Founded: 1861

Location: Seattle, WA

Phone: (206) 543-2100

E-mail: askuwadm@u.washington.edu

Web site: www.washington.edu

Number of Undergraduates: 26,310

Number of Graduate Students: 9,380

Cost: Approximately $13,500 per year in state; $26,000 out of state

Application Deadline: January 15

Rating:
Selective

Notable Majors/Programs:
Business, Architecture,
Life Sciences, Engineering

Size:

○ Small   ○ Medium   ● Large

Location:

● Urban   ○ Suburban   ○ Rural

On a Saturday, students talk about academics:

○ Always   ● Sometimes   ○ Never

Nightlife:

○ Intense   ● Moderate   ○ Laid-back

Politically, UW leans:

○ Left   ○ Right   ● Split

Diversity:

● High   ○ Low   ○ Medium

PAC Ten: Yes!

Students describe University of Washington in five words:
- Beautiful location; something for everyone
- Nicely big, lotsa resources, uber-Northwestern

From the School

The academic core of the University of Washington is its College of Arts and Sciences; the teaching and research of the University's many professional schools provide essential complements to these programs in the arts, humanities, social sciences, and natural and mathematical sciences. Programs in law, medicine, forest resources, oceanography and fisheries, library science, and aeronautics are offered exclusively (in accord with state law) by the University of Washington. . . . The schools and colleges of architecture and urban planning, business administration, education, engineering, nursing, pharmacy, public affairs, and social work have a long tradition of educating students for service to the region and the nation.

—www.washington.edu

If you're interested in University of Washington, you may also be interested in:
CU–Boulder, U. Mass, U. Michigan, UC Berkeley, UC Santa Cruz, UW–Madison

Name: Natasha

Hometown: Ft. Lewis, Washington

Class Year: Freshman

Major: Nursing

Extracurriculars: Intramural volleyball team, Black Student Union, Knitting Club

Career Goal: I plan to enter nursing school in 2006 and graduate in 2008. Then I want to get a job as a registered nurse working in the neonatal unit and then possibly go back to school to become a nurse practitioner.

How would you describe UW's reputation?

Well to people in Washington, our school is just the main public university in Seattle. And it's huge. People who know about it, know that it's actually one of the best research institutions in the nation. We don't really have a party school reputation, except for that one incident when the frats on Greek row went crazy and smashed cars and made the news.

Is this reputation accurate?

Yeah our reputation's accurate because we are a huge school and a heck of a lot of research goes on here and I don't think we party any more than any other public universities.

What would an admissions officer at UW probably not tell a prospective student? What aspect of your school would a prospective student probably not see on a campus tour?

They probably wouldn't tell a prospective student that the balconies of one the residence halls are locked during finals week because there is a supposed rise in possible suicides during that time. Such are the rumors. They also might not mention that some of your vital classes could be in the Fisheries or Health Sciences buildings, which could be a twenty- to thirty-minute walk, depending. They also probably wouldn't show you a room in some of the residence halls because they are super-small and look like dungeons.

The Institution

This school is *the* classic, out-of-the-movies university. It has a beautiful campus, with the classic lawn at the center of the campus, where everything goes down: rallies, protests, concerts, and more.

The weather in Seattle is not too hot and not too cold. It only snows maybe one week a year here and it rarely gets above 80 degrees (at least during the school year). We have a reputation for rain, which is true—but it doesn't rain nonstop. It'll break and have sun, then rain again. There's also a lot of fog.

Being a school of forty thousand students, the campus is huge. Be prepared to walk, bike, or even skateboard. One really great item is your U-PASS, which allows you to hop on any metro bus for a one-time fee paid quarterly.

The Education

Most people here are hard-working, and take school seriously. I've had all positive experiences with faculty. Most seem to care about their students and have as much contact with them as you can have in class of two or three hundred. I haven't witnessed the competitiveness that I expected. It's definitely not like an Ivy League school where everyone is out for blood and will do anything at all costs to get ahead of everyone else. Most people are laid-back. It's nice.

The Students

This campus, as well as the Seattle area in general, is very liberal. Just about everyone is a Democrat. The Republicans finally came out of hiding when Bush won the election, but you would not even know they existed if he didn't win. The campus isn't very diverse in race. It's mostly Caucasian and Asian with a small percentage of African Americans, Native Americans, Hispanics, and others. There are a lot of cliques within races as well as Greeks. Most students are from the state of Washington, but there are others from around the country. Upper- and underclassmen mix. Most people are very friendly with people on their dorm floors.

The Activities

With the exception of this year, football games are popular. Basketball games are all sold-out and because we have the number one Division I volleyball team in the nation, many people attend volleyball games. We have the best athletic facilities ever—and they've been recently renovated. The IMA has four floors, an indoor track, dance studios, tons of treadmills, state of the art work-out equipment, weights, an indoor climbing wall, at least four basketball courts, a few volleyball courts, racquetball courts, tennis courts, soccer and football fields, pool, a lounge with a big screen TV, and much more. It's awesome. There's always something like classes or team sports going on. You won't get out of shape if you make the short walk there.

Everyone reads *The Daily,* which is the school paper. There are many religious groups and plenty of services to attend. Many people do community service, especially to get into grad school. On sunny days there are definitely the people who sit on the grass between classes and read, some throw Frisbees, and three out of five people walk around with some type of headphones on playing music usually from an iPod.

The Social Scene

There's always a party going on, especially on Greek row where all the sororities and fraternities are. They live such a different lifestyle than those who dorm or commute. Different types of people definitely party differently. Alcohol is abundant no matter what age you are.

This isn't one of those campuses where you're going to know everyone. Not at all. But most people are friendly and hold the door and will say "hi" to complete strangers. It's up the individual on whether they want to get out and meet people. You aren't forced to, but there is plenty of opportunity. Dorm life is cool. You get to know people on your floor or in your cluster, even if it's just seeing them in the bathroom.

Name: Amelia
Hometown: Sonoma, California
Class Year: Senior
Major: English, with a creative writing emphasis
Extracurriculars: None under the UW umbrella—
  I take dance classes off campus and have worked throughout college. That keeps me pretty busy.
Career Goal: To make a decent living by contributing in some capacity to the literary arts.

How would you describe UW's reputation?

People tend to think that admissions to UW are very competitive for out-of-state applicants (which I was), and are generally impressed by its size, stature, and importance as a research institution.

Is this reputation accurate?

Mmm, it's difficult to say, as a person who was granted admission, how common or impressive a feat that is. I could probably tell you a lot more about their admission standards had I been re-

jected. I've definitely met a disturbing number of boneheads at UW, many of them from out of state, as well as some extraordinarily bright people. I guess when it comes to the student body, it's a wash. The university's contributions to scientific research cannot be denied, nor can its commitment to providing its students with a textured and interdisciplinary education.

What would an admissions officer at UW probably not tell a prospective student? What aspect of your school would a prospective student probably not see on a campus tour?

You definitely learn the hard way that at UW, no one—not your R.A., not your admissions counselor, and no one in your chosen department, will know or care who you are unless you beat them over the head with your own interest in your scholastic future. And even then, they will only be able to find your file or remember your name by referencing your seven-digit student number. In other words, guidance at this school is a joke. As one of thirty-five thousand students, you are utterly alone at the helm of your education, so you need to get real comfortable with being proactive about it—real quick. This atmosphere inspires some students to greatness and completely shuts others out of the process. Bear this in mind. However, if you are aggressive about securing the education that you want and deserve, you will find some extraordinary professors here, who will take an interest in you specifically, and they may even change your life.

The Institution

I chose UW partly because of its enormous student body, and resultant opportunities for personal anonymity. Coming from a very small town, I relished the idea of going about my business on campus all day without ever once running into a familiar face. And that's the reality here. Though like any social institution anonymity becomes less and less possible over time. There is a real lack of community on campus, however, which can leave you feeling somewhat adrift and lonely at times.

Seattle is a great city, with lots to do whether your preference be camping in the evergreens or camping out on a local bar stool. I've found the population slightly disappointing—Seattle has a reputation as a liberal city, and I suppose growing up in the San Francisco area, I have a slightly skewed definition of what is liberal, but many

Washingtonians I've met have freaked me out with their conservative backgrounds. Even the political correctness in the Northwest can come off as closed-minded at times.

School spirit definitely revolves around the football season: the Huskies (even when they're "rebuilding") nearly always pack Husky Stadium, which is a massive, gorgeous sporting facility right on Lake Washington. Few things in life are more fun than an Apple Cup (the annual game against UW's rival Washington State, or "Wazoo" to locals) in Seattle.

The weather in Seattle, and there is no way of getting around this, absolutely sucks 75 percent of the time. It is freezing, overcast, dark, and pisses rain day after day after day, from September to June. The summer months are phenomenally beautiful, and in a city with as much natural beauty as Seattle, a nice day can literally take your breath away. Especially after enduring nine months of grossness.

Campus is huge, so if you have a class in the Fisheries building right before a class in the Art building, you will have to run (but never run through Red Square when it's wet—you will slip, and it will be humiliating). And you'll still be late. But most profs are surprisingly understanding.

The dorms are very institutional, with tiny hospital-esque rooms in huge, ugly buildings. But almost all of my college friends were a direct result of living in the dorms my freshman year, and I found them to be a nearly perfect segue from adolescence to "adulthood." It is sort of uncool to spend more than one year on campus, especially considering the wealth of off campus housing opportunities and the über-strict campus cops (an actual division of the Seattle PD, with full police powers), but freshman year on campus was crucial for me in terms of meeting people and figuring out campus life. When it comes to moving off campus, I have the following piece of advice: get out of the U-District! Rents near campus are insanely inflated for what are largely crappy, ill-maintained, tiny apartments in a dirty, somewhat dangerous area. Neighboring Wallingford (my favorite), Wedgewood, Greenlake, Sand Point, Fremont, Ballard, and Montlake are all easy bus rides (UW students ride public transportation for free) from campus and offer much more pleasant accommodations.

The Education

Certain departments at the UW (read: sciences) are very well funded, extraordinarily staffed, and have seemingly limitless resources for their students. I, however, was an English major, who over four years watched class sizes in my department grow exponentially (which in a discipline that relies on active participation in class discussions, can be a virtual death to students' experience), courses slashed from the schedule en masse, and instructors' salaries cut back to the point where many had to leave for positions at more adequately funded private schools. Communications, one of the most popular majors at UW, was stricken from the roster entirely. Humanities classes became so competitive that half the time only those in the major in question could even register for them, making it prohibitively difficult to round-out your schedule with any degree of variety. Meanwhile, new buildings were going up all over campus for computer science, chemistry, and engineering students to more comfortably pursue their chosen disciplines. I found the favoritism toward those students who were (statistically) destined for more lucrative careers (with the accompanying disposable incomes flush enough to make donations to the alma mater possible) reprehensible and disappointing. That being said, I want to honestly commend those humanities professors who work under those constraints, because they are among the most dedicated and generous people I have worked with in college.

The Students

The student body at the UW is largely white and Asian, and doesn't have much diversity among social classes—mainly middle-class, mainly protestant, mainly West Coast in origin. There are a lot of campus groups, but with so many students, it is almost impossible for any of them to be very recognizable or have much of an impact on the campus as a whole.

One nice thing about UW, and Seattle in general, is that almost everyone wears what amounts to pajamas every day. You never feel out of place showing up to class grubby and sleepy, because everyone else is too. People are generally very laid-back and friendly.

The Activities

This has been the smallest part of my college experience. Almost everyone I know found their activities and social groups off campus. *The Daily* is the campus newspaper, and is pretty widely read, though not very good. You can learn about what's going on campus from reading that.

- Since 1989:
  - Five faculty members have won Nobel prizes in physics and medicine,
  - A faculty member in the English department won the 1990 National Book Award for fiction,
  - And there have been nine Macarthur (genius) fellows.

The Social Scene

The frat scene is huge at the UW. That is where most underage students get their party on during their freshman/sophomore years. All girls are welcome and drink for free, and guys can usually get in if they've got some ladies with them. Those parties are really just meat markets for the frat boys, but when they're your only option, they're all right. There are typically a number of house parties on any weekend night around the U-District, but a lot of times you end up wandering the streets in the rain in search of some vague, phantom keg. Once people turn twenty-one, they tend to disperse. I mainly go out in my neighborhood (Wallingford/ Fremont), which has a decent nightlife. "The Ave," the main drag of the U-District, has a number of popular dive bars where everyone goes occasionally to get wasted for cheap, but I try to limit the time I spend there. The dating scene is pretty paltry. Maybe the endless rain does something to the motivation, but most people I know are mainly single or in long-term relationships.

Name: Sarah
Hometown: Renton, Washington
Class Year: Junior
Major: Anthropology, biology
Extracurriculars: Vice president of UNICEF, undergraduate research, University Chorale, volunteer at Woodland Park Zoo, and campus tour guide
Career Goal: I would like to stay in the collegiate atmosphere—either teaching, advising, or in an administrative capacity.

How would you describe your school's reputation?

We are a highly ranked research university known for many different departments. Our programs vary over many different areas of study. We are a very large state school that supports the education of Washingtonians.

Is this reputation accurate?

Very—we are a state school and very large. We have amazing departments that do some amazing research.

What would an admissions officer at UW probably not tell a prospective student?

An admissions officer at UW will not tell a student whether or not they are in.

The Institution

The University of Washington is a large school, but that doesn't mean there can't be school spirit—in fact, I think there's more! The Friday night at 9:00 p.m. before a home football game, the marching band will start at the north campus residence halls and rally the students through the north campus. Police stop traffic to allow the band and following students to march up to the Greek houses, then all the students finish the rally in Red Square. This is one of my fondest memories of living in the residence halls. I think that it really brings people together to share in the school spirit of Washington. When you first think of Seattle, you think *rain*. Of course it does rain here, but I think people are misled to believe that it is raining 363 days of the year. It doesn't rain that much. One of the best things about Seattle weather is that you can experience all four seasons.

The Education

I often get asked by prospective students, "are there research opportunities for undergrads?" Yes! As soon as I figured out what I wanted to focus on in my studies, I met my professor whom I am currently doing research with. She was willing to advise me on my research and even let me work on her project! On top of being able to work directly with these professors, we have amazing scholarships to promote undergraduate research. This helps encourage students to focus on their research and not have to worry about money.

The Students

The UW campus has been one of the most diverse environments I have ever been in. I think you can find people here of all personalities and interests. It is exciting when students debate in Red Square or in front of the HUB over political or moral issues. I like that this academic environment is one where students can debate in public while respecting the other person's point of view. In fact, there is a communications class that requires you to debate in Red Square.

The Activities

There are over 450 different student organizations—and this number is growing every year! Don't ever tell me you can't find something to do here, or someone to do it with. There are so many organizations to get involved with in Seattle that a student shouldn't have a problem finding a place to volunteer their time. I think that there are a lot of volunteer clubs, but the majority of students choose to volunteer on their own and not through clubs.

The Social Scene

To describe our social scene, I want to take the residence halls as an example of the campus itself.

Each of the residence halls has different living situations: single gender floor, co-ed floor, cluster/suite and half male half female. Students have so many options as to what their preference is. There is also special interest housing such as the SAFE house (Substance and Alcohol Free Environment), international floor, outdoor floor, honors floor, and the list goes on! Oftentimes people worry about the partying, but you don't have to be involved with it if you choose not to. Students can really choose what kind of living situation you want, and that will help to find other students who have similar interests.

Notable UW Alumni Include:
Bruce Lee, martial arts film actor
Chuck Close, artist
Dawn Wells, actress
George Hitchings, biochemist
George Stigle, economist
Hank Ketcham, creator of Dennis the Menace

WASHINGTON UNIVERSITY IN ST. LOUIS

Founded: 1853
Location: St. Louis, MO
Phone: (800) 638-0700
E-mail: admissions@wustl.edu
Web site: www.wustl.edu

Number of Undergraduates: 7,219
Number of Graduate Students: 4,639
Cost: Approximately $39,000 per year
Application Deadline: January 15
Early Decision: November 15

Rating:	Notable Majors/Programs:
Most Selective	Engineering, Business, Biology, German

Size:
○ Small ● Medium ○ Large

Location:
○ Urban ● Suburban ○ Rural

On a Saturday, students talk about academics:
○ Always ● Sometimes ○ Never

Nightlife:
● Intense ○ Moderate ○ Laid-back

Politically, Wash U. leans:
● Left ○ Right ○ Split

Diversity:
○ High ○ Low ● Medium

Students describe Wash U. in five words:
- Historic, beautiful, preppy, traditional, southern
- Growing more prestigious each year

From the School

Washington University's educational mission is the promotion of learning—learning by students and by faculty.

Central to our mission are our goals, which are to foster excellence in our teaching, research, scholarship, and service; to prepare students with the attitudes, skills, and habits of lifelong learning and with leadership skills, enabling them to be useful members of a global society; and to be an exemplary institution in our home community of St. Louis, as well as in the nation and in the world.
—www.wustl.edu

If you're interested in Wash U., you may also be interested in:
Claremont McKenna, Cornell, Duke, Princeton, Stanford, Vanderbilt

Name: Sarah
Hometown: Rockville Centre, New York
Class Year: Freshman
Major: I'm not sure yet—I'm thinking I'll major in either marketing, accounting, or international business
Extracurriculars: Student Admissions Committee, Pi Beta Phi sorority, Each One Teach One tutoring group

How would you describe Wash U.'s reputation?

Washington University in St. Louis is an extremely prestigious and highly respected national university. Last year, *U.S. News & World Report* ranked us the eleventh best school in the nation. (Down from ninth the year before.)

Is this reputation accurate?

Absolutely. The academic and social experiences you'll have at Wash U. are, in a word, incredible. In the past, only students and alumni knew what a special place this was. Now, because our ranking has skyrocketed, lots of people are in on the secret.

What aspect of your school would a prospective student not see on a campus tour?

Frat Row—a main component of WUSTL's social life—would probably be downplayed on a campus tour. Ask lots of questions about it. If you decide to come here it will be a big part of your life, and you deserve to know exactly what that will mean.

The Institution

Wash U. has an extremely pretty and well-designed campus. It's really easy to get from one place to another. Most on-campus housing is grouped together in a beautiful area called the "South Forty." The main campus, which has classrooms, lecture halls, and dining halls, is just a short walk from there. If you want to get off campus, for whatever reason, Wash U. also provides frequent shuttles that go here, there, and the other place.

Wash U. always had really nice dorms. Lately, though, the nice traditional-style dorms have been overshadowed by newly built Hilton-style dorms. They are ridiculous. They're like hotels. Gorgeous. So, at Wash U., you have the option of living in a nice dorm, or a *gorgeous* one.

It's not cheap to come to Wash U.—our tuition, while comparable to what other top schools charge, is still kind of outrageous—but, once you get here, you live well. As I said, our dorms are palatial, our teachers are some of the leaders in their fields. Our campus is pretty. It's safe—we have our very own Wash U. police department. The food here is delicious, too, we have an on-campus Starbucks, a Krispy Kreme, Kaldis Coffee, a stir-fry place, a cool eating place said to be modeled after The Max from *Saved by the Bell*. And, fantastically, there aren't any set eating hours. Any time you're hungry, you can go to a dining hall and they'll serve you food. Late night hunger pangs? No problem, everything is open until 1:00 a.m. on weekdays and 3:00 a.m. on weekends.

I love this place. It's the only college I applied to outside of the East Coast, where I'm from. And to get here and back, I have to take a plane. I hate planes. Every time I get on a plane, I'm certain it's going to crash and I'm going to die a terrible death. The fact that I fly back and forth several times a year, just to go to Wash U., really says something about this place. If I was having an average academic and social experience, or a very good one, or even a great one, I think it wouldn't have been worth my anxiety and I would have transferred. Luckily (I suppose) I'm having an extraordinary time here.

The Education

Classes at Wash U. are mostly small. Yes, you will have lecture-based classes, but those will all break down into smaller groupings run by very knowledgeable TAs, and after class both the professors and TAs have office hours that you can go to if you need extra help. Students respect their professors here, because they tend to be so accomplished, but the in-class atmosphere is still notably relaxed. My microeconomics teacher wears Converse sneakers to class. My accounting professor once brought the new OutKast CD into class and used it as background music for his Power Point presentations. Students at Wash U. do compete with one another. We're all used to being at the top of our class, we can't help it. We compare grades, we try to do better than the next person. But it's never malicious or overwhelming or uncomfortable. It's just a vague aura of everyone trying to do their personal best. That is, unless the people in question are premed students, and then it's a whole different ball game—and from what I hear, it can get nasty.

The Students

Most students at Wash U. are wealthy. But that doesn't mean that they're stuck up—everyone gets along, there are no rules about what to wear (I wear sweatpants to class all the time), what to listen to, what to believe in. We're not a follow-the-leader type of campus, or a social-climber campus. It's more laid-back and chilled out than that. Most students are pretty open-minded, I'd say 65 percent of us are liberals, 35 percent are conservatives. It makes for lively debate. There are also a *lot* of Jewish students here, and the Jewish student groups are big and vocal.

The Activities

There are about 5 billion clubs that you can join at Wash U., and if you want to start a new one, it couldn't be easier—you just have to get another student to stand next to you while you declare yourselves a club. The school will probably give you money, and if you put up posters around campus, other students will probably sign up for it. Community service is a big thing on our campus, as are holding fund-raisers. One of the first things freshman do after arriving on campus is go to Service First, a day of community service activities that serves as an introduction to the St. Louis community. And every year Wash U. puts on a twelve-hour Relay for Life and a twelve-hour Dance Marathon that raise money to help fight cancer.

Sports aren't a huge thing at Wash U.—we're a Division III school—but our women's volleyball team recently won the NCAA Division III championship. And Red Alert (a popular student group) sends out e-mails to students about our sports games, gives out tickets, free pizza, and T-shirts, and generally does a good job of getting everyone psyched and cheering for our teams. This enhances our already considerable school pride.

On any given sunny day, Wash U.'s campus is buzzing. Kids are hanging out by the sand volleyball court, in the Swamp (that's what we call the field by the residence halls), and the basketball courts are full of kids shooting hoops. Frisbees fly everywhere. Hammocks are set up all over campus by the administration, and someone is always reading in one.

The Social Scene

Wash U. students spend a lot of time doing work. But they also spend a lot of time partying. On any given night of the week, the bars are packed. Every weekend, the campus comes alive with fraternity parties, suite parties, and apartment parties. The fraternity parties get particularly wild, and over 25 percent of the student body goes Greek. If going Greek isn't your thing but you still like to get sloshed every now and again, don't worry—Greek parties are usually open to all.

Strangely enough, even though St. Louis is a great place, most Wash U. students don't have much to do with it. There's so much going on right near campus, and on campus, that we're otherwise occupied!

Name: Ashley
Hometown: Des Moines, Iowa
Class Year: Sophomore
Major: Biology and German
Extracurriculars: Pi Beta Phi sorority, The Amateurs coed a cappella group, PEMRAP undergraduate research associate, intramural tennis
Career Goal: I'd like to become an orthodontist.

How would you describe Wash U.'s reputation?

WUSTL is known for being full of hard-working rich kids—a lot of whom are premed.

Is this reputation accurate?

Extremely accurate. Students at WUSTL work hard to be the best, and they tend to have a lot of money—our campus parking lot sometimes looks like a BMW dealership. Also, while our school has its fair share of premeds—and our premed program is absolutely top-notch—our humanities departments are also stellar. I think humanities are the hidden gem of WUSTL.

What would an admissions officer at your school probably not tell a prospective student?

WUSTL is a school in flux. Lately, it's become more selective and more well known—WUSTL is consistently ranked among the top ten schools in America now, which means its ranked only a stone's throw away from schools like Harvard and Princeton. I think WUSTL's administration definitely wants WUSTL to be closer than a stone's throw away—it wants to be rubbing shoulders with those big boys. But they're not entirely sure how to get there. At the moment, I think they're making our academics more difficult as one inroad. They're also (misguidedly) making it more difficult to study abroad (through our new distribution system, we can't have credits from foreign universities count as elective credits). I don't know. More and more, students are starting to describe the administration as "cryptic" and "self-involved."

The Institution

Okay, I chose to come to WUSTL because it's *beautiful*. Our classrooms are state of the art, our dorms are some of the biggest and nicest in the country, and we have plenty of dining options to choose from for every meal. That said, I haven't spent much of my time at WUSTL enjoying the campus's beauty, or in my dorm, or in classrooms, or eating in the dining halls. I've spent most of my time in the library. Reading, studying, writing. Reading, studying, and writing so much that I'm kind of bitter. Yes, I'll leave WUSTL having received a great education, and I'll leave WUSTL more prepared for med school than my peers from other universities will be. But I studied so much that I feel like I missed out on the typical college experience. I didn't have time to socialize or goof around. The premed curriculum is really cutthroat here. The exams are incredibly difficult, not because they have to be (the material is challenging, but not overly so), but because WUSTL wants to appear dedicated to fighting grade inflation, and because it wants to weed out the weak to keep up its stellar reputation. On the plus side, if you do survive at WUSTL as a premed and get good grades, you're almost assured a spot in one of the nation's most elite medical schools. But I just feel like I could have learned as much useful stuff and *also* had a college experience if my professors were more focused on my personal development and less focused on making the curriculum so difficult.

The Education

As I'm sure you gathered from that rant, if you're premed, WUSTL is very, very difficult. That said, not all students are psycho premeds, toiling away in classes with one to four hundred other students in them. There are plenty of humanities students here, and they have a lovely time. Their classes are small and intimate. Their work is far less cutthroat. My friends who are in the humanities

only have great things to say. The German department here is also fantastic—classes in the department are varied and interesting, and German professors truly take the time to get to know their students and understand them. WUSTL also makes it incredibly easy for students to get involved in research as an undergraduate. I know a lot of schools will say "undergraduates are involved in research," sure, but the reality is, at most schools undergraduates simply wash test tubes and enter data into logbooks. That's not the case here. At WUSTL, undergraduates are given meaningful research to do, and while they're doing it they become extremely close with their professors.

> "There's *always* construction on campus—partially because the school's large endowment allows it to continuously improve its facilities."
>
> ✦ John, senior

The Students

Students at WUSTL are mostly East Coast, liberal, self-styled "intellectuals." This is to my great dissapointment—it's rough being the lone midwestern Republican, forced to constantly swallow the vocal liberal drivel. Most students are also either upper-middle-class or just plain rich. When someone says "Oh, I'm just a poor college student" at WUSTL, it means they were only able to afford *one* new Gucci handbag, instead of the two they were originally planning on buying. This isn't to say there are no middle-class students here—there are, they're just aren't many of them. Also, although there are a fair number of Black, Latino, and Asian students on campus, they *are not* integrated—there are groups of ethnic minorities, and the groups of white kids. I really don't understand this. There is no visible hostility. Neither group seems opposed to mixing with the other, there's no feeling that mixing would be unwelcome. But still, minorities and white students keep to themselves. It's weird.

The Activities

Kids at WUSTL don't really play typical sports like football, baseball, and basketball. Instead, they play a lot of preppy sports like tennis and volleyball.

Those are both big scenes on campus. Community service is also widely encouraged and participated in. Any kind of community service that excites you, it's already happening and you can jump into the middle of it.

The Social Scene

When (non premed) WUSTL students party, they party hard. The administration, lately, has cracked down on underage drinking, but this has just made students more creative. If you're smart, and you want to drink here, it's not really a problem. I'd say the biggest party places on campus are the frat houses. Everyone on campus goes to Greek parties to dance, drink, happily make fools of themselves, and generally forget about that paper they've been working on all week and should be writing right then. Around junior year, some kids get sick of the frat party scene and start hanging out and drinking in small groups, or heading to nearby bars in St. Louis.

Lastly—it seems like everyone here has a boyfriend or girlfriend. *Everyone.* I guess having a significant other makes the stressful workload more manageable—there's someone there to cuddle up to when you come home from the library at 2:00 a.m. So, yeah. If you come to WUSTL, I'd bet money that you'll find yourself a partner, too.

Name: Dani
Hometown: Rye Neck, New York
Class Year: Freshman
Major: Fashion design and marketing
Extracurriculars: Greek life, Campus Programming Council
Career Goal: Fashion designer/buyer

How would you describe Wash U.'s reputation?

WUSTL is an academic school that still has a good social scene. You know the drill. We work hard, we play hard.

Is this reputation accurate?

Pretty much. This school has high academic standards that force students to work hard, but when it's time to relax and have fun we know how to do that, too. I'd venture to say some students take their social lives as seriously as they do their educations.

What aspect of your school would a prospective student not see on a campus tour?

If you like to party, and get yourself involved in the Wash U. social scene, you'll have a great time. So long as you're not premed, you'll party lots, you'll party rambunctiously, you'll party with plenty of alcohol on hand. Most prospective students visit Wash U. during the day with their parents, so they don't see this.

The Institution

I chose to come to Wash U. because it seemed like it offered a perfect balance between work and play. Its academics have led to Wash U. being ranked among the top fifteen schools in America—and its party scene has caused some of my friends to say "I've never been drunk so many consecutive nights in my life," just before they're about to get drunk again. The school is also a good size—small enough so you'll run into the same people all the time (which means you can develop some good friendships), but large enough so that you'll see new people every single time you go out. And because students don't leave campus very much, Wash U. does feel like a community. It's kind of like going to sleep-away camp and staying there for four years. All the dorms are laid out in a circle around a huge field, like it's a little village, you're always surrounded by kids your age, everyone stays up late. In the middle of a week when you don't have much work due, it's sleep-away camp with alcohol, or it's like living in a happy commune with less tie-dye.

The Education

During the week, students at Wash U. work hard. We know (ostensibly) we're here to learn, and we actually want to learn. So we hit the books.

If you're a disciplined person, you can spend a few hours a day in class, a few hours a day in the library doing schoolwork, and still have plenty of time each night to enjoy yourself. This is what most people do. Unless you're a premed student. Our premed program is one of the best programs in the nation. Those kids work, and then work, and then work some more.

Also, Wash U. doesn't have a core per se, but every student does have to fill distribution requirements by taking some courses in the natural sciences, some in the social and behavioral sciences, some in history and literature, and some in cultural studies.

The Students

Wash U. isn't very diverse. Most students are white, most students are wealthy, a lot of students are Jewish. Yes, there are still nonwhite, non-wealthy, non-Jews here. But they're in the minority.

Students at Wash U. are doers, they take on a lot. Almost everyone double majors, or gets a dual degree. Kids involve themselves in everything from Greek life to the Student Council to a comedy group to singing in a choir—and often, a student will involve themselves in all of those things at once. Greek life is really big at Wash U., and if you like to party lots, then you'll find yourself pledging a frat here faster than you can blink. If Greek life isn't your thing, that's fine too. You'll just have a less hardcore time on weekends.

The Social Scene

When the weekend arrives at Wash U. most students force learning and classes from their minds, and prepare to have a blast. The Wash U. social scene can't possibly compare to that of a big state school with twenty thousand kids, but we try our hardest to come close! We party just about every weekend, and, really, if you know where to look, on every weekday. (I'm not sure what people who don't party do because, well, I don't tend to ever see them.) Frats tend to host the most parties, and there are also small parties in dorms on the South Forty, and lots of off-campus parties hosted by upperclassmen.

Most people at Wash U. are friendly and outgoing, and when you go out you'll see all your friends and, if you want to, you can always meet new people as well. If it's not a weekend but you don't have work to do and you want to have fun, most kids bar hop. On Tuesday nights, nearby Duffy's has great karaoke, and the place is always packed with Wash U. students. Monday, Wednesday, and Thursday nights the Landing is the place to be. And, luckily, bars close at two. So students always make it back to campus at a reasonable hour, ready to get up for classes bright and early the next morning.

Lastly—St. Louis hosts the second biggest Mardi Gras celebration in the country, and everyone goes to Soulard and parties all day and into the night. It's no New Orleans, but it's still great fun. Go WUSTL!

Notable Wash U. Alumni Include:
Daniel Nathans, Nobel Prize winner, medicine
Tennessee Williams, playwright
Carolyne Roehme, fashion designer
Aaron Rosenberg, composer
Harold Ramis, film writer, director, actor
Mary Wickes, actress

WASHINGTON AND LEE UNIVERSITY

Founded: 1749
Location: Lexington, VA
Phone: (540) 458-8400
E-mail: admissions@wlu.edu
Web site: www.wlu.edu

Number of Undergraduates: 1,730
Number of Graduate Students: 10
Cost: Approximately $32,500 per year
Application Deadline: January 15
Early Decision: December 1

Rating:	Notable Majors/Programs:
Most Selective	Business, Engineering, Life Sciences, English

Size:
● Small　○ Medium　○ Large

Location:
○ Urban　● Suburban　○ Rural

On a Saturday, students talk about academics:
○ Always　● Sometimes　○ Never

Nightlife:
● Intense　○ Moderate　○ Laid-back

Politically, Washington & Lee leans:
○ Left　● Right　○ Split

Diversity:
○ High　○ Low　● Medium

Students describe Washington and Lee in five words:
- Bucolic, elite, conservative, athletic, academic
- Gentile, respectful of tradition, rigorous, fratty!

From the School

For more than 250 years, this institution's mission has been to develop intellectual growth in its students in an environment of learning which stresses both the importance of individual honor and integrity and the responsibility to serve society through the productive use of one's talents and education.

—www2.wlu.edu

If you're interested in Washington and Lee, you may also be interested in:
Davidson, Duke, UNC at Chapel Hill, Vanderbilt, U. Virginia, Wake Forest

Name: Jessica
Hometown: Rockville, Maryland
Class Year: Junior
Major: Biochemistry, and considering a double in English
Extracurriculars: Women's Leadership Group, Women's Studies Advisory Board, peer counselor, Kappa Alpha Theta (sorority), Alpha Epsilon Delta (premed honor society), volunteer at local hospital ER
Career Goal: I want to be a sports orthopedist, specializing in knees.

How would you describe Washington and Lee's reputation?

People consider W&L the last bastion of the Reagan-loving, church-going, wealthy southern conservative.

Is this reputation accurate?

W&L is a conservative campus—the largest organization at school is the College Republicans—but, while most students are fiscally conservative, the student body is pretty socially liberal. I think, as a whole, people here are prepared to accept alternative lifestyles, even if they don't engage in them.

What aspect of Washington and Lee would a prospective student not see on a campus tour?

If you don't envision yourself being able to coexist with a vibrant and visible Greek system, W&L might not be the place for you. If you come to W&L, the word *fratty* will creep into your vocabulary. It's slang for all things that fit the traditional stereotype of the fraternity lifestyle—a southern guy wearing a collared shirt with khaki pants and loafers without socks, who drives an SUV, and drinks plenty of Southern Comfort with his fraternity brothers. He often affects an attitude of indifference even though they're plenty of issues on his mind, because it's fratty not to care. The fratty guy, however, is a consummate gentleman around campus. He's polite to parents, has good manners, always holds doors open, and loves the Honor Code. You'll see a lot of young men who fit this description at W&L.

The Institution

I adore Washington & Lee now, but it took me a while. I came from a very liberal, diverse high school in Maryland to a campus that I perceived as overwhelmingly white, conservative, and southern. I felt very isolated. With time, things changed—I made better friends, I became more engaged in extracurriculars, I found academic departments that really challenged me. A major factor that helped me come to love W&L was joining my sorority. I hadn't planned to go Greek when I came here, but I gave it a shot, and I have no regrets. The Greek system works at this school; joining a fraternity or sorority is a legitimate way to make real, lasting social connections with a variety of people you might not otherwise meet. Honestly, though, what I appreciate most about W&L right now is the sense of community that one finds on a small campus in the country. I stayed at W&L during the summer before my junior year to do chemistry research. I was involved in a freak car accident that July, with four other students, that led to one fatality and sent the rest of us to the emergency room. We were there until 2:00 a.m., and in that time, the dean of freshmen, the dean of multicultural affairs, the head of security, and my research adviser and his wife all came to the emergency room to offer their support. In the days that followed, all four of us experienced an outpouring of care, concern, and condolences from the entire community. The dean of students baked us a pie with blueberries she picked herself, and she delivered it personally to the off-campus apartment where we were all staying. It's that kind of campus—we're family—and after the tragedy of that accident, I could not be more thankful.

The Education

Washington & Lee has a 12-12-6 week calendar. The short, six-week spring term is wonderful. You only take two classes—yeah, they're pretty intense as far as reading load and the rapid-fire nature of assignments coming at you—but it's worth it because you invariably have much more flexibility with your time during spring term. Because there's less time in the classroom then, I'm able to volunteer and generally be much more involved on campus and in the community. Also, as a science major, spring term is pretty much the only time I can go abroad, which I plan to do before I graduate.

The faculty here is a huge draw. We don't have TAs; all of my classes have been taught be professors with Ph.D.s. In the classroom, they're uniformly very engaging, insightful lecturers. There are a few terminally boring professors at W&L—but for every mediocre professor, there are about four great ones. Moreover, the faculty is exceptionally supportive of student endeavors beyond the classroom: if you want to do independent research, it's easy to find a professor to advise you; if you don't know where to apply for grad school, professors are happy to make suggestions and even contact potential institutions directly to put in a good word. Professors here are not prima donnas—they all have office hours and they will bend over backward to encourage motivated students. W&L doesn't attract professors who want to be the hardest-core researchers, we attract professors who love working with undergraduates.

Also, while the student body as a whole definitely works hard and strives to do well, there is very little unhealthy competition here. I hear stories of academic sabotage from my friends at other schools, but nothing like that goes on here. On a whole, students are extremely cooperative in their work and are almost always willing to help each other out.

> "A shirt you'll find often on campus bears the quote, 'Washington & Lee: We're not snobs, we're just better than you!'"
> ✦ Laurel, senior

The Students

I had never seen so many wealthy, white, southern people in the same place in my life—until I came here! That said, though the students here all tend to look the same, there is a diversity of viewpoints on this campus. I came to W&L leaning to the political left, but going to school here has made me much more vocal about being liberal—someone has to stand up to all of those conservatives. Honestly, I can't imagine being a minority on this campus, not because I think there is much outright discrimination or prejudice, but because it seems like it would be very isolating. The student body is almost entirely straight, white, and Christian, and I think it would be very hard for a minority student to have classes or live in a hall where he or she was the only one who didn't have the same sexual orientation, skin color, and religious affiliation. If I could change something about this campus, I would make it more multicultural.

The Activities

There's not a ton to do in Lexington, Virginia. You might like big malls with great shopping, museums with wing after wing of seemingly endless collections, and cavernous movie theaters with a dozen screens, but you won't find any of those here! To make up for the lack of other options, lots of students volunteer in the community, play sports, and take an active role in campus organizations. W&L is small enough that if you have an idea to improve the quality of life on campus, the administration will pretty much do all they can to help you get it off the ground. And, if worse comes to worst, Wal-Mart is open twenty-four hours.

The Social Scene

Here is the quintessential W&L party: a crowded frat basement, cases of cheap beer, a decent '80s cover band, lots of dancing, and, ultimately, two hundred people considering the finer points of hooking up. The hookup scene is alive and well at W&L; it appears that the dating scene is on life-support. Our social scene centers around our fraternities and around drinking. Most people consider it a party when you combine the two. As a nondrinker, I enjoy the parties in moderation, but they can become tedious. However, there are plenty of other opportunities: our film society brings in great movies, the Student Activities board brings bands and sponsors field trips to do cool stuff like skiing or visiting D.C., and you can always drive forty-five minutes to UVA and Charlottesville to see what's going on there.

Name: Laura
Hometown: Savannah, Georgia
Class Year: Sophomore
Major: English and business administration
Extracurriculars: varsity tennis team, tour guide, kathekon (alumni relations board) VP of publicity Students Activities board, peer tutor, social chairman Kappa Alpha Theta, entertainment cochair fancy dress committee
Career Goal: I really want to work in the music/entertainment industry. I know more school is in my future and I eventually want to teach one day (preferably at W&L!).

How would you describe Washington and Lee's reputation?

A hidden gem. Some people have never heard

of W&L, but when you ask any professional circle about this university, it is known instantly as a great school. Honorable and academically challenging we have a high acceptance rate into grad schools and are known to be a great place for making connections.

Is this reputation accurate?

Yes.

> "The biggest controversy on campus is whether or not people should wear their collars up on polo shirts."
>
> ✦ James, junior

What aspect of Washington and Lee would a prospective student not see on a campus tour?

Well, we party. A lot. So I won't say things on tours when parents are there because they worry (that's what parents do). W&L is definitely a work hard, play hard atmosphere—and if I got to talk to parents about it, I'd tell them that I think this attitude is the strength not weakness of the school. Another common misconception of W&L is the perceived southerness of the school. Some people think that because Robert E. Lee is buried on our front lawn, we are a Confederate flag wavin', the-south-will-rise-again institution. Not true. A large percentage of students do hail from southern states, but we all behave as polite ladies and gentlemen—true southern hospitality. If that makes us southern, so be it.

The Institution

On big-time football (or lack thereof): even though we don't have the big-time football or basketball in "Lexvegas," the school spirit is the same, if not stronger, as larger universities. You aren't cheering for some obscure guy who got into your school for the sole purpose of being an athlete—you are cheering for the guy or girl who sits next to you in multivariable calculus, who is in your sorority or frat, or who is a campus leader that happens to be good at football, basketball, tennis, or whatever sport we're cheering for. I've seen whole fraternities or sororities come out with cowbells and signs for one guy or girl from their organization who plays on the team.

The school size on paper appears small in comparison to other universities. However, the best piece of advice I received about a small school was from an alumni in my hometown: at big schools, the schools are just that, big, and you need to break down into much smaller groups in order to not be swallowed. At a smaller school, you aren't just going to know the hundred people in your sorority or frat, by the time you graduate you are going to know at least two thousand people, and know them well. You aren't going to know that many people well at a big school even if you might *see* them as many times every day. My favorite traditions: dressing up in sundresses and ties/shorts for game days, speaking tradition, streaking the colonnade (I've heard . . .), Fancy Dress, Homecoming, Mock Con, Christmas Weekend, spring term, and the list goes on.

Our campus is beautiful—if you like red brick, white columns, and rolling grassy knolls, then you will love W&L. Complete blending of traditional with current: Lee Chapel (where the general is buried) is ivy covered, while the new commons is three stories, with dining hall, café, wireless capabilities, a movie theater, and student offices. The town in one word: charming. I initially came here and thought it was stuck in 1945, but the town prides itself on maintaining its historical charm. After being in Lexington for five minutes, I never wanted to leave—it truly is the quintessential American small town with interesting restaurants and boutiques and no commercial bombardment.

> "The honor system really works. Don't be fooled by other schools with an 'honor code.' Theirs isn't nearly the same."
>
> ✦ Michael, sophomore

The Education

When I was doing the college tour thing I went to one school and the first thing the admissions guy said to me with his smug little face was, "you come here [insert dramatic pause] you will be knocked down a peg." He went on jabbering how everyone here was a valedictorian, varsity captain, national science fair winner, and managed to build an orphanage all at the same time. Right, so, I wasn't going to subject myself to cutthroat competition among peers. I came to W&L instead. Are the students here valedictorians, varsity captains, national science fair–winning orphanage builders? Of course. Would you know it? Not because they told you. The atmosphere here is competitive, but it's in such a way that your peers and professors want you to do well—it's more of an inspiring atmosphere, as opposed to pasty academics clutching notes to their chests for fear of giving an advantage to someone else. Study sessions are the norm, not the exception.

The general course requirements are an important part of any liberal arts experience. Taking classes in more than one discipline is the only way to truly have a complete and well-rounded college education. Other than the general education courses and major courses, a student has roughly one-fourth of their classes to take as electives. This means you also end up with roughly one-fourth of the students in a typical class from different majors. A biology major like me can take classes in politics, philosophy, or the huge range of other topics. It also makes double majoring an option. This allows students to really pursue what they are passionate about while extending beyond the range of their major. A science student at W&L has an edge over his contemporaries at other schools. Because we have no graduate school (besides law), students are directly involved in faculty research and get to have extensive paid experience working in their field. In my time at W&L (both during the summer and school year), I've done tree frog research in Ecuador, salamander research in the mountains of Virginia, and biological weapons research for the Defense Department.

And because of the liberal arts focus here, there aren't too many differences between science majors and humanities students. Liberal arts really brings people out of their particular major and puts them together in a class they otherwise might not have other taken.

The Students

You aren't going to see people picketing, ever. Students are politically interested (and mostly Republican) but you aren't going to see protesters against Columbus Day because he took America from the natives (I've heard it, that really has happened at other schools).

Average student, male: shaggy hair, owns a lot of Polo, Lacoste, J. Crew, Patagonia, North Face, Kavu, Croakies, and the appropriate sunglasses; utterly fratastic. Female: well dressed (black pants a must at this school), pearls are common, owns a lot of Patagonia, North Face, Burberry, Polo, Kate Spade: sratastic, but a little more variance than the guy's uniform. For the most part, the students are well dressed and love to party.

The Activities

This is not a suitcase campus. People rarely go home or to another school, except on breaks. Something is always going on even if you don't dig the frat basement band thing.

I am a big music fan and the smallness of the town made me think I wasn't going to get to see my bands. However, I was extremely wrong. Student organizations have brought bands such as Widespread Panic, Leftover Salmon, String Cheese Incident, and North Mississippi Allstars. And Richmond, Roanoke, and Charlottesville are a short drive. Speakers are the same way. This school does not allow the town to stay small to its students.

> "We are the country club of the South, but everyone is not rich, white, preppy, Republican. There are some Democrats here, I promise! I miss my hippie clothing, but the school really does teach you to be presentable."
>
> ✦ Lia, junior

The Social Scene

Wednesday, Friday, and Saturday are the big nights when the majority of the people go out, usually to a frat party in town (at the house) or a party in the country. In-town parties are completely open (no guest lists, no armbands, no cover price—if you are a girl here, you will pretty much never pay for anything if you go out), at least one band playing a weekend night, but usually two or three. In the country, parties have free beer (and water), and there are usually at least one or two a night. The Halloween party at Windfall Hill is huge. Another interesting aspect of W&L is that all the off-campus houses are named, so instead of telling Traveler (the school-provided sober van circuit) "I want to go to 435 Main Street," you say the party's at Utah, Munster, Candyland, Northpole, Sponge, Batcave—every house has a name. You live in university housing for two years (this includes frat and sorority houses), then you have the option to live off campus, which most students do (in the country or in town).

Name: Nick
Hometown: San Antonio, Texas
Class Year: Junior
Major: Biology and environmental studies
Extracurriculars: Student recruitment committee (tour guides), dorm counselor, Outing Club, cycling team, research assistant
Career Goal: First, to go to medical school and then to specialize as an oncologist.

How would you describe Washington and Lee's reputation?

W&L is a small school with extremely good academics that enriches students through a liberal arts education. We have the facilities and faculty of a large research university, but the personal feel and community of a small liberal arts school.

Is this reputation accurate?

Yes. Washington & Lee is the best of both worlds; a great academic education that leaves students ready for successful careers in the real world, but without the problem of students feeling lost in the crowd. At W&L, every student is important and never anonymous.

What would an admissions officer at Washington and Lee probably not tell a prospective student?

An admissions officer might leave out the huge number of leadership opportunities available at W&L. Every student has the opportunity to be the big man on campus due to the huge number of extracurricular clubs and activities. Students are taught to be leaders in and out of the classroom. This aspect is difficult sometimes to quantify or demonstrate to perspective students, but will make a huge difference once you're here.

The Institution

Many students choose Washington & Lee over other colleges and universities because of its mix of great academics and small size. We have a huge course catalog and small classes where a student is not a number, but an individual. The size and tightness of the community give a real feeling of family, where everyone knows everybody else and is interested in their success.

I choose my school because of its exceptional premed program—90 percent of all applicants are accepted out of college—and for the unique ability to do meaningful undergraduate research. Of equal importance was the honor system and the feeling of community it inspires. You will not find a more civil, or friendly student body anywhere. The honor system also provides a unique relationship between townspeople and the school that is vastly different from most college towns (students interact with the community through extensive service and employment opportunities). The cornerstone of Washington & Lee is our unique honor system. A legacy of General Robert E. Lee, it is among the very best in the nation and of the utmost importance to students, alumni, and faculty. W&L does not just talk about honor; we live by it and expect it in all of our students both in and out of the classroom.

Located in the Shenandoah Valley, the beauty of Washington & Lee as a campus is matched only in the surrounding mountains and streams. Caught between two national forests, W&L provides students with the unique ability to hike, cycle, mountain bike, fly fish, and kayak with only a short car trip.

The Education

Washington & Lee provides a good mix of academics and social/extracurricular activities. Classes are demanding and have to be our number one priority, but it is understood that outside experiences can be just as important.

Our small semester, spring term, offers a unique educational experience where students take highly specialized classes that could not be offered in a normal term. As far as majors are concerned, students tend to polarize in our business school and journalism school. Of the top thirty national liberal arts colleges, W&L has the only two such programs. The sciences are also very popular, especially chemistry, biology, psychology, and geology.

As part of our liberal arts education, many students enrich their college education by studying abroad. Over half of W&L students spend some time outside the United States over their four years. Our 12-12-6 academic schedule allows all students (even preprofessional) to get away and experience education outside of the States.

The Students

Washington & Lee students hail from forty-four states and seventeen foreign countries, leaving students with the ability to learn from classmates about different ideas and cultures while on campus. Leading campus groups include the neighbors service league, the Outing Club, and the college Republicans and Democrats. Every four years, over 98 percent of students participate in the Mock Convention, which is covered by CSPAN and MSNBC. W&L has accurately predicted the outcome of each party's presidential nominee eighteen of the last twenty-three times (the most accurate in the nation).

The Activities

All students do some type of extracurricular activity that adds to life at W&L in some way. The Outing Club has trips that occur at least once a week, if not more, and Neighbors Service League are the largest campus organizations. Athletics are very prevalent. W&L dominates the Old Dominion Athletic Conference (Division III) in men's and women's lacrosse, field hockey, tennis, volleyball, and several others. Most government, including the administration of the honor system, is student-run and free of administrative oversight. Students really do lead the school.

The Social Scene

Most social activities revolve around Greek life. Sorority and fraternity life on campus is dominant, but not overwhelming. What's more, all students are invited to all social functions, regardless of Greek affiliation. Our biggest social event is the Fancy Dress Ball, where students put on four days of activities, including a black-tie ball, using the over eighty thousand dollars earmarked for the event.

Notable Washington and Lee Alumni Include:

Pat Robertson, founder, Christian Broadcasting Network

Robert Mosbacher, former secretary of commerce

Terry Brooks, author

Tom Robbins, author

Tom Wolfe, journalist

Ninety-four alumni have been congressmen, thirty-one have been governors, and four have been U.S. Supreme Court justices.

WELLESLEY COLLEGE

Founded: 1870
Location: Wellesley, MA
Phone: (781) 283-1000
E-mail: admission@wellesley.edu
Web site: www.wellesley.edu

Number of Undergraduates: 2,290
Number of Graduate Students: 0
Cost: Approximately $39,000 per year
Application Deadline: January 15
Early Decision: November 1

Rating:	Notable Majors/Programs:
Very Selective	Social Sciences, Life Sciences

Size:
● Small ○ Medium ○ Large

Location:
○ Urban ● Suburban ○ Rural

On a Saturday, students talk about academics:
● Always ○ Sometimes ○ Never

Nightlife:
○ Intense ○ Moderate ● Laid-back

Politically, Wellesley leans:
● Left ○ Right ○ Split

Diversity:
● High ○ Low ○ Medium

All Women's: Yes!

Students describe Wellesley in five words:
- Beautiful, intellectual, open-minded, career-oriented strength
- Empowered, politically correct, scholarly women

From the School

The mission of Wellesley College is to provide an excellent liberal arts education for women who will make a difference in the world. Wellesley is a college for the student who has high personal, intellectual, and professional expectations. Beyond this common ground, there is no typical Wellesley student. Students come from all over the world, from different cultures and backgrounds, and they have prepared for Wellesley at hundreds of different secondary schools.

—www.wellesley.edu

If you're interested in Wellesley, you may also be interested in:
Amherst, Barnard, Bryn Mawr, Harvard, Smith, Spelman

Name: Sophie

Hometown: Audubon, Pennsylvania

Class Year: Freshman

Major: Considering doubling in economics and international relations

Extracurriculars: College Government (Student Senate), Dorm Vice President of Administration

Career Goal: Originally, medicine. Now, either law or business.

How would you describe Wellesley's reputation?

Wellesley is definitely one of the most prestigious schools in the country, but the funny thing is, a lot of people hear its name and go, "huh?" until I say something like "Hillary Clinton went there," and then all of a sudden, realization dawns on them (sometimes). It's quite funny, actually. We also have a strangely split reputation for both being very conservative as a women's college (by those who don't know us well), and for being very liberal (by those who do know us well). People who don't understand Wellesley tend to see us as elitist feminists who are determined to rule the world.

Is this reputation accurate?

Granted, we're all highly motivated and ambitious women, but we have fun just like everyone else. In some ways, we are still very conservative, both in terms of administrative views and by the minor fact that we're still a strictly women's college. However, in terms of the student body and our views, we couldn't be more liberal. The entire college, though nonpartisan, is definitely dominated by Democratic beliefs. But we do respect other beliefs—and I think that type of respect, in a sense, makes us more liberal than most schools.

What would an admissions officer at Wellesley probably not tell a prospective student? What aspect of your school would a prospective student not see on a campus tour?

Every school has a party scene. Many prospective students might be shocked that an all girls school can have fun, but we do, and a lot of times, it's not through substance (ab)use. Also not mentioned on your official visit is the fact that stress here is *rampant*. Everyone at Wellesley has some strength (or two or ten) that placed her at the top of her high school classes, and it's often an odd realization that she may not be at the pinnacle any-

more. So the stress can get a bit overwhelming at times. But hey, we're all still here!

The Institution

With our rolling hills, Lake Waban, and the old, gothic architecture of our residence halls and academic buildings, Wellesley looks and feels exactly like what college is supposed to be—you won't find a prettier campus anywhere.

In terms of traditions, Marathon Monday is probably my favorite here. The Boston Marathon takes place right next to Wellesley, outside of Munger Hall, and we've become famous for our insane energy and spirit, and for our crazy, newsworthy "Scream Tunnel," through which we shout nonstop, encouraging the runners. So much energy, so much spirit, it's no wonder runners love us so much. Munger Hall (my dorm!) sets up a huge line of posters, and we offer the runners oranges and water along their tiring route. It makes me proud to be a part of that.

The meal plan is also amazing. One simple plan: unlimited food. That's right, unlimited. As a junk food addict, I love it. We eat as much as we want, whenever we want, and the only drawback is that the dining hall hours end early.

The weather is—New England weather. It gets frightfully cold here in the winter, and it snows like crazy, but luckily the dorms have radiators in each room. I'd suggest investing in a heavy coat and boots, though, because while inside it will be warm, the trek to class every day in the late November/early December weather can be brutal. Some girls I know from the West Coast were shocked to discover that their winter coats just couldn't deal with the true Bostonian winters.

Campus security (lovingly nicknamed Campus Po by the students) are fabulous. Many of the officers are parents of Wellesley students, and those who are not, take care of us as if we were family. Shuttle services run at all hours of the night from various areas of campus such as the library and the science center back to individual dorms, and in general, there is a very kind attitude toward maintaining safety on campus.

The Education

Don't let the fun-loving aspect of Wellesley women fool you: we are *hardcore* students. Why? Simple: the workload is intense. College at first seemed as if it would be much easier than high school, since it requires fewer classes per semester. However, you quickly find that the workload for each class is insanely more than you imagined. We study and talk about class after school, on nights, and on weekends. One of my favorite things to do on a Sunday afternoon is to walk into the town of Wellesley, sit in the Starbucks with my friends, and do some homework or read while sipping a Frappuccino.

"The 'Official' List of 50 things to do at Wellesley before you graduate:

1. Run naked across Severance Green
2. Get twelve hours of sleep in one night
3. Go Step Singing
4. See the campus from the top of Galenstone Tower
5. Walk around Lake Waban with a friend
6. Have a party in your room for no reason and invite everyone you know
7. Skinny dip in Lake Waban
8. Read a book that isn't required and that doesn't have anything to do with your major
9. Pull a nonacademic all-nighter
10. Go traying on Severance Green (traying is sledding on a cafeteria tray)
11. Write a letter to the editor
12. Attend one sporting event for each Wellesley athletic team
13. Admit you don't know everything
14. Have a little too much to drink at a department party and start a singalong with your favorite professor
15. Eat nachos at the Hoop
16. Get a Little Sister
17. Eat in all the dining halls in one day.
18. Send an e-mail to someone who is sitting in the same room
19. Buy candy in El Table to eat during class
20. Let a prospective student sleep on your floor
21. Become the ultimate fan of at least one Wellesley sports team
22. Stay for winter session
23. Be the subject of a psychology experiment
24. Nominate a professor for the Pinanski Prize
25. Swing next to the Chapel
26. Attend Senate, say something
27. Go tunneling
28. Try dorm or class crew on the lake
29. Visit the observatory
30. Become a regular at Mobile Mart/CVS
31. Go to a Shakespeare Society production
32. Go ice skating on Paramecium Pond
33. Declare your own personal Lake Day
34. Go trick-or-treating at President Walsh's house
35. Nap in the library
36. Start a dorm war
37. Stage a protest
38. Join an organization
39. Go to a frat party
40. Write a paper in thirteen-point New York
41. Learn to fake a Boston accent
42. Attend an on-campus party
43. Voluntarily attend a lectrure
44. Take a day off and be a tourist in Boston
45. Primal scream
46. Cheer at the Boston Marathon
47. Go to a commencement other than your own
48. See at least one a cappella concert
49. Listen to WZLY
50. Ride in a Campus Po car. Lights and sirens are a bonus."

✦ Sophie, junior

Competition is definitely present. I mean, it's a campus of 2,300 brilliant, hormonal, perfectionistic, anal-retentive, and stressed women. Just imagine us during finals! However, the great (and admittedly kind of contradictory) thing is that the stress often doesn't make us more competitive, it makes us more willing to give and receive help, because we know what it's like to need it.

Most of the classes I've taken are lecture-based, but more so in the science departments. The humanities, especially seminars of course, are more discussion-oriented. As the college is undergrad, and almost all classes are taught by professors, TAs and student tutors are used just for additional help.

There are at least fifty-two majors, including several interdepartmental ones, and on top of that, you can create your own major if you can't find one out of the fifty-two that suits you. The core curriculum provides you with a very solid liberal arts foundation, but the classes are so varied that you can find many courses to satisfy those requirements.

The Honor Code is fabulous. Truthfully, I was skeptical at first because it's unwritten and places so much trust in everyone, not just the students. But what I love about Wellesley is that everyone appreciates that trust and it's seldom abused. This policy allows us to have self-scheduled take-home

> "There's kind of a joke on campus: 'so which one are you going to be: doctor, lawyer, or businesswoman?'"
> ✦ Micki, sophomore

exams and makes for a much more welcoming and warm environment in which to live and to learn.

The Students

Some people say that Wellesley can't be all that diverse, considering we're all girls. That's utterly wrong. You'd be surprised by the different kinds of people here—not only in terms of their varying perspectives and interests, but also in terms of economic backgrounds, traditions, racial/cultural/etc. beliefs. Wellesley is very diverse. There is a lot of support for LGBT people, groups and politics on campus. I'd say the campus is mostly Democratic, though there are definitely many other political beliefs out there. There isn't much separating upper- and lowerclasswomen; some of my closest friends this first year are seniors and juniors, and I'm definitely sad to see them leave. Upperclasswomen tend to be some of the most supporting people you meet here, and they never cease to amuse, tease, help, and encourage the incoming students. Since it's a campus of women, emotions tend to sometimes run high. There are people who like to provoke others, and there is some level of cattiness, but that can be said of every school environment.

The Activities

The schools near us are BU, Brandeis, MIT, Babson College, and Harvard, and we interact most with the latter three. We cross register at MIT and Babson, thus activities span all those campuses. MIT opened all its rush events to Wellesley students, and often we get discounts on the activities on other campuses.

A cappella groups are very popular, as are cultural organizations and their annual cultural shows. The Greek life is very minute, with only four official sororities on campus, but that doesn't mean there's any shortage of parties—you'll find they're simply sponsored by different organizations. The *Wellesley News* is read by practically everyone, mostly because it is provided free everywhere. Theater is also very big, as are the club sports like rugby, tennis, and ultimate Frisbee. College Government plays a role in all sides of student life here, and is probably the biggest force on campus. As a senator in College Government, I've seen debates and legislation ranging from constituting new organizations to grade inflation, fees and fines to the planning of Spring Concert.

If it's 3 a.m. on a Wednesday night, I'm most likely doing last-minute work while online with half of the Wellesley community. Real college students go to bed with the dawn. Sleep is for wimps, or for those who are lucky enough to get some.

The Social Scene

People mostly party off campus, or preparty on campus and then go off. We do have a lot of parties on campus, though, and most of these serve alcohol only to those with ID. Since Wellesley is a women's college, the dating scene is not that huge, unless you're LBGT. I know most of the girls who have boyfriends either have them from home or from MIT, Harvard, or another school in the area. It can sometimes get lonely, but that's what friends are for.

Dorm life is amazing, especially if you live in Munger! There are so many amazing women here who know how to have fun without guys, drugs, and/or drinks. Everyone is friendly for the most part, and it's not uncommon to have complete discussions with random strangers in your dorm, the dining halls, or the library. While meeting new people happens all the time, you'll also find that most people in your dorm, or your floor at least, will be familiar faces to you within the first month of school.

Name: Larsen
Hometown: Merced, California
Class Year: Sophomore
Majors: Theater studies and American studies (concentration in education)
Extracurriculars: Upstage, Shakespeare Society, Body and Soul
Career Goal: I want to be an artistic director of my own theater company.

How would you describe Wellesley's reputation?

Wellesley has a varied reputation. We are sometimes frat-ho man-hating lesbians, sometimes dynamic leaders, sometimes the epitome of *Mona Lisa Smile,* sometimes rebellious. Most importantly, we have a reputation for intelligence and competence.

Is this reputation accurate?

The school is different things to different people, but I'd say that every person at Wellesley is an intelligent human being. Every alumna that I've met is dazzling, despite what she majored in or has done with their life.

What would an admissions officer at Wellesley probably not tell a prospective student?

An admissions officer would probably not tell students about the housing crunch, or about the construction plans—they seem to think that students and construction can coexist happily, but this, my friend, is a falsehood.

> "On a campus tour, a prospie wouldn't see the compulsive overachievers, the people with eating disorders, the sex toy and porn parties (so fun!), the naked party or dyke ball but also the individual brilliance of each and every woman here and how powerful that makes you feel."
>
> ✦ Wendy, senior

The Institution

We are a sisterhood of intelligent, sometimes dorky, brilliant, and driven women who have come together to revel in the beauty of academia. Naturally, this sort of climate has bred an Old Girl's Network, and the opportunities afforded from it are amazing. This summer I was working at a theater festival in the Adirondacks in upstate New York and one night a Wellesley alumna there sought me out, and gave me her card and told me to call her and we'd do lunch. I know very few people who don't have a story about an alumna taking care of her sisters beyond the Wellesley Bubble.

The campus is a beautiful respite with proximity to Boston, complete with a lake and an arboretum and many grassy knolls. (Though it's also at water level, so on some really gross rainy days, half the campus becomes a pond.)

Our Honor Code is amazing: you can usually leave your stuff unlocked and it will still be there—I left my Discman in the Hoop (the campus café) and it was still exactly where I left it two days later.

The Education

I think what makes Wellesley consistently so highly ranked for its academics is that the people who apply here are all geeks of some fashion or another. Most students here are into being at school and learning, and actually enjoy spending time in the library and working themselves to the bone. My breakfast conversation this morning consisted of some bitching about the library not being open yet and how we'd be the first in line to enter. All of my friends know so much about their field, which adds to both classes and the overall vibe of the school. It's a great place to be an egghead.

We have distribution requirements, and classes are sorted by type (quantitative reasoning; music, art, performance; social and behavioral analysis; etc.) and you have to take a certain amount of each type of course. But it's generally pretty easy to fulfill these requirements.

You can do an independent study on pretty much whatever you want and get credit for it, if you find a professor willing to advise you. If you're looking to do research with a professor, which I personally haven't, you can do it over the summer. About a third of students go abroad their junior year for a semester or a year. Students are highly encouraged to go abroad.

The Students

There is a lot of diversity on campus, but I think the problem with all the ethnic student unions is that they can serve to put the ethnic diversity into boxes. Republicans feel left out a lot of the time, as most of the campus is liberal and relatively vocal about it. I think it's a bigger deal to be a Republican on campus than a lesbian. It feels like most students are from California, Massachusetts, and New York, and then everywhere else. We have a high representation of people from all over the world, but the majority seems to come from those three states. Overall it's a pretty safe and intelligent environment, and everyone mixes.

The Activities

We have good sports and good extracurriculars. People are devoted to the organizations they are in. It's also pretty easy to organize groups and events, mostly due to the college's addiction to FirstClass, our e-mail server. I've been the vice president of Upstage, the student theater organization, and it really provides great opportunities for people like me who want to go into theater. The organization provides funds and space for six student run/produced productions a year. You have to apply the year before to get a show slot, but not that many schools have a program where it's so easy to get in as a designer or director. If you are up at 3 a.m., it is most likely because you're pulling an all-nighter to get your work done—and procrastinating by reading and posting on FirstClass.

The Social Scene

People party in many different ways—some people go to Boston every weekend to hit up the frat parties, or go to clubs, or just to hang with their friends there. Some people stay on campus and attend the immense amount of things (theater, dance, movies, concerts, hanging out with friends) available over any given weekend.

Dorm life is interesting—each dorm has a distinct personality. There are societies on campus, each of which has an academic aim: Phi Sigma is lecture, Tau Zeta Epsilon is arts and music, Zeta Alpha is literary, and Shakespeare is obviously Shakespeare. The Shakespeare Society puts on a Shakespeare play every semester. Almost everyone lives on campus, and the campus itself is very friendly.

Name: Leslie
Hometown: Fresno, California
Class Year: Freshman
Major: English, premed
Extracurriculars: In-depth editor for *Generasians* (Asian/Asian American Awareness Magazine), Senior reception coordinator for Students of Asian Descent, house council secretary, Japan Club secretary, cochairperson for the Formal for the Class of 2007, member of the Hippocratic Society, Mei Mei Jei Jei big sister, one of the Buddhist representatives on MultiFaith Council
Career Goal: I hope to become either a physician, focusing on neuroradiology, or be somehow involved with hospital administration.

How would you describe Wellesley's reputation?

In the New England area, it seems that socially, Wellesley College has a soiled reputation in regards to the character of its students. Some magazines (*Rolling Stone, Playboy*) helped give Wellesley women the reputation of easy young girls, who are just waiting for the weekend to let loose on Boston. Elsewhere—from my home state of California, say—they either have no idea what or where Wellesley is, or they assume that it's like the *Mona Lisa Smile* portrayal of the fictional 1950s Wellesley, conservative and constrictive.

Is this reputation accurate?

Sure there are a few sexual animals on the prowl, but at what college aren't there? And here, they're definitely in the minority. Yes, Wellesley College is very quiet on the weekends because many go into Boston, but not everyone goes in search of parties, clubs, and men (despite the fact our nighttime buses have been nicknamed "f*ck trucks")—many go just to have dinner at restaurants, see museums, experience urban life (something that the little town of Wellesley does not provide). Whether or not Wellesley is known to the general public doesn't matter as much as the fact that employers and graduate schools recognize and know Wellesley College for our good academics and networking opportunities.

What would an admissions officer at Wellesley probably not tell a prospective student? What aspect of your school would a prospective student not see on a campus tour?

The town of Wellesley seems to die after 7:00 p.m. on weekdays, 9:00 p.m. on weekends. Boston dies after midnight—forcing many to go to frat parties if they don't have other connections already planned. Also, the transportation to and from Wellesley is not stellar. Many times, the buses break down, have standing room only, and take forty to forty-five minutes to get into Boston (the brochures make it seem as if Boston is twenty minutes away).

Institution

In between Tower Court East and Severance Hall are the infamous suicide rooms. It's been said that before we came (we modern girls, that is), the Wellesley students were able to bring maids with them, and these suicide rooms were the rooms of the students' maids. These are three teeny windowless rooms with one solitary lightbulb, a dresser, a closet, and a cot. One day, the three maids decided to hang themselves in their rooms. Now, students can walk up the crickety stairs in between the two dorms and peer under the doors to the locked rooms, the dresser, the cot, the closet. They are locked, but the maids' ghosts may still walk the halls.

> "At first I missed guys for all the clowning around they do, but then I realized that I could become the class clown for once—and it's been great ever since!"
>
> ✦ Wendy, senior

The Education

Most of my classes have been lecture-based, though the professor always allows time for questions and discussion. I definitely receive personal attention from professors. They all provide office hours, and even if you don't go to office hours, they are almost always in their office throughout the week. I have visited professors at seven in the morning to ten at night. I came to this school intimidated by the small class sizes and the personability of professors (I came from a high school with forty people in a class), but I now have tea with my English professors, have lunch with my adviser to Students of Asian Descent, and I've even borrowed my adviser's car! I often find myself chatting online with my professors.

I came from a high school where I was what most would call above average, and then I come to this school and I find myself average (a lot of my Wellesley friends would concur, not about me necessarily, but about having experience this themselves). It's a very humbling feeling, but it gives

you a perspective that makes you work a lot harder than you're used to. I spend a lot of time on schoolwork outside of class. I don't know when I have time to breathe.

The Students

Students are definitely Democrats! Being even a liberal Republican, I find myself hiding my political association because of the political ardor many students have. The religious experience is important to me, and it's been supportive here. We have a MultiFaith Council that has an open forum for all faiths. Representatives discuss the basics of their religions in a living room situation. It's comfortable, supportive, and I always find myself learning new things and opening myself to new perspectives. The student body is fairly diverse, and the Asian/Asian-American population is significant (over a quarter of the student body). As a result, I find that the majority of my friends are of Asian descent. I came from a high school that was very diverse—but now at Wellesley, I find that cultural groups socialize with similar cultural groups when in large cliques. Individually, however, many students socialize with others of different ethnicities.

Currently, students of Asian descent are attempting to institutionalize an Asian-American studies major. We have faced many challenges in the past four years and although there has been some success (one course each in the English, religion, and history departments as well as an adviser), we're going to keep pushing!

Activities

We go into Boston for dinner and coffee. Sometimes we'll stop by an MIT fraternity we've become friendly with, but we usually chill around Cambridge in search of new stores, restaurants, and people. If we're not up to battling the forces of the f*ck truck, we stay at Wellesley, walk to a few nearby restaurants, or rent a movie and order takeout. We have fun just by ourselves.

The Social Scene

Friday and Saturday nights are pretty dead at Wellesley College, but there's a party here every other weekend (almost). Societies host decent parties that bring busloads of boys to the school. There also is a pub that hosts bands frequently—it's a good spot for anyone to come relax while listening to good music. Our Tower Court is supposedly the biggest party on campus, where U-Hauls dump loads of boys from around the New England area, but Dyke Ball is the place to be!

The dating scene is pretty nonexistent for first years and even sophomores. I find that many girls come to Wellesley with boyfriends already, or they are dating guys that they already knew. But if you're straight and want to find someone, your only decent option is to go to frat parties and just hang out and chat with the guys—and even then, it may not be the most suitable situation because they're usually intoxicated or attached, or the girls from the other schools have the upper hand because they have class with the guys. Plus, you have the competition of twenty other girls who have decided to attend the frat parties in search of the very same thing you are searching for.

Notable Wellesley Alumni Include:
Cokie Roberts, journalist
Diane Sawyer, broadcast journalist
Hillary Rodham Clinton, United States senator and former First Lady
Katharine Lee Bates, author of the words to "America the Beautiful"
Madeleine K. Albright, former U.S. secretary of State
Nora Ephron, writer

WESLEYAN UNIVERSITY

Founded: 1831

Location: Middletown, CT

Phone: (860) 685-3000

E-mail: admissions@wesleyan.edu

Web site: www.wesleyan.edu

Number of Undergraduates: 2,750

Number of Graduate Students: 200

Cost: Approximately $40,000 per year

Application Deadline: January 1

Early Decision: November 15

Rating:	Notable Majors/Programs:
Most Selective	English, Life Sciences, Social Sciences, Film

Size:
- ○ Small
- ● Medium
- ○ Large

Location:
- ○ Urban
- ● Suburban
- ○ Rural

On a Saturday, students talk about academics:
- ● Always
- ○ Sometimes
- ○ Never

Nightlife:
- ○ Intense
- ● Moderate
- ○ Laid-back

Politically, Wesleyan leans:
- ● Left
- ○ Right
- ○ Split

Diversity:
- ● High
- ○ Low
- ○ Medium

Five-College school: Yes!

Students describe Wesleyan in five words:
- Liberal, prestigious, personalized, top-notch academics
- Most creative/intellectual/political/artistic student body in America

From the School

Wesleyan is a community of active learners. Our faculty bring their scholarship and creative work to their teaching and engage students as creators of knowledge. We enhance capacities for critical and imaginative thinking that can address unfamiliar and changing circumstances, engender a moral sensibility that can weigh consequence beyond the self; and establish an enduring love of learning for its own sake.

—www.wesleyan.edu

If you're interested in Wesleyan, you may also be interested in:

Amherst, Brown, Carleton, Oberlin, Reed, Vassar, Yale

Name: Michael
Hometown: Kansas City, Missouri
Class Year: Junior
Major: Biology, premed
Extracurriculars: What *don't* I do? Everyone at Wes tries everything at least once.
Career Goal: I'd like to become a doctor.

How would you describe Wesleyan's reputation?

Wesleyan is known as an elite, top ten liberal arts college. It's frequently named the most political/activist school in country. Wesleyan students are known as extremely creative artist/intellectual types, who see multiple sides to every issue and take great joy in debating every one of those sides for hours and hours on end. In high school, my friends regarded Wesleyan as the best school in America for combining artistic freethinkers with prestigious top-notch academics.

Is this reputation accurate?

Wesleyan defies easy categorization. It's everything mentioned above, but it's also much more. It's a school full of creative types, drawn to Wesleyan's top-notch English, studio arts, and film majors. (Speaking of, Wesleyan has the best film program in the country right now.) Then, studying right alongside these creative types are brilliant scientists—Wesleyan gets more federal research funds than any liberal arts college in America, students do really important research, and nine of every ten graduates gets into their top-choice medical school. We also have lots of econ majors, in addition to people who major in totally random things but land investment banking gigs upon graduation, and this is only a fraction of our student body. Tons of kids—most of us, probably—have *no* idea what our professional focus will be, but, nonetheless, we really love learning for its own sake.

What's coolest is that nobody actually breaks down into categories like the ones above. Wes kids are good at many things, and interested in even more. One of my housemates is a concert pianist who started a nonprofit in high school and double majors in film and econ here. Another is a compsci and philosophy double major who started his own company while still in college. A third is the captain of the track team who farms during the summer, and also dances here and does interdisciplinary psych research on con men. And they probably all have hidden accolades and oddball talents that I don't even know about—sometimes even your closest friends can surprise you. Just when you think someone couldn't have a more diverse range of interests and accomplishments, you discover something that blows you away all over again. *That's* Wesleyan for you.

What would an admissions officer at Wesleyan probably not tell a prospective student?

An admissions officer wouldn't tell visitors just how politically active Wesleyan students are—particularly against Wesleyan's own administration. In the recent past, our big bad administration has made many decisions in an attempt to chip away at Wesleyan's liberal and quirky reputation. So good-bye Art House, where for years on end students threw the beloved, twice-yearly Naked Party. Good-bye sidewalk chalking, which students used to get out all sorts of political messages. Hello newly admitted students—you're more mainstream and normal each year. Luckily, Wesleyan students fight back. That's who we are, how we've been taught to think. A Wesleyan education teaches you to challenge authority, to think critically—and to act. So when Art House was first shut down, we threw the Naked Party elsewhere. When they said we couldn't use sidewalk chalk, we got hundreds of faculty members to support us and went out there and chalked anyway. I think we're probably the only elite school that's constantly this passionate and involved, this fiery. We love this place, and we refuse to be steamrolled.

The Institution

Wesleyan's a great place to be if you're ready for it. You have to be motivated, because there's a ton of work. You have to be creative, because Wesleyan is in small-town Connecticut, and you have to make the most of what's around. You have to be friendly, because there are a lot of lovely people to meet, but there are some lonely people, too. Life moves pretty fast. Be ready to live in extremes: we work hard, protest hard, party hard. But we certainly know how to mellow out—the breaks between the extremes are just as enjoyable as the extremes themselves.

Sometimes I walk around our campus with a big grin on my face, because it's so beautiful. I love how the varied and sometimes stunning architecture reflects the institution itself. On the one hand you have Olin Library, a traditional brick and marble structure designed by the architect of the Lincoln Memorial, a building as gorgeous as you'd find at any institution in America. We have College Row, a beautiful area with brownstone administration buildings, criss-crossing walkways, and tons of trees. Then on the other end of campus you have the Center for the Arts, a scattering of stark gray bunker-like structures built to look like they'd survived some kind of nuclear explosion. And there's every type of architecture in between, including the Foss Hill dorms, which look like '70s-style brownstone motels—but are nonetheless quite functional.

Speaking of dorms, housing at Wesleyan is pretty good. Every student is guaranteed housing all four years, almost everyone lives on campus through senior year, and plenty of freshman get either singles or two-room doubles. Rooms tend to be pretty big, functional if not pretty. Most freshmen live in Clark (the oldest dorm, just renovated to be ultramodern with elevators and too-heavy-to-steal leather furniture), the Foss Hill dorms (Nicholson, Hewitt), WestCo (an artsy/hippie/hipster dorm), or the Butterfields (quieter dorms because they were designed to be riot-proof [thank your parents' generation for that], but you're even more likely to get a single). As you get older, housing options get bigger and nicer. And no matter where you live, you'll never be far from your friends—Wesleyan is only about a ten-minute walk from one end to the other.

The Education

Wesleyan is probably the least competitive school you'll find—there's no academic warfare here. Students do well because they're personally driven. I'm sure all the schools you're considering are full of really smart kids. They might even have smart kids who work hard and love learning. But take a minute to ponder the difference between "smart," "hard-working," and "intellectual." Being intellectual isn't just about liking academics; it's about a deep commitment to rigorous inquiry. It's about a passion for books, numbers, and theories that goes beyond anything measurable by average SAT scores or number of hours spent studying. If you scratch beneath the surface on your college tours, you'll find that surprisingly few top schools actually have deeply intellectual environments. Wesleyan does. What Weslyan doesn't have is a core curriculum. There are vague "Expectations" in the humanities, social sciences, and math and sci-

ence, but if you don't want to take them, you don't have to. Thirty percent of students opt out and there's absolutely no penalty.

Wesleyan faculty members tend to split their time about fifty fifty between teaching and research (all tenure-track faculty is required to do both.) Most faculty members only teach two courses at a time, so when they're teaching, you get their full attention. And when they're researching, there's only one hundred and fifty to two hundred graduate students at Wesleyan (mostly in the sciences), which means the vast majority of lab research comes from undergraduates, who get to play in all the research facilities with our fun and expensive equipment, and then sometimes get coauthorship credit for their work when it's published.

A big reason I came to Wesleyan was because the admissions office talked a lot about the strong science and econ departments. They said something like 25 percent of kids major in the sciences, which is a huge number for a liberal arts school. And our economics department is ranked second best of any liberal arts college in the nation. Which is damn good. I mean, our econ profs are truly inspiring, and I'm usually pretty reticent to say stuff like that.

Forty-five percent of students at Wesleyan study abroad, which is pretty cool. But the coolest is where we go: approximately half the students who study abroad do it somewhere outside western Europe. Which is a massive percentage compared to our peer institutions, and says volumes about Wes. We're aware of the world, not just the world around us. We have 125 preapproved programs, and you pay standard Wesleyan tuition (yes, financial aid even carries over) to go on any of them. Want to go somewhere that's not already on that list of 125 programs? You just petition and—poof!—if you have sound academic justification, it'll be approved. You can go anywhere in the world. Wesleyan's big enough to offer tons of resources; small and accommodating enough that you can make them your own.

> "There is no average student on campus: there are artsy-hipster-too-cool-for-school kids, jocks, hippies, activists, preppies, etc. Sometimes we mix, sometimes we don't."
> ✦ Ann, sophomore

The Students

Our campus is overwhelmingly liberal, but not overwhelmingly radical. However, there are a few radicals, and they get absorbed by their politics to a ridiculous extent. You'll see the same kid screaming and yelling and crying one day for the plight of the janitors, the next day refusing to eat to save the undomesticated rabbits, on a third day wearing a shroud, dressed all in black because he's decided that's the best way to protest SUVs, and by the end of the week he's standing naked in the library to speak out against sweatshop labor. To the casual onlooker, these activists make Wesleyan seem kind of "cause of the week," but, like I said, they're in the minority. For the most part, wild protesting, hunger strikes, sit-ins, and anarchy are rare.

The queer groups, propeace and anticorporation groups, music groups, and a couple athletic teams (women's rugby, especially) are hyper-involved in campus life. There are also large ethnicity-based or geographical-based groups, like Ujamaa (African American), Ajua Campos (Latino), and the Midwest club. I could develop a miles-long list of the identity groups here. There isn't as much racial integration as one would hope, but there is little to no animosity between racial groups. Wesleyan may be Diversity University, but we also have a lot of wealthy white students.

The bathroom walls here are great: besides the typical lists of hot frosh, they churn up some good discussions; they're one of the few places on campus anyone, homophobes and conservatives included, can feel comfortable saying what they feel. It's kind of weird to be in a place where the gay kids are out and proud and abundant and dominant—in large, large numbers—and it's the Republicans who are in the closet.

The Activities

Athletics are taken very seriously by the people who do them. We're Division III, so you can play more than one sport, but we're also a NESCAC school, which means we're quite competitive. Including intramurals (and being Wes, we have some pretty ridiculous ones), 80 percent of Wes students participate in athletics at some point. Also, Wesleyan is in Connecticut—two hours from New York and Boston, and a half hour from New Haven and Hartford (but nobody goes to Hartford, unless they're picking a friend up at the airport). New Haven has lots of concerts and lectures that might be worth the half-hour drive, but Yalies are there, and they're kind of annoying. Unless they're our friends, in which case it's cool that they're so close. Some professors teach at both Yale and Wesleyan, and sometimes Yale has a lecture worth traveling to.

Then we come to Middletown, where Wesleyan's located. Wes doesn't have a grand gated entrance to campus—our campus is part of the Middletown community and sometimes I think Wes students wish that weren't so. Middletown gets a bad rap because it's not a yuppified, quaint college town. It's over 350 years old, and it's gritty. It's even more diverse than Wesleyan's student body, and it's got people from all socioeconomic classes who just go about their business living there. A lot of students wish Middletown felt safer, or looked prettier (read: more gentrified). I *like* that Middletown is here to puncture the Wesleyan Bubble every so often—I think it's good to be grounded in the real world.

The Social Scene

I'd say that this is a work hard, play hard school, but there really isn't a separation between the two. When you're up until 5:00 a.m. on a Tuesday night, the discussion flipping from Kierkegaard to toe-jam to the band jamming next door and back to your paper on postcolonialist ethnographies, are you working or playing? And when it's 8 p.m. on a Saturday night and you're at the Science in Society majors' cocktails, taking an Action Potential Shot while discussing the social implications of this nonlaboratory experimentation, are you socializing or are you learning? Get my point yet? Wesleyan's like that.

Name: Cameron
Hometown: Sanford, Maine
Class Year: Senior
Major: European history
Extracurriculars: Varsity Baseball, Senior interviewer, gospel choir, tour guide. Also, every intramural sport possible, and extreme picnicking.
Career Goal: To become someone who's interesting to talk to.

How would you describe your school's reputation?

Extremely liberal and accepting of everything—except for intolerance.

Is this reputation accurate?

Sure.

What aspect of your school would a prospective student not see on a campus tour?

We are supposedly Diversity University but a prospective student might not recognize this if they didn't know where to look. Unfortunately, diverse is not a synonym for integrated. We are working on this.

The Institution

In the campus center bathrooms you can always find interesting political ideas and poetry written alongside and often in response to ignorant scribbling, requests for sex, and borderline pornographic cartoons ranging from fair to excellent in ability. The most difficult part of being a freshman here is that you will not sleep. There is too much to do. If you are sleeping, then you are missing out.

I chose Wesleyan because I had never met such an incredible group of interesting and interested people in my life. This includes both professors and students. This was not just the naïve perception of an eighteen year old, four years later I feel the exact same way.

> "People love Wesleyan, but not in the traditional sense. We sing our fight song with gusto (and a note of irony): it's heard at women's rugby games, on the first night of freshman orientation, and just randomly on Foss Hill."
>
> ✦ Rebecca, senior

The Education

Yes, I do talk about my classes on a Saturday night. Unfortunately I am usually incoherent after about 11:00 p.m. This is especially bad when I am at a professor's house, or they are at my house. Professors do take a special interest in students, even starting as a freshman, but don't expect to go to dinner with them until at least junior year.

None of my classes are taught by TAs, although some classes do have optional after-class TA sessions that can prove very useful both in learning the material and making friends. About half my classes were discussion-based and half lecture-based as an underclassman, but as an upperclassman almost all of my classes have been discussion-based, except for dance.

We don't have a core curriculum at Wesleyan—instead we have "general education expectations." If you don't fulfill the general education expectations and only take the classes you want, nothing happens. More than a quarter of students graduate without fulfilling them and you can still get honors and everything. Seriously. If you don't believe me, ask an administrator at Wesleyan. I don't ever cheat here. I know people who do, and they get caught and end up hiding from their parents, tending bar, and begging to come back to Wesleyan. I spend about two or three hours on homework every night. This is an average, as I sometimes don't do any work for days/weeks at a time. However, when I don't do work for days/weeks at a time I am punished by painful all-nighters that I am forced to hold frequently over the last few weeks of school.

The Students

. . . are fantastic.

The Activities

There are student groups of every type imaginable. Everyone's part of a group and these groups are what form the larger Wesleyan community. Think you have a new group idea that doesn't exist already? Think again. Chances are there are already three of them. Good try with your new hotshot-transgendered-midget-eskimo-lawndart championship group. We already have it, and everyone's a member. Did I say "a group"? Don't even try being in only one group. It won't happen.

Upset about something? Stage a protest. Or wait a week and there will be one that you like, you can join in. You'd better have an opinion. And yes, it ought to be a liberal opinion. Conservatives and liberals are the groups least likely to mix on this campus. This is mostly due to the fact that conservatives are bunch of fat stupidheads who don't see the big picture and generally don't think very clearly. We'll have to put up with them for the rest of our lives, why should we have to deal with them while we're in college? I'm a varsity athlete, I dance, sing, give tours, and try to get involved in theater. Theater is supposed to be very accessible at Wesleyan but that hasn't been my experience. Our student newspaper, *The Argus,* is a dirty gossip rag, flirting with obscenity and libel twice a week. Needless to say, it is very popular.

The Social Scene

There are as many parties here as you want there to be. They take place in dorm rooms, apartments, student houses, and late nights in the squash courts. Parties rule, if you're into that sort of thing. Everyone has a good time. I have a better time though, my parties almost always involve drinking. Isn't the point of a party to unwind with your friends while enjoying fine music and a cool beverage of your choice? Everyone deserves this choice and at Wesleyan they can exercise it. You don't have to "fight for your right to party" or anything like that. That is a bunch of contrived Beastie Boy hogwash. I think there is a drinking policy at Wesleyan, but it's never stopped me from drinking, or anyone else I know—students party how they want to party and no one stops them. Frats exist on campus, but don't dominate—they're mostly liberal hippie frats. Go to frat parties, they give away lots of booze. You can also do other things besides drink on weekends, there's absolutely no pressure to do things you don't want to. Go to plays, lectures, concerts, dance shows, or seminars—there's always something going on. Dating, let's see: where could you go on a date at Wesleyan? Go to a play or a movie, then see each other out at a house party and hook up. There are two secret societies on Wesleyan's campus, but I can't tell you about them because they're old and powerful and secret.

> "Wesleyan has no core curriculum. You only take the classes you want."
> ✦ Peter, junior

Name: Alix
Hometown: Willington, Connecticut
Class Year: Sophomore
Major: English
Extracurriculars: Steel band!
Career Goal: I want to write. I write poetry, fiction, and everything in between, so contributing anything to a major publication, preferably a magazine or journal, would be amazing.

How would you describe your school's reputation?

Wesleyan has a reputation for being extremely politically active. As Wes students, we're purportedly angry, motivated, and ready to get down and dirty for our respective causes. We also have a reputation for being funky, fashionable, and sexually liberated. Essentially, as far as any outsider knows, Wesleyan students live on the cutting edge of liberal life.

Is this reputation accurate?

Wesleyan is not as politically active as everybody thinks it is. A handful of ultra-activists fight vehemently for chalking, reproductive rights, queer liberation, vegetarianism, and any other cause you can dream of. However, the fact is most Wes students are average college kids who attend rallies and marches because they're social events. If you're like me and want to ignore 70 percent of the political fervor going on here, you certainly can. Of course, most Wes students—being the passionate, intelligent people they are—cherish a spirited political debate.

What would an admissions officer at your school probably not tell a prospective student? What aspect of your school would a prospective student not see on a campus tour?

An admissions officer at Wes would never tell a prospective student about crime in Middletown. In the recent past, there were an alarming number of incidents, and while the administration took action and it's gotten much better, I think it has left a lot of people on edge. Additionally, students who choose to live off campus are given no guidance as to which locations are safe and which are definitely not. No matter how nice Wesleyan is, Middletown remains—for the most part—pretty sketchy.

The Institution

The best thing about Wesleyan is that anybody can find a niche. This is a home away from home awaiting every type of person, whether queer, straight, black, white, athletic, artistic, loquacious, or painfully shy. I've never met anybody who couldn't find at least a dozen kindred souls at Wes. Besides, even the rare student who continues to feel awkward and out of place after a month or two at Wes will find that everything changes after the biannual Wesleyan Naked Party (no longer what it once was since the administration shut down its host, Art House). One of Wesleyan's most cherished traditions, the Naked Party draws Wes-heads of all creeds and colors for a night of body paint, dancing, and jollifying to the tunes of Wesleyan's very own naked ska band. The school that gets naked together stays together.

Wesleyan winters are unbearably cold, especially for native Californians. A scarf, hat, mittens, and heavy jacket are essential just to get to class without dying on the coldest of February days. However, the cold weather also means plenty of snowstorms, and Wesleyan happens to have Foss Hill—the best sledding hill ever—on its premises. That means that after any big snowfall you can go to The Hill and watch half-drunken Wesleyan students waging snowball wars, building snow-transvestites, and fashioning sleds out of everything from meal trays and laundry baskets to bed frames and recycling bins. Is the crazy snow scene worth the abominable weather? I think so.

> "In addition to being quirky and cool:
> - *Vanity Fair* has called Wesleyan a hot film school on the rise. In Hollywood, there's a 'Wesleyan Mafia'—almost any film you watch has some Wes connection.
> - Our Economics Department is top three among liberal arts colleges.
> - Wes has the top-ranked undergraduate astronomy program in the country.
> - We rank second among all liberal arts colleges for sending students on to earn doctoral degrees in scientific fields.
> - We receive more federal funds for scientific research than any of the top twenty liberal arts schools.
> - Wesleyan faculty report student coauthors in 46 percent of their research publications.
> - Our ethnomusicology department is supposed to be one of the best in the world."
>
> ✦ Jacob, sophomore

The Education

Classes here are amazing, and yes we talk about them all the time. Not because we're just geeky

(though we're that, too), but because we love ideas and love sharing them—Wesleyan is a truly intellectual place. The professors are accessible, enthusiastic, and brilliant. Extremely challenging courses are the norm at Wes, and the majority of students manage difficult course loads in addition to extracurricular activities and a thriving social life. It's possible to find classes that require little to no work, but the best courses tend to be the most demanding.

This semester I chose to take four writing-intensive English classes, and, consequently, I'm swamped with work, but in the past I've never found myself too overwhelmed. The English Department features an all-star cast of inspiring professors, and for a writer like me it's a dream come true to be sitting in a poetry class taught by one of your favorite poets, surrounded by nine other students, each one just as thrilled to be there as you are. Wesleyan has a lot of great interdisciplinary programs, which really underscores how we do liberal arts here. Wesleyan professors really believe that everything you learn is somehow related to everything else you learn. An American studies class contextualizes what you're reading in a history class, which provides background for your queer theory course. In your science in society classes, you'll learn to question the philosophy and social contexts of the lab research you're doing for your work-study job. That's what learning is like here.

Everybody at Wesleyan, no matter how physically fit, should take a dance class at some point (and many people do). Wes offers everything from ballet to South Indian to West African, and both expert and inexperienced dancers can take any class. The Film Department is marvelous, and there are a lot of really stellar majors you wouldn't expect here. I've found the sciences at Wesleyan can be frustrating, however, for artsy literature types like myself. Every student, even English majors, is *supposed* to take three math or science courses before they graduate to fulfill our general education expectations. But the easier courses geared toward nonmajors fill up fast. For those Wes students (like me) who never got past pre-calculus in high school, it can be a real challenge to find an interesting science/math course within the range of my abilities to fill the requirement However, the natural sciences here are really excellent for those who do decide to major in them, and there's a ton of research that everyone and their cousin gets involved in.

The Students

The students at Wesleyan are passionate, intelligent, crazy, and fun-loving. There's been an influx of "normal" people lately—I don't know what that's all about, but hopefully they'll be less normal and boring by the time they leave. At Wes there are two major types of people: the hippies and the hipsters. The hippies smoke pot, wear long skirts, hemp necklaces, and Birkenstocks, and sit on Foss Hill all day. The hipsters listen to obscure bands you've never heard of, wear bowling shoes, ripped jeans, and aviator glasses, and belong to Eclectic, an aptly named coed quasi-frat. The hippies and the hipsters are battling right now for possession of Wesleyan. But I'm noticing a new trend that looks promising: the hippie-hipster hybrid. I belong to this category. These people listen to Radiohead, wear Doc Martens, hoodies, and hoop earrings, and float freely from Womanist house to Alpha-Delt. I'm hoping that the hybrids will take over soon enough.

The Activities

I'm overwhelmed just thinking about all the activities offered at Wesleyan. Boogie Club members wear shower caps and sporadically surprise dining students with a break-dancing contest or interpretive dance. *The Argus* (more up my alley) is the witty campus newspaper featuring notorious Wespeaks, editorials in which Wesleyan students rant about the issue of the week. There are hundreds of activities to choose from, and if you don't find what you're looking for, it's always cool to start your own club. I'm thinking of starting a group in the fall. It's going to meet twice a week, and I'll name it "The Knitters Who Love Falafel, Movies from the '80s, and Making Poems out of Cut-up-Magazines Club." Honestly, though, I could probably get funding for that club. That's what it's like at Wes.

The Social Scene

First of all, there's the drinking, dancing, and general mayhem that occurs from Wednesday night to Saturday night. Lots of Wes kids choose to go out on weekends, but staying in is definitely not reserved for bookworms only. In fact, some of the most fun I've had at Wesleyan has been during quiet weekends, watching a movie from the Wesleyan Film Series or playing Scrabble with my housemates and baking cookies until 2:00 a.m. However, if it's partying you seek, Wesleyan is well equipped. Wednesdsay night everybody flocks to The Gatekeeper, a tiny dive bar hidden in the sketchiest part of Middletown. The parties every weekend night exist mainly in crowded senior houses with loud bands and long lines to get to the keg. The handful of frats at Wes throw amazing parties sometimes, and you can always get a beer there if you want, but it's easy to ignore that scene entirely. (I do.) The famous Wesleyan theme parties are, in my opinion, the best part of the weekend scene. Some of the annual big-name parties include the Halloween Party, the Sex Party, the Willy-Wonka Party, the Robot Party, Zonker-Harris Day, the Sexy Astronauts Party, Uncle Duke Day, the Naked Party, and Bob Marley's Birthday Party.

Notable Wesleyan Alumni Include:

Bill Belichick, head coach, New England Patriots
Bradley Whitford, actor
Eliza Leighton, cofounder, Stand for Children
Herb Kelleher, founder and chairman, Southwest Airlines
Joshua Boger, president and CEO, Vertex Pharmaceuticals
Walter Wrinston, former chairman and CEO, Citibank

WHITMAN COLLEGE

Founded: 1883

Location: Walla Walla, WA

Phone: (509) 527-5111

E-mail: admission@whitman.edu

Web site: www.whitman.edu

Number of Undergraduates: 1,420

Number of Graduate Students: 0

Cost: Approximately $34,500 per year

Application Deadline: January 15

Early Decision: November 15

Rating:	Notable Majors/Programs:
Selective	Politics, English, Life Sciences, Social Sciences

Size:
● Small   ○ Medium   ○ Large

Location:
○ Urban   ○ Suburban   ● Rural

On a Saturday, students talk about academics:
○ Always   ● Sometimes   ○ Never

Nightlife:
○ Intense   ○ Moderate   ● Laid-back

Politically, Whitman leans:
● Left   ○ Right   ○ Split

Diversity:
○ High   ● Low   ○ Medium

Students describe Whitman in five words:
- Dorky, driven, bare-footed, camplike college
- Politically active, outdoorsy, inspiring—and fun

From the School

Learning is a process of stretching, exploring, and thinking critically—not memorization and feeding facts back to professors on multiple choice quizzes and exams. At Whitman you are challenged to write, to debate, to participate actively in small classes and seminars, to conduct independent research, to examine existing theories, tear them apart, and put them back together again.

—www.whitman.edu

If you're interested in Whitman, you may also be interested in:
UC Santa Cruz, Lewis & Clark, Pomona, Reed, Stanford, University of Washington

Name: Emily
Hometown: Eugene, Oregon
Class Year: Freshman
Major: Pre-Engineering
Extracurriculars: Varsity Volleyball, IM sports, rock climbing, theater
Career Goal: To be an environmental engineer

How would you describe Whitman's reputation?

I think we are known as an academically rigorous school. Some have called it the "Harvard of the Northwest." I think it also has a reputation as being a rich white kids who wish they were hippies school.

Is this reputation accurate?

In some ways, like most reputations. I think that Whitman has a very homogenous population. This campus has a very distinct attitude, or personality. There are a lot of outdoorsy students, and there's a lot of environmental awareness. It is a very academic school, but I don't think its environment is intense in the same way as a place like Harvard. I feel like students' lives here are much more balanced. We study hard, but we know how to play hard, too.

What would an admissions officer at Whitman probably not tell a prospective student?

We have a very lenient alcohol policy, which I don't think the admission office likes to advertise to parents—although I feel it makes a lot of sense, and is probably safer than a more strict policy.

The Institution

Campus is beautiful!! The nicest in our conference, and one of the best I've seen. It's fairly classic, centered around Ankeny Field and radiating out from there, with a mixture of older brick buildings and more modern designs. The only ugly architecture is the athletic facility's cement fortress. All the housing, especially for upperclassmen and the all girls dorm, is really nice in comparison to other campuses I've been on, and our rooms are reasonably sized. The landscaping here is beautiful and varies from hedges and rose gardens to relative wilderness with paths and benches winding through it. The president has made it a goal to put a lot of artwork on campus, so there are sculptures all over (though some people don't agree with his tastes).

Walla Walla is a cute city, and the wheat fields that surround the area can be beautiful at times, or brown and ugly at others. But they do provide wonderful stargazing opportunities. Downtown is quaint, but there's not a lot there, especially if you're a shopper. There are a lot of restaurants, banks, and your basic Wal-Mart, Safeway, and Taco Bell type stores but people don't often leave campus to get into Walla Walla unless they need something. People are proud of being here, but there's not a big rah rah crowd (it probably doesn't help that our mascot is the missionaries, though). I don't think Whitman students are snobby about the school. We're all here because we know it's good, but we're not snobby about it. Our president has a special relationship with students. He reads bedtime stories in dorms, hands out cookies in the library during midterms, comes into classes to talk with students about plans—it's nice.

The Education

Whitman is rigorous, but it's not unmanageable. People have tons of homework, spend a lot of time in office hours with teachers, and have to work hard—but there is time in the day to do your schoolwork and still be extremely involved, as most students are. Friday and Saturday nights, most people go out and play—but not to an extent that would jeopardize their schoolwork. There is hardly any competition; people are very collaborative. It's common to hear people discussing their paper topics and helping each other study. We peer edit a lot in the dorms. And because freshmen take the same core class, we are all reading the same thing at the same time—so you'll always hear people discussing the reading and work together.

I'm not sure academic experiences vary much across majors, because we all have to take the same core classes; humanities people are taking science classes for distribution purposes and vice versa. Right now only half my classes are going toward my major. I really enjoy the wide variety of classes offered here. It's not like high school where you can only take basic philosophy, or basic history. They have classes like Environmental Aesthetics or Criminal Delinquency, things you would never be offered in a high school setting.

The Students

Whitman, although the admissions office tries its hardest, is not a very racially diverse population. I would say a majority of students are middle- to upper-class Caucasians from the Northwest. However, there is a lot of energy devoted by clubs and individuals to raise cultural awareness. Black Student Union, Club Latino, and the Asian groups put on several activities throughout the year, including dances, fund-raisers, speakers, foreign food nights in the dining halls. The LGBT group is also rather active. We just finished Drag Fest, a week full of activities, speakers, and movies to raise awareness about sexual orientation. I would say the biggest issue on campus is the environment. There's a push to make things cleaner and more efficient on campus. Politically, there are probably more Democrats than anything, but the Republicans make themselves heard and there is very little pressure to conform to any norm. My favorite part of Whitman is the overall student attitude. Whitties know how to work really hard, and then play really hard. There is stress, yes, and we pull all-nighters like every other college student, but we know when it's time to relax. People are pretty laid-back, casual: wear whatever you want, be into whatever you want.

> "I hate our mascot. I don't think it's appropriate to have a missionary carrying a gun and a Bible to symbolize our school. We are not at all a religious institution."
> ✦ Michelle, senior

The Activities

We're really out in the middle of nowhere, but the school does an amazing job of bringing entertainment to us. Every single night of the week I have the dilemma of having to decide what I'll go see and what I just can't make this time. Movies, speakers, acts, concerts, and on-campus performances are happening constantly. I have friends who go to school in Portland, and near Seattle, and they have less to do than I do way out here in wheat fields! The dorms all have activities as well and every Wednesday night, the staffs plan study breaks. There's hardly ever time to be bored.

People here love the sun. If it's nice out, everyone's out doing homework on blankets, playing Frisbee, playing lacrosse or rugby, foot bagging, anything. The Greek system is pretty active, but they're not imposing, and they have a lot of open functions. And when there are large, popular all-campus events like concerts or speakers, or there's

a slip-and-slide on Ankeny, people from all different interest groups and social groups come together without problems. There is a huge diversity of activities at Whitman, and people are always trying to get everyone else to participate. The outdoor program has opportunities to learn to rock climb and kayak, and they love when people with zero experience come out.

I'd say it's hard to be a Division III student athlete. No strings get pulled like they do in Division I schools for you. We get some fans out to games, but there is generally more support at intramural football than volleyball games, though we do have some regulars, and a lot of faculty and staff come, which is great.

The Social Scene

People party every weekend. There's almost always somewhere to go dance, and usually somewhere to find a keg. Sometimes people will party on weeknights, but it's usually a small group, and pretty low key. Most parties are open to everyone who wants to come. Even cast parties end up being all-campus events. It's easy to meet people, but I guess sometimes it's hard to get to know people because there really isn't anywhere to be alone with someone on campus. Most people I know from having lived with them or been in class with them. Dorms are so much fun to live in. I would recommend them to every freshman. It's definitely part of the experience.

Name: Kara
Hometown: Mendon, Massachusetts
Class Year: Junior
Major: Politics with a gender studies minor
Extracurriculars: President of FACE (Feminists Advocating Change and Empowerment) and secretary for Coalition against Homophobia, archery instructor, Girl Scout
Career Goal: Uncertain

How would you describe Whitman's reputation?

Whitman has a decent reputation on the West Coast; however, very few people have heard of Whitman on the East Coast.

Is this reputation accurate?

When trying to decide between Smith and Whitman, I asked my high school principal (a West Coaster) what Whitman's reputation was like in comparison with Smith's. He said—"Whitman is a good school; I haven't been here long enough to know Smith." For me, Smith was a rather well-known school, so I thought that said a lot about Whitman.

What would an admissions officer at Whitman probably not tell a prospective student?

The thing probably most hidden, and yet the most obvious, is the homogeneity at Whitman. We have a very low diversity rate, and the admissions office will spout all sorts of figures as to how they are rectifying it, but it simply hasn't worked.

The Institution

I chose Whitman because of the feeling that I got when I visited—it's hard to describe, but I suppose the closest thing would be somewhere between contentment and nirvana. I believe it comes from the people—everyone who goes to Whitman was a giant dork in high school. So then, when you come to college, everyone is proud of their dorkiness and that makes for a great, interested and interesting student body.

I'm not exactly sure where the busiest bathroom on campus is—although living in a hallway full of girls, the bathroom was pretty busy at eight in the morning. The RA pasted up jokes and random facts on the wall. It was good. There also is a plaque on one of the urinals in one of the academic buildings, in memory of a professor. We still aren't quite sure what that's all about.

The Education

Professors are awesome. One of the reasons I picked Whitman was because the students and professors have a great rapport. My core professor invited us to his house for a party—we watched movies, sang karaoke, and went in his hot tub. This isn't far from the norm—professors are interested in their students, and students in their professors. Quite simply, they care.

Classes in the social sciences and humanities are tiny—generally capped at thirty-five. I think intro-level science classes might be bigger. The professor of one of my history classes took one class day a week to divide us up into three smaller groups so that we could have more intimate discussion.

The Students

In terms of activism, Whitman has a very excitable student body. There are always debates over the student listserv, and so on. Sometimes the problem seems to me the lack of initiative. There are groups of dedicated students who generally run things—put on events, head clubs, and so on. Students love to attend these events, however, they are not so interested in planning them.

Most students are from the West Coast. It was difficult for me, being from Massachusetts, to meet people freshman year and have them say "Hi! I'm Suzy from Corvallis." I do, however, know the geography of the Northwest far better now.

The Activities

The Greek system at Whitman is just another club. There aren't nasty people who say "I don't like her because she isn't Greek," or anything of that sort. There are friendly rivalries, like the Greek choral competition in the spring—and indie kids get shirts with the Greek letters of GDI (god damned independents).

Varsity athletics exist on campus, but I only know this because my friend is an athletic trainer. Club and intramural sports are far more popular, and it's great, because you don't have to be insane about it every day.

FACE, Feminists Advocating Change and Empowerment, is a wonderful group of people (and not just girls! we have guy members too!), and we do a lot on campus. We are responsible, in conjunction with the administration, for getting safety whistles to the student body (distributed every fall to first years and transfers). We also host Take Back the Night every year. We also have Masturbation Workshops, which is not so much a hands-on thing as it is deconstructing the taboos and assumptions behind masturbation. Coalition is also an awesome group of people. We're integral in putting on events for the campus that increase gender/sexuality awareness on campus through panels, dances, movies, whatever we can do to get people's attention.

If I was awake at 3:00 a.m. on a Wednesday night, I'd be playing Frisbee golf, making Annie's macaroni and cheese in the lounge with friends, generally gabbing—though halls have quiet hours when you need to be considerate of other people. Don't have parties in the halls, do it in a room!

The Social Scene

You can tell the first years by the fact that they say "hi!" to everyone they pass. Generally people will smile at you, since Whitman is so small—everyone can at least remember faces if not names.

Name: Ben
Hometown: Sammamish, Washington
Class Year: Freshman
Major: Environmental studies/geology combo
Extracurriculars: Wind Ensemble, Jazz Ensemble 1, Jazz Combo, Trombone quartet, Whitman Mentors Program, Office of Admissions student caller, Shalom Student Group, Frisbee golf
Career Goal: Coming into Whitman, I was set on majoring in chemistry and going to dental school. Since then, I've rethought my goals and remapped my next four years at Whitman. I have decided to just follow my passions and interests and see where they take me. I am confident that I don't necessarily have to have a career in my field of major.

How would you describe Whitman's reputation?

My school has a reputation for academically pushing its students, and for having an incredibly strong bond between the president, faculty members, and the students.

> "I think the distribution requirements are ridiculously narrow and I wish the school were more open to conservative thoughts."
> ✦ D. F., senior

Is this reputation accurate?

This reputation is extremely accurate. Last semester I wrote a total of twenty-nine papers! I was pushed really hard in my writing class. And during finals week, Tom Cronin, the president of the college, came into the library and passed out cookies, wishing students good luck. I have also been to three of my professor's homes after only a couple semesters here, and don't hesitate to schedule meetings with any of them.

What aspect of Whitman would a prospective student not see on a campus tour?

On a tour, you wouldn't see the student body "in action," playing Frisbee, reading, or doing intramural sports. Usually the tours are in the mornings when students are sleeping, or in classes.

The Institution

My college search was intense—I researched 150 small liberal arts colleges around the nation, and slowly narrowed my list by talking to students from the schools. At Whitman, I couldn't find a single thing that people complain about. Everyone is happy, there is a lot of school pride, and campus opens up events to community members—it's amazing!

The relationship between students and administration is amazing. I haven't heard of any problems. They go out of their way to help students. No red tape whatsoever. Whitman offers interest houses, such as the Fine Arts House, the Writing House, La Casa Hispana, the Outdoor House, the German House, the French House, the Asian Studies House, and more!

I really like the tradition of DuckFest. Students have the opportunity to make their down ducks any way they like (the more creative the better), and then place them around campus. A campus duck map is made for students to go on the walking tour, and then the president of the college judges the ducks. I absolutely love this school.

The Education

Even on Saturday nights, students talk about school. One reason why I came to Whitman was because of the lack of competition between students for good grades. Sure, all students want to get grades, and most work extremely hard for good grades, but students here really work together to solve problems. There is no competition whatsoever. Outside of class, I spend about two hours a night on homework during the school week, but about ten hours on the weekends. This is my own choice, though—because I am so busy during the week with all my other activities, I choose to put off most of my work until the weekend. At Whitman, besides writing theses, students have to pass written finals and oral finals. Furthermore, all freshmen take Core Class (Antiquity and Modernity), a class studying Western thought. Everyone takes the class at the same time, three days out of the week. There are multiple research opportunities for undergraduates.

The Students

Most students are from the Northwest, but that is because Whitman is not too widely known on the East Coast. If Whitman spreads its name around, there's no doubt there will be a huge East Coast population coming to the school. I looked at many East Coast schools and, frankly, Whitman was better.

Most students are Democrats, but there is definitely a strong Republican student group on campus. The average Whitman student is laid-back, works very hard on schoolwork, but is also involved in three or four activities or groups on campus. Everyone's pretty balanced here.

> "People here are really outgoing and accepting, so be ready for people to want to be your friend. We like to include everybody here, so if you are shy it might be a little shocking."
>
> ✦ Juliana, junior

The Activities

Over 70 percent of students participate in intramural sports! Every week, multiple music events are put on by both students and faculty members! Music is really big on campus. There are pianos in every residence hall. This year, we had the grandson of Gandhi give a speech on campus. Among other speakers, we also had Ben Stein come and talk to us. Internships are huge here. Internship initiative is encouraged, and there is a very useful database of Whitman alumni, with their majors and their current occupations.

The Social Scene

Usually people party on weekends, if they feel like it. What's neat about a lot of the parties is that they're not based around alcohol. And there is no pressure whatsoever to drink if you don't want to. Whitman students are very responsible with their drinking. Usually things start picking up on Friday nights around nine-thirty or ten. There is absolutely no division between the Greek system and regular residence life. Everyone gets along. The campus is very friendly. People who I don't even know say "hi" to me. It's extremely uncommon to walk across campus without at least one person saying "hello." People also hold doors open for each other. Some would say Whitman's a pretty chill place, but I've found the atmosphere to be quite warm, actually.

Notable Whitman Alumni Include:

John Markoff, *New York Times* journalist
Karen Glover, managing partner of Preston Gates & Ellis LLP, director of Adaptis
Ralph Cordiner, former CEO of General Electric
Ryan Crocker, former U.S. ambassador to Lebanon, Syria, Kuwait, and Afghanistan
Walter Brattain, Nobel Prize–winning physicist
William O. Douglas, U.S. Supreme Court justice

COLLEGE OF WILLIAM AND MARY

Founded: 1693
Location: Williamsburg, VA
Phone: (757) 221-4000
E-mail: admiss@wm.edu
Web site: www.wm.edu

Number of Undergraduates: 5,690
Number of Graduate Students: 1,410
Cost: Approximately $13,000 per year in state; $28,000 out of state
Application Deadline: January 5
Early Decision: November 1

Rating:	Notable Majors/Programs:
Selective	Premed, English, Business, Psychology

Size:
○ Small ● Medium ○ Large

Location:
○ Urban ○ Suburban ● Rural

On a Saturday, students talk about academics:
○ Always ● Sometimes ○ Never

Nightlife:
● Intense ○ Moderate ○ Laid-back

Politically, William and Mary leans:
○ Left ● Right ○ Split

Diversity:
○ High ● Low ○ Medium

Students describe William and Mary in five words:
- Intellectual, traditional, friendly, little community
- Antediluvian, rigorous, provoking tribe pride!

From the School

The College of William and Mary, one of the nation's premier state-assisted liberal arts universities, believes that excellence in teaching is the key to unlocking intellectual and personal possibilities for students. Dedicated to this philosophy and committed to limited enrollment, the College provides high-quality undergraduate, graduate and professional education that prepares students to make significant contributions to the Commonwealth of Virginia and the nation. In recognition, the media have included William and Mary among the nation's prestigious "Public Ivys," and ranked it first among state institutions in terms of commitment to teaching.

—www.wm.edu

If you're interested in William and Mary, you may also be interested in:
U. Chicago, Davidson, Emory, Haverford, U. Virginia, Williams

Name: Matthew
Hometown: Cherry Hill, New Jersey
Class Year: Sophomore
Majors: English, government
Extracurriculars: cofounder of William and Mary Tae Kwon Do club, juggling club, Lutheran Student Association, Science Fiction and Fantasy club, college Republicans
Career Goal: English professor, writer

How would you describe William and Mary's reputation?

Students are considered to be bookish, loving all things academically rigorous, and to have an easygoing attitude.

Is this reputation accurate?

Our reputation as a rigorous academic environment is absolutely accurate, although it doesn't elucidate what great activities apart from scholastics our campus offers. The social environment is diverse, with scores of student organizations.

What would an admissions officer at William and Mary probably not tell a prospective student?

They're not likely to tell the student about the poor housing for roughly half the sophomore class—it is several miles from campus, albeit with a busing service—but there are plans to build more centralized housing, thank goodness. Nor will you hear about the tradition of getting drunk on the last day of classes, a festivity dubbed "Blowout." Participation is not mandatory; some love it, some hate it. In recent years, teetotaler students lined up on Blowout to blow a 0.00 BAC on a breathalyzer.

The Institution

William and Mary's body consists of several thousand students and I feel it is a comfortable size. It's a medium-sized school. I chose my school because of its academic reputation, its cost-effectiveness, and its beauty. It fit my expectations perfectly. I have many close friendships with student and townie friends who I met through various social groups. I have great "Tribe Pride," as our school spirit is dubbed. A great majority of my friends echo this sentiment. In addition to the tradition of Blowout, there's also the Triathlon which includes streaking in our beautiful Sunken Gardens, swimming in the murky waters of our Crim Dell, and illegally hopping the governor's wall in Colonial Williamsburg. Some people have been banned from Colonial Williamsburg after being caught by the police.

Nothing expresses so accurately the character of an institution as its bathroom graffiti can. Apart from the banal, coarse turpitude that people engrave on bathroom walls the world over, our campus bathrooms are rife with witticisms, debates, and adages. Certain vulgarities are even subject to grammar correction.

The campus is historic and beautiful. Old bosky trails cut across most of campus and in a beautiful hiking trail behind it. We have a lovely bridge know as the Crim Dell whereupon couples engaging in a tryst seal their love as eternal in midnight osculation. The physical layout of the campus, with its winding, tranquil paths, is for me the most appealing aspect. Be prepared and willing to take that scenic route, as library renovations currently proscribe students from making a straight line across campus via the direct path behind the library. It's been like that for years, and will probably continue forever. Our campus admissions office likes to talk of "tradition and innovation"—yup, William and Mary possesses a long tradition of innovating the darned road behind this darned library.

The Education

This is known for being a really academically intense place. I talk about classes all the time with classmates. Most of my classes are discussion-based, but that depends more on the major than anything else. The professors are active socially, and I number several friends among my professors. There are many research opportunities for undergraduates, especially during the summer. The grad school affects me little, except for providing me with a friend or two. The core curriculum is not so bad if you get it out of the way early so you can focus on discovering the department(s) you wish to concentrate in. I haven't found a weak department yet. Study abroad programs are excellent.

The Students

Our campus is relatively apolitical compared to many others. There are political groups, but few big rallies or tight organizations. One thing I can say about our college is that we are tolerant people. I'm a bit of a quirky oddball myself, and feel no pressure to convert to any standard. We all know we're smart people, and respect each other. As a public school, we get people from all walks of life, not just the richest of the Right. The three core groups geographically are northern Virginia, the rest of the state, and the out-of-state students.

The Activities

We don't interact with other schools apart from sports. Personally, I'm involved in the tae kwon do club, juggling club, the Lutheran Student Association, and above all else, the Sci-Fi (Skiffy) Club. Skiffy has Nerf games in academic buildings at night, an activity approved by the administration and campus police because it keeps many students from drinking on a Saturday night in what some consider a boring town. (I don't consider it as such.) The administration is willing to work with students to help achieve excellent organizations and activities. Juggling is great fun, as is my martial art and my religious organization. For more serious athletes, political activists, or service-oriented students, there are organizations for everyone. We get great speakers like Antonin Scalia, Henry Kissinger, and Ralph Nader.

The Social Scene

People party at the frats or the local drinking establishments. Our campus has a standard alcohol policy that follows laws coherently. The Greek scene is large on campus, about a third of students, but those who elect not to participate are not shunned or isolated by their peers. In essence, everyone is tolerant of each other's social interests. It's easy to meet new people, in or out of a Greek family. Drinking occurs mostly at the frats, but there are plenty of alternatives in what some consider a boring tourist town because students and the administration have broad interests and create fun alternatives.

Name: Angela
Hometown: Nairobi, Kenya
Class Year: Sophomore
Major: English
Extracurriculars: Alpha Phi Omega Service Fraternity, National Society of Collegiate Scholars, Student Advisory Committee for English, and Mused—Creative Writing Club
Career Goal: To be a writer and work in publishing as a day job.

How would you describe William and Mary's reputation?

It is known for being very studious school. It is known for having difficult classes and students who strive to achieve in these classes. Also, it has the reputation for its history—it's one of the oldest schools in the nation, and a sense of history here is heightened by the fact that William and Mary is on the doorstep of Colonial Williamsburg. Tourists often mistake the college for one of the colonial displays.

Is this reputation accurate?

Fairly. The classes are hard, but not unmanageable, and most of the students work hard to achieve high marks. But while the library is usually full, students have fun as well—the library is not the only place that is full on a Saturday night. And indeed, "1693" bears its mark on many a William and Mary sweatshirt.

What would an admissions officer at William and Mary probably not tell a prospective student?

There have been a lot of tragedies, a few fatal accidents and suicides, at the school in the past couple of years; this would probably not be something discussed with prospective students. Understandably so—an accident is an accident, and telling first-time visitors about it tends to leave a needlessly negative impression of the school. The campus traditions that involve alcohol and partying and the lack of diversity on campus is not mentioned to students visiting the school either.

The Institution

I chose to attend William and Mary after only one visit because, unlike the other schools, I could easily imagine living there. I loved the campus and thought that it was incredibly beautiful; there were trees everywhere and pretty much everything was green. The buildings were made of a beautiful brick and matched well with their surroundings. I could well imagine reading beneath the trees and studying in the austere buildings.

Some people are very spirited, infused with the green and yellow Tribe Pride, and others are not. But pride is something that you feel inside, not something that you show by attending events (especially when you're not the biggest fan of football or Yule Log ceremonies). Personally, my inner pride in William and Mary vacillates. When I'm doing well and I'm happy with my life overall, I love William and Mary to death. When I'm not doing so well, well, you know.

The Education

As an English major, most of my classes are very discussion-oriented. I've found that professors will usually accept views differing from their own, as long as they are well supported by specific references to the text of a work. I find this very encouraging in that it shows that most professors do not view themselves as being so intelligent that they won't listen to students' ideas.

I do not talk about classes on Saturday nights, Sunday nights, or really any nights at all, unless I'm incredibly stressed out. I think about school when I'm doing work and when I'm in class, but not on my downtime. When I'm not working, I prefer to do more interesting things like gossip, write stories, read, or watch movies.

The Students

"Where are you from?" "NOVA (Northern Virginia)" is a dialogue you hear quite a lot here. Indeed, one of my major complaints about the school is its almost complete lack of diversity. As an international student and a person who has spent a great deal of time traveling, this can be incredibly frustrating. Although there are definitely people from different countries and different walks of life on William and Mary's campus, they are simply few and far between.

Also, many students join fraternities and sororities or other self-involved clubs or groups that to me seem to create a clique mentality and limit the meshing of students. Personally, I feel that social Greek organizations are unhealthy for their members because it seems they encourage people to meld themselves to a specific mold, they'd probably disagree with me on this, though.

Most of the students who are preprofessionally oriented are premed. While this does not necessarily imply that they have less contact with other students, it does in a sense separate them. Premed students have classes together the entire time they are here, so it's logical that they've got a special bond.

The Activities

There are many traditions and activities here, most of which, I must admit, I don't involve myself in. As someone uninvolved with athletics, it does not play a large role in my life at William and Mary. However, there is decent attendance for those teams.

The most widely attended events are the concerts given by outside groups often given in the Sunken Gardens, a sunken field frequently used by students for studying or playing Frisbee, Cake came to our school last year and gave a concert in one of the halls. Tickets were only fifteen dollars and it was widely attended by the student body.

Community Service is fairly popular at William and Mary. One of the largest groups on campus, which I am in fact a member of, is Alpha Phi Omega, a service fraternity. Members have to perform a specific amount of service a semester, so with APO I have helped maintain campus escort, escorting people safely across campus after dark, and have participated in various other activities benefiting the campus and the community surrounding it. However, while the group is beneficial to campus, I feel that it is also somewhat cliquey, so I've been less involved as of late.

I leave campus fairly frequently. I often take long walks or go to the supermarket to buy supplements to our generally unsatisfactory cafeteria food. Other times, if I travel with friends who have cars, I go to the beach or to the very small mall located in Newport News. Sometimes I take the buses provided to students, and travel to the Prime Outlets or to the Williamsburg Crossing movie theater. Leaving campus by bus is no problem but coming back is usually a bit more difficult.

The Social Scene

Due to a recent change in the school's policy and the new Alcohol Task Force, people have been partying less. However, there are still fraternity parties, and alcohol is still available. While it is slightly harder to procure, almost everyone knows at least one person who is in a fraternity or above the age of twenty-one. People usually party on the weekends, but can start as early as Thursday's Happy Hour.

Name: Cecily
Hometown: Arlington, Virginia
Class Year: Junior
Majors: French and psychology
Extracurriculars: Tour guide, social sorority, tutoring, intramural soccer and volleyball, theater
Career Goal: Teacher

How would you describe William and Mary's reputation?

Really, really academic.

Is this reputation accurate?

Yes, we definitely deserve it! The schoolwork here can be very intense, but I would qualify that by saying that we work hard *and* we play hard.

What would an admissions officer at William and Mary probably not tell a prospective student?

I doubt an admissions officer even knows the kind of socializing that goes on during the weekends, though they assumedly were once in college as well. It always surprises me that for the amount of students who come out of here successfully, a remarkable number maintaining a very rigorous social schedule—which attests to their abilities, I suppose!

> "The College has a very comprehensive core curriculum; I wish it were looser and had more options (particularly in my weaker areas, of course!). With the current budget cuts and general financial malaise in Virginia, I find it a little ridiculous that a Middle Eastern Studies/Women's Studies major has to take a life science, a physical science, and a lab with one of the two."
>
> ✦ Roni, freshman

The Institution

This school is the absolute perfect size. I can walk from "Ancient Campus"—the original Wren building—to the furthest building on New Campus, and pass along the way three of my good friends, ten acquaintances, twenty students I recognize by face, and a hundred more I have never seen in my life. I can feel comfortable in the group of friends I have found, and never cease to meet new friends every week. William and Mary has incredible diversity—not in a racial sense, but rather in the type of student that it seems to attract. People come with so many different areas of interest that even if you meet someone during a volunteer project meeting, you may find yourself joining a jam session with them, or going to see their favorite obscure punk rock show. Anything goes and somehow all the col-

ors flow together. Sure there are those who flip their collars up, but that is just as acceptable as being known for playing the bagpipes. I have never been to a place where people are accepted for being so beautifully quirky as they are here.

Warning, in case you visit when there's bad weather: when it rains, it pours—and this campus turns into one giant lake. More than one of my friends have invested in rubber boots to avoid the games of hopscotch on two-hundred-year-old bricks.

The Education

You know you are with a William and Mary student when they break out a fact about the nutrients in the salad you are eating at dinner, or the chemical composition of your loose-leaf paper. I have even heard guys walk up to girls at parties and start conversations with "Hey, aren't you in my advanced chem section?" The best part is that we are all able to laugh at ourselves and always have that to fall back on as an excuse for supposedly dorky behavior: "Hey, I'm a William and Mary student, it comes with being here."

One thing that surprises people when they hear how academic this school is the lack of cutthroat competition. I have never walked out of a classroom surrounded by a chorus of "What did you get on the exam? I got a better grade then you." Students here are unquestionably driven—I think that's prerequisite for being accepted—but the wonderful thing about this place is that we all recognize the kind of pressure we each are under. We put ourselves under that pressure, and we get it from professors and from parents, and I think we are all aware that that's quite enough; in fact, I think it makes us more supportive of each other. Last spring I was cramming late-night style in the library for an exam the next morning. A girl walked up to me with a box of donut holes and said, "Here, it's going to be a long night, this'll help get you through." I had never seen her before in my life.

I totally support the system of General Education Requirements the college requires for graduation. So many students come in not knowing what they want to concentrate in, and it provides them with the opportunity to explore each possible area of study in the liberal arts program. And for those who know exactly what they want to study, there are classes that will reflect their interests in almost every department.

The Students

Students here can be described as very involved—the college gives so many opportunities with its organizations for students to pursue non-academic interests that people can't but help take advantage of that and be exposed to the wide array of backgrounds and interests of other students. I think this campus tries very hard to be politically correct. There are about eight different church denominations surrounding the campus, and the college does not associate itself with any one religion in particular. The school makes a clear point to embrace them all—from Catholic Campus Ministry to the Buddhist society. You can be as involved in Fellowship for Christian Athletes as you want, and not be judged any differently by someone who may be part of the Democratic students organization. I think one would have to try awfully hard to *not* mix with people they are different from, even extremely so—whether in different areas of academic concentration, part of the Greek community or not, politically involved or not. The one thing that unites students across the board is their love for this school—multiple rallies for support of higher education in Virginia, even organized trips to Richmond to lobby before the lieutenant governor have clearly shown that.

The Activities

Community service is huge at William and Mary. There is by no means any sort of requirement to get involved, but students really can't avoid it. Each Greek organization throws philanthropies each semester that are open to the entire campus and draw students and staff alike. One of the most popular takes place every spring: campus golf. For a small entrance fee, any group of people interested in grabbing a beat-up golf club and worn-out tennis ball can play on courses set up all over campus. The day always starts off with Timmy J. (our president, Timothy Sullivan) and a group of selected students teeing off in the Sunken Gardens. People can get really into it—from crazy plaids to extreme clown costumes, it's a great excuse to enjoy your friends, raise money for a philanthropy, enjoy a beautiful day, and laugh at everyone's pathetic or impressive attempts to play golf (clearly no experience needed).

One of the wonderful things about William and Mary's location is the proximity to the beach. Only a five-minute drive away, I have spent many a day at Jamestown beach, studying in the sand and working on my tan. But if I didn't want to drive anywhere on a sunny day, I could take my beach blanket out to the Sunken Gardens to join the Frisbee or football throwers, readers, nappers—even people who bring out laptops to make use of the wireless Internet connection there.

The Social Scene

William and Mary can have a somewhat erratic weekend scene: some weekends I can't find enough time to partake in everything that's going on, while others it's easy to stay in and watch a movie. Any given weekend will have at least one fraternity party hopping—sometimes three each night—and a lecture series to attend. One of the things I appreciate about this school is that it's campus oriented. People generally stay on campus for the weekends, so even if there is no specific party you might be interested in attending, you can find a group of people who want to create their own fun—from midnight ultimate Frisbee games to star-gazing and playing guitar out at Lake Matoaka. The college does an impressive job of bringing activities onto campus, though—hypnotists, comedians, newly released movies, even big-name bands like Guster, Cake, Pat McGee, and Sister Hazel. But when you do want to go off campus, it's a good thing we're close to Norfolk's bars and nightclubs (though they often resemble the fraternity parties here, so why bother?).

Notable William and Mary Alumni Include:
Glenn Close, actress
James Monroe, former president
John Marshall, former Chief Justice
Jon Stewart, comedian
Perry Ellis, fashion designer
Thomas Jefferson, former president

WILLIAMS COLLEGE

Founded: 1793

Location: Williamstown, MA

Phone: (413) 597-2211

E-mail: admissions@williams.edu

Web site: www.williams.edu

Number of Undergraduates: 1,970

Number of Graduate Students: 60

Cost: Approximately $40,000 per year

Application Deadline: January 1

Early Decision: November 10

Rating:	Notable Majors/Programs:
Most Selective	Life Sciences, Social Sciences, Art History

Size:
- ● Small ○ Medium ○ Large

Location:
- ○ Urban ○ Suburban ● Rural

On a Saturday, students talk about academics:
- ○ Always ● Sometimes ○ Never

Nightlife:
- ● Intense ○ Moderate ○ Laid-back

Politically, Williams leans:
- ○ Left ○ Right ● Split

Diversity:
- ● High ○ Low ○ Medium

Students describe Williams in five words:
- Isolated, elite, preppy, outdoorsy, rigorous
- Intellectual, hard-working, close-knit, over-committed, tiny

From the School

At Williams, with a spectacularly talented and devoted faculty and staff, great physical and financial wealth, and the absolute finest students in all of American higher education, we are obligated to realize a vision of educational excellence worthy of our extraordinary resources. That vision undoubtedly involves the optimal use of new technologies and a commitment to redouble our efforts to educate our students in an environment that reflects the great strength of our diverse society and to keep the precious prize of a Williams education open to the most talented students in the nation regardless of family background.

—www.williams.edu

If you're interested in Williams, you may also be interested in:
Amherst, Bowdoin, Dartmouth, Haverford, Middlebury, Princeton

Name: Chris
Hometown: Honolulu, Hawaii
Class Year: Freshman
Majors: Biology, economics
Extracurriculars: Cross Country/Track, photographer for the yearbook
Career Goal: Ask me again in a couple of years.

How would you describe Williams's reputation?

When you tell people you go to Williams, you either get "oh. . . . umm. . . . where's that?" or the less frequent "Wow! That's a great school!" So, for those who have heard of our little college out in the backwoods of Massachusetts, we have the reputation for being a school which rivals the Ivies in academics, while also supporting the one of the best Division III sports programs in the country (as well as having the most interesting, diverse, and friendly students around!). However, there are always nagging rumors that there's nothing to do "out there in the woods" and that, consequently, you spend every spare moment drinking your life away.

Is this reputation accurate?

All—except for that last bit.

What would an admissions officer at Williams probably not tell a prospective student?

If you come from warmer climes, you will probably be completely uninformed as to how long winter lasts up here! Boy, was I in for a surprise.

> "Athletics at Williams is a big issue. People say that the very stringent criteria used in the admissions process for most students are relaxed for athletes."
>
> ✦ Rebecca, sophomore

The Institution

As a first-year student, I cannot believe how easy it was to transition to the independent life of a college student. With the orientation week, the amazing JAs (junior advisers), and the supportive and understanding professors, Williams does an amazing job at making you feel like you're at home right from the beginning. Of course, as a first-year you'll get those passing bouts of home-sickness (some people more than others), but I have found that these rarely last long, given the familylike atmosphere fostered by everyone around you. For me, the most difficult part of the college transition was not in making friends or in managing my time, but in learning how to do my own laundry!

The Education

The advantages of an education at a small school such as Williams become abundantly clear when you see the close interaction that students maintain with their professors. Because there are no graduate students, the professors are focused solely on us. All my profs have been absolutely brilliant, almost always available to meet and go over questions and course material, and to top it all off they are really cool! It is not unheard of to be invited to a prof's house for dinner just to hang out and talk. Opportunities for further study are often presented and encouraged—upperclass students in the sciences, for example, are cowriting papers with their professors and getting published, which is something that you almost never would be able to do in a larger institution.

Students here are academically brilliant, but are not stuck up about it. It's amazing to sit down at the TV and listen in on the commercial-break conversations—everyone knows so much about everything (and we're not just talking pop culture here, although they have demonstrated proficiency in that area as well!). Being here is certainly humbling, but in a very good way.

Well, one tiny gripe: the advising system for freshmen could use some improvement. When you're assigned to a faculty member who'll help you choose courses, you usually expect some degree of helpful insight. Some lucky students find it. Some, like me, get an adviser who simply agrees to your class choices without offering much constructive input. And some, like my friend, get the track coach, who, although exceptionally skilled at training speedy tracksters, is utterly at a loss to distinguish between the Fun and Games Club and the course on game theory.

The Students

School spirit is through the roof—although we tend to take our loyalty with a healthy dose of humor. C'mon, we're called the "Ephs." And we do have a purple cow for a mascot, after all. The prestige of the college is as understated by the students as the udders are overstated in our mascot. But overall, I think the attitude and personality of the student body was summed up best by my dad when he visited me at the beginning of the year: "They're all so nice!" Nothing could be closer to the truth. And as far as the myth of getting to know everyone in a month because of the small size of the school: there is an amazingly diverse student body, and if you wanted, you could certainly meet a new and totally interesting and talented person every single day.

> "The Berkshires is a wonderful place to spend four years."
> ✦ Rebecca, sophomore

The Activities

Of course, athletics are a very big part of campus life (let's just say that I think there might be ten overweight people on this entire campus). WUFO (Williams Ultimate Frisbee Organization) members are almost a cult, but boy-oh-boy, do they really know how to have a good time! But there are other major campus groups, too. And the a cappella groups are the campus boy (and girl) bands, complete with their personal armies of groupies. And the Queer Student Union throws the best party of the year by far. It's still amazing to me that the entire student body always comes out in force to cheer/support/participate in almost every event that happens throughout the year. Now that's true "team spirit"! I've never once felt like I was missing out on anything because of Williams's location— but if you have a hankering for some urban living—New York is only three hours away.

The Social Scene

There are always parties. And there is almost always alcohol. But I have never found there to be any peer pressure to drink—people respect your decisions, and you can still have a good time without getting plastered. Of course, there are always going to be the guys upstairs who are either intoxicated or detoxing. But they have never caused an inconvenience to me—in fact, they came in the other night and asked if their music was too loud, and offered to turn it down—and even though they couldn't remember my name, it was nice of them to ask!

Name: Jessica
Hometown: Los Angeles, California
Class Year: Sophomore
Major: Art history and psych
Extracurriculars: Tour guide, rugby, tennis, tae kwon do, squash
Career Goal: Possibly advertising, law, or museum education.

How would you describe Williams's reputation?
A walking J. Crew catalog.

Is this reputation accurate?
Not entirely. There are lots of other people here who hardly resemble the reputation at all. Williams has a greater population of people wearing Lili Pulitzer and jetting off to Hamptons retreats than, say, my hometown, but we're not overrun by pink and green polos—it just comes with the northeastern territory. I'm sure we'd have more sun-loving, hardcore flip-flop fanatic So Cal girls like me if we were in L.A. I have learned to play squash, and they have learned to say "hi" to people from Indiana. But I have yet to own a pair of khakis.

What would an admissions officer at Williams probably not tell a prospective student? What aspect of your school would a prospective student not see on a campus tour?
Not tell: You will have a hard time saying no to the millions of ways to distract yourself and procrastinate, which is a problem considering how much reading can accumulate over only two days.

Not see: How weary we all get during exams and how we become crazed vampires when trying to function on only two hours of sleep a night for a week. Your snooze button has never looked so alluring.

The Institution

I wanted to experience the quintessential New England college experience in all its glory. What better place than Williams? This school knows that a good education incorporates diverse learning styles and subjects. You might be leading a discussion in the morning and stomping through muddy woods in the afternoon. Williams looks so much like the quintessential New England college that it would make a Hollywood location scout drool. We're all pretty humble compared to what you might think after being listed as number one in the big rankings. After all, most people still haven't heard of us.

Williams has the best housing I have ever seen for undergrads. I will have lived in a single all four years, and this year I share a bathroom with only one other person. Each floor has free cable and our basement houses a full-size pool table. We live like royalty compared to other places. All you have to do is provide Mardi Gras beads and Scarface posters. Almost everyone lives on campus, and whatever is technically "off campus" is still more or less on campus. Williamstown is pretty much Williams College, save the Stop & Shop we all migrate to for ramen noodles (it's a nationwide epidemic). But enjoy this while you can; you can venture into the real world of housing later. One of the best programs at Williams, hands down, is the Junior Advisory (JA) system. Two juniors, a male and a female, live with an "entry" of about twenty-five to thirty frosh and simply help them through the year. They are not there to enforce college rules—they aren't even paid. Rather, they are a crutch, an inspiration, even a foundation that can help you with anything from picking classes to holding back your hair. You are essentially given a Williams family, having just left your own, as a support system to both learn from and teach to.

Here at Williams you never fret about traipsing around at 4 a.m. Aside from an early "walk-of-shamer" or bloated snack bar patron, the most worrisome creature you might encounter in the middle of the night is a fox or stag. Security is incredibly helpful and is, er, very skilled at recovering repeatedly lost dorm keys. They'll even drive you to your dorm after 2:00 a.m., which is a handy resource when you've gone blind from an all-nighter in the computer lab and it's raining buckets. Just learn to distinguish campus security from Williamstown Police. In certain circumstances, one will drive you to the health center, and the other will drive you to jail.

Everything is bikeable. As long as you look both ways and have some sort of muscle on those thighs, you'll be on your way to a shorter commute. Take the term "commute" loosely, though, as you can literally roll down a hill from some dorms to your classes. And given that we're a *tad*

smaller than state universities, you're really lazy if you think anything on campus is far. Some places require campus buses, so suck it up and walk, you baby.

I am from California, so I miss being spoiled, but the seasons here are unparalleled, especially our fall. For about a week and a half, the whole Berkshire area becomes a study in color; the valley is ablaze with every color from auburn to fire-engine red and, with the help of some crisp fall air, Shangri La reaches our bucolic little town. We get enough snow to make the mountains fifteen minutes away a perfect afternoon ski destination, and the spring does serve to revive hope in us all that shorts and flip-flops will be practical again. You also learn to value the term "above freezing."

The Education

Semester/Term System: We are spoiled. Among other treats, in two semesters we get a month-long "Winter Study" and a two-week spring break. Winter Study is essentially a month of one fun elective-type class where we all order pizza, stay up even later, and fashion igloos out of ice. Watch for snowballs while doing all three. And who knew an all-nighter could revolve around a James Bond movie marathon instead of a poli sci term paper? You see, the administration figures it's too cold to force us to be productive, so we get to choose just how ambitious we want to be. You can intern in New York, leave campus for an independent "99" project, or just roll around in wool sweaters, mittens, and earmuffs while trying to forge your way through a snowbank. On another note, Williams adds in little freebie days like Mountain Day, where we are literally given a day off from classes to hike up Mount Greylock and enjoy some free cider and donuts.

Since Williams is so small, when you graduate you are a perennial member of an exclusive secret society: few people know about it, but those who do are the ones who matter when you're trying to get a job or interview. We have ever-so-quietly infiltrated every major job market. Case in point? The Williams "Art Mafia." We have a giddily ridiculous number of alumni running the nation's major art museums. Summer research and other internship opportunities abound, so if you're in Williamstown over the summer, you're not alone. Rather than become a ghost town, summer in Williamstown is host to the high-profile Williams

Theater Festival, as well as tons of current and future (summer program) students. Summer listservs and events keep things interesting and there's always New York or Beantown when you need to see a high-rise and maybe even some traffic. With so many resources here, it's also possible for a prof to set you up with research in another city of your choice.

We don't have a core curriculum, just divisional requirements that are easy and generally fun to complete. Most students voluntarily go out of their way to diversify their classes in order to get more out of Williams than a few poli sci seminars or bio labs. I am only a science hobbyist here, but I suspect (and have heard) that the majors find the campus very accommodating. We truly do have amazing facilities and great research opportunities. For a liberal arts college, we sure know how to pack in the frog legs and zygotes.

Williams also has Oxford-style tutorials where you and a fellow student meet with your professors once a week, write papers, and critique each other's work. They're offered in nearly every department and are very popular.

The Students

I'm involved in many multicultural organizations on campus, which I guess is at odds with the fact that, being a white girl from Beverly Hills, I am not exactly the poster child for the issues I confront, support, and identify with. The minority population is really an untapped resource for many students on campus; there is such a wealth of culture that we should be experiencing and sharing on a broader level. The minority students have been an integral, active part of changing and expanding the school's curriculum. We are working on maintaining and strengthening the Asian, African American, Jewish, and Latino studies program. A fall Tolerance Rally and Latino, student lobbying and demonstration for academic programs, put diversity issues at the forefront of Williams's politics. The school has since gotten on board and is now committed to finding professors in all fields of multicultural academics. The moral of the story is that Williams is a dynamic institution that actually takes student input to heart. If you fight for it, it will happen.

Perhaps more quietly divisive on campus than race/ethnicity is socioeconomic status. Truth be told, there are a lot of wealthy kids here. There are also a lot on financial aid. We don't talk about it, but the difference exists and we sometimes socially function by it.

The Activities

No other schools are that close, but they're not that far either; we're part of the "Little Three" with Amherst and Wesleyan.

The Lehman Council is our community service body. Lots of students participate and there are also many opportunities in the area. We also frequently put on events such as walks, runs, and other fund-raisers whose profits are donated to charities in the area. On a sunny day, there are: people playing Frisbee, people doing work, girls tanning in bikinis, and guys playing football. Some groups head down to the river for a dip and others stay a bit closer and lounge on Chapin "Beach" (the steps).

> "On Mountain Day, students are roused at 7:00 a.m. with ringing church bells. Classes are cancelled, allowing students to climb three miles of a nearby mountain where they are greeted with a cappella and hot cider."
>
> ✦ Alexis, sophomore

The Social Scene

Visitors are sometimes surprised to find that Williams College students definitely know how to party. Aside from whatever you do with friends, there's always a big two or three at the row houses along Main Sreet (they used to be frat houses back in the day), and you can drop by the pub or the Red Herring for something other than keg beer. Thursday is the new Saturday, and Tuesday is the new Thursday. Go figure. There are always other options such as performances and movies to go to.

Name: Alexis
Hometown: Cherry Valley, New York
Class Year: Sophomore
Major: Political science, environmental studies
Extracurriculars: Greensense (environmental advocacy organization), model United Nations team, Penpals (community service)

Career Goal: To be an environmental lawyer, specifically in the international sector

How would you describe Williams's reputation?

I think a couple people still hold on to the old stereotype that Williams is just another elitist, Ivy League–type breeding ground for future cocktail-drinking snobs. In reality, however, as more and more people hear about the real Williams, they discover that it is actually a very diverse school with students who balance intense academic and social lives. Williams is getting more and more academic and athletic recognition every year.

Is this reputation accurate?

Students do wear a lot of J. Crew, fewer than half are on financial aid, and fewer than half are from public school; however, these statistics do not manifest themselves in any outward stereotype. Williams is actually an extremely accepting school where students are genuinely interested in what their peers do and love.

What aspect of Williams would a prospective student not see on a campus tour?

One thing that most Williams students complain about is the advising system. I was lucky enough to have a very good experience with the system and have an adviser who perfectly matched my interests. But some advisers may have no experience with the student's interests and activities. The administration and College Council are working to modify the advising system to better adapt it to the students. As the system now stands, however, many students are left alone to work on class selection and scheduling.

The Institution

Williams has an indescribable spirit. I don't know where it comes from, but most people that I talk to recall "something special about the place." Williams is small in population, so students get to know each other, and they also interact a great deal with their teachers; even in some larger classes (one hundred students), teachers will learn students' names. The administration is constantly looking for ways to improve campus life, so they always ask for student advice and input. This overriding cooperative atmosphere makes the students very proud and spirited—and you can see this during, say, a Williams versus Amherst basketball game, which will inevitably be bathed in a sea of purple-and-yellow screaming fans.

To add to the spirit of Williams are certain traditions like Mountain Day, when students are roused on a random Friday in October at 7:00 a.m. with ringing church bells. Classes are cancelled, allowing students to climb three miles of a nearby mountain where they are greeted with a cappella and hot cider. What a way to enjoy the foliage before the snows come!

The Education

One of the best aspects of Williams is its winter study program. Students spend three weeks in January taking one course, which can be anything from marble carving to the *Illiad*. This is a great time to meet new people, catch up with your friends, and try something new for a few weeks. My freshman year I was even able to travel to Boston for three days to visit the courts and learn about public policy! Some students are lucky enough to get enrolled in a study away course, such as Eye Care in Nicaragua or Carpets in Turkey. Nonfreshmen can design their own courses, allowing students to explore a particular aspect of Williams or travel abroad.

There is a surprisingly small amount of competition between students. Most people do not discuss grades at all; we all understand that our peers are intelligent and motivated in different ways. Everyone works very hard—in the classroom and beyond. For those students who are particularly comfortable with a subject, there are many opportunities to help others, like becoming a teaching assistant (where you won't actually teach—just hold help sessions) or a writing tutor. Professors are extremely accessible and willing to speak after class, write e-mails, and hold special help meetings.

The Students

I have often heard, and agree with, the statement that Williams students are the greatest aspect of the college. There is a large contingency from the Northeast, and about half are from public schools and less than half are on financial aid. A little less than half play a varsity sport. No one seems to care about wealth or public versus private high school. As most students see it, we all got accepted to Williams and we all deserve to be here. People mostly focus on students' varied and interesting talents.

Students here have some very interesting histories and interests. An amazing number have won national awards or have a significant accomplishment. One of my friends is an all-state nordic skier, one is a national roller-skating champion, one has published chemistry research, one is an all-American pianist. And they all act like normal people!

The average student is a middle-class suburbanite who has played a sport sometime in his/her life but who also has a quirky interest in something else. He/she enjoys many disciplines (hence attendance at a liberal arts college) but is focused on law, medicine, or business (those are Williams's most popular fields of study). The average student works hard but makes it a priority to socialize and take advantage of the many concerts, speakers, and parties at Williams.

The Activities

There's a plethora of campus organizations, from a sushi club to a prochoice group. An inordinate amount of students are involved in some form of community service as well as outing activities and performance groups. For some reason, learning how to swing dance has become a sort of rite of passage for Williams students. Most people entered Williams with some type of artistic experience, as is indicated by high attendance at theater, music, and dance performances. I think over 90 percent of students have actually participated in a performance group at some time during their Williams career. The religious and activist organizations are pretty vocal, especially the Queer Student Union, Student Global AIDS Campaign, the Anti-War Community Taskforce, the Williams Christian Fellowship, and the Garfield Republican Club. The student newspaper, *The Record,* is widely read and contributed to, as are other publications like the satire magazine (*The Mad Cow*) and *The Literary Review*. There seems to be every type of cultural/racial group available, and they frequently hold cultural weekends and dinners. Even though Williams is small, the students are proud of their heritages and want to show them off.

The Social Scene

There really are no other colleges around Williams, so we've cultivated our own social scene. While there is a large party scene concentrated in a few places on campus, there is no pressure to drink or party every weekend. Many people value any rest they can get and welcome a weekend of movie watching. I definitely have logged some late nights discussing politics or having water fights. Students do not lie when they say there is no shortage of things to do. If worse came to worst, we could always catch up on the readings for class!

The campus party scene is pretty open, although it can become exclusive at times because of the tight friendships people form and the bonds between sports teams. Nevertheless, I feel there is more social mobility than at other schools just because Williams strictly outlaws fraternities and sororities. There is usually a good mix of small and large parties so people are not stuck with one or the other.

Notable Williams Alumni Include:
Chuck Fruit, chief marketing officer and senior VP of Coca-Cola
James N. Wood, director of the Art Institute of Chicago
Martha Williamson, producer
Stephen Sondheim, lyricist and composer
Steve Case, founder of America Online
Thomas Krens, director of Guggenheim Museums Worldwide

UNIVERSITY OF WISCONSIN—MADISON

Founded: 1848
Location: Madison, WI
Phone: (608) 262-1234
E-mail: onwisconsin@admissions.wisc.edu
Web site: www.wisc.edu

Number of Undergraduates: 39,340
Number of Graduate Students:
Cost: Approximately $12,000 per year in state; $26,000 out of state
Application Deadline: February 1

Rating:	Notable Majors/Programs:
Selective	Education, Life Sciences, Journalism, Business

Size:
○ Small ○ Medium ● Large

Location:
● Urban ○ Suburban ○ Rural

On a Saturday, students talk about academics:
○ Always ● Sometimes ○ Never

Nightlife:
● Intense ○ Moderate ○ Laid-back

Politically, UW–Madison leans:
○ Left ○ Right ● Split

Diversity:
○ High ● Low ○ Medium

Big Ten School: Yes!

Students describe UW–Madison in five words:
- Challenging, beautiful, busy, spirited, large
- Strong research; lots of Wisconsinites

From the School

As hard as it may be to define a "typical" student at UW-Madison, it is even harder to describe a typical student experience. UW–Madison offers instruction in more than one hundred fields, with more than 8,700 courses listed each year. Learning opportunities can vary from traditional classroom lectures to individualized laboratory projects to work experiences in the community. And that doesn't even begin to encompass the multitude of extracurricular opportunities for growth—anything from participation in one of more than 700 student clubs and organizations to living in one of UW-Madison's unique residential learning communities.

—www.uc.wisc.edu

If you're interested in UW–Madison, you may also be interested in:
UC Berkeley, Case Western, CU–Boulder, U. Mich, Northwestern, University of Washington

Name: Tiff

Hometown: Eau Claire, Wisconsin

Class Year: Sophomore

Majors: Biochemistry and philosophy

Extracurriculars: Soccer club president, Tri-Beta Biological Honor Society officer, POP (People Opposing Prejudice) member

Career Goal: Not sure—probably going to get a degree in law and a science Ph.D. after undergrad work.

How would you describe UW–Madison's reputation?

I think we are known as a party school, but a party school where everybody still works hard and is studious. It's also a top-flight public university with some strong research programs.

Is this reputation accurate?

To an extent. The academics are certainly top-tier if that's the experience you seek, and parties, and drinking, are a big part of the UW campus. But the thing that I didn't know when I came here was whatever you feel like doing on a Saturday night, somebody else will be doing the exact same thing. I've done laundry on a Saturday night with friends, and I've also gone out the week before a big test with friends. There really are all types at Madison, and there will be people like you every step of the way.

What would an admissions officer at UW–Madison probably not tell a prospective student?

They would probably downplay the amount of drinking, and they would also probably not describe how difficult it is for freshmen to register for classes. These are what I found misrepresented when I visited—understandably, though, because the parents don't want to hear about drinking or about how their kid is not going to get into the classes that they want right away.

The Institution

I like how my school is prestigious but not. There are lots of people around that were all really good students in high school, but there doesn't seem to be a snotty attitude that I saw at other selective schools. Things at Madison (with exceptions of course) stay pretty down to earth, despite the quality of the programs that are offered.

I chose my school because it is a great value: it's a selective university, known for many top programs, especially in the sciences. It is also near a lake, and near downtown Madison. I can go shopping or go for a run next to a lake. It just seemed to me like everything would be at my fingertips at Madison.

I love our school's size. There are always new people to meet, you can find people to get close to, and you can also slump into class in your pajamas without being noticed. For me, it is the best environment. I do know, however, that for people who need more guidance and personal attention, that this campus may not be the best fit. You do have to watch out for yourself, and seek out people, because the school isn't always searching you out individually and making sure that you are doing everything that you are supposed to. As far as campus size, the 80 free bus is really helpful, especially when it is cold out (I hate winter!). However, usually class is not that far away, and I've only had to use the 80 to get to work.

My favorite tradition at Madison is Halloween—although it is unbelievably loud and unbelievably filled with non-Madisonites, it is the craziest thing you have ever seen. It can get scary, and you have to watch out, but it is the most entertaining thing I have seen around here. You can only imagine . . .

There are some quite interesting statements in our bathrooms, especially at our most popular library, College Library. Check it out. The most entertaining that I have seen recently are intense political debates. It gets intense, intellectual, and interesting.

> "Madison is known for three things: sports, alcohol, and research. What you might not know is, bordered by two lakes, Mendota and Monona, our campus is one of the most beautiful in the country. Go Badgers!"
> ✦ Sarah, sophomore

The Education

I talk about classes with my friends all the time. Madison is different than I expected it to be because I thought that college would be a little easier! The classes are a lot of work, and although you may only have class for two hours a day, you will have a full day of work. I spend about twenty to thirty hours on schoolwork outside of class. It never seems to end! The competition is tough, especially in certain majors. The Business School, the School of Education, the Pharmacy School, and the Journalism School are all highly selective, and people have to work hard to get in. Everybody earned their way here, and the curves reflect that each grade has to be earned.

The TAs are great here—they are really intelligent, really open to working with you out of class, and they really increase the amount of learning. The professors are also usually good—of course there are always some who are boring, or too preoccupied to talk out of class, but in my classes they have always been really available.

There are research opportunities for anybody who wants to do research. Many seniors do theses and projects, and many professors work very closely with students on their theses. There are a lot of science lab jobs and summer research opportunities here. It is amazing how involved in real science I already am. I feel like my job is actually making a difference in the real world.

I have taken a course on the history of rock and roll that was amazing, and I am currently taking a philosophy course called Theories of Evil. There are always interesting classes here and it's a pity I won't be able to take them all before I graduate.

> "The average UW student, I would describe as very determined, friendly, carefree, and very open to new ideas."
> ✦ Laura, senior

The Students

I would say the average student on campus is white, from the Midwest, and planning on going to professional school. Overall, the campus is pretty liberal, but there are all types around. You'll see Catholic movements, socialist movements, and lots of diversity programs. Overall, we still are a white majority school, and the school is working on fixing that. It also depends on where you spend your time: I am white, but I have friends who are African American, Nigerian, Indian, Vietnamese, Chinese, Icelandic, and Cuban; some people, however, stay with their own group, so you see clusters of white people, clusters of Asian people, and clusters of black people.

The Activities

There are several technical colleges around, and there is a private university, Edgewood, which is really close to our campus. Although many of their students hang out at the UW campus, and many of us also volunteer or work at Edgewood, we don't interact with them much. Athletics are big here, especially football. Basketball and hockey are also really popular here. There are also a lot of concerts and theater going on. There are so many amazing performers and speakers that come here, you always feel guilty for not being able to see them all. No matter what you are interested in, there will be people speaking on it. Our school papers are read a lot, and they are provided all around campus. Greek life is not very big on our campus, although they are around. Many people volunteer and the opportunities are endless. There are tutoring programs, political organizations, too many to describe. I rarely leave campus, and when I do it is usually to go to the mall, to a movie, or to a grocery store.

The Social Scene

There are always people partying on campus. The busiest nights are Thursday, Friday, and Saturday, and the least busy nights are Sunday and Monday. There are people here who party every night of the week, and there are people here who have never drank before. But yes, you will encounter drinking here—it's just part of the social scene on campus.

It doesn't matter at all here if you join a sorority or a frat—there is no pressure, but they are around if you want to join. I definitely don't know everyone on campus—I can't even imagine knowing that many people. Dorm life is squished, and there isn't a lot of privacy. It's not too bad, although I do miss having a private bathroom and my own kitchen to cook and store stuff in! I am glad that I lived in the dorms for two years, because I met some amazing people here, but I am also looking forward to having my own apartment next year with my friends. We usually don't say "hi" to strangers on the sidewalk here—there are so many people around, you would never get anywhere on time if you did! People do usually hold open doors for others though.

Name: Joel
Hometown: Silver Spring, Maryland
Class Year: Junior

Majors: Management and human resources/pre-med

Extracurriculars: Sigma Chi Fraternity, Alpha Epsilon Delta Pre-Medical Fratenity

Career Goal: Plastic surgeon

How would you describe UW–Madison's reputation?

Hard drinkers in a cold, bleak world.

Is this reputation accurate?

Absolutely. Weather is questionable at best but the bars are always warm.

What aspect of UW–Madison would a prospective student not see on a campus tour?

The amazing diversity—in places to drink: dorms, frats, house parties, bars.

The Institution

A world-class education with a well-earned reputation for partying. Wisconsin students *love* Wisconsin, and Bucky, and beer, and brats. During football season, Saturdays are devoted to waking up early, mixing no-name vodka into bloody Marys and seeing how many two-story beer bongs can be kept down on the hike to Camp Randall where win or lose the bars are guaranteed to packed with beer-soaked undergrads decked out in red.

The Education

Interesting and engaging courses are readily available and the required core curriculum doesn't force students to take anything unbearable—but as a first- or second-year student, registering for the better, or in some unfortunate cases, required, courses can be an exercise in futility. A good solution is to track down an older student with a low credit load and get them to hold a class or two for you with their high credit priority. You figure out how to work the system here.

The Students

Wisconsin is extremely diverse—the student population is made up of white students from all over the world and from every walk of life. The only color you're likely to see is on the East Coast sorority girls who stay in the tanning beds a little too long when they go fake-baking in February. The students from the East Coast are stereotypically cliquish and segregate themselves by living in the private residence halls. A reciprocity agreement with Minnesota and our proximity to Chicago brings in students representing a wide variety of socioeconomic backgrounds, but this rarely factors into people's choice of social groups. In most cases, friendships formed in the freshman dorms last and provide the source of most second- and third-year roommates.

The Activities

Intramural sports are extremely popular; there are three levels of varying competitiveness and anyone interested can get involved.

The Social Scene

Pick a night in Madison and any student over nineteen can name the bar and drink special that draws the largest crowd. With State Street centrally located near campus and home to well over thirty bars, a friendly crowd is always just around the corner. If the bar scene isn't for you, or you don't have an ID that remotely resembles you, opportunities to party are still nearly limitless with fraternities and off-campus student housing hosting parties Wednesday through Saturday. A weekend not wasted is a wasted weekend.

Name: Henry
Hometown: West Allis, Wisconsin
Class Year: Junior
Major: Sociology
Extracurriculars: Midwest Asian American Student Union (committee chair), Asian Pacific American Council (current program coordinator and former chair), MAASU Conference Committee (committee chair), Asian American Studies Program Faculty Board (student representative)
Career Goal: Consulting or Asian Pacific American related

How would you describe UW–Madison's reputation?

We're known for low diversity rates and high drinking culture. It's because of these two factors that my family was a little worried about me attending Madison.

Is this reputation accurate?

The reputation is simultaneously accurate and inaccurate. Number-wise, the diversity rate is low, but the school administration does direct a lot of time and money toward diversity. Most of the students in Madison are suburban white kids who are not racist, but rather ignorant of diversity issues. As for the drinking culture in Madison, the reputation is accurate. In the state where beer reigns supreme, it seems only natural that the students mimic the adults.

What would an admissions officer at UW–Madison probably not tell a prospective student?

If I were an admissions officer I would not tell a prospective student, especially a prospective student of color, the chance they might experience a racist episode is very high. This is due to, in my personal opinion, the number of white students who drink and their drunken interaction with people unlike them.

The Institution

I feel that Madison is the best university out there. There is so much to do on this campus. The size of the school is one of the most appealing things about the university; the campus actually makes up the city's downtown. I also like the fact that it's right next to a lake. If you ever spent a summer on campus, you would realize how calm the summers are compared to the rest of the school year. There is a huge sense of pride here, which is quite elevated by our sports. Come game night, the streets are packed with red and white. It is because of our school spirit that we were rated by *Sport Illustrated* as the number one college sports town. I may speak negatively about my campus's lack of diversity, but I do love this place, and think it is still a work in progress. With so many resources available to students who want to make a change, I really want Madison to be a campus that I want to send my kids to.

The Education

This is where size really matters: in the classroom. Before becoming a sociology major, I was an engineering major. All my classes were lectures and the personal attention from professors was minimal. Additionally, interaction and compassion from my engineering/science/math professors wasn't, well, present. I felt frustrated and grew to disdain my classes, professors, and the people around me. It just felt like I was detached from the real world and caught up in a world of intellectual bookworm snobs who did not care about anything else but the advancement of their grades and their potential jobs. Switching to sociology was the best move I ever made. The classes were smaller and were taught by professors, not TAs. The issues seemed real and the people around me were informed about what was going on in life. The best part was feeling how the tools I learn in sociology can make a difference in my life. It connected my extracurricular social justice work with my professional life.

The Students

The campus of Madison may be known for its liberalism, but that's just a remembrance of the campus's history in the 70s movement. The reality is that there are a lot of conservatives on campus or even worse, a lot of students who are apathetic to it all. Most of the students are from suburbs and do not care about diversity or social justice issues. People still protest and rally from time to time

The Activities

The student groups that are most strong are not the frats, but the students of color organizations. Even though our numbers are small, our voices are loud. As mentioned before, it is the sway over our school resources that empowers students of color groups to make visible changes on campus. For instance, my organization just put together a free conference for eight hundred students from the Big Ten and Midwest to learn and interact about Asian-Pacific-American issues. It was the best thing that I've done in college and would not be possible without the backing of the university.

The Social Scene

The social scene depends on your personal preference. If you're underage and living in the dorms, you go to house parties. If you're twenty-one, you hit up the bars. The relationship to alcohol and partying goes hand and hand. The best time to go out during the year is Halloween, when the downtown scene is packed with crazy and drunk people, and during our annual street block party.

Notable UW–Madison Alumni Include:
Charles Lindbergh, aviator
Frank Lloyd Wright, architect
Greta Van Susteren, journalist
John Muir, naturalist
Stephen Ambrose, historian
Four Nobel laureates

YALE UNIVERSITY

Founded: 1701

Location: New Haven, CT

Phone: (203) 432-9316

E-mail: undergraduate.admissions@yale.edu

Web site: www.yale.edu/admit

Number of Undergraduates: 5,339

Number of Graduate Students: 4,877

Cost: Approximately $37,000 per year

Application Deadline: December 31

Early Decision: November 1

Rating:	Notable Majors/Programs:
Most Selective	Biology, History, Economics, English

Size:
○ Small ● Medium ○ Large

Location:
● Urban ○ Suburban ○ Rural

On a Saturday, students talk about academics:
○ Always ● Sometimes ○ Never

Nightlife:
○ Intense ● Moderate ○ Laid-back

Politically, Yale leans:
● Left ○ Right ○ Split

Diversity:
● High ○ Low ○ Medium

Ivy League: Yes!

Students describe Yale in five words:
- Traditional, influential, gorgeous Ivy League
- So much better than Harvard

From the School

In our complex and rapidly changing world, a sound education can never be considered finished or complete. Yale strives to develop in its students the practical abilities they need to contribute to society while ensuring that their education will enable them to deal with the unexpected turns society will take. At its most fundamental level, however, Yale's purpose is to instill in its students an affection for learning that leads to development of their intellectual, creative, and moral capacities throughout the whole of their lives.

—www.yale.edu/admit/freshmen

If you're interested in Yale, you may also be interested in:
Amherst, Brown, Harvard, Stanford, Wesleyan, Williams

Name: Matthew
Hometown: Rocklin, California
Class Year: Sophomore
Major: Biology
Extracurriculars: Yale Heavyweight Crew, Athletes in Action, and I teach science to third graders
Career Goal: To become a doctor

How would you describe Yale's reputation?

Put simply, Yale is reputed to be among the best universities in the world.

Is this reputation accurate?

I'll just say that everyone I've spoken with at Yale feels so incredibly lucky, and so blessed, to be here. It's a privilege to be a Yalie. Sometimes as a student, after a year or two, you begin settling into things and Yale simply becomes the place where you're spending your day-to-day life. When that happens you have to pinch yourself and remember just how lucky you are.

What aspect of your school would a prospective student not see on a campus tour?

Yale has a "Residential College" system, which is a bit difficult to understand. The system essentially means Yale is divided into twelve smaller residential colleges (like Oxford and Cambridge). Every student is affiliated with one residential college, and that's where students live, eat meals, and bond most closely with other students. Each residential college has its own academic dean and master in charge of student life. A few times every semester the master will have an official tea, where they'll invite prominent politicians, actors, artists, entertainers, and/or CEOs to speak to the students in their particular college. This is great, because it lets students in each college have personal contact with really prominent figures! It also breeds a lot of college pride—Yalies love their college from the time it's first assigned till years after they graduate. As a Yalie, even into your middle age, when you hear someone else went to Yale the first thing you'll say is "Great—but what college were you in?"

The Institution

The residential colleges at Yale are absolutely breathtaking. Each college has a courtyard with old oak trees, big, Gothic buildings, spiral staircases, wood and stone carvings, ivy growing on the walls, and beautiful bell towers overlooking it all. You really do live in castles. Sometimes, I feel like I'm right back in the 1800s. Another plus—the residential colleges allow students to feel like they're members of a small school within the big school that is Yale University. Students get to know their college dean and college master extremely well, and the deans and masters introduce students to very important people. Just this last year, both Bill Clinton and Al Gore gave lectures to members of my college! And really, just the chance to know your fellow Yale students is a blessing. If the achievements of the overwhelming number of past Yale grads is any indication, more than half the kids in your dorm will wind up becoming prominent figures in some segment of American society! Needless to say, I love Yale. Really, I bleed blue. I'm actually a transfer student—I spent my freshman year at UCLA, a gigantic public school—so I feel like I can really appreciate the uniqueness of Yale, having first spent time somewhere else. I mean, there's this thing call the "Yale Moment" that happens here, when you're walking around on campus and you suddenly stop yourself and go "My lord. I'm at Yale. *I'm at Yale.*"

On a more practical note, in the winter, Connecticut gets cold, particularly if you're a native Californian like me. If you come to Yale, buy a good goose-down jacket and a pair of boots. Steel yourself to start loving snow, because we get quite a bit of it. I guess snow is exciting for a few weeks, but then it turns into slush. Year-round good weather is one thing UCLA definitely does have over Yale.

The Education

Students at Yale do compete against one another, because everyone is used to being number one. When you have a class where everyone was their high school valedictorian, no student will happily settle for now being the second best—even when the harsh reality is, *someone* in the room is going to *have* to be second best, and third best, and so on. So, if you come here, be prepared to study, and study, and study, and learn to like feeling pressure to get every answer right and read every book you can.

I'd say most classes here are discussion based, and in larger classes you'll break up into smaller discussion groups, where you really get to hear what other students think. People are *very* well prepared for class, and I've found most conversations with my peers to be both intelligent and well informed.

Yale has a core curriculum, too, which has to be fulfilled during your first two years here. Every student has to take two years of a foreign language, two courses in language and literature, two courses in history, two courses in the social sciences, and two courses in the natural sciences.

Also, every student at Yale has a professor who's their undergraduate adviser. This professor reviews all your course choices with you, and helps you put together a list of classes that's appropriate, demanding, and rewarding. I've found the advising at Yale to be excellent, and my adviser has helped me define my academic goals and set out a plan to achieve them.

Lastly—I thought I was working hard in high school. I took quite a few AP classes, and did several varsity sports. To make a long story short, I had no idea how much harder I would be working at Yale. Sleeping eight hours a night? Yeah right. Try five on a good night.

The Students

Yale has students of every race, religion, sexuality, and nationality. It's probably the most diverse place I've ever been. On a given day, I can walk through my residential college and hear a large handful of languages spoken, debating any number of ideas.

Yale students are highly political, and both conservatives and liberals feel free to scream their viewpoints until they're blue in the face.

Most Yale students go on to graduate school. Most Yale students read both the *New York Times* and the *Yale Daily News*. The most anticipated publication of the year is the issue of the campus magazine *Rumpus* entitled "Yale's 50 Most Beautiful People." And yes, as I'm sure you've heard, there *are* secret societies at Yale. But I can't tell you if I'm in one, or talk about them, because they'd come after me, you know. You'd find me floating facedown in some lake somewhere, a knife in my back, just kidding. Yale secret societies exist, but they're mostly just for fun. *Mostly.*

The Activities

A vast, vast, vast amount of Yale students are involved in community service. Really, the number is something like 75 percent of us. We think it's important to give back to the surrounding community any way we can. I go to an inner-city elementary school once a week and help teach third grade kids about science.

Most Yale students stay on campus on weekends, but I'm lucky because I live in a very well-endowed residential college (as you'll learn, some residential colleges have more money—and arguably more prestige—than others). Because my residential college has cash to spare, the master organizes New York culture nights and takes four students every single week to see a Broadway show or play or ballet, and then they'll go out to dinner. The last time I went, transportation should have cost me $20, my ticket for the opera should have cost $210, and my dinner should have cost $75. I paid nothing. Yale footed the entire bill.

The Social Scene

Yalies have the reputation of spending their lives in the library, studying incredibly hard. And we do spend a lot of time in the library doing just that. But we also have a lot of fun. There are parties all over campus every weekend, and once a year each of the twelve residential colleges throws a massive bash, spending thousands and thousands of dollars. Really, Yale parties do kick ass. Sorry, big state schools. When it comes down to it, Yale is better at partying, too.

Name: Thomas
Hometown: San Francisco, California
Class Year: Junior
Major: American studies
Extracurriculars: Japanese American Students Union, Freestyle Expressions Breakdancing Crew, Asian American Student Alliance, Korean American Students at Yale
Career Goal: I plan on dedicating my life to public service in LA or Washington, D.C.

How would you describe Yale's reputation?

People say Yale is one of the best, if not the best, college in the United States. People also probably say Yale is a holding pen for stuck-up, white, East Coast prep school kids, who think that they are better than everyone else and will rule the world in no time.

Is this reputation accurate?

Sort of. Yes, Yale is one of the best schools in the nation. And yes, there are a lot of white, stuck-up prep school kids here. But there are also lots of minority students, and students from less well-off backgrounds, and kids from parts of America that aren't the East Coast. Really, I think Yale has a very diverse campus.

What would an admissions officer probably not tell a prospective student?

An admissions officer won't tell a prospective student that there will be times during their Yale career when they won't sleep for seventy-two hours straight because of work. You will study until sunrise many times.

The Institution

Everyone here has a ridiculous amount of Yale pride. We hate Harvard with a vengeance, wear Yale T-shirts and hoodies whenever possible, and revel in the fact that a Yalie is in the White House, even though most of us probably didn't vote for him.

One bad thing is that Yale separates itself from New Haven. At Yale, there's lots of idealism, privilege, history. And then blocks away there's "dangerous" and poor New Haven, which freshmen are told to steer clear of. I suspect Yale is afraid of New Haven because most New Haven residents are minorities. I guess it's scary for naïve freshman to walk into a black or Hispanic neighborhood—whatever. I've found New Haven to be perfectly safe, and think Yale and New Haven should become far more integrated in the future.

The Education

Yale professors are, as one might expect, stellar. They're also interesting characters. The best class I took here was Formation of Modern American Culture from 1920–present, with this gay socialist prof who lectured entirely in spoken-word. The final paper for the class was on Tupac's song "Changes," and how it reflected American urban and mainstream society. Tell me, where else could you write a final paper, under a distinguished professor, on the rapper Tupac Shakur?

And while Yalies work hard, we also know how to have fun. Saturday nights, we party, no work-talk allowed. Really, just because Yale is an Ivy League school doesn't mean we're all nerds. Everyone needs release every now and again!

The Students

Yalies love politics, and Yale conservatives and liberals generally argue to the death. They scream, shout, get red in the face, make up, shake hands,

and then go home thinking "I hate so-and-so, they're so closed-minded and backward! Tomorrow, I'll show them the error of their ways, and they'll come around." Arguments are on literally every issue, from race, class, and the next president, to whether *He-Man* or *Thundercats* was the more sophisticated '80s cartoon show.

And a lot of these arguments will take place in the Commons, which is a ridiculously grand dining hall on Yale's campus that looks exactly like something out of a Harry Potter film. The only caveat is that despite there being lots of diversity at Yale, students self-segregate. If you glance at where students are sitting in the Commons, and who they're sitting with, it really hits you how divided Yale can be. There's the Asian table, the football team table, the black table, the chemistry table, and so on. We all get along in a broad sense, we all talk to one another, but when it comes down to it everyone forms little cliques and befriends those who are most like them.

> "The only complaint that I heard about Yale before matriculating was about New Haven, which is unjustified. New Haven is a vibrant city with many wonderful parks, ethnic restaurants, and a thriving arts scene."
> ✦ Hae Jin, senior

The Activities

For the most part, Yale students don't interact with students from other schools. There are a couple of small colleges nearby, and their students will sometimes come to New Haven to party at Toad's place, where we'll encounter them. But these kids conspicuously stand out, they dress really scantily, very "un-Yale," and we keep our distance. I guess the big exceptions would be Harvard—we sometimes have joint activities with inferior students from that school, and Harvard students will come to New Haven, or we'll go to Boston—and Wesleyan University is a half hour away, so sometimes Yalies will go to Middletown to visit friends from their prep school days, or Wesleyan kids will trek down to New Haven. I think a lot of Yale professors teach at Wesleyan sometimes, too.

Personally, I leave campus as much as I can. Why? Because there's a train station in New Haven that will take you to New York City for under twenty dollars, and you'll arrive in Grand Central Station in less than an hour and a half. Really, if you don't take advantage of New York City while you're at Yale, I think you've wasted your four years. It's not that Yale isn't interesting—it is—but this is Manhattan, center of the world, a brief hour-and-a-half train ride from your doorstep! You might wonder, why go to Yale if you love New York City so much? Why don't you just go to Columbia? I guess the answer is that New York City is amazing, and distracting, so I couldn't go to Columbia and get any work done. I'd always be enticed to hop on a subway and explore. At Yale, you're far enough away to focus on your work when you need to. But you're still close enough to get your city buzz whenever you want it!

At 3:00 a.m. on a Wednesday night at Yale, I'm still awake. I may be working on papers, I may have just gotten back from a late night snack run to Mamouns with my friends, I may be sitting around talking, watching a movie, playing PS2. Before I got to sleep, I'll probably grab my cell and call my friends on the West Coast, who should still be awake.

The Social Scene

So, every single weekend Yalies party. No questions, no exceptions. Different people party differently, though—some will pregame in their room, taking shots of cheap vodka, tequila, and SoCo. Others will head to different nightclubs around campus that have open bars on the weekend. Some will go straight to clubs and lounges and drink nothing at all. Yet more people will put together a courtyard party in their residential college. In the end, most will drink some, dance lots, cause some trouble, maybe find someone to kiss and cuddle with, then finally call it a night around 3:00 or 4:00 a.m., passing out in their bed knowing they had fun!

Name: Annabelle
Hometown: Bronxville, New York
Class Year: Junior
Major: Physics
Extracurriculars: Safety Mix Comedy Troupe, Yale Glee Club, photography for *Rumpus* (the campus tabloid), musical theater. For a while I sang a cappella, but never again!
Career Goal: I'm trying to find a way to do something creative that still incorporates the physical sciences.

How would you describe Yale's reputation?

Yale is known for being filled to the brim with brilliant, enthusiastic students. It's said that the beauty of our campus only accentuates the ugliness and terror of the city we're located in, New Haven. I've heard Yale students never date, but they drink substantially and spend much of their time on the stage doing theater or singing a cappella. Supposedly many Yalies are gay, and most Yalies hang on to the far end of left-wing politics. Adding to the mix, Yalies are supposed to be rich and self-absorbed. And Yale professors are said to be blindingly brilliant, often verging on snobby, but still more accessible than they would be if they taught at Harvard.

Is this reputation accurate?

Well, most Yalies are, indeed, brilliant and enthusiastic, but not all of them are. There are definitely some slackers here (and most view the slackers with a mix of condescension and admiration). Our campus is gorgeous, but no school is complete without its token ugly buildings, and we have a few of those (Morse, Stiles, and the A&A building). New Haven is actually a lovely place to be, although every student is heckled for change by homeless people several times a day. The Yale dating scene *is* lacking—Yale men, for some reason, are petrified to ask Yale women out on dates. Most of the dates I've heard of have been initiated by the women. Yale *is* something of a drinking school, but not in a binge-drinking sort of way. There's just lots of casual social drinking, sometimes some marijuana smoking. There's tons and tons of theater going on, and oppressive amounts of a cappella. There are also a lot of gay students, and they're 100 percent accepted, so come here if you're gay and looking for a welcoming atmosphere. Students on the whole lean to the left, but most would probably say they're left-leaning rather than left-wing. While there are a lot of rich students here, there are also a lot of poor people—in short, economic diversity. Lastly, I'd say professors are both brilliant and approachable, for the most part—but bad teachers, too, slip through the cracks.

What would an admissions officer at Yale probably not tell a prospective student? What aspect of your school would a prospective student not see on a campus tour?

There is a lot of on-campus bitterness toward the a cappella groups—there are too damn many of them!

Most of the campus also doesn't have much respect for right-wingers or the very religious. And on-campus food isn't the greatest, though the Thai and Indian food in New Haven can't be beat.

Bright College Years
H. S. Durand '81, Carl Wilhelm

Bright college years with pleasure rife,
The shortest, gladdest years of life;
How swiftly are ye gliding by!
Oh, why does time so quickly fly!
The seasons come, the seasons go,
The earth is green or white with snow,
But time and change shall naught avail
To break the friendships formed at Yale.

In afteryears, should troubles rise
To cloud the blue of sunny skies,
How bright will seem through mem'ry's
     haze,
Those happy, golden, by-gone days!
Oh, let us strive that ever we
May let these words our watchcry be,
Where'er upon life's seas we sail:
"For God, for Country, and for Yale!"

The Institution

Yale is a world of its own. As a student, you're surrounded by secret society buildings, statues of famous alumni, visiting successful graduates, pictures in local restaurants of former award-winning Yale sports teams. It's hard to explain, but it's an atmosphere that's unique to Yale. Once you've been through all this, you have a lifelong understanding with other Yale grads, who have been through it, too.

Also, I need to talk about the strike. This year, the dining hall and custodial workers at Yale went on strike for better labor contracts. Yale the institution is sometimes big and insulated and wealthy and evil, and evidently it wasn't doing the right thing by its workers. Things are now settled (kind of), but labor relations are still really strained, and the average custodial worker will not have the best things to say about Yale's bureaucracy. Because labor strikes affected every Yale student, most Yalies are now pretty well-read on labor laws and local Connecticut politics that impact the situation.

The Education

Yes, yes, I talk about my classwork on Saturday nights. Not everyone does—actually, most people don't—but my friends and I do. We're really into our academics, and jabber on about them as much as possible. Everyday conversations between me and my buddies almost always factor in our readings or personal philosophies, and we love to have witty pun wars (hush you! pun wars require brilliance!).

In the physics major, students frequently get together to hash out problem sets before they're due—we'll meet in my room to help each other out, rifle through textbooks, and generally talk back and forth until we have all the answers right. Then we'll all go to Yorkside (the popular pizza/diner place) and sarcastically congratulate one another on our collective brilliance. The physics major, because we have these sessions, and because it's relatively small, has a really tight-knit group of students in it.

The best physics class I've taken here is the now defunct Intermediate Physics with Professor David DeMille. Professor DeMille consistently turned what would could have been a rote and boring physics class into a fascinating discussion of physical principles and their hypothetical uses. Everyone always came out of his class feeling like they really understood the (daunting) material. Two more memorable classes: Writing Comedy with Mark O'Donnell (who recently won a Tony for writing the book for *Hairspray*), where students wrote songs and workshopped them with the rest of the class and Mania and Mass Psychology, with Eric Schwab, where we read impenetrable philosophy, watched bizarre films, and had to, as our final project, "do something relevant." One student decided to go to England, watched the May Day riots, and wrote about them. I went to the New Orleans Mardi Gras and wrote a twenty-two-page paper on breast flashing and voyeurism.

The Students

There are lots of big, loud, influential student groups at Yale. Recently, a Christian group took out full-page ads in the *Yale Daily News* telling everyone about the things Christ could offer them. The Af-Am house and La Casa are both respected and beloved institutions that hold frequent concerts, parties, and discussions. The LGBT community is, well, hardly a community. Gay and lesbian students are so accepted at Yale, they often don't need a support group—they live like everyone else, and there are enough LGBT kids they'll come into contact with in their classes and dorms that they don't need LGBT exclusive spaces to meet people to date. Yale students come from all over the world, literally from every corner of the entire world, but a disproportionate amount of students come from the parts of the world called New York, Connecticut, and California. That said, my roommate is from West Virginia, and two of the boys upstairs are from Zimbabwe, another from Bulgaria.

Students are fairly political, although not all are actively political. We had about 160 people attend the March for Women's Lives. The *Yale Daily News* is a generally respected paper, although the students mock it for poor reporting. On most issues, students at Yale are sure that they are right, and they'll try to prove this by arguing louder and then louder. It seems like people argue here just for the sake of it.

The Activities

The a cappella community is probably the most infamous community at Yale. To get into an a cappella group, you enter into the rush process (akin to frat rushing, but without the hazing), which takes the entire month of December and leaves both freshmen and group members exhausted and often disillusioned. Many Yalies love a cappella, I've found it to be time-sapping and cultish.

On the other hand, I've loved my time with the Yale Glee Club, a less exclusive/catty group that sings better music, in my opinion. We went on a fun, fun tour through the Midwest and will be going to the Southwest and Australia next year. Safety Mix, my improv troupe, has also been a lot of fun. We're a bit more casual than most of the troupes, and I find every rehearsal to be therapeutic. There's always theater going up at Yale. Come late spring, there are about seven shows every weekend, I kid you not. People mostly stick around campus on the weekend at Yale. There's always so much you can do and so much you have to do on any given day. It's easy to keep yourself busy with academics, extracurriculars, and friends' performances.

The Social Scene

I'm not very into the party scene here. I'd much rather sit around in a quiet room with friends and chat or watch *The Family Guy* than go into a loud, crowded, dark room with strangers and a keg. However, if loud, crowded, dark rooms with kegs are your thing, there's plenty of them to be found at Yale.

It's somewhat difficult to be a nondrinker at Yale, but if you develop a healthy attitude (i.e., you don't mind being around people who drink even if you don't drink yourself) it's not too bad. Seeing other people's shows is a big part of the social scene. Chilling at local restaurants (like Yorkside, go Yorkside!) is also a big part of the social scene. The Residential College system fosters strong friendship at Yale; I've met about a third of my friends through my residential college. The other ones I've met through classes (my physics crowd) or my extracurricular activities (improv, glee club).

While many parts of Yale have been wonderful, I have to say I'm somewhat disappointed with college life thus far. College hasn't swept me off my feet the way TV told me it would. I guess, at Yale, there's just not enough time in the day to do anything fully, you can never devote your all to academics, extracurriculars, and friends at the same time, and because of it you always feel like key parts of your life are lacking. I've also been very frustrated with the lack of a dating scene at Yale, as I'm looking for a boyfriend but can't find one no matter how hard I try, and this isn't a "me" thing, it's a Yale thing. No one dates. At all. It's either random hookups, or nothing. People are even reluctant to make intimate, close friends at Yale, too many students are too focused on maintaining an image of perfection, and if they let someone in, that someone might see their flaws, which, for many Yalies, would be considered personally disastrous.

Notable Yale Alumni Include:
George Bush, forty-first U.S. president
George W. Bush, forty-third U.S. president
Clarence Thomas, Supreme Court justice
John Fenn, Nobel Prize–winning chemist
Raymond Davis, Nobel Prize–winning physicist
Edward Norton, actor

Have Your Say

We know it seems far off, but one day you, too, will be a college student. And when that day arrives, we want to hear what *you* have to say about your school. What are the academics like? What aren't prospective students seeing on campus tours? What's going on in your dorm at three a.m. on a Wednesday night?

Log on at www.studentsguide.com/colleges/haveyoursay. Take a half hour and tell us anything about your school—the good, the bad, the just plain weird. *Students' Guide to Colleges* will be rereleased yearly by Penguin Books, and, in a future edition, you could become one of the three students selected to represent your school in print.